REPAIR MANUAL

DATSUN/NISSAN PICK-UPS and PATHFINDERS 1970-89

All U.S. and Canadian models of Pick-Ups and Pathfinders
2- and 4-wheel Drive • Gasoline and Diesel Engines

Sr. Vice President	Ronald A. Hoxter
Publisher and Editor-In-Chief	Kerry A. Freeman, S.A.E.
Managing Editors	Peter M. Conti, Jr. □ W. Calvin Settle, Jr., S.A.E.
Assistant Managing Editor	Nick D'Andrea
Senior Editors	Richard J. Rivele, S.A.E. □ Ron Webb
Director of Manufacturing	Mike D'Imperio
Manager of Manufacturing	John F. Butler
Editor	Dean F. Morgantini, S.A.E.

CHILTON BOOK COMPANY

*ONE OF THE **DIVERSIFIED PUBLISHING COMPANIES**,*
*A PART OF **CAPITAL CITIES/ABC, INC.***

CONTENTS

1 GENERAL INFORMATION and MAINTENANCE

2 ENGINE PERFORMANCE and TUNE-UP

3 ENGINE and ENGINE OVERHAUL

4 EMISSION CONTROLS

5 FUEL SYSTEM

6 CHASSIS ELECTRICAL

DRIVE TRAIN

SUSPENSION and STEERING

BRAKES

BODY

MECHANIC'S DATA

SAFETY NOTICE

Proper service and repair procedures are vital to the safe, reliable operation of all motor vehicles, as well as the personal safety of those performing repairs. This book outlines procedures for servicing and repairing vehicles using safe, effective methods. The procedures contain many NOTES, CAUTIONS and WARNINGS which should be followed along with standard safety procedures to eliminate the possibility of personal injury or improper service which could damage the vehicle or compromise its safety.

It is important to note that repair procedures and techniques, tools and parts for servicing motor vehicles, as well as the skill and experience of the individual performing the work vary widely. It is not possible to anticipate all of the conceivable ways or conditions under which vehicles may be serviced, or to provide cautions as to all of the possible hazards that may result. Standard and accepted safety precautions and equipment should be used when handling toxic or flammable fluids, and safety goggles or other protection should be used during cutting, grinding, chiseling, prying, or any other process that can cause material removal or projectiles.

Some procedures require the use of tools specially designed for a specific purpose. Before substituting another tool or procedure, you must be completely satisfied that neither your personal safety, nor the performance of the vehicle will be endangered.

Although the information in this guide is based on industry sources and is as complete as possible at the time of publication, the possibility exists that the manufacturer made later changes which could not be included here. While striving for total accuracy, Chilton Book Company cannot assume responsibility for any errors, changes, or omissions that may occur in the compilation of this data.

PART NUMBERS

Part numbers listed in this reference are not recommendations by Chilton for any product by brand name. They are references that can be used with interchange manuals and aftermarket supplier catalogs to locate each brand supplier's discrete part number.

SPECIAL TOOLS

Special tools are recommended by the vehicle manufacturer to perform their specific job. Use has been kept to a minimum, but where absolutely necessary, they are referred to in the text by the part number of the tool manufacturer. Datsun special tools referred to in this guide are available through Kent-Moore Corporation, 29784 Little Mack, Roseville, Michigan 48066. For Canada, contact Kent-Moore of Canada, LTD., 2395 Cawthra Mississauga, Ontario, Canada L5A, 3Ps., or an equivalent tool can be purchased locally from a tool supplier or parts outlet.

ACKNOWLEDGMENTS

Chilton Book Company expresses appreciation to the Nissan Motor Corporation in the U.S.A., Carson, California 90248 for their generous assistance.

Published in Radnor, Pennsylvania 19089, by Chilton Book Company

Manufactured in the United States of America
67890 876543

Chilton's Repair Manual: Datsun/Nissan Pick-Ups and PathFinder 1970–89
ISBN 0-8019-7932-3 pbk.
Library of Congress Catalog Card No. 88-43174

General Information and Maintenance

1

HOW TO USE THIS BOOK

Chilton's Repair Manual for Datsun/Nissan Trucks is intended to teach you about the inner workings of your truck and save you money on its upkeep.

The first two chapters will be the most used, since they contain maintenance and tune-up information and procedures. Studies have shown that a properly tuned and maintained truck can get at least 10% better gas mileage (which translates into lower operating costs) and periodic maintenance will catch minor problems before they turn into major repair bills. The other chapters deal with the more complex systems of your truck. Operating systems from engine through brakes are covered to the extent that the average do-it-yourselfer becomes mechanically involved. This book will not explain such things as rebuilding the differential for the simple reason that the expertise required and the investment in special tools make this task impractical and uneconomical. It will give you the detailed instructions to help you change your own brake pads and shoes, tune-up the engine, replace spark plugs and filters, and do many more jobs that will save you money, give you personal satisfaction and help you avoid expensive problems.

A secondary purpose of this book is a reference guide for owners who want to understand their truck and/or their mechanics better. In this case, no tools at all are required. Knowing just what a particular repair job requires in parts and labor time will allow you to evaluate whether or not you're getting a fair price quote and help decipher itemized bills from a repair shop.

Before attempting any repairs or service on your truck, read through the entire procedure outlined in the appropriate chapter. This will give you the overall view of what tools and supplies will be required. There is nothing more frustrating than having to walk to the bus stop on Monday morning because you were short one gasket on Sunday afternoon. So read ahead and plan ahead. Each operation should be approached logically and all procedures thoroughly understood before attempting any work. Some special tools that may be required can often be rented from local automotive jobbers or places specializing in renting tools and equipment. Check the yellow pages of your phone book.

All chapters contain adjustments, maintenance, removal and installation procedures, and overhaul procedures. When overhaul is not considered practical, we tell you how to remove the failed part and then how to install the new or rebuilt replacement. In this way, you at least save the labor costs. Backyard overhaul of some components (such as the alternator or water pump) is just not practical, but the removal and installation procedure is often simple and well within the capabilities of the average truck owner.

Two basic mechanic's rules should be mentioned here. First, whenever the LEFT side of the truck or engine is referred to, it is meant to specify the DRIVER'S side of the truck. Conversely, the RIGHT side of the truck means the PASSENGER'S side. Second, all screws and bolts are removed by turning counterclockwise, and tightened by turning clockwise.

Safety is always the most important rule. Constantly be aware of the dangers involved in working on or around an automobile and take proper precautions to avoid the risk of personal injury or damage to the vehicle. See the section in this chapter, Servicing Your Vehicle Safely, and the SAFETY NOTICE on the acknowledgment page before attempting any service procedures and pay attention to the instructions provided. There are 3 common mistakes in mechanical work:

1. Incorrect order of assembly, disassembly

or adjustment. When taking something apart or putting it together, doing things in the wrong order usually just costs you extra time; however it CAN break something. Read the entire procedure before beginning disassembly. Do everything in the order in which the instructions say you should do it, even if you can't immediately see a reason for it. When you're taking apart something that is very intricate (for example a carburetor), you might want to draw a picture of how it looks when assembled at one point in order to make sure you get everything back in its proper position. We will supply exploded views whenever possible, but sometimes the job requires more attention to detail than an illustration provides. When making adjustments (especially tune-up adjustments), do them in order. One adjustment often affects another and you cannot expect satisfactory results unless each adjustment is made only when it cannot be changed by any other.

2. Overtorquing (or undertorquing) nuts and bolts. While it is more common for overtorquing to cause damage, undertorquing can cause a fastener to vibrate loose and cause serious damage, especially when dealing with aluminum parts. Pay attention to torque specifications and utilize a torque wrench in assembly. If a torque figure is not available remember that, if you are using the right tool to do the job, you will probably not have to strain yourself to get a fastener tight enough. The pitch of most threads is so slight that the tension you put on the wrench will be multiplied many times in actual force on what you are tightening. A good example of how critical torque is can be seen in the case of spark plug installation, especially where you are putting the plug into an aluminum cylinder head. Too little torque can fail to crush the gasket, causing leakage of combustion gases and consequent overheating of the plug and engine parts. Too much torque can damage the threads or distort the plug, which changes the spark gap at the electrode. Since more and more manufacturers are using aluminum in their engine and chassis parts to save weight, a torque wrench should be in any serious do-it-yourselfer's tool box.

There are many commercial chemical products available for ensuring that fasteners won't come loose, even if they are not torqued just right (a very common brand is Loctite®). If you're worried about getting something together tight enough to hold, but loose enough to avoid mechanical damage during assembly, one of these products might offer substantial insurance. Read the label on the package and make sure the product is compatible with the materials, fluids, etc. involved before choosing one.

3. Crossthreading. This occurs when a part such as a bolt is screwed into a nut or casting at the wrong angle and forced, causing the threads to become damaged. Crossthreading is more likely to occur if access is difficult. It helps to clean and lubricate fasteners, and to start threading with the part to be installed going straight in, using your fingers. If you encounter resistance, unscrew the part and start over again at a different angle until it can be inserted and turned several times without much effort. Keep in mind that many parts, especially spark plugs, use tapered threads so that gentle turning will automatically bring the part you're threading to the proper angle if you don't force it or resist a change in angle. Don't put a wrench on the part until it's been turned in a couple of times by hand. If you suddenly encounter resistance and the part has not seated fully, don't force it. Pull it back out and make sure it's clean and threading properly.

Always take your time and be patient; once you have some experience, working on your truck will become an enjoyable hobby.

TOOLS AND EQUIPMENT

Naturally, without the proper tools and equipment it is impossible to properly service your vehicle. It would be impossible to catalog each tool that you would need to perform each or every operation in this book. It would also be unwise for the amateur to rush out and buy an expensive set of tools and the theory that he may need one or more of them at sometime.

The best approach is to proceed slowly, gathering together a good quality set of those tools that are used most frequently. Don't be misled by the low cost of bargain tools. It is far better to spend a little more for better quality. Forged wrenches, 6– or 12–point sockets and fine tooth ratchets are by far preferable to their less expensive counterparts. As any good mechanic can tell you, there are few worse experiences than trying to work on a truck with bad tools. Your monetary savings will be far outweighed by frustration and mangled knuckles.

Certain tools, plus a basic ability to handle tools, are required to get started. A basic mechanics tool set, a torque wrench, and, for 1976 and later models, a Torx® bits set. Torx® bits are hexlobular drivers which fit both inside and outside on special Torx® head fasteners used in various places on some trucks.

Begin accumulating those tools that are used most frequently; those associated with routine maintenance and tune-up.

In addition to the normal assortment of screwdrivers and pliers you should have the following tools for routine maintenance jobs (your truck, depending on the model year, uses both SAE and metric fasteners):

1. SAE/Metric wrenches, sockets and combination open end/box end wrenches in sizes from ⅛″ to ¾″ and 3mm to 19mm, and a spark plug socket ($^{13}/_{16}$″ or ⅝″). If possible, buy various length socket drive extensions. One break in this department is that the metric sockets available in the U.S. will all fit the ratchet handles and extensions you may already have (¼″, ⅜″, and ½″ drive).
2. Jackstands for support.
3. Oil filter wrench.
4. Oil filler spout or funnel.
5. Grease gun for chassis lubrication.
6. Hydrometer for checking the battery.
7. A low flat pan for draining oil.
8. Lots of rags for wiping up the inevitable mess.

In addition to the above items there are several others that are not absolutely necessary, but handy to have around. These include oil-dry, a transmission fluid funnel and the usual supply of lubricants, antifreeze and fluids, although these can be purchased as needed. This is a basic list for routine maintenance, but only your personal needs and desires can accurately determine your list of necessary tools.

The second list of tools is for tune-ups. While the tools involved here are slightly more sophisticated, they need not be outrageously expensive. There are several inexpensive tach/dwell meters on the market that are every bit as good for the average mechanic as a $100.00 professional model. Just be sure that it goes to at least 1200–1500 rpm on the tach scale and that it works on 4, 6 and 8 cylinder engines. A basic list of tune-up equipment could include:

1. Tach-dwell meter
2. Spark plug wrench
3. Timing light (a DC light that works from the truck's battery is best, although an AC light that plugs into 110V house current will suffice at some sacrifice in brightness)
4. Wire spark plug gauge/adjusting tools
5. Set of feeler blades.

Here again, be guided by your own needs. A feeler blade will set the point gap as easily as dwell meter will read dwell, but slightly less accurately. And since you will need a tachometer anyway ... well, make your own decision.

In addition to these basic tools, there are several other tools and gauges you may find useful. These include:

1. A compression gauge. The screw-in type is slower to use, but eliminates the possibility of a faulty reading due to escaping pressure
2. A manifold vacuum gauge
3. A test light
4. An induction meter. This is used for determining whether or not there is current in a wire. These are handy for use if a wire is broken somewhere in a wiring harness.

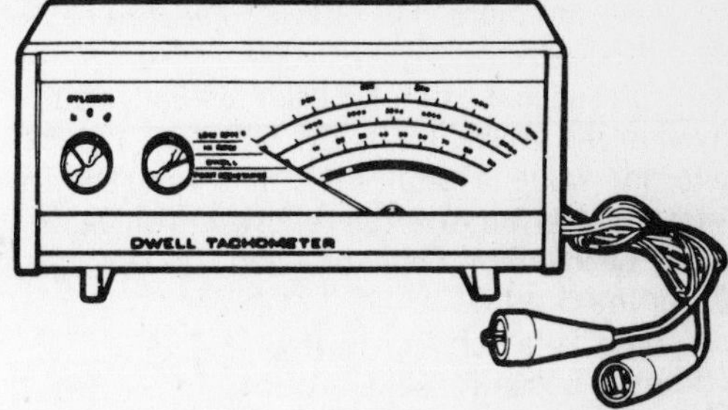

A dwell/tachometer is useful for tune-up work; you won't need a dwell meter if your car has electronic ignition

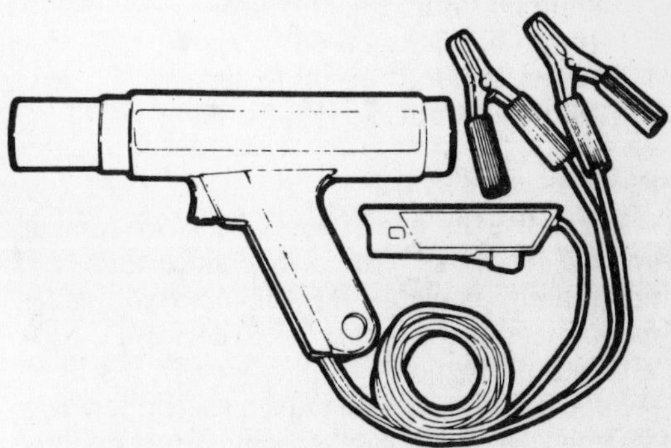
An inductive pickup simplifies timing light connection to the spark plug wire

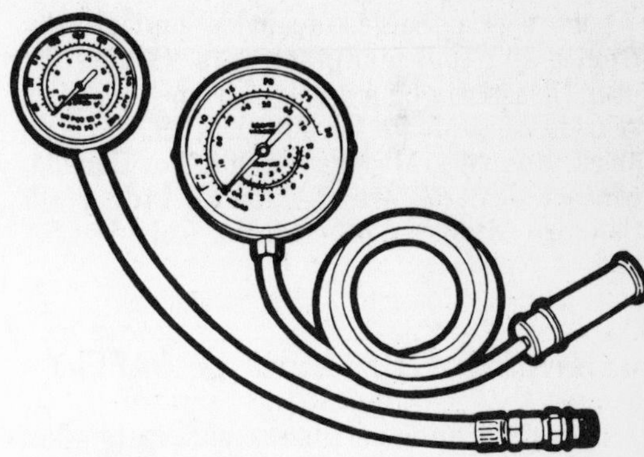
A compression gauge and a combination vacuum/fuel pressure gauge are handy for troubleshooting and tune-up work

As a final note, you will probably find a torque wrench necessary for all but the most basic work. The beam type models are perfectly adequate, although the newer click (breakaway) type are more precise, and you don't have to crane your neck to see a torque reading in awkward situations. The breakaway torque wrenches are more expensive and should be recalibrated periodically.

Torque specification for each fastener will be given in the procedure in any case that a specific torque value is required. If no torque specifications are given, use the following values as a guide, based upon fastener size:

Bolts marked 6T

6mm bolt/nut: 5–7 ft. lbs.
8mm bolt/nut: 12–17 ft. lbs.
10mm bolt/nut: 23–34 ft. lbs.
12mm bolt/nut: 41–59 ft. lbs.
14mm bolt/nut: 56–76 ft. lbs.

Bolts marked 8T

6mm bolt/nut: 6–9 ft. lbs.
8mm bolt/nut: 13–20 ft. lbs.
10mm bolt/nut: 27–40 ft. lbs.
12mm bolt/nut: 46–69 ft. lbs.
14mm bolt/nut: 75–101 ft. lbs.

Special Tools

Normally, the use of special factory tools is avoided for repair procedures, since these are not readily available for the do-it-yourselfer mechanic. When it is possible to perform the job with more commonly available tools, it will be pointed out, but occasionally, a special tool was designed to perform a specific function and should be used. Before substituting another tool, you should be convinced that neither your safety nor the performance of the vehicle will be compromised.

Some special tools are available commercially from major tool manufacturers. Others for your Nissan can be purchased from you dealer or from Kent-Moore Corporation, 29784 Little Mack, Roseville, Michigan 48066. For Canada, contact Kent-Moore of Canada, Ltd., 2395 Cawthra Mississauga, Ontario, Canada L5A 3P2.

SERVICING YOUR VEHICLE SAFELY

It is virtually impossible to anticipate all of the hazards involved with automotive maintenance and service but care and common sense will prevent most accidents.

The rules of safety for mechanics range from "don't smoke around gasoline," to "use the proper tool for the job." The trick to avoiding injuries is to develop safe work habits and take every possible precaution.

Do's

- Do keep a fire extinguisher and first aid kit within easy reach.
- Do wear safety glasses or goggles when cutting, drilling, grinding or prying. If you wear glasses for the sake of vision, then they should

Always support the car on jackstands when working under it

be made of hardened glass that can serve also as safety glasses, or wear safety goggles over your regular glasses.

- Do shield your eyes whenever you work around the battery. Batteries contain sulfuric acid. In case of contact with the eyes or skin, flush the area with water or a mixture of water and baking soda and get medical attention immediately.
- Do use safety stands for any under-truck service. Jacks are for raising vehicles; safety stands are for making sure the vehicle stays raised until you want it to come down. Whenever the vehicle is raised, block the wheels remaining on the ground and set the parking brake.
- Do use adequate ventilation when working with any chemicals. Asbestos dust resulting from brake lining wear cause cancer.
- Do disconnect the negative battery cable when working on the electrical system.
- Do follow manufacturer's directions whenever working with potentially hazardous materials. Both brake fluid and antifreeze are poisonous if taken internally.
- Do properly maintain your tools. Loose hammerheads, mushroomed punches and chisels, frayed or poorly grounded electrical cords, excessively worn screwdrivers, spread wrenches (open end), cracked sockets, slipping ratchets, or faulty droplight sockets can cause accidents.
- Do use the proper size and type of tool for the job being done.
- Do when possible, pull on a wrench handle rather than push on it, and adjust you stance to prevent a fall.
- Do be sure that adjustable wrenches are tightly adjusted on the nut or bolt and pulled so that the face is on the side of the fixed jaw.
- Do select a wrench or socket that fits the nut or bolt. The wrench or socket should sit straight, not cocked.
- Do strike squarely with a hammer. avoid glancing blows.

• Do set the parking brake and block the wheels if the work requires that the engine be running.

Don'ts

• Don't run an engine in a garage or anywhere else without proper ventilation – EVER! Carbon monoxide is poisonous. It is absorbed by the body 400 times faster than oxygen. It takes a long time to leave the human body and you can build up a deadly supply of it in your system by simply breathing in a little every day. You may not realize you are slowly poisoning yourself. Always use power vents, windows, fans or open the garage doors.

• Don't work around moving parts while wearing a necktie or other loose clothing. Short sleeves are much safer than long, loose sleeves. Hard-toed shoes with neoprene soles protect your toes and give a better grip on slippery surfaces. Jewelry such as watches, fancy belt buckles, beads, or body adornment of any kind is not safe while working around a truck. Long hair should be hidden under a hat or cap.

• Don't use pockets for toolboxes. A fall or bump can drive a screwdriver deep into you body. Even a wiping cloth hanging from the back pocket can wrap around a spinning shaft or fan.

• Don't smoke when working around gasoline, cleaning solvent or other flammable material.

• Don't smoke when working around the battery. When the battery is being charged, it gives off explosive hydrogen gas.

• Don't use gasoline to wash your hands. There are excellent soaps available. Gasoline may contain lead, and lead can enter the body through a cut, accumulating in the body until you are very ill. Gasoline also removes all the natural oils from the skin so that bone dry hands will suck up oil and grease.

• Don't service the air conditioning system unless you are equipped with the necessary tools and training. The refrigerant, R–12, is extremely cold and when exposed to the air, will instantly freeze any surface it comes in contact with, including your eyes. Although the refrigerant is normally non-toxic, R–12 becomes a deadly poisonous gas in the presence of an open flame. One good whiff of the vapors from burning refrigerant can be fatal.

SERIAL NUMBER IDENTIFICATION

Vehicle Identification Number

The vehicle serial number is stamped on a plate found in the upper center portion of the

The VIN plate is located on the firewall—1970–78

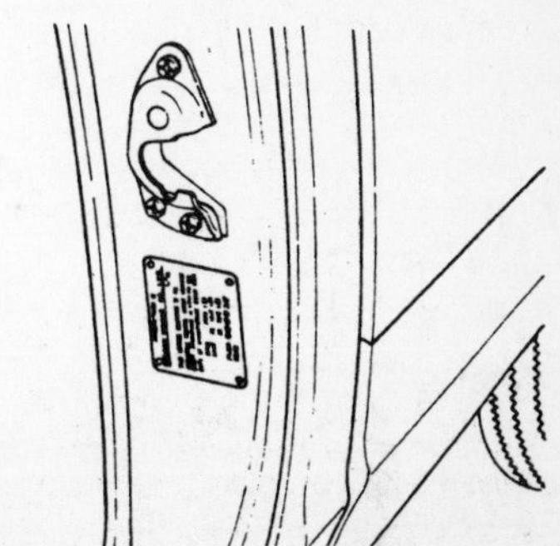

The vehicle identification number is also found on the driver's side door pillar—1970–78

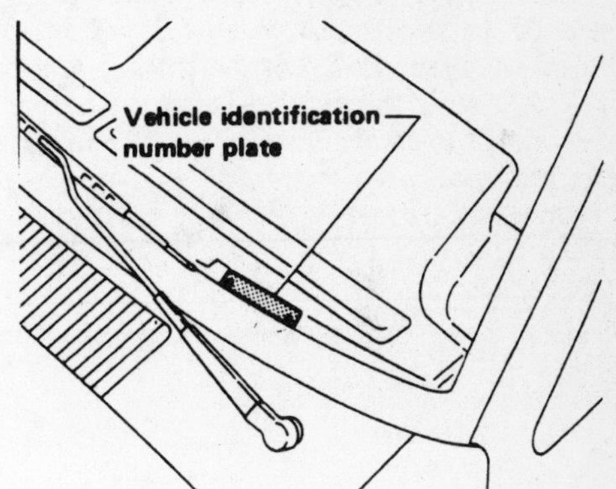

The vehicle identification number can be found on the left side of the instrument panel, visible through the windshield—1979–89

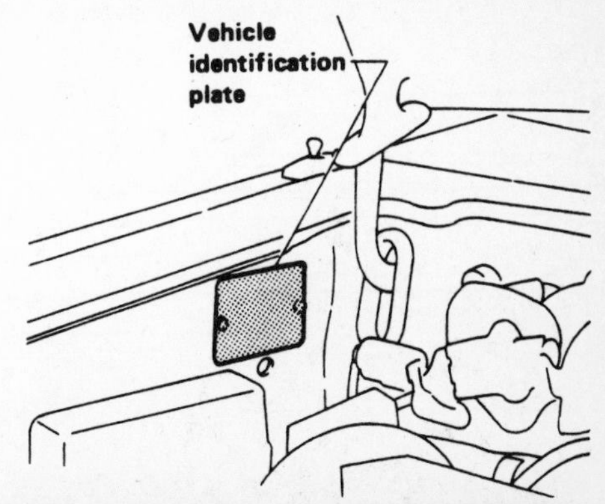

The VIN plate is located on the right front fender apron—1979–89

firewall on 1970–78 models. It can also be found stamped on a metal tag, fastened to the driver's side door pillar (all models).

On 1979–89 models, the number is located on the right front fender apron in the engine compartment (behind the wheel arch).

All 1979–89 models also have the vehicle identification number stamped on a plate attached to the left side of the instrument panel. The plate is visible through the windshield.

The vehicle identification (model variation codes) may be interpreted as follows:

- 1970–71: All models are marked PL521TU. The first letter, P, indicates the L16 engine. The second letter, L, means left hand drive, 521 is the model number. The first suffix letter, T, indicates a floor shift. The second suffix letter, U, indicates a U.S. and Canada specification model.
- 1972: All models are marked PL620TU.

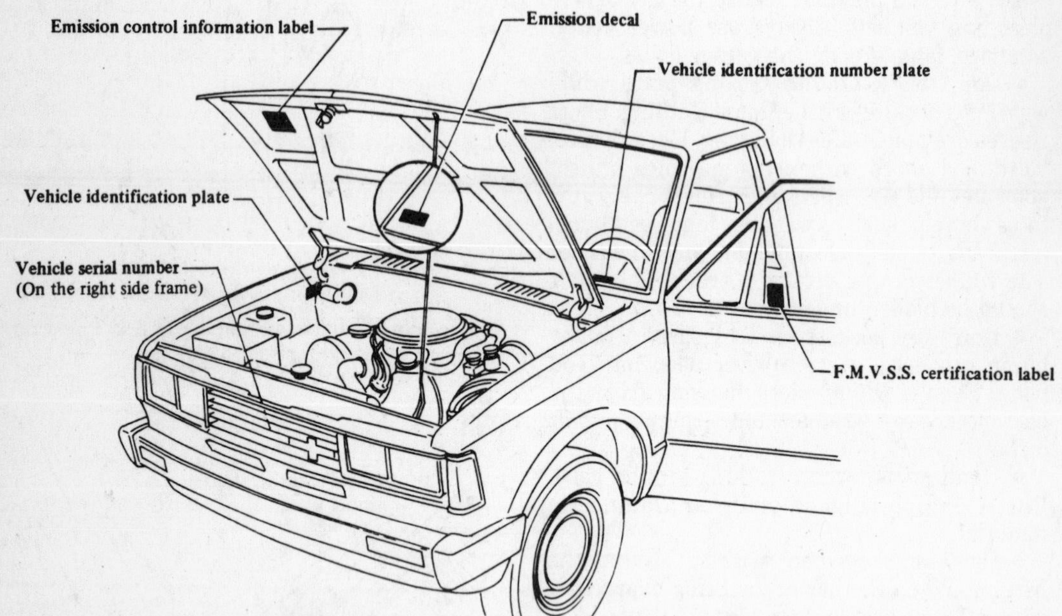

Serial number locations—1979–86 models (720-D series)

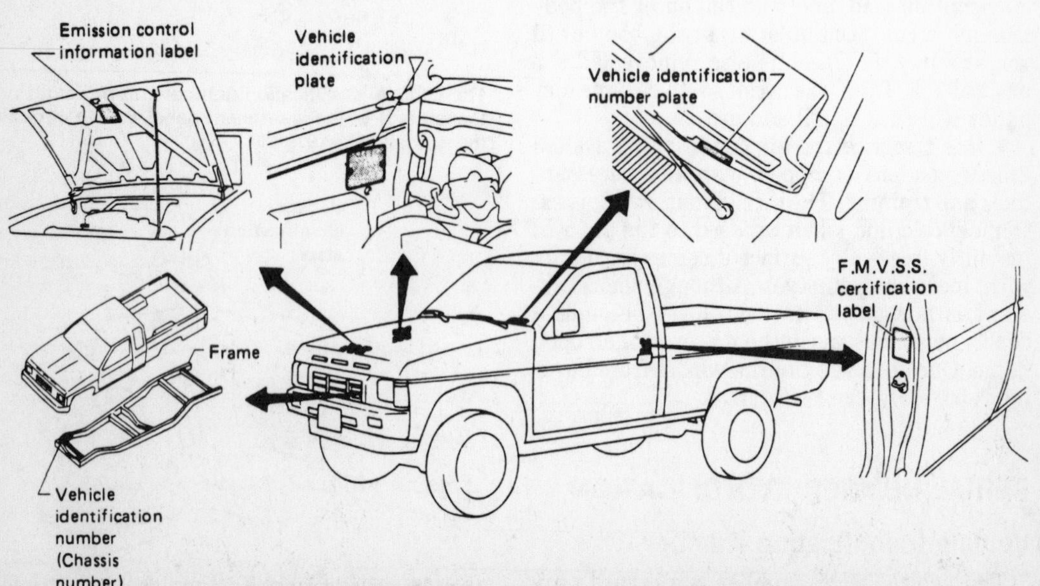

Serial number locations—1986–89 models (D21-D series)

The only change from 1970–71 is the model number, 620.

- 1973–74: The prefix letters remain the same, PL, with P indicating the 1600cc engine through mid 1973, or the 1800cc engine thereafter. The next three numbers, 620 are the model number. Four suffix letters are used. The first is either a K or a blank; K indicates an automatic transmission. The second and third suffix letter are T and U, with the same meaning as in earlier year. The fourth suffix letter is an H or blank; H indicates that no heater is installed.
- 1975–76: Three prefix letters and four suffix letters are used. The first letter is an H, for the L20B engine. The second letter is L, for left hand drive. The third letter is either a G or a blank; G is for long wheelbase (long bed) trucks.

Vehicle Identification

Model/Type	Year	Identification Number
Pick-Up/L16	1970–72	PL521
Pick-Up/L18 L20B	1973–74 1975–78	PL620
Pick-Up/L20B Z20 Z22 Z24 SD22 SD25	1979–86	720-D
Pick-Up & Pathfinder/ Z24 Z24i VG30i SD25	1986½– 1989	D21-D

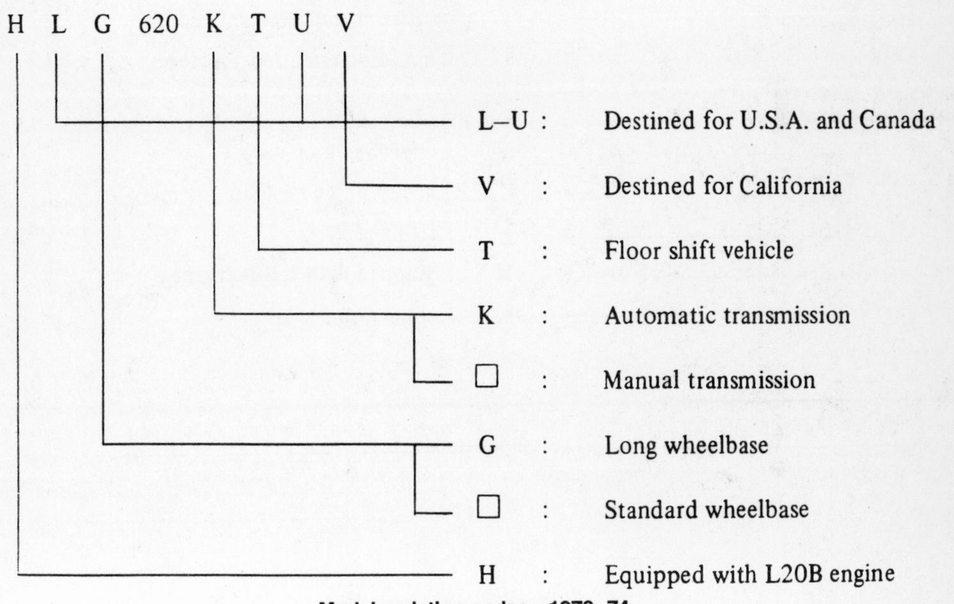

Model variation codes—1973–74

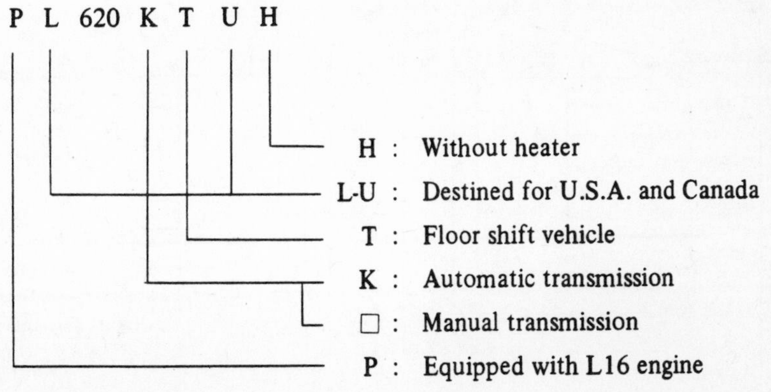

Model variation codes—1975–76

The next three numbers, 620, are the model number. The four suffix letters remain the same as in 1973–74, with the exception of the last letter in 1976, which may be a V or a blank; V indicates a California model.

- 1977–79: Four prefix and four suffix letter are used. The first letter is a K or a bland; K indicates a king cab model. The second, third, and fourth letters are the same as those used in 1975–76. The next three numbers are the model number, 620. The first suffix letter is either a K, an F, or a blank; K indicates automatic transmission, F indicates a 5-speed, a blank indicates a 4-speed. The second and third suffix

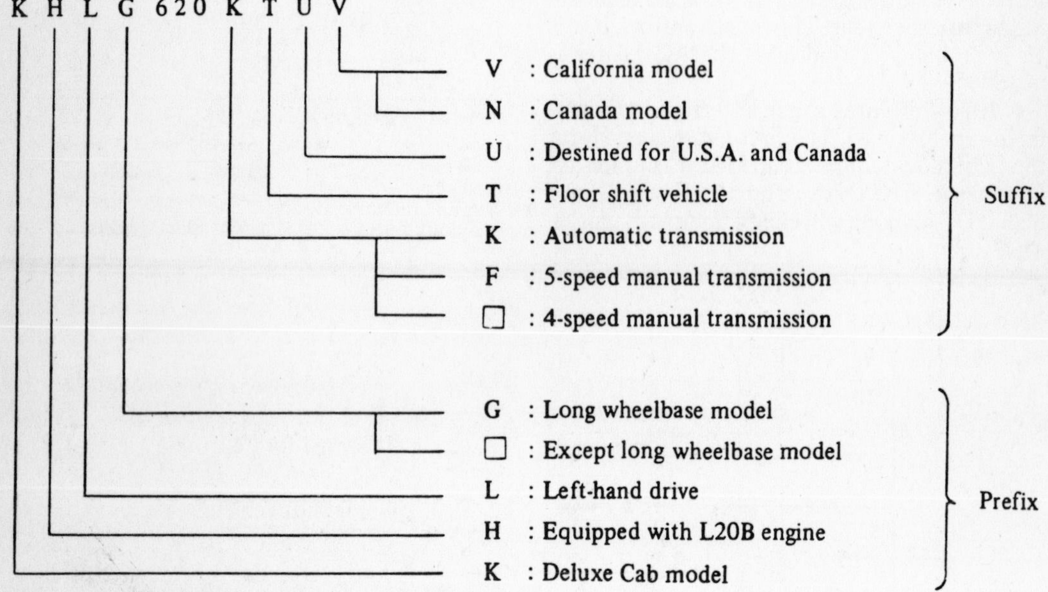

Model variation codes—1977–79

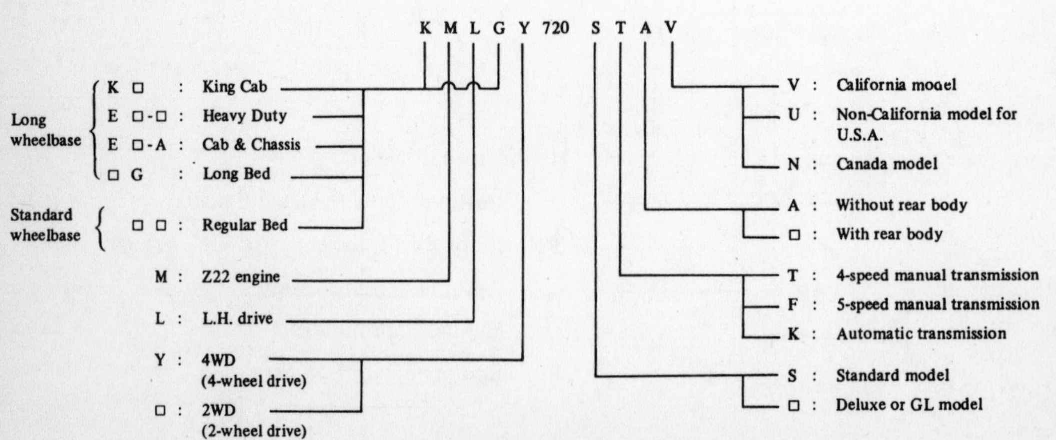

Model variation codes—1980–81

letter, T and U, have the same meaning as in earlier years. The last letter is either a V, an N, or a blank; V indicates a California model, N indicates a Canada model, a blank indicates a 49 States model.

• 1980–81: A four letter prefix for 2-wheel drive models and a five letter prefix for 4-wheel drive models followed by a three digit code denoting the truck series is used. The suffix for these years is either four letters for 2-wheel drive or two letters for 4-wheel drive.

• 1982–83: All truck models use a five letter prefix followed by the model designation, then a four letter suffix explained in the illustration.

• 1984–86 (720 Series): All truck models use a five letter prefix followed by the model desig-

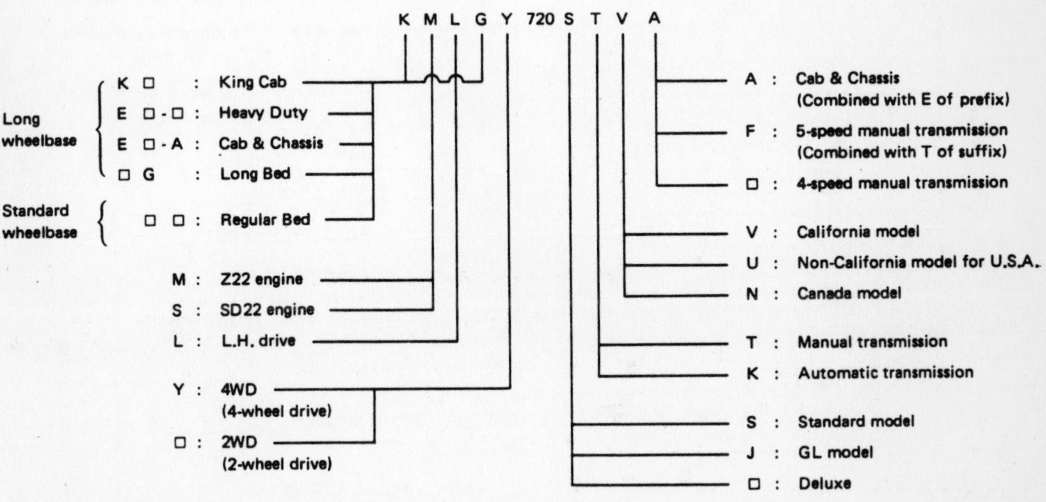

Model variation codes—1982–83

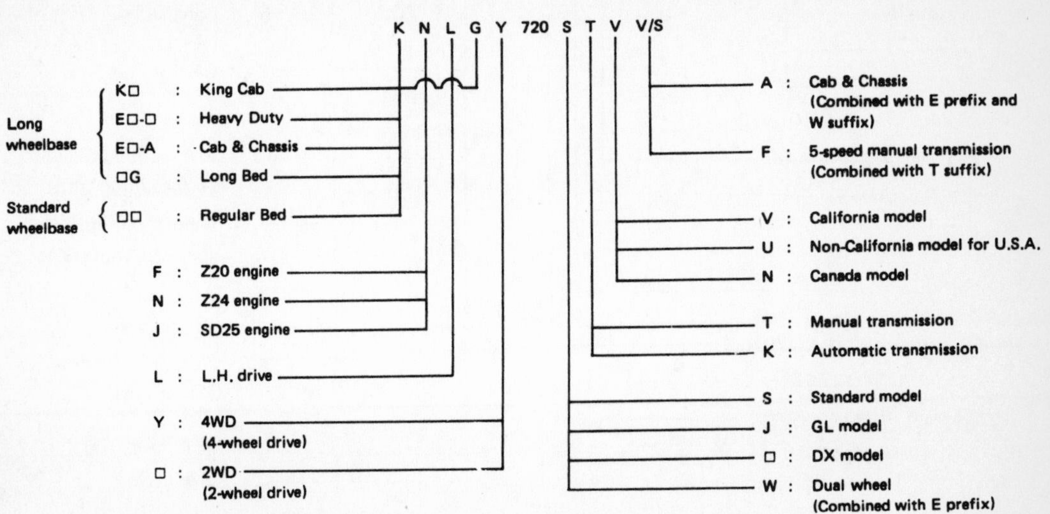

Model variation codes—1984–86 (720-D series)

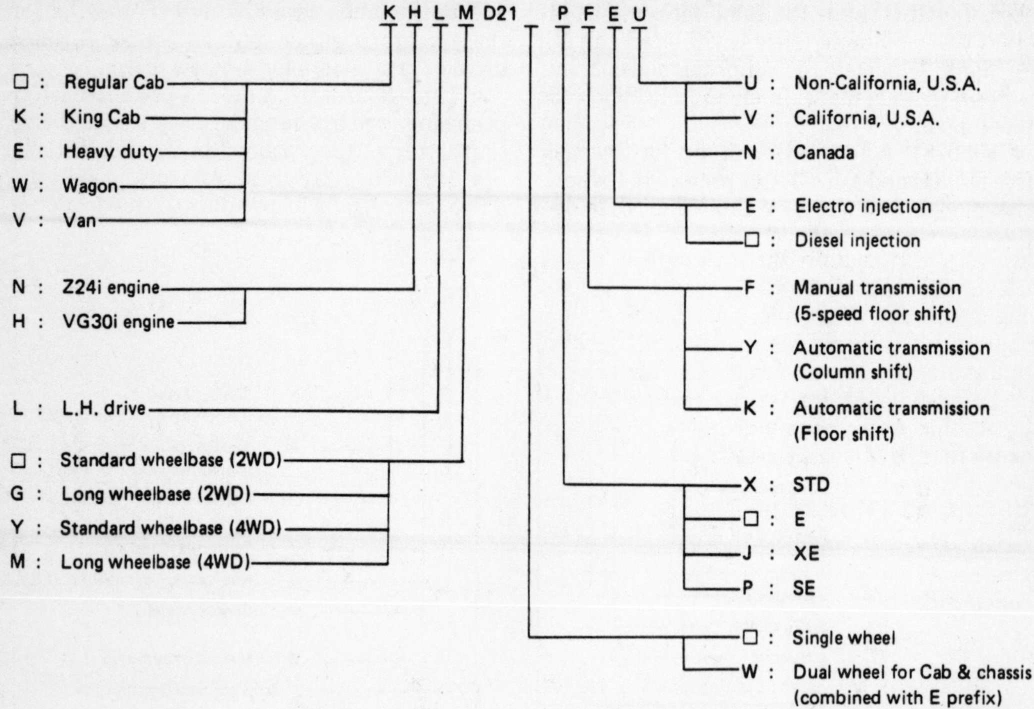

K H L M D21 _ P F E U
□ : Regular Cab
K : King Cab
E : Heavy duty
W : Wagon
V : Van
N : Z24i engine
H : VG30i engine
L : L.H. drive
□ : Standard wheelbase (2WD)
G : Long wheelbase (2WD)
Y : Standard wheelbase (4WD)
M : Long wheelbase (4WD)
U : Non-California, U.S.A.
V : California, U.S.A.
N : Canada
E : Electro injection
□ : Diesel injection
F : Manual transmission (5-speed floor shift)
Y : Automatic transmission (Column shift)
K : Automatic transmission (Floor shift)
X : STD
□ : E
J : XE
P : SE
□ : Single wheel
W : Dual wheel for Cab & chassis (combined with E prefix)

Model variation codes—1986–88 (D21-D series)

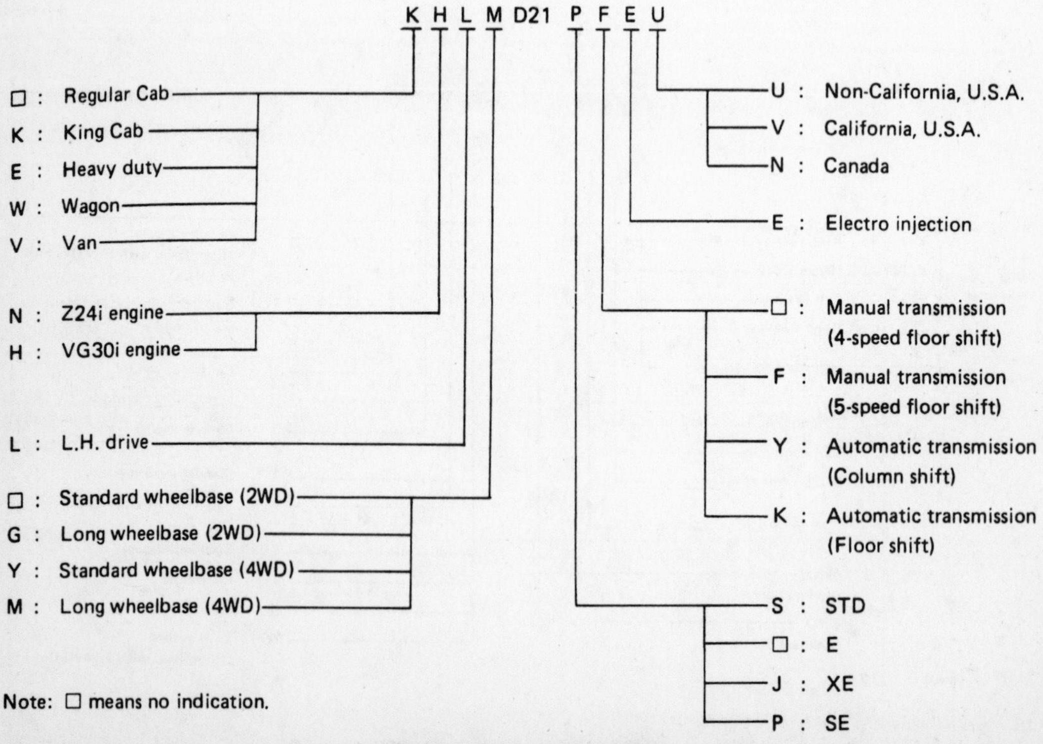

K H L M D21 P F E U
□ : Regular Cab
K : King Cab
E : Heavy duty
W : Wagon
V : Van
N : Z24i engine
H : VG30i engine
L : L.H. drive
□ : Standard wheelbase (2WD)
G : Long wheelbase (2WD)
Y : Standard wheelbase (4WD)
M : Long wheelbase (4WD)
U : Non-California, U.S.A.
V : California, U.S.A.
N : Canada
E : Electro injection
□ : Manual transmission (4-speed floor shift)
F : Manual transmission (5-speed floor shift)
Y : Automatic transmission (Column shift)
K : Automatic transmission (Floor shift)
S : STD
□ : E
J : XE
P : SE
Note: □ means no indication.

Model variation codes—1989

nation, then a five letter suffix; the last two letters separated by a slash, explained in the illustration.

- 1986–89 (D21 Series): All truck models use a four letter prefix followed by the model designation, then a five letter suffix (four on 1989 models) explained in the illustration.

The serial number on all 1970–80 models consists of a series identification (see chart) followed by a six digit production number. The serial number on all 1981–88 models has been changed to the 17-digit format. The first three digits are the World Manufacturer Identification number. The next five digits are the Vehicle Description Section (same as the series identification number above). The remaining nine digits are the production numbers.

Engine Serial Number

The engine serial number consists of an engine series identification number followed by a six digit production number.

L16, L18 and L20B Engines

The serial number is stamped on the right side of the cylinder block, just below No. 4 spark plug.

Z20, Z22, Z24 and Z24i Engines

The serial number is stamped on the left side of the cylinder block, below the No. 3 and No. 4 spark plugs.

VG30i Engines

The serial number is stamped on the cylinder block, below the rear of the right side cylinder head.

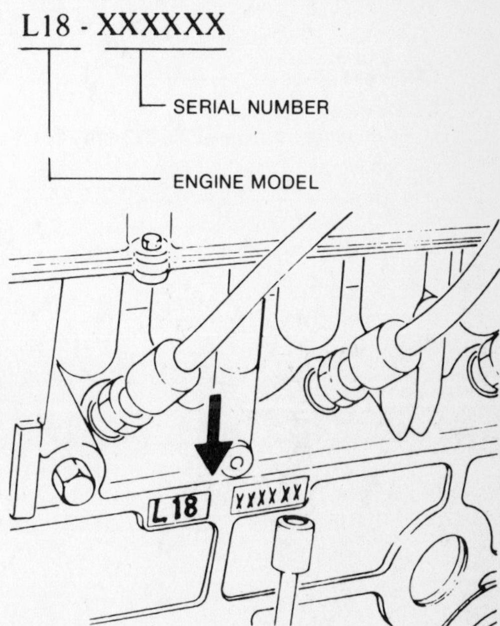

Engine serial number location—L16, L18 and L20B engines

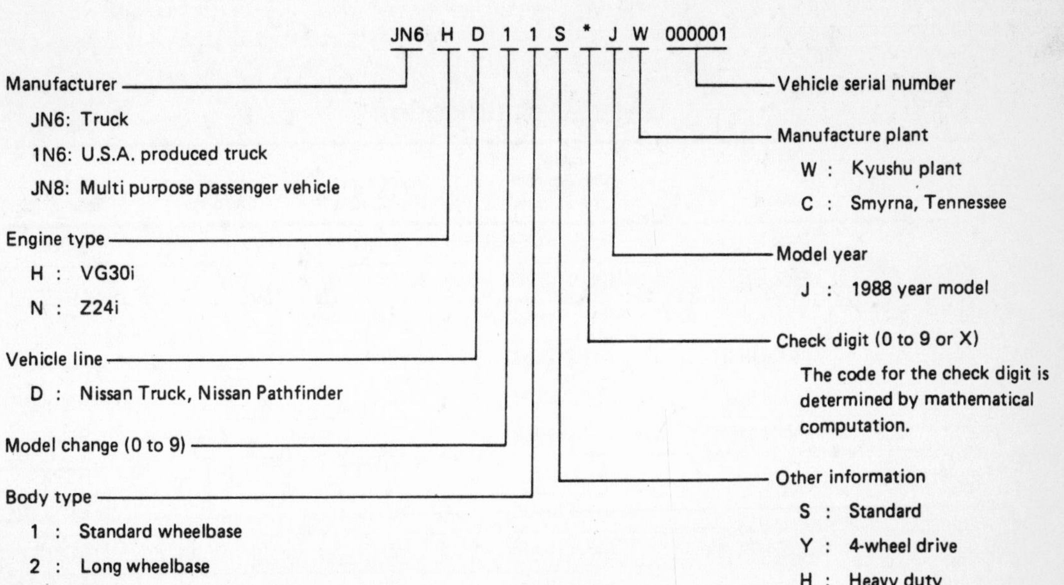

The new 17-digit VIN is used on all 1981–89 models

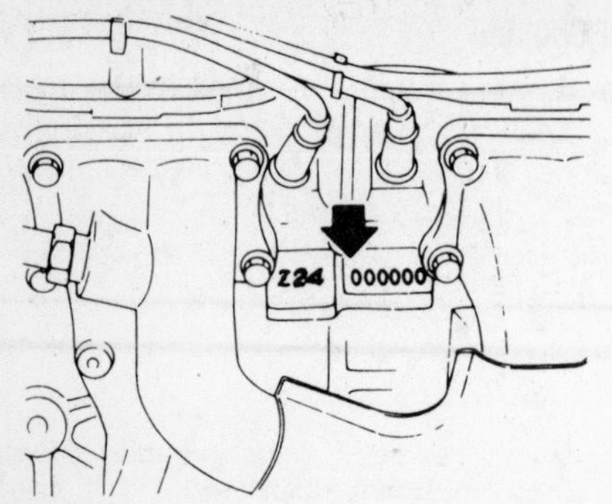

Engine serial number location—Z20, Z22 and Z24 engines

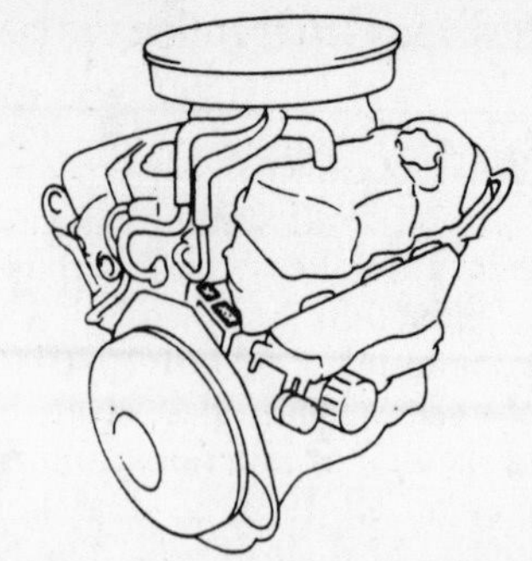

Engine serial number location—VG30i engines

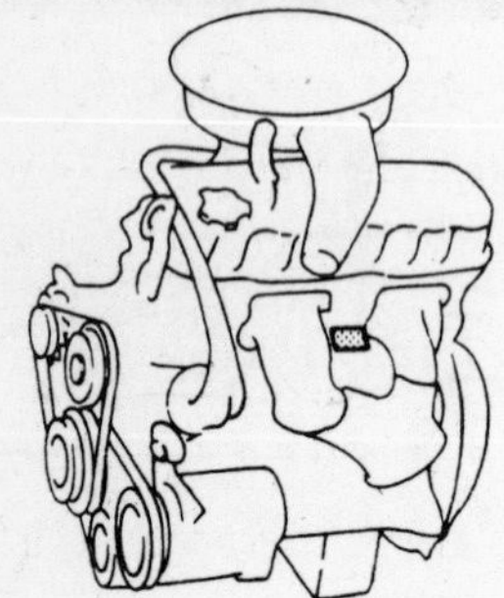

Engine serial number location—Z24i enqines

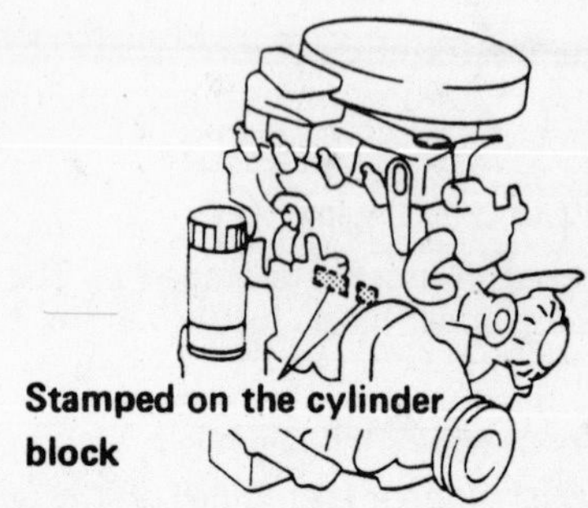

Engine serial number location—SD22 and SD25 engines

Engine Identification

Year	Model	Engine Displacement cu. in. (cc)	Engine Series Identification	No. of Cylinders	Engine Type
1970–72	Pick-Up	97.3 (1595)	L16	4	SOHC
1973–74	Pick-Up	108.0 (1770)	L18	4	SOHC
1975–80	Pick-Up	119.1 (1952)	L20B	4	SOHC
1981–83	Pick-Up	133.5 (2187)	Z22	4	SOHC
		132.0 (2164)	SD22	4	Diesel/SOHC
1984–86	Pick-Up	119.8 (1952)	Z20	4	SOHC
		146.8 (2389)	Z24	4	SOHC
		152.0 (2488)	SD25	4	Diesel/SOHC
1986½–89	Pick-Up/Pathfinder	146.8 (2389)	Z24	4	SOHC
		146.8 (2389)	Z24i	4	SOHC
		181.0 (2960)	VG30i	6	SOHC
		152.0 (2488)	SD25	4	Diesel/SOHC

SOHC: Single Overhead Camshaft

SD22 and SD25 Diesel Engines

On these engines the serial number is stamped on the right side of the cylinder block, behind the injection pump.

Transmission

The transmission serial number is stamped on the front upper face of the transmission case on manual transmissions, or on the right side of the transmission case on automatic transmissions.

Automatic transmission serial number location—1986–89 (D21-D series) exc. RE4R01A

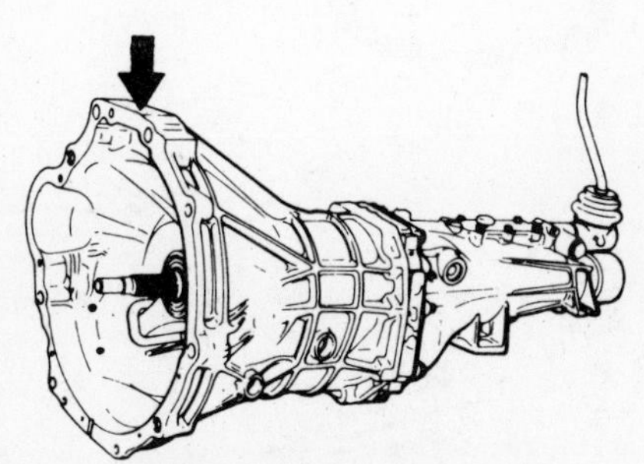

Manual transmission serial number location—1970–86

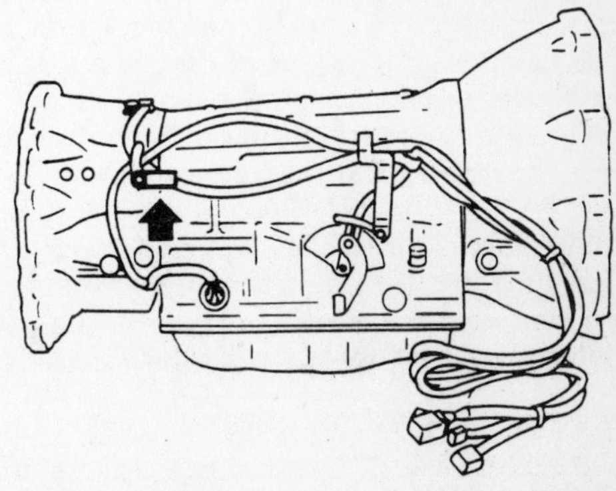

Automatic transmission serial number location—1988–89 RE4R01A

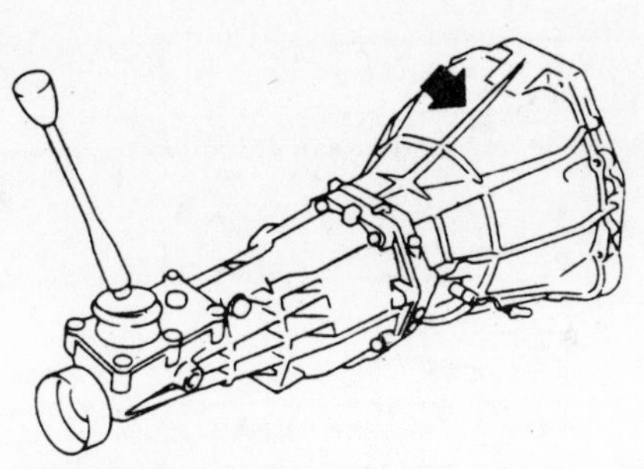

Manual transmission serial number location—1986–89 (D21-D series)

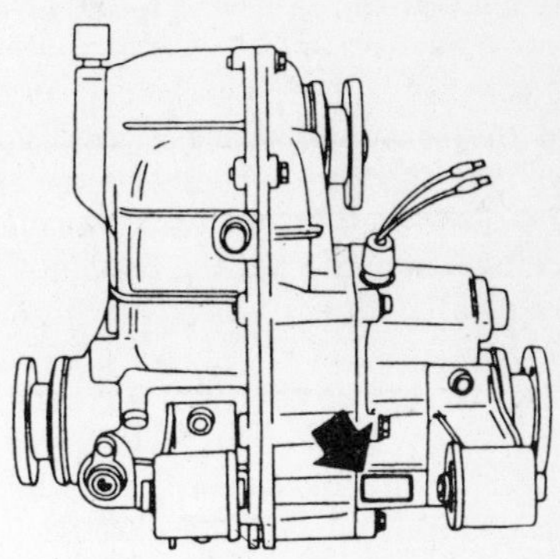

Transfer case identification number location, all except D21 series

Automatic transmission serial number location—1974–86

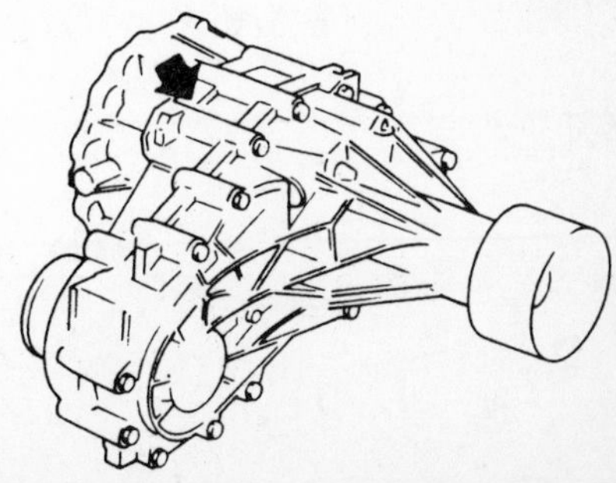

Transfer case identification number location, D21 series

ROUTINE MAINTENANCE

Air Cleaner

REMOVAL AND INSTALLATION

The element should be replaced at the recommended intervals shown in the Maintenance Intervals chart later in this chapter. If your truck is operated under severely dusty conditions or severe operating conditions, more frequent changes will certainly be necessary. Inspect the element at least twice a year. Early spring and early fall are always good times for inspection. Remove the element and check for any perforations or tears in the filter. Check the cleaner housing for signs of dirt or dust that may have leaked through the filter element or in through the snorkel tube. Position a droplight on one side of the element and look through the filter at the light. If no glow of light can be seen through the element material, replace the filter. If holes in the filter element are apparent or signs of dirt seepage through the filter are evident, replace the filter.

Air Cleaner Assembly (Housing)

1. Disconnect all hoses, ducts and vacuum tubes from the air cleaner assembly.
2. Remove the top cover wing nut (two on later models) and grommet (if equipped). Most models will also utilize three or four side clips to further secure the top of the assembly, simply pull the wire tab and release the clip; in fact air cleaners on a few engines are secured solely by means of clips (air box-to-cleaner housing). Remove the cover and lift out the filter element.
3. Remove any side mount brackets and/or retaining bolts and lift off the air cleaner assembly.
4. Clean or replace the filter element as detailed previously. Wipe clean all surfaces of the air cleaner housing and cover. Check the condition of the mounting gasket and replace it if it appears worn or broken.
5. Reposition the air cleaner assembly and install the mounting bracket and/or bolts.
6. Reposition the filter element in the case and install the cover being careful not to overtighten the wingnut(s). On round-style cleaners, be certain that the arrows on the cover lid and the snorkel match up properly.

NOTE: *Filter elements on many engines have a TOP and BOTTOM side, be sure they are inserted correctly.*

7. Reconnect all hoses, ductwork and vacuum lines.

NOTE: *Never operate the engine without the air filter element in place.*

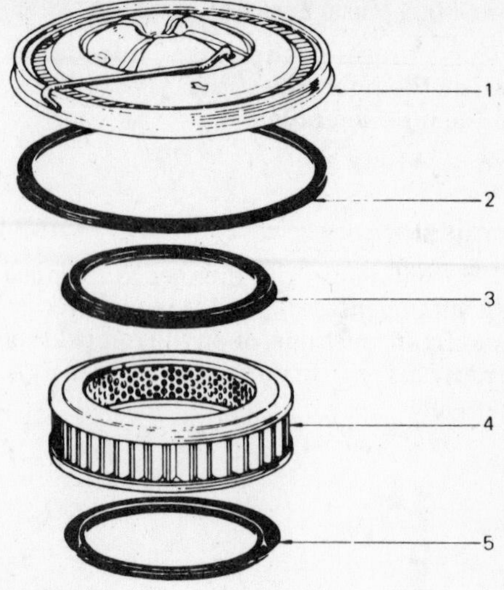
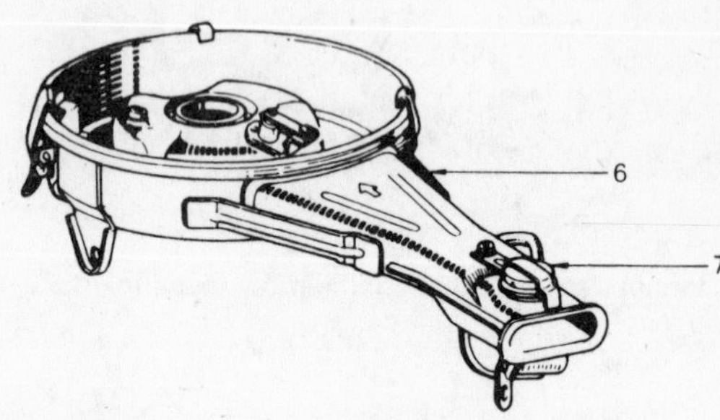

1. Cover
2. Gasket
3. Gasket
4. Cleaner element
5. Gasket
6. Case
7. Hot air intake diaphragm

Typical air cleaner element and housing assembly

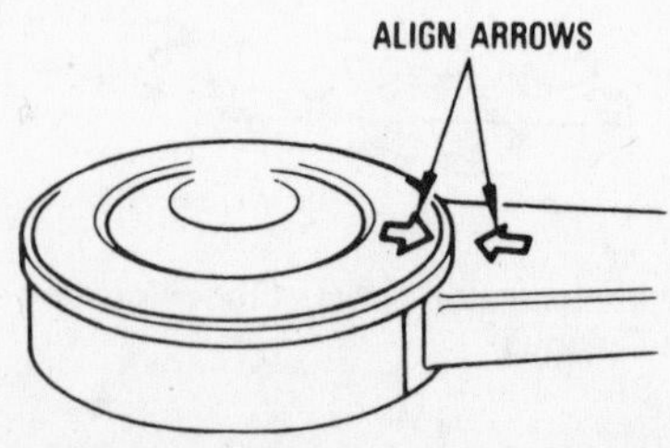

Many air cleaner assemblies have arrows on the housing and lid; always make sure they align

Sometimes the air filter can be cleaned with low pressure compressed air

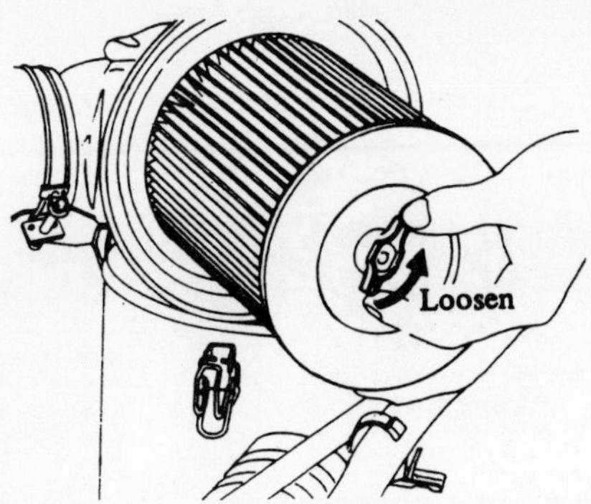

Air filter element—SD22 engines

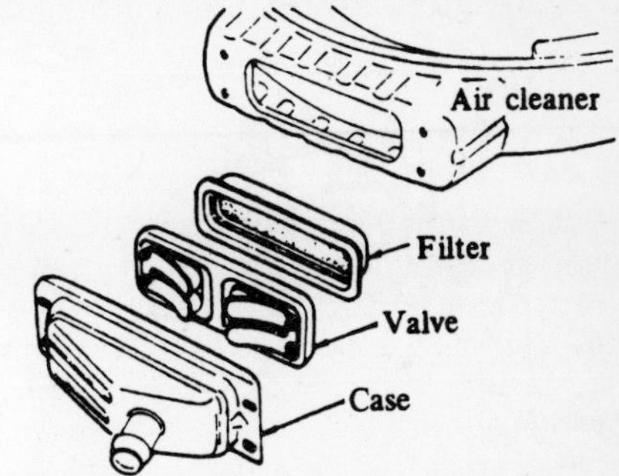

Air induction/injector valve filter—1981–86 carbureted models

Air Cleaner Element

The element can, in most cases be replaced by removing the wingnut(s) and side clips as already detailed.

On the SD22 engine, the filter element is removed with the air cleaner housing lid. Remove the wing nut at the bottom of the element and disconnect it from the lid.

Crankcase Ventilation Filter

Certain models may also utilize a cleaner-mounted crankcase ventilation filter, if so, it should also be cleaned or replaced at the same time as the regular filter element. To replace the filter, remove the air cleaner top cover and pull the filter from its housing on the side of the cleaner assembly. Push a new filter into the housing and reinstall the cover. If the filter and plastic holder need replacement, remove the clip mounting the feeder tube to the cleaner housing and then remove the assembly from the air cleaner.

Air Induction/Injection Valve Filter

1981–86 CARBURETED ENGINES

These models utilize an additional filter in the air cleaner housing and it is easily replaced. Unscrew the mounting screws and remove the valve filter case. Pull the valve out and remove the filter that lies underneath it. Install the new filter and then the valve. Pay particular attention to which way the valve is facing so that the exhaust gases will not flow backward through the system. Install the valve case.

Fuel Filter

REMOVAL AND INSTALLATION

CAUTION: *NEVER SMOKE WHEN WORKING AROUND OR NEAR GASOLINE! MAKE SURE THAT THERE IS NO ACTIVE IGNITION SOURCE NEAR YOUR WORK AREA!*

1970–83 Carbureted Engines

The fuel filter is located on the right inner fender in the engine compartment. It is a disposable cartridge type.

1. Using a pair of pliers, expand the hose clamp on one side of the filter, and slide the clamp further down the hose, past the point to which the filter pipe extends. Remove the other clamp in the same manner.
2. Grasp the hoses near the ends and twist them gently to pull them free from the filter pipes.

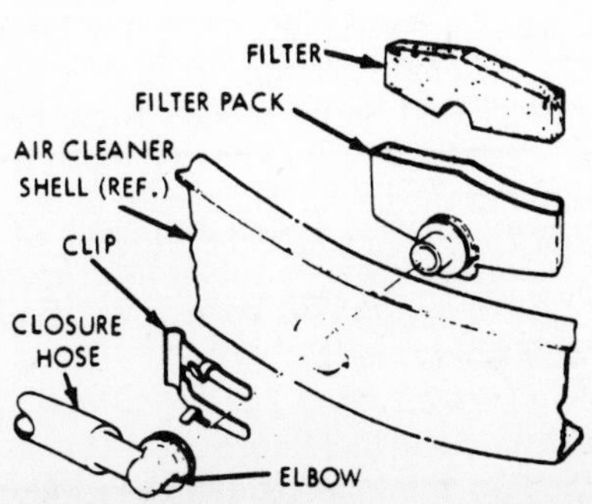

Crankcase ventilation filter

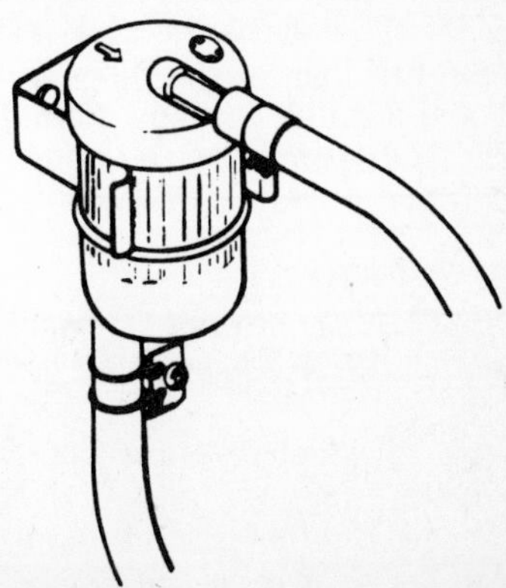
Fuel filter—1970–79

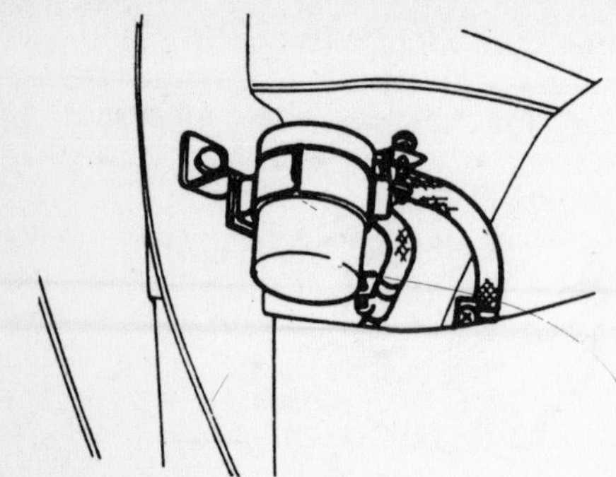

Fuel filter—1980–83

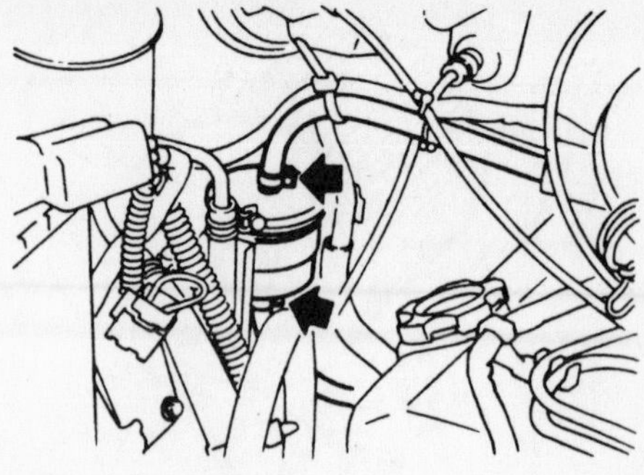

Fuel filter—1986–89 VG30i

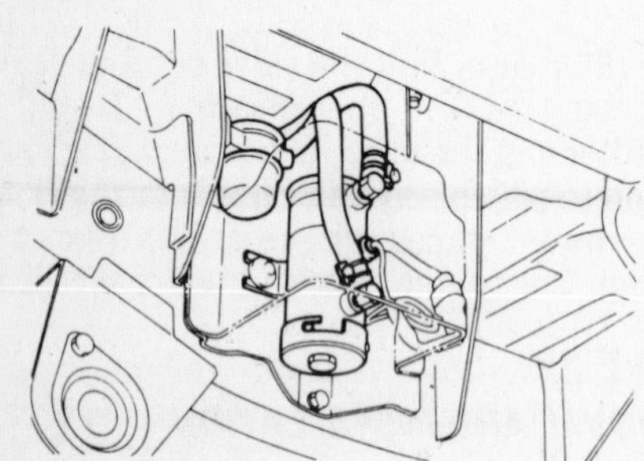

Fuel filter—1984–86

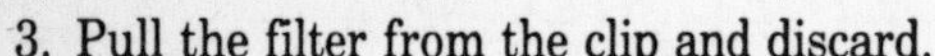

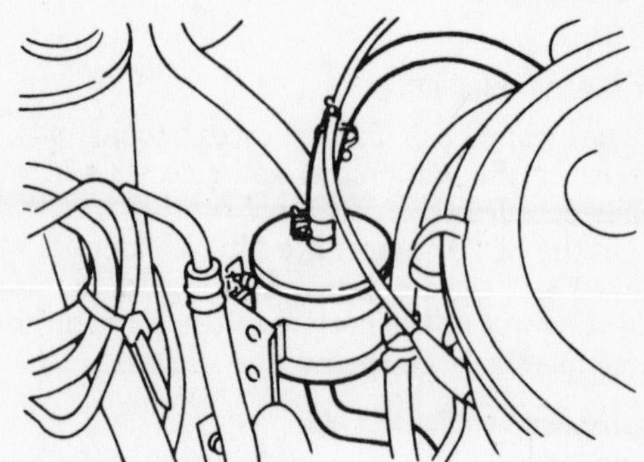

Fuel filter—1986—89 Z24i

3. Pull the filter from the clip and discard.
4. Install the new filter into the clip. Push the hoses onto the filter pipes, and slide the clamps back into position. Start the engine and check for leaks.

1984–86 Carbureted Engines

The fuel filter is located on the inside of the frame above the left rear spring front shackle.

Changing the filter is VERY awkward. Since it is inline and below tank level, fuel will pour from the fuel lines when they are disconnected from the filter. The only way of preventing this, is to siphon all of the gasoline from the tank before replacing the filter. It would, therefore, be a good idea to run the tank almost dry before changing the filter. Once the tank is dry, disconnect the fuel lines at the filter, unbolt the old filter and install a new one. Reconnect the fuel lines, fill the tank, start the engine and check for leaks.

Fuel Injected Engines

WARNING: *Never attempt to remove the fuel filter without first relieving the fuel system pressure!*

1. Release the fuel pressure from the fuel line as follows:
   a. Remove the fuel pump fuse at the fuse box.
   b. Start the engine.
   c. After the engine stalls, crank the engine two or three times to make sure that the fuel pressure is released.
   d. Turn the ignition switch off and reinstall the fuel pump fuse.
2. Loosen the hose clamps at the fuel inlet and outlet lines and slide each line off the filter nipples.
3. Remove the fuel filter.
4. Replace the fuel filter. Always be sure to use new hose clamps.

Diesel Engines

Two filters are used in the fuel system on 1981–86 720 Series models; a large spin-on type and a smaller inline type. The larger filter, called the main filter, is located on the right front fender inner liner. The smaller filter, called the primary filter, is located on the firewall, in the engine compartment.

On 1986–87 D20 Series models there is one filter and a sedimentor/fuel heater. Both units can be found in the back right corner of the engine compartment, in a bracket attached to the firewall.

1981–86 720 SERIES MAIN FILTER

1. Disconnect the fuel filter sensor connector (if equipped) at the lower end of the filter.
2. Drain the fuel from the filter (see Chapter

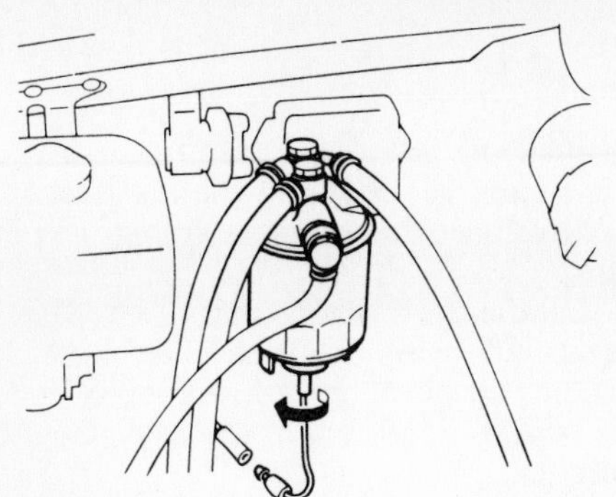

Fuel filter (main)—1981–86 SD22 and SD25 engines (720-D series)

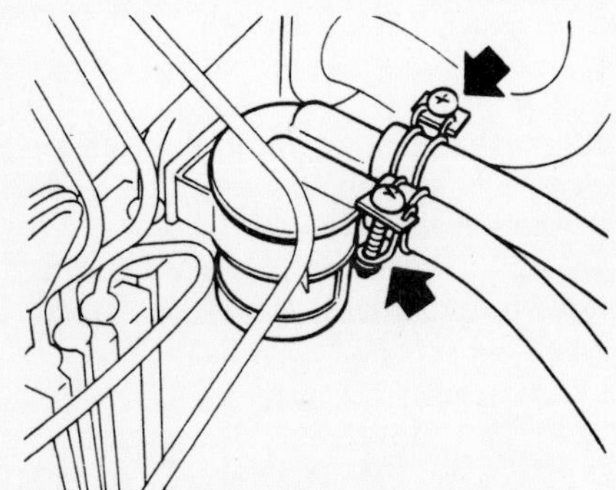

Fuel filter (primary)—1981–83 SD22 engines

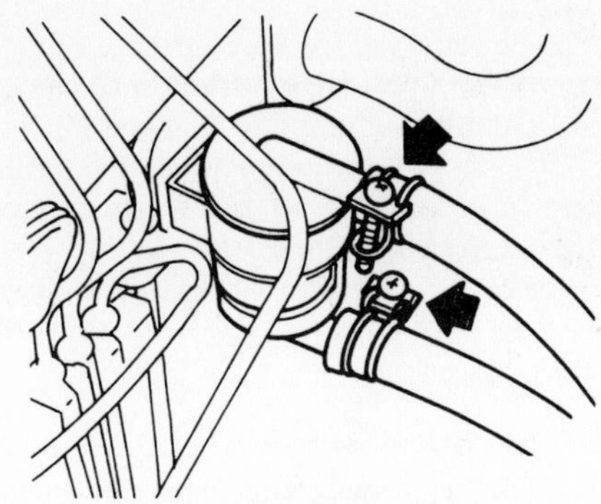

Fuel filter (primary)—1984–86 SD25 engine (720-D series)

When installing the primary filter on 1984–86 SD25 engines (720-D series), be sure that the word UPPER faces upward

5), loosen the two mounting bolts and remove the filter.

3. Unscrew the filter from the housing. An oil filter strap wrench may come in handy when removing the filter.

4. Coat the filter gasket lightly with diesel fuel and then screw it in hand tight. Next, use the strap wrench and turn the filter ¾ turn more.

5. Mount the filter assembly, tighten the bolts and connect the sensor switch.

6. Bleed the fuel system.

7. Using the priming pump on the injection pump, fill the filter with fuel and check for leaks.

1981–86 720 SERIES
PRIMARY FILTER

1. Using a pair of pliers, expand the hose clamp on one side of the filter, and slide the clamp further down the hose, past the point to which the filter pipe extends. Remove the other clamp in the same manner.

2. Grasp the hoses near the ends and twist them gently to pull them free from the filter pipes.

3. Pull the filter from the clip and discard.

4. Install the new filter into the clip. Push the hoses onto the filter pipes, and slide the clamps back into position. Start the engine and check for leaks.

NOTE: *On the SD25, be sure to install the primary fuel filter with the word UPPER facing upward!*

1986–87 D21 SERIES

1. Position a rag underneath the filter and remove the fuel line.

2. Drain the fuel from the filter as detailed in Chapter 5.

3. Unscrew the fuel filter from the bracket head. It should come off with your hands. If not, use an oil filter strap wrench to help it along, but be careful!

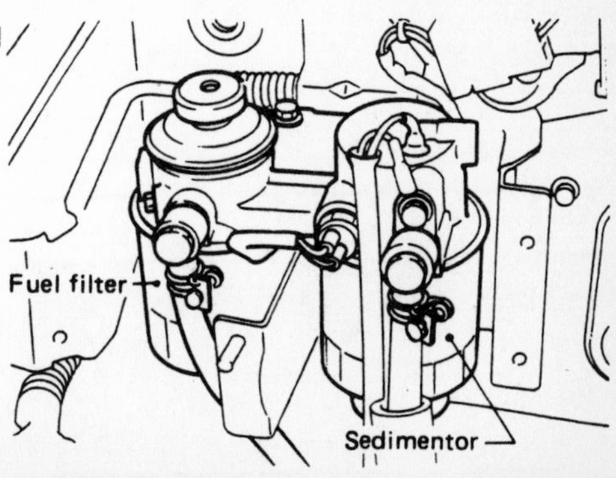

Fuel filter and sedimentor—1986–87 SD25 engines (D21-D series)

4. Clean the fuel filter mounting surface on the bracket. Coat the rubber gasket on a new filter with diesel fuel and then screw it into the bracket until it is snug. Tighten it an additional $^2/_3$ turn. Do not use a strap wrench for installation!

5. Bleed the fuel system, start the engine and check for any leaks.

DRAINING THE DIESEL FUEL FILTER

WARNING: *When the fuel filter warning light or buzzer comes on, the water in the fuel filter must be drained immediately.*

1. Raise the hood and position a small pan or jar underneath the main filter to catch the water about to be released.

2. Reach under the fuel filter and, on 1981–83 models, remove the fuel filter sensor connector. On 1984–87 models, simply loosen the drain valve under the filter 4 or 5 times until the water begins to come out. DO NOT remove the drain valve/connector on 1984–87 models.

3. Depressing the priming pump will usually speed the removal of water from the filter. Its on the side of the injection pump housing on 1981–86 models (720 series) and on top of the filter mounting bracket on 1986–87 models (D21 series). Pump the priming pump until fuel is the only substance being forced out.

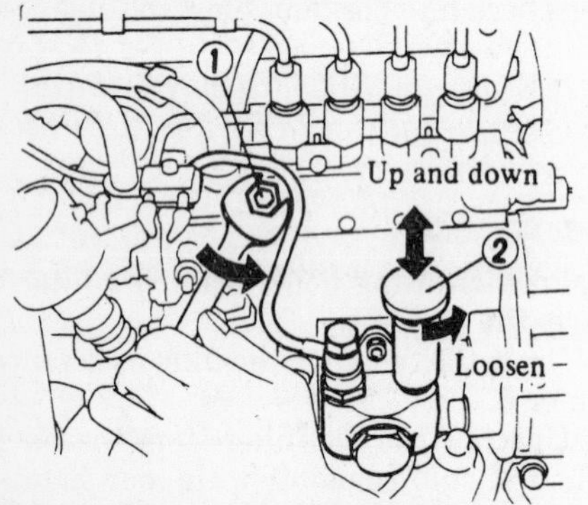

Priming pump (2) and air vent screw (1)—1981–86 SD22 and SD25 engines (720-D series)

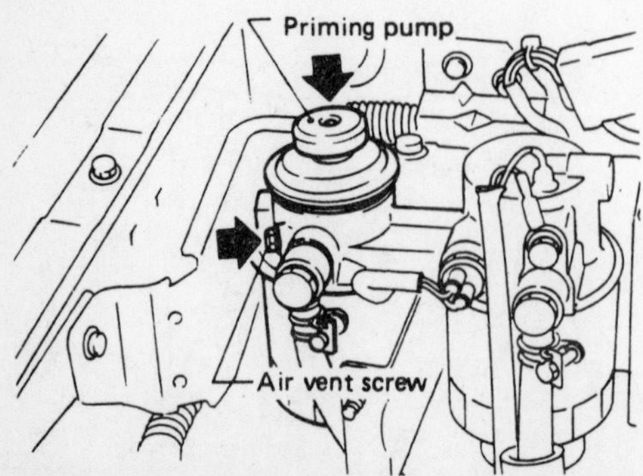

Priming pump and air vent screw—1986–87 SD25 engines (D21-D series)

BLEEDING THE FUEL SYSTEM

Air should be bled from the fuel system on diesel engines whenever the system has been opened.

1. Locate the priming pump. On 1981–86 models (720 series), its on the side of the injection pump (remove the cap); on 1986–87 models (D21 series), its on top of the filter mounting bracket.

2. Rotate the priming pump counterclockwise (720 series only) and then loosen the air vent screw on the side of the injection pump housing (720 series) or on the side of the filter mounting bracket (D21 series).

NOTE: *SD22 engines utilize two (2) air vent screws.*

3. Pump the priming pump until all air has been expelled through the vent hole and then tighten the air vent screw.

4. On 720 series models, press the priming pump down and turn it clockwise. Install the pump cap.

PCV Valve

The PCV valve regulates crankcase ventilation during various engine operating conditions. At high vacuum (idle speed and partial load range) it will open slightly and at low vacuum (full throttle) it will open fully. This causes vapor to be removed from the crankcase by the engine vacuum and then sucked into the combustion chamber where it is dissipated.

NOTE: *The PCV system will not function properly unless the oil filler cap is tightly sealed. Check the gasket on the cap and be certain it is not leaking. Replace the cap or gasket or both if necessary to ensure proper sealing.*

REMOVAL AND INSTALLATION

1. Check the ventilation hoses and lines for leaks or clogging. Clean or replace as necessary.

2. With the engine running at idle, locate the

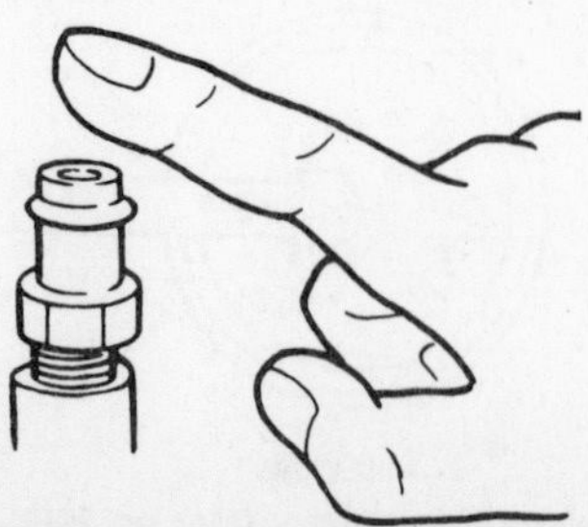

A strong suction should be felt when a finger is placed over the PCV valve with the engine idling

PCV valve and remove the ventilation hose from the valve; a strong hissing sound should be heard as air passes through the valve.

3. With the engine still idling, place your finger over the valve; a strong vacuum should be felt.

4. If the PCV valve failed either of the preceding two checks, it will require replacement.

5. Locate the PCV valve in the cylinder head cover or intake manifold and remove it by unscrewing it and then pulling it upward.

6. To install, simply slip the hose back onto the proper end of the PCV valve and then press it into the retaining grommet or screw it back in.

7. An additional check without removing the valve could be: with the engine running, remove the ventilator hose from the PCV valve. If the valve is working, a hissing noise will be heard as air passes through the valve and a strong vacuum should be felt immediately when the valve inlet is blocked with a finger. If the valve is suspected of being plugged, it should be replaced.

8. For further information on the PCV system, please refer to Chapter 4.

Air Injection/Induction Valve Filter

REMOVAL AND INSTALLATION

1975–80 Carbureted Engines
1986–89 Fuel Injected Engines

Regular maintenance for this component includes a check of the drive belt tension at the specified interval, and replacement of the air pump air filter every 24,000 miles (40,000 km). The air filter case is located in the left front of the engine compartment on most models. To replace the air filter, simply unscrew the wing nut(s) securing the cover to the case, withdraw the old filter, install the new one, and reinstall the case. More information on the air pump system can be found in Chapter 4.

1981–86 Carbureted Engines

These models utilize an air cleaner-mounted valve and filter. Removal and installation procedures are detailed in the Air Cleaner section.

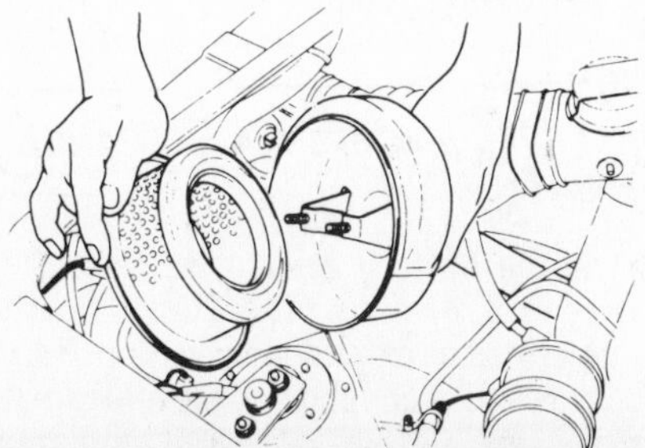

Air pump filter—1975–80 carbureted engines

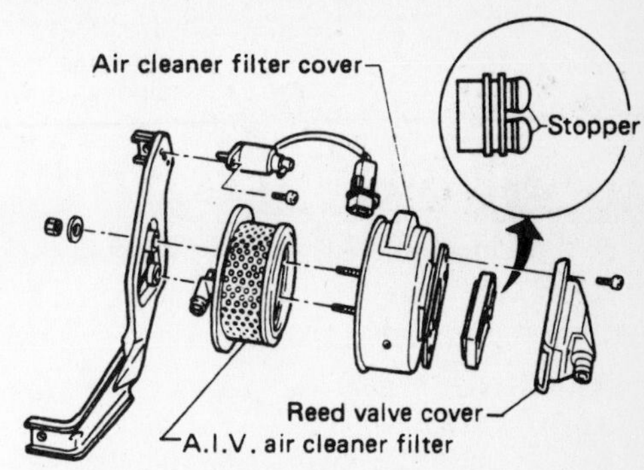

Air pump filter—1986–89 fuel injected engines

Evaporative Canister

SERVICING

Gasoline Engines Only

Check the evaporation control system every 15,000 miles (24,000 km). Check the fuel and vapor lines and hoses for proper connections and correct routing as well as condition. Replace damaged or deteriorated parts as necessary. Remove and check the operation of the check valve on 1970–75 models in the following manner:

1. With all the hoses disconnected from the valve, apply air pressure to the fuel tank side of the valve. The air should flow through the valve and exit the crankcase side of the valve. If the valve does not behave in the above manner, replace it.

2. Apply air pressure to the crankcase side of the valve. Air should not pass to either of the other two outlets.

3. When air pressure is applied to the carburetor side of the valve, the air should pass through to exit out the fuel tank and/or the crankcase side of the valve.

On 1975–89 models, the flow guide valve is replaced with a carbon filled canister which stores fuel vapors until the engine is started,

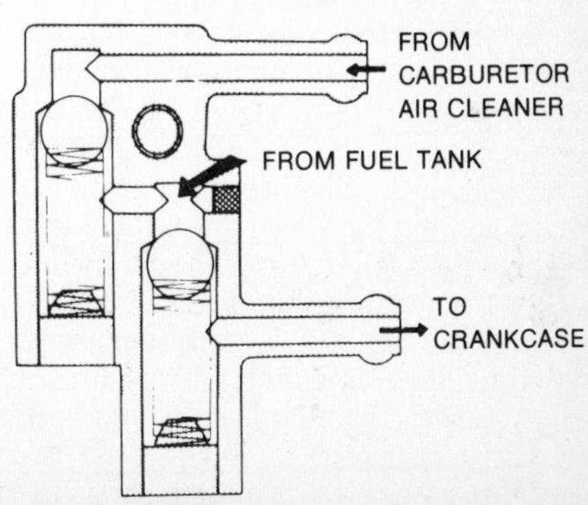

Diagram of the evaporative emission check valve

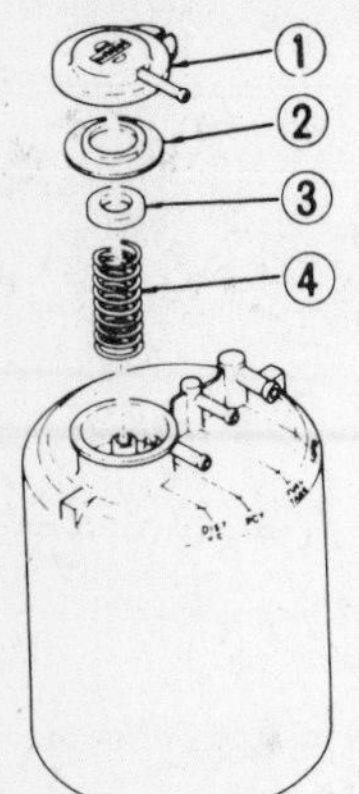

1. Cover
2. Diaphragm
3. Retainer
4. Spring

Components of the carbon canister purge control valve—1975 and later models

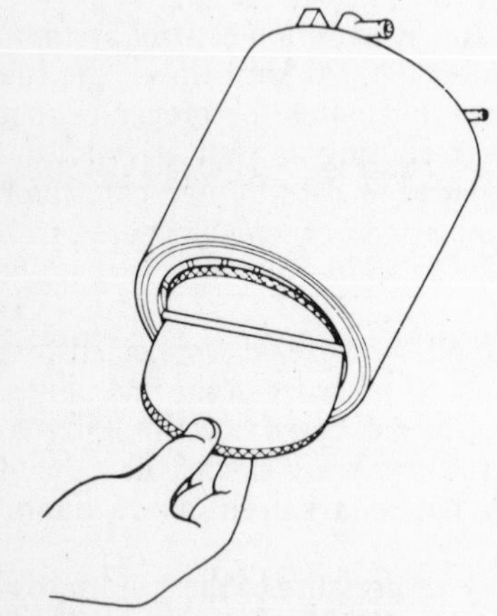

Replacing the carbon canister filter

the vapors are then drawn into the combustion chambers and burned.

To check the operation of the carbon canister purge control valve, disconnect the rubber hose between the canister control valve and the T-fitting, at the T-fitting. Apply vacuum to the hose leading to the control valve. The vacuum condition should be maintained indefinitely. If the control valve leaks, remove the top cover of the valve and check for a dislocated or cracked diaphragm. If the diaphragm is damaged, a repair kit containing a new diaphragm, retainer, and spring is available and should be installed.

The carbon canister has an air filter in the bottom of the canister. Most filters are replaceable. The filter element should be checked once a year or every 15,000 miles (24,000 km); more frequently if the truck is operated in dusty areas. Replace the filter by pulling it out of the bottom of the canister and installing a new one.

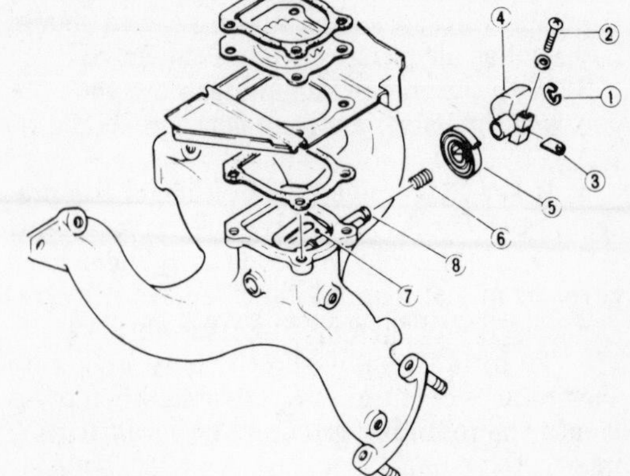

1. Snap ring
2. Lock bolt
3. Key
4. Counterweight
5. Thermostatic spring
6. Coil spring
7. Heat control shaft
8. Valve shaft

Components of the heat control valve

Heat Riser

SERVICING

The heat control valve (heat riser) is a thermostatically operated valve used on gasoline engines in the exhaust manifold. It is used only on 1975–77 trucks. It opens when the engine is warming up, to direct hot exhaust gases to the intake manifold, in order to preheat the incoming air/fuel mixture. If it sticks shut, the result will be frequent stalling during warm-up, especially in cold or damp weather. If it sticks open, the result will be a rough idle after the engine is warm.

The heat control valve should be checked for free operation every six months or 6000 miles (9600 km). Simply give the counterweight a twirl (engine cold) to ascertain that no binding exists. If the valve sticks, apply a heat control solvent specially formulated for the purpose to the ends of the shaft. This solvent is available at most auto parts stores. Sometimes lightly rapping the end of the shaft with a plastic mallet (engine hot) will break it loose. If this fails, the components will have to be removed from the truck for further repairs.

Battery

FLUID LEVEL (EXCEPT MAINTENANCE FREE BATTERIES)

Check the battery electrolyte level at least once a month, or more often in hot weather or during periods of extended operation. The level can be checked through the case on translucent polypropylene batteries; the cell caps must be removed on other models. The electrolyte level

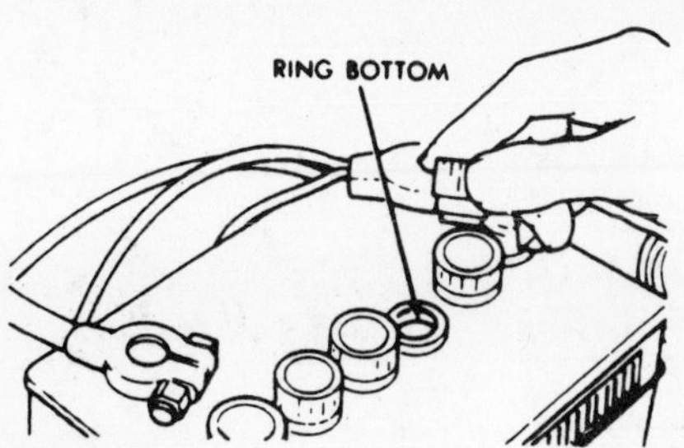

Fill each battery cell to the bottom of the split ring with distilled water

in each cell should be kept filled to the split ring inside, or the line marked on the outside of the case.

If the level is low, add only distilled water, or colorless, odorless drinking water, through the opening until the level is correct. Each cell is completely separate from the others, so each must be checked and filled individually.

If water is added in freezing weather, the truck should be driven several miles to allow the water to mix with the electrolyte. Otherwise, the battery could freeze.

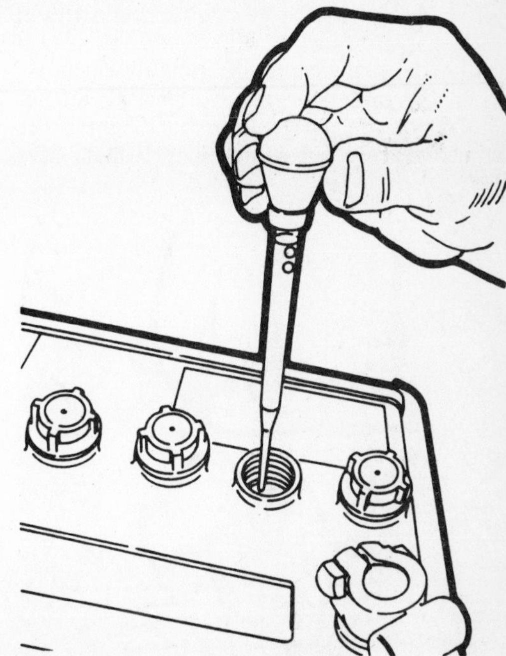

The specific gravity of the battery can be checked with a simple float-type hydrometer

SPECIFIC GRAVITY (EXCEPT MAINTENANCE FREE BATTERIES)

At least once a year, check the specific gravity of the battery. It should be between 1.20 in.Hg and 1.26 in.Hg at room temperature.

The specific gravity can be check with the use of an hydrometer, an inexpensive instrument available from many sources, including auto parts stores. The hydrometer has a squeeze bulb at one end and a nozzle at the other. Battery electrolyte is sucked into the hydrometer until the float is lifted from its seat. The specific gravity is then read by noting the position of the float. Generally, if after charging, the specific gravity between any two cells varies more than 50 points (0.50), the battery is bad and should be replaced.

It is not possible to check the specific gravity in this manner on sealed (maintenance-free) batteries. Instead, the indicator built into the top of the case must be relied on to display any signs of battery deterioration. If the indicator is dark, the battery can be assumed to be OK. If the indicator is light, the specific gravity is low, and the battery should be charged or replaced.

Battery State of Charge at Room Temperature

Specific Gravity Reading	Charged Condition
1.260–1.280	Fully Charged
1.230–1.250	¾ Charged
1.200–1.220	½ Charged
1.170–1.190	¼ Charged
1.140–1.160	Almost no Charge
1.110–1.130	No Charge

CABLES AND CLAMPS

Once a year, the battery terminals and the cable clamps should be cleaned. Loosen the clamps and remove the cables, negative cable first. On batteries with posts on top, the use of a puller specially made for the purpose is recommended. These are inexpensive, and available in auto parts stores. Side terminal battery cables are secured with a bolt.

Clean the cable lamps and the battery terminal with a wire brush, until all corrosion, grease, etc., is removed and the metal is shiny. It is especially important to clean the inside of the clamp thoroughly, since a small deposit of foreign material or oxidation there will prevent a sound electrical connection and inhibit either starting or charging. Special tools are available for cleaning these parts, one type for conventional batteries and another type for side terminal batteries.

Before installing the cables, loosen the battery holddown clamp or strap, remove the battery and check the battery tray. Clear it of any debris, and check it for soundness. Rust should be wire brushed away, and the metal given a coat of anti-rust paint. Replace the battery and tighten the holddown clamp or strap securely, but be careful not to overtighten, which will crack the battery case.

After the clamps and terminals are clean, reinstall the cables, negative cable last; do not hammer on the clamps to install. Tighten the clamps securely, but do not distort them. Give

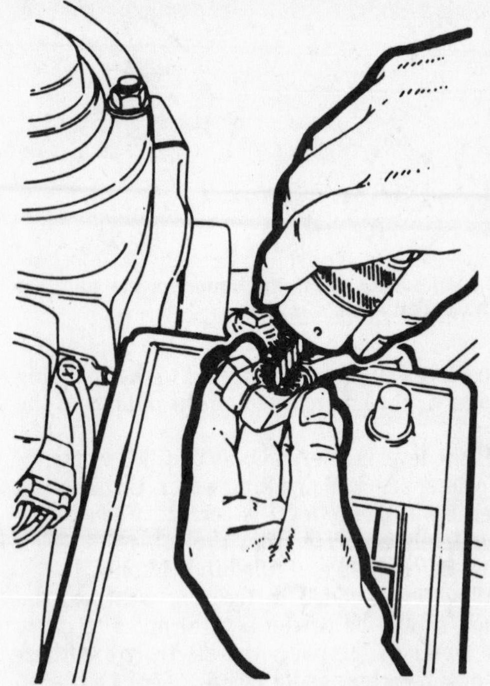

Clean the inside of the clamps with a wire brush, or the special tool

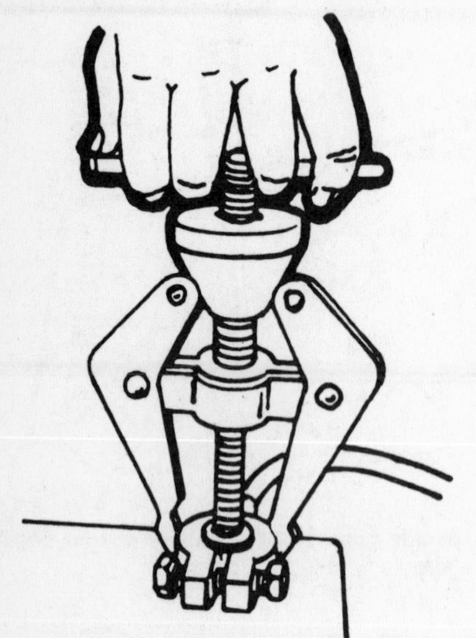

Special pullers are available to remove cable clamps

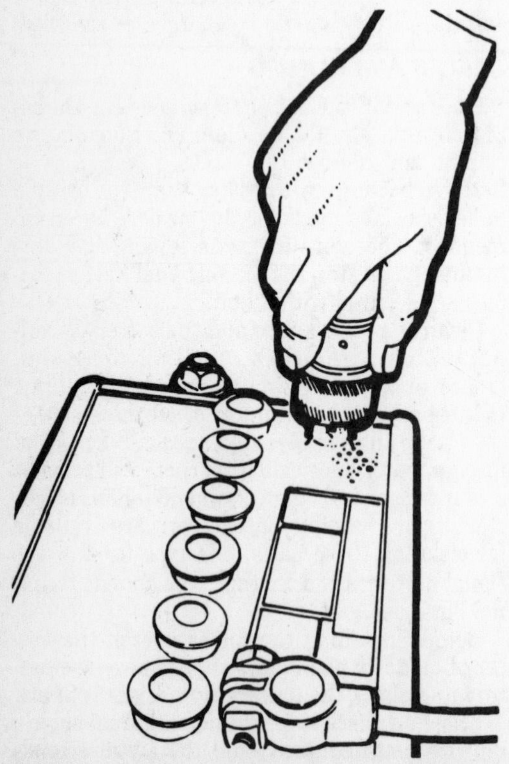

Clean the battery posts with a wire brush, or the special tool shown

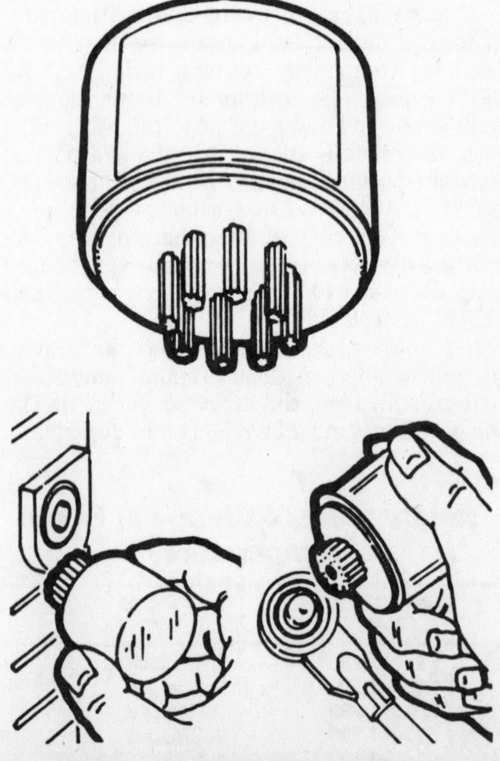

Special tools are also available for cleaning the posts and clamps on side terminal batteries

the clamps and terminals a thin external coat of grease after installation, to retard corrosion.

Check the cables at the same time that the terminals are cleaned. If the cable insulation is cracked or broken, or if the ends are frayed, the cable should be replaced with a new cable of the same length and gauge.

CAUTION: *Keep flame or sparks away from the battery; it gives off explosive hydrogen gas! Battery electrolyte contains sulphuric acid! If you should splash any on your skin or in your eyes, flush the affected area with plenty of clear water. If it lands in your eyes, get medical help immediately!*

REPLACEMENT

When it becomes necessary to replace the battery, be sure to select a new battery with a cold cranking power rating equal to or greater than the battery originally installed. Deterioration, embrittlement and just plain aging of the battery cables, starter motor and associated wires makes the battery's job all the more difficult in successive years. The slow increase in electrical resistance over time makes it prudent to install a new battery with a greater capacity than the old. Details on battery removal and installation are covered in Chapter 3.

Drive Belts

Check the condition of the drive belts and check the belt tension at least every 15,000 miles (24,000 km).

1. Inspect the belts for signs of glazing or cracking. A glazed belt will be perfectly smooth from slippage, while a good belt will have a slight texture of fabric visible. Cracks will generally start at the inner edge of the belt and run outward. Replace the belt at the first sign of cracking or if the glazing is severe.
2. Belt tension does not refer to play or droop. By placing your thumb midway between the two pulleys, it should be possible to depress the belt ¼–½". If any of the belts can be depressed more than this, or cannot be depressed this much, adjust the tension. Inadequate tension will always result in slippage or wear, while

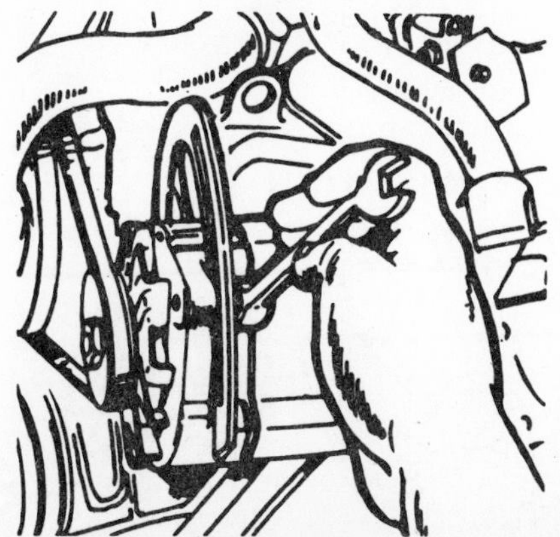

To adjust belt tension or to replace belts, first lossen the components mounting and adjusting bolts slightly

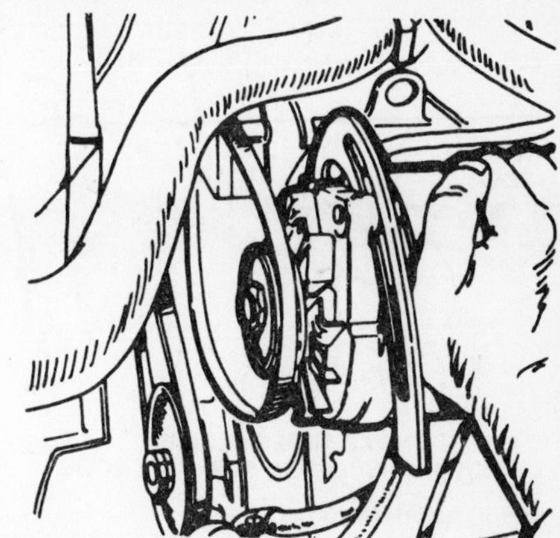

Push the component toward the engine and slip off the belt

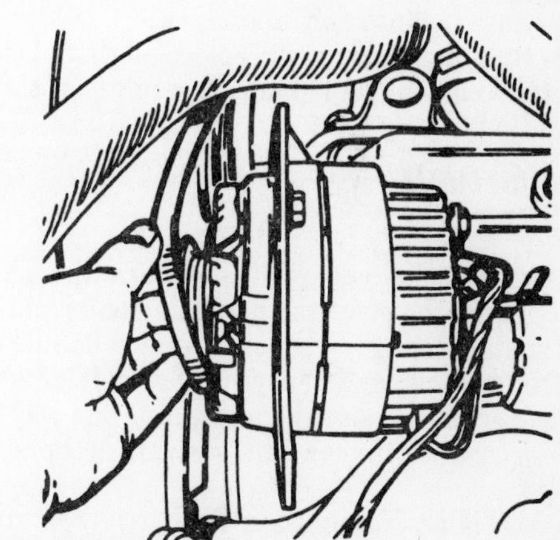

Slip the new belt over the pulley

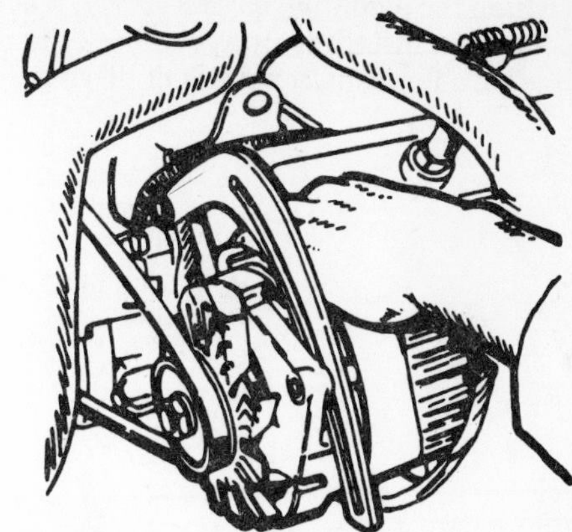

Pull outward on the component and tighten the mounting bolts

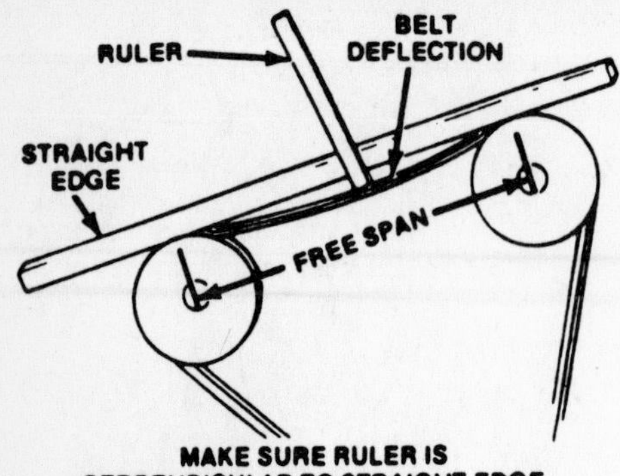

Measuring belt deflection

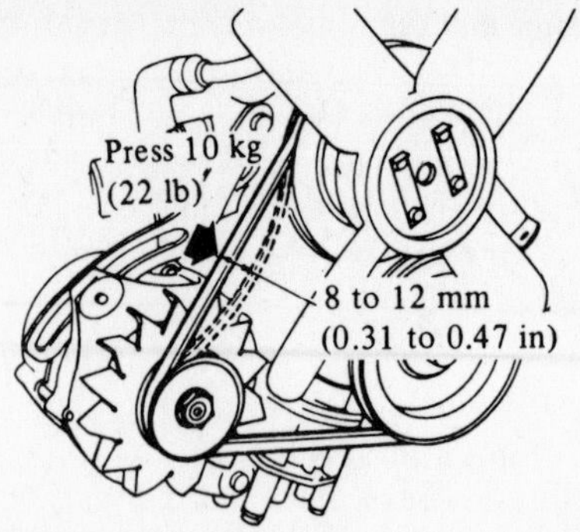

Checking the drive belt tension—1970–74

excessive tension will damage pulley bearings and cause belts to fray and crack.

3. Its not a bad idea to replace all drive belts at 60,000 miles (96,000 km) regardless of their condition.

ADJUSTMENT

Alternator

To adjust the tension of the alternator drive belt, loosen the pivot and mounting bolts on the alternator. Using a wooden hammer handle or a broomstick, or even your hand if you're strong enough, move the alternator one way or the other until the tension is within acceptable limits.

CAUTION: *Never use a screwdriver or any other metal device such as a prybar, as a lever when adjusting the alternator belt tension!*

Tighten the mounting bolts securely. If a new belt has been installed, always recheck the tension after a few hundred miles of driving.

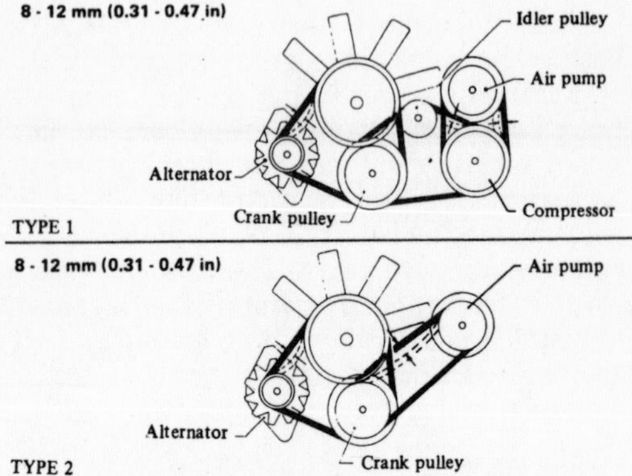

Checking the drive belt tension—1980

Air Conditioning Compressor

A/C compressor belt tension can be adjusted by turning the tension adjusting bolt which is located on the compressor tensioner bracket. Turn the bolt clockwise to tighten the belt and counterclockwise to loosen it.

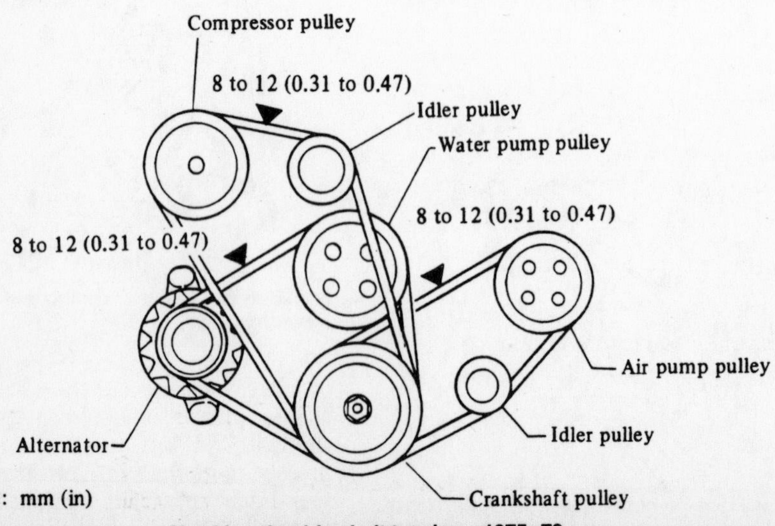

Checkign the drive belt tension—1975–79

Air Pump

To adjust the tension of the air pump drive belt, loosen the adjusting lever bolt and then the pivot bolt. Move the pump in or out until the desired tension is achieved.

NOTE: *The tension should always be checked between the air pump and the crankshaft pulley on all trucks without air conditioning. On trucks with air conditioning, tension should be checked between the A/C compressor and the crankshaft pulley.*

Power Steering Pump

Tension on the power steering belt is adjusted by means of an idler pulley. Turn the adjusting bolt on the idler pulley until the desired ten-

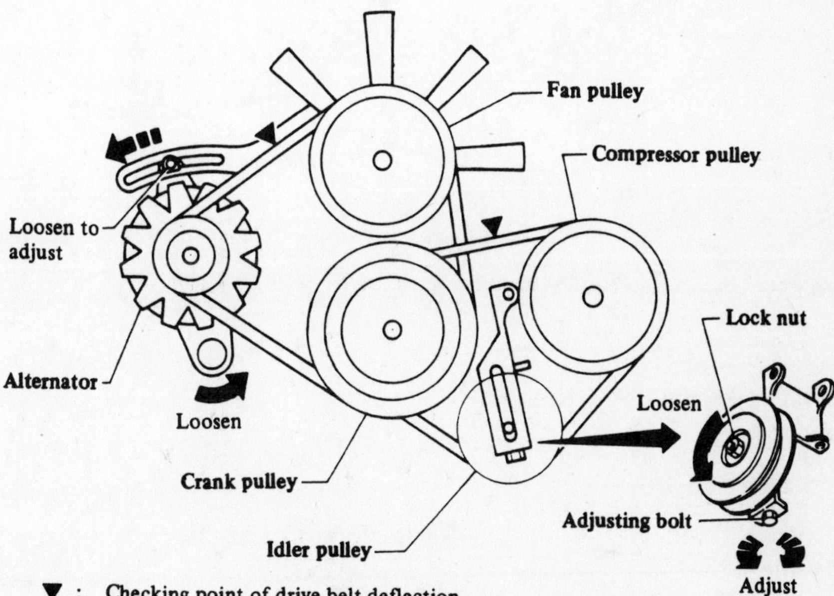

Checking the drive belt tension—1981–83

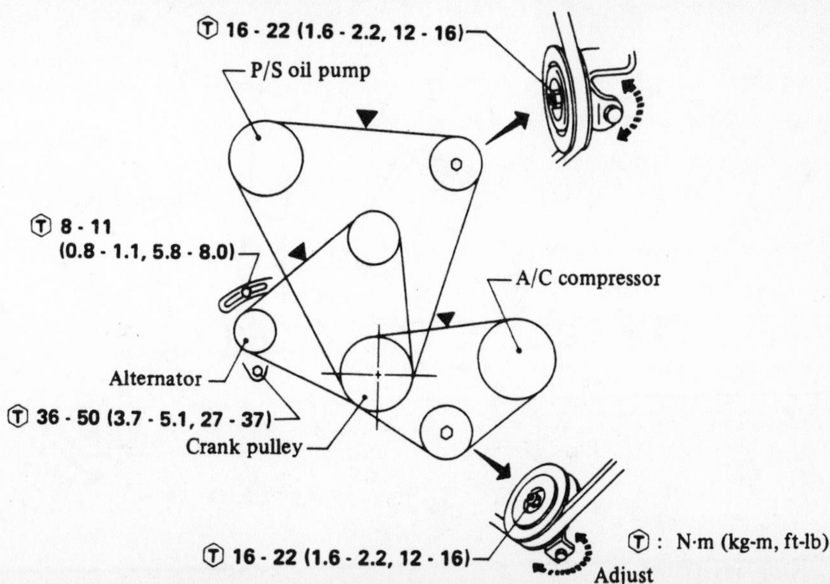

Checking the drive belt tension—1984–86 (720-D series)

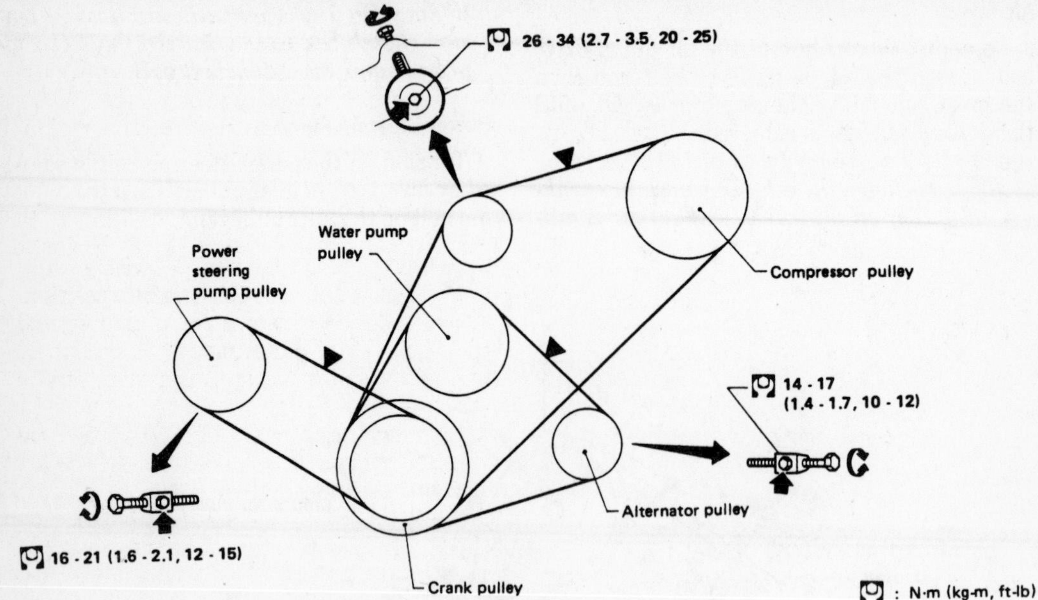

Checking the drive belt tension—1986–89 VG30i

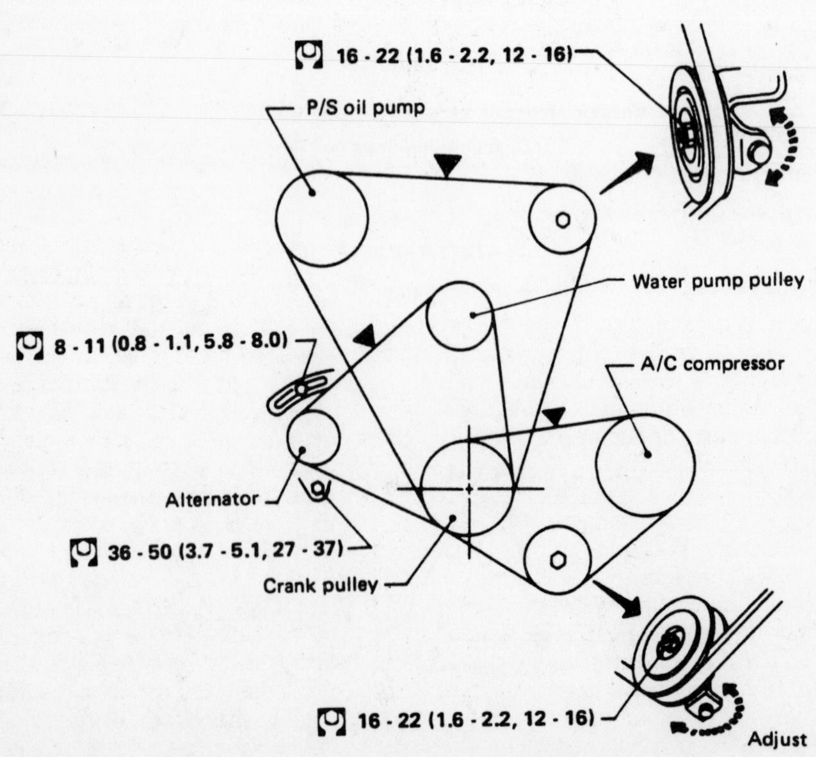

: N·m (kg-m, ft-lb)

Checking the drive belt tension—1986–89 Z24i

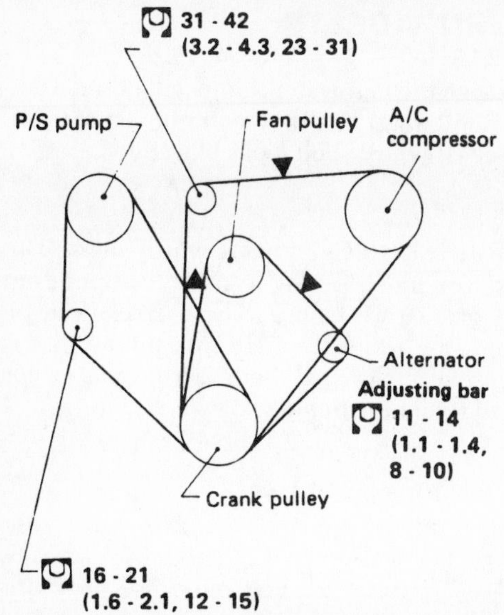

Checking the drive belt tension—1986–87 SD25

sion is achieved and the retighten the idler pulley lockbolt.

Hoses

CAUTION: *On models equipped with an electric cooling fan, disconnect the negative battery cable, or fan motor wiring harness connector before replacing any radiator/heater hose. The fan may come on, under certain circumstances, even though the ignition is Off.*

REPLACEMENT

Inspect the condition of the radiator and heater hoses periodically. Early spring and at the beginning of the fall or winter, when you are performing other maintenance, are good times. Make sure the engine and cooling system are cold. Visually inspect for cracking, rotting or collapsed hoses, replace as necessary. Run your hand along the length of the hose. If a weak or swollen spot is noted when squeezing the hose wall, replace the hose.

1. Drain the cooling system into a suitable container (if the coolant is to be reused).

CAUTION: *When draining the coolant, keep in mind that cats and dogs are attracted by the ethylene glycol antifreeze, and are quite likely to drink any that is left in an uncovered container or in puddles on the ground. This will prove fatal in sufficient quantity. Always drain the coolant into a sealable container. Coolant should be reused unless it is contaminated or several years old.*

2. Loosen the hose clamps at each end of the hose that requires replacement.
3. Twist, pull and slide the hose off the radiator, water pump, thermostat or heater connection.
4. Clean the hose mounting connections. Position the hose clamps on the new hose.
5. Coat the connection surfaces with a water resistant sealer and slide the hose into position. Make sure the hose clamps are located beyond the raised bead of the connector (if equipped) and centered in the clamping area of the connection.
6. Tighten the clamps to 20–30 in. lbs. Do not overtighten.
7. Fill the cooling system.
8. Start the engine and allow it to reach normal operating temperature. Check for leaks.

Air Conditioning System

GENERAL SERVICING PROCEDURES

The most important aspect of air conditioning service is the maintenance of pure and adequate charge of refrigerant in the system. A refrigeration system cannot function properly if a significant percentage of the charge is lost. Leaks are common because the severe vibration encountered in an automobile can easily cause a sufficient cracking or loosening of the air conditioning fittings. As a result, the extreme operating pressures of the system force refrigerant out.

The problem can be understood by considering what happens to the system as it is operated with a continuous leak. Because the expansion valve regulates the flow of refrigerant to the evaporator, the level of refrigerant there is fairly constant. The receiver/drier stores any excess of refrigerant, and so a loss will first appear there as a reduction in the level of liquid. As this level nears the bottom of the vessel, some refrigerant vapor bubbles will begin to appear in the stream of liquid supplied to the expansion valve. This vapor decreases the capacity of the expansion valve very little as the valve opens to compensate for its presence. As the quantity of liquid in the condenser decreases, the operating pressure will drop there and throughout the high side of the system. As the R–12 continues to be expelled, the pressure available to force the liquid through the expansion valve will continue to decrease, and, eventually, the valve's orifice will prove to be too much of a restriction for adequate flow even with the needle fully withdrawn.

At this point, low side pressure will start to drop, and severe reduction in cooling capacity,

HOW TO SPOT WORN V-BELTS

V-Belts are vital to efficient engine operation—they drive the fan, water pump and other accessories. They require little maintenance (occasional tightening) but they will not last forever. Slipping or failure of the V-belt will lead to overheating. If your V-belt looks like any of these, it should be replaced.

Cracking or weathering

This belt has deep cracks, which cause it to flex. Too much flexing leads to heat build-up and premature failure. These cracks can be caused by using the belt on a pulley that is too small. Notched belts are available for small diameter pulleys.

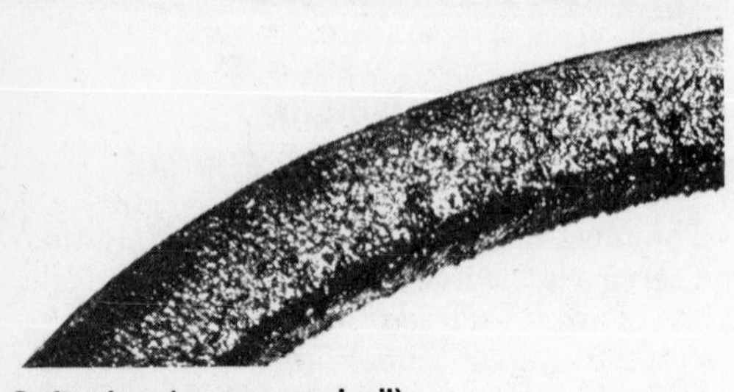

Softening (grease and oil)

Oil and grease on a belt can cause the belt's rubber compounds to soften and separate from the reinforcing cords that hold the belt together. The belt will first slip, then finally fail altogether.

Glazing

Glazing is caused by a belt that is slipping. A slipping belt can cause a run-down battery, erratic power steering, overheating or poor accessory performance. The more the belt slips, the more glazing will be built up on the surface of the belt. The more the belt is glazed, the more it will slip. If the glazing is light, tighten the belt.

Worn cover

The cover of this belt is worn off and is peeling away. The reinforcing cords will begin to wear and the belt will shortly break. When the belt cover wears in spots or has a rough jagged appearance, check the pulley grooves for roughness.

Separation

This belt is on the verge of breaking and leaving you stranded. The layers of the belt are separating and the reinforcing cords are exposed. It's just a matter of time before it breaks completely.

HOW TO SPOT BAD HOSES

Both the upper and lower radiator hoses are called upon to perform difficult jobs in an inhospitable environment. They are subject to nearly 18 psi at under hood temperatures often over 280°F., and must circulate nearly 7500 gallons of coolant an hour—3 good reasons to have good hoses.

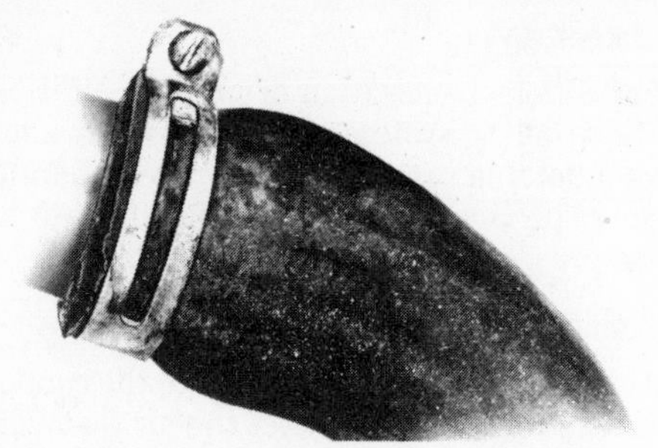

Swollen hose

A good test for any hose is to feel it for soft or spongy spots. Frequently these will appear as swollen areas of the hose. The most likely cause is oil soaking. This hose could burst at any time, when hot or under pressure.

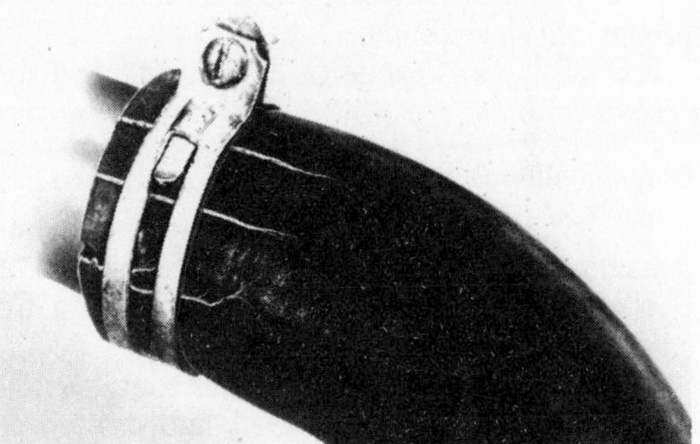

Cracked hose

Cracked hoses can usually be seen but feel the hoses to be sure they have not hardened; a prime cause of cracking. This hose has cracked down to the reinforcing cords and could split at any of the cracks.

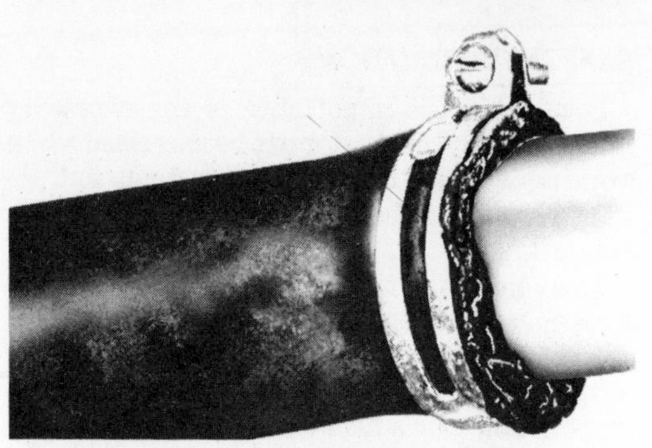

Frayed hose end (due to weak clamp)

Weakened clamps frequently are the cause of hose and cooling system failure. The connection between the pipe and hose has deteriorated enough to allow coolant to escape when the engine is hot.

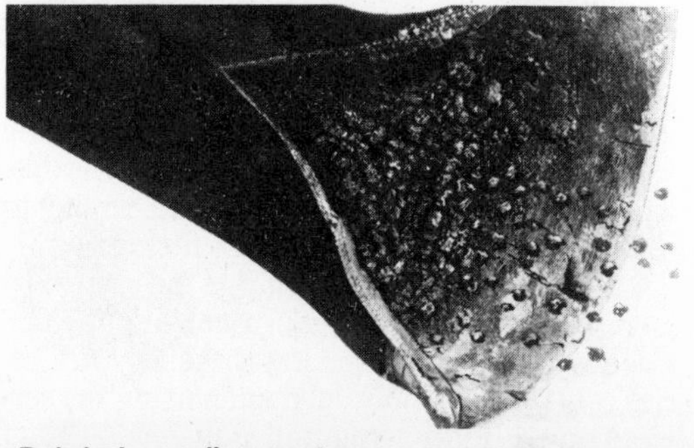

Debris in cooling system

Debris, rust and scale in the cooling system can cause the inside of a hose to weaken. This can usually be felt on the outside of the hose as soft or thinner areas.

marked by freeze-up of the evaporator coil, will result. Eventually, the operating pressure of the evaporator will be lower than the pressure of the atmosphere surrounding it, and air will be drawn into the system wherever there are leaks in the low side.

Because all atmospheric air contains at least some moisture, water will enter the system and mix with the R-12 and the oil. Trace amounts of moisture will cause sludging of the oil, and corrosion of the system. Saturation and clogging of the filter/drier, and freezing of the expansion valve orifice will eventually result. As air fills the system to a greater and greater extend, it will interfere more and more with the normal flows of refrigerant and heat.

A list of general precautions that should be observed while doing this follows:

1. Keep all tools as clean and dry as possible.
2. Thoroughly purge the service gauges and hoses of air and moisture before connecting them to the system. Keep them capped when not in use.
3. Thoroughly clean any refrigerant fitting before disconnecting it, in order to minimize the entrance of dirt into the system.
4. Plan any operation that requires opening the system beforehand in order to minimize the length of time it will be exposed to open air. Cap or seal the open ends to minimize the entrance of foreign material.
5. When adding oil, pour it through an extremely clean and dry tube or funnel. Keep the oil capped whenever possible. Do not use oil that has not been kept tightly sealed.
6. Use only refrigerant 12. Purchase refrigerant intended for use in only automotive air conditioning system. Avoid the use of refrigerant 12 that may be packaged for another use, such as cleaning, or powering a horn, as it is impure.
7. Completely evacuate any system that has been opened to replace a component, other than when isolating the compressor, or that has leaked sufficiently to draw in moisture and air. This requires evacuating air and moisture with a good vacuum pump for at least one hour.

WARNING: *If a system has been open for a considerable length of time it may be advisable to evacuate the system for up to 12 hours (overnight).*

8. Use a wrench on both halves of a fitting that is to be disconnected, so as to avoid placing torque on any of the refrigerant lines.

ADDITIONAL PREVENTIVE MAINTENANCE CHECKS

Antifreeze

In order to prevent heater core freeze-up during A/C operation, it is necessary to maintain permanent type antifreeze protection of +15°F (−9°C) or lower. A reading of −15°F (−26°C) is ideal since this protection also supplies sufficient corrosion inhibitors for the protection of the engine cooling system.

NOTE: *The same antifreeze should not be used longer than the manufacturer specified.*

Radiator Cap

For efficient operation of an air conditioned truck's cooling system, the radiator cap should have a holding pressure which meets manufacturer's specifications. A cap which fails to hold these pressure should be replaced.

Condenser

Any obstruction of or damage to the condenser configuration will restrict the air flow which is essential to its efficient operation. It is therefore, a good rule to keep this unit clean and in proper physical shape.

NOTE: *Bug screens are regarded as obstructions.*

Condensation Drain Tube

This single molded drain tube expels the condensation, which accumulates on the bottom of the evaporator housing, into the engine compartment.

If this tube is obstructed, the air conditioning performance can be restricted and condensation buildup can spill over onto the vehicle's floor.

SAFETY PRECAUTIONS

Because of the importance of the necessary safety precautions that must be exercised when working with air conditioning systems and R-12 refrigerant, a recap of the safety precautions are outlined.

1. Avoid contact with a charged refrigeration system, even when working on another part of the air conditioning system or vehicle. If a heavy tool comes into contact with a section of copper tubing or a heat exchanger, it can easily cause the relatively soft material to rupture.
2. When it is necessary to apply force to a fitting which contains refrigerant, as when checking that all system couplings are securely tightened, use a wrench on both parts of the fitting involved, if possible. This will avoid putting torque on refrigerant tubing. (It is advisable, when possible, to use tube or line wrenches when tightening these flare nut fittings.)
3. Do not attempt to discharge the system by merely loosening a fitting, or removing the service valve caps and cracking these valves. Precise control is possibly only when using the service gauges. Place a rag under the open end of the center charging hose while discharging the

system to catch any drops of liquid that might escape. Wear protective gloves when connecting or disconnecting service gauge hoses.

4. Discharge the system only in a well ventilated area, as high concentrations of the gas can exclude oxygen and act as an anesthesia. When leak testing or soldering, this is particularly important, as toxic gas is formed when R–12 contacts any flame.

5. Never start a system without first verifying that both service valves are backseated, if equipped, and that all fittings are throughout the system are snugly connected.

6. Avoid applying heat to any refrigerant line or storage vessel. Charging may be aided by using water heated to less than +125°F (+51°C) to warm the refrigerant container. Never allow a refrigerant storage container to sit out in the sun, or near any other source of heat, such as a radiator.

7. Always wear goggles when working on a system to protect the eyes. If refrigerant contacts the eye, it is advisable in all cases to see a physician as soon as possible.

8. Frostbite from liquid refrigerant should be treated by first gradually warming the area with cool water, and then gently applying petroleum jelly. A physician should be consulted.

9. Always keep refrigerant can fittings capped when not in use. Avoid sudden shock to the can which might occur from dropping it, or from banging a heavy tool against it. Never carry a can in the passenger compartment of a truck.

10. Always completely discharge the system before painting the vehicle (if the paint is to be baked on), or before welding anywhere near the refrigerant lines.

TEST GAUGES

Most of the service work performed in air conditioning requires the use of a set of two gauges, one for the high (head) pressure side of the system, the other for the low (suction) side.

The low side gauge records both pressure and vacuum. Vacuum readings are calibrated from 0 to 30 in.Hg and the pressure graduations read from 0 to no less than 60 psi.

The high side gauge measures pressure from 0 to at last 600 psi.

Both gauges are threaded into a manifold that contains two hand shut-off valves. Proper manipulation of these valves and the use of the attached test hoses allow the user to perform the following services:

1. Test high and low side pressures.
2. Remove air, moisture, and contaminated refrigerant.
3. Purge the system (of refrigerant).
4. Charge the system (with refrigerant).

The manifold valves are designed so that they have no direct effect on gauge readings, but serve only to provide for, or cut off, flow of refrigerant through the manifold. During all testing and hook-up operations, the valves are kept in a close position to avoid disturbing the refrigeration system. The valves are opened only to purge the system or refrigerant or to charge it.

INSPECTION

CAUTION: *The compressed refrigerant used in the air conditioning system expands into the atmosphere at a temperature of −21.7°F (−29.8°C) or lower. This will freeze any surface, including your eyes, that it contacts. In addition, the refrigerant decomposes into a poisonous gas in the presence of a flame. Do not open or disconnect any part of the air conditioning system.*

Sight Glass Check

You can safely make a few simple checks to determine if your air conditioning system needs service. The tests work best if the temperature is warm (about +70°F [21°C]).

NOTE: *If your vehicle is equipped with an aftermarket air conditioner, the following system check may not apply. You should contact the manufacturer of the unit for instructions on systems checks.*

1. Place the automatic transmission in Park or the manual transmission in Neutral. Set the parking brake.
2. Run the engine at a fast idle (about 1500 rpm) either with the help of a friend or by temporarily readjusting the idle speed screw.
3. Set the controls for maximum cold with the blower on High.
4. Locate the sight glass in one of the system lines. Usually it is on the left alongside the top of the radiator.
5. If you see bubbles, the system must be recharged. Very likely there is a leak at some point.
6. If there are no bubbles, there is either no refrigerant at all or the system is fully charged. Feel the two hoses going to the belt-driven compressor. If they are both at the same tempera-

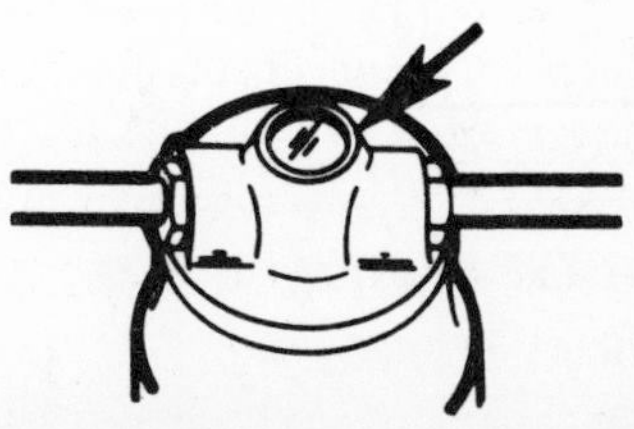

Arrow points to the sight glass on top of the air conditioner's receiver dehydrator

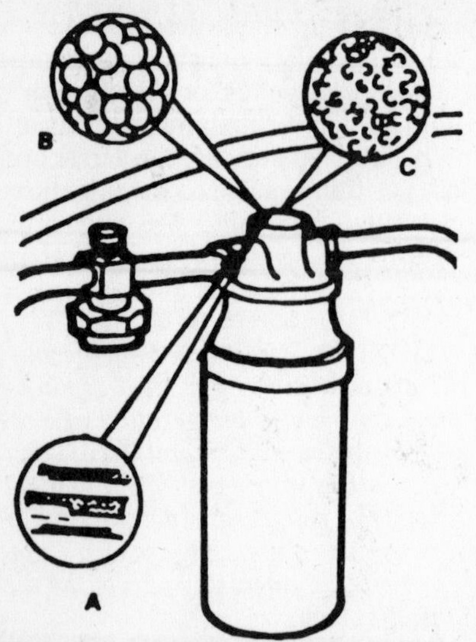

Oil streaks (A), constant bubbles (B) or foam (C) indicate there is not enough refrigerant in the system. Occasional bubbling during initial operation is normal. A clear sight glass indicates a proper charge of refrigerant or no refrigerant at all, which can be determined by the presence of cold air at the outlets of the car. If the glass is clouded with a milky white substance, have the receiver/drier checked

ture, the system is empty and must be recharged.

7. If one hose (high pressure) is warm and the other (low pressure) is cold, the system may be all right. However, you are probably making these tests because you think there is something wrong, so proceed to the next step.
8. Have an assistant in the truck turn the fan control on and off to operate the compressor clutch. Watch the sight glass.
9. If bubbles appear when the clutch is disengaged and disappear when it is engaged, the system is properly charged.
10. If the refrigerant takes more than 45 seconds to bubble when the clutch is disengaged, the system is overcharged. This usually causes poor cooling at low speeds.

CAUTION: *If it is determined that the system has a leak, it should be corrected as soon as possible. Leaks may allow moisture to enter and cause a very expensive rust problem.*

NOTE: *Exercise the air conditioner for a few minutes, every two weeks or so, during the cold months. This avoids the possibility of the compressor seals drying out from lack of lubrication.*

TESTING THE SYSTEM

1. Connect a gauge set.
2. Close (clockwise) both gauge set valves.
3. Mid-position both service valves.
4. Park the vehicle in the shade. Start the engine, set the parking brake, place the transmission in NEUTRAL and establish an idle of 1500 rpm.
5. Run the air conditioning system for full cooling, but NOT in the **MAX** or **COLD** mode.
6. Insert a thermometer into the center air outlet.
7. Use the accompanying performance chart for a specifications reference. If pressures are abnormal, refer to the accompanying Pressure Diagnosis Chart.

ISOLATING THE COMPRESSOR

It is not necessary to discharge the system for compressor removal. The compressor can be

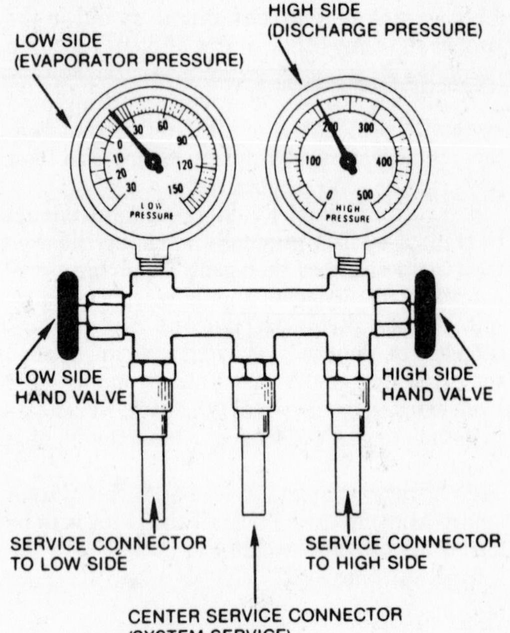

Typical manifold gauge set

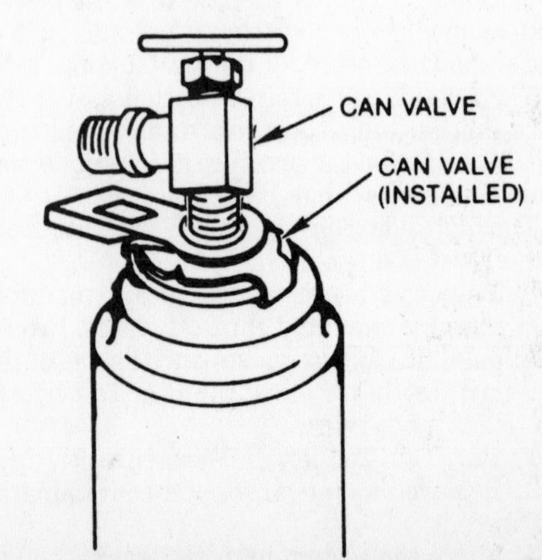

One pound R-12 can with opener valve connencted

Troubleshooting Basic Air Conditioning Problems

Problem	Cause	Solution
There's little or no air coming from the vents (and you're sure it's on)	• The A/C fuse is blown • Broken or loose wires or connections • The on/off switch is defective	• Check and/or replace fuse • Check and/or repair connections • Replace switch
The air coming from the vents is not cool enough	• Windows and air vent wings open • The compressor belt is slipping • Heater is on • Condenser is clogged with debris • Refrigerant has escaped through a leak in the system • Receiver/drier is plugged	• Close windows and vent wings • Tighten or replace compressor belt • Shut heater off • Clean the condenser • Check system • Service system
The air has an odor	• Vacuum system is disrupted • Odor producing substances on the evaporator case • Condensation has collected in the bottom of the evaporator housing	• Have the system checked/repaired • Clean the evaporator case • Clean the evaporator housing drains
System is noisy or vibrating	• Compressor belt or mountings loose • Air in the system	• Tighten or replace belt; tighten mounting bolts • Have the system serviced
Sight glass condition		
Constant bubbles, foam or oil streaks	• Undercharged system	• Charge the system
Clear sight glass, but no cold air	• No refrigerant at all	• Check and charge the system
Clear sight glass, but air is cold	• System is OK	
Clouded with milky fluid	• Receiver drier is leaking dessicant	• Have system checked
Large difference in temperature of lines	• System undercharged	• Charge and leak test the system
Compressor noise	• Broken valves • Overcharged • Incorrect oil level • Piston slap • Broken rings • Drive belt pulley bolts are loose	• Replace the valve plate • Discharge, evacuate and install the correct charge • Isolate the compressor and check the oil level. Correct as necessary. • Replace the compressor • Replace the compressor • Tighten with the correct torque specification
Excessive vibration	• Incorrect belt tension • Clutch loose • Overcharged • Pulley is misaligned	• Adjust the belt tension • Tighten the clutch • Discharge, evacuate and install the correct charge • Align the pulley
Condensation dripping in the passenger compartment	• Drain hose plugged or improperly positioned • Insulation removed or improperly installed	• Clean the drain hose and check for proper installation • Replace the insulation on the expansion valve and hoses
Frozen evaporator coil	• Faulty thermostat • Thermostat capillary tube improperly installed • Thermostat not adjusted properly	• Replace the thermostat • Install the capillary tube correctly • Adjust the thermostat
Low side low—high side low	• System refrigerant is low • Expansion valve is restricted	• Evacuate, leak test and charge the system • Replace the expansion valve
Low side high—high side low	• Internal leak in the compressor—worn	• Remove the compressor cylinder head and inspect the compressor. Replace the valve plate assembly if necessary. If the compressor pistons, rings or

Troubleshooting Basic Air Conditioning Problems (cont.)

Problem	Cause	Solution
Low side high—high side low (cont.)		cylinders are excessively worn or scored replace the compressor
	• Cylinder head gasket is leaking	• Install a replacement cylinder head gasket
	• Expansion valve is defective	• Replace the expansion valve
	• Drive belt slipping	• Adjust the belt tension
Low side high—high side high	• Condenser fins obstructed	• Clean the condenser fins
	• Air in the system	• Evacuate, leak test and charge the system
	• Expansion valve is defective	• Replace the expansion valve
	• Loose or worn fan belts	• Adjust or replace the belts as necessary
Low side low—high side high	• Expansion valve is defective	• Replace the expansion valve
	• Restriction in the refrigerant hose	• Check the hose for kinks—replace if necessary
	• Restriction in the receiver/drier	• Replace the receiver/drier
	• Restriction in the condenser	• Replace the condenser
Low side and high side normal (inadequate cooling)	• Air in the system	• Evacuate, leak test and charge the system
	• Moisture in the system	• Evacuate, leak test and charge the system

isolated from the rest of the system, eliminating the need for recharging.

1. Connect a manifold gauge set.
2. Close both gauge hand valves and mid-position (crack) both compressor service valves.
3. Start the engine and turn on the air conditioning.
4. Turn the compressor suction valve slowly clockwise towards the front-seated position. When the suction pressure drops to zero, stop the engine and turn off the air conditioning. Quickly front-seat the valve completely.
5. Front-seat the discharge service valve.
6. Loosen the oil level check plug to remove any internal pressure.

The compressor is now isolated and the service valves can now be removed.

DISCHARGING THE SYSTEM

1. Connect the manifold gauge set.
2. Conect the red charging hose (high pressure side) of the manifold gauge to the service valve on the liquid line. Connect the blue charging hose (low pressure side) to the suction line.
3. Place the free end of the center hose into a suitable container.
4. Slowly open the high pressure hand valve to adjust the refrigerant flow. Open the valve slightly.

NOTE: *If you allow the refrigerant to rush out, it will take some refrigerant oil with it!*

5. Check the container to make sure that no oil is being discharged. If there is oil present in the container, partially close the hand valve.
6. After the manifold gauge reading drops below 50 psi, slowly open the low pressure valve.
7. As the system pressure drops, gradually open both high and low valves until both gauges read 0 psi.

EVACUATING AND CHARGING THE SYSTEM

NOTE: *This procedure requires the use of a vacuum pump.*

1. Connect the manifold gauge set.
2. Connect the center hose to the vacuum pump inlet.
3. Turn the vacuum pump on and then open both hand valves.
4. Allow the vacuum pump to operate for approximately 10 minutes. Check that the low pressure gauge reads more than 600mm Hg (23.62 in.Hg/80.0 kPa) of vacuum.

NOTE: *If the reading on the gauges is not more than 600mm Hg, close both valves and shut off the vacuum pump. Inspect the system for leaks and repair as necessary.*

5. After the low pressure gauge shows a vacuum of more than 700mm Hg, continue evacuating for approximately 15 more minutes.
6. Close the manifold gauge valves and shut off the vacuum pump.
7. Install the refrigerant container tap valve.
8. Connect the center hose to the valve fitting.
9. Turn the handle clockwise to make a hole in the sealed tap.

10. Turn the handle fully counterclockwise to fill the center hose with air. Do not open the high and low pressure valve.

11. Loosen the center hose nut connected to the center fitting of the manifold gauge until a hiss can be heard. Allow air to escape for a few seconds and then tighten the nut.

NOTE: *After finishing evacuation of the system, always check for leaks.*

12. Install the refrigerant can tap valve.

13. Open the high pressure valve to charge the system with refrigerant vapor.

14. When the low pressure gauge reads 1 kg cm^2 (14 psi), close the high pressure valve.

15. Leak-test the system.

LEAK TESTING

Some leak tests can be performed with a soapy water solution. There must be at least a ½ lb charge in the system for a leak to be detected. The most extensive leak tests are performed with either a Halide flame type leak tester or the more preferable electronic leak tester.

In either case, the equipment is expensive, and, the use of a Halide detector can be **extremely** hazardous!

Windshield Wipers

For maximum effectiveness and longest element lift, the windshield and wiper blades should be kept clean. Dirt, tree sap, road tar and so on will cause streaking, smearing and blade deterioration if left on the glass. It is advisable to wash the windshield carefully with a commercial glass cleaner at least once a month. Wipe off the rubber blades with the wet rag af-

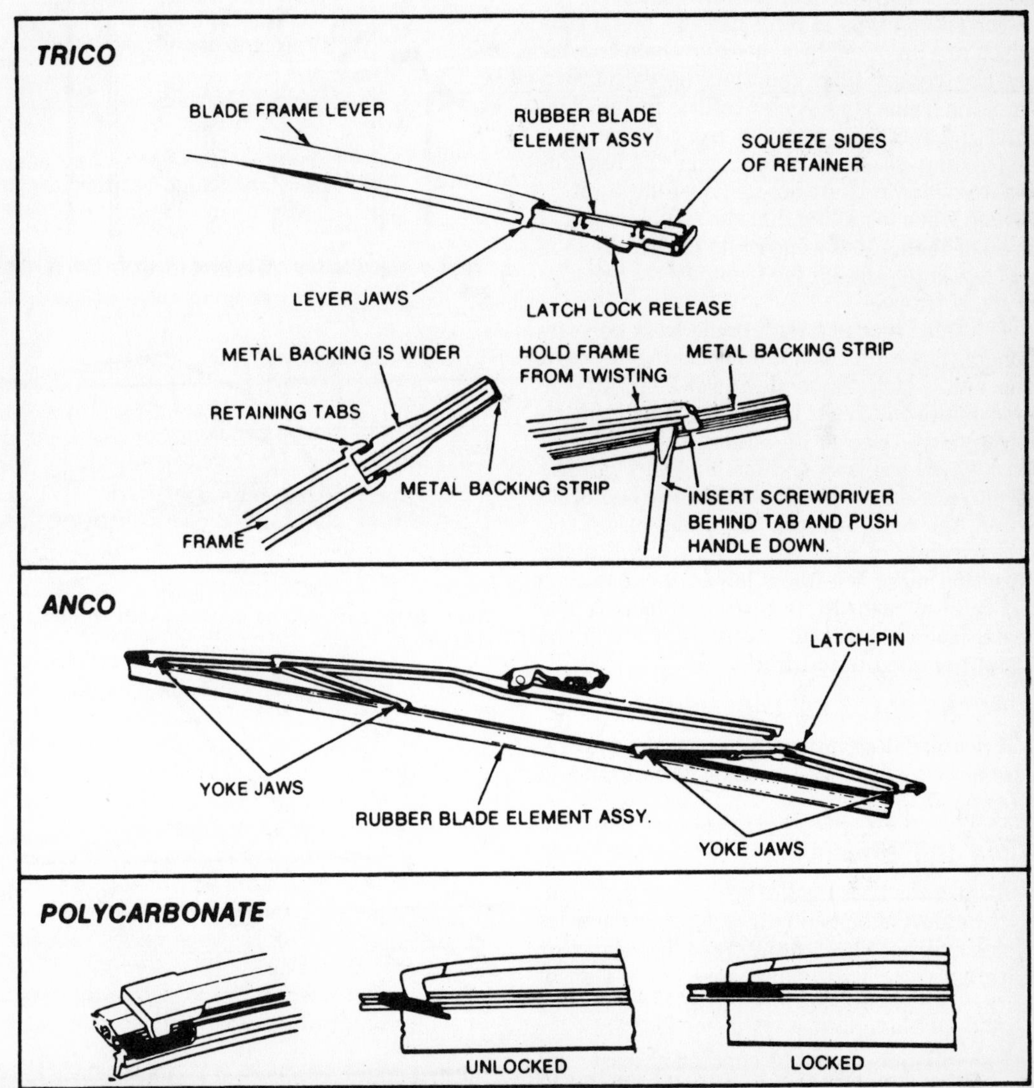

The three types of wiper element retention

terwards. Do not attempt to move the wipers by hand; damage to the motor and drive mechanism will result.

If the blades are found to be cracked, broken or torn, they should be replaced immediately. Replacement intervals will vary with usage, although ozone deterioration usually limits blade lift to about one year. If the wiper pattern is smeared or streaked, or if the blade chatters across the glass, the elements should be replaced. It is easiest and most sensible to replace the elements in pairs.

There are basically three different types of refills, which differ in their method of replacement. One type has two release buttons, approximately ⅓ of the way up from the ends of the blade frame. Pushing the buttons down releases a lock and allows the rubber filler to be removed from the frame. The new filler slides back into the frame and locks in place.

The second type of refill has two metal tabs which are unlocked by squeezing them together. The rubber filler can then be withdrawn from the frame jaws. A new refill is installed by inserting the refill into the front frame jaws and sliding it rear ward to engage the remaining frame jaws. There are usually four jaws. Be certain when installing that the refill is engaged in all of them. At the end of its travel, the tabs will lock into place on the front jaws of the wiper blade frame.

The third type is a refill made from polycarbonate. The refill has a simple locking device at one end which flexes downward out of the groove into which the jaws of the holder fit, allowing easy release. By sliding the new refill through all the jaws and pushing through the slight resistance when it reaches the end of its travel, the refill will lock into position.

Regardless of the type of refill used, make sure that all of the frame jaws are engaged as the refill is pushed into place and locked. The metal blade holder and frame will scratch the glass if allowed to touch it.

ARM AND BLADE REPLACEMENT

A detailed description and procedures for replacing the wiper arm and blade is found in Chapter 6.

Tires and Wheels

Inspect the tires regularly for wear and damage. Remove stones or other foreign particles which may be lodged in the tread. If tread wear is excessive or irregular it could be a sign of front end problems, or simply improper inflation.

The inflation should be checked at least once per month and adjusted if necessary. The tires must be cold (driven less than one mile) or an inaccurate reading will result. Do not forget to check the spare.

The correct inflation pressure for your vehicle can be found on a decal mounted to the truck. Depending upon model and year, the decal can be located at the driver's door, the passenger's door or the glove box. If you cannot

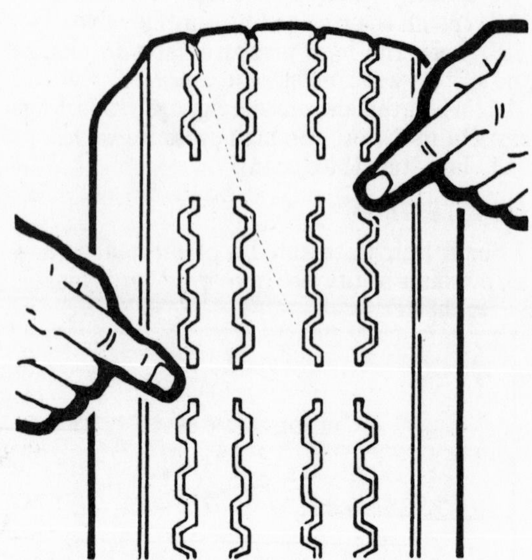

Tread wear indicators will appear when the tire is worn out

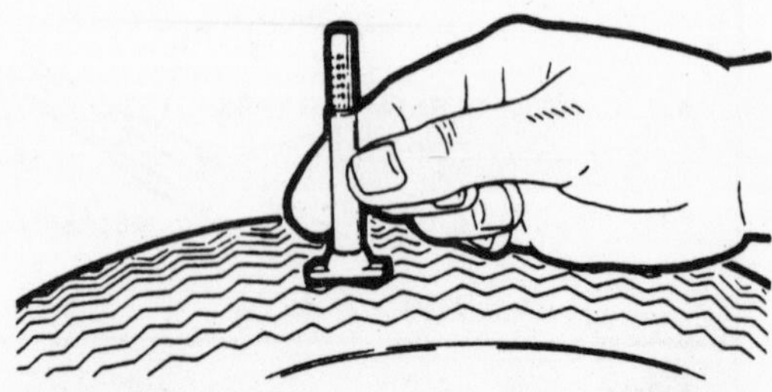

Tread depth can also be checked with an inexpensive gauge

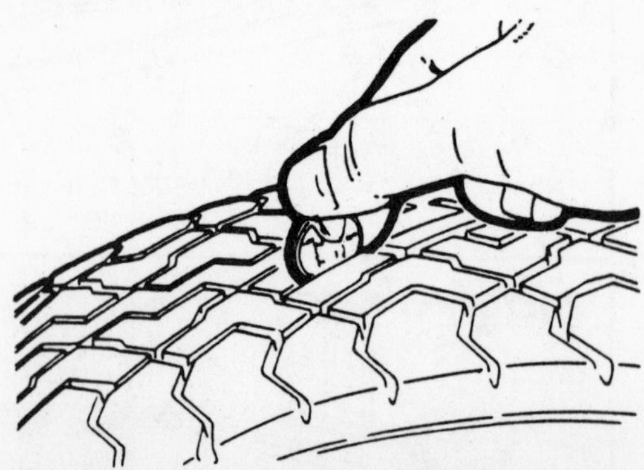

A penny works as well as anything when checking tread depth; when the top of Lincoln's head is visible, it's time for new tires

find the decal a local automobile tire dealer can furnish you with information.

Inspect tires for uneven wear that might indicate the need for front end alignment or tire rotation. Tires should be replaced when a tread wear indicator appears as a solid band across the tread.

When you buy new tires, give some thought to these points, especially if you are switching to larger tires or to another profile series (50, 60, 70, 78):

1. The wheels must be the correct width for the tire. Tire dealers have charts of tire and rim compatibility. A mismatch can cause sloppy handling and rapid tread wear. The old rule of thumb is that the tread width should match the rim width (inside bead to inside bead) within an inch. For radial tires, the rim width should be 80% or less of the tire (not tread) width.

2. The height (mounted diameter) of the new tires can greatly change speedometer accuracy, engine speed at a given road speed, fuel mileage, acceleration, and ground clearance. Tire makers furnish full measurement specifications. Speedometer drive gears are available from Nissan dealers for correction.

NOTE: *Dimensions of tires marked the same size may vary significantly, even among tires from the same maker.*

3. The spare tire should be usable, at least for low speed operation, with the new tires.

4. There shouldn't be any body interference when loaded, on bumps, or in turning.

The only sure way to avoid problems with these points is to stick to tire and wheel sizes available as factory options.

TIRE ROTATION

The rotation is recommended every 6000 miles (9600 km) or so, to obtain maximum tire wear. The pattern you use depends on whether or not your truck has a usable spare. Radial tires should not be cross-switched (from one side of the truck to the other); they last longer if their direction of rotation is not changed. Snow tires sometimes have directional arrows molded into the side of the carcass; the arrow shows the direction of rotation. They will wear very rapidly if the rotation is reversed. Studded tires will lose their studs if their rotational direction is reversed.

NOTE: *Mark the wheel position or direction of rotation on radial tires or studded snow tires before removing them.*

If your truck is equipped with tires having different load ratings on the front and the rear, the tires should not be rotated front to rear. Rotating these tires could affect tire life (the tires with the lower rating will wear faster, and could become overloaded), and upset the handling of the truck.

TIRE USAGE

The tires on your truck were selected to provide the best all around performance for normal operation when inflated as specified. Oversize tires (Load Range D) will not increase the maximum carrying capacity of the vehicle, although they will provide an extra margin of tread life. Be sure to check overall height before using larger size tires which may cause interference with suspension components or wheel wells.

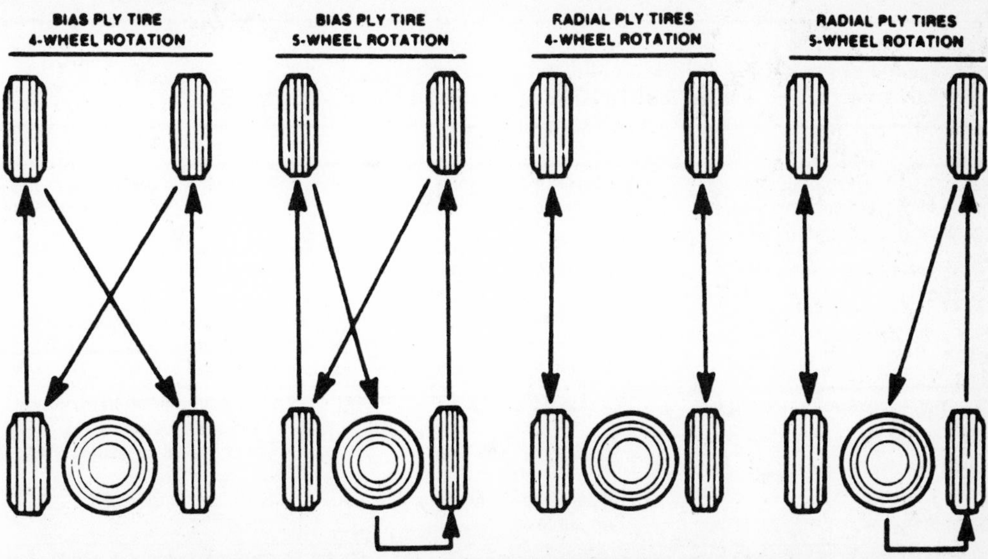

Tire rotation diagrams; note that radials should not be cross-switched

When replacing conventional tire sizes with other tire size designations, be sure to check the manufacturer's recommendations. Interchangeability is not always possible because of differences in load ratings, tire dimensions, wheel well clearances, and rim size. Also due to differences in handling characteristics, 70 Series and 60 Series tires should be used only in pairs on the same axle; radial tires should be used only in sets of four.

The wheels must be the correct width for the tire. Tire dealers have charts of tire and rim compatibility. A mismatch can cause sloppy handling and rapid tread wear. The old rule of thumb is that the tread width should match the rim width (inside bead to inside bead) within an inch. For radial tires, the rim width should be 80% or less of the tire (not tread) width.

The height (mounted diameter) of the new tires can greatly change speedometer accuracy, engine speed at a given road speed, fuel mileage, acceleration, and ground clearance. Tire manu-

Troubleshooting Basic Wheel Problems

Problem	Cause	Solution
The car's front end vibrates at high speed	• The wheels are out of balance • Wheels are out of alignment	• Have wheels balanced • Have wheel alignment checked/adjusted
Car pulls to either side	• Wheels are out of alignment • Unequal tire pressure • Different size tires or wheels	• Have wheel alignment checked/adjusted • Check/adjust tire pressure • Change tires or wheels to same size
The car's wheel(s) wobbles	• Loose wheel lug nuts • Wheels out of balance • Damaged wheel • Wheels are out of alignment • Worn or damaged ball joint • Excessive play in the steering linkage (usually due to worn parts) • Defective shock absorber	• Tighten wheel lug nuts • Have tires balanced • Raise car and spin the wheel. If the wheel is bent, it should be replaced • Have wheel alignment checked/adjusted • Check ball joints • Check steering linkage • Check shock absorbers
Tires wear unevenly or prematurely	• Incorrect wheel size • Wheels are out of balance • Wheels are out of alignment	• Check if wheel and tire size are compatible • Have wheels balanced • Have wheel alignment checked/adjusted

Troubleshooting Basic Tire Problems

Problem	Cause	Solution
The car's front end vibrates at high speeds and the steering wheel shakes	• Wheels out of balance • Front end needs aligning	• Have wheels balanced • Have front end alignment checked
The car pulls to one side while cruising	• Unequal tire pressure (car will usually pull to the low side) • Mismatched tires • Front end needs aligning	• Check/adjust tire pressure • Be sure tires are of the same type and size • Have front end alignment checked
Abnormal, excessive or uneven tire wear See "How to Read Tire Wear"	• Infrequent tire rotation • Improper tire pressure • Sudden stops/starts or high speed on curves	• Rotate tires more frequently to equalize wear • Check/adjust pressure • Correct driving habits
Tire squeals	• Improper tire pressure • Front end needs aligning	• Check/adjust tire pressure • Have front end alignment checked

facturers furnish full measurement specifications. Speedometer drive gears are available for correction.

NOTE: *Dimensions of tires marked the same size may vary significantly, even among tires from the same manufacturer.*

The spare tire should be usable, at least for low speed operation, with the new tires.

TIRE DESIGN

For maximum satisfaction, tires should be used in sets of five. Mixing or different types (radial, bias-belted, fiberglass belted) should be avoided. Conventional bias tires are constructed so that the cords run bead-to-bead at an angle. Alternate plies run at an opposite angle. This type of construction gives rigidity to both tread and sidewall. Bias-belted tires are similar in construction to conventional bias ply tires. Belts run at an angle and also at a 90° angle to the bead, as in the radial tire. Tread life is improved considerably over the conventional bias tire. The radial tire differs in construction, but instead of the carcass plies running at an angle of 90° to each other, they run at an angle of 90° to the bead. This gives the tread a great deal of rigidity and the sidewall a great deal of flexibility and accounts for the characteristic bulge associated with radial tires.

Radial tire are recommended for use on all Nissan trucks. If they are used, tire sizes and wheel diameters should be selected to maintain ground clearance and tire load capacity equivalent to the minimum specified tire. Radial tires should always be used in sets of five, but in an emergency radial tires can be used with caution

Tire Size Comparison Chart

"Letter" sizes			Inch Sizes	Metric-inch Sizes		
"60 Series"	"70 Series"	"78 Series"	1965–77	"60 Series"	"70 Series"	"80 Series"
			5.50-12, 5.60-12	165/60-12	165/70-12	155-12
		Y78-12	6.00-12			
		W78-13	5.20-13	165/60-13	145/70-13	135-13
		Y78-13	5.60-13	175/60-13	155/70-13	145-13
			6.15-13	185/60-13	165/70-13	155-13, P155/80-13
A60-13	A70-13	A78-13	6.40-13	195/60-13	175/70-13	165-13
B60-13	B70-13	B78-13	6.70-13	205/60-13	185/70-13	175-13
			6.90-13			
C60-13	C70-13	C78-13	7.00-13	215/60-13	195/70-13	185-13
D60-13	D70-13	D78-13	7.25-13			
E60-13	E70-13	E78-13	7.75-13			195-13
			5.20-14	165/60-14	145/70-14	135-14
			5.60-14	175/60-14	155/70-14	145-14
			5.90-14			
A60-14	A70-14	A78-14	6.15-14	185/60-14	165/70-14	155-14
	B70-14	B78-14	6.45-14	195/60-14	175/70-14	165-14
	C70-14	C78-14	6.95-14	205/60-14	185/70-14	175-14
D60-14	D70-14	D78-14				
E60-14	E70-14	E78-14	7.35-14	215/60-14	195/70-14	185-14
F60-14	F70-14	F78-14, F83-14	7.75-14	225/60-14	200/70-14	195-14
G60-14	G70-14	G77-14, G78-14	8.25-14	235/60-14	205/70-14	205-14
H60-14	H70-14	H78-14	8.55-14	245/60-14	215/70-14	215-14
J60-14	J70-14	J78-14	8.85-14	255/60-14	225/70-14	225-14
L60-14	L70-14		9.15-14	265/60-14	235/70-14	
	A70-15	A78-15	5.60-15	185/60-15	165/70-15	155-15
B60-15	B70-15	B78-15	6.35-15	195/60-15	175/70-15	165-15
C60-15	C70-15	C78-15	6.85-15	205/60-15	185/70-15	175-15
	D70-15	D78-15				
E60-15	E70-15	E78-15	7.35-15	215/60-15	195/70-15	185-15
F60-15	F70-15	F78-15	7.75-15	225/60-15	205/70-15	195-15
G60-15	G70-15	G78-15	8.15-15/8.25-15	235/60-15	215/70-15	205-15
H60-15	H70-15	H78-15	8.45-15/8.55-15	245/60-15	225/70-15	215-15
J60-15	J70-15	J78-15	8.85-15/8.90-15	255/60-15	235/70-15	225-15
	K70-15		9.00-15	265/60-15	245/70-15	230-15
L60-15	L70-15	L78-15, L84-15	9.15-15			235-15
	M70-15	M78-15				255-15
		N78-15				

Note: Every size tire is not listed and many size comparisons are approximate, based on load ratings. Wider tires than those supplied new with the vehicle, should always be checked for clearance.

on the rear axle only. If this is done, both tires on the rear should be of radial design.

NOTE: *Radial tires should never be used on only the front axle.*

STORAGE

Store the tires at the proper inflation pressure if they are mounted on wheels. Keep them in a cool dry place, laid on their sides. If the tires are stored in the garage or basement, do not let them stand on a concrete floor; set them on strips of wood.

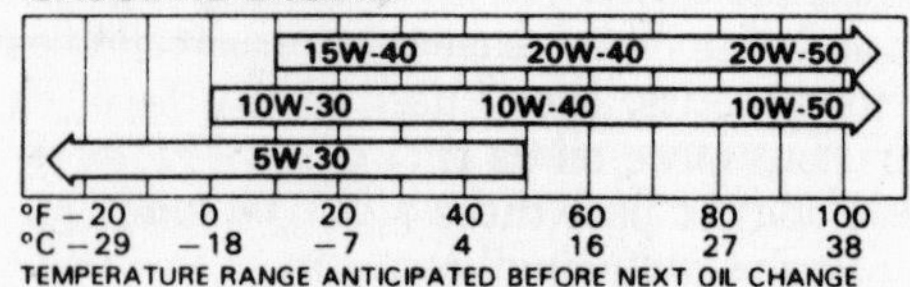

Oil viscosity chart—gasoline engines

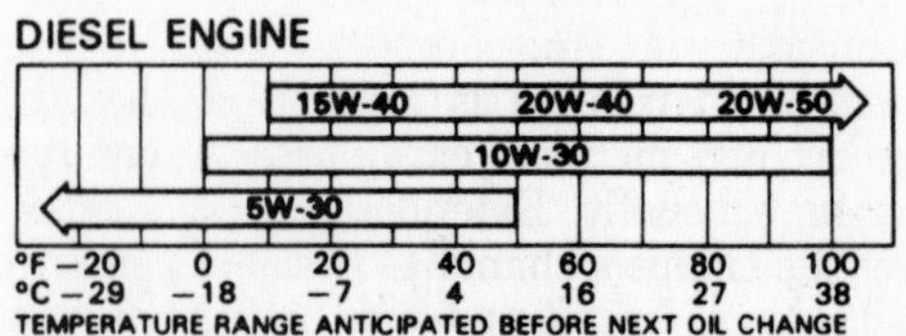

Oil viscosity chart—diesel engines

FLUIDS AND LUBRICANTS

Oil and Fuel Recommendations

OIL

The SAE (Society of Automotive Engineers) grade number indicates the viscosity of the engine oil; its resistance to flow at a given temperature. The lower the SAE grade number, the lighter the oil. For example, the mono-grade oils begin with SAE 5 weight, which is a thin light oil, and continue in viscosity up to SAE 80 or 90 weight, which are heavy gear lubricants. These oils are also known as "straight weight", meaning they are of a single viscosity, and do not vary with engine temperature.

Multi-viscosity oils offer the important advantage of being adaptable to temperature extremes. These oils have designations such as 10W-40, 20W-50, etc. The "10W-40" means that in winter (the "W" in the designation) the oil acts like a thin 10 weight oil, allowing the engine to spin easily when cold and offering rapid lubrication. Once the engine has warmed up, however, the oil acts like a straight 40 weight, maintaining good lubrication and protection for the engine's internal components. A 20W-50 oil would therefore be slightly heavier than and not as ideal in cold weather as the 10W-40, but would offer better protection at higher rpm and temperatures because when warm it acts like a 50 weight oil. Whichever oil viscosity you choose when changing the oil, make sure you are anticipating the temperatures your engine will be operating in until the oil is changed again. Refer to the oil viscosity chart for oil recommendations according to temperature.

The API (American Petroleum Institute) designation indicates the classification of engine oil used under certain given operating conditions. Only oils designated for use "Service SF" should be used. Oils of the SF type perform a variety of functions inside the engine in addition to the basic function as a lubricant. Through a balanced system of metallic detergents and polymeric dispersants, the oil prevents the formation of high and low temperature deposits and also keeps sludge and particles of dirt in suspension. Acids, particularly sulfuric acid, as well as other by-products of combustion, are neutralized. Both the SAE grade number and the APE designation can be found on top of the oil can.

Diesel engines also require SF engine oil. In addition, the oil must qualify for a CC rating. The API has a number of different diesel engine ratings, including CB, CC, and CD. Any of these other oils are fine as long as the designation CC appears on the can along with them. Do not use oil labeled only SF or only CC. Both designations must always appear together.

For recommended oil viscosities, refer to the chart. Note that 10W-30 and 10W-40 grade oils are not recommended for sustained high speed driving when the temperature rises above the indicated limit.

Synthetic Oil

There are many excellent synthetic and fuel-efficient oils currently available that can provide better gas mileage, longer service life, and in some cases better engine protection. These benefits do not come without a few hitches, however; the main one being the price of synthetic oils, which is three or four times the price per quart of conventional oil.

Synthetic oil is not for every truck and every type of driving, so you should consider your engine's condition and your type of driving. Also, check your truck's warranty conditions regarding the use of synthetic oils.

Both brand new engines and older, high mileage engines are the wrong candidates for synthetic oil. The synthetic oils are so slippery that they can prevent the proper break-in of new engines; most manufacturers recommend that you wait until the engine is properly broken in

(3000 miles) before using synthetic oil. Older engines with wear have a different problem with synthetics: they "use" (consume during operation) more oil as they age. Slippery synthetic oils get past these worn parts easily. If your engine is "using" conventional oil, it will use synthetics much faster. Also, if your truck is leaking oil past old seals you'll have a much greater leak problem with synthetics.

Consider your type of driving. If most of your accumulated mileage is high speed, highway type driving, the more expensive synthetic oils may be a benefit. Extended highway driving gives the engine a chance to warm up, accumulating less acids in the oil and putting less stress on the engine over the long run. Under these conditions, the oil change interval can be extended (as long as your oil filter can last the extended life of the oil) up to the advertised mileage claims of the synthetics. Trucks with synthetic oils may show increased fuel economy in highway driving, due to less internal friction. However, many automotive experts agree that 50,000 miles (80,000 km) is too long to keep any oil in your engine.

Trucks used under harder circumstances, such as stop-and-go, city type driving, short trips, or extended idling, should be serviced more frequently. For the engines in these trucks, the much greater cost of synthetic or fuel-efficient oils may not be worth the investment. Internal wear increase much quicker on these trucks, causing greater oil consumption and leakage.

NOTE: *The mixing of conventional and synthetic oils is not recommended. If you are using synthetic oil, it might be wise to carry two or three quarts with you no matter where you drive, as not all service stations carry this type of lubricant.*

Non-detergent or straight mineral oils must never be used.

FUEL

Gasoline Engines

It is important to use fuel of the proper octane rating in your truck. Octane rating is based on the quantity of anti-knock compounds added to the fuel and it determines the speed at which the gas will burn. The lower the octane rating, the faster it burns. The higher the octane, the slower the fuel will burn and a greater percentage of compounds in the fuel prevent spark ping (knock), detonation and preignition (dieseling).

As the temperature of the engine increases, the air/fuel mixture exhibits a tendency to ignite before the spark plug is fired. If fuel of an octane rating too low for the engine is used, this will allow combustion to occur before the piston has completed its compression stroke, thereby creating a very high pressure very rapidly.

Fuel of the proper octane rating, for the compression ratio and ignition timing of your truck, will slow the combustion process sufficiently to allow the spark plug enough time to ignite the mixture completely and smoothly. Many non-catalyst models are designed to run on regular fuel. The use of some super-premium fuel is no substitution for a properly tuned and main-

Recommended Lubricants

Component	Lubricant
Engine Oil	API SF/CC
Manual Transmission	API GL-4, SAE 75W-90 or 80W-90 ①
Automatic Transmission	ATF DEXTRON® II
Transfer Case	API GL-4, SAE 75W-90 or 80W-90
Differentials	API GL-5, SAE 80W-90
Brake Master Cylinder	DOT 3, SAE J1703
Clutch Master Cylinder	DOT 3, SAE J1703
Power Steering	ATF DEXTRON® II
Steering Gear	API GL-4, SAE 75W-90 or 80W-90
Steering Knuckle	NLGI #2
Ball Joints	NLGI #1 or #2
Wheel Bearings	NLGI #2
Coolant	Ethylene Glycol-Based Antifreeze

① Diesel Engines: API GL-3 or GL-4 90W or 140W

tained engine. Chances are that if your engine exhibits any signs of spark ping, detonation or pre-ignition when using regular fuel, the ignition timing should be checked against specifications or the cylinder head should be removed for decarbonizing.

Vehicles equipped with catalytic converters must use UNLEADED GASOLINE ONLY. Use of unleaded fuel shortened the life of spark plugs, exhaust systems and EGR valves and can damage the catalytic converter. Most converter equipped models are designed to operate using unleaded gasoline with a minimum rating of 87 octane. Use of unleaded gas with octane ratings lower than 87 can cause persistent spark knock which could lead to engine damage.

Light spark knock may be noticed when accelerating or driving up hills. The slight knocking may be considered normal (with 87 octane) because the maximum fuel economy is obtained under condition of occasional light spark knock. Gasoline with an octane rating higher than 87 may be used, but it is not necessary (in most cases) for proper operation.

If spark knock is constant, when using 87 octane, at cruising speeds on level ground, ignition timing adjustment may be required.

NOTE: *Your engine's fuel requirement can change with time, mainly due to carbon buildup, which changes the compression ratio. If your engine pings, knocks or runs on, switch to a higher grade of fuel. Sometimes just changing brands will cure the problem. If it becomes necessary to retard the timing from specifications, don't change it more than a few degrees. Retarded timing will reduce power output and fuel mileage and will increase the engine temperature.*

Diesel Engines

Diesel engines require the use of diesel fuel. At no time should gasoline be substituted. Two grades of diesel fuel are manufactured, #1 and #2, although #2 grade is generally more available. Better fuel economy results from the use of #2 grade fuel. In some northern parts of the U.S. and in most parts of Canada, #1 grade fuel is available in the winter or a winterized blend of #2 grade is supplied in winter months. When the temperature falls below 20°F (−7°C), #1 grade or winterized #2 grade fuel are the only fuels that can be used. Cold temperatures cause unwinterized #2 to thicken (it actually gels), blocking the fuel lines and preventing the engine from running.

DIESEL CAUTIONS:

- Do not use home heating oil in your truck.
- Do not use ether or starting assist fluids in your truck.
- Do not use any fuel additives recommended for use in gasoline engines.

It is normal that the engine noise level is louder during the warm-up period in winter. It is also normal that whitish/blue smoke may be emitted from the exhaust after starting and during warm-up. The amount of smoke depends upon the outside temperature.

OPERATION IN FOREIGN COUNTRIES

If you plan to drive your truck outside the United States or Canada, there is a possibility that fuels will be too low in anti-knock quality and could produce engine damage. It is wise to consult with local authorities upon arrival in a foreign country to determine the best fuels available.

Engine

CAUTION: *Prolonged and repeated skin contact with used engine oil, with no effort to remove the oil, may be harmful. Always follow these simple precautions when handling used motor oil:*

- Avoid prolonged skin contact with used motor oil.
- Remove oil from skin by washing thoroughly with soap and water or waterless hand cleaner. Do not use gasoline, thinners or other solvents.
- Avoid prolonged skin contact with oil-soaked clothing.

OIL LEVEL CHECK

Every time you stop for fuel, check the engine oil as follows:

1. Park the truck on level ground.
2. When checking the oil level it is best for the engine to be at operating temperature, although checking the oil immediately after a stopping will lead to a false reading. Wait a few minutes after turning off the engine to allow the oil to drain back into the crankcase.
3. Open the hood and locate the dipstick which is on the left side (L16, L18, L20B, SD22 and SD25 engines) or the right side (Z20, Z22, Z24, Z24i and VG301 engines). Pull the dipstick from its tube, wipe it clean and reinsert it.

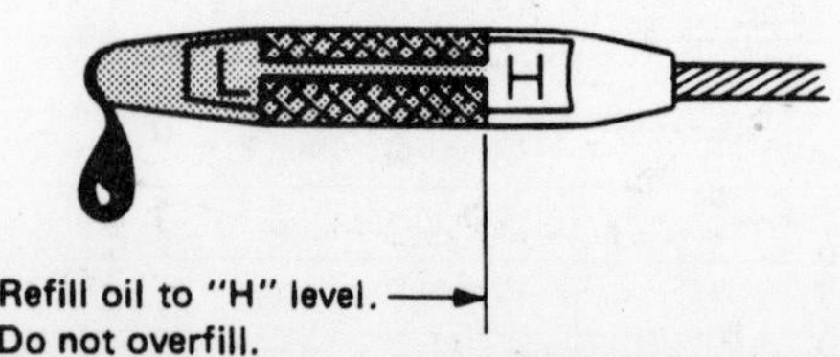

The oil level indicated on the dipstick should never be below the "L" line or above the "H" line

4. Pull the dipstick out again and, holding it horizontally, read the oil level. The oil should be between the **H** and **L** marks on the dipstick. If the oil is below the **L** mark, add oil of the proper viscosity through the capped opening on the top of the cylinder head cover. See the "Oil and Fuel Recommendations" chart in this chapter for the proper viscosity ad rating of oil to use.

5. Replace the dipstick and check the oil level again after adding any oil. Be careful not to overfill the crankcase. Approximately one quart of oil will raise the level from the **L** to the **H**. Excess oil will generally be consumed at an accelerated rate.

OIL AND FILTER CHANGE

The oil should be changed every 6000 miles (9600 km) on models built between 1970–77. All 1978–89 models should have the oil changed every 7500 miles (12,000 km).

CAUTION: *Prolonged and repeated skin contact with used engine oil, with no effort to remove the oil, may be harmful. Always follow these simple precautions when handling used motor oil.*

- Avoid prolonged skin contract with used motor oil.
- Remove oil from skin by washing thoroughly with soap and water or waterless hand cleaner. Do not use gasoline, thinners or other solvents.
- Avoid prolonged skin contact with oil-soaked clothing.

The oil drain plug is located on the bottom, rear of the oil pan (bottom of the engine, underneath the truck). The oil filter is located on the right side of the engine on all models.

The mileage figures given are the Nissan recommended intervals assuming normal driving and conditions. If your truck is being used under dusty, polluted or off-road conditions, change the oil and filter more frequently than specified. The same goes for trucks driven in stop-and-go traffic or only for short distances. Always drain the oil after the engine has been running long enough to bring it to normal operating temperature. Hot oil will flow easier and more contaminants will be removed along with the oil than if it were drained cold. To change the oil and filter:

CAUTION: *The EPA warns that prolonged contact with used engine oil may cause a number of skin disorders, including cancer! You should make every effort to minimize your exposure to used engine oil. Protective gloves should be worn when changing the oil. Wash your hands and any other exposed skin areas as soon as possible after exposure to used engine oil. Soap and water, or waterless hand cleaner should be used.*

1. Run the engine until it reaches normal operating temperature.
2. Jack up the front of the truck and support it on safety stands.

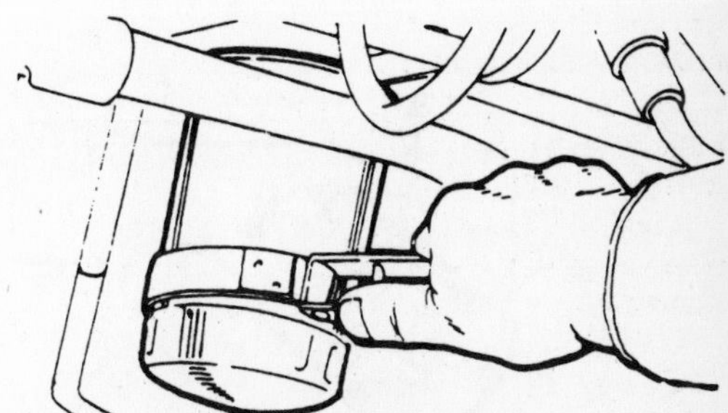

Remove the oil filter with a strap wrench

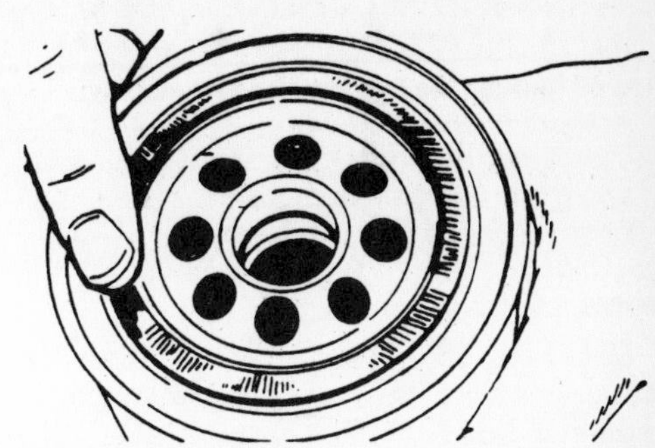

Lubricate the gasket on the new filter with clean engine oil. A dry gasket may not make a good seal and will allow the filter to leak

By keeping an inward pressure on the drain plug as you unscrew it, the oil won't escape past the threads

Install the new oil filter by hand

3. Slide a drain pan of at least 6 quarts capacity under the oil pan.

4. Loosen the drain plug. Turn the plug out by hand. By keeping an inward pressure on the plug as you unscrew it, oil won't escape past the threads and you can remove it without being burned by hot oil.

NOTE: *1984–87 models (720 series) with the SD25 diesel engine utilize two oil drain plugs. One at the front of the oil pan and the other on the right rear side.*

5. Allow the oil to drain completely and then install the drain plug(s). Don't overtighten the plug(s), or you'll be buying a new pan or a trick replacement plug for stripped threads.

6. Using a strap wrench, remove the oil filter; on Z24i and VG30i engines, use a cap-type filter removal tool. Keep in mind that it's holding about one quart of dirty, hot oil. The filter on diesel engines is mounted upside down so be sure that all oil has been drained!

7. Empty the old filter into the drain pan and dispose of the filter.

8. Using a clean rag, wipe off the filter adapter on the engine block. Be sure that the rag doesn't leave any lint which could clog an oil passage.

9. Coat the rubber gasket on the filter with fresh oil. Spin it onto the engine by hand; when the gasket touches the adapter surface give it another ½–¾ turn. No more, or you'll squash the gasket and it will leak.

10. Refill the engine with the correct amount of fresh oil. See the "Capacities" chart.

11. Check the oil level on the dipstick. It is normal for the level to be a bit above the full mark. Start the engine and allow it to idle for a few minutes.

CAUTION: *Do not run the engine above idle speed until it has built up oil pressure, indicated when the oil light goes out.*

12. Shut off the engine, allow the oil to drain for a few minutes, and check the oil level. Check around the filter and drain plug for any leaks, and correct as necessary.

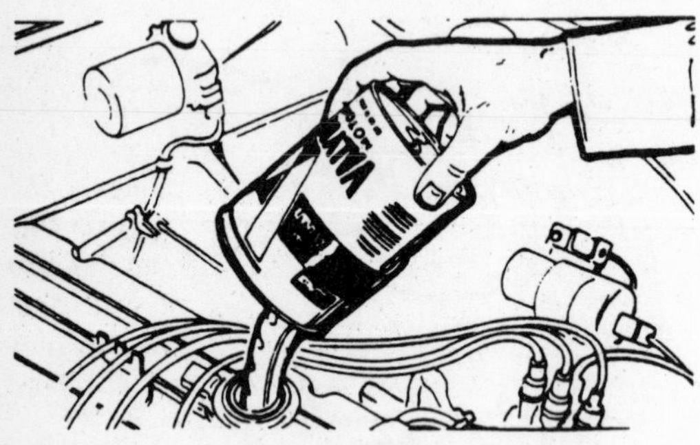

Add oil through the cylinder head cover only

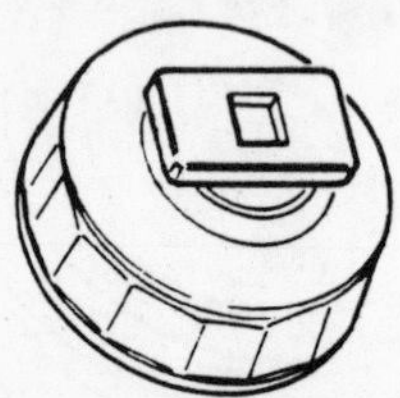

Use a cap-type oil filter removal tool on fuel injected engines

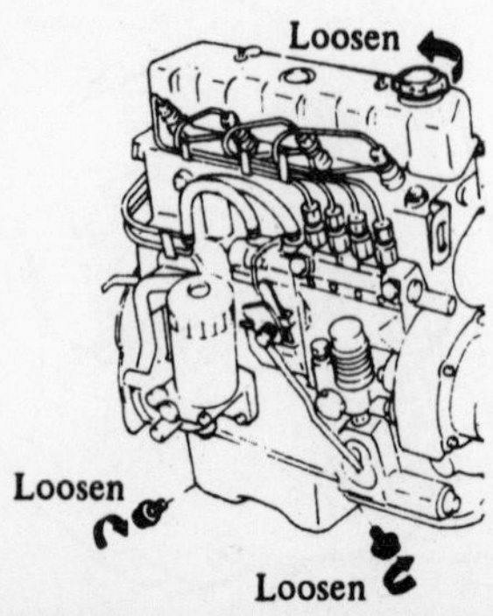

1984–87 SD25 engines use two (2) oil drain plugs

Manual Transmission

FLUID RECOMMENDATIONS

- Pick-Ups and Pathfinders with gasoline engines: multipurpose gear oil API GL-4; SAE 75W-90 or 80W-90
- Pick-Ups with diesel engines: multipurpose gear oil API GL-3 or GL-4; SAE 90W or SAE 140W.

FLUID LEVEL CHECK

The oil in the manual transmission should be checked at least every 7500 miles (12,000 km) for 1970–78, or 15,000 miles (24,000 km) for 1979–89 and replaced every 25,000–30,000 miles (40,000–48,000 km), even more frequently if driven in deep water.

1. With the truck parked on a level surface, remove the filler plug (square head on some

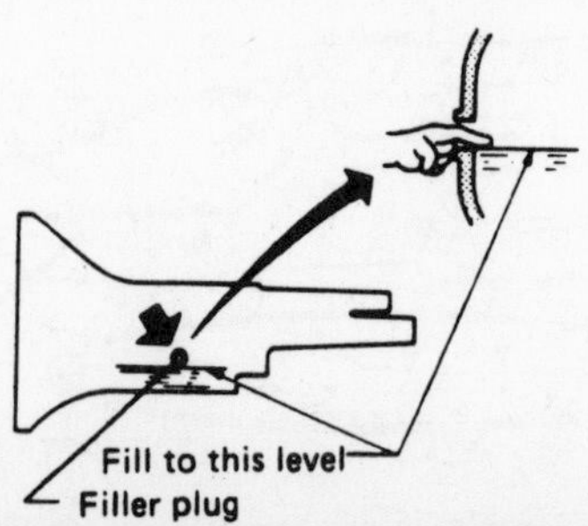

The oil level in the manual transmission should be up to the bottom of the filler (upper) plug

models, Allen head on others) from the left side of the transmission housing.

2. If the lubricant begins to trickle out of the hole, there is enough. Otherwise, carefully insert your finger (watch out for sharp threads!) and check to see if the oil is up to the edge of the hole.

CAUTION: *Prolonged and repeated skin contact with used engine oil, with no effort to remove the oil, may be harmful. Always follow these simple precautions when handling used motor oil.*

- Avoid prolonged skin contact with used motor oil.
- Remove oil from skin by washing thoroughly with soap and water or waterless hand cleaner. Do not use gasoline, thinners or other solvents.
- Avoid prolonged skin contact with oil-soaked clothing.

3. If not, add oil through the hole until the level is at the edge of the hole. Most gear lubricants come in a plastic squeeze bottle with a nozzle; making additions simple. You can also use a common everyday kitchen baster.

4. Replace the filler plug, run the engine and check for leaks.

DRAIN AND REFILL

Once every 24,000 miles (40,000 km) for 1970–78, or once every 30,000 miles (48,000 km) for 1979–89, the oil in the manual transmission should be changed.

1. The transmission oil should be hot before it is drained. If the engine is at normal operating temperature, the transmission oil should be hot enough.

2. Raise the truck and support it properly on jackstands so that you can safely work underneath. You will probably not have enough room to work if the truck is not raised.

3. The drain plug is located on the bottom of the transmission. Place a pan under the drain plug and remove it. Keep a slight upward pressure on the plug while unscrewing it, this will keep the oil from pouring out until the plug is removed.

CAUTION: *The oil will be HOT! Be careful when you remove the plug so that you don't take a bath in hot gear oil.*

4. Allow the oil to drain completely. Clean off the plug and replace it, tightening it until it is just snug.

5. Remove the filler plug from the side of the transmission case. It is on the driver's (left) side. There is usually a gasket underneath this plug. Replace it if damaged.

6. Fill the transmission with gear oil through the filler plug hole as detailed previously. Refer to the Capacities Chart for the amount of oil needed to refill your transmission.

7. The oil level should come right up to the edge of the hole. You can stick your finger in to verify this. Watch out for sharp threads!

8. Replace the filler plug and gasket, lower the truck, and check for leaks. Dispose of the old oil in the proper manner.

CHECKING WATER ENTRY

1986–89 4WD Models Only

After having driven in deep water or mud, the clutch housing should always be checked for water entry. There is a small rubber gasket at the bottom of the left side leading edge of the transmission case where it mates with the rear of the engine block, carefully pry it out and let any water that has collected in the clutch housing seep out.

Automatic Transmission

FLUID RECOMMENDATIONS

- All models: DEXRON®II ATF

FLUID LEVEL CHECK

Check the automatic transmission fluid level at least every 6000 miles (9600 km) for 1973–79; 15,000 miles (24,000 km) for 1980–89.The dipstick is in the right rear of the engine compartment. The fluid level should be checked only when the transmission is hot (normal operating temperature). The transmission is considered hot after about 20 miles of highway driving.

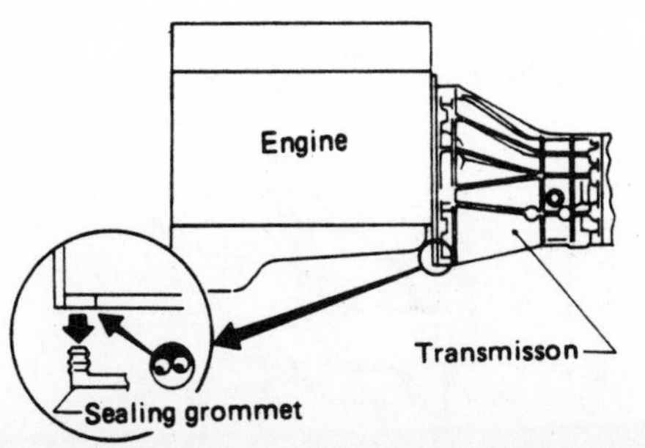

Checking the housing for water entry—1986–89 4WD

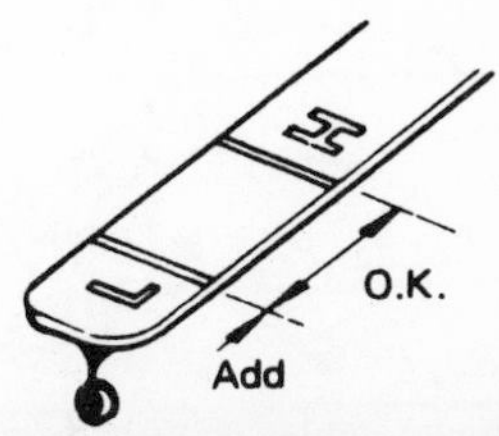

Automatic transmission dipstick—1973–87

1. Park the truck on a level surface with the engine idling. Shift the transmission into **P** and set the parking brake.

2. Remove the dipstick, wipe it clean and reinsert if firmly. Be sure that it has been pushed all the way in. Remove the dipstick and check the fluid level while holding it horizontally. With the engine running, the fluid level should be between the **H** and **L** marks on 1973–87 models. 1988–89 models have a HOT and a COLD side to the dipstick. On 2wd models, the fluid level should be between the two hash marks on the HOT side or between the two notches on the COLD side. On 4wd models, the fluid level should be within the cross-hatched area on the HOT or COLD sides.

3. If the fluid level is below the **L** mark on 1973–87 models, below the lower hash mark (HOT) or lower notch (COLD) on 1988–89 2wd models, or not within the cross-hatched area on either side of the dipstick on 1988–89 4wd models, pour DEXRON®II ATFinto the dipstick tube. This is easily done with the aid of a funnel. Check the level often as you are filling the transmission. Be extremely careful not to overfill it. Overfilling will cause slippage, seal damage and overheating. Approximately one pint of ATF will raise the level from one notch to the other.

NOTE: *Always use the proper transmission fluid when filling your truck's transmission. All models use DEXRON®II. Always check with the owner's manual to be sure. NEVER use Type F in a transmission requiring DEXRON® or vice versa, as severe damage will result.*

CAUTION: *The fluid on the dipstick should always be a bright red color. It if is discolored (brown or black), or smells burnt, serious transmission troubles, probably due to overheating, should be suspected. The transmission should be inspected by a qualified service technician to locate the cause of the burnt fluid.*

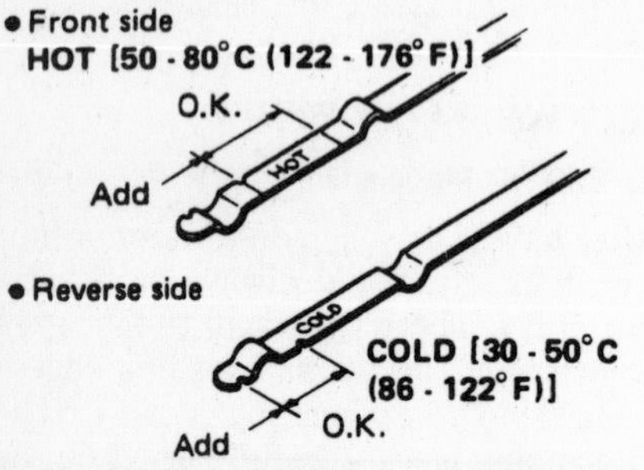

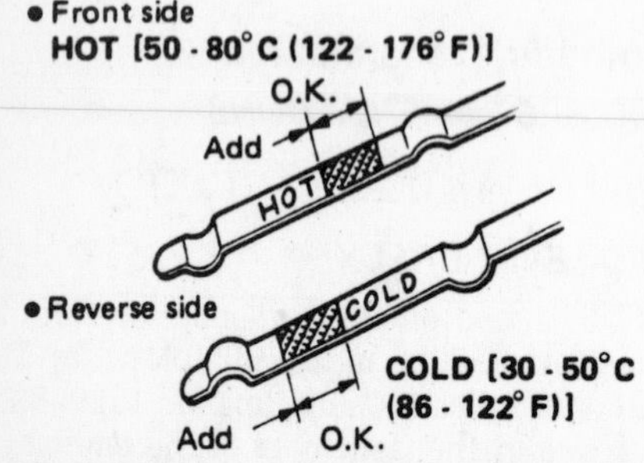

Automatic transmission dipstick—1988–89 2WD

Automatic transmission dipstick—1988–89 4WD

DRAIN AND REFILL

The automatic transmission fluid should be changed at least every 25,000–30,000 miles (40,000–48,000 km). If the truck is normally used in severe service, such as stop-and-go driving, trailer towing or the like, the interval should be halved. The fluid should be hot before it is drained; a 20 minute drive will accomplish this.

Pan and Filter Service

1. There is no drain plug; the fluid pan must be removed. Partially loosen the pan retaining screws until the pan can be pulled down at one corner. Lower a corner of the pan and allow all fluid to drain out.

2. After the pan has drained completely, remove the pan retaining screws and then remove the pan and gasket.

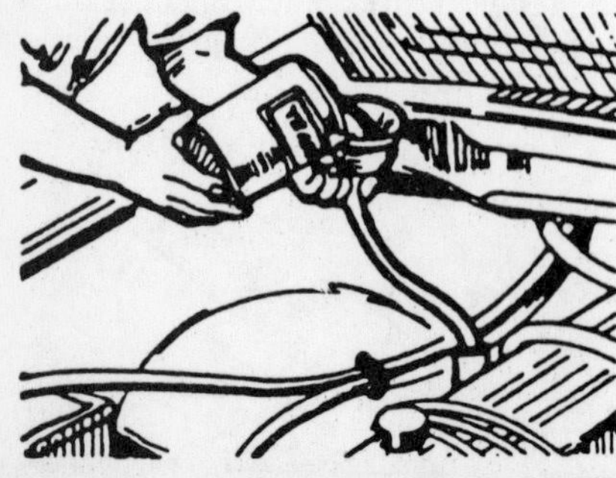

Add automatic transmission fluid through the dipstick tube

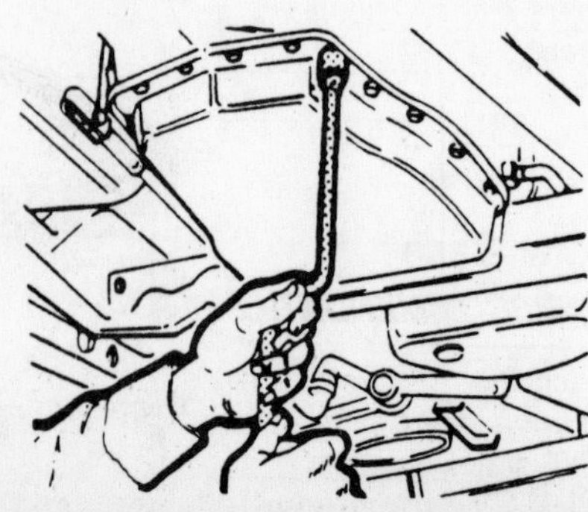

Removing the pan on the automatic transmission

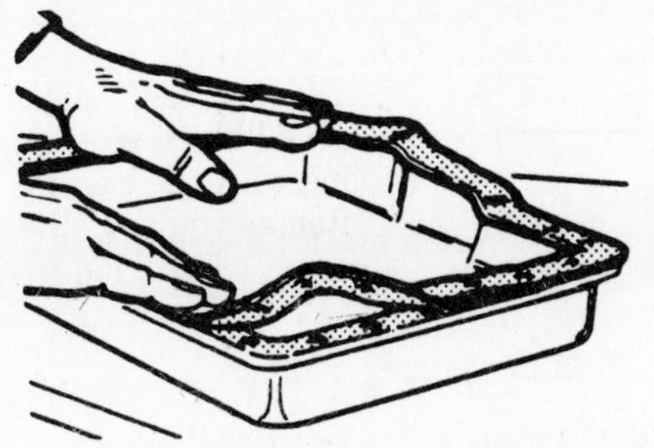

Always replace the gasket when installing the pan

3. Clean the pan thoroughly and allow it to air dry. If you wipe it out with a rag you run the risk of leaving bits of lint in the pan which will clog the tiny hydraulic passages in the transmission.

4. Install the pan using a new gasket. If you decide to use sealer on the gasket, apply it only in a very thin bead running to the outside of the pan screw holes. Tighten the pan screws evenly in rotation from the center outwards, to 3–5 ft. lbs.

5. It is a good idea to measure the amount of fluid drained from the transmission to determine the correct amount of fresh fluid to add. This is because some parts of the transmission may not drain completely and using the dry refill amount specified in the "Capacities" chart could lead to overfilling. Fluid is added only through the dipstick tube. Use only the proper automatic transmission fluid; do not overfill.

6. Replace the dipstick after filling. Start the engine and allow it to idle. DO NOT race the engine.

7. After the engine has idled for a few minutes, shift the transmission slowly through the gears and then return it to **P**. With the engine still idling, check the fluid level on the dipstick. If necessary, add more fluid to raise the level to where it is supposed to be.

CAUTION: *Check the fluid in the drain pan, it should always be a bright red color. It if is discolored (brown or black), or smells burnt, serious transmission troubles, probably due to overheating, should be suspected. The transmission should be inspected by a qualified service technician to locate the cause of the burnt fluid.*

Transfer Case

FLUID RECOMMENDATIONS

- Pick-Ups and Pathfinder with gasoline engines: multipurpose gear oil API GL-4; SAE 75W-90 or 80W-90
- Pick-Ups with diesel engines: multipurpose gear oil API GL-4; SAE 90W.

FLUID LEVEL CHECK

The oil in the transfer case should be checked at least every 15,000 miles (24,000 km) and replaced every 25,000–30,000 miles (40,000–48,000 km), even more frequently if driven in deep water or mud.

1. With the truck parked on a level surface, remove the filler plug from the side of the transfer case housing on 1980–86 models (720 series), or the rear of the housing on 1986–89 models (D21 series).

2. If the lubricant begins to trickle out of the hole, there is enough. Otherwise, carefully insert your finger (watch out for sharp threads!) and check to see if the oil is up to the edge of the hole.

CAUTION: *Prolonged and repeated skin contact with used engine oil, with no effort to remove the oil, may be harmful. Always follow these simple precautions when handling used motor oil.*

- Avoid prolonged skin contact with used motor oil.
- Remove oil from skin by washing thoroughly with soap and water or waterless hand cleaner. Do not use gasoline, thinners or other solvents.
- Avoid prolonged skin contact with oil-soaked clothing.

3. If not, add oil through the hole until the level is at the edge of the hole. Most gear lubricants come in a plastic squeeze bottle with a nozzle; making additions simple. You can also use a common everyday kitchen baster.

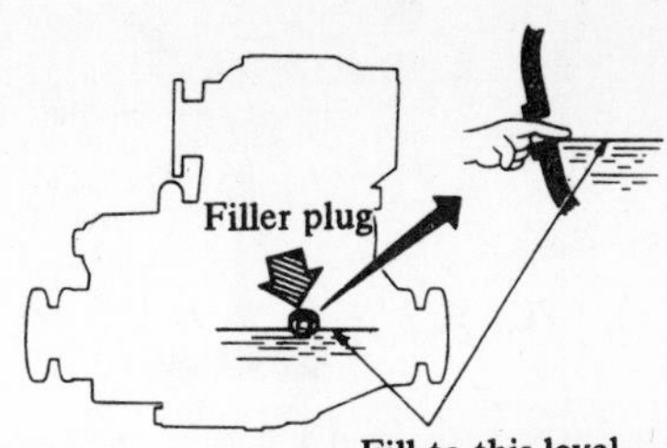

Transfer case filler plug location—1980–86 (720-D series)

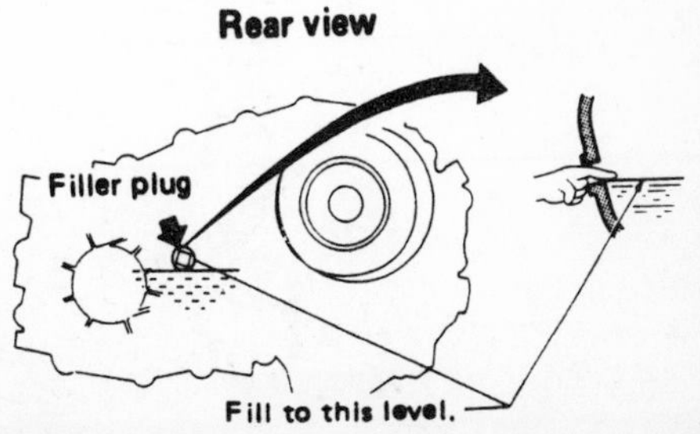

Transfer case filler plug location—1986–89 (D21-D series)

4. Replace the filler plug, run the engine and check for leaks.

DRAIN AND REFILL

Once every every 30,000 miles (48,000 km), the oil in the transfer case should be changed.

1. The transfer case oil should be hot before it is drained. If the engine is at normal operating temperature, the oil should be hot enough.
2. Raise the truck and support it properly on jackstands so that you can safely work underneath. You will probably not have enough room to work if the truck is not raised.
3. The drain plug is located on the bottom of the transfer case. Place a pan under the drain plug and remove it. Keep a slight upward pressure on the plug while unscrewing it, this will keep the oil from pouring out until the plug is removed.

CAUTION: *The oil will be HOT. Be careful when you remove the plug so that you don't take a bath in hot gear oil.*

4. Allow the oil to drain completely. Clean off the plug and replace it, tightening it until it is just snug.
5. Remove the filler plug from the side of the case. There will be a gasket underneath this plug. Replace it if damaged.
6. Fill the transfer case with gear oil through the filler plug hole as detailed previously. Refer to the Capacities Chart for the amount of oil needed to refill your transfer case.
7. The oil level should come right up to the edge of the hole. You can stick your finger in to verify this. Watch out for sharp threads.
8. Replace the filler plug and gasket, lower the truck, and check for leaks. Dispose of the old oil in the proper manner.

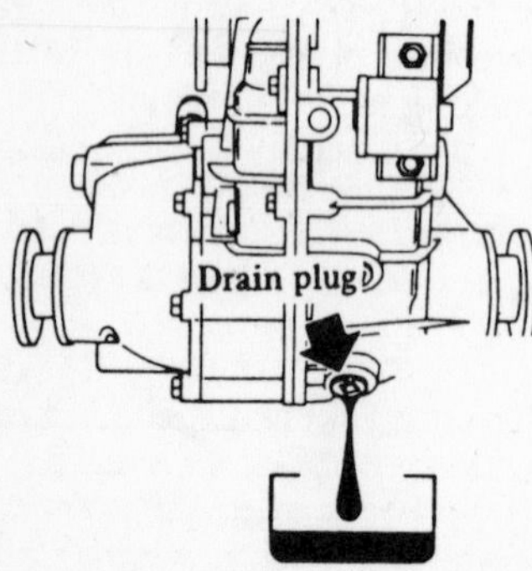

Transfer case drain plug location—1980–86(720-D series)

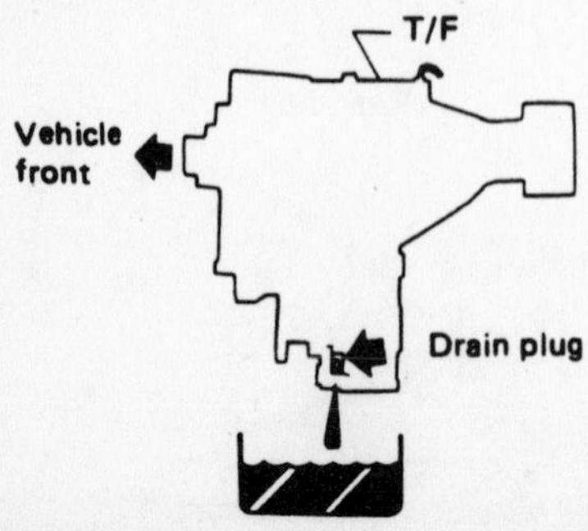

Transfer case drain plug location—1986–89 (D21-D series)

Drive Axles (Differentials)

FLUID RECOMMENDATIONS

- All models: Hypoid gear oil API GL-5; below 0°F (−18°C): SAE 90W, above 0°F (−18°C): SAE 80W or 80W-90.

FLUID LEVEL CHECK

The oil in the front and/or rear differential should be checked at least every 15,000 miles (24,000 km) and replaced every 25,000–30,000 miles (40,000–48,000 km). If driven in deep water it should be replaced immediately.

1. With the truck parked on a level surface, remove the filler plug from the back of the differential.

NOTE: *The plug on the bottom is the drain plug on rear differentials. The lower of the two plugs on the back of the housing is the drain plug on front differentials.*

2. If the oil begins to trickle out of the hole, there is enough. Otherwise, carefully insert your finger (watch out for sharp threads!) into

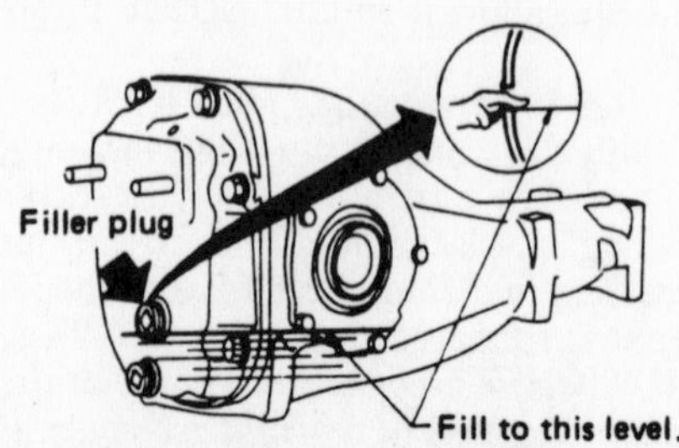

Checking the fluid level in the front differential

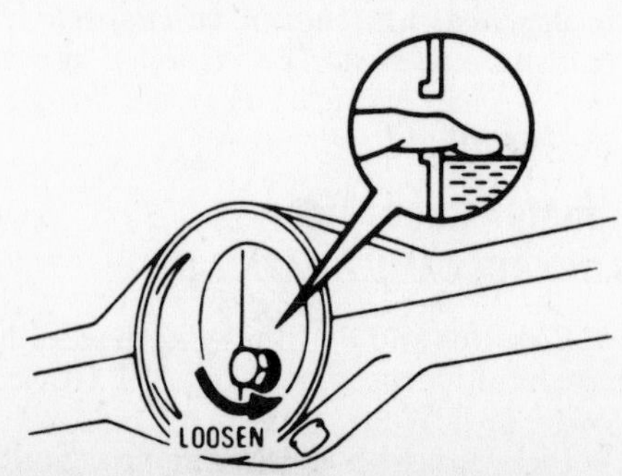

Checking the fluid level in the rear differential

the hole and check to see if the oil is up to the bottom edge of the filler hole.

3. If not, add oil through the hole until the level is at the edge of the hole. Most gear oils come in a plastic squeeze bottle with a nozzle, making additions simple. You can also use a common kitchen baster. Use standard GL-5 hypoid type gear oil; SAE 90 or SAE 80 if you live in a particularly cold area.

4. Replace the filler plug and drive the truck for a while. Stop the truck and check for leaks.

DRAIN AND REFILL

The gear oil in the front or rear axle should be changed at least every 25,000–30,000 miles (40,000–48,000 km); immediately if driven in deep water.

To drain and fill the differential, proceed as follows:

1. Park the vehicle on a level surface. Set the parking brake.
2. Remove the filler (upper) plug. Place a container which is large enough to catch all of the differential oil, under the drain plug.
3. Remove the drain (lower) plug and gasket, if so equipped. Allow all of the oil to drain into the container.
4. Install the drain plug. Tighten it so that it will not leak, but do not overtighten.

NOTE: *Its usually a good idea to replace the drain plug gasket at this time.*

5. Refill with the proper grade and viscosity of axle lubricant (see "Recommended Lubricants" chart). Be sure that the level reaches the bottom of the filler plug. DO NOT overfill.

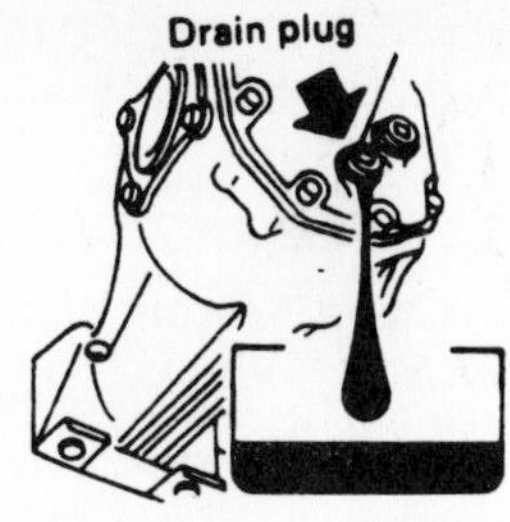

Drain plug location in the front differential

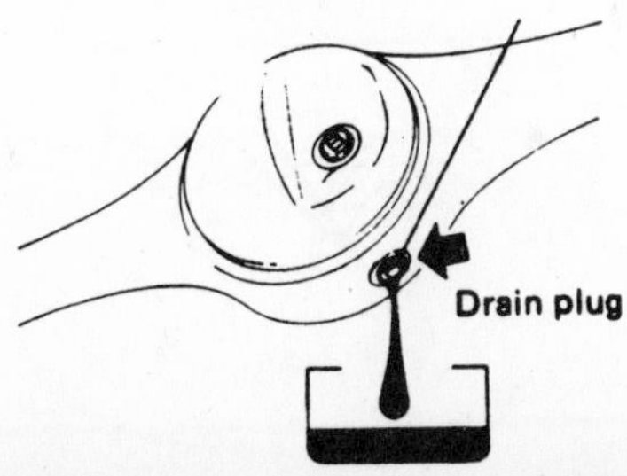

Drain plug location in the rear differential

6. Install the filler plug and check for leakage.

Cooling System

FLUID RECOMMENDATIONS

When additional coolant is required to maintain the proper level, always add a 50/50 mixture of ethylene glycol antifreeze/coolant and water.

FLUID LEVEL CHECK

Dealing with the cooling system can be a tricky matter unless the proper precautions are observed. It is best to check the coolant level in the radiator when the engine is cold. This is done by removing the radiator cap and seeing that the coolant is within ¾" of the bottom of the filler neck. On later models, the cooling system has, as one of its components, an expansion tank. If coolant is visible above the **Low** or **Min** mark on the tank, the level is satisfactory. Always be certain that the filler caps on both the radiator and the reservoir are tightly closed.

In the event that the coolant level must be checked when the engine is warm or on engines without the expansion tank, place a thick rag over the radiator cap and slowly turn the cap counterclockwise until it reaches the first detent. Allow all the hot steam to escape. This will allow the pressure in the system to drop gradually, preventing an explosion of hot coolant. When the hissing noise stops, remove the cap the rest of the way.

It's a good idea to check the coolant every time that you stop for fuel. If the coolant level is low, add equal amount of ethylene glycol based antifreeze and clean water. On models without an expansion tank, add coolant through the radiator filler neck. Fill the expansion tank to the **Full** or **Max** level on trucks with that system.

CAUTION: *Never add cold coolant to a hot engine unless the engine is running, to avoid cracking the engine block.*

Avoid using water that is known to have a high alkaline content or is very hard, except in emergency situations. Drain and flush the cool-

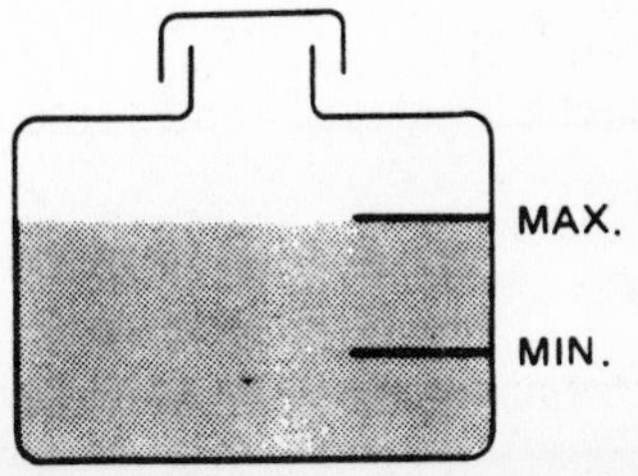

The coolant level should never fall below the MIN mark on models with an expansion tank

ing system as soon as possible after using such water.

The radiator hoses and clamps and the radiator cap should be checked at the same time as the coolant level. Hoses which are brittle, cracked, or swollen should be replaced. Clamps should be checked for tightness (screwdriver tight only! Do not allow the clamp to cut into the hose or crush the fitting). The radiator cap gasket should be checked for any obvious tears, cracks or swelling, or any signs of incorrect seating in the radiator neck.

DRAIN AND REFILL

CAUTION: *When draining the coolant, keep in mind that cats and dogs are attracted by the ethylene glycol antifreeze, and are quite likely to drink any that is left in an uncovered container or in puddles on the ground. This will prove fatal in sufficient quantity. Always drain the coolant into a sealable container. Coolant should be reused unless it is contaminated or several years old.*

Completely draining and refilling the cooling system every two years at least will remove accumulated rust, scale and other deposits.

NOTE: *Use a good quality antifreeze with water pump lubricants, rust inhibitors and other corrosion inhibitors along with acid neutralizers. Use a permanent type coolant that meets specification ESE-M97B44A or the equivalent.*

1. Drain the existing antifreeze and coolant. Open the radiator and engine drain petcocks (models equipped), or disconnect the bottom radiator hose, at the radiator outlet. Set the heater temperature controls to the full HOT position.

NOTE: *Before opening the radiator petcock, spray it with some penetrating lubricant.*

2. Close the petcock or reconnect the lower hose and fill the system with water.
3. Add a can of quality radiator flush. Be sure the flush is safe to use in engines having aluminum components.
4. Idle the engine until the upper radiator hose gets hot.
5. Drain the system again.
6. Repeat this process until the drained water is clear and free of scale.
7. Close all petcocks and connect all the hoses.
8. If equipped with a coolant recovery system, flush the reservoir with water and leave empty.
9. Determine the capacity of your cooling system (see Capacities specifications). Add a 50/50 mix of quality antifreeze (ethylene glycol) and water to provide the desired protection.

SYSTEM INSPECTION

Most permanent antifreeze/coolant have a colored dye added which makes the solution an excellent leak detector. When servicing the cooling system, check for leakage at:

- All hoses and hose connections.
- Radiator seams, radiator core, and radiator draincock.
- All engine block and cylinder head freeze (core) plugs, and drain plugs.
- Edges of all cooling system gaskets (head gaskets, thermostat gasket).
- Transmission fluid cooler.
- Heating system components, water pump.
- Check the engine oil dipstick for signs of coolant in the engine oil.
- Check the coolant in the radiator for signs of oil in the coolant.

Investigate and correct any indication of coolant leakage.

Check the Radiator Cap

While you are checking the coolant level, check the radiator cap for a worn or cracked gasket. If the cap doesn't seal properly, fluid will be lost and the engine will overheat.

A worn cap should be replaced with a new one.

Clean Radiator of Debris

Periodically clean any debris such as leaves, paper, insects, etc., from the radiator fins. Pick the large pieces off by hand. The smaller pieces can be washed away with water pressure from a hose.

Carefully straighten any bent radiator fins with a pair of needle nose pliers. Be careful, the fins are very soft. Don't wiggle the fins back and forth too much. Straighten them once and try not to move them again.

CHECKING SYSTEM PROTECTION

A 50/50 mix of coolant concentrate and water will usually provide protection to −35°F (−37°C). Freeze protection may be checked by using a cooling system hydrometer. Inexpen-

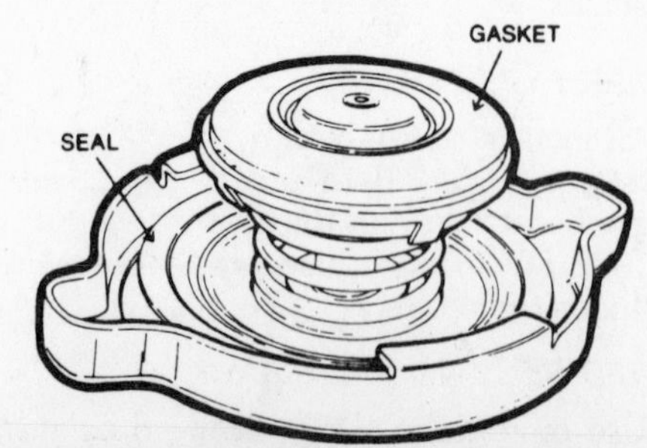

Check the radiator cap seal and gasket condition

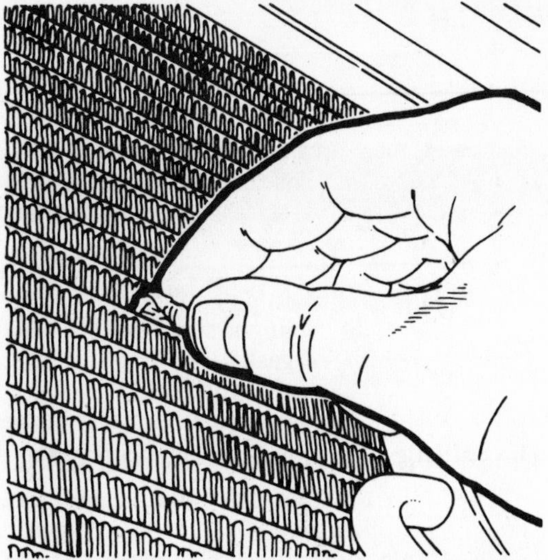
Clean the radiator fins of any debris which impedes air flow

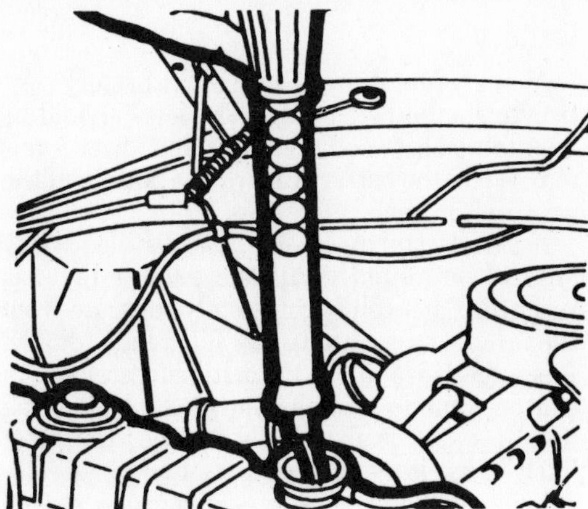
The freezing protection rating can be checked with an antifreeze tester

sive hydrometers (floating ball types) may be obtained from a local department store (automotive section) or an auto supply store. Follow the directions packaged with the coolant hydrometer when checking protection.

Master Cylinders

All models utilize both a brake and a clutch master cylinder. Both are located above the brake booster unit at the driver's side firewall.

1972–80 models utilize two (2) brake master cylinder reservoirs.

FLUID RECOMMENDATIONS

Use only Heavy Duty Brake fluid meeting DOT 3 or SAE J1703 specifications.

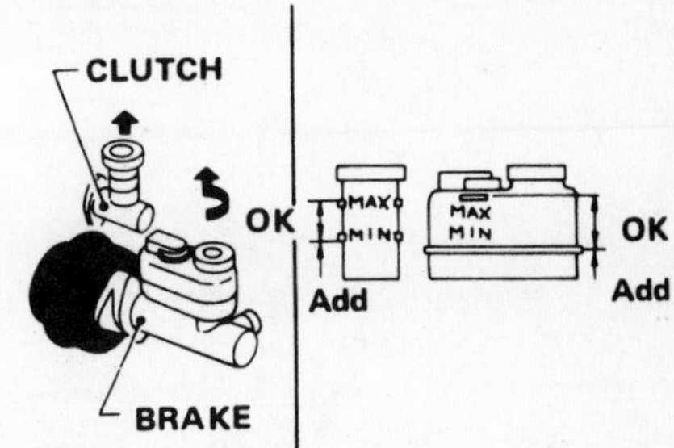

Brake and clutch master cylinders—typical

FLUID LEVEL CHECK

The fluid in the brake and/or clutch master cylinders should be checked every 6 months or 6000 miles (9600 km).

Check the fluid level on the side of the reservoir. If fluid is required, remove the screw on the and remove the filler cap and gasket from the master cylinder. Fill the reservoir to the full line in the reservoir. Install the filler cap, making sure the gasket is properly seated in the cap.

NOTE: *It is normal for the fluid level to fall as the disc brake pads wear. However, if the master cylinder requires filling frequently, you should check the system for leaks in the hoses, master cylinder, or wheel cylinders. Brake fluid dissolves paint. It also absorbs moisture from the air; never leave a container or the master cylinder or the clutch cylinder uncovered any longer than necessary. The clutch master cylinder uses the same fluid as the brakes, and should be checked at the same time as the brake master cylinder.*

Power Steering Pump

FLUID RECOMMENDATIONS

- Use only DEXRON®II ATF in the power steering system.

FLUID LEVEL CHECK

Check the power steering fluid level every 6 months or 6000 miles (9600 km).

1. Park the vehicle on a level surface. Run the engine until normal operating temperature is reached.
2. Turn the steering all the way to the left and then all the way to the right several times. Center the steering wheel and shut off the engine.
3. Open the hood and check the power steering reservoir fluid level.
4. Remove the filler cap and wipe the dipstick attached clean.
5. Re-insert the dipstick and tighten the cap. Remove the dipstick and note the fluid level indicated on the dipstick.

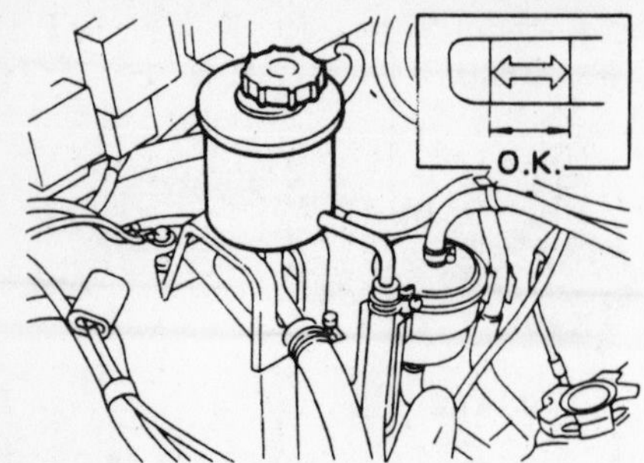

Power steering pump dipstick

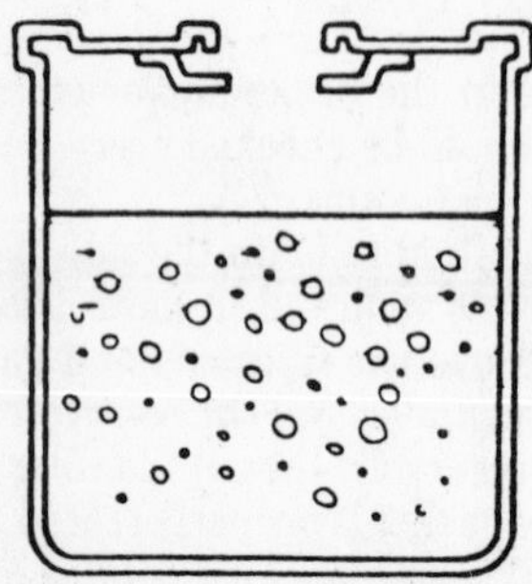

Foaming or emulsification indicates air in the system

6. The level should be at any point below the upper hash mark, but not below the lower hash mark (in the HOT or COLD ranges).
7. Add fluid as necessary. Do not overfill.

Steering Gear

FLUID RECOMMENDATIONS

Use standard hypoid-type gear oil GL-4, SAE 90W when refilling the steering gear.

FLUID LEVEL CHECK

Every year or 15,000 miles (24,000 km) you should check the steering gear housing lubricating oil. The filler plug is on top of the housing and requires a 14mm wrench for removal. The level should be at or near the top of the housing.

Checking the steering gear fluid level

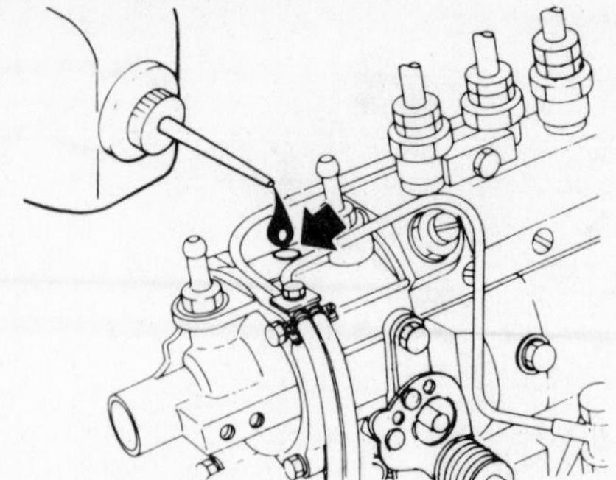

Filling the diesel injection pump reservoir

Diesel Injection Pump Diaphragm Oil

The oil in the injection pump diaphragm should be checked every 5,000 miles. To check the level, remove the filler plug located at the governor end of the pump and fill the reservoir to the plug level. The proper lubricant is cod liver oil.

Battery

At every fuel stop the level of the battery electrolyte should be checked. The level should be maintained between the upper and lower levels marked on the battery case or the bottom of the vent well in each cell.

If the electrolyte level is low, distilled water should be added until the proper level is reached. Each cell is completely separate from the others, so each must be filled individually. It is a good idea to add the distilled water with a squeeze bulb to avoid having electrolyte splash out. If water is frequently needed, the most likely cause is overcharging, caused by a faulty voltage regulator. If any acid solution should escape, it can be neutralized with a baking soda and water solution, but don't let the stuff get in the battery. In winter, add water only before driving to prevent the battery from freezing and cracking. When replacing a battery, it is important that the replacement have an out put rating equal to or greater than original equipment. See Chapter 3 for details on battery replacement.

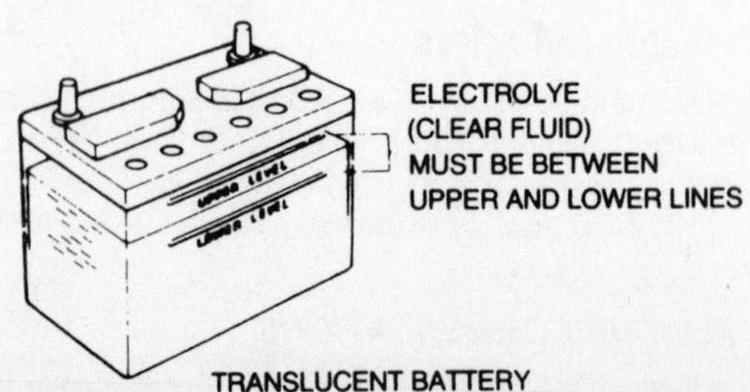

Some batteries have level indicator lines on their sides

CAUTION: *If you get acid on you skin or in your eyes, rinse it off immediately with lots of water. Go to a doctor if it gets in you eyes. The gases formed inside the battery cells are highly explosive. Never check the level of the electrolyte in the presence of flame or while smoking.*

Chassis Greasing

Complete chassis greasing should include an inspection of all rubber suspension bushings, lubrication of all body hinges, as well as proper greasing of the front suspension upper and lower ball joints and control arm bushings. To provide correct operation, the chassis should be greased every 6 months or 6000 miles (9600 km) on 1970–78 trucks. The 1979–89 trucks should be greased every 7500 miles (12,000 km).

If you wish to perform this operation yourself you should purchase a cartridge type grease gun and several cartridges of multipurpose lithium base grease. You will also need to purchase grease fittings from your Nissan dealer, as certain front end components are fitted with screw-in plugs to prevent entry of foreign material.

Remove the plug and install the grease fitting (if necessary). Push the nozzle of the grease gun down firmly onto the fitting and while applying pressure, force the new grease into the boot. Force sufficient grease into the fitting to cause the old grease to be expelled. When this has been accomplished, remove the fitting and replace the plug. Follow this procedure on each front suspension lubrication point.

Certain models have a two piece driveshaft which must be greased at the same 6 month/7,500 mile interval. The driveshaft is equipped with a grease fitting, located on the shaft just behind the center support bearing. Simply wipe off the fitting and pump in two or three shots of grease. There is no built in escape hole for the old grease to exit, so don't keep pumping in grease until the seal gives way.

MANUAL TRANSMISSION AND CLUTCH LINKAGE

On models so equipped, apply a small amount of chassis grease to the pivot points of the transmission and clutch linkage as per the chassis lubrication diagram.

AUTOMATIC TRANSMISSION LINKAGE

On models so equipped, apply a small amount of 10W engine oil to the kickdown and shift linkage at the pivot points.

PARKING BRAKE LINKAGE

At yearly intervals or whenever binding is noticeable in the parking brake linkage, lubricate the cable guides, levers and linkage with a suitable chassis grease.

Wheel Bearings

NOTE: *The following procedures are for 2wd only. For wheel bearing procedures on 4wd vehicles, please refer to the Front Drive Axle section in Chapter 7.*

ADJUSTMENT AND LUBRICATION

Only the front wheel bearings require periodic service. The lubricant to use is high temperature disc brake wheel bearing grease meeting NLGI No. 2 specifications. (This grease should be used even if the truck is equipped with drum brakes; it has superior protection characteristics.) This service is recommended at the specified period in the Maintenance Intervals chart or whenever the truck has been driven in water up to the hub.

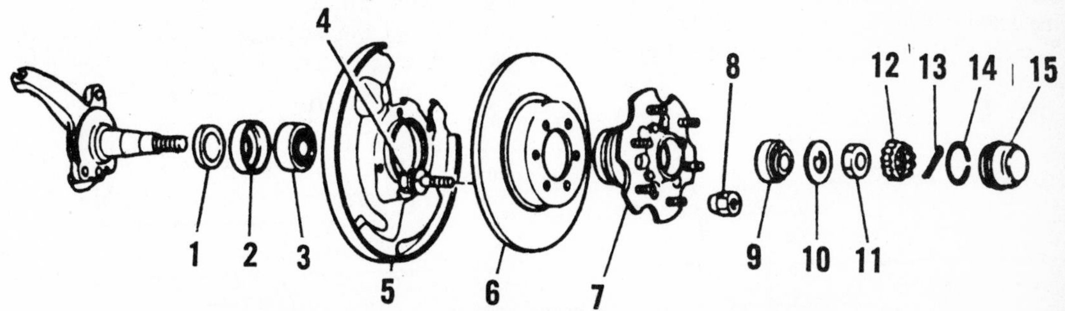

1. Spacer
2. Grease seal
3. Inner bearing
4. Hub bolt
5. Backing plate
6. Disc (rotor)
7. Hub
8. Lug nut
9. Outer bearing
10. Washer
11. Adjusting nut
12. Lock (castle) nut
13. Cotter pin
14. O-ring
15. Grease cap

Exploded view of the 2-wd hub and bearings with disc brakes. Drum brakes are similar

Before handling the bearings there are a few things that you should remember:

Remember to DO the following:

1. Remove all outside dirt from the housing before exposing the bearing.
2. Treat a used bearing as gently as you would a new one.
3. Work with clean tools in clean surroundings.
4. Use clean, dry canvas gloves, or at least clean, dry hands.
5. Clean solvents and flushing fluids are a must.
6. Use clean paper when laying out the bearings to dry.
7. Protect disassembled bearings from rust and dirt. Cover them up.
8. Use clean rags to wipe bearings
9. Keep the bearings in oil-proof paper when they are to be stored or are not in use.
10. Clean the inside of the housing before replacing the bearings.

Do NOT do the following:

1. Don't work in dirty surroundings.
2. Don't use dirty, chipped, or damaged tools.
3. Try not to work on wooden work benches or use wooden mallets.
4. Don't handle bearings with dirty or moist hands.
5. Do not use gasoline for cleaning; use a safe solvent.
6. Do not spin dry bearings with compressed air. They will be damaged.
7. Do not spin unclean bearings.
8. Avoid using cotton waste or dirty cloths to wipe bearings.
9. Try not to scratch or nick bearing surfaces.
10. Do not allow the bearing to come in contact with dirt or rust at any time.

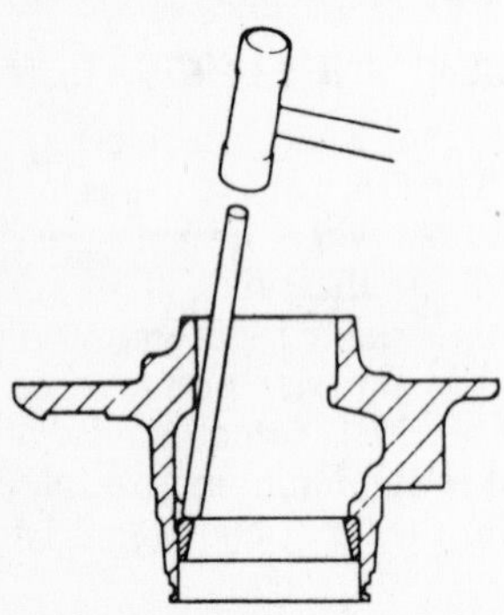

Drive worn bearing cups from the hub with a soft drift and a hammer

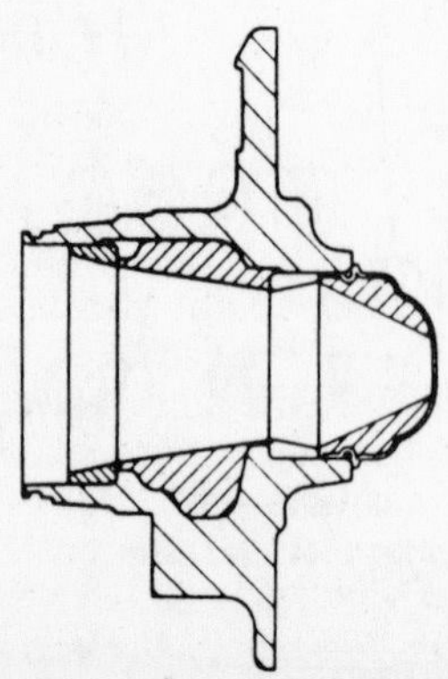

Fill the shaded portion of the hub and grease cap with grease; also coat the cups with grease

2-Wheel Drive

You will need a special claw type puller for this job to remove the inner bearing and the steering knuckle grease retainer if you truck has drum brakes.

Procedures are basically the same for either disc or drum brakes.

1. Remove the bake drum or brake caliper, following the procedure outlined in Chapter 9.
2. It is not necessary to remove the drum or disc from the hub. The outer wheel bearing will come off with the hub. Simply pull the hub and disc or drum assembly towards you off the spindle. Be sure to catch the bearing before it falls to the ground.
3. Drum brakes: The inner bearing and grease retainer must be pulled from the spindle with the claw puller. Be sure that the fingers of the tool pull on the seal, and not on the bearing itself. Discard the grease retainer.

   Disc brakes: The inner bearing will have to be driven from the hub along with the oil seal. Use a brass rod as a drift and carefully drive the inner bearing cone out. Remove the bearing and the oil seal. Discard the seal.
4. Clean the bearings in solvent and allow to air dry. You risk leaving bits of lint in the races if you dry them with a rag. Clean the bearing cups in the hub.
5. Inspect the bearings carefully. If they are worn, pitted, burned, or scored, they should be replaced, along with the bearing cups in which they run.
6. You can use a brass rod as a drift, or a large socket or piece of pipe to drive the inner and outer bearing cups out of the hub.
7. Install the new inner cup, and then the outer cup, in that order, into the hub, using either the brass drift or socket method outlined earlier.

   NOTE: *Use care not to cock the bearing cups in the hub. If they are not fully seated, the bearings will be impossible to adjust properly.*
8. Drum brakes: Press a new grease retainer onto the spindle. Place a large glob of grease

into one palm and force the edge of the inner bearing into it so that the grease fills the bearing. Do this until the whole bearing is packed. Press the inner bearing into the spindle, seating it firmly against the grease retainer.

Disc brakes: Coat the inner bearing cup with grease. Pack the inner bearing with grease as outlined for drum brakes, and press the inner bearing into the cup. Press a new oil seal into place on top of the bearing. You may have to give the seal a few gentle raps with a soft drift to get it to seat properly.

9. Install the hub and drum or disc assembly onto the spindle. With drum brakes, first thoroughly coat the inner cup with grease.

10. Coat the outer bearing cup with grease. Pack the outer bearing with grease and install into the cup.

11. Pack the grease cap with grease and set it aside. It will be replaced last, after the preload adjustment. You can put the grease away now.

12. Install the lock washer, and castellated nut (lock washer, nut, and adjusting castle nut with disc brakes) loosely, and go on to the preload adjustment following.

BEARING PRELOAD ADJUSTMENT

1. While turning the hub forward, tighten the castellated nut (plain nut on disc brakes) to 25–29 ft. lbs. (34–39 Nm).

2. Rotate the hub a few more times to snug down the bearings.

3. Retighten the nut to the above specification. Unscrew it $\frac{1}{6}$ of a turn and lock it in place with a new cotter pin. On disc brakes, snug the adjusting nut up against the nut and then back it off the required distance to insert a new cotter pin. You should not have to back it off more than $\frac{1}{6}$ of a turn.

4. Install the grease cap, and wipe off any grease that oozes out.

5. Install the front wheel and a couple of lug nuts. Check the axial play of the wheel by shaking it back and forth; the bearing freeplay should feel close to zero, but the wheel should spin freely. With drum brakes, be sure that the shoes are not dragging against the drum.

6. If the bearing play is correct with drum brakes you can install the rest of the lug nuts. With disc brakes, remove the wheel, replace the caliper, then install the wheel.

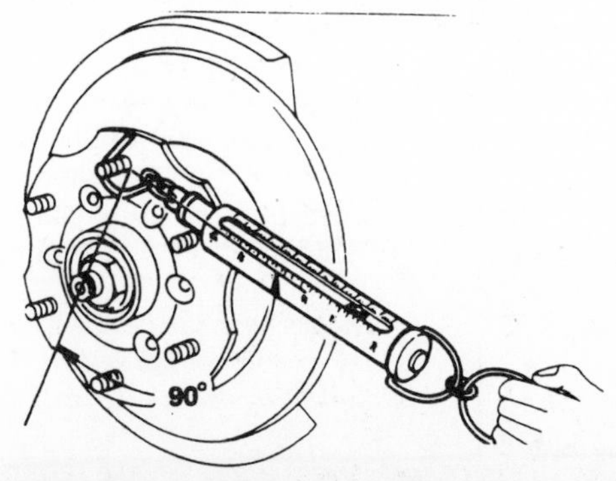

Checking the wheel bearing preload

4-Wheel Drive

NOTE: *For wheel bearing procedures on 4wd vehicles, please refer to the Front Drive Axle section in Chapter 7.*

OUTSIDE VEHICLE MAINTENANCE

Lock Cylinders

Apply graphite lubricant sparingly thought the key slot. Insert the key and operate the lock several times to be sure that the lubricant is worked into the lock cylinder.

Door Hinges and Hinge Checks

Spray a silicone lubricant on the hinge pivot points to eliminate any binding conditions. Open and close the door several times to be sure that the lubricant is evenly and thoroughly distributed.

Tailgate

Spray a silicone lubricant on all of the pivot and friction surfaces to eliminate any squeaks or binds. Work the tailgate to distribute the lubricant

Body Drain Holes

Be sure that the drain holes in the doors and rocker panels are cleared of obstruction. A small screwdriver can be used to clear them of any debris.

PUSHING AND TOWING

WARNING: *Push-starting is not recommended for trucks equipped with a catalytic converter. Raw gas collecting in the converter may cause damage. Jump starting is recommended.*

To push-start your manual transmission equipped Nissan (automatic transmission models cannot be push started), make sure of bumper alignment. If the bumper of the vehicle pushing does not match with your truck's bumper, it would be wise to tie an old tire either on the back of your truck, or on the front of the pushing vehicle. Switch the ignition to **ON** and depress the clutch pedal. Shift the transmission to third gear and hold the accelerator pedal about halfway down. signal the push vehicle to pro-

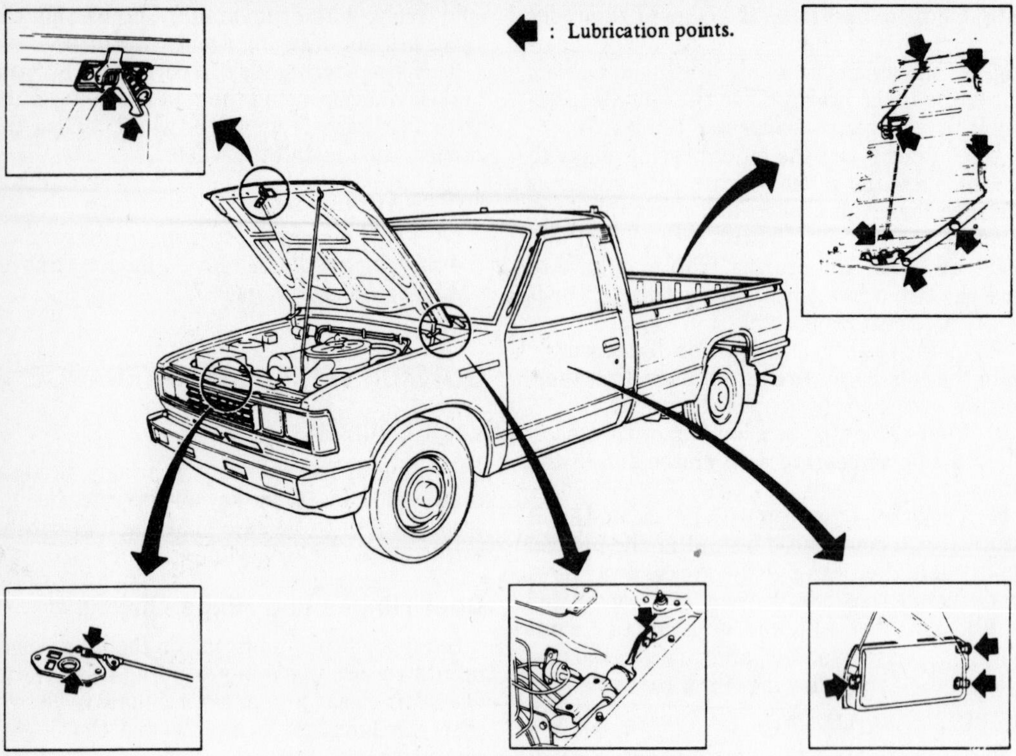

: Lubrication points.

Body lubrication points—1980–86 (720-D series)

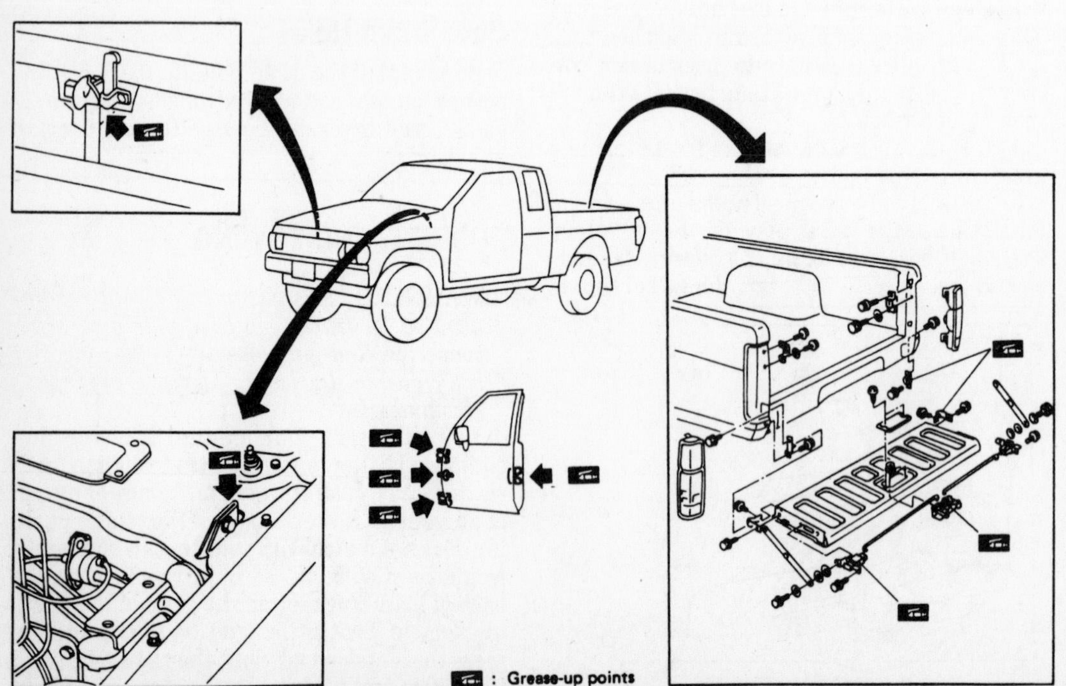

Body lubrication points—1986–87 (D21-D series)

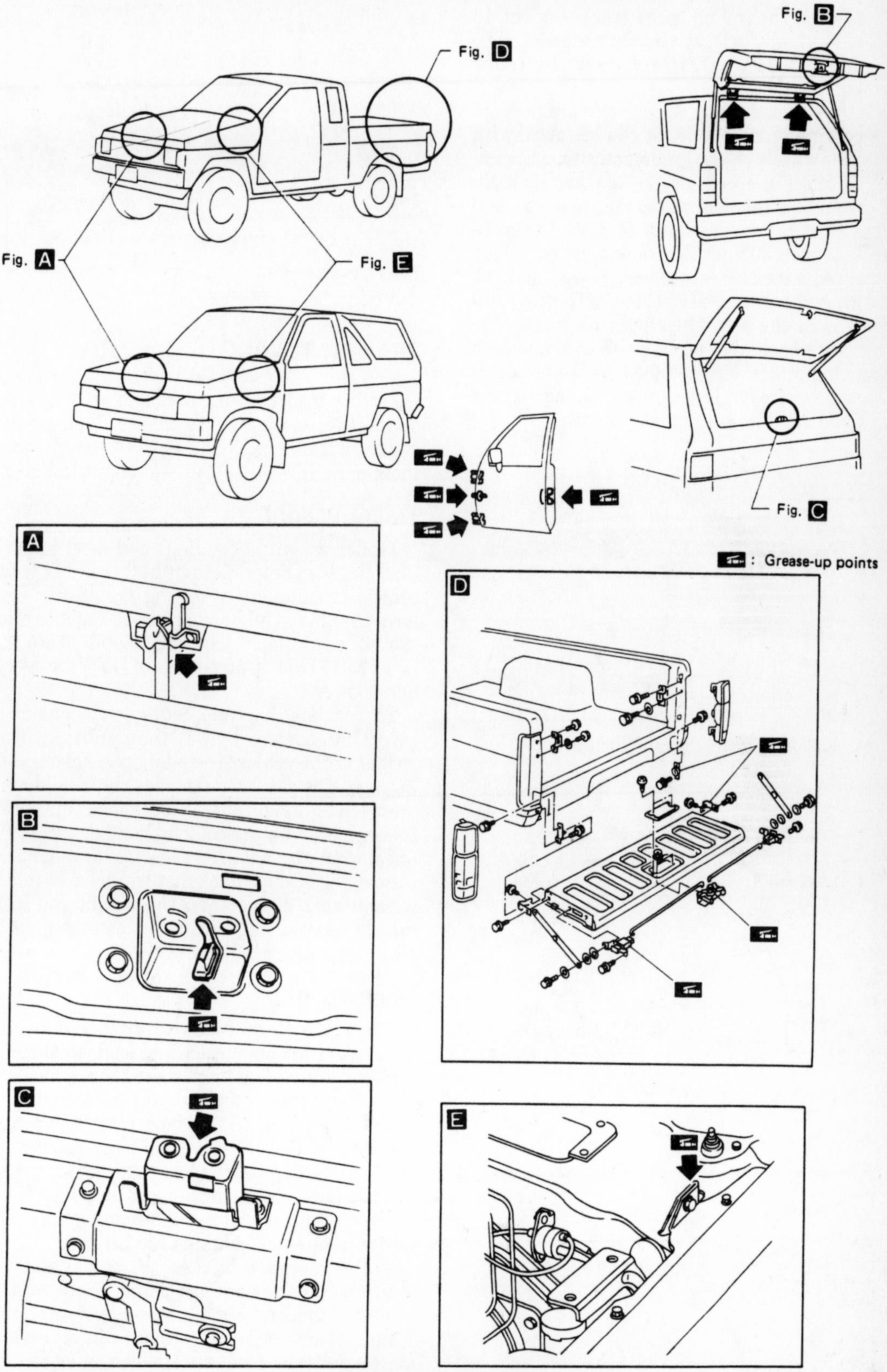

Body lubrication points—1988–89

ceed, when the rolling speed reaches about 10 mph, gradually release the clutch pedal. The engine should start, if not have the truck towed.

If the transmission and rear axle are in proper working order, the truck can be towed with the rear wheels on the ground for distances under 15 miles at speeds no greater then 30 mph. If the transmission or rear is known to be damaged or if the truck has to be towed over 15 miles or over 30 mph the truck must be dollied or towed with the rear wheels raised and the steering wheel secured so that the front wheels remain in the straight-ahead position. The steering wheel must be clamped with a special clamping device designed for towing service. If the key controlled lock is used damage to the lock and steering column may occur.

Recommended towing methods—2wd

Recommended towing methods—4wd

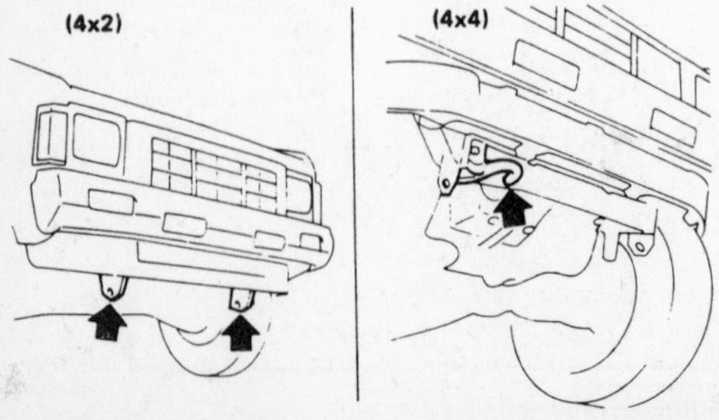

Towing points—2wd

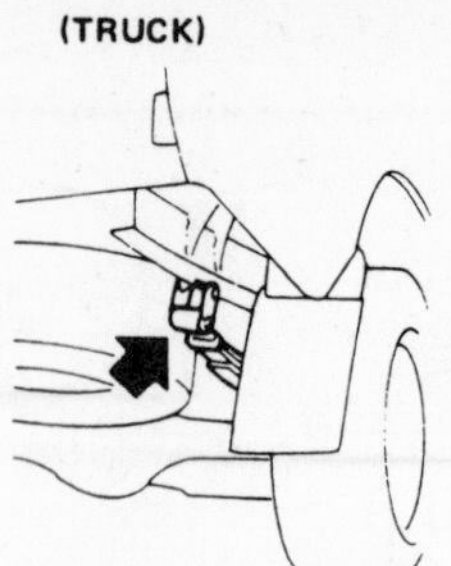

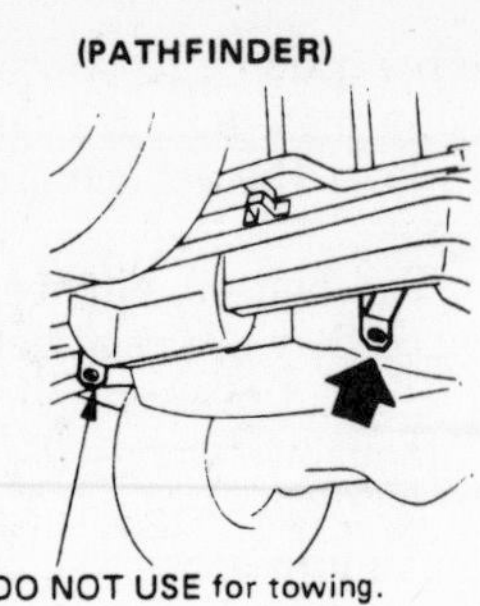

Towing points—4wd

TRAILER TOWING

Factory trailer towing packages are available on most Nissan trucks. However, if you are installing a trailer hitch and wiring on your truck, there are a few thing that you ought to know.

Trailer Weight

Trailer weight is the first, and most important, factor in determining whether or not your vehicle is suitable for towing the trailer you have in mind. The horsepower-to-weight ratio should be calculated. The basic standard is a ratio of 35:1. That is, 35 pounds of GVW for every horsepower.

To calculate this ratio, multiply you engine's rated horsepower by 35, then subtract the weight of the vehicle, including passengers and luggage. The resulting figure is the ideal maximum trailer weight that you can tow. One point to consider: a numerically higher axle ratio can offset what appears to be a low trailer weight. If the weight of the trailer that you have in mind is somewhat higher than the weight you just calculated, you might consider changing your rear axle ratio to compensate.

Hitch Weight

There are three kinds of hitches: bumper mounted, frame mounted, and load equalizing.

Bumper mounted hitches are those which attach solely to the vehicle's bumper. Many states prohibit towing with this type of hitch, when it attaches to the vehicle's stock bumper, since it subjects the bumper to stresses for which it was not designed. Aftermarket rear step bumpers, designed for trailer towing, are acceptable for use with bumper mounted hitches.

Frame mounted hitches can be of the type which bolts to two or more points on the frame, plus the bumper, or just to several points on the frame. Frame mounted hitches can also be of the tongue type, for Class I towing, or, of the receiver type, for Classes II and III.

Load equalizing hitches are usually used for

large trailers. Most equalizing hitches are welded in place and use equalizing bars and chains to level the vehicle after the trailer is hooked up.

The bolt-on hitches are the most common, since they are relatively easy to install.

Check the gross weight rating of your trailer. Tongue weight is usually figured as 10% of gross trailer weight. Therefore, a trailer with a maximum gross weight of 2000 lb. will have a maximum tongue weight of 200 lb. Class I tarilers fall into this category. Class II trailers are those with a gross weight rating of 2000–3500 lb., while Class III trailers fall into the 3500–6000 lb. category. Class IV trailers are those over 6000 lb. and are for use with fifth wheel trucks, only.

When you've determined the hitch that you'll need, follow the manufacturer's installation instructions, exactly, especially when it comes to fastener torques. The hitch will subjected to a lot of stress and good hitches come with hardened bolts. Never substitute an inferior bolt for a hardened bolt.

Wiring

Wiring your Nissan for towing is fairly easy. There are a number of good wiring kits available and these should be used, rather than trying to design your own. All trailers will need brake lights and turn signals as well as tail lights and side marker lights. Most states require extra marker lights for overly wide trailers. Also, most states have recently required back-up lights for trailers, and most trailer manufacturers have been building trailers with back-up lights for several years.

Additionally, some Class I, most Class II and just about all Class III trailers will have electric brakes.

Add to this number an accessories wire, to operate trailer internal equipment or to charge the trailer's battery, and you can have as many as seven wires in the harness.

Determine the equipment on your trailer and buy the wiring kit necessary. The kit will contain all the wires needed, plus a plug adapter set which included the female plug, mounted on

Recommended Equipment Checklist

Equipment	Class I Trailers Under 2,000 pounds	Class II Trailers 2,000-3,500 pounds	Class III Trailers 3,500-6,000 pounds	Class IV Trailers 6,000 pounds and up
Hitch	Frame or Equalizing	Equalizing	Equalizing	Fifth wheel Pick-up truck only
Tongue Load Limit**	Up to 200 pounds	200-350 pounds	350-600 pounds	600 pounds and up
Trailer Brakes	Not Required	Required	Required	Required
Safety Chain	3/16" diameter links	1/4" diameter links	5/16" diameter links	—
Fender Mounted Mirrors	Useful, but not necessary	Recommended	Recommended	Recommended
Turn Signal Flasher	Standard	Constant Rate or heavy duty	Constant Rate or heavy duty	Constant Rate or heavy duty
Coolant Recovery System	Recommended	Required	Required	Required
Transmission Oil Cooler	Recommended	Recommended	Recommended	Recommended
Engine Oil Cooler	Recommended	Recommended	Recommended	Recommended
Air Adjustable Shock Absorbers	Recommended	Recommended	Recommended	Recommended
Flex or Clutch Fan	Recommended	Recommended	Recommended	Recommended
Tires	***	***	***	***

NOTE: The information in this chart is a guide. Check the manufacturer's recommendations for your car if in doubt.

*Local laws may require specific equipment such as trailer brakes or fender mounted mirrors. Check your local laws. Hitch weight is usually 10-15% of trailer gross weight and should be measured with trailer loaded.

**Most manufacturer's do not recommend towing trailers of over 1,000 pounds with compacts. Some intermediates cannot tow Class III trailers.

***Check manufacturer's recommendations for your specific car/ trailer combination.

—Does not apply

the bumper or hitch, and the male plug, wired into, or plugged into the trailer harness.

When installing the kit, follow the manufacturer's instructions. The color coding of the wires is standard throughout the industry.

One point to note, most imported vehicles, have separate turn signals. On most domestic vehicles, the brake lights and rear turn signals operate with the same bulb. For those vehicles with separate turn signals, you can purchase an isolation unit so that the brake lights won't blink whenever the turn signals are operated, or, you can go to your local electronics supply house and buy four diodes to wire in series with the brake and turn signal bulbs. Diodes will isolate the brake and turn signals. The choice is yours. The isolation units are simple and quick to install, but far more expensive than the diodes. The diodes, however, require more work to install properly, since they require the cutting of each bulb's wire and soldering in place of the diode.

One final point, the best kits are those with a spring loaded cover on the vehicle mounted socket. This cover prevents dirt and moisture from corroding the terminals. Never let the vehicle socket hang loosely. Always mount it securely to the bumper or hitch.

Cooling

ENGINE

One of the most common, if not THE most common, problem associated with trailer towing is engine overheating.

With factory installed trailer towing packages, a heavy duty cooling system is usually included. Heavy duty cooling systems are available as optional equipment on most Nissans, with or without a trailer package. If you have one of these extra-capacity systems, you shouldn't have any overheating problems.

If you have a standard cooling system, without an expansion tank, you'll definitely need to get an aftermarket expansion tank kit, preferably one with at least a 2 quart capacity. These kits are easily installed on the radiator's overflow hose, and come with a pressure cap designed for expansion tanks.

Another helpful accessory is a Flex Fan. These fan are large diameter units are designed to provide more airflow at low speeds, with blades that have deeply cupped surfaces. The blades then flex, or flatten out, at high speed, when less cooling air is needed. These fans are far lighter in weight than stock fans, requiring less horsepower to drive them. Also, they are far quieter than stock fans.

If you do decide to replace your stock fan with a flex fan, note that if your truck has a fan clutch, a spacer between the flex fan and water pump hub will be needed.

Aftermarket engine oil coolers are helpful for prolonging engine oil life and reducing overall engine temperatures. Both of these factors increase engine life.

While not absolutely necessary in towing Class I and some Class II trailers, they are recommended for heavier Class II and all Class III towing.

Engine oil cooler systems consist of an adapter, screwed on in place of the oil filter, a remote filter mounting and a multi-tube, finned heat exchanger, which is mounted in front of the radiator or air conditioning condenser.

TRANSMISSION

An automatic transmission is usually recommended for trailer towing. Modern automatics have proven reliable and, of course, easy to operate, in trailer towing.

The increased load of a trailer, however, causes an increase in the temperature of the automatic transmission fluid. Heat is the worst enemy of an automatic transmission. As the temperature of the fluid increases, the life of the fluid decreases.

It is essential, therefore, that you install an automatic transmission cooler.

The cooler, which consists of a multi-tube, finned heat exchanger, is usually installed in front of the radiator or air conditioning compressor, and hooked inline with the transmission cooler tank inlet line. Follow the cooler manufacturer's installation instructions.

Select a cooler of at least adequate capacity, based upon the combined gross weights of the truck and trailer.

Cooler manufacturers recommend that you use an aftermarket cooler in addition to, and not instead of, the present cooling tank in your radiator. If you do want to use it in place of the radiator cooling tank, get a cooler at least two sizes larger than normally necessary.

NOTE: *A transmission cooler can, sometimes, cause slow or harsh shifting in the transmission during cold weather, until the fluid has a chance to come up to normal operating temperature. Some coolers can be purchased with or retrofitted with a temperature bypass valve which will allow fluid flow through the cooler only when the fluid has reached operating temperature, or above.*

JACKING AND HOISTING

Your truck is equipped with either a scissors type jack, or a bumper jack. The scissor-type jack is placed under the side of the truck so that

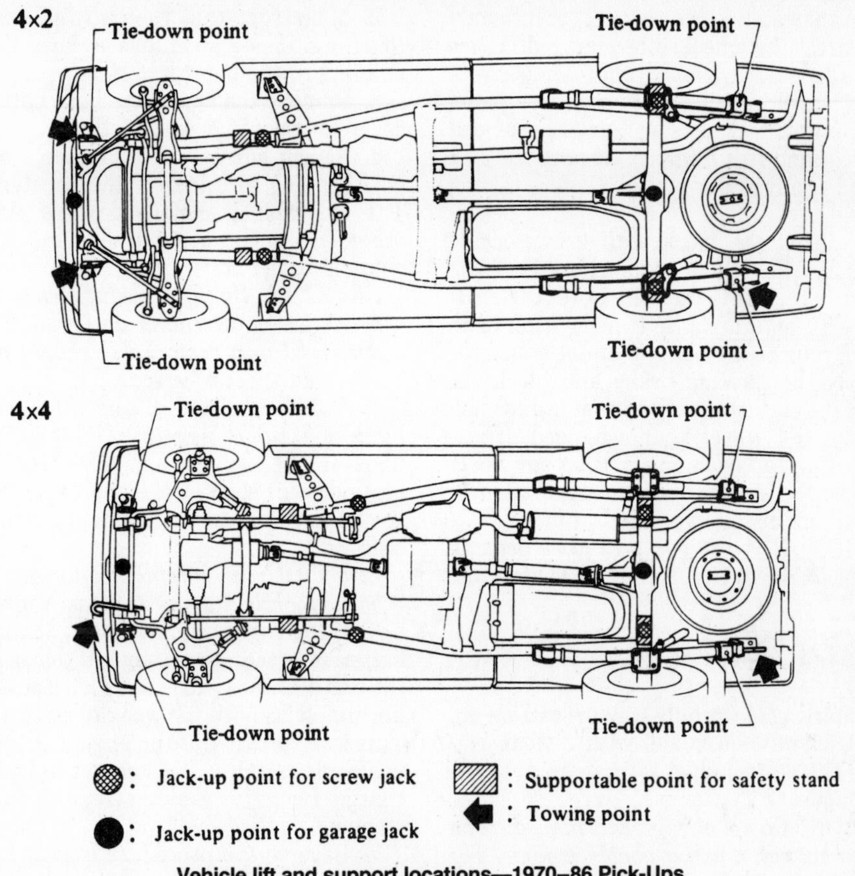

Vehicle lift and support locations—1970–86 Pick-Ups

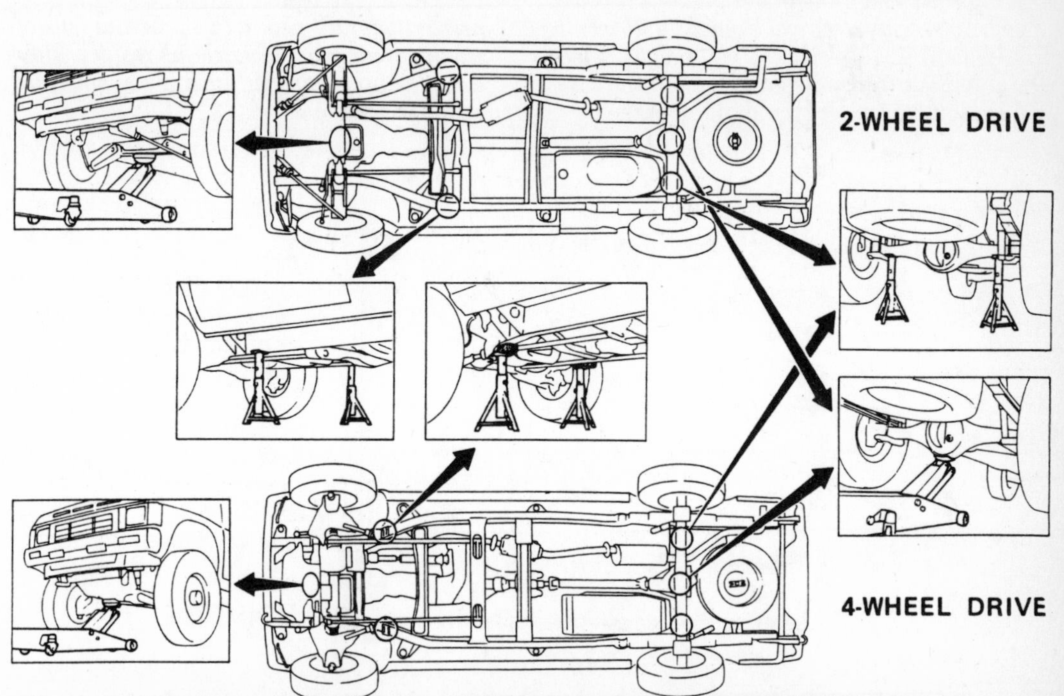

Vehicle lift and support locations—1986—89 Pick-Ups and Pathfinders

it fits into the notch in the vertical rocker panel flange nearest the wheel to be changed. These jacking notches are located approximately 8″ from the wheel opening on the rocker panel flanges. Bumper jack slots or flats are provided on the front and rear bumper. Be sure the jack is inserted firmly and is straight before raising the vehicle.

When raising the truck with a scissors or bumper jack follow these precautions: Park the truck on level spot, put the selector in **P** (PARK) with an automatic transmission or in reverse if your truck has a manual transmission, apply the parking brake and block the front and the back of the wheel that is diagonally opposite the wheel being changed. These jacks are fine for changing a tire, but never crawl under the truck when it is supported only by the scissors or bumper jack.

CAUTION: *If you're going to work beneath the vehicle, always support it on jackstands.*

JUMP STARTING

Jump starting is the only way to start an automatic transmission model with a weak battery, and the best method for a manual transmission model.

CAUTION: *Do not attempt this procedure on a frozen battery, it will probably explode. The battery in the other vehicle must be a 12 volt, negatively grounded one. Do not attempt to jump start your Datsun with a 24 volt power source; serious electrical damage will result.*

1. Turn off all electrical equipment. Place the automatic transmission in Park or the manual in Neutral and set the parking brake.
2. Make sure that the two vehicles are not touching. It is a good idea to keep the engine running in the booster vehicle.
3. Remove the caps from both batteries and cover the openings with cloths.
4. Attach one end of a jumper cable to the positive (+) terminal of the booster battery. The red cable is usually positive. Attach the other end to the positive terminal of the discharged battery.

CAUTION: *Be very careful about these connections! An alternator and regulator can be destroyed in a remarkably short time if battery polarity is reversed.*

5. Attach one end of the other cable (the black one) to the negative (−) terminal of the booster battery. Attach the other end to a ground point such as the engine lift bracket of the truck being started. Do not connect it to the battery.

CAUTION: *Be careful not to lean over the battery while making this last connection!*

6. If the engine will not start, disconnect the batteries as soon as possible. If this is not done, the two batteries will soon reach a state of equilibrium, with both too weak to start an engine. This is no problem if the engine of the booster vehicle is running fast enough to keep up the charge. Lengthy cranking can also damage the starter.
7. Reverse the procedure exactly to remove the jumper cables. Discard the rags, because they may have acid on them.

NOTE: *It is recognized that some or all of the precautions outlined in this procedure are often ignored with no harmful results. However, the procedure outlined is the only fully safe, foolproof one.*

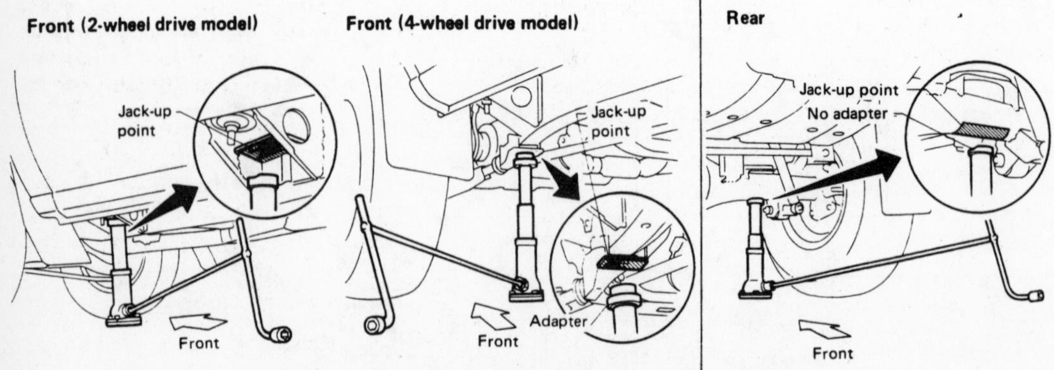

Screw jack locations—1986–89 Pick-Ups and Pathfinders

JUMP STARTING A DEAD BATTERY

The chemical reaction in a battery produces explosive hydrogen gas. This is the safe way to jump start a dead battery, reducing the chances of an accidental spark that could cause an explosion.

Jump Starting Precautions

1. Be sure both batteries are of the same voltage.
2. Be sure both batteries are of the same polarity (have the same grounded terminal).
3. Be sure the vehicles are not touching.
4. Be sure the vent cap holes are not obstructed.
5. Do not smoke or allow sparks around the battery.
6. In cold weather, check for frozen electrolyte in the battery. Do not jump start a frozen battery.
7. Do not allow electrolyte on your skin or clothing.
8. Be sure the electrolyte is not frozen.

CAUTION: *Make certain that the ignition key, in the vehicle with the dead battery, is in the OFF position. Connecting cables to vehicles with on-board computers will result in computer destruction if the key is not in the OFF position.*

Jump Starting Procedure

1. Determine voltages of the two batteries; they must be the same.
2. Bring the starting vehicle close (they must not touch) so that the batteries can be reached easily.
3. Turn off all accessories and both engines. Put both cars in Neutral or Park and set the handbrake.
4. Cover the cell caps with a rag—do not cover terminals.
5. If the terminals on the run-down battery are heavily corroded, clean them.
6. Identify the positive and negative posts on both batteries and connect the cables in the order shown.
7. Start the engine of the starting vehicle and run it at fast idle. Try to start the car with the dead battery. Crank it for no more than 10 seconds at a time and let it cool off for 20 seconds in between tries.
8. If it doesn't start in 3 tries, there is something else wrong.
9. Disconnect the cables in the reverse order.
10. Replace the cell covers and dispose of the rags.

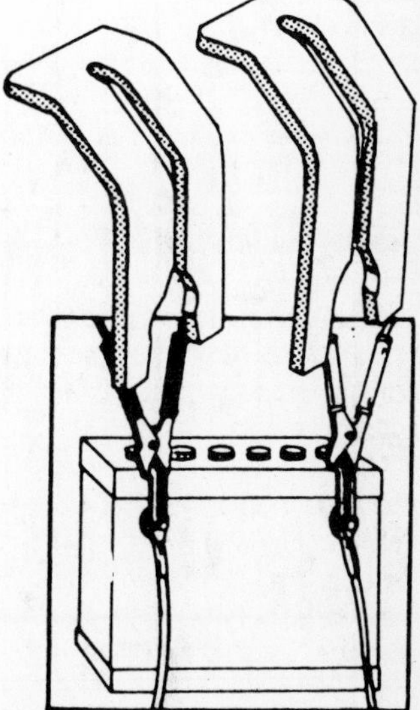

Side terminal batteries occasionally pose a problem when connecting jumper cables. There frequently isn't enough room to clamp the cables without touching sheet metal. Side terminal adaptors are available to alleviate this problem and should be removed after use.

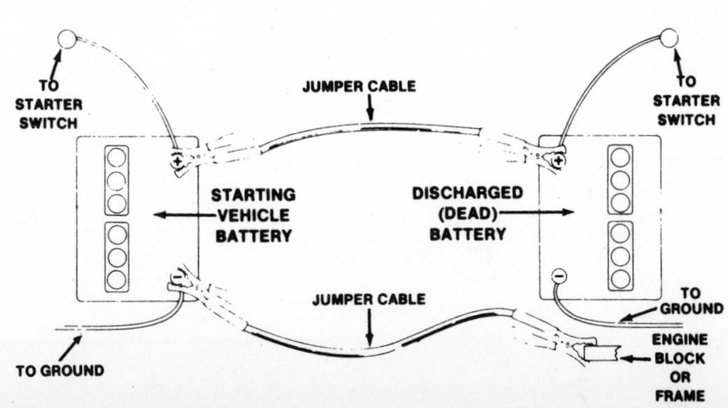

Make certain vehicles do not touch. This hook-up for negative ground cars only

Capacities

Year	Model	Engine	Engine Displacement Cu. In. (cc)	Engine Crankcase (qts) With Filter	Engine Crankcase (qts) Without Filter	Transmission (pts) Manual 4-spd	Transmission (pts) Manual 5-spd	Transmission (pts) Automatic	Transfer Case (qts)	Drive Axle (qts) Front	Drive Axle (qts) Rear	Gasoline Tank (gals)	Cooling System (qts)
1970	Pick-Up	L16	97.3 (1595)	4.4	3.6	4.2	—	—	—	—	1.7	11	7.2
1971	Pick-Up	L16	97.3 (1595)	4.4	3.6	4.2	—	—	—	—	1.7	11	7.2
1972	Pick-Up	L16	97.3 (1595)	4.4	3.6	4.2	—	—	—	—	2.1	12	6.3
1973	Pick-Up	L18	108.0 (1770)	5.0	4.5	3.6	—	—	—	—	2.1	12	6.3
1974	Pick-Up	L18	108.0 (1770)	5.0	4.5	3.6	—	11.7	—	—	2.1	12	6.3
1975	Pick-Up	L20B	119.1 (1952)	5.0	4.5	3.6	—	11.7	—	—	2.1	12	6.3
1976	Pick-Up	L20B	119.1 (1952)	5.0	4.5	3.6	4.2	11.7	—	—	2.1	12	8.5
1977	Pick-Up	L20B	119.1 (1952)	5.0	4.5	3.6	4.2	11.7	—	—	2.1	12	8.5
1978	Pick-Up	L20B	119.1 (1952)	5.0	4.5	3.6	4.2	11.7	—	—	2.1	12	9.3
1979	Pick-Up	L20B	119.1 (1952)	4.5	4.0	3.6	4.2	11.7	—	—	2.1	13 ①	9.3
1980	Pick-Up	L20B	119.1 (1952)	4.5	4.0	3.6	4.2	11.7	3.0	2.1	2.6	13.2 ①	9.3
1981	Pick-Up	Z22	133.5 (2187)	4.6	4.0	3.6	4.2	11.7	3.0	2.1	2.6	②	10.75
		SD22	132.0 (2164)	5.8	5.0	—	4.2	—	—	—	2.6	15.8 ③	10.5
1982	Pick-Up	Z22	133.5 (2187)	4.6	4.0	3.6	4.2	11.7	3.0	2.1	2.6	②	10.75
		SD22	132.0 (2164)	6.4	5.9	—	4.2	—	—	—	2.6	15.8 ③	10.5
1983	Pick-Up	Z22	133.5 (2187)	4.6	4.0	3.6	4.2	11.7	3.0	2.1	2.6	②	10.75
		SD22	132.0 (2164)	5.3	4.8	—	4.2	—	—	—	2.6	15.8 ③	10.5
1984	Pick-Up (2WD)	Z20	119.0 (1952)	4.4	3.9	—	4.2	11.7	—	—	2.6	②	10.75
		Z24	146.8 (2389)	4.4	3.9	—	4.2	11.7	—	—	2.6 ④	②	10.75
		SD25	152.0 (2488)	5.4	4.9	—	4.2	—	—	—	2.6	②	11.2
	Pick-Up (4WD)	Z24	146.8 (2389)	4.5	4.0	—	4.2	11.7	3.0	2.1	2.6	②	10.75
1985	Pick-Up (2WD)	Z20	119.0 (1952)	3.9	3.4	—	4.2	11.7	—	—	2.6	②	10.75
		Z24	146.8 (2389)	3.9	3.4	—	4.2	11.7	—	—	2.6 ④	②	10.75

Year	Model	Engine	Displacement cu. in. (cc)										
		SD25	152.0 (2488)	5.75	4.9	—	4.2	—	—	—	2.6	②	11.2
	Pick-Up (4WD)	Z24	146.8 (2389)	4.25	3.75	—	4.2	11.7	3.0	2.1	2.6	②	10.75
1986	Pick-Up (2WD)	Z20	119.0 (1952)	3.9	3.4	—	4.2	11.7	—	—	2.6	②	10.75
		Z24	146.8 (2389)	3.9	3.4	—	4.2	11.7	—	—	2.6 ④	②	10.75
		Z24i	146.8 (2389)	4.0	3.5	—	4.2	14.7	—	—	⑥	15.9 ⑦	8.6
		VG30i	181.0 (2960)	4.2	3.8	—	5.0	14.7	—	—	⑥	15.9 ⑦	10.5
		SD25	152.0 (2488)	4.25	3.75	—	4.2	—	—	—	2.6	②	11.2
	Pick-Up (4WD) ⑨	Z24	146.8 (2389)	3.9	3.4	—	4.2	11.7	3.0	2.1	2.6	②	10.75
		Z24i	146.8 (2389)	4.5	4.0	—	7.6	14.7	4.6	⑤	⑥	15.9 ⑦	8.6
		VG30i	181.0 (2960)	3.9	3.2	—	8.5	14.7	4.6	⑤	⑥	15.9 ⑦	10.5
1987	Pick-Up (2WD)	Z24i	146.8 (2389)	4.0	3.5	—	4.2	14.7	—	—	⑥	15.9 ⑦	8.6
		VG30i	181.0 (2960)	4.2	3.8	—	5.0	15.6	—	—	⑥	15.9 ⑦	10.5
		SD25	152.0 (2488)	7.9	7.2	—	4.2	11.7	—	—	2.6	15.9 ⑦	12.9
	Pick-Up (4WD) ⑨	Z24i	146.8 (2389)	4.5	4.0	—	8.5	14.7	4.6	⑤	⑥	15.9 ⑦	8.6
		VG30i	181.0 (2960)	3.9	3.2	—	8.5	15.6	4.6	⑤	⑥	15.9 ⑦	10.5
1988	Pick-Up (2WD)	Z24i	146.8 (2389)	4.0	3.5	NA	4.2	14.7	—	—	⑥	15.9	8.6
		VG30i	181.0 (2960)	4.2	3.8	—	5.1	14.7	—	—	⑥	21.1 ⑧	10.5
	Pick-Up (4WD) ⑨	Z24i	146.8 (2389)	4.5	4.0	—	8.5	16.0	4.6	⑤	⑥	15.9	8.6
		VG30i	181.0 (2960)	3.9	3.2	—	7.9	16.0	4.6	⑤	⑥	21.1 ⑧	10.5
1989	Pick-Up (2WD) ⑨	Z24i	146.8 (2389)	4.0	3.5	3.8	4.2	14.7	—	—	⑥	15.9	8.6
		VG30i	181.0 (2960)	4.2	3.8	—	5.1	14.7	—	—	⑥	21.1 ⑧	10.5
	Pick-Up (4WD) ⑨	Z24i	146.8 (2389)	4.5	4.0	—	8.5	18.0	4.6	⑤	⑥	15.9	8.6
		VG30i	181.0 (2960)	3.9	3.2	—	7.9	18.0	4.6	⑤	⑥	21.1 ⑧	10.5

NA: Not available
① LongBed: 17
② 2WD Std. Wheelbase: 13.2
4WD Std. Wheelbase: 15.8
2WD Long Wheelbase: 16.8
4WD Long Wheelbase: 19.8
③ Long Wheelbase: 16.8
④ Dual Rear Wheels: 2.75
⑤ R180A: 2.7
R200A: 3.1
⑥ C200: 2.7
H190A: 3.1
H233B: 5.8
⑦ King Cab & Heavy Duty: 21.2
⑧ 2WD SE & 4WD Regular Cab SE: 15.9
⑨ Includes Pathfinder

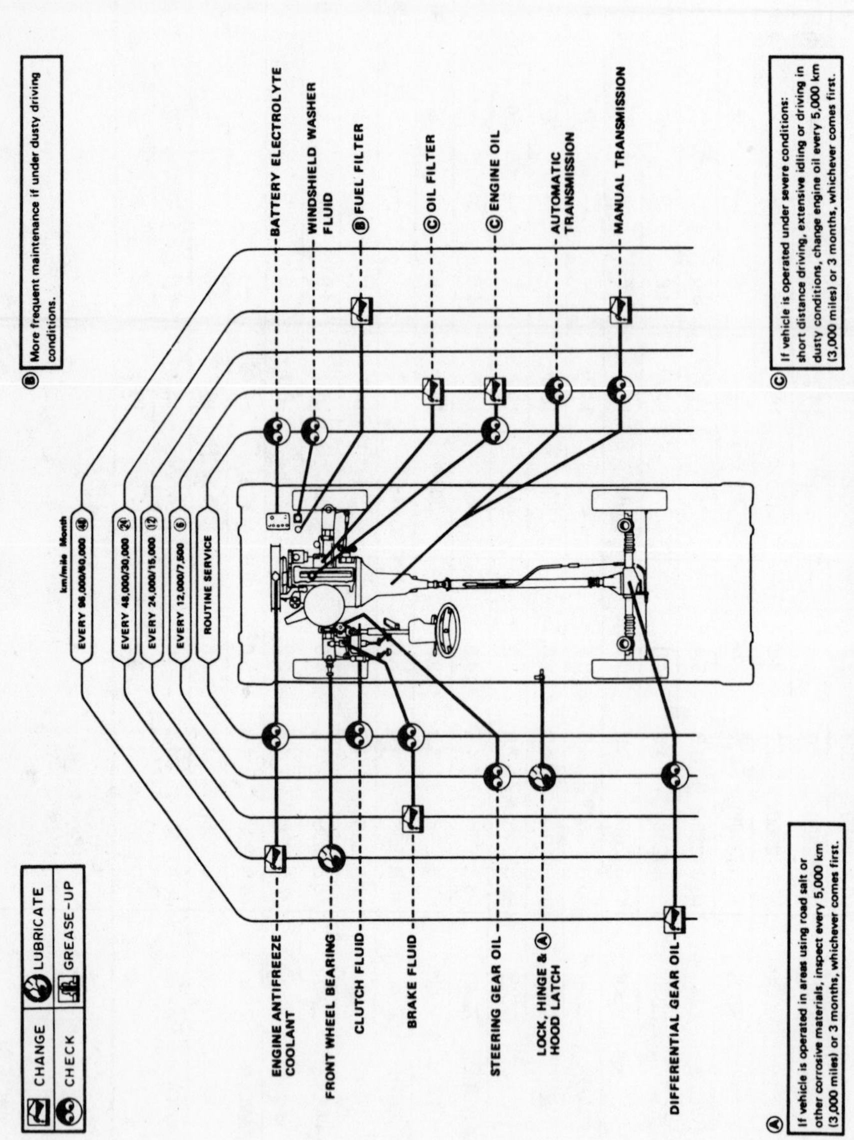

Vehicle maintenance and lubrication chart—1979

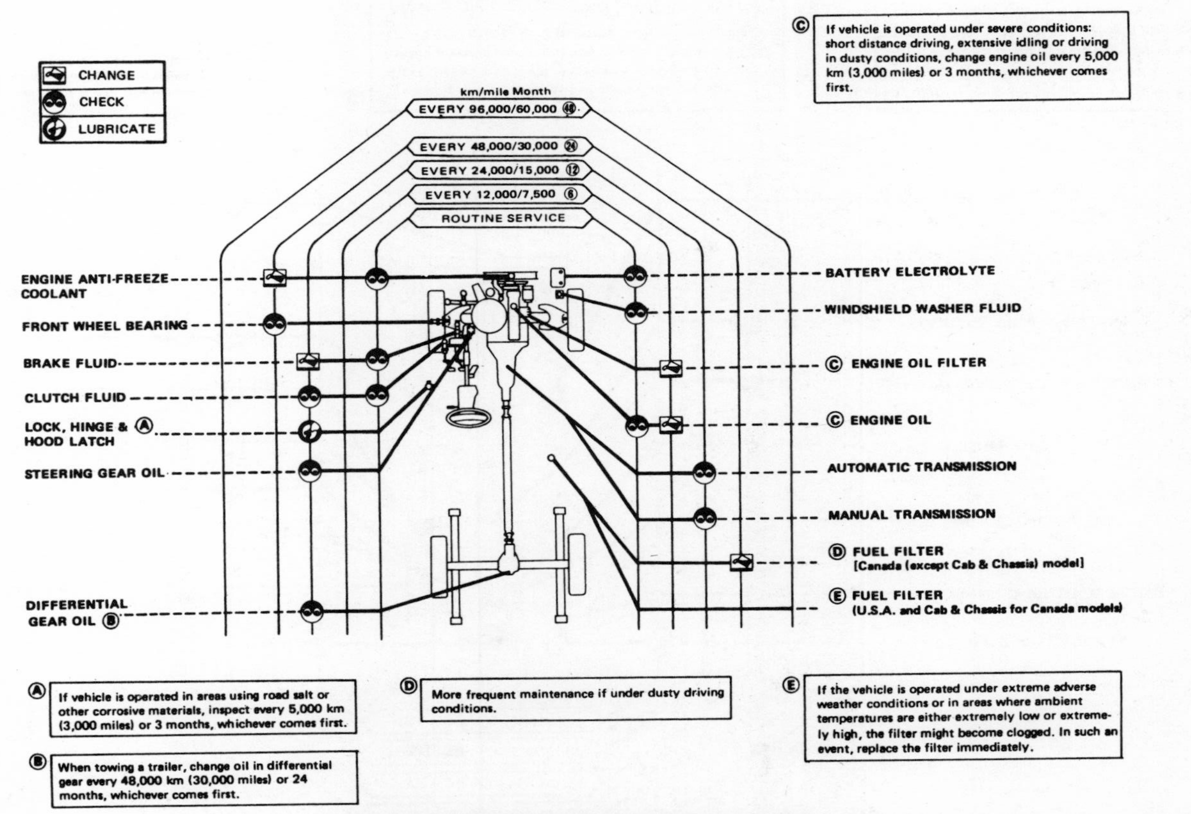

Vehicle maintenance and lubrication chart—1980

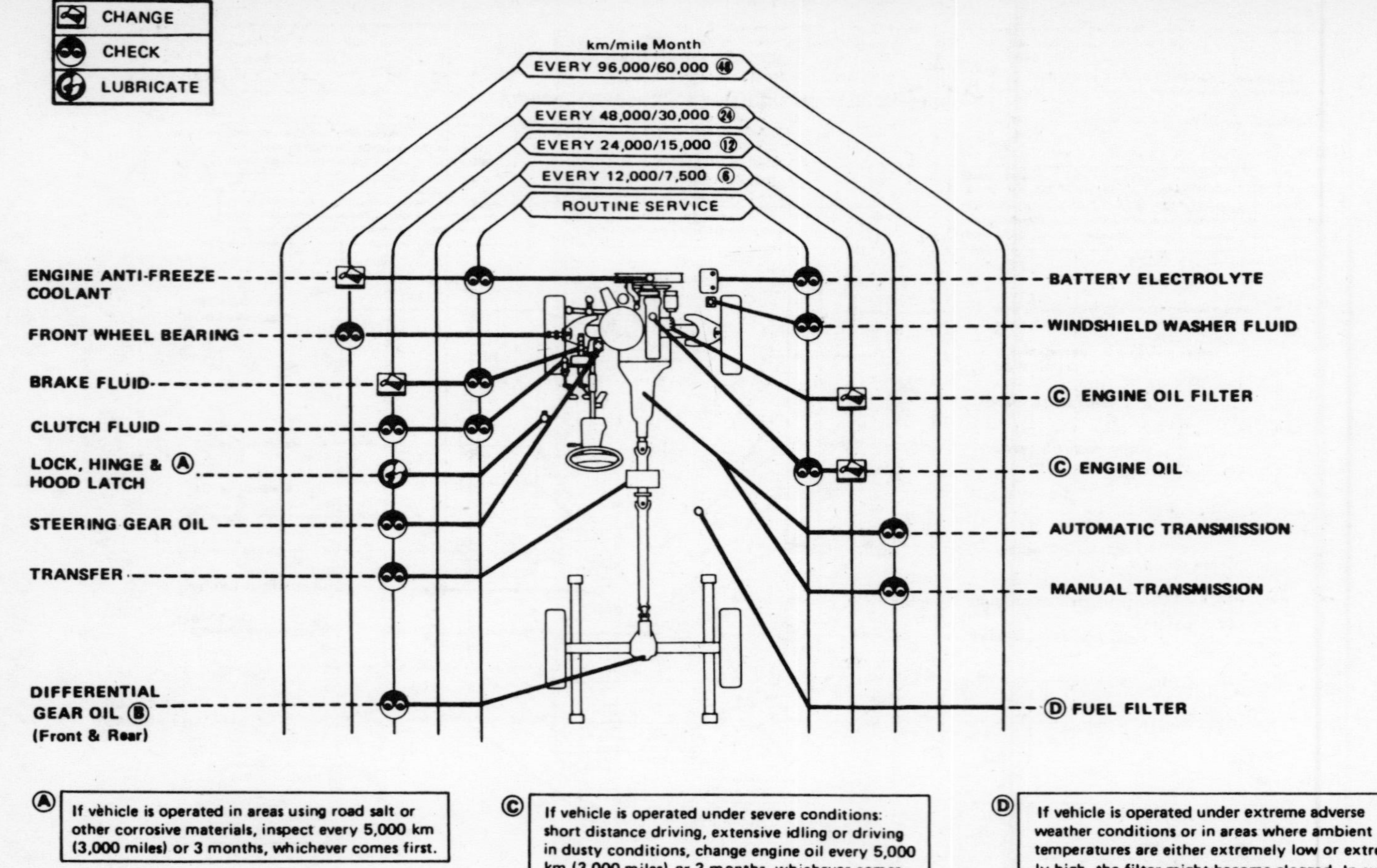

Ⓐ If vehicle is operated in areas using road salt or other corrosive materials, inspect every 5,000 km (3,000 miles) or 3 months, whichever comes first.

Ⓑ When towing a trailer, change oil in differential gear every 48,000 km (30,000 miles) or 24 months, whichever comes first.

Ⓒ If vehicle is operated under severe conditions: short distance driving, extensive idling or driving in dusty conditions, change engine oil every 5,000 km (3,000 miles) or 3 months, whichever comes first.

Ⓓ If vehicle is operated under extreme adverse weather conditions or in areas where ambient temperatures are either extremely low or extremely high, the filter might become clogged. In such an event, replace the filter immediately.

Vehicle maintenance and lubrication chart—1981

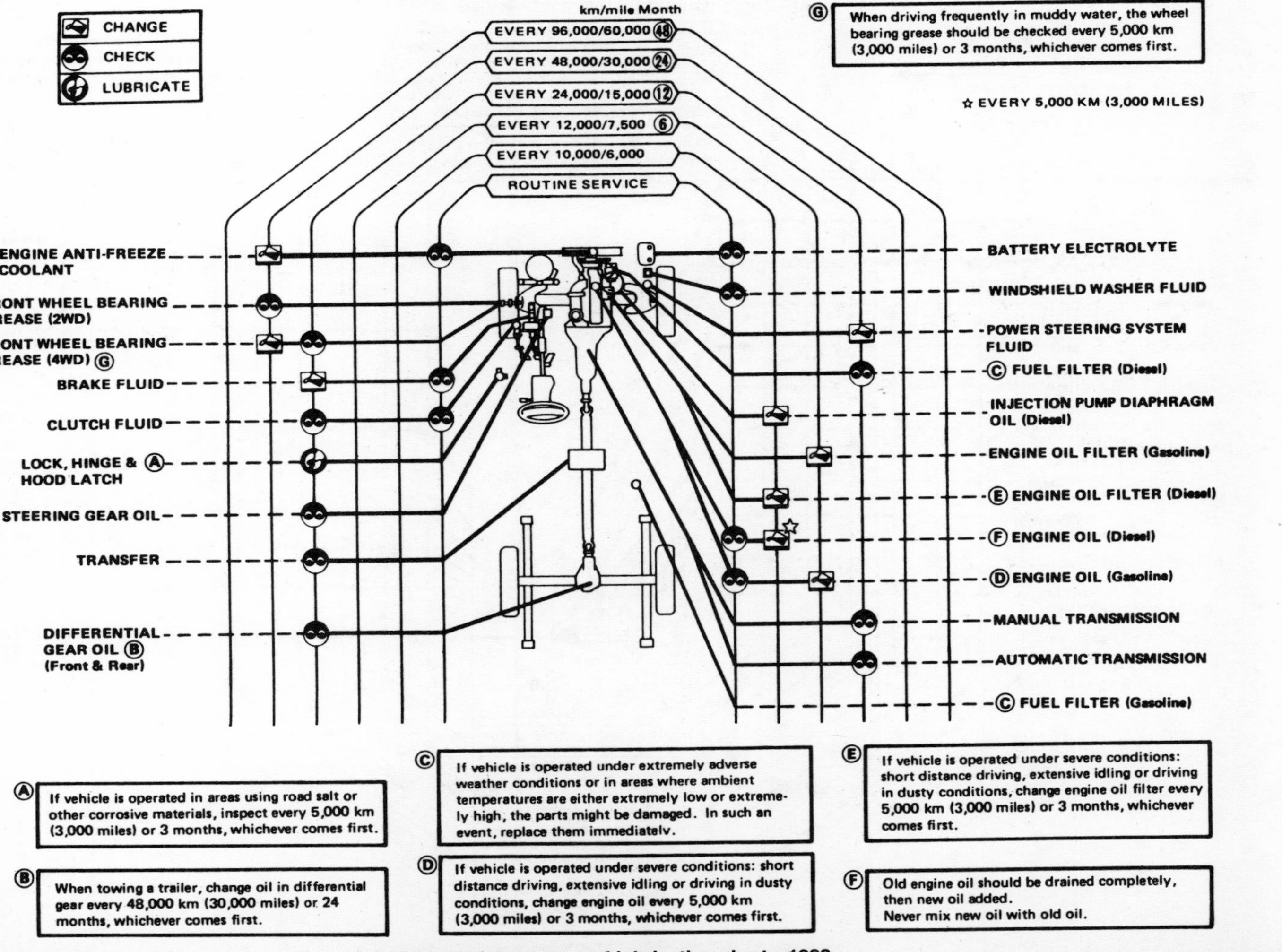

Vehicle maintenance and lubrication chart—1982

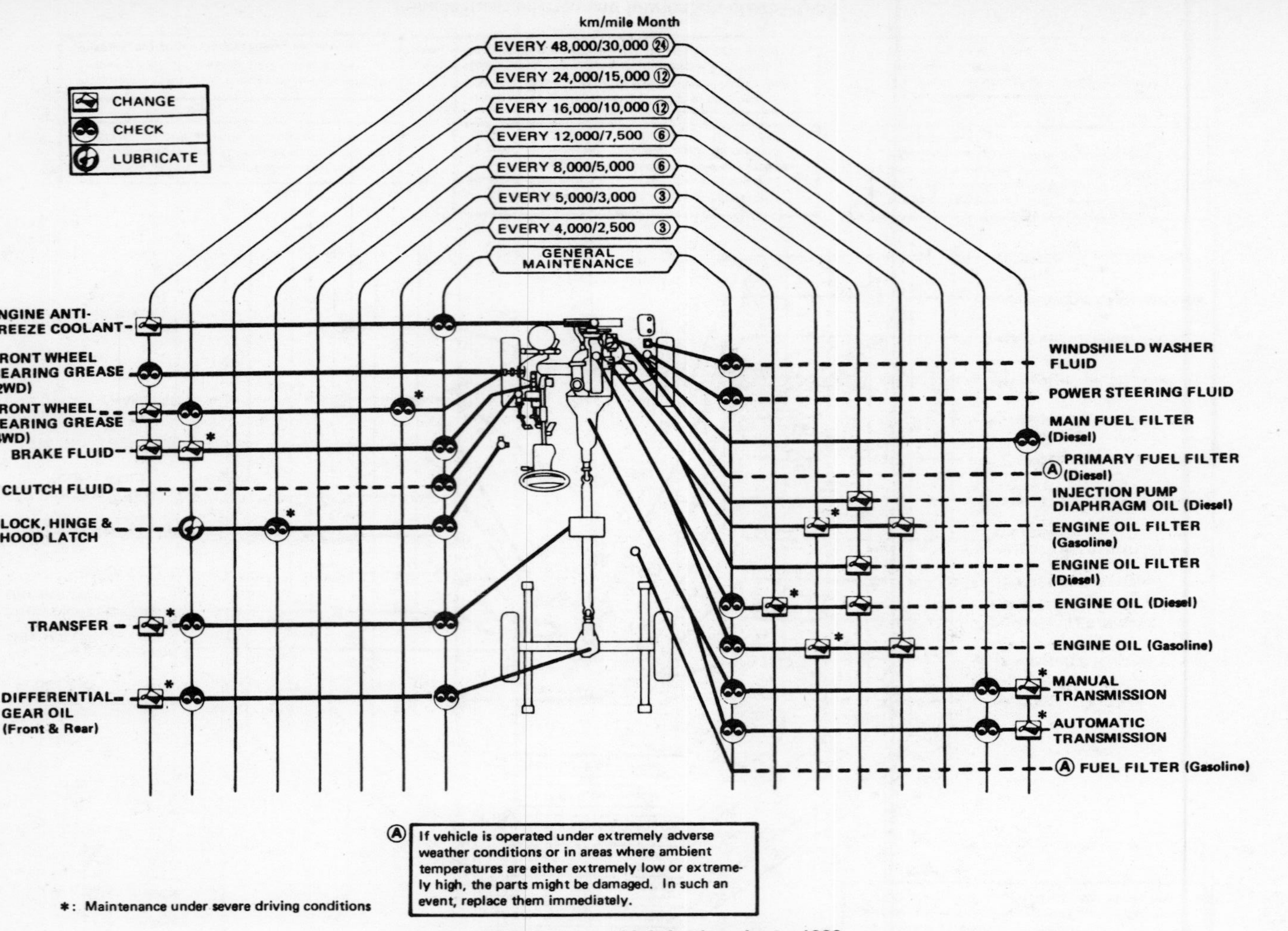

Vehicle maintenance and lubrication chart—1983

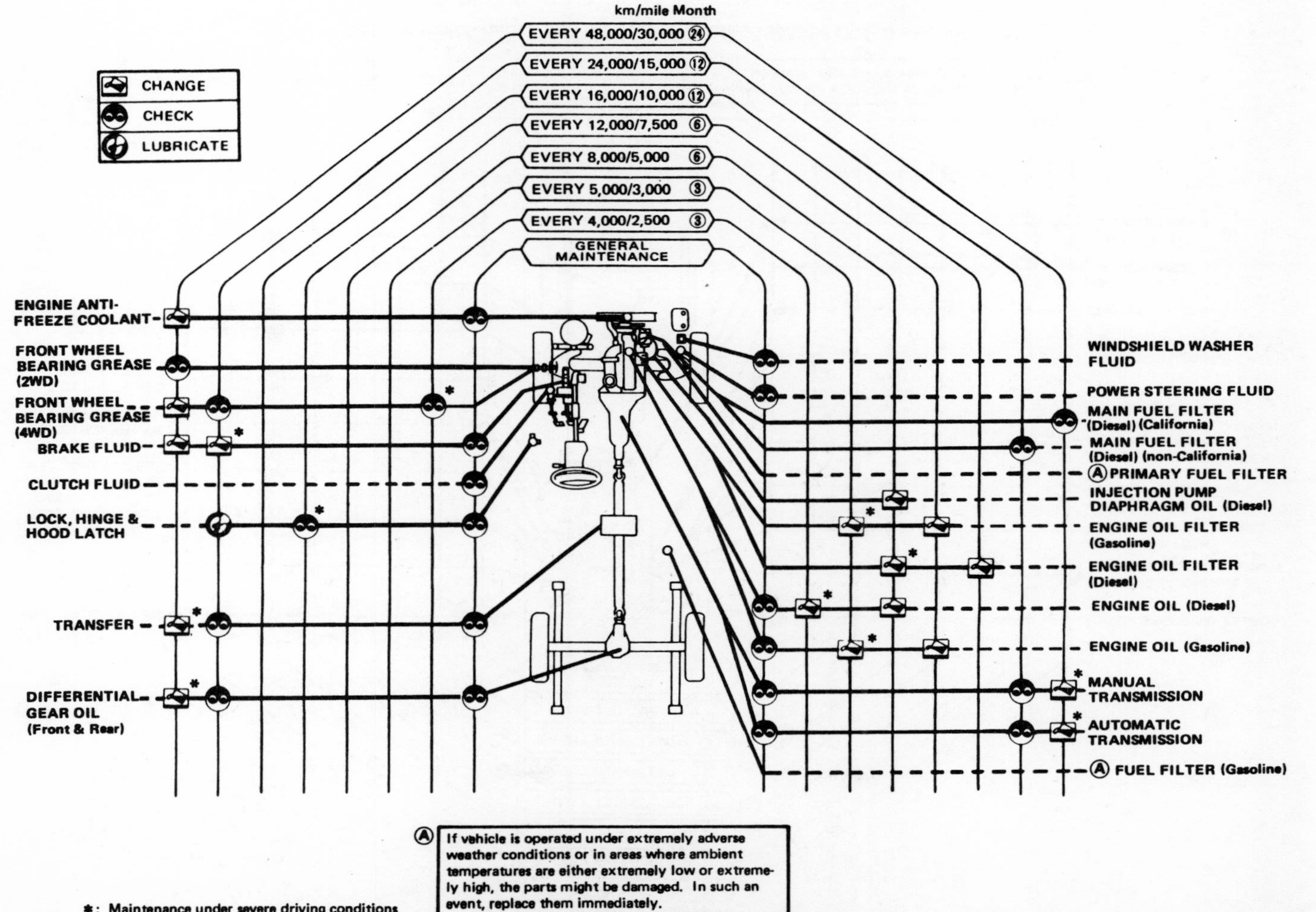

Vehicle maintenance and lubrication chart—1984

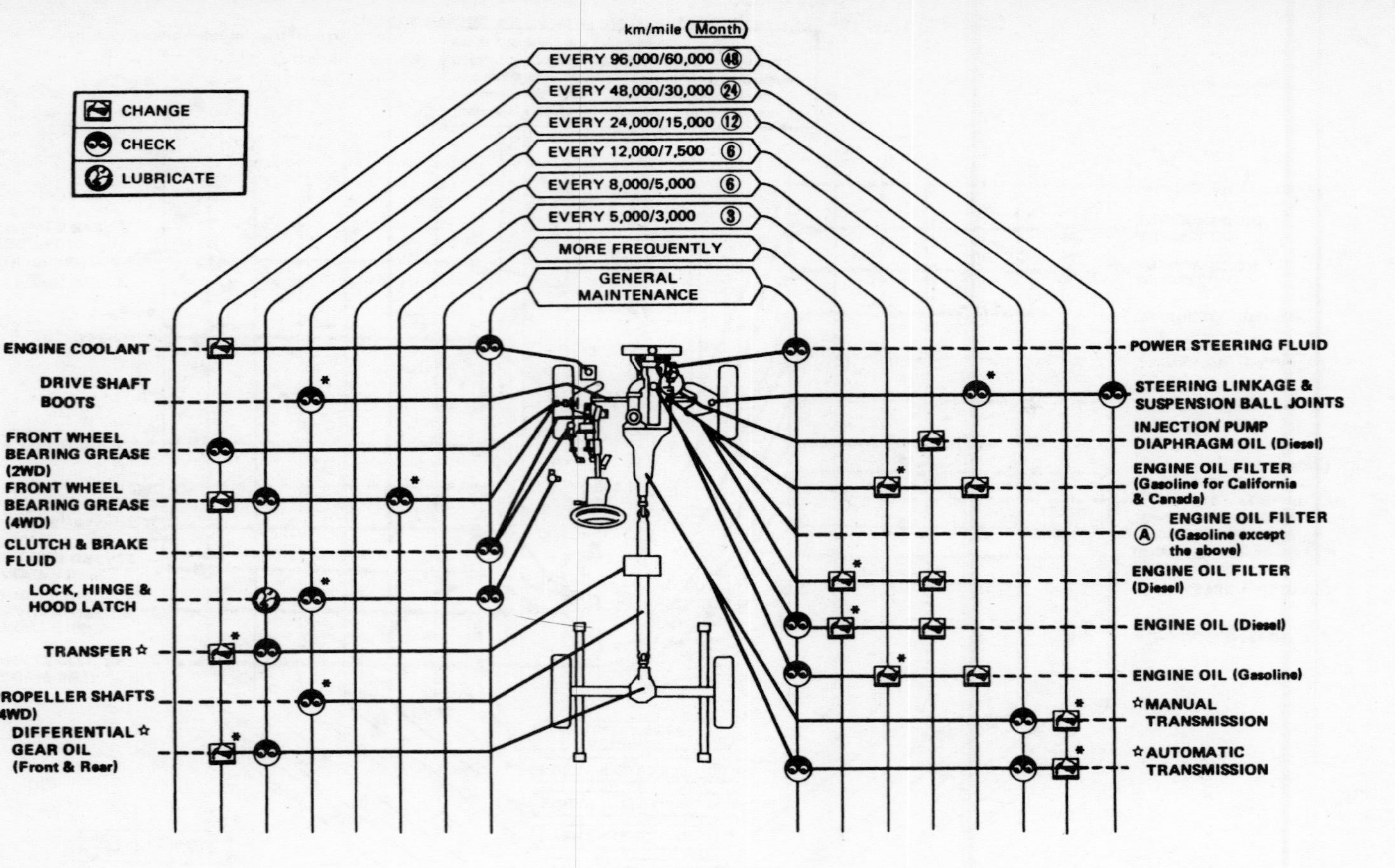

Vehicle maintenance and lubrication chart—1985–86 (720-D series)

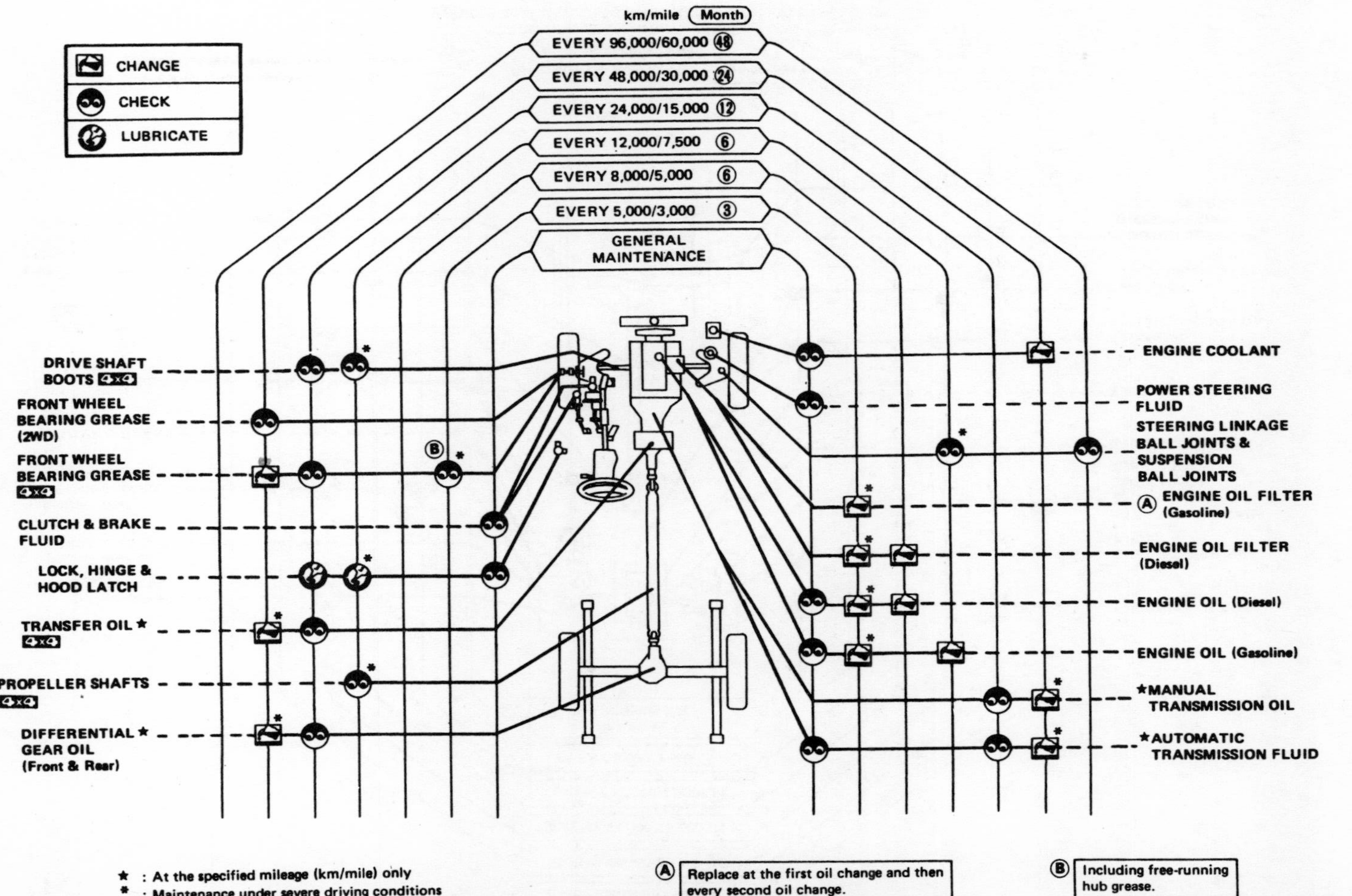

Vehicle maintenance and lubrication chart—1986–87 (D21-D series)

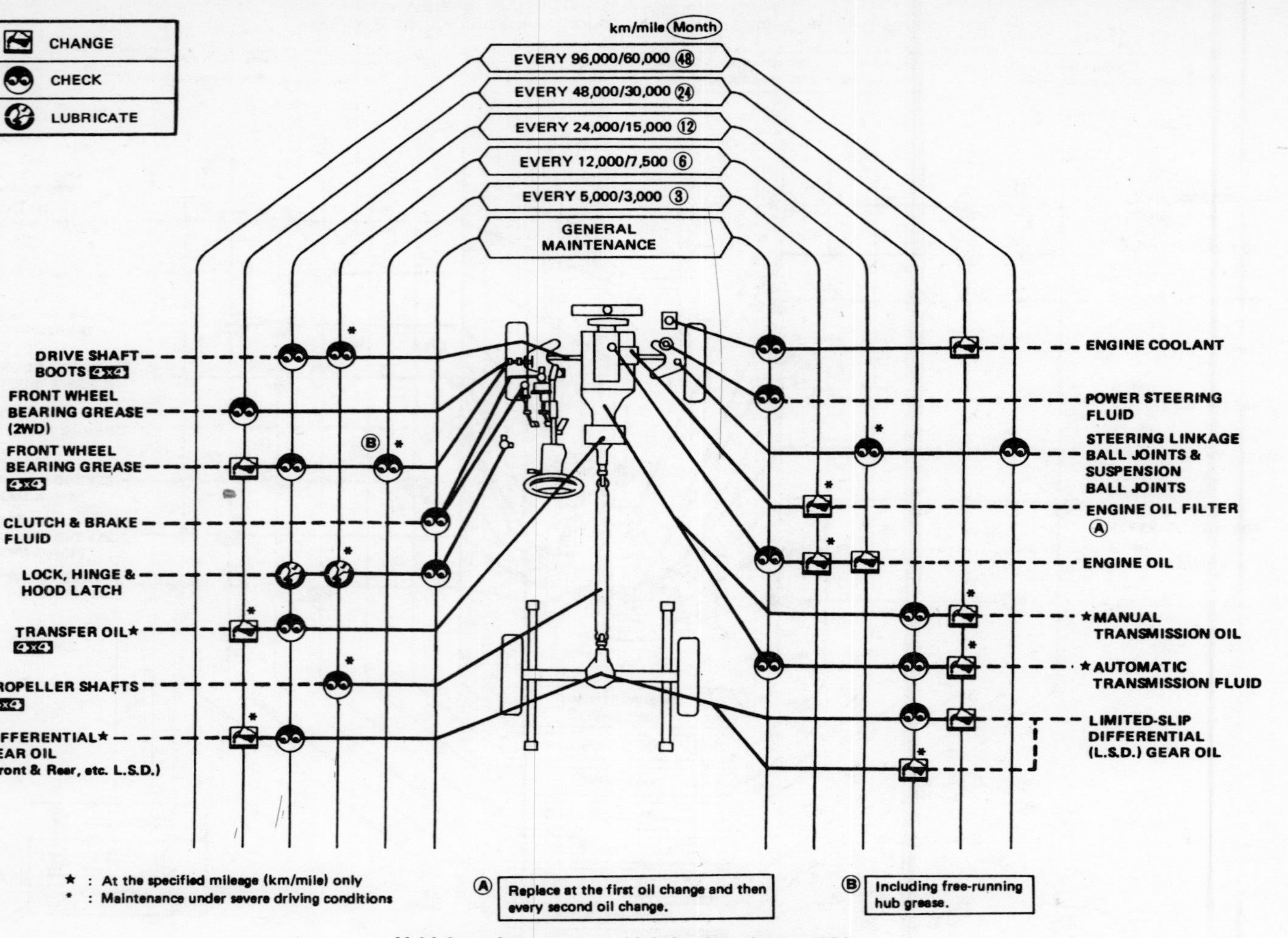

Vehicle maintenance and lubrication chart—1988

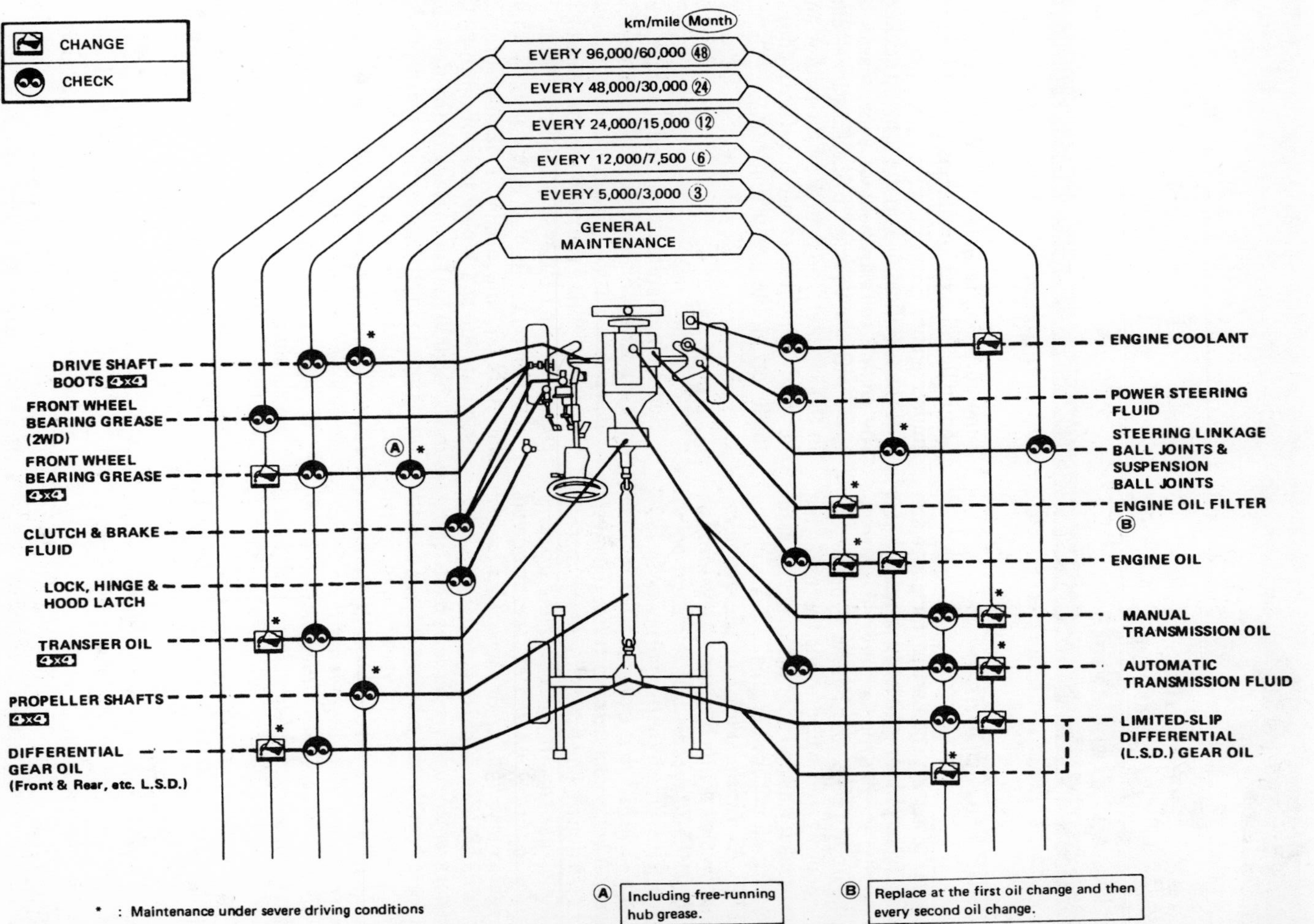

Vehicle maintenance and lubrication chart—1989

Engine Performance and Tune-Up

2

TUNE-UP PROCEDURES

In order to extract the best performance and economy from your engine it is essential that it be properly tuned at regular intervals. A regular tune-up will keep your Nissan's engine running smoothly and will prevent the annoying minor breakdowns and poor performance associated with an untuned engine.

NOTE: *All Nissan Pick-Ups use a conventional breaker points ignition system through 1975. 1970–73 models utilize a dual points system for emission control purposes. In 1976 Nissan switched to a transistorized ignition system. This system was much like the previous system with one basic difference; instead of the breaker points switching the primary current to the coil on and off, they triggered an igniter which did it for them. This igniter contains two transistors and an assortment of resistors which together serve as a switching device to turn the coil primary current on and off. The advantage of this type of circuitry is a reduced current through the distributor breaker points, thus prolonging their expected life and reducing scheduled maintenance.*

In 1976, a few models sold in California came equipped with a fully transistorized electronic ignition system. 1976–77 49 States and Canada models use the single breaker points system used in all models in 1974–75. In 1978, this system became standard on all models.

A complete tune-up should be performed every 15,000 miles (24,000 km) or twelve months, whichever comes first. This interval should be halved if the truck is operated under severe conditions, such as trailer towing, prolonged idling, continual stop and start driving, or if starting or running problems are noticed. It is assumed that the routine maintenance described in Chapter 1 has been kept up, as this will have a decided effect on the results of a tune-up. All of the applicable steps of a tune-up should be followed in order, as the result is a cumulative one.

If the specifications on the tune-up sticker in the engine compartment of your Nissan disagree with the "Tune-Up Specifications" chart in this chapter, the figures on the sticker must be used. The sticker often reflects changes made during the production run.

Spark Plugs

Spark plugs ignite the air and fuel mixture in the cylinder as the piston reaches the top of the compression stroke. The controlled explosion that results forces the piston down, turning the crankshaft and the rest of the drive train.

The average life of a spark plug is 15,000 miles (24,000 km), although manufacturers are now claiming spark plug lives of up to 30,000 miles (48,000 km) or more with the new platinum tipped plugs. This is, however, dependent on a number of factors: the mechanical condition of the engine; the type of fuel; the driving conditions; and the driver.

When you remove the spark plugs, check their condition. They are a good indicator of the condition of the engine. It is a good idea to remove the spark plugs every 6000 miles (9600 km) or so to keep an eye on the mechanical state of the engine.

A small deposit of light tan or gray material (or rust red with unleaded fuel) on a spark plug that has been used for any period of time is to be considered normal. Any other color, or abnormal amounts of deposit, indicates that there is something amiss in the engine.

The gap between the center electrode and the side or ground electrode can be expected to increase not more than 0.025mm every 1,000 miles (1600 km) under normal conditions.

When a spark plug is functioning normally or, more accurately, when the plug is installed

Troubleshooting Engine Performance

Problem	Cause	Solution
Hard starting (engine cranks normally)	• Binding linkage, choke valve or choke piston	• Repair as necessary
	• Restricted choke vacuum diaphragm	• Clean passages
	• Improper fuel level	• Adjust float level
	• Dirty, worn or faulty needle valve and seat	• Repair as necessary
	• Float sticking	• Repair as necessary
	• Faulty fuel pump	• Replace fuel pump
	• Incorrect choke cover adjustment	• Adjust choke cover
	• Inadequate choke unloader adjustment	• Adjust choke unloader
	• Faulty ignition coil	• Test and replace as necessary
	• Improper spark plug gap	• Adjust gap
	• Incorrect ignition timing	• Adjust timing
	• Incorrect valve timing	• Check valve timing; repair as necessary
Rough idle or stalling	• Incorrect curb or fast idle speed	• Adjust curb or fast idle speed
	• Incorrect ignition timing	• Adjust timing to specification
	• Improper feedback system operation	• Refer to Chapter 4
	• Improper fast idle cam adjustment	• Adjust fast idle cam
	• Faulty EGR valve operation	• Test EGR system and replace as necessary
	• Faulty PCV valve air flow	• Test PCV valve and replace as necessary
	• Choke binding	• Locate and eliminate binding condition
	• Faulty TAC vacuum motor or valve	• Repair as necessary
	• Air leak into manifold vacuum	• Inspect manifold vacuum connections and repair as necessary
	• Improper fuel level	• Adjust fuel level
	• Faulty distributor rotor or cap	• Replace rotor or cap
	• Improperly seated valves	• Test cylinder compression, repair as necessary
	• Incorrect ignition wiring	• Inspect wiring and correct as necessary
	• Faulty ignition coil	• Test coil and replace as necessary
	• Restricted air vent or idle passages	• Clean passages
	• Restricted air cleaner	• Clean or replace air cleaner filler element
	• Faulty choke vacuum diaphragm	• Repair as necessary
Faulty low-speed operation	• Restricted idle transfer slots	• Clean transfer slots
	• Restricted idle air vents and passages	• Clean air vents and passages
	• Restricted air cleaner	• Clean or replace air cleaner filter element
	• Improper fuel level	• Adjust fuel level
	• Faulty spark plugs	• Clean or replace spark plugs
	• Dirty, corroded, or loose ignition secondary circuit wire connections	• Clean or tighten secondary circuit wire connections
	• Improper feedback system operation	• Refer to Chapter 4
	• Faulty ignition coil high voltage wire	• Replace ignition coil high voltage wire
	• Faulty distributor cap	• Replace cap
Faulty acceleration	• Improper accelerator pump stroke	• Adjust accelerator pump stroke
	• Incorrect ignition timing	• Adjust timing
	• Inoperative pump discharge check ball or needle	• Clean or replace as necessary
	• Worn or damaged pump diaphragm or piston	• Replace diaphragm or piston

Troubleshooting Engine Performance (cont.)

Problem	Cause	Solution
Faulty acceleration (cont.)	• Leaking carburetor main body cover gasket	• Replace gasket
	• Engine cold and choke set too lean	• Adjust choke cover
	• Improper metering rod adjustment (BBD Model carburetor)	• Adjust metering rod
	• Faulty spark plug(s)	• Clean or replace spark plug(s)
	• Improperly seated valves	• Test cylinder compression, repair as necessary
	• Faulty ignition coil	• Test coil and replace as necessary
	• Improper feedback system operation	• Refer to Chapter 4
Faulty high speed operation	• Incorrect ignition timing	• Adjust timing
	• Faulty distributor centrifugal advance mechanism	• Check centrifugal advance mechanism and repair as necessary
	• Faulty distributor vacuum advance mechanism	• Check vacuum advance mechanism and repair as necessary
	• Low fuel pump volume	• Replace fuel pump
	• Wrong spark plug air gap or wrong plug	• Adjust air gap or install correct plug
	• Faulty choke operation	• Adjust choke cover
	• Partially restricted exhaust manifold, exhaust pipe, catalytic converter, muffler, or tailpipe	• Eliminate restriction
	• Restricted vacuum passages	• Clean passages
	• Improper size or restricted main jet	• Clean or replace as necessary
	• Restricted air cleaner	• Clean or replace filter element as necessary
	• Faulty distributor rotor or cap	• Replace rotor or cap
	• Faulty ignition coil	• Test coil and replace as necessary
	• Improperly seated valve(s)	• Test cylinder compression, repair as necessary
	• Faulty valve spring(s)	• Inspect and test valve spring tension, replace as necessary
	• Incorrect valve timing	• Check valve timing and repair as necessary
	• Intake manifold restricted	• Remove restriction or replace manifold
	• Worn distributor shaft	• Replace shaft
	• Improper feedback system operation	• Refer to Chapter 4
Misfire at all speeds	• Faulty spark plug(s)	• Clean or replace spark plug(s)
	• Faulty spark plug wire(s)	• Replace as necessary
	• Faulty distributor cap or rotor	• Replace cap or rotor
	• Faulty ignition coil	• Test coil and replace as necessary
	• Primary ignition circuit shorted or open intermittently	• Troubleshoot primary circuit and repair as necessary
	• Improperly seated valve(s)	• Test cylinder compression, repair as necessary
	• Faulty hydraulic tappet(s)	• Clean or replace tappet(s)
	• Improper feedback system operation	• Refer to Chapter 4
	• Faulty valve spring(s)	• Inspect and test valve spring tension, repair as necessary
	• Worn camshaft lobes	• Replace camshaft
	• Air leak into manifold	• Check manifold vacuum and repair as necessary
	• Improper carburetor adjustment	• Adjust carburetor
	• Fuel pump volume or pressure low	• Replace fuel pump
	• Blown cylinder head gasket	• Replace gasket
	• Intake or exhaust manifold passage(s) restricted	• Pass chain through passage(s) and repair as necessary
	• Incorrect trigger wheel installed in distributor	• Install correct trigger wheel

Troubleshooting Engine Performance (cont.)

Problem	Cause	Solution
Power not up to normal	• Incorrect ignition timing • Faulty distributor rotor • Trigger wheel loose on shaft • Incorrect spark plug gap • Faulty fuel pump • Incorrect valve timing • Faulty ignition coil • Faulty ignition wires • Improperly seated valves • Blown cylinder head gasket • Leaking piston rings • Worn distributor shaft • Improper feedback system operation	• Adjust timing • Replace rotor • Reposition or replace trigger wheel • Adjust gap • Replace fuel pump • Check valve timing and repair as necessary • Test coil and replace as necessary • Test wires and replace as necessary • Test cylinder compression and repair as necessary • Replace gasket • Test compression and repair as necessary • Replace shaft • Refer to Chapter 4
Intake backfire	• Improper ignition timing • Faulty accelerator pump discharge • Defective EGR CTO valve • Defective TAC vacuum motor or valve • Lean air/fuel mixture	• Adjust timing • Repair as necessary • Replace EGR CTO valve • Repair as necessary • Check float level or manifold vacuum for air leak. Remove sediment from bowl
Exhaust backfire	• Air leak into manifold vacuum • Faulty air injection diverter valve • Exhaust leak	• Check manifold vacuum and repair as necessary • Test diverter valve and replace as necessary • Locate and eliminate leak
Ping or spark knock	• Incorrect ignition timing • Distributor centrifugal or vacuum advance malfunction • Excessive combustion chamber deposits • Air leak into manifold vacuum • Excessively high compression • Fuel octane rating excessively low • Sharp edges in combustion chamber • EGR valve not functioning properly	• Adjust timing • Inspect advance mechanism and repair as necessary • Remove with combustion chamber cleaner • Check manifold vacuum and repair as necessary • Test compression and repair as necessary • Try alternate fuel source • Grind smooth • Test EGR system and replace as necessary
Surging (at cruising to top speeds)	• Low carburetor fuel level • Low fuel pump pressure or volume • Metering rod(s) not adjusted properly (BBD Model Carburetor) • Improper PCV valve air flow • Air leak into manifold vacuum • Incorrect spark advance • Restricted main jet(s) • Undersize main jet(s) • Restricted air vents • Restricted fuel filter • Restricted air cleaner • EGR valve not functioning properly • Improper feedback system operation	• Adjust fuel level • Replace fuel pump • Adjust metering rod • Test PCV valve and replace as necessary • Check manifold vacuum and repair as necessary • Test and replace as necessary • Clean main jet(s) • Replace main jet(s) • Clean air vents • Replace fuel filter • Clean or replace air cleaner filter element • Test EGR system and replace as necessary • Refer to Chapter 4

Gasoline Engine Tune-Up Specifications

When analyzing compression test results, look for uniformity among cylinders, rather than specific pressures.

Year	Engine Type	Spark Plugs		Distributor		Ignition Timing (deg)▲		Compression Pressure (psi)**	Fuel Pump Pressure (psi)	Idle Speed (rpm)▲		Valve Clearance (in.)‡	
		Type	Gap (in.)	Point Dwell (deg)	Point Gap (in.)	MT	AT			MT	AT	In	Ex
1970	L16	B6ES	0.033	52	0.020	10B	—	171	2.6–3.4	700	—	0.010	0,012
1971	L16	B6ES	0.033	52	0.020	10B	—	171	2.6–3.4	700	—	0.010	0.012
1972	L16	B6ES	0.032	52	0.020	7B	—	171	2.6–3.4	700	—	0.010	0.012
1973	L16	B6ES	0.030	52	0.020	8B	—	171	2.6–3.4	800	—	0.010	0.012
	L18	B6ES	0.030	52	0.020	5B	5B	171	2.6–3.4	800	650	0.010	0.012
1974	L18	B6ES	0.030	52	0.020	12B	12B	171	2.6–3.4	800	650	0.010	0.012
1975	L20B	BP6ES	0.034	52	0.020	12B ①	12B	171	2.8–3.8	750	650	0.010	0.012
1976	L20B	②	③	④	④⑤	12B ①	12B	171	2.8–3.8	750	650	0.010	0.012
1977	L20B	②	③	④	④⑤	12B ①	12B	171	2.8–3.8	750	650	0.010	0.012
1978	L20B	BP6ES-11	0.041	—	⑤	12B	12B	171	3.0–3.9 ⑦	600	600	0.010	0.012
1979	L20B	BP6ES-11	0.041	—	⑥	12B	12B	171	3.0–3.9 ⑦	650	630	0.010	0.012
1980	L20B	BP6ES-11	0.041	—	⑥	12B ①	12B	171	3.0–3.9 ⑦	600	600	0.010	0.012
1981	Z22	BP6ES ⑧	0.033	—	⑥	5B	5B	171	3.0–3.9	650 ⑨	650	0.012	0.012
1982	Z22	⑩	0.033	—	⑥	3B	3B	171	3.0–3.9	650 ⑨	650	0.012	0.012
1983	Z22	⑩	0.033	—	⑥	3B	3B	171	3.0–3.9	650 ⑨	650	0.012	0.012
1984	Z20	⑩	0.033	—	⑥	5B	—	171	2.7–3.4	600	—	0.012	0.012
	Z24	⑩	0.033	—	⑥	3B	3B	171	2.7–3.4	700 ⑪	650	0.012	0.012
1985	Z20	⑩	0.033	—	⑥	5B	—	171	2.7–3.4	600	—	0.012	0.012
	Z24	⑩	0.033	—	⑥	3B	3B	171	2.7–3.4	700 ⑪	650	0.012	0.012
1986	Z20	⑩	0.033	—	⑥	5B	—	171	2.7–3.4	600	—	0.012	0.012
	Z24	⑩	0.033	—	⑥	3B	3B	171	2.7–3.4	700 ⑪	650	0.012	0.012
	Z24i	BPR5ES	0.033	—	—	5B	5B	173	36	900	650	0.012	0.012
	VG30i	BCPR5ES-11	0.041	—	—	12B	12B	173	36	800	700	Hyd.	Hyd.

1987	Z24i	BPR5ES	0.033	—	—	10B	10B	173	36	800	750	0.012	0.012
	VG30i	BCPR5ES-11	0.041	—	—	12B	12B	173	36	800	700	Hyd.	Hyd.
1988	Z24i	BPR5ES	0.033	—	—	10B	10B	173	36	800	650	0.012	0.012
	VG30i	BCPR5ES-11	0.041	—	—	12B	12B	173	36	800	700	Hyd.	Hyd.
1989	Z24i	BPR5ES	0.033	—	—	10B	10B	173	36	800	650	0.012	0.012
	VG30i	BCPR5ES-11	0.041	—	—	12B	12B	173	36	800	700	Hyd.	Hyd.

NOTE: The underhood specifications sticker often reflects tune-up specification changes made while the car is in production. Sticker figures must be used if they disagree with those in this chart.
▲With the manual transmission in Neutral and the automatic transmission in Drive (D)
** Lowest reading must be at least 80% of highest
‡ Valve clearances checked with the engine HOT
MT Manual Transmission
AT Automatic Transmission
B Before top dead center
In Intake
Ex Exhaust
① 1975–77 Calif. & 1980 Calif. Heavy Duty: 10B
② Point-type (exc. 1977 Canada): BP6ES
1977 Canada: BPR6ES
Transistorized: BP6ES-11
③ Point-type: 0.033
Transistor-type: 0.041
④ Point-type: Dwell—52; Gap—0.020
⑤ Air gap: 0.008–0.016
⑥ Air gap: 0.012–0.020
⑦ W/electric fuel pump (A/C models): 4.6 or less
⑧ Canada: BPR6ES
⑨ 4WD: 800
⑩ Intake: BPR6ES
Exhaust: BPR5ES
⑪ 4WD: 800
2WD Canada: 650

Diesel Engine Tune-Up Specifications

Year	Injector Opening Pressure (psi)	Low Idle (rpm)	Dashpot Speed (rpm)	Valve Clearance (in.)		Intake Valve Opens (deg.)	Injection Timing rpm	Firing Order
				Intake	Exhaust			
1981–83	1422.5	550–700	1280–1350	.014	.014	28	20 BTDC	1-3-4-2
1984–86	1422.5	650–800	1280–1350	.014	.014	28	18 BTDC	1-3-4-2

in an engine that is functioning properly, the plugs can be taken out, cleaned, regapped, and reinstalled in the engine without doing the engine any harm.

When, and if, a plug fouls and begins to misfire, you will have to investigate, correct the cause of the fouling, and either clean or replace the plug.

There are several reasons why a spark plug will foul and you can learn which is at fault by just looking at the plug. Refer to the color "Spark Plug Diagnosis" section in the center of this manual for illustrations of these problems and information on their cure.

Spark plugs suitable for use in your Nissan's engine are offered in a number of different heat ranges. The amount of heat which the plug absorbs is determined by the length of the lower insulator. The longer the insulator the hotter the plug will operate; the shorter the insulator, the cooler it will operate. A spark plug that absorbs (or retains) little heat and remains too cool will accumulate deposits of lead, oil, and carbon, because it is not hot enough to burn them off. This leads to fouling and consequent misfiring. A spark plug that absorbs too much heat will have no deposits, but the electrodes will burn away quickly and, in some cases, preignition may result. Preignition occurs when the spark plug tips get so hot that they ignite the air/fuel mixture before the actual spark fires. This premature ignition will usually cause a pinging sound under conditions of low speed and heavy load. In severe cases, the heat may become high enough to start the air/fuel mixture burning throughout the combustion chamber rather than just to the front of the plug. In this case, the resultant explosion will be strong enough to damage pistons, rings, and valves.

In most cases the factory recommended heat range is correct; it is chosen to perform well under a wide range of operating conditions. However, if most of your driving is long distance, high speed travel, you may want to install a spark plug one step colder than standard. If most of your driving is of the short trip variety, when the engine may not always reach operating temperature, a hotter plug may help burn off the deposits normally accumulated under those conditions.

REMOVAL

1. Number the wires so that you won't cross them when you replace them.
2. Remove the wire from the end of the spark lug by grasping the wire by the rubber boot. If the boot sticks to the plug, remove it by twisting and pulling at the same time. Do not pull wire itself or you will damage the core.
3. Use a $^{13}/_{16}''$ spark plug socket to loosen all of the plugs about two turns.

NOTE: *The cylinder head is cast from aluminum. Remove the spark plugs when the engine is cold, if possible, to prevent damage to the threads.*

If removal of the plugs is difficult, apply a

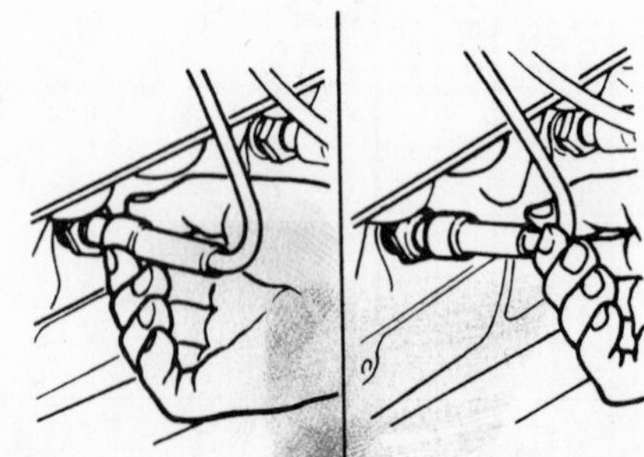

Twist and pull on the rubber boot to remove the spark plug wires; never pull on the wire itself

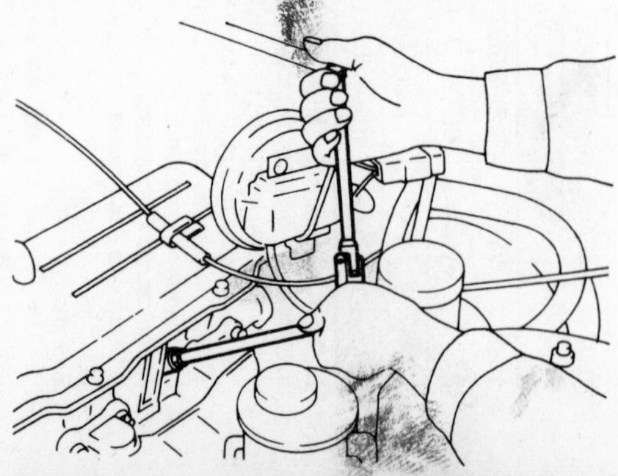

Plugs are removed using the proper combination of socket wrench, universals, and extensions

few drops of penetrating oil or silicone spray to the area around the base of the plug, and allow it a few minutes to work.

4. If compressed air is available, apply it to the area around the spark plug holes. Otherwise, use a rag or a brush to clean the area. Be careful not to allow nay foreign material to drop into the spark plug holes.

5. Remove the plugs by unscrewing them the rest of the way from the engine.

INSPECTION

Check the plugs for deposits and wear (see the "Spark Plug Diagnosis" color section in the center of this book). If they are not going to be replaced, clean the plugs thoroughly. Remember that nay kind of deposit will decrease the efficiency of the plug. Plugs can be cleaned on a spark plug cleaning machine, which can sometimes be found in service stations, or you can do an acceptable job of cleaning with a stiff brush. If the plugs are cleaned, the electrodes must be filed flat. Use an ignition points file, not an emery board or the like, which will leave deposits. The electrodes must be filed perfectly flat with sharp edges; rounded edges reduce the spark plug voltage by as much as 50%.

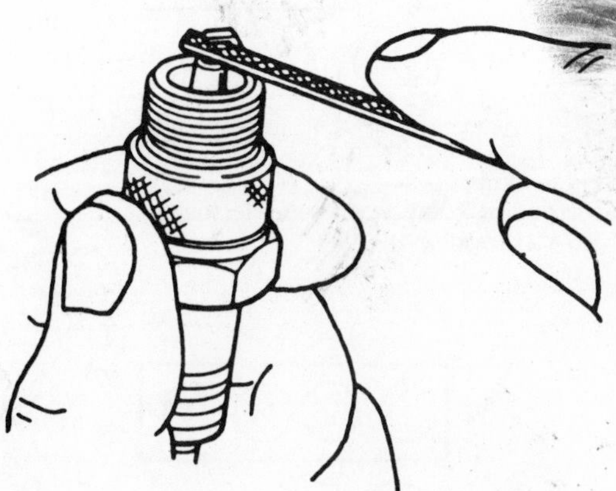

Plugs in good condition can be filed and reused

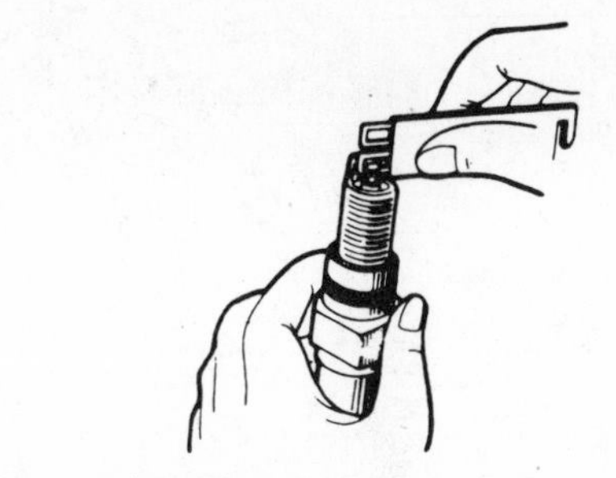

Check the spark plugs with a wire feeler gauge

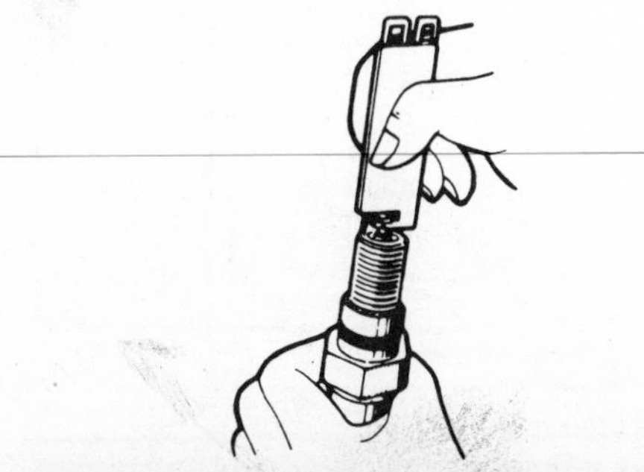

Bend the side electrode to adjust the gap

Check spark plug gap before installation. The ground electrode (the L-shaped one connected to the body of the plug) must be parallel to the center electrode and the specified size wire gauge (see "Tune-Up Specifications").

CAUTION: *NEVER adjust the gap on a used platinum tipped spark plug!*

Always check the gap on new plugs, too; they are not always set correctly at the factory. Do not use a flat feeler gauge when measuring the gap, because the reading will be inaccurate. Wire gapping tools usually have a bending tool attached. Use that to adjust the side electrode until the proper distance is obtained Absolutely never bend the center electrode. Also, be careful not to bend the side electrode too far or too often; it may weaken and break off within the engine, requiring removal of the cylinder head to retrieve it.

INSTALLATION

1. Lubricate the threads of the spark plugs with a drop of oil. Install the plugs and tighten them hand tight. Take care not to cross-thread them.

2. Tighten the spark plugs with the socket. Do not apply the same amount of force you would use for a bolt; just snug them in. If a torque wrench is available, tighten to 11–15 ft. lbs.

3. Install the wires on their respective plugs. Make sure the wires are firmly connected. You will be able to feel them click into place.

Spark Plug Wires

CHECKING AND REPLACEMENT

At every tune-up, visually inspect the spark plug cables for burns cuts, or breaks in the insulation. Check the boots and the nipples on the distributor cap and coil. Replace any damaged wiring.

Every 36,000 miles (58,000 km) or so, the resistance of the wires should be checked with an ohmmeter. Wires with excessive resistance will cause misfiring, and may make the engine difficult to start in damp weather. Generally, the

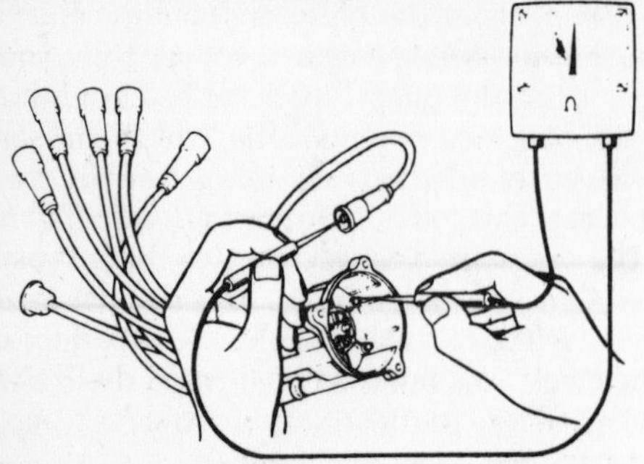

Checking plug wire resistance with an ohmmeter

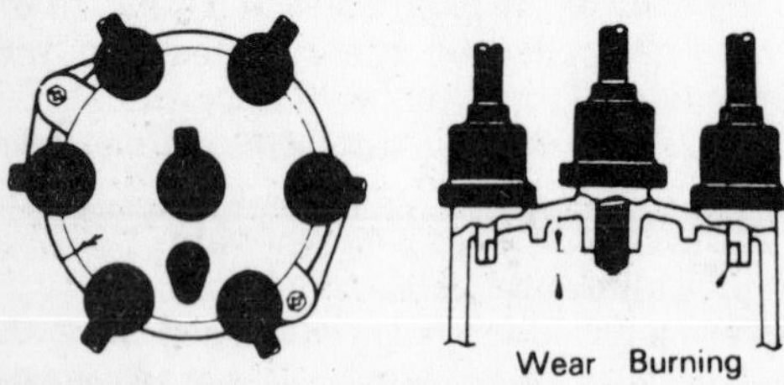

Check the distributor cap for cracks; check the cable ends for wear

useful life of the cables is 36,000–50,000 miles (58,000–80,000 km).

To check resistance, remove the distributor cap, leaving the wires attached. Connect one lead of an ohmmeter to an electrode within the cap; connect the other lead to the corresponding spark plug terminal (remove it from the plug for this test). Replace any wire which shows a resistance over 25,000 ohms (Ω). Test the high tension lead from the coil by connecting the ohmmeter between the center contact in the distributor cap and either of the primary terminals of the coil. If resistance is more than 25,000 ohms (Ω), remove the cable from the coil and check the resistance of the cable alone. Anything over 15,000 ohms (Ω) is cause for replacement. It should be remembered that resistance is also a function of length; the longer the cable, the greater the resistance. Thus, if the cables on your truck are longer than the factory originals, resistance will be higher, quite possibly outside these limits.

When installing new cables, replace them one at a time to avoid mixups. Start by replacing the longest one first. Install the boot firmly over the spark plug. Route the wire over the same path as the original. Insert the nipple firmly into the tower on the cap or the coil.

FIRING ORDERS

To avoid confusion, always replace the spark plug wires one at a time.

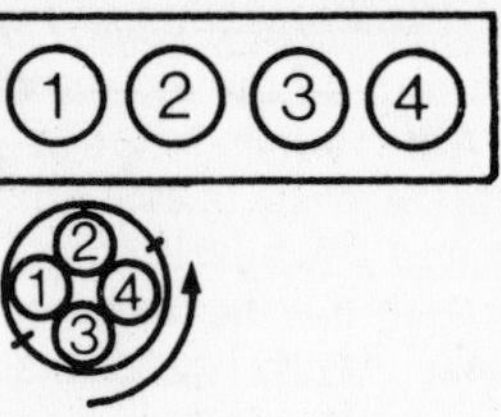

Firing Order: 1–3–4–2
Distributor Rotation: Counterclockwise
1970–73 L16 and L18 engines

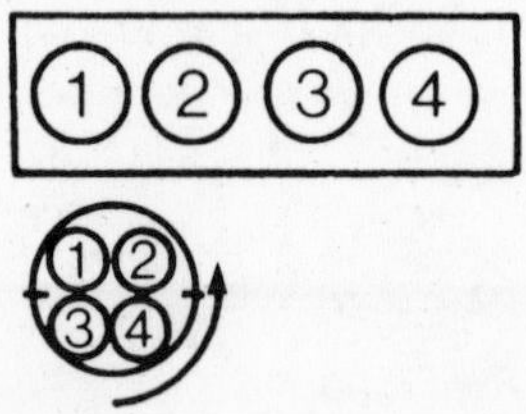

Firing Order: 1–3–4–2
Distributor Rotation: Counterclockwise
1974 L18 engines

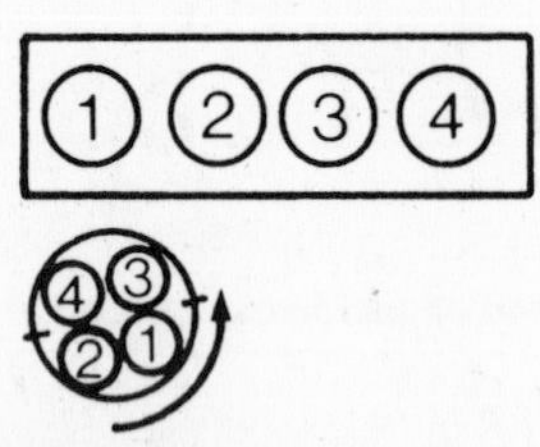

Firing Order: 1–3–4–2
Distributor Rotation: Counterlcockwise
1975–80 L20B engines

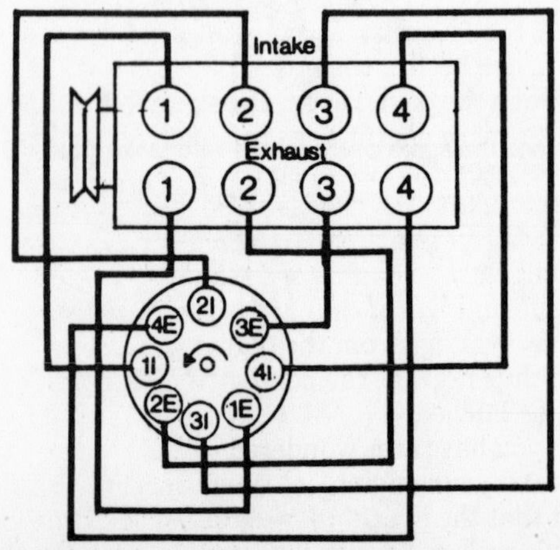

Firing Order: 1–3–4–2
Distributor Rotation: Counterclockwise
1981–89 Z20, Z22, Z24 and Z24i engines

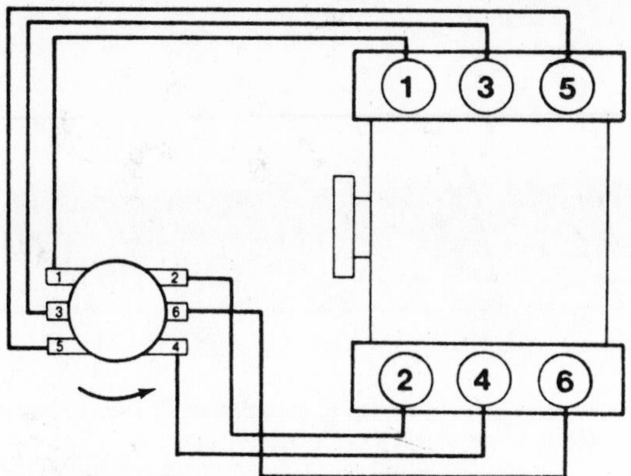

Firing Order: 1–2–3–4–5–6
Distributor Rotation: Counterclockwise
1986–89 VG30i engines

Breaker Points and Condenser

The points function as a circuit breaker for the primary circuit of the ignition system. The ignition coil must boost the 12 volts of electrical pressure supplied by the battery to as much as 25,000 volts in order to fire the plugs. To do this, the coil depends on the points and the condenser to make a clean break in the primary circuit.

The coil has both primary and secondary circuits. When the ignition is turned on, the battery supplies voltage through the coil and onto the points. The points are connected to ground, completing the primary circuit. As the current passes through the coil, a magnetic field is created in the iron center core of the coil. When the cam in the distributor turns, the points open, breaking the primary circuit. The magnetic field in the primary circuit of the coil then collapses and cuts through the secondary circuit windings around the iron core. Because of the physical principle called electromagnetic induction, the battery voltage is increased to a level sufficient to fire the spark plugs.

When the points open, the electrical charge in the primary circuit tries to jump the gap created between the two open contacts of the points If this electrical charge were not transferred elsewhere, the metal contacts of the points would start to change rapidly.

The function of the condenser is to absorb excessive voltage from the points when they open and thus prevent the points from becoming pitted or burned.

If you have ever wondered why it is necessary to tune your engine occasionally, consider the fact that the ignition system must complete the above cycle each time a spark plug fires. On a 4-cylinder, 4-cycle engine, two of the four plugs must fire once for every engine revolution. If the idle speed of your engine is 800 revolutions per minute (800 rpm), the breaker points open and close two times for each revolution. For every minute your engine idles, your points open and close 1600 times (2 x 800 = 1600). And that is just at idle. What about at 3000 rpm?

There are two ways to check breaker point gap; with a feeler gauge or with a swell meter. Either way you set the points, you are adjusting the amount of time (in degrees of distributor rotation) that the points will remain open. If you adjust the points with a feeler gauge, you are setting the maximum amount the points will open when the rubbing block on the points is on a high point of the distributor cam. When you adjust the points with a swell meter, you are measuring the number of degrees (of distributor cam rotation) that points will remain closed before they start to open as a high point of the distributor cam approaches the rubbing block of the points.

If you still do not understand how the points function, take a friend, go outside, and remove the distributor cap from your engine. Have your friend operate the starter (make sure that the transmission is not in gear) as you look at the exposed parts of the distributor.

There are two rules that should always be followed when adjusting or replacing points. The points and condenser are a matched set; never replace one without replacing the other. If you change the point gap or swell of the engine, you also change the ignition timing. Therefore, if you adjust the points, you must also adjust the timing.

INSPECTION AND CLEANING

The breaker points should be inspected and cleaned at 6000 mile (9600 km) intervals. To do so, perform the following steps:

1. Disconnect the high tension lead from the coil.
2. Unsnap the two distributor cap retaining clips and lift the cap straight up. Leave the leads connected to the cap and position it out of the way.
3. Remove the rotor and dust cover by pulling them straight up.
4. Place a screwdriver against the breaker points and pry them open. Examine their condition. If they are excessively worn, burned, or pitted, they should be replaced.
5. Polish the points with a point file. Do not use emery cloth or sandpaper; these may leave particles on the points causing them to arc.
6. Clean the distributor cap and rotor with alcohol. Inspect the cap terminals for looseness and corrosion. Check the rotor tip for excessive burning. Inspect both cap and rotor for cracks.

Replace either if they show any of the above signs of wear or damage.

7. Check the operation of the centrifugal advance mechanism by turning the rotor clockwise. Release the rotor; it should return to its original position. If it doesn't, check for binding parts.

8. Check the vacuum advance unit, but removing the plastic cap and pressing on the octane selector. It should return to its original position. Check for binding if it doesn't.

9. If the points do not require replacement, proceed with the adjustment section below. Otherwise perform the point and condense replacement procedures.

REMOVAL AND INSTALLATION

1. Mark or tag then remove the coil high tension wire from the top of the distributor cap. Remove the distributor cap and place it out of the way. Remove the rotor from the distributor shaft by pulling up.

2. On single point distributors, remove the condenser from the distributor body. On early dual point distributors, you will find that one condenser is virtually impossible to reach without removing the distributor from the engine. To do this, first note and mark the position of the distributor on the small timing scale on the front of the distributor. Then mark the position of the rotor in relation to the distributor body. Do this by simply replacing the rotor on the distributor shaft and marking the spot on the distributor body where the rotor is pointing. Be careful not to turn the engine over while performing this operation.

3. Remove the distributor on dual point models by removing the small bolt at the rear of the distributor. Lift the distributor out of the block. It is now possible to remove the rear condenser. Do not crank the engine with the distributor removed.

4. On single point distributors, remove the points assembly attaching screws and then remove the points. A magnetic screwdriver or one

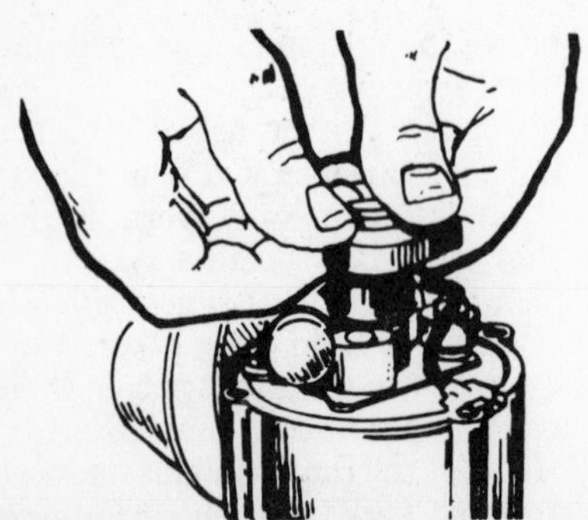

Pull the rotor straight up to remove it

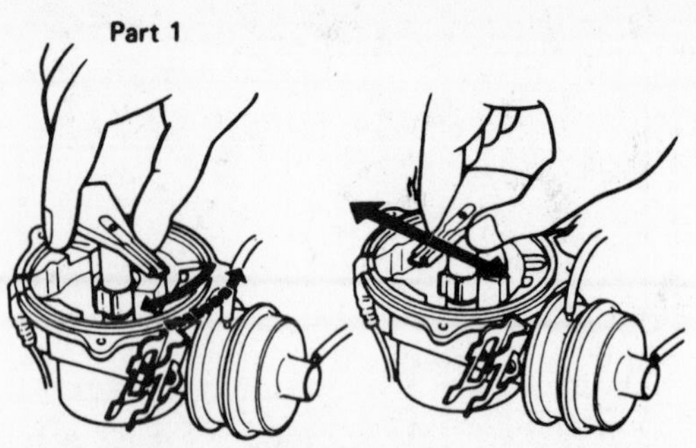

The rotor should return to its original position when rotated slightly and then let go

On dual point distributors, #1 and #2 are the mounting screws. Do not loosen #3, the phase adjusting screw

with a holding mechanism will come in handy here, so that you don't drop a screw into the distributor and have to remove the entire distributor to retrieve it. After the points are removed, wipe off the cam and apply new cam lubricant. If you don't, the points will wear out in a few thousand miles.

5. On dual point distributors, you will probably find it easier to simply remove the points assemblies while the distributor is out of the engine. Install the new points and condensers. You can either set the point gap now or later after you have reinstalled the distributor.

6. On dual point models, install the distributor, making sure the marks made earlier are lined up. Note that the slot for the oil pump drive is tapered and will only fit one way.

7. On single point distributors, slip the new set of points onto the locating dowel and install the screws that hold the assembly onto the plate. Don't tighten them all the way yet, since you'll only have to loosen them to set the point gap.

8. Install the new condenser on single point models and attach the condenser lead to the points.

9. Set the point gap and dwell (see the following sections).

ADJUSTMENT OF THE BREAKER POINTS WITH A FEELER GAUGE

Single Point Distributor

1. If the contact points of the assembly are not parallel, bend the stationary contact so that they make contact across the entire surface of the contacts. Bend only the stationary bracket part of the point assembly; not the movable contact.

2. Turn the engine until the rubbing block of the points is on one of the high points of the distributor cam. You can do this by either turning the ignition switch to the start position and releasing it quickly (bumping the engine) or by using a wrench on the bolt which holds the crankshaft pulley to the crankshaft.

3. Place the correct size feeler gauge between the contacts (see the Tune-Up Specifications

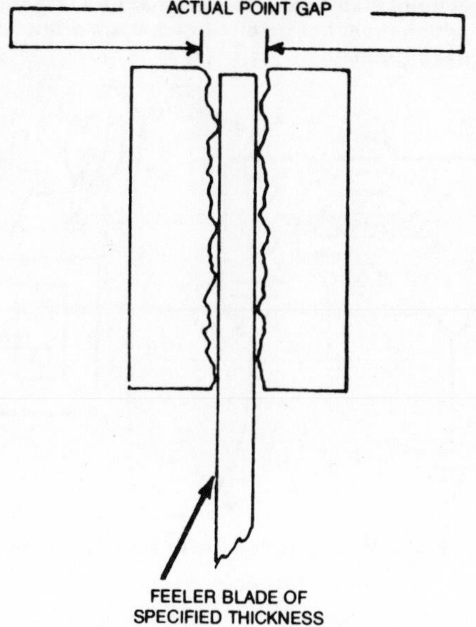

The feeler gauge method of checking point gap is less accurate than the dwell meter method

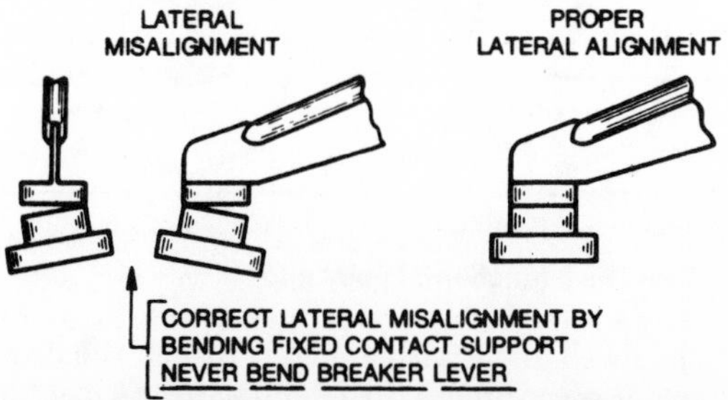

Check the points for proper alignment after installation

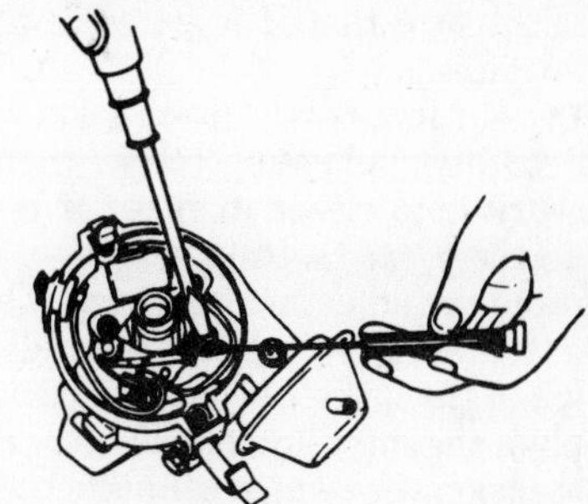

All single point distributor gaps are adjusted with the eccentric screw

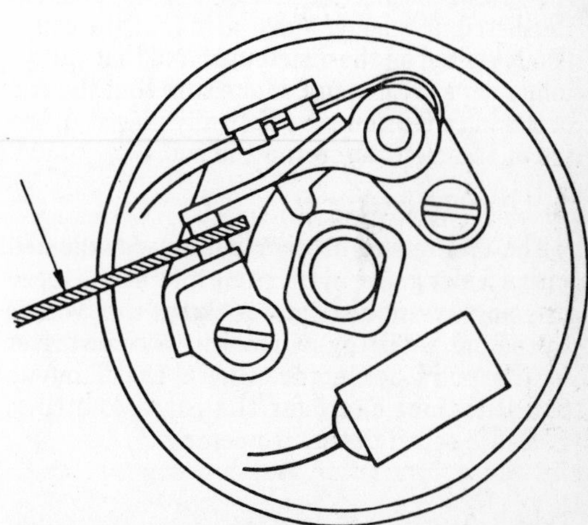

The arrow indicates the flat feeler gauge used to measure the point gap. Be sure that the rubbing block rests on the high spot of the cam, as shown.

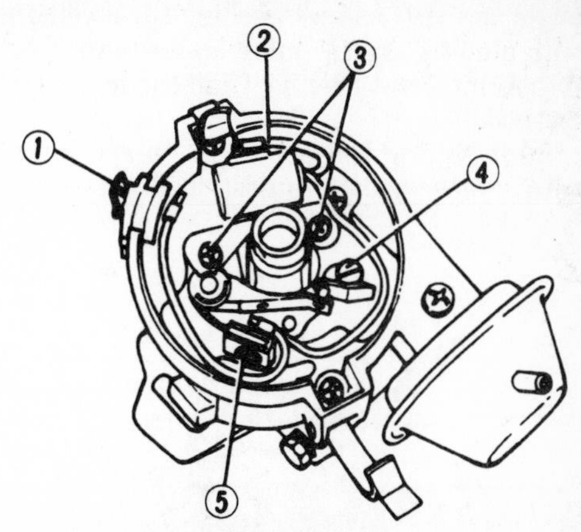

1. Primary lead terminal
2. Ground lead wire
3. Set screw
4. Adjuster
5. Screw

Single point distributor

chart). Make sure that it is parallel with the contact surfaces.

4. With your free hand, insert a screwdriver into the eccentric adjusting screw, then twist the screwdriver to either increase or decrease the gap to the proper setting.

5. Tighten the adjustment lockscrew and recheck the contact gap to make sure that didn't change when the lockscrew was tightened.

6. Replace the rotor and distributor cap, and the high tension wire which connects the top of the distributor and the oil. Make sure that the rotor is firmly seated all the way onto the distributor shaft and that the tab of the rotor is aligned with notch in the shaft. Align the tab in the base of the distributor cap with the notch in the distributor body. Make sure that the cap is firmly seated on the distributor and that the retainer clips are in place. Make sure that the end of the high tension wire is firmly placed in the top of the distributor and the coil.

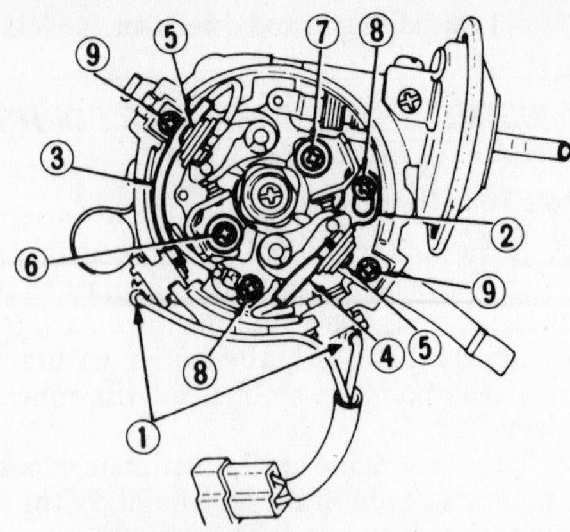

1. Lead wire terminal set screws
2. Adjuster plate
3. Primary lead wire—advanced points
4. Primary lead wire—retarded points
5. Primary lead wire set screw
6. Set screw—advanced points
7. Set screw—retarded points
8. Adjuster plate set screws
9. Breaker plate set screws

Dual point distributor. This view shows two screws (8) which must not be disturbed when adjusting or replacing points

Dual Point Distributor

The two sets of breaker points are adjusted with a feeler gauge in the same manner as those in a single point distributor, except that you do the actual adjusting by twisting a screwdriver in the point set notch. Check the Tune-up Specifications chart for the correct setting. Both are set to the same opening.

Dwell Angle

The dwell angle or cam angle is the number of degrees that the distributor cam rotates while the points are closed. There is an inverse relationship between dwell angle and point gap. Increasing the point gap will decrease the dwell angle and vice versa. Checking the dwell angle with a meter is a far more accurate method of measuring point opening than the feeler gauge method.

After setting the point gap to specification with a feeler gauge as described above, check the dwell angle with a meter. Attach the dwell meter according to the manufacturer's instruction sheet. The negative lead is grounded and the positive lead is connected to the primary

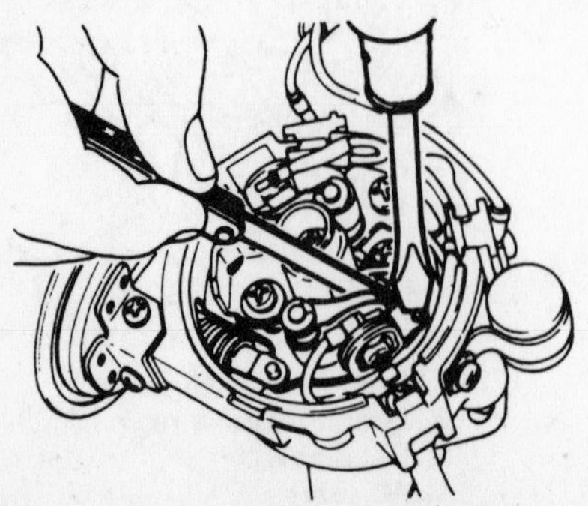

Point gap on the dual point distributor is adjusted by twisting a screwdriver in the notch

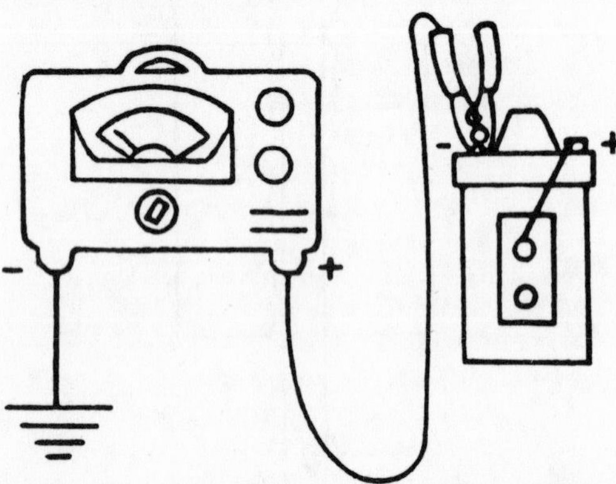

Dwell meter connections with transistorized ignition

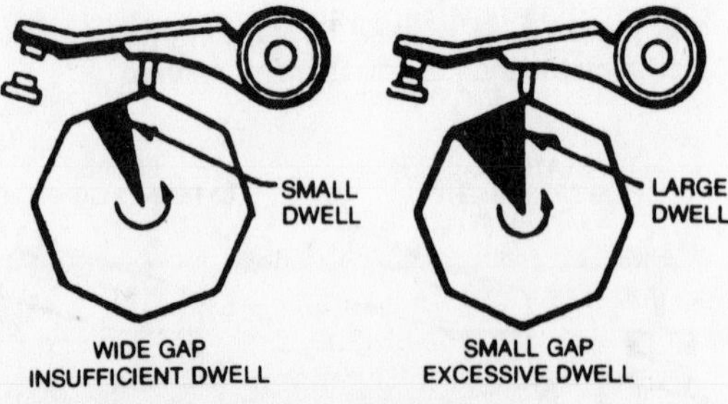

Dwell as a function of point gap

wire terminal which runs from the coil to the distributor. Start the engine, let it idle and reach operating temperature, and observe the dwell on the meter. The reading should fall within the allowable range. If it does not, the gap will have to be reset or the breaker points will have to be replaced.

ADJUSTMENT OF THE BREAKER POINTS WITH A DWELL METER

Dwell can be checked with the engine running or cranking. Decrease dwell by increasing the point gap; increase by decreasing the gap. Dwell angle is simply the number of degrees of distributor shaft rotation during which the points stay closed. Theoretically, if the point gap is correct, the dwell should also be correct or nearly so. Adjustment with a dwell meter produces more exact, consistent results since it is a dynamic adjustment. If dwell varies more than 3° from idle speed to 1,750 engine rpm, the distributor is worn.

Single Point Distributor

1. Adjust the points with a feeler gauge as previously described.
2. Connect the dwell meter to the ignition circuit as according to the manufacturer's instructions. One lead of the meter is connected to a ground and the other lead is connected to the distributor post on the coil. An adapter is usually provided for this purpose.
3. If the dwell meter has a set line on it, adjust the meter to zero the indicator.
4. Start the engine.

NOTE: *Be careful when working on any vehicle while the engine is running. Make sure that the transmission is in Neutral and that the parking brake is applied. Keep hands, clothing, tools and the wires of the test instruments clear of the rotating fan blades.*

5. Observe the reading on the dwell meter. If the reading is within the specified range, turn off the engine and remove the dwell meter.

NOTE: *If the meter does not have a scale for 4 cylinder engines, multiply the 8 cylinder reading by two.*

6. If the reading is above the specified range, the breaker point gap is too small. If the reading is below the specified range, the gap is too large. In either case, the engine must be stopped and the gap adjusted in the manner previously covered. After making the adjustment, start the engine and check the reading on the dwell meter. When the correct reading is obtained, disconnect the dwell meter.
7. Check the adjustment of the ignition timing.

Use the terminals provided (arrows) for jumper wire connection

Dual Point Distributor

Adjust the point gap of a dual point distributor with a dwell meter as follows:

1. Mark and disconnect the wiring harness of the distributor from the engine wiring harness.
2. Using a jumper wire, connect the black wire of the engine side of the harness to the black wire of the distributor side of the harness (advance points).
3. Start the engine and observe the reading on the dwell meter. Shut the engine off and adjust the points accordingly as previously outlined for single point distributors.
4. Disconnect the jumper wire from the black wire of the distributor side of the wiring harness and connect it to the yellow wire (retard points).
5. Adjust the point gap as necessary.
6. After the dwell of both sets of points is correct, remove the jumper wire and connect the engine-to-distributor wiring harness securely.

Electronic Ignition

CARBURETED ENGINES

Datsun pick-ups sold in California beginning in 1976 are equipped with electronic ignition, and all 1978 and later trucks are equipped with the system. The 1978 system differs somewhat from the earlier system; the 1979 and later system is markedly different.

The electronic ignition differs from its conventional counterpart only in the distributor component area. The secondary side of the ignition system is the same as a conventional breaker points system.

Located in the distributor, in addition to the normal ignition rotor, is a four spoke rotor (reluctor) which rests on the distributor shaft where the breaker points cam is found on earlier systems. A pick-up coil, consisting of a magnet, coil, and wiring, rests on the breaker plate next to the reluctor. The system also uses a transistor ignition unit, located on the right side of the firewall in the passenger compartment, through 1978, 1979–80 models have an integrated circuit (IC) ignition unit, which is mounted on the side of the distributor. In addition, 1979–80 models use a ring-type pick-up coil, which surrounds the reluctor, rather than the arm-type coil used through 1978.

When a reluctor spoke is not aligned with the pick-up coil, it generates large lines of flux between itself, the magnet, and the pick-up coil. This large flux variation results in high generated voltage in the pick-up coil. preventing current from flowing to the pick-up coil. When a reluctor spoke lines up with the pick-up coil, the flux variation is low, thus, zero voltage is generated, allowing current to flow to the pick--up coil. Ignition primary current is then cut off by the electronic unit, allowing the field in the ignition coil to collapse, inducing high secondary voltage in the conventional manner. The high voltage then flows through the distributor to the spark plug, as usual.

Because no points or condenser are used, and because dwell is determined by the electronic unit, no adjustments are necessary. Ignition timing is checked in the usual way, but unless the distributor is disturbed it is not likely to ever change very much.

1981 and later models are equipped with a slightly different ignition system and do not utilize a pick-up coil. This system uses two ignition coils and each cylinder has two spark plugs which fire simultaneously. In this manner the engine is able to consume large quantities of recirculated exhaust gas which would cause a single spark plug cylinder to misfire and idle roughly.

FUEL INJECTED ENGINES

The Electronic Concentrated Engine Control System is used on these engines. This system employs a microcomputer which controls fuel injection, spark timing, exhaust gas recirculation (EGR), idle speed, fuel pump operation and mixture ratio feedback. Electrical signals from each sensor are fed into the computer and each actuator is controlled by an electrical pulse with a duration that is computed in the microcomputer. There are some basic tests that may be performed to check the ignition system as outlined under Troubleshooting below, however, when engine malfunctions occur, the use of an ECCS analyzer is necessary to accurately diagnose the problem.

The ECCS analyzer monitors several input and output signals that are emitted in response to various engine operating and stopped conditions. Input signals are compared to computerized signal values stored in the Central Electronic Control Unit (CECU) while output signals are monitored to ensure they are properly attuned before they are emitted from the CECU unit to the actuators. In other words, this analyzer analyzes all electrical signals that are transmitted to and from the CECU unit.

Since this analyzer would be very expensive to purchase, any suspected malfunction of the engine cannot be corrected by an obvious visual inspection, this should be left to a qualified repair shop that contains this equipment.

DISTRIBUTOR SERVICE

Service consists of inspection of the distributor cap, rotor, and ignition wires, replacing when necessary. These parts can be expected to last for at least 40,000 miles. In addition, the reluctor air gap should be checked periodically.

Carbureted Engines Only

1976–80

1. The distributor cap is held on by two clips. Release them with a screwdriver and lift the cap straight up and off, with the wires attached. Inspect the cap for cracks, carbon tracks, or a worn center contact. Replace it if necessary, transferring the wires one at a time from the old cap to the new.
2. Pull the ignition rotor (not the spoked reluctor) straight up to remove. Replace it if its contacts are worn, burned, or pitted. Do not file the contacts. To replace, press it firmly onto the shaft. It only goes on one way, so be sure it is fully seated.
3. Before replacing the ignition rotor, check the reluctor air gap. Use a non-magnetic feeler gauge. Rotate the engine until a reluctor spoke is aligned with the pick-up coil (either bump the engine around with the starter, or turn it with a wrench on the crankshaft pulley bolt). The gap should measure 0.20–0.40mm through 1978, or 0.30–0.50mm for 1979–80. Adjustment, if necessary, is made by loosening the pick-up coil mounting screws and shifting its position on

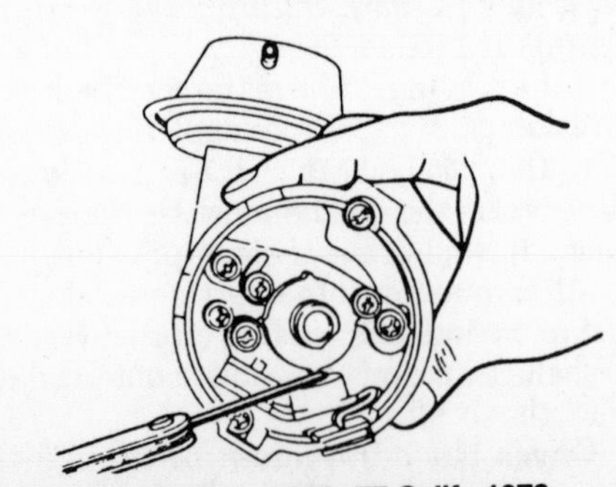

Air gap adjustment—1976–77 Calif.; 1978

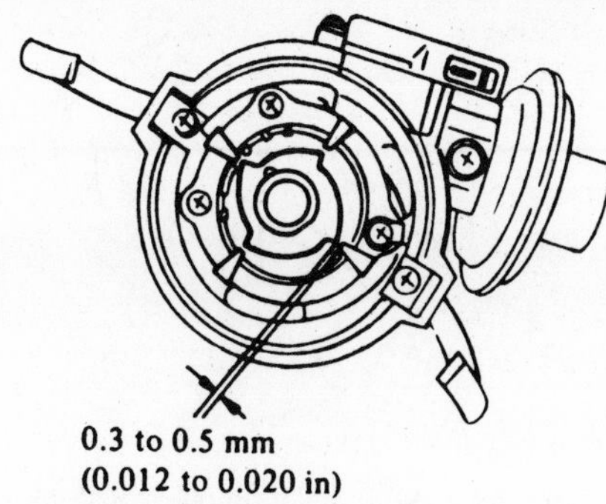

Air gap adjustment—1979–80

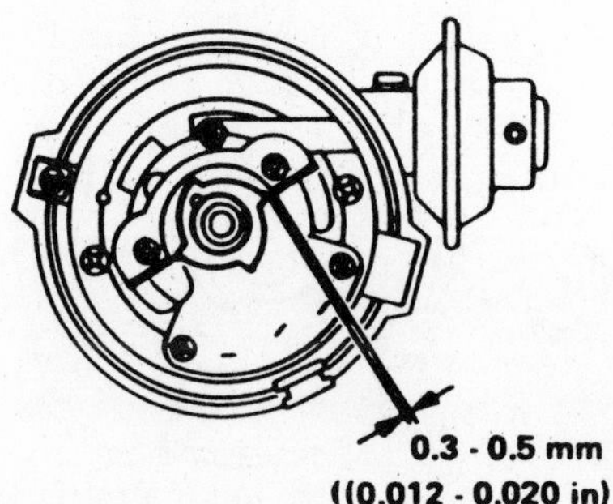

Air gap adjustment—1981–86 carbureted models

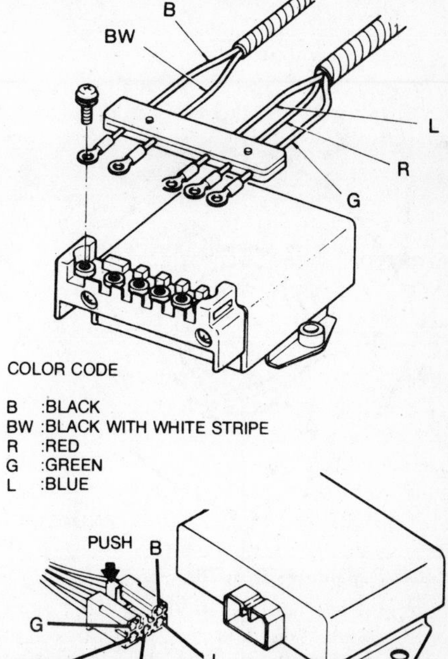

Electronic control unit connections: Upper, 1976–77; Lower, 1978.

the breaker plate either closer to or farther from the reluctor. On 1979–80 models, center the pick-up coil (ring) around the reluctor. Tighten the screws and recheck the gap.

4. Inspect the wires for cracks or brittleness. Replace them one at a time to prevent crosswiring, carefully pressing the replacement wires into place. The cores of electronic wires are more susceptible to breakage than those of standard wires, so treat them gently.

1981–86

1. Remove the distributor cap then remove the rotor retaining screw.
2. Adjust the air gap between the reluctor and stator. The air gap should be 0.30–0.50mm.
3. Inspect the wires, cap and rotor as outlined in the above procedure.

PICK-UP COIL AND RELUCTOR REPLACEMENT

Carbureted Engines Only

1976-78

The reluctor cannot be removed on some early models. It is an integral part of the distributor shaft. Non-removable reluctors can be distinguished by the absence of a roll pin (retaining pin) which locks the reluctor in place on the shaft.

To replace the pick-up coil on all 1976–78 models:

1. Remove the distributor cap by releasing the two spring clips. Remove the ignition rotor by pulling it straight up and off the shaft.
2. Disconnect the distributor wiring harness at the terminal block.
3. Remove the two pick-up coil mounting screws. Remove the screws retaining the wiring harness to the distributor.
4. Remove the pick-up coil.

When replacing the the pick-up coil leave the mounting screws slightly loose to facilitate air gap adjustment.

To replace the reluctor on models with a roll pin:

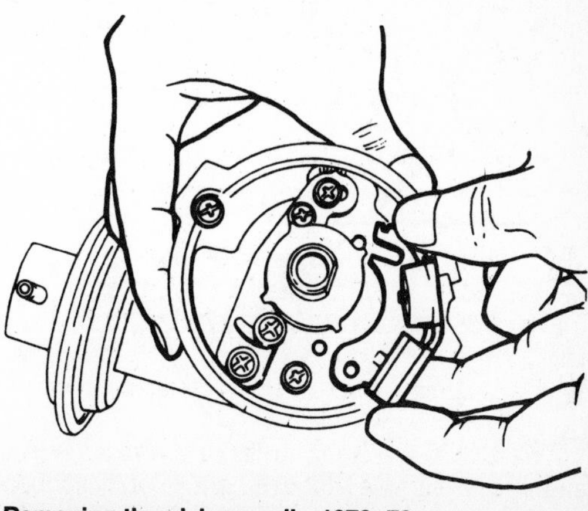
Removing the pick-up coil—1976–78

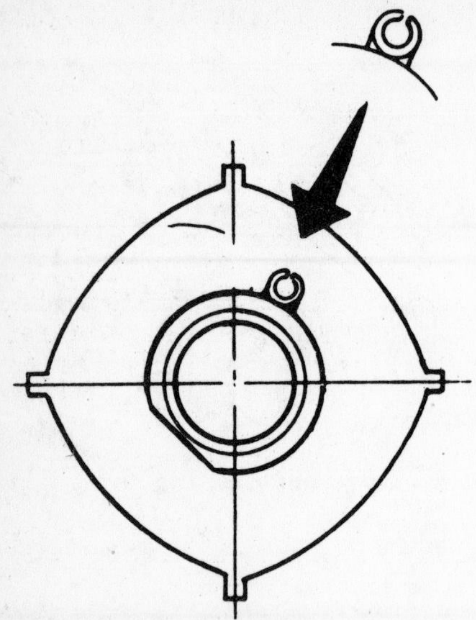
Roll pin installation—1976–78

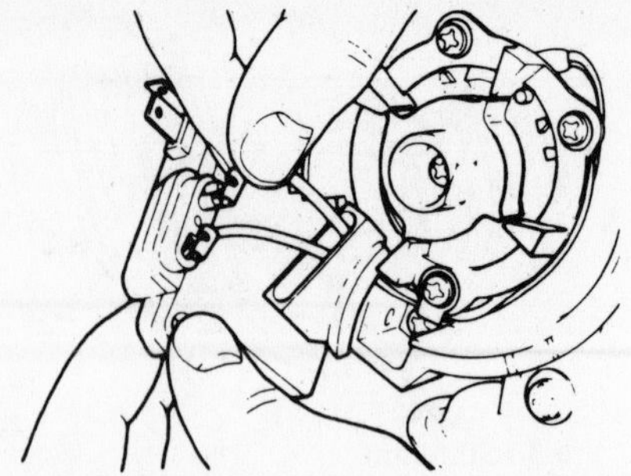
Connecting the pick-up coil terminal—1979–80

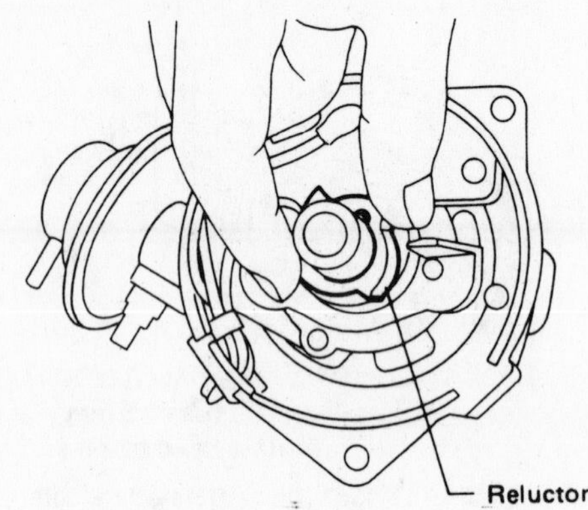

Removing the reluctor—1979–86

1. Remove the distributor cap, ignition rotor and the pick-up coil.
2. Use two screwdrivers or pry bars to pry the reluctor from the distributor shaft. Be extremely careful not to damage the reluctor teeth. Remove the roll pin.
3. To replace, press the reluctor firmly onto the shaft. Install a new roll pin with the slit facing away from the distributor shaft. Do not reuse the old roll pin.

1979–86

1. Remove the distributor cap. Remove the ignition rotor by pulling the rotor straight up and off the shaft.
2. Use a pair of needle nose pliers to disconnect the pick-up coil spade connectors from the ignition unit. Do not pull on the pick-up coil wires themselves.
3. Remove the toothed stator and the ring magnet underneath it by removing the three mounting screws.

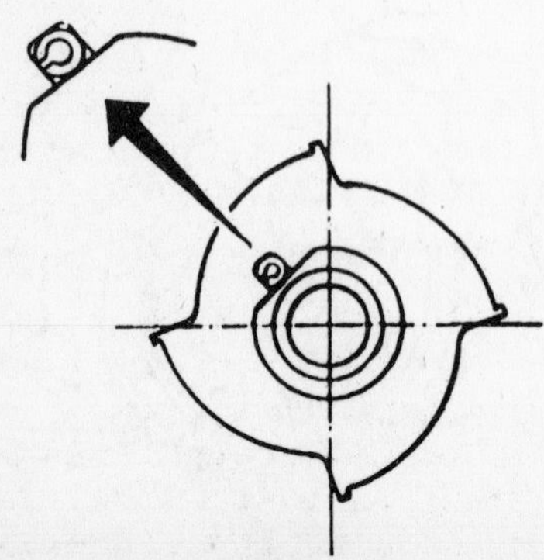
Roll pin installation—1979–86

4. Remove the reluctor by prying it from the distributor shaft with two small pry bars or a small puller. Be careful not to damage any of the reluctor teeth. Remove the roll pin.
5. Remove the screw retaining the pick-up coil wiring harness to the distributor. Remove the pick-up coil.
6. Install the pick-up coil into place in the distributor body. Replace the wiring harness retainer.
7. Press the reluctor firmly into place on the shaft. Install a new roll pin with the slit in the pin parallel to the flat on the shaft.
8. Install the magnet and stator, and center the stator around the reluctor. Check the air gap.
9. Press the pick-up coil spade connectors onto the ignition unit terminals with your fingers. The proper connections can be determined from the color code marked on the grommet. Replace the ignition rotor and the distributor cap.

RELUCTOR AND IC IGNITION UNIT

Carbureted Engines Only

1. Remove the distributor cap and rotor. The rotor is held to the distributor shaft by a retaining screw, which must be removed.
2. Remove the wiring harness and the vacuum controller from the housing.

3. Using 2 flat bladed screwdrivers, place one on each side of the reluctor and pry it from the distributor shaft.

NOTE: *When removing the reluctor, be careful not to damage or distort the teeth.*

4. Remove the roll pin from the reluctor.

NOTE: *To remove the IC unit, mark and remove the breaker plate assembly and separate the IC unit from it. Be careful not to loose the spacers when you remove the IC unit.*

5. Install the IC unit to the breaker plate assembly.

6. Install the wiring harness and the vacuum controller to the distributor housing. When you install the roll pin into the reluctor position the cutout direction of the roll pin in parallel with the notch in the reluctor. Make sure that the harness to the IC ignition unit is tightly secured, then adjust the air gap between the reluctor and the stator. Refer to the exploded views of the distributor in this book.

TROUBLESHOOTING

NOTE: *This book contains simple testing procedures for your truck's electronic ignition. More comprehensive testing on this system and other electronic control systems on your Datsun can be found in CHILTON'S GUIDE TO ELECTRONIC ENGINE CONTROLS, book part number 7535, available at your local retailer.*

1976–78 Carbureted Engines Only

The main differences between the 1976–77 and 1978 systems are: (1) the 1976–77 system uses an external ballast resistor located next to the ignition coil, and (2) the earlier system uses a wiring harness with individual eyelet connectors to the electronic unit, while the later system uses a multiple plug connector. You will need an accurate voltmeter and ohmmeter for these test, which must be performed in the order given.

1. Check all connections for corrosion, looseness, breaks, etc., and correct if necessary. Clean and gap the spark plugs.

2a. Disconnect the harness (connector or plug) from the electronic unit. Turn the ignition switch **ON**. Set the voltmeter to the DC 50v range. Connect the positive (+) voltmeter lead to the black/white wire terminal, and the negative (−) lead to the black wire terminal. Battery voltage should be obtained. If not, check the black/white and black wires for continuity; check the battery terminals for corrosion; check the battery state of charge.

2b. Next, connect the voltmeter (+) lead to the blue wire and the (−) lead to the black wire. Battery voltage should be obtained. If not, check the blue wire for continuity; check the ignition coil terminals for corrosion or looseness; check the coil for continuity. On 1976–77 models, also check the external ballast resistor.

3. Disconnect the distributor harness wires from the ignition coil ballast resistor on 1976–77 models, leaving the ballast resistor-to-coil wires attached. On 1978 models, disconnect the ignition coil wires. Connect the leads of an ohmmeter to the ballast resistor outside terminals (at each end) through 1977; resistance should be 1.6–2.0Ω. In 1978, connect the ohmmeter to the coil terminals: resistance should be 0Ω. If more than 2.0Ω, 1976–77, or 1.8Ω, 1978, replace the coil.

4. Disconnect the harness from the electronic control unit. Connect an ohmmeter to the red and the green wire terminals. Resistance should be 720Ω. If far more or far less, replace the distributor pick-up coil.

5. Disconnect the anti-dieseling solenoid connector (see Chapter 4). Connect a voltmeter to the red and green terminals of the electronic control harness. When the starter is cranked, the needle should deflect slightly. If not, replace the distributor pick-up coil.

6. Reconnect the ignition coil and the electronic control unit. Leave the anti-dieseling solenoid wire disconnected. Unplug the high tension lead (coil-to-distributor) from the distributor and hold it 3–6mm from the cylinder head with a pair of insulated pliers and a heavy glove. BE CAREFUL! When the engine is cranked, a spark should be observed. If not, check the lead, and replace the electronic control unit.

7. Reconnect all wires.

- 1976–77: connect the voltmeter (+) lead to the blue electronic control harness connector and the (−) lead to the black wire. The harness should be attached to the control unit.
- 1978: connect the voltmeter (+) lead to the (−) terminal of the ignition coil and the (−) lead to the ground.

As soon as the ignition switch is turned **ON**, the meter should indicate battery voltage. If not, replace the electronic control unit.

1979–80 Carbureted Engines Only

1. Make a check of the power supply circuit. Turn the ignition **OFF**. Disconnect the connector from the top of the IC unit. Turn the ignition **ON**. Measure the voltage at each terminal of the connector in turn by touching the probe of the positive lead of the voltmeter to one of the terminals, and touching the probe of the negative lead of the voltmeter to a ground, such as the engine. In each case, battery voltage should be indicated. If not, check all wiring, the ignition switch, and all connectors for breaks, corrosion, discontinuity, etc., and repair as necessary.

2. Check the primary windings of the ignition coil. Turn the ignition **OFF**. Disconnect the harness connector from the negative coil terminals. Use a ohmmeter to measure the resistance between the positive and negative terminals on the coil. If resistance is 0.84–1.02Ω, the coil is OK. Replace if far from this range.

If the power supply, circuits, wiring, and coil are in good shape, check the IC unit and pick-up coil, as follows:

3. Turn the ignition **OFF**. Remove the distributor cap and ignition rotor. Use an ohmmeter to measure the resistance between the two terminals of the pick-up coil, where they attach to the IC unit. Measure the resistance by reversing the polarity of the probes. If approximately 400Ω are indicated, the pick-up coil is OK, but the IC unit is bad and must be replaced. If other than 400Ω are measured, go to the next step.

4. Be certain the 2-pin connector to the IC unit is secure. Turn the ignition **ON**. Measure the voltage at the ignition coil negative terminal. Turn the ignition **OFF**.

WARNING: *Remove the tester probe from the coil negative terminal before switching the ignition OFF, to prevent burning out the tester.*

If zero voltage is indicated, the IC unit is bad and must be replaced. If battery voltage is indicated, proceed.

5. Remove the IC unit from the distributor:

a. Disconnect the battery ground (negative) cable.

b. Remove the distributor cap and ignition rotor.

c. Disconnect the harness connector at the top of the IC unit.

d. Remove the two screws securing the IC unit to the distributor.

e. Disconnect the two pick-up coil wires from the IC unit.

NOTE: *Pull the connectors free with a pair of needlenosed pliers. Do not pull on the wires to detach the connectors.*

f. Remove the IC unit.

6. Measure the resistance between the terminals of the pick-up coil. It should be approximately 400Ω. If so, the pick-up coil is OK, and the IC unit is bad. If not approximately 400Ω, the pick-up coil is bad and must be replaced.

7. With a new pick-up coil installed, install the IC unit. Check for a spark at one of the spark plugs. If a good spark is obtained, the IC unit is OK. If not, replace the IC unit.

1981–86 Carbureted Engines Only

BATTERY VOLTAGE (NO LOAD)

With the ignition key in the **OFF** position, connect a voltmeter to the positive and negative terminals of the battery. The reading should not be below 11.5 volts. A lower reading indicates a faulty battery, charging or starting system.

BATTERY CRANKING VOLTAGE

1. Connect a voltmeter to the battery and set to the appropriate scale.

2. Remove the coil wire from the distributor cap and ground it.

3. Crank the engine for approximately 15 seconds. The voltage reading should not be less than 9.6 volts while cranking. A lower reading indicates a faulty battery, charging or starting system.

SECONDARY WIRING TEST

With the distributor cap removed, connect an ohmmeter to each end of the spark plug cables. The resistance readings should be less than 30,000Ω. If the resistance readings are greater than 30,000Ω, replace the distributor cap and/or plug wires.

IGNITION COIL SECONDARY CIRCUIT

With the ignition key in the **OFF** position, and the coil wire removed from the coil, connect an ohmmeter with one probe to the coil wire socket and the other to the negative terminal. Check both coils. The resistance reading should be between 7,000–11,000Ω. If not, replace the ignition coil.

POWER SUPPLY CIRCUIT

1. Connect a voltmeter with the positive probe to the **B** terminal (power source) and the negative probe to the distributor housing.

2. Turn the ignition key to the **ON** position.

3. The reading should be between 11.5–12.5 volts. If below 11.5 volts, check the wiring between the ignition switch and the I.C. unit.

POWER SUPPLY CIRCUIT (CRANKING)

1. Connect a voltmeter as in Step 1 above.

2. Pull the coil wire from the distributor cap and ground it.

3. Turn the key to the **START** position and observe the voltmeter while the engine is cranking.

4. If the voltage reading is more than 1 volt below battery cranking voltage and/or is below 8.6 volts, check the ignition switch and wiring from the switch to the I.C. unit.

IGNITION PRIMARY CIRCUIT

1. Connect a voltmeter negative probe to the **I** terminal and the negative voltmeter probe to the distributor housing.

2. Turn the ignition key to the **ON** position. If the reading is between 11.5–12.5 volts proceed to Step 3. If the reading is below 11.5 volts

proceed to the Ignition Coil Primary Circuit test which follows.

3. Connect the voltmeter positive probe to the **E** terminal and the negative voltmeter probe the distributor housing.

4. Turn the ignition key to the **ON** position. If the reading is between 11.5–12.5 volts proceed to the I.C. Unit Ground Circuit test. If the reading is below 11.5 volts proceed to the Ignition Coil Primary Circuit test.

IGNITION COIL PRIMARY CIRCUIT

1. Place the ignition key in the **OFF** position.

2. Remove the coil wire from the coil.

3. Measure the resistance between the two terminals of the coil. The resistance should be between 1.04–1.27Ω. If not the ignition coil is defective and should be replaced.

I.C. UNIT GROUND CIRCUIT

1. Connect the positive probe of a voltmeter to the housing of the distributor.

2. Connect the negative probe of a voltmeter to the negative terminal of the battery.

3. Pull out the coil wire from the distributor cap and ground it.

4. Turn the key to the **START** position and observe the voltmeter while cranking.

5. If the voltmeter reading is 0.05 volts or less, replace the IC ignition unit assembly.

6. If the voltmeter reading is more than 0.5 volts, check the distributor ground, wiring from the chassis ground to the battery including battery cable connections.

1986–89 Fuel Injected Engines

Troubleshooting procedures for these engines should be left to a certified service technician.

Ignition Timing

Ignition timing is the measurement in degrees of crankshaft rotation of the instant the spark plugs in the cylinders fire, in relation to the location of the piston, while the piston is on its compression stroke.

Ignition timing is adjusted by loosening the distributor locking device and turning the distributor in the engine.

Ideally, the air/fuel mixture in the cylinder will be ignited (by the spark plug) and just beginning its rapid expansion as the piston passes top dead center (TDC) of the compression stroke. If this happens, the piston will be beginning the power stroke just as the compressed (by the movement of the piston) air/fuel mixture starts to expand. The expansion of the air/fuel mixture will then force the piston down on the power stroke and turn the crankshaft.

It takes a fraction of a second for the spark from the plug to completely ignite the mixture in the cylinder. Because of this, the spark plug must fire before the piston reaches TDC, if the mixture is to be completely ignited as the piston passes TDC. This measurement is given in degrees (of crankshaft rotation) before the piston reaches top dead center (BTDC). If the ignition timing setting for your engine is seven (7°) BTDC, this means that the spark plug must fire at a time when the piston for that cylinder is 7° before top dead center of its compression stroke. However, this only holds true while your engine is at idle speed.

As you accelerate from idle, the speed of your engine (rpm) increases. The increase in rpm means that the pistons are now traveling up and down much faster. Because of this, the spark plugs will have to fire even sooner if the mixture is to be completely ignited as the piston passes TDC. To accomplish this, the distributor incorporates means to advance the timing of the spark as engine speed increases.

The distributor in your Nissan has two means of advancing the ignition timing. One is called centrifugal advance and is actuated by weights in the distributor. The other is called vacuum advance and is controlled by that larger circular housing on the side of the distributor.

In addition, some distributors have a vacuum retard mechanism which is contained in the same housing on the side of the distributor as the vacuum advance. The function of this mechanism is to retard the timing of the ignition spark under certain engine conditions. This causes more complete burning of the air/fuel mixture in the cylinder and consequently lowers exhaust emissions.

Because these mechanisms change ignition timing, it is necessary to disconnect and plug the one or two vacuum lines from the distributor when setting the basic ignition timing.

NOTE: *On all fuel injected models (VG30i and Z24i) a crankangle sensor in the distributor is used. This sensor controls ignition timing and has other engine control functions. There is no vacuum or centrifugal advance all timing settings are controlled by the E.C.U.*

If ignition timing is set too far advanced (BTDC), the ignition and expansion of the air/fuel mixture in the cylinder will try to force the piston down the cylinder while it is still traveling upward. This causes engine "ping", a sound which resembles marbles being dropped into an empty tin can. If the ignition timing is too far retarded (after, or ATDC), the piston will have already started down on the power stroke when the air/fuel mixture ignites and expands. This will cause the piston to be forced down only a portion of its travel. This will result in poor engine performance and lack of power.

Ignition timing adjustment is checked with a timing light. This instrument is connected to the number one (No. 1) spark plug of the engine. The timing light flashes every time an electrical current is sent from the distributor, through the No. 1 spark plug wire, to the spark plug. The crankshaft pulley and the front cover of the engine are marked with a timing pointer and a timing scale. When the timing pointer is aligned with the **0** mark on the timing scale, the piston is the No. 1 cylinder is at TDC of its compression stroke. With the engine running, and the timing light aimed at the timing pointer and timing scale, the stroboscopic flashes from the timing light will allow you to check the ignition timing setting of the engine. The timing light flashes every time the spark plug in the No. 1 cylinder of the engine fires. Since the flash from the timing light makes the crankshaft pulley seem stationary for a moment you will be able to read the exact position of the piston in the No. 1 cylinder on the timing scale on the front of the engine.

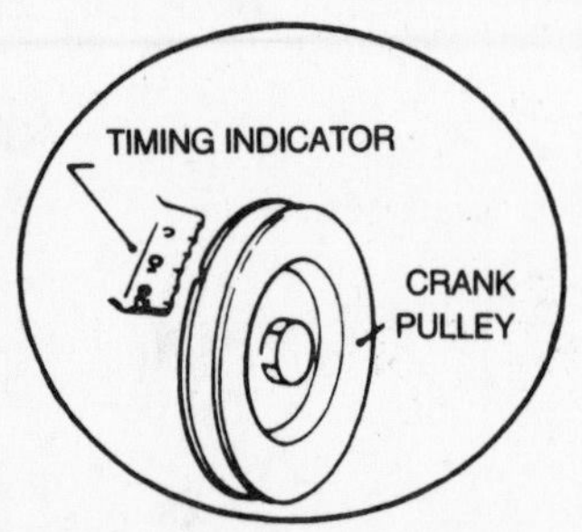

Typical timing indicator-to-pulley relationship

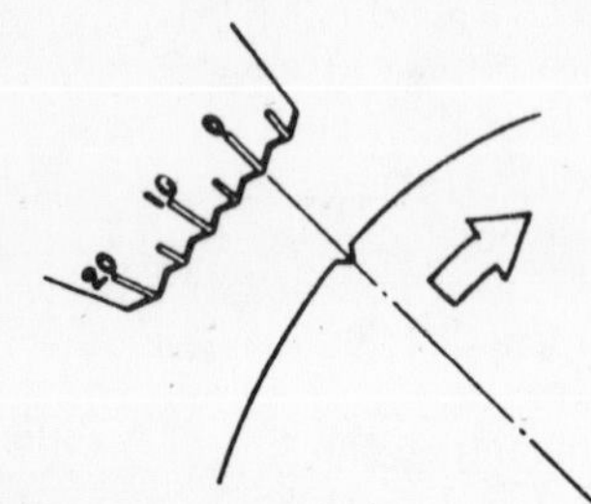

Timing marks—typical

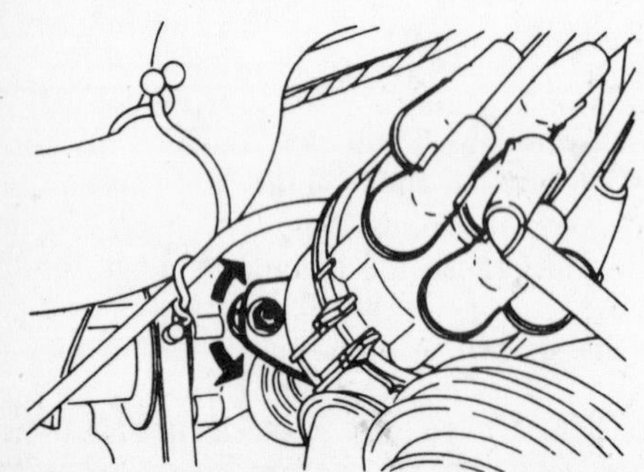

Loosen the distributor lockbolt and turn the distributor slightly to advance (upper arrow) or retard (lower arrow) the timing—1970–80

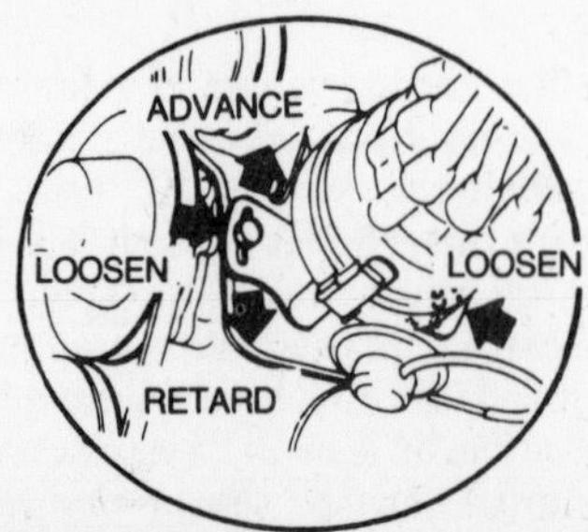

Adjusting the ignition timing—1981–86 carbureted engines

There are three basic types of timing lights available. The first is a simple neon bulb with two wire connections (one for the spark plug and one for the plug wire, connecting the light in series). This type of light is quite dim, and must be held closely to the marks to be seen, but it is inexpensive. The second type of light operates from the battery. Two alligator clips connect to the battery terminals, while a third wire connects to the spark plug with an adapter. This type of light is more expensive, but the xenon bulb provides a nice bright flash which can even be seen in sunlight. The third type replaces the battery source with 110 volt house current. Some timing lights have other functions built into them, such as dwell meters, tachometers, or remote starting switches. These are convenient, in that they reduce the tangle of wires under the hood, but may duplicate the functions of tools you already have.

If your Nissan has electronic ignition, you should use a timing light with an inductive pickup. This pickup simply clamps onto the No. 1 plug wire, eliminating the adapter. It is not susceptible to crossfiring or false triggering, which may occur with a conventional light, due to the greater voltages produced by electronic ignition.

CHECKING AND ADJUSTMENT

1970–86 Carbureted Engines

NOTE: *Refer to Chapter 5 for the procedure to time diesel engines and to check and adjust the phase timing of the two sets of points in 1970–73 models.*

If the underhood emissions decal differs from the information given below, always use the information on the decal as this reflects the latest changes made during production.

1. Set the dwell of the breaker points to the

proper specification, on those trucks so equipped.

2. Locate the timing marks on the crankshaft pulley and the front of the engine.

3. Clean off the timing marks, so that you can see them.

4. Use chalk or white paint to color the mark on the crankshaft pulley and the mark on the scale which will indicate the correct timing when aligned with the notch on the crankshaft pulley.

5. Attach a tachometer to the engine.

6. Attach a timing light to the engine, according to the manufacturer's instructions. If the timing light has three wires, one, usually green or blue, is attached to the No. 1 spark plug with an adapter. The other wires are connected to the battery. The red wire goes to the positive side of the battery and the black wire is connected to the negative terminal of the battery. If the truck has electronic ignition use an inductive timing light as described above.

7. Leave the vacuum line connected to the distributor vacuum diaphragm on models through 1980. On 1982–86 models disconnect the distributor vacuum hose from the vacuum controller and plug the hose. Also on Canadian Z24 engines disconnect the air injection hoses and cap the injection pipes.

CAUTION: *Keep fingers, clothes, tools, hair, and leads clear of the spinning engine fan. Be sure that you are running the engine in a well ventilated area!*

7. Allow the engine to run at the specified idle speed with the gearshift in Neutral with manual transmission and Drive (D) with automatic transmission.

CAUTION: *Be sure that the parking brake is set and that the front wheels are blocked to prevent the truck from rolling forward, especially when Drive is selected with an automatic!*

8. Point the timing light at the marks indicated in the chart and illustrations. With the engine at idle, timing should be at the specification given on the "Tune-Up Specifications" chart at the beginning of the chapter.

9. If the timing is not at the specification, loosen the pinch bolt (holddown bolt) at the base of the distributor just enough so that the distributor can be turned. Turn the distributor to advance or retard the timing as required. Once the proper marks are seen to align with the timing light, timing is correct.

10. Stop the engine and tighten the pinch bolt. Start the engine and recheck the timing. Stop the engine; disconnect the tachometer and timing light.

11. Tighten the distributor lockbolt and recheck the timing.

1986–89 Fuel Injected Engines

NOTE: *When checking ignition timing on air conditioner equipped trucks, make sure that the air conditioner is OFF when proceeding with the check. Refer to Idle Speed And Mixture Adjustments section in this chapter.*

CAUTION: *Automatic transmission equipped models should be shifted into D for idle speed checks. When in Drive, the parking brake must be fully applied and both front and rear wheels chocked. When racing the engine on automatic transmission equipped models, make sure that the shift lever is in the N or P position and remove the wheel chocks.*

1. Run the engine until it reaches normal operating temperature.

2. Open the hood, and race the engine at 2000 rpm for about 2 minutes under no-load (all accessories **OFF**).

3. Run the engine at idle speed..

4. Race the engine two or three times under no-load, then run the engine for one minute at idle.

5. Check the idle speed. Adjust the idle speed to specifications by turning the idle speed adjusting screw. Refer to the Tune Up Specifications Chart.

6. Connect a timing light according to the light manufacturer's instructions. Adjust the timing by loosening the distributor holddown bolts and turning the distributor clockwise to advance and counterclockwise to retard.

Injection Pump Timing

DIESEL ENGINES

For information and procedures regarding injection pump timing, please refer to Chapter 5.

Valve Lash

As part of every major tune-up or once every 6000 miles (1970–74) 12,500 miles (1975–78), and 15,000 miles (1979–89) the valve clearance should be checked and adjusted if necessary.

Valve lash is one factor which determines how far the intake and exhaust valves will open into the cylinder.

If the valve clearance is too large, part of the lift of the camshaft will be used up in removing the excessive clearance, thus the valves will not be opened far enough. This condition has two effects, the valve train components will emit a tapping noise as they take up the excessive clearance, and the engine will perform poorly, since the less the intake valves open, the smaller the amount of air/fuel mixture admitted to the cylinders will be. The less the exhaust valves open, the greater the back-pressure in the cylinder which prevents the proper air/fuel mixture from entering the cylinder.

If the valve clearance is too small, the intake and exhaust valves will not fully seat on the cylinder head when they close. When a valve seats on the cylinder head it does two things; it seals the combustion chamber so none of the gases in the cylinder can escape and it cools itself by transferring some of the heat it absorbed from the combustion process through the cylinder head and into the engine cooling system. Therefore, if the valve clearance is too small, the engine will run poorly (due to gases escaping from the combustion chamber), and the valves will overheat and warp (since they cannot transfer heat unless they are touching the seat in the cylinder head).

NOTE: *Although Nissan recommends that the valve lash on certain models be set while the engine is running, we feel that for the average owner/mechanic it is more convenient to adjust the valves statically (engine off). Thus, running valve lash and adjustment procedures have been omitted from the manual.*

While all valve adjustments must be as accurate as possible, it is better to have the valve adjustment slightly loose than slightly tight, as burnt valves may result from overly tight adjustments.

ADJUSTMENTS

1970–80 L16, L18 and L20B Engines

1. The valves are adjusted with the engine at normal operating temperature. Oil temperature, and the resultant parts expansion, is much more important than water temperature. Run the engine for at least fifteen minutes to ensure that all the parts have reached their full expansion. After the engine is warmed up, shut it off.

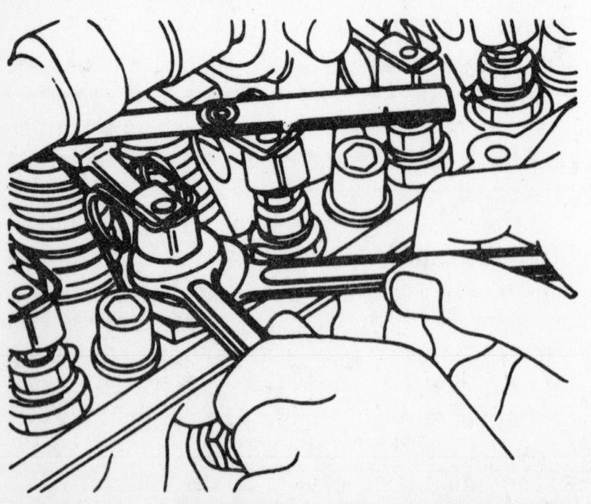

Loosen the locknut and turn the pivot adjuster to adjust the valve clearance—L16, L18 and L20B engines

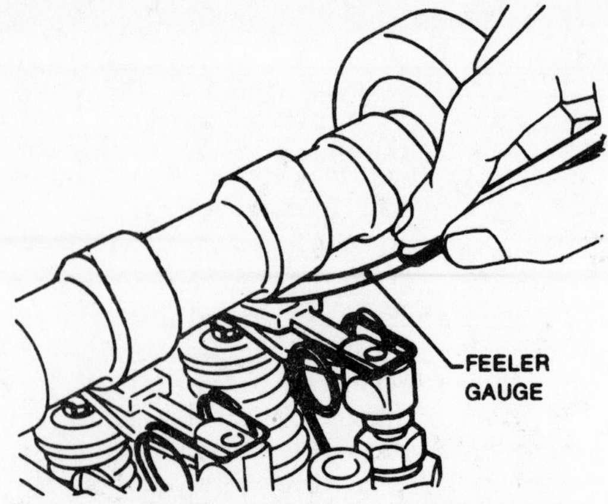

Checking the valve clearance with a flat feeler gauge—L16, L18 and L20B engines

2. Purchase either a new gasket or some silicone gasket seal before remove the cylinder head cover. Note the location of any wires and hoses which may interfere with cover removal, disconnect them and move them aside. Then remove the bolts which hold the cylinder head cover in place and remove the cover.
3. Place a wrench on the crankshaft pulley bolt and turn the engine over until the valves for the No. 1 cylinder are closed. When both camshaft lobes are pointing up, the valves are closed. If you have not done this before, it is a good idea to turn the engine over slowly several times and watch the valve action until you have a clear idea of just when the valve is closed.
4. Check the clearance of the intake and exhaust valves. You can differentiate between them by lining them up with the tubes of the intake and exhaust manifolds. The correct size feeler gauge should pass between the base circle of the camshaft and the rocker arm with just a slight drag. Be sure the feeler gauge is inserted straight and not on an angle.
5. If the valves need adjustment, loosen the locking nut and then adjust the clearance with the adjusting screw. You will probably find it necessary to hold the locking nut while you turn the adjuster. After you have the correct clearance, tighten the locking nut and recheck the clearance. Remember, its better to have them too loose than too tight, especially exhaust valves.
6. Repeat this procedure until you have checked and/or adjusted all the valves. Keep in mind that all that is necessary is to have the valves closed and the camshaft lobes pointing up. It is not particularly important what stroke the engine is on.
7. Install the cam cover gasket, the cam cover, and any wires and hoses which were removed.

1981–82 Z22 Engines

1. The valves must be adjusted with the engine warm, so start the truck and run the engine until the needle on the temperature gauges reaches the middle of the gauge. After the engine is warm, shut it off.

2. Purchase either a new gasket or some silicone gasket sealer before removing the cylinder head cover. Counting on the old gasket to be in good shape is a losing proposition; always use new gaskets. Note the location of any wires and hoses which may interfere with cylinder head cover removal, disconnect them and move them to one side. Remove the bolts holding the cover in place and remove the cover. Remember, the engine will be hot, so be careful!

3. Place a wrench on the crankshaft pulley bolt and turn the engine over until the first cam lobe behind the camshaft timing chain sprocket is pointing straight down.

NOTE: *If you decide to turn the engine by bumping it with the starter, be sure to disconnect the high tension wire from the coil(s) to prevent the engine from accidentally starting and spewing oil all over the engine compartment.*

CAUTION: *Never attempt to turn the engine by using a wrench on the camshaft sprocket bolt; there is a one to two turning ratio between the camshaft and the crankshaft which will put a tremendous strain on the timing chain.*

4. See the illustration marked FIRST, and check valves (1), (4), (6) and (7) to 0.3mm using a flat bladed feeler gauge. The feeler gauge should pass between the valve stem end and the rocker arm screw with a very slight drag. Insert the feeler gauge straight, not at an angle.

5. If the clearance is not within specified value, loosen the rocker arm lock nut and turn the rocker arm screw to obtain the proper clearance. After correct clearance is obtained, tighten the locknut.

6. Turn the engine over so that the first cam lobe behind the camshaft timing chain sprocket is pointing straight up and check the valves marked (2), (3), (5) and (8) in the SECOND illustration. They, too, should have a clearance of 0.3mm. Adjust as necessary.

7. Install the cylinder head cover gasket, the

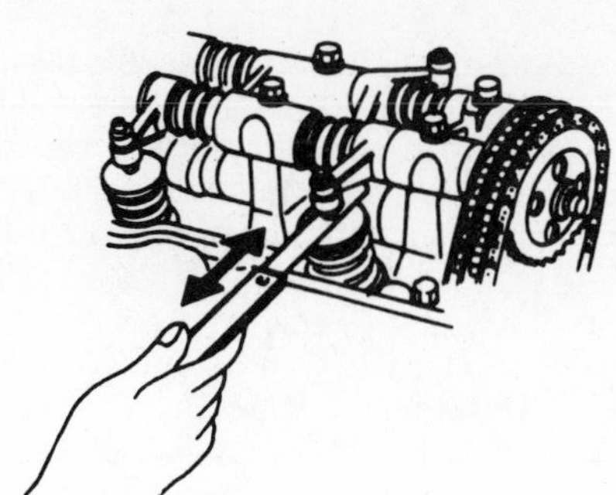

Checking the valve clearance with a flat feeler gauge—1981–82 Z22 engines

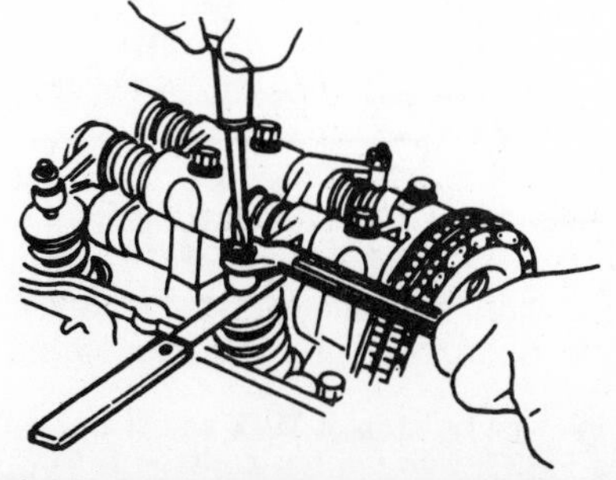

Loosen the locknut and turn the adjusting screw to adjust the valve clearance—1981–82 Z22 engines

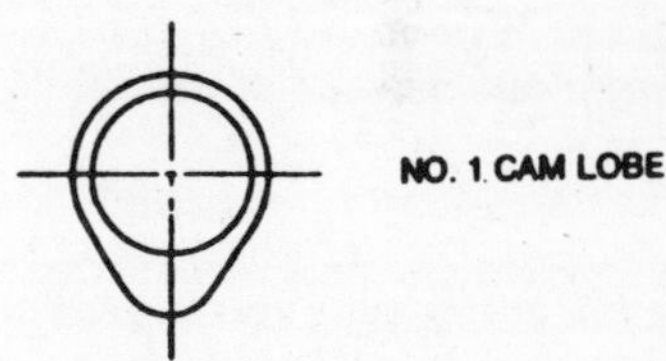

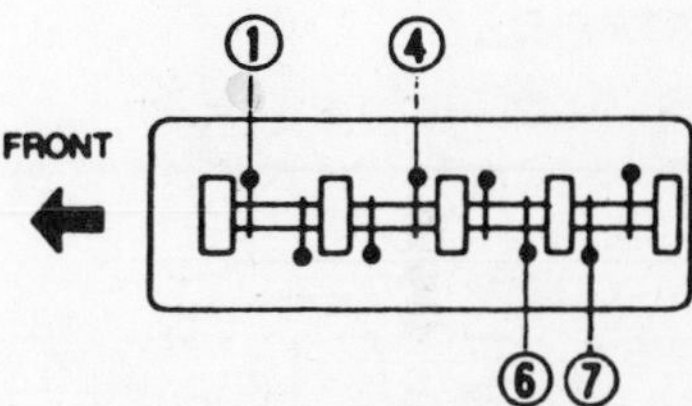

With the camshaft lobe pointing down, adjust these valves FIRST—1981–82 Z22 engines

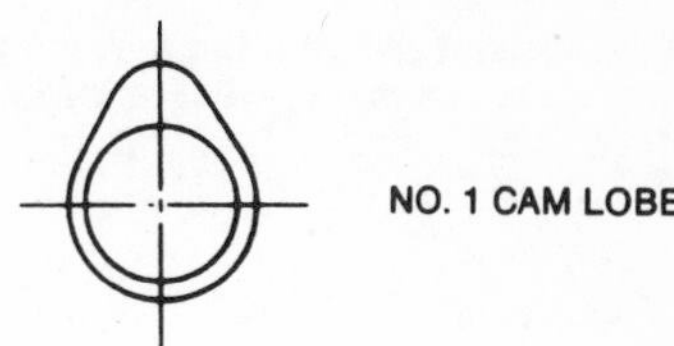

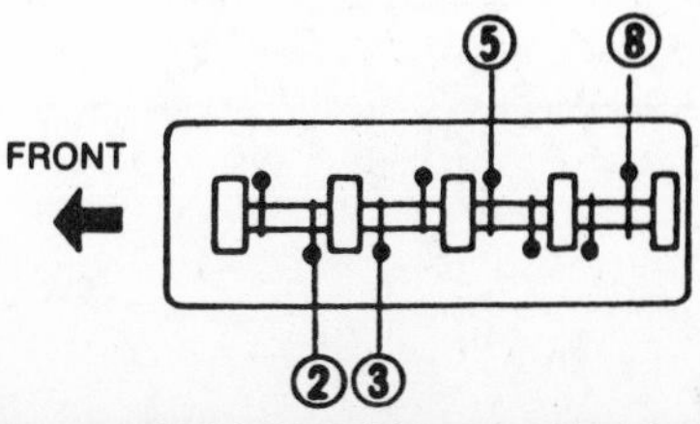

With the camshaft lobe poiting up, adjust these valves SECOND—1981–82 Z22 engines

cover itself and any wires and hoses which were removed.

1983–89 Z20, Z22, Z24 and Z24i Gasoline Engines 1981–87 SD22 and SD25 Diesel Engines

1. The valves must be adjusted with the engine warm, so start the truck and run the engine until the needle on the temperature gauges reaches the middle of the gauge. After the engine is warm, shut it off.

2. Purchase either a new gasket or some silicone gasket sealer before removing the cylinder head cover. Counting on the old gasket to be in good shape is a losing proposition; always use new gaskets. Note the location of any wires and hoses which may interfere with cylinder head cover removal, disconnect them and move them to one side. Remove the bolts holding the cover in place and remove the cover. Remember, the engine will be hot, so be careful!

3. Rotate the crankshaft until the timing marks indicate that the No. 1 piston is at TDC of the compression stroke. If you're not sure of which stroke you're on, remove the No. 1 spark plug and hold your thumb over the hole. Pressure will be felt as the piston starts up on the compression stroke.

4. See the illustration marked FIRST, and

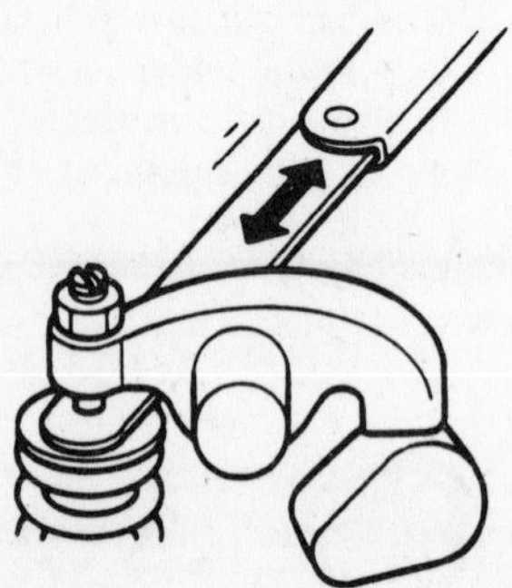

Checking the valve clearance with a flat feeler gauge—1983–89 Z20, Z22, Z24 and Z24i engines

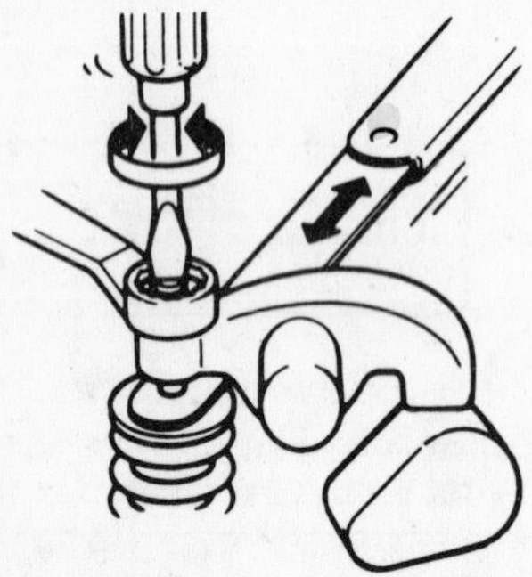

Loosen the locknut and turn the adjusting screw to adjust the valve clearance—1983–89 Z20, Z22, Z24 and Z24i engines

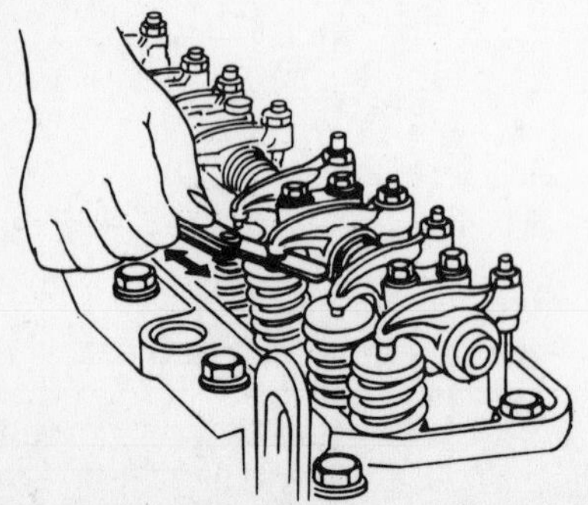

Checking the valve clearance with a flat feeler gauge—SD22 and SD25 engines

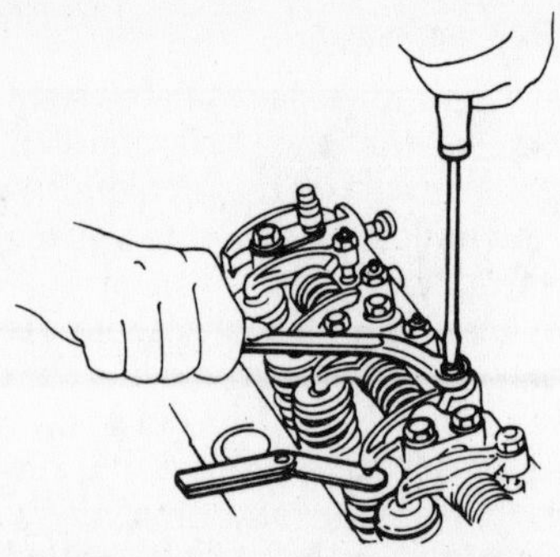

Loosen the locknut and turn the adjusting screw to adjust the valve clearance—SD22 and SD25 engines

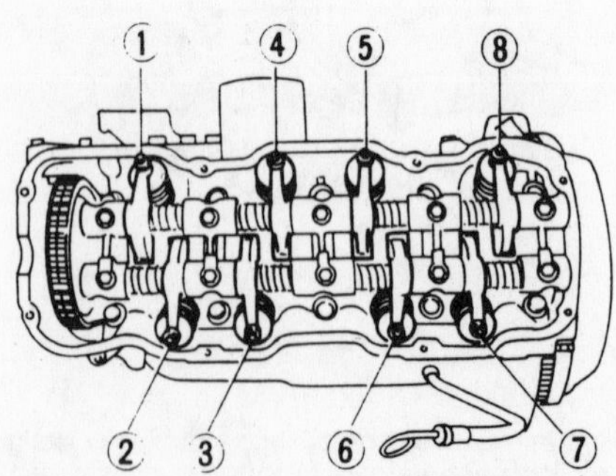

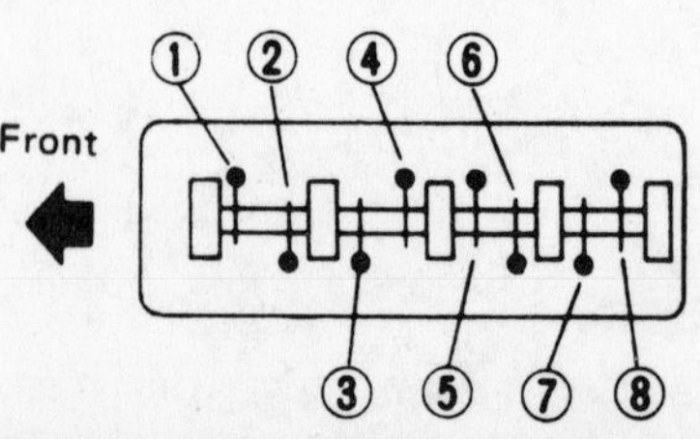

With the No. 1 piston at TDC, adjust the top set of valves FIRST; with the No. 4 piston at TDC, adjust the bottom set of valves SECOND—1983–89 Z20, Z22, Z24 and Z24i engines

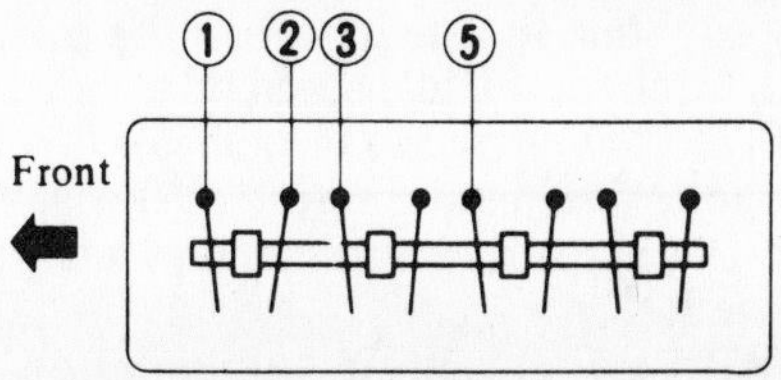

With the No. 1 piston at TDC, adjust these valves FIRST—SD22 and SD25 engines

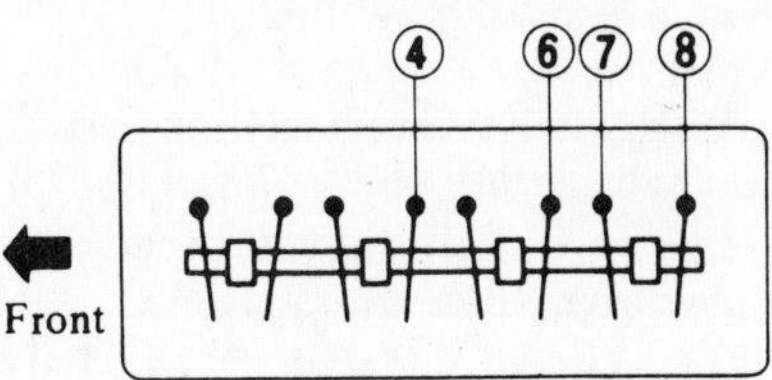

With the No. 4 piston at TDC, adjust these valves SECOND—SD22 and SD25 engines

check valves (1), (2), (4) and (6)—gasoline engines, or (1), (2), (3) and (5)—diesel engines using a flat bladed feeler gauge. The feeler gauge should pass between the valve stem end and the rocker arm screw with a very slight drag. Insert the feeler gauge straight, not at an angle.

5. If the clearance is not within specified value, loosen the rocker arm lock nut and turn the rocker arm screw to obtain the proper clearance. After correct clearance is obtained, tighten the locknut.

6. Rotate the crankshaft until the timing marks indicate that the No. 4 piston is at TDC of the compression stroke. If you're not sure of which stroke you're on, remove the No. 4 spark plug and hold your thumb over the hole. Pressure will be felt as the piston starts up on the compression stroke.

7. See the illustration marked SECOND, and check valves (3), (5), (7) and (8)—gasoline engines, or (4), (6), (7) and (8)—diesel engines. Check and adjust valve clearance as detailed in Step 4–5.

8. Install the cylinder head cover gasket, the cover itself and any wires and hoses which were removed.

1986–89 VG30i Engines

These models utilize hydraulic valve lifters. Periodic adjustment is neither necessary or possible.

Carburetor

This section contains only carburetor adjustments as they normally apply to engine tune-up. Descriptions of the carburetor and complete adjustment procedures can be found in Chapter 5.

When the engine in your Nissan is running, air/fuel mixture from the carburetor is being drawn into the engine by a partial vacuum which is created by the downward movement of the pistons on the intake stroke of the 4-stroke cycle of the engine. The amount of air/fuel mixture that enters the engine is controlled by throttle plates in the bottom of the carburetor. When the engine is not running, the throttle plates are closed, completely blocking off the bottom of the carburetor from the inside of the engine. The throttle plates are connected, through the throttle linkage, to the gas pedal in the passenger compartment of the truck. After you start the engine and put the transmission in gear, you depress the gas pedal to start the truck moving. What you actually are doing when you depress the gas pedal is opening the throttle plate in the carburetor to admit more of the air/fuel mixture to the engine. The further you open the throttle plates in the carburetor, the higher the engine speed becomes.

As previously stated, when the engine is not running, the throttle plates in the carburetor are closed. When the engine is idling, it is necessary to open the throttle plates slightly. To prevent having to keep your foot on the gas pedal when the engine is idling, an idle speed adjusting screw was added to the carburetor. This screw has the same effect as keeping your foot slightly depressed on the gas pedal. The idle speed adjusting screw contacts a lever (the throttle lever) on the outside of the carburetor. When the screw is turned in, it opens the throttle plate on the carburetor, raising the idle speed of the engine. This screw is called the curb idle adjusting screw, and the procedures in this section tell you how to adjust it.

Since it is difficult for the engine to draw the air/fuel mixture from the carburetor with the small amount of throttle plate opening that is present when the engine is idling, an idle mixture passage is provided in the carburetor. This passage delivers air/fuel mixture to the engine from a hole which is located in the bottom of the carburetor below the throttle plates. This idle mixture passage contains an adjusting screw which restricts the amount of air/fuel mixture that enters the engine at idle.

IDLE SPEED AND MIXTURE ADJUSTMENT

1970–81

1. Start the engine and run it until it reaches operating temperature.

2. Allow the engine idle speed to stabilize by running the engine at idle for at least 1 minute.

3. If it hasn't already been done, check and adjust the ignition timing to the proper setting.

4. Turn off the engine and connect a tachometer to the engine.

5. Disconnect and plug the air hose between the three way connector and check valve, if equipped. Start the engine. With the transmission in **N**, check the idle speed on the tachometer. If the reading on the tachometer is correct, turn the idle adjusting screw clockwise to increase the idle speed and counterclockwise to decrease it.

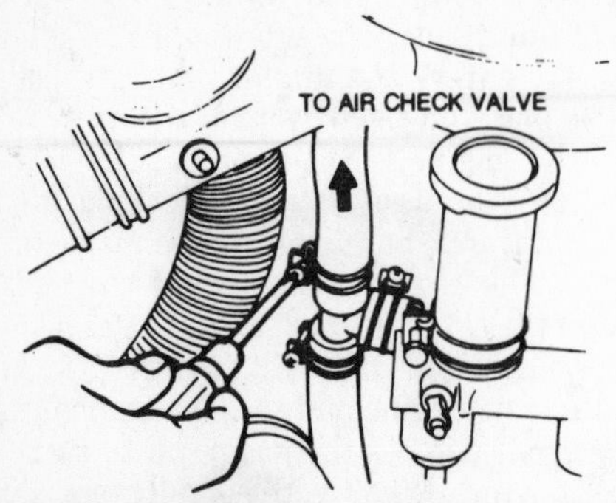

Disconnect the air hose between the three way connector and the check valve—1970–81

Mixture screw (arrow). Note limiter tab

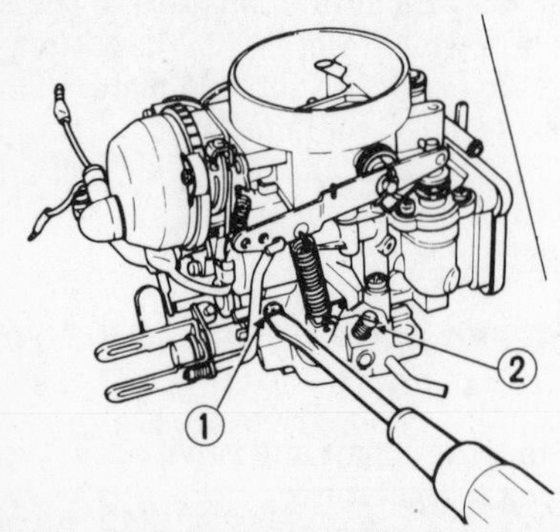

1. Idle speed adjusting screw
2. Air/fuel mixture adjusting screw

Idle speed and mixture adjustment screws—1970–8

6. With an automatic transmission in **D** (wheels chocked and parking brake applied) or a manual transmission in **N**, turn the mixture screw out until the engine rpm starts to drop due to an overly rich mixture.

7. Turn the screw in past the starting point until the engine rpm start to drop because of a too lean mixture. On 1975–77 models, turn the mixture screw in until the idle speed drops 60–70 rpm with manual transmission, or 15–25 rpm with automatic transmission (in **D**). On 1978 models, the rpm drop should be 45–55 rpm for all trucks. For 1979–81 models the rpm drop should be 45–55 rpm with manual transmission, or 25–35 rpm with automatic transmission (in **D**). If the mixture limiter cap will not allow this adjustment, remove it, make the adjustment, and reinstall it. Go on to Step 10 for 1975–81 trucks.

8. On 1970–74 models, turn the mixture screw back out to the point midway between the two extreme positions where the engine began losing rpm to achieve the fastest and smoothest idle.

9. Adjust the curb idle speed to the proper specification on 1970–74 models.

10. Install the air hose. If the engine speed increases, reduce it with the idle speed screw.

NOTE: *To be sure that the vehicle is complying with emission laws, have the exhaust checked with a CO meter. The percentages of CO should be 3% for 1970–71, 2% 1972, 1.5% 1973–74, 2% 1975–77, and 1% 1978–81 at idle speed.*

Idle limiter caps are installed on the mixture adjusting screws so that an incorrect adjustment cannot be made. If a satisfactory idle cannot be obtained within the range of the limiter caps, remove them and make the adjustment as outlined above. Reinstall the limiter caps so that the cap can be turned only ⅛ of a turn counterclockwise before it reaches the stop. Have the engine checked with a CO meter after making the adjustment.

1982–86

NOTE: *These models require the use of a CO Meter to adjust their mixture ratios, therefore only idle speed adjustments are given.*

1. Connect a tachometer according to the manufacturer's instructions.

2. Turn all the accessories and lights **OFF**. Make sure that the wheels are straight ahead on models with power steering.

Idle speed adjustment—1982–86 carbureted engines

3. Run the engine at 2000 rpm for 2 minutes with the transmission in **P** or **N**.

4. Run the engine at normal idle speed for 1 minute in **P** or **N**.

5. Check the idle speed with the automatic transmission in **D**, wheel blocked and the parking brake on using the figures provided on your underhood sticker. If the indicated idle speed does not agree with the specified speed, adjust the idle by turning the throttle adjusting screw at the carbuertor.

Electronic Fuel Injection (EFI)

These trucks use a rather complex electronic fuel injection system which is controlled by a series of temperature, altitude (for California) and air flow sensors which feed information into a central control unit. The control unit then relays an electronic signal to the injector nozzle at each cylinder, which allows a predetermined amount of fuel into the combustion chamber. To adjust the mixture controls on these units requires a CO meter and several special Datsun/Nissan tools. Therefore, we will confine ourselves to idle speed adjustment.

IDLE SPEED ADJUSTMENT

1. Turn off the: headlights, heater blower, air conditioning, and rear window defogger. If the truck has power steering, make sure the wheel is in the straight ahead position. The ignition timing must be correct to get an effective idle speed adjustment. Connect a tachometer (a special adapter harness may be needed, SST# EG11170000) according to the instrument manufacturer's directions.

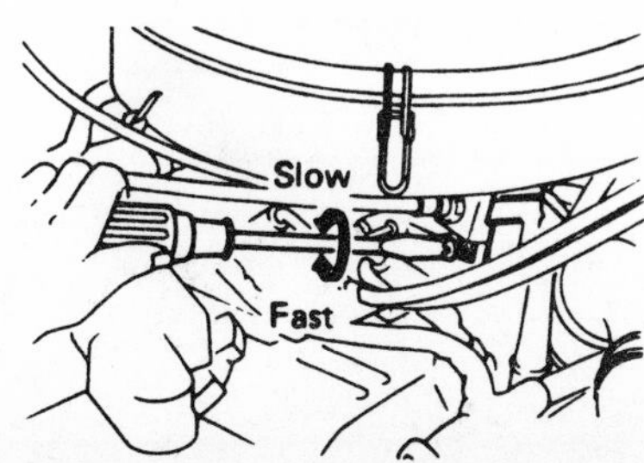

Idle seed adjustment—VG30i engines

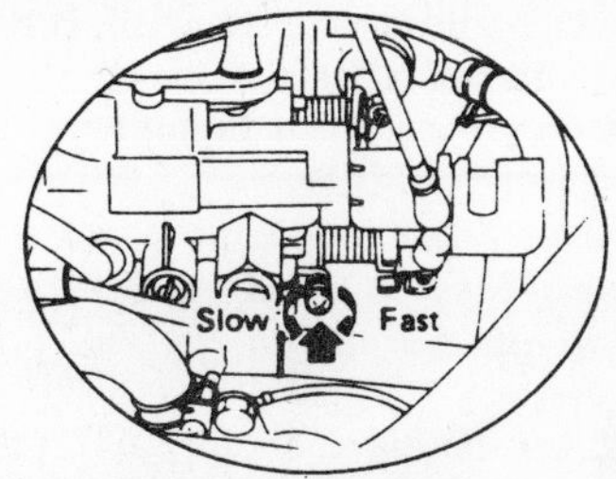

Idle speed adjustment—Z24i engines

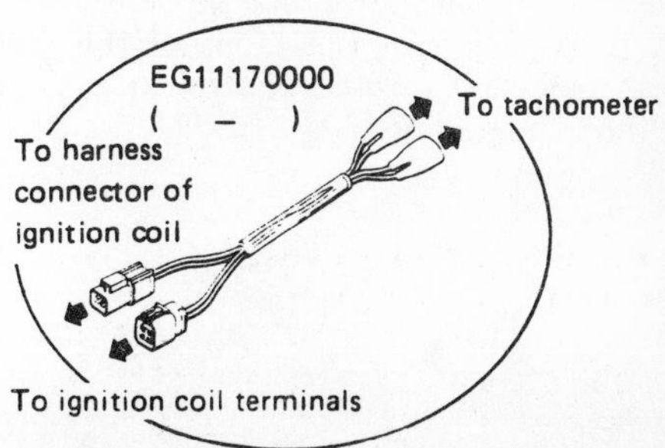

A special harness is used for tachometer connection on fuel injected engines

2. Start the engine and warm the engine so it reaches normal operating temperature. The water temperature indicator should be in the middle of the gauge.

3. Run engine at 2000 rpm for about 2 minutes under no load.

4. Race the engine to 2000–3000 rpm a few times under no load and then allow it to return to idle speed.

5. Apply the parking brake securely and then put the transmission into **D**, if the truck has an automatic. Adjust the idle speed to the figure shown in the Tune-Up Specifications Chart by turning the idle speed adjusting screw shown in the appropriate illustration.

6. Turn the engine off and remove the tachometer. Road test for proper operation.

Diesel Fuel Injection

IDLE SPEED ADJUSTMENT

NOTE: *A special diesel tachometer will be required for this procedure. A normal tachometer will not work.*

1. Make sure all electrical accessories are turned off.

2. Start the engine and run it until it reaches the normal operating temperature.

3. The automatic transmission (if so

equipped) should be in D with the parking brake on and the wheels blocked.

4. Attach the diesel tachometer's pick-up to the No. 1 injection tube.

NOTE: *In order to obtain a more accurate reading of the idle speed, you may wish to remove all the clamps on the No. 1 injection tube.*

5. Run the engine at about 2000 rpm for two minutes under no-load conditions.

6. Slow the engine down to idle speed for about 1 min. and then check the idle.

7. If the engine is not idling at the proper speed, push the throttle control knob (under dash) all the way in on the SD22.

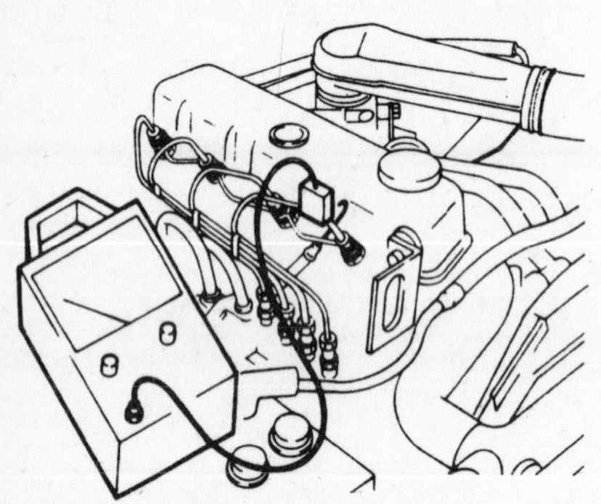

Connect a diesel tachometer to the No. 1 injection tube

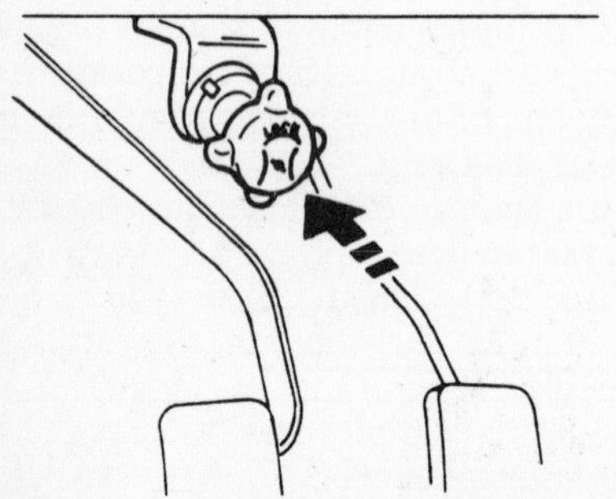

Push the throttle control knob all the way in—SD22 engines

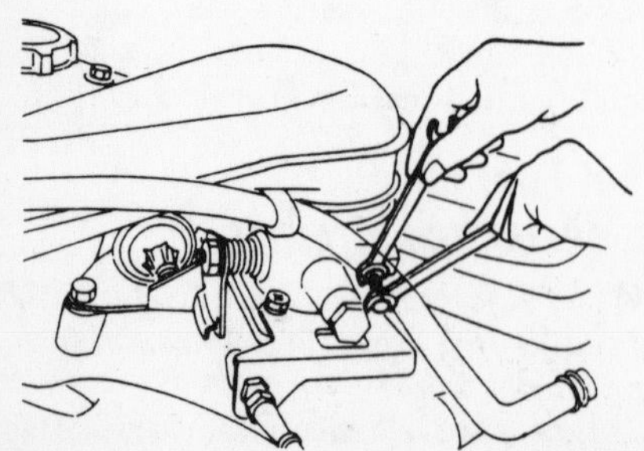

Idle speed adjustment—SD22 and SD25 (720-D series) engines

Idle speed adjustment—SD25 (D21-D series) engines

8. Loosen the idle screw lock nut. Start the engine again and turn the adjusting screw until the proper idle is obtained. Stop the engine.

9. Tighten the idle adjusting screw lock nut and then disconnect the tachometer.

DASH POT ADJUSTMENT

NOTE: *A special diesel tachometer will be required for this procedure. A normal tachometer will not work.*

1. Make sure all electrical accessories are turned off.

2. Start the engine and run it until it reaches the normal operating temperature.

3. The automatic transmission (if so equipped) should be in D with the parking brake on and the wheels blocked.

4. Attach the diesel tachometer's pick-up to the No. 1 injection tube.

NOTE: *In order to obtain a more accurate reading of the idle speed, you may wish to remove all the clamps on the No. 1 injection tube.*

5. Loosen the dash pot lock nut.

6. With the engine speed at 1280–1350 rpm, operate and adjust the dash pot so that the control lever tip contacts the dash pot tip.

7. Tighten the lock nut, disconnect the tachometer and road test the truck.

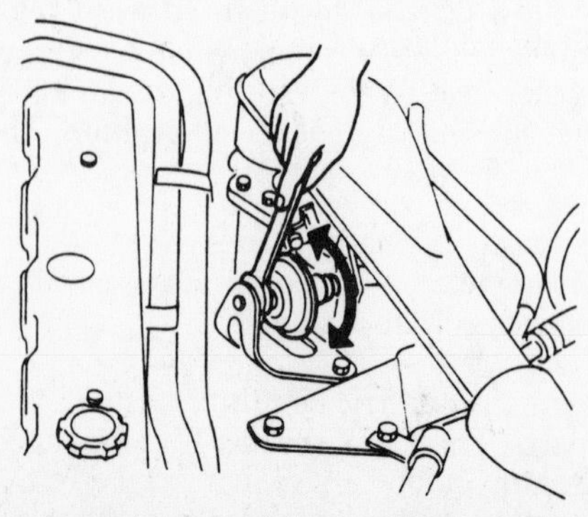

Dash pot adjustment—SD22 and SD25 engines

Engine and Engine Overhaul

3

UNDERSTANDING BASIC ELECTRICITY

Understanding the basic theory of electricity makes electrical troubleshooting much easier. Several gauges are used in electrical troubleshooting to see inside the circuit being tested. Without a basic understanding, it will be difficult to understand testing procedures.

Electricity is the flow of electrons, hypothetical particles thought to constitute the basic "stuff" of electricity. In a comparison with water flowing in a pipe, the electrons would be the water. As the flow of water can be measured, the flow of electricity can be measured. The unit of measurement is amperes, frequently abbreviated "amps". An ammeter will measure the actual amount of current flowing in the circuit.

Just as the water pressure is measured in units such as pounds per square inch, electrical pressure is measured in volts. When a voltmeter's two probes are placed on two "live" portions of an electrical circuit with different electrical pressures, current will flow through the voltmeter and produce a reading which indicates the difference in electrical pressure between the two parts of the circuit.

While increasing the voltage in a circuit will increase the flow of current, the actual flow depends not only on voltage, but on the resistance of the circuit. The standard unit for measuring circuit resistance is an ohm, measured by an ohmmeter. The ohmmeter is somewhat similar to an ammeter, but incorporates its own source of power so that a standard voltage is always present.

An actual electric circuit consists of four basic parts. These are: the power source such as a generator or battery; a hot wire, which conducts the electricity under a relatively high voltage to the component supplied by the circuit; the load, such as a lamp, motor, resistor, or relay coil; and the ground wire, which carries the current back to the source under very low voltage. In such a circuit the bulk of the resistance exists between the point where the hot wire is connected to the load, and the point where the load is grounded. In an automobile, the vehicle's frame, which is made of steel, is used as a part of the ground circuit for many of the electrical devices.

Remember that, in electrical testing, the voltmeter is connected in parallel with the circuit being tested (without disconnecting any wires) and measures the difference in voltage between the locations of the two probes; that the ammeter is connected in series with the load (the circuit is separated at one point and the ammeter inserted so it becomes a part of the circuit); and the ohmmeter is self-powered, so that all the power in the circuit should be off and the portion of the circuit to be measured contacted at either end by one of the probes of the meter.

For any electrical system to operate, it must make a complete circuit. This simply means that the power flow from the battery must make a complete circle. When an electrical component is operating, power flows from the battery to the component, passes through the component causing it to perform its function (lighting a light bulb) and then returns to the battery through the ground of the circuit. This ground is usually (but not always) the metal part of the truck on which the electrical component is mounted.

Perhaps the easiest way to visualize this is to think of connecting a light bulb with two wires attached to it to your battery. The battery in your truck has two posts (negative and positive). If one of the two wires attached to the light bulb was attached to the negative post of the battery and the other wire was attached to the positive post of the battery, you would have a complete circuit. Current from the battery would flow out one post, through the wire attached to it and then to the light bulb, where it would pass through causing it to light. It would then leave the light bulb, travel through the other wire, and return to the other post of the battery.

The normal automotive circuit differs from this simple example in two ways. First, instead of having a return wire from the bulb to the battery, the light bulb returns the current to the battery through the chassis of the vehicle. Since the negative battery cable is attached to the chassis and the chassis is made of electrically conductive metal, the chassis of the vehicle can serve as a ground wire to complete the circuit. Secondly, most automotive circuits contain switches to turn components on and off.

Some electrical components which require a large amount of current to operate also have a relay in their circuit. Since these circuits carry a large amount of current, the thickness of the wire in the circuit (gauge size) is also greater. If this large wire were connected from the component to the control switch on the instrument panel, and then back to the component, a voltage drop would occur in the circuit. To prevent this potential drop in voltage, an electromagnetic switch (relay) is used. The large wires in the circuit are connected from the battery to one side of the relay, and from the opposite side of the relay to the component. The relay is normally open, preventing current from passing through the circuit. An additional, smaller, wire is connected from the relay to the control switch for the circuit. When the control switch is turned on, it grounds the smaller wire from the relay and completes the circuit. When the control switch is turned on, it grounds the smaller wire from the relay. If you were to disconnect the light bulb (from the previous example of a light bulb being connected to the battery by two wires) from the wires and touch the two wires together (please take our word for this; don't try it), the result will be a shower of sparks. A similar thing happens (on a smaller scale) when the power supply wire to a component or the electrical component itself becomes grounded before the normal ground connection for the circuit. To prevent damage to the system, the fuse for the circuit blows to interrupt the circuit, protecting the components from damage. Because grounding a wire from a power source makes a complete circuit, less the required component to see the power, the phenomenon is called a short circuit. The most common causes of short circuits are: the rubber insulation on the wire breaking or rubbing through to expose the current carrying core of the wire to a metal part of the truck, or a shorted switch.

Some electrical systems on the truck are protected by a circuit breaker which is, basically, a self-repairing fuse. When either of the above described events takes place in a system which is protected by a circuit breaker, the circuit breaker opens the circuit the same way a fuse does. However, when either the short is removed from the circuit or the surge subsides, the circuit breaker resets itself and does not have to be replaced as a fuse does.

The final protective device in the chassis electrical system is a fuse link. A fuse link is a wire that acts as a fuse. It is connected between the starter relay and the main wiring harness for the truck. This connection is under the hood, very near a similar fuse link which protects the engine electrical system. Since the fuse link protects all the chassis electrical components, it is the probably cause of trouble when none of the electrical components function, unless the battery is disconnected or dead.

Electrical problems generally fall into one of three areas:

1. The component that is not functioning is not receiving current.
2. The component itself is not functioning.
3. The component is not properly grounded.

Problems that fall into the first category are by far the most complicated. It is the current supply system to the component which contains all the switches, relays, fuses., etc.

The electrical system can be checked with a test light and a jumper wire. A test light is a device that looks like a pointed screwdriver with a wire attached to it. It has a light bulb in its handle. A jumper wire is a piece of insulated wire with an alligator clip attached to each end.

If a light bulb is not working, you must follow a systematic plan to determine which of the three causes is the villain.

1. Turn on the switch that controls the inoperable bulb.
2. Disconnect the power supply wire from the bulb.
3. Attach the ground wire on the test light to a good metal ground.
4. Touch the probe end of the test light to the end of the power supply wire that was disconnected form the bulb. If the bulb is receiving current, the test light will go on.

NOTE: *If the bulb is one which works only when the ignition key is turned on (turn signal), make sure the key is turned on.*

If the test light does not go on, then the problem is in the circuit between the battery and the bulb. As mentioned before, this includes all the switches, fuses, and relays in the system. Turn to the wiring diagram and find the bulb on the diagram. Follow the wire that runs back to the battery. The problem is an open circuit between the battery and the bulb. If the fuse is blown and, when replaced, immediately blows again, there is a short circuit in the system which must be located and repaired. If there is a switch in the system, bypass it with a jumper wire. This is done by connecting one end of the jumper wire to the power supply wire into the switch and the other end of the jumper wire to the wire coming out of the switch. Again, consult the wiring diagram. If the test light lights with the jumper wire installed, the switch or whatever was bypassed is defective.

NOTE: *Never substitute the jumper wire for the bulb, as the bulb is the component required to use the power from the power source.*

5. If the bulb in the test light goes on, then the current is getting to the bulb that is not working in the truck. This eliminates the first of the three possible causes. Connect the power supply wire and connect a jumper wire from the bulb to a good metal ground. Do this with the switch which controls the bulb turned on, and also the ignition switch turned on if it is required for the light to work. If the bulb works with jumper wire installed, then it has a bad ground. This is usually caused by the metal area on which the bulb mounts to the truck being coated with some type of foreign matter.

6. If neither test located the source of the trouble, then the light bulb itself is defective.

The above test procedure can be applied to any of the components of the chassis electrical system by substituting the component that is not working for the light bulb. Remember that for any electrical system to work, all connections must be clean and tight.

UNDERSTANDING THE ENGINE ELECTRICAL SYSTEM

The engine electrical system can be broken down into three separate and distinct systems:

1. The starting system.
2. The charging system.
3. The ignition system.

Battery and Starting System

The battery is the first link in the chain of mechanisms which work together to provide cranking of the automobile engine. In most modern trucks, the battery is a lead/acid electro-chemical device consisting of six two-volt (2V) subsections connected in series so the unit is capable of producing approximately 12V of electrical pressure. Each subsection, or cell, consists of a series of positive and negative plates held a short distance apart in a solution of sulfuric acid and water. The two types of plates are of dissimilar metals. This causes a chemical reaction to be set up, and it is this reaction which produces current flow from the battery when its positive and negative terminals are connected to an electrical appliance such as a lamp or a motor. The continued transfer of electrons would eventually convert sulfuric acid in the electrolyte to water, and make the two plates identical in chemical composition. As electrical energy is removed from the battery, its voltage output tends to drop. Thus, measuring battery voltage and battery electrolyte composition are two ways of checking the ability of the unit to supply power. During the starting of the engine, electrical energy is removed from the battery. However, if the charging circuit is in good condition and the operating conditions are normal, the power removed from the battery will be replaced by the generator (or alternator) which will force electrons back through the battery, reversing the normal flow, and restoring the battery to its original chemical state.

The battery and starting motor are linked by very heavy electrical cables designed to minimize resistant to the flow of current. Generally, the major power supply cable that leaves the battery goes directly to the starter, while other electrical needs are supplied by a smaller cable. During the starter operation, power flows from the battery to the starter and is grounded through the truck's frame and the battery's negative ground strap.

The starting motor is a specially designed, direct current electric motor capable of producing a very great amount of power for its size. One thing that allows the motor to produce a great deal of power is its tremendous rotating speed. It drives the engine through a tiny pinion gear (attached to the starter's armature), which drives the very large flywheel ring gear at a greatly reduced speed. Another factor allowing it to produce so much power is that only intermittent operation is required of it. Thus, little allowance for air circulation is required, and the windings can be built into a very small space.

The starter solenoid is a magnetic device which employs the small current supplied by the starting switch circuit of the ignition switch. The magnetic action moves a plunger which mechanically engages the starter and electrically closes the heavy switch which connects it to the battery. The starting switch circuit consists of the starting switch contained within the ignition switch, a transmission neutral safety switch or clutch pedal switch, and the wiring necessary to connect these with the starter solenoid or relay.

A pinion, which is a small gear, is mounted to a one-way drive clutch. This clutch is splined to the starter armature shaft. When the ignition switch is moved to the **Start** position, the solenoid plunger slides the pinion toward the flywheel ring gear via a collar and spring. If the teeth on the pinion and flywheel match properly, the pinion will engage the flywheel immediately. If the gear teeth butt one another, the spring will be compressed and will force the gears to mesh as soon as the starter turns far enough to allow them to do so. As the solenoid plunger reaches the end of its travel, it closes the contacts that connect the battery and starter and then the engine is cranked.

As soon as the engine starts, the flywheel ring gear begins turning fast enough to drive the pinion at an extremely high rate of speed. At this point, the one-way clutch begins allowing the pinion to spin faster than the starter shaft so that the starter will not operate at excessive speed. When the ignition switch is released from the starter position, the solenoid is de-energized, and a spring contained within the solenoid assembly pulls the gear out of mesh and interrupts the current flow to the starter.

Some starters employ a separate relay, mounted away from the starter, to switch the motor and solenoid current on and off. The relay thus replaces the solenoid electrical switch, but does not eliminate the need for a solenoid mounted on the starter used to mechanically engage the starter drive gears. The relay is used to reduce the amount of current the starting switch must carry.

The Charging System

The automobile charging system provides electrical power for operation of the vehicle's ignition and starting systems and all the electrical accessories. The battery serves as an electrical surge or storage tank, storing (in chemical form) the energy originally produced by the engine-driven generator. The system also provides a means of regulating generator output to protect the battery from being overcharged and to avoid excessive voltage to the accessories.

The storage battery is chemical device incorporating parallel lead plates in a tank containing a sulfuric acid/water solution. Adjacent plates are slightly dissimilar, and the chemical reaction of the two dissimilar plates produces electrical energy when the battery is connected to a load such as the starter motor. The chemical reaction is reversible, so that when the generator is producing a voltage (electrical pressure) greater than that produced by the battery, electricity is forced into the battery, and the battery is returned to its fully charged state.

The vehicle's generator is driven mechanically, through V-belts, by the engine crankshaft. It consists of two coils of fine wire, one stationary (the "stator"), and one moveable (the "rotor"). The rotor may also be known as the "armature," and consists of fine wire wrapped around an iron core which is mounted on the shaft. The electricity which flows through the two coils of wire (provided initially be the battery in some cases) creates an intense magnetic field around both the rotor and stator, and the interaction between the two fields creates voltage, allowing the generator to power the accessories and charge the battery.

There are two types of generators; the earlier is the direct current (DC) type. The current produced by the DC generator is generated in the armature and carried off the spinning armature by stationary brushes contacting the commutator. The commutator plates, which are separated by a very short gap, are connected to the armature circuits so that the current will flow in one direction only in the wires carrying the generator output. The generator stator consists of two stationary coils of wire which draw some of the output current of the generator to form a powerful magnetic field and create the interaction of fields which generates the voltage. The generator field is wired in series with the regulator.

Newer automobiles use alternating current generators because they are more efficient, can be rotated at higher speeds, and have fewer brush problems. In an alternator, the field rotates while all the current produced passes only through the stator windings. The brushes bear against continuous slip rings rather than a commutator. This causes the current produced to periodically reverse the direction of its flow. Diodes (electrical one-way switches) block the flow of current from traveling in the wrong direction. A series of diodes is wired together to permit the alternating flow of the stator to be converted to a pulsating, but unidirectional flow at the alternator output. The alternator's field is wired in series with the voltage regulator.

The regulator consists of several circuits. Each circuit has a core, or magnetic coil of wire, which operates a switch. Each switch to ground through one or more resistors. The coil of wire responds directly to system voltage. When the voltage reaches the required level, the magnetic field created by the winding of wire closes the switch and inserts a resistance into the generator field circuit, thus reducing the output. The contacts of the switch cycle open and close many times each second to precisely control voltage.

While alternators are self-limiting as far as maximum current is concerned, DC generators employ a current regulating circuit which responds directly to the total amount of current flowing through the generator circuit rather than to the output voltage. The current regulator is similar to the voltage regulator except that all system current must flow through the energizing coil on its way to the various accessories.

SAFETY PRECAUTIONS

Observing these precautions will ensure safe handling of the electrical systems components and will avoid damage to the vehicle's electrical system:

a. Be absolutely sure of the polarity of a booster battery before making connections. Connect the cables positive to positive, and negative to negative. Connect positive cables first and then make the last connection to a ground on the body of the booster vehicle so that arcing cannot ignite hydrogen gas that may have accumulated near the battery. Even momentary connection of a booster battery with the polarity reversed will damage alternator diodes.

b. Disconnect both vehicle battery cables before attempting to charge a battery.

c. Never ground the alternator or generator output or battery terminal. Be cautious when using metal tools around a battery to avoid creating a short circuit between the terminals.

d. Never ground the field circuit between the alternator and regulator.

e. Never run an alternator or generator without load unless the field circuit is disconnected.

f. Never attempt to polarize an alternator.

g. Keep the regulator cover in place when taking voltage and current limiter readings.

h. Use insulated tools when adjusting the regulator.

i. Whenever DC generator-to-generator wires have been disconnected, the generator *must* be re-polarized. To do this with an externally grounded, light duty generator, momentarily place a jumper wire between the battery terminal and the generator terminal of the regulator. With an internally grounded heavy duty unit, disconnect the wire to the regulator field terminal and touch the regulator battery terminal with it.

Ignition Coil

TESTING

Primary Resistance Check

In order to check the coil primary resistance, you must first disconnect all wires from the ignition coil terminals. Using an ohmmeter, check the resistance between the positive (15) and the negative (1) terminals on the coil. The resistance should be:

- L16 and L18 – 1.17–1.43Ω
- L20B (1975) – 1.17–1.43Ω

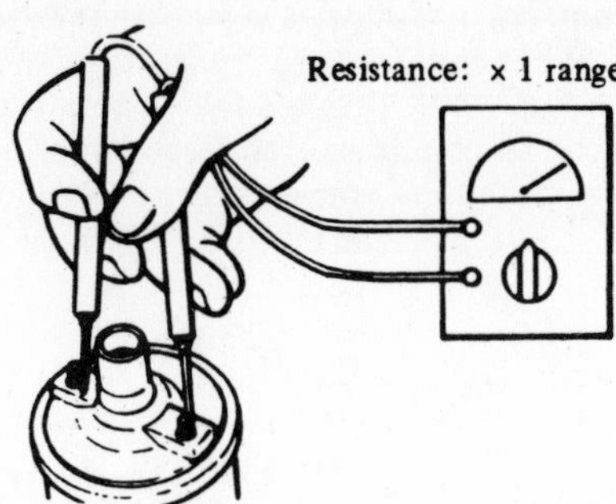

Checking the coil primary resistance—1970–86

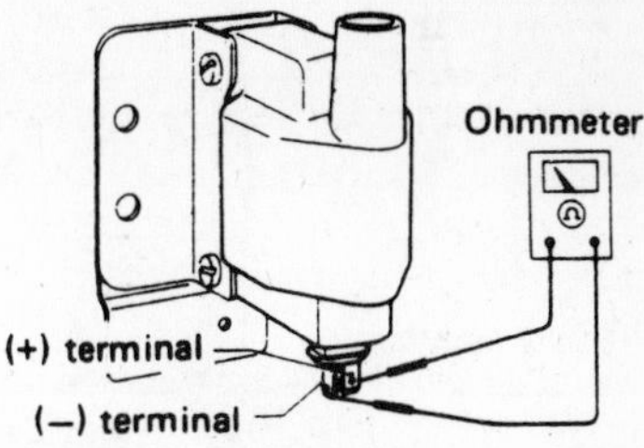

Checking the coil primary resistance—1986–89 Z24i (VG30i similar)

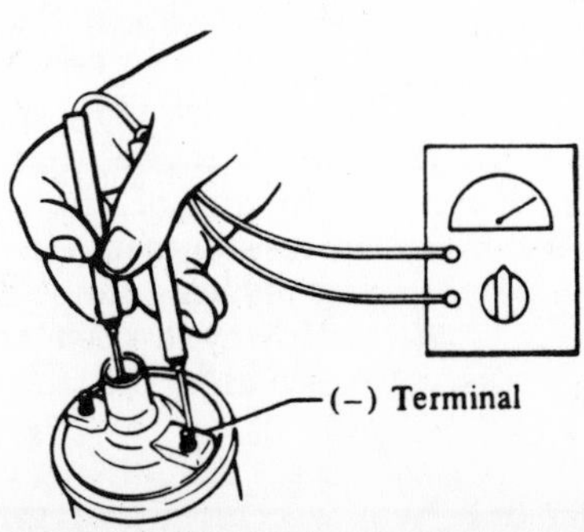

Checking the coil secondary resistance—1970–86

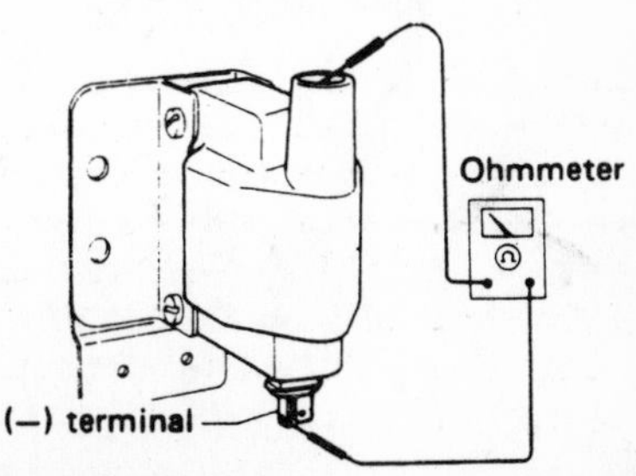

Checking the coil secondary resistance—1986–89 Z24i (VG30i similar)

- L20B (1976 Fed.) – 1.17–1.43Ω
- L20B (1977 Fed.) – 1.08–1.32Ω
- L20B (1976-77 Calif.) – 0.45–0.55Ω
- L20B (1978-80) – 0.84–1.02Ω
- Z22 (1981-83) – 1.04–1.27Ω
- Z20 (1984-86) – 0.84–1.02Ω
- Z24 (1984-87) – 1.05–1.27Ω
- Z24i (1986-89) – 0.80–1.00Ω
- VG30i (1986-89) – 0.80–1.00Ω

NOTE: *Remember that all Z20, Z22, Z24 and Z24i engines have 2 ignition coils; check them both!*

If the resistance is not within these tolerances, the coil will require replacement.

Secondary Resistance Check

In order to check the coil secondary resistance, you must first disconnect all wires from the ignition coil terminals. Using an ohmmeter, check the resistance between the positive (15) terminal and the coil wire (4) terminal. The resistance should be:

- L16 and L18 – 11,200–16,800Ω
- L20B (1975) – 11,200–16,800Ω
- L20B (1976 Fed.) – 11,200–16,800Ω
- L20B (1977 Fed.) – 8,240–12,400Ω
- L20B (1976-77 Calif.) – 8,500–12,700Ω
- L20B (1978-80) – 8,200–12,400Ω
- Z22 (1981-83) – 7,300–11,000Ω
- Z20 (1984-86) – 8,300–12,600Ω
- Z24 (1984-87) – 8,400–12,600Ω
- Z24i (1986-89) – 7,600–11,400Ω
- VG30i (1986-89) – 7,600–11,400Ω

NOTE: *Remember that all Z20, Z22, Z24 and Z24i engines have 2 ignition coils; check them both!*

If the resistance is not within these tolerances, the coil will require replacement.

REMOVAL AND INSTALLATION

1. Disconnect the negative battery cable.
2. Tag and disconnect all electrical leads at the coil.
3. Remove the two mounting bolts and lift off the ignition coil.
4. Install the coil in position and tighten the mounting bolts.
5. Connect all wires.
6. Connect the negative battery cable.

Distributor

REMOVAL

To remove the distributor, proceed in the following
order:

1. Unfasten the retaining clips and lift the distributor cap straight off. It will be easier to install the distributor if the wiring is left connected to the cap. If the wires must be removed from the cap, mark their positions to aid in installation.

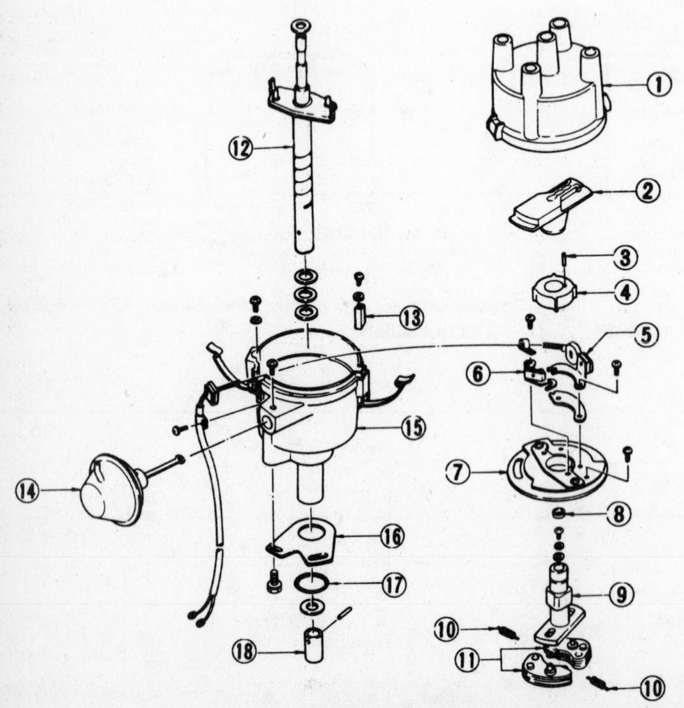

1 Cap assembly
2 Rotor head assembly
3 Roll pin
4 Reluctor
5 Pick-up coil
6 Contactor
7 Breaker plate assembly
8 Packing
9 Rotor shaft
10 Governor spring
11 Governor weight
12 Shaft assembly
13 Cap setter
14 Vacuum controller
15 Housing
16 Fixing plate
17 O-ring
18 Collar

Exploded view of the distributor—1976–78

2. Remove the dust cover and mark the position of the rotor relative to the distributor body; then mark the position of the body relative to the block.

3. Disconnect the coil primary wire and the vacuum lines, mark which is which for installation.

4. Remove the pinch-bolt and lift the distributor straight out, away from the engine. The rotor and body are marked so that they can be returned to the position from which they were removed. Do not turn or disturb the engine (unless absolutely necessary, such as for engine rebuilding), after the distributor has been removed.

INSTALLATION
TIMING NOT DISTURBED

1. Insert the distributor in the block and align the matchmarks made during removal.

2. Engage the distributor driven gear with the distributor drive.

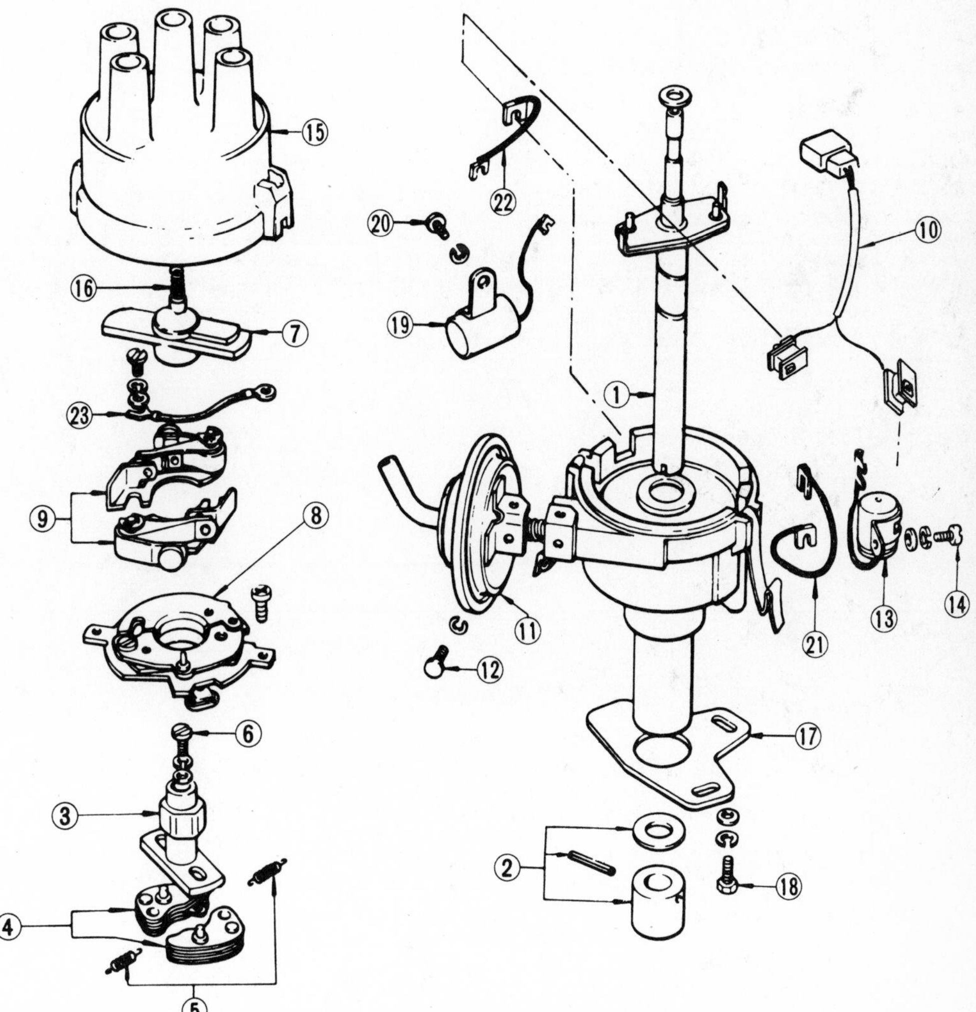

1. Shaft assembly
2. Collar set assembly
3. Cam assembly
4. Governor weight assembly
5. Governor spring set
6. Screw
7. Rotor head assembly
8. Breaker assembly
9. Contact set
10. Connector assembly
11. Vacuum control assembly
12. Screw
13. Condenser assembly (for advanced points)
14. Screw
15. Distributor cap assembly
16. Carbon point assembly
17. Fixing plate
18. Bolt
19. Condenser assembly (for retarded points)
20. Screw
21. Lead wire assembly (for advanced points)
22. Lead wire assembly (for retarded points)
23. Ground wire assembly

Exploded view of the distributor—1970–73

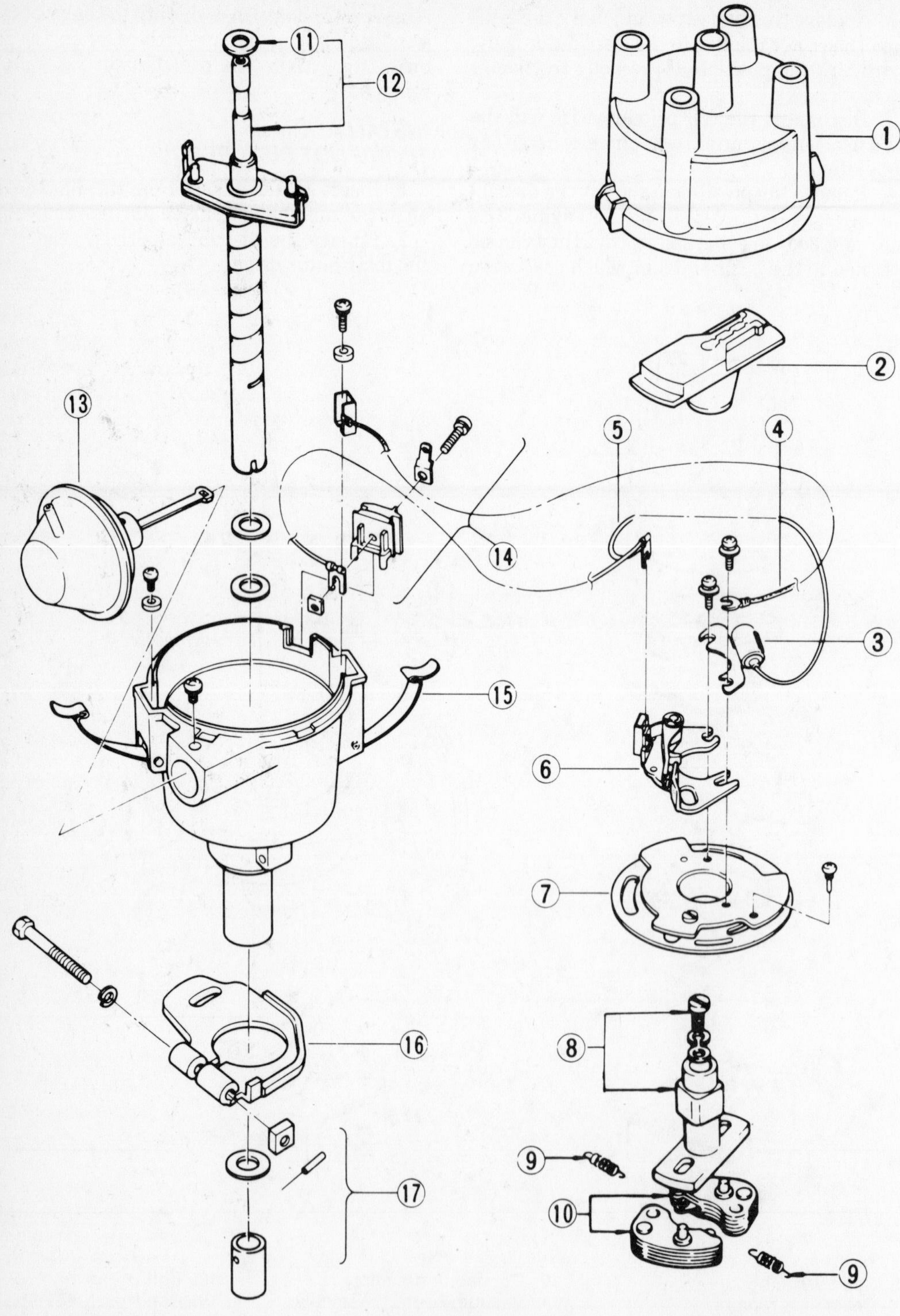

1. Cap assembly
2. Rotor head assembly
3. Condenser assembly
4. Ground wire assembly
5. Lead wire assembly
6. Contact set
7. Breaker plate assembly
8. Cam assembly
9. Governor spring
10. Governor weight
11. Thrust washer
12. Shaft assembly
13. Vacuum control assembly
14. Terminal assembly
15. Clamp
16. Fixing plate
17. Collar set

Exploded view of the distributor—1974; later models with points are similar except for the fixing plate

3. Install the distributor clamp and secure it with the pinch-bolt.

4. Install the cap, primary wire, and vacuum line(s).

5. Install the spark plug leads. Consult the marks made during removal to be sure that the proper lead goes to each plug. Install the high tension wire if it was removed.

6. Start the engine. Check the timing and adjust it if necessary.

INSTALLATION TIMING LOST

If the engine has been cranked, dismantled, or the timing otherwise lost, proceed as follows:

1. It is necessary to place the No. 1 cylinder in the firing position to correctly install the distributor. To locate this position, the ignition timing marks on the crankshaft front pulley are used.

2. Remove the No. 1 cylinder spark plug. Turn the crankshaft until the piston in the No. 1 cylinder is moving up on the compression stroke. This can be determined by placing your thumb over the spark plug hole and feeling the air being forced out of the cylinder. Stop turning the crankshaft when the timing marks indicate **TDC** or **0**.

3. Oil the distributor housing lightly where the distributor bears on the cylinder block.

4. Install the distributor so that the rotor, which is mounted on the shaft, points toward the No. 1 spark plug terminal tower position when the cap is installed. Of course you won't be able to see the direction in which the rotor is pointing if the cap is on the distributor. Lay the

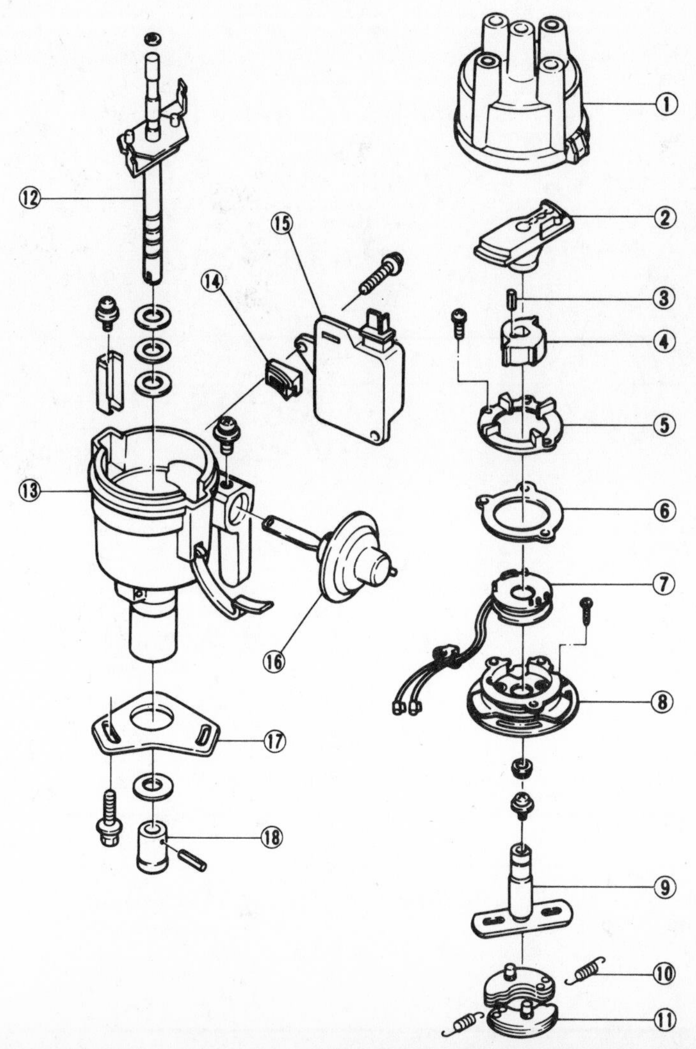

1 Cap assembly
2 Rotor head assembly
3 Roll pin
4 Reluctor
5 Stator
6 Magnet assembly
7 Pick-up coil assembly
8 Breaker plate assembly
9 Rotor shaft assembly
10 Governor spring
11 Governor weight
12 Shaft assembly
13 Housing assembly
14 Grommet
15 IC ignition unit
16 Vacuum controller
17 Fixing plate
18 Collar

Exploded view of the distributor—1979–80

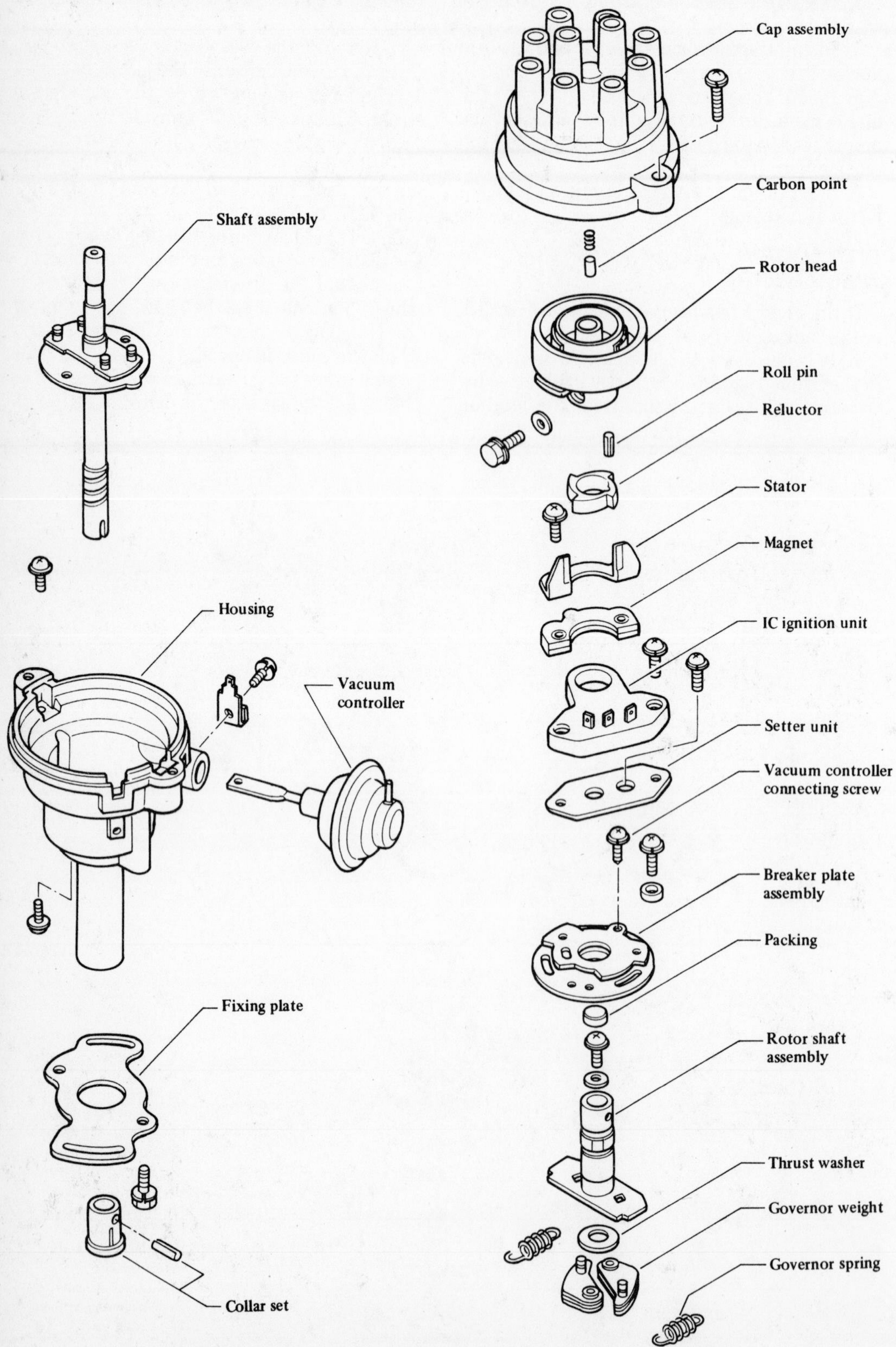

Exploded view of the distributor—1981–86 Z20, Z22 and Z24 engines

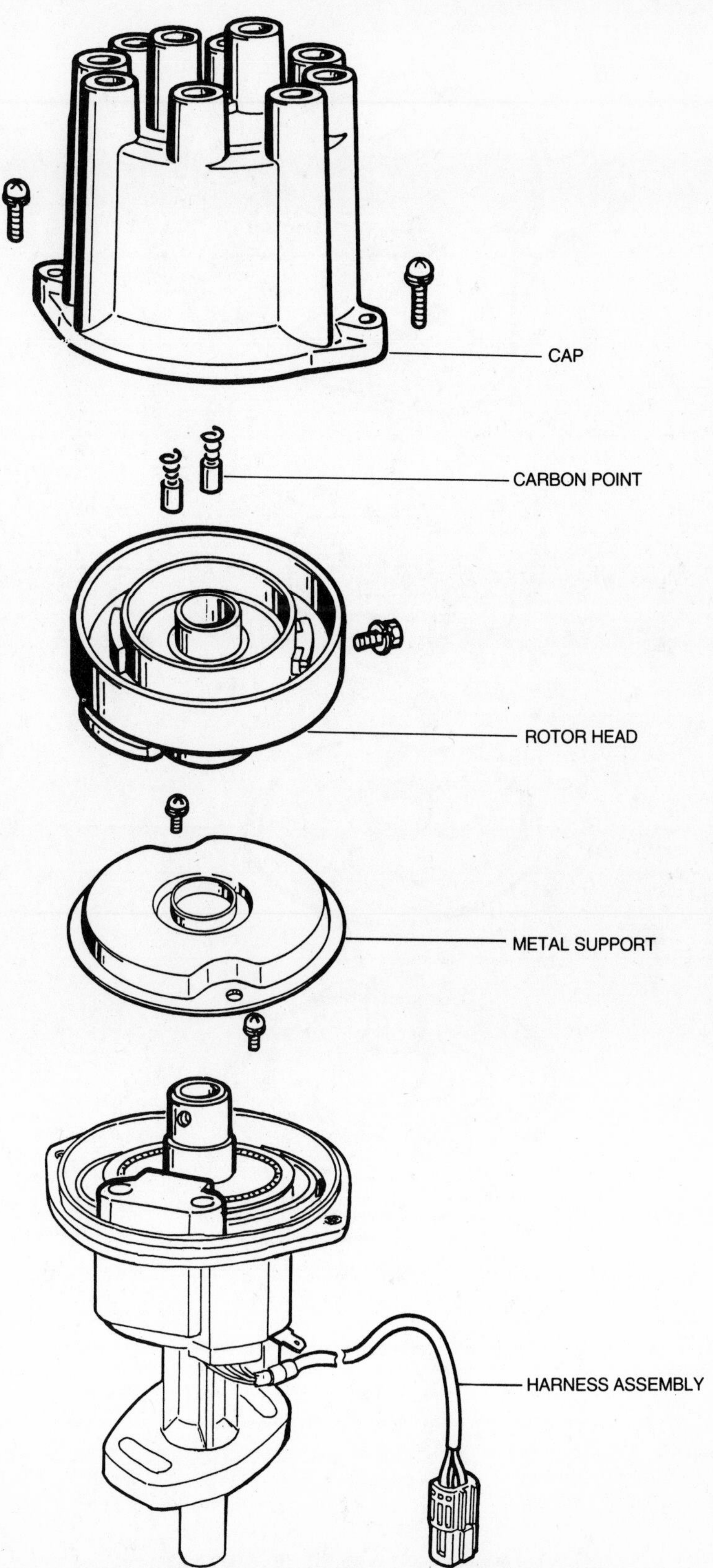

Exploded view of the distributor—1986–89 Z24i engines

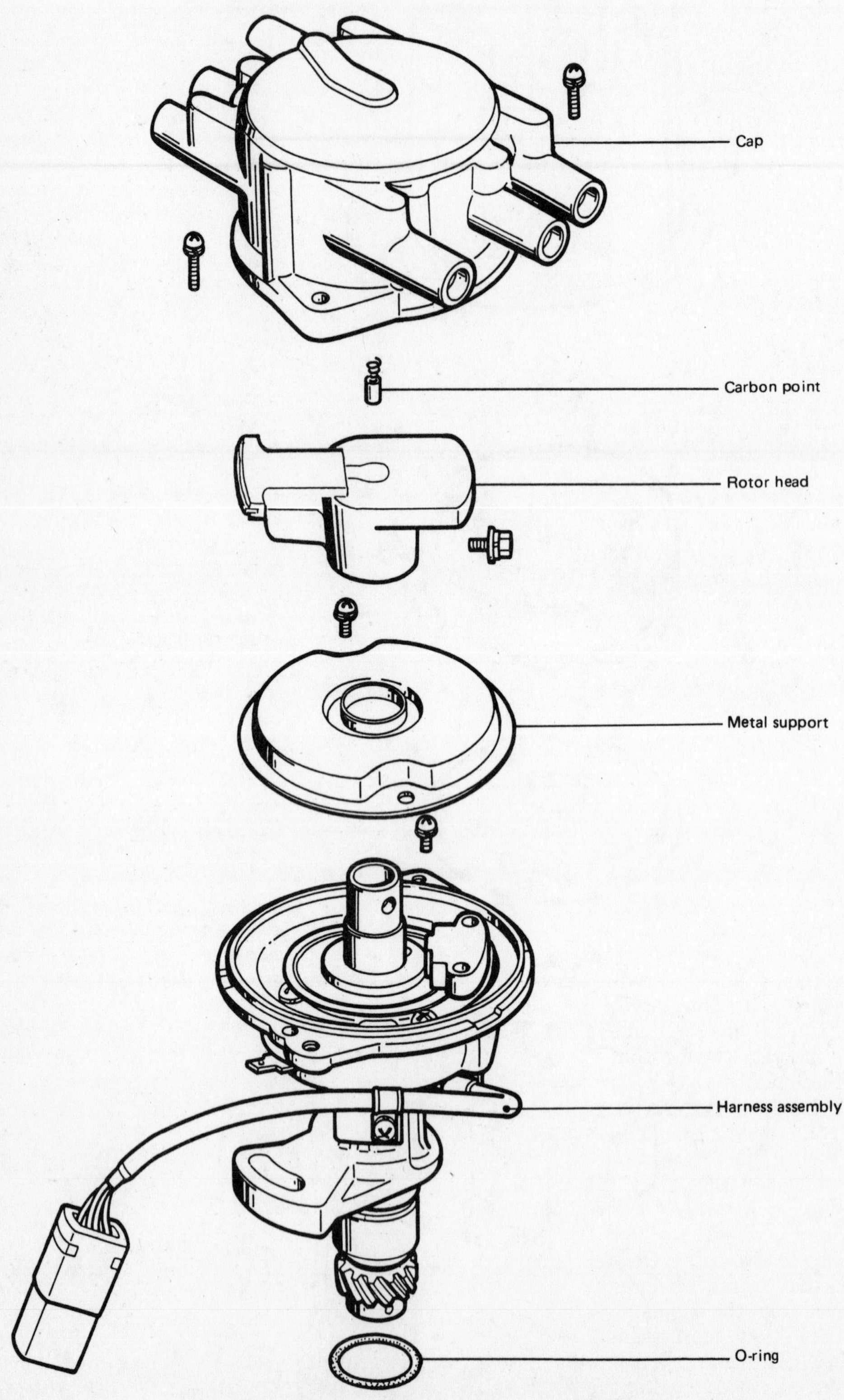

Exploded view of the distributor—1986–89 VG30i engines

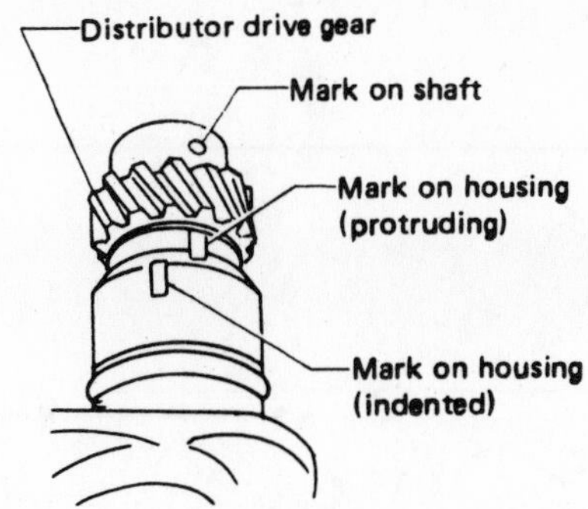

Align the mark on the housing with the mark on the shaft—VG30i

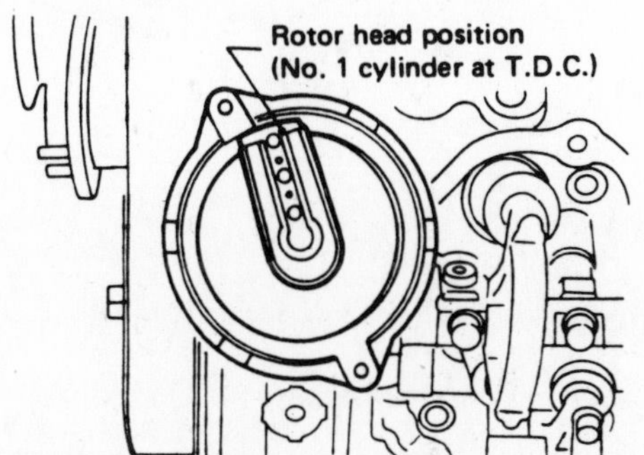

After the distributor has been installed, the rotor should be in this position—VG30i

cap on the top of the distributor and make a mark on the side of the distributor housing just below the No.1 spark plug terminal plug terminal. Make sure that the rotor points toward that mark when you install the distributor.

On the VG30i, align the mark on the distributor shaft with the *protruding* mark on the housing.

5. When the distributor shaft has reached the bottom of the hole, move the rotor back and forth slightly until the driving lug on the end of the shaft enter the slots cut in the end of the oil pump shaft and the distributor assembly slides down into place.

6. When the distributor is correctly installed, the breaker points should be in such a position that they are just ready to break contact with each other or a lobe of the reluctor is aligned with the stator contact. This is accomplished by rotating the distributor body after it has been installed in the engine. Once again, line up the marks that you made before the distributor was removed from the engine.

On the VG30i, the distributor rotot should be in the 11:25 o'clock position.

7. Install the distributor holddown bolt.

8. Install the spark plug into the No. 1 spark plug hole and continue from Step 3 of the distributor installation procedure.

Alternator

The alternator converts the mechanical energy supplied by the drive belt into electrical energy by a process of electromagnetic induction. When the ignition switch is turned on, current flows from the battery through the charging system light (or ammeter) to the voltage regulator, and finally to the alternator. When the engine is started, the drive belt turns the rotating field (rotor) in the stationary windings (stator), inducing alternating current. This alternating current is converted into usable direct current by the diode rectifier. Most of this current is used to charge the battery and to supply power for the vehicle's electrical accessories. A small part of this current is returned to the field windings of the alternator enabling it to increase its power output. When the current in the field windings reaches a predetermined level, the voltage regulator grounds the circuit preventing any further increase. The cycle is continued so that the voltage supply remains constant.

All models use a 12 volt alternator. Amperage ratings vary according to the year and model. 1970-77 models utilize a separate, adjustable regulator, while 1978-89 models have a transistorized, nonadjustable regulator, integral with the alternator.

ALTERNATOR PRECAUTIONS

To prevent damage to the alternator and regulator, the following precautionary measures must be taken when working with the electrical system.

1. Never reverse the battery connections. Always check the battery polarity visually. This is to be done before any connections are made to ensure that all of the connections correspond to the battery ground polarity of the truck.
2. Booster batteries must be connected properly. Make sure the positive cable of the booster battery is connected to the positive terminal of the battery which is getting the boost.
3. Disconnect the battery cables before using a fast charger; the charger has a tendency to force current through the diodes in the opposite direction for which they were designed.
4. Never use a fast charger as a booster for starting the truck.
5. Never disconnect the voltage regulator while the engine is running, unless as noted for testing purposes.
6. Do not ground the alternator output terminal.
7. Do not operate the alternator on an open circuit with the field energized.
8. Do not attempt to polarize the alternator.
9. Disconnect the battery cables and remove

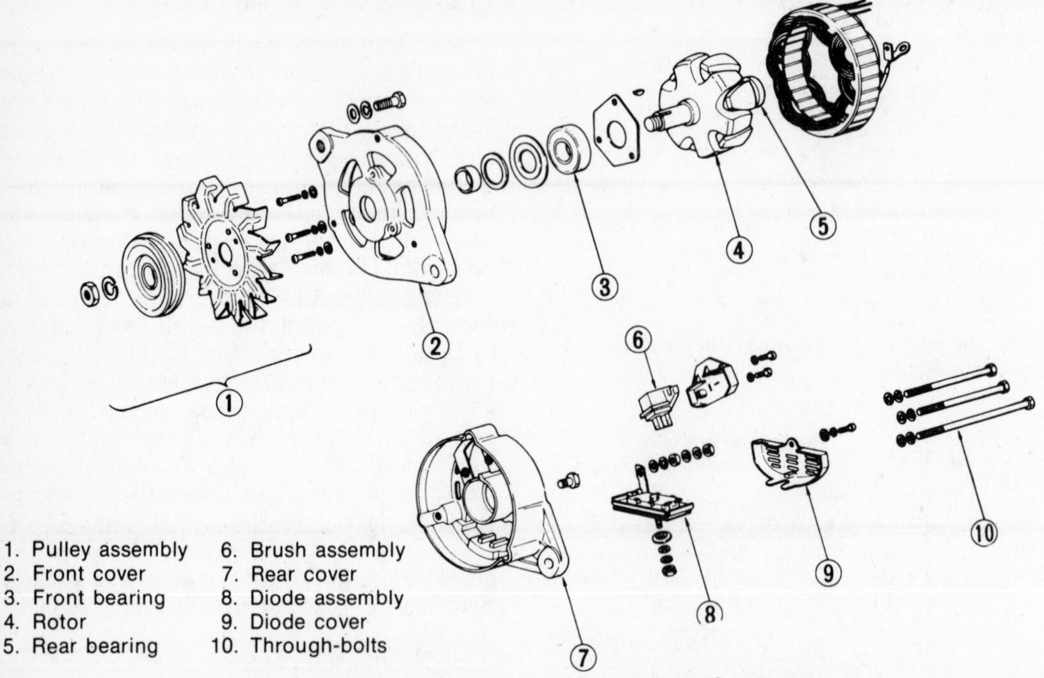

1. Pulley assembly
2. Front cover
3. Front bearing
4. Rotor
5. Rear bearing
6. Brush assembly
7. Rear cover
8. Diode assembly
9. Diode cover
10. Through-bolts

Exploded view of the alternator—1970–77 (LT-135-13B shown)

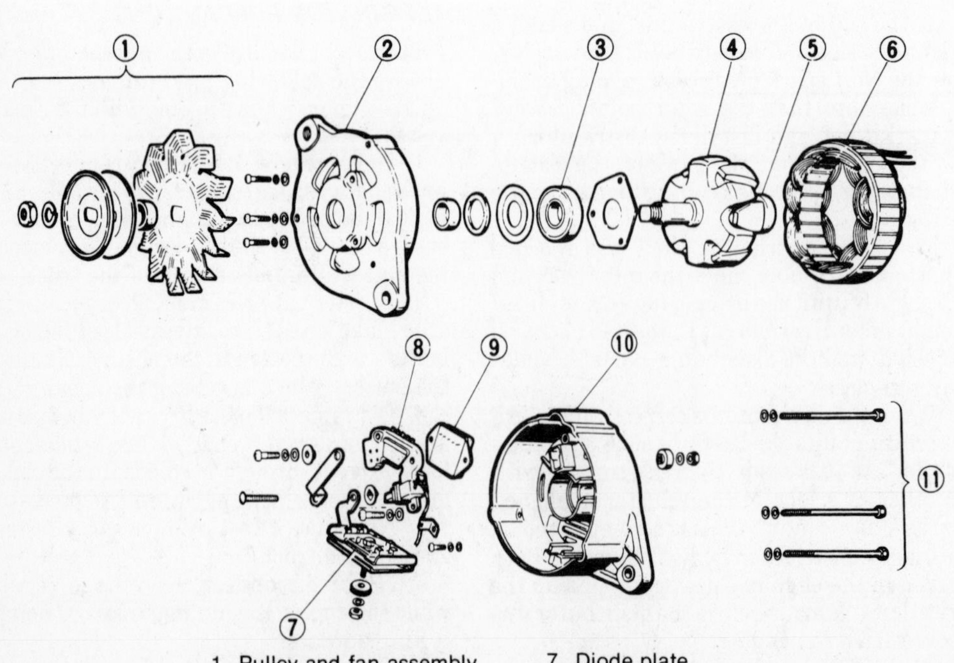

1. Pulley and fan assembly
2. Front cover
3. Front bearing
4. Rotor
5. Rear bearing
6. Stator
7. Diode plate
8. Brush assembly
9. Regulator
10. Rear cover
11. Through bolts

Exploded view of the alternator—1978–80

the alternator before using an electric arc welder on the truck.

10. Protect the alternator from excessive moisture. If the engine is to be steam cleaned, cover or remove the alternator.

REMOVAL AND INSTALLATION

NOTE: *On some models, the alternator is mounted very low on the engine. On these models, it may be necessary to remove the*

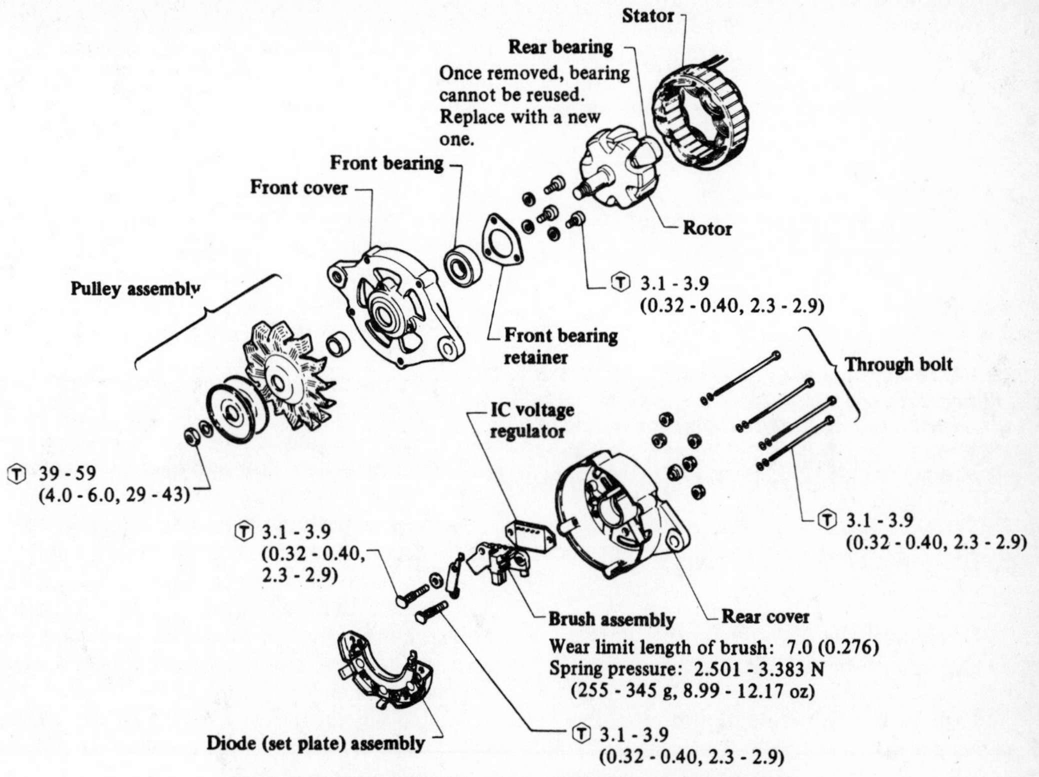

Stator
Rear bearing
Once removed, bearing cannot be reused. Replace with a new one.
Front bearing
Front cover
Rotor
Pulley assembly
Ⓣ 3.1 - 3.9 (0.32 - 0.40, 2.3 - 2.9)
Front bearing retainer
Through bolt
IC voltage regulator
Ⓣ 39 - 59 (4.0 - 6.0, 29 - 43)
Ⓣ 3.1 - 3.9 (0.32 - 0.40, 2.3 - 2.9)
Ⓣ 3.1 - 3.9 (0.32 - 0.40, 2.3 - 2.9)
Brush assembly
Rear cover
Wear limit length of brush: 7.0 (0.276)
Spring pressure: 2.501 - 3.383 N (255 - 345 g, 8.99 - 12.17 oz)
Diode (set plate) assembly
Ⓣ 3.1 - 3.9 (0.32 - 0.40, 2.3 - 2.9)

Exploded view of the alternator—1981–89 gasoline engines

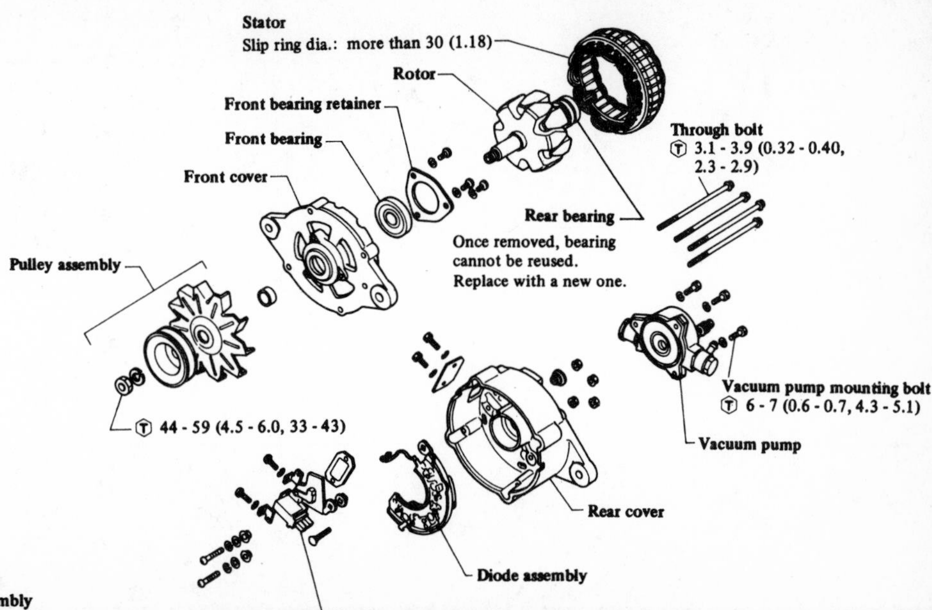

Exploded view of the alternator—SD22 engines

gravel shield and work from beneath the truck in order to gain access to the alternator.

1. Disconnect the negative battery cable.
2. Remove the alternator pivot bolt. Push the alternator in and remove the drive belt.
3. Pull back the rubber boots and disconnect the wiring from the back of the alternator.
4. Remove the alternator mounting bolt and then withdraw the alternator from its bracket.
5. Position the alternator in its mounting bracket and lightly tighten the mounting and adjusting bolts.
6. Connect the electrical leads at the rear of the alternator.
7. Adjust the belt tension as detailed in Chapter 1.

Regulator

All 1970-77 models are equipped with a separate, adjustable regulator. 1978-89 models are equipped with a transistorized regulator which is attached to the brush assembly on the side of the alternator housing. If faulty, it must be replaced; there are no adjustments which can be made.

REMOVAL AND INSTALLATION

1970-77

1. Disconnect the negative battery cable.
2. Disconnect the wiring harness connector at the back of the regulator.
3. Remove the regulator mounting bolts.
4. Remove the regulator.
5. Install the regulator and tighten the mounting bolts.
6. Connect the wiring harness and the negative battery cable.

1978-89

The transistorized regulator is soldered to the brush assembly inside the alternator. It is non-adjustable, and must be replaced together with the brush assembly if faulty.

1. Remove the alternator.
2. Remove the thru-bolts and separate the front cover from the stator housing.
3. Unsolder the wire connecting the diode plate to brush at the brush terminal.
4. Remove the bolt retaining the diode plate to the rear cover.
5. Remove the nut securing the battery terminal bolt.
6. Lift the stator slightly, together with the diode plate, to gain access to the diode plate screw. Remove the screw.
7. Separate the stator and diode, and remove the brush and regulator assembly.
8. On assembly, apply soldering heat sparingly, carrying out the operation as quickly as possible, to avoid heat damage to transistors and diodes. Before assembling the alternator halves, bend a piece of wire into an L-shape and slip it through the rear cover next to the brushes. Use the wire to hold the brushes in a retracted position until the case halves are as-

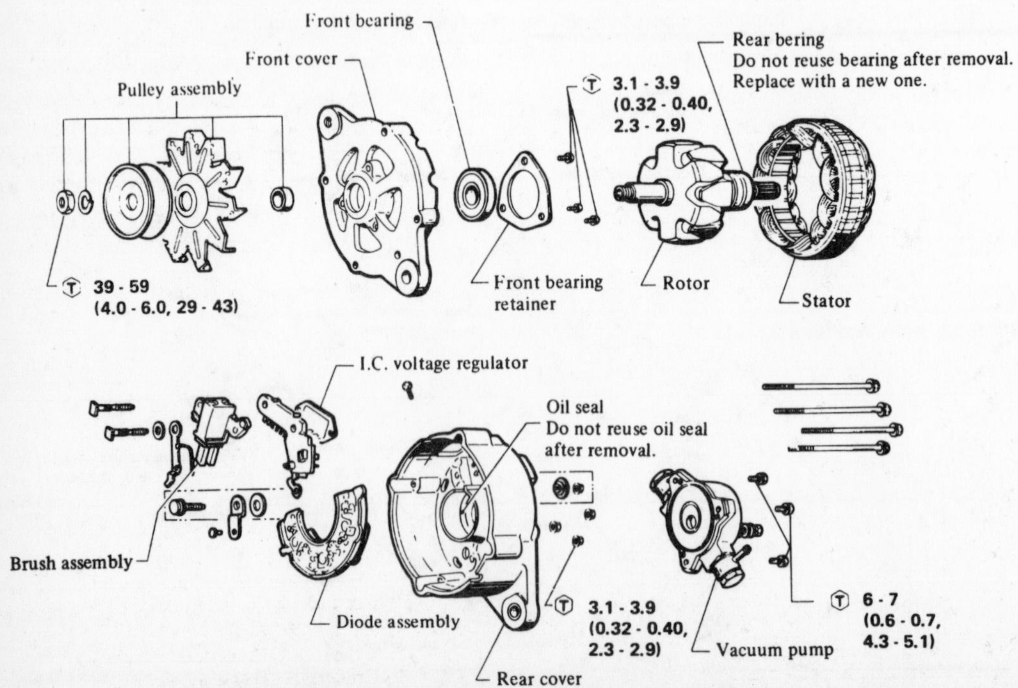

Exploded view of the alternator—SD25 engines

sembled. Remove the wire carefully, to prevent damage to the slip rings.

ADJUSTMENT

1970-72

1. Operate the alternator long enough to raise the temperature of the regulator to normal operating temperature.
2. Adjust the back gap of the voltage regulator coil by loosening the armature set screw and sliding the armature. The gap should be 0.035–0.039 in. (0.89–1.00mm).
3. Adjust the air gap of the voltage regulator coil by bending the primary contact support to the right or left with a pair of needlenose pliers. The gap should be 0.032–0.047 in. (0.80–1.20mm).
4. Adjust the point gap by bending the secondary contact support to the right or left with pliers. The gap should be 0.016–0.020 in. (0.40–0.50mm).
5. Adjust the pilot lamp relay coil yoke gap by loosening the armature set screw, adjusting the gap and retightening the set screw. The gap should be 0.008 in. (0.20mm).
6. Adjust the pilot lamp relay coil air gap by loosening the contact set screw and inserting a screwdriver in the hole provided and moving the points up or down. The gap should be 0.020–0.024 in. (0.50–0.60mm).
7. Adjust the pilot lamp relay coil point gap by loosening the contact point retaining screw and inserting a screwdriver in the hole provided and moving the point contact either up or down. The gap should be between 0.016–0.020 in.(0.40–0.50mm).
8. Adjust the voltage valve by bending the stopper on the voltage regulator coil. The regulated voltage should be between 14–15 volts at 4000 alternator rpm.

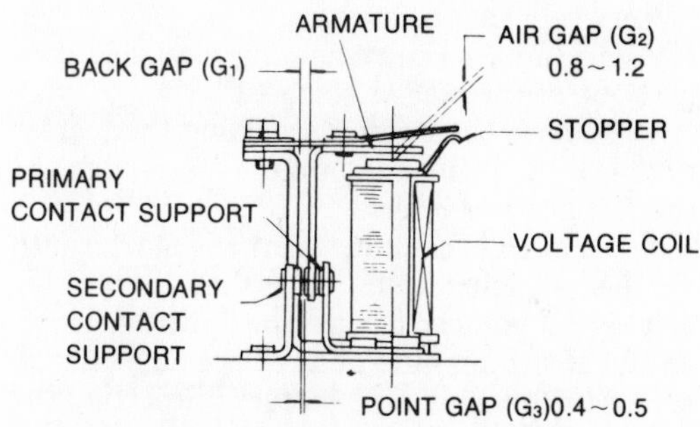

Voltage regulator coil adjustment—1970-72

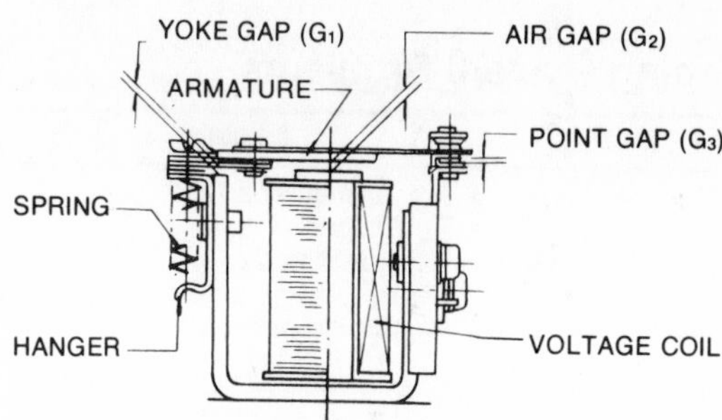

Pilot lamp relay adjustment—1970-72

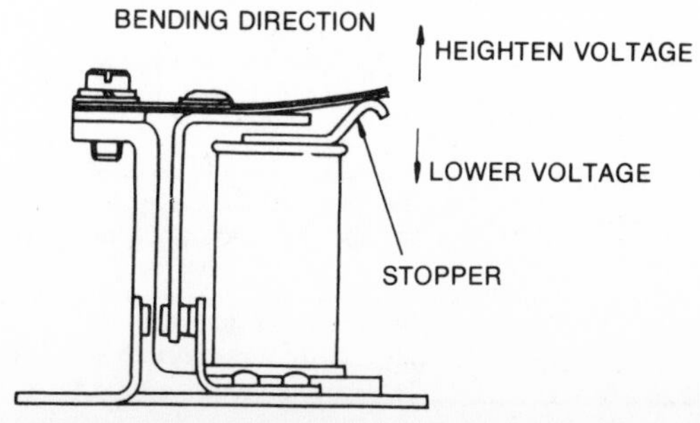

Voltage value adjustment—1970-72

1973-77

1. Adjust the voltage regulator core gap by loosening the screw which is used to secure the contact set on the yoke, and move the contact up or down as necessary. Retighten the screw. The gap should be 0.024–0.039 in. (0.60–1.00mm).
2. Adjust the point gap of the voltage regulator coil by loosening the screw used to secure the upper contact and move the upper contact up or down. The gap should be 0.012–0.016 in. (0.30–0.40mm) for 1973-75 models or 0.014–0.018 in. (0.35–0.45mm) for 1976-77 models.
3. The core gap and point gap on the charge relay coil is or are adjusted in the same manner as previously outlined for the voltage regulator coil. The core gap is to be set at 0.032–0.039 in. (0.80–1.00mm) and the point gap adjusted to 0.016–0.024 in. (0.40–0.60mm).

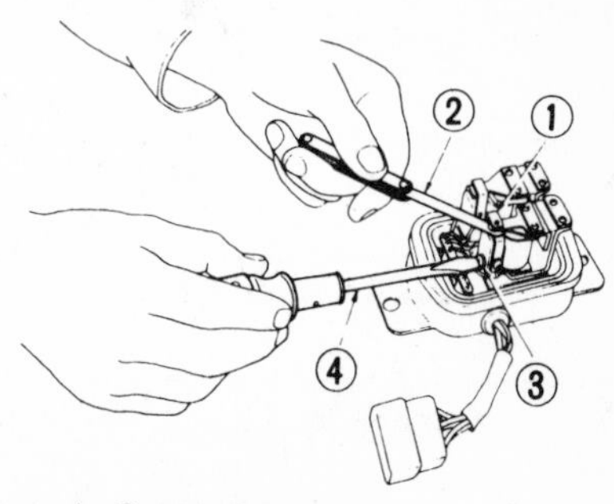

1. Contact set
2. Thickness gauge
3. 4 mm (0.1575 in.) dia. screw
4. Crosshead screwdriver

Voltage regulator core gap adjustment—1973-77

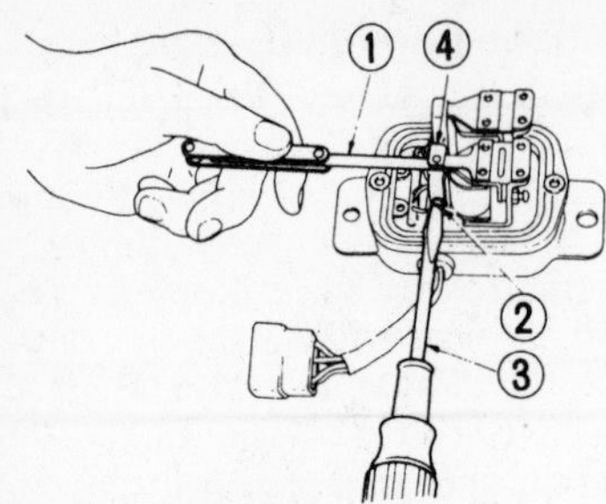

1. Thickness gauge
2. 3 mm (0.1181 in.) dia. screw
3. Crosshead screwdriver
4. Upper contact

Voltage regulator coil point gap adjustment—1973–77

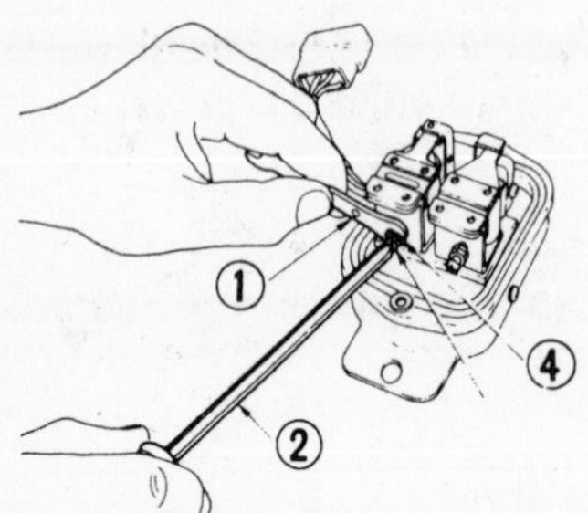

1. Wrench
2. Phillips screwdriver
3. Adjusting screw
4. Locknut

Regulated voltage adjustment—1973–77

4. The regulated voltage is adjusted by loosening the locknut and turning the adjusting screw clockwise to increase, or counterclockwise to decrease the regulated voltage. The voltage should be between 14.3–15.3 volts at 68°F (20°C).

1978-89

Regulators on these models are not adjustable.

Starter

REMOVAL AND INSTALLATION

NOTE: *On some models with automatic transmission, it may be necessary to disconnect the throttle rod.*

1. Disconnect the negative (–) battery cable at the battery, then disconnect the positive (+) battery cable at the starter.
2. Disconnect the remaining electrical connections at the starter solenoid.
3. Remove the two nuts holding the starter to the bell housing and pull the starter toward the front of the vehicle.
4. To install the unit, insert the starter into the bell housing being sure that the starter drive is not jammed against the flywheel. Tighten the attaching nuts and replace all electrical connections making the battery connection the last.

Troubleshooting Basic Charging System Problems

Problem	Cause	Solution
Noisy alternator	• Loose mountings • Loose drive pulley • Worn bearings • Brush noise • Internal circuits shorted (High pitched whine)	• Tighten mounting bolts • Tighten pulley • Replace alternator • Replace alternator • Replace alternator
Squeal when starting engine or accelerating	• Glazed or loose belt	• Replace or adjust belt
Indicator light remains on or ammeter indicates discharge (engine running)	• Broken fan belt • Broken or disconnected wires • Internal alternator problems • Defective voltage regulator	• Install belt • Repair or connect wiring • Replace alternator • Replace voltage regulator
Car light bulbs continually burn out—battery needs water continually	• Alternator/regulator overcharging	• Replace voltage regulator/alternator
Car lights flare on acceleration	• Battery low • Internal alternator/regulator problems	• Charge or replace battery • Replace alternator/regulator
Low voltage output (alternator light flickers continually or ammeter needle wanders)	• Loose or worn belt • Dirty or corroded connections • Internal alternator/regulator problems	• Replace or adjust belt • Clean or replace connections • Replace alternator or regulator

OVERHAUL

Solenoid Replacement

1. Remove the starter.
2. Unscrew the two solenoid switch (magnetic switch) retaining screws.
3. Remove the solenoid. In order to unhook the solenoid from the starter drive lever, lift it up at the same time that you are pulling it out of the starter housing.
4. Installation is in the reverse order of removal. Make sure that the solenoid switch is properly engaged with the drive lever before tightening the mounting screws.

Brush Replacement

NON-REDUCTION GEAR TYPE

1. Remove the starter.
2. Remove the solenoid (magnetic switch).
3. Remove the two end frame cap mounting bolts and remove the end frame cap.
4. Remove the O-ring and lock plate from the armature shaft groove and then slide the shims off the shaft.

Alternator and Regulator Specifications

	Alternator		Voltage Regulator						
			Charge Indicator Relay			Voltage Regulator			
Year	Manufacturer and/or Part Number	Output @ Generator rpm	Back Gap (in.)	Air Gap (in.)	Point Gap (in.)	Back Gap (in.)	Air Gap (in.)	Point Gap (in.)	Regulated Voltage
1970–72	Hitachi LT130–41	22 Amp @ 2500 (14 volts)	0.007	0.022	0.018	0.037	0.039	0.014	14–15
1973	Hitachi LT135–13B	28 Amp @ 2500 (14 volts)	—	0.035	0.020	—	0.032	0.014	14–15
1974	Hitachi LT135–13B	28 Amp @ 2500 (14 volts)	—	0.035	0.020	—	0.032	0.014	14–15
1975	Hitachi LT135–13B LT135–19B ①	28 Amp @ 2500 (14 volts)	—	0.035	0.020	—	0.032	0.014	14–15
1976	Hitachi LT135–13B LT135–19B ①	28 @ 2500	—	0.035	0.020	—	0.032	0.016	14.3–15.3
1977	Hitachi LT135–36B LT138–01B ①	28 @ 2500 30 @ 2500	—	0.035	0.020	—	0.032	0.016	14.3–15.3
1978–80	Hitachi LR135–44 LR138–01 ①	27.5 @ 2500 30.0 @ 2500	—Transistorized Non-Adjustable Relay—						14.4–15.0
1981–84	Hitachi LR150–98 LR160–78 LR150–52 LR160–78	50 @ 5000 60 @ 5000 50 @ 5000 60 @ 5000	—Transistorized Non-Adjustable Relay—						14.4–15.0
1985–89	Hitachi LR150–98B LR150–197B LR160–78B LR160–140B LR150–177 LR150–194B LR160–120 LR160–151 LR160–154 LR160–422B LR150–403 LR155–401	50 @ 5000 50 @ 5000 60 @ 5000 60 @ 5000 50 @ 5000 50 @ 5000 60 @ 5000 60 @ 5000 60 @ 5000 60 @ 5000 50 @ 5000 55 @ 5000	—Transistorized Non-Adjustable Relay—						14.4–15.0 ②

① With air conditioning —Non applicable
② LR160–151: 14.1–14.7

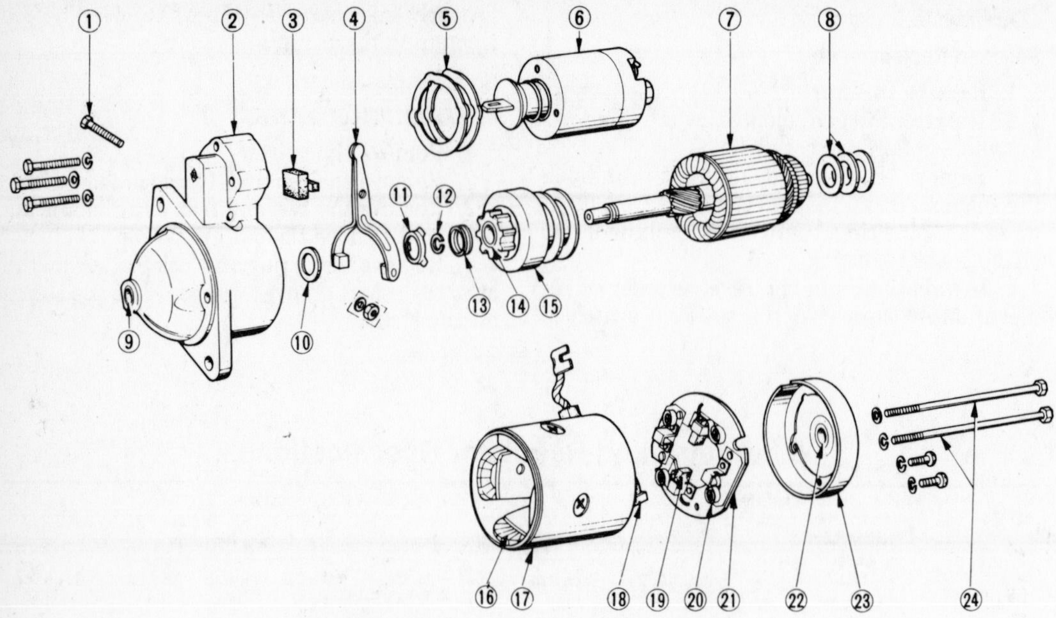

1. Shift lever pin
2. Gear case
3. Dust cover
4. Shift lever
5. Dust cover
6. Magnetic switch
7. Armature
8. Thrust washer
9. Metal
10. Thrust washer
11. Stopper washer
12. Stopper clip
13. Pinion stopper
14. Pinion
15. Overrunning clutch
16. Field coil
17. Yoke
18. Brush (+)
19. Brush (−)
20. Brush spring
21. Brush holder
22. Metal
23. Rear cover
24. Through-bolt

Exploded view of a starter—non-reduction gear

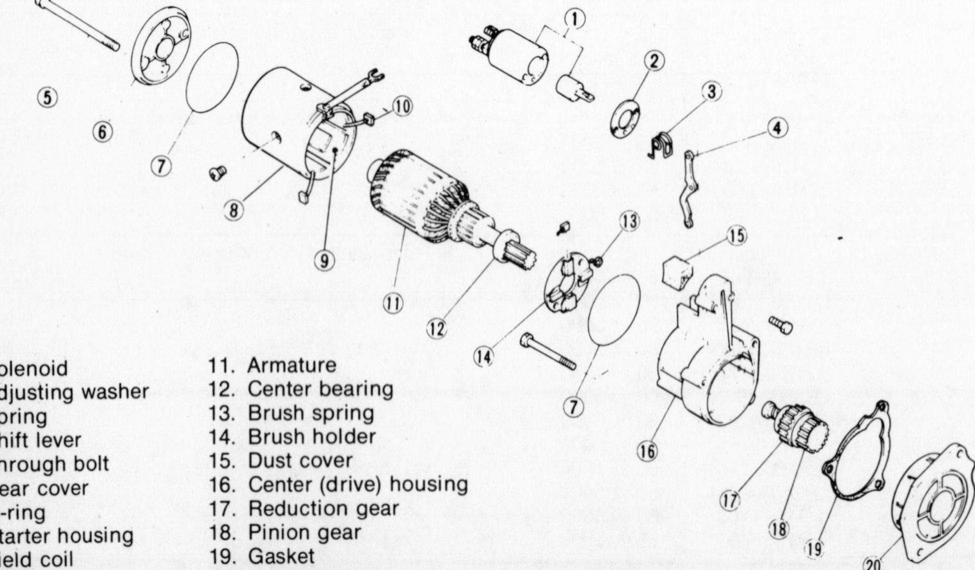

1. Solenoid
2. Adjusting washer
3. Spring
4. Shift lever
5. Through bolt
6. Rear cover
7. O-ring
8. Starter housing
9. Field coil
10. Brush
11. Armature
12. Center bearing
13. Brush spring
14. Brush holder
15. Dust cover
16. Center (drive) housing
17. Reduction gear
18. Pinion gear
19. Gasket
20. Front cover

Exploded view of a starter—reduction gear

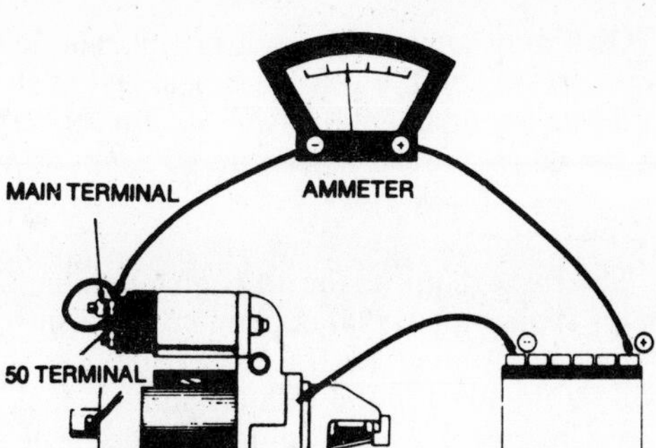

Simplified no-load test

5. Unscrew the two long housing screws (they are found at the front of the starter) and carefully pull off the end plate.
6. Using a screwdriver, separate the brushes from the brush holder.
7. Slide the brush holder off of the armature shaft.
8. Crush the old brushes off of the copper braid and file away any remaining solder.
9. Fit the new brushes to the braid and spread the braid slightly.

NOTE: *Use a soldering iron of at least 250 watts.*

10. Using a radio-grade solder, solder the brush to the braid. Grip the copper braid with flat pliers to prevent the solder from flowing down its length.
11. File off any extra solder and then repeat the procedure for the remaining three brushes.
12. Installation is in the reverse order of removal.

NOTE: *When installing the brush holder, make sure that the brushes line up properly.*

REDUCTION GEAR TYPE

1. Remove the starter. Remove the solenoid.
2. Remove the thru-bolts and the rear cover. The rear cover can be pried off with a screwdriver, but be careful not to damage the O-ring.
3. Remove the starter housing, armature, and brush holder from the center housing. They can be removed as an assembly.
4. Remove the positive side brush from its holder. The positive brush is insulated from the brush holder, and its lead wire is connected to the field coil.
5. Carefully lift the negative brush from the commutator and remove it form the holder.
6. Installation is in the reverse order of removal.

Starter Drive Replacement

NON-REDUCTION GEAR TYPE

1. With the starter motor removed from the vehicle, remove the solenoid from the starter.
2. Remove the two through-bolts and separate the gear case from the yoke housing.
3. Remove the pinion stopper clip and the pinion stopper.
4. Slide the starter drive off the armature shaft.
5. Install the starter drive and reassemble the starter in the reverse order of removal.

REDUCTION GEAR TYPE

1. Remove the starter.
2. Remove the solenoid and the shift lever.
3. Remove the bolts securing the center housing to the front cover and separate the parts.
4. Remove the gears and starter drive.
5. Installation is in the reverse order of removal.

Battery

Refer to Chapter 1 for details on battery maintenance.

REMOVAL AND INSTALLATION

1. Disconnect the negative battery cable from the terminal, then disconnect the positive cable. Special pullers are available to remove the clamps.

NOTE: *To avoid sparks, always disconnect the negative cable first and reconnect it last.*

2. Unscrew and remove the battery holddown clamp.
3. Remove the battery, being careful not to spill any of the acid.

NOTE: *Spilled acid can be neutralized with a baking soda and water solution. If you somehow get acid into your eyes, flush it out with lots of clean water and get to a doctor as quickly as possible.*

4. Clean the battery posts thoroughly before reinstalling or when installing a new one.
5. Clean the cable clamps using the special tools or a wire brush, both inside and out.
6. Install the battery, and the holddown clamp. Connect the positive and then the negative cable. Do not hammer them into place. The terminals should be coated with grease to prevent corrosion.

CAUTION: *Make absolutely sure that the battery is connected properly before you turn on the ignition switch. Reversed polarity can burn out our alternator and regulator in a matter of seconds.*

ENGINE MECHANICAL

Engine Overhaul Tips

Most engine overhaul procedures are fairly standard. In addition to specific parts replacement procedures and complete specifications for your individual engine, this chapter also is a guide to accept rebuilding procedures. Examples of standard rebuilding practice are shown and should be used along with specific details concerning your particular engine.

Competent and accurate machine shop services will ensure maximum performance, reliability and engine life. Procedures marked with the symbol shown above should be performed by a competent machine shop, and are provided so that you will be familiar with the procedures necessary to a successful overhaul.

In most instances it is more profitable for the do-it-yourself mechanic to remove, clean and inspect the component, buy the necessary parts and deliver these to a shop for actual machine work.

On the other hand, much of the rebuilding work (crankshaft, block, bearings, piston rods, and other components) is well within the scope of the do-it-yourself mechanic.

TOOLS

The tools required for an engine overhaul or parts replacement will depend on the depth of your involvement. With a few exceptions, they will be the tools found in a mechanic's tool kit (see Chapter 1). More in-depth work will require any or all of the following:

- a dial indicator (reading in thousandths) mounted on a universal base
- micrometers and telescope gauges
- jaw and screw type pullers
- scraper
- valve spring compressor

Battery and Starter Specifications

		Battery			Starter						
					Lock Test			No Load Test			Brush Spring Tension
Year	Engine	Amp Hour Capacity	Volts	Ground	Amps	Volts	Torque (ft. lbs.)	Amps	Volts	RPM	(oz)
1970–72	L16	①	12	Neg	350	10.5	7.95	60	12	7000+ ②	28
1973	L16	①	12	Neg	Not Recommended			60	12	7000+ ②	56
1973–74	L18	①	12	Neg	Not Recommended			60	12	7000+ ②	56
1975–80	L20B	①	12	Neg	Not Recommended			60	12	7000+ ②	56
1981–83	Z20, 22, 24	①	12	Neg	Not Recommended			60 ③	11.5 ④	6000–7000	56
	SD22, 25	①	12	Neg	800	5.0	21.0	55	12	6500	123.2
1984–86	Z20, Z24, SD25 (720 series)	⑤	12	Neg	Not Recommended			⑥	⑦	⑧	⑨
1986–89	Z24i, VG30i, SD25 (D21 series)	⑩	12	Neg	Not Recommended			⑪	⑫	⑬	⑭

① 40, 50, or 69 amp hour batteries were available
② 6000+ if equipped with automatic transmission
③ Canada: 100
④ Canada: 11.0
⑤ U.S.A.: 60 amp., (65 optional)
Canada: 65 amp.
Diesel: 80 amp.
⑥ U.S.A.: 60 amp.
Canada: 100 amp.
Diesel: 150 amp.
⑦ U.S.A.: 11.5 volt
Canada: 11 volt
Diesel: 12 volt
⑧ U.S.A. w/A.T.: 6,000 rpm
U.S.A. w/M.T.: 7,000 rpm
Canada: 3,900 rpm
Diesel: 3,500 rpm
⑨ U.S.A.: 72 oz.
Canada: 64 oz.
Diesel: 128 oz.
⑩ U.S.A.: 60 amp
Canada: Z24i—65 amp.,
VG30i—70 amp.,
Diesel—65 amp.
⑪ VG30i eng: 90 amp.
2WD (4 cyl.): 60 amp.
4WD (4 cyl.): 100 amp.
Diesel: 160 amp.
⑫ VG30i eng: 11.0
2WD (4 cyl.): 11.5
4WD (4 cyl.): 11.0
Diesel: 11.0
⑬ VG30i: 2,650 rpm
2WD w/M.T: 7,000 rpm
2WD w/A.T: 6,000 rpm
4WD: 3,900 rpm
Diesel: 3,900 rpm
⑭ 2WD: 72 oz.
4WD: 64 oz.
Diesel: 104 oz.

- ring groove cleaner
- piston ring expander and compressor
- ridge reamer
- cylinder hone or glaze breaker
- Plastigage®
- engine stand

Use of most of these tools is illustrated in this chapter. Many can be rented for a one-time use from a local parts jobber or tool supply house specializing in automotive work.

Occasionally, the use of special tools is called for. See the information on Special Tools and Safety Notice in the front of this book before substituting another tool.

INSPECTION TECHNIQUES

Procedures and specifications are given in this chapter for inspecting, cleaning and assessing the wear limits of most major components. Other procedures such as Magnaflux® and Zyglo® can be used to locate material flaws and stress cracks. Magnaflux® is a magnetic process applicable only to ferrous materials. The Zyglo® process coats the material with a flourescent dye penetrant and can be used on any material Check for suspected surface cracks can be more readily made using spot check dye. The dye is sprayed onto the suspected area, wiped off and the area sprayed with a developer. Cracks will show up brightly.

OVERHAUL TIPS

Aluminum has become extremely popular for use in engines, due to its low weight. Observe the following precautions when handling aluminum parts:

- Never hot tank aluminum parts (the

Troubleshooting Basic Starting System Problems

Problem	Cause	Solution
Starter motor rotates engine slowly	• Battery charge low or battery defective	• Charge or replace battery
	• Defective circuit between battery and starter motor	• Clean and tighten, or replace cables
	• Low load current	• Bench-test starter motor. Inspect for worn brushes and weak brush springs.
	• High load current	• Bench-test starter motor. Check engine for friction, drag or coolant in cylinders. Check ring gear-to-pinion gear clearance.
Starter motor will not rotate engine	• Battery charge low or battery defective	• Charge or replace battery
	• Faulty solenoid	• Check solenoid ground. Repair or replace as necessary.
	• Damage drive pinion gear or ring gear	• Replace damaged gear(s)
	• Starter motor engagement weak	• Bench-test starter motor
	• Starter motor rotates slowly with high load current	• Inspect drive yoke pull-down and point gap, check for worn end bushings, check ring gear clearance
	• Engine seized	• Repair engine
Starter motor drive will not engage (solenoid known to be good)	• Defective contact point assembly	• Repair or replace contact point assembly
	• Inadequate contact point assembly ground	• Repair connection at ground screw
	• Defective hold-in coil	• Replace field winding assembly
Starter motor drive will not disengage	• Starter motor loose on flywheel housing	• Tighten mounting bolts
	• Worn drive end busing	• Replace bushing
	• Damaged ring gear teeth	• Replace ring gear or driveplate
	• Drive yoke return spring broken or missing	• Replace spring
Starter motor drive disengages prematurely	• Weak drive assembly thrust spring	• Replace drive mechanism
	• Hold-in coil defective	• Replace field winding assembly
Low load current	• Worn brushes	• Replace brushes
	• Weak brush springs	• Replace springs

caustic hot-tank solution will eat the aluminum.

- Remove all aluminum parts (identification tag, etc.) from engine parts prior to the tanking.
- Always coat threads lightly with engine oil or antiseize compounds before installation, to prevent seizure.
- Never overtorque bolts or spark plugs especially in aluminum threads.

Stripped threads in any component can be repaired using any of several commercial repair kits (Heli-Coil®, Microdot®, Keenserts®, etc.).

When assembling the engine, any parts that will be frictional contact must be prelubed to provide lubrication at initial start up. Any product specifically formulated for this purpose can be used, but engine oil is not recommended as a prelube.

When semipermanent (locked, but removable) installation of bolts or nuts is desired, threads should be cleaned and coated with Loctite® or other similar, commercial nonhardening sealant.

REPAIRING DAMAGED THREADS

Several methods of repairing damaged threads are available. Heli-Coil® (shown here), Keenserts® and Microdot® are among the most widely used. All involve basically the same principle, drilling out stripped threads, tapping the hole and installing a prewound insert, making welding, plugging and oversize fasteners unnecessary.

Two types of thread repair inserts are usually supplied: a standard type for most Inch Coarse, Inch Fine, Metric Course and Metric Fine thread sizes and a spark lug type to fit most spark plug port sizes. Consult the individual manufacturer's catalog to determine exact applications. Typical thread repair kits will contain a selection of prewound threaded inserts, a tap (corresponding to the outside diameter threads of the insert) and an installation tool.

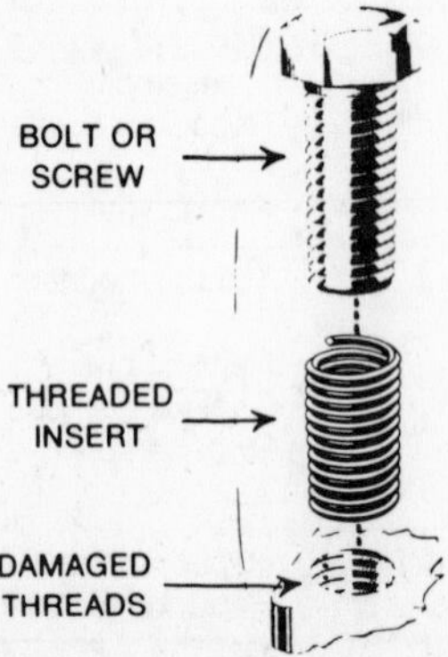

Damaged bolt holes can be repaired with thread repair inserts

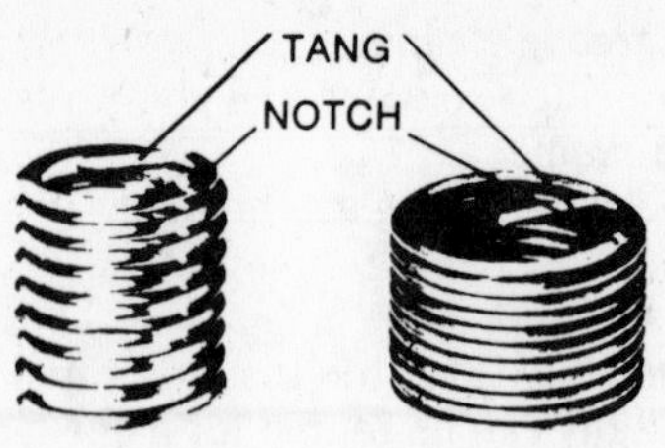

Standard thread repair insert (left) and spark plug thread insert (right)

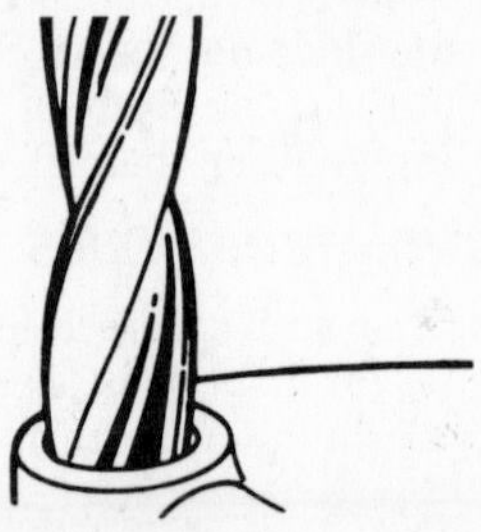

Drill out the damaged threads with specified drill. Drill completely through the hole or to the bottom of a blind hole

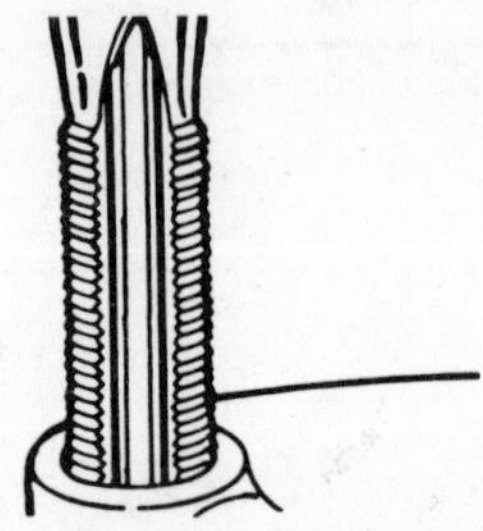

With the tap supplied, tap the hole to receive the thread insert. Keep the tap well oiled and back it out frequently to avoid clogging the threads

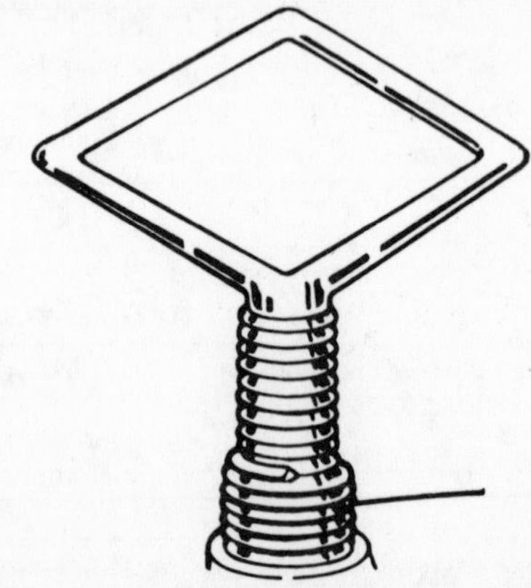

Screw the threaded insert onto the installation tool until the tang engages the slot. Screw the insert into the tapped hole until it is ¼–½ turn below the top surface. After installation break off the tang with a hammer and punch

Spark plug inserts usually differ because they require a tap equipped with pilot threads and a combined reamer/tap section. Most manufacturers also supply blister packed thread repair inserts separately in addition to a master kit containing a variety of taps and inserts plus installation tools.

Before effecting a repair to a threaded hole, remove any snapped, broken or damaged bolts or studs. Penetrating oil can be used to free frozen threads; the offending item can be removed with locking pliers or with a screw or stud extractor. After the hole is clear, the thread can be repaired, as follows:

Checking Engine Compression

A noticeable lack of engine power, excessive oil consumption and/or poor fuel mileage measured over an extended period are all indicators of internal engine war. Worn piston rings, scored or worn cylinder bores, blown head gaskets, sticking or burnt valves and worn valve seats are all possible culprits here. A check of each cylinder's compression will help you locate the problems.

As mentioned in the Tools and Equipment section of Chapter 1, a screw-in type compression gauge is more accurate that the type you simply hold against the spark plug hole, although it takes slightly longer to use. It's worth it to obtain a more accurate reading. Follow the procedures below for gasoline and diesel engined trucks.

GASOLINE ENGINES

1. Warm up the engine to normal operating temperature.
2. Remove all spark plugs.
3. Disconnect the high tension lead from the ignition coil.
4. On carbureted trucks, fully open the throttle either by operating the carburetor throttle linkage by hand or by having an assistant floor the accelerator pedal. On fuel injected trucks, disconnect the cold start valve and all injector connections.
5. Screw the compression gauge into the No. 1 spark plug hole until the fitting is snug.

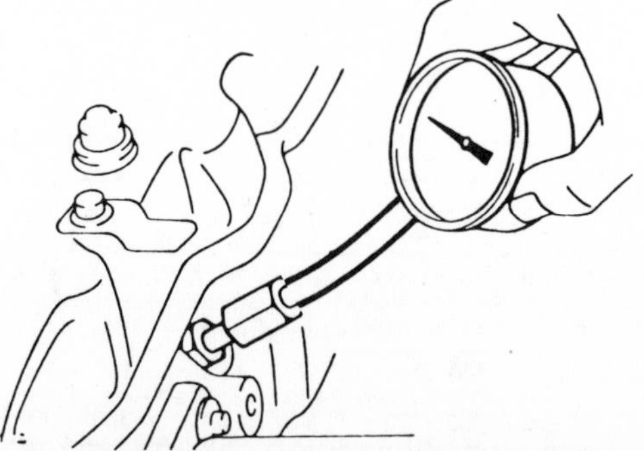

The screw-in type compression gauge is more accurate

NOTE: *Be careful not to crossthread the plug hole. On aluminum cylinder heads use extra care, as the threads in these heads are easily ruined.*

6. Ask an assistant to depress the accelerator pedal fully on both carbureted and fuel injected trucks. Then, while you read the compression gauge, ask the assistant to crank the engine two or three times in short bursts using the ignition switch.
7. Read the compression gauge at the end of each series of cranks, and record the highest of these readings. Repeat this procedure for each of the engine's cylinders. Compare the highest reading of each cylinder to the compression pressure specification in the Tune-Up Specifications chart in Chapter 2. The specs in this chart are maximum values.

A cylinders compression pressure is usually acceptable if it is not less than 80% of maximum. The difference between each cylinder should be no more than 12–14 lbs.

8. If a cylinder is unusually low, pour a tablespoon of clean engine oil into the cylinder through the spark plug hole and repeat the compression test. If the compression comes up after adding the oil, it appears that the cylinder's piston rings or bore are damaged or worn. If the pressure remains low, the valves may not be seating properly (a valve job is needed), or the head gasket may be blown near that cylinder. If compression in any two adjacent cylinders is low, and if the addition of oil doesn't help the compression, there is leakage past the head gasket. Oil and coolant water in the combustion chamber can result from this problem. There may be evidence of water droplets on the engine dipstick when a had gasket has blown.

DIESEL ENGINES

Checking cylinder compression on diesel engines is basically the same procedure as on gasoline engines except for the following:

1. A special compression gauge adaptor suitable for diesel engines (because these engines have much greater compression pressures) must be used.

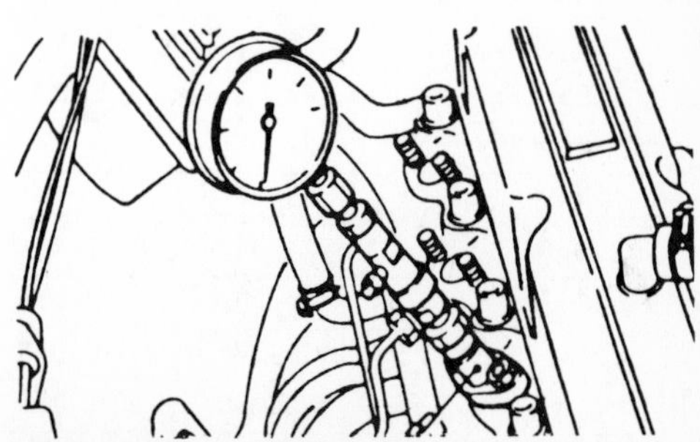

Diesel engines require a special compression gauge adaptor

Standard Torque Specifications and Fastener Markings

In the absence of specific torques, the following chart can be used as a guide to the maximum safe torque of a particular size/grade of fastener.

- There is no torque difference for fine or coarse threads.
- Torque values are based on clean, dry threads. Reduce the value by 10% if threads are oiled prior to assembly.
- The torque required for aluminuın components or fasteners is considerably less.

U.S. Bolts

SAE Grade Number	1 or 2			5			6 or 7		
Number of lines always 2 less than the grade number.									
Bolt Size	Maximum Torque			Maximum Torque			Maximum Torque		
(Inches)—(Thread)	Ft./Lbs.	Kgm	Nm	Ft./Lbs.	Kgm	Nm	Ft./Lbs.	Kgm	Nm
¼—20	5	0.7	6.8	8	1.1	10.8	10	1.4	13.5
—28	6	0.8	8.1	10	1.4	13.6			
5/16—18	11	1.5	14.9	17	2.3	23.0	19	2.6	25.8
—24	13	1.8	17.6	19	2.6	25.7			
⅜—16	18	2.5	24.4	31	4.3	42.0	34	4.7	46.0
—24	20	2.75	27.1	35	4.8	47.5			
7/16—14	28	3.8	37.0	49	6.8	66.4	55	7.6	74.5
—20	30	4.2	40.7	55	7.6	74.5			
½—13	39	5.4	52.8	75	10.4	101.7	85	11.75	115.2
—20	41	5.7	55.6	85	11.7	115.2			
9/16—12	51	7.0	69.2	110	15.2	149.1	120	16.6	162.7
—18	55	7.6	74.5	120	16.6	162.7			
⅝—11	83	11.5	112.5	150	20.7	203.3	167	23.0	226.5
—18	95	13.1	128.8	170	23.5	230.5			
¾—10	105	14.5	142.3	270	37.3	366.0	280	38.7	379.6
—16	115	15.9	155.9	295	40.8	400.0			
⅞— 9	160	22.1	216.9	395	54.6	535.5	440	60.9	596.5
—14	175	24.2	237.2	435	60.1	589.7			
1— 8	236	32.5	318.6	590	81.6	799.9	660	91.3	894.8
—14	250	34.6	338.9	660	91.3	849.8			

Metric Bolts

Relative Strength Marking	4.6, 4.8			8.8		
Bolt Markings						
Bolt Size	Maximum Torque			Maximum Torque		
Thread Size x Pitch (mm)	Ft./Lbs.	Kgm	Nm	Ft./Lbs.	Kgm	Nm
6 x 1.0	2–3	.2–.4	3–4	3–6	.4–.8	5–8
8 x 1.25	6–8	.8–1	8–12	9–14	1.2–1.9	13–19
10 x 1.25	12–17	1.5–2.3	16–23	20–29	2.7–4.0	27–39
12 x 1.25	21–32	2.9–4.4	29–43	35–53	4.8–7.3	47–72
14 x 1.5	35–52	4.8–7.1	48–70	57–85	7.8–11.7	77–110
16 x 1.5	51–77	7.0–10.6	67–100	90–120	12.4–16.5	130–160
18 x 1.5	74–110	10.2–15.1	100–150	130–170	17.9–23.4	180–230
20 x 1.5	110–140	15.1–19.3	150–190	190–240	26.2–46.9	160–320
22 x 1.5	150–190	22.0–26.2	200–260	250–320	34.5–44.1	340–430
24 x 1.5	190–240	26.2–46.9	260–320	310–410	42.7–56.5	420–550

2. Remove the injector tubes and remove the injectors from each cylinder.

NOTE: *Don't forget to remove the washer underneath each injector; otherwise, it may get lost when the engine is cranked.*

3. When fitting the compression gauge adaptor to the cylinder head, make sure the bleeder of the gauge (if equipped) is closed.

4. When reinstalling the injector assemblies, install new washers underneath each injector.

General Engine Specifications

Year	Engine Type	Engine Displacement Cu. In. (cc)	Carburetor Type	Horsepower (@ rpm)	Torque @ rpm (ft. lbs.)	Bore x Stroke (in.)	Compression Ratio	Oil Pressure @ rpm (psi)
1970	L16	97.3 (1595)	2 bbl	96 @ 5600	100 @ 3600	3.27 x 2.90	8.5:1	47 @ 2000
1971	L16	97.3 (1595)	2 bbl	96 @ 5600	100 @ 3600	3.27 x 2.90	8.5:1	47 @ 2000
1972	L16	97.3 (1595)	2 bbl	96 @ 5600	100 @ 3600	3.27 x 2.90	8.5:1	47 @ 2000
1973	L16	97.3 (1595)	2 bbl	96 @ 5600	100 @ 3600	3.27 x 2.90	8.5:1	47 @ 2000
	L18	108.0 (1770)	2 bbl	100 @ 5600	100 @ 3600	3.35 x 3.07	8.5:1	47 @ 2000
1974	L18	108.0 (1770)	2 bbl	100 @ 5600	100 @ 3600	3.35 x 3.07	8.5:1	47 @ 2000
1975	L20B	119.1 (1952)	2 bbl	112 @ 5600	108 @ 3200	3.35 x 3.39	8.5:1	53 @ 2000
1976	L20B	119.1 (1952)	2 bbl	112 @ 5600	108 @ 3200	3.35 x 3.39	8.5:1	53 @ 2000
1977	L20B	119.1 (1952)	2 bbl	112 @ 5600	108 @ 3200	3.35 x 3.39	8.5:1	53 @ 2000
1978	L20B	119.1 (1952)	2 bbl	112 @ 5600	108 @ 3200	3.35 x 3.39	8.5:1	53 @ 2000
1979	L20B	119.1 (1952)	2 bbl	97 @ 5600	102 @ 3200	3.35 x 3.39	8.5:1	53 @ 2000
1980	L20B	119.1 (1952)	2 bbl	97 @ 5600	102 @ 3200	3.35 x 3.39	8.5:1	53 @ 2000
1981	Z22	133.5 (2187)	2 bbl	98 @ 4000	117 @ 1800	3.43 x 3.62	8.5:1	60 @ idle
	SD22	132.0 (2164)	DFI	61 @ 4000	102 @ 1800	3.27 x 3.94	21.6:1	60 @ idle
1982	Z22	133.5 (2187)	2 bbl	98 @ 4000	117 @ 1800	3.43 x 3.62	8.5:1	60 @ idle
	SD22	132.0 (2164)	DFI	61 @ 4000	102 @ 1800	3.27 x 3.94	21.6:1	60 @ idle
1983	Z22	133.5 (2187)	2 bbl	98 @ 4000	117 @ 1800	3.43 x 3.62	8.5:1	60 @ idle
	SD22	132.0 (2164)	DFI	61 @ 4000	102 @ 1800	3.27 x 3.94	21.6:1	60 @ idle
1984	Z20	119.0 (1952)	2 bbl	97 @ 5600	102 @ 3200	3.35 x 3.39	9.4:1	60 @ idle
	Z24	146.8 (2389)	2 bbl	103 @ 4800	134 @ 2800	3.50 x 3.78	8.3:1	60 @ idle
	SD25	152.0 (2488)	DFI	70 @ 4000	115 @ 2000	3.50 x 3.94	21.4:1	60 @ idle

General Engine Specifications (cont.)

Year	Engine Type	Engine Displacement Cu. In. (cc)	Carburetor Type	Horsepower (@ rpm)	Torque @ rpm (ft. lbs.)	Bore x Stroke (in.)	Compression Ratio	Oil Pressure @ rpm (psi)
1985	Z20	119.0 (1952)	2 bbl	97 @ 5600	102 @ 3200	3.35 x 3.39	9.4:1	60 @ idle
	Z24	146.8 (2389)	2 bbl	103 @ 4800	134 @ 2800	3.50 x 3.78	8.3:1	60 @ idle
	SD25	152.0 (2488)	DFI	70 @ 4000	115 @ 2000	3.50 x 3.94	21.4:1	60 @ idle
1986	Z20	119.0 (1952)	2 bbl	97 @ 5600	102 @ 3200	3.35 x 3.39	9.4:1	60 @ idle
	Z24	146.8 (2389)	2 bbl	103 @ 4800	134 @ 2800	3.50 x 3.78	8.3:1	60 @ idle
	Z24i	146.8 (2389)	EFI	103 @ 4800	134 @ 2800	3.50 x 3.78	8.3:1	60 @ idle
	VG30i	181.0 (2960)	EFI	152 @ 5200	162 @ 3600	3.43 x 3.27	9.0:1	60 @ idle
	SD25	152.0 (2488)	DFI	70 @ 4000	115 @ 2000	3.50 x 3.94	21.4:1	60 @ idle
1987	Z24i	146.8 (2389)	EFI	103 @ 4800	134 @ 2800	3.50 x 3.78	8.3:1	60 @ idle
	VG30i	181.0 (2960)	EFI	152 @ 5200	162 @ 3600	3.43 x 3.27	9.0:1	60 @ idle
	SD25	152.0 (2488)	DFI	70 @ 4000	115 @ 2000	3.50 x 3.94	21.4:1	60 @ idle
1988	Z24i	146.8 (2389)	EFI	106 @ 4800	137 @ 2400	3.50 x 3.78	8.3:1	60 @ idle
	VG30i	181.0 (2960)	EFI	145 @ 4800	166 @ 2800	3.43 x 3.27	9.0:1	60 @ idle
1989	Z24i	146.8 (2389)	EFI	106 @ 4800	137 @ 2400	3.50 x 3.78	8.3:1	60 @ idle
	VG30i	181.0 (2960)	EFI	145 @ 4800	166 @ 2800	3.43 x 3.27	9.0:1	60 @ idle

EFI Electronic Fuel Injection
DFI Diesel Fuel Injection

Valve Specifications

Year	Engine Type	Seat Angle (deg)	Face Angle (deg)	Spring Test Pressure (lbs)		Spring Installed Height (in.)		Stem-to-Guide Clearance (in.)▲		Stem Diameter (in.)	
				Inner	Outer	Inner	Outer	Intake	Exhaust	Intake	Exhaust
1971	L16	45	45	27 @ 1.38	64 @ 1.53	1.77	2.05	0.0006–0.0018	0.0016–0.0028	0.3136–0.3142	0.3128–0.3134
1972	L16	45	45	27 @ 1.38	64 @ 1.53	1.77	2.05	0.0006–0.0018	0.0016–0.0028	0.3136–0.3142	0.3128–0.3134
1973	L16	45	45	27 @ 1.38	64 @ 1.53	1.77	1.97	0.0008–0.0021	0.0016–0.0029	0.3136–0.3142	0.3128–0.3134
	L18	45	45	27 @ 1.38	47 @ 1.58	1.77	1.97	0.0008–0.0021	0.0016–0.0029	0.3136–0.3142	0.3128–0.3134
1974	L18	45	45	27 @ 1.38	47 @ 1.58	1.77	1.97	0.0008–0.0021	0.0016–0.0029	0.3136–0.3142	0.3128–0.3134

Valve Specifications (cont.)

Year	Engine Type	Seat Angle (deg)	Face Angle (deg)	Spring Test Pressure (lbs)		Spring Installed Height (in.)		Stem-to-Guide Clearance (in.)▲		Stem Diameter (in.)	
				Inner	Outer	Inner	Outer	Intake	Exhaust	Intake	Exhaust
1975	L20B	45	45	27 @ 1.38	47 @ 1.58	1.77	1.97	0.0008–0.0021	0.0016–0.0029	0.3136–0.3142	0.3128–0.3134
1976	L20B	45	45	27 @ 1.38	47 @ 1.58	1.77	1.97	0.0008–0.0021	0.0016–0.0029	0.3136–0.3142	0.3128–0.3134
1977	L20B	45	45	27 @ 1.38	47 @ 1.58	1.77	1.97	0.0008–0.0021	0.0016–0.0029	0.3136–0.3142	0.3128–0.3134
1978	L20B	45	45.5	27 @ 1.38	47 @ 1.58	1.77	1.97	0.0008–0.0021	0.0016–0.0029	0.3136–0.3142	0.3128–0.3134
1979	L20B	45	45.5	27 @ 1.38	47 @ 1.58	1.77	1.97	0.0008–0.0021	0.0016–0.0029	0.3136–0.3142	0.3128–0.3134
1980	L20B	45	45.5	27 @ 1.38	47 @ 1.58	1.77	1.97	0.0008–0.0021	0.0016–0.0029	0.3136–0.3142	0.3128–0.3134
1981	Z22	45.5	45.5	51 @ 1.575	51 @ 1.378	1.74	1.96	0.0008–0.0021	0.0016–0.0029	0.3136–0.3142	0.3128–0.3134
	SD22	45	45	—	33 @ 1.634	—	1.93	0.0006–0.0018	0.0016–0.0028	0.3137–0.3143	0.3137–0.3143
1982	Z22	45.5	45.5	51 @ 1.575	51 @ 1.378	1.74	1.96	0.0008–0.0021	0.0016–0.0029	0.3136–0.3142	0.3128–0.3134
	SD22	45	45	—	33 @ 1.634	—	1.93	0.0006–0.0018	0.0016–0.0028	0.3137–0.3143	0.3137–0.3143
1983	Z22	45.5	45.5	51 @ 1.575	51 @ 1.378	1.74	1.96	0.0008–0.0021	0.0016–0.0029	0.3136–0.3142	0.3128–0.3134
	SD22	45	45	—	33 @ 1.634	—	1.93	0.0006–0.0018	0.0016–0.0028	0.3137–0.3143	0.3137–0.3143
1984	Z20	45.5	45.5	57 @ 0.98	115 @ 1.18	1.57	1.38	0.0008–0.0021	0.0016–0.0029	0.3136–0.3142	0.3128–0.3134
	Z24	45.5	45	57 @ 0.98	115 @ 1.18	1.57	1.38	0.0008–0.0021	0.0016–0.0029	0.3136–0.3142	0.3128–0.3134
	SD25	45	45	—	148 @ 1.224	—	1.56	0.0006–0.0018	0.0016–0.0028	0.3138–0.3144	0.3128–0.3134
1985	Z20	45.5	45.5	57 @ 0.98	115 @ 118	1.57	1.38	0.0008–0.0021	0.0016–0.0029	0.3136–0.3142	0.3128–0.3134
	Z24	45.5	45	57 @ 0.98	115 @ 1.18	1.57	1.38	0.0008–0.0021	0.0016–0.0029	0.3136–0.3142	0.3128–0.3134
	SD25	45	45	—	148 @ 1.224	—	1.56	0.0006–0.0018	0.0016–0.0028	0.3138–0.3144	0.3128–0.3134
1986	Z20	45.5	45.5	57 @ 0.98	115 @ 1.18	1.57	1.38	0.0008–0.0021	0.0016–0.0029	0.3136–0.3142	0.3128–0.3134
	Z24	45.5	45	57 @ 0.98	115 @ 1.18	1.57	1.38	0.0008–0.0021	0.0016–0.0029	0.3136–0.3142	0.3128–0.3134
	Z24i	45.5	45.5	24 @ 1.378	51 @ 1.575	1.57	1.38	0.0008–0.0021	0.0016–0.0029	0.3136–0.3142	0.3128–0.3134
	VG30i	45.5	45.5	57 @ 0.984	118 @ 1.181	0.98	1.18	0.0008–0.0021	0.0012–0.0018	0.2742–0.2748	0.3136–0.3138
	SD25	45	45	—	148 @ 1.224	—	1.56	0.0006–0.0018	0.0016–0.028	0.3138–0.3144	0.3128–0.3134
1987	Z24i	45.5	45.5	24 @ 1.378	51 @ 1.575	1.57	1.38	0.0008–0.0021	0.0016–0.0029	0.3136–0.3142	0.3128–0.3134

Valve Specifications (cont.)

Year	Engine Type	Seat Angle (deg)	Face Angle (deg)	Spring Test Pressure (lbs) Inner	Spring Test Pressure (lbs) Outer	Spring Installed Height (in.) Inner	Spring Installed Height (in.) Outer	Stem-to-Guide Clearance (in.)▲ Intake	Stem-to-Guide Clearance (in.)▲ Exhaust	Stem Diameter (in.) Intake	Stem Diameter (in.) Exhaust
1987	VG30i	45.5	45.5	57 @ 0.984	118 @ 1.181	0.98	1.18	0.0008–0.0021	0.0012–0.0018	0.2742–0.2748	0.3136–0.3138
	SD25	45	45	—	148 @ 1.224	—	1.56	0.0006–0.0018	0.0016–0.0028	0.3138–0.3144	0.3128–0.3134
1988	Z24i	45.5	45.5	24 @ 1.378	51 @ 1.575	1.57	1.38	0.0008–0.0021	0.0016–0.0029	0.3136–0.3142	0.3128–0.3134
	VG30i	45.5	45.5	57 @ 0.984	118 @ 1.181	0.98	1.18	0.0008–0.0021	0.0016–0.0029	0.2742–0.2748	0.3128–0.3134
1989	Z24i	45.5	45.5	24 @ 1.378	51 @ 1.575	1.57	1.38	0.0008–0.0021	0.0016–0.0029	0.3136–0.3142	0.3128–0.3134
	VG30i	45.5	45.5	57 @ 0.984	118 @ 1.181	0.98	1.18	0.0008–0.0021	0.0016–0.0029	0.2742–0.2748	0.3128–0.3134

Camshaft Specifications

(All measurements in inches)

Year	Engine	Journal Diameter 1	Journal Diameter 2	Journal Diameter 3	Journal Diameter 4	Bearing Clearance	Lobe Lift Intake	Lobe Lift Exhaust	Camshaft End Play
1970	L16	1.8877–1.8883	1.8877–1.8883	1.8877–1.8883	1.8877–1.8883	0.0015–0.0026	0.275	0.275	0.003–0.015
1971	L16	1.8877–1.8883	1.8877–1.8883	1.8877–1.8883	1.8877–1.8883	0.0015–0.0026	0.275	0.275	0.003–0.015
1972	L16	1.8877–1.8883	1.8877–1.8883	1.8877–1.8883	1.8877–1.8883	0.0015–0.0026	0.275	0.275	0.003–0.015
1973	L16	1.8877–1.8883	1.8877–1.8883	1.8877–1.8883	1.8877–1.8883	0.0015–0.0026	0.275	0.275	0.003–0.015
	L18	1.8877–1.8883	1.8877–1.8883	1.8877–1.8883	1.8877–1.8883	0.0015–0.0026	0.275	0.275	0.003–0.015
1974	L18	1.8877–1.8883	1.8877–1.8883	1.8877–1.8883	1.8877–1.8883	0.0015–0.0026	0.275	0.275	0.003–0.015
1975	L20B	1.8877–1.8883	1.8877–1.8883	1.8877–1.8883	1.8877–1.8883	0.0015–0.0026	0.275	0.275	0.003–0.015
1976	L20B	1.8877–1.8883	1.8877–1.8883	1.8877–1.8883	1.8877–1.8883	0.0015–0.0026	0.275	0.275	0.003–0.015
1977	L20B	1.8877–1.8883	1.8877–1.8883	1.8877–1.8883	1.8877–1.8883	0.0015–0.0026	0.275	0.275	0.003–0.015
1978	L20B	1.8877–1.8883	1.8877–1.8883	1.8877–1.8883	1.8877–1.8883	0.0015–0.0026	0.275	0.275	0.003–0.015
1979	L20B	1.8877–1.8883	1.8877–1.8883	1.8877–1.8883	1.8877–1.8883	0.0015–0.0026	0.275	0.275	0.003–0.015
1980	L20B	1.8877–1.8883	1.8877–1.8883	1.8877–1.8883	1.8877–1.8883	0.0015–0.0026	0.275	0.275	0.003–0.015
1981	Z22	1.2967–1.2974	1.2967–1.2974	1.2967–1.2974	1.2967–1.2974	0.0018–0.0035	0.218	0.218	0.004–0.012
	SD22	1.7887–1.7892	1.7282–1.7287	1.6228–1.6233	—	①	—	—	0.019–0.020

Camshaft Specifications (cont.)

(All measurements in inches)

Year	Engine	Journal Diameter 1	2	3	4	Bearing Clearance	Lobe Lift Intake	Exhaust	Camshaft End Play
1982	Z22	1.2967–1.2974	1.2967–1.2974	1.2967–1.2974	1.2967–1.2974		0.218	0.218	0.004–0.012
	SD22	1.7887–1.7892	1.7282–1.7287	1.6228–1.6233	—	①	—	—	0.019–0.020
1983	Z22	1.2967–1.2974	1.2967–1.2974	1.2967–1.2974	1.2967–1.2974		0.218	0.218	0.004–0.012
	SD22	1.7887–1.7892	1.7282–1.7287	1.6228–1.6233	—	①	—	—	0.019–0.020
1984	Z20	1.2967–1.2974	1.2967–1.2974	1.2967–1.2974	1.2967–1.2974		0.218	0.218	0.004–0.012
	Z24	1.2967–1.2974	1.2967–1.2974	1.2967–1.2974	1.2967–1.2974		0.218	0.218	0.004–0.012
	SD25	1.7887–1.7892	1.7282–1.7287	1.6228–1.6233	—	①	—	—	0.003–0.011
1985	Z20	1.2967–1.2974	1.2967–1.2974	1.2967–1.2974	1.2967–1.2974		0.218	0.218	0.004–0.012
	Z24	1.2967–1.2974	1.2967–1.2974	1.2967–1.2974	1.2967–1.2974		0.218	0.218	0.004–0.012
	SD25	1.7887–1.7892	1.7282–1.7287	1.6228–1.6233	—	①	—	—	0.003–0.011
1986	Z20	1.2967–1.2974	1.2967–1.2974	1.2967–1.2974	1.2967–1.2974	0.0018–0.0035	0.218	0.218	0.004–0.012
	Z24	1.2967–1.2974	1.2967–1.2974	1.2967–1.2974	1.2967–1.2974	0.0018–0.0035	0.218	0.218	0.004–0.012
	Z24i	1.2961–1.2968	1.2961–1.2968	1.2961–1.2968	1.2961–1.2968	0.0024–0.0041	—	—	—
	VG30i	②	②	②	②	0.0018–0.0035	—	—	0.0012–0.0024
	SD25	1.7887–1.7892	1.7282–1.7287	1.6228–1.6233	—	①	—	—	0.003–0.011
1987	Z24i	1.2961–1.2968	1.2961–1.2968	1.2961–1.2968	1.2961–1.2968	0.0024–0.0041	—	—	—
	VG30i	②	②	②	②	0.0018–0.0035	—	—	0.0012–0.0024
	SD25	1.7887–1.7892	1.7282–1.7287	1.6228–1.6233	—	①	—	—	0.003–0.011
1988	Z24i	1.2961–1.2968	1.2961–1.2968	1.2961–1.2968	1.2961–1.2968	0.0024–0.0041	—	—	—
	VG30i	②	②	②	②	0.0018–0.0035	—	—	0.0012–0.0024
1989	Z24i	1.2961–1.2968	1.2961–1.2968	1.2961–1.2968	1.2961–1.2968	0.0024–0.0041	—	—	—
	VG30i	②	②	②	②	0.0018–0.0035	—	—	0.0012–0.0024

① #1, 3: 0.0009–0.0040
#2: 0.0015–0.0045

② #1 (left side only): 1.8866–1.8874
#2, 3 & 4: 1.8472–1.8480
#5: 1.6701–1.6709

Crankshaft and Connecting Rod Specifications

All measurements are given in inches

		Crankshaft				Connecting Rod		
Year	Engine Type	Main Brg Journal Dia	Main Brg Oil Clearance	Shaft End-Play	Thrust on No.	Journal Diameter	Oil Clearance	Side Clearance
1970	L16	2.1631–2.1636	0.0008–0.0028	0.0020–0.0059	3	1.9670–1.9675	0.0006–0.0026	0.0079–0.0118
1971	L16	2.1631–2.1636	0.0008–0.0028	0.0020–0.0059	3	1.9670–1.9675	0.0006–0.0026	0.0079–0.0118
1972	L16	2.1631–2.1636	0.0008–0.0028	0.0020–0.0059	3	1.9670–1.9675	0.0006–0.0026	0.0079–0.0118
1973	L16	2.1631–2.1636	0.0008–0.0024	0.0020–0.0071	3	1.9670–1.9675	0.0010–0.0022	0.0079–0.0118
	L18	2.1631–2.1636	0.0008–0.0024	0.0020–0.0071	3	1.9670–1.9675	0.0010–0.0022	0.0079–0.0118
1974	L18	2.1631–2.1636	0.0008–0.0024	0.0020–0.0071	3	1.9670–1.9675	0.0010–0.0022	0.0079–0.0118
1975	L20B	2.3599–2.3600	0.0008–0.0024	0.0020–0.0071	3	1.9670–1.9675	0.0010–0.0022	0.0079–0.0118
1976	L20B	2.3599–2.3600	0.0008–0.0024	0.0020–0.0071	3	1.9670–1.9675	0.0010–0.0022	0.0079–0.0118
1977	L20B	2.3599–2.3600	0.0008–0.0024	0.0020–0.0071	3	1.9670–1.9675	0.0010–0.0022	0.0079–0.0118
1978	L20B	2.3599–2.3600	0.0008–0.0024	0.0020–0.0071	3	1.9670–1.9675	0.0010–0.0022	0.0079–0.0118
1979	L20B	2.1631–2.1636	0.0008–0.0024	0.0020–0.0071	3	1.9670–1.9675	0.0010–0.0022	0.0080–0.0120
1980	L20B	2.1631–2.1636	0.0008–0.0024	0.0020–0.0071	3	1.9670–1.9675	0.0010–0.0022	0.0080–0.0120
1981	Z22	2.1631–2.1636	0.0008–0.0024	0.0020–0.0071	3	1.9670–1.9675	0.0010–0.0022	0.0080–0.0120
	SD22	2.7916–2.7921	0.0014–0.0037	0.0024–0.0055	4	2.0832–2.0837	0.0014–0.0034	0.0039–0.0079
1982	Z22	2.1631–2.1636	0.0008–0.0024	0.0020–0.0071	3	1.9670–1.9675	0.0010–0.0022	0.0080–0.0120
	SD22	2.7916–2.7921	0.0014–0.0037	0.0024–0.0055	4	2.0832–2.0837	0.0014–0.0034	0.0039–0.0079
1983	Z22	2.1631–2.1636	0.0008–0.0024	0.0020–0.0071	3	1.9670–1.9675	0.0010–0.0022	0.0080–0.0120
	SD22	2.7916–2.7921	0.0014–0.0037	0.0024–0.0055	4	2.0832–2.0837	0.0014–0.0034	0.0039–0.0079
1984	Z20	2.1631–2.1636	0.0008–0.0024	0.0020–0.0071	3	1.9670–1.9675	0.0010–0.0022	0.0080–0.0120
	Z24	2.1631–2.1636	0.0008–0.0024	0.0020–0.0071	3	1.9670–1.9675	0.0010–0.0022	0.0080–0.0120
	SD25	2.7916–2.7921	0.0014–0.0034	0.0024–0.0055	4	2.0832–2.0837	0.0014–0.0032	0.0039–0.0079
1985	Z20	2.1631–2.1636	0.0008–0.0024	0.0020–0.0071	3	1.9670–1.9675	0.0010–0.0022	0.0080–0.0120
	Z24	2.1631–2.1636	0.0008–0.0024	0.0020–0.0071	3	1.9670–1.9675	0.0010–0.0022	0.0080–0.0120
	SD25	2.7916–2.7921	0.0014–0.0034	0.0024–0.0055	4	2.0832–2.0837	0.0014–0.0032	0.0039–0.0079

Crankshaft and Connecting Rod Specifications (cont.)

All measurements are given in inches

Year	Engine Type	Crankshaft: Main Brg Journal Dia	Crankshaft: Main Brg Oil Clearance	Crankshaft: Shaft End-Play	Crankshaft: Thrust on No.	Connecting Rod: Journal Diameter	Connecting Rod: Oil Clearance	Connecting Rod: Side Clearance
1986	Z20	2.1631–2.1636	0.0008–0.0024	0.0020–0.0071	3	1.9670–1.9675	0.0010–0.0022	0.0080–0.0120
	Z24	2.1631–2.1636	0.0008–0.0024	0.0020–0.0071	3	1.9670–1.9675	0.0010–0.0022	0.0080–0.0120
	Z24i	2.3599–2.3604	①	0.0020–0.0071	3	1.9670–1.9675	0.0005–0.0021	0.0080–0.0120
	VG30i	2.4790–2.4793	0.0011–0.0022	0.0020–0.0067	4	1.9670–1.9675	0.0004–0.0020	0.0079–0.0138
	SD25	2.7916–2.7921	0.0014–0.0034	0.0024–0.0055	4	2.0832–2.0837	0.0014–0.0032	0.0039–0.0079
1987	Z24i	2.3599–2.3604	①	0.0020–0.0071	3	1.9670–1.9675	0.0005–0.0021	0.0080–0.0120
	VG30i	2.4790–2.4793	0.0011–0.0022	0.0020–0.0067	4	1.9670–1.9675	0.0004–0.0020	0.0079–0.0138
	SD25	2.7916–2.7921	0.0014–0.0034	0.0024–0.0055	4	2.0832–2.0837	0.0014–0.0032	0.0039–0.0079
1988	Z24i	2.3599–2.3604	①	0.0020–0.0071	3	1.9670–1.9675	0.0005–0.0021	0.0080–0.0120
	VG30i	2.4790–2.4793	0.0011–0.0022	0.0020–0.0067	4	1.9667–1.9675	0.0006–0.0021	0.0079–0.0138
1989	Z24i	2.3599–2.3604	①	0.0020–0.0071	3	1.9670–1.9675	0.0006–0.0019	0.0080–0.0120
	VG30i	2.4790–2.4793	0.0011–0.0022	0.0020–0.0067	4	1.9667–1.9675	0.0006–0.0021	0.0079–0.0138

① #1, 5: 0.0008–0.0024
#2, 3 & 4: 0.0008–0.0030

Piston and Ring Specifications

(All measurements in inches)

Year	Engine Type	Piston Clearance 68°F	Ring Gap: Top Compression	Ring Gap: Bottom Compression	Ring Gap: Oil Control	Ring Side Clearance (Ring to Land): Top Compression	Ring Side Clearance (Ring to Land): Bottom Compression	Ring Side Clearance (Ring to Land): Oil Control
1970	L16	0.0010–0.0018	0.0091–0.0150	0.0059–0.0118	0.0059–0.0118	0.0018–0.0031	0.0012–0.0025	0.0010–0.0025
1971	L16	0.0010–0.0018	0.0091–0.0150	0.0059–0.0118	0.0059–0.0118	0.0018–0.0031	0.0012–0.0025	0.0010–0.0025
1972	L16	0.0010–0.0018	0.0091–0.0150	0.0059–0.0118	0.0059–0.0118	0.0018–0.0031	0.0012–0.0025	0.0010–0.0025
1973	L16	0.0010–0.0018	0.0098–0.0157	0.0059–0.0118	0.0118–0.0354	0.0016–0.0031	0.0012–0.0028	snug
	L18	0.0010–0.0018	0.0138–0.0217	0.0118–0.0197	0.0118–0.0354	0.0018–0.0031	0.0012–0.0028	snug
1974	L18	0.0010–0.0018	0.0098–0.0157	0.0118–0.0197	0.0118–0.0354	0.0016–0.0029	0.0012–0.0028	snug
1975	L20B	0.0010–0.0018	0.0098–0.0157	0.0118–0.0197	0.0118–0.0354	0.0016–0.0029	0.0012–0.0028	snug

Piston and Ring Specifications (cont.)

(All measurements in inches)

Year	Engine Type	Piston Clearance 68°F	Ring Gap			Ring Side Clearance (Ring to Land)		
			Top Compression	Bottom Compression	Oil Control	Top Compression	Bottom Compression	Oil Control
1976	L20B	0.0010–0.0018	0.0098–0.0157	0.0118–0.0197	0.0118–0.0354	0.0016–0.0029	0.0012–0.0028	snug
1977	L20B	0.0010–0.0018	0.0098–0.0157	0.0118–0.0197	0.0118–0.0354	0.0016–0.0029	0.0012–0.0028	snug
1978	L20B	0.0010–0.0018	0.0098–0.0157	0.0118–0.0197	0.0118–0.0354	0.0016–0.0029	0.0012–0.0028	snug
1979	L20B	0.0010–0.0018	0.0098–0.0157	0.0118–0.0197	0.0118–0.0354	0.0016–0.0029	0.0012–0.0028	snug
1980	L20B	0.0010–0.0018	0.0098–0.0157	0.0118–0.0197	0.0118–0.0354	0.0016–0.0029	0.0012–0.0028	snug
1981	Z22	0.0010–0.0018	0.0098–0.0157	0.0059–0.0118	0.0118–0.0354	0.0016–0.0029	0.0012–0.0025	snug
	SD22	0.0016–0.0043	0.0118–0.0177	0.0079–0.0138	0.0059–0.0118	0.0024–0.0039	0.0016–0.0032	0.0008–0.0024
1982	Z22	0.0010–0.0018	0.0098–0.0157	0.0059–0.0118	0.0118–0.0354	0.0016–0.0029	0.0012–0.0025	snug
	SD22	0.0016–0.0043	0.0118–0.0177	0.0079–0.0138	0.0059–0.0118	0.0024–0.0039	0.0016–0.0032	0.0008–0.0024
1983	Z22	0.0010–0.0018	0.0098–0.0157	0.0059–0.0118	0.0118–0.0354	0.0016–0.0029	0.0012–0.0025	snug
	SD22	0.0016–0.0043	0.0118–0.0177	0.0079–0.0138	0.0059–0.0118	0.0024–0.0039	0.0016–0.0032	0.0008–0.0024
1984	Z20	0.0010–0.0018	0.0098–0.0157	0.0059–0.0118	0.0118–0.0354	0.0016–0.0029	0.0012–0.0025	snug
	Z24	0.0010–0.0018	0.0098–0.0157	0.0059–0.0118	0.0118–0.0354	0.0016–0.0029	0.0012–0.0025	snug
	SD25	0.0031–0.0041	0.0118–0.0177	0.0079–0.0138	0.0059–0.0118	0.0024–0.0039	0.0016–0.0032	0.0008–0.0024
1985	Z20	0.0010–0.0018	0.0098–0.0157	0.0059–0.0118	0.0118–0.0354	0.0016–0.0029	0.0012–0.0025	snug
	Z24	0.0010–0.0018	0.0098–0.0157	0.0059–0.0118	0.0118–0.0354	0.0016–0.0029	0.0012–0.0025	snug
	SD25	0.0031–0.0041	0.0118–0.0177	0.0079–0.0138	0.0059–0.0118	0.0024–0.0039	0.0016–0.0032	0.0008–0.0024
1986	Z20	0.0010–0.0018	0.0098–0.0157	0.0059–0.0118	0.0118–0.0354	0.0016–0.0029	0.0012–0.0025	snug
	Z24	0.0010–0.0018	0.0098–0.0157	0.0059–0.0118	0.0118–0.0354	0.0016–0.0029	0.0012–0.0025	snug
	Z24i	0.0010–0.0018	0.0110–0.0150	0.0098–0.0138	0.0079–0.0236	0.0016–0.0029	0.0012–0.0025	snug
	VG30i	0.0010–0.0018	0.0083–0.0134	0.0071–0.0173	0.0079–0.0299	0.0016–0.0029	0.0012–0.0025	0.0006–0.0073
	SD25	0.0031–0.0041	0.0118–0.0177	0.0079–0.0138	0.0059–0.0118	0.0024–0.0039	0.0016–0.0032	0.0008–0.0024
1987	Z24i	0.0010–0.0018	0.0110–0.0150	0.0098–0.0138	0.0079–0.0236	0.0016–0.0029	0.0012–0.0025	snug
	VG30i	0.0010–0.0018	0.0083–0.0134	0.0071–0.0173	0.0079–0.0299	0.0016–0.0029	0.0012–0.0025	0.0006–0.0073

Piston and Ring Specifications (cont.)

(All measurements in inches)

Year	Engine Type	Piston Clearance 68°F	Ring Gap			Ring Side Clearance (Ring to Land)		
			Top Compression	Bottom Compression	Oil Control	Top Compression	Bottom Compression	Oil Control
1987	SD25	0.0031–0.0041	0.0118–0.0177	0.0079–0.0138	0.0059–0.0118	0.0024–0.0039	0.0016–0.0032	0.0008–0.0024
1988	Z24i	0.0010–0.0018	0.0110–0.0150	0.0098–0.0138	0.0079–0.0236	0.0016–0.0029	0.0012–0.0025	snug
	VG30i	0.0010–0.0018	0.0083–0.0134	0.0071–0.0173	0.0079–0.0299	0.0016–0.0029	0.0012–0.0025	0.0006–0.0073
1989	Z24i	0.0010–00018	0.0110–0.0150	0.0098–0.0138	0.0079–0.0236	0.0016–0.0029	0.0012–0.0025	snug
	VG30i	0.0010–0.0018	0.0083–0.0173	0.0071–00173	0.0079–0.0299	0.016–0.0029	0.0012–0.0025	0.0006–0.0075

Torque Specifications

(All readings in ft. lbs.)

Year	Engine Type	Cylinder Head Bolts	Rod Bearing Bolts	Main Bearing Bolts	Crankshaft Pulley Bolt	Flywheel to Crankshaft Bolts	Manifold	
							Intake	Exhaust
1970	L16	40 ①	23	36	122	72	11	11
1971	L16	40 ①	23	36	122	72	11	11
1972	L16	40①	23	36	122	72	11	11
1973	L16	43 ①	25	37	102	109	11	11
	L18	55 ②	37	37	102	109	11	11
1974	L18	55 ②	37	37	102	109	11	11
1975	L20B	61 ③	37	37	102	109	11	11
1976	L20B	61 ③	37	37	102	109	11	11
1977	L20B	61 ③	37	37	102	109	11	11
1978	L20B	61 ③	37	37	102	109	11	11
1979	L20B	61 ③	37	37	102	109	11	11
1980	L20B	61 ③	37	37	102	109	11	11
1981	Z22	58 ③	37	37	102	109	15	15
	SD22	⑤	40	127	239	33	13	13
1982	Z22	58 ③	37	37	102	109	15	15
	SD22	⑤	40	127	239	33	13	13
1983	Z22	58 ③	37	37	102	109	15	15
	SD22	⑤	40	127	239	33	13	13
1984	Z20	④	37	37	102	109	15	15
	Z24	④	37	37	102	109	15	15
	SD25	⑥	50	125	239	123	13	13
1985	Z20	④	37	37	102	109	15	15
	Z24	④	37	37	102	109	15	15
	SD25	⑥	50	125	239	123	13	13

Torque Specifications (cont.)

(All readings in ft. lbs.)

Year	Engine Type	Cylinder Head Bolts	Rod Bearing Bolts	Main Bearing Bolts	Crankshaft Pulley Bolt	Flywheel to Crankshaft Bolts	Manifold	
							Intake	Exhaust
1986	Z20	④	37	37	102	109	15	15
	Z24	④	37	37	102	109	15	15
	Z24i	④	37	37	110	109	13	13
	VG30i	44	37	70	94	76	13 ⑦	14
	SD25	⑥	50	125	239	123	13	13
1987	Z24i	④	37	37	110	109	13	13
	VG30i	44	37	70	94	76	13 ⑦	14
	SD25	⑥	50	125	239	123	13	13
1988	Z24i	④	37	37	110	109	13	13
	VG30i	⑧	41	70	94	76	13 ⑦	14
1989	Z24i	④	37	37	110	109	13	13
	VG30i	⑧	41	70	94	76	13 ⑦	14

① Tighten to 33 ft. lbs., then to specification
② Tighten to 23 ft. lbs., then to specification
③ Tighten to 29 ft. lbs., then 43 ft. lbs., then specification
④ Tighten to 22 ft. lbs., then 58 ft. lbs., loosen all bolts completely, then tighten to 22 ft. lbs., then 61 ft. lbs.
⑤ Small bolts: 42 ft. lbs.
Large bolts: 98 ft. lbs.
⑥ Small bolts: 37 ft. lbs.
Large bolts: 91 ft. lbs.
⑦ Nut: 18 ft. lbs.
⑧ Tighten to 22 ft. lbs., then 43 ft. lbs., loosen all bolts completely, then tighten to 22 ft. lbs., then 61 ft. lbs.

Troubleshooting Engine Mechanical Problems

Problem	Cause	Solution
External oil leaks	• Fuel pump gasket broken or improperly seated	• Replace gasket
	• Cylinder head cover RTV sealant broken or improperly seated	• Replace sealant; inspect cylinder head cover sealant flange and cylinder head sealant surface for distortion and cracks
	• Oil filler cap leaking or missing	• Replace cap
	• Oil filter gasket broken or improperly seated	• Replace oil filter
	• Oil pan side gasket broken, improperly seated or opening in RTV sealant	• Replace gasket or repair opening in sealant; inspect oil pan gasket flange for distortion
	• Oil pan front oil seal broken or improperly seated	• Replace seal; inspect timing case cover and oil pan seal flange for distortion
	• Oil pan rear oil seal broken or improperly seated	• Replace seal; inspect oil pan rear oil seal flange; inspect rear main bearing cap for cracks, plugged oil return channels, or distortion in seal groove
	• Timing case cover oil seal broken or improperly seated	• Replace seal
	• Excess oil pressure because of restricted PCV valve	• Replace PCV valve
	• Oil pan drain plug loose or has stripped threads	• Repair as necessary and tighten
	• Rear oil gallery plug loose	• Use appropriate sealant on gallery plug and tighten

Troubleshooting Engine Mechanical Problems (cont.)

Problem	Cause	Solution
	• Rear camshaft plug loose or improperly seated • Distributor base gasket damaged	• Seat camshaft plug or replace and seal, as necessary • Replace gasket
Excessive oil consumption	• Oil level too high • Oil with wrong viscosity being used • PCV valve stuck closed • Valve stem oil deflectors (or seals) are damaged, missing, or incorrect type • Valve stems or valve guides worn • Poorly fitted or missing valve cover baffles • Piston rings broken or missing • Scuffed piston • Incorrect piston ring gap • Piston rings sticking or excessively loose in grooves • Compression rings installed upside down • Cylinder walls worn, scored, or glazed • Piston ring gaps not properly staggered • Excessive main or connecting rod bearing clearance	• Drain oil to specified level • Replace with specified oil • Replace PCV valve • Replace valve stem oil deflectors • Measure stem-to-guide clearance and repair as necessary • Replace valve cover • Replace broken or missing rings • Replace piston • Measure ring gap, repair as necessary • Measure ring side clearance, repair as necessary • Repair as necessary • Repair as necessary • Repair as necessary • Measure bearing clearance, repair as necessary
No oil pressure	• Low oil level • Oil pressure gauge, warning lamp or sending unit inaccurate • Oil pump malfunction • Oil pressure relief valve sticking • Oil passages on pressure side of pump obstructed • Oil pickup screen or tube obstructed • Loose oil inlet tube	• Add oil to correct level • Replace oil pressure gauge or warning lamp • Replace oil pump • Remove and inspect oil pressure relief valve assembly • Inspect oil passages for obstruction • Inspect oil pickup for obstruction • Tighten or seal inlet tube
Low oil pressure	• Low oil level • Inaccurate gauge, warning lamp or sending unit • Oil excessively thin because of dilution, poor quality, or improper grade • Excessive oil temperature • Oil pressure relief spring weak or sticking • Oil inlet tube and screen assembly has restriction or air leak • Excessive oil pump clearance • Excessive main, rod, or camshaft bearing clearance	• Add oil to correct level • Replace oil pressure gauge or warning lamp • Drain and refill crankcase with recommended oil • Correct cause of overheating engine • Remove and inspect oil pressure relief valve assembly • Remove and inspect oil inlet tube and screen assembly. (Fill inlet tube with lacquer thinner to locate leaks.) • Measure clearances • Measure bearing clearances, repair as necessary
High oil pressure	• Improper oil viscosity • Oil pressure gauge or sending unit inaccurate • Oil pressure relief valve sticking closed	• Drain and refill crankcase with correct viscosity oil • Replace oil pressure gauge • Remove and inspect oil pressure relief valve assembly
Main bearing noise	• Insufficient oil supply	• Inspect for low oil level and low oil pressure

Troubleshooting Engine Mechanical Problems (cont.)

Problem	Cause	Solution
Main bearing noise (cont.)	• Main bearing clearance excessive	• Measure main bearing clearance, repair as necessary
	• Bearing insert missing	• Replace missing insert
	• Crankshaft end play excessive	• Measure end play, repair as necessary
	• Improperly tightened main bearing cap bolts	• Tighten bolts with specified torque
	• Loose flywheel or drive plate	• Tighten flywheel or drive plate attaching bolts
	• Loose or damaged vibration damper	• Repair as necessary
Connecting rod bearing noise	• Insufficient oil supply	• Inspect for low oil level and low oil pressure
	• Carbon build-up on piston	• Remove carbon from piston crown
	• Bearing clearance excessive or bearing missing	• Measure clearance, repair as necessary
	• Crankshaft connecting rod journal out-of-round	• Measure journal dimensions, repair or replace as necessary
	• Misaligned connecting rod or cap	• Repair as necessary
	• Connecting rod bolts tightened improperly	• Tighten bolts with specified torque
Piston noise	• Piston-to-cylinder wall clearance excessive (scuffed piston)	• Measure clearance and examine piston
	• Cylinder walls excessively tapered or out-of-round	• Measure cylinder wall dimensions, rebore cylinder
	• Piston ring broken	• Replace all rings on piston
	• Loose or seized piston pin	• Measure piston-to-pin clearance, repair as necessary
	• Connecting rods misaligned	• Measure rod alignment, straighten or replace
	• Piston ring side clearance excessively loose or tight	• Measure ring side clearance, repair as necessary
	• Carbon build-up on piston is excessive	• Remove carbon from piston
Valve actuating component noise	• Insufficient oil supply	• Check for: (a) Low oil level (b) Low oil pressure (c) Plugged push rods (d) Wrong hydraulic tappets (e) Restricted oil gallery (f) Excessive tappet to bore clearance
	• Push rods worn or bent	• Replace worn or bent push rods
	• Rocker arms or pivots worn	• Replace worn rocker arms or pivots
	• Foreign objects or chips in hydraulic tappets	• Clean tappets
	• Excessive tappet leak-down	• Replace valve tappet
	• Tappet face worn	• Replace tappet; inspect corresponding cam lobe for wear
	• Broken or cocked valve springs	• Properly seat cocked springs; replace broken springs
	• Stem-to-guide clearance excessive	• Measure stem-to-guide clearance, repair as required
	• Valve bent	• Replace valve
	• Loose rocker arms	• Tighten bolts with specified torque
	• Valve seat runout excessive	• Regrind valve seat/valves
	• Missing valve lock	• Install valve lock
	• Push rod rubbing or contacting cylinder head	• Remove cylinder head and remove obstruction in head
	• Excessive engine oil (four-cylinder engine)	• Correct oil level

Troubleshooting the Cooling System

Problem	Cause	Solution
High temperature gauge indication—overheating	• Coolant level low • Fan belt loose • Radiator hose(s) collapsed • Radiator airflow blocked • Faulty radiator cap • Ignition timing incorrect • Idle speed low • Air trapped in cooling system • Heavy traffic driving • Incorrect cooling system component(s) installed • Faulty thermostat • Water pump shaft broken or impeller loose • Radiator tubes clogged • Cooling system clogged • Casting flash in cooling passages • Brakes dragging • Excessive engine friction • Antifreeze concentration over 68% • Missing air seals • Faulty gauge or sending unit • Loss of coolant flow caused by leakage or foaming • Viscous fan drive failed	• Replenish coolant • Adjust fan belt tension • Replace hose(s) • Remove restriction (bug screen, fog lamps, etc.) • Replace radiator cap • Adjust ignition timing • Adjust idle speed • Purge air • Operate at fast idle in neutral intermittently to cool engine • Install proper component(s) • Replace thermostat • Replace water pump • Flush radiator • Flush system • Repair or replace as necessary. Flash may be visible by removing cooling system components or removing core plugs. • Repair brakes • Repair engine • Lower antifreeze concentration percentage • Replace air seals • Repair or replace faulty component • Repair or replace leaking component, replace coolant • Replace unit
Low temperature indication—undercooling	• Thermostat stuck open • Faulty gauge or sending unit	• Replace thermostat • Repair or replace faulty component
Coolant loss—boilover	• Overfilled cooling system • Quick shutdown after hard (hot) run • Air in system resulting in occasional "burping" of coolant • Insufficient antifreeze allowing coolant boiling point to be too low • Antifreeze deteriorated because of age or contamination • Leaks due to loose hose clamps, loose nuts, bolts, drain plugs, faulty hoses, or defective radiator • Faulty head gasket • Cracked head, manifold, or block • Faulty radiator cap	• Reduce coolant level to proper specification • Allow engine to run at fast idle prior to shutdown • Purge system • Add antifreeze to raise boiling point • Replace coolant • Pressure test system to locate source of leak(s) then repair as necessary • Replace head gasket • Replace as necessary • Replace cap
Coolant entry into crankcase or cylinder(s)	• Faulty head gasket • Crack in head, manifold or block	• Replace head gasket • Replace as necessary
Coolant recovery system inoperative	• Coolant level low • Leak in system • Pressure cap not tight or seal missing, or leaking • Pressure cap defective • Overflow tube clogged or leaking • Recovery bottle vent restricted	• Replenish coolant to FULL mark • Pressure test to isolate leak and repair as necessary • Repair as necessary • Replace cap • Repair as necessary • Remove restriction

Troubleshooting the Cooling System (cont.)

Problem	Cause	Solution
Noise	• Fan contacting shroud • Loose water pump impeller • Glazed fan belt • Loose fan belt • Rough surface on drive pulley • Water pump bearing worn • Belt alignment	• Reposition shroud and inspect engine mounts • Replace pump • Apply silicone or replace belt • Adjust fan belt tension • Replace pulley • Remove belt to isolate. Replace pump. • Check pulley alignment. Repair as necessary.
No coolant flow through heater core	• Restricted return inlet in water pump • Heater hose collapsed or restricted • Restricted heater core • Restricted outlet in thermostat housing • Intake manifold bypass hole in cylinder head restricted • Faulty heater control valve • Intake manifold coolant passage restricted	• Remove restriction • Remove restriction or replace hose • Remove restriction or replace core • Remove flash or restriction • Remove restriction • Replace valve • Remove restriction or replace intake manifold

NOTE: *Immediately after shutdown, the engine enters a condition known as heat soak. This is caused by the cooling system being inoperative while engine temperature is still high. If coolant temperature rises above boiling point, expansion and pressure may push some coolant out of the radiator overflow tube. If this does not occur frequently it is considered normal.*

Troubleshooting the Serpentine Drive Belt

Problem	Cause	Solution
Tension sheeting fabric failure (woven fabric on outside circumference of belt has cracked or separated from body of belt)	• Grooved or backside idler pulley diameters are less than minimum recommended • Tension sheeting contacting (rubbing) stationary object • Excessive heat causing woven fabric to age • Tension sheeting splice has fractured	• Replace pulley(s) not conforming to specification • Correct rubbing condition • Replace belt • Replace belt
Noise (objectional squeal, squeak, or rumble is heard or felt while drive belt is in operation)	• Belt slippage • Bearing noise • Belt misalignment • Belt-to-pulley mismatch • Driven component inducing vibration • System resonant frequency inducing vibration	• Adjust belt • Locate and repair • Align belt/pulley(s) • Install correct belt • Locate defective driven component and repair • Vary belt tension within specifications. Replace belt.
Rib chunking (one or more ribs has separated from belt body)	• Foreign objects imbedded in pulley grooves • Installation damage • Drive loads in excess of design specifications • Insufficient internal belt adhesion	• Remove foreign objects from pulley grooves • Replace belt • Adjust belt tension • Replace belt
Rib or belt wear (belt ribs contact bottom of pulley grooves)	• Pulley(s) misaligned • Mismatch of belt and pulley groove widths • Abrasive environment • Rusted pulley(s) • Sharp or jagged pulley groove tips • Rubber deteriorated	• Align pulley(s) • Replace belt • Replace belt • Clean rust from pulley(s) • Replace pulley • Replace belt

Troubleshooting the Serpentine Drive Belt (cont.)

Problem	Cause	Solution
Longitudinal belt cracking (cracks between two ribs)	• Belt has mistracked from pulley groove • Pulley groove tip has worn away rubber-to-tensile member	• Replace belt • Replace belt
Belt slips	• Belt slipping because of insufficient tension • Belt or pulley subjected to substance (belt dressing, oil, ethylene glycol) that has reduced friction • Driven component bearing failure • Belt glazed and hardened from heat and excessive slippage	• Adjust tension • Replace belt and clean pulleys • Replace faulty component bearing • Replace belt
"Groove jumping" (belt does not maintain correct position on pulley, or turns over and/or runs off pulleys)	• Insufficient belt tension • Pulley(s) not within design tolerance • Foreign object(s) in grooves • Excessive belt speed • Pulley misalignment • Belt-to-pulley profile mismatched • Belt cordline is distorted	• Adjust belt tension • Replace pulley(s) • Remove foreign objects from grooves • Avoid excessive engine acceleration • Align pulley(s) • Install correct belt • Replace belt
Belt broken (Note: identify and correct problem before replacement belt is installed)	• Excessive tension • Tensile members damaged during belt installation • Belt turnover • Severe pulley misalignment • Bracket, pulley, or bearing failure	• Replace belt and adjust tension to specification • Replace belt • Replace belt • Align pulley(s) • Replace defective component and belt
Cord edge failure (tensile member exposed at edges of belt or separated from belt body)	• Excessive tension • Drive pulley misalignment • Belt contacting stationary object • Pulley irregularities • Improper pulley construction • Insufficient adhesion between tensile member and rubber matrix	• Adjust belt tension • Align pulley • Correct as necessary • Replace pulley • Replace pulley • Replace belt and adjust tension to specifications
Sporadic rib cracking (multiple cracks in belt ribs at random intervals)	• Ribbed pulley(s) diameter less than minimum specification • Backside bend flat pulley(s) diameter less than minimum • Excessive heat condition causing rubber to harden • Excessive belt thickness • Belt overcured • Excessive tension	• Replace pulley(s) • Replace pulley(s) • Correct heat condition as necessary • Replace belt • Replace belt • Adjust belt tension

Engine

REMOVAL AND INSTALLATION

1970-83

It is much easier to remove the engine and the transmission together as an assembly than to remove only the engine from the engine compartment. After the engine and transmission are removed from the vehicle, the two can be separated.

1. Disconnect the battery ground cable. Remove the battery.
2. Mark the location of the hood hinges on the body in order to facilitate installation and remove the hood.
3. Remove the air cleaner after disconnecting the PCV hose from the rocker cover.
4. Drain the radiator of coolant and the engine crankcase of oil.

CAUTION: *When draining the coolant, keep*

in mind that cats and dogs are attracted by the ethylene glycol antifreeze, and are quite likely to drink any that is left in an uncovered container or in puddles on the ground. This will prove fatal in sufficient quantity. Always drain the coolant into a sealable container. Coolant should be reused unless it is contaminated or several years old.

5. Disconnect the upper and lower radiator hoses from the engine. Disconnect and plug the automatic transmission cooler lines at the radiator, if so equipped. Use a flare nut wrench if one is available.
6. Remove the four bolts securing the radiator and remove the radiator from the vehicle.
7. Disconnect the engine ground cable at the cylinder head.
8. Disconnect the electrical leads at the starter, alternator, distributor, the high tension ignition coil cable, and the oil pressure and temperature sending units' wires.
9. Disconnect the fuel line at the fuel pump (or filter on electric pump models), the heater hose at the engine side, and the choke wire and accelerator cable at the carburetor. Disconnect the emission hoses or wires to the carbon canister, air pump, B.C.D.D. solenoid, and fuel cut solenoid; the vacuum hose to the brake booster (on models so equipped), and any other wires or hoses running to the engine. Tag all wires as they are disconnected for assembly.
10. Remove the transmission control linkage from the transmission; in the case of an automatic transmission, remove the cross-shaft assembly from the transmission. Remove the selector rod from the selector lever on the automatic transmission. On manual transmissions, lift the rubber boot and remove the nut or C-clip from the shift lever and detach the shift lever from the transmission.
11. Remove the two bolts securing the clutch slave cylinder. Disconnect the clutch slave cylinder and the flexible tubing as an assembly.
12. Disconnect the speedometer cable and the back-up light wiring (and neutral switch, if equipped) from the rear section of the transmission.
13. Disconnect the exhaust pipe from the exhaust manifold.
14. Disconnect the driveshaft center bearing bracket from the third crossmember of the frame. Disconnect the driveshaft at the differential housing. Remove the driveshaft assembly from the vehicle and plug the rear end of the transmission extension housing to prevent loss of transmission lubricant.
15. Attach a suitable lifting device to the engine and lift the engine slightly.
16. Remove the front engine mount bolts on both sides of the engine.

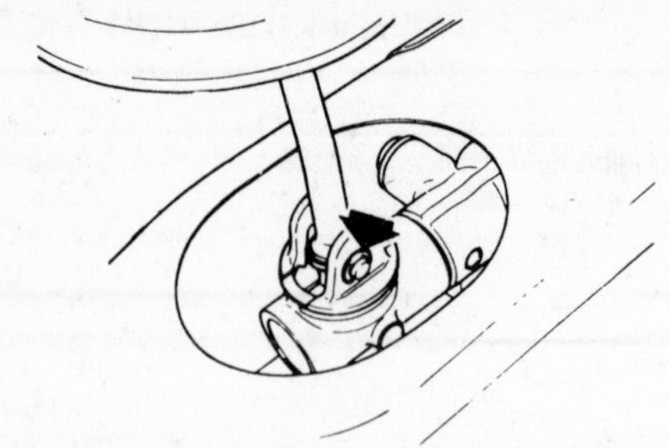

Remove the C-clip and pin on later models—1970–83

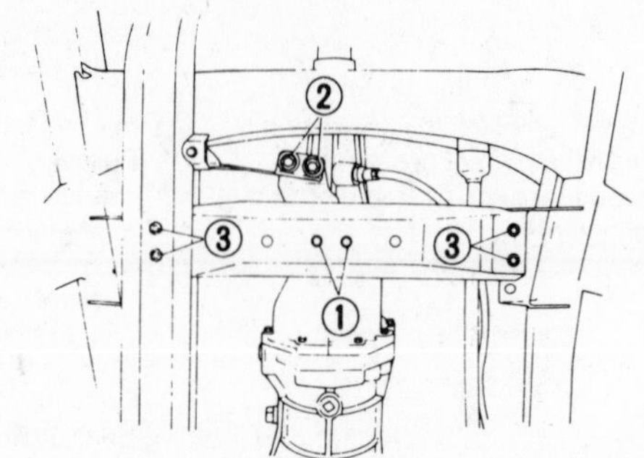

Crossmember removal—1972–83

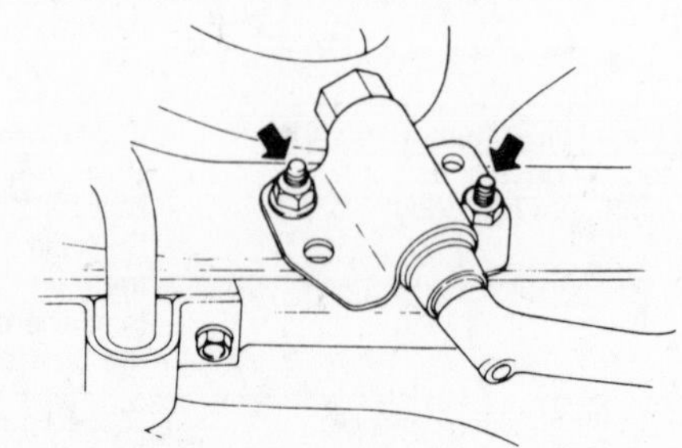

Idler arm removal—1976–83

17. Place a jack under the transmission and lift it slightly.
18. Loosen the two combination engine rear mounting/transmission mounting bolts. On models with a catalytic converter, loosen the two exhaust pipe hanger bolts.
19. On 1972 and later models, remove the four bolts (two on each side) securing the engine rear mounting/transmission support side member and detach the support from the frame.
20. On 1976 and later models, remove the bolts securing the idler arm to the frame, and push down the tie rod.
21. Pull the engine toward the front as far as possible and carefully raise the engine with the transmission up and out of the vehicle.

22. Install the engine in the reverse order of removal, taking note of the following:

- Do not connect any parts of the engine or transmission until the engine and transmission are in place on the engine/transmission mounts and secured by the mounting bolts.
- Secure the rear support first and then the front engine mounts, using the upper bolt hole as a guide.

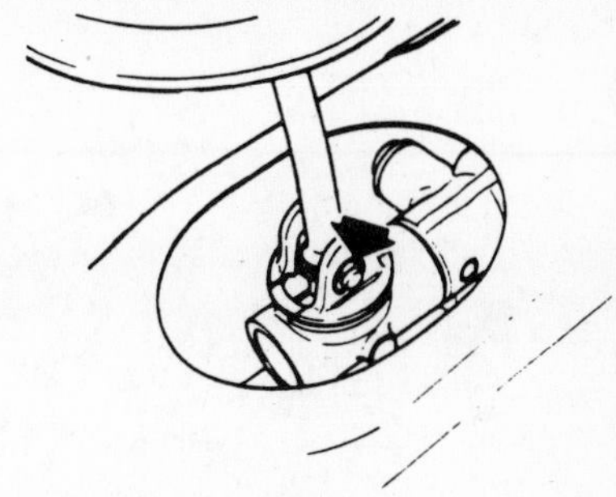

Removing the transmission control linkage—1984-86 Z20 and Z24 engines (w/MT)

1984-86 720-D Series

1. Disconnect the negative battery cable.
2. Remove the engine undercover.
3. Disconnect the windshield washer hose and then remove the hood. Scribe matchmarks around the hinges for easy installation.
4. Drain the engine oil. Drain the engine coolant from the radiator and the cylinder block.

   CAUTION: *When draining the coolant, keep in mind that cats and dogs are attracted by the ethylene glycol antifreeze, and are quite likely to drink any that is left in an uncovered container or in puddles on the ground. This will prove fatal in sufficient quantity. Always drain the coolant into a sealable container. Coolant should be reused unless it is contaminated or several years old.*
5. Drain the automatic transmission fluid on models so equipped.
6. Disconnect the air cleaner hose and then remove the air cleaner.
7. Remove the radiator and shroud as detailed later in this chapter. On models with automatic transmission oil coolers, disconnect and plug the oil lines at the radiator
8. Remove the coupling fan.
9. Disconnect the two heater hoses at the engine.
10. Remove the drive belts.
11. Remove the power steering pump from its bracket (if equipped). Disconnect the ground strap from the bracket.
12. On models with air conditioning, loosen the drive belt and remove the air conditioning compressor. Position it out of the way with the refrigerant lines still attached.
13. Remove the transmission control linkage.
14. Disconnect the speedometer cable. Tag and disconnect any electrical leads at the transmission.
15. On models with manual transmission, remove the clutch release cylinder and its bracket from the transmission. Position it aside without disconnecting the hydraulic lines.
16. Remove the bolts and disconnect the exhaust pipe at the manifold.
17. Disconnect and remove the parking brake cable at the brake lever side.
18. Matchmark the rear driveshaft to the

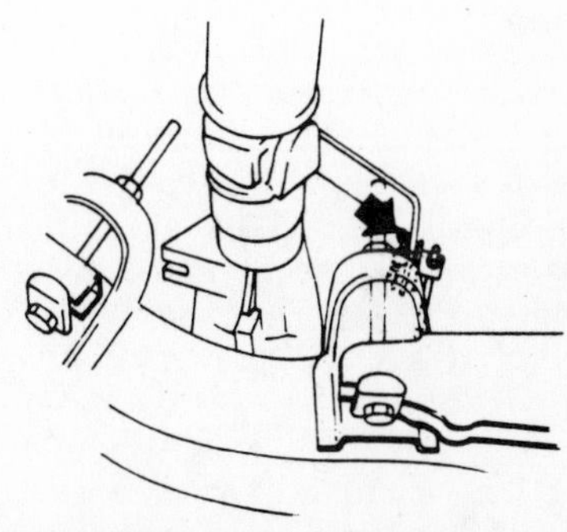

Removing the transmission control linkage—1984-86 Z20 and Z24 engines (w/AT)

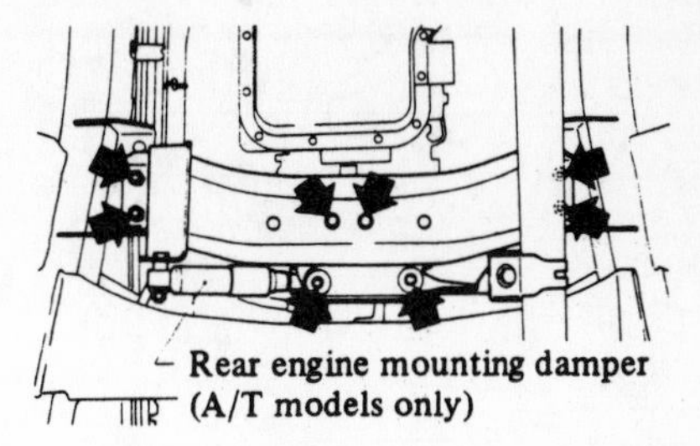

Removing the rear engine mount support—1984-86

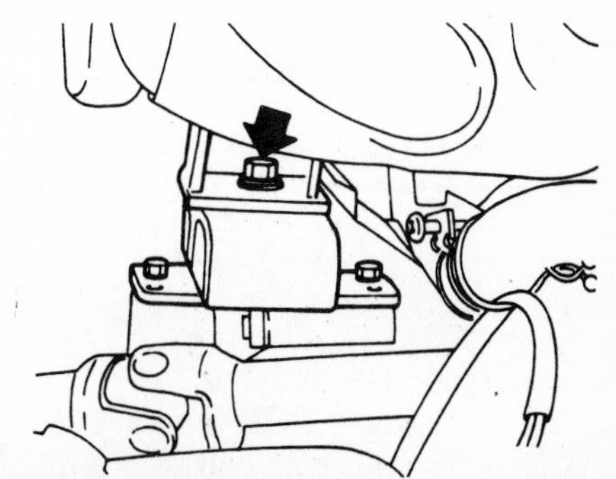

Front engine mount (left)—1984-86 Z20 and Z24 engines

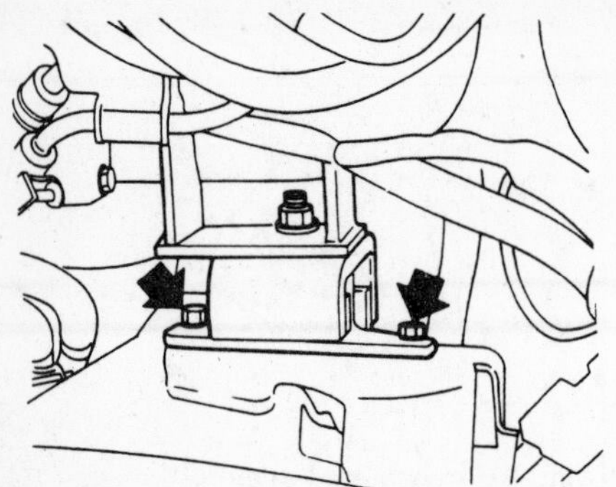
Front engine mount (right)—1984–86 Z20 and Z24 engines

Front engine mount (left)—1984–86 SD25 engines

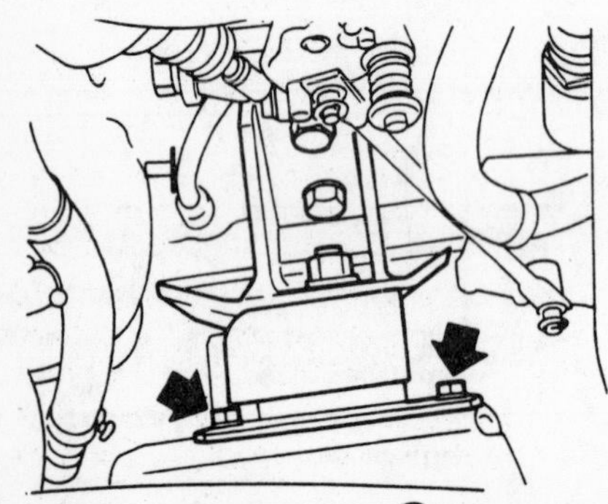
Front engine mount (right)—1984–86 SD25 engines

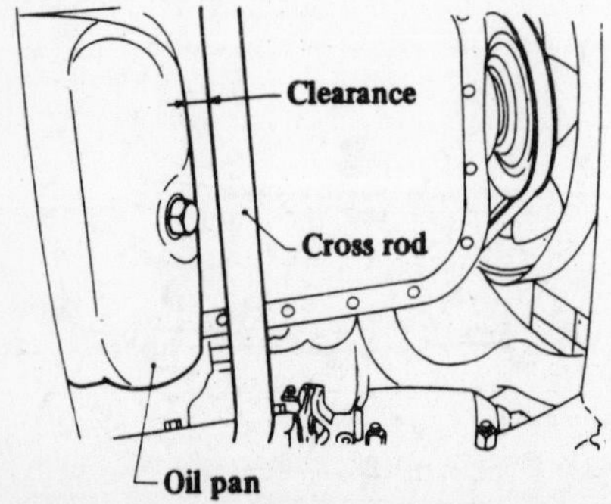

On models with an SD25 engine, make sure there is sufficient clearance between the cross rod and oil pan

transmission flange and then remove the driveshaft. Be sure to plug the hole in the extension housing.

19. Matchmark the front driveshaft (4wd models) to the transfer case flange and then remove the front driveshaft.

20. Attach an engine hoist chain to the lifting brackets on the engine and then raise the engine just enough to ease the weight on the front and rear engine mount insulators.

21. On models with 4wd, carefully slide a floor jack underneath the front differential carrier and remove the front mounting bolt. Remove the rear mounting bolts and crossmember and then slowly lower the carrier.

22. On models with automatic transmission, remove the rear engine mount support-to-body bolts.

23. Remove the mounting bolts for the front engine mount.

24. On models with a diesel engine, turn the steering wheel lock-to-lock a few times and check that there is sufficient clearance between the cross rod and the oil pan.

25. Tighten the engine hoist chain and carefully lift the engine/transmission assembly up and out of the truck. Be very careful not to bump into anything as the engine comes out of the engine compartment.

To install:

1. Slowly lower the engine/transmission assembly into the engine compartment.

2. Raise the transmission onto the crossmember with a floor jack.

3. Align the holes in the engine mounts and the frame, install the bolts and then remove the engine hoist chain.

4. On models with automatic transmission, install the rear engine mount support-to-body bolts.

5. On models with 4wd, carefully raise the floor jack underneath the front differential carrier and install the rear mounting bolts and crossmember. Install the front mounting bolt.

6. Install the front driveshaft (4wd models) to the transfer case flange.

7. Remove the plug in the extension housing and the connect the rear driveshaft to the transmission flange.

8. Connect and install the parking brake cable.

9. Install the the exhaust pipe at the manifold.

engine.

10. Install the clutch release cylinder and its bracket at the transmission.

11. Connect the speedometer cable. Reconnect any electrical leads at the transmission (check the tags you made in Step 14).

12. Install the transmission control linkage.

13. Install the air conditioning compressor and drive belt.
14. Install the power steering pump and its bracket (if equipped). Be sure to connect the ground strap to the bracket.
15. Install the drive belts.
16. Connect the heater hoses.
17. Install the coupling fan.
18. Install the radiator and shroud. Unplug the automatic transmission oil cooler lines and connect them (if equipped).
19. Install the air cleaner.
20. Refill the engine and automatic transmission with fluid.
21. Install and adjust the hood.
22. Install the engine undercover.
23. Connect the negative battery cable, start the truck and road test it.

1986-89 D21-D Series

1. Disconnect the negative battery cable.
2. Remove the engine undercover.
3. Disconnect the windshield washer hose and then remove the hood. Scribe matchmarks around the hinges for easy installation.
4. Drain the engine oil. Drain the engine coolant from the radiator and the cylinder block.

CAUTION: *When draining the coolant, keep in mind that cats and dogs are attracted by the ethylene glycol antifreeze, and are quite likely to drink any that is left in an uncovered container or in puddles on the ground. This will prove fatal in sufficient quantity. Always drain the coolant into a sealable container. Coolant should be reused unless it is contaminated or several years old.*

5. Drain the automatic transmission fluid on models so equipped.
6. Disconnect the air cleaner hose and then remove the air cleaner.
7. Remove the radiator and shroud as detailed later in this chapter. On models with automatic transmission oil coolers, disconnect and plug the oil lines at the radiator
8. Remove the coupling fan.
9. Disconnect the two heater hoses at the engine.
10. Remove the drive belts.
11. Remove the power steering pump from its bracket (if equipped). Disconnect the ground strap from the bracket.
12. On models with air conditioning, loosen the drive belt and remove the air conditioning compressor. Position it out of the way with the refrigerant lines still attached.
13. Remove the transmission control linkage.
14. On 4wd models, disconnect the starter leads and remove the starter. On 2wd models disconnect the starter motor leads.
15. Disconnect the speedometer cable. Tag and disconnect any electrical leads at the transmission.
16. On models with manual transmission, remove the clutch release cylinder and its bracket from the transmission. Position it aside without disconnecting the hydraulic lines.
17. Remove the bolts and disconnect the exhaust pipe at the manifold.
18. On 4wd models, matchmark the front driveshaft (4wd models) to the transfer case flange and then remove the front driveshaft.
19. On models with 4wd, carefully slide a floor jack underneath the front differential carrier and remove the front mounting bolt. Remove the rear mounting bolts and crossmember and then slowly lower the carrier.
20. On 4wd models, remove the transmission-to-engine bracket mounting nuts.
21. On 4wd models, remove the mounting bolts for the front engine mounts.
22. Attach an engine hoist chain to the lifting brackets on the engine and then raise the engine just enough to ease the weight on the front and rear engine mount insulators.
23. On 4wd models, remove the front differential carrier.
24. On 2wd models, matchmark the rear driveshaft to the transmission flange and then remove the driveshaft. Be sure to plug the hole in the extension housing.
25. On 2wd models, remove the transmission-to-rear engine mount bracket bolts.
26. On 2wd models, remove the transmission member.
27. On 4wd models, remove the transmission-to-engine mounting bolts.
28. Tighten the engine hoist chain and carefully lift the engine (4wd) or engine/transmission (2wd) assembly up and out of the truck. Be very careful not to bump into anything as the engine comes out of the engine compartment.

To install:

1. Slowly lower the engine/transmission assembly into the engine compartment.
2. Raise the transmission onto the crossmember with a floor jack.
3. Align the holes in the engine mounts and the frame, install the bolts and then remove the engine hoist chain.
4. On 4wd models, install the transmission-to-engine mounting bolts. Tighten the 16mm and 25mm bolts to 22–29 ft. lbs. (29–39 Nm).
5. On 2wd models, install the transmission member.
6. On 2wd models, install the transmission-to-rear engine mount bracket bolts and tighten to 30–38 ft. lbs. (41–52 Nm).
7. On 2wd models, install the rear driveshaft to the transmission flange.

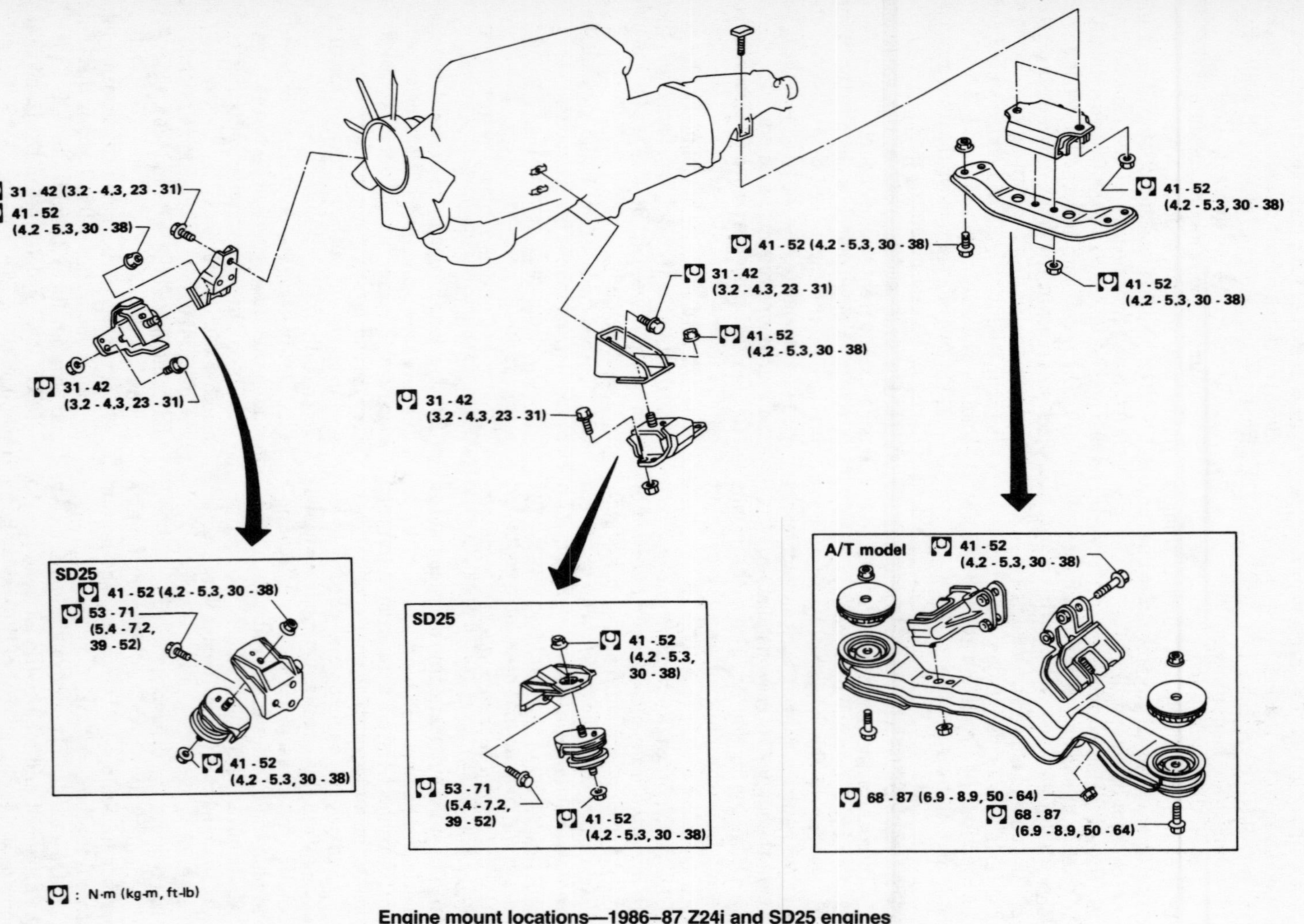

Engine mount locations—1986–87 Z24i and SD25 engines

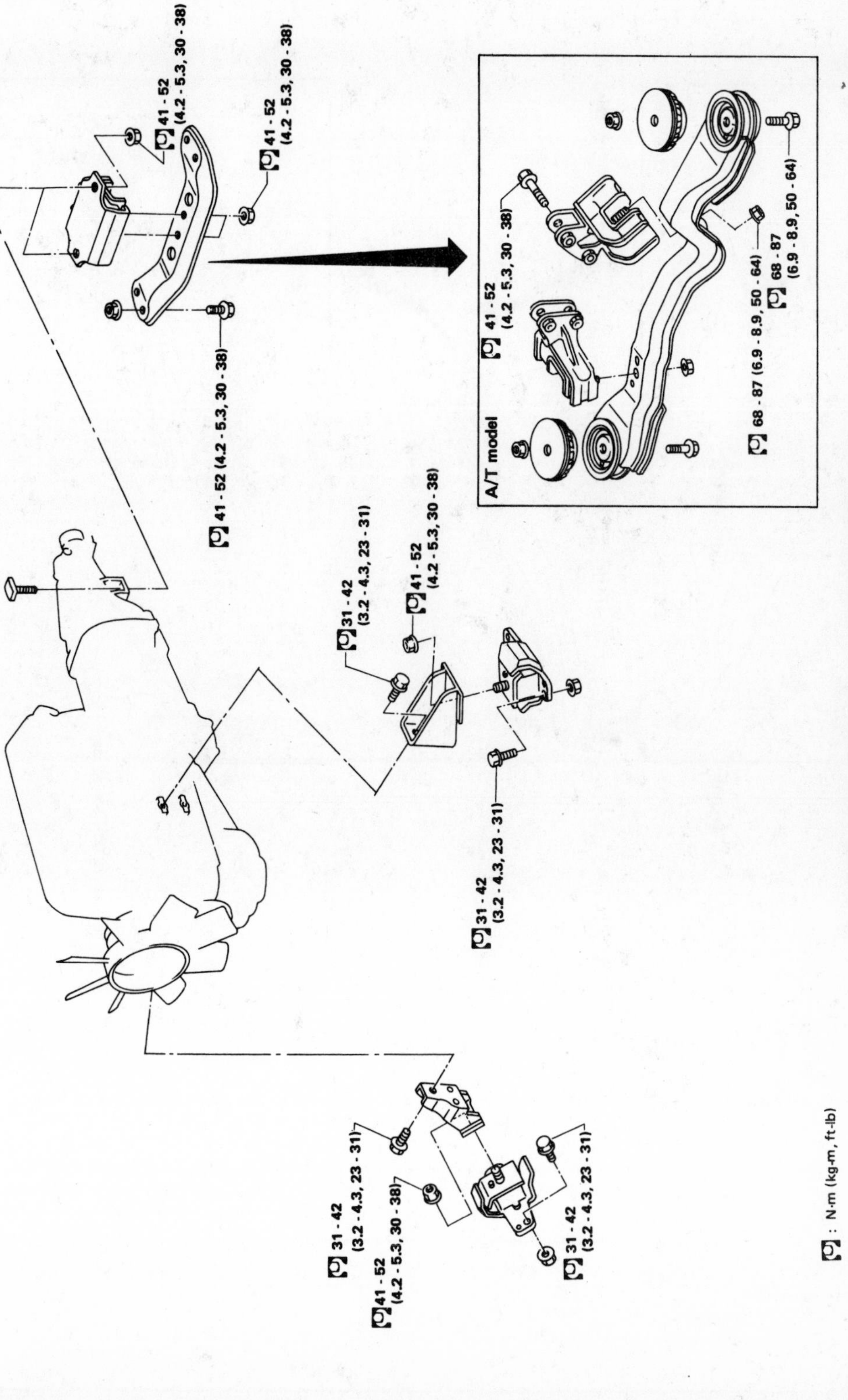

Engine mount locations—1988–89 Z24i engines

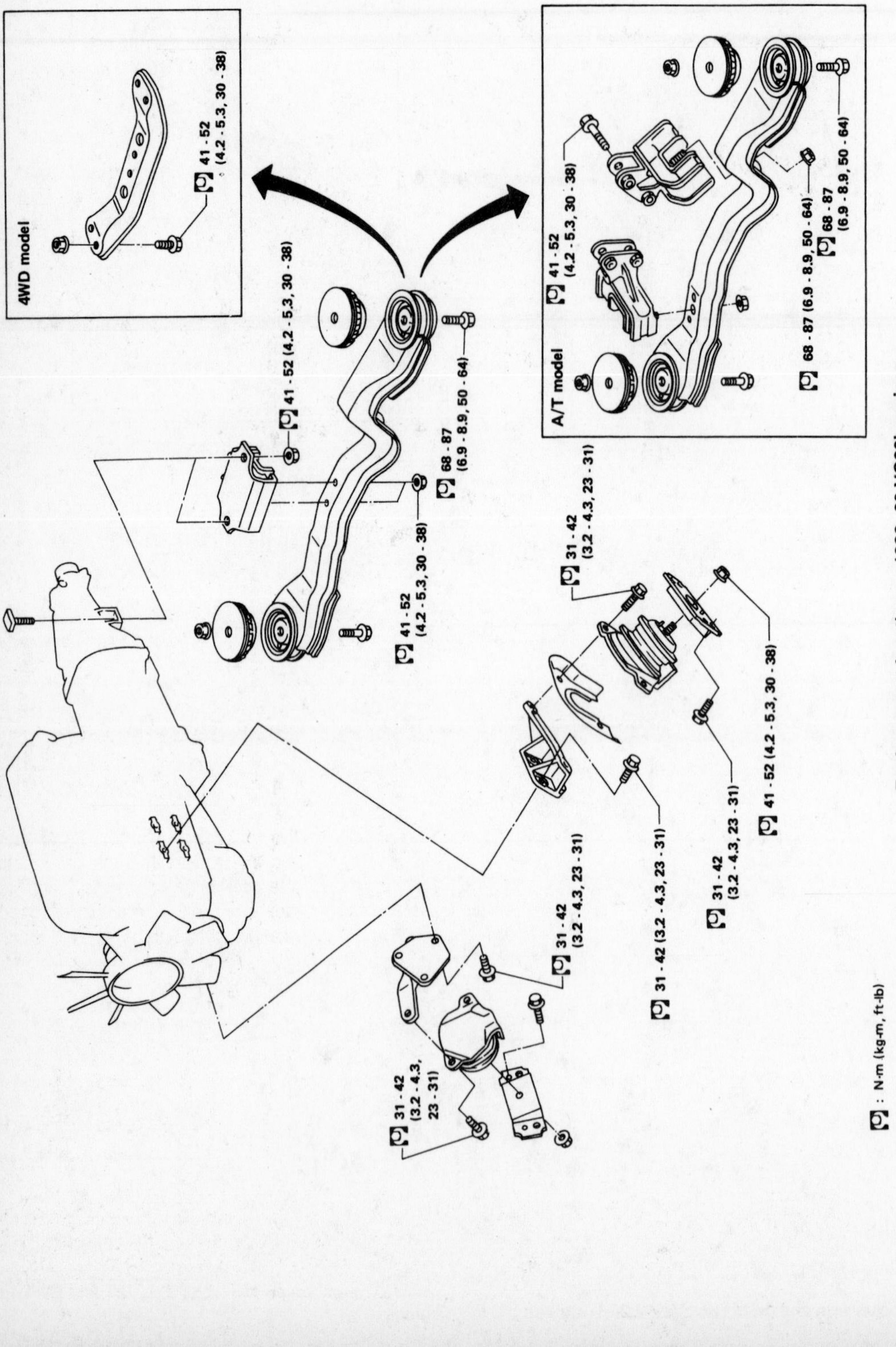

4WD model

41 - 52 (4.2 - 5.3, 30 - 38)

A/T model

41 - 52 (4.2 - 5.3, 30 - 38)

68 - 87 (6.9 - 8.9, 50 - 64)

68 - 87 (6.9 - 8.9, 50 - 64)

68 - 87 (6.9 - 8.9, 50 - 64)

41 - 52 (4.2 - 5.3, 30 - 38)

68 - 87 (6.9 - 8.9, 50 - 64)

41 - 52 (4.2 - 5.3, 30 - 38)

41 - 52 (4.2 - 5.3, 30 - 38)

31 - 42 (3.2 - 4.3, 23 - 31)

31 - 42 (3.2 - 4.3, 23 - 31)

31 - 42 (3.2 - 4.3, 23 - 31)

41 - 52 (4.2 - 5.3, 30 - 38)

31 - 42 (3.2 - 4.3, 23 - 31)

31 - 42 (3.2 - 4.3, 23 - 31)

31 - 42 (3.2 - 4.3, 23 - 31)

: N·m (kg-m, ft-lb)

Engine mount locations—1986–89 VG30i engines

8. On 4wd models, install the front differential carrier.

9. On 4wd models, install the mounting bolts for the front engine mounts and tighten to 23–31 ft. lbs. (31–42 Nm). On models with a diesel engine, tighten the right side to 30–38 ft. lbs. (41–52 Nm) and the left side to 39–52 ft. lbs. (53–71 Nm).

10. On 4wd models, install the transmission-to-engine bracket mounting nuts and tighten to 30–38 ft. lbs. (41–52 Nm).

11. On 4wd models, align the matchmarks on the front driveshaft to those on the transfer case flange and then install the front driveshaft.

12. Connect the exhaust pipe to the manifold.

13. Install the clutch release cylinder and its bracket to the transmission.

14. Connect the speedometer cable. Connect any electrical leads at the transmission.

15. On 4wd models, connect the starter leads and install the starter. On 2wd models, connect the starter motor leads.

16. Install the air conditioning compressor and drive belt.

17. Install the power steering pump and its bracket (if equipped). Be sure to connect the ground strap to the bracket.

18. Install the drive belts.

19. Connect the heater hoses.

20. Install the coupling fan.

21. Install the radiator and shroud. Unplug the automatic transmission oil cooler lines and connect them (if equipped).

22. Refill the engine and automatic transmission with fluid.

23. Install and adjust the hood.

24. Install the engine undercover.

25. Connect the negative battery cable, start the truck and road test it.

Cylinder Head Cover

REMOVAL AND INSTALLATION

1. Remove the air cleaner assembly.

2. Disconnect the PCV hose(s) from the cylinder head cover.

3. Remove the nuts and washers. Lift the cover off the cylinder head. Cover the oil return hole in the head to prevent dirt or objects from falling in. Remove the gasket.

4. To install, replace the cover gasket if it shows any signs of damage, breaks or cracking. Tighten the nuts evenly, reconnect the PCV hose and install the air cleaner assembly.

Rocker Arms and Rocker Pivots

REMOVAL AND INSTALLATION

L16, L18 and L20B Engines

1. Remove the cylinder head cover.

2. Loosen the rocker pivot locknut. Lower the pivot by screwing it down into the cylinder head.

3. Remove the rocker arm by pressing down on the valve spring.

4. To remove the rocker pivots, loosen the locknut, then unscrew the pivot from the cylinder head.

5. Install the pivots and screw them into the cylinder head. Tighten the locknut.

6. Press down on the valve spring and install the rocker arm.

7. Install the cylinder head cover.

Rocker Arm/Shaft Assembly

REMOVAL AND INSTALLATION

Z20, Z22, Z24 and Z24i Engines

1. Remove the cylinder head cover. The rocker shaft assembly is removed by simply removing the retaining bolts.

NOTE: *When removing the bolts, DO NOT REMOVE THE NO.1 AND NO. 5 BRACKET BOLTS SINCE THE ROCKER SHAFT BRACKET AND ROCKER ARM WILL SPRING OUT!*

2. Remove the rocker shaft bracket and then slide the valve rockers and springs off of the rocker shaft. Be absolutely sure to keep all parts in the order in which they were removed; they must be reassembled in the same order.

3. Inspect the rocker arms and shaft for damage, replace as necessary.

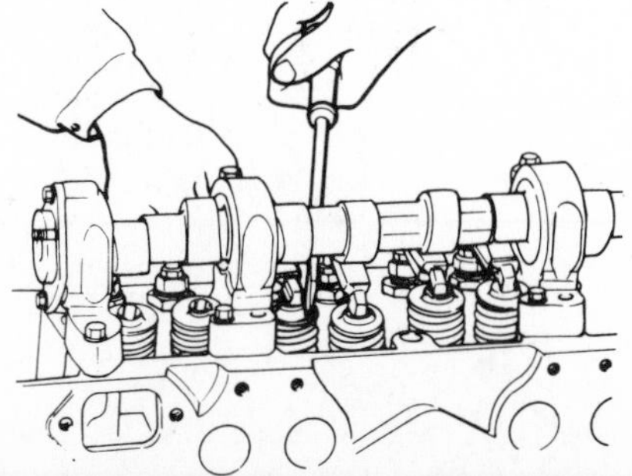

Rocker arm and pivot removal—L20B engines

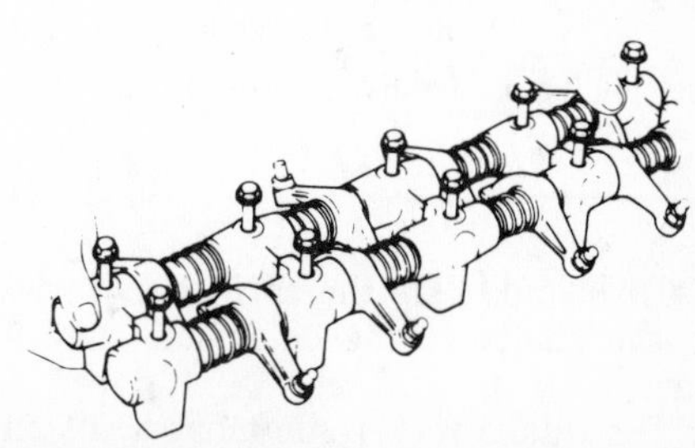

Rocker shaft assembly—Z20, Z22, Z24 and Z24i engines

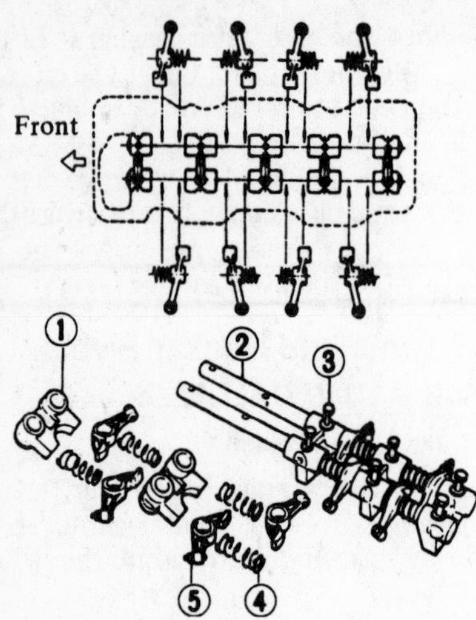

Rocker arm installation—Z20, Z22, Z24 and Z24i engines

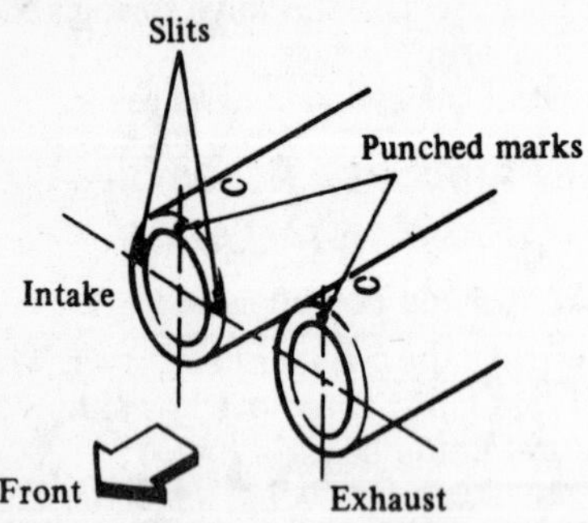

Rocker shaft installation—Z20, Z22, Z24 and Z24i engines

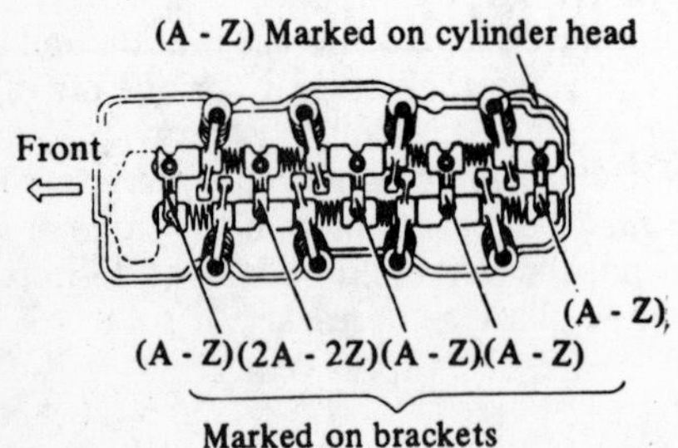

Rocker shaft/arm identification—Z20, Z22, Z24 and Z24i engines

4. To install, slide the springs and rockers onto the shafts in the oder that they were removed.

5. The intake rocker shaft has a slit on its leading edge, but the ehaust shaft does not. Additionally, each shaft has a punch mark on its leading edge. The shafts should be assembled with these marks facing upward as they are used for oil hole identification.

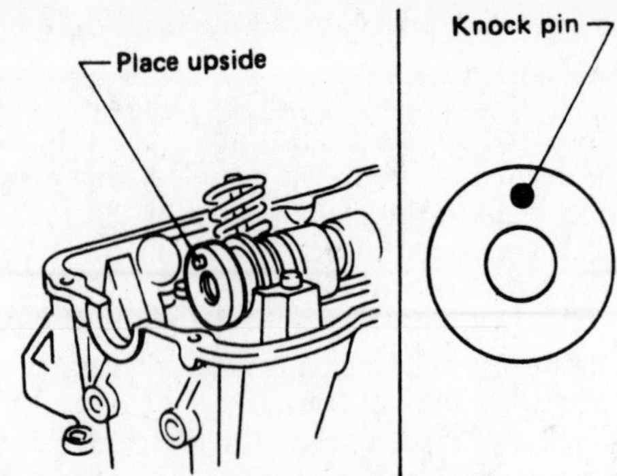

Make sure that the camshaft knockpin is in the UP position—Z20, Z22, Z24 and Z24i engines

6. The intake and exhaust rockers for the Nos. 1 and 3 cylinders are the same and are identified by the mark **1**. The same holds true for the rockers on Nos. 2 and 4 cylinders; they are identified with a **2**.

7. The rocker shaft brackets are also marked as to their original location; simply match them to the like marks on the cylinder head.

8. At this point, reinsert a bracket bolt into holes for the No. 1 and No. 5 brackets (any bolt is fine). This will insure that the assembly stays together while you mount it on the head.

9. Mount the rocker shaft assembly on the cylinder head in a manner that accommodates the camshaft knock pin and then tighten the retaining bolts gradually, in two or three stages to 11–18 ft. lbs. (15–25 Nm).

VG30i Engines

1. Remove the cylinder head covers.
2. Remove the rocker arm shaft-to-cylinder head bolts and lift the rocker arm/shaft assembly from the cylinder head.
3. Separate the rocker arms from the shaft.

NOTE: *When separating the rocker arms*

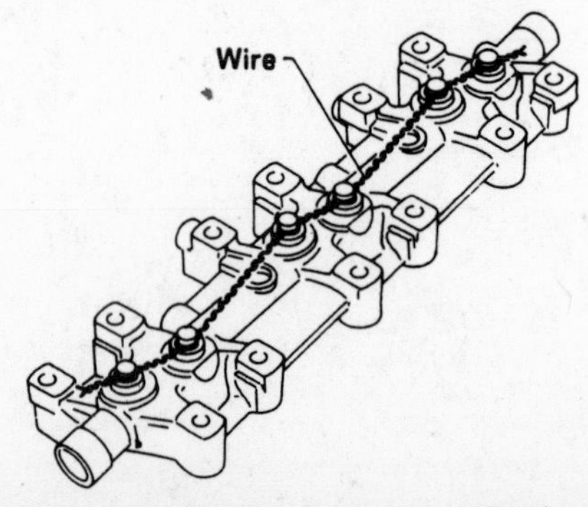

Hold the rockers together with wire—VG30i engines

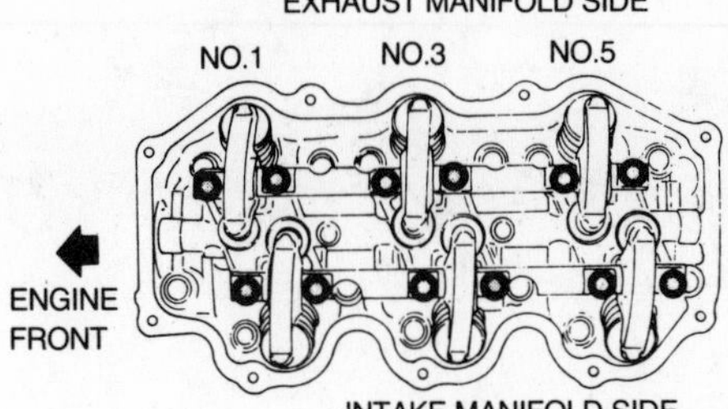

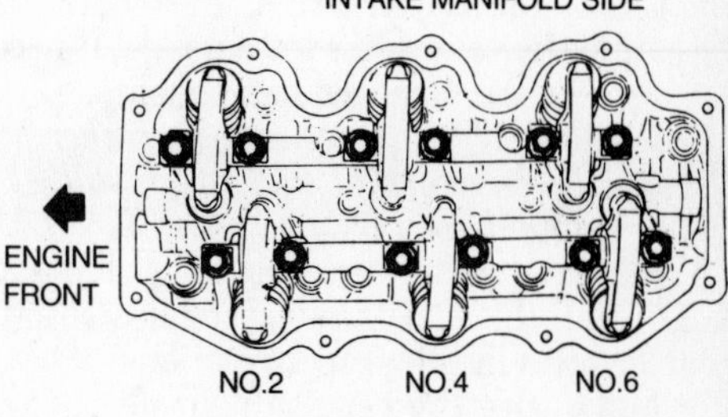

Rocker shaft installation direction—VG30i engines

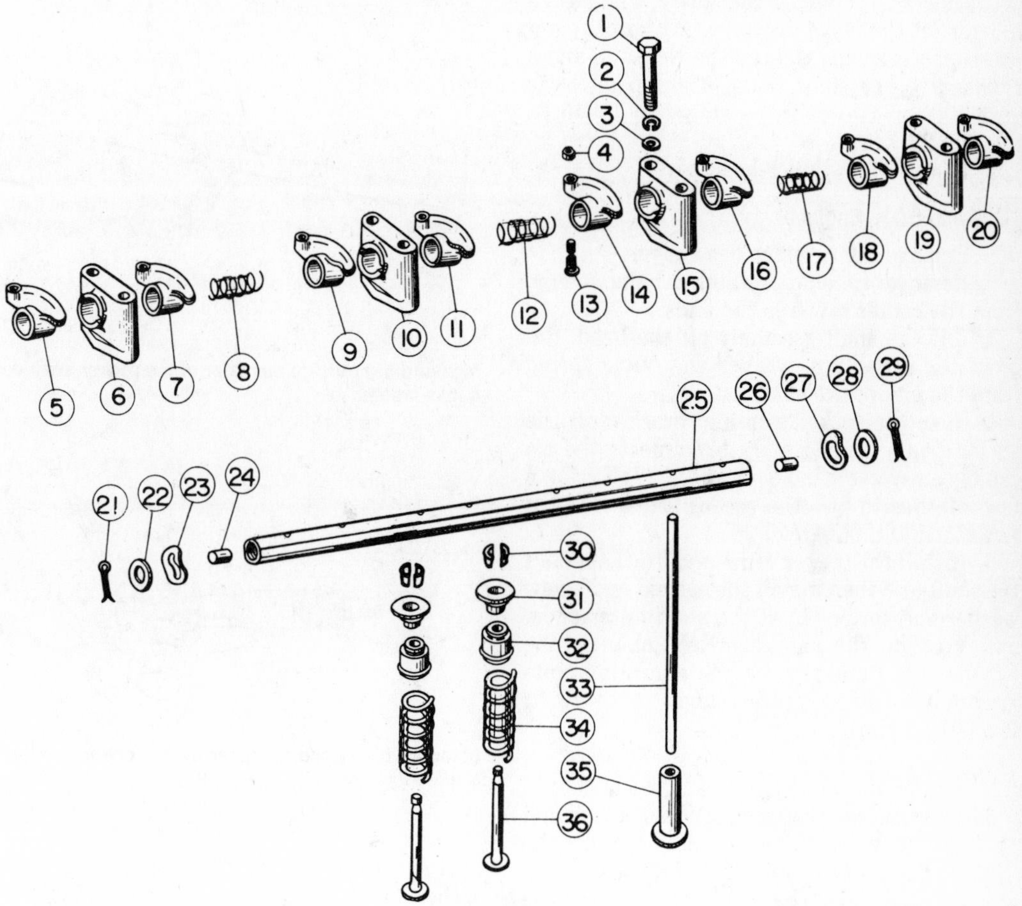

1. Bolt
2. Lock washer
3. Flat washer
4. Lock nut
5. Valve rocker A
6. Rocker shaft bracket
7. Valve rocker B
8. Inside spring
9. Valve rocker C
10. Rocker shaft bracket
11. Valve rocker D
12. Inside spring
13. Adjusting screw
14. Valve rocker A
15. Rocker shaft bracket
16. Valve rocker B
17. Inside spring
18. Valve rocker C
19. Rocker shaft bracket
20. Valve rocker D
21. Cotter pin
22. Washer
23. Outside spring
24. Plug
25. Rocker shaft
26. Plug
27. Outside spring
28. Washer
29. Cotter pin
30. Split collar
31. Spring seat
32. Valve stem seal
33. Push rod
34. Valve spring
35. Valve lifter
36. Valve

Exploded view of the rocker assembly—SD22 and SD25 engines

from the rocker arm shafts, be sure to keep the parts in order for reinstallation purposes.

4. Check the rocker arms, the shafts, the valves and the valve lifter for damage. If necessary, replace the damaged components.

CAUTION: *When installing the rocker arm shafts, be certain that they are installed in their original positions.*

5. Slide the rocker arms onto the shafts and then install the shaft/arm assemblies onto the cylinder head in the proper positions.
6. Make sure the camshaft knock pin is at the top of the camshaft and that the lobe is not in the lifted position. Set the No. 1 piston at TDC of its compression stroke and then tighten the rocker shaft bolts for the Nos. 2, 4 and 6 cylinders. Set the No. 4 piston at TDC of its compression stroke and tighten the Nos. 1, 3 and 5 cylinder rocker shaft bolts. Tighten all bolts gradually, in two or three stages to 13–16 ft. lbs. (18–22 Nm).
7. Install the cylinder head cover.

SD22 and SD25 Engines

1. Remove the cylinder head cover.
2. Remove the shaft retaining bolts evenly, from the center towards the ends.
3. Lift the shaft assembly off the head. Remove the cotter pin, washer and outer spring from the end of the shaft.
4. Slide the rocker arm and bracket off the shaft. It may be necessary to immerse the assembly in water heated to 160°F (71°C) for a few minutes to free the rocker arms. NEVER HAMMER THEM OFF!
5. Install the rocker arms and brackets onto the shaft and then install the soring, and a new washer and cotter pin at the shaft outer ends.
6. Position the shaft/arm assembly on the cylinder head and tighten the mounting bolts gradually, in two or three stages to 14–18 ft. lbs. (20–22 Nm).

INSPECTION

The oil clearance between the rocker arm and shaft is measured in two steps. Measure the outside diameter of the rocker shaft with a micrometer. Measure the inside diameter of the rocker arms with a dial indicator. The difference between the rocker arm inner diameter and the shaft outer diameter is the oil clearance. Clearance specs are as follows:

- Z20: 0.0003–0.0019 in. (0.008–0.050mm)
- Z22: 0.0003–0.0019 in. (0.008–0.050mm)
- Z24: 0.0003–0.0019 in. (0.008–0.050mm)
- Z24i: 0.0003–0.0019 in. (0.008–0.050mm)
- VG30i: 0.0003–0.0019 in. (0.008–0.050mm)
- SD22: 0.0008–0.0020 in. (0.02–0.05mm)
- SD25: 0.0008–0.0020 in. (0.02–0.05mm)

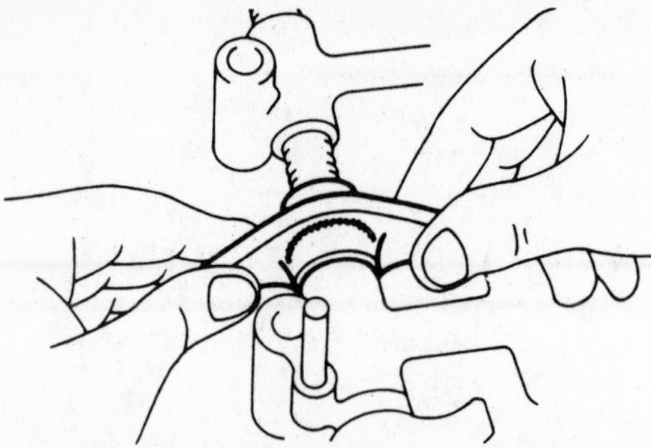

Check the rocker arm-to-shaft wear by wiggling the arm laterally on the shaft; little or no movement should be felt

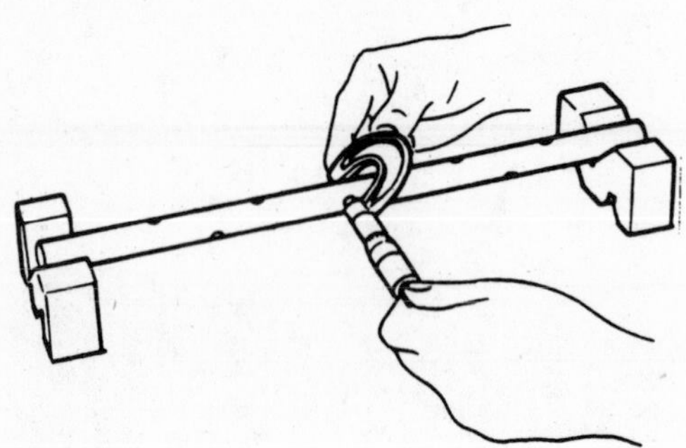

Measure the outside diameter of the rocker shaft with a micrometer

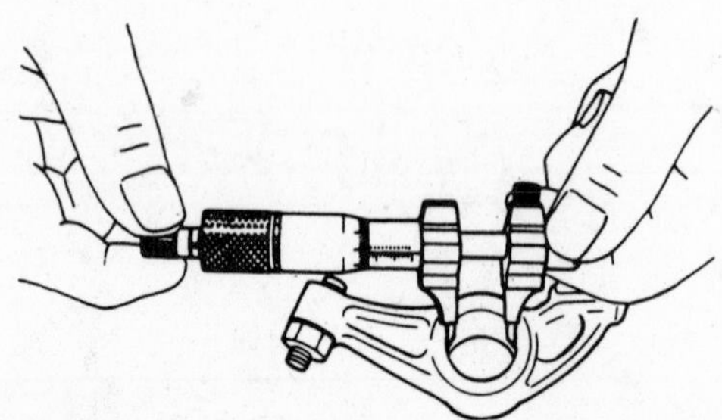

Measure the inside diameter of the rocker shaft with a dial indicator

If specs are not within these ranges, replace either the rocker shaft or rocker arm. Clearance can also be checked by moving the rocker arm laterally on the shaft when assembled. *There should be little or no movement.*

While disassembled, check the cam follower end (the flat end that contacts the camshaft) of the rocker arm for excess wear. The surface should be smooth and shiny. If excess wear is evident, check also the lobe of the camshaft, it may also be worn.

Reassemble the rocker shaft assemblies in the exact opposite order or removal. Accelerated camshaft wear and/or sloppy valve action will result if rocker arms are mixed and end up operating against the wrong cam lobes.

Thermostat

REMOVAL AND INSTALLATION

1. Drain the engine coolant into a clean container so that the level is below the thermostat housing.

CAUTION: *When draining the coolant, keep in mind that cats and dogs are attracted by the ethylene glycol antifreeze, and are quite likely to drink any that is left in an uncovered container or in puddles on the ground. This will prove fatal in sufficient quantity. Always drain the coolant into a sealable container. Coolant should be reused unless it is contaminated or several years old.*

2. Disconnect the upper radiator hose at the water outlet.

3. Loosen the two securing nuts and remove the water outlet, gasket, and the thermostat from the thermostat housing.

4. When installing the thermostat always use a new gasket with sealer and make sure the

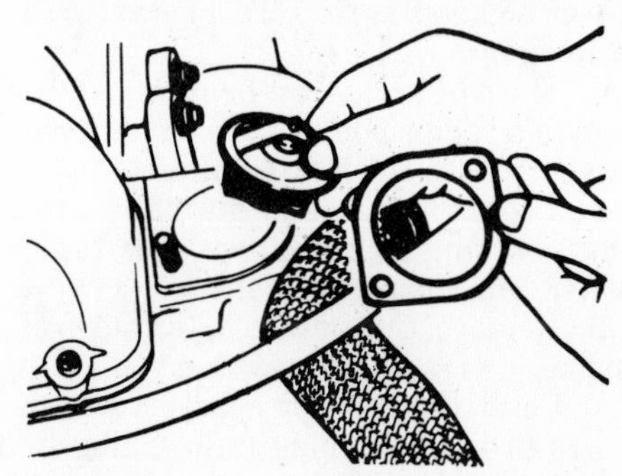

Thermostat removal—L16, L18 and L20B engines

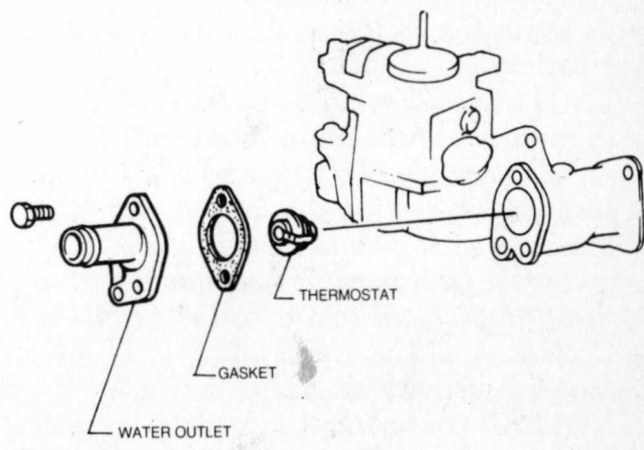

Thermostat removal—Z20, Z22, Z24 and Z24i engines

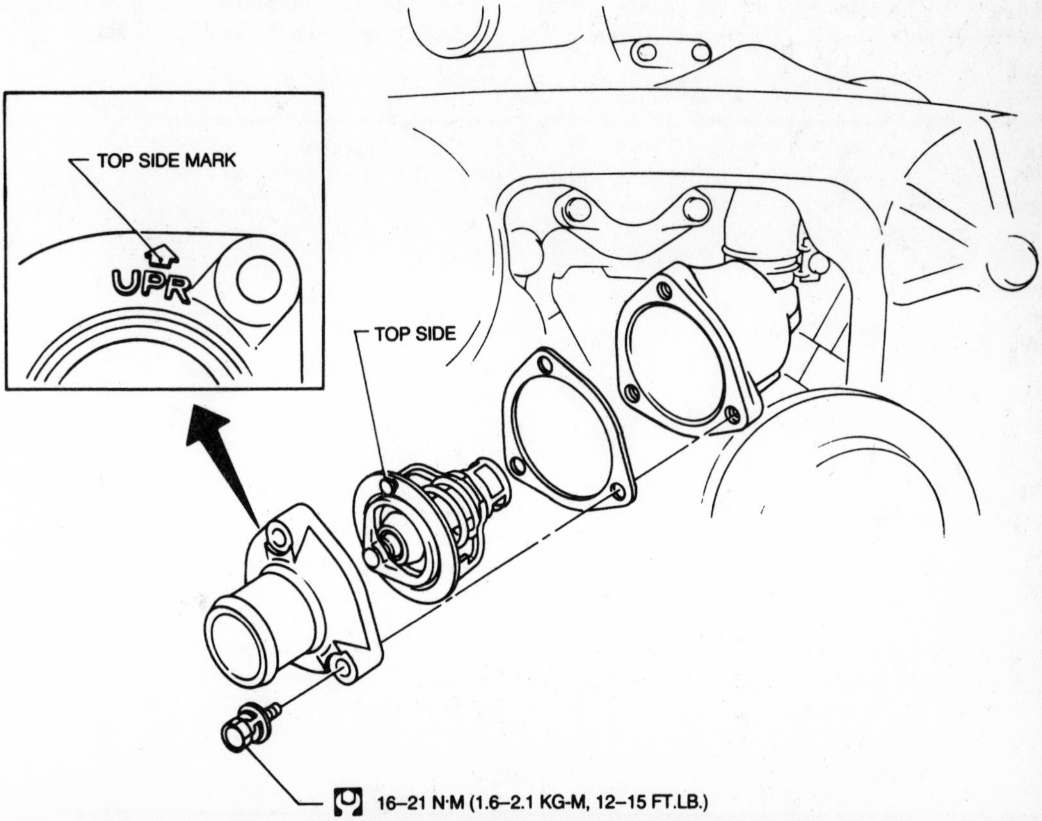

Thermostat removal—VG30i engines

thermostat spring is facing the inside of the engine. The factory installed thermostat opening temperature is 180°F (82°C) for trucks sold in the U.S., 190°F (88°C) for trucks sold in Canada.

Intake Manifold

REMOVAL AND INSTALLATION

L16, L18 and L20B Engines

1. Remove the air cleaner assembly together with all of the attending hoses. Remove the EGR tube on 1974-80 models.
2. Drain the cooling system and disconnect the battery.

CAUTION: *When draining the coolant, keep in mind that cats and dogs are attracted by the ethylene glycol antifreeze, and are quite likely to drink any that is left in an uncovered container or in puddles on the ground. This will prove fatal in sufficient quantity. Always drain the coolant into a sealable container. Coolant should be reused unless it is contaminated or several years old.*

NOTE: *It is important to replace the gasket whenever the intake manifold is removed. Because the intake and exhaust manifolds share a common gasket, whenever the intake manifold is removed, the exhaust manifold must also be removed, so that the gasket can be replaced.*

Intake manifold—L16, L18 and L20B engines

3. Disconnect the throttle linkage, fuel, and vacuum lines from the carburetor. Label all wires and hoses as they are removed to simplify installation.
4. The carburetor can be removed from the manifold at this point or can be removed as an assembly with the intake manifold.
5. Loosen the intake manifold attaching nuts, working from the two ends toward the center, and then remove them.
6. Remove the intake manifold from the engine.
7. Cover the cylinder head ports with shop cloths to keep anything from falling into the cylinder head or block.
8. When installing the intake manifold, always use a new gasket. Tighten the manifold bolts from the center outwards, in two progressive steps, to 9–12 ft. lbs. (12–16 Nm).

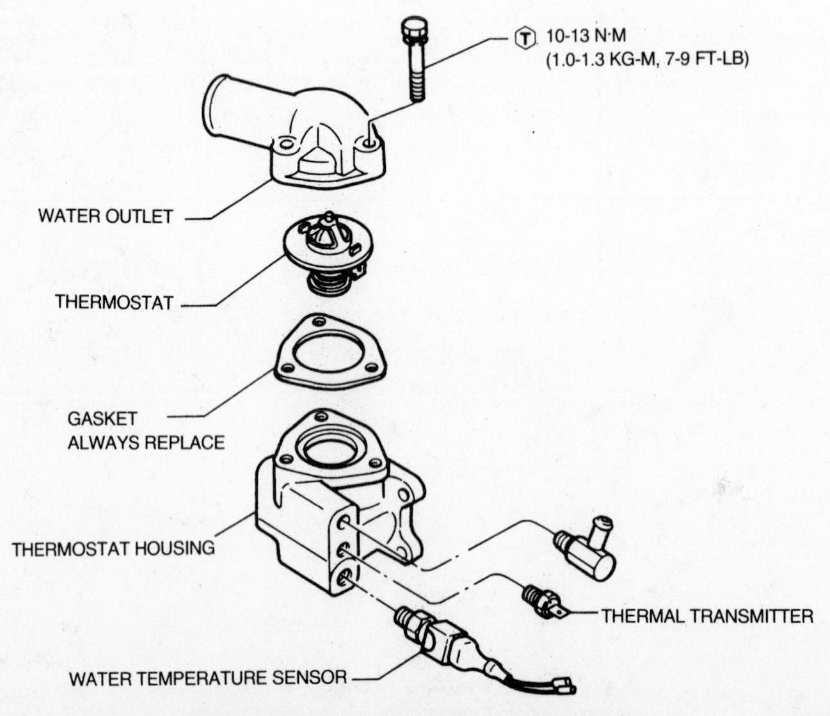

Thermostat removal—SD22 and SD25 engines

9. Connect all hoses and lines and install the carburetor (if removed). Install the air cleaner and fill the cooling system.

Z20, Z22, Z24 and Z24i Engines

NOTE: *Always release the fuel pressure on fuel injected engines before removing any fuel system component.*

1. Drain the coolant and disconnect the battery cable.

CAUTION: *When draining the coolant, keep in mind that cats and dogs are attracted by the ethylene glycol antifreeze, and are quite likely to drink any that is left in an uncovered container or in puddles on the ground. This will prove fatal in sufficient quantity. Always drain the coolant into a sealable container. Coolant should be reused unless it is contaminated or several years old.*

2. On the Z24i, remove the air cleaner hoses. On the Z20, Z22 and Z24, remove the air cleaner.
3. Remove the radiator hoses from the manifold.
4. On the Z20, Z22 and Z24, remove the fuel, air and vacuum hoses from the carburetor. Remove the throttle linkage and remove the carburetor.
5. Remove the throttle cable and disconnect the fuel pipe and the return fuel line on the Z24i. Plug the fuel pipe to prevent spilling fuel.

NOTE: *When unplugging wires and hoses, mark each hose and its connection with a piece of masking tape, then mark the two pieces of tape with the numbers 1, 2, 3, etc. When assembling, simply match the pieces of tape.*

6. Remove all remaining wires, tubes, the air cleaner bracket (Z20, Z22 and Z24) and the EGR and PCV tubes from the rear of the intake manifold. Remove the air induction pipe from the front of the engine (Z20, Z22 and Z24). Remove the manifold supports on the Z24i.
7. Unbolt and remove the intake manifold. On the Z24i, remove the manifold with injectors, EGR valve, fuel tubes, etc., still attached.
8. Clean the gasket mounting surfaces then install the intake manifold on the engine. Always use a new intake manifold gasket. Tighten the mounting bolts from the center, out, to 12–15 ft. lbs. (16–21 Nm)
9. Connect all electrical connections, tubes, the air cleaner bracket (Z20, Z22 and Z24) and the EGR and PCV tubes to the rear of the intake manifold. Install the air induction pipe to the front of the engine (Z20, Z22 and Z24). Install the manifold supports on the Z24i.
10. Install the throttle cable and reconnect

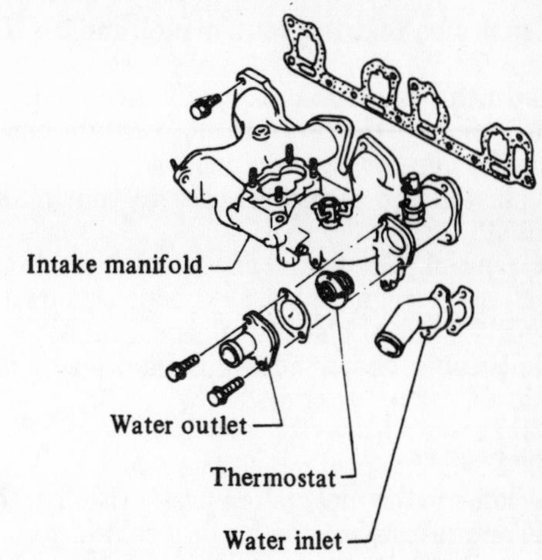

Intake manifold—Z20, Z22 and Z24 engines

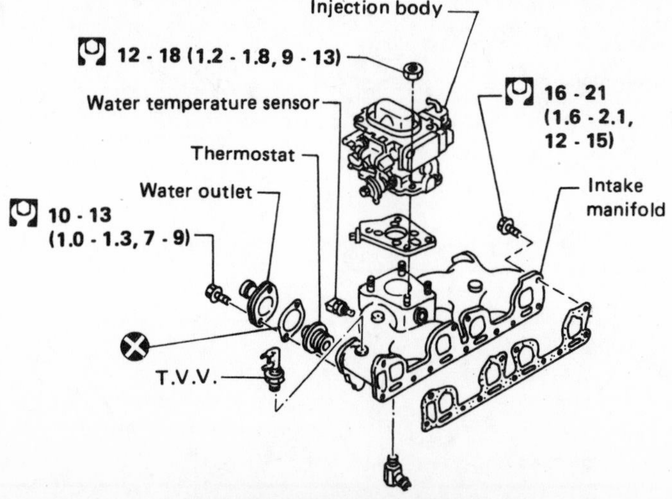

Intake manifold—Z24i engines

the fuel pipe and the return fuel line on the Z24i.

11. Install the carburetor and throttle linkage. Reconnect the fuel, air and vacuum hoses to the carburetor on these models.

12. Install the radiator hoses to the intake manifold.

13. On the Z24i, install the air cleaner hoses. On all other engines, install the air cleaner.

14. Refill the coolant level and connect the battery cable. Start the engine and check for leaks.

VG30i Engines

1. Release the fuel system pressure (Chapter One) and disconnect the battery cables.

2. Drain coolant by removing the drain plug on the left side of the cylinder block.

CAUTION: *When draining the coolant, keep in mind that cats and dogs are attracted by the ethylene glycol antifreeze, and are quite likely to drink any that is left in an uncovered container or in puddles on the ground. This will prove fatal in sufficient quantity. Always drain the coolant into a sealable container. Coolant should be reused unless it is contaminated or several years old.*

3. Disconnect all valves, lines, hoses, cables and or brackets to gain access to the collector cover and collector assembly retaining bolts.

4. Remove the collector cover. Remove the collector-to-intake manifold bolts in numerical order.

5. Remove the intake manifold and injection unit assembly. Loosen intake manifold bolts in the sequence shown.

6. Install the intake manifold and injection unit assembly with a new gasket to the engine. Tighten the manifold bolts and nuts in two or three stages, to 12–14 ft. lbs. (16–20 Nm) in the order shown.

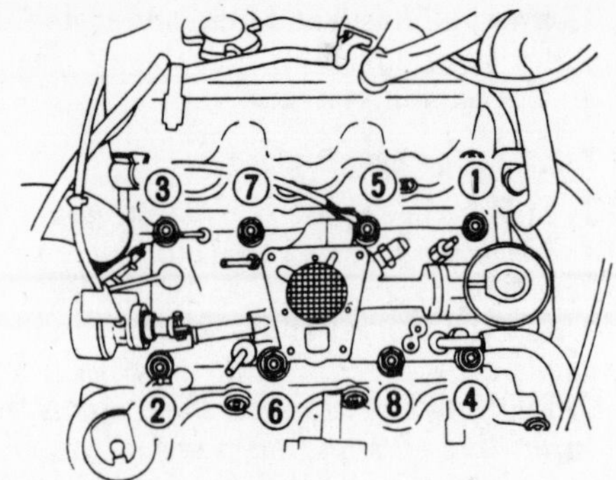

Intake manifold bolt loosening sequence—VG30i engines

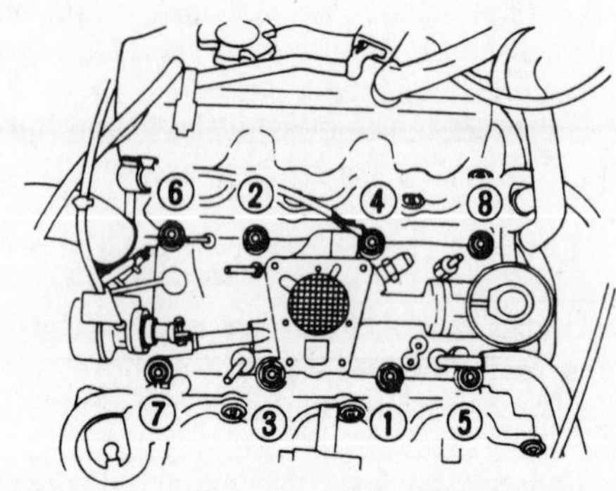

Intake manifold bolt tightening sequence—VG30i engines

7. Install the collector and collector cover with new gaskets. Tighten collector-to-intake manifold bolts in two or three stages, in the reverse order of removal.

8. Connect all valves, lines, hoses, cables and or brackets to the collector cover and collector assembly.

9. Refill the cooling system. Reconnect the battery cables.

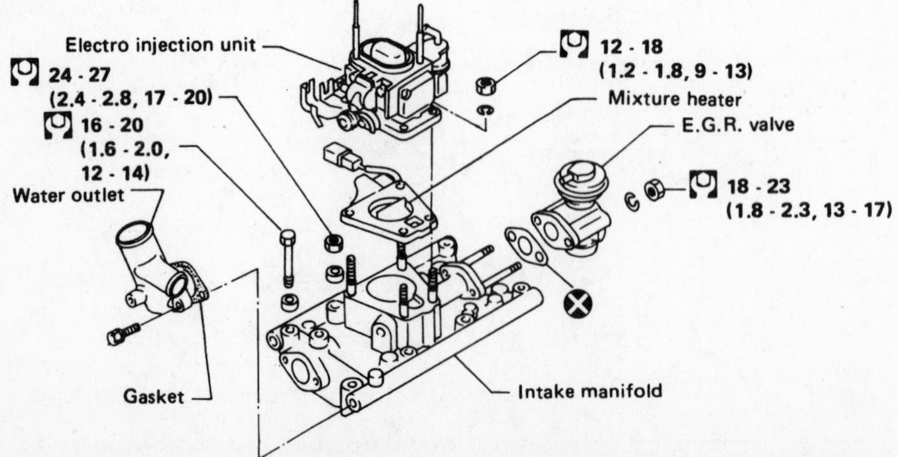

Intake manifold—VG30i engines

10. Check fluid levels , start the engine and check for leaks.

SD22 and SD25 Engines

1. Drain the coolant and disconnect the battery cable.

CAUTION: *When draining the coolant, keep in mind that cats and dogs are attracted by the ethylene glycol antifreeze, and are quite likely to drink any that is left in an uncovered container or in puddles on the ground. This will prove fatal in sufficient quantity. Always drain the coolant into a sealable container. Coolant should be reused unless it is contaminated or several years old.*

2. Tag and disconnect the lines and hoses at the throttle chamber/venturi, dropping resistor and breather. On California SD22 engines, disconnect the EGR pipe at the valve.
3. Disconnect and remove the dashpot from the intake manifold on SD22 engines (exhaust manifold – Calif.).
4. Remove the intake manifold.
5. Scrape any old gasket material off the cylinder head mounting surface and install the manifold using a new gasket. Tighten the bolts gradually, in two or three stages.
6. Install the dashpot and connect all lines, hoses and pipes.
7. Refill the cooling system.

Exhaust Manifold

REMOVAL AND INSTALLATION

All Except SD22, SD25 and VG30I Engines

NOTE: *You may find that removing the intake manifold will provide better access to the exhaust manifold on some early models.*

1. Remove the air cleaner assembly. Remove the heat shield.
2. Tag and disconnect the high tension wires from the spark plugs on the exhaust side of the engine.
3. Disconnect the exhaust pipe from the exhaust manifold.

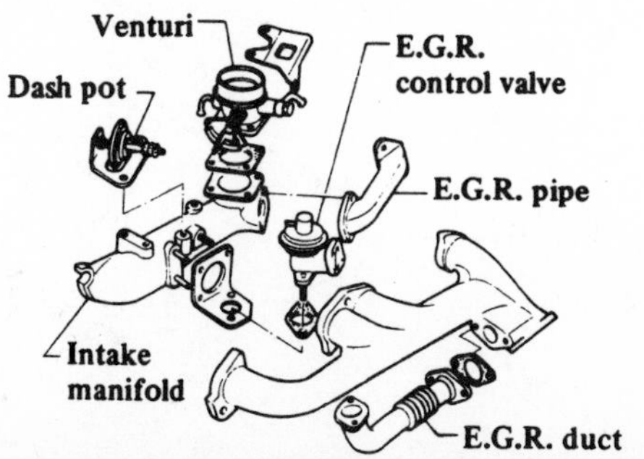

Intake and exhaust manifolds—Calif. SD22 engine shown; other diesels similar

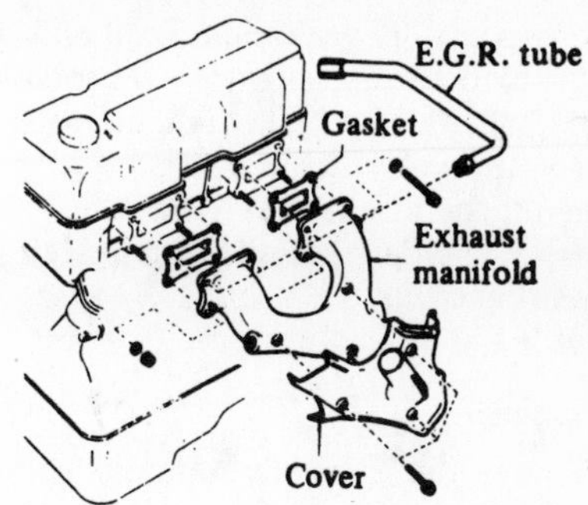

Exhaust manifold—Z20, Z22 and Z24 engines

NOTE: *Soak the exhaust pipe retaining bolts with penetrating oil if necessary to loosen them.*

4. On the carbureted models, remove the air induction and/or the EGR tubes from the exhaust manifold. On the Z24i, disconnect the exhaust gas sensor electrical connector.
5. Remove the exhaust manifold mounting nuts and then remove the manifold from the cylinder head.
6. Using a putty knife, clean the gasket mounting surfaces.
7. Install the manifold onto the engine, use new gaskets and, from the center working to the end, tighten the exhaust manifold nuts/bolts to 12–15 ft. lbs. (16–21 Nm)
8. Install the air induction and/or the EGR tubes to the exhaust manifold or the exhaust gas sensor electrical connector.
9. Reconnect exhaust pipe to the manifold.
10. Connect spark plug wires and air cleaner and any related hoses.
11. Start engine and check for exhaust leaks.

SD22 and SD25 Engines

1. Drain the coolant and disconnect the battery cable.

CAUTION: *When draining the coolant, keep in mind that cats and dogs are attracted by the ethylene glycol antifreeze, and are quite likely to drink any that is left in an uncovered container or in puddles on the ground. This will prove fatal in sufficient quantity. Always drain the coolant into a sealable container. Coolant should be reused unless it is contaminated or several years old.*

2. Tag and disconnect the lines and hoses at the throttle chamber/venturi, dropping resistor and breather. On California SD22 engines, disconnect the EGR pipe at the valve.
3. Disconnect and remove the dashpot from the intake manifold on SD22 engines (exhaust manifold – Calif.).
4. Remove the intake manifold and then remove the exhaust manifold.

5. Scrape any old gasket material off the cylinder head mounting surface and install the manifold using a new gasket. Tighten the bolts gradually, in two or three stages.
6. Install the intake manifold.
7. Install the dashpot and connect all lines, hoses and pipes.
8. Refill the cooling system.

VG30i Engines

1. Remove the exhaust manifold sub-cover and manifold cover. Remove the EGR tube from the right side exhaust manifold. Remove the exhaust manifold stay.
2. Disconnect the left side exhaust manifold at the exhaust pipe by removing retaining nuts and then disconnect the right side manifold from the connecting pipe.

NOTE: *Soak the exhaust pipe retaining bolts with penetrating oil if necessary to loosen them.*

3. Remove bolts for each manifold in the order shown.
4. Clean all gasket surfaces. Install new gaskets.
5. Install the manifold to the engine, tightening the mounting bolts alternately, in two stages, in the order shown. Tighten the left side bolts to 13–16 ft. lbs. (18–22 Nm); tighten the right side bolts to 16–20 ft. lbs. (22–27 Nm).
6. Reconnect the exhaust pipe and the connecting pipe. Be careful not break these bolts.
7. Install the exhaust manifold stay and the EGR tube to the right side manifold.

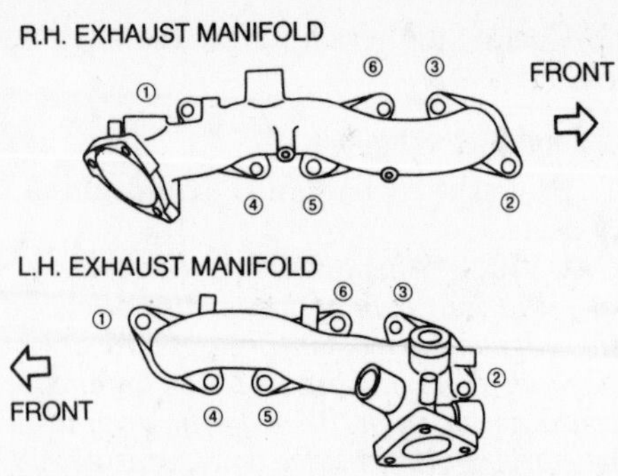

Exhaust manifold bolt loosening sequence—VG30i engines

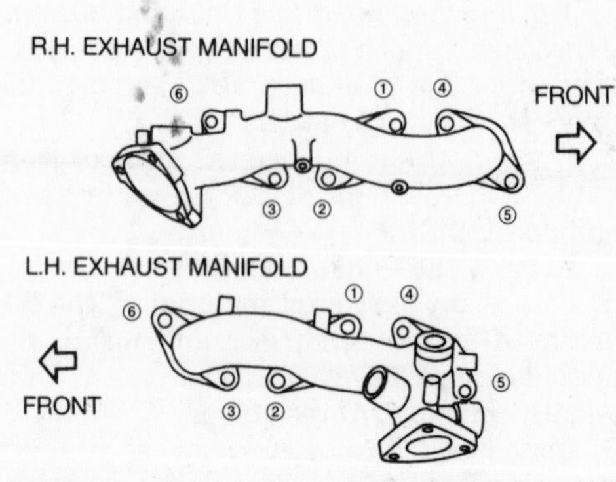

Exhaust manifold bolt tightening sequence—VG30i engines

8. Install the exhaust manifold covers. Start the engine and check for exhaust leaks.

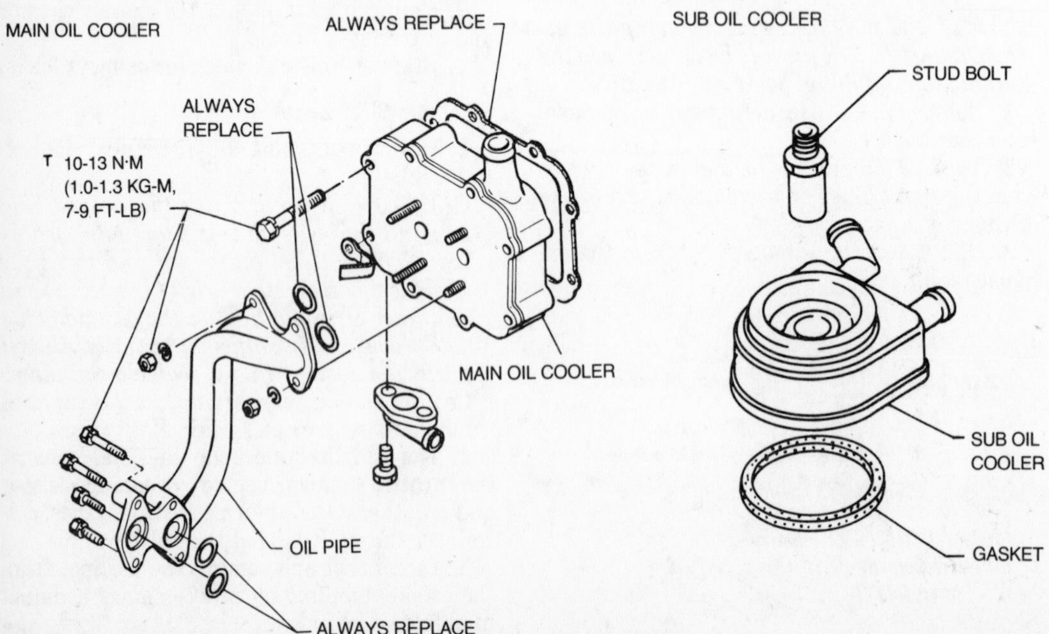

Oil cooler—SD22 and SD25 engines

Oil Cooler

REMOVAL AND INSTALLATION

SD22 and SD25 Engines

1. Drain the coolant until it is below the level of the oil cooler.

CAUTION: *When draining the coolant, keep in mind that cats and dogs are attracted by the ethylene glycol antifreeze, and are quite likely to drink any that is left in an uncovered container or in puddles on the ground. This will prove fatal in sufficient quantity. Always drain the coolant into a sealable container. Coolant should be reused unless it is contaminated or several years old.*

2. Remove the water hose from the cooler.
3. Remove the mounting bolts and lift he cooler from the block.

NOTE: *Have a drip pan ready, since some oil will drain out.*

4. Install the oil cooler and tighten the bolts to 7–9 ft. lbs. Use new O-rings and rubber gaskets.

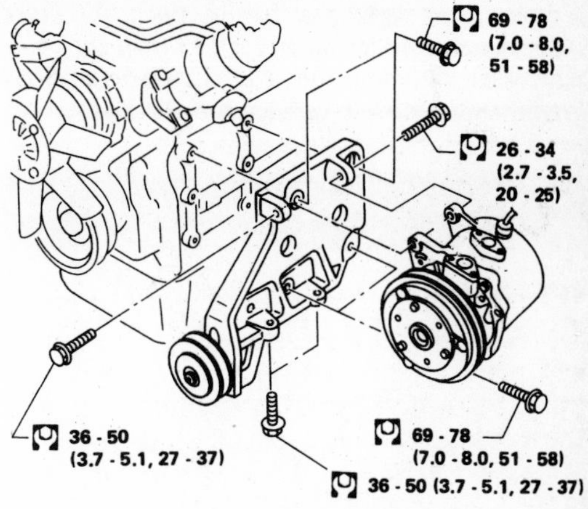

A/C compressor mounting—Z20, Z22, Z24 and Z24i engines

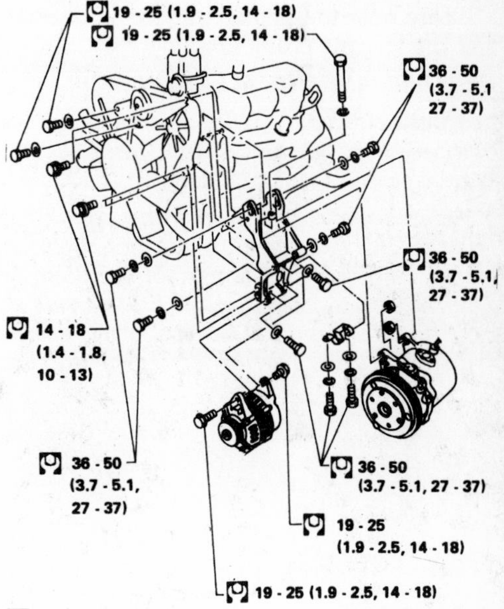

A/C compressor mounting—VG30i engines

Air Conditioning Compressor

Please refer to Chapter One for all Charging and Discharging procedures.

REMOVAL AND INSTALLATION

All Models

CAUTION: *The compressed refrigerant used in the air conditioning system expands into the atmosphere at a temperature of –2°F or lower. This will freeze any surface, including your eyes, that it contacts. In addition, the refrigerant decomposes into a poisonous gas in the presence of a flame. Do not open or disconnect any part of the air conditioning system until you have read the SAFETY WARNINGS section in Chapter One.*

1. Disconnect the negative battery cables.
2. Remove all the necessary equipment in order to gain access to the compressor mounting bolts.
3. Remove the compressor drive belt.

NOTE: *To facilitate removal of the compressor belt, remove the idler pulley and bracket as an assembly beforehand from the underside of the truck.*

4. Discharge the air conditioning system.
5. Disconnect and plug the refrigerant lines with a clean shop towel.

NOTE: *Be sure to use 2 wrenches (one to loosen fitting—one to hold fitting in place) when disconnecting the refrigerant lines.*

6. Tag and disconnect all electrical connections.
7. Remove the compressor mounting bolts. Remove the compressor from the vehicle.
8. Install the compressor on the engine and evenly tighten all the mounting bolts equally.
9. Connect all the electrical connections and unplug and reconnect all refrigerant lines.
10. Install all the necessary equipment in order to gain access to the compressor mounting bolts.
11. Install and adjust the drive belt.
12. Connect the negative battery cable.
13. Evacuate and charge the system as required. Make sure the oil level is correct for the compressor.

NOTE: *Do not attempt to the leave the com-*

pressor on its side or upside down for more than a couple minutes, as the oil in the compressor will enter the low pressure chambers. Always be sure to replace the O-rings.

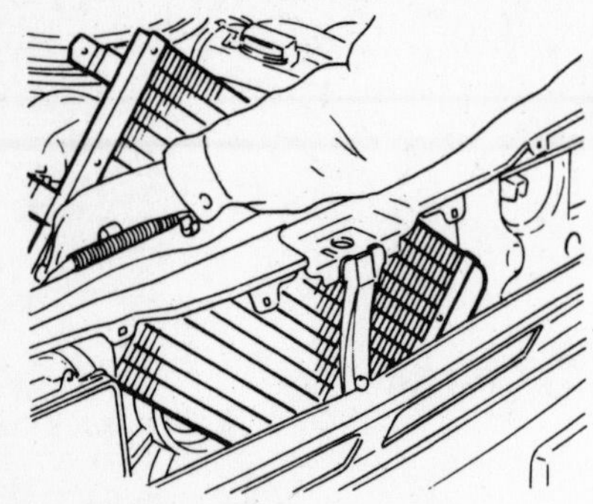

Removing the condenser

Air Conditioning Condenser

Please refer to Chapter One for all Charging and Discharging procedures.

REMOVAL AND INSTALLATION

All Models

CAUTION: *The compressed refrigerant used in the air conditioning system expands into the atmosphere at a temperature of −2°F or lower. This will freeze any surface, including your eyes, that it contacts. In addition, the refrigerant decomposes into a poisonous gas in the presence of a flame. Do not open or disconnect any part of the air conditioning system until you have read the SAFTEY WARNINGS section in Chapter One.*

1. Disconnect the negative battery cables.
2. Remove the necessary components in order to gain access to the condenser retaining bolts. If equipped, remove the condenser fan motor, as necessary.
3. Discharge the system. Remove the condenser refrigerant lines and plug them with a clean shop towel.

NOTE: *On the some models the receiver/drier assembly should be removed before removing the condenser.*

4. Remove the condenser retaining bolts. Remove the condenser from the vehicle.
5. Install the condenser in the vehicle and evenly tighten all the mounting bolts equally.

NOTE: *Always use new O-rings in all refrigerant lines.*

6. Reconnect all the refrigerant lines.
7. Install all the necessary equipment in order to gain access to the condenser mounting bolts. Install the condenser fan motor if removed.
8. Connect the negative battery cable.
9. Evacuate and charge the system as required.

Radiator

REMOVAL AND INSTALLATION

NOTE: *On some models, it may be necessary to remove the grille before removing the radiator. The cooling system can be drained by opening the drain cock at the bottom of the ra-*

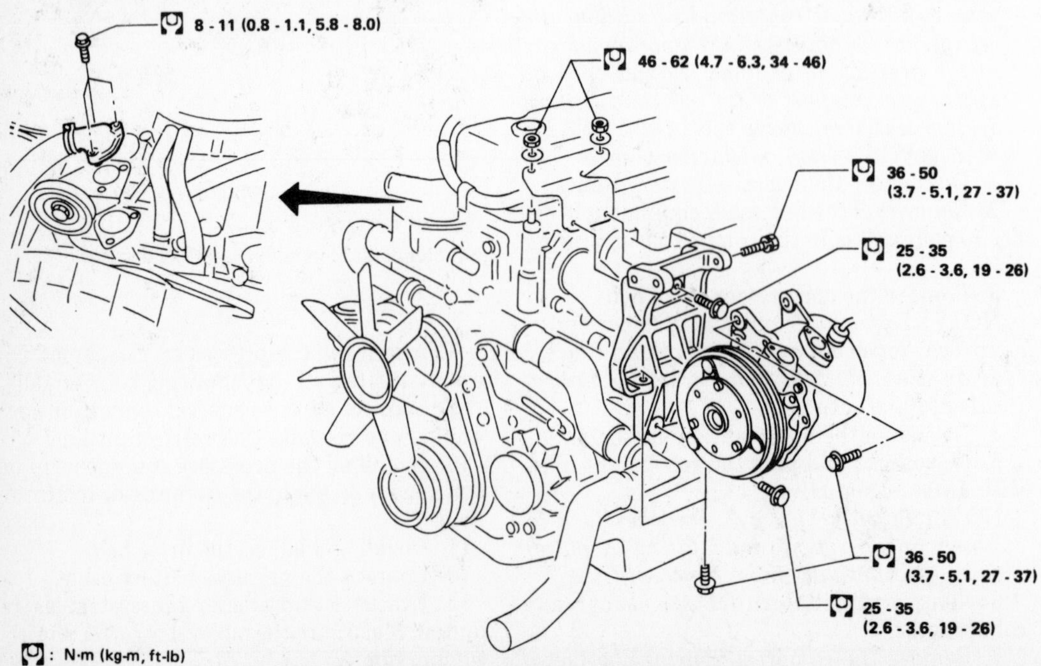

A/C compressor mounting—SD25 engines

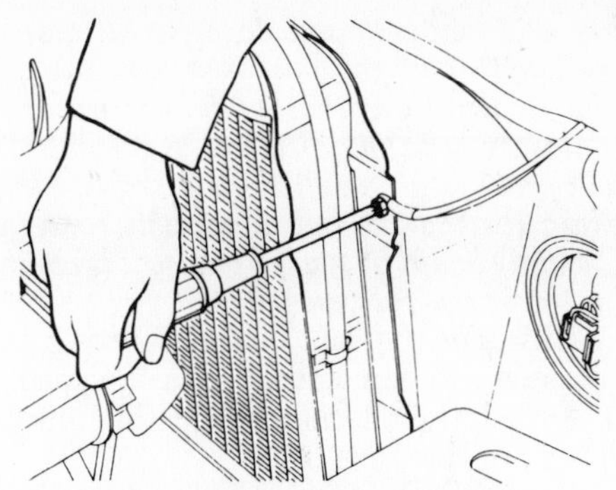

Removing the radiator securing bolts

diator or by removing the lower radiator hose. Be careful not to damage the fins or core tubes when removing and installing the radiator. NEVER OPEN THE RADIATOR CAP WHEN HOT!

1. Drain the engine coolant into a clean container. On fuel injected models, remove the air cleaner inlet pipe.

CAUTION: *When draining the coolant, keep in mind that cats and dogs are attracted by the ethylene glycol antifreeze, and are quite likely to drink any that is left in an uncovered container or in puddles on the ground. This will prove fatal in sufficient quantity. Always drain the coolant into a sealable container. Coolant should be reused unless it is contaminated or several years old.*

2. Disconnect the upper and lower radiator hoses and the coolant reserve tank hose.
3. Disconnect the automatic transmission oil cooler lines if so equipped. Plug the lines to keep dirt from entering them.
4. If the radiator has a fan shroud, unbolt the shroud and move it back. Hang it over the fan.
5. Remove the radiator mounting bolts and the radiator.
6. Install the radiator in the vehicle and tighten the mounting bolts evenly.
7. If equipped with an automatic transmission, connect the cooling lines at the radiator.
8. Connect the upper and lower hoses and the coolant reserve tank hose.
9. Refill the cooling system (refer to Chapter One) and automatic transmission if necessary, operate the engine until warm and then check the coolant level. Check also for any leaks.

Water Pump

REMOVAL AND INSTALLATION

1. Drain the cooling system.

CAUTION: *When draining the coolant, keep*

FAN
PUMP GASKET (ALWAYS REPLACE)
WATER PUMP WITH FAN COUPLING
FAN BELT

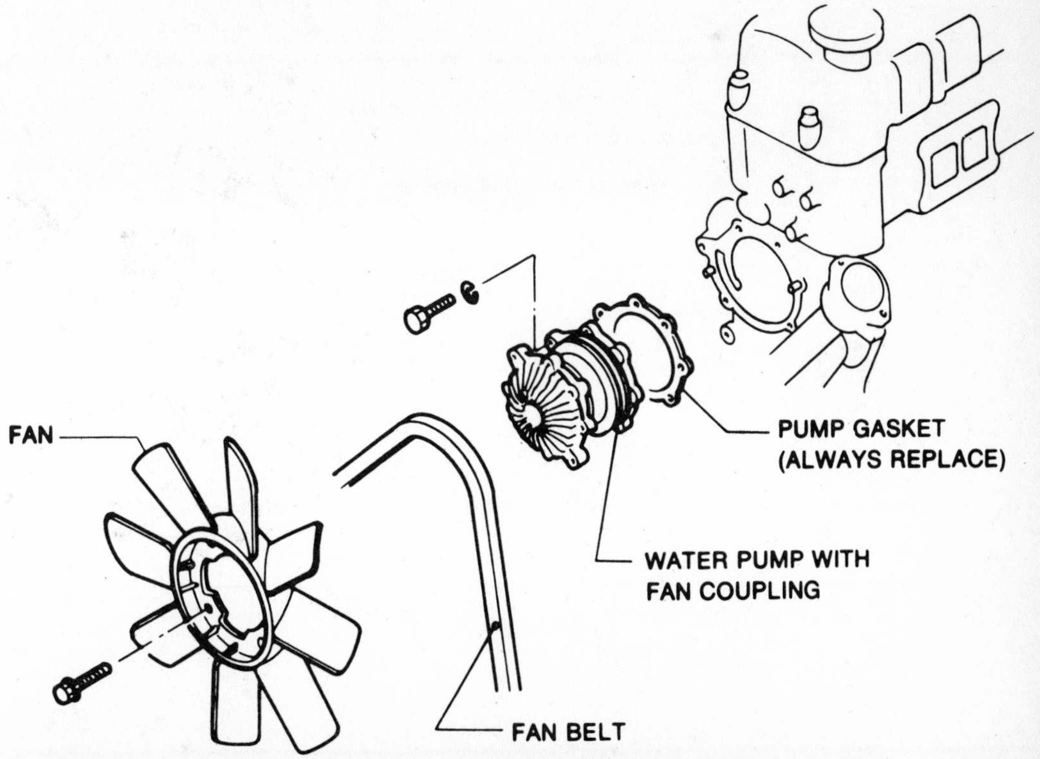

Water pump—4 cylinder gasoline engines

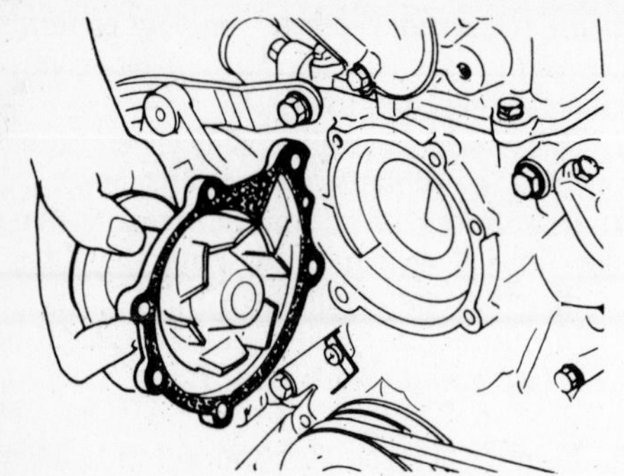

Removing the water pump—4 cylinder gasoline engines

in mind that cats and dogs are attracted by the ethylene glycol antifreeze, and are quite likely to drink any that is left in an uncovered container or in puddles on the ground. This will prove fatal in sufficient quantity. Always drain the coolant into a sealable container. Coolant should be reused unless it is contaminated or several years old.

2. Unfasten the fan shroud securing bolts and remove the fan shroud, if so equipped.

3. Loosen the alternator adjusting link bolt and remove the drive belt.

4. Repeat Step 3 for the air and/or power steering pump drive belt, if so equipped.

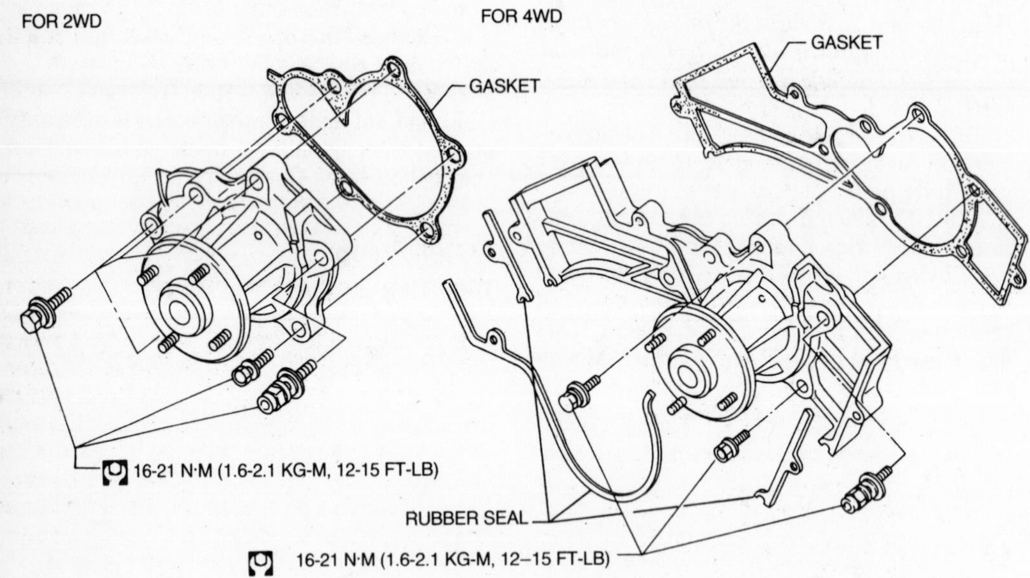

Water pump—VG30i engines

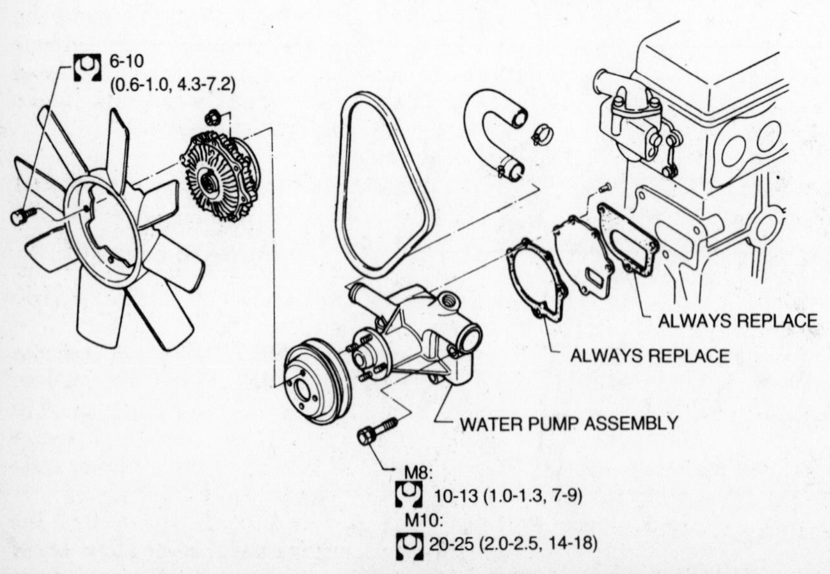

Water pump—SD22 and SD25 engines

5. On the SD22 and SD25, detach the bypass hose from the water pump.

6. Unfasten the water pump retaining bolts (note the different size bolts on the VG30i) and remove the water pump and fan assembly, using care not to damage the radiator with the fan.

CAUTION: *If the fan is equipped with a fluid coupling, do not tip the fan/pump assembly on its side, as the fluid will run out.*

7. Remove all traces of gasket and/or sealant from the pump-to-cover mounting surfaces. Install the water pump and tighten the M6mounting bolts to 3–7 ft. lbs. (4–10 Nm) and the M8 bolts to 7–12 ft. lbs. (10–16 Nm) on 4 cylinder gasoline engines; the M6 bolts to 7-9 ft. lbs. (10–13 Nm) and the M8 bolts to 14–18 ft. lbs. (20–25 Nm) on SD22 and SD25 engines; and, 12–15 ft. lbs. (16–21 Nm) on the VG30i. Always use a new gasket between the pump body and its mounting.

8. Install the drive belt and adjust the tension.

9. Refill the cooling system, start the engine and check for leaks.

Cylinder Head

REMOVAL AND INSTALLATION

L16, L18 and L20B Engines

1. Crank the engine until the No. 1 piston is at TDC of the compression stroke and disconnect the negative battery cable, drain the cooling system, and remove the air cleaner and attending hoses.

CAUTION: *When draining the coolant, keep in mind that cats and dogs are attracted by the ethylene glycol antifreeze, and are quite likely to drink any that is left in an uncovered container or in puddles on the ground. This will prove fatal in sufficient quantity. Always drain the coolant into a sealable container. Coolant should be reused unless it is contaminated or several years old.*

2. Remove the alternator.

3. If equipped with air conditioning, unbolt the compressor and move it aside onto the fender. Do not detach any of the compressor lines; the escaping refrigerant will freeze any surface it contacts, including your skin.

4. Disconnect the carburetor throttle linkage, the fuel line and any other vacuum lines or electrical leads, and remove the carburetor.

5. Disconnect the exhaust pipe from the exhaust manifold.

6. Remove the fan and fan pulley.

7. Remove the spark plugs to protect them from damage. Lay the spark plugs aside and out of the way.

8. Remove the cylinder head cover.

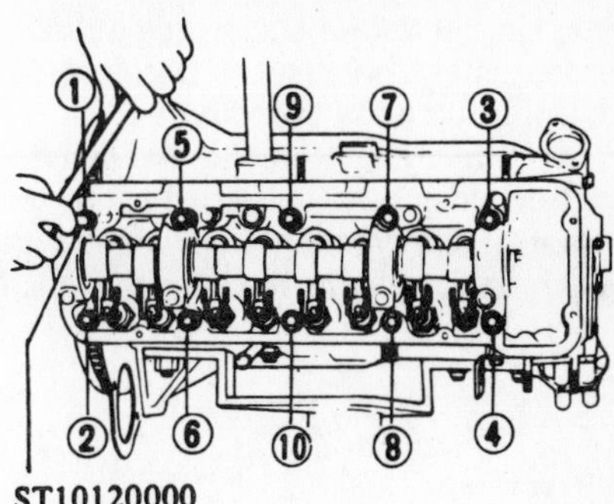

Cylinder head bolt loosening sequence—L16, L18 and L20B engines

9. Remove the water pump.

10. Om models with a mechanicalfuel pump, remove the pump from the cylinder head.

11. Remove the fuel pump drive cam.

12. Mark the relationship of the camshaft sprocket to the timing chain with paint or chalk. If this is done, it will not be necessary to locate the factory timing marks. Before removing the camshaft sprocket, it will be necessary to wedge the chain in place so that it will not fall down into the front cover. The factory procedure is to wedge the timing chain in place with the wooden wedge shown here. The problem with this is that it may allow the chain tensioner to move out far enough to cock itself against the chain. If this happens, you'll find that the chain won't go back over the sprocket after you've put the sprocket back on. In this case, you'll have to remove the front cover and push the tensioner back. After installing the wedge, unbolt and remove the camshaft sprocket.

13. Loosen and remove the cylinder head bolts, gradually and in the order shown. You will need a 10mm Allen wrench to remove the head bolts. Keep the bolts in order, because they are different sizes. Lift the cylinder head assembly from the engine. Remove the intake and exhaust manifolds as necessary.

To install:

1. Thoroughly clean the cylinder block and head mating surfaces. Check the block and head for flatness before installing the head. Install a new cylinder head gasket. Do not use sealer on the cylinder head gasket of 1973-80 models. Use sealer on all other models.

2. With the crankshaft turned so that the No. 1 piston is at TDC of the compression stroke (if not already done so as mentioned in Step 1), make sure that the camshaft sprocket timing mark and the oblong groove in the camshaft retaining plate are aligned.

3. Place the cylinder head in position on the cylinder block, being careful not to allow any of the valves to come in contact with any of the

pistons. Do not rotate the crankshaft or camshaft separately because of possible damage which might occur to the valves.

4. Temporarily tighten the two center right and left cylinder head bolts to 14.5 ft. lbs.

5. Install the camshaft sprocket together (with the timing chain) to the camshaft. Make sure that the marks you made earlier line up. If the chain will not stretch over the sprocket, the problem lies in the tensioner. See Timing Chain Removal and Installation for timing procedure, if necessary.

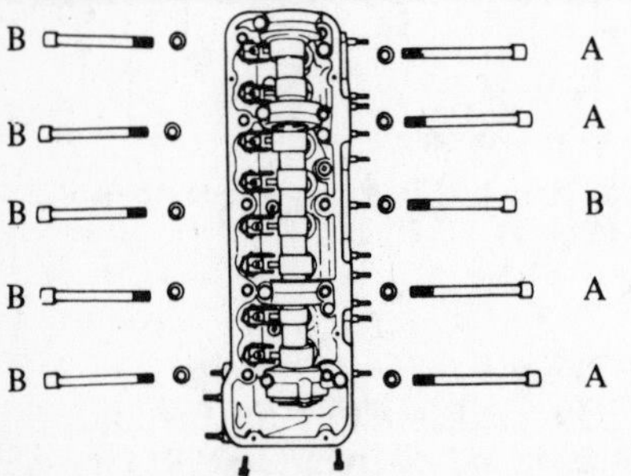

Different size cylinder head bolts—L16, L18 and L20B engines

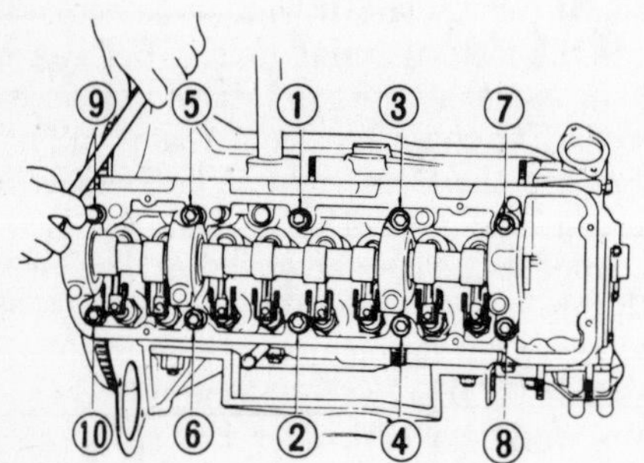

Cylinder head bolt tightening sequence—L16, L18 and L20B engines

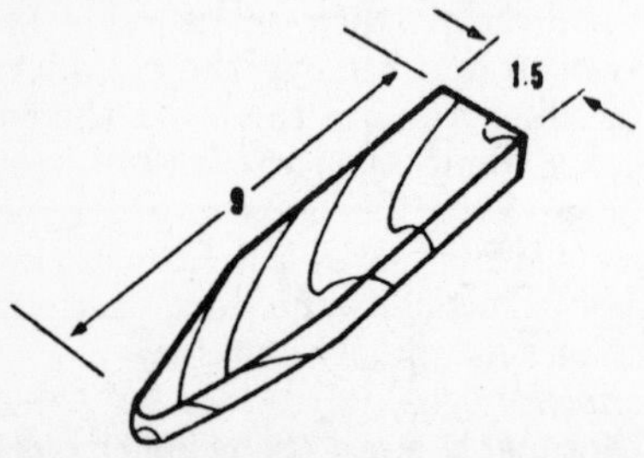

Dimensions for fabricating the wooden wedge used in support the timing chain—L16, L18 and L20B engines (Z-series engine similar)

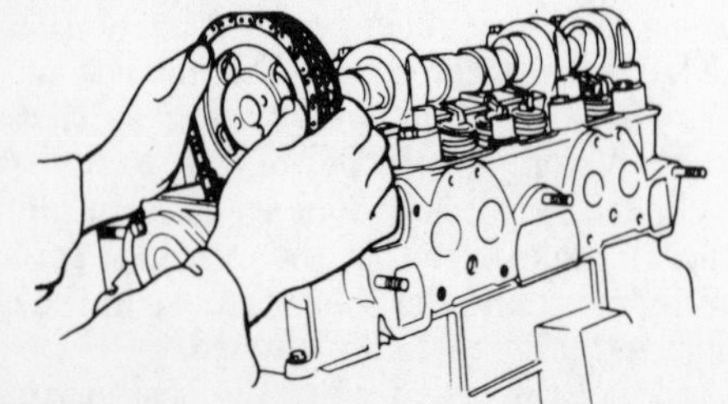

Removing the camshaft sprocket and chain—L16, L18 and L20B engines

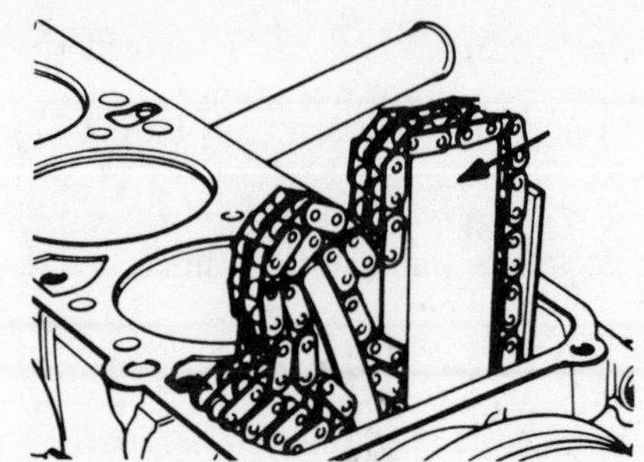

Support the timing chain with a wedge—L16, L18 and L20B engines

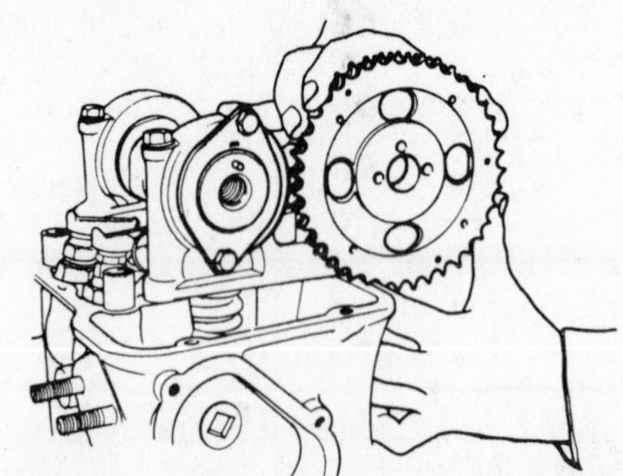

Installing the camshaft sprocket—L16, L18 and L20B engines

6. Install the cylinder head bolts. Note that there are two sizes of bolts used; the longer bolts are installed on the driver side of the engine with a smaller bolt in the center position. The remaining small bolts are installed on the opposite side of the cylinder.

7. Tighten the cylinder head bolts in three stages on 1973-80 models: first to 29 ft. lbs., second to 43 ft. lbs., and lastly to 47–62 ft. lbs. On 1970-72 models, tighten the cylinder head bolts to 36–43 ft. lbs. in three progressive steps. Tighten the cylinder head bolts on all models in the proper sequence.

8. Install the fuel pump assembly, water pump and cylinder head cover.

9. Clean and regap the spark plugs then install plugs into the cylinder head. DO NOT OVER-TORQUE THE SPARK PLUGS!

10. Install the fan pulley and cooling fan. Connect the exhaust pipe to the exhaust manifold.

11. Install the carburetor and connect the carburetor throttle linkage, the fuel line and any other vacuum lines or electrical leads.

12. Install the alternator and its electrical connections. Install the drive belt and adjust the tension.

13. Adjust the valves. Fill the cooling system and then start the engine and run it until it reaches normal operating temperature. Retighten the cylinder head bolts to specifications. Readjust the valves. Retighten the cylinder head bolts again after 600 miles, and readjust the valves at that time.

Z20, Z22, Z24 and Z24i Engines

1. Complete Steps 1–6 for the L16, L18 and L20B engines.
2. Disconnect the throttle linkage, the air cleaner or its intake hose assembly (fuel injection). Disconnect the fuel line, the return fuel line and any other vacuum lines or electrical leads. Remove the carburetor (Z20, Z22 and Z24) to avoid damaging it while removing the head.

NOTE: *A good rule of thumb when disconnecting the rather complex engine wiring of today's automobiles is to put a piece of masking tape on the wire or hose and on the connection you removed the wire or hose from, then mark both pieced of tape 1, 2, 3, etc. When replacing wiring, simply match the pieces of tape.*

3. Remove the EGR tube from around the rear of the engine.
4. Remove the exhaust air induction tubes from around the front of the engine and from the exhaust manifold.
5. Unbolt the exhaust manifold from the exhaust pipe. Remove the fuel pump.
6. Remove the intake manifold supports from under the manifold. Remove the PCV valve from around the rear of the engine if necessary.
7. Remove the spark plugs to protect them from damage. Remove the cylinder head cover.

NOTE: *The spark plug leads should be marked, however it would be wise to mark them yourself, especially the dual spark plug models.*

8. Mark the relationship of the camshaft sprocket to the timing chain with paint or chalk. If this is done, it will not be necessary to

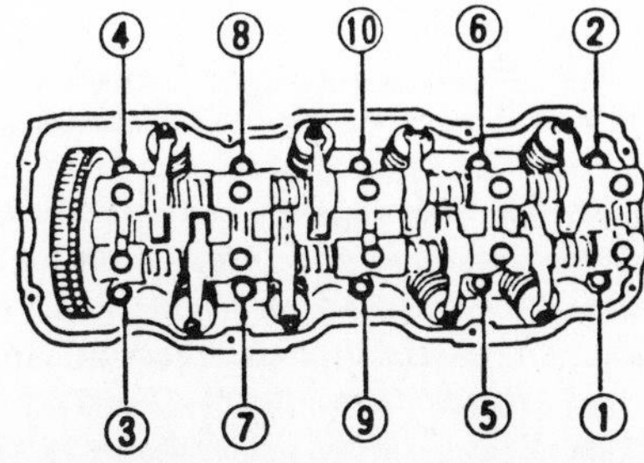

Cylinder head bolt loosening sequence—Z20, Z22, ZS24 and Z24i engines

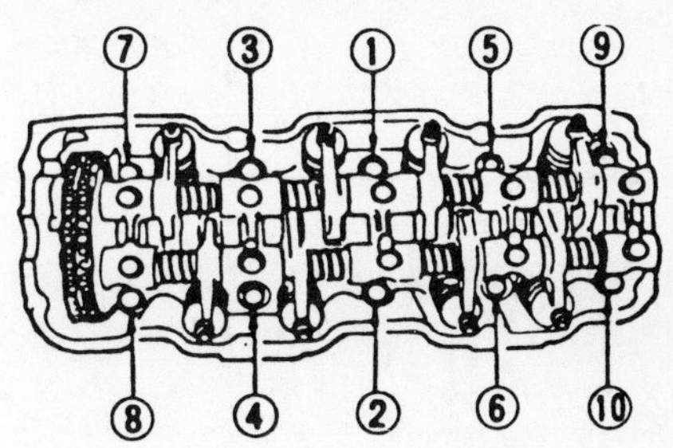

Support the timing chain—Z24i engines

locate the factory timing marks. Before removing the camshaft sprocket, it will be necessary to wedge the chain in place so that it will not fall down into the front cover. The factory procedure is to wedge the timing chain in place with the wooden wedge shown here. The problem with this procedure is that it may allow the chain tensioner to move out far enough to cock itself against the chain. If this happens, you'll find that the chain won't go back over the sprocket after you've put the sprocket back on. In this case, you'll have to remove the front cover and push the tensioner back. After you've wedged the chain, unbolt the camshaft sprocket and remove it.

9. Working from both ends in, loosen the cylinder head bolts and remove them. Remove the bolts securing the cylinder head to the front cover assembly.
10. Lift the cylinder head off the engine block. It may be necessary to tap the head lightly with a rubbermallet to loosen it.

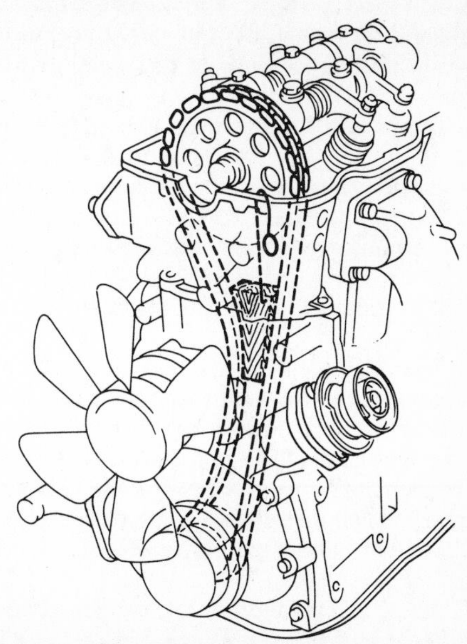

Cylinder head bolt tightening sequence—Z20, Z22, Z24 and Z24i engines

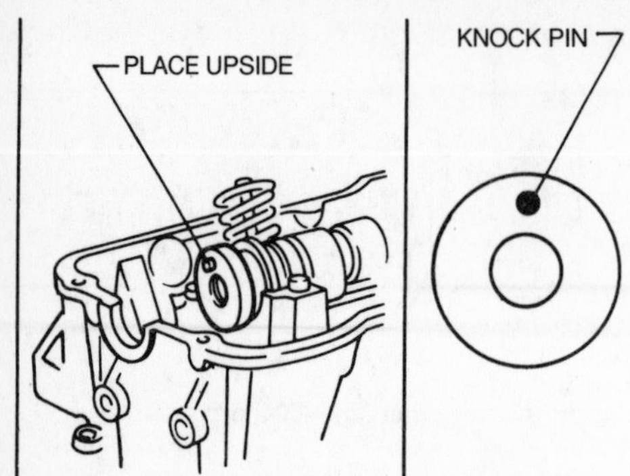

Camshaft knockpin positioning—Z24i engines

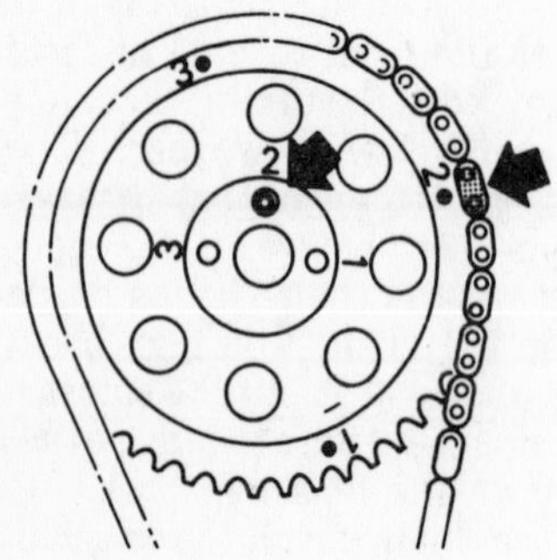

Camshaft sprocket alignment—Z24i engines

To install:

1. Thoroughly clean the cylinder block and head surfaces and check both for warpage.
2. Fit the new head gasket. Don't use sealant. Make sure that no open valves are in the way of raised pistons, and *never* rotate the crankshaft or camshaft separately because of possible damage which might occur to the valves.
3. Temporarily tighten the two center right and left cylinder head bolts to 14 ft. lbs.
4. Install the camshaft sprocket together with the timing chain to the camshaft. Make sure the marks you made earlier line up with each other. If you get into trouble, see Timing Chain Removal and Installation for timing procedures.

On the Z24i, confirm that the No. 1 cylinder is set at TDC on its compression stroke. Make sure that the front knock pin is positioned at the upper surface of the camshaft. Set the chain on the camshaft sprocket by aligning each mating mark. Then install the camshaft sprocket to the camshaft and tighten to 87–116 ft. lbs. (118–157 Nm)

NOTE: *The camshaft sprocket should be installed by fitting the knock pin of the camshaft into its No. 2 hole. And the No. 2 timing mark must also be used.*

Apply sealant to the sealant point of the cylinder head and install the rubber plug.

5. Install the cylinder head bolts and torque them to 22 ft. lbs. (29 Nm), then 40 ft. lbs., and then 58 ft. lbs. (78 Nm). Loosen all bolts completely and retighten 22 ft. lbs. (29 Nm), and then to 54–61 ft. lbs. (74–83 Nm); or, if you have an angle torque wrench, give all bolts a final turn of 90–95 degrees. Tighten all bolts gradually, in the order shown.
6. Clean and regap the spark plugs then install them in the cylinder head. DO NOT OVER-TORQUE THE SPARK PLUGS!
7. Install the cylinder head cover with a new gasket.
8. Install the intake manifold supports from under the manifold. Install the PCV valve if it was removed.
9. Connect the exhaust pipe to exhaust manifold. Install the fuel pump.
10. Install the exhaust air induction tubes to the front of the engine or to the exhaust manifold.
11. Install the EGR tube from around the rear of the engine.
12. Install the carburetor (Z20, Z22 and Z24). Connect the throttle linkage, the air cleaner or its intake hose assembly (Z24i). Reconnect the fuel line, the return fuel line and any other vacuum lines or electrical leads.
13. Install the power steering pump if so equipped and correctly adjust the drive belt.
14. Install the air conditioning compressor and correctly adjust the drive belt.
15. Install the alternator mounting bracket, alternator, electrical connections to the alternator and adjust the drive belt.
16. Reconnect the heater and radiator hoses.
17. Refill the cooling system. Adjust the valves.
18. Start the engine and it until it reaches normal operating temperature, check for the correct coolant level.
19. Check for leaks and roadtest vehicle for proper operation.

NOTE: *It is always wise to drain the crankcase oil after the cylinder head has been installed to avoid coolant contamination.*

VG30i Engines

NOTE: *To remove or install the cylinder head, you'll need a special hex head wrench ST10120000 (J24239-01) or equivalent. The collector assembly and intake manifold have special bolt sequence for removal and installation. The distributor assembly is located in the left cylinder head mark and remove it if necessary.*

1. Release the fuel pressure. See the procedure in this chapter for timing belt removal. Set

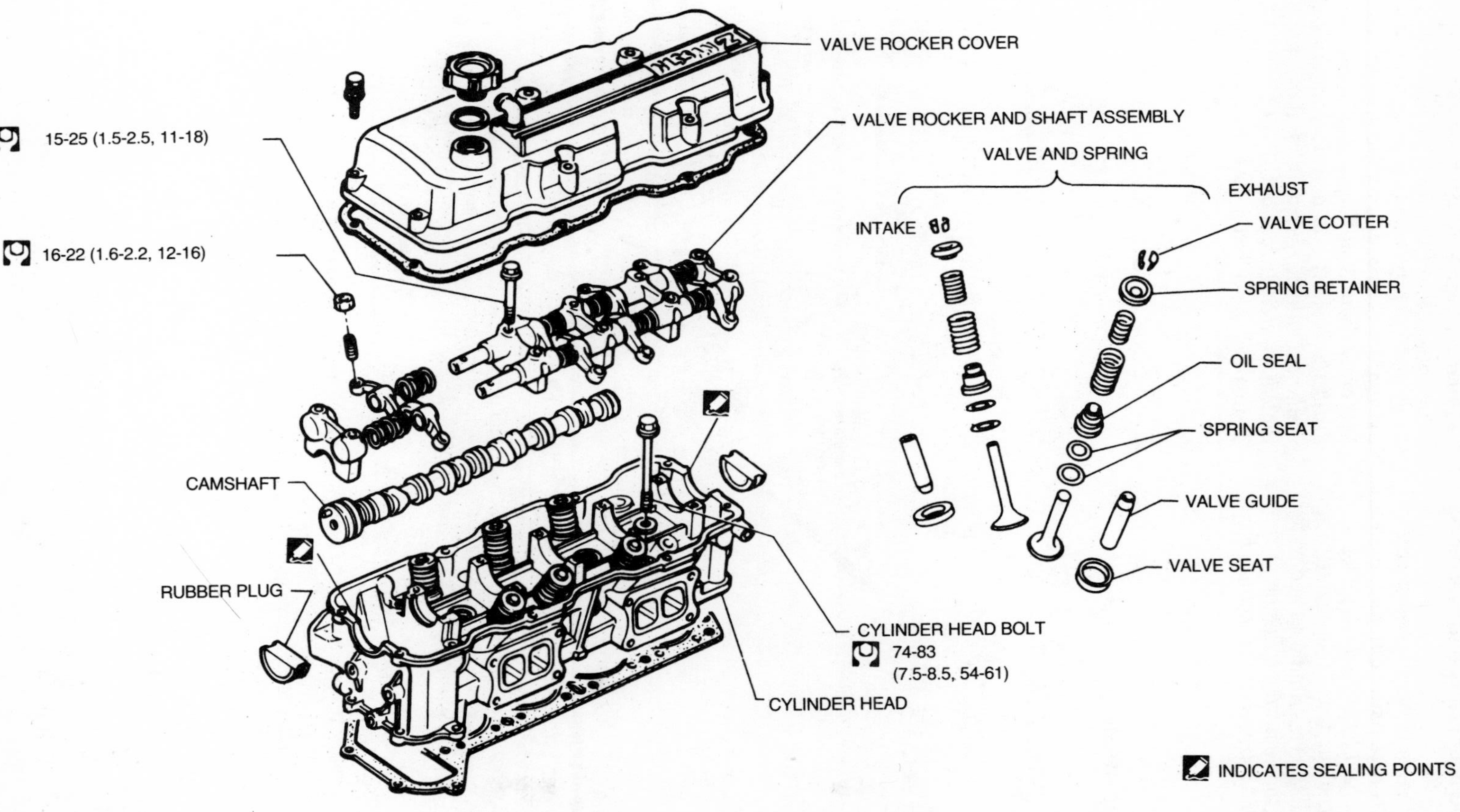

Exploded view of the cylinder head—Z20, Z22, Z24 and Z24i engines (L-series engines similar)

: N·M (KG-M, FT-LB)

the engine to TDC and then remove the timing belt.

NOTE: *Do not rotate either the crankshaft or camshaft from this point onward, or the valves could be bent by hitting the pistons.*

2. Drain the coolant from the engine. Tag and disconnect all the vacuum hoses and water hoses connected to the intake collector.

CAUTION: *When draining the coolant, keep in mind that cats and dogs are attracted by the ethylene glycol antifreeze, and are quite likely to drink any that is left in an uncovered container or in puddles on the ground. This will prove fatal in sufficient quantity. Always drain the coolant into a sealable container. Coolant should be reused unless it is contaminated or several years old.*

3. Remove the collector cover and the collec-

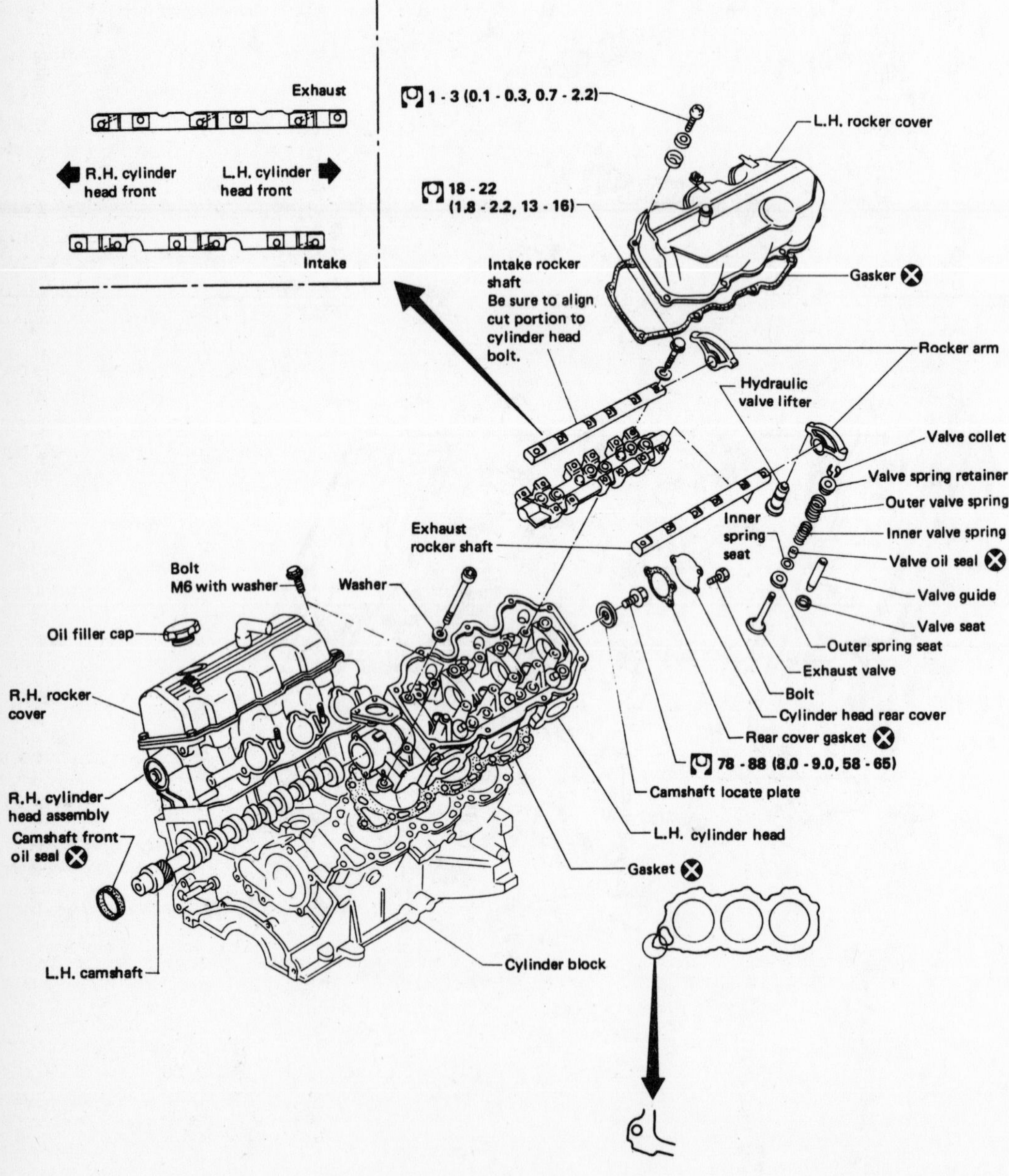

Exploded view of the cylinder head—VG30i engines

tor. Refer to the section Intake Manifold Removal And Installation for correct bolt removal sequence.

4. Remove the intake manifold and fuel tube assembly.

5. Remove the exhaust collector bracket. Remove the exhaust manifold covers. Disconnect the exhaust manifold when it connects to the exhaust pipe (three bolts).

6. Remove the camshaft pulleys and the rear timing cover securing bolts.

7. Loosen the cylinder head bolts a little at a time, in the order shown.

8. Remove the cylinder head with the exhaust manifold attached. If you need to remove the exhaust manifold, refer to the procedure in this section.

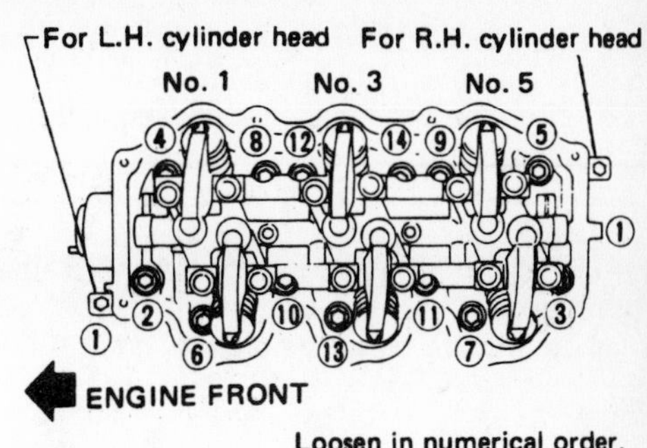

Cylinder head bolt loosening sequence—1988–89 VG30i engines

Loosen in numerical order.

Cylinder head bolt loosening sequence—1986–87 VG30i engines

To install:

1. Check the positions of the timing marks and camshaft sprockets to make sure they have not shifted. The mark on the crankshaft should be aligned with the one on the oil pump body and the camshaft knockpin should be at the top.

2. Install the head with a new gasket. Apply clean engine oil to the threads and seats of the bolts and install the bolts with washers (beveled edges up) in the correct position. Note that

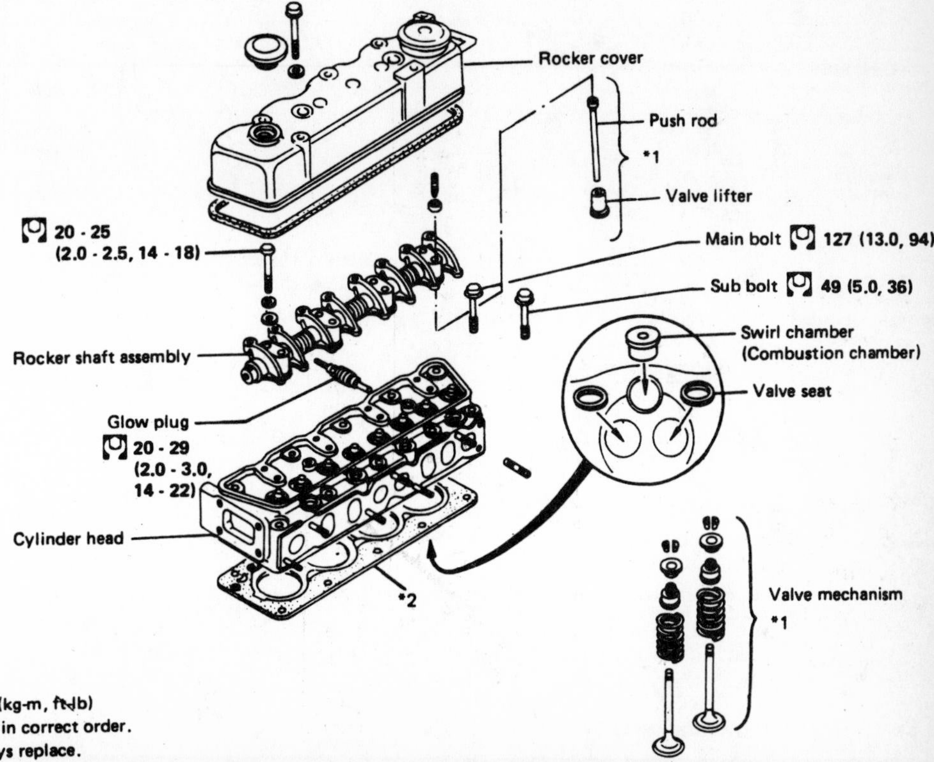

Exploded view of the cylinder head—SD25 engines (SD22 engines similar)

bolts 4, 5, 12 and 13 (5.00 in.) are longer than the others. Other bolts are 4.17 in.

3. Tighten the bolts in the proper sequence, in the following stages:

a. Tighten all bolts, in order, to 22 ft. lbs. (29 Nm)

b. Tighten all bolts, in order, to 43 ft. lbs. (59 Nm)

c. Loosen all bolts completely.

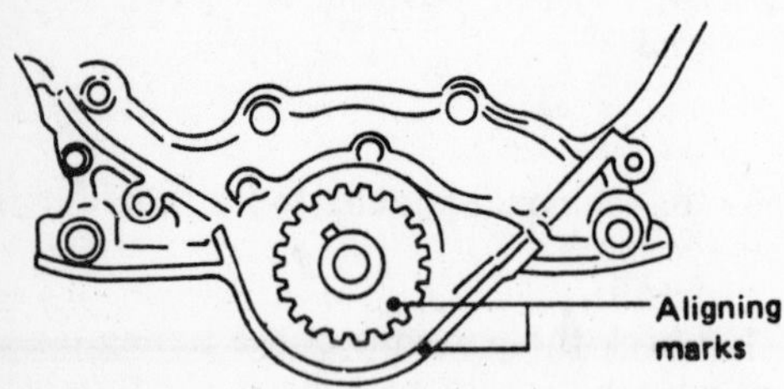

Crankshaft sprocket alignment—VG30i engines

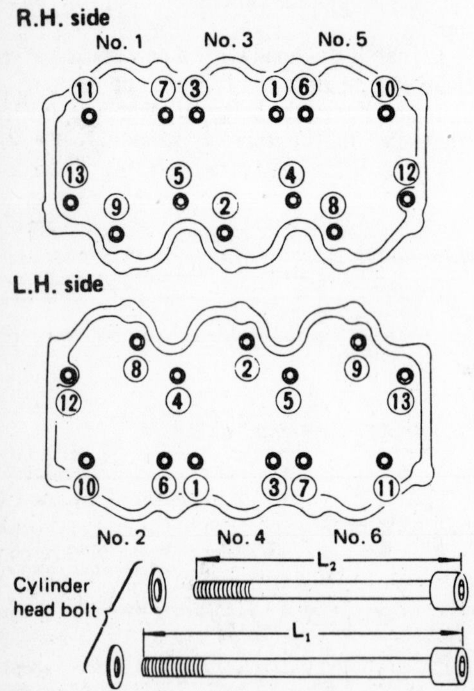

Cylilnder head bolt tightening sequence—VG30i engines

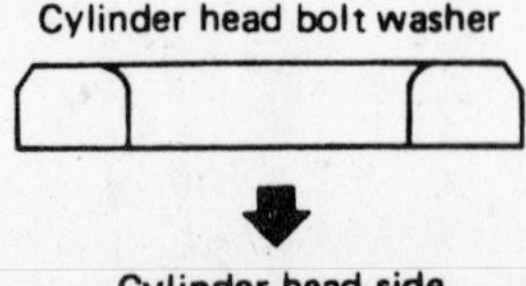

Install the cylinder head bolt washer this way—VG30i engines

d. Tighten all bolts, in order, to 22 ft. lbs. (29 Nm)

e. Tighten all bolts, in order, to 40–47 ft. lbs. (54–64 Nm). Or, if you have an angle torque wrench available, tighten them 60–65 degrees tighter rather than the final torque.

4. Install the rear timing cover bolts. Install the camshaft pulleys. Make sure the pulley marked **R3** goes on the right and that marked **L3** goes on the left.

5. Align the timing marks if necessary and then install the timing belt and adjust the belt tension.

6. Install the front upper and lower belt covers.

7. Make sure that the cylinder head cover bolts, trays and washers are free of oil. Then, install the cylinder head covers.

8. Install the intake manifold and fuel tube.

9. Install the exhaust manifold if removed from the cylinder head.

10. Connect the exhaust manifold to the exhaust pipe connection. Install the exhaust collector bracket.

11. Install the collector and collector cover. Refer to the section for Intake Manifold Remov-

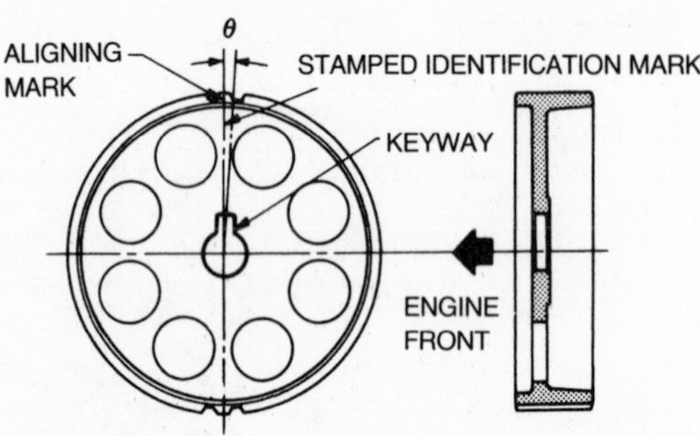

Camshaft sprocket installation and positioning—VG30i engines

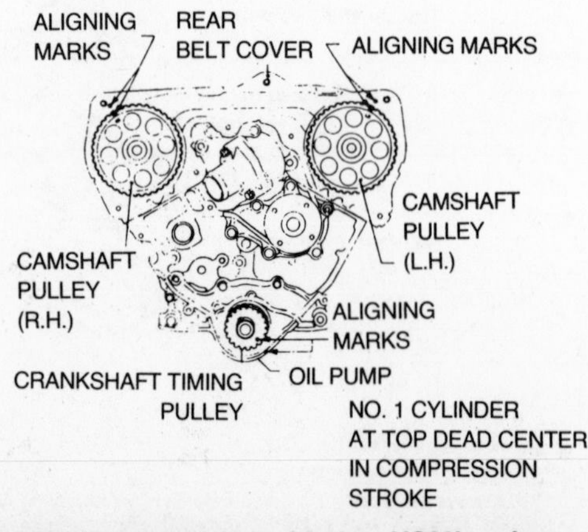

Camshaft sprocket timing marks—VG30i engines

al And Installation for the correct torque pattern.

12. Connect all the vacuum hoses and water hoses to the intake collector.

13. Refill the cooling system. Start the engine and then check the engine timing. After the engine reaches the normal operating temperture, check for the correct coolant level.

14. Roadtest the vehicle for proper operation.

SD22 and SD25 Engines

1. Remove the air cleaner.
2. Remove the crankcase vent hose and remove the intake and exhaust manifolds. These are bolted together.
3. Remove the alternator, bracket and belts.
4. Disconnect the coolant hose between the head and the oil cooler.
5. Remove the fuel filter assembly.
6. Disconnect the injection lines from the pump and the injectors. Cap all openings at once.
7. Remove the bypass hoses between the coolant pump and the thermostat housing.
8. Remove the fan.
9. Remove the rocker arm cover.
10. Remove the rocker arm shaft assembly.
11. Remove the pushrods and keep them in order.
12. Remove the fuel return lines.
13. Remove the injection nozzles from the cylinder head.
14. Remove the cylinder head bolts gradually, in the sequence shown.
15. Attach a hoist to the head and lift it clear of the block. On occasion, the precombustion chambers may fall out, especially if the head is bumped or handled roughly. Take care that they are returned to their original positions if this occurs.

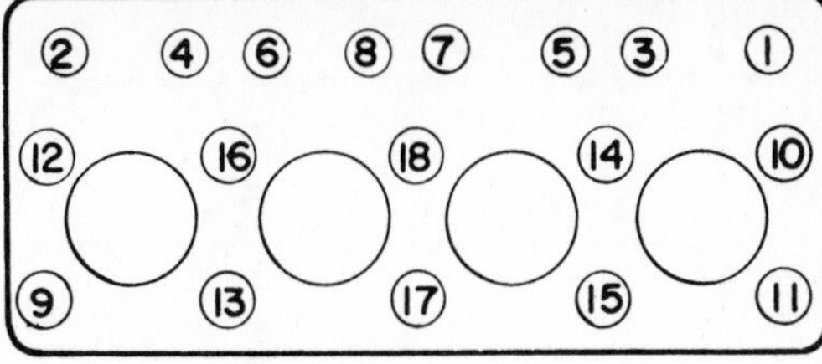

Cylinder head bolt loosening sequence—SD22 and SD25 engines

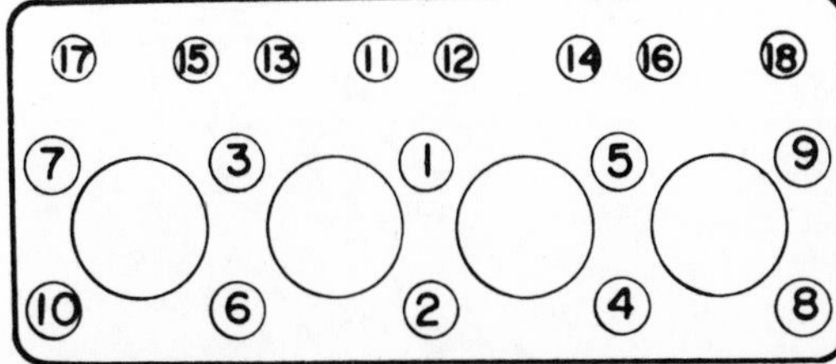

Cylinder head bolt tightening sequence—SD22 and SD25 engines

To Install:

1. Remove the head gasket and O-rings.
2. Clean and inspect all parts.
3. Check the head with a straightedge. Maximum warpage is 0.0079 in. (0.2mm). Do not remove more than 0.011 in. (0.28mm) from the head.
4. Place a new cylinder head gasket on the block with the stainless steel inset side facing up.
5. Install the O-rings around the water and oil passages.
6. Position the cylinder head on the engine block.
7. Coat the head bolts with clean engine oil and tighten them in sequence, in stages as follows:
   a. Tighten the main (large) bolts to 43–58 ft. lbs. (59–78 Nm)
   b. Tighten the sub (small) bolts to 14–22 ft. lbs. (20–29 Nm)
   c. Tighten the main bolts to 87–94 ft. lbs. (118–127 Nm)
   d. Tighten the sub bolts yo 33–40 ft. lbs. (44–54 Nm)
8. Install the pushrods, pressing down and turning them to be sure of proper seating.
9. Install the rocker arm shaft assembly, tighten the bolts to 18 ft.lb. in sequence from the center to each end.
10. Install the injection nozzles.
11. Install the remaining components as they were removed.

CLEANING AND INSPECTION

When the rocker assembly and valve train have been removed from the cylinder head (see Valves and Springs below), set the cylinder head on two wooden blocks on the bench, combustion chamber side up. Using a scraper or putty knife, carefully scrape away any gasket material that may have stuck to the head-to-block mating surface when the head was removed. Make sure you DO NOT gouge the mating surface with the tool.

Using a wire brush chucked into your electric drill, remove the carbon in each combustion chamber. Make sure the brush is actually removing the carbon and not merely burnishing it.

Clean all the valve guides using a valve guide brush (available at most auto parts or auto tool shops) and solvent. A fine-bristled rifle bore cleaning brush also works here.

Inspect the threads of each spark plug hole by

screwing a plug into each, making sure it screws down completely. Heli-coil® any plug hole this is damaged.

CAUTION: *DO NOT hot tank the cylinder head! The head material on most engines is aluminum, which is ruined if subjected to the hot tank solution. Some of the early engines were equipped with cast iron heads, which can be hot-tanked (a service performed by most machine shops which immerses the head in a hot, caustic solution for cleaning). To be sure your engine's cylinder head is aluminum, check around its perimeter with a magnet. Your engine has an iron head if the magnet sticks.*

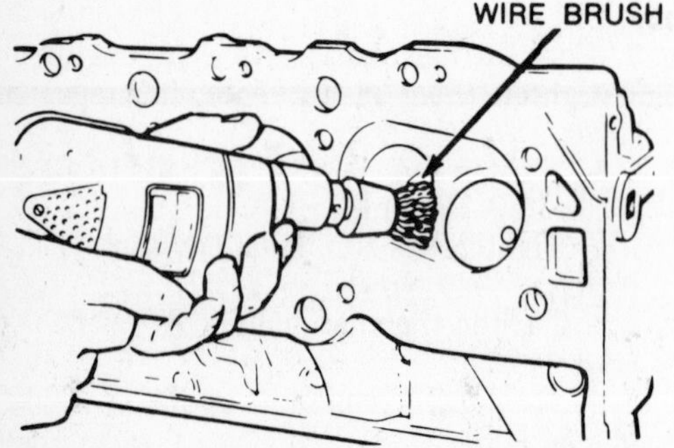

Remove the carbon from the cylinder head with a wire brush and electric drill

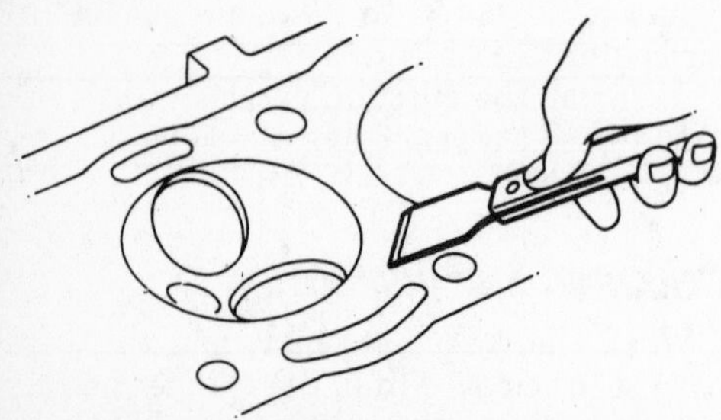

Do not scratch the cylinder head mating surface when removing the old gasket material

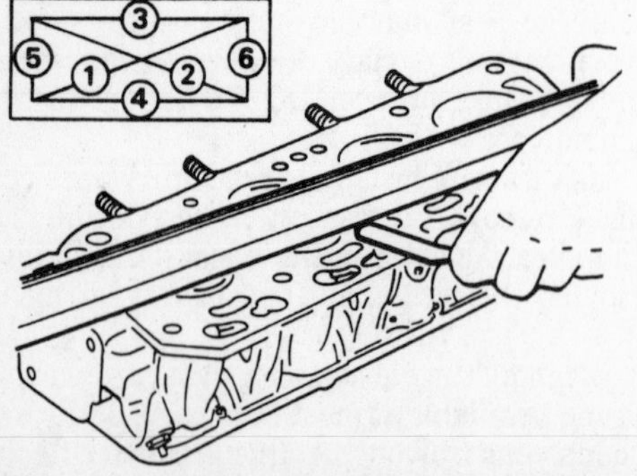

Check the cylinder head mating surface straightness with a precision straightedge and a feeler gauge

NOTE: *Before hot-tanking any overhead cam head, check with the machine shop doing the work. Some cam bearings are easily damaged by the hot tank solution.*

Finally, go over the entire head with a clean shop rag soaked in solvent to remove any grit, old gasket particles, etc. Blow out the bolt holes, coolant galleys, intake and exhaust ports, valve guides and plug holes with compressed air.

RESURFACING

While the head is removed, check the head-to-block mating surface for straightness. If the engine has overheated and blown a head gasket, this must be done as a matter of course. A warped mating surface must be resurfaced (milled); this is done on a milling machine and is quite similar to planing a piece of wood.

Using a precision steel straightedge and a blade-type feeler gauge, check the surface of the head across its length, width and diagonal length as shown in the illustrations. Also check the intake and exhaust manifold mating surfaces and cam cover (all) mating surfaces. If warpage exceed 0.08mm in a 152mm span, or 0.15mm over the total length, the head must be milled. If warpage is highly excessive, the head must be replaced. Again, consult the machine shop operator on head milling limitations.

CYLINDER BLOCK CLEANING

While the cylinder head is removed, the top of the cylinder block and pistons should also be cleaned. Before you begin, rotate the crank-

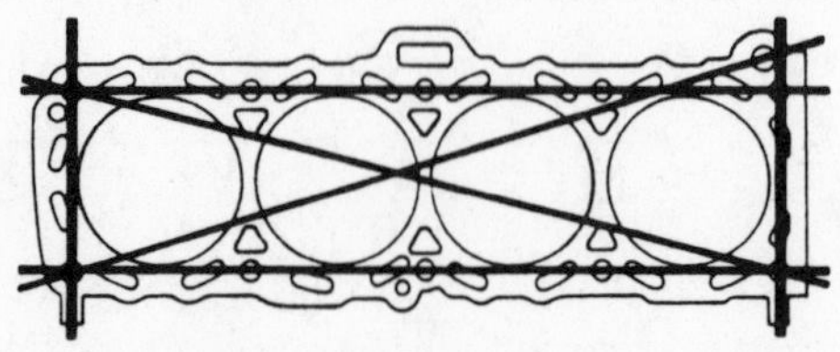

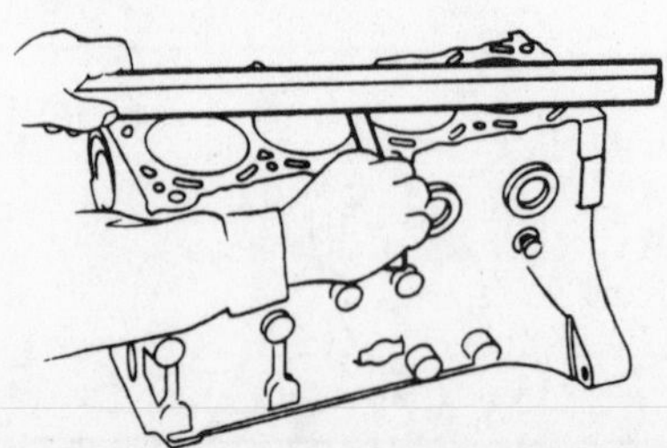

Check the cylinder block mating surface straightness with a precision straightedge and a feeler gauge

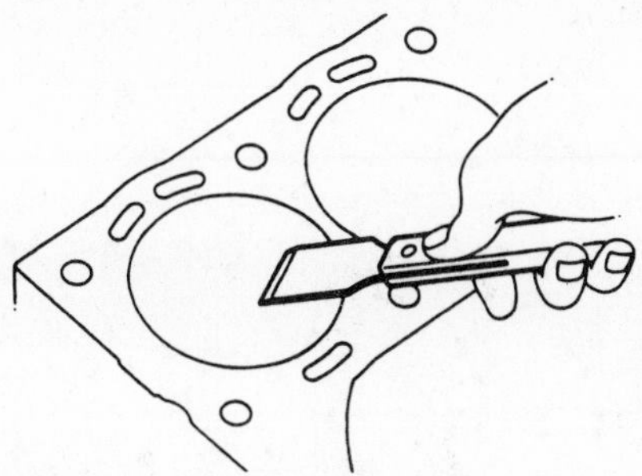

Removing carbon from the piston tops; do not scratch the pistons

shaft until one or more pistons are flush with the top of the block (on the four cylinder engines, you will either have Nos. 1 and 4 up, or Nos. 2 and 3 up). Carefully stuff clean rags into the cylinders in which the pistons are down. This will help keep grit and carbon chips out during cleaning. Using care not to gouge or scratch the block-to-head mating surface and the piston top(s), clean away any old gasket material with a wire brush and/or scraper. On the piston tops, make sure you are actually removing the carbon and not merely burnishing it.

Remove the rags from the down cylinders after you have wiped the top of the block with a solvent soaked rag. Rotate the crankshaft until the other pistons come up flush with the top of the block, and clean those pistons.

NOTE: *Because you have rotated the crankshaft, you will have to re-time the engine following the procedure listed under the Timing Chain/Timing Belt removal.*

Make sure you wipe out each cylinder thoroughly with a solvent-soaked rag, to remove all traces of grit, before the head is reassembled to the block.

Valves and Springs

ADJUSTMENT (AFTER ENGINE SERVICE)

The valves on all engines covered here must be adjusted following any valve train disassembly. Follow the procedure listed in Chapter Two for valve adjustment.

REMOVAL AND INSTALLATION

A valve spring compressor is needed to remove the valves and springs; these are available at most auto parts and auto tool shops. A small magnet is very helpful for removing the keepers and spring seats.

Set the head on its side on the bench. Install the spring compressor so that the fixed side of the tool is flat against the valve head in the combustion chamber, and the screw side is against the retainer. Slowly turn the screw in

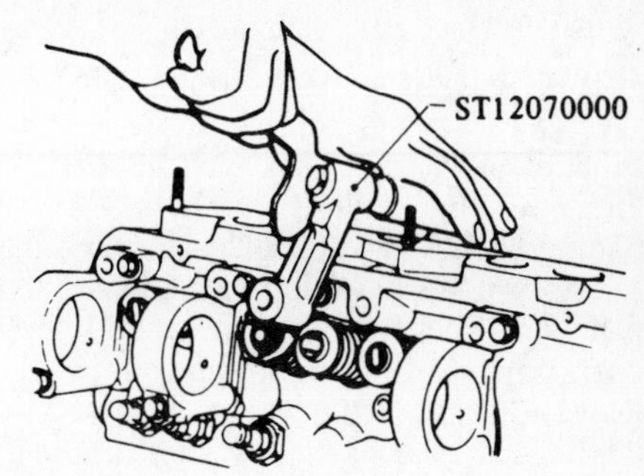

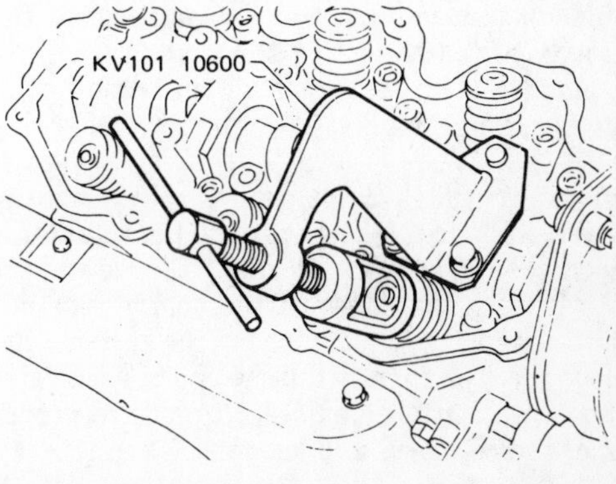

Compressing the valve springs—all 4 cylinder gasoline engines

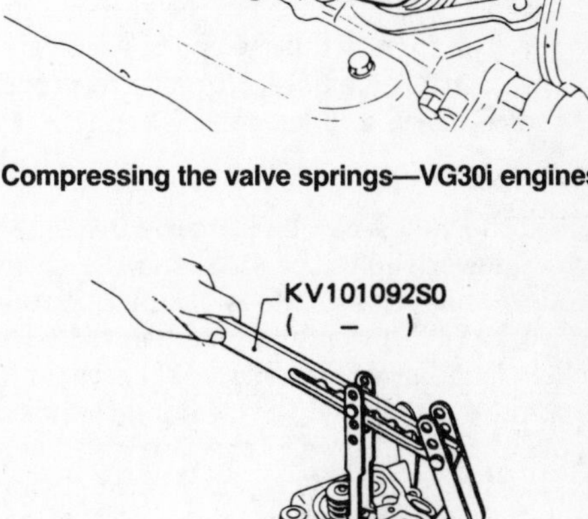

Compressing the valve springs—VG30i engines

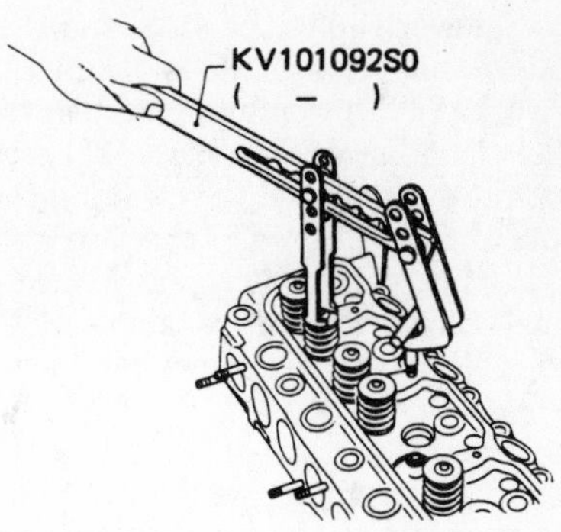

Compressing the valve springs—SD22 and SD25 engines

towards the head, compressing the spring. As the spring compresses, the keepers will be revealed; pick them off of the valve stem with the magnet as they are easily fumbled and lost. When the keepers are removed, back the screw out and remove the retainers and springs. Remove the compressor and pull the valves out of the head from the other side. Remove the valve seals by hand and remove the spring seats with the magnet.

Since it is very important that each valve and its spring, retainer, spring seat and keepers is reassembled in its original location, you must keep these parts in order. The best way to do this to to cut either eight (four cylinder) or twelve (six cylinder) holes in a piece of heavy cardboard or wood. Label each hole with the cylinder number and either **IN** or **EX**, corresponding to the location of each valve in the head. As you remove each valve, insert it into the holder, and assemble the seats, springs, keepers and retainers to the stem on the labeled side of the holder. This way each valve and its attending parts are kept together, and can be put back into the head in their proper locations.

After lapping each valve into its seat (see Valve Lapping below), oil each valve stem, and install each valve into the head in the reverse order of removal, so that all parts except the keepers are assembled on the stem. Always use new valve stem seals. Install the spring compressor, and compress the retainer and spring until the keeper groove on the valve stem is fully revealed. Coat the groove with a wipe of grease (to hold the keepers until the retainer is released) and install both keepers, wide end up. Slowly back the screw of the compressor out until the spring retainer covers the keepers. Remove the tool. Lightly tap the end of each valve stem with a rubber hammer to ensure proper fit of the retainers and keepers.

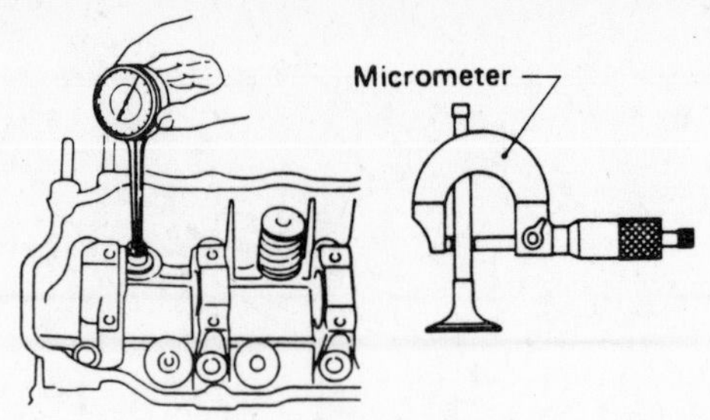

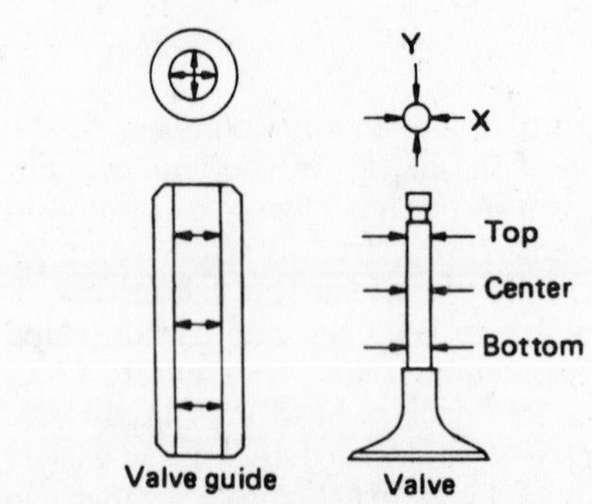

Checking the stem-to-guide clearance

INSPECTION

Before the valves can be properly inspected, the stem, lower end of the stem and the entire valve face and head must be cleaned. An old valve works well for chipping carbon from the valve head, and a wire brush, gasket scraper or putty knife can be used for cleaning the valve face and the area between the face and lower stem. Do not scratch the valve face during cleaning. Clean the entire stem with a rag soaked in thinners to remove all varnish and gum.

Thorough inspection of the valves requires the use of a micrometer, and a dial indicator is needed to measure the inside diameter of the

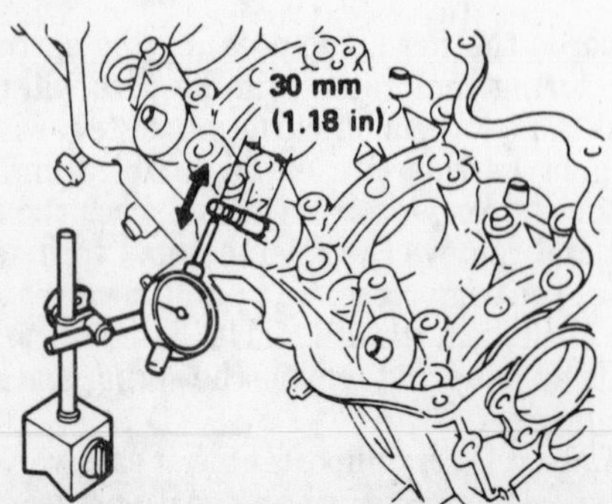

Use a dial indicator to check valve guide deflection

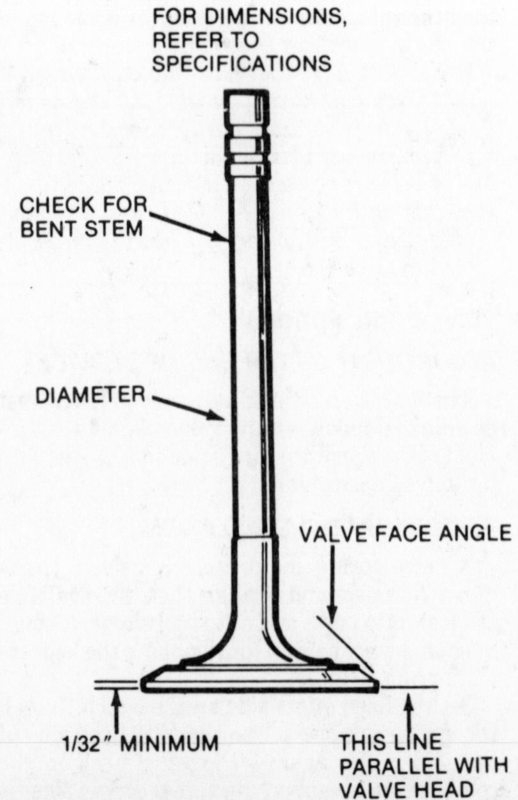

Critical valve dimensions

valve guides. If there instruments are not available to you, the valves and head can be taken to a reputable machine ship for inspection. Refer to the Valve Specifications chart for valve stem and stem-to-guide specifications.

If the above instruments are at your disposal, measure the diameter of each valve stem at the locations illustrated. Jot these measurements down. Using the dial indicator, measure the inside diameter of the valve guides at their bottom, top and midpoint 90° apart. Jot these measurements down also. Subtract the valve stem measurement from the valve guide inside measurement; if the clearance exceed that listed in the specifications chart under Stem-to-Guide Clearance, replace the valve(s). Stem-to-guide clearance can also be checked at a machine shop, where a dial indicator would be used.

Check the top of each valve stem for pitting and unusual wear due to improper rocker adjustment, etc. The stem tip can be ground flat if it is worn, but no more than 0.50mm can be removed; if this limit must be exceeded to make the tip flat and square, then the valve must be replaced. If the valve stem tips are ground, make sure you fix the valve securely into a jig designed for this purpose, so the tip contacts the grinding wheel squarely at exactly 90°. Most machine shops that handle automotive work are equipped for this job.

Check the valve seat concentricity with a dial gauge

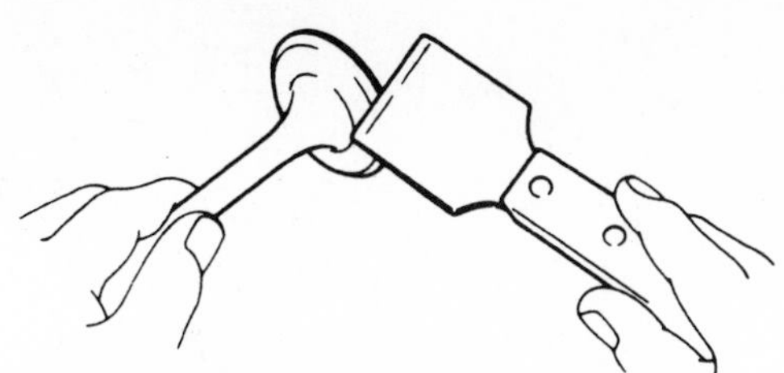

Carefully scrape carbon from the valve head

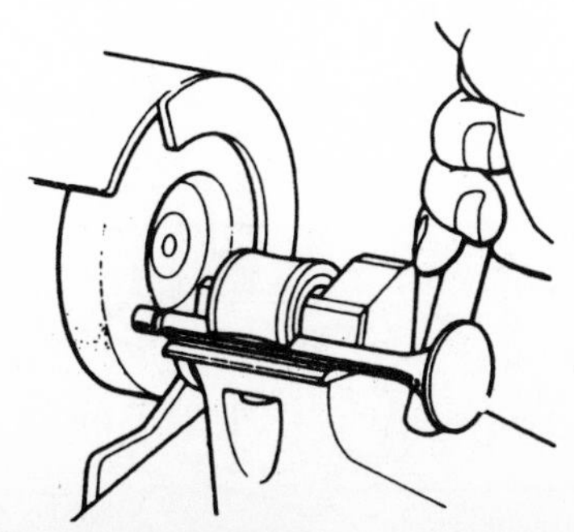

Grinding the valve stem tip

REFACING

Valve refacing should only be handled by a reputable machine shop, as the experience and equipment needed to do the job are beyond that of the average owner/mechanic. During the course of a normal valve job, refacing is necessary when simply lapping the valves into their seats will not correct the seat and face wear. When the valves are reground (resurfaced), the valve seats must also be recut, again requiring special equipment and experience.

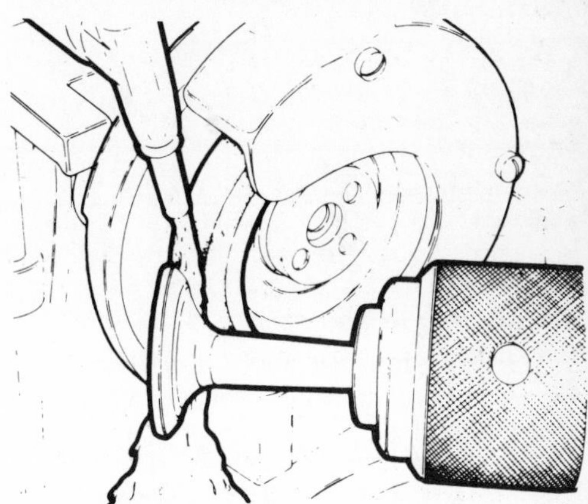

Valve grinding by machine

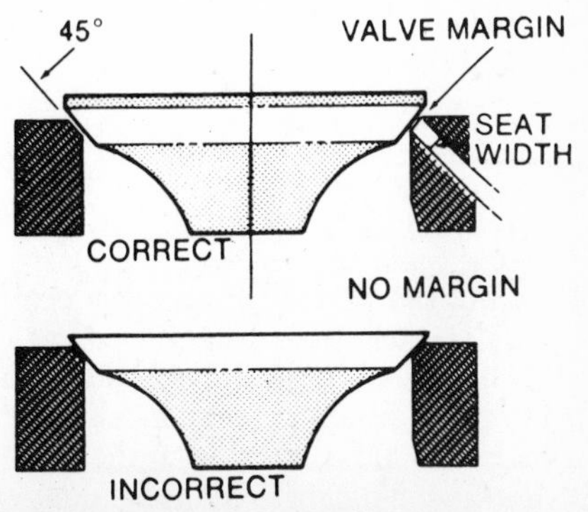

Valve seat width and centering

Lapping the valves by hand

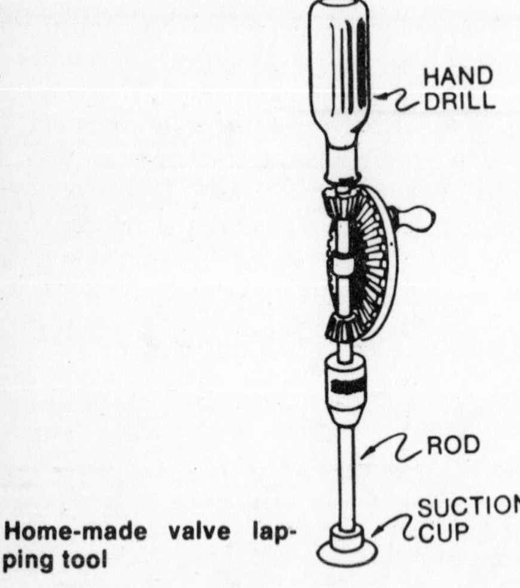

Home-made valve lapping tool

VALVE LAPPING

The valves must be lapped into their seats after resurfacing, to ensure proper sealing. Even if the valves have not been refaced, they should be lapped into the head before reassembly.

Set the cylinder head on the workbench, combustion chamber side up. Rest the head on wooden blocks on either end, so there are two or three inches between the tops of the valve guides and the bench.

1. Lightly lube the valve stem with clean engine oil. Coat the valve seat completely with valve grinding compound. Use just enough compound that the full width and circumference of the seat are covered.
2. Install the valve in its proper location in the head. Attach the suction cup end of the valve lapping tool to the valve head. It usually helps to put a small amount of saliva into the suction cup to aid it sticking to the valve.
3. Rotate the tool between the palms, changing position and lifting the tool often to prevent grooving. Lap the valve in until a smooth, evenly polished seat and valve face are evident.
4. Remove the valve from the head. Wipe away all traces of grinding compound from the valve face and seat. Wipe out the port with a solvent soaked rag, and swab out the valve guide with a piece of solvent soaked rag to make sure there are no traces of compound grit inside the guide. This cleaning is important.
5. Proceed through the remaining valves, one at a time. Make sure the valve faces, seats, cylinder ports and valve guides are clean before reassembling the valve train.

Valve Springs

INSPECTION

Valve spring squareness, length and tension should be checked while the valve train is disassembled. Place each valve spring on a flat surface next to a steel square. Measure the length of the spring, and rotate it against the edge of the square to measure distortion. If spring length varies (by comparison) by more than 1.6mm or if distortion exceeds 1.6mm, replace the spring.

Spring tension must be checked on a spring tester. Springs used on most engines should be within one pound of each other when tested at their specified installed heights.

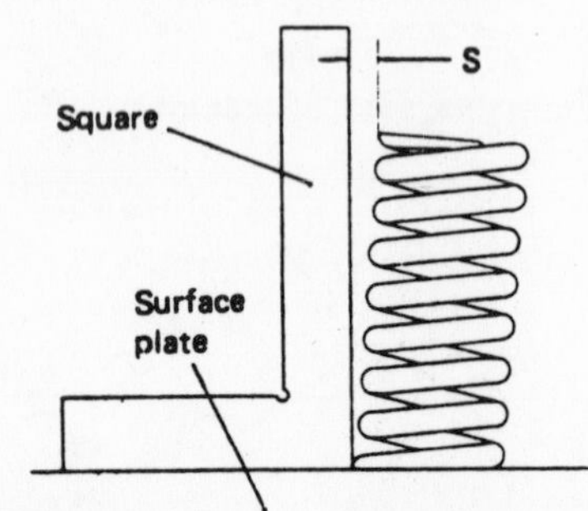

Check the valve spring length and squareness with a steel square

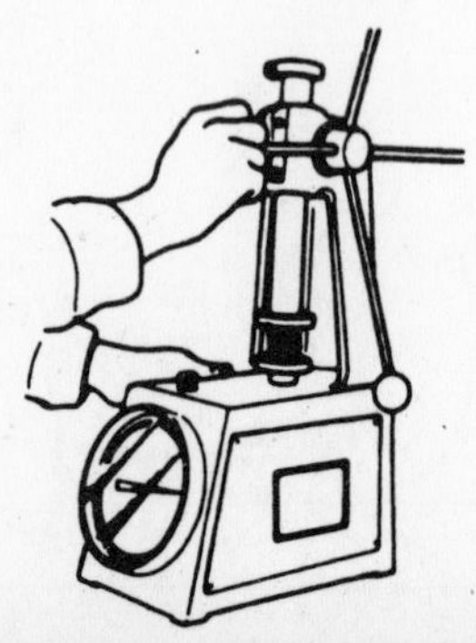

Have the spring tension checked at a machine shop

Valve Seats

REMOVAL AND INSTALLATION

Gasoline Engines

1. With the cylinder head removed from the engine and the valves removed from the cylinder head, old valve seat inserts can be removed by boring them out until they collapse. Be careful that the boring doesn't continue beyond the bottom face of the insert recess in the cylinder head.
2. Select the suitable valve seat insert and check its outside diameter.
3. Machine the cylinder head recess using the center of the valve guide as the center of the valve seat insert so that the insert will have the correct fit.
4. Ream the cylinder head recess at room temperature.
5. Heat the cylinder head to 302–392°F (150–200°C).
6. Fit the insert, making sure that it seats fully in the recess in the cylinder head. Peen the insert with a punch in at least four places equally spaced around its circumference.
7. Grind the valve seats to the proper angle.
8. Lap the valves with lapping compound to each seat to which they are to be mated. Thoroughly clean both the valves and the seat of all lapping compound before installing the valves.

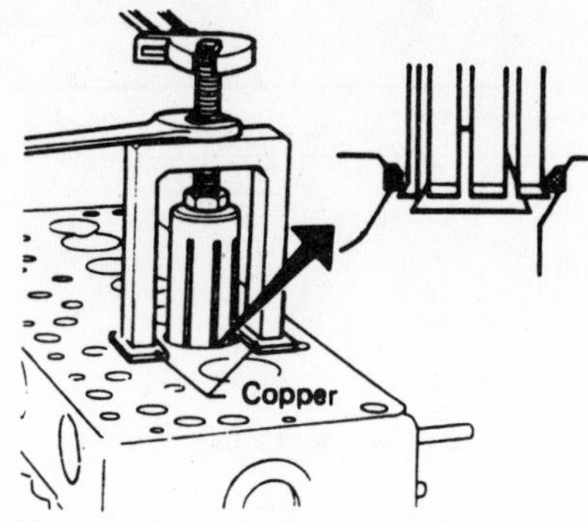

Bore out the old valve seal until it collapses

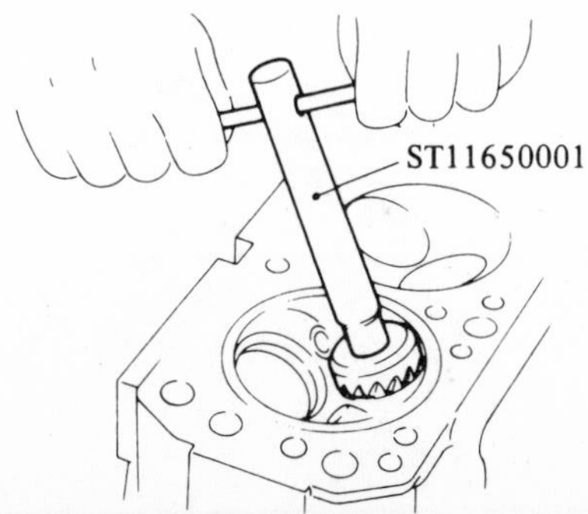

Reaming the valve seats

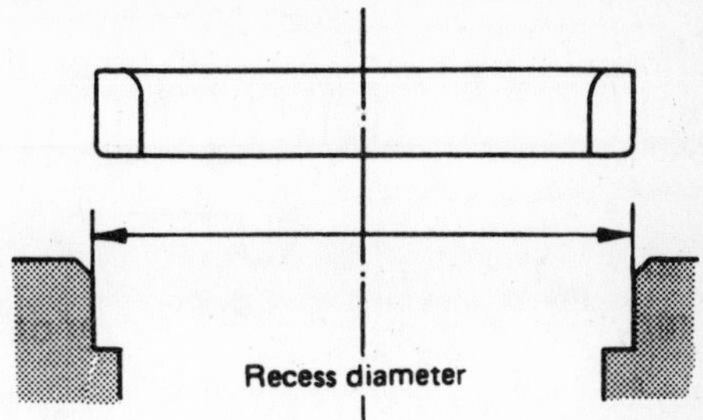

Valve seat replacement

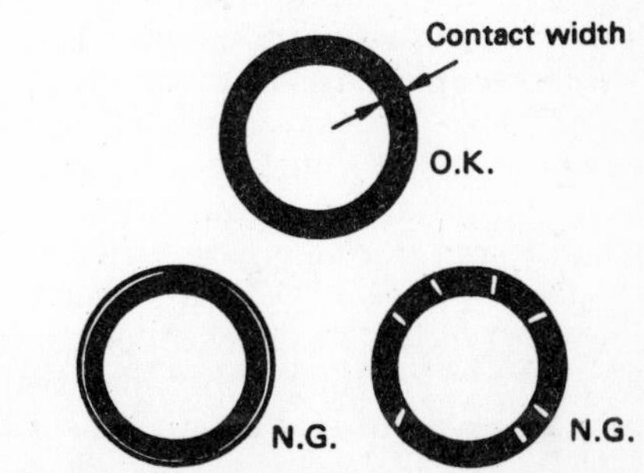

Check the valve seat contact surface

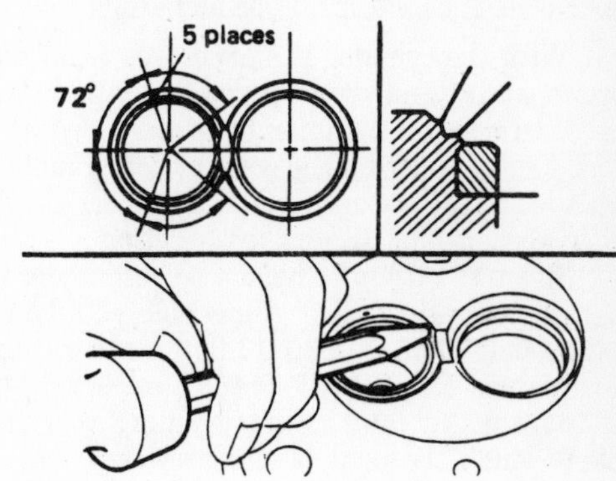

On the diesel, stake the exhaust valve seat in five places with a punch

Diesel Engines

1. Turn the head upside down in water at 175°F (79°C) while at the same time cool the valve seat in dry ice, for about 5–10 minutes.
2. Crack the seat with a cold chisel and remove it.
3. Chill the new seats in dry ice and install them in the head. Reface and lap the seats according to specifications.

Valve Guides

INSPECTION

Valve guides should be cleaned as outlined earlier, and checked when valve stem diameter and stem-to-guide clearance is checked. Gener-

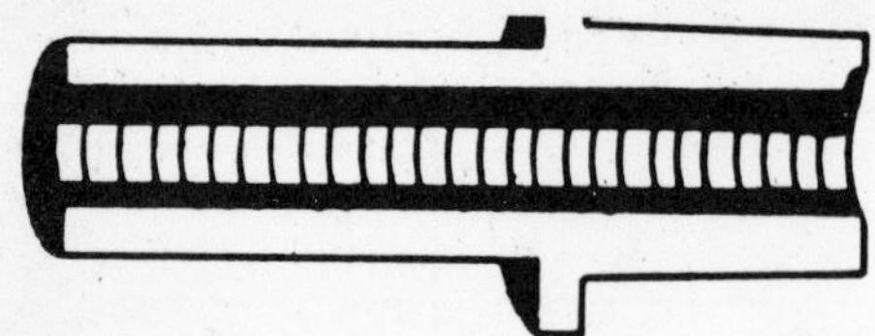

Cross-section of a knurled valve guide

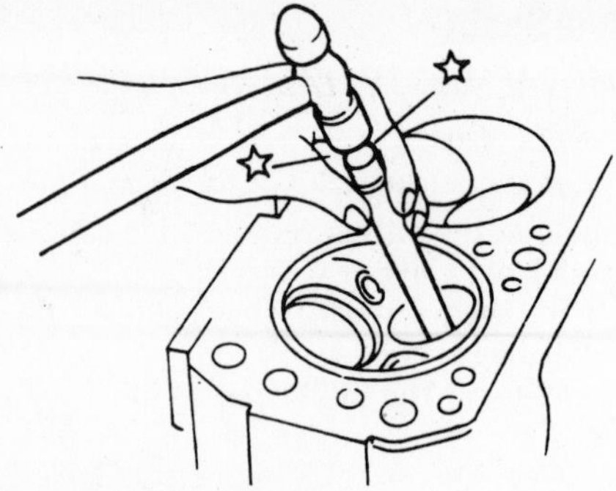

Driving out the valve guide

ally, if the engine is using oil through the guides (assuming the valve seals are OK) and the valve stem diameter is within specification, it is the guides that are worn and need replacing.

Valve guides which are not excessively worn or distorted may, in some cases, be knurled rather than replaced. Knurling is a process in which metal inside the valve guide bore is displaced and raised (forming a very fine cross-hatch pattern), thereby reducing clearance. Knurling also provides for excellent oil control. The possibility of knurling rather than replacing the guides should be discussed with a machinist.

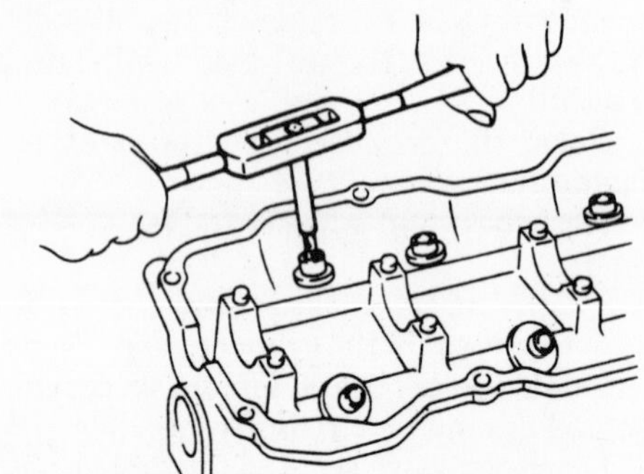

Reaming the cylinder head valve guide hole

REMOVAL AND INSTALLATION

All Engines Except SD22, SD25 and VG30i

1. With the cylinder head removed from the engine, and the valves removed from the head, use a drift and a hammer or press. Drive the valve guides out from the combustion chamber side toward the rocker cover side. A heated cylinder head will facilitate the operation.
2. Ream the cylinder head side guide hole at room temperature. The guide hole should be 0.4719–0.4723 in. (11.989–11.996mm) for standard valves and 0.4797–0.4802 in. (12.184–12.197mm) for 0.0079 in. (0.2mm) oversize valves which are available for service.
3. After heating the cylinder head to 302–392°F (150–200°C); 302–320°F (150–160°C) on the Z24i, press the new valve guide carefully into the cylinder head. The top of the valve guide should protrude out the top of the guide hole 0.4173 in. (10.5mm).
4. Ream the bore of the valve guide with the valve guide pressed into the cylinder head. The standard valve guide bore size is 0.3150–0.3157 in. (8.00–8.02mm).
5. Assemble the cylinder head and install it on the engine.

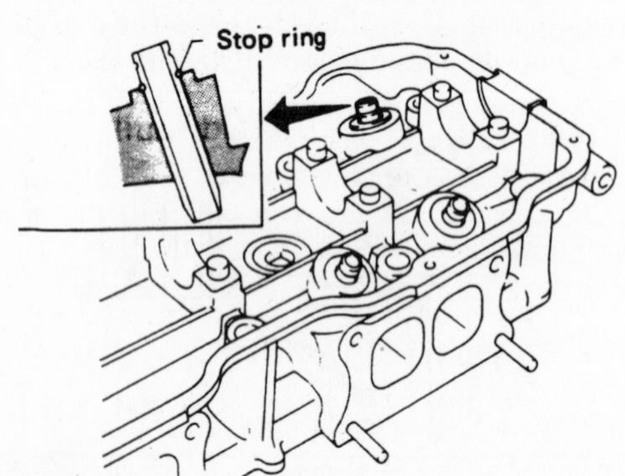

Pressing in the replacement valve guide—4 cylinder gasoline engines

VG30i Engines

1. Remove the valve springs.
2. Heat the cylinder head to at least 320°F (160°C), then drive out the guide using an arbor press or a hammer and drift punch.

NOTE: *Drive the valve guides toward the rocker arm cover side of the cylinder head.*

3. With the valve guides removed, ream the

Pressing in the replacement valve guide—VG30i engines

cylinder head valve guide hole (inside diameter) to:

a. Intake: 0.4400–0.4408 in. (11.176–11.196mm)
b. Exhaust: 0.4793–0.4802 in. (12.174–12.197mm)

4. Heat the cylinder to at least 320°F (160°C) and press the service valve guide onto the cylinder head.
5. Ream the valve guide (inside diameter) to:

a. Intake: 0.2756–0.2763 in. (7.000–7.018mm)
b. Exhaust: 0.3150–0.3157 in. (8.000–8.019mm)

6. To install, use new gaskets, valve guide seals and reverse the removal procedures.

SD22 and SD25 Engine

Valve guides are not replaceable.

Oil Pan

REMOVAL AND INSTALLATION

1970-86 (720-D Series)

To remove the oil pan it will be necessary to unbolt the motor mounts and jack the engine to gain clearance. On the diesel it will be necessary to remove the crossmember, the oil filter, the injection pump rear bracket and oil tube, and the main and secondary oil coolers. It is also helpful, on the diesel, to have the steering wheel in either the full left or right position. Remove the stabilizer bar or any other suspension or member that may make access easier to remove the pan. Drain the oil and remove the attaching screw and remove the oil pan and gasket. Apply a thin bead of silicone seal to the engine block at the junction of the block and front cover, and the junction of the block and the main bearing cap. Then apply a thin coat of silicone seal to the new oil pan gasket, install the gasket to the block, and install the pan. Tighten the pan bolts in a circular pattern from the center of the ends, to 4–7 ft. lbs. Overtightening will distort the pan lip, causing leakage.

1986-89 (D21-D Series)

Z24I ENGINES

1. Remove the engine under cover and drain the engine oil.
2. Remove the bolt from the front differential carrier member on 4wd models.
3. On 4wd models, position a floor jack under the front differential carrier and remove the mounting bolts.
4. On 2wd models, remove the front crossmember.
5. On 4wd models, remove the transmission-to-rear engine mount bracket nuts.
6. On 4wd models, remove the engine mount nuts and bolts.
7. On 4wd models, attach and engine hoist and raise the engine slightly.
8. Remove the oil pan mounting bolts. Insert a seal cutter tool between the cylinder block and the oil pan and tap it around the circumference of the pan with a hammer. Remove the oil pan.

NOTE: *Be careful not to drive the seal cutter into the oil pump or rear oil seal retainer as you will damage the aluminum mating surface.*

9. Remove all traces of gasket material from the pan and block mating surfaces.
10. Apply a continuous bead of sealant (3.5–4.5mm) to the oil pan mating surface. Be sure to trace the sealant bead to the inside of the bolt holes where there is no groove.
11. Install the pan and tighten all bolts in the reverse order of removal. Tighten the bolts to 4–5 ft. lbs. (4–7 Nm).
12. Wait at least 30 minutes and then refill the engine with oil. Run the engine until it reaches normal operating temperature and then check for leaks.

VG30I ENGINES

1. Remove the engine under cover and drain the engine oil.
2. On 2wd models, remove the stabilizer bar bracket bolts.
3. On 4wd models, remove the front driveshaft and disconnect the halfshafts at the transfer case. Position a floor jack under the front differential carrier and remove the mounting bolts.
4. On 2wd models, remove the front crossmember.
5. Remove the idler arm.
6. Remove the starter motor.
7. On 4wd models, remove the transmission-to-rear engine mount bracket nuts.
8. On 4wd models, remove the engine mount nuts and bolts.
9. Remove the engine gussets.
10. On 4wd models, attach and engine hoist and raise the engine slightly.
11. Remove the oil pan mounting bolts in the order shown. Insert a seal cutter tool between the cylinder block and the oil pan and tap it around the circumference of the pan with a hammer. Remove the oil pan.

NOTE: *Be careful not to drive the seal cutter into the oil pump or rear oil seal retainer as you will damage the aluminum mating surface.*

12. Remove all traces of gasket material from the pan and block mating surfaces.
13. Apply sealant to the oil pump and oil seal retainer gasket.

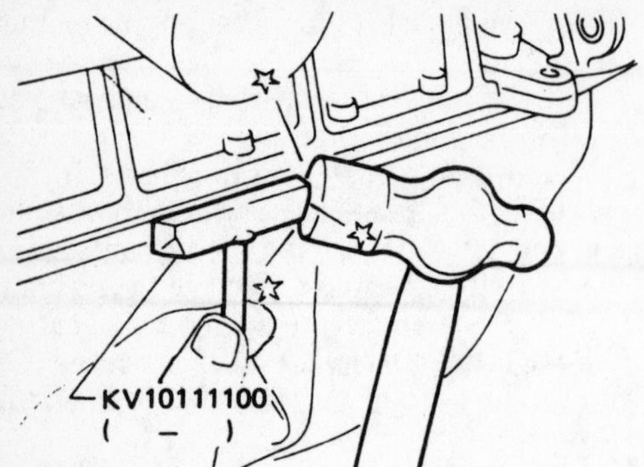

Using a seal cutter to separate the oil pan from the cylinder block

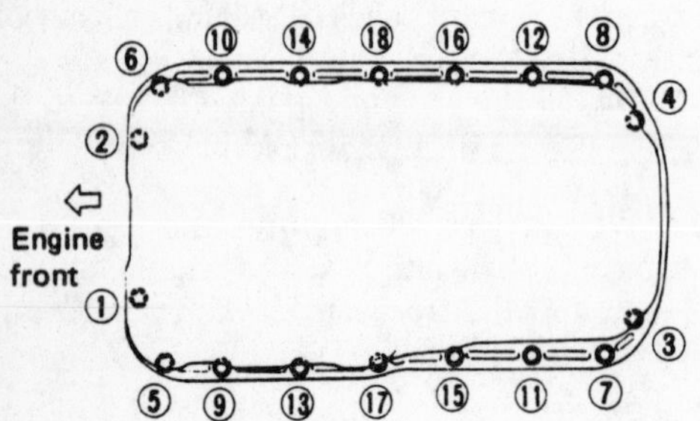

Oil pan bolt loosening sequence—VG30in engines

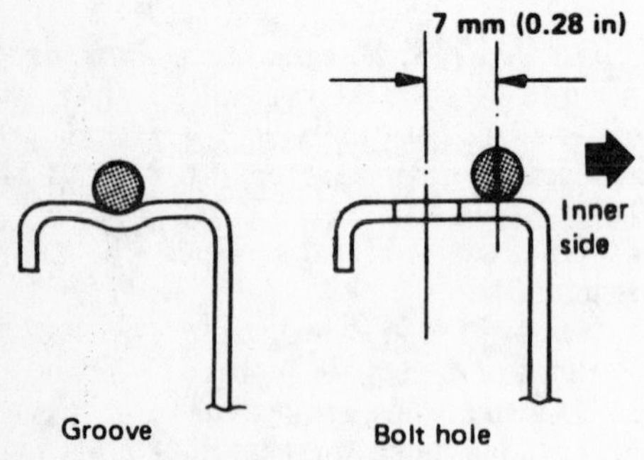

Apply the bead of sealant like this

14. Apply a continuous bead of sealant (3.5–4.5mm) to the oil pan mating surface. Be sure to trace the sealant bead to the inside of the bolt holes where there is no groove.
15. Install the pan and tighten all bolts in the reverse order of removal. Tighten the bolts to 4–5 ft. lbs. (4–7 Nm).
16. Wait at least 30 minutes and then refill the engine with oil. Run the engine until it reaches normal operating temperature and then check for leaks.

SD25 ENGINES

1. Remove the engine under cover and drain the engine oil.
2. Remove the stabilizer bar bracket bolts.
3. Remove the front crossmember.
4. Remove the idler arm.
5. Remove the oil pan mounting bolts in the order shown. Insert a seal cutter tool between the cylinder block and the oil pan and tap it around the circumference of the pan with a hammer. Remove the oil pan.

NOTE: *Be careful not to drive the seal cutter into the oil pump or rear oil seal retainer as you will damage the aluminum mating surface.*

6. Remove all traces of gasket material from the pan and block mating surfaces.
7. Apply a continuous bead of sealant (3.5–4.5mm) to the oil pan mating surface. Be sure to trace the sealant bead to the inside of the bolt holes where there is no groove.
8. Install the pan and tighten all bolts in the reverse order of removal. Tighten the bolts to 4–5 ft. lbs. (4–7 Nm).
9. Wait at least 30 minutes and then refill the engine with oil. Run the engine until it reaches normal operating temperature and then check for leaks.

Oil Pump

REMOVAL AND INSTALLATION

All Four Cylinder Gasoline Engines

The oil pump is mounted externally on the engine, eliminating the need to remove the oil pan in order to remove the oil pump.

1. Remove the distributor.
2. Drain the engine oil.
3. Remove the front stabilizer bar.
4. Remove the splash shield board.
5. Loosen the mounting bolts and remove the oil pump body with the drive spindle assembly.
6. Before installing the oil pump in the engine, turn the crankshaft so that the No. 1 piston is at TDC of the compression stroke.
7. Fill the pump housing with engine oil,

Removing the oil pump, four cylinder gasoline engines

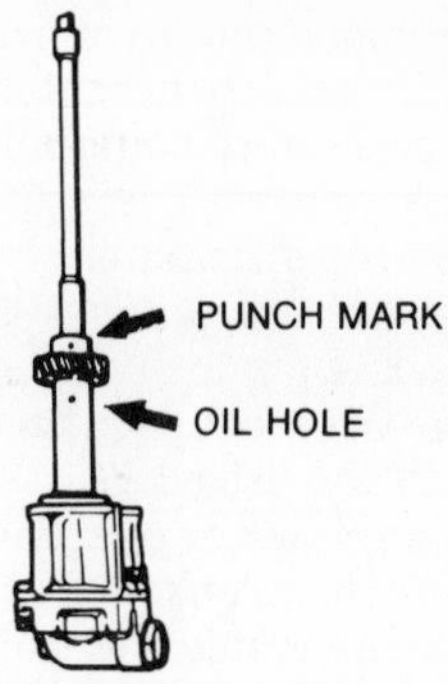

Aligning the punch mark on the spindle with the hole in the oil pump, four cylinder gasoline engines

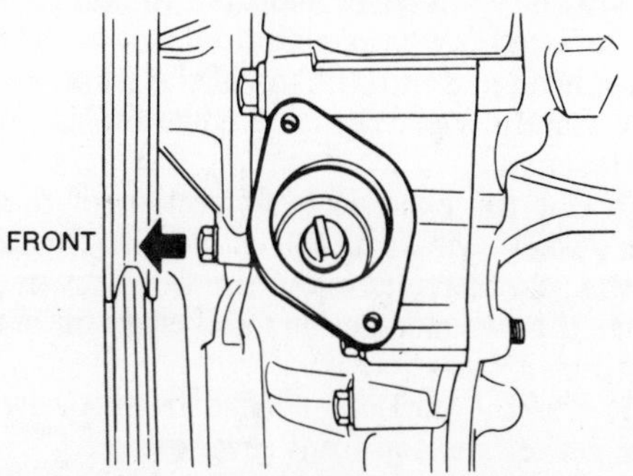

The projection on the top of the oil pump drive spindle located in the 11:25 O'clock position. The smaller cresent formed by the notch faces forward, four cylinder gasoline engines

then align the punch mark on the spindle with the hole in the oil pump.

8. With a new gasket placed over the drive spindle, install the oil pump and drive spindle assembly so that the projection on the top of the drive spindle is located in the 11:25 o'clock position.

9. Install the distributor with the metal tip of the rotor pointing toward the No. 1 spark plug tower of the distributor cap.

10. Install the splash shield and front stabilizer bar.

11. Refill the engine with oil. Start the engine, check ignition timing and check for oil leaks.

VG30i Engines

1. Remove the oil pan. Remove the timing belt.

2. Remove the crankshaft timing sprocket (it may be necessary to use a puller) and the timing belt plate.

3. Remove the oil pump strainer and pick-up tube from the oil pump.

4. Loosen the oil pump retaining bolts and then remove the oil pump.

5. To install, use new gaskets (use silicone

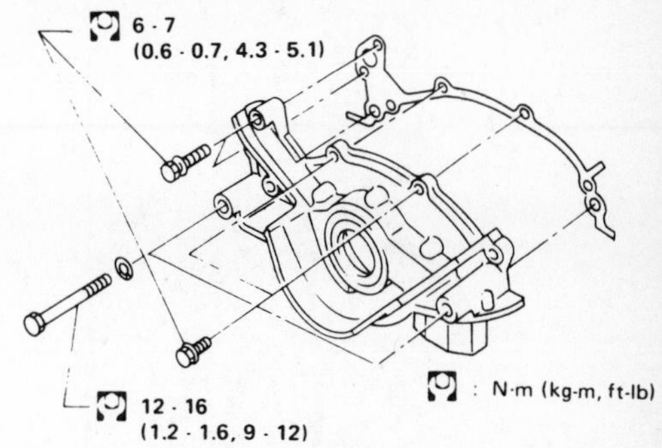

Oil pump installation—V6 engine

sealant), an new oil seal. Tighten the 6mm bolts to 4–5 ft. lbs. (6–7 Nm) and the 8mm bolts to 9–12 ft. lbs. (12–16 Nm). Refill the engine with oil.

NOTE: *Before installing the oil pump, be sure to pack the pump's cavity with petroleum jelly, then make sure the O-ring is properly fitted.*

6. Connect the oil strainer and pick-up tube to the pump body.

7. Install the timing belt plate and the crankshaft pulley.

8. Install the timing belt and front cover. Start the engine and check for any leaks.

SD22 and SD25 Engines

1. Remove the oil pump drive spindle.

2. Remove the oil pan.

3. Unbolt and remove the oil pump. Discard the gasket.

4. Using a new gasket, install the oil pump. Tighten the bolts to 7–9 ft. lbs. (10–12 Nm) on the SD22 and 9–14 ft. lbs. (13–19 Nm) on the SD25

5. Install the drive spindle by aligning it with the oil pump driveshaft groove in the cylinder block and the camshaft oil pump drive gear.

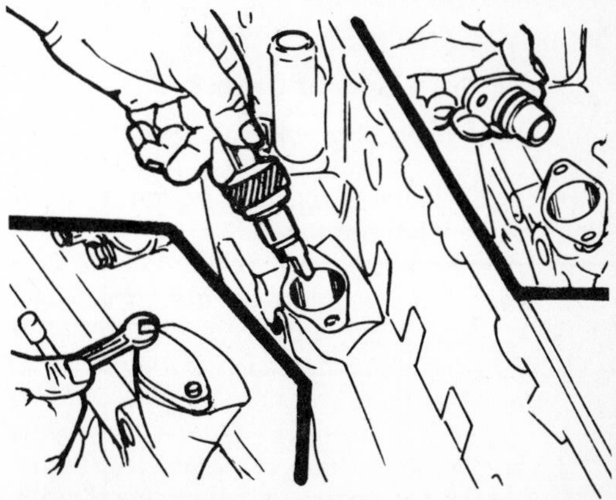

Removing the oil pump drive spindle—SD22 and SD25 engines

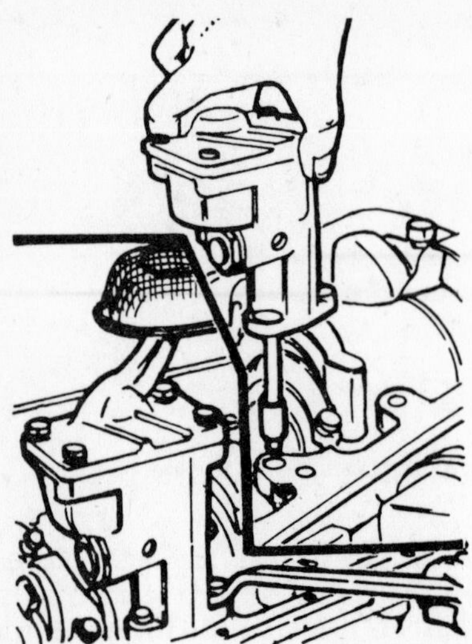

Removing the oil pump—SD22 and SD25 engines

6. Place a new O-ring on the spindle support and bolt it to the block.

7. Install the oil pan and fill the engine with oil. Start the engine and check for leaks.

Oil Filter Canister Assembly

REMOVAL AND INSTALLATION

SD22 and SD25 Engines

1. Remove the bolts at the oil filter end of the oil inlet and outlet lines.

2. Remove the four filter assembly mounting bolts and separate the filter from the block.

NOTE: *Have a drip pan ready, since some oil will drain out.*

3. Installation is easy, simply position the cannister and connect the inlet and outlet lines. Tighten the mounting bolts to 14–18 ft. lbs.

Timing Chain Cover

REMOVAL AND INSTALLATION

All Four Cylinder Gasoline Engines

1. Disconnect the negative battery cable from the battery, drain the cooling system, and remove the radiator together with the upper and lower radiator hoses.

CAUTION: *When draining the coolant, keep in mind that cats and dogs are attracted by the ethylene glycol antifreeze, and are quite likely to drink any that is left in an uncovered container or in puddles on the ground. This will prove fatal in sufficient quantity. Always drain the coolant into a sealable container. Coolant should be reused unless it is contaminated or several years old.*

2. Loosen the alternator drive belt adjusting screw and remove the drive belt. Remove the bolts which attach the alternator bracket to the engine and position the alternator aside out of the way.

3. Remove the distributor.

4. Remove the oil pump attaching screws, and take out the pump and its drive sprindle.

5. Remove the cooling fan and the fan pulley together with the drive belt.

6. Remove the water pump.

7. Remove the crankshaft pulley bolt and then remove the crankshaft pulley.

8. Remove the bolts holding the front cover to the front of the cylinder block, the four bolts which retain the front of the oil pan to the bottom of the front cover and the two bolts which are screwed down through the front of the cylinder head and into the top of the front cover.

9. Carefully pry the front cover off the front of the engine.

10. Cut the exposed front section of the oil pan gasket away from the oil pan. Do the same to the gasket at the top of the front cover. Remove the two side gaskets and clean all of the mating surfaces.

11. Cut the portions needed from a new oil pan gasket and top front cover gasket.

12. Apply sealer to all of the gaskets and position them on the engine in their proper places.

13. Apply a light coating of oil to the crankshaft oil seal and carefully mount in the front cover to the front of the engine and install all of the mounting bolts. Tighten the 8mm bolts to 7–12 ft. lbs. (10–16 Nm) and the 6mm bolts to 3–7 ft. lbs. (4–10 Nm). Tighten the oil pan attaching bolts to 4–7 ft. lb. (6–8 Nm).

14. Before installing the oil pump, place the gasket over the shaft and make sure that the mark on the drive spindle faces (aligned with) the oil pump hole. Install the oil pump so that the projection on the top of the shaft is located in the exact position as when it was removed or, at the 11:25 o'clock when the piston in the No.

Removing the timing chain cover—all 4 cylinder gasoline engines

1 cylinder is placed at TDC on the compression stroke, if the engine was disturbed since disassembly. Tighten the oil pump attaching screws to 8–10 ft. lbs. (11–15 Nm).

15. Install the crankshaft pulley and bolt. Tighten the bolt to 87–116 ft. lbs. (118–157 Nm).

16. Install the water pump with a new gasket. Install the fan pulley and cooling fan. Install the drive belt and adjust the belt to the correct tension.

17. Install the distributor in the correct position. Reconnect the alternator bracket and alternator if it was removed. Install the drive belt and adjust the belt to the correct tension.

18. Install the radiator, reconnect the upper and lower radiator hoses and refill the cooling system.

19. Reconnect the negative battery cable. Start the engine, check ignition timing and check for leaks.

Timing Belt Cover

REMOVAL AND INSTALLATION

VG30i Engines

NOTE: *The front oil seal is a part of the oil pump assembly. To replace the oil pump seal, refer to the Oil Pump Removal and Installation procedures, in this section and replace the oil seal.*

1. Remove the radiator shroud, the fan and the pulleys.

2. Drain the coolant from the radiator and remove the water pump hose.

CAUTION: *When draining the coolant, keep in mind that cats and dogs are attracted by the ethylene glycol antifreeze, and are quite likely to drink any that is left in an uncovered container or in puddles on the ground. This will prove fatal in sufficient quantity. Always drain the coolant into a sealable container. Coolant should be reused unless it is contaminated or several years old.*

3. Remove the power steering, A/C compressor and alternator drive belts.

4. Remove the suction pipe bracket and then remove the lower hose from the suction pipe.

5. Remove the spark plugs.

6. Set the No. 1 piston at TDC of its compression stroke and the remove the idler bracket for the compressor drive belt.

7. Remove the crankshaft pulley.

8. Loosen all bolts and remove the upper and lower timing belt covers.

9. Install the two timing belt covers and tighten the mounting bolts to 2–4 ft. lbs. (3–5 Nm).

10. Press the crankshaft pulley onto the crankshaft and tighten the bolt to 90–98 ft. lbs. (123–132 Nm). Install the spark plugs.

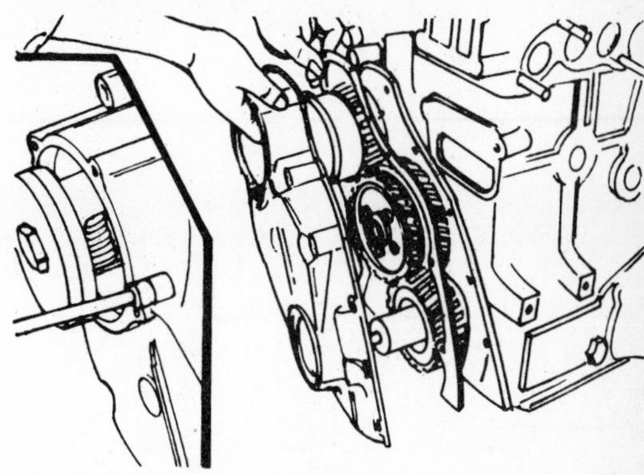

Removing the timing chain cover—SD22 and SD25 engines

11. Install the A/C compressor idler bracket.

12. Install the suction pipe bracket and connect the lower hose. Install all drive belts and adjust their tension.

13. Reconnect the water pump hose and fill the engine with coolant. Install the fan shroud and pulleys. Start the engine and check for any leaks.

Timing Gear Cover

REMOVAL AND INSTALLATION

SD22 and SD25 Engines

NOTE: *A 41mm (1.614 in.) socket is needed for this procedure.*

1. Remove the fan and pulley.

2. Remove the water pump by-pass hose and allow the cooling system to drain below the level of the water pump.

CAUTION: *When draining the coolant, keep in mind that cats and dogs are attracted by the ethylene glycol antifreeze, and are quite likely to drink any that is left in an uncovered container or in puddles on the ground. This will prove fatal in sufficient quantity. Always drain the coolant into a sealable container. Coolant should be reused unless it is contaminated or several years old.*

3. Remove the three bolts and lift the water pump and gasket off the block. Discard the gasket.

4. Remove the crankshaft pulley nut with a 41mm socket.

5. Drive the pulley from the crankshaft with a wooden or plastic mallet.

6. Remove the 5 bolts and lift the timing gear cover from the case.

7. Install the timing gear cover to the cylinder block. Always replace the cover oil seal and

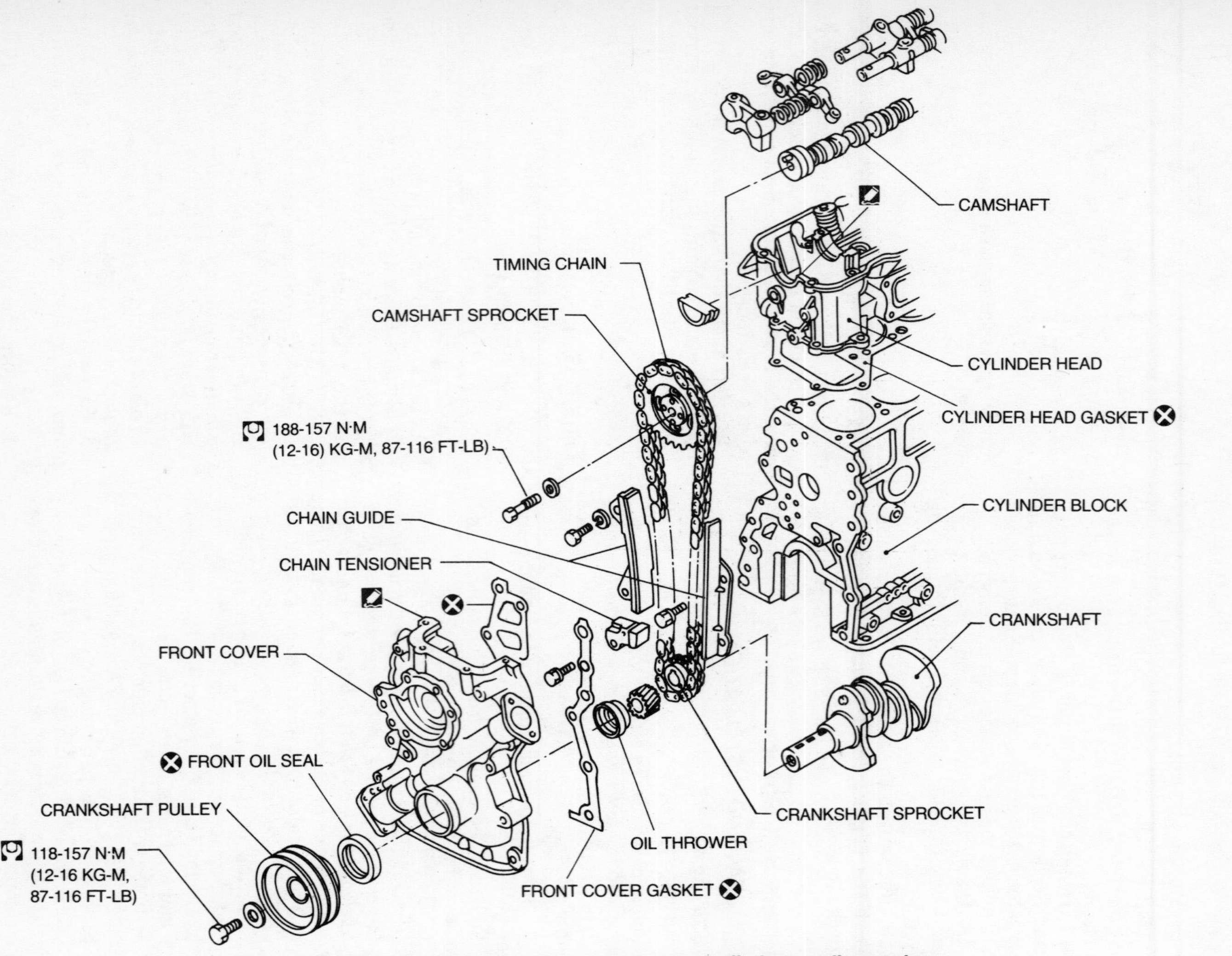

Exploded view of the timing chain assembly—all 4 cylinder gaosline engines

use a new cover gasket. Tighten the cover mounting bolts to 7–9 ft. lbs. (10–13 Nm).

8. Install the crankshaft pulley and tighten the nut to 217–239 ft. lbs. (294–324 Nm).

9. Install the water pump.

NOTE: *Do not tighten the water pump bolts until the belt adjuster is installed when install the alternator.*

10. Install the water pump by-pass hose, the pulley and cooling fan. Refill the engine with coolant, start the engine and check for leaks.

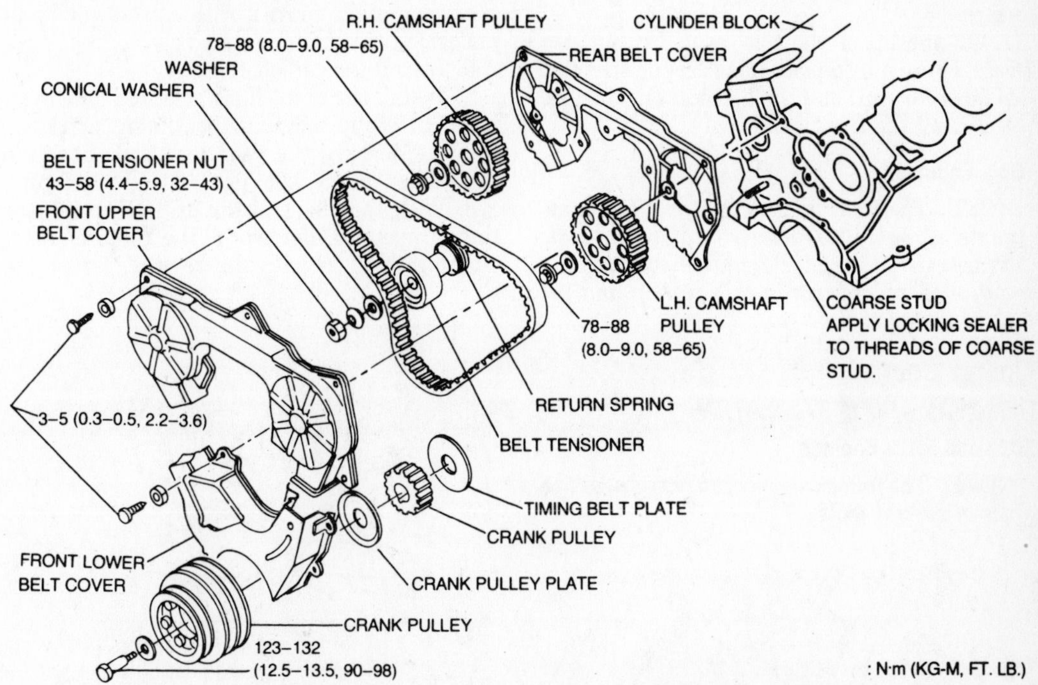

Exploded view of the timing belt assembly—VG30i engines

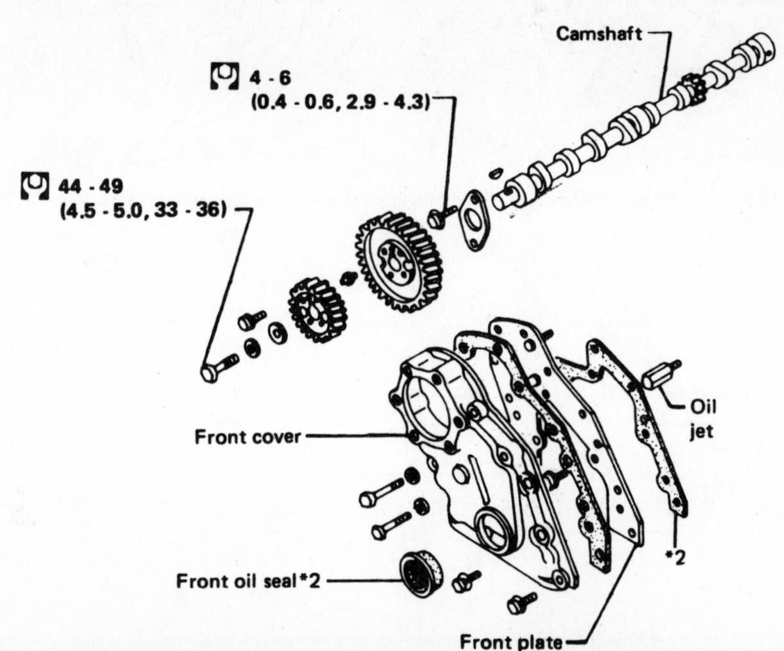

Exploded view of the timing gear assembly—SD22 and SD25 engines

Front Oil Seal

REMOVAL AND INSTALLATION

Four Cylinder Engines

1. Remove the front cover.
2. Pry the old seal from the cover with a pointed piece of plastic or wood. Do not use a screwdriver to avoid scratching the seal surface.
3. Oil the lip of the new seal. Do not use grease. Press it into place, making sure the flat side faces forward and the lip faces the engine.
4. Install the front cover.

VG30i Engines

NOTE: *The front oil seal is a part of the oil pump assembly. To replace the oil pump seal, please refer to the Oil Pump Removal and Installation procedures in this section and replace the oil seal.*

Timing Gears

REMOVAL AND INSTALLATION

SD22 and SD25 Engines

NOTE: *The following procedure requires the use of special tools.*

1. Remove the timing gear cover.
2. Remove the timing gear round nut.
3. Using timer extractor #57926-581, thread the tool into the timer weight holder. Remove the timing gear assembly by threading the extractor tool bolt.
4. Unbolt and remove the camshaft gear set.
5. Remove the oil slinger. Unbolt the crankshaft gear and remove it with a two-armed gear puller.
6. Install the camshaft gear.
7. Install the crankshaft gear and oil slinger while carefully aligning the timing marks as shown. Measure the gear backlash. Backlash should be 0.0028–0.0079 in. (0.071–0.200mm).
8. With the No. 1 piston at TDC, mesh the timing gear and idler gear at the **Y** marks. After aligning the gear with the keyway, secure the

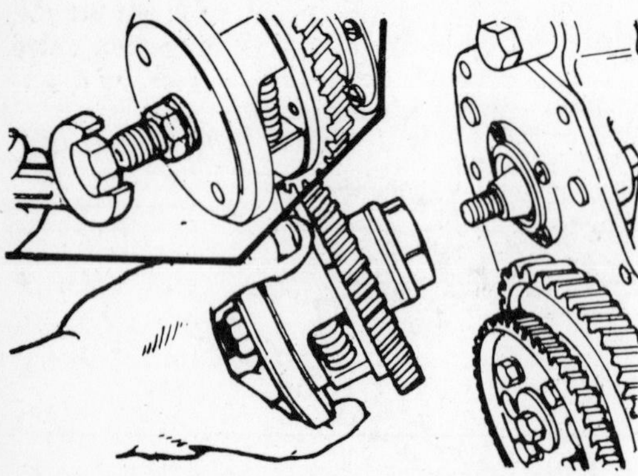

Timer removal and installation—SD22 and SD25 engines

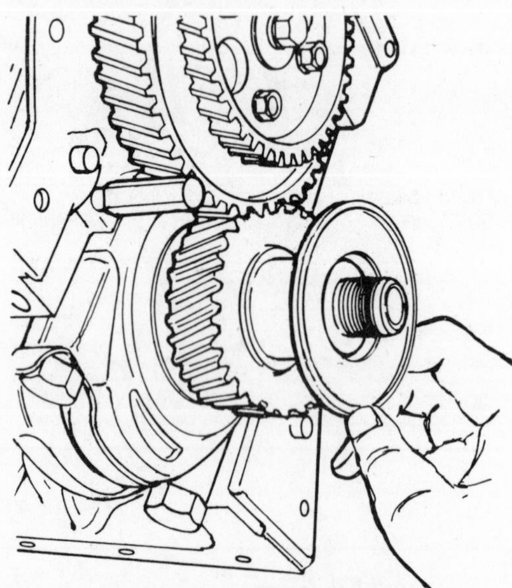

Oil slinger installation—SD22 and SD25 engines

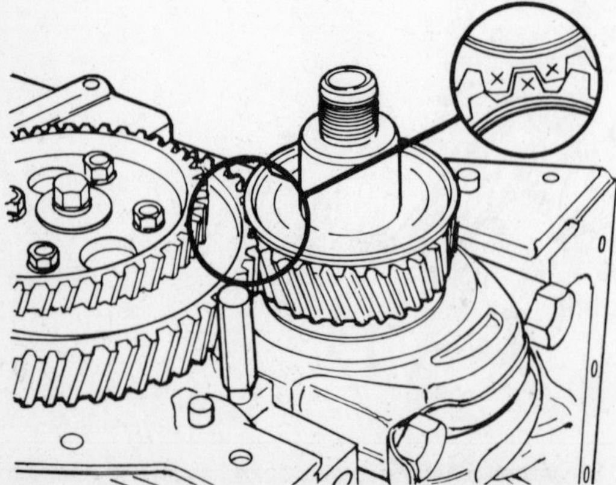

Timing mark alignment—SD22 and SD25 engines

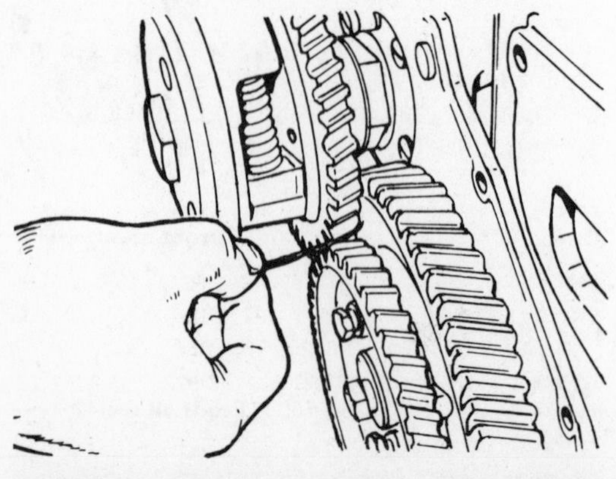

Measuring the timing gear backlash—SD22 and SD25 engines

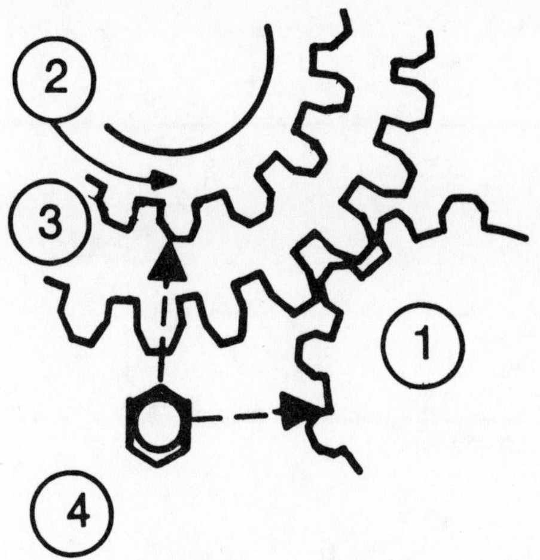

1. Crankshaft gear
2. Idle gear
3. Camshaft gear
4. Oil jet

Oil jet orientation—SD22 and SD25 engines

timer assembly with a lock washer and the round nut. Tighten the nut to 50–58 ft. lbs.

9. Install the timing gear cover.

NOTE: *If the gear case oil jet was removed, install in the relationship as shown.*

Timing Chain and Tensioner

REMOVAL AND INSTALLATION

All 4 Cylinder Gasoline Engines

1. Before beginning any disassembly procedures, position the No. 1 piston at TDC on the compression stroke.
2. Remove the timing chain cover. Remove the cylinder head cover.
3. With the No. 1 piston at TDC, the timing marks on the camshaft sprocket and the timing chain should be visible. Mark both of them with paint. Also mark the relationship of the camshaft sprocket to the camshaft. At this point you will see that there are three sets of timing marks and locating holes in the sprocket. They are for making adjustments to compensate for timing chain stretch. See the Timing Chain Adjustment section following for details.
4. With the timing marks on the camshaft sprocket clearly marked, locate and mark the timing marks on the crankshaft sprocket. Also mark the chain timing mark. Of course, if the chain is not to be reused, marking it is useless.
5. Unbolt the camshaft sprocket and remove the sprocket along with the chain. As you remove the chain, hold it where the chain tensioner contacts it. When the chain is removed, the tensioner is going to come apart. *Hold on to it and you won't lose any of the parts!* The crankshaft sprocket can be removed with a puller, if necessary. There is no need to remove the chain guide unless it is being replaced.
6. Install the timing chain and the camshaft sprocket together after first positioning the chain over the crankshaft sprocket. Position the sprocket so that the marks made previously line up. This is assuming that the engine has not been disturbed. The camshaft and the crankshaft keys should both be pointing upward. If a new chain and/or gear is being installed, position the sprocket so that the timing marks on the chain align with the marks on the sprocket (with both keys pointing up). The marks are on the right hand side of the sprockets as you face the engine. 1970-73 L16 and L18 engines have 42 pins between the mating marks of the chain and sprockets when the chain is installed correctly. 1974-80 L18 and L20B engines have 44 pins.

NOTE: *The factory refers to the pins as links, but in American terminology this is incorrect. Count the pins. There are two (2) pins per chain link. This is an important step! If you do not get the exact number of pins between the timing marks, valve timing will be incorrect, and the engine will either not run at all or run very badly.*

Z20, Z22, Z24 and Z24i engines do not use the pin counting method for finding correct valve timing. Instead, set the timing chain by align-

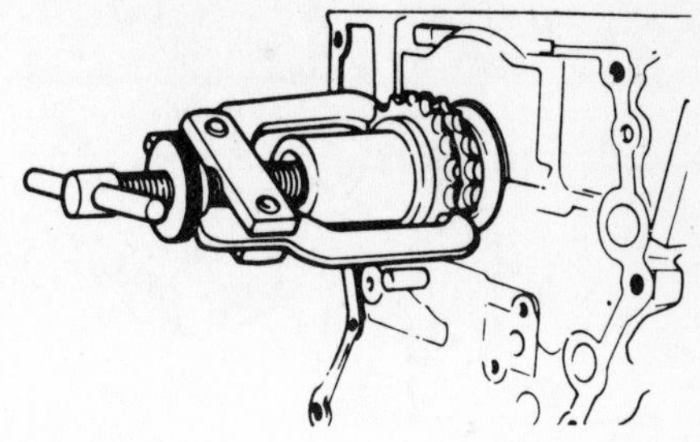

Crankshaft sprocket removal—all 4 cylinder gasoline engines

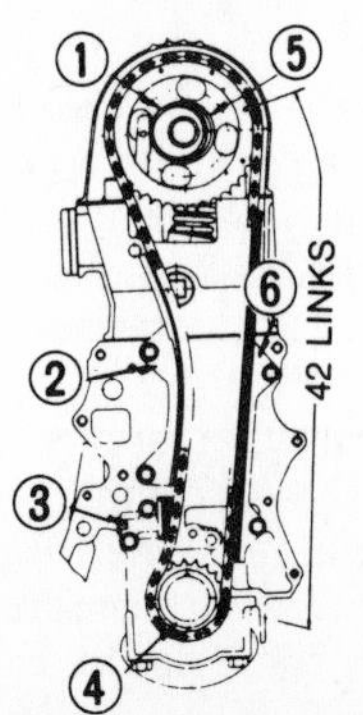

1. Fuel pump drive cam
2. Chain guide
3. Chain tensioner
4. Crank sprocket
5. Cam sprocket
6. Chain guide

When installing the timing chain, count the number of links—L16, L18 and L20B engines

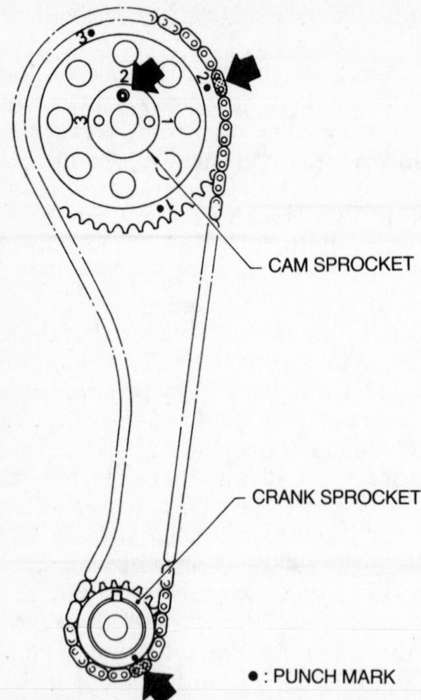

Timign chain and sprocket alignment—Z20, Z22, Z24 and Z24i engines

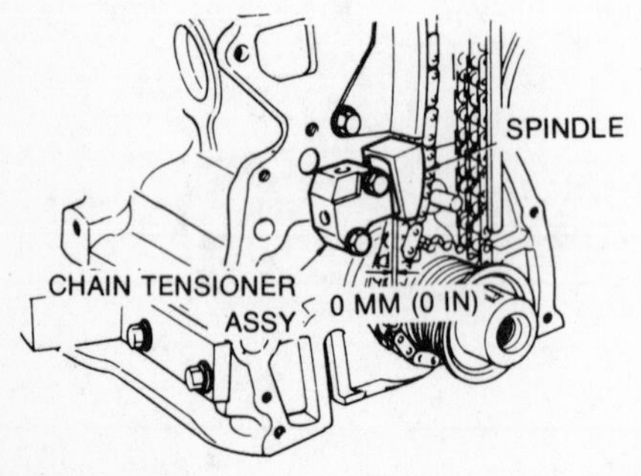

Installing the timing chain tensioner—all 4 cylinder gasoline engines

ing its mating marks with those of the crankshaft sprocket and camshaft sprocket. The camshaft sprocket should be installed by fitting the knock pin of the camshaft into its No. 2 hole. And the No. 2 timing mark must also be used.

7. Install the camshaft sprocket bolt and tighten it to 87–116 ft. lbs. (118–157 Nm).

8. Install the chain guide and tensioner. Adjust the protrusion of the chain tensioner spindle to zero clearance. Tighten the bolts to 4–7 ft. lbs. (6–10 Nm).

9. With a new seal installed in the timing chain cover and a light coat of oil applied to the

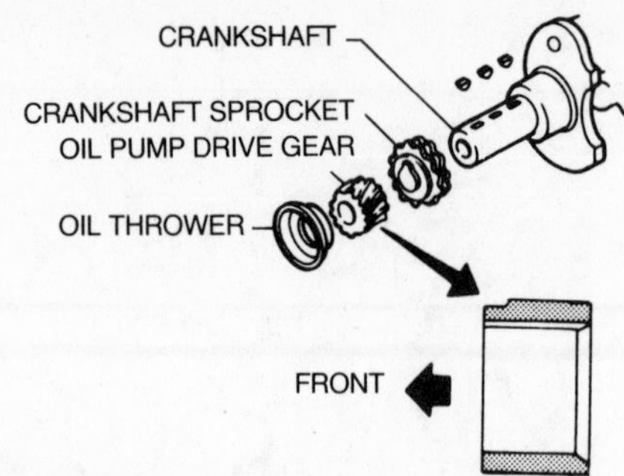

Crankshaft sprocket installation—Z20, Z22, Z24 and Z24i engines

seal, install the timing cover. Start the engine and check for any leaks. Check the ignition timing.

TIMING CHAIN ADJUSTMENT

L16, L18 and L20B Engines

When the timing chain stretches excessively, the valve timing will be adversely affected. There are two camshaft sprocket locating holes provided to correct the valve timing. Actually there are three sets of holes and timing marks on the camshaft sprocket; the third hole and timing mark are for 6 cylinder Datsun engines and in the case of the Datsun pick-ups, these are obviously ignored.

If the stretch of the chain roller links is excessive, adjust the camshaft sprocket location by transferring the camshaft set position of the camshaft sprocket from the factory position of the No. 1 to the No. 2 as follows:

1. Turn the crankshaft until the No. 1 piston is at TDC on its compression stroke. Examine whether the camshaft sprocket location notch is to the left of the oblong groove on the camshaft retaining plate. If the notch in the sprocket is to the left of the groove in the retaining plate, then the chain is stretched and needs adjusting.

2. Remove the camshaft sprocket and timing chain and then reinstall the sprocket and chain with the locating dowel on the camshaft inserted into the No. 2 hole of the sprocket and the timing mark on the timing chain aligned with the No. 2 marks on the sprocket. The amount of modification is 4° of crankshaft rotation.

3. Recheck the valve timing as outlined in Step 1. The notch in the sprocket should be to the right of the groove in the camshaft retaining plate.

4. If and when the notch cannot be brought to the right of the groove with the sprocket installed in the No. 2 hole, the timing chain must be replaced to gain the proper valve timing.

Timing Belt

REMOVAL AND INSTALLATION

VG30i Engines

1. Remove the upper and lower timing belt covers.
2. Turn the crankshaft so that the No. 1 cylinder is at the TDC of the compression stroke.
3. Using chalk or paint, mark the relationship of the timing belt to the camshaft and the crankshaft sprockets; also, mark the timing belt's direction of rotation.
4. Loosen the timing belt tensioner and return spring, then remove the timing belt.

CAUTION: *Before installing the timing belt, confirm that the No. 1 cylinder is set at the TDC of the compression stroke.*

5. Remove both cylinder head covers and loosen all rocker arm shaft retaining bolts.

NOTE: *The rocker arm shaft bolts MUST be loosened so that the correct belt tension can be obtained.*

6. Install the tensioner and the return spring. Using a hexagon wrench, turn the tensioner clockwise and temporarily tighten the lock nut.

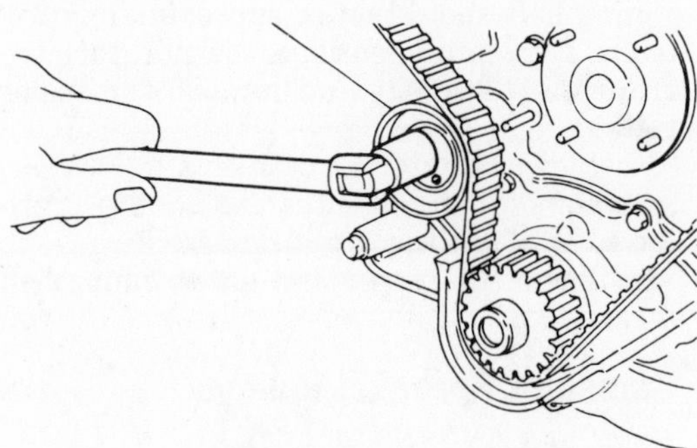

Loosening the timing belt tensioner—VG30i engines

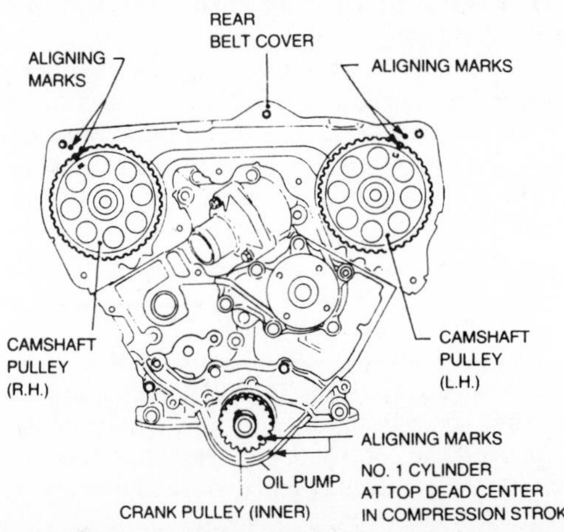

Camshaft and crankshaft sprocket alignment—VG30i engines

7. Make sure that the timing belt is clean and free from oil or water.
8. When installing the timing belt align the white lines on the belt with the punchmarks on the camshaft and crankshaft sprockets. Have the arrow on the timing belt pointing toward the front belt covers.

NOTE: *A good way (although rather tedious!) to check for proper timing belt instal-*

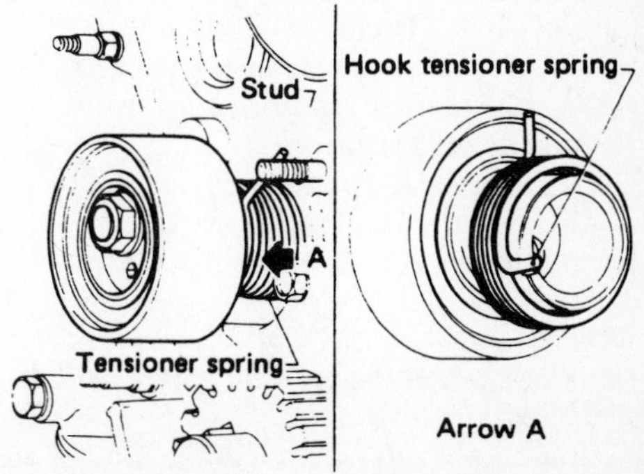

Timing belt tensioner and return spring installation—VG30i engines

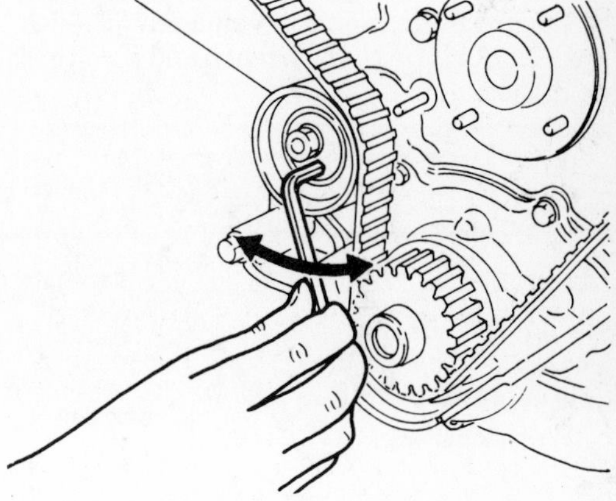

Tighten the tensioner locknut—VG30i engines

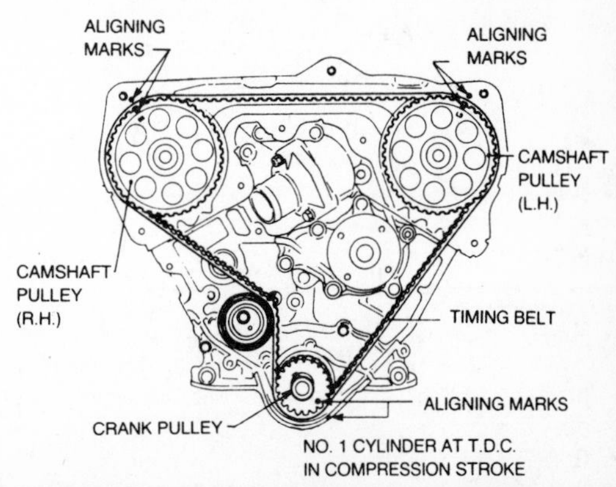

Timign belt-to-sprocket alignment—VG30i engines

lation is to count the number of belt teeth between the timing marks. There are 133 teeth on the belt; there should be 40 teeth between the timing marks on the left and right side camshaft sprockets, and 43 teeth between the timing marks on the left side camshaft sprocket and the crankshaft sprocket.

1986-87 Engines:

9. Using a hexagon wrench, loosen the tensioner lock bolt, set the tensioner and then slowly turn the tensioner clockwise and counterclockwise 2–3 times.

NOTE: *If the coarse tensioner stud has been removed, be sure to apply locking sealer to the threads before installing it.*

10. Tighten the tensioner lock nut to 32–43 ft. lbs. (43–58 Nm). Tighten the rocker arm shaft retaining bolts (in 2–3 stages) to 13–16 ft. lbs. (18–22 Nm).

NOTE: *Before tightening, be sure to set the camshaft lobe at the position where the lobe is not lifted.*

11. Install the upper and lower timing belt covers.

1988-89 Engines:

12. While keeping the tensioner steady, loosen the locknut with a hexagon wrench.

13. Turn the tension approximately 70–80 degrees clockwise with the wrench and then tighten the locknut.

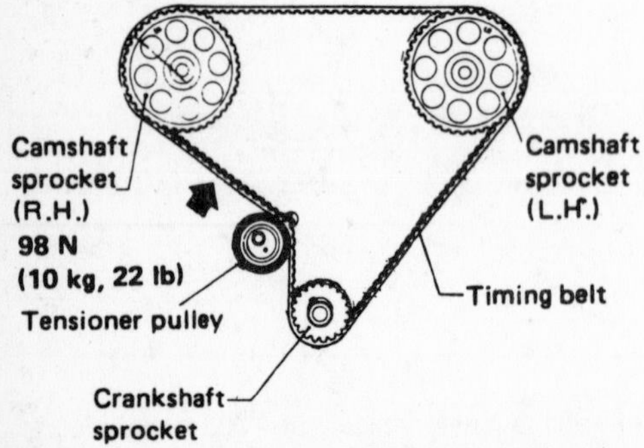

Check the timing belt tension—1988–89 VG30i engines

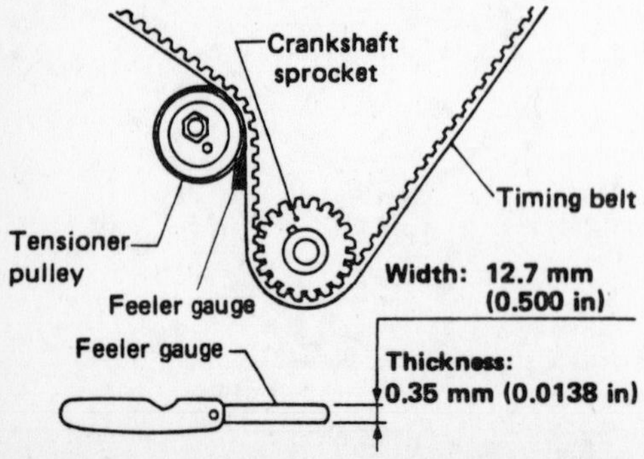

Feeler gauge positioning—1988–89 VG30i engines

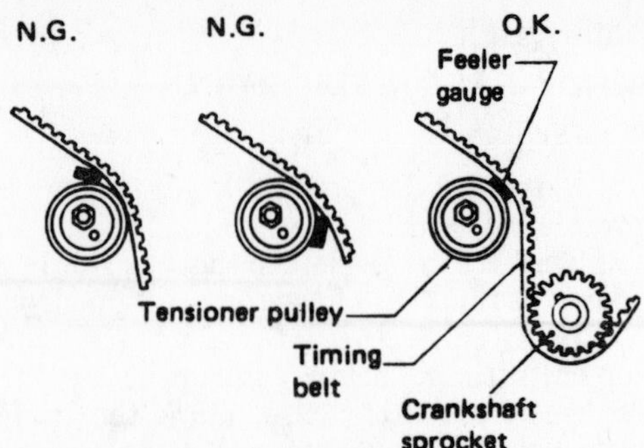

Turn the crankshaft until the feeler gauge is in this position—1988–89 VG30i engines

14. Turn the crankshaft in a clockwise direction several times and then *slowly* set the No. 1 piston to TDC of the compression stroke.

15. Apply 22 lbs. of pressure (push it in!) to the center span of the timing belt between the right side camshaft sprocket and the tensioner pulley and then loosen the tensioner locknut.

16. Using a 0.0138 in. (0.35mm) feeler gauge (the actual width of the blade *must* be ½ in. thick!) positioned as shown in the illustration, turn the crankshaft clockwise (*slowly!*). The timing belt should move approximately 2½ teeth. Tighten the tensioner locknut, turn the crankshaft slightly and remove the feeler gauge.

17. Slowly rotate the crankshaft clockwise several more times and then set the No. 1 piston to TDC of the compression stroke.

18. Install the upper and lower timing belt covers.

Camshaft Sprocket/Pulleys

REMOVAL AND INSTALLATION

All 4 Cylinder Gasoline Engines

1. Remove the timing chain with the camshaft sprocket.

NOTE: *The engines are designed so that the camshaft sprocket MUST be removed at the same time that the timing chain is removed.*

2. To install, use new gaskets and reverse the removal procedures. If necessary, adjust the timing chain.

VG30i Engines

1. Remove the timing belt.

2. Using an adjustable spanner wrench (to hold the camshaft pulley) and a socket wrench, remove the camshaft pulley bolt and washer.

3. Pull the camshaft pulley(s) from the camshaft(s). Be careful not to loose the woodruff key.

NOTE: *The right and left camshaft pulleys are different parts. Install them in their cor-*

rect positions. The right pulley has an R3 identification mark and the left pulley has an L3.

4. To install the camshaft pulleys, perform the following:
   a. Remove the cylinder head covers.
   b. Loosen the rocker arm shaft assembly bolts.
   c. Remove the spark plugs.
   d. Install the camshaft pulleys.
5. Install and adjust the timing belt.
6. Install the timing belt covers.

Camshaft

REMOVAL AND INSTALLATION

L16, L18 and L20B Engines

NOTE: *Removal of the cylinder head from the engine is optional. Mark and keep all parts in order for correct installation.*

1. Remove the camshaft sprocket from the camshaft together with the timing chain. Refer to the Timing Chain procedures if necessary.
2. Loosen the valve rocker pivot locknut and remove the rocker arm by pressing down on the valve spring.
3. Remove the two retaining nuts on the camshaft retainer plate at the front of the cylinder head and carefully slide the camshaft out (towards the front of the vehicle) of the camshaft carrier.
4. Check camshaft runout, endplay, wear and journal clearance as described in this chapter.
5. Lightly coat the camshaft bearings with clean motor oil and carefully slide the camshaft into place in the camshaft carrier.
6. Install the camshaft retainer plate with the oblong groove in the face of the plate facing toward the front of the engine.
7. Check the valve timing as outlined under Timing Chain Removal and Installation and install the timing sprocket on the camshaft, tightening the bolt together with the fuel pump cam (gasoline engines only) to 86–116 ft. lbs.
8. Install the rocker arms by pressing down the valve springs with a screwdriver and install the valve rocker springs.
9. Install the cylinder head, if it was removed, and assemble the rest of the engine.
10. Start the engine and run it until it reaches

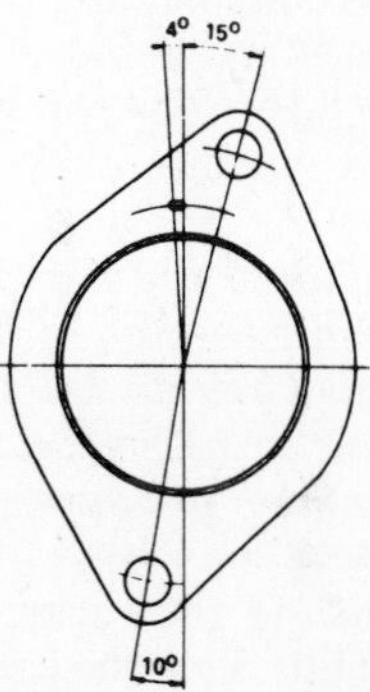

Camshaft locating plate—L16, L18 and L20B engines

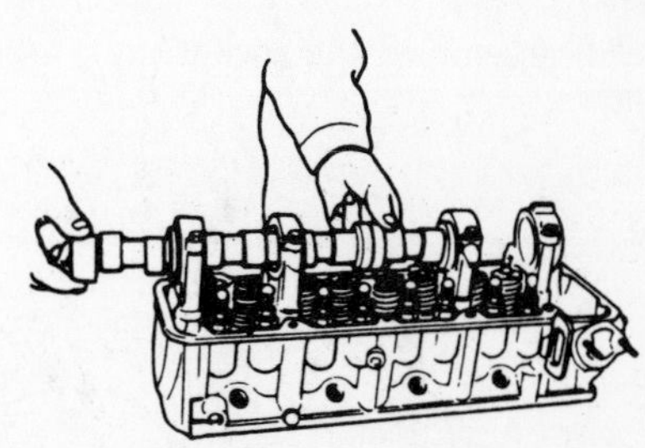

Removing the camshaft—all 4 cylinder gasoline engines

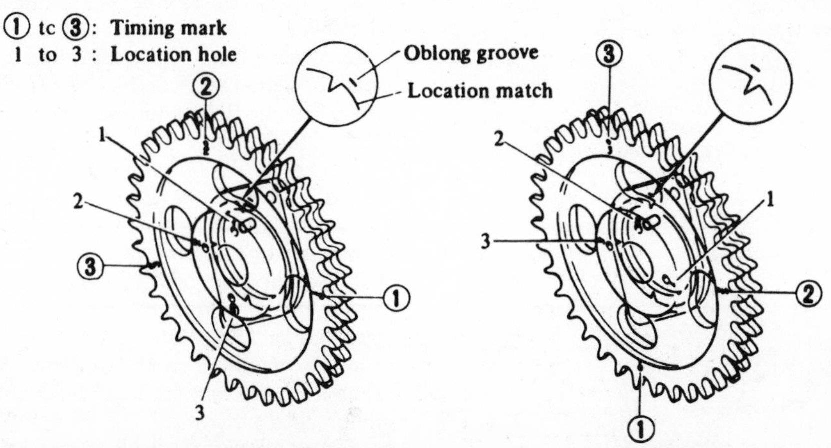

Adjusting the camshaft sprocket location—L16, L18 and L20B engines

normal operating temperature. Remove cylinder head cover, check and adjust valves if necessary. Install the cylinder head cover with a new gasket and check for oil leaks.

Z20, Z22, Z24 and Z24i Engines

NOTE: *Removal of the cylinder head from the engine is optional. Mark and keep all parts in order for correct installation.*

1. Set the No. 1 piston at TDC on its compression stroke and then remove the camshaft sprocket from the camshaft together with the timing chain.
2. Loosen the bolts holding the rocker shaft assembly in place and remove the six center bolts. Do not pull the four end bolts out of the rocker assembly because they hold the unit together.

NOTE: *When loosening the bolts, work from the ends in and loosen all of the bolts a little at a time so that you do not strain the camshaft or the rocker assembly. Remember, the camshaft is under pressure from the valve springs!*

3. After removing the rocker assembly, remove the camshaft. Slide the camshaft carefully out of the front of the vehicle.

NOTE: *Mark and keep the disassembled parts in order.*

If you disassembled the rocker unit, assemble as follows:

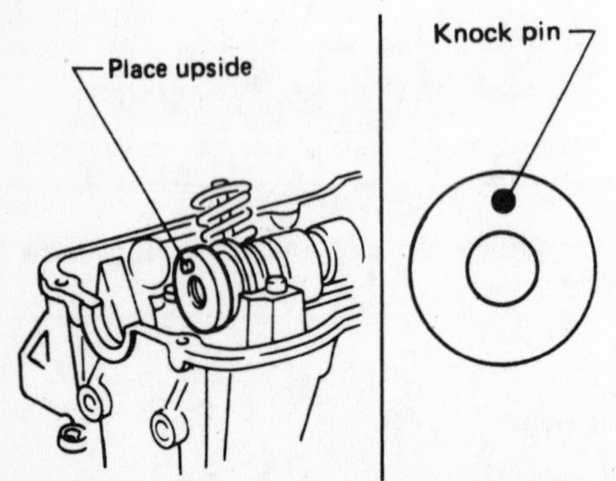

Make sure that the camshaft is installed with the knockpin UP—Z20, Z22, Z24 and Z24i engines

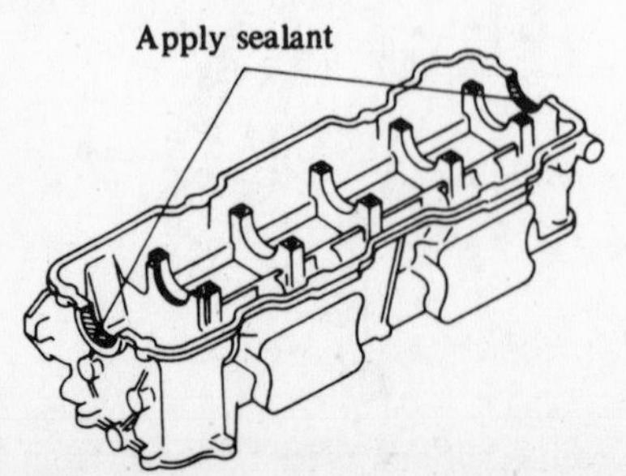

Apply sealer here—Z20, Z22, Z24 and Z24i engines

4. Install the mounting brackets, valve rockers and springs observing the following considerations:
   a. The two rocker shafts are different. Both have punch marks in the ends that face the front of the engine. The rocker shaft that goes on the side of the intake manifold has two slits in its end just below the punch mark. The exhaust side rocker shaft does not have slits.
   b. The rocker arms for the intake and exhaust valves are interchangeable between cylinders one and three and are identified by the mark **1**. Similarly, the rockers for cylinders two and four are interchangeable and are identified by the mark **2**.
   c. The rocker shaft mounting brackets are also coded for correct placement with either an **A** or a **Z** plus a number code.
5. Check camshaft runout, endplay wear and journal clearance as described in this chapter.
6. Apply sealant to the end camshaft saddles as shown in the accompanying illustration. Place the camshaft on the head with its knockpin pointing up.
7. Fit the rocker assembly on the head, making sure you mount it on its knock pin.
8. Tighten the bolts to 11–18 ft. lbs. (15–25 Nm), in several stages working from the middle bolts and moving outwards on both sides.

NOTE: *Make sure that the engine is at TDC of the compression stroke for the No. 1 piston or you may damage some valves.*

9. Adjust the valves.

VG30i Engines

NOTE: *Nissan recommends that the cylinder heads be removed from the engine, with the engine mounted in the vehicle, before removing the camshafts.*

1. Remove the timing belt. Remove the cylinder head.
2. With cylinder head mounted on a suitable workbench, remove the rocker shafts with rocker arms. Bolts should be loosened in two or three stages.

NOTE: *Hold the valve lifters with wire so that they will not drop from the lifter guide. Put an identification mark on the lifters to avoid mixing them up.*

3. At the rear of the cylinder head, remove the cylinder head rear cover, the camshaft bolt and the locating plate.
4. Remove the camshaft front oil seal and then slide the camshaft out the front of the cylinder head assembly.
5. Install camshaft, locater plate, cylinder head rear cover and front oil seal. Set the camshaft knock pin at the 12:00 o'clock position

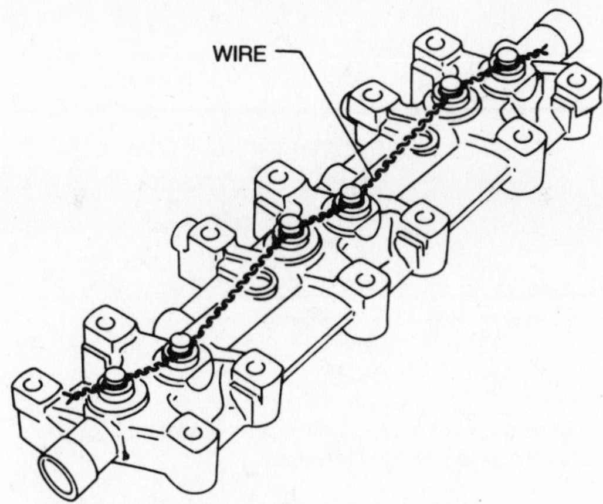

Hold the valve lifters with wire—V6 engine

Hold the rocker arms with wire when removing them—VG30i engines

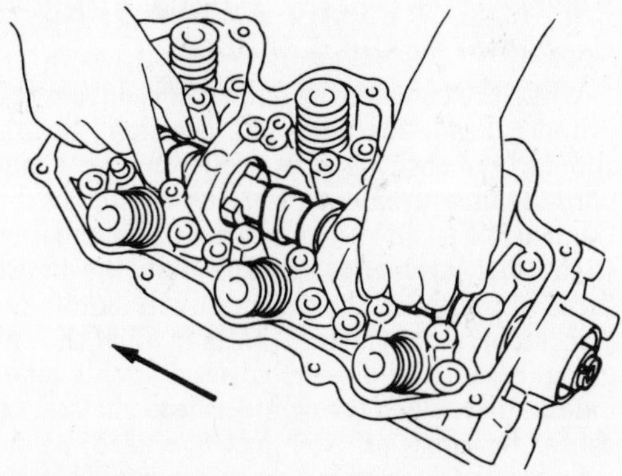

Remove the camshaft in the direction of the arrow—VG30i engines

(straight up). Install cylinder head with new gasket to engine.

6. Install valve lifter guide assembly, being sure to assemble the valve lifters in their original positions. After installing them in the correct location, remove the wire holding them in lifter guide.

7. Install the rocker shafts in position with their rocker arms. Tighten the bolts in two or three stages to 13–16 ft. lbs (18–22 Nm). Before tightening, be sure to set the camshaft lobe in a position where the lobe is not lifted or the valve closed. You can set each cylinder one at a time or follow the procedure below (the timing belt must be installed in the correct position):

a. Set the No. 1 piston at TDC of its compression stroke and tighten the rocker shaft bolts for the No. 2, No. 4 and No. 6 cylinders.

b. Set the No. 4 piston at TDC of its compression stroke and tighten the rocker shaft bolts for the No. 1, No. 3 and No. 5 cylinders.

c. Tighten the rocker shaft retaining bolts to 13–16 ft. lbs. (18–22 Nm).

8. Install the rear timing belt cover and camshaft sprocket. The left and right camshaft sprockets are different parts. Install the correct sprocket in the correct position.

NOTE: *The right and left camshaft sprockets are different parts. Install them in their correct positions. The right sprocket has an R3 identification mark and the left has an L3.*

9. Install the timing belt.

SD22 and SD25 Engines

1. Remove the cylinder head.
2. Remove the valve lifters and mark them for reasssembly.
3. Remove the front case and timing gear cover.
4. Remove the tachometer drive support nuts.
5. Remove the timer round nut.
6. Thread the timer extractor, ST #57926-581, into the timer weight holder. Remove the timer assembly by tightening the extractor bolt.
7. Remove the oil pump drive spindle.
8. Remove the camshaft locating plate bolts and carefully slide the camshaft from the engine.
9. Coat the camshaft with clean engine oil and carefully slide it into the block. Install the locating plate.
10. Install the oil pump drive spindle by aligning the oil pump driveshaft groove and the camshaft oil pump drive gear with the spindle.

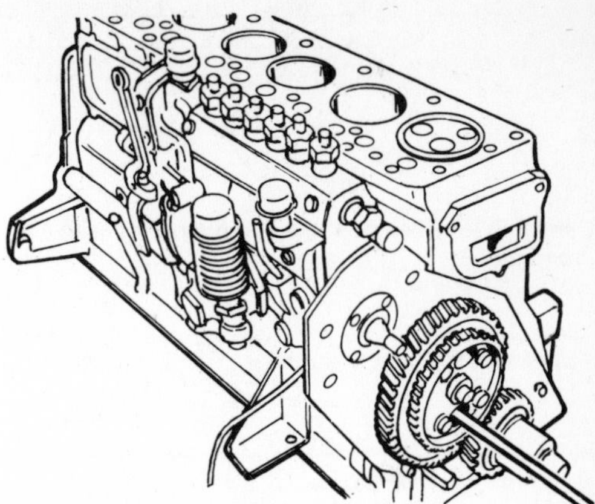

Removing the camshaft locating bolts—SD22 and SD25 engines

CHECKING CAMSHAFT RUNOUT

Camshaft runout should be checked when the camshaft has been removed from the engine. An accurate dial indicator is needed for

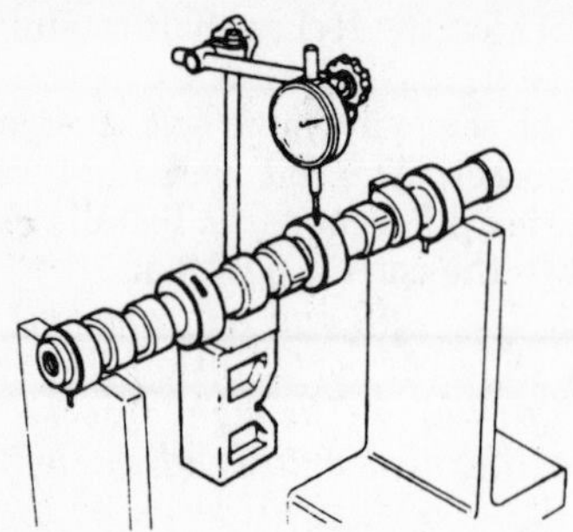

Camshaft run-out must be measured with a dial indicator

this procedure; engine specialists and most machine shops have this equipment. If you have access to a dial indicator, or can take your camshaft to someone who does, measure the camshaft bearing journal runout. The maximum (limit) runout on the L16, L18, L20D, Z20, Z22, Z24 and Z24i camshafts is 0.0008 in. (0.2mm). The runout limit on the SD22 and SD25 camshafts is 0.0024 in. (0.06mm). The maximum (limit) runout on the VG30i camshaft is 0.0039 in. (0.1mm) If the runout exceeds the limit replace the camshaft.

CHECKING CAMSHAFT LOBE HEIGHT

Use a micrometer to check camshaft (lobe) height, making sure the anvil and the spindle of the micrometer are positioned directly on the heel and tip of the camshaft lobe as shown in the accompanying illustration.

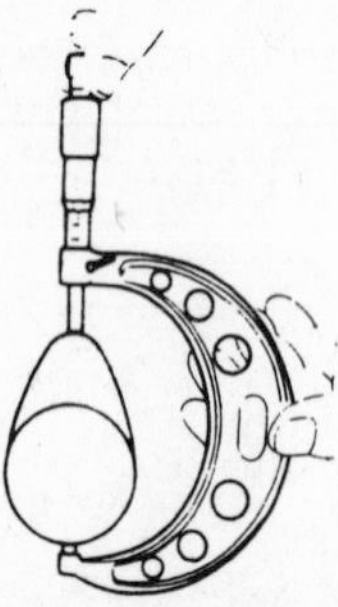

Camshaft lobe height should be measured with a micrometer

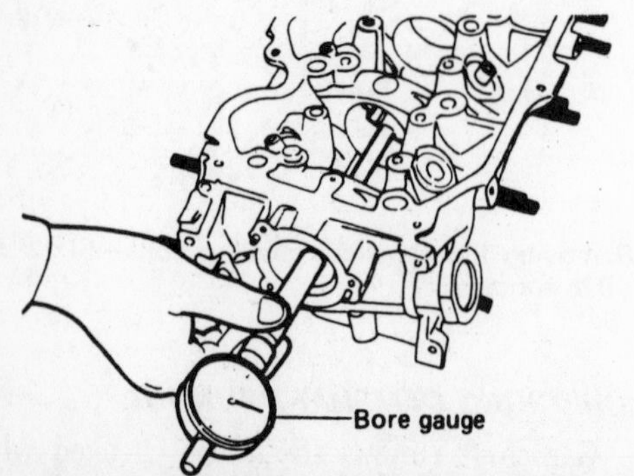

Measuring the inside diameter of the camshaft saddles to determine journal clearance

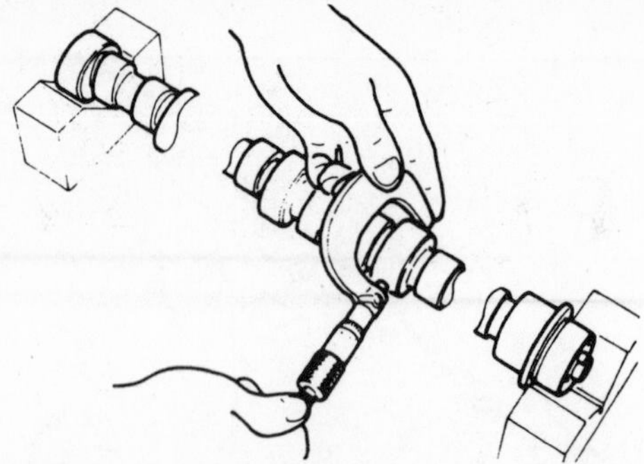

Measuring outside diameter of the camshaft journals to determine journal clearance

CHECKING CAMSHAFT JOURNALS AND CAMSHAFT BEARING SADDLES

While the camshaft is still removed from the cylinder head, the camshaft bearing journals should be measured with a micrometer. Compare the measurements with those listed in the Camshaft Specifications chart in this chapter. If the measurements are less than the limits listed in the chart, the camshaft will require replacement, since the camshafts in all of the engines (except the diesels) covered in this manual run directly on the cylinder head surface; no actual bearings or bushings are used, so no oversize bearings or bushings are available.

Using an inside dial gauge or inside micrometer, measure the inside diameter of the camshaft saddles (the camshaft mounts that are either integrally cast as part of the cylinder head, or are a bolted on, one piece unit. The Z-series engines use a saddle-and-cap arrangement. The inside diameter of the saddles on all engines is 1.8898–1.8904 in. On the VG30i engine, contact a Nissan dealer or local machine shop for that specification. The camshaft journal oil clearances are listed in the Camshaft Specifications chart in this chapter. If the saddle inside diameters exceed those listed above, the cylinder head must be replaced (again, because oversize bearings or bushings are not available).

On the SD22 and SD25, the camshaft runs in bushings. Measure the inside diameter of the camshaft bushing with a dial gauge and the outside diameter of the camshaft journal with a micrometer. The diference between the two measurements should be:

- Front – 0.0009–0.0040 in. (0.024–0.102mm)
- Center – 0.0015–0.0045 in. (0.037–0.115mm)

• Rear—0.0009–0.0040 in. (0.024–0.102mm)

• The limit on all should be a maximum of 0.0059 in. (0.15mm)

Bushing Replacement

SD22 AND SD25 ENGINES

NOTE: *This procedure will require the use of Nissan special tools #ST16650010, ST16650020, ST16650030 and ST16650040.*

1. Remove the rear camshaft plug.
2. Working from the front side of the engine, press out the camshaft bushings.
3. Install new bushings with the tool so that the beveled ends face forward (front of the engine). Be sure that the oil passage hole in the cylinder block and the oil hole in the bushing are in alignment.
4. Check the bushing oil clearance.
5. Coat a *new* rear plug with liquid sealant and install it with a brass drift.

CHECKING CAMSHAFT ENDPLAY

After the camshaft has been installed, endplay should be checked. The camshaft sprocket should *not* be installed on the cam. Use a dial gauge to check the endplay, by moving the camshaft forward and backward in the cylinder head. Endplay specifications should be as noted in the Camshaft Specifications chart.

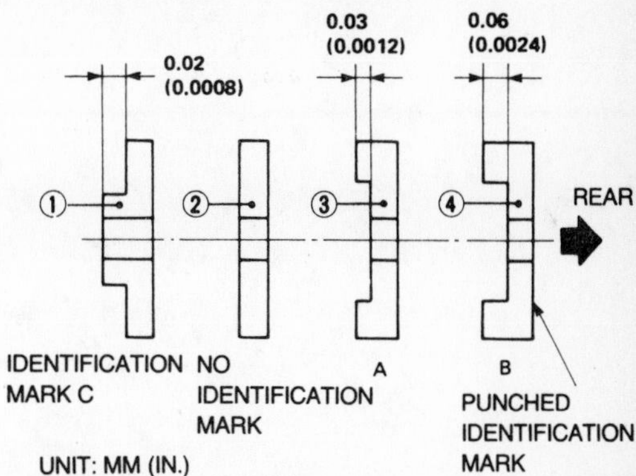

Adjust the camshaft endplay with shims—VG30i engines

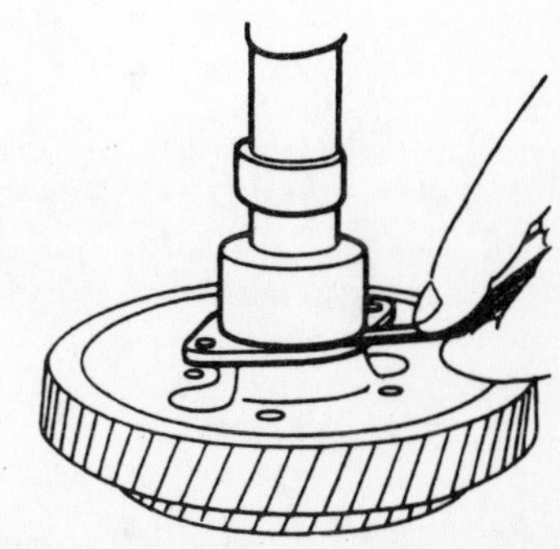

Measuring the camshaft endplay—SD22 and SD25 engines

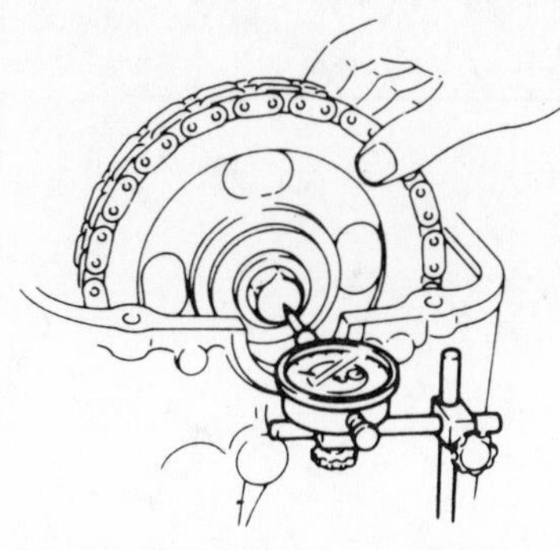

Measuring the camshaft endplay—all 4 cylinder gasoline engines

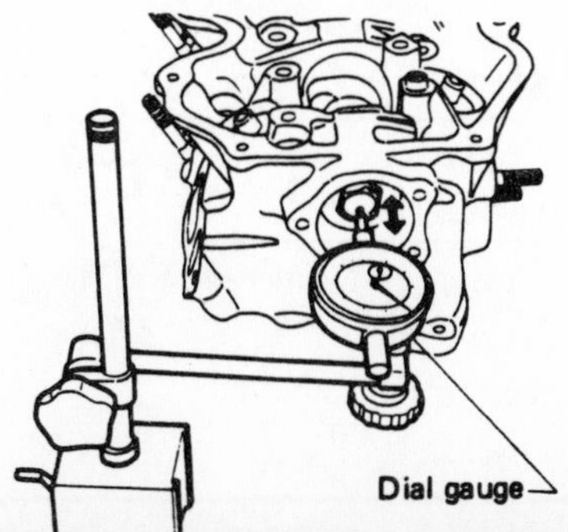

Measuring the camshaft endplay—VG30i engines

Pistons and Connecting Rods

REMOVAL AND INSTALLATION

All Engines

NOTE: *Before removing the piston assemblies, connecting rod bearing clearance and side clearance should be checked. Refer to the Connecting Rod Inspection procedure in this chapter.*

1. Remove the cylinder head as outlined in the appropriate preceding section.
2. Remove the oil pan and pump.
3. Position a cylinder ridge reamer into the top of the cylinder bore. Keeping the tool square, ream the ridges from the top of the bore. Clean out the ridge material with a solvent-soaked rag, or blow it out with compressed air.
4. Remove the oil strainer if it is in the way. Unbolt the connecting rod caps, after match marking each cap to its connecting rod.
5. Place pieces of rubber hose over the rod bolts, to protect the cylinder walls and crank journals from scratches. Push the connecting

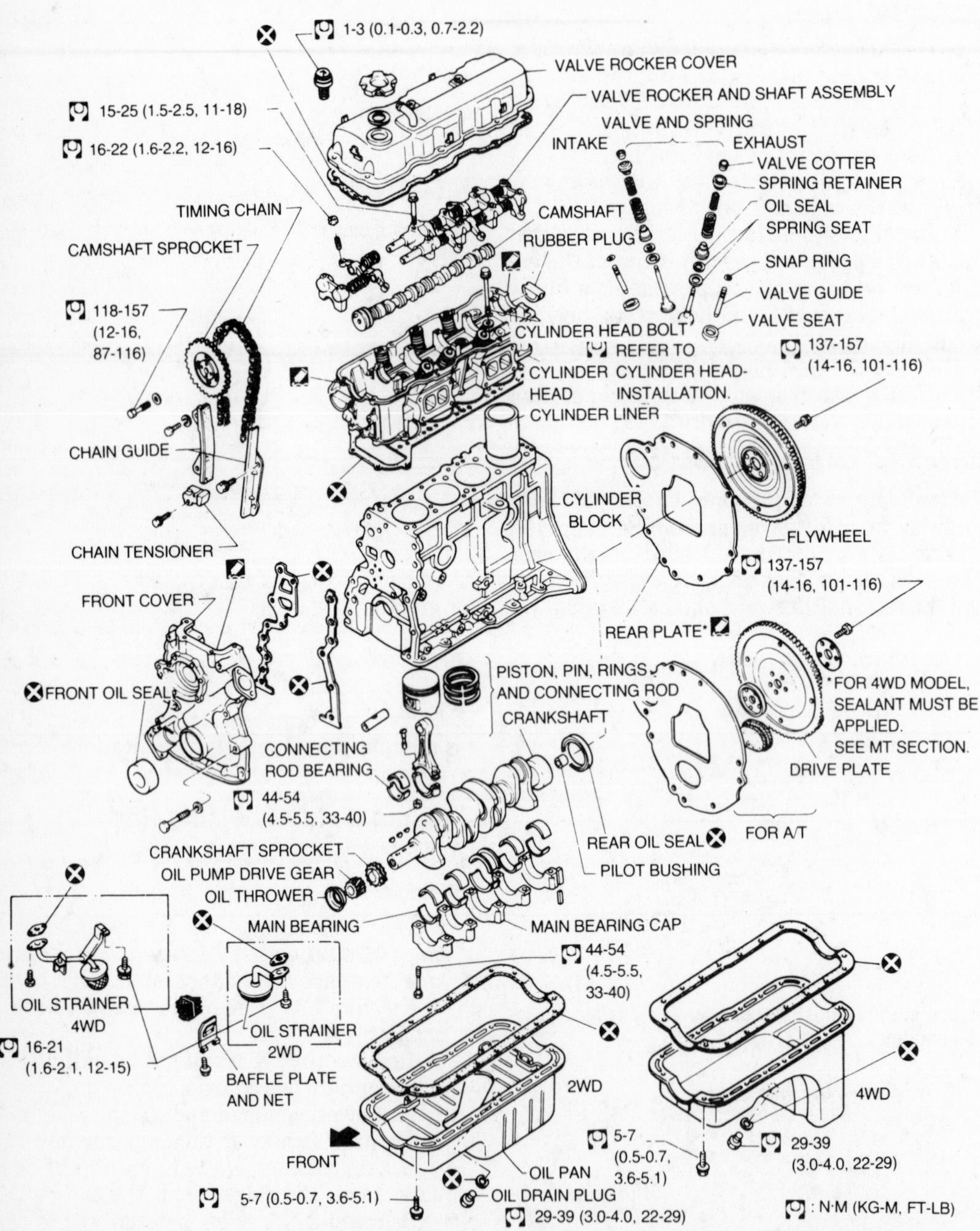

Exploded view of the cylinder block—Z20, Z22, Z24 and Z24i engines (L-series engines similar)

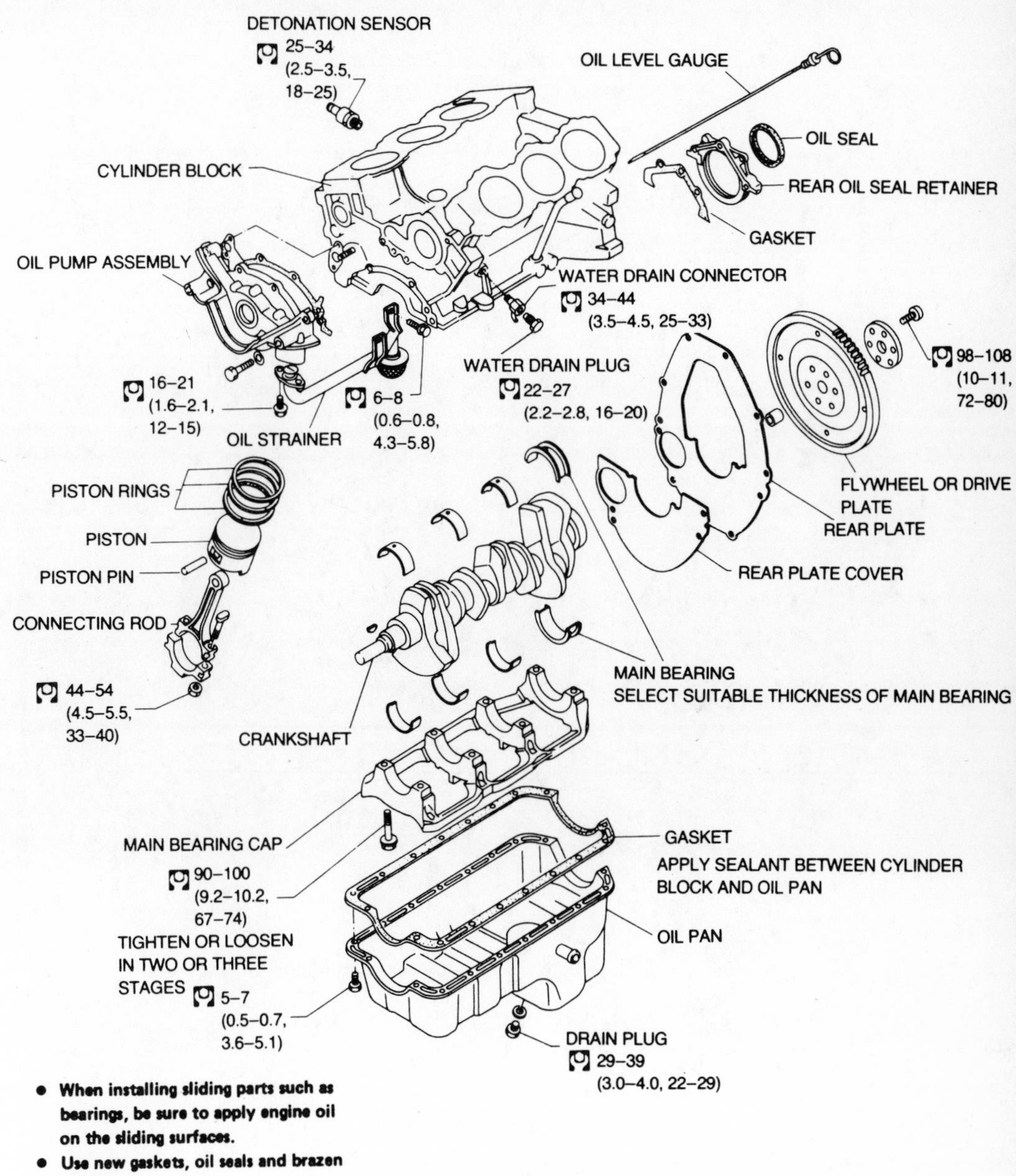

Exploded view of the cylinder block—VG30i engines

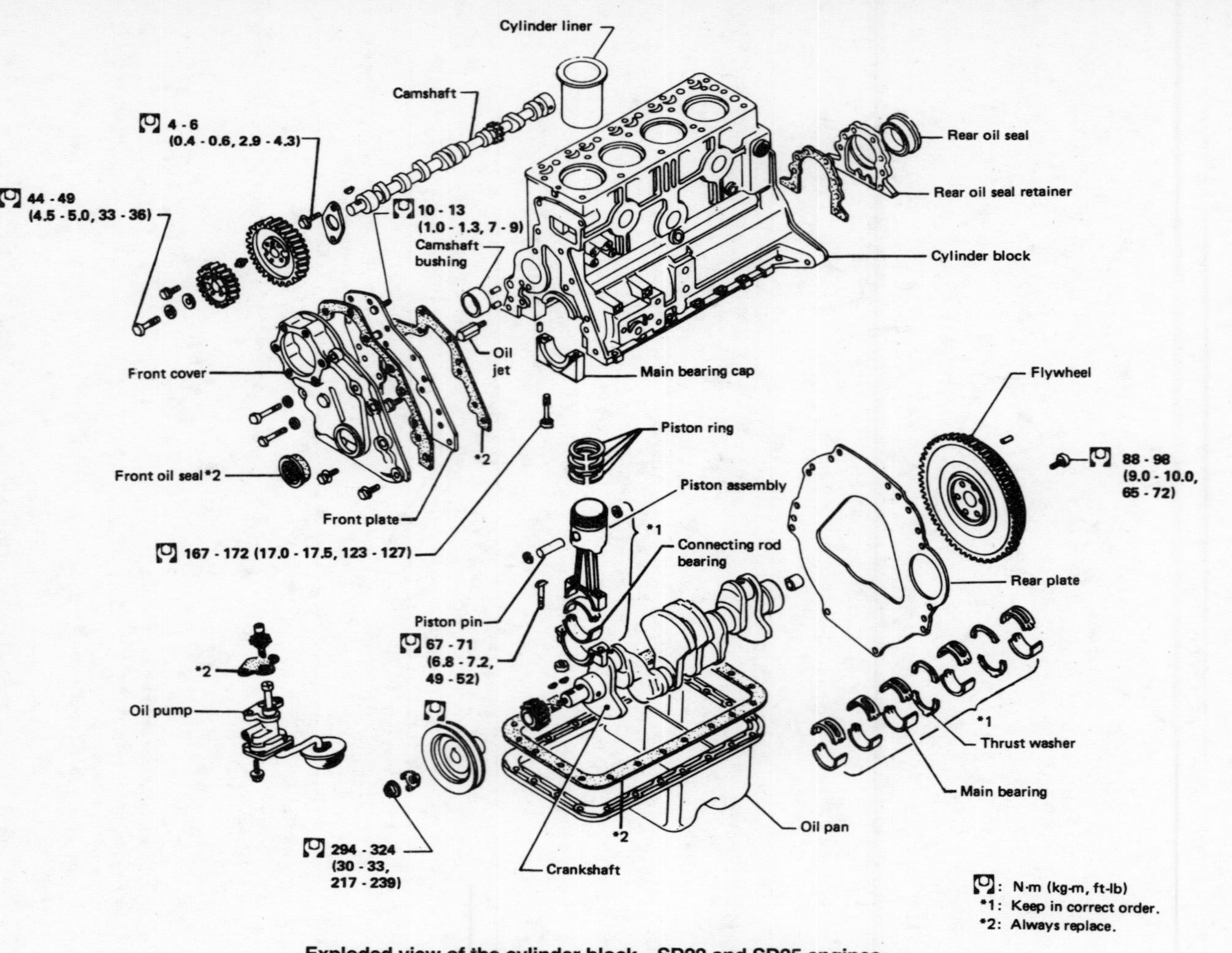

Exploded view of the cylinder block—SD22 and SD25 engines

rod and piston up and out of the cylinder from the bottom using a wooden hammer handle.

CAUTION: *Use care not to scratch the crank journals or the cylinder walls.*

6. Mark each connecting rod with the number of the cylinder from which it was removed. Number stamps are available at most hardware or auto supply stores.

Installation is performed in the following order:

1. Apply a light coating of engine oil to the pistons, rings, and outer ends of the wrist pins.
2. Examine the piston to ensure that it has been assembled with its parts positioned correctly. (See the illustrations.) Be sure that the ring gaps are not pointed toward the thrust face of the piston and that they do not overlap.
3. Place pieces of rubber hose over the connecting rod bolts, to keep the threads from damaging the crank journal and cylinder bore. Install the pistons, using a ring compressor, into the cylinder bore. Be sure that the appropriate marks on the piston are facing the front of the cylinder. (see Identification And Positioning)

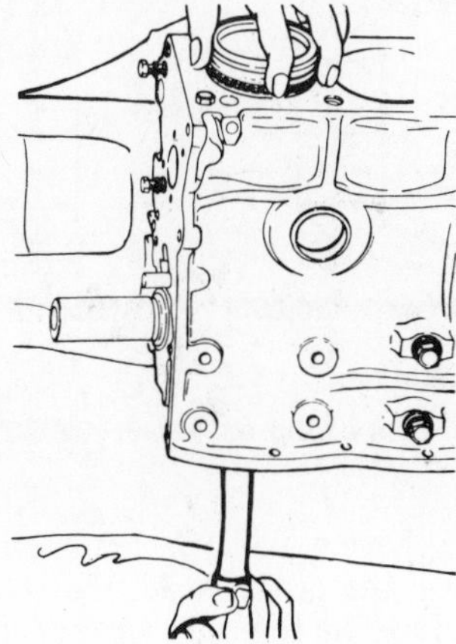

Removing the piston and connecting rod assembly from the cylinder block

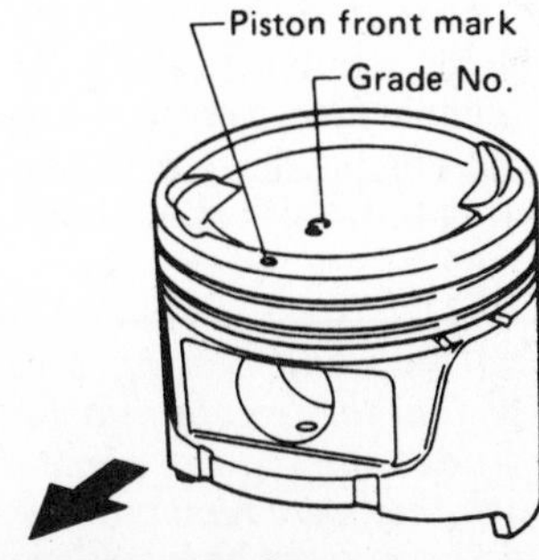

Installing the piston and connecting rod

NOTE: *It is important that the pistons, rods, bearing, etc., be returned to the same cylinder bore from which they were removed.*

4. Install the connecting rod bearing caps and tighten them to the torque figures given in the Torque Specifications chart.

NOTE: *Be sure that the mating marks on the connecting rods and rod bearing caps are aligned.*

5. Install the oil pump. Install the oil pan.
6. Install the cylinder head.

IDENTIFICATION AND POSITIONING

The pistons used in gasoline engines are marked with a notch in the piston head. When installed in the engine, the notch markings *must* be facing towards the front of the engine.

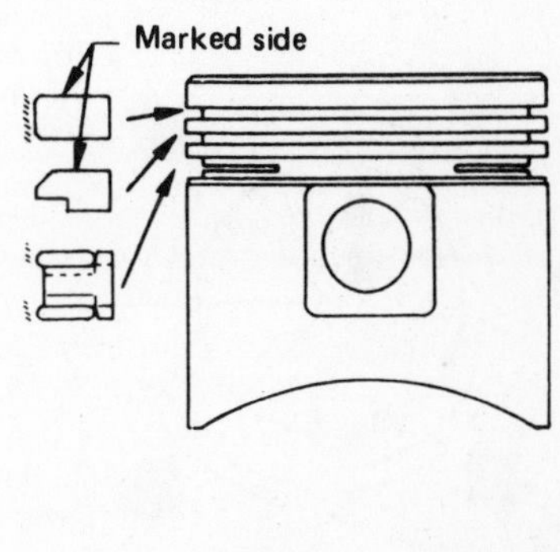

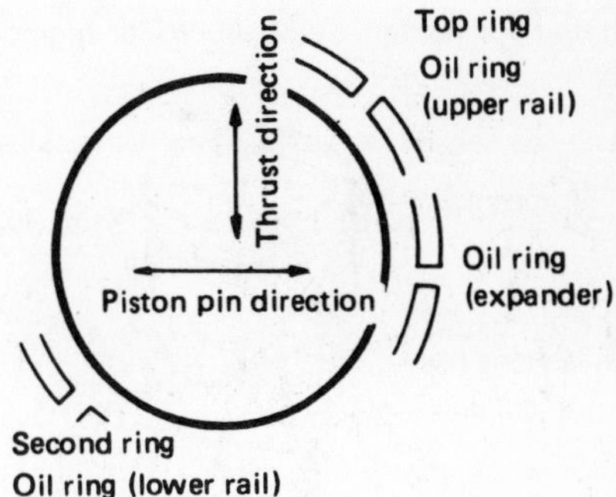

Piston ring positioning—L16, L18, L20B, Z20, Z22, Z24 and Z24i engines

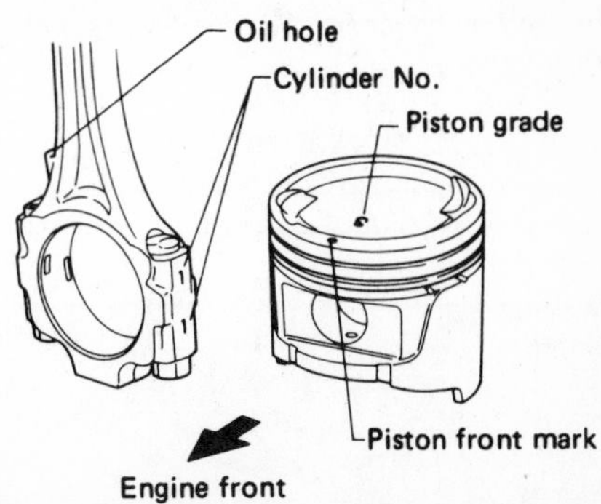

Piston and connecting rod positioning—all gasoline engines

Additionally, late model VG30i engines have a **W** mark on the piston skirt and this must face forward. The pistons used in diesel engines are less fortunate–they have no marking–in-

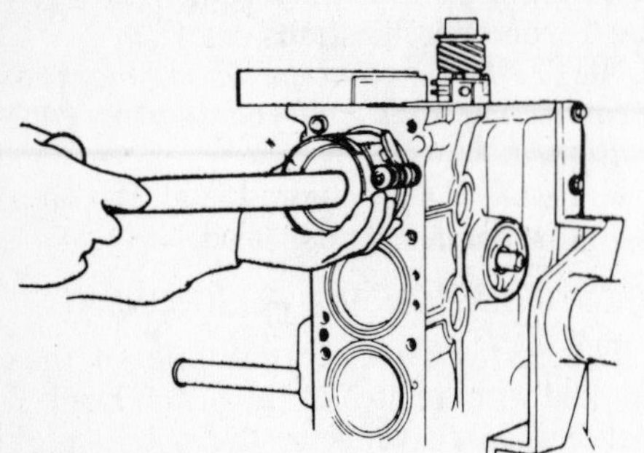

Piston ring positioning—1986–87 VG30i engines

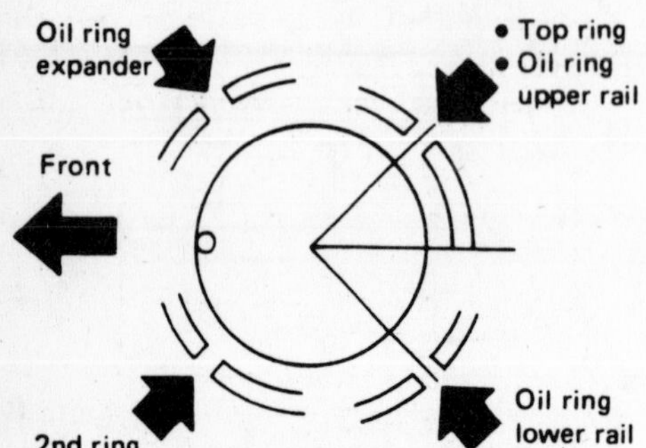

Piston ring positioning—1988–89 VG30i engine

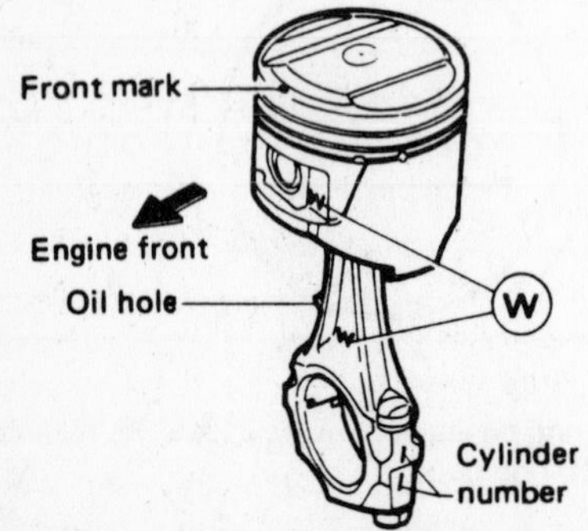

Piston and connecitng rod positioning—1988–89 VG30i engines

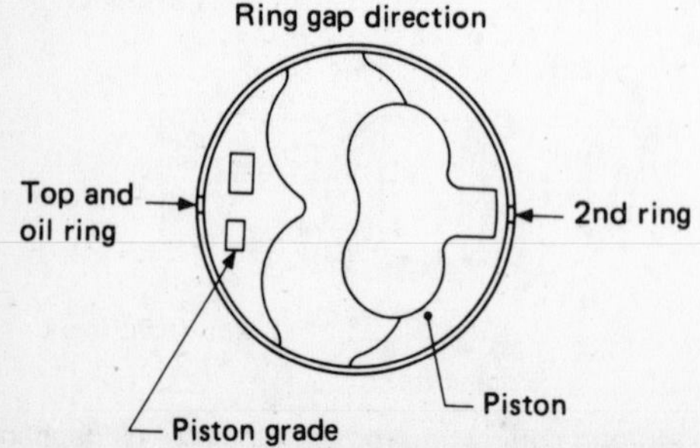

Piston ring positioning—SD22 and SD25 engines

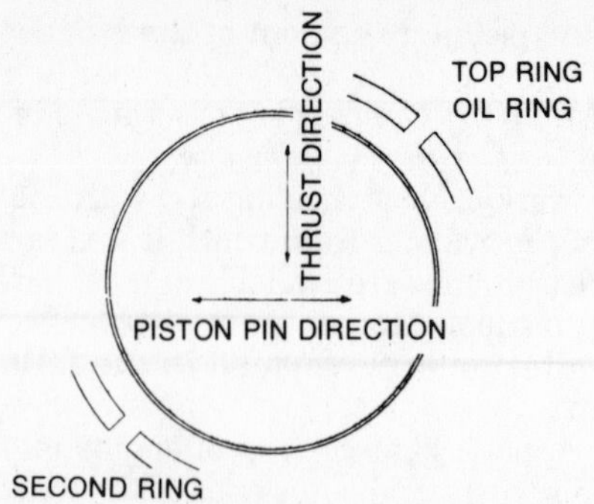

Piston and connecting rod positioning—SD22 and SD25 engines

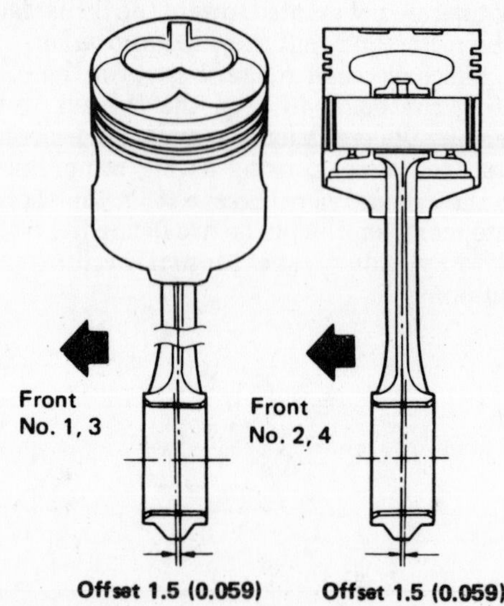

Piston and connecting rod offset—SD22 and SD25 engines

stead, they have a leaf-type combustion chamber cut into the piston head, the stem of this leaf must face the the right (passenger) side of the truck.

The connecting rods should be installed in the engine with oil hole facing the right side of the engine. *Most* connecting rods also have the cylinder number stamped into the side of the rod and cap, these numbers should face the left side of the engine. Also, as with the pistons, late model VG30i engines have a **W** stamped into the connecting rod which should face the front of the engine..

NOTE: *It is advisable to number the pistons, connecting rods and bearing caps in some manner so that they can be reinstalled in the same cylinder, facing the same direction, from which they were removed.*

The piston rings must be installed with their gaps in the same position as shown in the illustrations below.

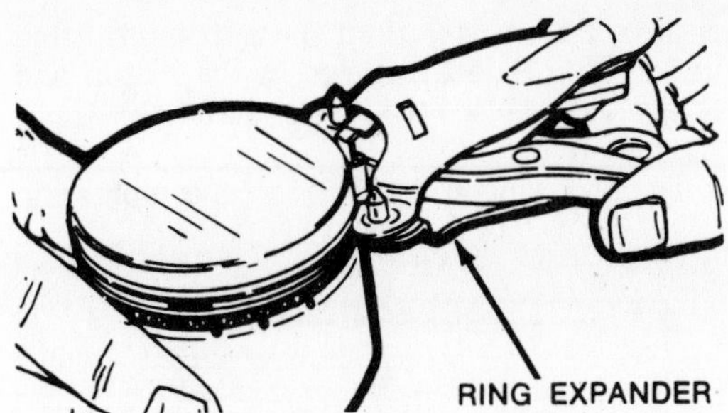

Removing the piston rings

When fully heated, the wrist pin should be able to be pushed into place by hand

PISTON RING REPLACEMENT

NOTE: *The cylinder walls must be de-glazed (honed) when the piston rings are replaced. De-glazing ensures proper ring seating and oil retention.*

Using a piston ring expander, remove the rings one by one. Always remove and replace the rings of each piston before going on to the next. This helps avoid mixing up the rings. When the rings have been removed from each piston, perform the end gap and piston inspection and cleaning procedure detailed below (Cleaning and Inspection). The rings are marked on one side, the mark denoting the up side for installation.

Install the rings using the ring expander, starting with the top compression ring and working down. Make sure the marks are facing up on each ring. Position the rings so that the ring and gaps are set as in the illustrations. Never align the end gaps!

WRIST PIN REMOVAL AND INSTALLATION

Wrist pin and/or connecting rod small-end bushing wear can be checked by rocking the piston at a right angle to the wrist pin by hand. If more than very *slight* movement is felt, the pin and/or rod busing must be replaced.

The pistons on the engines covered here must be heated in hot water to expand them before the wrist pins can be removed and installed. The four cylinder pistons must be heated to 176°F (80°C), and all six cylinder pistons must be heated to 140°F (60°C). This job can be performed at a machine shop if the idea of boiling pistons in the kitchen doesn't appeal to you. If you decide to do it, however, remember that each piston, pin and connecting rod assembly is a matched set and must be kept together until reassembly.

1. Using needlenose or snapring pliers, remove the snaprings from the piston (if so equipped).
2. Heat the piston(s) in hot water (as noted above depending on engine).
3. Using a plastic-faced hammer and driver, lightly tap the wrist pin out of the piston. Remove the piston from the connecting rod.
4. Assembly is in the opposite order of disassembly. The piston must again be heated to install the wrist pin and rod; it should be able to be pushed into place with your thumb when heated. When assembling, make sure the marks on the piston and connecting rod are aligned on the same side as shown.

CLEANING AND INSPECTION

Clean the piston after removing the rings, by first scraping any carbon from the piston top. Do not scratch the piston in any way during cleaning. Use a broken piston ring or ring cleaning tool to clean out the ring grooves. Clean the entire piston with solvent and a brush (NOT a wire brush).

Once the piston is thoroughly cleaned, insert

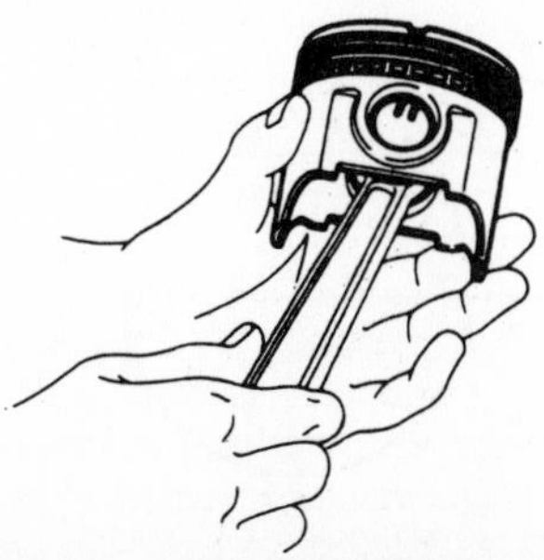
Rock the piston at a right angle to the wrist pin to check pin and small end bushing wear

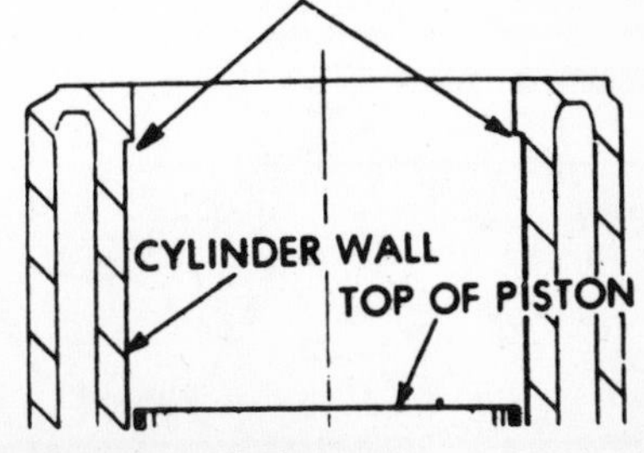

Ridge caused by cylinder wear

the side of a good piston ring (both No. 1 and No. 2 compression on each piston) into its respective groove. Using a feeler gauge, measure the clearance between the ring and its groove. If clearance is greater than the maximum listed under Ring Side Clearance in the Piston and Ring chart, replace the ring(s) and if necessary, the piston.

To check ring end-gap, insert a compression

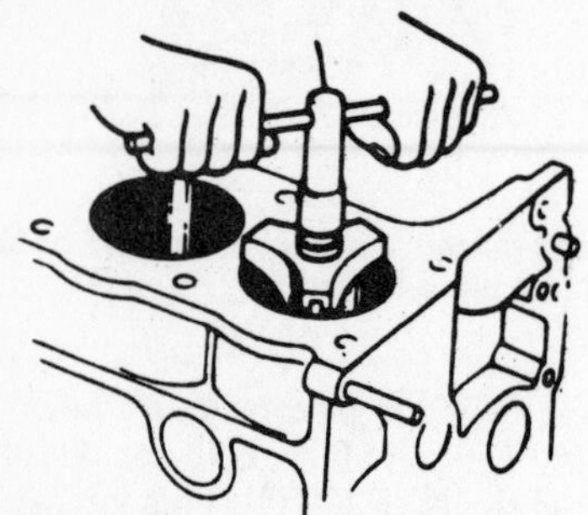

Removing the ridge with a ridge reamer

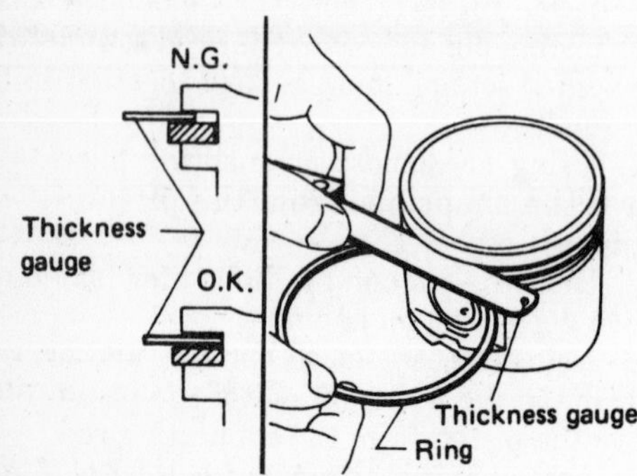

Check the piston ring side clearance

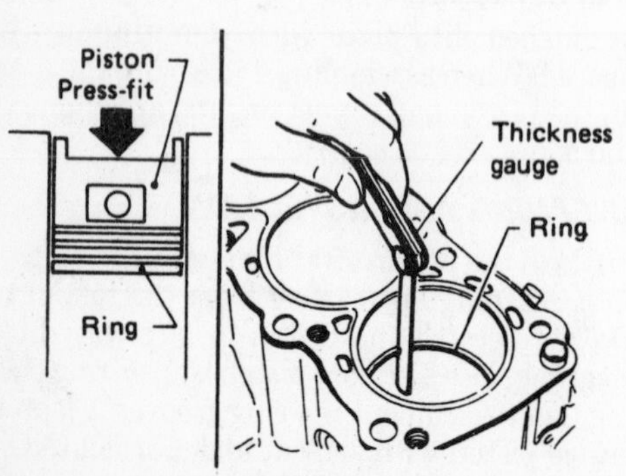

Check the piston ring end gap

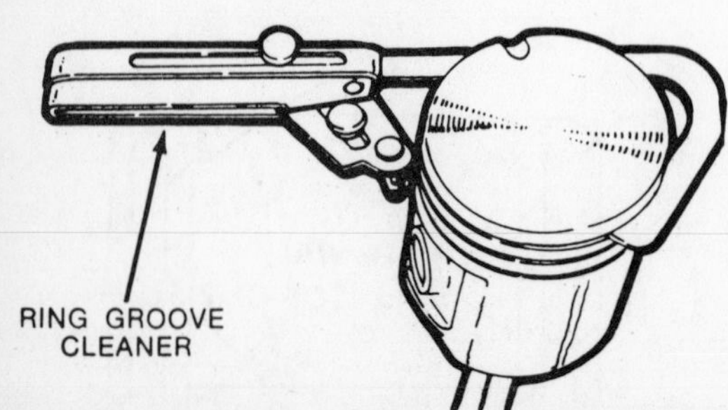

Clean the piston ring grooves

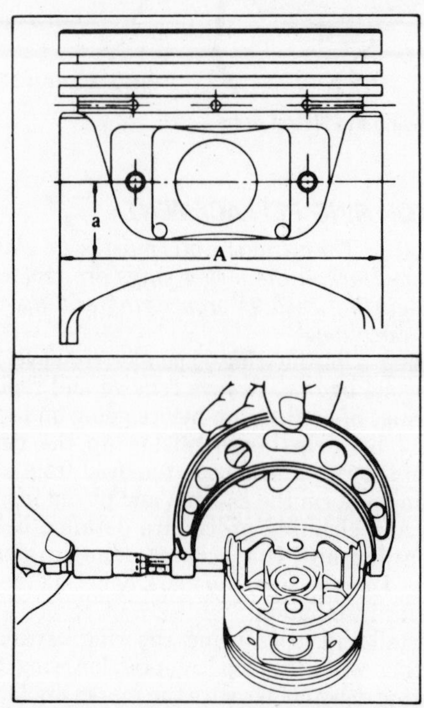

Measuring the piston. A is the skirt dimension

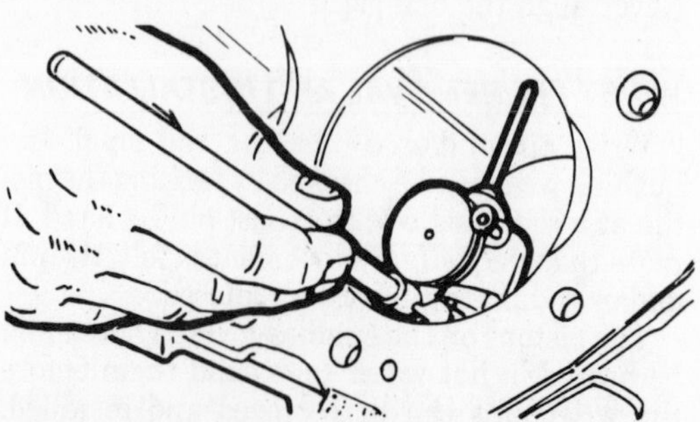

Measure the cylinder bore with a dial gauge

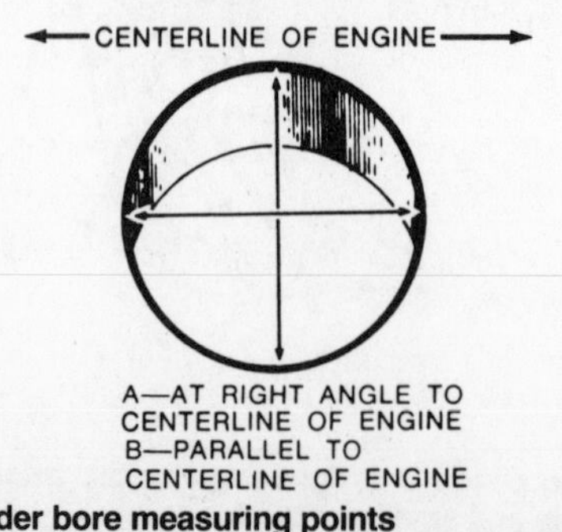

Cylinder bore measuring points

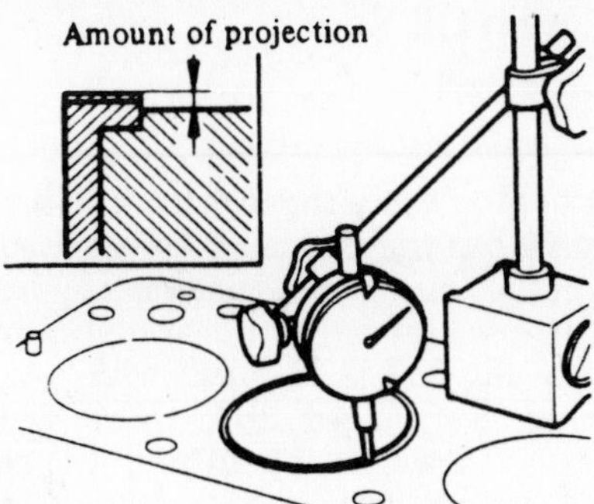

Measuring the cylinder liner projection on the diesel engine.

ring into the cylinder. Lightly oil the cylinder bore and push the ring down into the cylinder with a piston, to the bottom of its travel. Measure the ring end-gap with a feeler gauge. If the gap is not within specification, replace the ring; DO NOT file the ring ends.

CYLINDER BORE INSPECTION

Place a rag over the crankshaft journals. Wipe out each cylinder with a clean, solvent-soaked rag. Visually inspect the cylinder bores for roughness, scoring or scuffing; also check the bores by feel. Measure the cylinder bore diameter with an inside micrometer, or a telescope gauge and micrometer. Measure the bore at points parallel and perpendicular to the engine centerline at the top (below the ridge) and bottom of the bore. Subtract the bottom measurements from the top to determine cylinder taper.

Measure the piston diameter with a micrometer; since this micrometer may not be part of your tool kit as it is necessarily large, you have to have the pistons miked at a machine shop. Take the measurements at right angles to the wrist pin center line, about an inch down the piston skirt from the top. Compare this measurement to the bore diameter of each cylinder. The difference is the piston clearance. If the clearance is greater than that specified in the Piston and Ring Specifications chart, have the cylinders honed or rebored and replace the pistons with an oversize set. Piston clearance can also be checked by inverting a piston into an oiled cylinder, and sliding in a feeler gauge between the two.

CONNECTING ROD INSPECTION AND BEARING REPLACEMENT

Connecting rod side clearance and big-end bearing inspection and replacement should be performed while the rods are still installed in the engine. Determine the clearance between the connecting rod sides and the crankshaft using a feeler gauge. If clearance is below the minimum tolerance, check with a machinist about machining the rod to provide adequate clearance. If clearance is excessive, substitute an unworn rod and recheck; if clearance is still outside specifications, the crankshaft must be welded and reground, or replaced.

To check connecting rod big-end bearing clearances, remove the rod bearing caps one at a time. Using a clean, dry shop rag, thoroughly clean all oil from the crank journal and bearing insert in the cap.

NOTE: *The Plastigage® gaging material you will be using to check clearances with is soluble in oil; therefore any oil on the journal or bearing could result in an incorrect reading.*

Lay a strip of Plastigage® along the full length of the bearing insert (along the crank journal if the engine is out of the truck and inverted). Reinstall the cap and torque to specifications listed in the Torque Specifications chart.

Remove the rod cap and determine the bearing clearance by comparing the width of the now flattened Plastigage® to the scale on the Plastigage® envelope. Journal taper is determined by comparing the width of the Plastigage® strip near its ends. Rotate the crankshaft 90° and retest, to determine journal eccentricity.

NOTE: *Do not rotate the crankshaft with the Plastigage® installed.*

If the bearing insert and crank journal appear intact and are within tolerances, no further service is required and the bearing caps

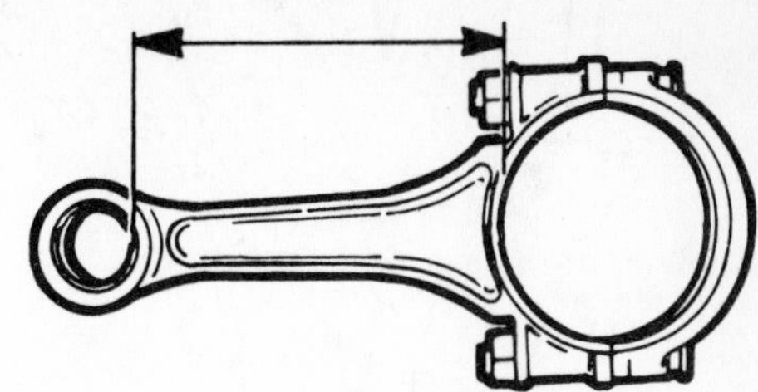

Check the connecting rod length (arrow)

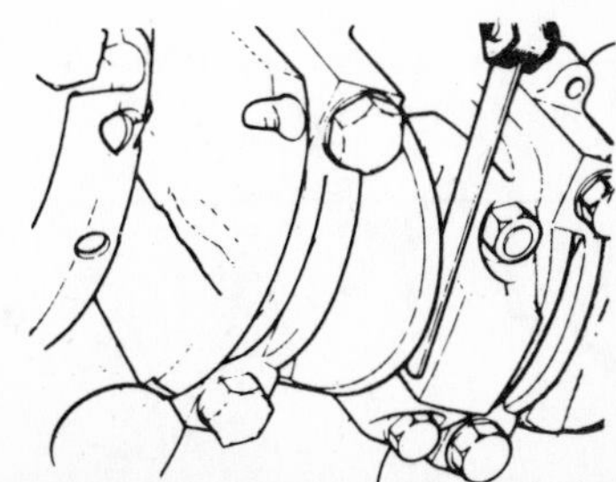

Check the connecting rod side clearance with a feeler gauge

can be reinstalled (remove Plastigage® before installation). If clearances are not within tolerances, the bearing inserts in both the connecting rod and rod cap must be replaced with undersize inserts, and/or the crankshaft must be reground. To install the bearing insert halves, press them into the bearing caps and connecting rods. Make sure the tab in each insert fits into the notch in each rod and cap. Lube the face of each insert with engine oil prior to installing each rod into the engine.

The connecting rods can be further inspected when they are removed from the engine and separated from their pistons. Rod alignment (straightness and squareness) must be checked by a machinist, as the rod must be set in a special fixture. Many machine shops also perform a Magnafluxing service, which is a process that shows up any tiny cracks that you may be unable to see.

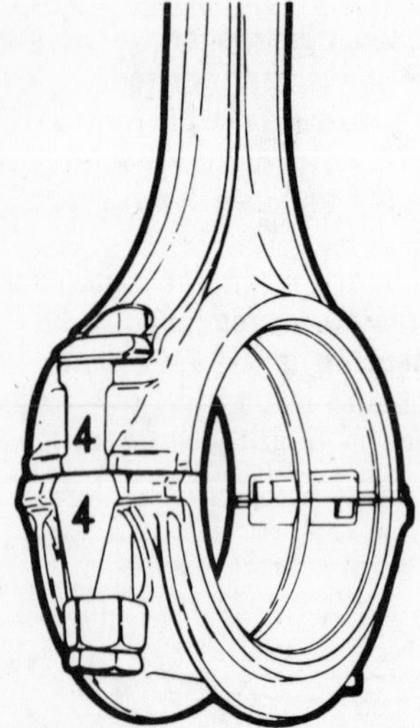

Match the connecting rod to the cylinder with a number stamp

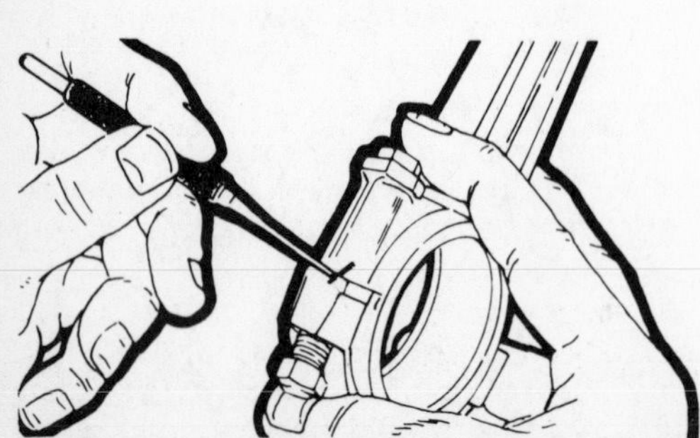

Match the connecting rod and cap with scribe marks

Rear Main Oil Seal

REPLACEMENT

All 4 Cylinder Gasoline Engines

In order to replace the rear main oil seal, the rear main bearing cap must be removed. Removal of the rear main bearing cap requires the use of a special rear main bearing cap puller. Also, the oil seal is installed with a special crankshaft rear oil seal drift. Unless these or similar tools are available to you, it is recommended that the oil seal be replaced by a Nissan/Datsun service center or an independent shop that has the proper equipment.

1. Remove the engine and transmission assembly from the vehicle.
2. Remove the transmission from the engine. Remove the oil pan.
3. Remove the clutch from the flywheel.
4. Remove the flywheel from the crankshaft.
5. Remove the rear main bearing cap together with the bearing cap side seals.
6. Remove the rear main oil seal from around the crankshaft.
7. Apply lithium grease around the sealing lip of the oil seal and install the seal around the crankshaft using a suitable tool.
8. Apply sealer to the rear main bearing cap as indicated, install the rear main bearing cap,

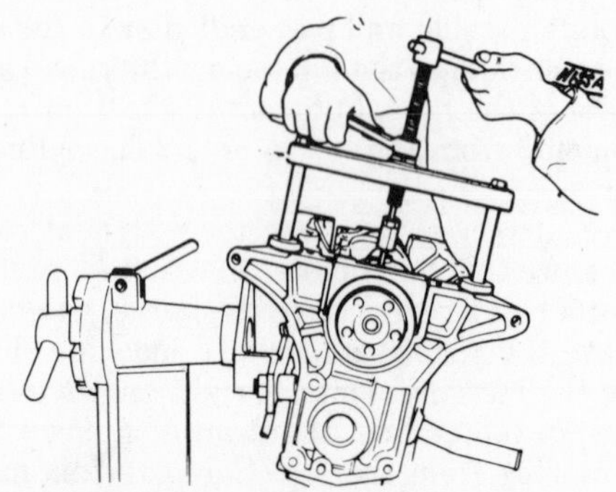

Removing the rear main bearing cap

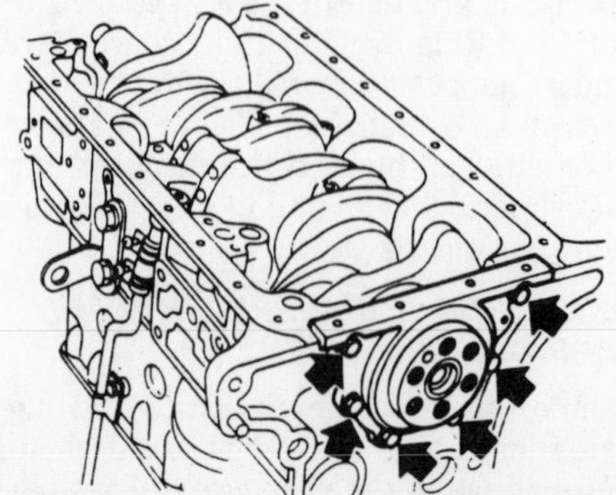

Removing the rear main seal retainer—SD22 and SD25 engines

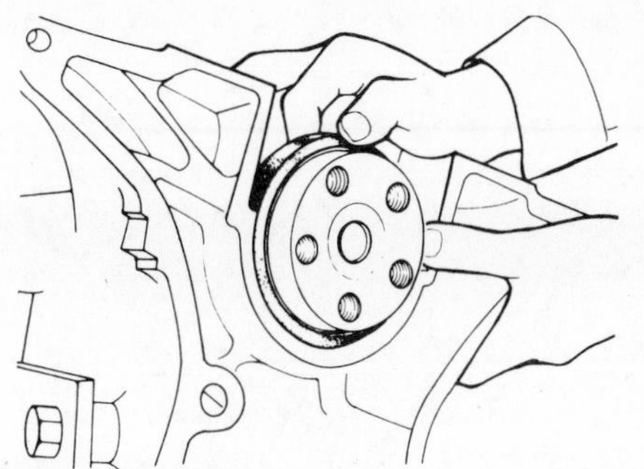
Removing the rear main seal retainer—all 4 cylinder gasoline engine

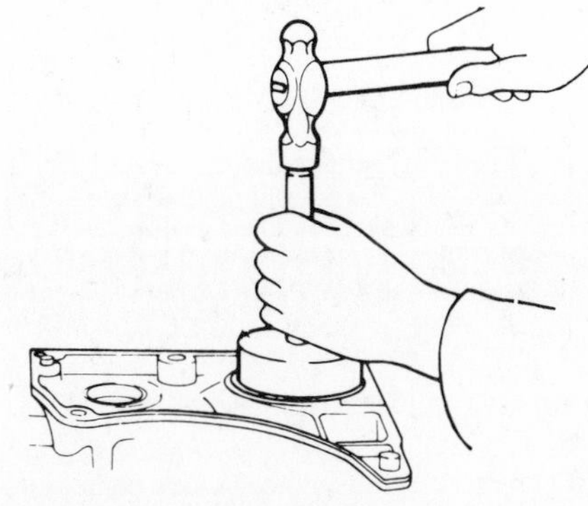
Installing the rear main seal

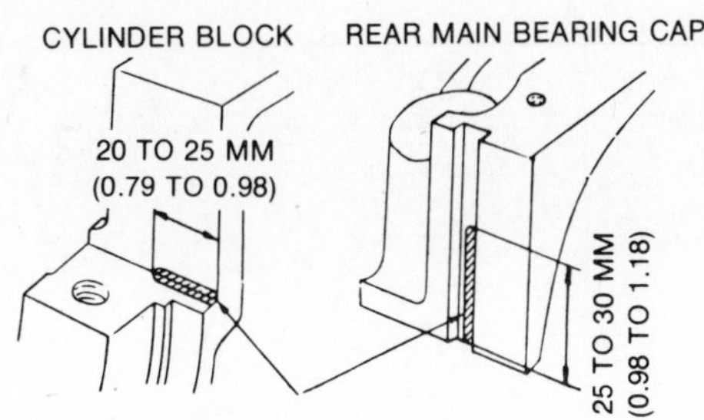

Application of sealer to the rear main bearing cap

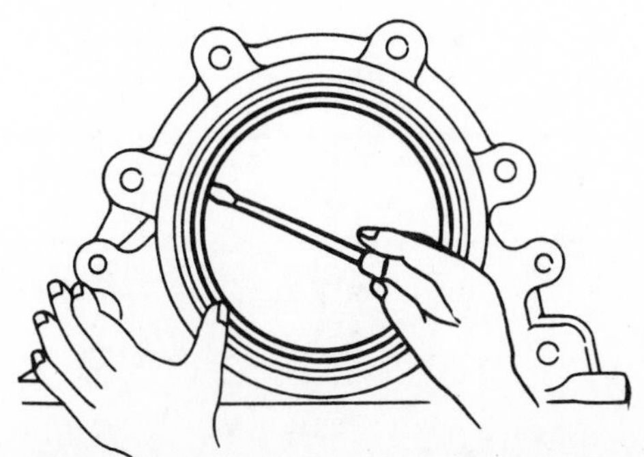
Removing the rear main seal—VG30i, SD22 and SD25 engines

and tighten the cap bolts to 33–40 ft. lbs. (44–54 Nm)

9. Apply sealant to the rear main bearing cap side seals and install the side seals, driving the seals into place with a suitable drift.

10. Install the oil pan with a new gasket.

11. Install the flywheel and clutch assembly.

12. Install the transmission to the engine and install the engine/transmission assembly in the vehicle. Refer to the Engine Removal and Installation procedure.

13. Check all fluid levels, start the engine and check for any leaks. Roadtest the vehicle for proper operation.

SD22, SD25 and VG30i Engines

1. Refer to the Engine, Removal and Installation procedures, in this section and remove the engine/transmission from the vehicle.

2. Separate the transmission from the engine.

3. Remove the clutch assembly from the flywheel (MT) or the torque converter from the drive plate (AT).

4. Remove the flywheel or the drive plate from the crankshaft, then secure the engine to a workstand.

5. If not having done so, drain the oil from the crankcase, then remove the oil pan.

6. Remove the rear oil seal retainer from the rear of the engine.

7. Using a medium pry bar (or even a pair of pliers), pry the oil seal from the oil seal retainer.

8. Using a putty knife, clean the gasket mounting surfaces.

9. Apply oil to the sealing lip and the mounting surface of the new oil seal, then press the seal into the oil seal retainer. Install the oil seal retainer/seal around the crankshaft.

10. To complete the installation, use new gaskets and reverse the removal procedures. Refill the crankcase and the cooling system; if equipped with an automatic transmission, check the fluid.

Crankshaft and Main Bearing

REMOVAL AND INSTALLATION

NOTE: *Before removing the crankshaft, check main bearing clearances as described under Main Bearing Clearance Check below.*

1. Remove the piston and connecting rod assemblies following the procedure in this chapter.

2. Check crankshaft thrust clearance (end play) before removing the crank from the block. Using a pry bar, pry the crankshaft the extent of its travel forward, and measure thrust clearance at the center main bearing (No. 4 bearing on V6 and diesel engines, No. 3 on 4 cylinder

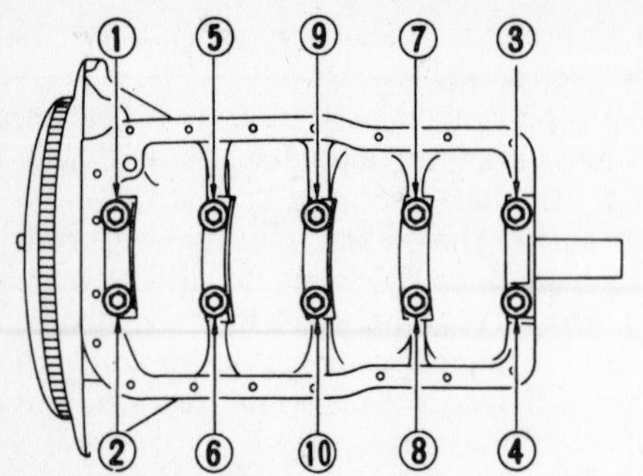

Main bearing cap bolt loosening sequence—all 4 cylinder gasoline engines

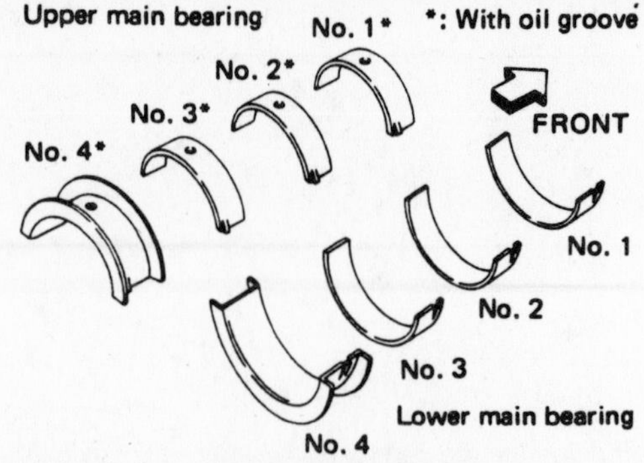

Main bearing positioning—VG30i engines

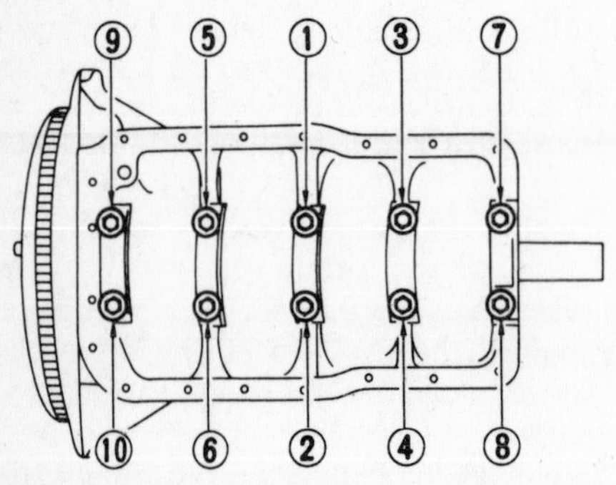

Main bearing cap bolt tightening sequence—all 4 cylinder gasoline engines

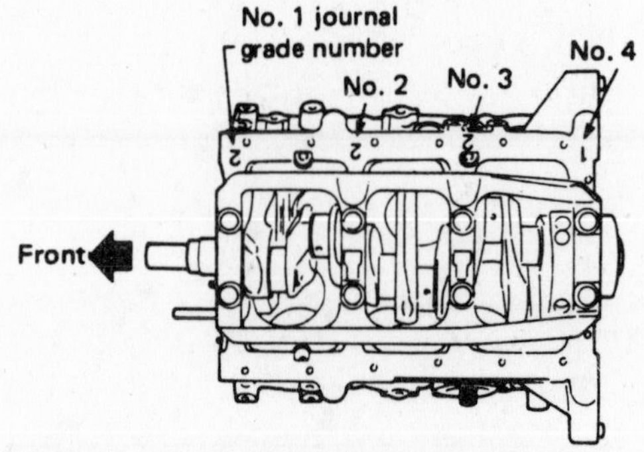

The grade mark of the cylinder block main journal is stamped on the block—VG30i engines

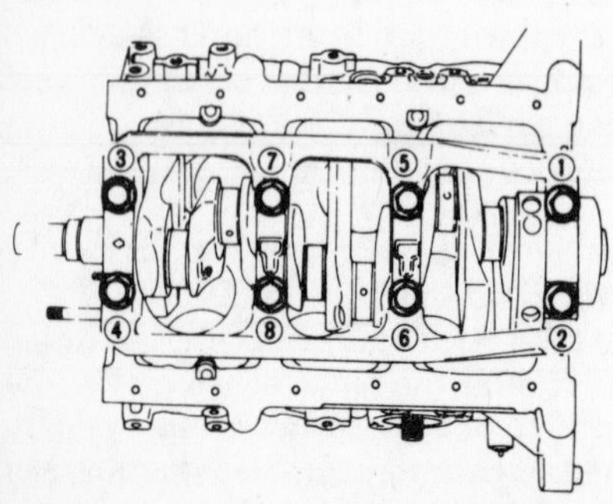

Main bearing cap bolt loosening sequence—VG30i engines

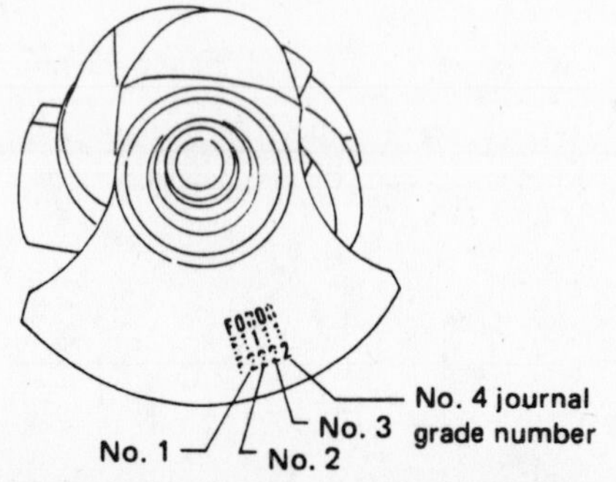

The grade mark of the crankshaft main journal is stamped on the crankshaft—VG30i engines

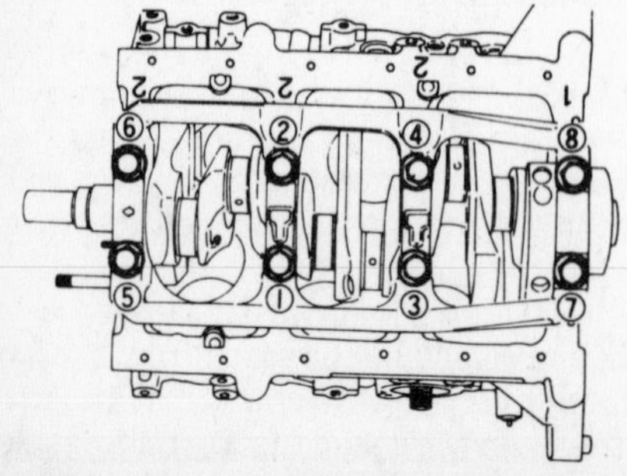

Main bearing cap bolt tightening sequence—VG30i engines

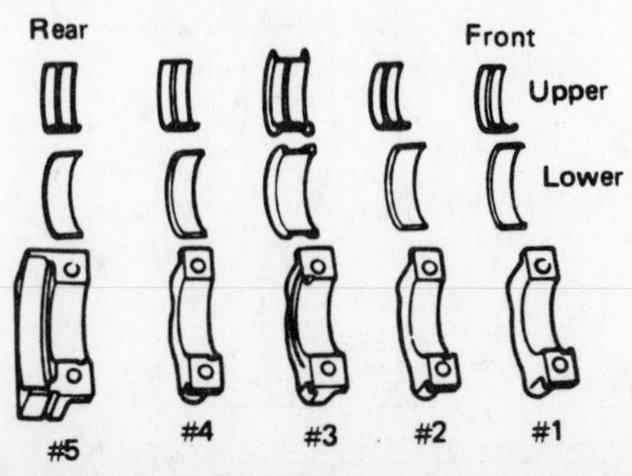

Main bearing positioning—Z20, Z22, Z24 and Z24i engines (L-series engines similar)

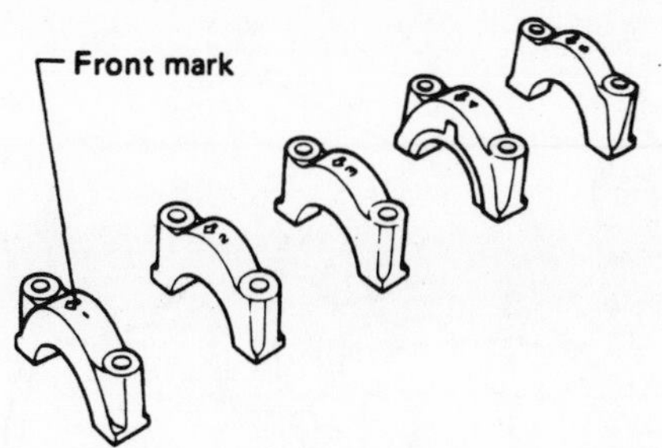

Main bearing cap positioning—SD22 and SD25 engines

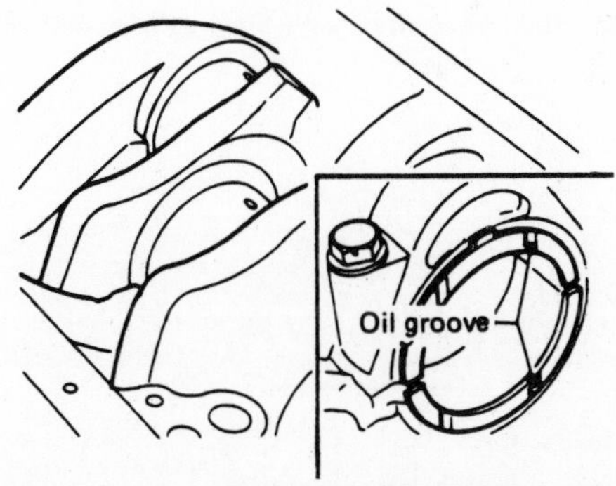

Thrust washer positioning—SD22 and SD25 engines

gasoline engines) with a feeler gauge. Pry the crankshaft the extent of its rearward travel, and measure the other side of the bearing. If clearance is greater than that specified, the thrust washers must be replaced (see main bearing installation, below).

3. Using a punch, mark the corresponding main bearing caps and saddles according to position: one punch on the front main cap and saddle, two on the second, three on the third, etc. This ensures correct reassembly.

4. Remove the main bearing caps after they have been marked.

5. Remove the crankshaft form the block.

6. Follow the crankshaft inspection, main bearing clearance checking and replacement procedures below before reinstalling the crankshaft.

INSPECTION

Crankshaft inspection and servicing should be handled exclusively by a reputable machinist, as most of the necessary procedures require a dial indicator and fixing jig, a large micrometer, and machine tools such as a crankshaft grinder. While at the machine shop, the crankshaft should be thoroughly cleaned (especially the oil passages). Magnafluxed (to check for minute cracks) and the following checks made: main journal diameter, crank pin (connecting rod journal) diameter, taper and out-of-round, and run-out. Wear, beyond specification limits, in any of these areas means the crankshaft must be reground or replaced.

MAIN BEARING CLEARANCE CHECK

Checking main bearing clearances is done in the same manner as checking connecting rod big-end clearances.

1. With the crankshaft installed, remove the main bearing cap. Clean all oil form the bearing insert in the cap and from the crankshaft journal, as the Plastigage® material is oil-soluble.

2. Lay a strip of Plastigage® along the full width of the bearing cap (or along the width of the crank journal if the engine is out of the truck and inverted).

3. Install the bearing cap and torque to specification.

NOTE: *Do not rotate the crankshaft with the Plastigage® installed.*

4. Remove the bearing cap and determine bearing clearance by comparing the width of the now-flattened Plastigage® with the scale on the Plastigage® envelope. Journal taper is determined by comparing the width of the Plastigage® strip near its ends. Rotate the crankshaft 90° and retest, to determine journal eccentricity.

5. Repeat the above for the remaining bearings. If the bearing journal and insert appear in good shape (with not unusual wear visible) and are within tolerances, no further main bearing service is required. If unusual wear is evident and/or the clearances are outside specifications, the bearings must be replaced and the cause of their wear found.

MAIN BEARING REPLACEMENT

Main bearings can be replaced with the crankshaft both in the engine (with the engine still in the truck) and out of the engine (with the engine on a work stand or bench). Both procedures are covered here. The main bearings must be replaced if the crankshaft has been reground; the replacement bearing being available in various undersize increments from most auto parts jobbers or your local Nissan dealer.

Engine Out of Truck

1. Remove the crankshaft from the engine block.

2. Remove the main bearing inserts from the bearing caps and from the main bearing saddles. Remove the thrust washers from the No. 3 (4 cylinder gasoline engines) or No. 4 (V6 and diesel engines) crank journal.

3. Thoroughly clean the saddles, bearing caps, and crankshaft.

4. Make sure the crankshaft has been fully

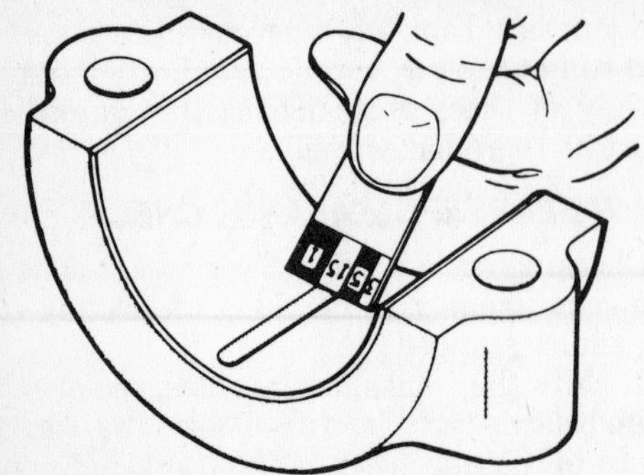

Measure Plastigage® to determine main bearing clearance

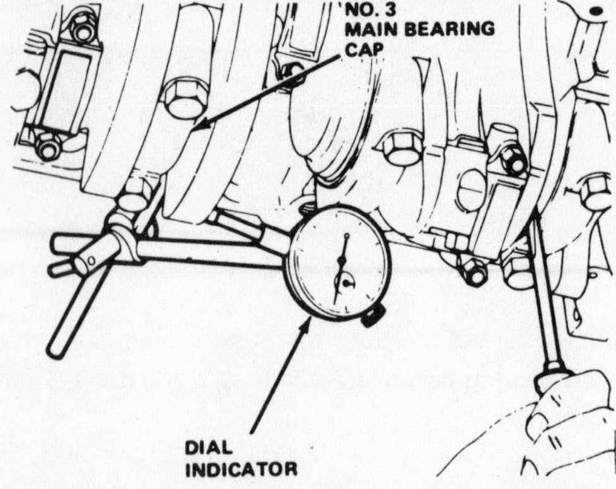

Check the crankshaft end-play with a dial indicator

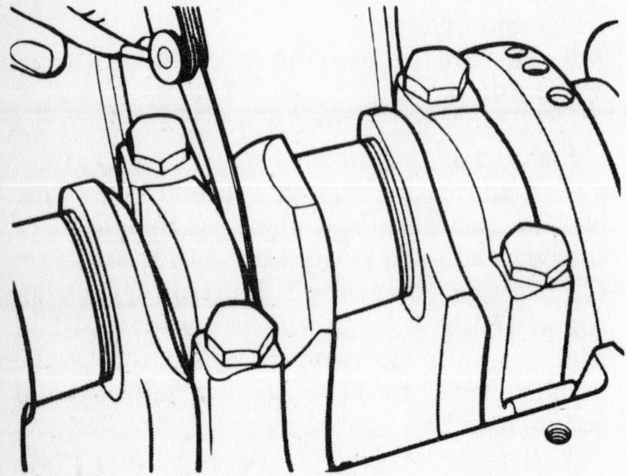

Check the crankshaft end-play with a feeler gauge

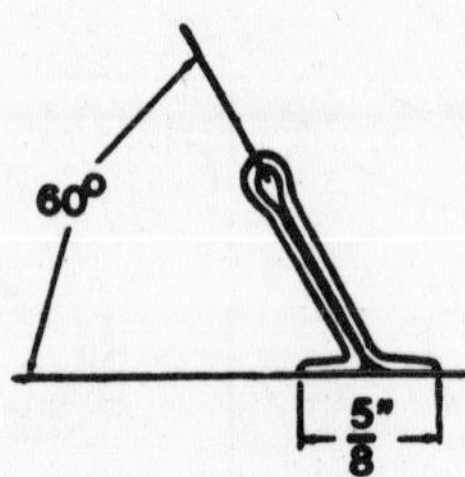

Home-made bearing roll-out pin

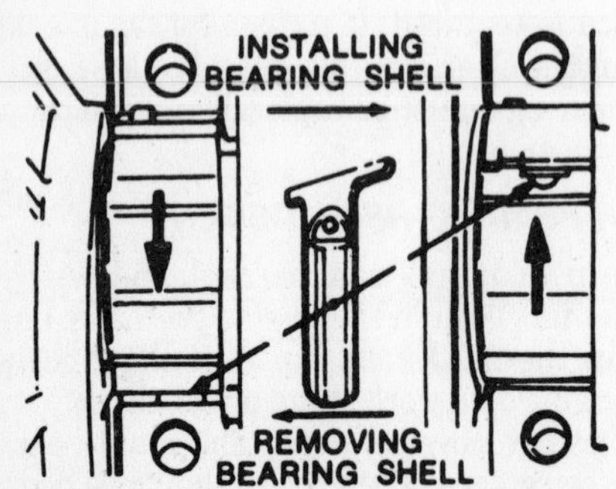

Upper bearing insert installation and removal

checked and is ready for reassembly. Place the upper main bearings in the block saddles so that the oil grooves and/or oil holes are correctly aligned with their corresponding grooves or holes in the saddles.

5. Install the thrust washers on the center main bearing, with the oil grooves facing out.

6. Lubricate the faces of all bearings with clean engine oil, and place the crankshaft in the block.

7. Install the main bearing caps in numbered order with the arrows or any other orientation marks facing forward. Torque all bolts except the center cap bolts in sequence in two or three passes to the specified torque. Rotate the crankshaft after each pass to ensure even tightness.

8. Align the thrust bearing by prying the

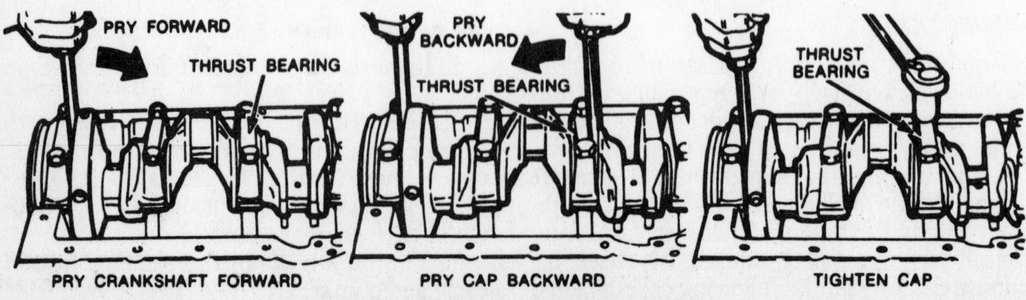

Aligning the crankshaft thrust bearing

crankshaft the extent of its axial travel several times with a pry bar. On last movement hold the crankshaft toward the front of the engine and torque the thrust bearing cap to specifications. Measure the crankshaft thrust clearance (end play) as previously described in this chapter. If clearance is outside specifications (too sloppy), install a new set of oversize thrust washers and check clearance again.

Engine And Crankshaft Installed

1. Remove the main bearing caps and keep them in order.
2. Make a bearing roll-out pin from a cotter pin as shown.
3. Carefully roll out the old inserts from the upper side of the crankshaft journal, noting the positions of the oil grooves and/or oil holes so the new inserts can be correctly installed.
4. Roll each new insert into its saddle after lightly oiling the crankshaft-side face of each. Make sure the notches and/or oil holes are correctly positioned.
5. Replace the bearing inserts in the caps with new inserts. Oil the face of each, and install the caps in numbered order with the arrows or other orientation marks facing forward. Torque the bolts to the specified torque in two or three passes in the sequence shown.

Flywheel and Ring Gear

REMOVAL AND INSTALLATION

All Engines

NOTE: *The clutch cover and the pressure plate are balanced as an assembly; if replacement of either part becomes necessary, replace both parts as an assembly. If vehicle is equipped with a automatic transmission use this procedure as a guide. See exploded view of engine assembly for flywheel/drive plate installation and quick torque reference.*

1. Remove the transmission, if the engine is installed in the truck.
2. Remove the clutch assembly, if equipped.
3. Remove the flywheel.
4. To install, use new flywheel bolts. Torque the bolts in a criss-cross pattern to the torque specified in the chart in this chapter.

EXHAUST SYSTEM

Safety Precautions

For a number of reasons, exhaust system work can be dangerous. Always observe the following precautions:

1. Support the vehicle securely by using jackstands or equivalent under the frame of the vehicle.
2. Wear safety goggles to protect your eyes from metal chips that may fly free while working on the exhaust system.
3. When using a torch, be careful not to come close to any fuel lines.
4. Always use the proper tool for the job.
5. NEVER WORK ON A HOT EXHAUST SYSTEM!!

Special Tools

A number of special exhaust tools can be rented or bought from a local auto parts store. It may also be quite helpful to use solvents designed to loosen rusted nuts or bolts. Remember that these products are often flammable, apply only to parts after they are cool.

Front Pipe

REMOVAL AND INSTALLATION

1. Support the vehicle securely by using jackstands or equivalent under the frame of the vehicle.
2. Remove the exhaust pipe clamps and any front exhaust pipe shield.
3. Soak the exhaust manifold front pipe mounting studs with penetrating oil. Remove attaching nuts and gasket from the manifold.

NOTE: *If these studs snap off, while removing the front pipe the manifold will have to be removed and the stud will have to be drill out and the hole tapped.*

4. Remove any exhaust pipe mounting hanger or bracket.
5. Remove front pipe from the muffler/catalytic converter.
6. Install the front pipe on the manifold with seal if so equipped.
7. Connect the pipe to the muffler/catalytic converter. Assemble all parts loosely and position the pipe to insure proper clearance from body of vehicle.
8. Tighten mounting studs, bracket bolts on exhaust clamps.
9. Install exhaust pipe shield.
10. Start engine and check for exhaust leaks.

Catalytic Converter

REMOVAL AND INSTALLATION

1. Remove the converter lower shield.
2. Disconnect converter from front pipe.
3. Disconnect converter from center pipe or tail pipe assembly.
4. Remove catalytic converter.

NOTE: *Assemble all parts loosely and position the converter before tightening the exhaust clamps.*

5. To install, reverse the removal procedures. Always use new clamps and exhaust seals, start the engine and check for leaks.

Tailpipe And Muffler

REMOVAL AND INSTALLATION

1. Disconnect the tailpipe at the center pipe, catalytic converter or front pipe.
2. Remove all brackets and exhaust clamps.
3. Remove the tailpipe from muffler. On some models the tailpipe and muffler are one piece.
4. To install reverse the removal procedures. Always use new clamps and exhaust seals, start engine and check for leaks.

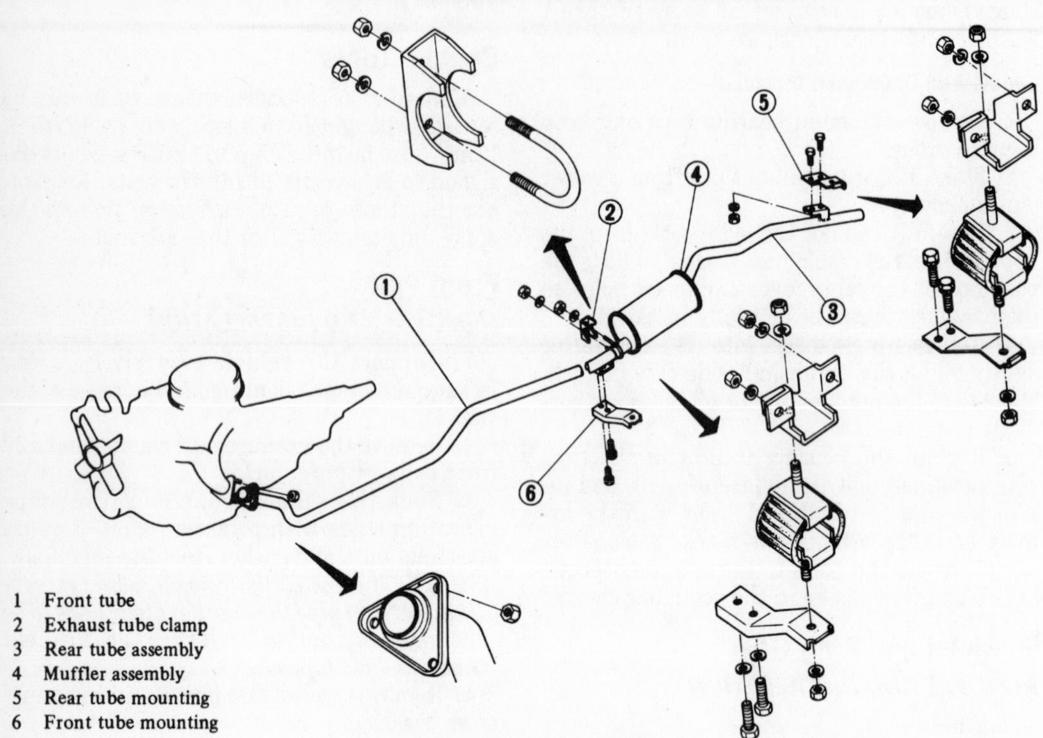

Typical exhaust system—1973–75

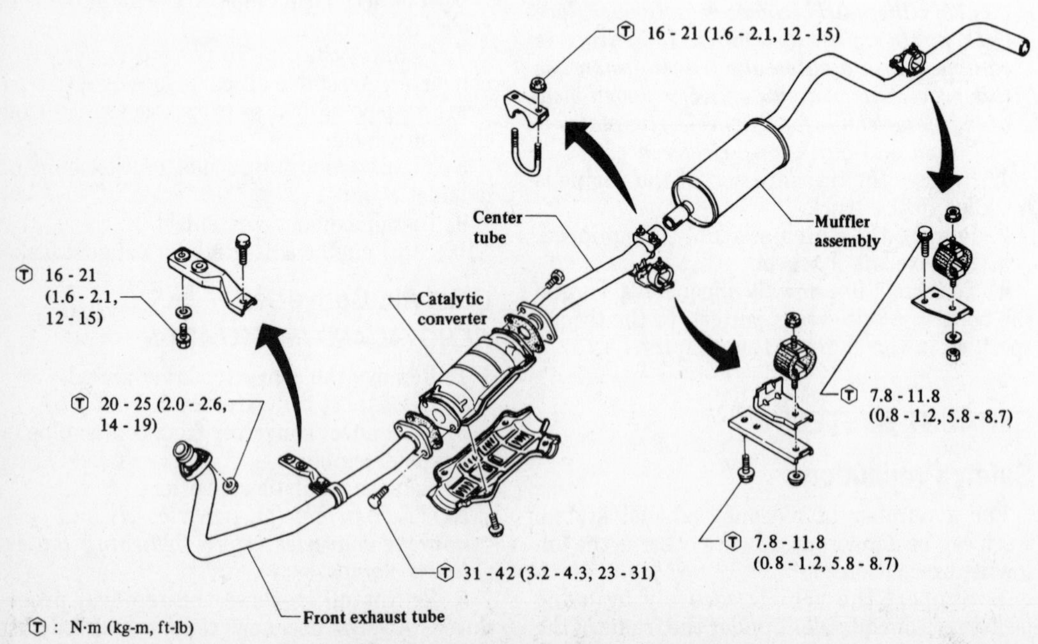

Typical exhaust system—1980 US models

Non-California model

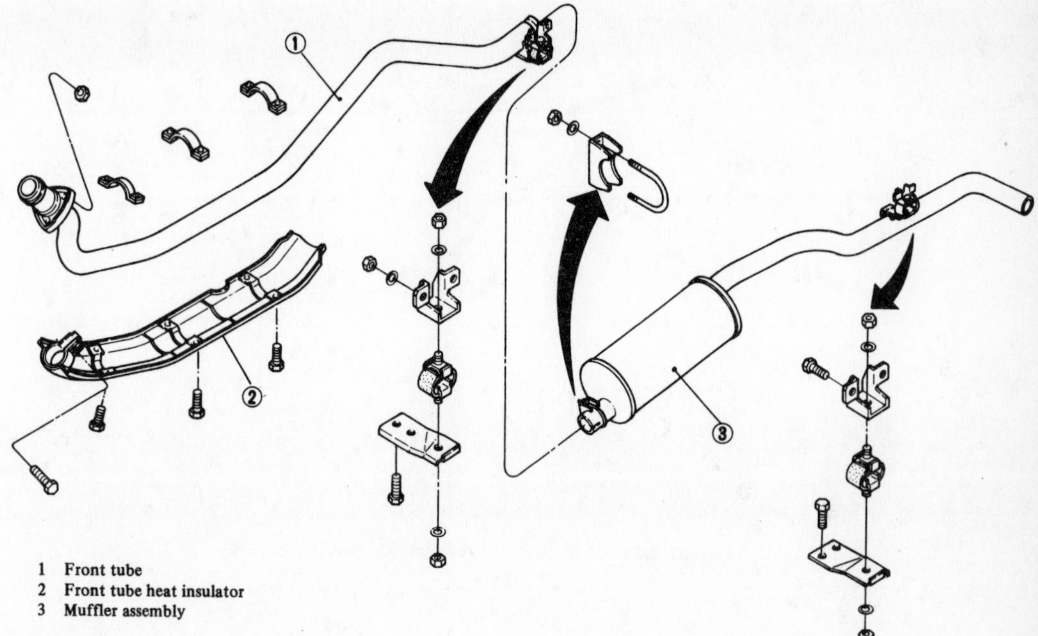

California model

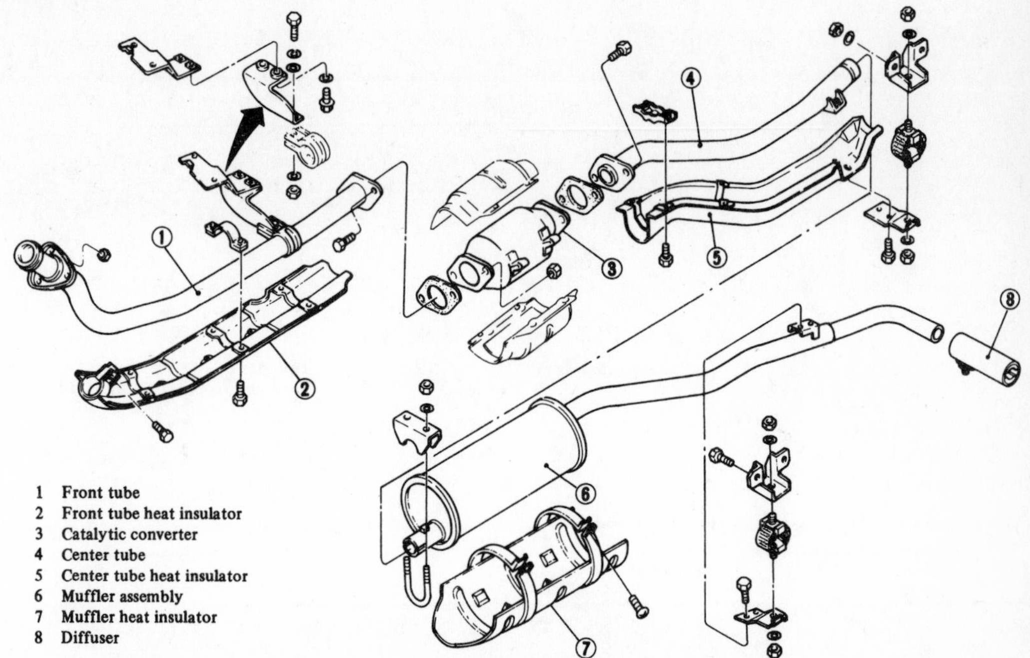

Typical exhaust system—1976–79

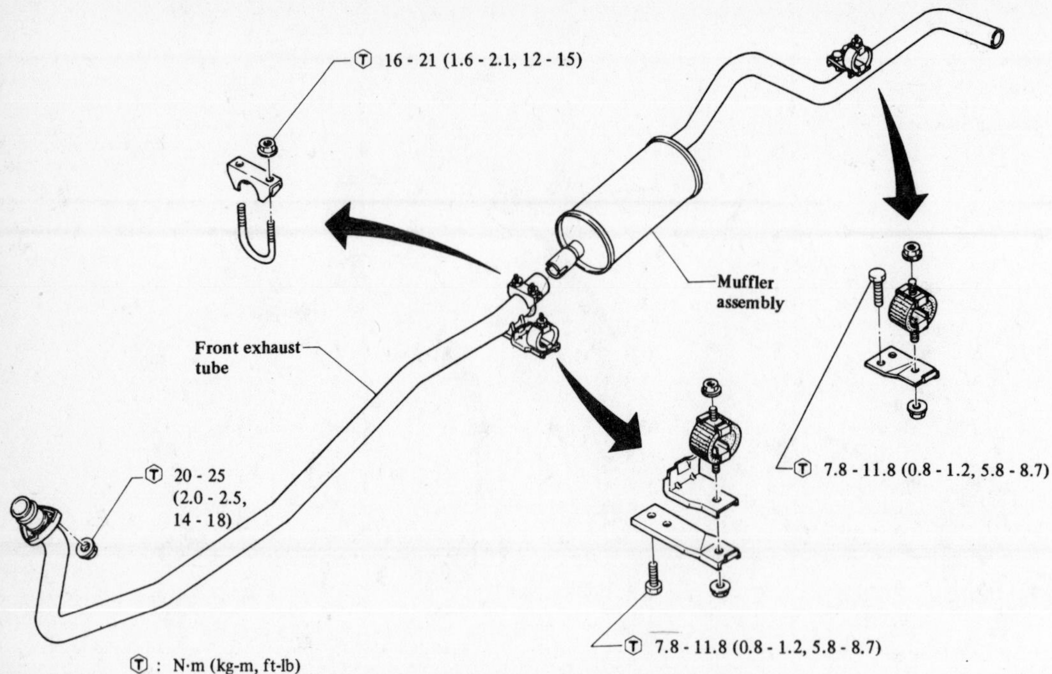

Typical exhaust system—1980 Canada models

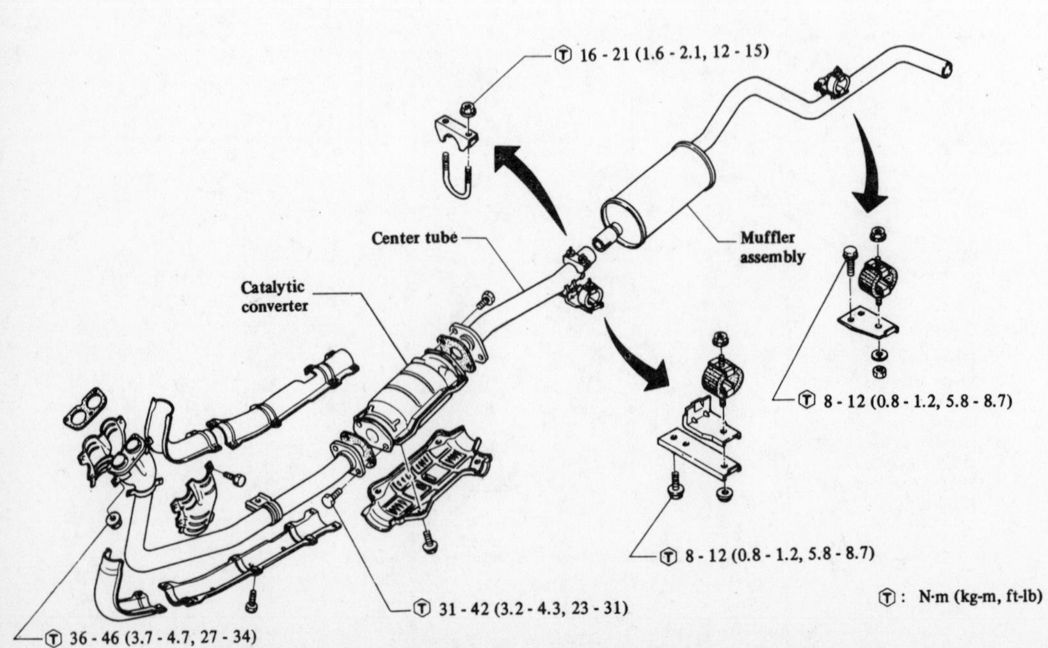

Typical exhaust system—1981–83 2wd models with Z22 engines (exc. HD)

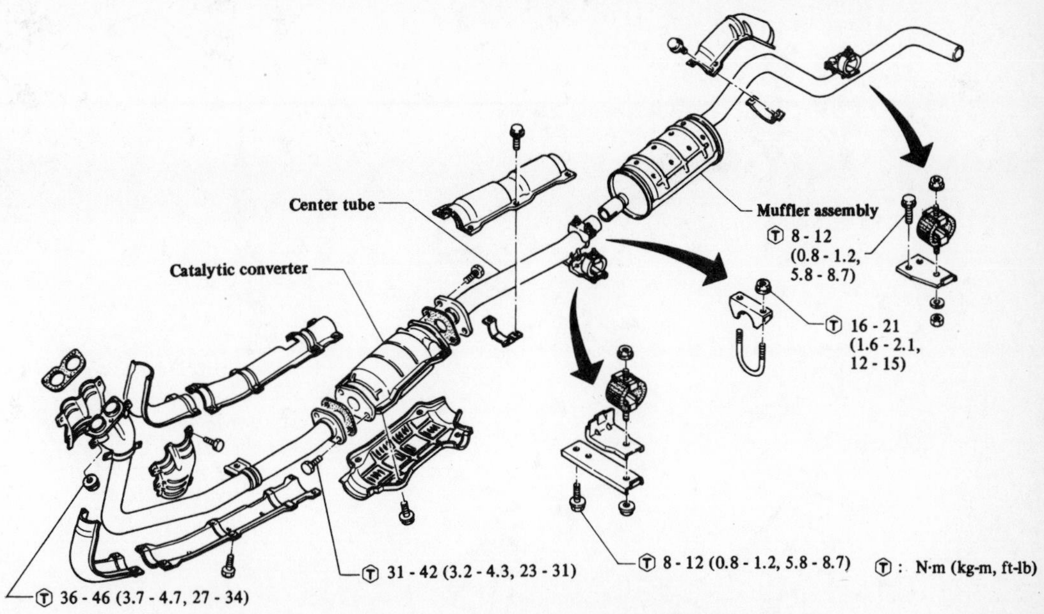

Typical exhaust system—1981–83 2wd models with Z22 engines (HD)

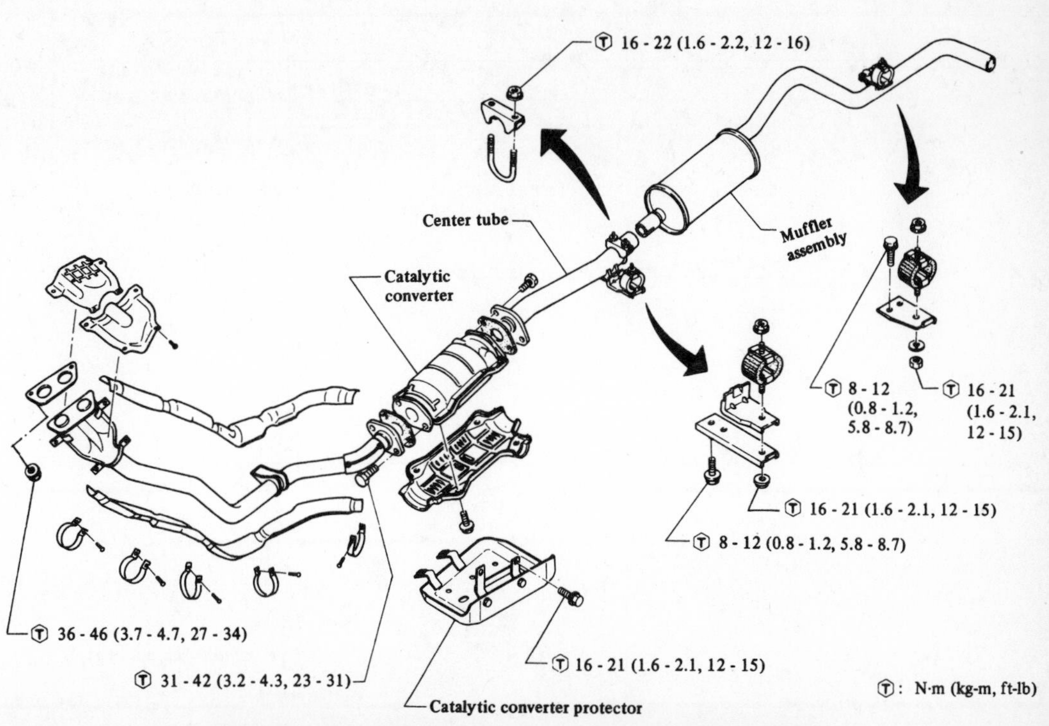

Typical exhaust system—1981–83 4wd models with Z22 engines

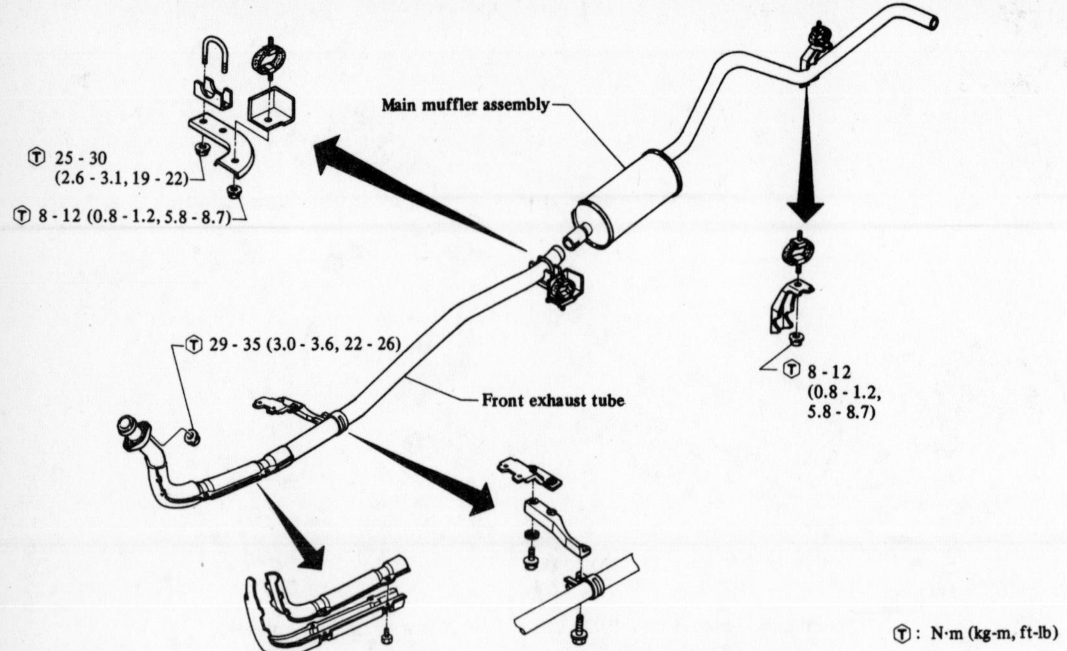

Main muffler assembly
T 25 - 30
(2.6 - 3.1, 19 - 22)
T 8 - 12 (0.8 - 1.2, 5.8 - 8.7)
T 29 - 35 (3.0 - 3.6, 22 - 26)
Front exhaust tube
T 8 - 12
(0.8 - 1.2,
5.8 - 8.7)
T : N·m (kg-m, ft-lb)

Typical exhaust system—1981–83 models with SD22 engines

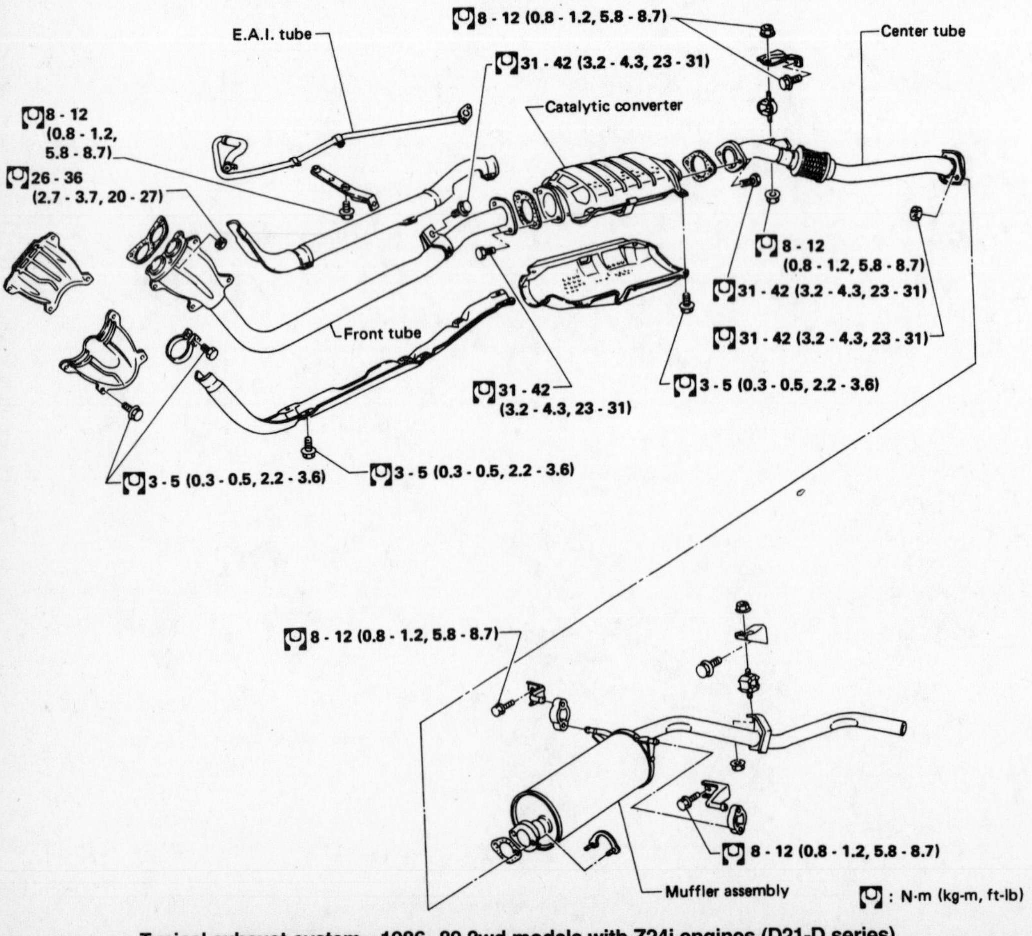

8 - 12 (0.8 - 1.2, 5.8 - 8.7)
E.A.I. tube
31 - 42 (3.2 - 4.3, 23 - 31)
Center tube
Catalytic converter
8 - 12
(0.8 - 1.2,
5.8 - 8.7)
26 - 36
(2.7 - 3.7, 20 - 27)
8 - 12
(0.8 - 1.2, 5.8 - 8.7)
31 - 42 (3.2 - 4.3, 23 - 31)
31 - 42 (3.2 - 4.3, 23 - 31)
Front tube
31 - 42
(3.2 - 4.3, 23 - 31)
3 - 5 (0.3 - 0.5, 2.2 - 3.6)
3 - 5 (0.3 - 0.5, 2.2 - 3.6)
3 - 5 (0.3 - 0.5, 2.2 - 3.6)
8 - 12 (0.8 - 1.2, 5.8 - 8.7)
8 - 12 (0.8 - 1.2, 5.8 - 8.7)
Muffler assembly
: N·m (kg-m, ft-lb)

Typical exhaust system—1986–89 2wd models with Z24i engines (D21-D series)

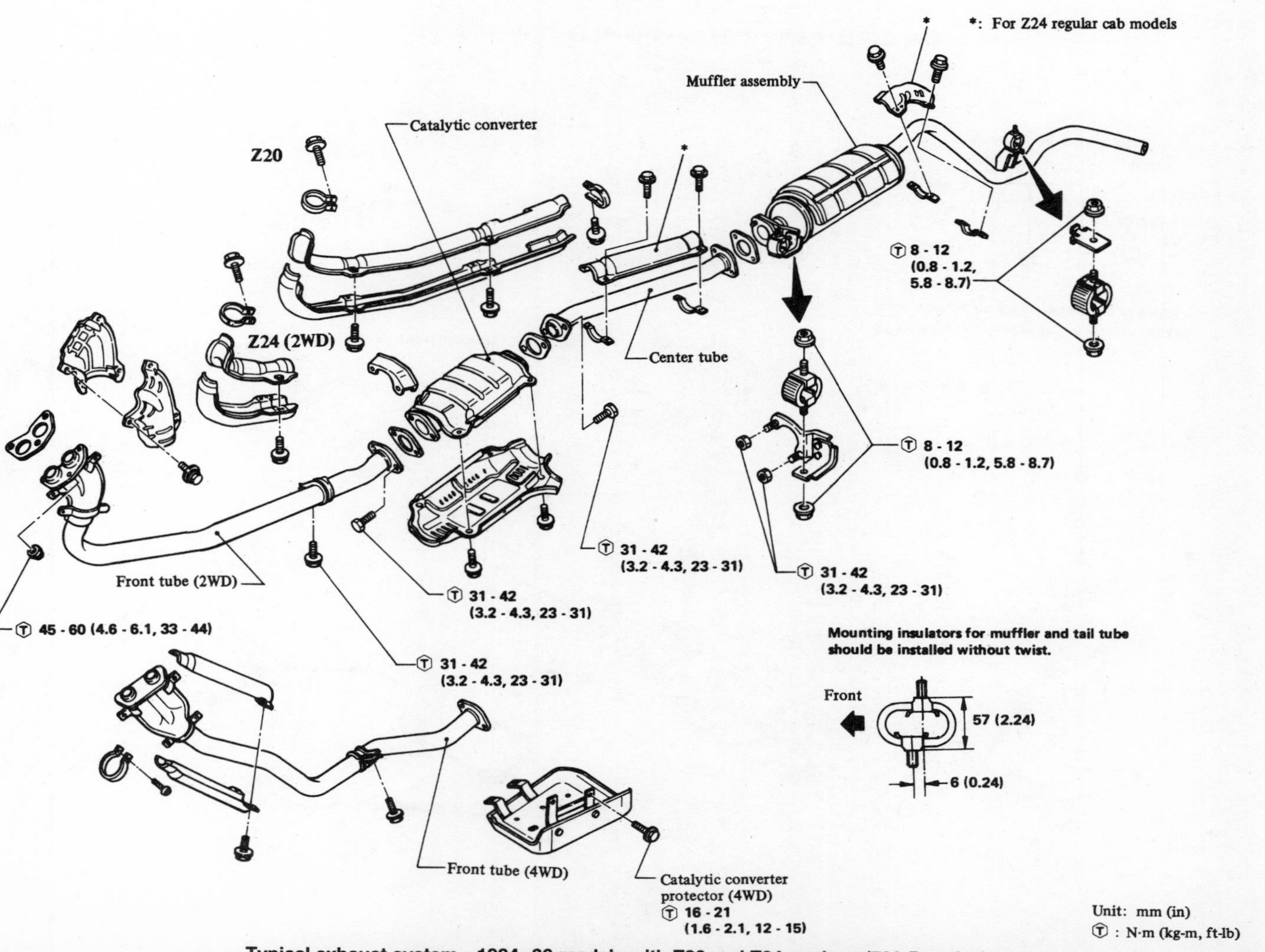

Typical exhaust system—1984–86 models with Z20 and Z24 engines (720-D series)

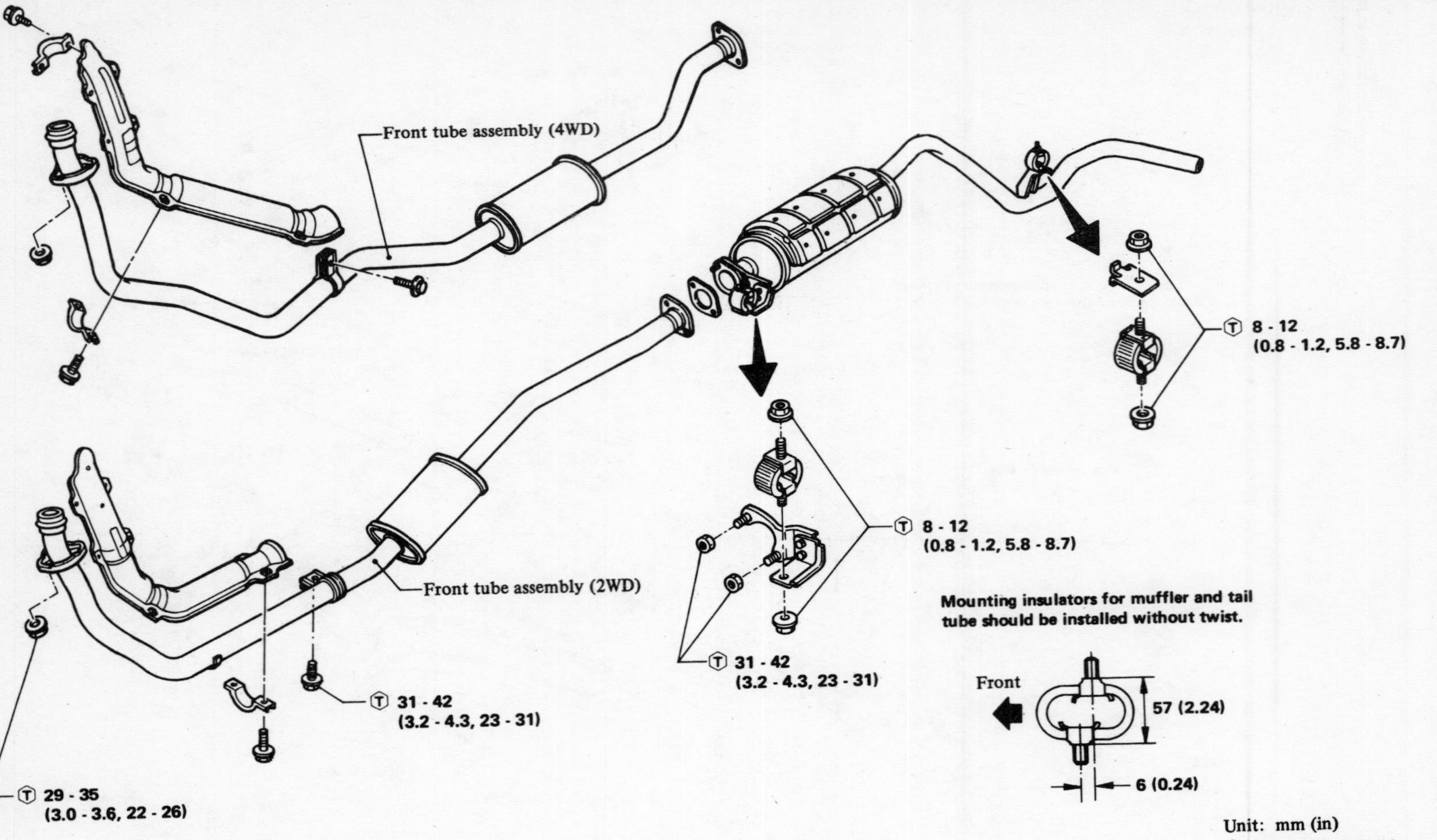

Typical exhaust system—1984–86 models with SD25 engines (720-D series)

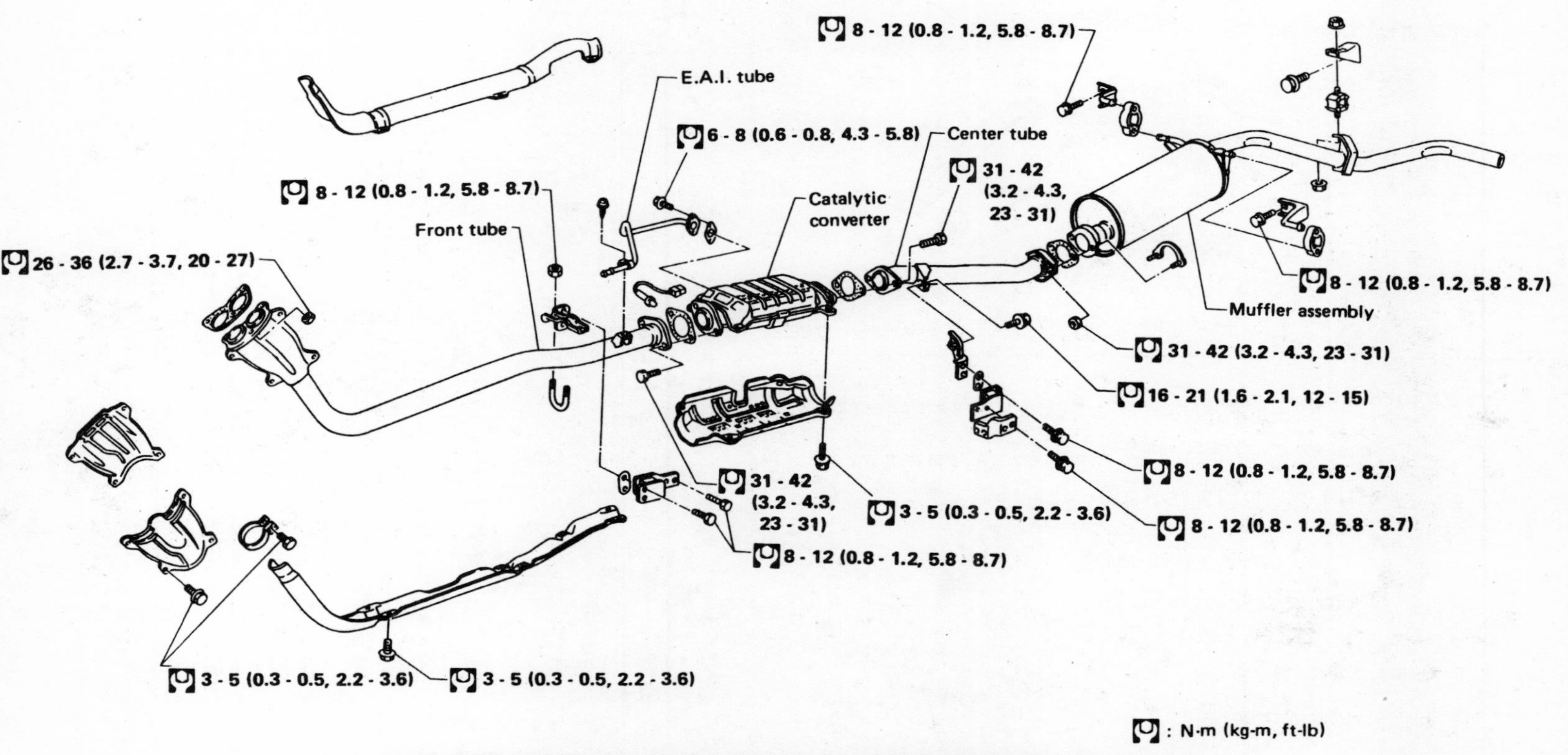

Typical exhaust system—1986–89 4wd models with Z24i engines (D21-D series)

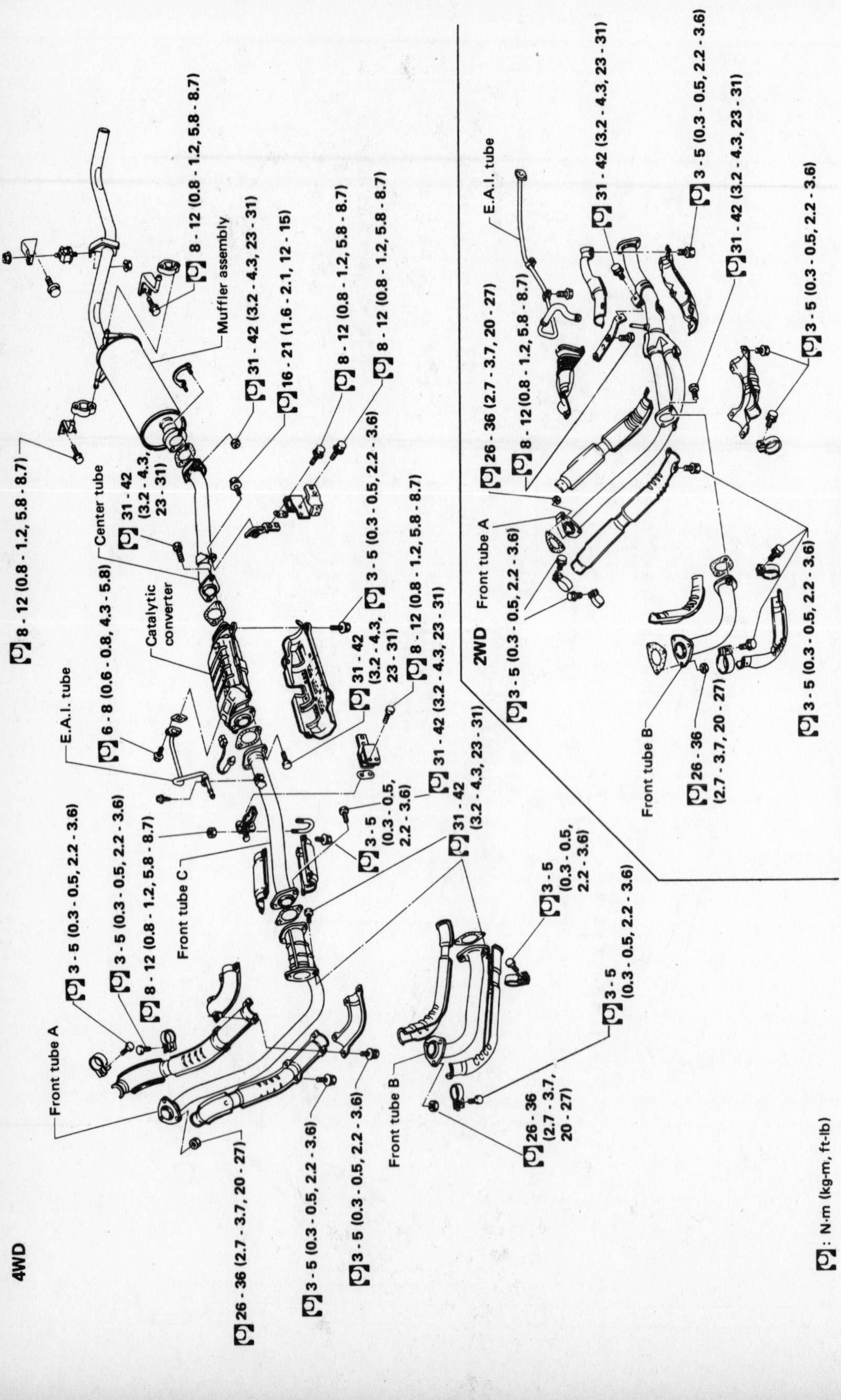

4WD

Front tube A
3 - 5 (0.3 - 0.5, 2.2 - 3.6)
3 - 5 (0.3 - 0.5, 2.2 - 3.6)
8 - 12 (0.8 - 1.2, 5.8 - 8.7)
Front tube C
E.A.I. tube
6 - 8 (0.6 - 0.8, 4.3 - 5.8)
Catalytic converter
8 - 12 (0.8 - 1.2, 5.8 - 8.7)
Center tube
31 - 42 (3.2 - 4.3, 23 - 31)
Muffler assembly
8 - 12 (0.8 - 1.2, 5.8 - 8.7)
31 - 42 (3.2 - 4.3, 23 - 31)
16 - 21 (1.6 - 2.1, 12 - 15)
8 - 12 (0.8 - 1.2, 5.8 - 8.7)
8 - 12 (0.8 - 1.2, 5.8 - 8.7)
3 - 5 (0.3 - 0.5, 2.2 - 3.6)
31 - 42 (3.2 - 4.3, 23 - 31)
8 - 12 (0.8 - 1.2, 5.8 - 8.7)
31 - 42 (3.2 - 4.3, 23 - 31)
3 - 5 (0.3 - 0.5, 2.2 - 3.6)
31 - 42 (3.2 - 4.3, 23 - 31)
3 - 5 (0.3 - 0.5, 2.2 - 3.6)
26 - 36 (2.7 - 3.7, 20 - 27)
3 - 5 (0.3 - 0.5, 2.2 - 3.6)
3 - 5 (0.3 - 0.5, 2.2 - 3.6)
Front tube B
26 - 36 (2.7 - 3.7, 20 - 27)
3 - 5 (0.3 - 0.5, 2.2 - 3.6)
3 - 5 (0.3 - 0.5, 2.2 - 3.6)

2WD

Front tube A
26 - 36 (2.7 - 3.7, 20 - 27)
8 - 12 (0.8 - 1.2, 5.8 - 8.7)
E.A.I. tube
31 - 42 (3.2 - 4.3, 23 - 31)
3 - 5 (0.3 - 0.5, 2.2 - 3.6)
31 - 42 (3.2 - 4.3, 23 - 31)
3 - 5 (0.3 - 0.5, 2.2 - 3.6)
3 - 5 (0.3 - 0.5, 2.2 - 3.6)
3 - 5 (0.3 - 0.5, 2.2 - 3.6)
Front tube B
26 - 36 (2.7 - 3.7, 20 - 27)
3 - 5 (0.3 - 0.5, 2.2 - 3.6)

: N·m (kg-m, ft-lb)

Typical exhaust system—1986—89 models with VG30i engines

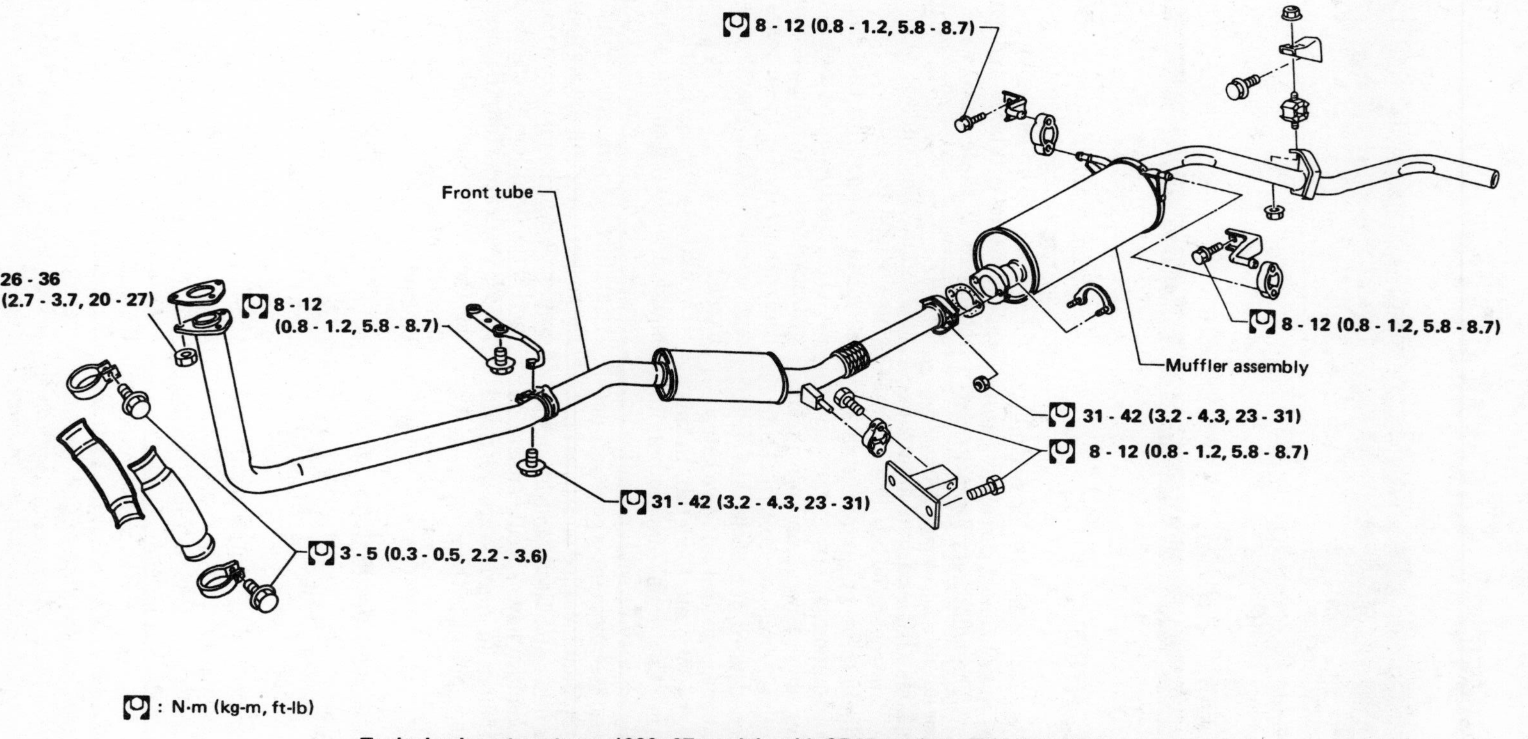

Typical exhaust system—1986–87 models with SD25 engines (D21-D series)

Emission Controls

4

EMISSION CONTROLS

There are three sources of automotive pollutants; crankcase fumes, exhaust gases, and gasoline evaporation. The pollutants formed from these substances fall into three categories: unburnt hydrocarbons (HC), carbon monoxide (C), and oxides of nitrogen (NOx). The equipment used to limit these pollutants is called emission control equipment.

Due to varying state, federal, and provincial regulations, specific emission control equipment have been devised for each. The U.S. emission equipment is divided into two categories: California and 49 State (Federal). In this section, the term "California" applies only to trucks originally built to be sold in California. California emissions equipment is generally not shared with equipment installed on trucks built to be sold in the other 49 States. Models built to be sold in Canada also have specific emissions equipment, although in most years 49 State and Canadian equipment is the same.

Positive Crankcase Ventilation (PCV) System

OPERATION

The crankcase emission control equipment consists of a positive crankcase ventilation valve (PCV), a closed or open oil filler cap and hoses to connect this equipment.

NOTE: *The crankcase emission control system on diesel engines is basically the same as that which is on the gasoline engine. Its major difference is the crankcase emission control valve. Although its function is the same as the gasoline engine's PCV valve, it's shape and location are different.*

When the engine is running, a small portion of the gases which are formed in the combustion chamber during combustion leak by the piston rings and enter the crankcase. Since these gases are under pressure they tend to escape from the crankcase and enter into the atmosphere. If these gases were allowed to remain in the crankcase for any length of time, they would contaminate the engine oil and cause sludge to build up. If the gases are allowed to escape into the atmosphere, they would pollute the air, as they contain unburned hydrocarbons. The crankcase emission control equipment recycles these gases back into the engine combustion chamber where they are burned.

Crankcase gases are recycled in the following manner: while the engine is running, clean filtered air is drawn into the crankcase through the air filter and then through a hose leading to the rocker cover. As the air passes through the crankcase it picks up the combustion gases and carries them out of the crankcase, up through the PCV valve and into the intake manifold. After they enter the intake manifold they are drawn into the combustion chamber and burned.

The most critical component in the system is the PCV valve. This vacuum controlled valve regulates the amount of gases which are recycled into the combustion changer. At low engine speeds the valve is partially closed, limiting the flow of gases into the intake manifold. As engine speed increases, the valve opens to admit greater quantities of the gases into the intake manifold. If the valve should become blocked or plugged, the gases will be prevented from escaping from the crankcase by the normal route. Since these gases are under pressure, they will find their own way out of the crankcase. This alternate route is usually a weak oil seal or gasket in the engine. As the gas escapes by the gasket it also creates an oil leak. Besides causing oil leaks, a clogged PCV valve also allows these gases to remain in the crank-

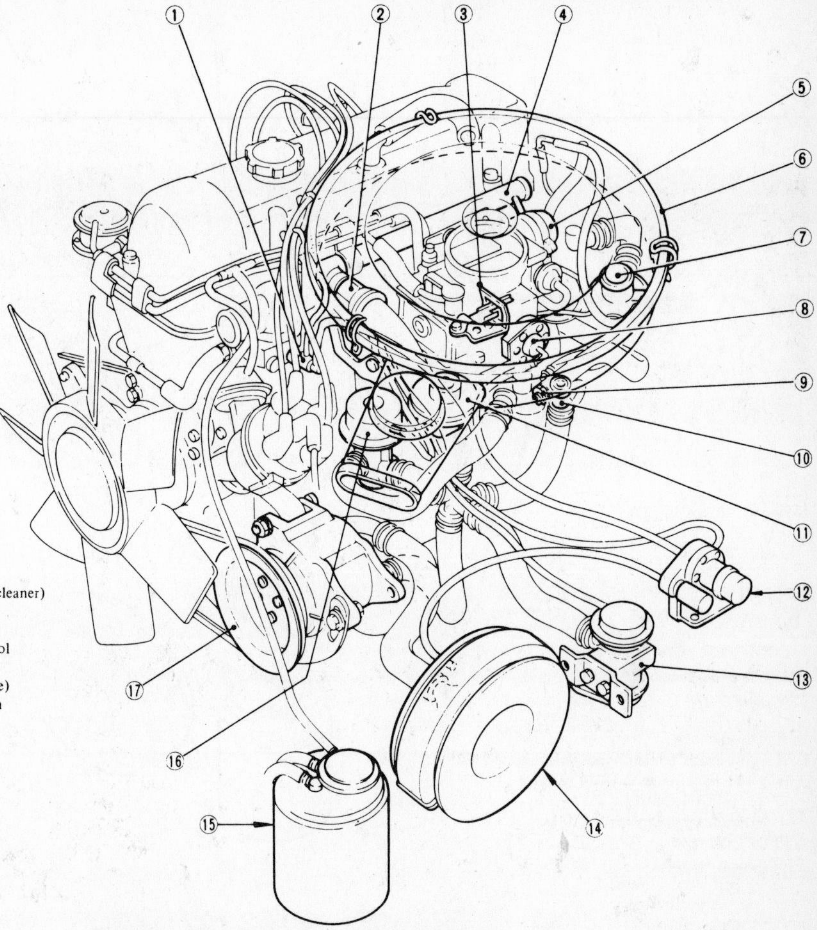

1 Thermal vacuum valve
2 Check valve
3 Altitude compensator (in air cleaner)
4 Air gallery pipe
5 Auto-choke
6 Automatic temperature control air cleaner
7 Anti-Backfire valve (A.B. valve)
8 Boost Controlled Deceleration Device (B.C.D.D.)
9 P.C.V. valve
10 Air relief valve
11 E.G.R. control valve
12 B.C.D.D. control valve and solenoid valve
13 Emergency air relief valve
14 Air pump air cleaner
15 Carbon canister
16 Air control valve
17 Air pump

Emission control system—1975–77 (Calif.)

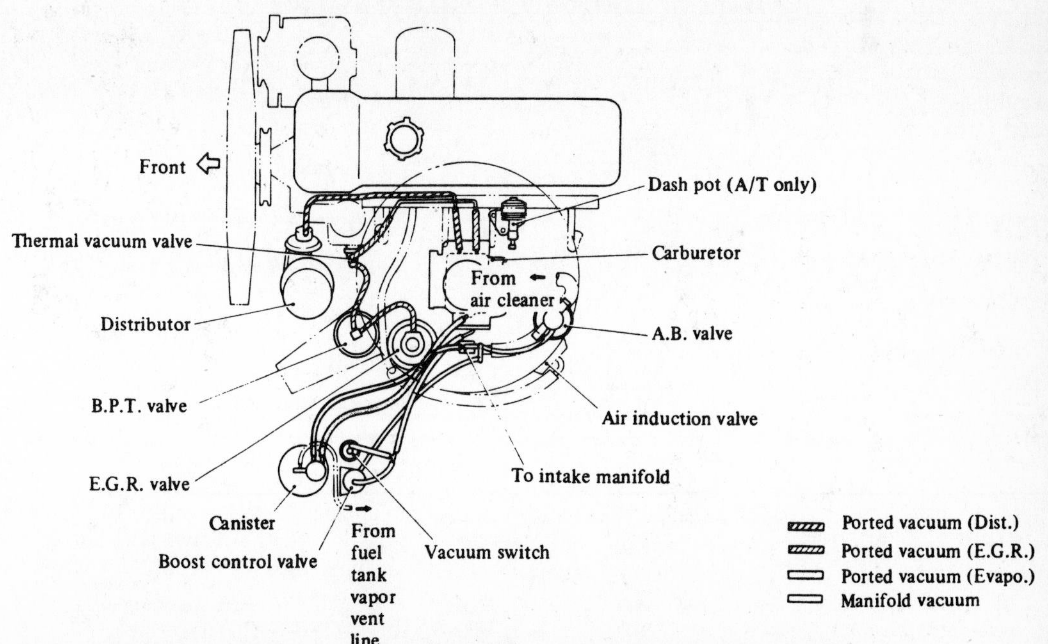

Emission control system vacuum diagram—1977–80 (49 State & Can. Cab/Chassis)

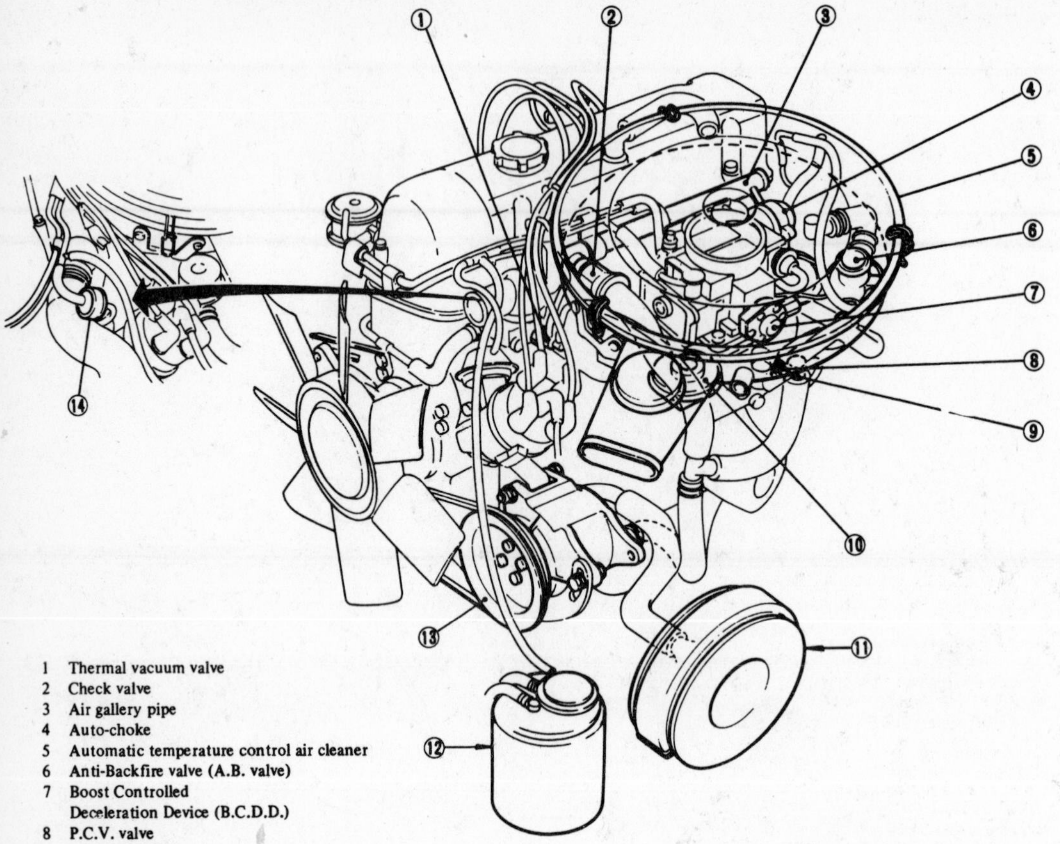

1 Thermal vacuum valve
2 Check valve
3 Air gallery pipe
4 Auto-choke
5 Automatic temperature control air cleaner
6 Anti-Backfire valve (A.B. valve)
7 Boost Controlled Deceleration Device (B.C.D.D.)
8 P.C.V. valve
9 Air relief valve
10 E.G.R. control valve
11 Air pump air cleaner
12 Carbon canister
13 Air pump
14 Spark delay valve (A/T models)

Emission control system—1975–77 (49 State & Canada)

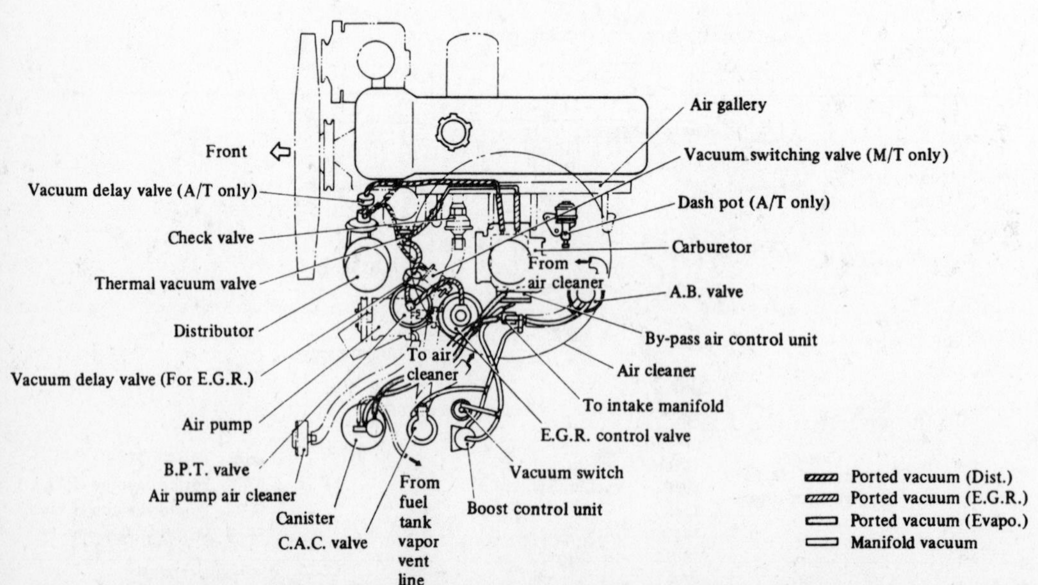

Emission control system vacuum diagram—1977–80 (Calif. exc. Heavy Duty)

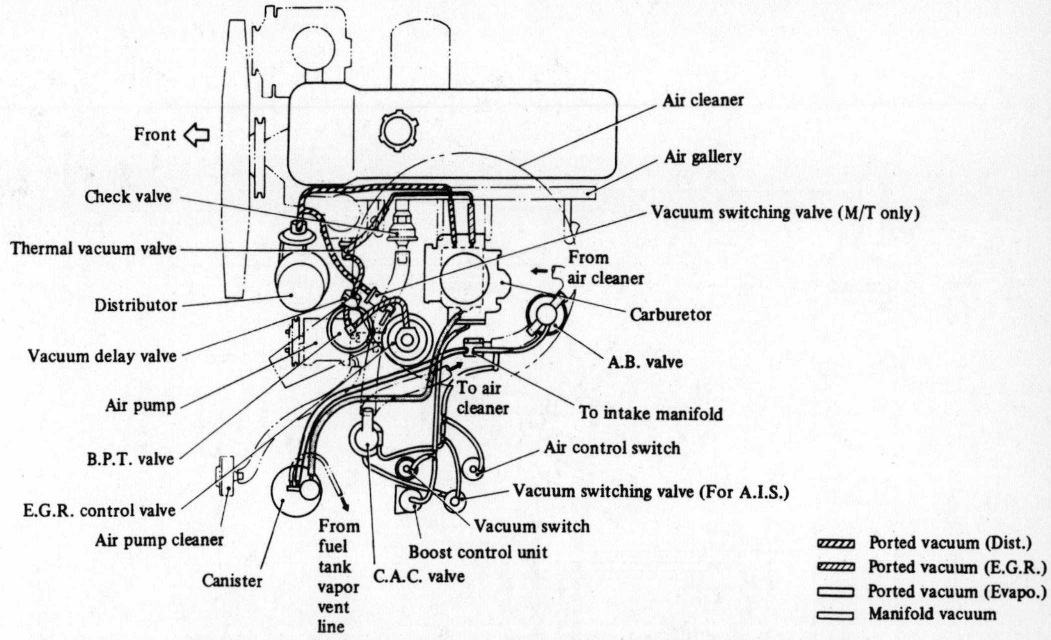

Emission control system vacuum diagram—1977–80 (Calif. Heavy Duty)

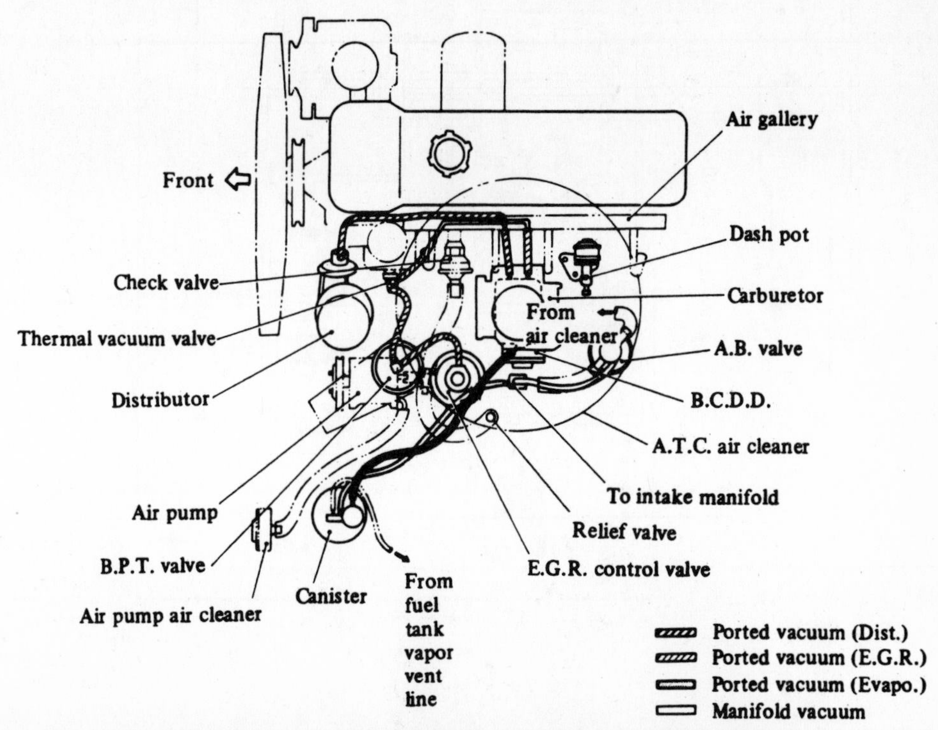

Emission control system vacuum diagram—1977–80 (Can. exc. Cab/Chassis)

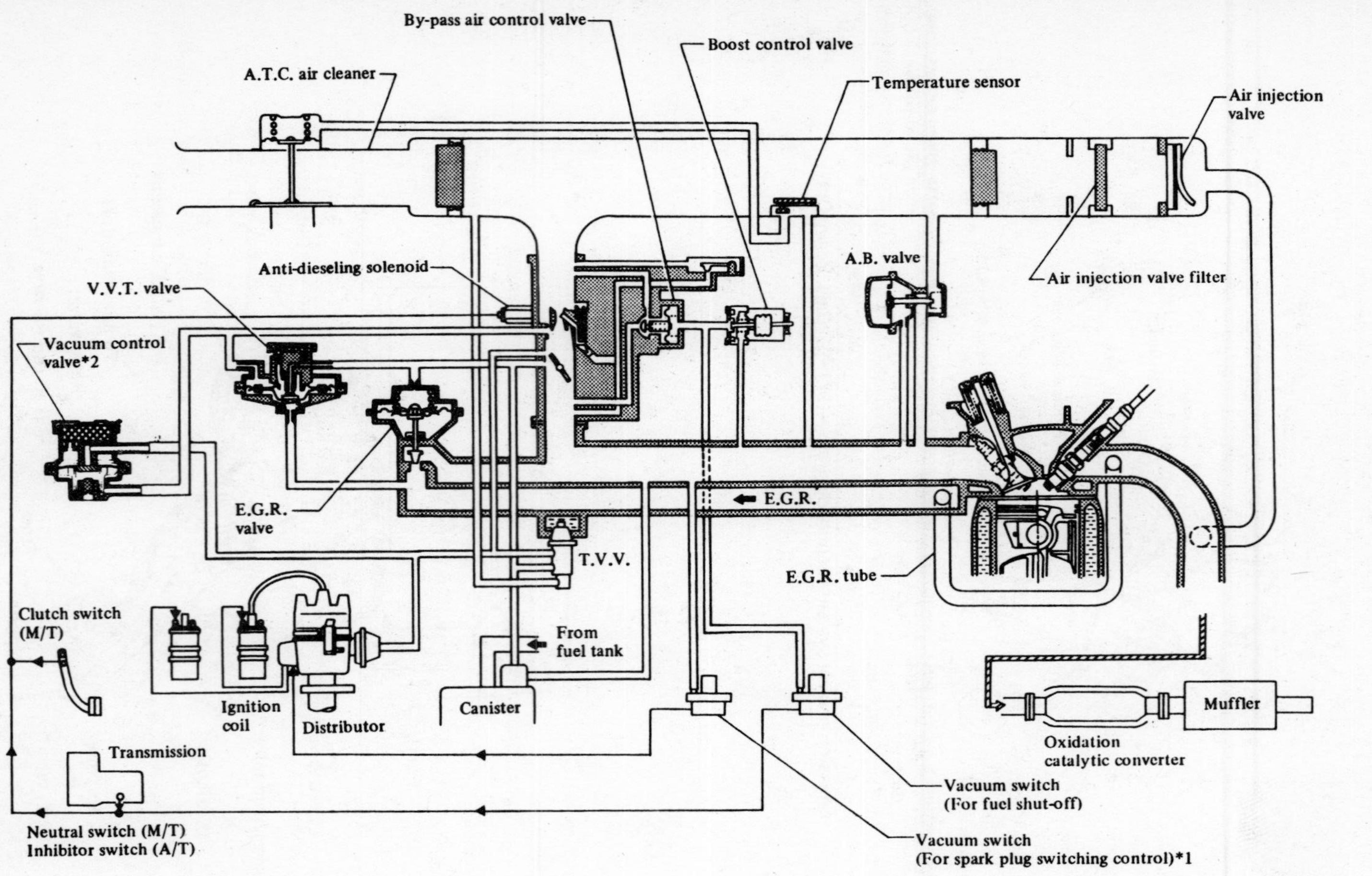

Emission control system—1981–83 (49 State & Canada)

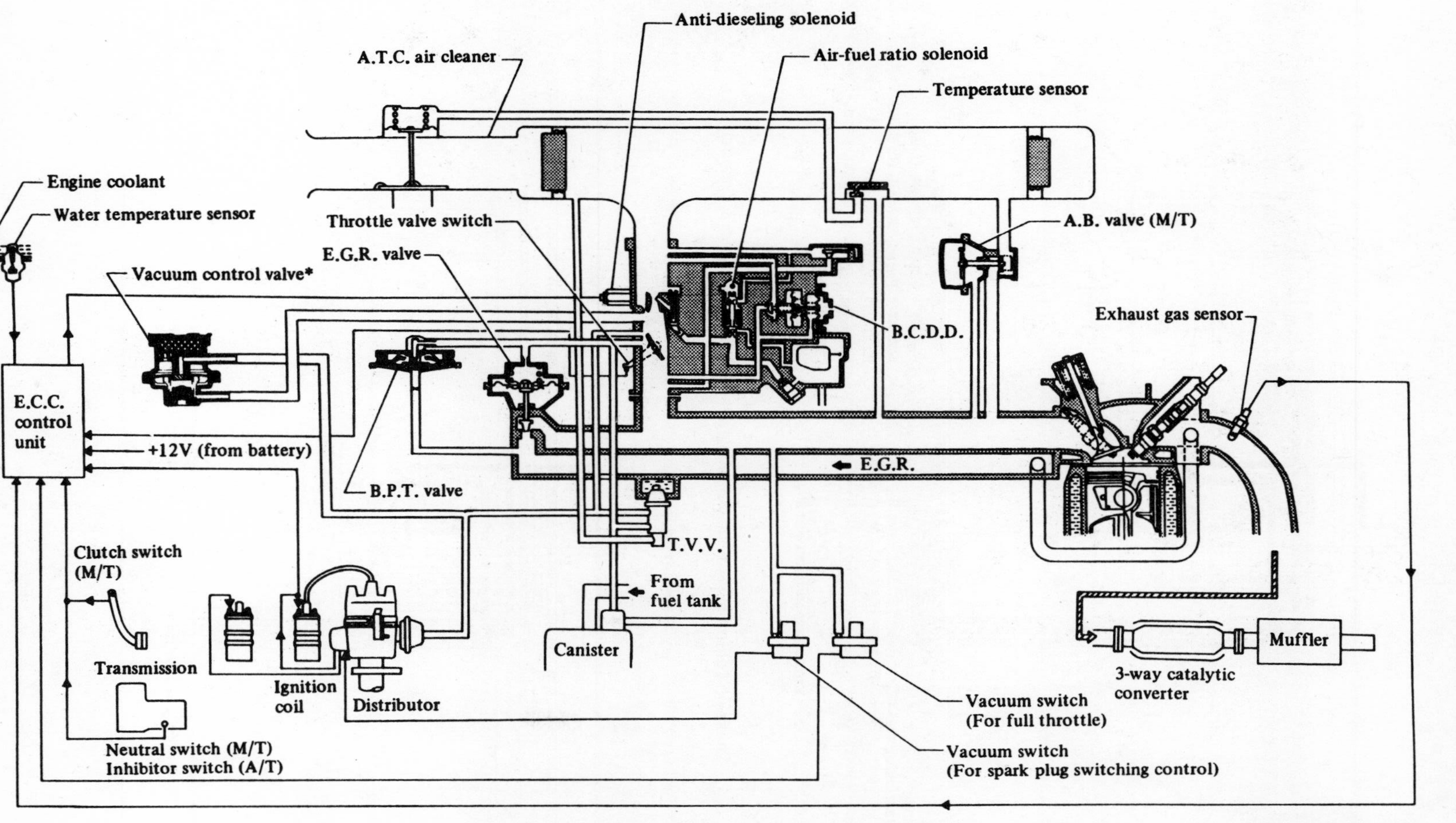

Emission control system—1981–83 (Calif.)

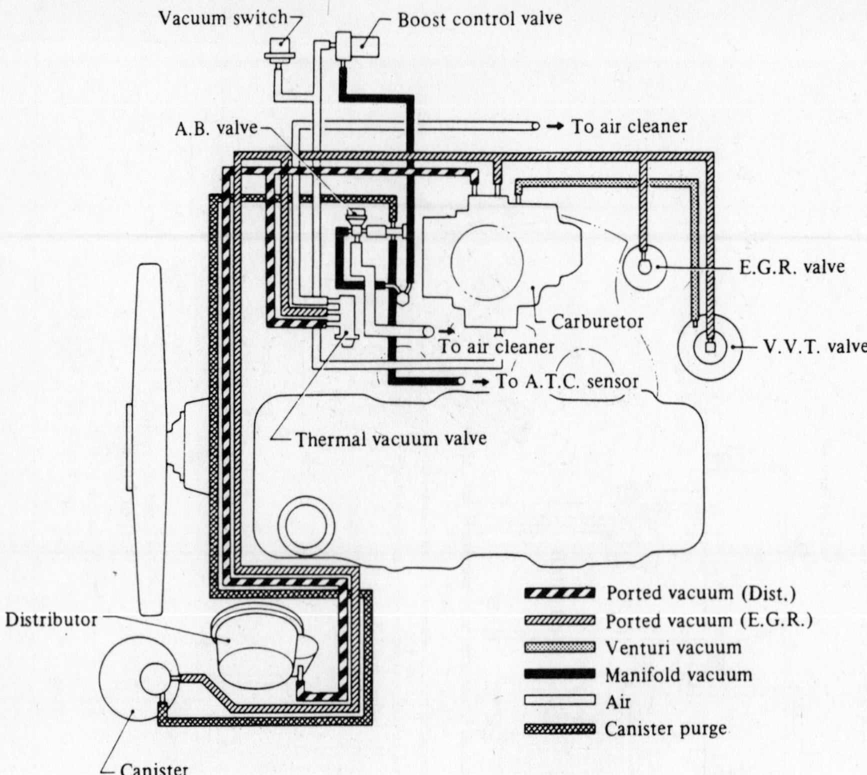

Emission control system vacuum diagram—1984 Z20 (49 State & Canada)

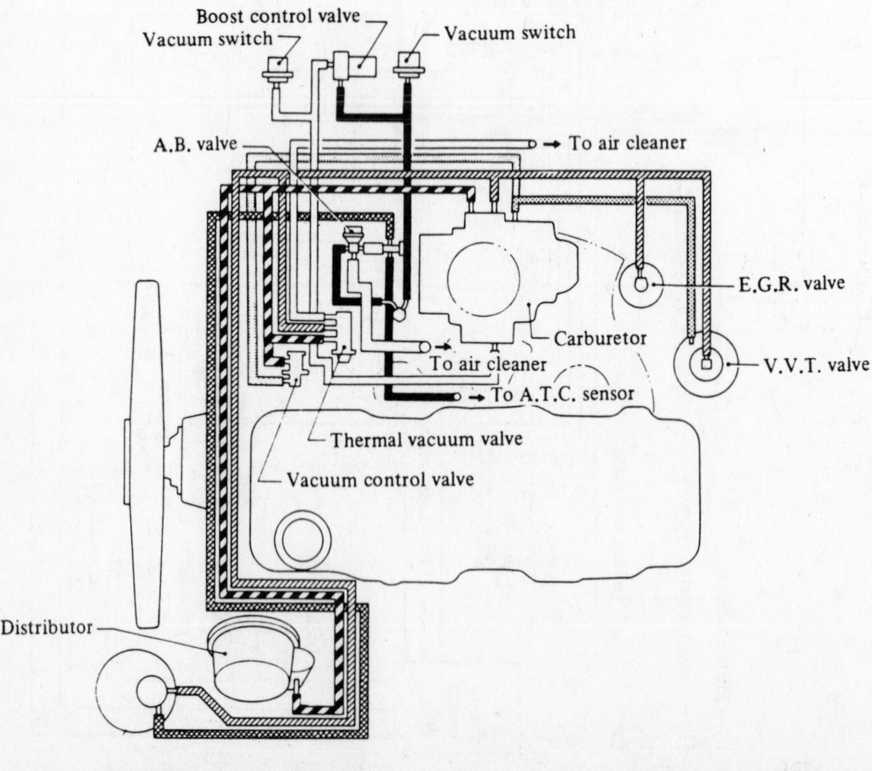

Emission control system vacuum diagram—1984 Z24 (49 State & Canada exc. High Alt.)

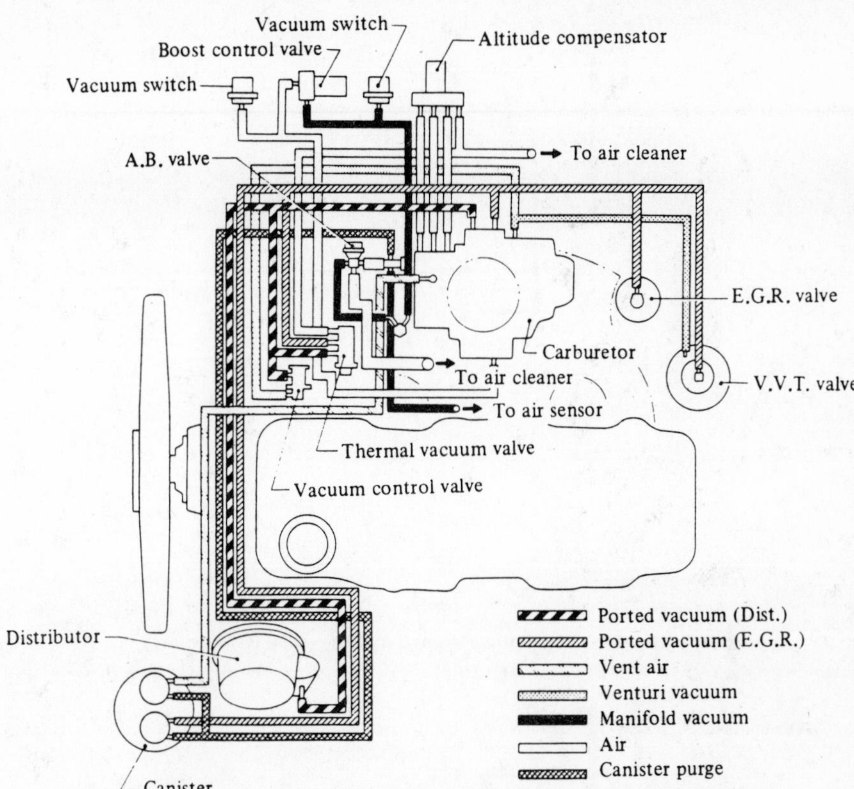

Emission control system vacuum diagram—1984 Z24 (49 State High Alt.)

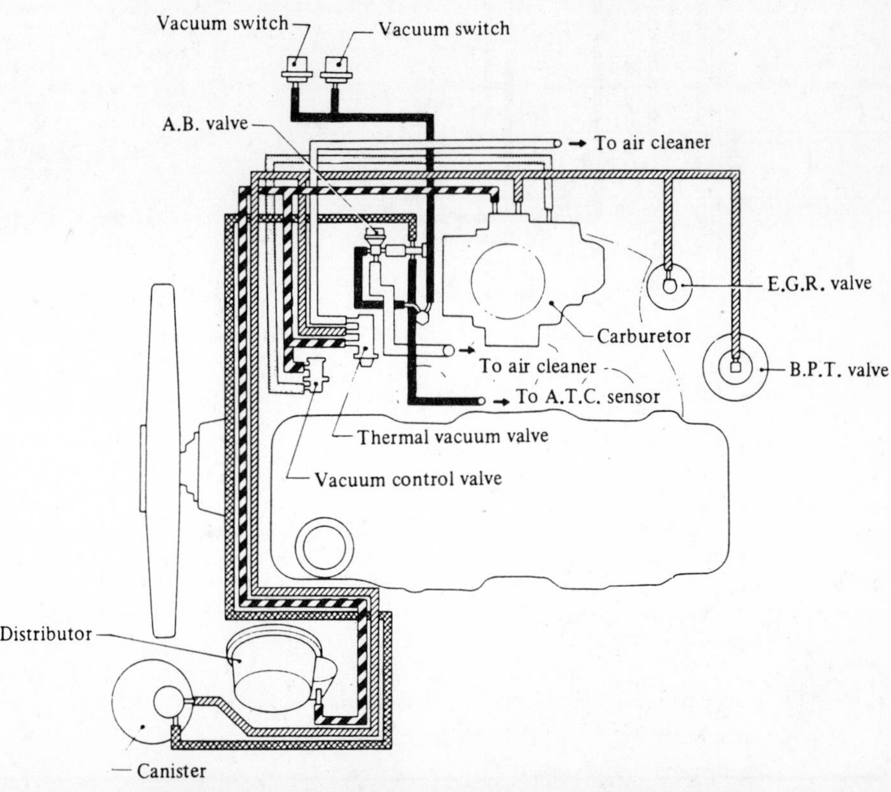

Emission control system vacuum diagram—1984 (Calif. w/MT)

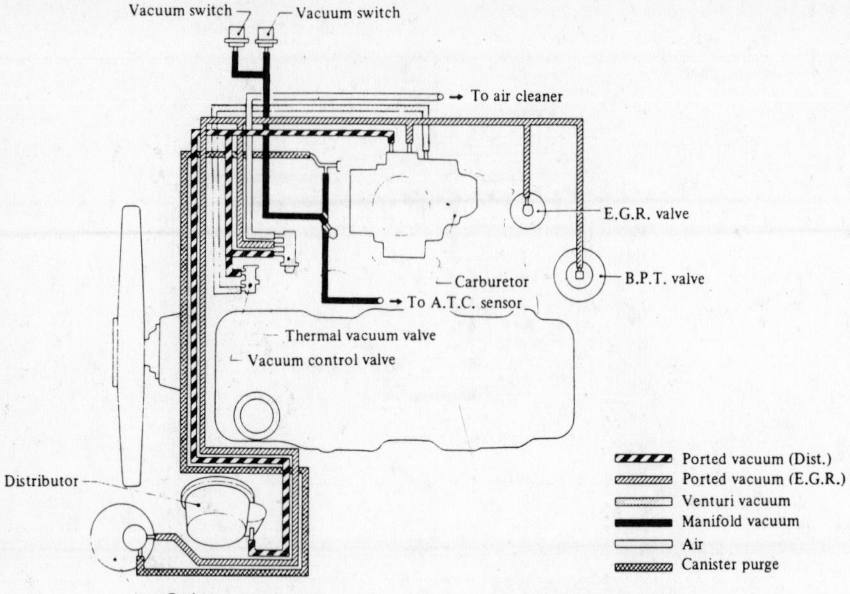

Vacuum switch
Vacuum switch
To air cleaner
E.G.R. valve
B.P.T. valve
Carburetor
To A.T.C. sensor
Thermal vacuum valve
Vacuum control valve
Distributor
Canister
Ported vacuum (Dist.)
Ported vacuum (E.G.R.)
Venturi vacuum
Manifold vacuum
Air
Canister purge

Emission control system vacuum diagram—1984 (Calif. w/MT)

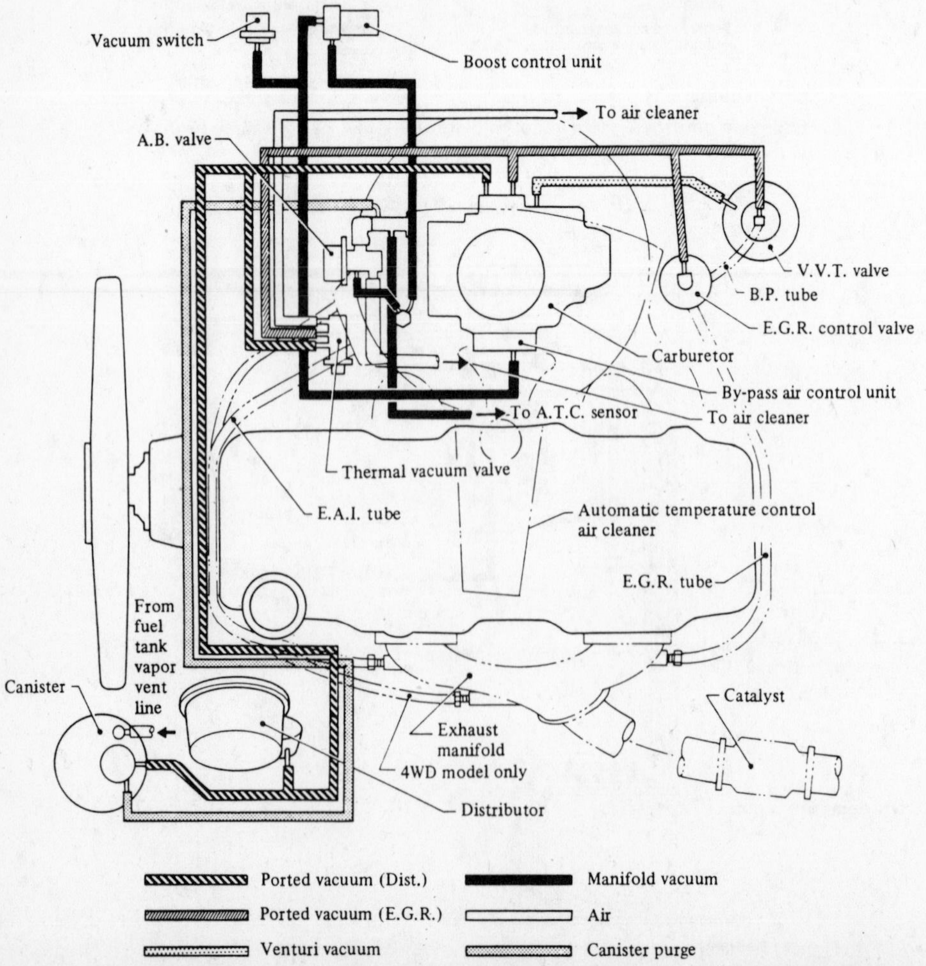

Vacuum switch
Boost control unit
To air cleaner
A.B. valve
V.V.T. valve
B.P. tube
E.G.R. control valve
Carburetor
By-pass air control unit
To A.T.C. sensor
To air cleaner
Thermal vacuum valve
E.A.I. tube
Automatic temperature control air cleaner
E.G.R. tube
From fuel tank vapor vent line
Canister
Catalyst
Exhaust manifold
4WD model only
Distributor
Ported vacuum (Dist.)
Ported vacuum (E.G.R.)
Venturi vacuum
Manifold vacuum
Air
Canister purge

Emission control system vacuum diagram—1981–83 Z22 (49 State & Canada exc. High Alt.)

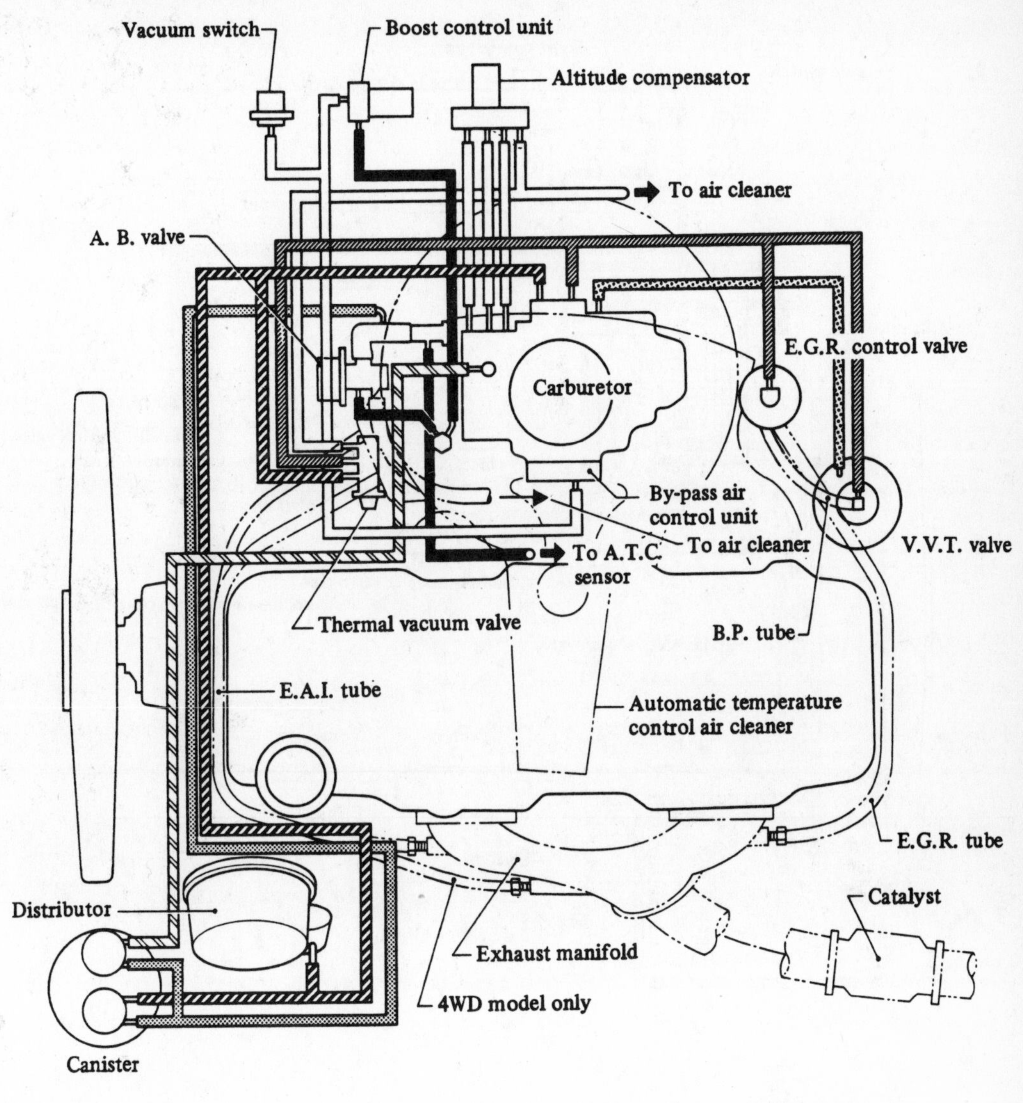

Emission control system vacuum diagram—1981–83 Z22 (49 State & Canada High Alt.)

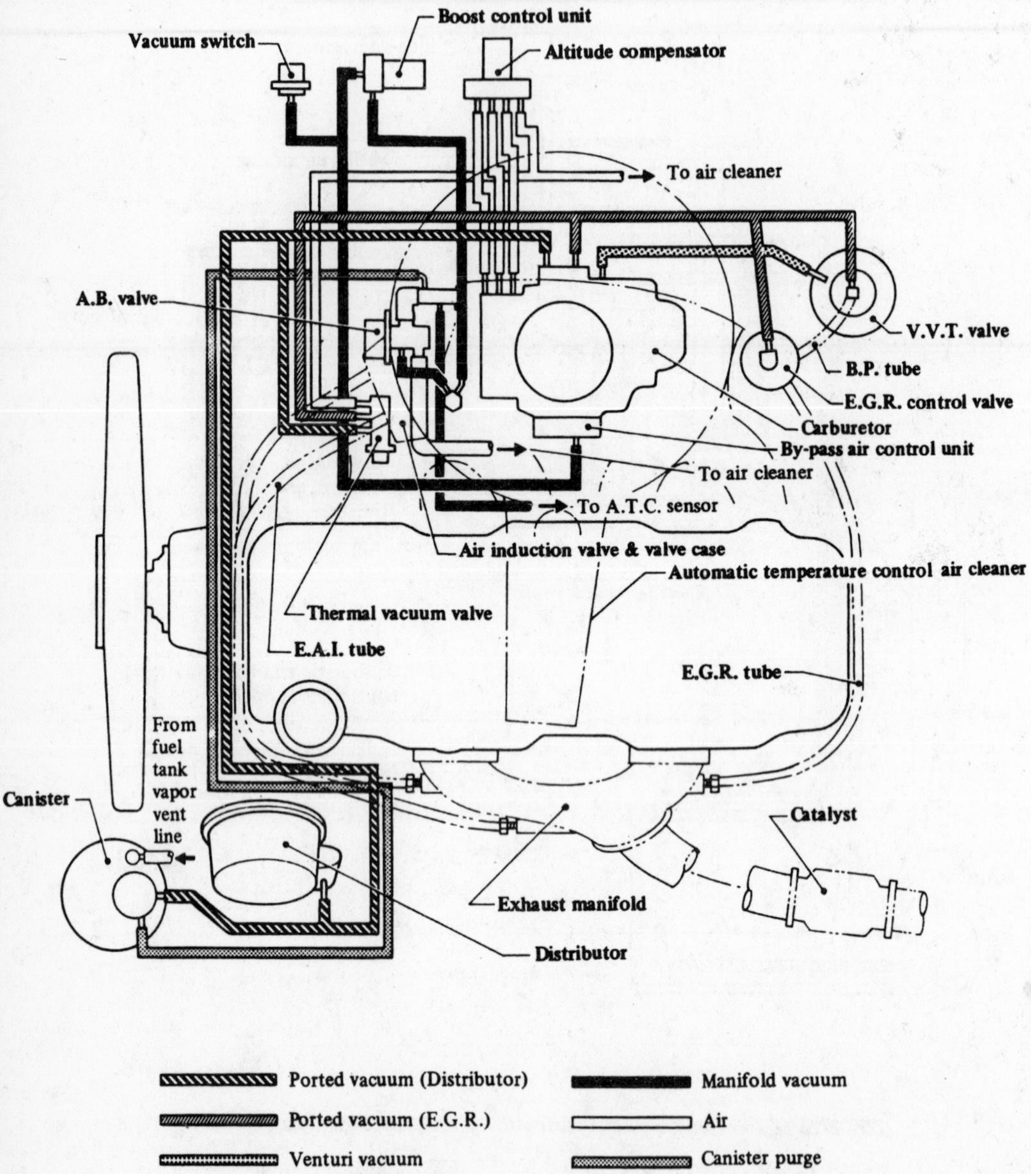

Boost control unit
Vacuum switch
Altitude compensator
To air cleaner
A.B. valve
V.V.T. valve
B.P. tube
E.G.R. control valve
Carburetor
By-pass air control unit
To air cleaner
To A.T.C. sensor
Air induction valve & valve case
Automatic temperature control air cleaner
Thermal vacuum valve
E.A.I. tube
E.G.R. tube
From fuel tank vapor vent line
Canister
Catalyst
Exhaust manifold
Distributor
Ported vacuum (Distributor)
Ported vacuum (E.G.R.)
Venturi vacuum
Manifold vacuum
Air
Canister purge

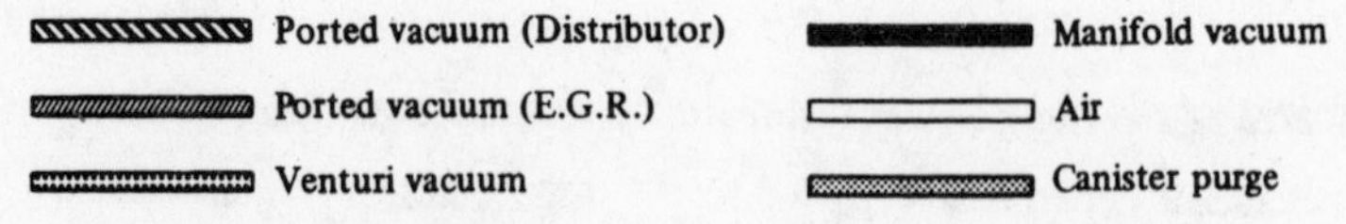

Emission control system vacuum diagram—1981–83 Z22 (Calif.)

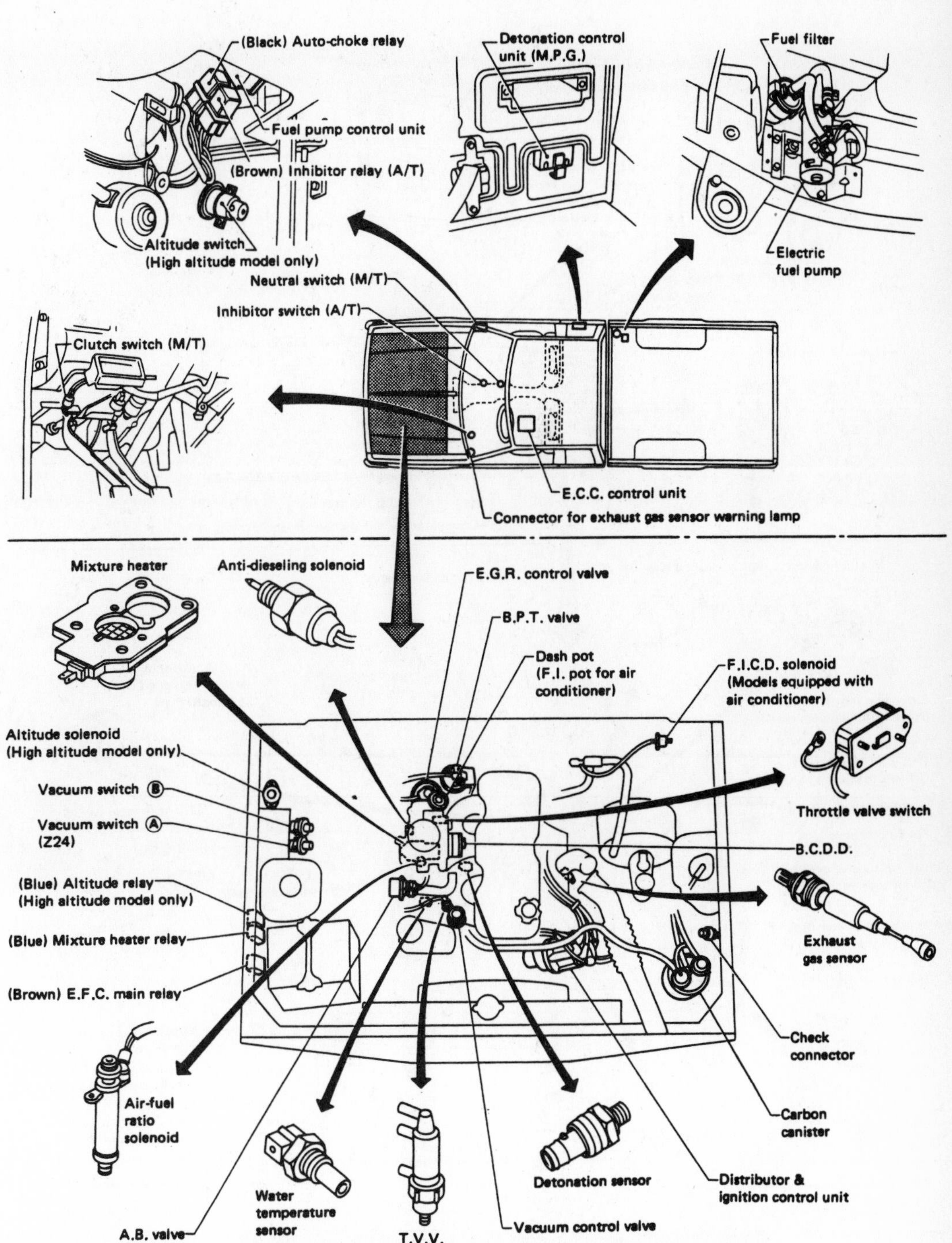

Emission control system components—1985 Z20 and Z24 (USA)

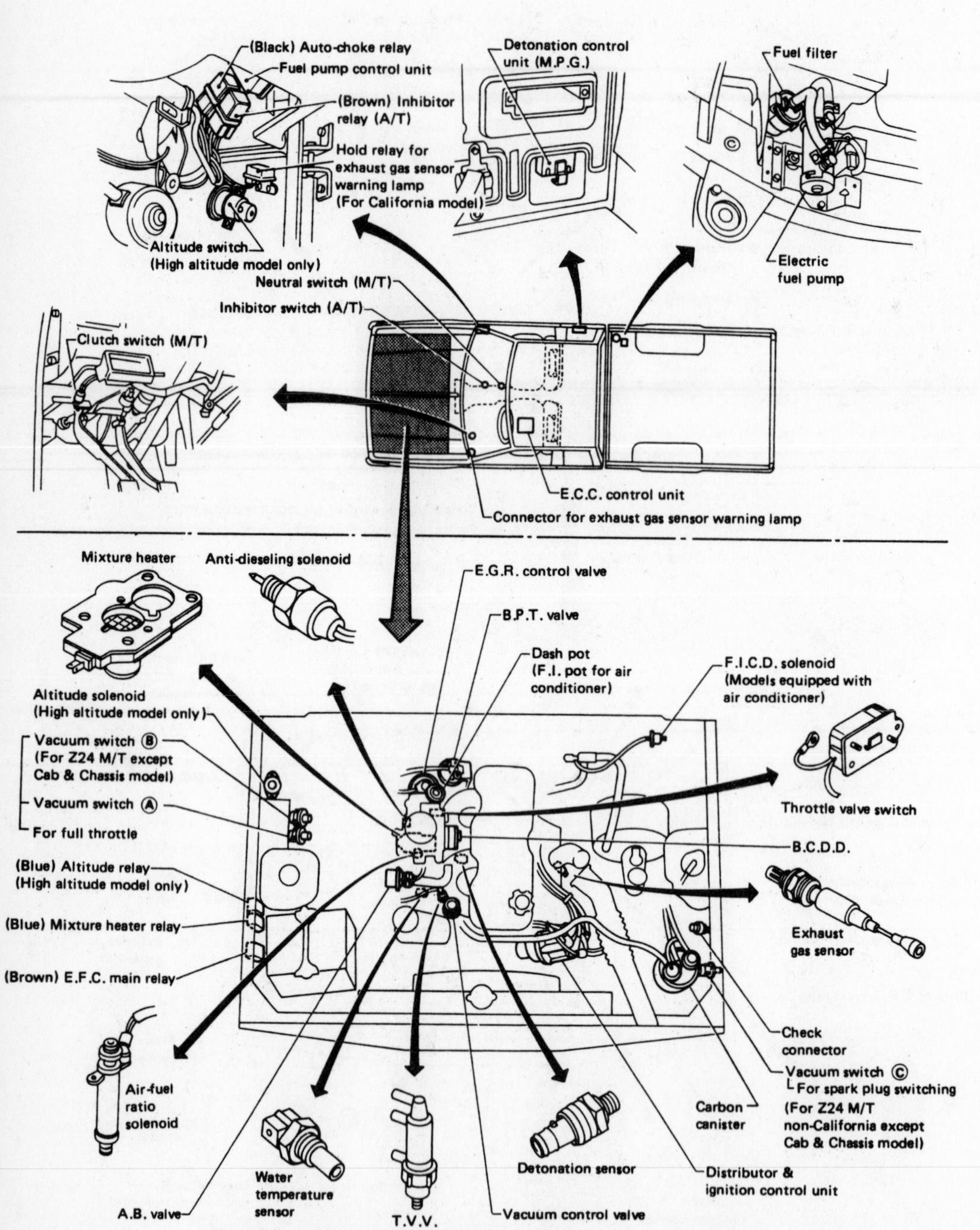

Emission control system components—1986 Z20 and Z24 (USA)

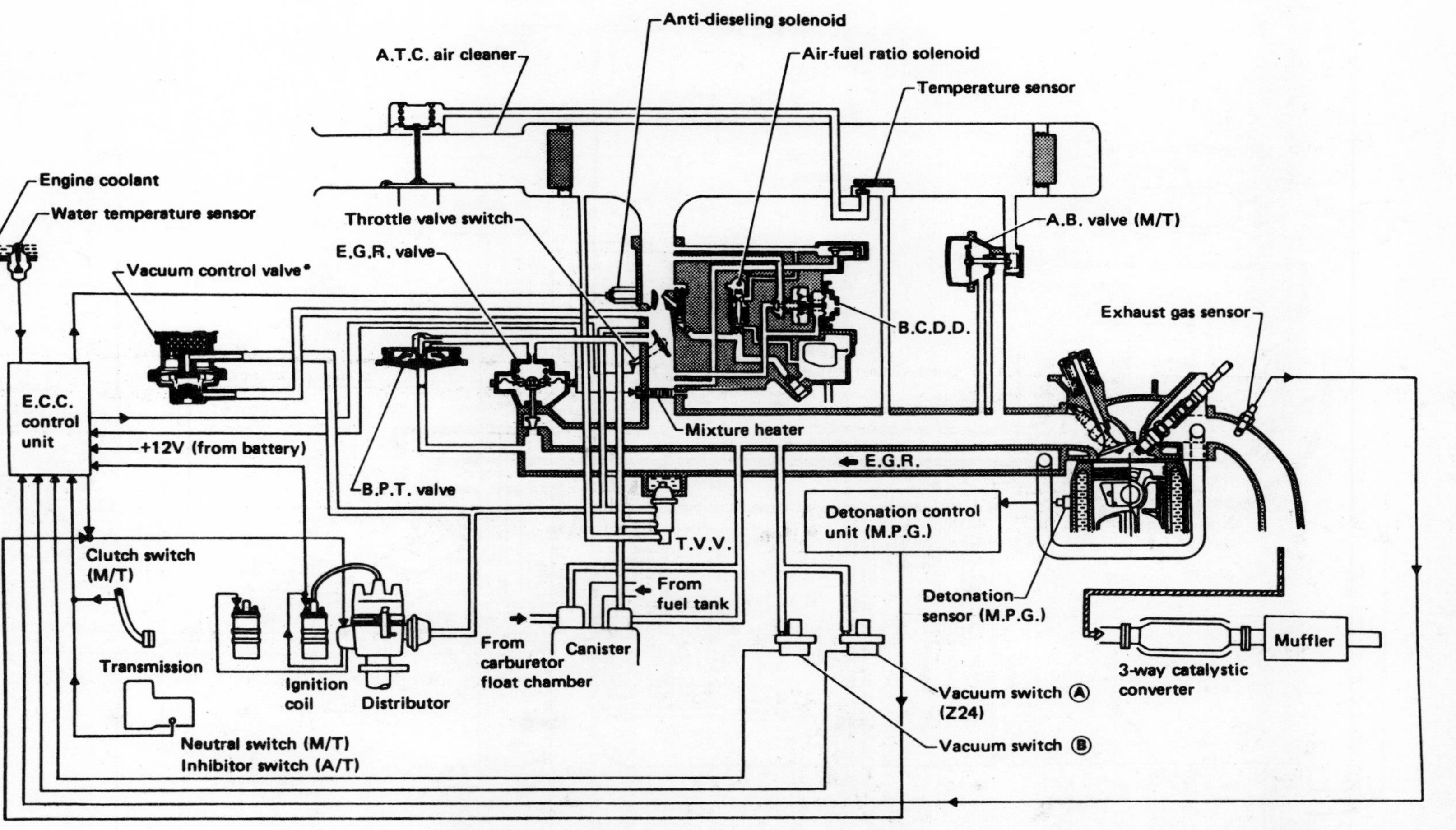

Emission control system—1985 Z20 and Z24 (USA)

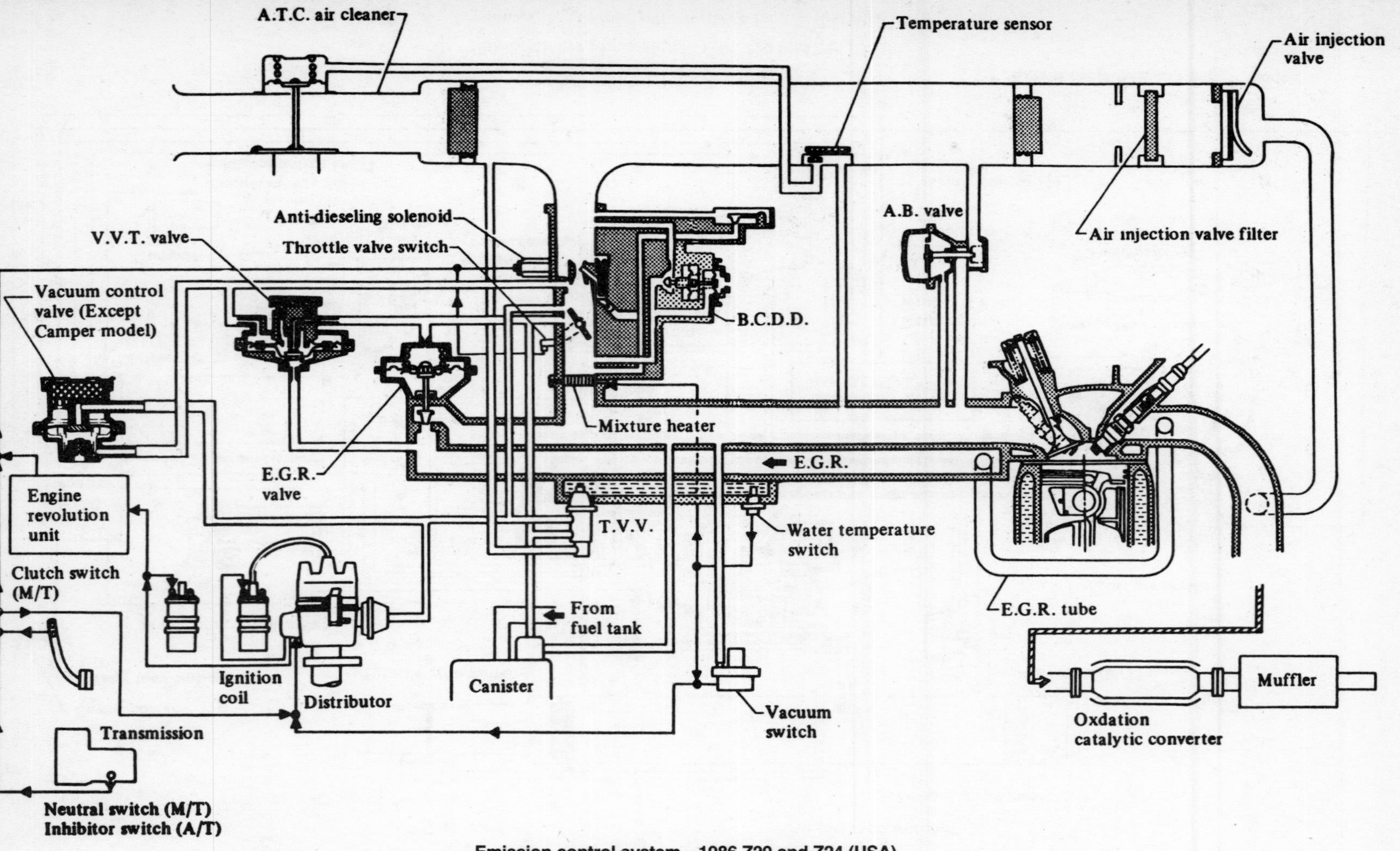

Emission control system—1986 Z20 and Z24 (USA)

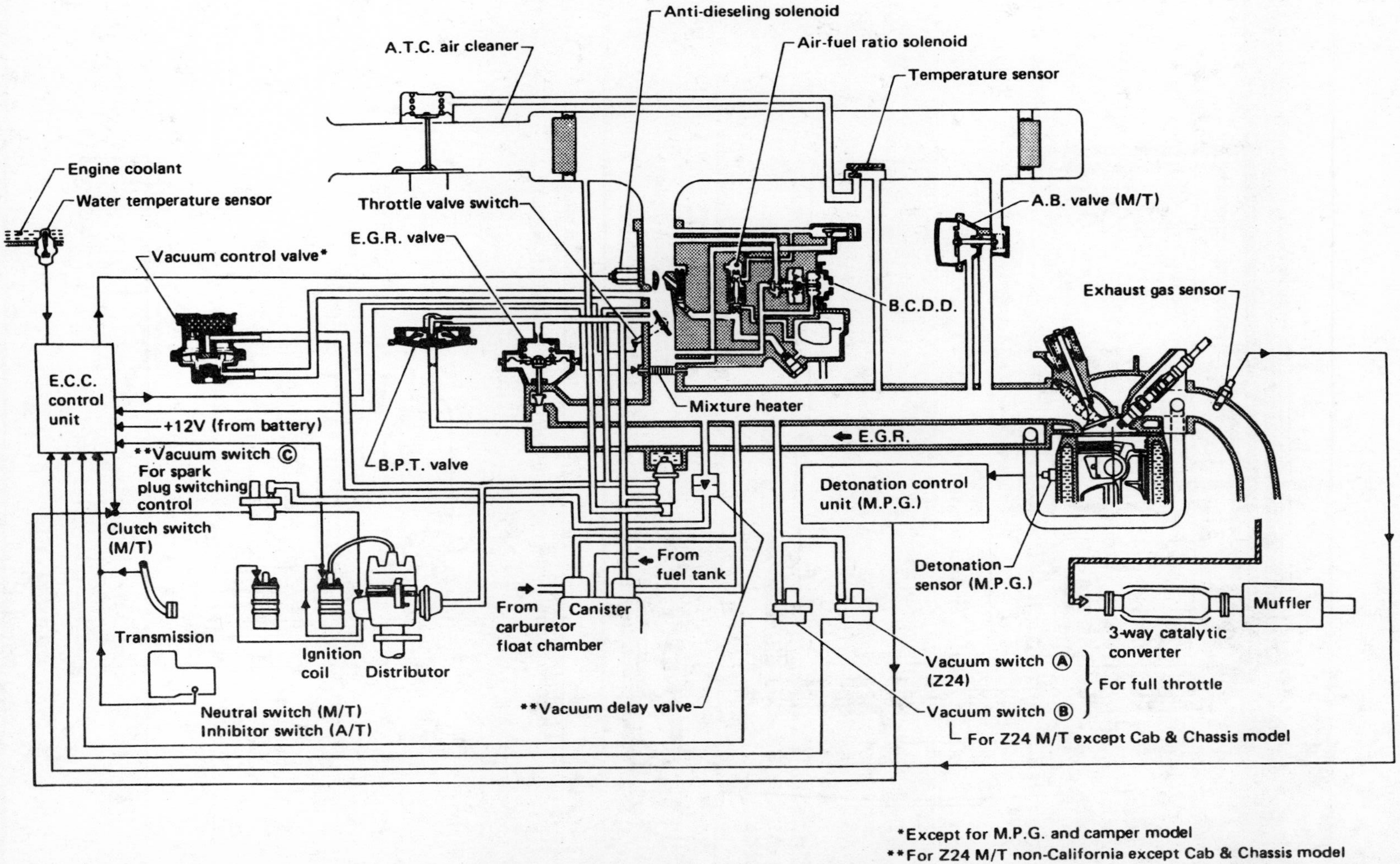

*Except for M.P.G. and camper model
**For Z24 M/T non-California except Cab & Chassis model

Emission control system—1985–86 Z24 (Canada)

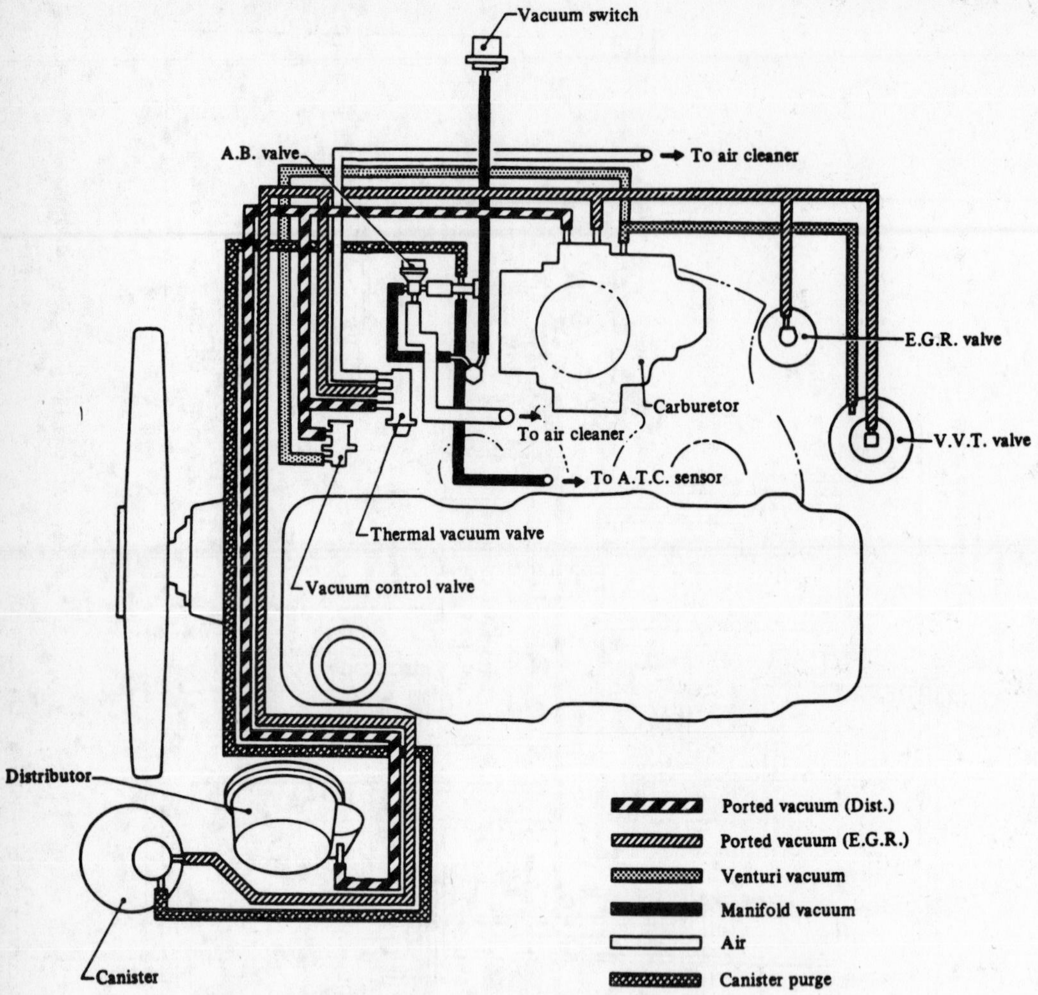

Vacuum switch
A.B. valve
To air cleaner
E.G.R. valve
Carburetor
To air cleaner
V.V.T. valve
To A.T.C. sensor
Thermal vacuum valve
Vacuum control valve
Distributor
Canister
Ported vacuum (Dist.)
Ported vacuum (E.G.R.)
Venturi vacuum
Manifold vacuum
Air
Canister purge

Emission control system vacuum diagram—1985–86 Z24 (Canada)

1 Seal type oil level gauge
2 Baffle plate
3 Filter
4 P.C.V. valve
5 Steel net
6 Baffle plate
Fresh air
Blow-by gas

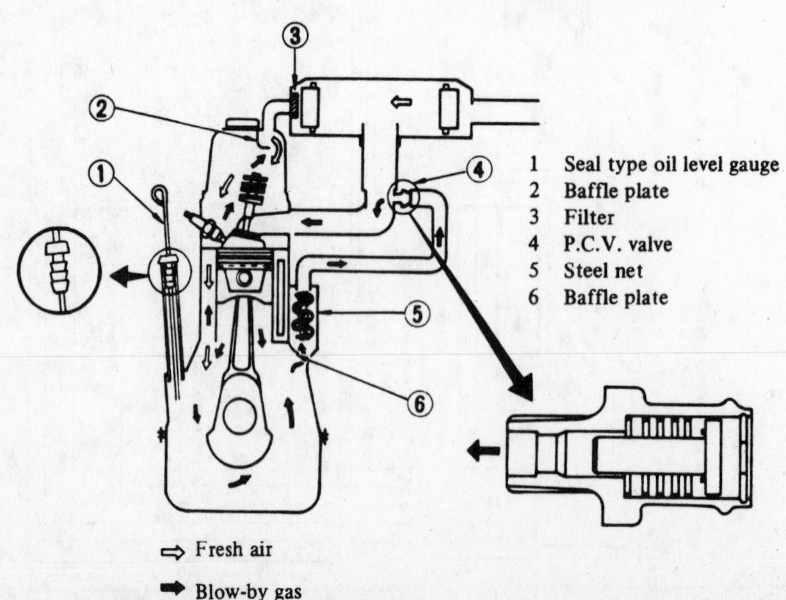

Positive crankcase ventilation system—1977–80 L20B engines

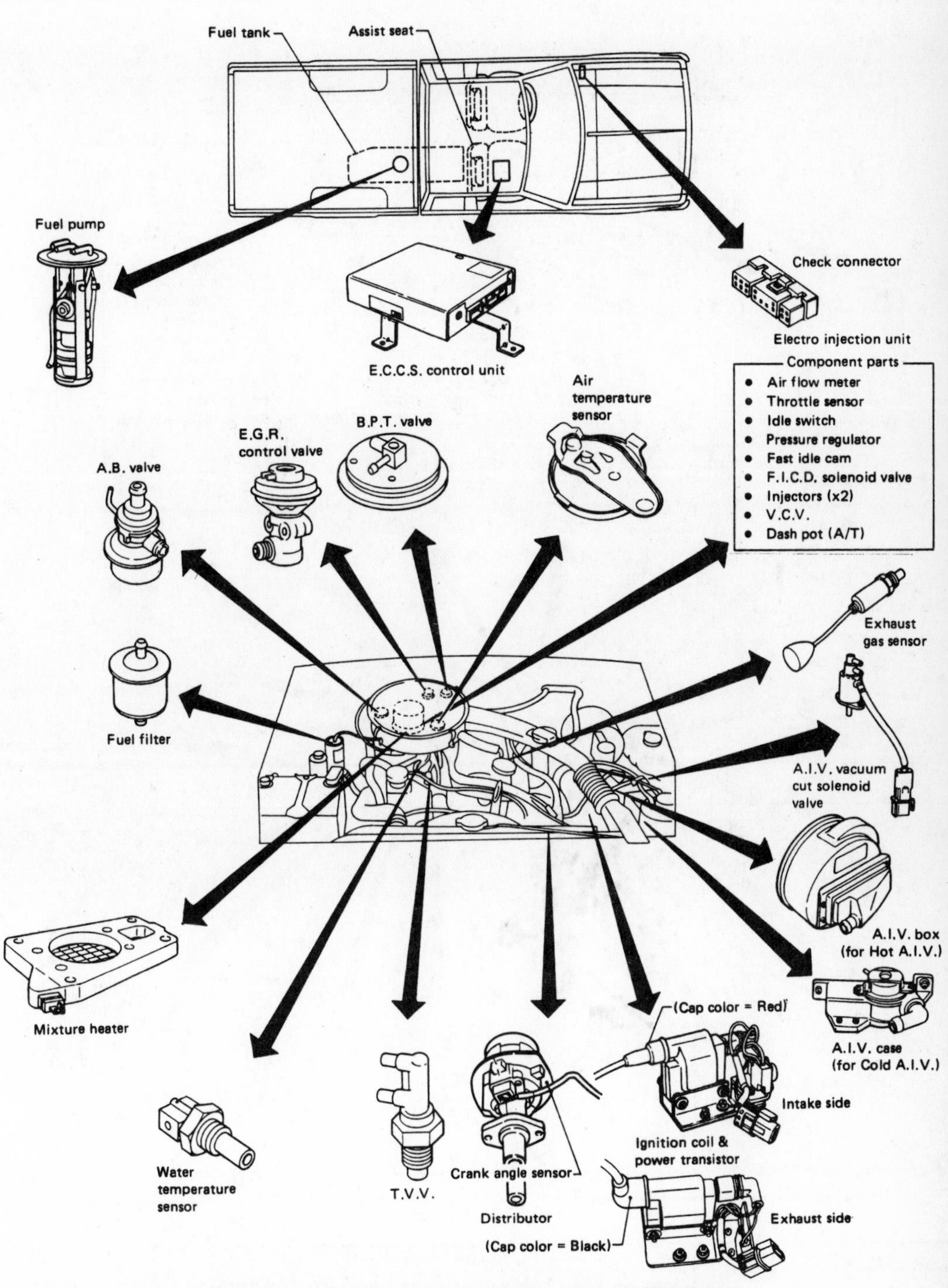

Emission control system components—1986–87 Z24i (USA)

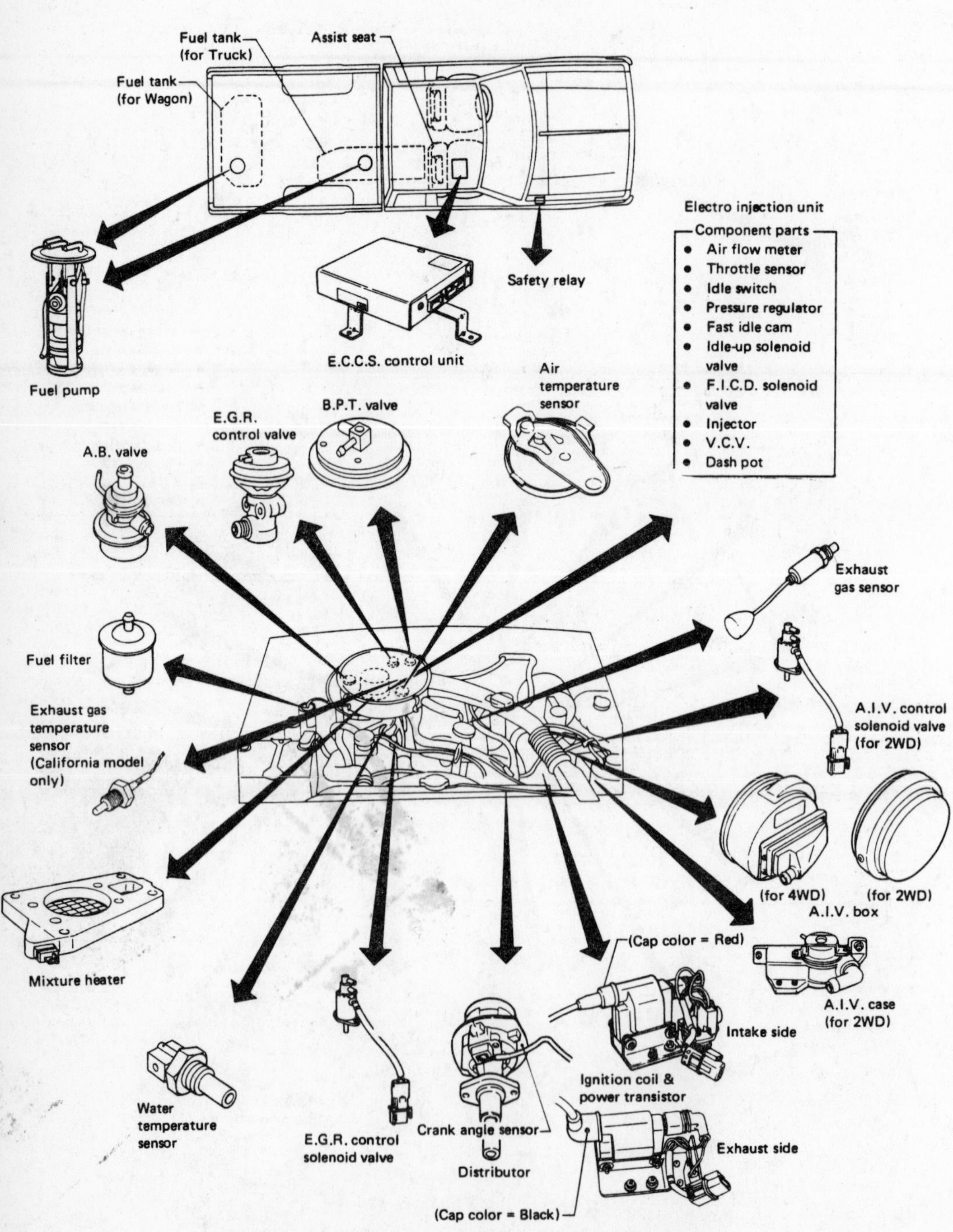

Emission control system components—1988–89 Z24i (USA)

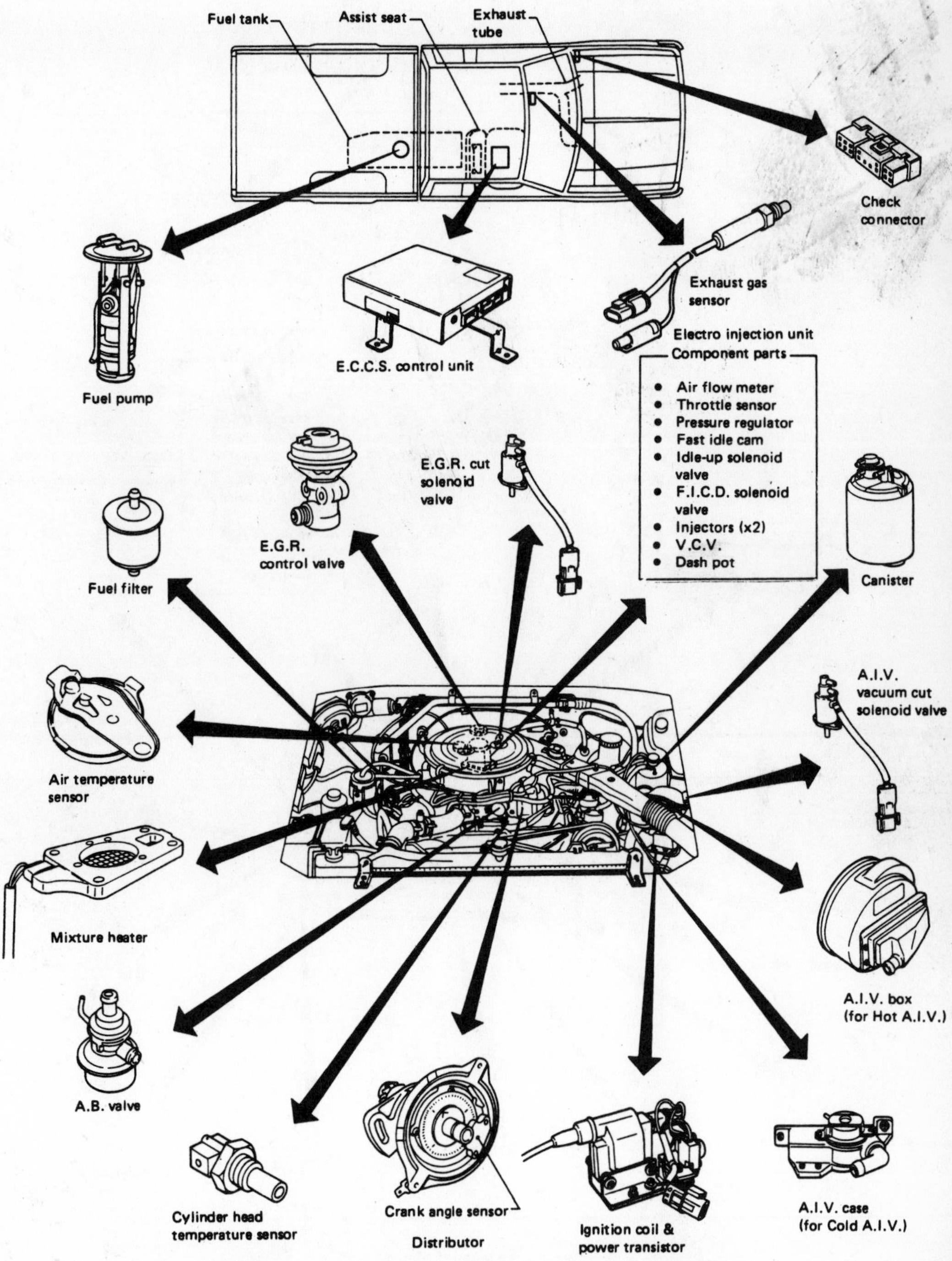

Fuel tank
Assist seat
Exhaust tube
Check connector
Fuel pump
E.C.C.S. control unit
Exhaust gas sensor

Electro injection unit
Component parts

- Air flow meter
- Throttle sensor
- Pressure regulator
- Fast idle cam
- Idle-up solenoid valve
- F.I.C.D. solenoid valve
- Injectors (x2)
- V.C.V.
- Dash pot

E.G.R. cut solenoid valve
E.G.R. control valve
Fuel filter
Canister
A.I.V. vacuum cut solenoid valve
Air temperature sensor
Mixture heater
A.I.V. box (for Hot A.I.V.)
A.B. valve
Cylinder head temperature sensor
Crank angle sensor
Distributor
Ignition coil & power transistor
A.I.V. case (for Cold A.I.V.)

Emission control system components—1986–87 VG30i (USA)

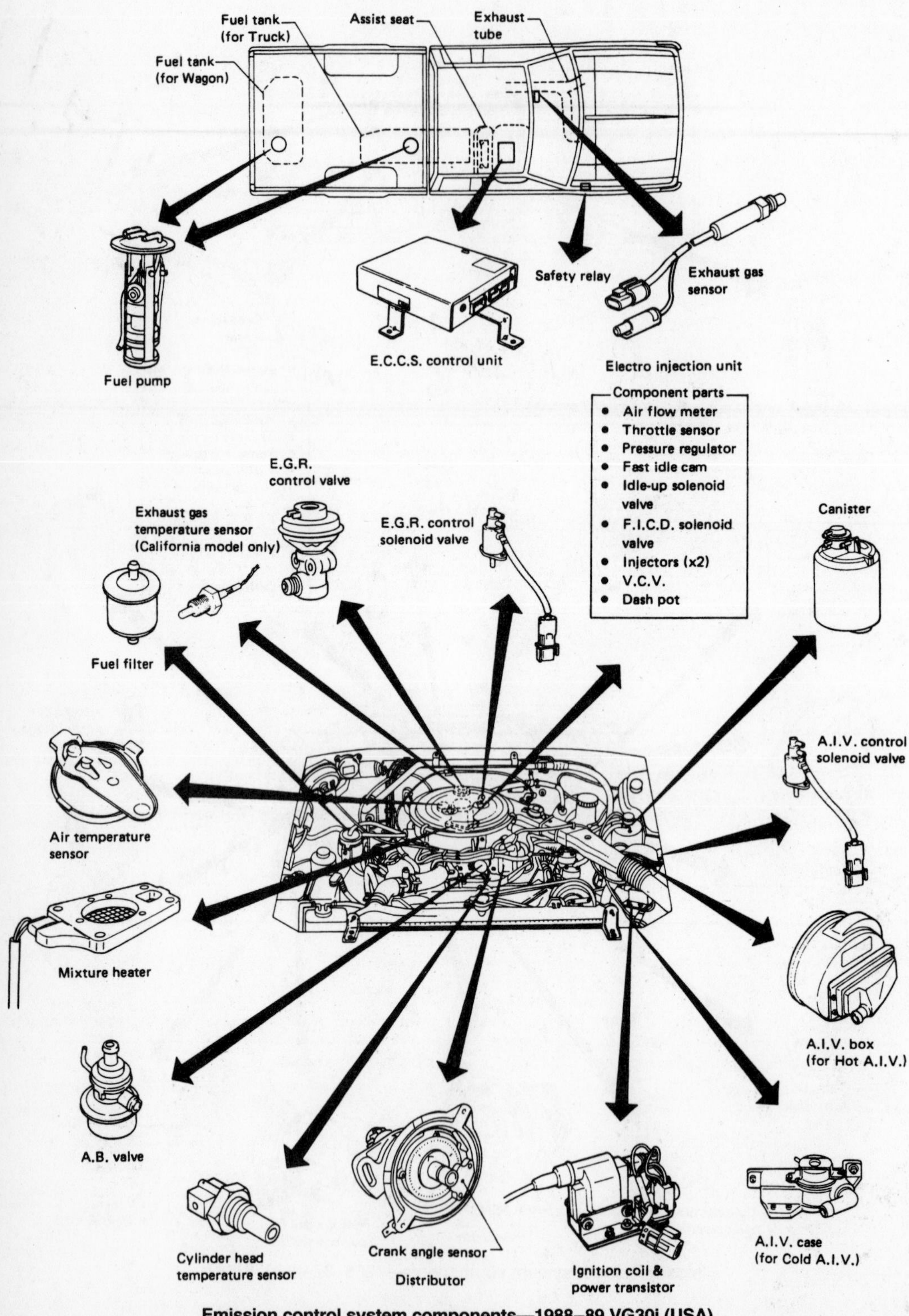

Emission control system components—1988–89 VG30i (USA)

case for an extended period of time, promoting the formation of sludge in the engine.

NOTE: *The PCV system will not function properly unless the oil filler cap is tightly sealed. Check the gasket on the cap and be certain it is not leaking. Replace the cap or gasket or both if necessary to ensure proper sealing.*

The above explanation and the troubleshooting procedure which follows applies to all engines with PCV systems.

TESTING

Check the PCV system hoses and connections, to see that there are no leaks. Then replace or tighten, as necessary.

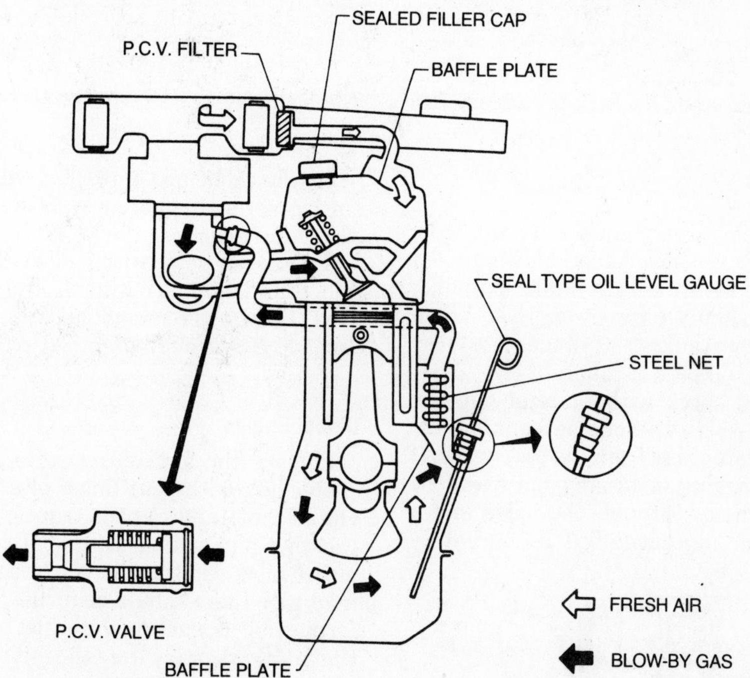

Positive crankcase ventilation system—1981–86 Z20, Z22 and Z24 engines

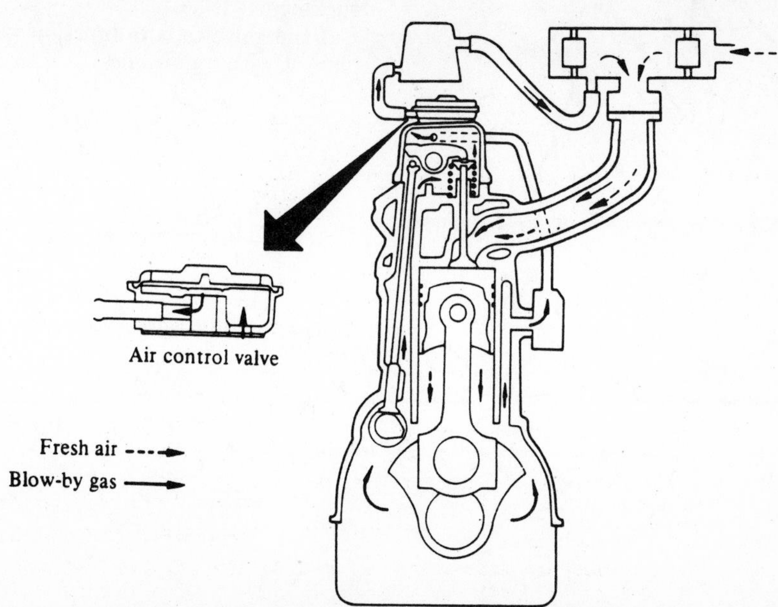

Positive crankcase ventilation system—SD25 engines

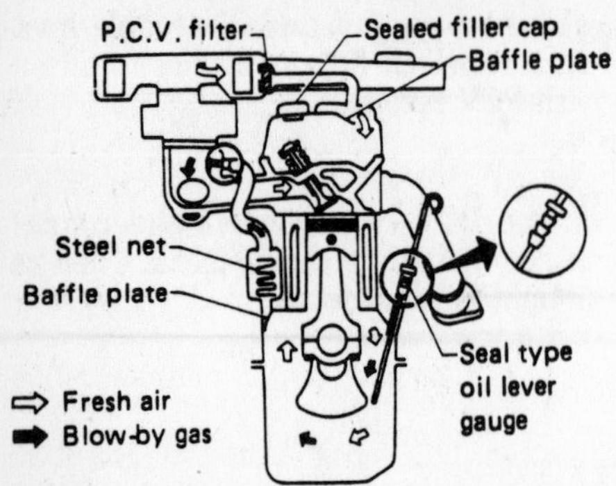

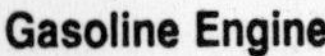

Positive crankcase ventilation system—1986–89 Z24i engines

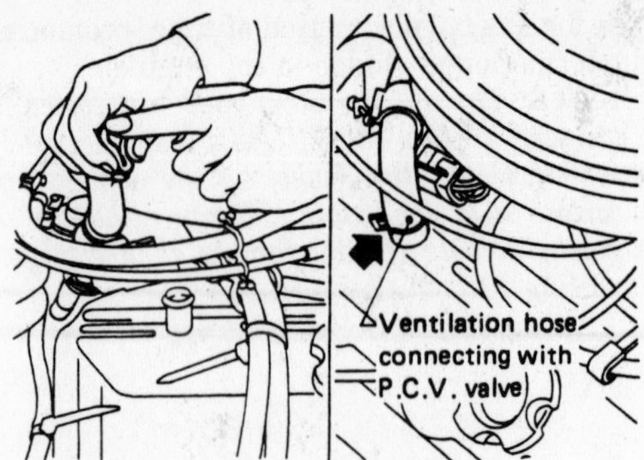

Testing the PCV valve—VG30i engines

Gasoline Engine

To check the valve, remove it and blow through both of its ends. When blowing from the side which goes toward the intake manifold, very little air should pass through it. When blowing from the crankcase (cylinder head cover) side, air should pass through freely.

An additional check without removing the valve could be—with the engine running, remove the ventilator hose from the PCV valve. If the valve is working, a hissing noise will be heard as air passes through the valve and a strong vacuum should be felt immediately when the valve inlet is blocked with a finger. If the valve is suspected of being plugged, it should be replaced.

Replace the valve with a new one if the valve fails to function as outlined.

NOTE: *Do not attempt to clean or adjust the valve. Replace it with a new one.*

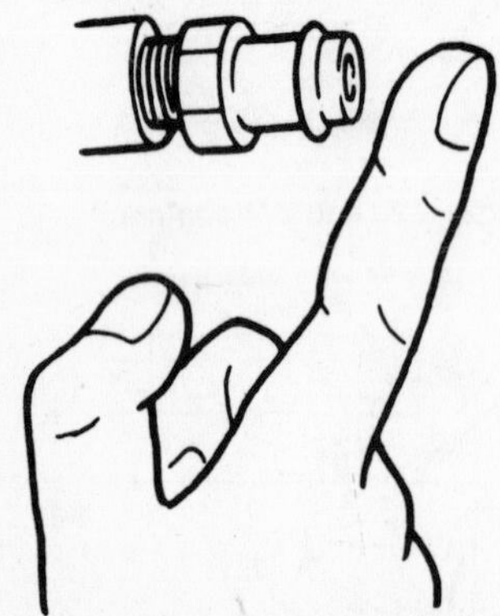

Testing the PCV valve—4 cylinder gasoline engines

Diesel Engine

Remove the air control valve and plug the center hole with your finger or a piece of tape. On 49 State and Canada trucks, blow air into the inlet pipe and check that it comes out the outlet pipe; additionally, when sucking on the inlet pipe there should be no air flow. On California models, suck on the outlet pipe and check that air flows freely from the inlt pipe; additionally, block the inlet pipe and then suck on the outlet pipe. You should be able to hear the diaphragm in the valve click open while you are sucking.

If the valve fails to function as detailed, replace it with a new one.

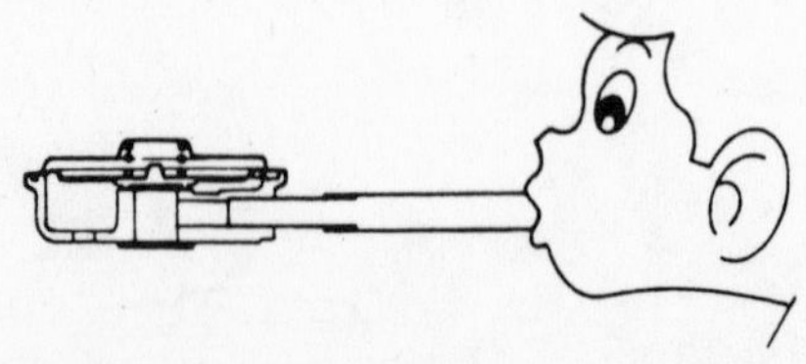

Testing the PCV valve—SD25 engines (49 state & Canada)

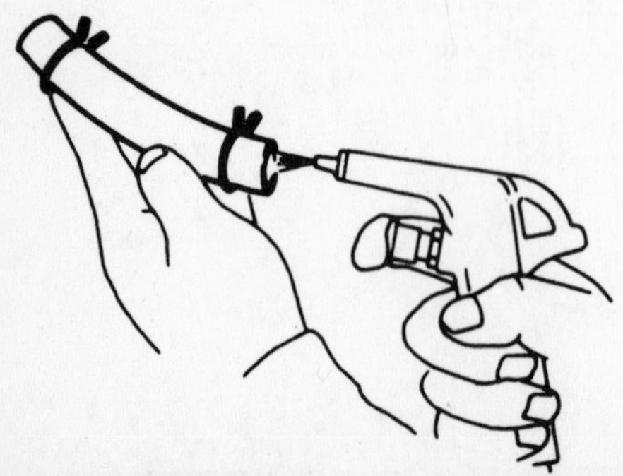

Clean out the PCV hose

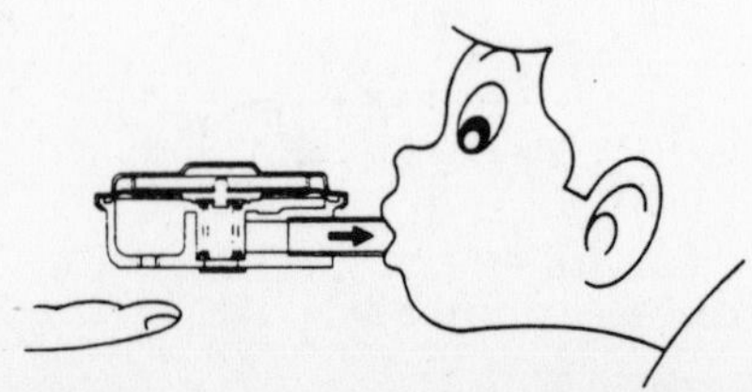

Testing the PCV valve—SD25 engines (Calif.)

REMOVAL AND INSTALLATION

Gasoline Engines

To remove the PCV valve, simply loosen the hose clamp and remove the valve from the manifold-to-crankcase hose and intake manifold; most valve pull right out, although some may require unscrewing. Install the PCV valve in the reverse order of removal.

Diesel Engines

Remove the cylinder head cover and press the air control valve out. To install it, simply press it in and replace the cylinder head cover.

Evaporative Emission Control System

When raw fuel evaporates, the vapors contain hydrocarbons. To prevent these fumes from escaping into the atmosphere, the fuel evaporative emission control system was developed.

There are two different evaporative emission control systems used on gasoline engined Datsun/Nissan trucks. The system used on 1970-1974 trucks consists of a sealed fuel tank, a vapor/liquid separator, a flow guide (check) valve, and all of the hoses connecting these components, in the above order, leading from the fuel tank to the PCV hose, which connects the crankcase to the PCV valve.

In operation, the vapor formed in the fuel tank passes through the vapor separator, into the flow guide valve and the crankcase. When the engine is not running, if the fuel vapor pressure in the vapor separator goes above 0.4 in. Hg, the flow guide valve opens and allows the vapor to enter the engine crankcase. Otherwise, the flow guide valve is closed to the vapor separator while the engine is not running. When the engine is running, and a vacuum is developed in

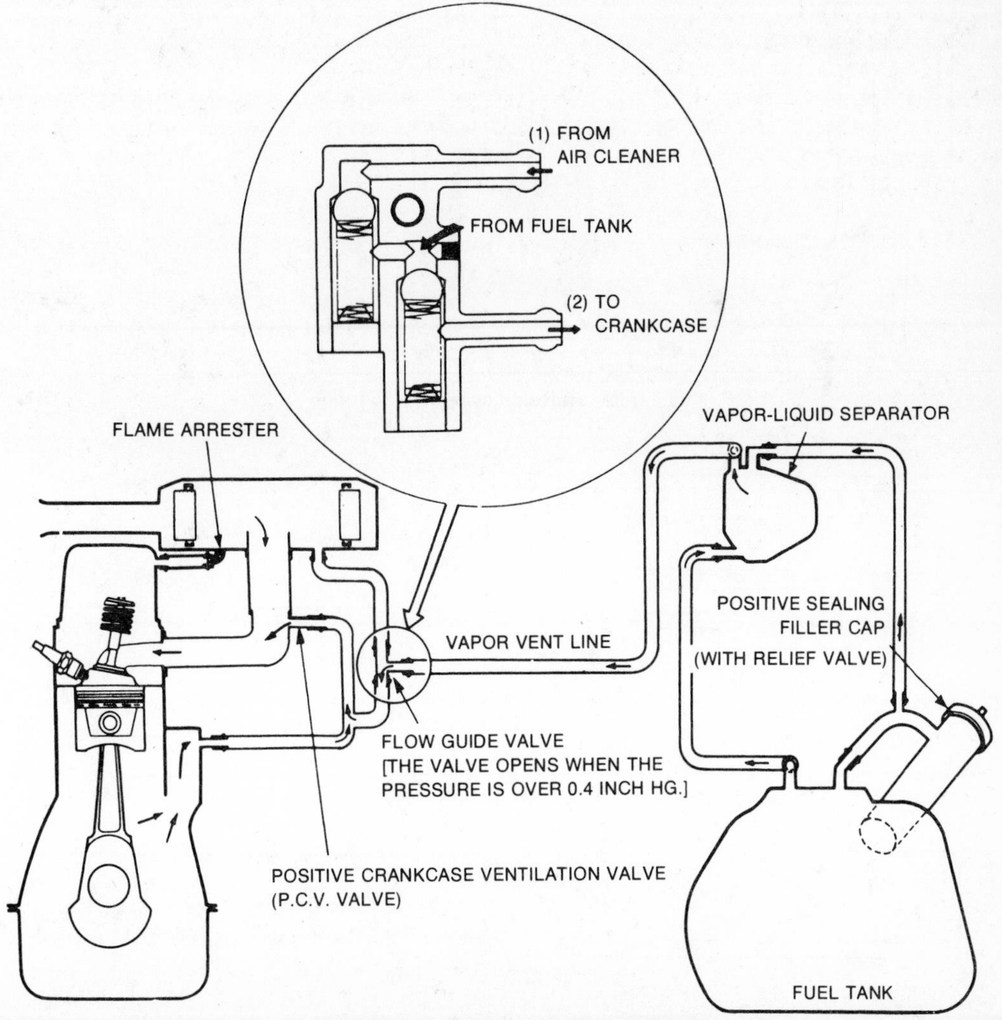

Evaporative emission system—1970–74

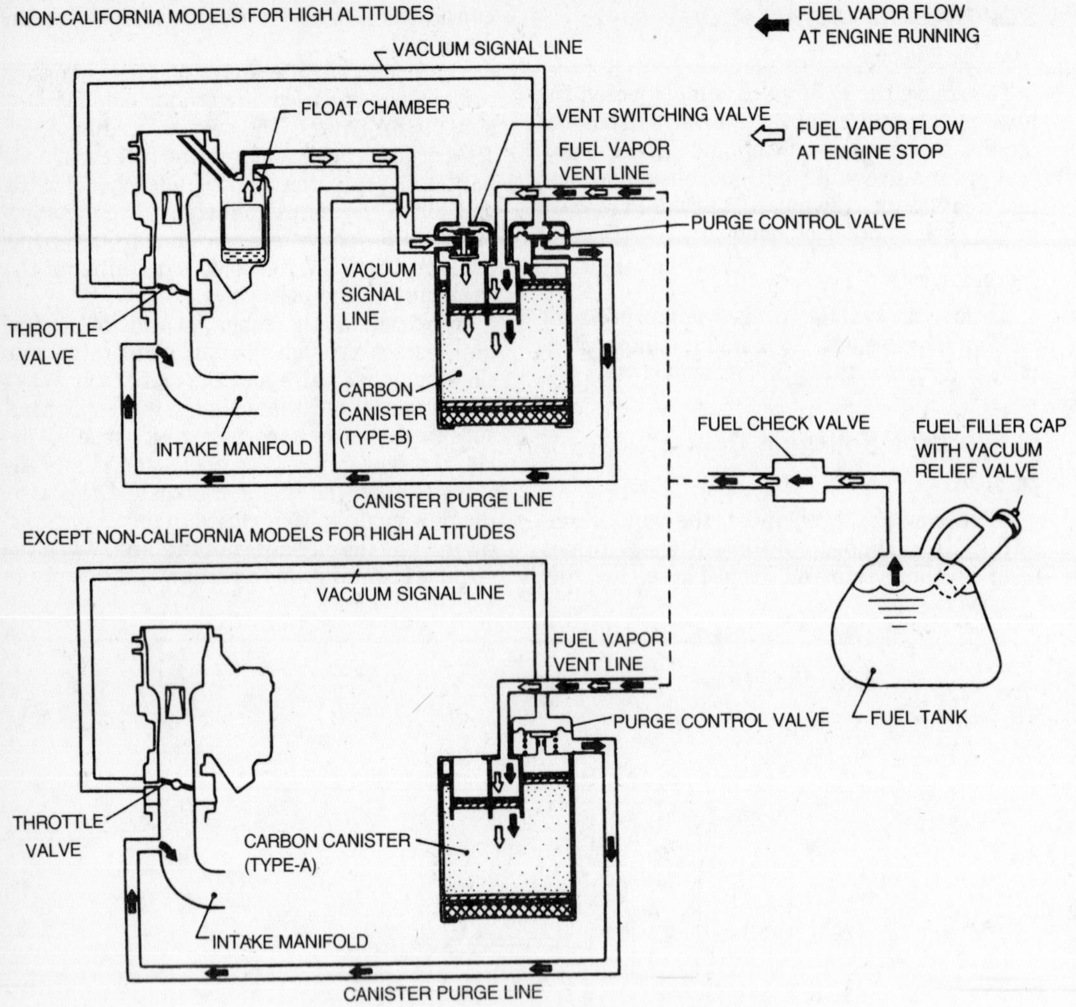

NON-CALIFORNIA MODELS FOR HIGH ALTITUDES
FUEL VAPOR FLOW AT ENGINE RUNNING
VACUUM SIGNAL LINE
FLOAT CHAMBER
VENT SWITCHING VALVE
FUEL VAPOR FLOW AT ENGINE STOP
FUEL VAPOR VENT LINE
PURGE CONTROL VALVE
VACUUM SIGNAL LINE
THROTTLE VALVE
CARBON CANISTER (TYPE-B)
INTAKE MANIFOLD
FUEL CHECK VALVE
FUEL FILLER CAP WITH VACUUM RELIEF VALVE
CANISTER PURGE LINE
EXCEPT NON-CALIFORNIA MODELS FOR HIGH ALTITUDES
VACUUM SIGNAL LINE
FUEL VAPOR VENT LINE
PURGE CONTROL VALVE
FUEL TANK
THROTTLE VALVE
CARBON CANISTER (TYPE-A)
INTAKE MANIFOLD
CANISTER PURGE LINE

Evaporative emission system—1981–84

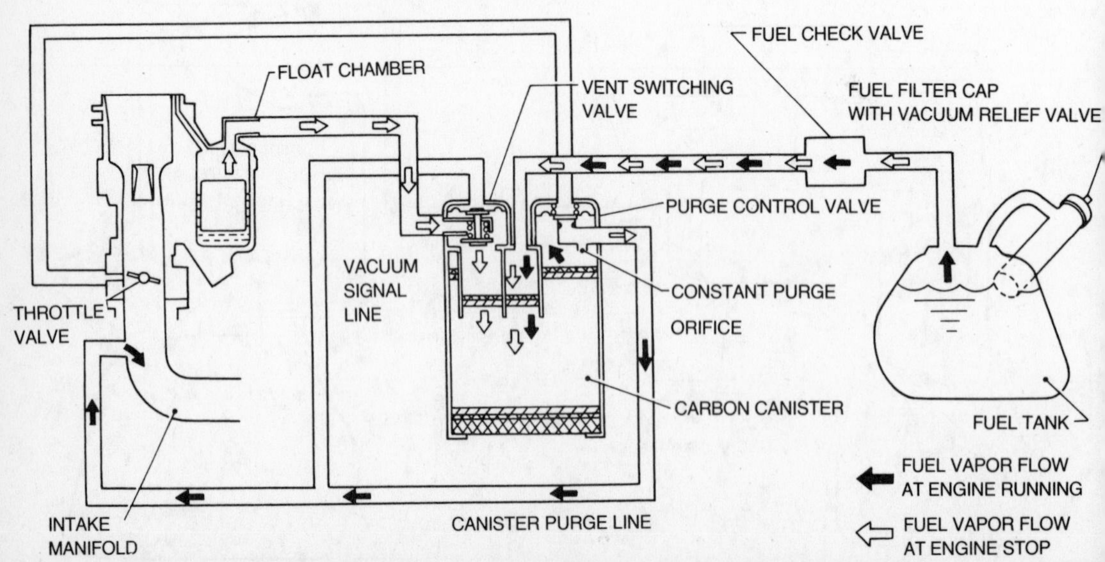

FUEL CHECK VALVE
FLOAT CHAMBER
VENT SWITCHING VALVE
FUEL FILTER CAP WITH VACUUM RELIEF VALVE
PURGE CONTROL VALVE
VACUUM SIGNAL LINE
CONSTANT PURGE ORIFICE
THROTTLE VALVE
CARBON CANISTER
FUEL TANK
FUEL VAPOR FLOW AT ENGINE RUNNING
INTAKE MANIFOLD
CANISTER PURGE LINE
FUEL VAPOR FLOW AT ENGINE STOP

Evaporative emission system—1985–86 Z20 and Z24 engines (USA)

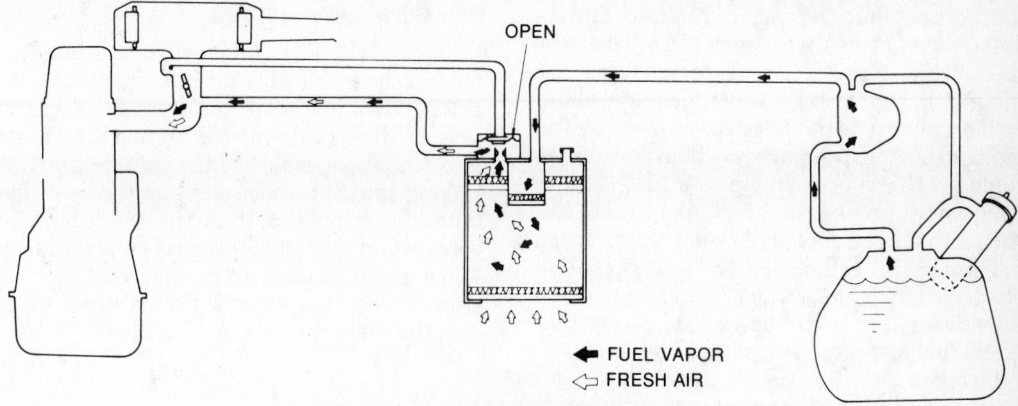

Evaporative emission system—1975–80

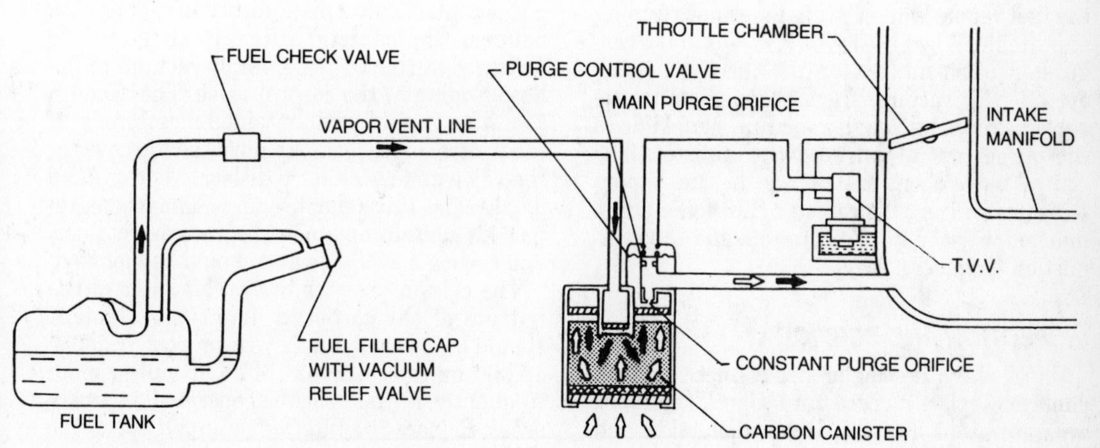

Evaporative emission system—1986–87 Z24i engines

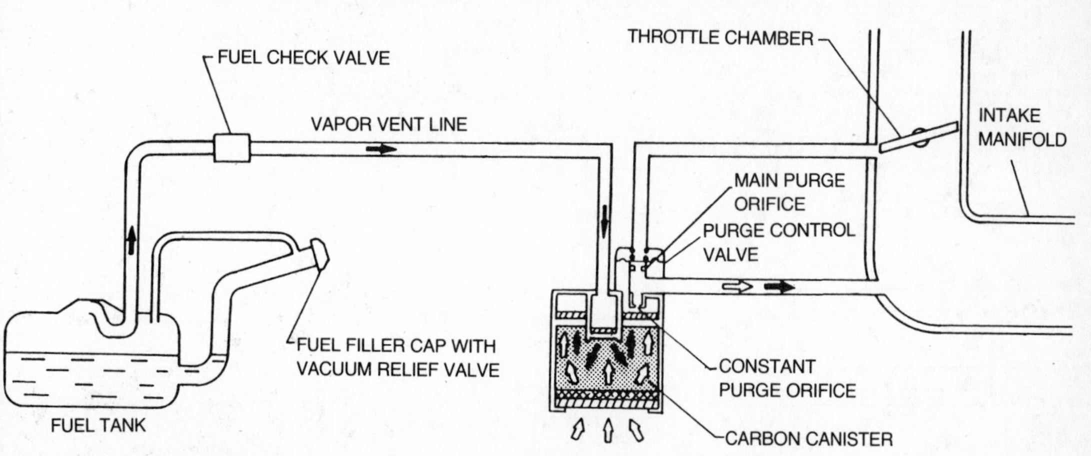

Evaporative emission system—1986–89 VG30i engines and 1988–89 Z24i engines

the fuel tank or in the engine crankcase and the difference of pressure between the relief side of the valve and the fuel tank or crankcase becomes 2 in. Hg, the relief valve opens and allows ambient air from the air cleaner into the fuel tank or the engine crankcase. This ambient air replaces the vapor within the fuel tank or crankcase, bringing the fuel tank or crankcase back into a neutral or positive pressure range.

The system used on 1975-89 trucks consists of a sealed fuel tank, a vapor/liquid separator, a vapor vent line, a carbon canister, a vacuum signal line and a canister purge line.

In operation, fuel vapors and/or liquid are routed to the liquid/vapor separator or check valve where liquid fuel is directed back into the fuel tank as fuel vapors flow into the charcoal filled canister. The charcoal absorbs and stores the fuel vapors when the engine is not running or is at idle. When the throttle valves in the carburetor (or air intakes for fuel injected models) are opened, vacuum from above the throttle valves is routed through a vacuum signal line to the purge control valve on the canister. The control valve opens and allows the fuel vapors to be drawn from the canister through a purge line and into the intake manifold and the combustion chambers.

INSPECTION AND SERVICE

Check the hoses for proper connections and damage. Replace as necessary. Check the vapor separator tank for fuel leaks, distortion and dents, and replace as necessary.

Flow Guide Valve—1970-75

Remove the flow guide valve and inspect it for leakage by blowing air into the ports in the valve. When air is applied from the fuel tank side, the flow guide valve is normal if air passes into the check side (crankcase side), but not leaking into the relief side (air cleaner side). When air is applied from the check side, the valve is normal if the passage of air is restricted. When air is applied from the relief side (air cleaner side), the valve is normal if air passes into the fuel tank side or into the check side.

Carbon Canister and Purge Control Valve—1975-89

To check the operation of the carbon canister purge control valve, disconnect the rubber hose between the canister control valve and the T-fitting, at the T-fitting. Apply vacuum to the hose leading to the control valve. The vacuum condition should be maintained indefinitely. If the control valve leaks, remove the top cover of the valve and check for a dislocated or cracked diaphragm. If the diaphragm is damaged, a repair kit containing a new diaphragm, retainer, and spring is available and should be installed.

The carbon canister has an air filter in the bottom of the canister. The filter element should be checked once a year or every 12,000–15,000 miles (19,200–24,000 km) miles; more frequently if the truck is operated in dusty areas, Replace the filter by pulling it out of the bottom of the canister and installing a new one.

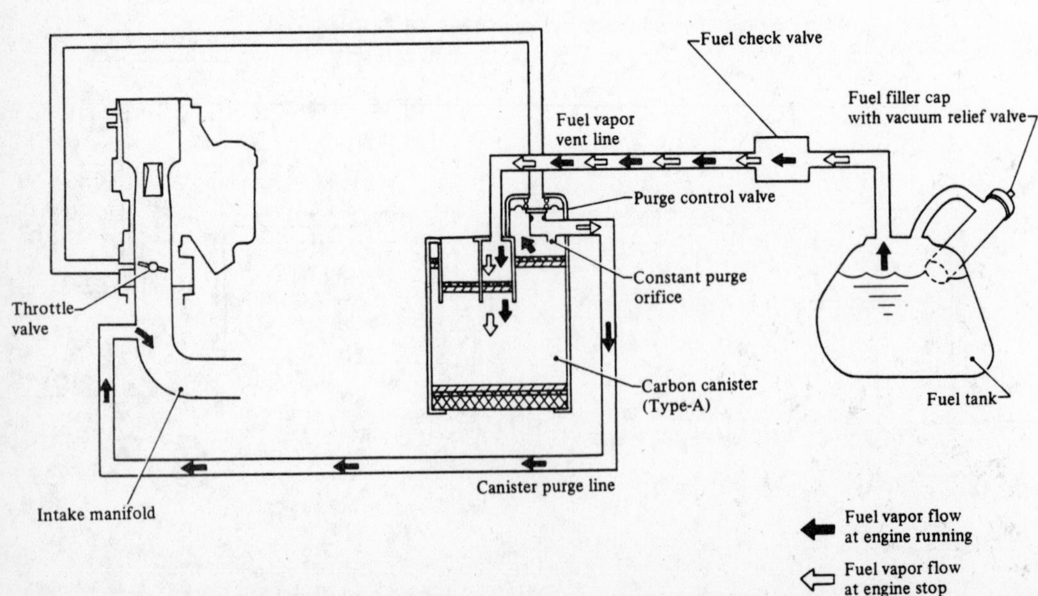

Evaporative emission system—1985–86 Z24 engines (Canada)

REMOVAL AND INSTALLATION

Removal and installation of the various evaporative emission control system components consists of disconnecting the hoses, loosening retaining screws, and removing the part which is to be replaced or checked. Installation is obvious. When replacing hoses, make sure that they are fuel and vapor resistant.

Dual Point Distributor

OPERATION

1970-73 Gasoline Engines Only

The dual point distributor has two sets of breaker points which operate independently of each other and are positioned with a relative phase angle of 5° (1970), 10° (1971), 7° (1972-73) apart. This makes one set the advanced points and the other set the retarded points.

The two sets of points, which mechanically operate continuously, are connected in parallel to the primary side of the ignition timing, depending on whether or not the retarded set of points is energized.

When both sets of points are electrically energized, the first set to open (the advanced set, 4° or 1° sooner) has no control over breaking the ignition coil primary circuit because the retarded set is still closed and maintaining a complete circuit to ground. When the retarded set of points opens, the advanced set is still open, and the primary circuit is broken causing the electromagnetic field in the coil to collapse and the ignition spark is produced.

When the retarded set of points is removed from the primary ignition circuit through the operation of a distributor relay inserted into the retarded points circuit, the advanced set of points controls the primary circuit. The retarded set of points is activated as follows:

On 1970 and 1971 models, the retarded set of points is activated only while cruising or accelerating with the throttle partially open and the transmission in 3rd gear. Under all other conditions, the retarded set of points is removed from the ignition circuit.

On 1972 models, the retarded set of points is activated only while cruising or accelerating with the throttle partially open, the transmission in 3rd gear, and with the ambient temperature above 50°F (10°C).

On 1973 models, the retarded set of points is activated only while the throttle is partially open, the temperature is above 50°F (10°C), and the transmission is in any gear but 4th.

NOTE: *When the ambient temperature is below 34°F (1°C), the retarded set of points is removed from the ignition circuit no matter what switch is on.*

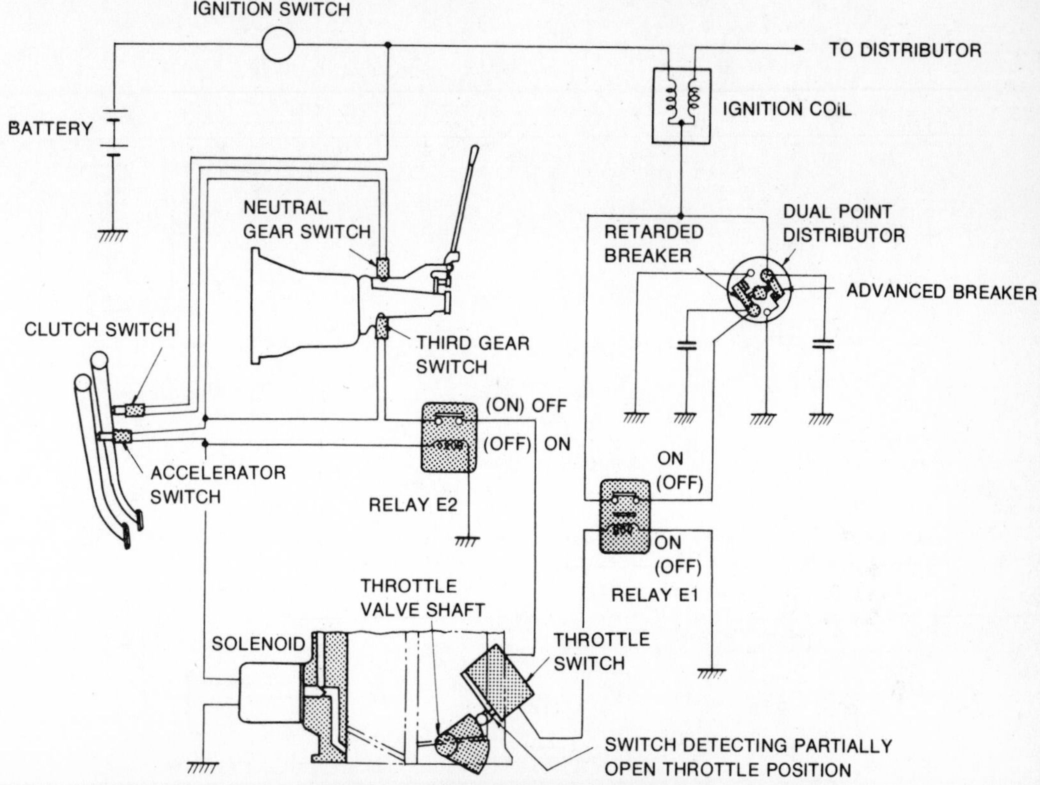

Dual point distributor system—1970–71

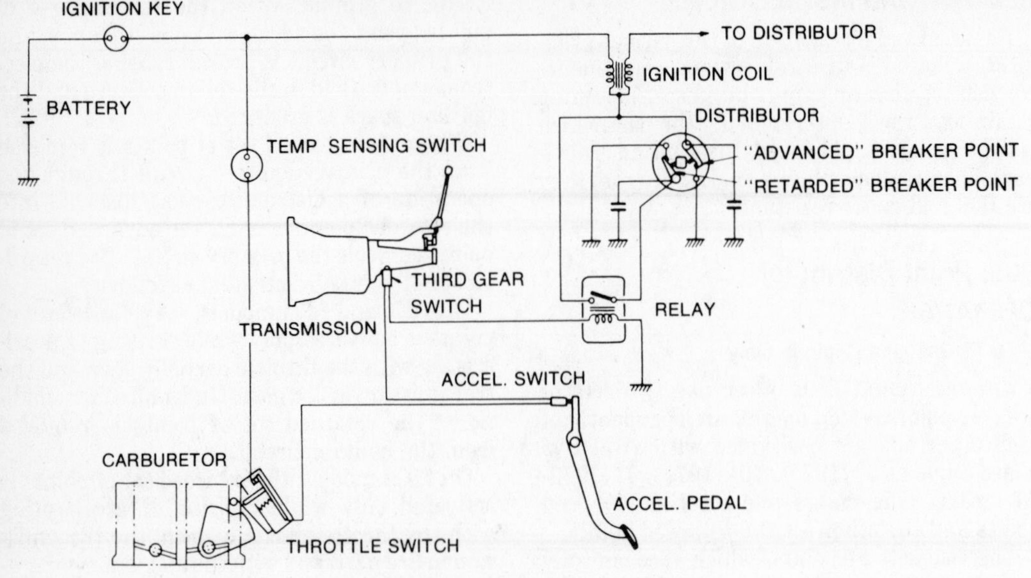

Dual point distributor system—1972 (MT)

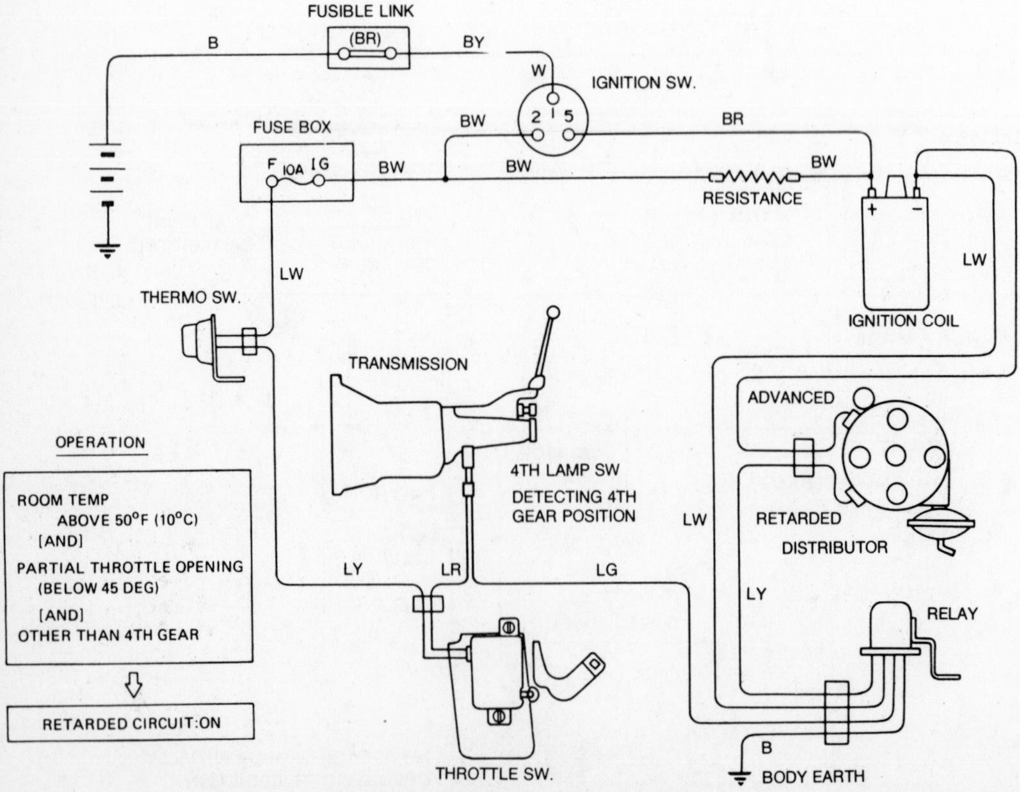

FUSIBLE LINK
(BR)
B
BY
W
IGNITION SW.
2 5
FUSE BOX
F 10A IG
BW
BW
BW
BR
BW
RESISTANCE
+ −
LW
B
LW
THERMO SW.
IGNITION COIL
TRANSMISSION
ADVANCED
OPERATION

ROOM TEMP
ABOVE 50°F (10°C)
[AND]
PARTIAL THROTTLE OPENING
(BELOW 45 DEG)
[AND]
OTHER THAN 4TH GEAR
⇩
RETARDED CIRCUIT:ON

4TH LAMP SW
DETECTING 4TH
GEAR POSITION
LW
RETARDED
DISTRIBUTOR
LY
LR
LG
LY
RELAY
B
BODY EARTH
THROTTLE SW.

Dual point distributor system—1973 (MT)

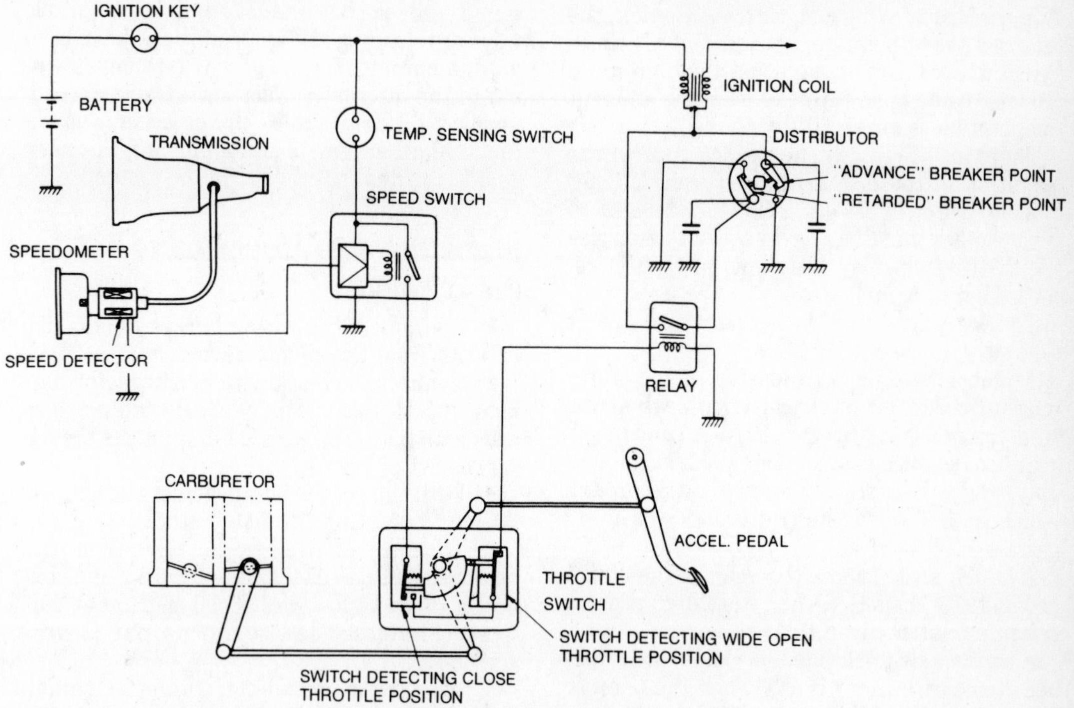

IGNITION KEY
BATTERY
TRANSMISSION
TEMP. SENSING SWITCH
IGNITION COIL
DISTRIBUTOR
"ADVANCE" BREAKER POINT
"RETARDED" BREAKER POINT
SPEED SWITCH
SPEEDOMETER
SPEED DETECTOR
RELAY
CARBURETOR
ACCEL. PEDAL
THROTTLE SWITCH
SWITCH DETECTING WIDE OPEN THROTTLE POSITION
SWITCH DETECTING CLOSE THROTTLE POSITION

Dual point distributor system—1972 (AT)

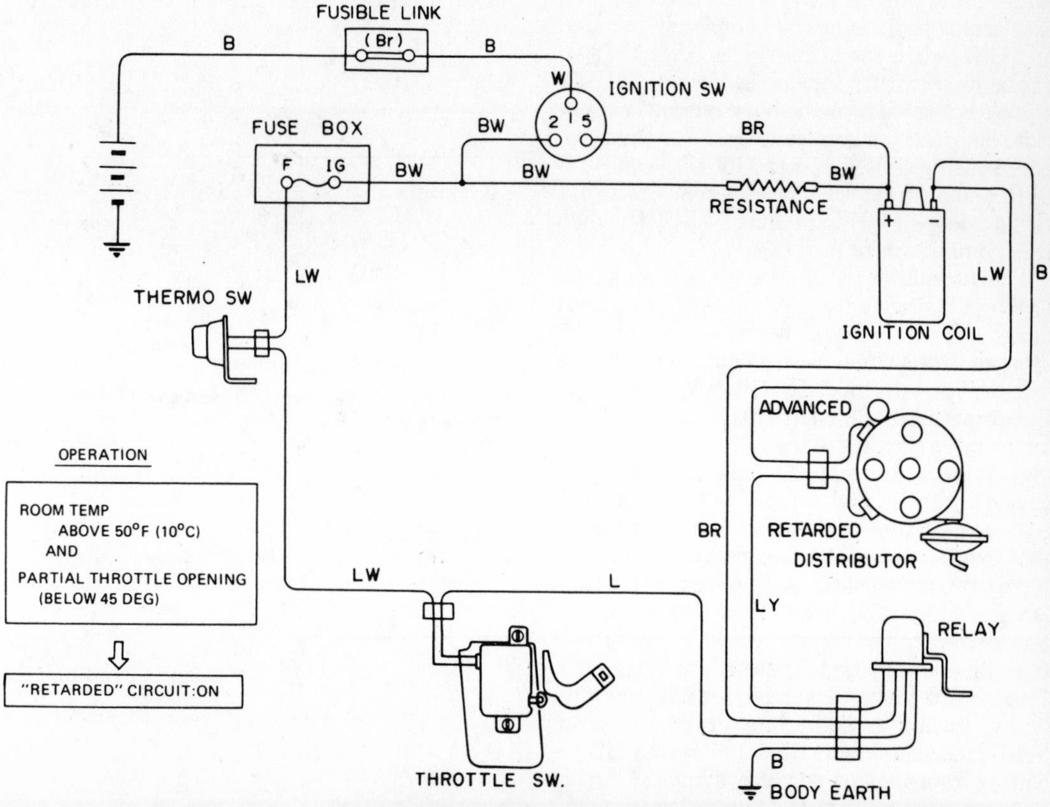

FUSIBLE LINK
B
(Br)
B
W
IGNITION SW
2 1 5
FUSE BOX
F IG
BW
BW
BW
BR
BW
RESISTANCE
+ −
LW
THERMO SW
LW
B
IGNITION COIL
ADVANCED
BR
RETARDED
DISTRIBUTOR
LW
L
LY
RELAY
THROTTLE SW.
B
BODY EARTH

OPERATION

ROOM TEMP
ABOVE 50°F (10°C)
AND
PARTIAL THROTTLE OPENING
(BELOW 45 DEG)

⇩

"RETARDED" CIRCUIT:ON

Dual point distributor system—1973 (AT)

In the case of an automatic transmission, the retarded set of points is activated at all times except under heavy acceleration and high speed cruising (wide open throttle) with the ambient temperature is above 50°F (10°C).

There are three switches which control the operation of the distributor relay on 1972-73 models; five switches on 1970-71 models. All of the switches must be **ON** in order to energize the distributor relay thus energizing the retarded set of points.

The switches and their operation are as follows:

A transmission switch located in the transmission closes an electrical circuit when the transmission is in 3rd gear (1970-72) and in any gear except 4th (1973). On 1970-71 models only, there is a transmission neutral switch which in **ON** when the transmission is in all gears except Neutral.

A clutch switch mounted against the clutch pedal (1970-71) is **ON** when the clutch pedal is released (clutch engaged).

A throttle switch located on the throttle linkage at the carburetor is **ON** when the throttle valve is moved within a predetermined angle: up to 35° on 1970-71 models, 40° on 1972 models, and 45° on 1973 models.

An accelerator switch mounted to the accelerator pedal linkage (1970-72) is **ON** when the accelerator pedal is nearly completely released and **OFF** when the pedal is opened farther.

The temperature sensing switch on 1972-73 models is located near the hood release lever inside the passenger compartment. The temperature sensing switch comes **ON** between 41°F (5°F) and 55°F (13°C) when the temperature is rising and goes **OFF** at about 34°F (1°C) when the temperature falls.

The distributor vacuum advance mechanism produces a spark advance based on the amount of vacuum in the intake manifold. With a high vacuum, less air/fuel mixture enters the engine cylinders and the mixture is therefore less highly compressed. Consequently, this mixture burns more slowly and the advance mechanism gives it more time to burn. This longer burning time results in higher combustion temperatures at peak pressure and hence, more time for nitrogen (N) to react with oxygen (O_2) and form nitrogen oxides (NOx). At the same time, this advance timing results in less complete combustion due to the greater area of cylinder wall (quench area) exposed at the instant of ignition. This cooled fuel will not burn as readily and hence, results in higher unburned hydrocarbons (HC). The production of NOx and HC resulting from vacuum advance is highest during idle and moderate acceleration in lower gears.

Retardation of the ignition timing is necessary to reduce NOx and HC emissions. Various ways of retarding the ignition spark have been used in automobiles, all of which remove vacuum to the distributor vacuum advance mechanism at different times under certain conditions. Another way of accomplishing the same goal is the dual point distributor system.

INSPECTION AND ADJUSTMENTS

Phase Difference

1. Disconnect the wiring harness of the distributor from the engine harness.
2. Connect the black wire of the engine harness with the black wire of the distributor harness with a jumper wire. This connects the advanced set of points.
3. With the engine idling, adjust the ignition timing by rotating the distributor.
4. Disconnect the jumper wire from the black wire of the distributor harness and connect it to the yellow wire of the distributor harness. The retarded set of points is now activated.
5. With the engine idling, check the ignition timing. The timing should be retarded from the advanced setting as follows: 5° for 1970; 10° for 1971; and 7° for 1972-73.
6. To adjust the out-of-phase angle of the ignition timing, loosen the adjuster plate set

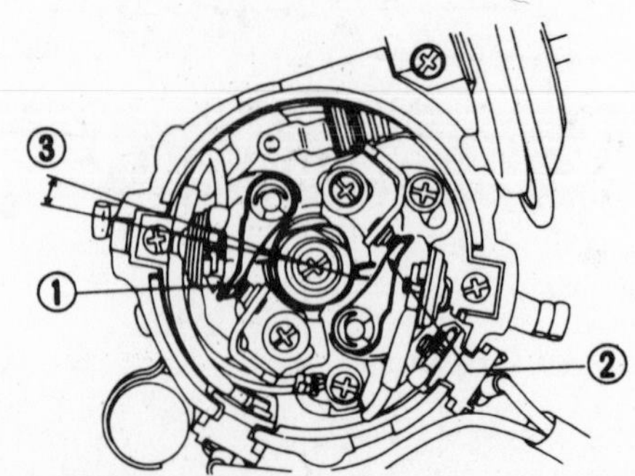

(1) Advance point set (2) Retarded point set (3) Phase difference

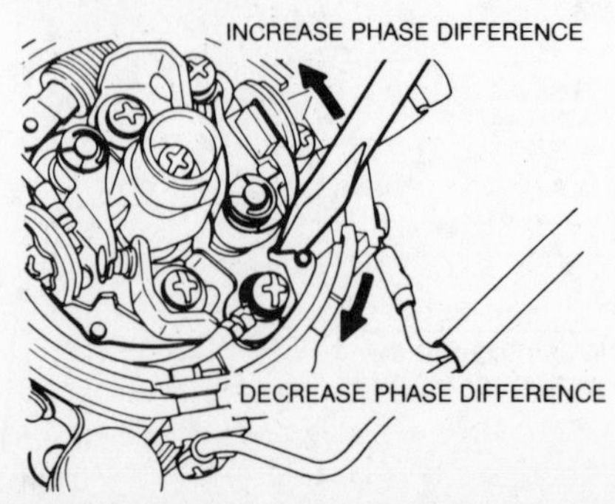

Adjusting the phase angle on a dual point distributor

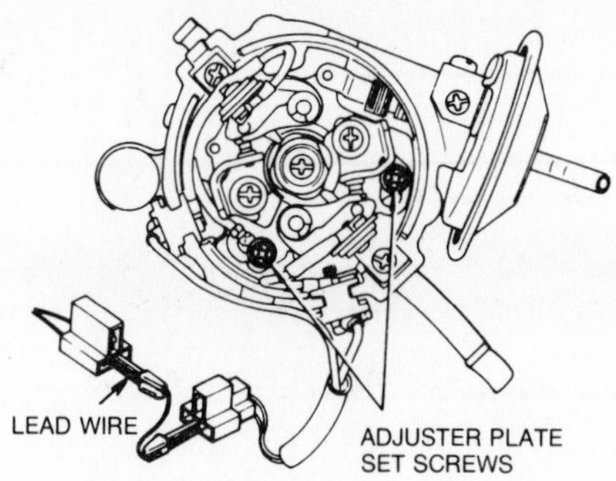

Connect a jumper wire between the two wiring harnesses to activate just one set of points

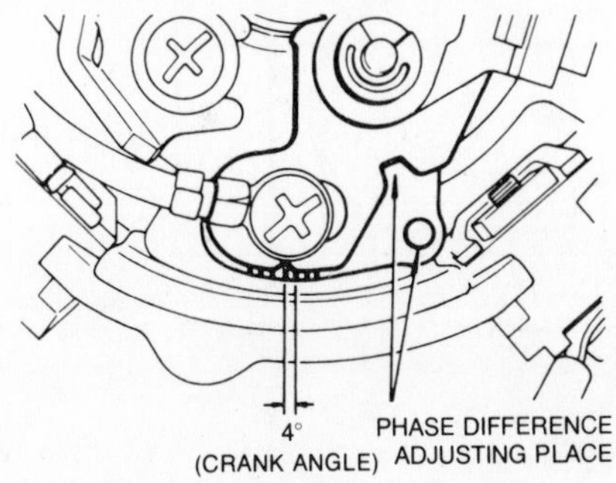

Phase angle adjusting scale

screws on the same side as the retarded set of points.

7. Place the blade of a screwdriver in the adjusting notch of the adjuster plate and turn the adjuster plate as required to obtain the correct retarded ignition timing specification. The ignition timing is retarded when the adjuster plate is turned counterclockwise. There are graduations on the adjuster plate to make the adjustment easier; one graduation is equal to 4° of crankshaft rotation.

8. Replace the distributor cap, start the engine, and check the ignition timing with the retarded set of points activated (yellow wire of the distributor wiring harness connected to the black wire of the engine wiring harness).

9. Repeat the steps above as necessary to properly set the retarded ignition timing.

Transmission Switch

Disconnect the electrical leads at the switch and connect a self-powered test light to the electrical leads. The switch should conduct electricity only when the gearshift is moved to the corresponding gear for that particular model year vehicle: 3rd gear on 1970-72 models and 4th gear on 1973 models. The neutral switch on 1970-71 models should conduct current when the transmission is shifted into **N**.

If the switch fails to perform in the above manner, replace it with a new one.

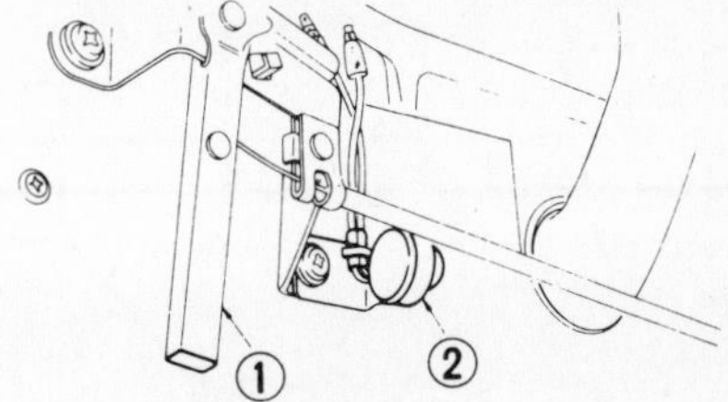

1. Hood release lever
2. Temperature sensing switch

Temperature sensing switch location

Clutch Switch

Test the clutch switch on 1970-71 models in the same manner as the transmission switch (self-powered test light). The switch should conduct current when the clutch pedal is released (clutch engaged).

Accelerator Switch

The accelerator switch is mounted on the accelerator pedal linkage (except 1973). It is checked with a self-powered test light in the same manner as outlined for the transmission switch. The switch should conduct current when the accelerator pedal is nearly completely released.

Throttle Switch

The throttle switch located on the throttle linkage at the carburetor is checked with a self-powered test light. Disconnect the electrical leads of the switch and connect the test light. The switch should not conduct current when the throttle valve is closed or opened as follows: The throttle valve opened up to 35° on 1970-71 models; 40° on 1972 models; and 45° on 1973 models. When the throttle is fully opened, the switch should conduct current.

Temperature Sensing Switch

The temperature sensing switch mounted in the passenger compartment (near the hood release lever) should not conduct current when the temperature is above 55°F (13°C) when connected to a self-powered test light as previously outlined for the throttle switch.

Dual Spark Plug Ignition System

OPERATION

Z20, Z22, Z24 and Z24i Engines

These engines have two spark plugs per cylinder. This arrangement allows the engine to burn large amounts of recirculated exhaust gases without affecting performance. In fact, the system works so well it improves gas mileage under most circumstances.

Both spark plugs fire simultaneously, which

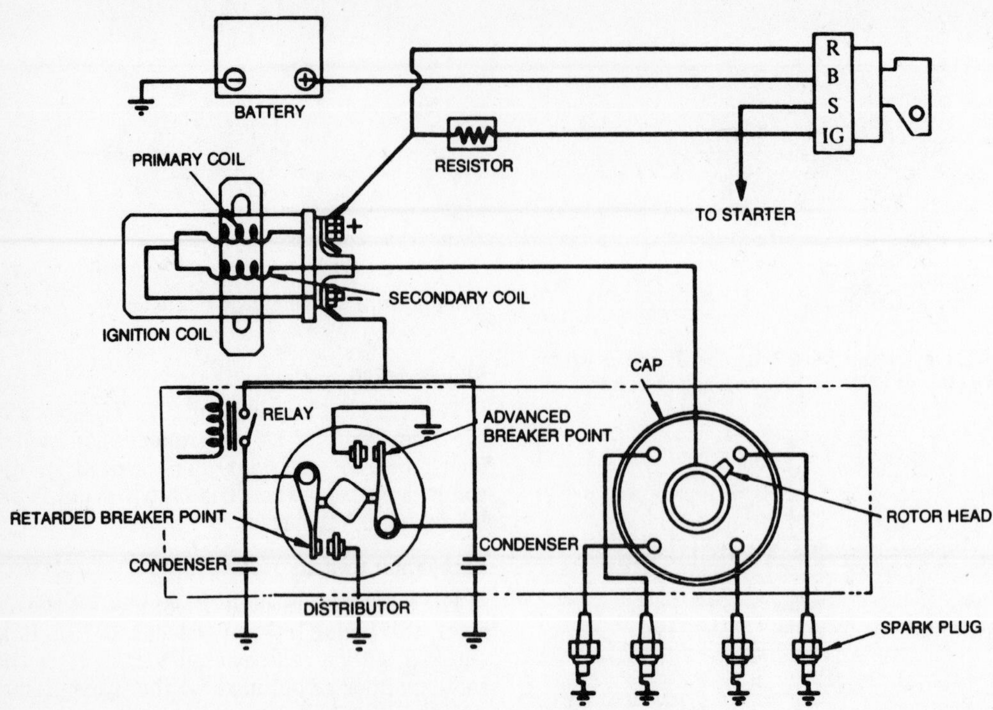

Dual point ignition system schematic

substantially shortens the time required to burn the air/fuel mixture when exhaust gases (EGR) are not being recirculated. When gases are being recirculated, the dual spark plug system brings the ignition level up to that of a single plug system which is not recirculating exhaust gases.

ADJUSTMENT

The only adjustments necessary are the tune-up and maintenance procedures outlined in Chapters 1 and 2.

Spark Timing Control System

OPERATION

Gasoline Engines Only

There are actually two different versions of this system, the first is utilized on many 1975-80 trucks and the second can be found on 1981-86 trucks (720-D series). The 1975-80 system controls distributor vacuum advance, giving full vacuum advance when the transmission is in 4th or 5th, and partial advance in the first three gears. This provides better control of the combustion process, lowering emissions of HC and NOx.

The system components include a top gear detecting switch, installed in the transmission, and a vacuum switching valve spliced into the distributor vacuum advance hose by means of a 3-way connector. When the transmission is shifted into either of the two top gears, the transmission switch goes on, activating the vacuum switching valve which closes its air bleed, giving full advance. Shifting into any gear but 4th and 5th turns the transmission switch off, deactivating the vacuum switching valve. The valve opens a vacuum leak, providing only partial vacuum advance to the distributor.

The 1981-86 system replaces the earlier system but is very similar. The major difference is that it works solely from engine water temperature changes rather than a transmission mounted switch. The system includes a thermal vacuum valve, a vacuum delay (control) valve, and attendant hoses. It performs the same function as the earlier system. To retard full spark advance at times when high levels of pollutants would otherwise be given off.

INSPECTION AND ADJUSTMENTS

1975-80 Engines

1. Check all hoses and electrical wires for proper connections, leaks or corrosion, and so on.

2. Check the distributor vacuum advance unit for proper operation. This can be checked by hooking up a timing light, starting the engine, then increasing engine speed and observing whether or not the timing marks advance. If not, the advance unit must be checked for binding or leaks.

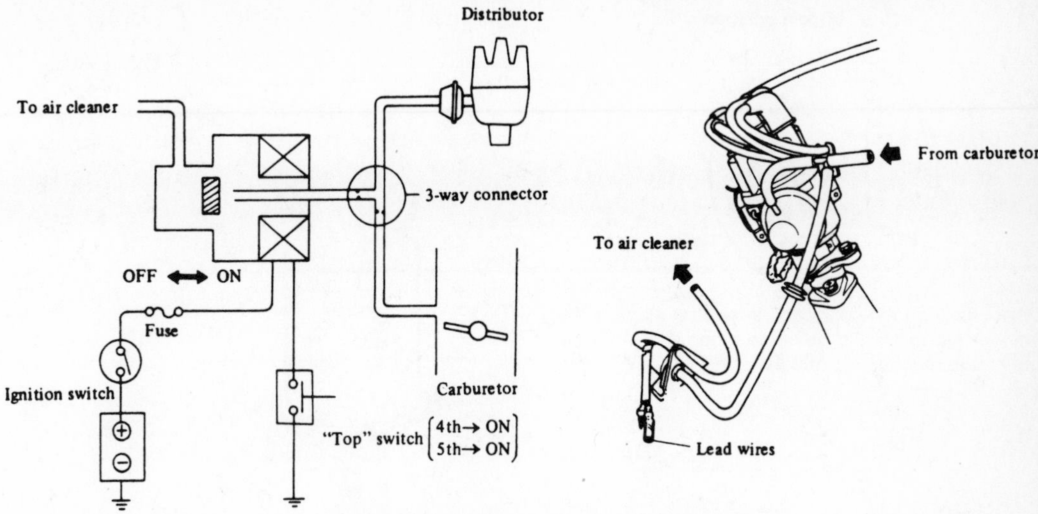

Spark timing control system—1979–80

3. With the timing light installed, increase the engine speed to 2000 rpm. Have an assistant disengage the clutch, then shift between 3rd, 4th and 5th, then back down and into neutral. Spark timing should vary when the transmission is in 4th or 5th (advance should be greater). If this is not the case, check the vacuum switching valve.

VACUUM SWITCHING VALVE

1. Disconnect the valve's electrical connectors. With the timing light installed, run the engine up to about 2000 rpm and keep it there. Check the timing.

2. Connect the valve's electrical connectors directly to the battery with a pair of jumper wires. Be sure to observe correct polarity. If spark timing varies, the valve is ok. If not, replace it.

TOP GEAR TRANSMISSION SWITCH

The switch can be checked easily with an ohmmeter. Connect the ohmmeter leads to the switch leads on the transmission. Shift back and forth between either 4th or 5th and one of the other gears. If the resistance does not change, replace the switch.

1981-86 Engines

Connect a timing light and check the ignition timing while the temperature gauge is in the cold position. Write down the reading. Allow

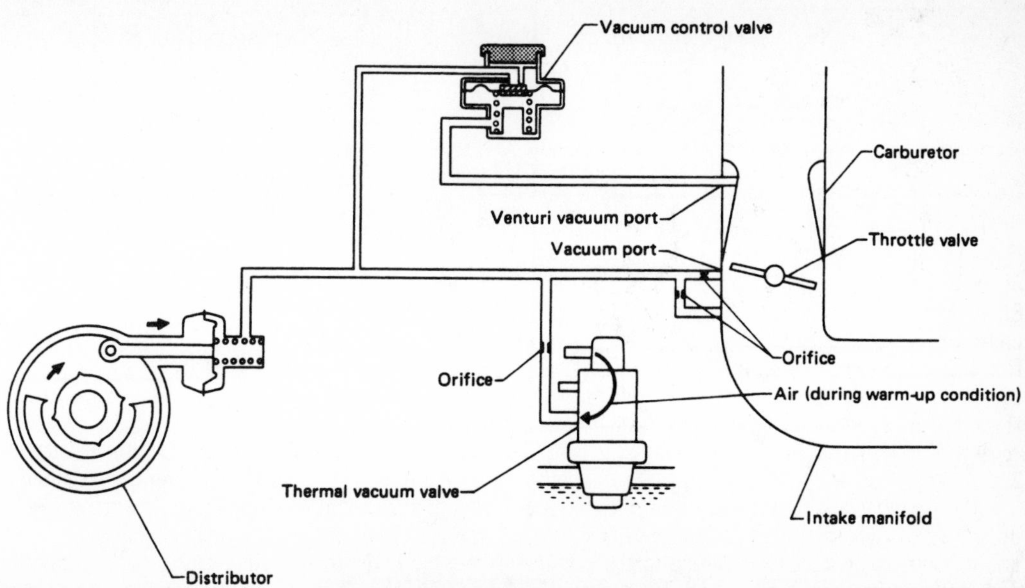

Spark timing control system—1981–86

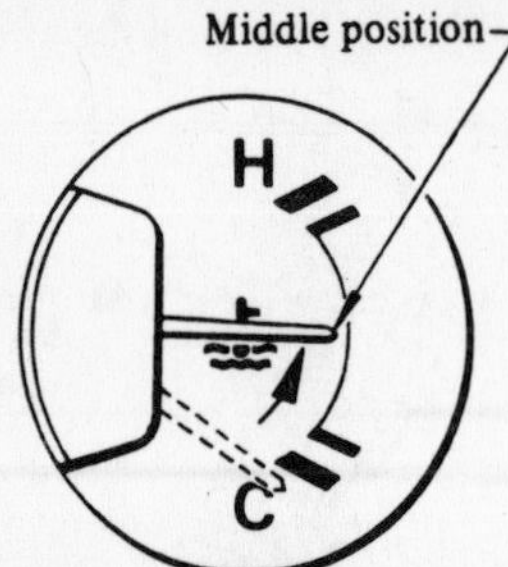

When checking the spark timing control system, the ignition timing should advance when the temperature gauge reaches the middle—1981–86

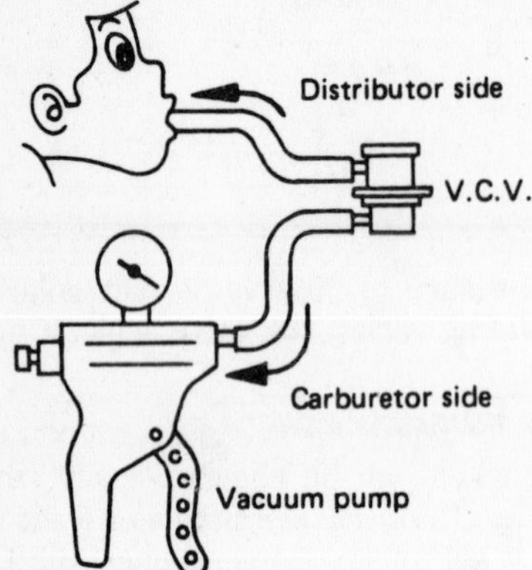

Checking the vacuum control valve—1981–86

the engine to run with the timing light attached until the temperature needle reaches the center of the gauge. As the engine is warming up, check with the timing light to make sure the ig-

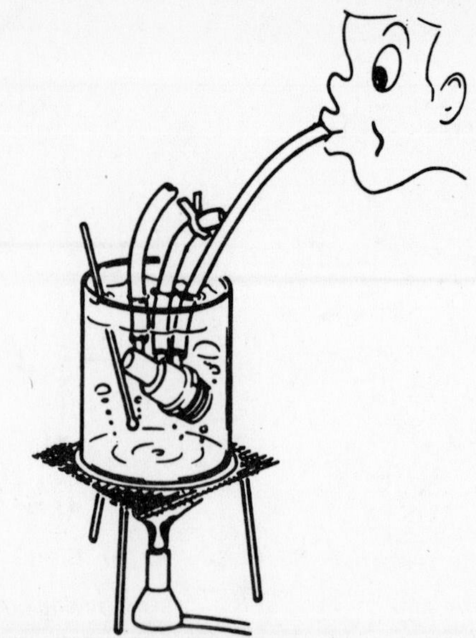

Checking the thermal vacuum valve—1981–86

nition timing retards. When the temperature needle is in the middle of the gauge, the ignition timing should advance from its previous position. If the ignition timing does not change, replace the thermal vacuum valve.

Spark Plug Switching Control System

OPERATION

This system, used only on the 1984-86 Canadian trucks (Z24), is designed to change the ig-

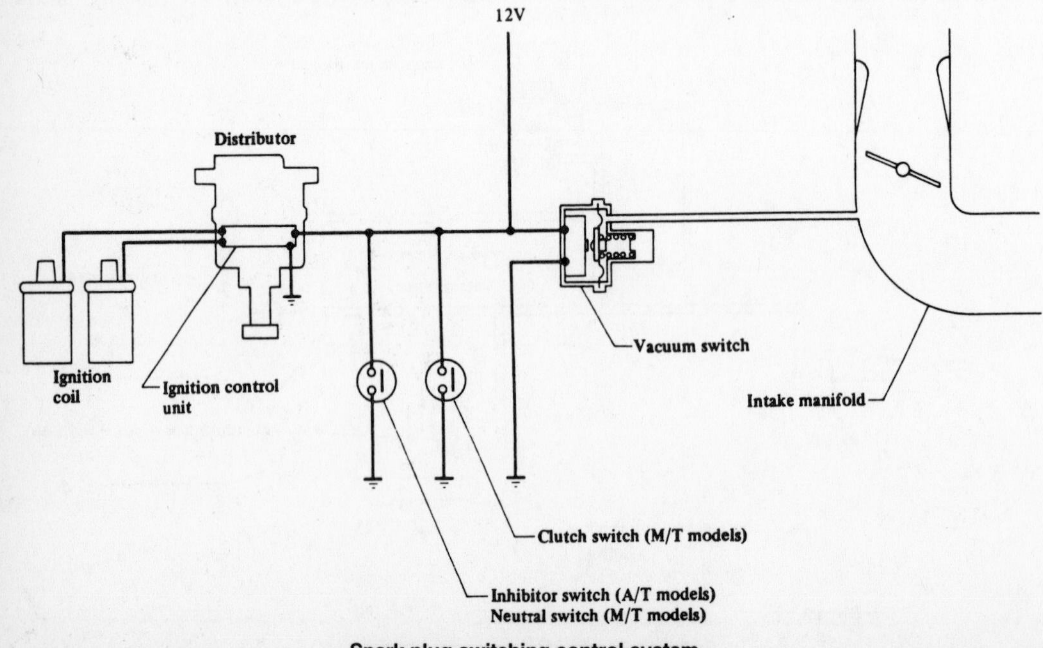

Spark plug switching control system

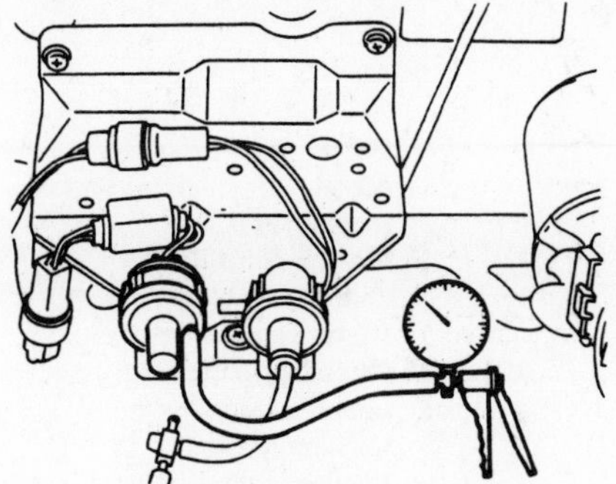

Testing the spark plug switching control system

nition system from 2-plug ignition to 1-plug ignition during heavy load driving conditions in order to reduce engine noise. The system also functions to advance ignition timing by the proper amount during 1-plug ignition.

Th system is composed of an ignition control unit installed in the distributor. The unit has a switching function which allows it to change from 2-plug to 1-plug operation by means of a vacuum switch in the intake manifold.

Early Fuel Evaporation System

OPERATION

Gasoline Engines Only

The early fuel evaporation system is used on certain 1973-77 L-series engines. The system's purpose is to heat the air/fuel mixture when the engine is below normal operating temperature. The L-series engines use a system much similar to the old style exhaust manifold heat riser. The only adjustment necessary is to occasionally lubricate the counterweight. Other than that, the system should be trouble-free.

Most later carbureted engines use coolant water heat instead of exhaust gas heat to prewarm the fuel mixture. This system should be trouble-free.

Boost Control Deceleration Device (BCDD)

OPERATION

Gasoline Engines Only

The BCDD reduces hydrocarbon emissions during coasting conditions. High manifold vacuum during coasting prevents the complete combustion of the air/fuel mixture because of the reduced amount of air. This condition will result in large HC emissions. Enriching the air/fuel mixture for a short time (during the high vacuum condition) will reduce the emission of HC in conjunction with the AIR system.

However, enriching the air/fuel mixture with only the mixture adjusting screw will cause poor engine idle, or invite an increase in the carbon monoxide (CO) content of the exhaust gases.

The BCDD consists of an independently operated auxiliary fuel system. This system functions when the engine is coasting to enrich the air/fuel mixture which minimizes the hydrocarbon content of the exhaust gases through more efficient combustion. This is accomplished without adversely affecting engine idle and the carbon monoxide content of the exhaust gases.

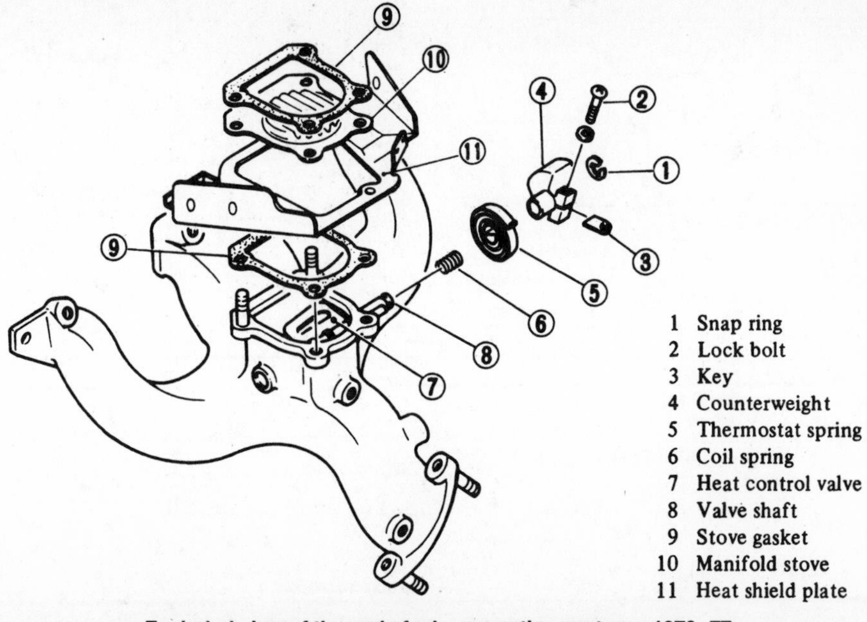

Exploded view of the early fuel evaporation system—1973–77

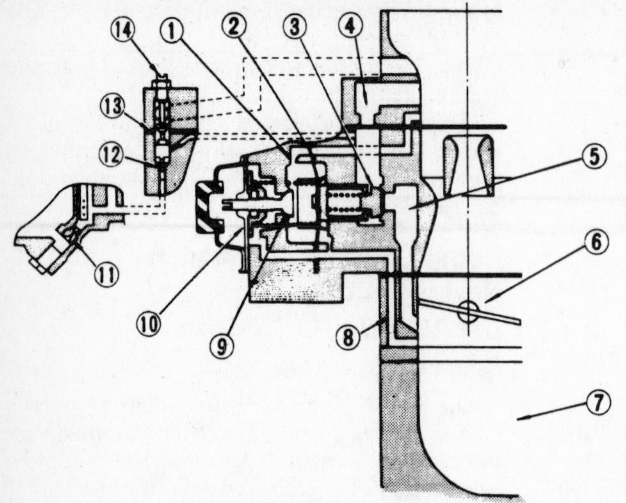

Cross view of the boost controlled deceleration system—1979–80

When intake manifold vacuum exceeds a predetermined value, a vacuum actuated diaphragm opens an air passage allowing additional air to enter the intake manifold. When the additional air passage is opened, vacuum is brought to bear on another diaphragm which opens a fuel passage allowing additional fuel to enter the intake manifold.

When the engine changes from a coasting condition to that of idling, the transmission speed sensor closes an electrical circuit, energizing the vacuum control solenoid valve. When energized, the vacuum control solenoid valve vents the intake manifold vacuum to the atmosphere, thus causing the two diaphragms to return to their normal positions, closing off the additional air and fuel mixture. The transmission switch is not used on 1978-79 models.

SERVICE

Normally, the BCDD never needs adjustment. However, if the need should arise because of suspected malfunction of the system, proceed as follows:

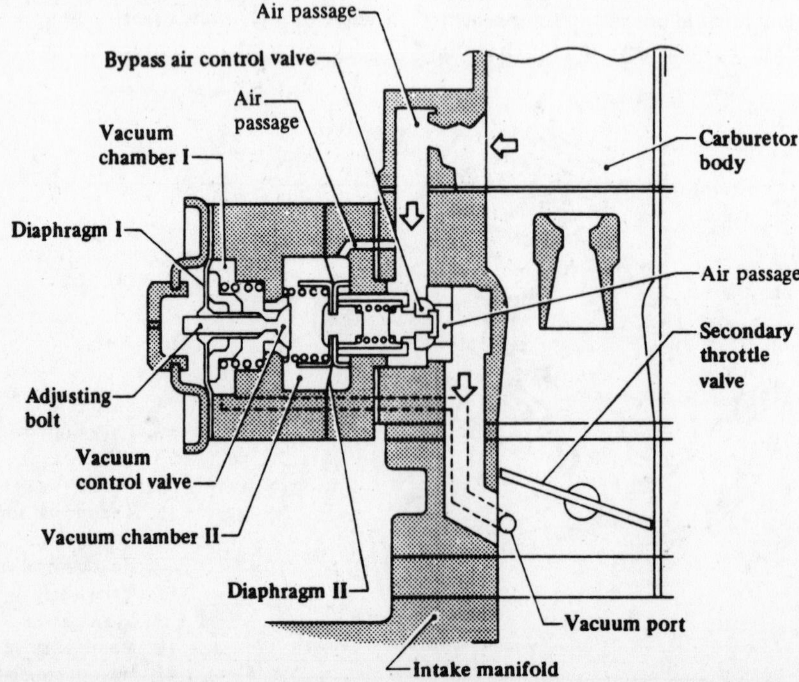

Cross view of the boost controlled deceleration system—1984–86 Z20 and Z24 engines

1. Connect a tachometer to the engine.

2. Connect a quick-response vacuum gauge to the intake manifold.

3. Disconnect the BCDD solenoid valve electrical leads.

4. Start and warm up the engine until it reaches normal operating temperature.

5. Adjust the idle speed to the proper specification.

6. Raise the engine speed to 3000–3500 rpm under no-load (transmission in **N** or **P**), then allow the throttle to close quickly. Take notice as to whether or not the engine rpm returns to idle speed and if it does, how long the fall in rpm is interrupted before it reaches idle speed.

At the moment the throttle is snapped closed at high engine rpm, the vacuum in the intake manifold reaches -27.7 in.Hg on pre-1975 vehicles and -23.6 in.Hg on 1975 and later models, and then gradually falls to about -16.5 in.Hg at idle speed. The process of the fall of intake manifold vacuum and engine rpm will take one of the following three forms:

a. When the operating pressure of the BCDD is too high, the system remains inoperative, and the vacuum in the intake manifold decreases without interruption just like that of an engine without a BCDD.

b. When the operating pressure is lower than that of the case given, but still higher than the properly set pressure, the fall of vacuum in the intake manifold is interrupted and kept constant at a certain level (operating pressure) for about 1 second and then gradually falls down to the normal vacuum at idle speed.

c. When the set operating pressure of the BCDD is lower than the intake manifold vacuum when the throttle is suddenly released, the engine speed will not lower to idle speed.

To adjust the set operating pressure of the BCDD, remove the adjusting screw cover from the BCDD mechanism mounted on the side of the carburetor.

The adjusting screw is a left-hand threaded screw. Turning the screw ⅛ of a turn in either

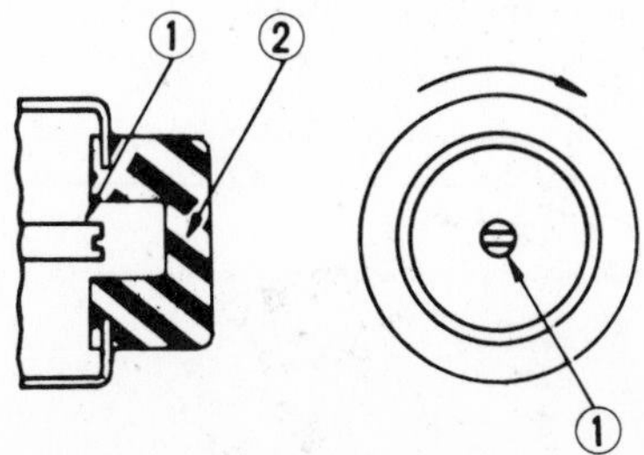

1. Adjusting screw "S"   2. Cover "C"

The operating pressure adjusting screw of the BCDD

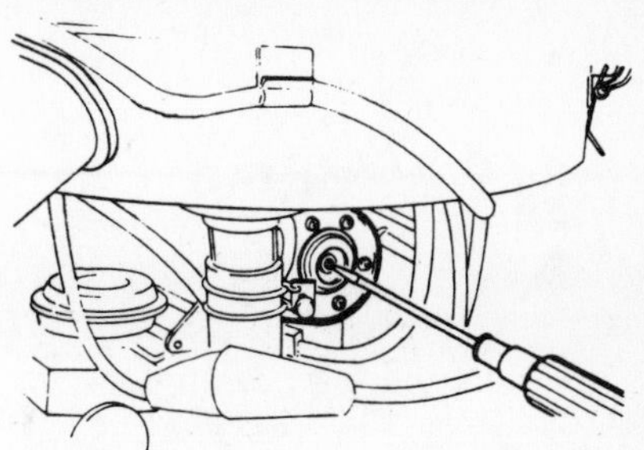

Adjusting the BCDD

direction will change the operation pressure about 0.79 in.Hg. Turning the screw counterclockwise will increase the amount of vacuum needed to operate the mechanism and turning the screw clockwise will decrease the amount of vacuum needed to operate the mechanism.

The operating pressure for the BCDD on a vehicle with a manual transmission is -19.7 ±0.79 in.Hg and for a vehicle with an automatic transmission -18.9 ±0.79 in.Hg through 1974. The decrease in intake manifold vacuum should be interrupted at these levels for about 1 second when the BCDD is operating correctly. The figures for later years are:

- 1975-76: 20.7 to -21.1 – manual transmission; 19.9 to -20.3 – automatic transmission
- 1977: 20.1 to -21.7 – manual transmission; 19.3 to -20.9 – automatic transmission
- 1978: 22.05 ± 0.79 – all models
- 1979 and later: 21.65 ± 0.75 – all models.

Don't forget to install the adjusting screw cover when the system is adjusted.

Intake Manifold Vacuum Control System

OPERATION

Gasoline Engines Only

This system, used in 1979-84, is designed to reduce the engine's oil consumption when the intake manifold vacuum increases to an extremely high level during deceleration. The system consists of two units. A boost control unit as the vacuum sensor, and a by-pass air control unit as an actuator. The boost control unit senses the manifold vacuum. When the level of the manifold vacuum increases above the predetermined value, the boost control valve opens and transmits the manifold vacuum to the bypass air control unit. The manifold vacuum then pulls the diaphragm in and opens the bypass air control valve, thereby causing the air to be bypassed to the intake manifold. After completion of the air by-pass, the manifold vacuum is lowered. This results in the closing of the boost control valve and then the closing of the

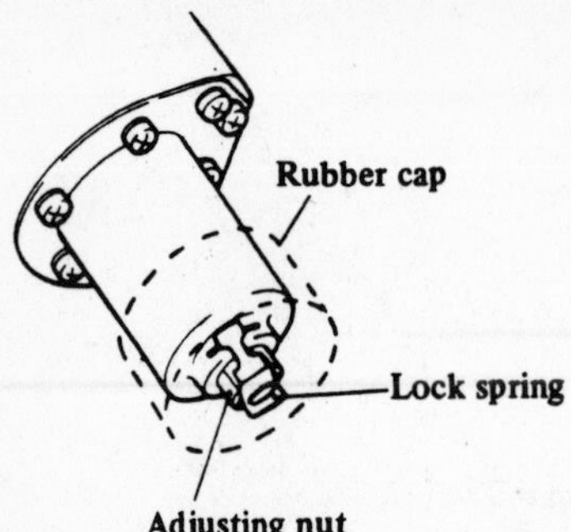

Intake manifold vacuum control system—boost control valve

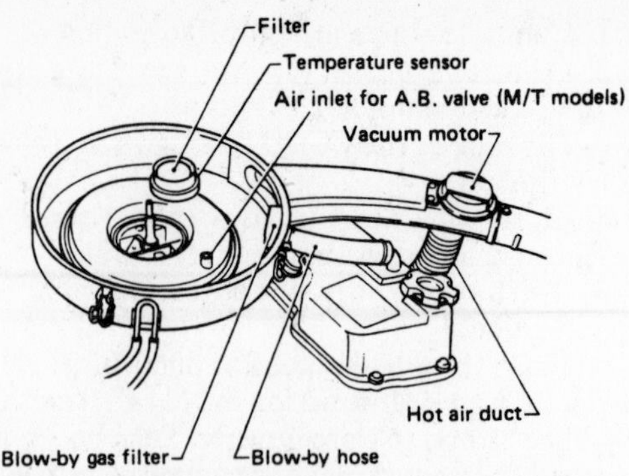

Automatic temperature control air cleaner—1985–86 Z20 and Z24 engines (USA)

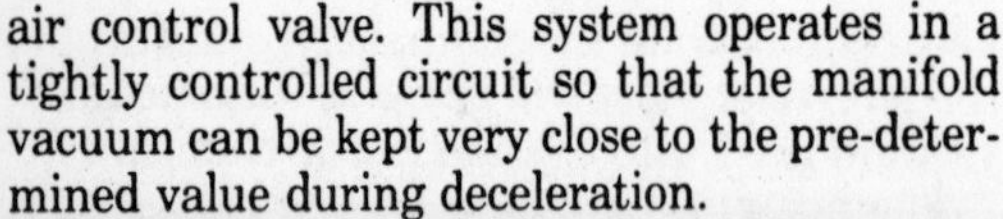

air control valve. This system operates in a tightly controlled circuit so that the manifold vacuum can be kept very close to the pre-determined value during deceleration.

Aside from a routine check of the hoses and their connections, no service or adjustments should ever be necessary on this system. If at some time you feel that an adjustment is required, it is suggested that you take the truck to a Nissan/Datsun dealer or an authorized service representative.

Automatic Temperature Controlled (ATC) Air Cleaner

OPERATION

The rate of fuel atomization varies with the temperature of the air with which the fuel is being mixed. The air/fuel ratio cannot be held con-

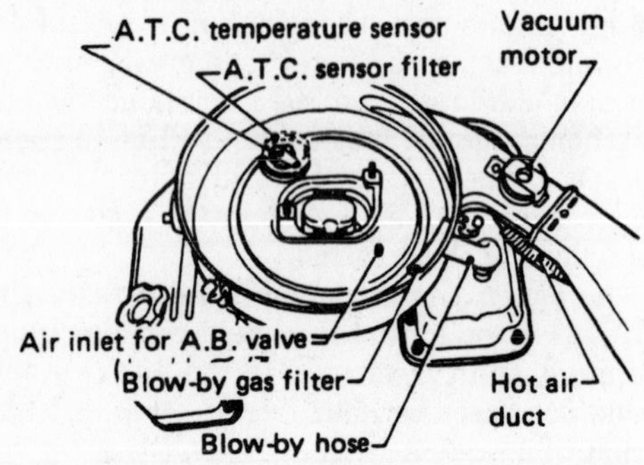

Automatic temperature control air cleaner—1986–89 Z24i engines

stant for efficient fuel combustion with a wide range of air temperatures. Cold air being drawn into the engine causes a denser and richer air/fuel mixture, inefficient fuel atomization,

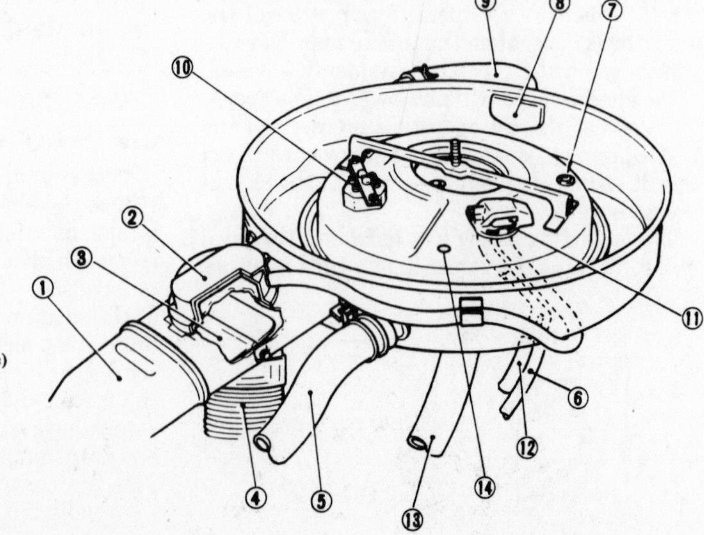

1. Fresh air duct (Except Canada)
2. Vacuum motor
3. Air control valve
4. Hot air duct
5. Air hose for A.I.S. (From C.A.C. valve) (Except Canada)
6. Vacuum tube from carbon canister
7. Air inlet for A.B. valve
8. Blow-by gas filter
9. Blow-by hose
10. Idle compensator
11. Temperature sensor assembly
12. Manifold vacuum
13. Air relief valve for air pump (Canada only)
14. Air inlet for T.C.S. (California only)

Automatic temperature control air cleaner—1977–80 (Calif. and Canada)

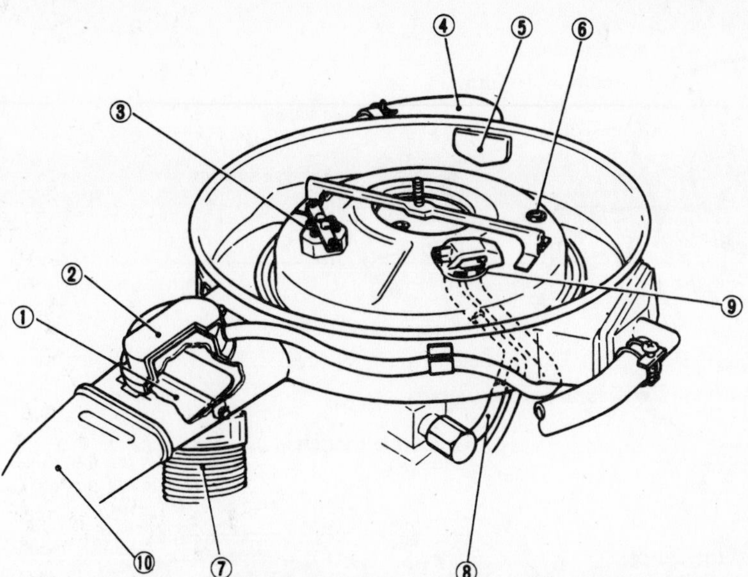

1 Air control valve
2 Vacuum motor
3 Idle compensator
4 Blow-by hose
5 Blow-by gas filter
6 Air inlet for A.B. valve
7 Hot air duct
8 Vacuum tube from intake manifold
9 Temperature sensor assembly
10 Fresh air duct

Automatic temperature control air cleaner—1977–80 (49 State)

and thus, more hydrocarbons in the exhaust gas. Hot air being drawn into the engine causes a leaner air/fuel mixture and more efficient atomization and combustion for less hydrocarbons in the exhaust gases.

The automatic temperature controlled air cleaner is designed so that the temperature of the ambient air being drawn into the engine is automatically controlled, to hold the temperature of the air and , consequently, the fuel/air ratio at a constant rate for efficient fuel combustion.

A temperature sensing vacuum switch controls vacuum applied to a vacuum motor operating a valve in the intake snorkel of the air cleaner. When the engine is cold or the air being drawn into the engine is cold, the vacuum motor opens the valve, allowing air heated by the

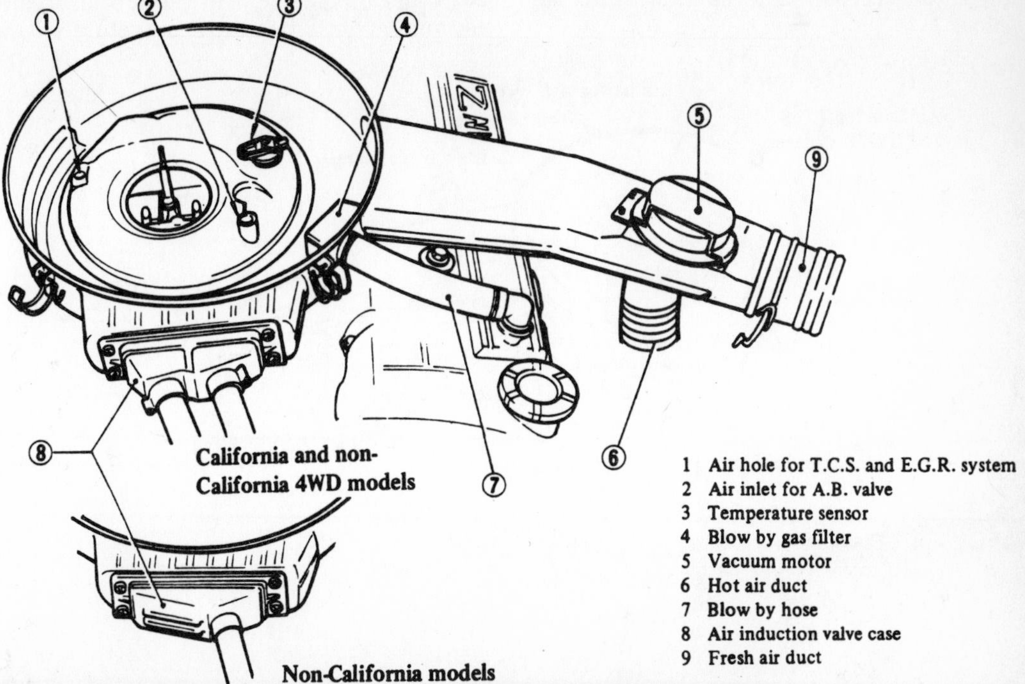

1 Air hole for T.C.S. and E.G.R. system
2 Air inlet for A.B. valve
3 Temperature sensor
4 Blow by gas filter
5 Vacuum motor
6 Hot air duct
7 Blow by hose
8 Air induction valve case
9 Fresh air duct

Automatic temperature control air cleaner—1981–83

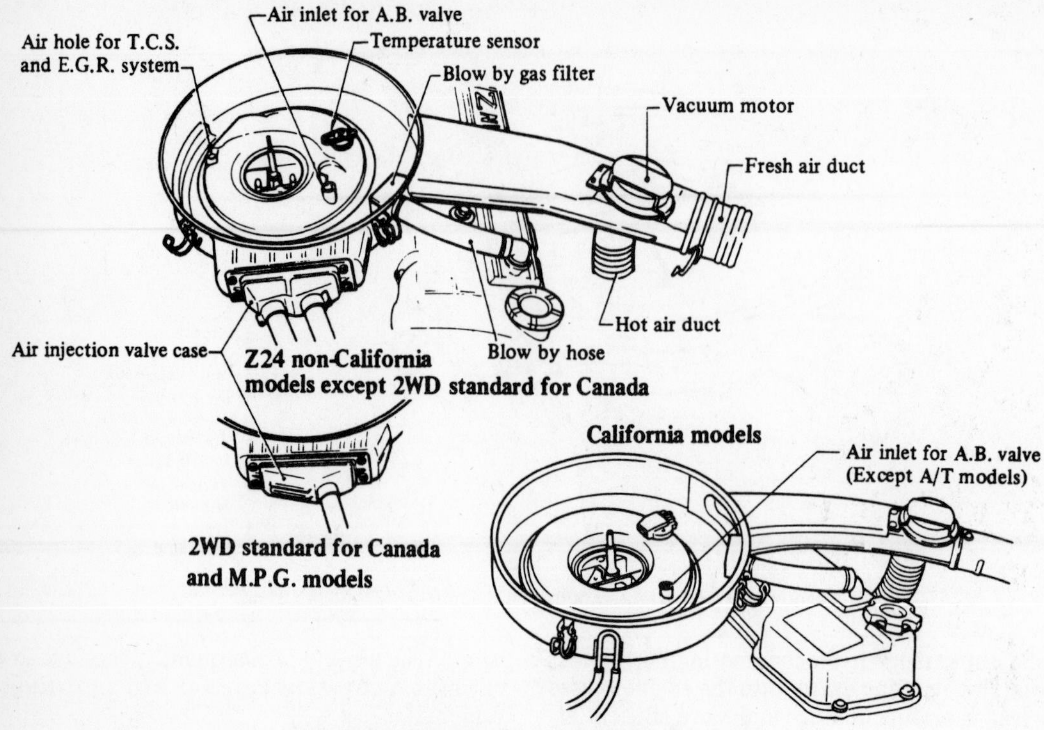

Automatic temperature control air cleaner—1984

exhaust manifold to be drawn into the engine. As the engine warms up, the temperature sensing unit shuts off the vacuum applied to the vacuum motor which allows the valve to close, shutting off the heated air and allowing cooler, outside (underhood) air to be drawn into the engine.

SERVICE

When the air around the temperature sensor of the unit mounted inside the air cleaner housing reaches 100°F (38°C), the sensor should block the flow of vacuum to the air control valve vacuum motor. When the temperature around

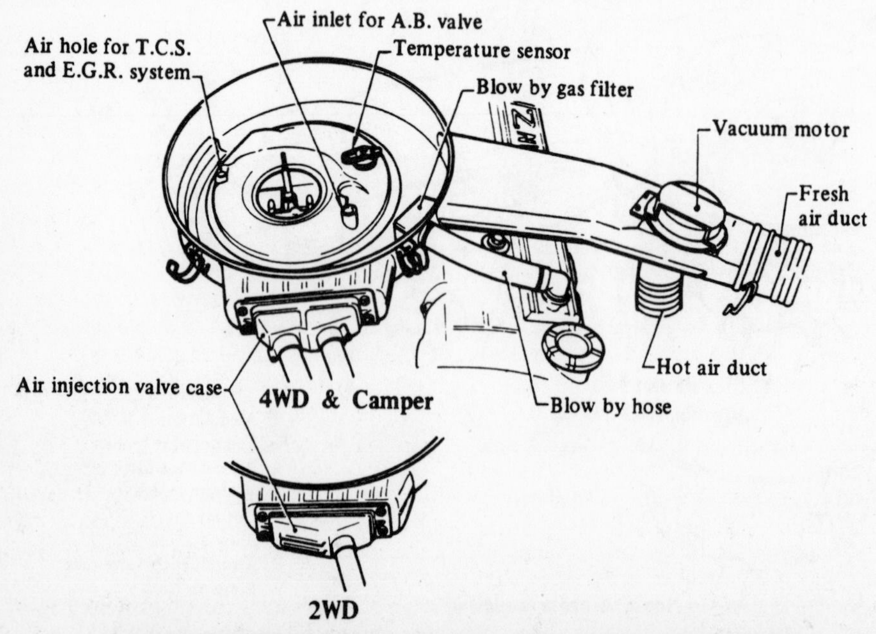

Automatic temperature control air cleaner—1985–86 Z24 engines (Canada)

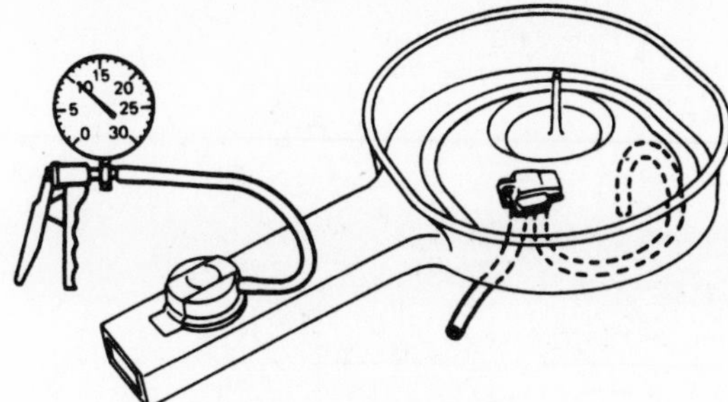

Testing the vacuum control motor

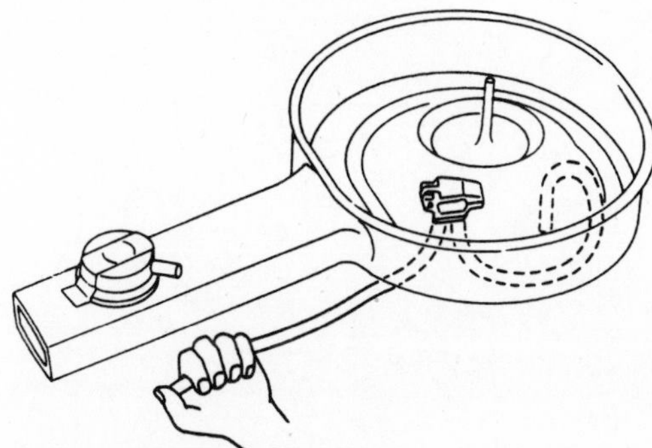
Testing the temperature sensor

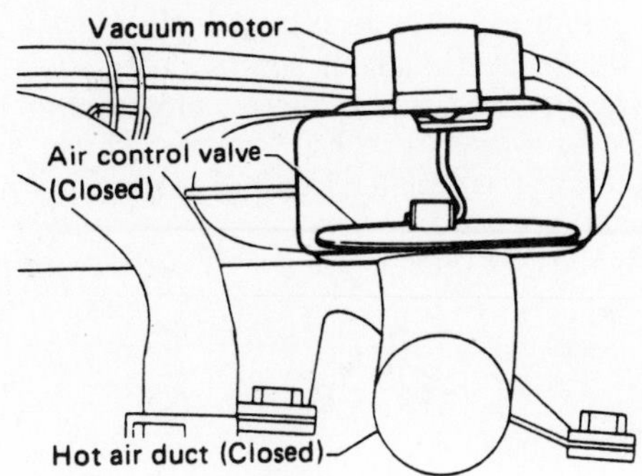

Air control valve—closed

the temperature sensor is below 100°F (38°C), the sensor should allow vacuum to pass onto the air valve vacuum motor, this blocking off the air cleaner snorkel to underhood (unheated) air.

When the temperature around the sensor is about 118°F (48°C), the air control valve should be completely open to underhood air.

When the engine is operating under a heavy load (wide open throttle acceleration), the air control valve fully opens to underhood air to obtain full power no matter what the temperature is around the temperature sensor.

If the air cleaner fails to operate correctly, check for loose or broken vacuum hoses. If the hoses are not the cause, replace the vacuum motor in the air cleaner.

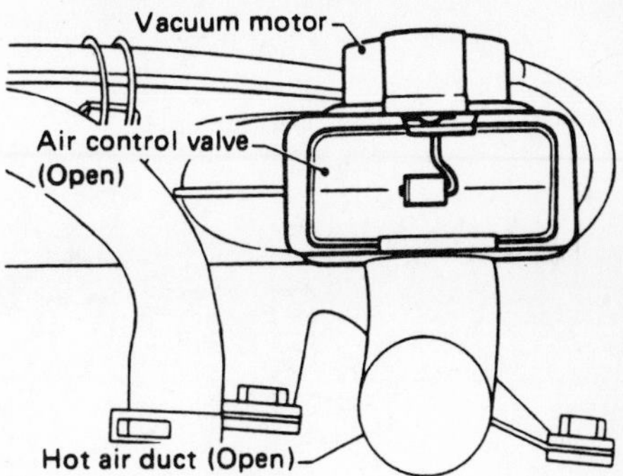

Air control valve—open

Exhaust Gas Recirculation (EGR) System

OPERATION

Gasoline Engines

Exhaust gas recirculation is used to reduce combustion temperatures in the engine, thereby reducing the oxides of nitrogen (NOx) emissions.

An EGR valve is mounted on the center of the intake manifold. The recycled exhaust gas is drawn into the bottom of the intake manifold riser portion through the exhaust manifold heat stove and EGR valve. A vacuum diaphragm is connected to a timed signal port at the carburetor flange.

As the throttle valve is opened, vacuum is applied to the EGR valve vacuum diaphragm. When the vacuum reaches about 2 in.Hg, the diaphragm moves against spring pressure and is in a fully up position at 8 in.Hg of vacuum. As the diaphragm moves up, it opens the exhaust gas metering valve which allows exhaust gas to be pulled into the engine intake manifold. The system does not operate when the engine is idling because the exhaust gas recirculation would cause a rough idle.

On 1974-75 models, an electrically operated solenoid is located in the vacuum line between the EGR valve and the carburetor. The operation of the solenoid is controlled by a temperature sensing switch mounted in the coolant outlet housing. When the temperature of the coolant is below normal operating temperature, the solenoid is electrically activated and blocks the vacuum line leading to the EGR valve, thus preventing exhaust gas recirculation. When the temperature of the engine coolant reaches operating temperature, the solenoid is deactivated and the vacuum is allowed to act upon the EGR valve diaphragm and exhaust gas recirculation takes place.

On 1975-86 models, a thermal vacuum valve inserted in the engine thermostat housing con-

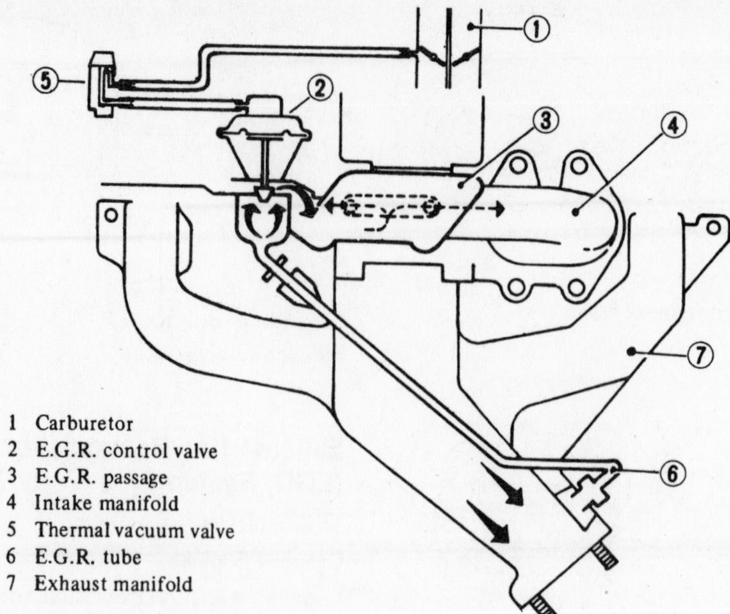

Exhaust gas recirculation system—1975–77

trols the application of vacuum to the EGR valve. When the engine coolant reaches a predetermined temperature, the thermal vacuum valve opens and allows vacuum to be routed to the EGR valve. Below the pre-determined temperature, the thermal vacuum valve closes and blocks vacuum to the EGR valve.

1978-80 and all 1986-86 models have a BPT valve installed between the EGR valve and the thermal vacuum valve. The BPT valve has a diaphragm raised or lowered by exhaust back pressure. The diaphragm opens or closes an air bleed, which is connected into the EGR vacuum line. High pressure results in higher levers of EGR, because the diaphragm is raised, closing off the air bleed, which allows more vacuum to reach and open the EGR valve. Thus, the amount of recirculated exhaust gas varies with exhaust pressure.

All 1981-84 models use a VVT valve (venturi

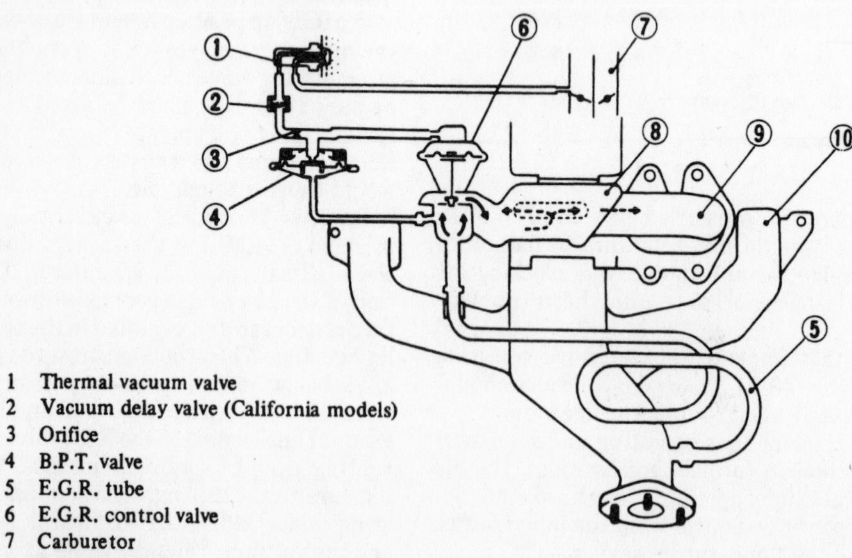

Exhaust gas recircuation system—1978–80

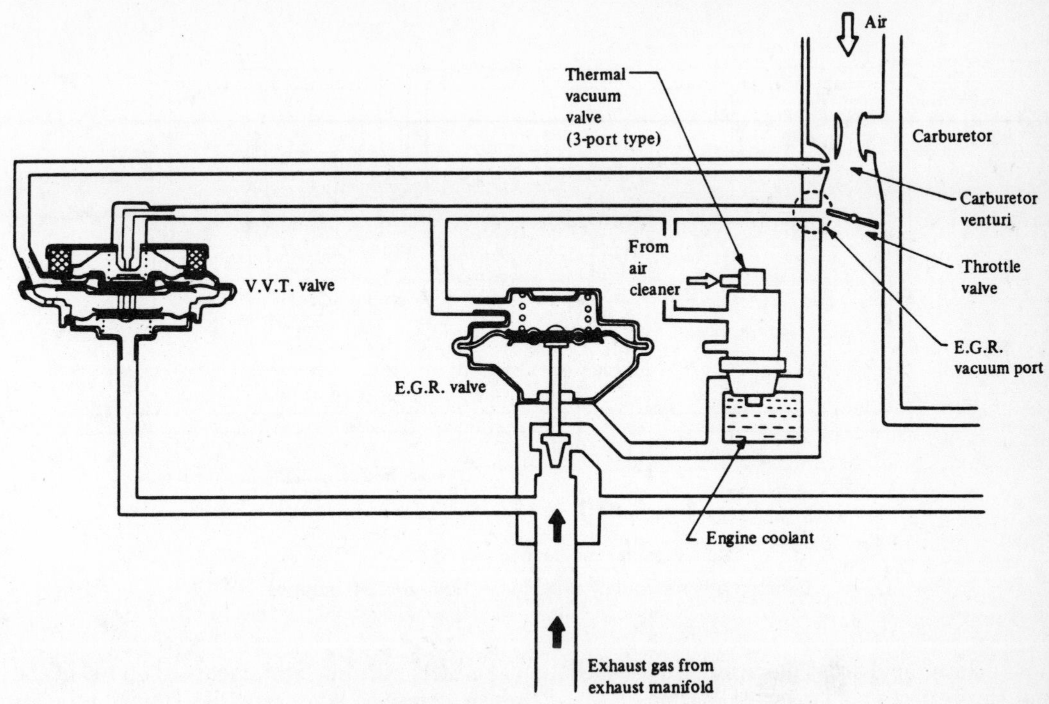

Exhaust gas recirculation system—1981–84

vacuum transducer valve) instead of the BPT valve. The VVT valve monitors exhaust pressure and carburetor vacuum in order to activate the diaphragm which controls the throttle vacuum applied to the EGR control valve. This system expands the operating range of the EGR flow rate as compared to the BPT unit.

1978-79 California models have a vacuum delay valve installed in the line between the thermal vacuum valve and the EGR valve. This

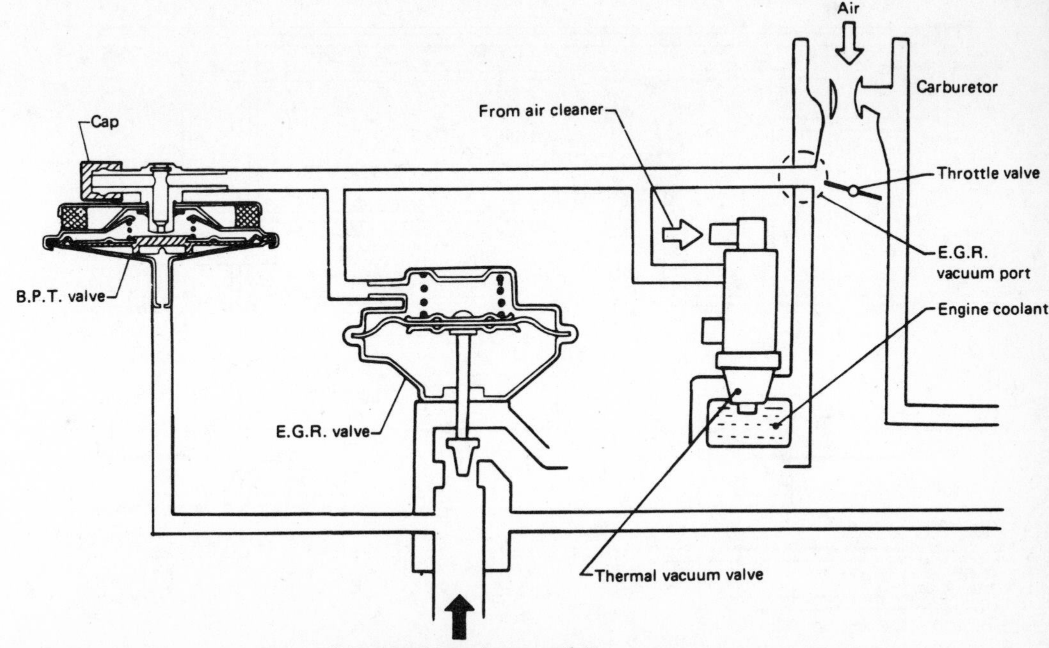

Exhaust gas recirculation system—1985–86 Z20 and Z24 engines

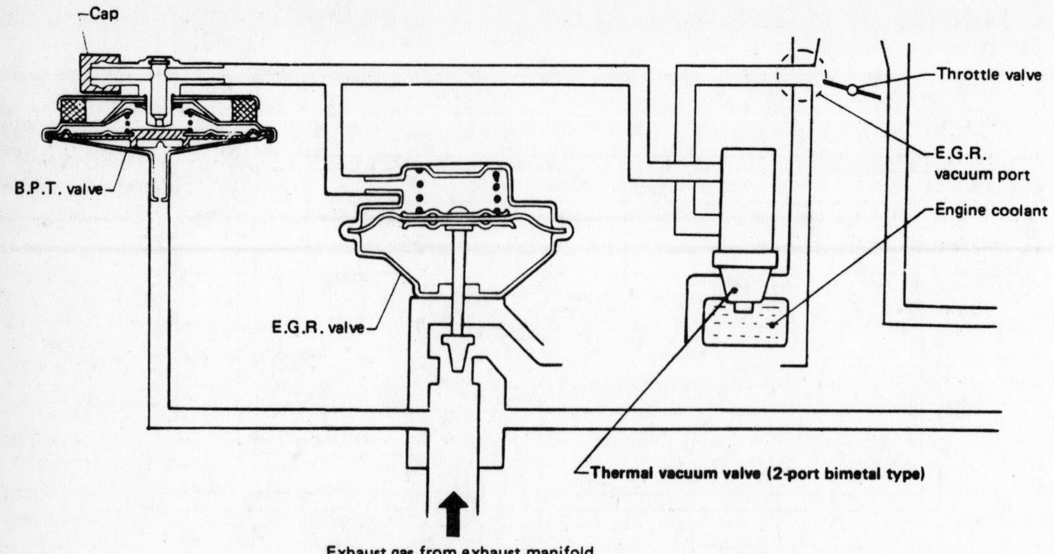

Exhaust gas recirculation system—1986–87 Z24i engines

valve delays rapid drops in vacuum in the EGR line, thus effecting a longer EGR time.

On all 1975 trucks (except Canadian models) and all 1976-77 49 States trucks, the EGR system is equipped with a warning system which monitors the distance the pick-up has traveled and activates a warning light when the EGR system must be checked and possibly serviced. The EGR warning light, mounted on top of the dash, comes on when a predetermined number of miles has been traveled and every time the starter is engaged as a check for a burned out bulb.

To reset the counter, which is mounted on the right fender apron under the hood, remove the grommet installed in the side of the counter

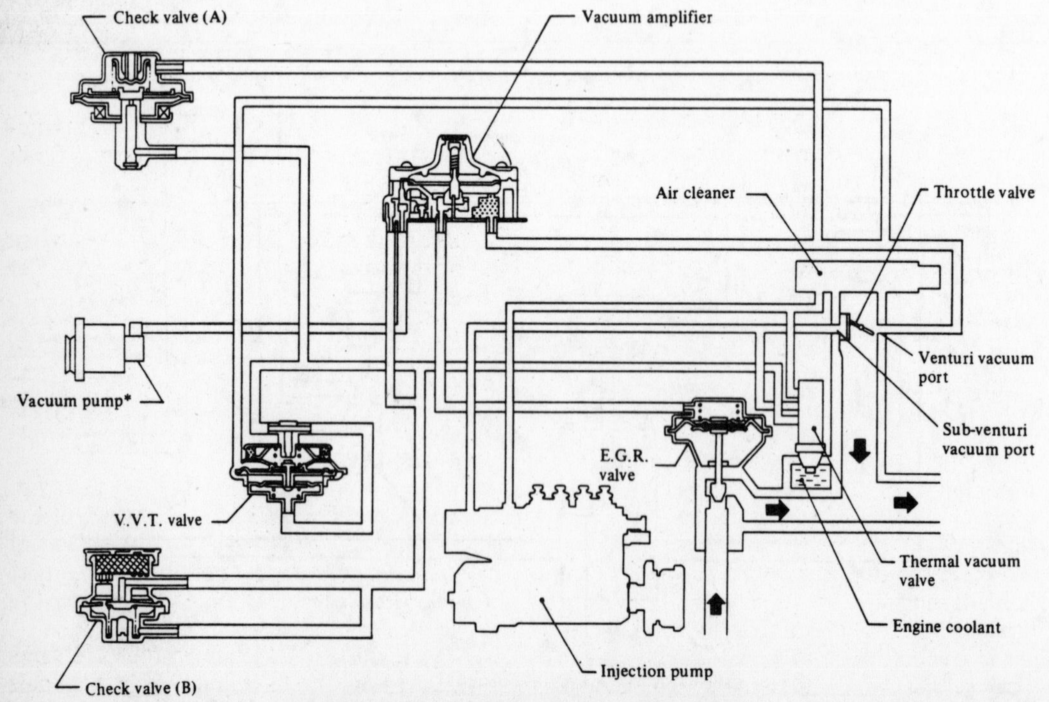

Exhaust gas recirculation system—SD25 engines

and insert the tip of a small screwdriver into the hole. Press down on the knob inside the hole. Reinstall the grommet.

Diesel Engines

This system is designed to control the formation of NOx emissions by recirculating the exhaust gas into the intake manifold passage through the control valve.

The EGR flow rate is controlled in three stages in accordance with the engine speed and load. The first stage, High EGR, is obtained through the combination of a closed throttle valve and an open EGR valve. The second stage, Low EGR, is obtained through the opening of the throttle valve. The third stage, Zero EGR, is obtained closing the EGR valve.

The engine load signal is picked up by the potentiometer installed on the injection pump control lever. The engine speed signal is transmitted by an electromagnetic revolution sensor attached to the front cover. The throttle diaphragm and the EGR valve are both actuated by vacuum generated at the vacuum pump. Solenoids are used to convert the electrical signal from the control unit into the vacuum signal.

The EGR system is deactivated under extremely high or low coolant temperatures in order to assure good driveability.

SERVICE

Gasoline Engines

1974-75

Check the operation of the EGR system as follows:

1. Visually inspect the entire EGR control system. Clean the mechanism so its free of oil and dirt. Replace any rubber hoses found to be cracked or broken.
2. Make sure that the EGR solenoid valve is properly wired.
3. Increase the engine speed from idling to 3000–3500 rpm. The plate of the EGR control valve diaphragm and the valve shaft should move upward as the engine speed is increased.
4. Disconnect the EGR solenoid valve electrical leads and connect them directly to the vehicle's 12V electrical supply (the battery!). Race the engine again with the EGR solenoid valve connected to a 12V power source (gues what that is!). The EGR control valve should remain stationary.
5. With the engine running at idle, push up the EGR control valve diaphragm by pressing it up with your finger. When this is done, the engine idle should become rough and uneven.

Inspect the two components of the EGR system as necessary in the following manner:

1. Remove the EGR control valve from the intake manifold.
2. Apply 4.7–5.1 in.Hg of vacuum to the EGR control valve by sucking on a tube attached to the outlet on top of the valve. The valve should move to the full up position. The valve should remain open for more than 30 seconds after the application of vacuum is discontinued and the vacuum hose is blocked.
3. Inspect the EGR valve for any signs of warpage or damage.
4. Clean the EGR valve seat with a brush and compressed air to prevent clogging.
5. Connect the EGR solenoid valve to a 12V DC power source and notice if the valve clicks when intermittently electrified. If the valve clicks, it is considered to be working properly.
6. Check the EGR temperature sensing switch by removing it from the engine and placing it in a container of water together with a thermometer. Connect a self-powered test light to the 2 electrical leads of the switch.
7. Heat the container of water.
8. The switch should conduct current when the water temperature is below 77°F (25°C) and stop conducting current when the water reaches a temperature somewhere between 88–106°F (31–41°C). Replace the switch if it behaves otherwise.

1975-89

1. Remove the EGR valve and apply enough vacuum to the diaphragm to open the valve.
2. The valve should remain open for over 30 seconds after the vacuum is removed.
3. Check the valve for damage, such as warpage, cracks, and excessive wear around the valve and seat.
4. Clean the seat with a brush and compressed air and remove any deposits from around the valve and port (seat).
5. To check the operation of the thermal vacuum valve, remove the valve from the engine and apply vacuum to the ports of the valve. The valve should not allow vacuum to pass.
6. Place the valve in a container of water with a thermometer and heat the water. When the temperature of the water reaches 134–145°F (57–63°C), remove the valve and apply vacuum to the ports; the valve should allow vacuum to pass through it.
7. To test the BPT valve, disconnect the two vacuum hoses from the valve. Plug one of the ports. While applying pressure to the bottom of the valve, apply vacuum to the unplugged port and check for leakage. If any exists, replace the valve.
8. To test the check valve installed in some models, remove the valve and blow into the side which connects to the EGR valve. Air should

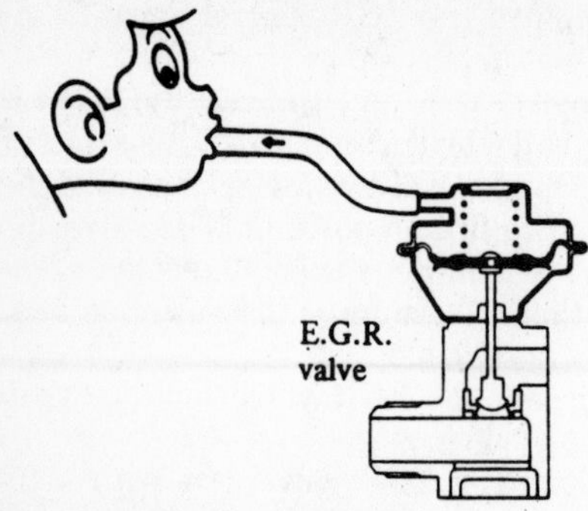

Testing the EGR valve—1975–89

Testing the thermal vacuum valve—1975–86

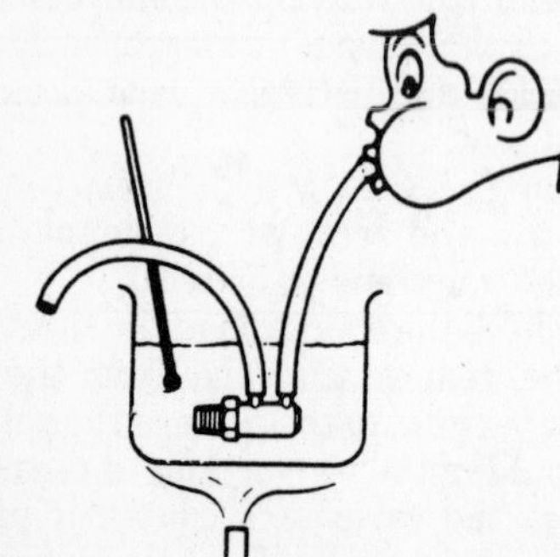

Testing the thermal vacuum valve—1987–89

flow. When air is applied to the other side, air flow resistance should be greater. If not, replace the valve.

9. To check the VVT valve, disconnect the top and bottom center hoses and apply vacuum to the top hose. Check for leaks. If a leak is present, replace the valve.

Diesel Engines

1. Visually inspect the entire EGR control system. Clean the mechanism so its free of oil

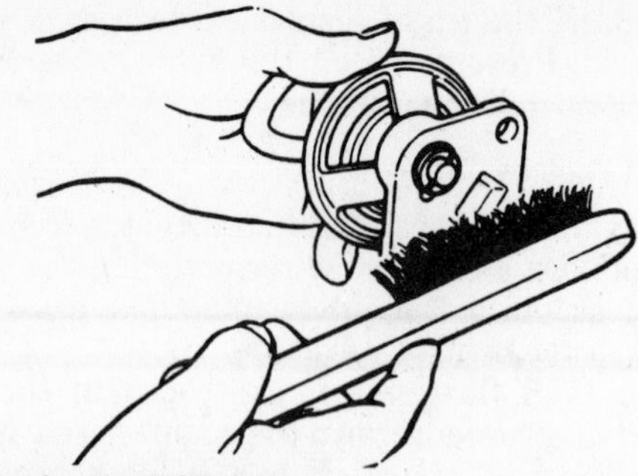

Cleaning the EGR valve

and dirt. Replace any rubber hoses found to be cracked or broken.

2. Remove the EGR valve and apply enough vacuum to the diaphragm to open the valve.

3. The valve should remain open for over 30 seconds after the vacuum is removed.

4. Check the valve for damage, such as warpage, cracks, and excessive wear around the valve and seat.

5. Clean the seat with a brush and compressed air and remove any deposits from around the valve and port (seat).

6. To check the operation of the thermal vacuum valve, remove the valve from the engine and apply vacuum to the ports of the valve. The valve should not allow vacuum to pass.

7. Place the valve in a container of water with a thermometer and heat the water. When the temperature of the water reaches 134–145°F (57–63°C), remove the valve and apply vacuum to the ports; the valve should allow vacuum to pass through it.

8. To check the VVT valve, block one vacuum port and suck from the other. There should be some initial air leakage which will gradually disappear. If not, replace the valve.

REMOVAL AND INSTALLATION

Gasoline Engines

1. Remove the nuts which attach the EGR tube and/or the BP tube to the EGR valve (if so equipped).

2. Unscrew the mounting bolts and remove the heat shield plate from the EGR control valve (if so equipped).

3. Tag and disconnect the EGR vacuum hose(s).

4. Unscrew the mounting bolts and remove the EGR control valve.

5. Install the EGR valve assembly with mounting bolts to intake manifold location.

6. Connect all vacuum hoses and install the heat shield if so equipped.

7. Connect EGR tube or BP tube to the EGR valve if so equipped.

NOTE: *Always be sure that the new valve is identical to the old one.*

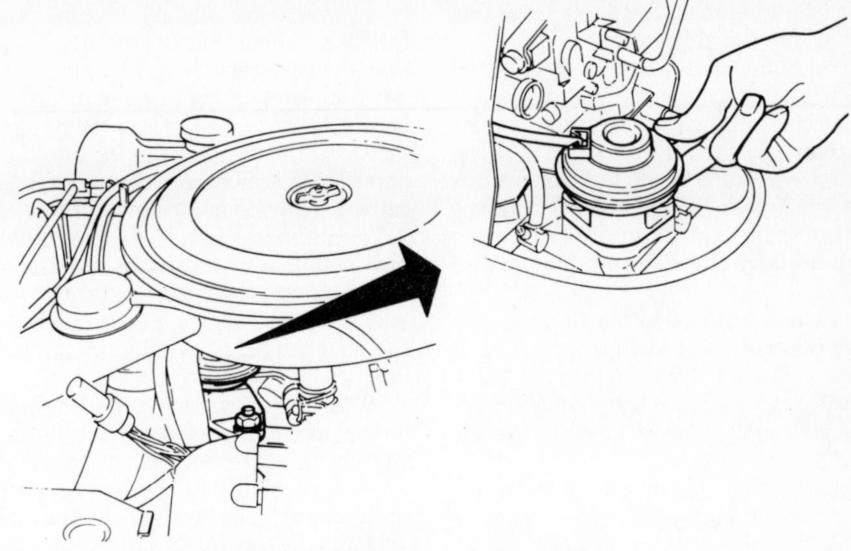

EGR valve—1980

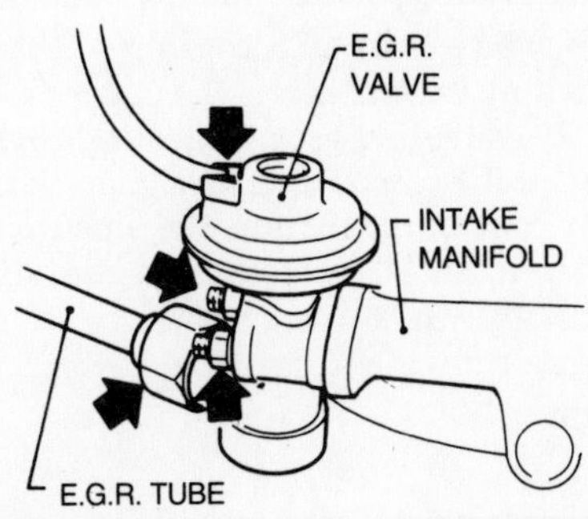

EGR valve—1981

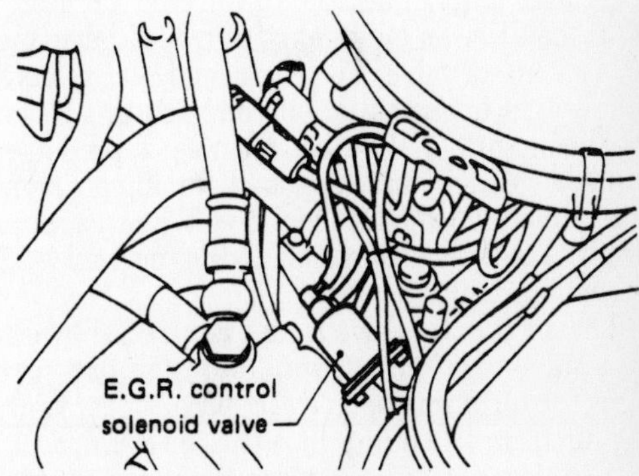

EGR valve—1986–89 Z24i engines

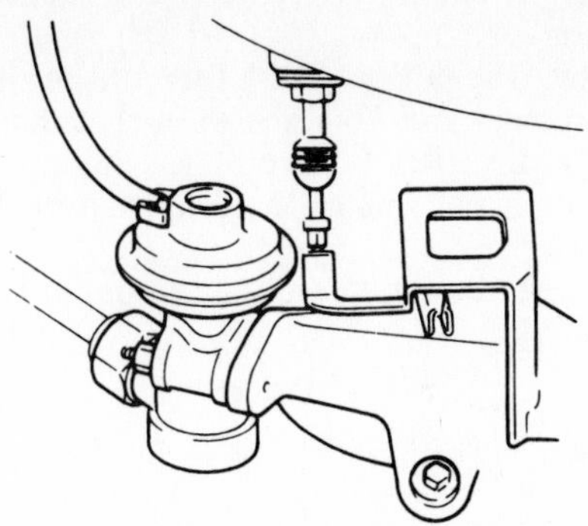

EGR valve—1982–86 Z20, Z22 and Z24 engines

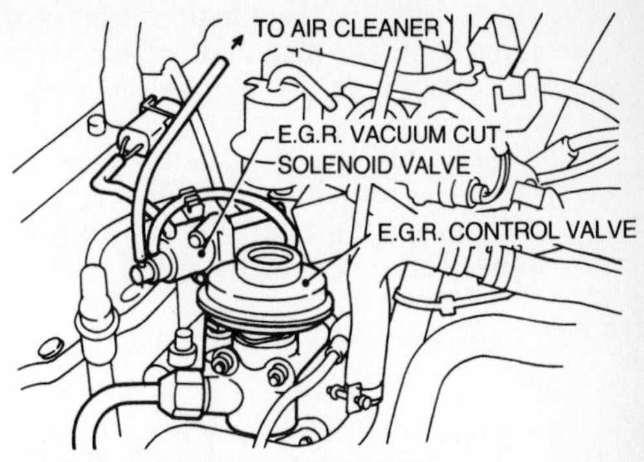

EGR valve—1986–89 VG30i engines

Diesel Engines

1. Remove the EGR duct and pipe bolts at the side of the control valve.
2. Disconnect the vacuum hose and remove the valve.
3. Install the valve and then connect the pipe and duct. Tighten the bolts to 19–26 ft. lbs. (25–35 Nm).

Air Injection System (AIS)

OPERATION

Gasoline Engines Only

In gasoline engines, it is difficult to burn the air/fuel mixture completely through normal combustion in the combustion chambers. Under certain operating conditions, unburned fuel is exhausted into the atmosphere.

The air injection reactor system is designed so that ambient air, pressurized by an air pump, is injected through the injection nozzles into the exhaust ports near each exhaust valve. The exhaust gases are at high temperatures and ignite when brought into contact with the oxygen of the ambient air. Thus, the unburned fuel is burned in the exhaust ports and manifold.

A check valve is installed in the air pump discharge line to prevent the airflow from reversing due to a broken drive belt, relief valve spring failure, or backfire in the exhaust manifold. Reversed airflow could damage the air pump.

The air pump relief valve bleeds off excess air from the pump at high speeds. The valve is mounted on the carburetor air cleaner.

Trucks with a catalytic converter have protection devices to prevent converter overheating due to large quantities of injected air. 1976-77 models use an emergency air relief valve and an air control valve. The emergency valve has a diaphragm operated by engine vacuum. When intake manifold vacuum reaches a predetermined level, the valve opens, diverting air from the pump into the atmosphere. When vacuum drops, the valve closes allowing normal AIS operation.

The air control valve is also controlled by engine vacuum. High vacuum and high pressure from the air pump open the control valve, venting air from the pump into the air cleaner.

1978-79 models have a combined air control valve instead of the relief valve, emergency valve, and air control valve. The combined air control valve regulates the amount of injected air according to intake manifold and air pump discharge pressure, to prevent the converter from overheating.

An anti-backfire valve is installed in an air delivery hose. The purpose of the valve is to prevent backfiring in the exhaust manifold during deceleration. When the throttle closes suddenly, an overly rich air/fuel mixture exists in the intake manifold due to the lack of air getting past the throttle valves. This rich mixture will not completely burn in the combustion chamber. If the unburned gases were to come in contact with the oxygen pumped into the exhaust ports by the air pump, they would ignite and cause backfiring and possible damage.

The anti-backfire valve is connected to the intake manifold by a vacuum line and when the vacuum rises, the valve opens a port in the intake manifold, allowing extra filtered air from the air chambers, leaning out the overly rich mixture.

1979 cab and chassis models have a transistorized programmed control unit, a vacuum switching valve, and an air control switch which govern air flow through the AIS. The air control switch, located between the intake manifold and the control unit, turns off when manifold vacuum is high, and on when vacuum is low. This provides a signal to the control unit, which determines when to turn the vacuum switching valve on or off accordingly. The vacuum switching valve controls the upper chamber of the CAC valve diaphragm, opening or closing the CAC valve according to signals received from the control unit. Thus, the amount of air injected into the AIS is monitored and adjusted as conditions warrant.

SERVICE

Air Pump

If the air pump makes an abnormal noise and cannot be corrected without removing the pump from the vehicle, check the following sequence:

1. Turn the pulley ¾ of a turn in the clockwise direction and ¼ of a turn in the counterclockwise direction. If the pulley is binding and if rotation is not smooth, a defective bearing is indicated.
2. Check the inner wall of the pump body,

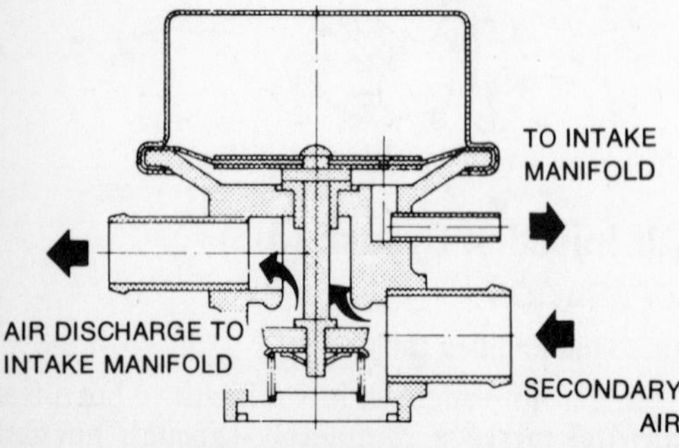

Anti-backfire valve—1975–86

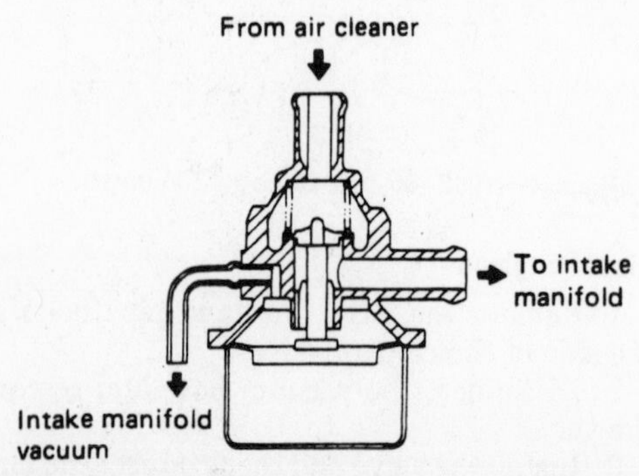

Anti-backfire valve—1986–89 Z24i and VG30i engines

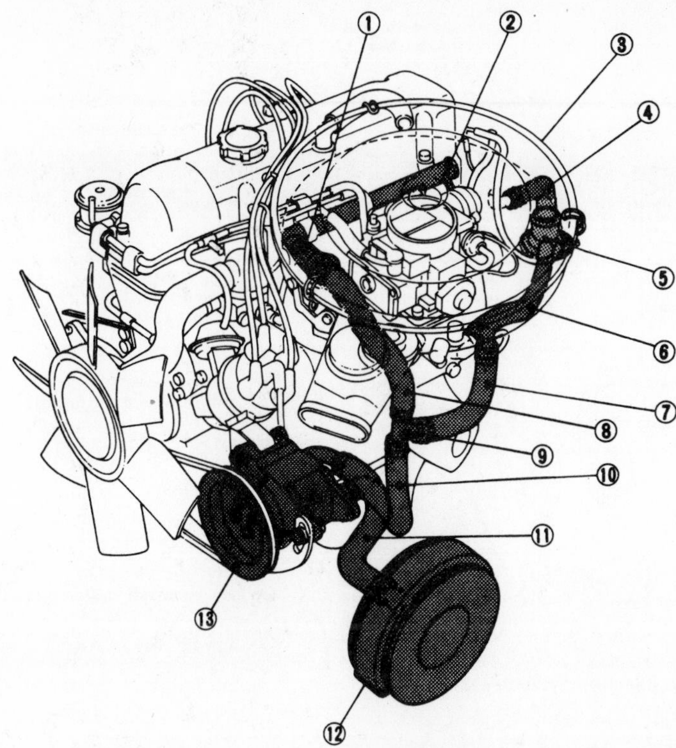

1 Check valve
2 Air gallery pipe
3 Automatic temperature control air cleaner
4 Air hose (carburetor air cleaner to A.B. valve)
5 Anti-backfire valve (A.B. valve)
6 Air hose (A.B. valve to intake manifold)
7 Air hose (carburetor air cleaner to air hose connector)
8 Air hose (check valve to air hose connector)
9 3-way connector
10 Air hose (air hose connector to air pump)
11 Air hose (air pump to air pump air cleaner)
12 Air pump air cleaner
13 Air pump

Air injection system—1975–77 (49 State)

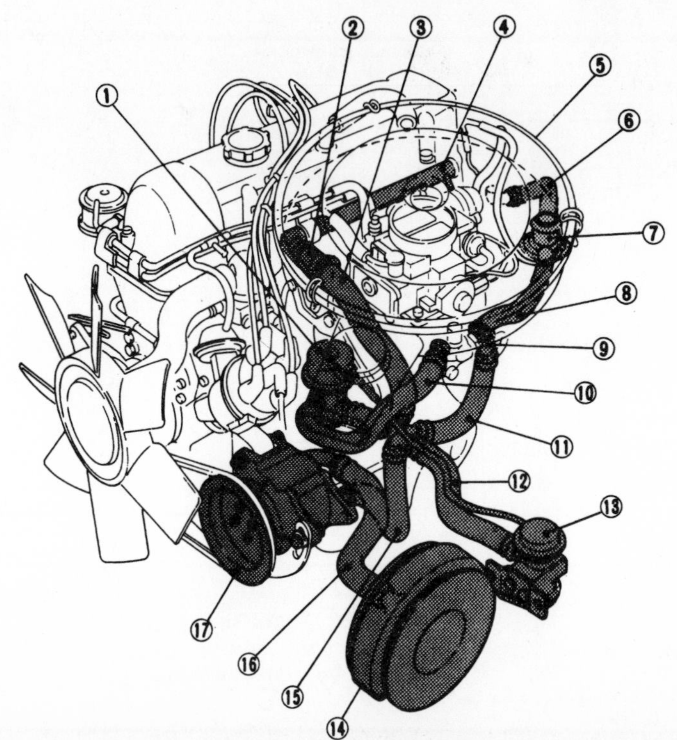

1 Air control valve
2 Check valve
3 Air hose (check valve to air hose connector)
4 Air gallery pipe
5 Automatic temperature control air cleaner
6 Air hose (carburetor air cleaner to A.B. valve)
7 Anti-backfire valve (A.B. valve)
8 Air hose (A.B. valve to intake manifold)
9 Air relief valve
10 Air hose (carburetor air cleaner to air control valve)
11 Air hose (air relief valve to air hose connector)
12 Air hose (air hose connector to emergency air relief valve)
13 Emergency air relief valve
14 Air pump air cleaner
15 Air hose (air hose connector to air pump)
16 Air hose (air pump to air pump air cleaner)
17 Air pump

Air injection system—1975–77 (Calif.)

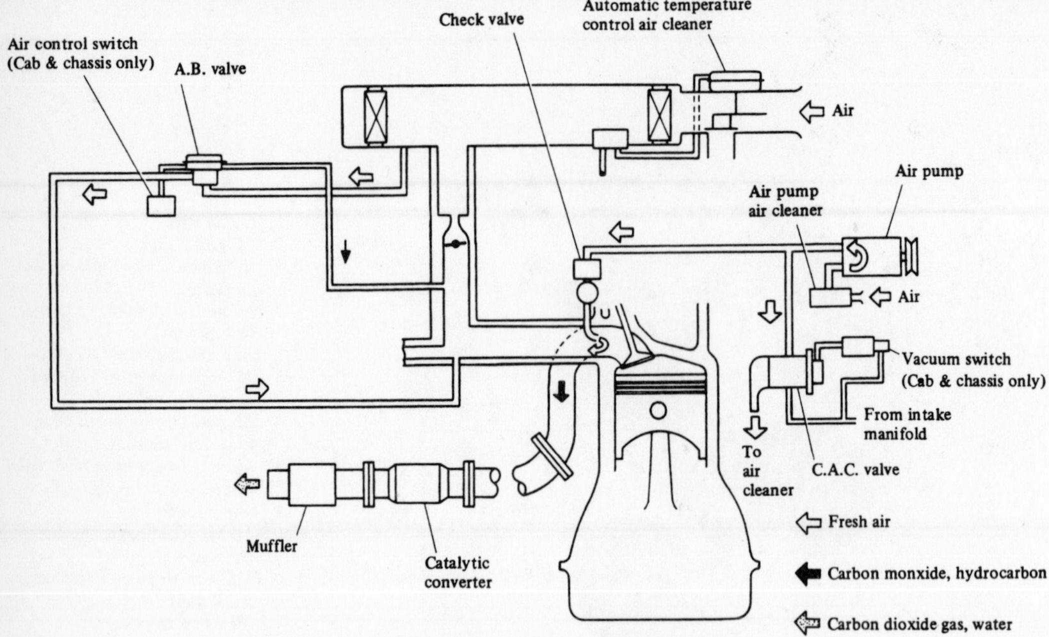

Air injection system—1978–80

vanes, and rotor for wear. If the rotor has abnormal wear, replace the air pump.

3. Check the needle roller bearing for wear and damage. If the bearings are defective, the air pump should be replaced.

4. Check and replace the rear side seal if abnormal wear or damage is noticed.

5. Check and replace the carbon shoes holding the vanes if they are found to be worn or damaged.

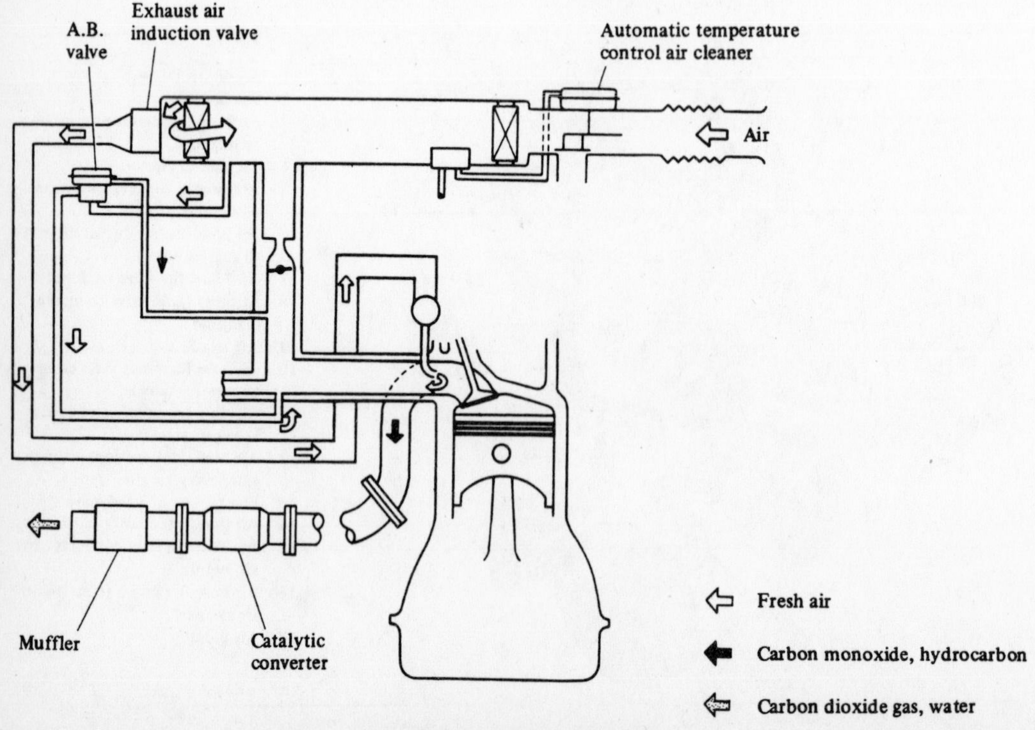

Air induction system—1978–80

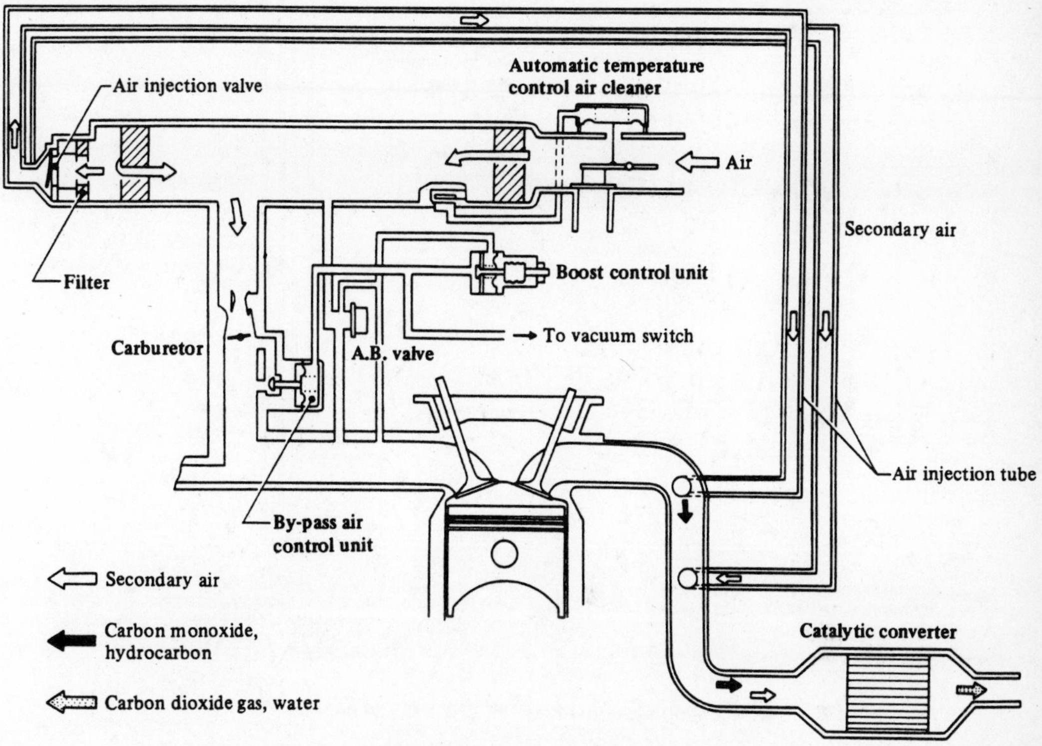

Air injection system—1981–84

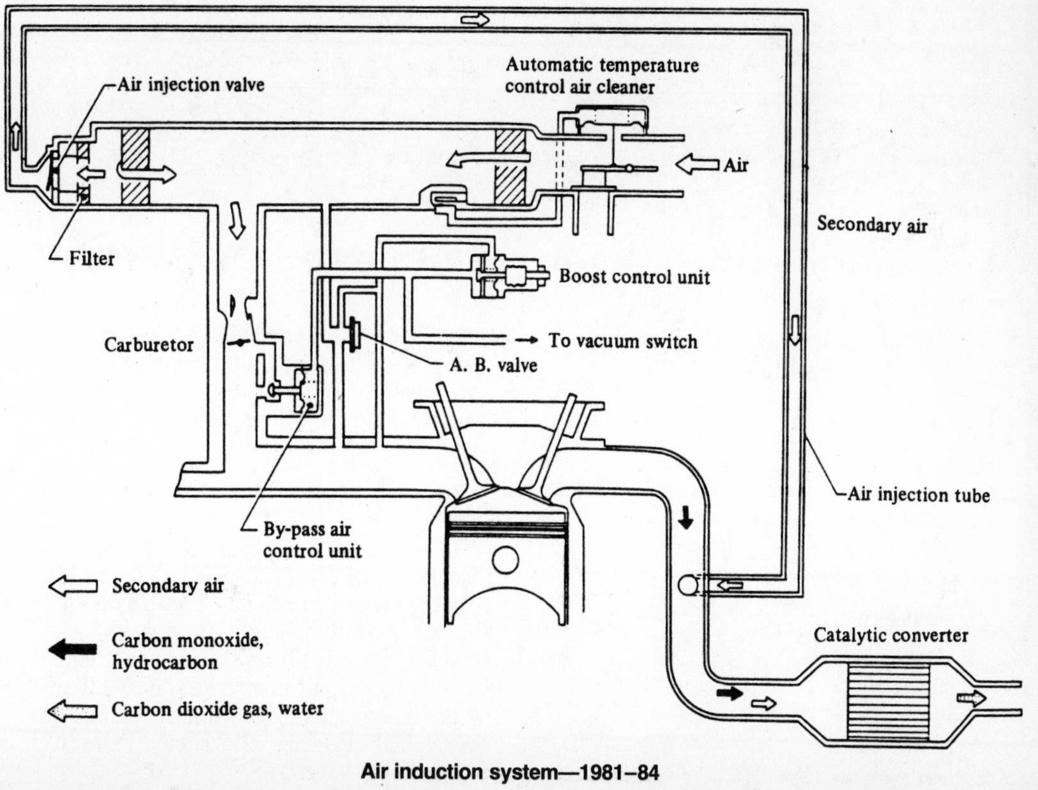

Air induction system—1981–84

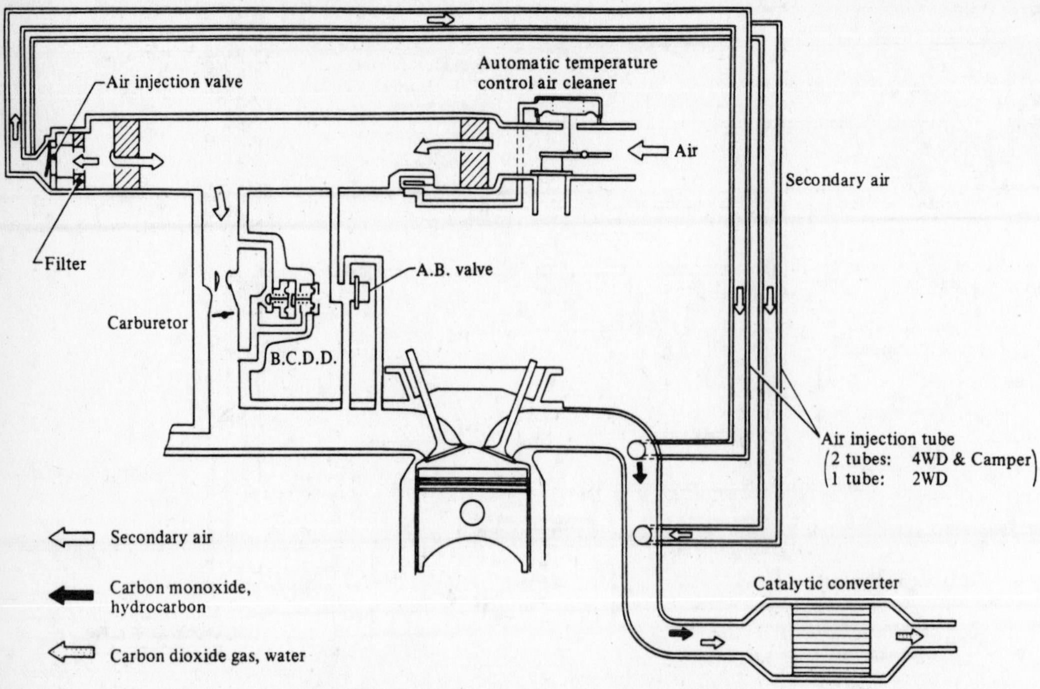

Air injection system—1985–86 Z20 and Z24 engines

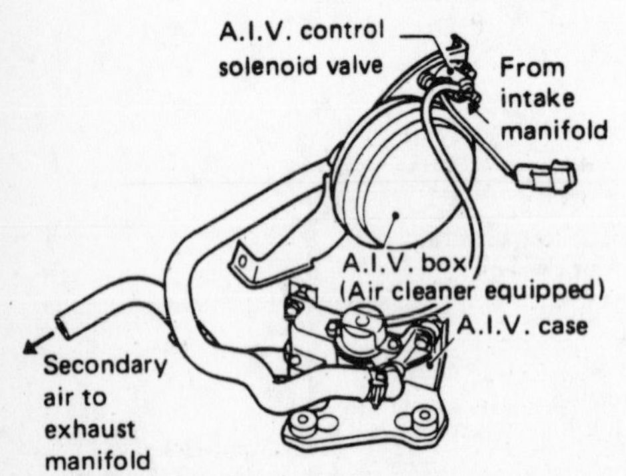

Air induction system—1986–89 Z24i engines (2wd)

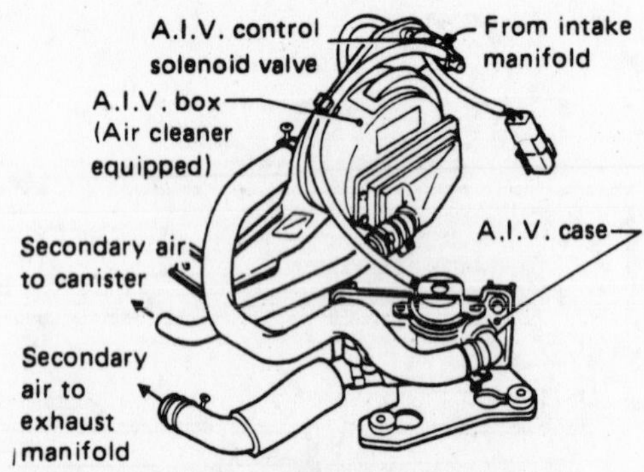

Air injection system—1986–89 VG30i engines

6. A deposit of carbon particles on the inner wall of the pump body and vanes is normal, but should be removed with compressed air before reassembling the air pump.

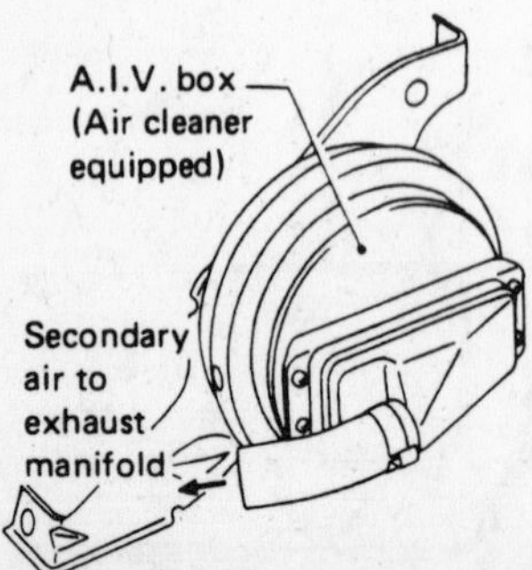

Air injection system—1986–89 Z24i engines (4wd)

Check Valve

Remove the check valve from the air pump discharge line. Test it for leakage by blowing air into the valve from the air pump side and from the air manifold side. Air should only pass through the valve from the air pump side if the valve is functioning normally. A small amount of air leakage from the manifold side can be overlooked. Replace the check valve if it is found to be defective.

Anti-Backfire Valve

To check the valve, disconnect the hose from the air cleaner and place a finger on the end. Run the engine up to about 3000 rpm, then quickly release the throttle. If the valve is performing correctly, suction should be felt at the end of the hose. If no suction is felt, replace the anti-backfire valve.

Air Pump Relief Valve

1. Disconnect the hoses leading to the check valve (on the air injection manifold) and the air control valve from the air hose connector. Plug the connector.

2. Start the engine and increase the engine speed to about 3000 rpm. Place you finger on the outlet of the relief valve (inside the air cleaner housing) and check for air discharge. If you do not feel any air coming out, the relief valve is faulty, and must be replaced.

Air Injection Nozzles

Check around the air manifold for air leakage with the engine running at 2000 rpm. If air is leaking form the eye joint bolt, retighten or replace the gasket. Check the air nozzles for restrictions by blowing air into the nozzles.

Hoses

Check and replace hoses if they are found to be weakened or cracked. Check all hose connections and clips. Be sure that the hoses are not in contact with other parts of the engine.

Emergency Air Relief Valve

1. Warm up the engine.

2. Check all hoses for leaks, kinks, improper connections, etc.

3. Run the engine up to 2000 rpm under no lead. No air should be discharged from the valve.

4. Disconnect the vacuum hose from the valve. This is the hose which runs to the intake manifold. Run the engine up to 2000 rpm. Air should be discharged from the valve. If not, replace it.

Combined Air Control Valve

1. Check all hoses for leaks, kinks, and improper connections.

2. Thoroughly warm up the engine.

3. With the engine idling, check for air discharge from the relief opening in the air cleaner case.

4. Disconnect and plug the vacuum hose from the valve. Air should be discharged from the valve with the engine idling. If the disconnected vacuum hose is not plugged. The engine will stumble.

5. Connect a hand operated vacuum pump to

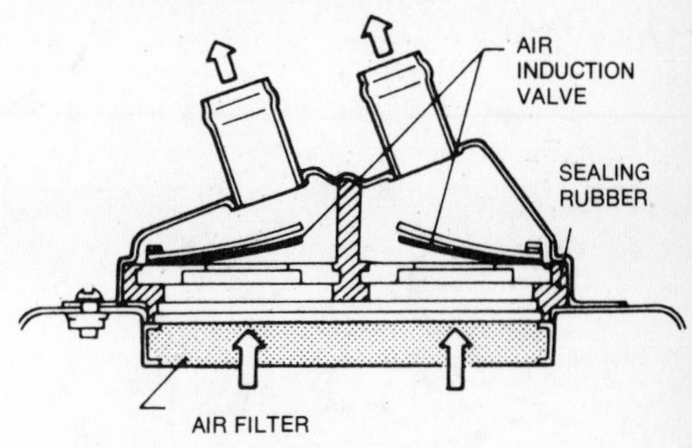

California type air induction case

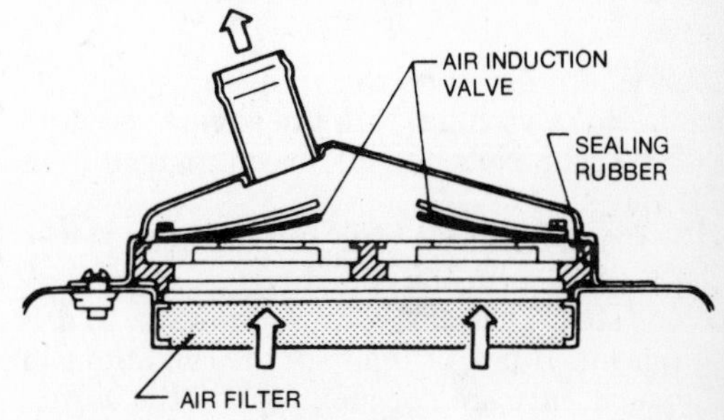

49 states air induction case

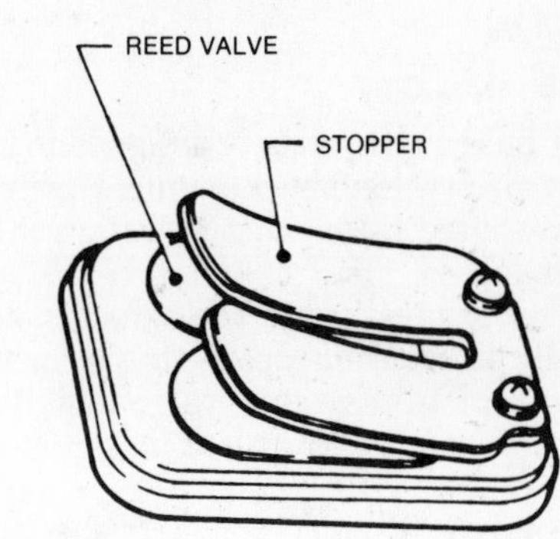

Air induction valve

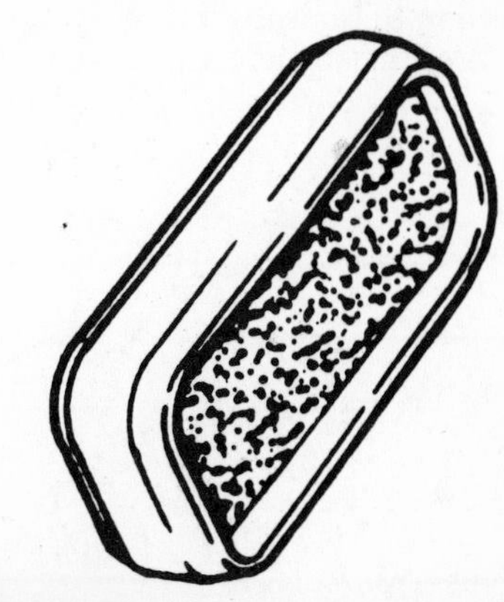

Air induction filter

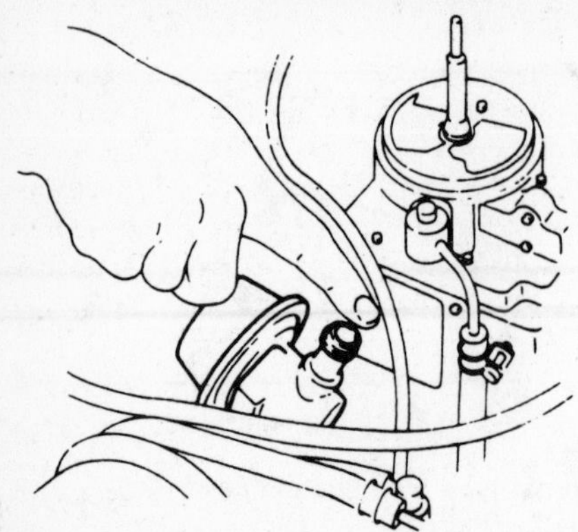
Checking the AB valve—1985–86 Z20 and Z24 engines

the vacuum fitting on the valve and apply 7.8–9.8 in.Hg of vacuum. Run the engine speed up to 3000 rpm. No air should be discharged from the valve.

6. Disconnect and plug the air hose at the check valve, with the conditions as in the preceding step. This should cause the valve to discharge air. If not, or if any of the conditions in this procedure are not met, replace the valve.

Air Induction System

OPERATION

Gasoline Engines Only

The air induction system is designed to send secondary air to the exhaust manifold, utilizing a vacuum caused by exhaust pulsation in the exhaust manifold.

The exhaust pressure in the exhaust manifold usually pulsates in response to the opening and closing of the exhaust valve and it decreases below atmospheric pressure periodically.

If a secondary air intake pipe is opened to he atmosphere under vacuum conditions, secondary air can be drawn into the exhaust manifold in proportion to the vacuum.

Therefore, the air induction system reduces CO and HC emissions in exhaust gases. The system consists of two air induction valves, a filter, hoses and E.A.I. tube(s).

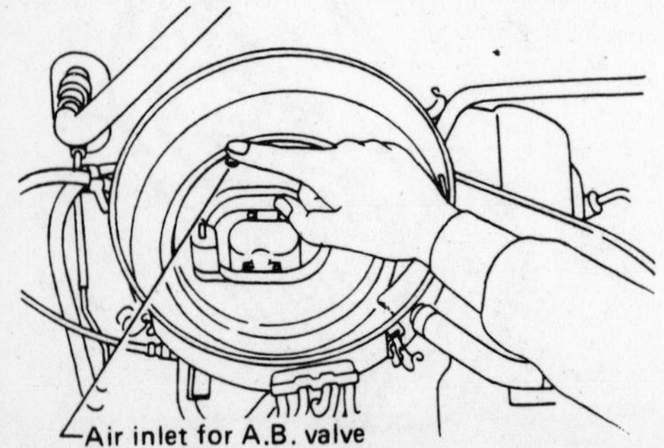

Checking the AB valve—1986–89 Z24i engines

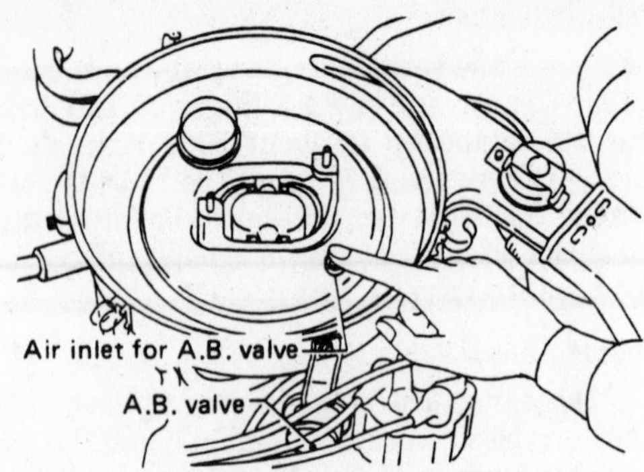

Checking the AB valve—1986–89 VG30i engines

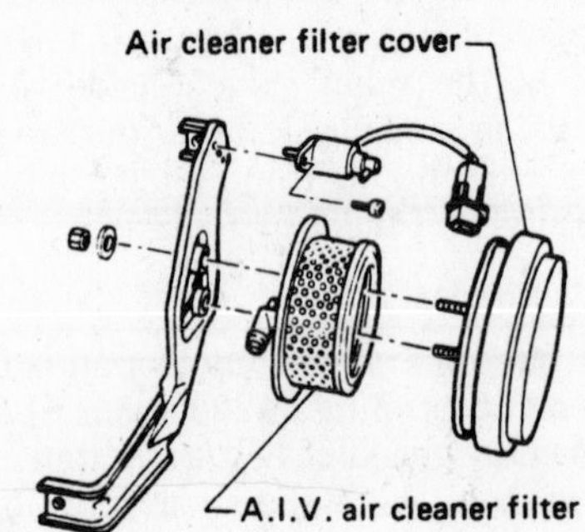

Exploded view of the air box—1986–89 Z24i engines (2wd)

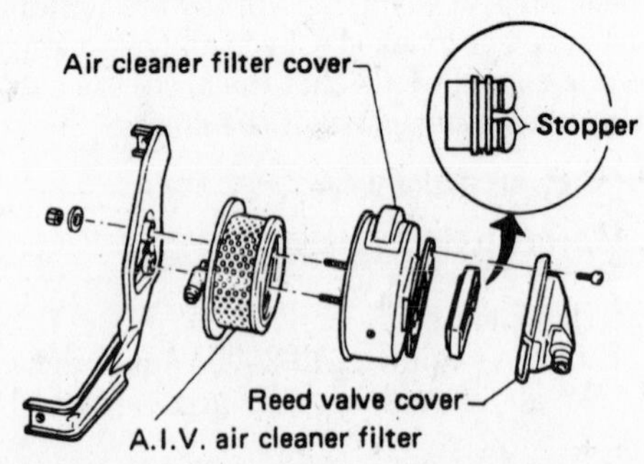

Exploded view of the air box—1986–89 Z24i engines (4wd)

AIR INDUCTION VALVE CASE

The air induction valve case consists of 2 reed valves, a rubber seal and a filter and is attached to the air cleaner. There are 2 types of air induction valve cases. Type A is equipped with 2 hose connectors and is installed on California models, while Type B is equipped with 1connector and is installed on non-California models.

AIR INDUCTION VALVE

Two reed valve type check valves are installed in the air cleaner. When the exhaust pressure is

Air cleaner filter cover
Stopper
Reed valve cover
A.I.V. air cleaner filter

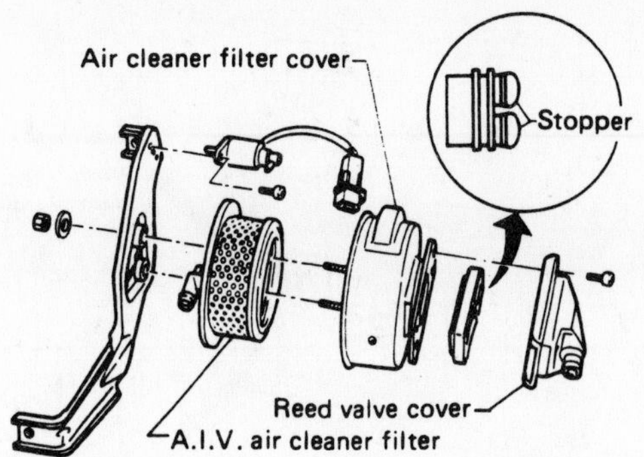

Exploded view of the air box—1986–89 VG30i engines

below atmospheric pressure (negative pressure), secondary air is sent to the exhaust manifold.

When the exhaust pressure is above atmospheric pressure, the reed valves prevent secondary air from being sent back to the air cleaner.

AIR INDUCTION VALVE FILTER

The air induction valve filter is installed at the dust side of the air cleaner. It purifies secondary air to be sent to the exhaust manifold.

AIR INDUCTION PIPE

The secondary air fed from the air induction valve goes through the EAI pipe to the exhaust manifold.

At this period, the mixture in the intake manifold becomes too rich to ignite and burn in the combustion chamber and burns easily in the exhaust system with injected air in the exhaust manifold.

The AB valve provides air to the intake manifold to make the air/fuel mixture leaner and prevents backfire.

The correct function of this valve reduces hydrocarbon emission during deceleration.

SERVICE

Air Induction Valve and Filter

Remove the valve and filter on the air cleaner. The air induction valve and valve filter can then be taken out easily. Installation is in the reverse sequence of removal.

AB Valve

1. Remove air cleaner.
2. Remove air hoses and vacuum tube. Then the AB valve can be taken out.

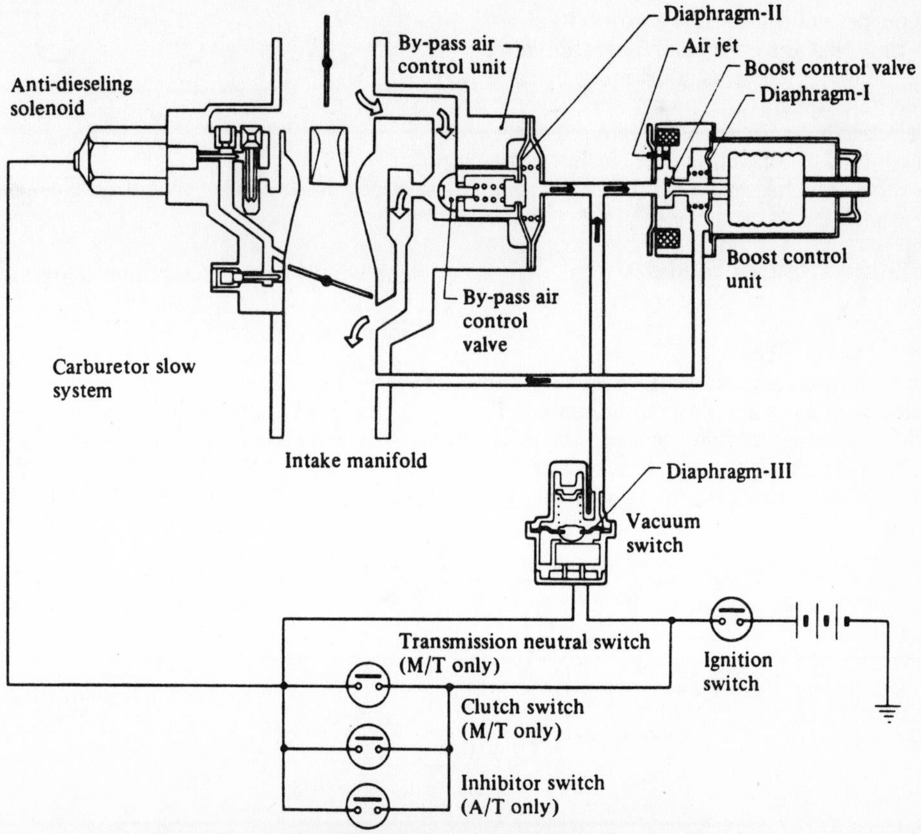

Diaphragm-II
By-pass air control unit
Air jet
Boost control valve
Diaphragm-I
Anti-dieseling solenoid
Boost control unit
By-pass air control valve
Carburetor slow system
Intake manifold
Diaphragm-III
Vacuum switch
Transmission neutral switch (M/T only)
Ignition switch
Clutch switch (M/T only)
Inhibitor switch (A/T only)

Fuel shut-off system—1979–84

Fuel Shut-Off System

OPERATION

Gasoline Engines

This system is designed to reduce HC emissions and also to improve fuel economy during deceleration.

The system is operated by an anti-dieseling solenoid valve in the carburetor which is controlled by a vacuum switch. When the intake manifold vacuum increases to an extremely high level (which it does during deceleration), the fuel flow of the slow system is shut off by the anti-dieseling solenoid valve. When the intake manifold vacuum drops to a low level again, the fuel flow the the slow system is resupplied.

The fuel shut-off system is further controlled by the clutch switch and gear position switches such as the neutral switch (manual transmission) and the inhibitor switch (automatic transmission) to ensure that fuel cannot be shut off even if the manifold vacuum is high enough to trigger the normal fuel shut-off operation.

Electric Choke

OPERATION

Gasoline Engines Only

The purpose of the electric choke is to shorten the time that the choke is in operation after the engine is started, thus shortening the time of high HC output.

An electric heater warms the bimetal spring which controls the opening and closing of the choke valve. The heater starts to heat as soon as the engine starts.

Detonation Control System

OPERATION

Gasoline Engines Only

This system is used on 1984-86 models and its purpose is to sense engine detonation or "knock". When detonation occurs in the cylinders, the sensor will detect the vibrations and send a signal to the detonation control unit which will in turn make minor adjustments to the ignition timing to keep engine performance at its optimum.

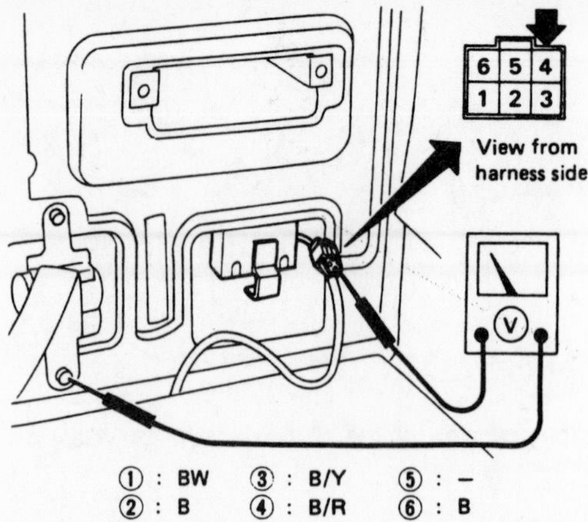

Checking the detonation control system ignition signal

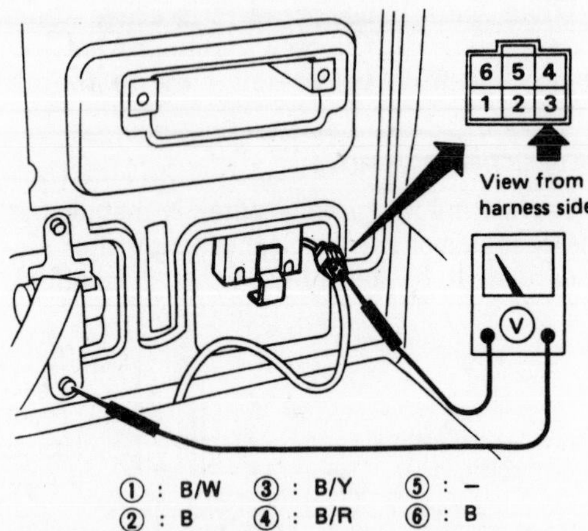

Checking the detonation control system output signal

SERVICE

1. Connect a timing light as per the manufacturer's instructions.
2. With engine speed at approximately 2200 rpm, disconnect the electrical lead at the deto-

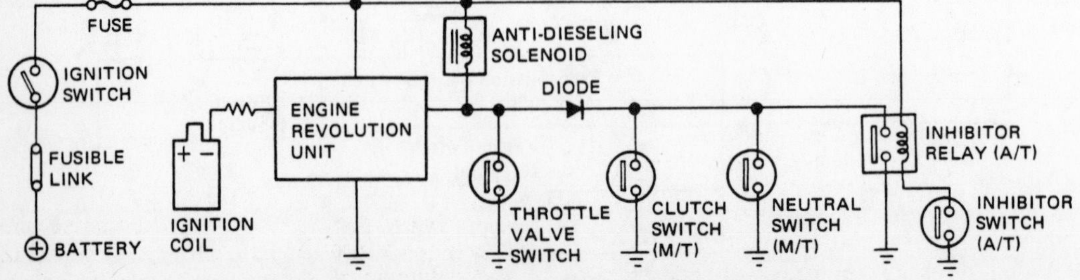

Fuel shut-off system—1985–86 Z24 engines (Canada)

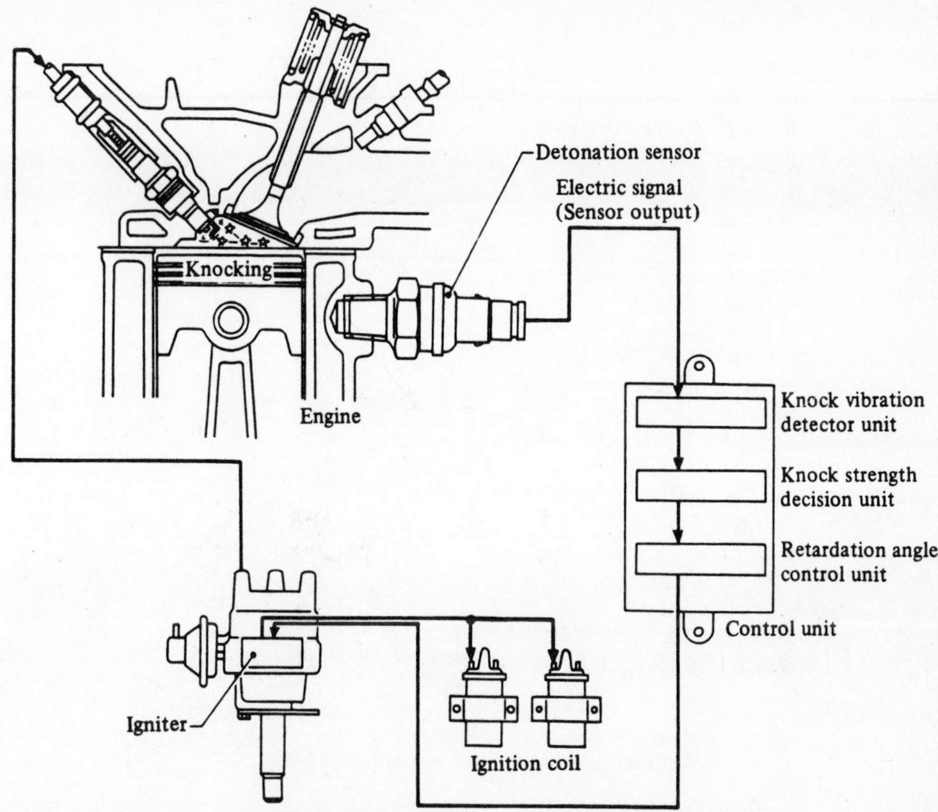

Detonation control system—1984–86 Z20 engines

nation sensor and check that the timing drops by approximately 10 degrees.

3. If the timing does not drop, check the distributor or the detonation control unit.

4. Locate the control unit behind the right side kick panel and connect a volt meter between ground and terminal **4**—make sure the engine is at 2200 rpm. Voltage should be 0.4–0.7V, if not, check the distributor and harness.

5. With the engine still idling at 2200 rpm and one voltmeter lead still grounded, insert the other lead into terminal **3**. Voltage should be 3.7–3.8V, if not, replace the control unit.

6. If both the distributor and control unit test properly, replace the sensor.

High Altitude Compensator System

OPERATION

Gasoline Engines Only

When the truck is operated at particularly high altitudes, where the air is thinner, the mixture ratio and intake manifold boost vary greatly; exhaust emissions also increase considerably. In order to decrease these emissions, an altitude compensation system is employed to correct the air/fuel ratio to that of sea level.

When the atmospheric pressure decreases (as altitude increases) to a certain value, an altitude switch is turned on, applying voltage to an altitude solenoid valve. When the solenoid valve turns on, additional air is let into the carburetor, allowing a leaner air/fuel ratio.

Mixture Heating System

OPERATION

Gasoline Engines Only

This system is 1983 California trucks with 4wd and certain Canada trucks. The system is employed to warm the air/fuel mixture after initial start-up. It is operated by means of a water temperature switch and a relay and consists of an heater/insulator plate positioned between the manifold and carburetor. It aids engine start-up ability and improves initial emisions discharge.

Catalytic Converter

OPERATION

Gasoline Engines Only

The catalytic converter is a muffler like container built into the exhaust system to aid in the reduction of exhaust emissions. The catalyst element consists of individual pellets or a

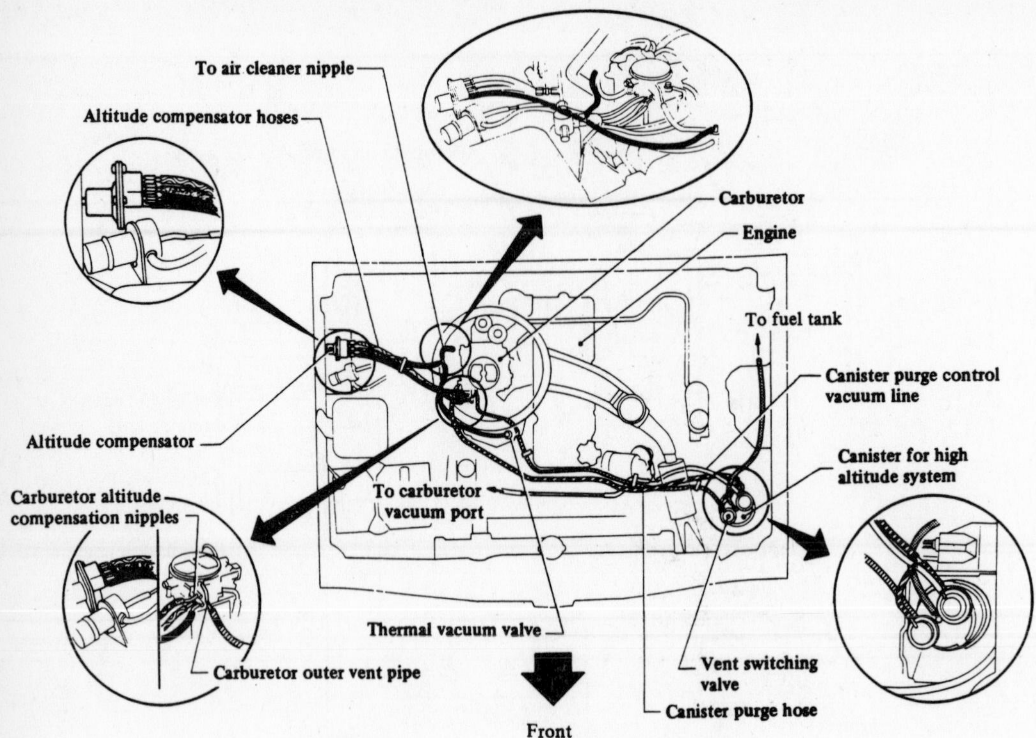

High altitude compensator system—1981–83

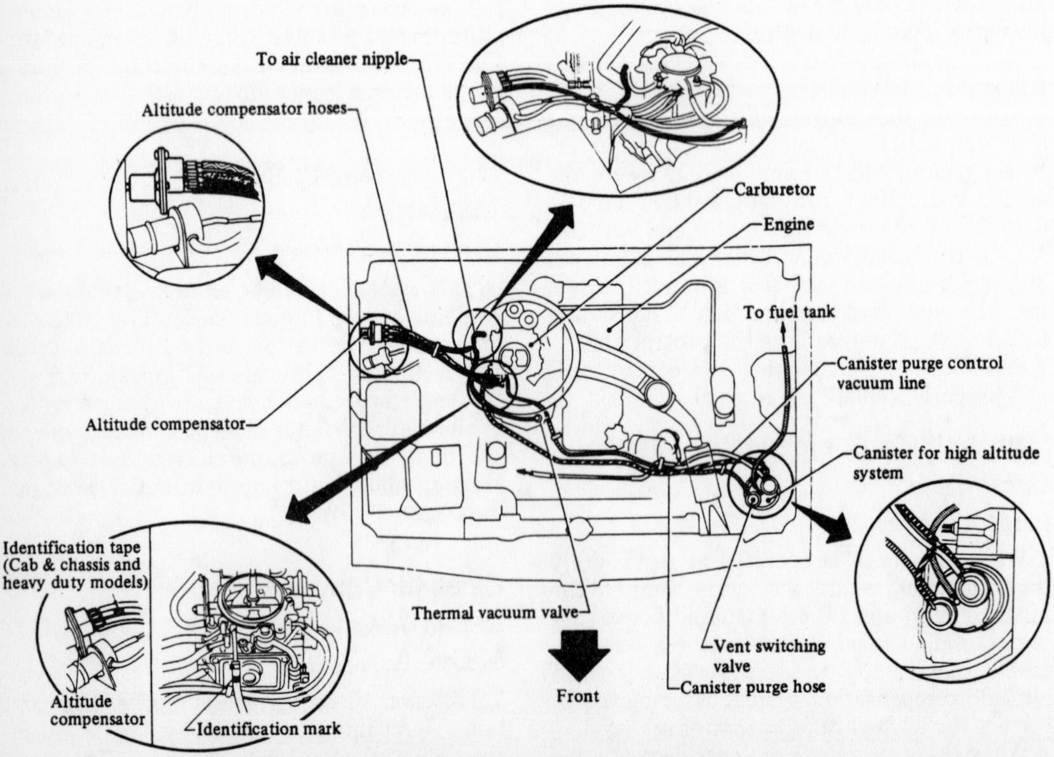

High altitude compensator system—1984

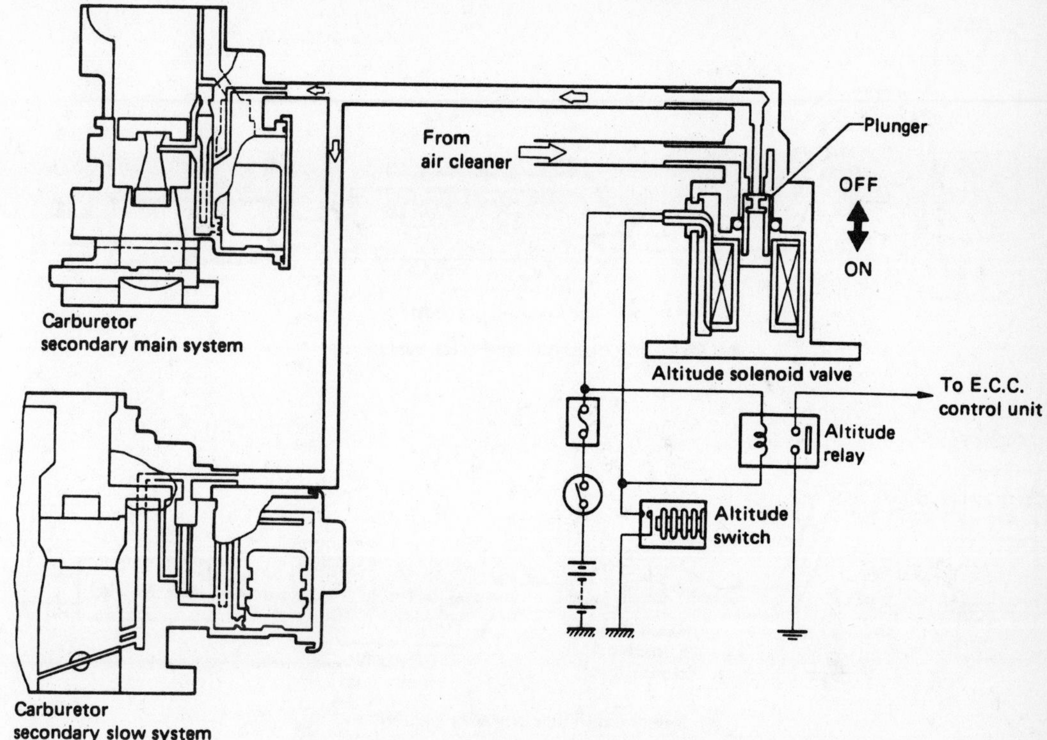

High altitude compensator system—1985–86

honeycomb monolithic substrate coated with a noble metal such as platinum, palladium, rhodium or a combination. When the exhaust gases come into contact with the catalyst, a chemical reaction occurs which will reduce the pollutants into harmless substances like water and carbon dioxide.

There are essentially two types of catalytic converters: an oxidizing type is used on many models. It requires the addition of oxygen to spur the catalyst into reducing the engine's HC and CO emissions into H_2O and CO_2. Because of this need for oxygen, the Air Injection system is used with all these models.

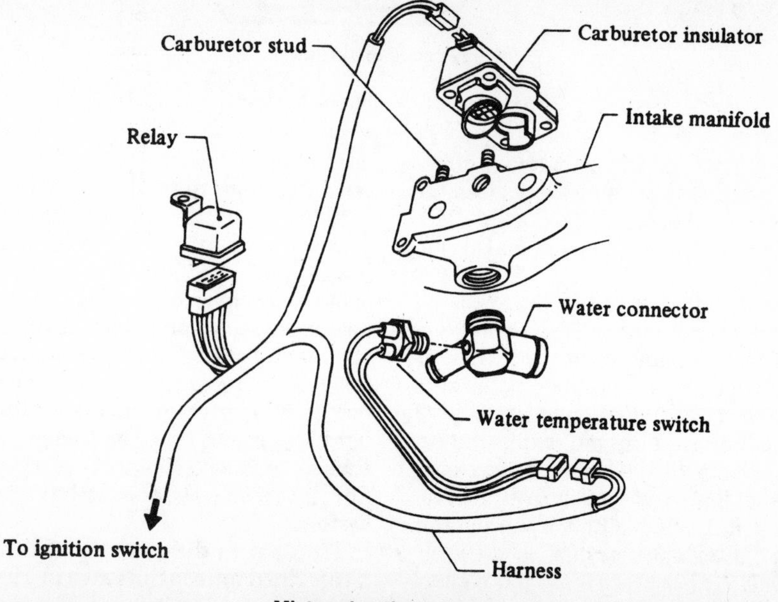

Mixture heating system

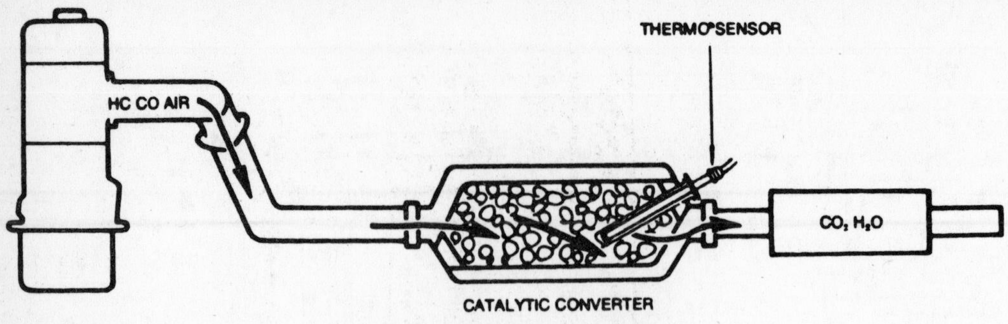

Oxidizing catalytic converter system

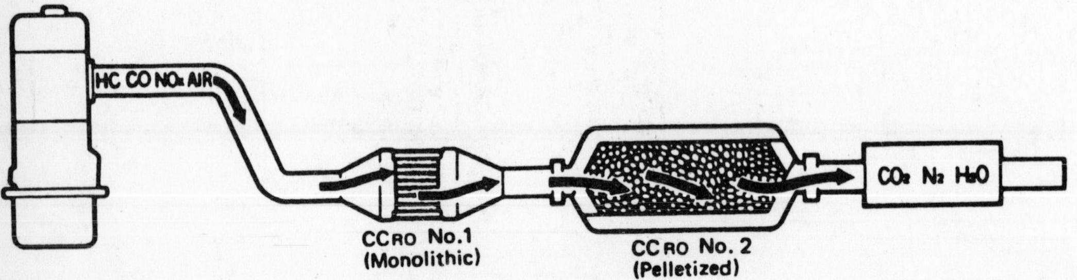

3-way catalytic converter system

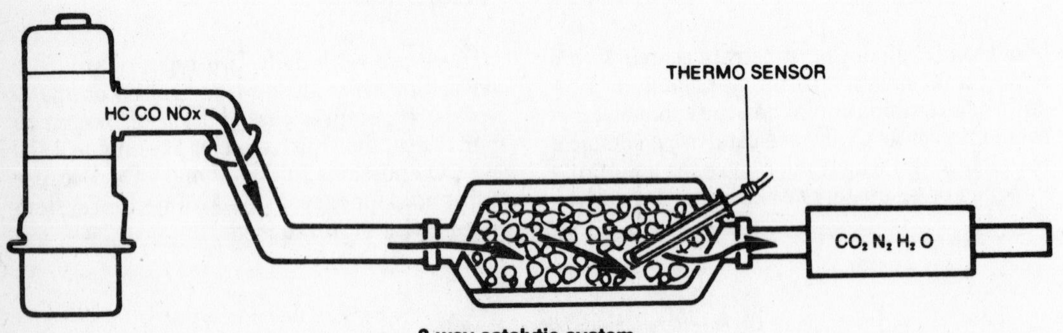

3-way catalytic system

Floor temperature warning system

The oxidizing catalytic converter, while effectively reducing HC and CO emissions, does little, if anything in the way of reducing NOx emissions. Thus, the three way catalytic converter.

The three way converter, unlike the oxidizing type, is capable of reducing HC, CO and NOx emissions; all at the same time. In theory, it seems impossible to reduce all three pollutants in one system since the reduction of HC and CO requires the addition of oxygen, while the reduction of NOx calls for the removal of oxygen. In actuality, the three way system really can reduce all three pollutants, but only if the amount of oxygen in the exhaust system is precisely controlled. Due to this precise oxygen control requirement, the three way converter system is used only in trucks equipped with an oxygen sensor system: the .

1976-78 models utilize a floor temperature warning system, consisting of a temperature sensor installed onto the floor of the truck above the converter, a relay, located under the passenger seat, and a light, installed on the instrument panel. The lamp illuminates when floor temperatures become abnormally high, due to converter or engine malfunction. The light also comes on when the ignition switch is turned to Start, to check its operation. 1979 and later models do not have the warning system.

Trucks with the catalytic converter also have a combined air control valve in 1978 and 1979, which control the amount of secondary air in-

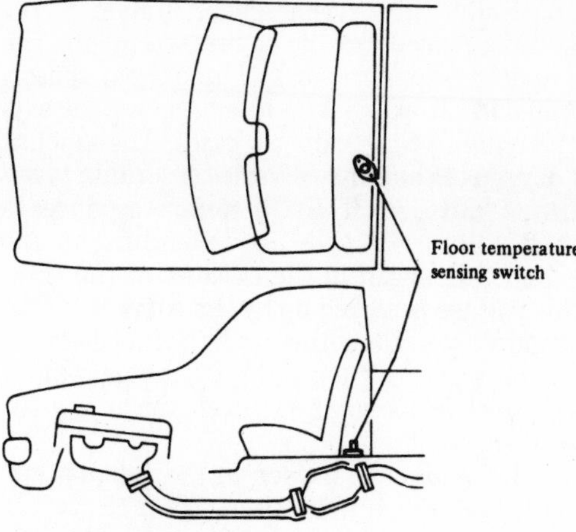

Pick-up existing caption

jected into the exhaust manifold. It is regulated by engine vacuum and air pump pressure, and works to keep the converter temperatures within proper limits. The combined air control valve replaces the air pump relief valve, found in the air pump system of trucks not equipped with a catalytic converter. 1976–77 models have an emergency air relief valve for catalyst protection. See the AIS section for a description.

All models with the three way converter have an oxygen sensor warning light on the dashboard, which illuminates at the first 30,000 mile interval, signaling the need for oxygen sensor replacement. The oxygen sensor is part of the Mixture Ratio Feedback System. The Feedback System uses the three way converter as one of its major components.

No regular maintenance is required for the catalytic converter system, except for periodic replacement of the Air Induction System filter (if so equipped). The Air Induction System is described earlier in this chapter. Filter replacement procedures are in Chapter 1. The Air Induction System is used to supply the catalytic converter with fresh air. Oxygen present in the air is used in the oxidation process.

PRECAUTIONS

1. Use only unleaded fuel.
2. Avoid prolonged idling. The engine should run on longer than 20 min. at curb idle and no longer than 10 min. at fast idle.
3. Do not disconnect any of the spark plug leads while the engine is running.
4. Make engine compression checks as quickly as possible.

TESTING

At the present time there is no known way to reliably test catalytic converter operation in the field. The only reliable test is a 12 hour and 40 min. soak test (CVS) which must be done in a laboratory.

An infrared HC/CO tester is not sensitive enough to measure the higher tailpipe emissions from a failing converter. Thus, a bad converter may allow enough emissions to escape so that the truck is no longer in compliance with Federal or state stands, but will still not cause the needle on a tester to move off zero.

The chemical reactions which occur inside a catalytic converter generate a great deal of heat. Most converter problems can be traced to fuel or ignition system problems which cause unusually high emissions. As a result of the increased intensity of the chemical reactions, the converter literally burns itself up.

A completely failed converter might cause a tester to show a slight reading. as a result, it is occasionally possible to detect one of these.

As long as you avoid severe overheating and the use of leaded fuels it is reasonably safe to assume that the converter is working properly. If you are in doubt, take the truck to a diagnostic center that has a tester.

NOTE: *If the catalytic converter becomes blocked the engine will not run. The converter has 5 year or 50,000 mile warranty contact your local Datsun/Nissan dealer for more information.*

Mixture Ratio Feedback System

OPERATION

Gasoline Engines Only

The need for better fuel economy coupled to increasingly strict emission control regulations dictates a more exact control of the engine air/fuel mixture. Datsun/Nissan has developed a Mixture Ratio Feedback System in response to these needs.

The principle of the system is to control the air/fuel mixture exactly, so that more complete combustion can occur in the engine, and more thorough oxidation and reduction of the exhaust gases can occur in the catalytic converter. The object is to maintain a stoichiometric air/fuel mixture, which is chemically correct for theoretically complete combustion. The stoichiometric ratio is 14.7:1 (air to fuel). At that point, the converter's efficiency is greatest in oxidizing and reducing HC, CO, and NOx into CO_2, H_2O, O_2, and N_2.

Components used in the system include an oxygen sensor, installed in the exhaust manifold upstream of the converter, a three way oxidation reduction catalytic converter, an electronic control unit, and the fuel injection system itself.

The oxygen sensor reads the oxygen content

of the exhaust gases. It generates an electric signal which is sent to the control unit. The control unit then decides how to adjust the mixture to keep it at the correct air/fuel ratio. For example, if the mixture is too lean, the control unit increases the fuel metering to the injectors. The monitoring process is a continual one, so that fine mixture adjustments are going on at all times.

The system has two modes of operation: open loop and closed loop. Open loop operation takes place when the engine is still cold. In this mode, the control unit ignores signals from the oxygen sensor and provides a fixed signal to the fuel injection unit. Closed loop operation takes place when the engine and catalytic converter have warmed to normal operating temperature. In closed loop operation, the control unit uses the oxygen sensor signals to adjust the mixture. The burned mixture's oxygen content is read by the oxygen sensor, which continues to signal the control unit, and so on. Thus, the closed loop mode is an interdependent system of information feedback.

Mixture is, of course, not readily adjustable in this system. All system adjustments require the use of a CO meter. Thus, they should be entrusted to a qualified dealer with access to the equipment and special training in the system's repair. The only regularly scheduled maintenance is replacement of the oxygen sensor at 30,000 mile intervals. This procedure is covered in the following section.

It should be noted that proper operation of the system is entirely dependent on the oxygen sensor. Thus, if the sensor is not replaced at the correct interval, or if the sensor fails during normal operation, the engine fuel mixture will be incorrect, resulting in poor fuel economy, starting problems, or stumbling and stalling of the engine when warm.

Oxygen Sensor

OPERATION

Gasoline Engines Only

The three-way catalytic converter, which is capable of reducing HC, CO and NOx into CO_2, H_2O, O_2 and N_2 can only function as long as the air/fuel mixture is kept within a critically precise range. The oxygen sensor system is what keeps the oxygen range in control.

Basically, the oxygen sensor system works like this: As soon as the engine warms up, the computer begins to work. The oxygen sensor, located in the exhaust manifold, senses the oxygen content of the exhaust gases. The amount of oxygen in the exhaust varies according to the air/fuel mixture. The O_2 sensor produces a small voltage that varies depending on the amount of oxygen in the exhaust at the time. This voltage is picked up by the computer. The computer works together with the fuel distributor and together they will vary the amount of fuel which is delivered to the engine at any given time.

If the amount of oxygen in the exhaust system is low, which indicates a rich mixture, the sensor voltage will be high. The higher the voltage signal sent to the computer, the more it will reduce the amount of fuel supplied to the engine. The amount of fuel is reduced until the amount of oxygen in the exhaust system increases, indicating a lean mixture. When the mixture is lean, the sensor will send a low voltage signal to the computer. The computer will then increase the quantity of fuel until the sensor voltage increases again and then the cycle will start all over.

REMOVAL AND INSTALLATION

1. Disconnect the negative battery cable.
2. Unplug the wiring connector leading from the O_2 sensor.

   NOTE: *Be careful not to bend the waterproof hose as the oxygen sensor will not function properly if the air passage is blocked.*
3. Unscrew the sensor from the exhaust manifold.
4. Coat the threads of the replacement sensor with a nickel base anti-seize compound. Do not use other types of compounds, since they may electrically insulate the sensor. Do not get compound on sensor housing. Install the sensor into the manifold. Installation torque for the sensor is about 18–25 ft. lbs. Connect the electrical lead. Be careful handling the electrical lead. It is easily damaged.
5. Reconnect the battery cable.

The oxygen sensor is installed in the exhaust manifold and is removed in the same manner as a spark plug. Exercise care when handling the sensor do not drop or handle the sensor roughly. Care should be used not to get compound on the sensor itself.

Fuel System

CARBURETED FUEL SYSTEM

Understanding the Fuel System

An automotive fuel system consists of everything between the fuel tank and the carburetor or fuel injection unit. This includes the tank itself, all the lines, one or more fuel filters, a fuel pump (mechanical or electric), and the carburetor or fuel injection unit.

With the exception of the carburetor or fuel injection unit, the fuel system is quite simple in operation. Fuel is drawn from the tank through the fuel line by the fuel pump, which forces it to the fuel filter, and from there to the carburetor where it is distributed to the cylinders.

Mechanical Fuel Pump

OPERATION

1970-76 – All Models
1977-83 – All Models Without A/C
1979-83 – All Models Except Cab/Chassis

The fuel pump is a mechanically operated, diaphragm type driven by the fuel pump eccentric cam on the front of the camshaft.

Design of the fuel pump permits disassembly,

Troubleshooting Basic Fuel System Problems

Problem	Cause	Solution
Engine cranks, but won't start (or is hard to start) when cold	• Empty fuel tank • Incorrect starting procedure • Defective fuel pump • No fuel in carburetor • Clogged fuel filter • Engine flooded • Defective choke	• Check for fuel in tank • Follow correct procedure • Check pump output • Check for fuel in the carburetor • Replace fuel filter • Wait 15 minutes; try again • Check choke plate
Engine cranks, but is hard to start (or does not start) when hot—(presence of fuel is assumed)	• Defective choke	• Check choke plate
Rough idle or engine runs rough	• Dirt or moisture in fuel • Clogged air filter • Faulty fuel pump	• Replace fuel filter • Replace air filter • Check fuel pump output
Engine stalls or hesitates on acceleration	• Dirt or moisture in the fuel • Dirty carburetor • Defective fuel pump • Incorrect float level, defective accelerator pump	• Replace fuel filter • Clean the carburetor • Check fuel pump output • Check carburetor
Poor gas mileage	• Clogged air filter • Dirty carburetor • Defective choke, faulty carburetor adjustment	• Replace air filter • Clean carburetor • Check carburetor
Engine is flooded (won't start accompanied by smell of raw fuel)	• Improperly adjusted choke or carburetor	• Wait 15 minutes and try again, without pumping gas pedal • If it won't start, check carburetor

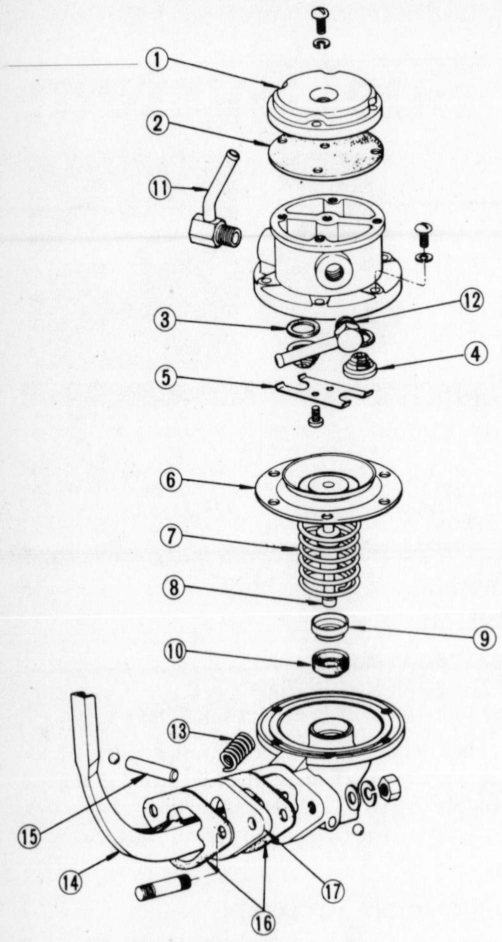

1. Fuel pump cap
2. Cap gasket
3. Valve packing
4. Fuel pump valve
5. Valve retainer
6. Diaphragm
7. Diaphragm spring
8. Pull rod
9. Lower body seal washer
10. Lower body seal
11. Inlet connector
12. Outlet connector
13. Rocker arm spring
14. Rocker arm
15. Rocker arm side pin
16. Fuel pump packing
17. Spacer—fuel pump to cylinder block

Exploded view of the mechanical fuel pump

cleaning, and repair or replacement of defective parts.

If the fuel pump is suspected of being faulty, tests for both pressure and volume should be performed. Never replace the pump without performing these simple tests first. Always check all hoses for leaks or clogs before testing the pump.

REMOVAL AND INSTALLATION

CAUTION: *Never smoke when working around gasoline! Avoid all sources of sparks or ignition. Gasoline vapors are EXTREMELY volatile!*

1. Disconnect the two fuel lines from the fuel pump. Be sure to keep the line leading from the fuel tank up high to prevent the excessive loss of fuel.
2. Remove the two fuel pump mounting nuts and remove the fuel pump assembly from the side of the engine.
3. Install the fuel pump using a new gasket and sealer on the mating surface.
4. Reconnect the two fuel lines.

TESTING

1. Disconnect the line between the carburetor and the fuel pump, at the carburetor.
2. Connect a fuel pump pressure gauge into the line.
3. Start the engine. The pressure should be between 3.0 and 3.9 psi (2.8–3.8 psi—early models). There is usually enough gas in the float bowl to perform this test.
4. If the pressure is ok, perform a capacity test. Remove the gauge from the line. Use a graduated container to catch the gas from the fuel line. Fill the carburetor float bowl with gas. Run the engine for one minute at about 1000 rpm. The pump should deliver 1000cc in one minute or less.

Electric Fuel Pump

OPERATION

1977-83—Models with A/C
1979-83—Cab/Chassis Models
1984-86—All Models

An electric fuel pump is used on these models. The pump is mounted on a bracket located on the right frame rail next to the fuel tank. There is a filter mounted in the body of the pump, which does not normally require service. The pump can be disassembled, if necessary, but all electronic parts within the body (one transistor, two diodes, and three resistors) must be replaced.

REMOVAL AND INSTALLATION

1. Disconnect the negative battery cable.
2. Remove the fuel pump protector.
3. Remove the inlet and outlet hoses, catching the fuel that escapes in a metal container.
4. Disconnect the wiring harness at the connector.
5. Remove the two bolts securing the pump to the bracket and remove the pump.
6. Unscrew the pump endcover and slide out

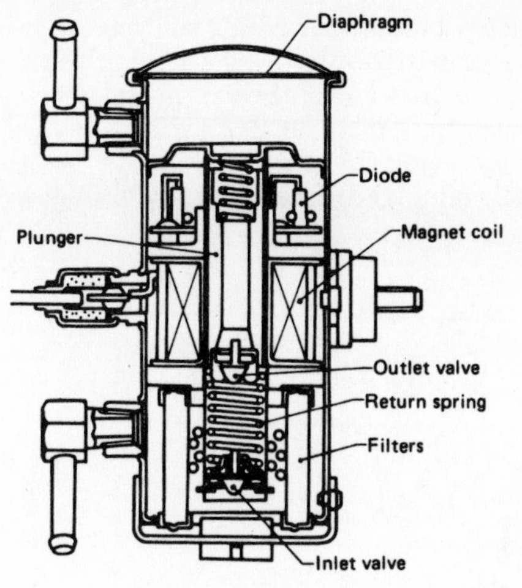

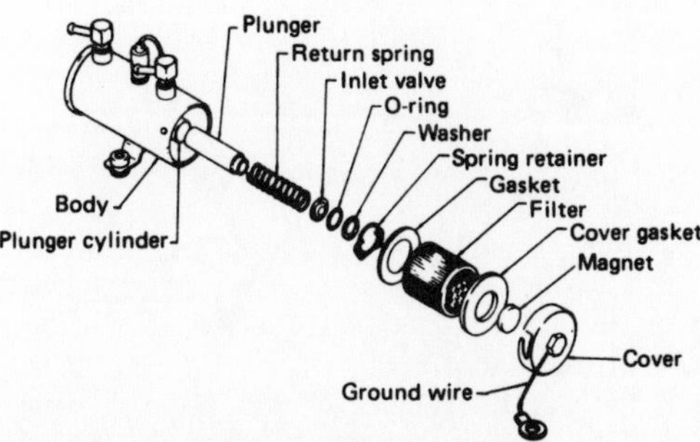

Exploded view of the electric fuel pump

the pump filter. Check that the filter is not clogged and then replace it.

7. Install the pump in the bracket and tighten the mounting screws.

8. Connect the wiring harness and the fuel lines.

9. Install the pump protector and reconnect the battery cable. Run the engine and check for leaks.

TESTING

1. Disconnect the hose from the pump outlet at the pump.

2. Connect a length of hose to the outlet. The

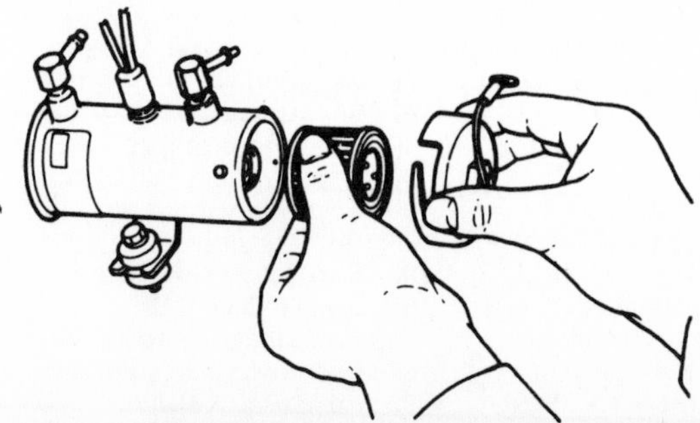

Removing the filter on the electric fuel pump

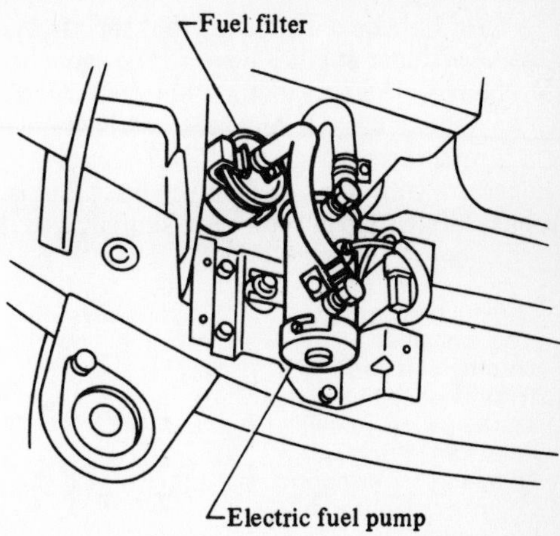

The electric fuel pump is located on the right frame rail

hose should have an inside diameter of 6mm (0.24 in.). The diameter of the hose is important for accurate measurements.

3. Raise the end of the hose above the level of the pump. Turn the ignition switch on and catch the gasoline in a graduated container. Pump output should be 1400cc in one minute or less.

4. Fuel pump pressure should be 4.6 psi through 1978, 3.1–3.8 psi for 1979-83 and 2.7–3.4 psi for 1984-86 models.

Carburetor

The carburetor is the most complex part of the entire fuel system. Carburetors vary greatly in construction, but they all operate basically the same way; their job is to supply the correct mixture of fuel and air to the engine in response to varying conditions.

Despite their complexity in operation, carburetors function because of a simple physical principle (the venturi principle). Air is drawn into the engine by the pumping action of the pistons. As the air enters the top of the carburetor, it passes through a venturi, which is nothing more than a restriction in the throttle bore. The air speeds up as it passes through the venturi, causing a slight drop in pressure. This pressure drop pulls fuel from the float bowl through a nozzle into the throttle bore, where it mixes with the air and forms a fine mist, which is distributed to the cylinders through the intake manifold.

There are six different systems (air/fuel circuits) in a carburetor that make it work; the Float system, Main Metering system, Idle and Low-Speed system, Accelerator Pump system, Power system, and the Choke system. The way these systems are arranged in the carburetor determines the carburetor's size and shape.

It's hard to believe that the 2 bbl carburetor used on 4 cylinder engines have all the same basic systems as the enormous 4 bbl carburetors used on V8 engines. Of course, the 4 bbls have more throttle bores ("barrels") and a lot of other hardware you won't find on the little 2 bbls. But basically, all carburetors are similar, and if you understand a simple 2 bbl, you can use that knowledge to understand a 4 bbl. If you'll study the explanations of the various systems on this stage, you'll discover that carburetors aren't as tricky as you thought they were. In fact, they're fairly simple, considering the job they have to do.

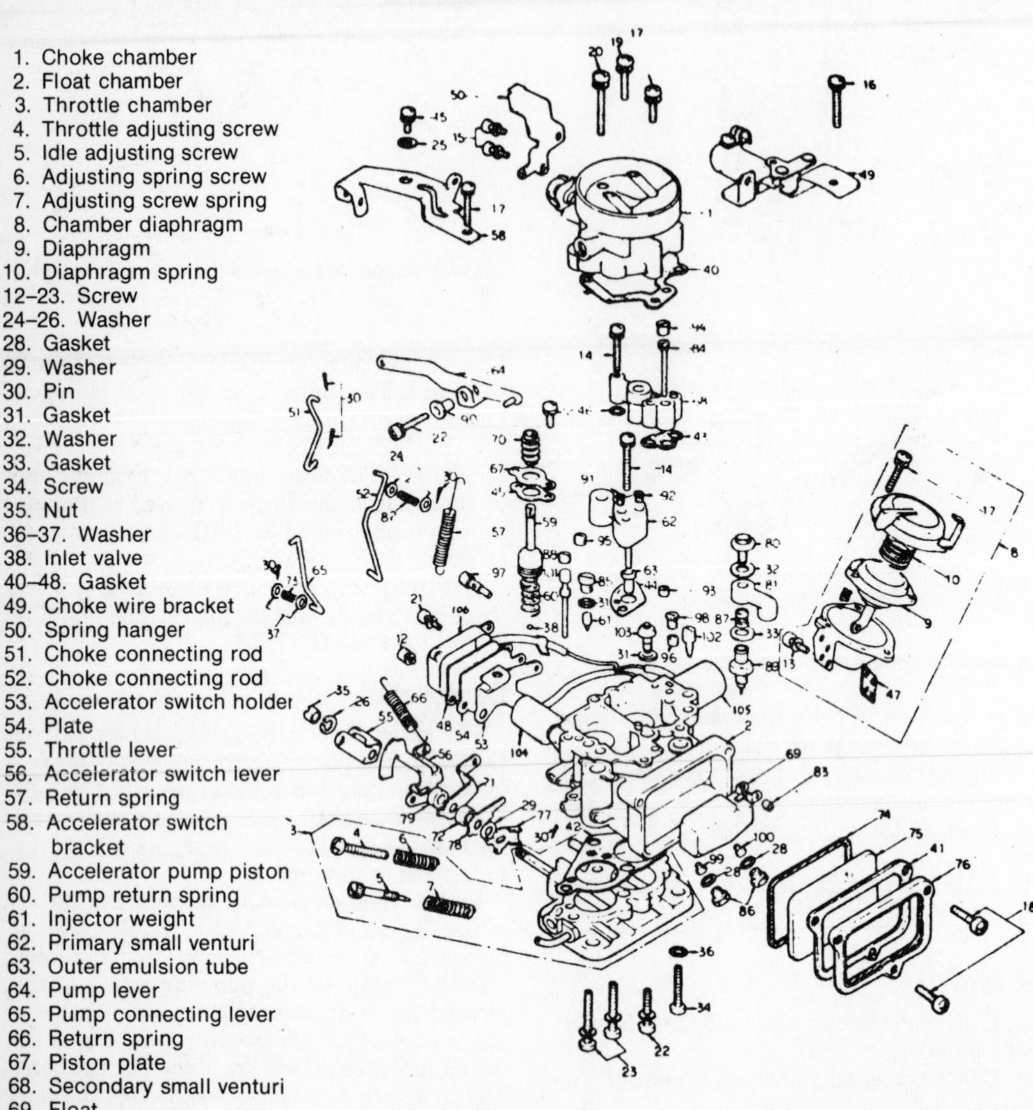

1. Choke chamber
2. Float chamber
3. Throttle chamber
4. Throttle adjusting screw
5. Idle adjusting screw
6. Adjusting spring screw
7. Adjusting screw spring
8. Chamber diaphragm
9. Diaphragm
10. Diaphragm spring

12–23. Screw
24–26. Washer
28. Gasket
29. Washer
30. Pin
31. Gasket
32. Washer
33. Gasket
34. Screw
35. Nut
36–37. Washer
38. Inlet valve
40–48. Gasket
49. Choke wire bracket
50. Spring hanger
51. Choke connecting rod
52. Choke connecting rod
53. Accelerator switch holder
54. Plate
55. Throttle lever
56. Accelerator switch lever
57. Return spring
58. Accelerator switch bracket
59. Accelerator pump piston
60. Pump return spring
61. Injector weight
62. Primary small venturi
63. Outer emulsion tube
64. Pump lever
65. Pump connecting lever
66. Return spring
67. Piston plate
68. Secondary small venturi
69. Float
70. Dust cover
71. Choke connecting lever
72. Sleeve (B)
73. Spring
74. Rubber seal
75. Level gauge
76. Level gauge cover
77. Adjust lever
78. Return plate
79. Sleeve (A)
80. Setscrew
81. Joint nipple
82. Spring
83. Float collar
84. Secondary emulsion tube
85. Injector weight plug
86. Main jet plug
87. Strainer
88. Primary slow jet plug
89. Float needle valve assy.
90. Collar
91. Primary main air bleed
92. Accelerator air bleed
93. Secondary slow air bleed
94. Secondary main air bleed
95. Primary slow air bleed
96. Coasting jet
97. Vacuum jet
98. Coasting air bleed
99. Primary main jet
100. Secondary main jet
101. Primary slow jet
102. Secondary slow jet
103. Power valve
104. Anti dieseling solenoid
105. Coasting valve solenoid
106. Accelerator switch

Exploded view of the carburetor—L16 and L18 engines

It's important to remember that carburetors seldom give trouble during normal operation. Other than changing the fuel and air filters and making sure the idle speed and mixture are OK at every tune-up, there's not much maintenance you can perform on the average carburetor.

The carburetors used on Nissan and Datsun pick-ups are conventional 2 bbl, downdraft types. The main circuits are: primary, for normal operational requirements; secondary, to supply high speed fuel needs; float, to supply fuel to the primary and secondary circuits; accelerator, to supply fuel for quick and safe ac-

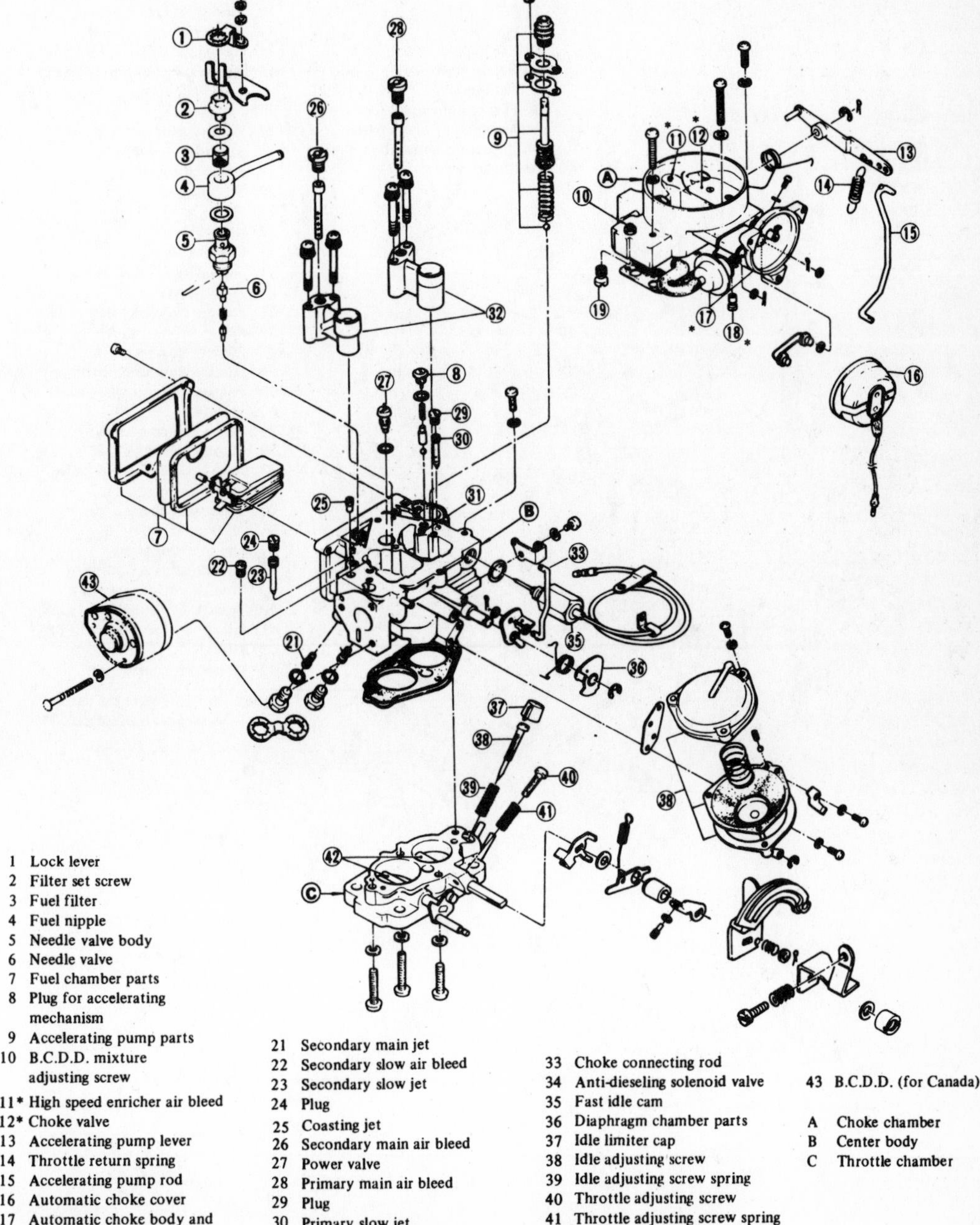

1 Lock lever
2 Filter set screw
3 Fuel filter
4 Fuel nipple
5 Needle valve body
6 Needle valve
7 Fuel chamber parts
8 Plug for accelerating mechanism
9 Accelerating pump parts
10 B.C.D.D. mixture adjusting screw
11* High speed enricher air bleed
12* Choke valve
13 Accelerating pump lever
14 Throttle return spring
15 Accelerating pump rod
16 Automatic choke cover
17 Automatic choke body and vacuum break diaphragm
18* Enricher jet
19* Coasting air bleed I
20 Primary main jet
21 Secondary main jet
22 Secondary slow air bleed
23 Secondary slow jet
24 Plug
25 Coasting jet
26 Secondary main air bleed
27 Power valve
28 Primary main air bleed
29 Plug
30 Primary slow jet
31 Primary slow air bleed
32 Primary and secondary small venturi
33 Choke connecting rod
34 Anti-dieseling solenoid valve
35 Fast idle cam
36 Diaphragm chamber parts
37 Idle limiter cap
38 Idle adjusting screw
39 Idle adjusting screw spring
40 Throttle adjusting screw
41 Throttle adjusting screw spring
42 Primary and secondary throttle valve
43 B.C.D.D. (for Canada)

A Choke chamber
B Center body
C Throttle chamber

Exploded view of the carburetor—L20B engines (Canada, typical)

celeration; choke, for reliable starting in cold weather; and power valve, for fuel economy. Although slight differences in appearance may be noted, these carburetors are basically alike. Of course, different jets and settings are demanded by the different engines to which they are fitted.

REMOVAL AND INSTALLATION

1. Disconnect the negative battery cable.
2. Loosen the radiator drain plug and drain the coolant into a suitable container.

CAUTION: *When draining the coolant, keep in mind that cats and dogs are attracted by*

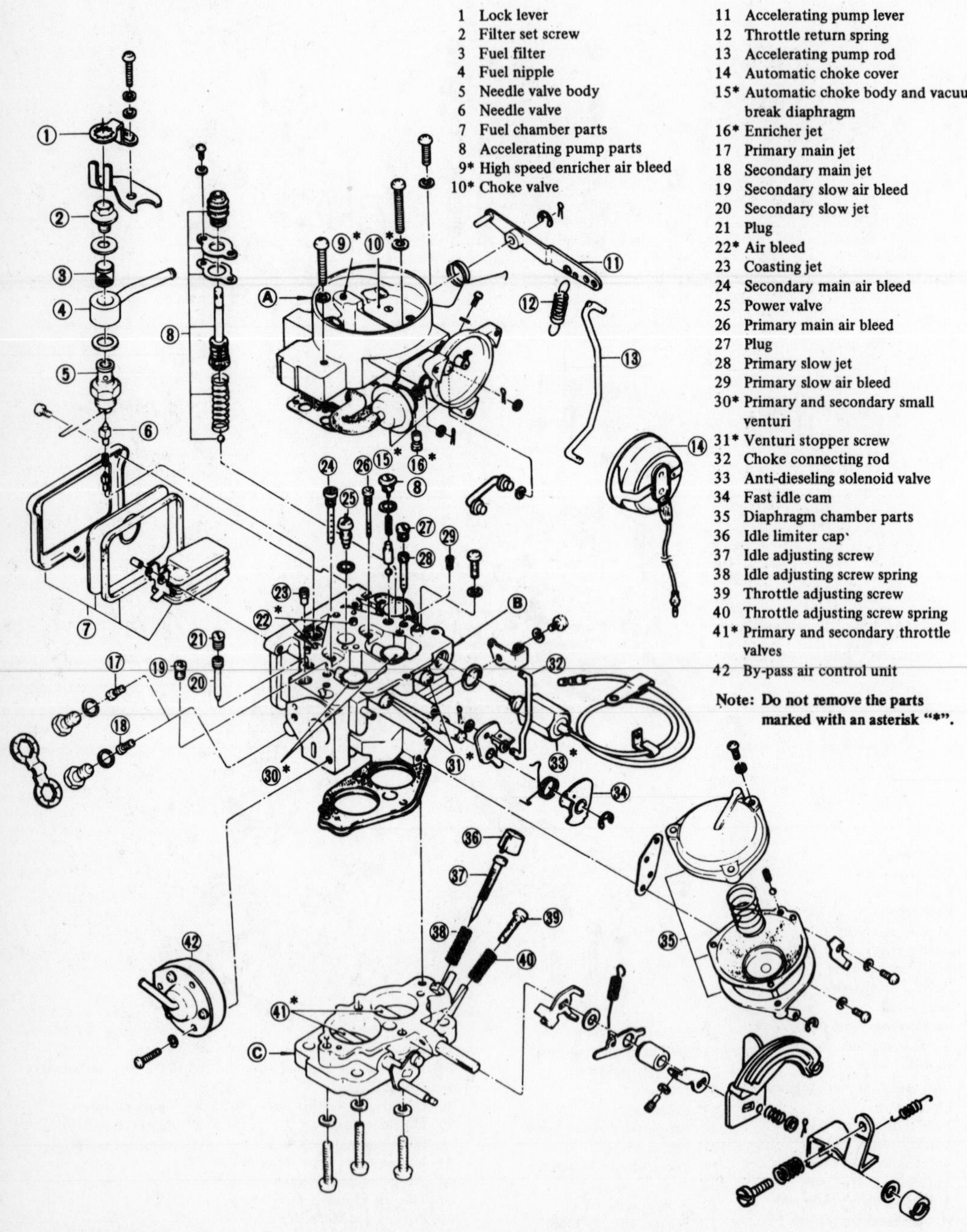

Exploded view of the carburetor—L20B engines (USA, typical)

the ethylene glycol antifreeze, and are quite likely to drink any that is left in an uncovered container or in puddles on the ground. This will prove fatal in sufficient quantity. Always drain the coolant into a sealable container. Coolant should be reused unless it is contaminated or several years old.

3. Unscrew the mounting screws and remove

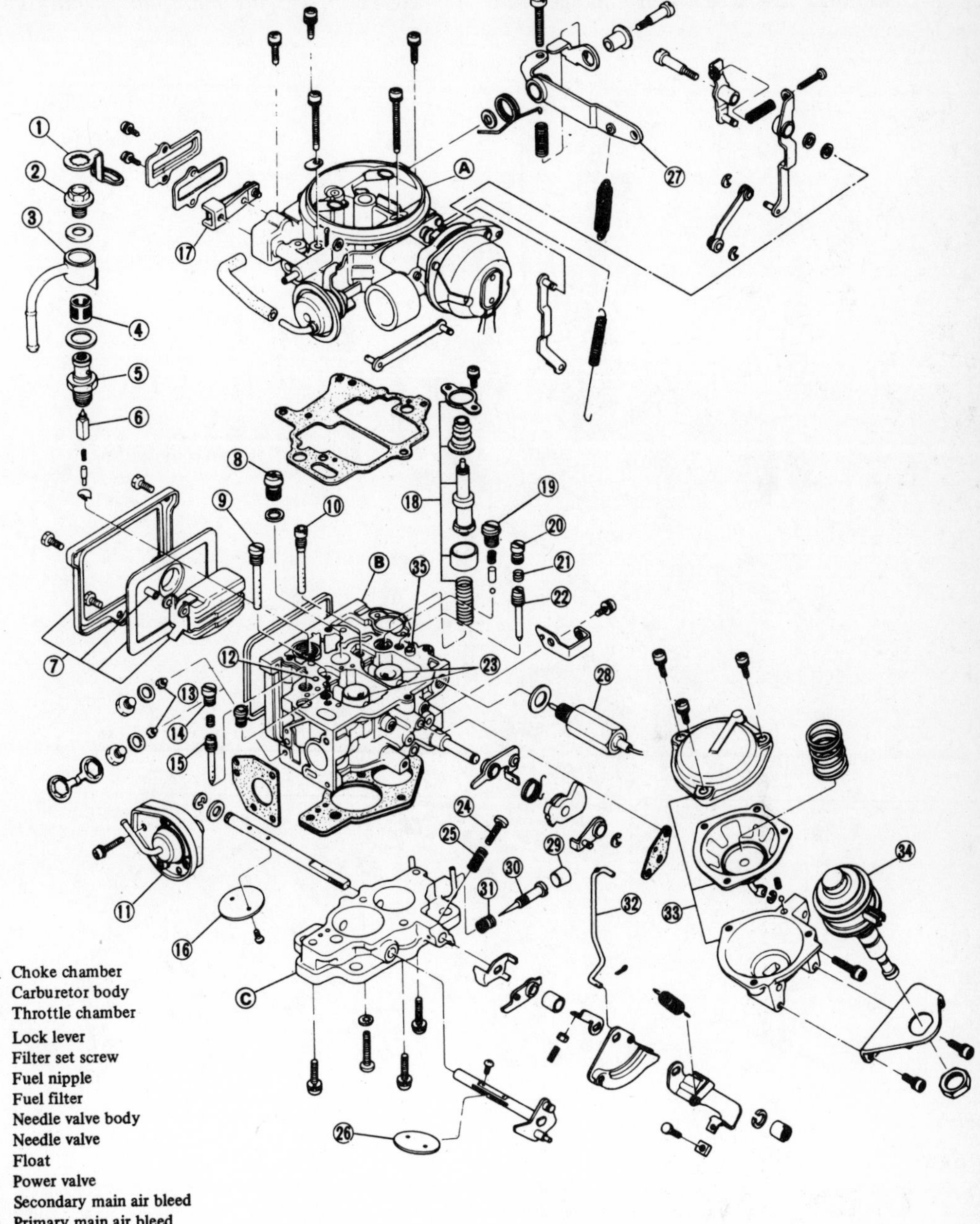

A Choke chamber
B Carburetor body
C Throttle chamber
1 Lock lever
2 Filter set screw
3 Fuel nipple
4 Fuel filter
5 Needle valve body
6 Needle valve
7 Float
8 Power valve
9 Secondary main air bleed
10 Primary main air bleed
11 B.C.D.D.
12 Secondary slow air bleed
13 Secondary main jet
14 Plug
15 Secondary slow jet
16 Primary throttle valve
17 Idle compensator
18 Accelerating pump parts
19 Plug for accelerating mechanism
20 Plug
21 Spring
22 Primary slow jet
23 Primary and secondary small venturi
24 Throttle adjusting screw
25 Throttle adjusting screw spring
26 Secondary throttle valve
27 Accelerating pump lever
28 Anti-dieseling solenoid valve
29 Blind plug
30 Idle adjusting screw
31 Idle adjusting screw spring
32 Choke connecting rod
33 Diaphragm chamber parts
34 Dash pot
35 Primary slow air bleed

Exploded view of the carburetor—Z22 engines

the air filter housing. Disconnect all hoses and lines leading from the air cleaner.

4. Tag and disconnect all fuel, vacuum, coolant and electrical lines or hoses leading from the carburetor.

5. Disconnect the accelerator linkage from the carburetor. On trucks equipped with an automatic transmission, disconnect the throttle cable linkage running from the transmission.

6. Remove the four carburetor mounting bolts and lift off the carburetor and its gasket.

NOTE: *Cover the manifold opening with a*

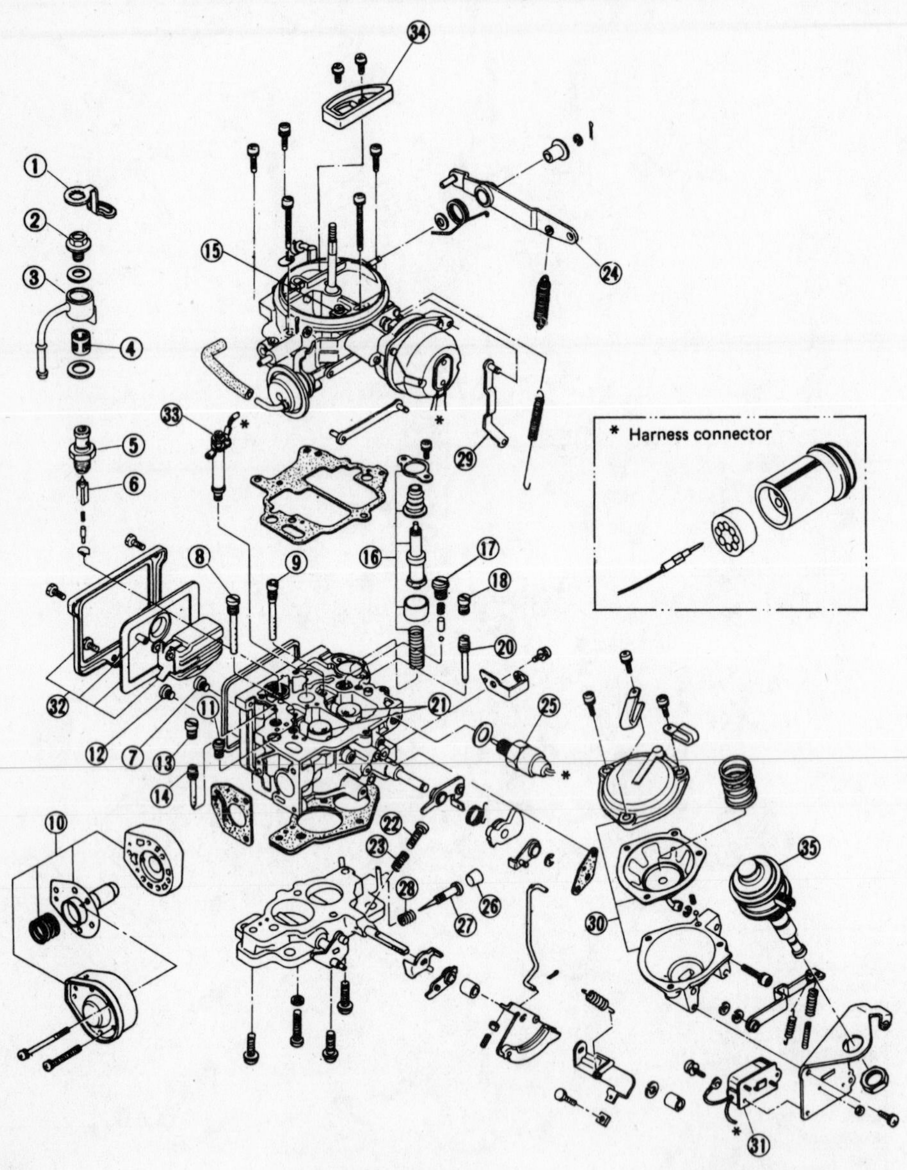

1 Lock plate
2 Filter set screw
3 Fuel nipple
4 Fuel filter
5 Needle valve body
6 Needle valve
7 Primary main jet
8 Secondary main air bleed
9 Primary main air bleed
10 B.C.D.D.
11 Secondary slow air bleed
12 Secondary main jet
13 Plug
14 Secondary slow jet
15 Idle compensator
16 Accelerating pump parts
17 Plug
18 Plug
20 Primary slow jet
21 Primary and secondary small venturi
22 Throttle adjusting screw
23 Throttle adjusting screw spring
24 Accelerating pump lever
25 Anti-dieseling solenoid valve
26 Blind plug
27 Idle adjusting screw
28 Idle adjusting screw spring
29 Choke connecting rod
30 Diaphragm chamber parts
31 Throttle valve switch
32 Float
33 Air-fuel ratio solenoid
34 Air vent cover
35 Dash pot

Exploded view of the carburetor—Z20 and Z24 engines

clean rag to prevent anything from falling into the engine.

7. Install the carburetor, tighten the mounting bolts and reconnect all linkage.

8. Start the engine and check for any leaks. Check the float level.

ADJUSTMENTS

Automatic Choke

1970-80

1. With the engine cold, make sure the choke is fully closed (press the gas pedal all the way to the floor and release, or pull the choke knob out on early models with that system).

2. Check the choke linkage for binding. The choke plate should be easily opened and closed with your finger. If the choke sticks or binds, it can usually be freed with a liberal application of a carburetor cleaner make for the purpose. A couple of quick shots from a spray can of this stuff normally does the trick. If not, the carburetor will have to be disassembled for repairs.

3. The choke is correctly adjusted when the index mark on the choke housing (notch) aligns with the center mark on the carburetor body. If the setting is incorrect, loosen the three screws clamping the choke body in place and rotate the choke cover left or right until the marks align. Tighten the screws carefully to avoid cracking the housing.

1981-86

These carburetors utilize an electric choke which cannot be adjusted. If the choke is not functioning properly, perform the following tests and replace the defective parts.

Choke Heater Circuit

CAUTION: *Use only those test leads illustrated.*

1. With the ignition off, check for continuity between leads **A** and **B** in the illustration.

2. If continuity is found, the heater is good. If continuity is not found, check for shorts or open wires.

3. With the engine at idle, check for voltage across **A** & **B**. A reading of 12 volts should be indicated. If not, check for a short or open circuit.

Choke Relay

1. Remove the relay, located on the right side of the firewall.

2. Check for continuity between **4** and **5**; and between **1** and **2**. Continuity should exist each time.

3. Check for continuity between **1** and **3**. There should be none.

4. Apply 12 volts across **4** and **5**. Continuity should now exist between **1** and **3**, but not between **1** and **2**.

5. If all these conditions are not met, replace the relay.

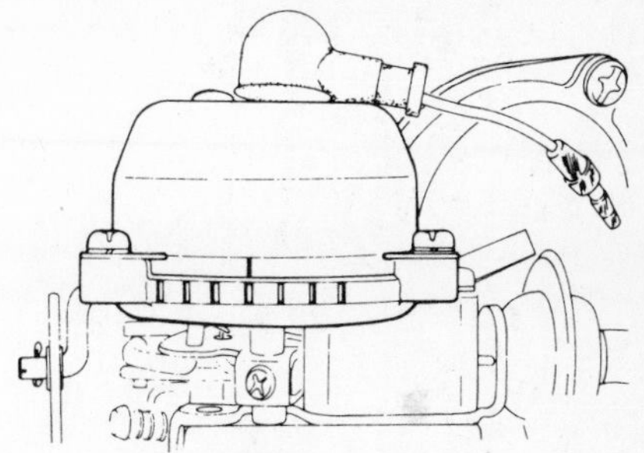

Align the choke cover mark with the center notch on the carburetor

Throttle Linkage

On all models, make sure the throttle is wide open when the accelerator pedal is floored. Some models have an adjustable accelerator pedal stop to prevent strain on the linkage.

Secondary Throttle Linkage

All Datsun/Nissan carburetors discussed in this book are two stage type carburetors. On this type of carburetor, the engine runs on the primary barrel most of the time, with the secondary barrel being used for acceleration purposes. When the throttle valve on the primary side opens to an angle of approximately 50 degrees (from its fully closed position), the sec-

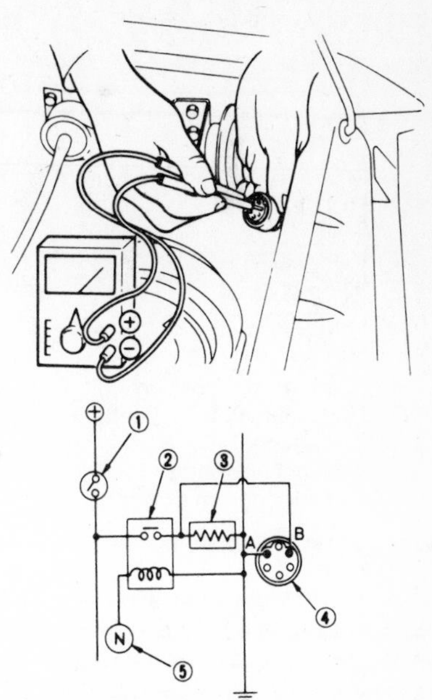

1. Ignition key
2. Automatic choke relay
   Engine stop : OFF
   Engine start : ON
3. Automatic choke heater
4. Function test connector
5. Alternator

Choke heater circuit test connections

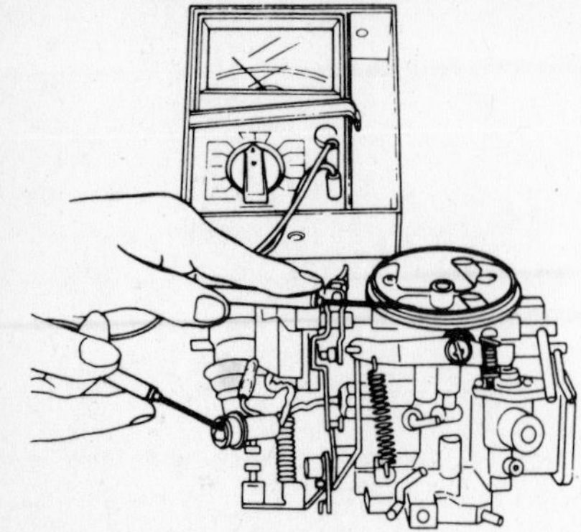

Choke coil test connections

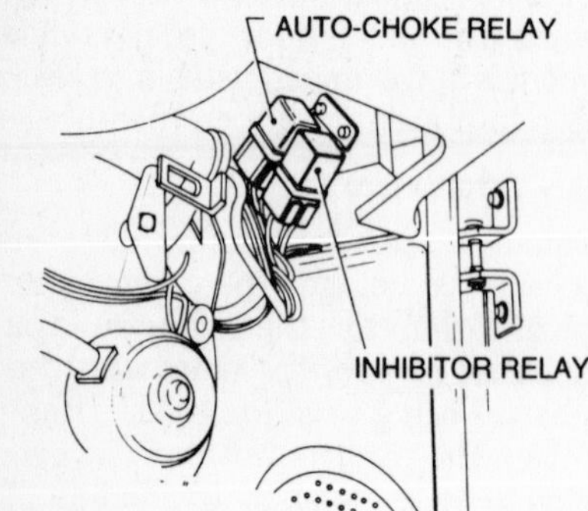

Choke relay

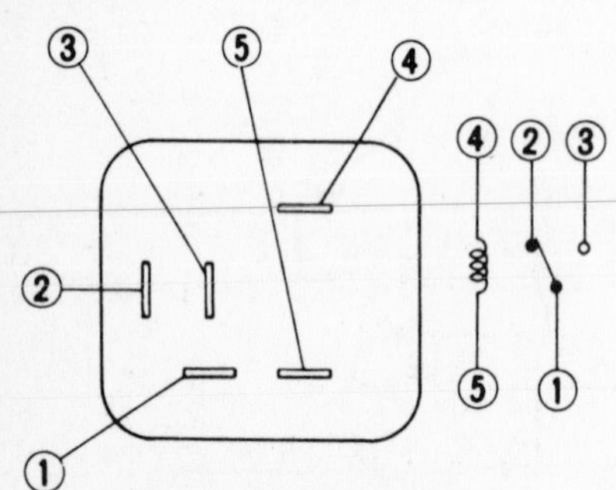

1. From "IG" position
2. To automatic choke heater
3. Useless
4. From alternator
5. From ignition switch

Choke relay test connections

ondary throttle valve is pulled open by the connecting linkage. The fifty degree angle of throttle valve opening works out to a clearance measurement of somewhere between 0.26–0.32 in. between the throttle valve and the carburetor body. The easiest way to measure this is to use a drill bit. Drill bits from size H to size P (standard letter size drill bits) should fit. Check the appendix in the back of the book for the exact size of the various drill bits. If an adjustment is necessary, bend the connecting link between the two linkage assemblies.

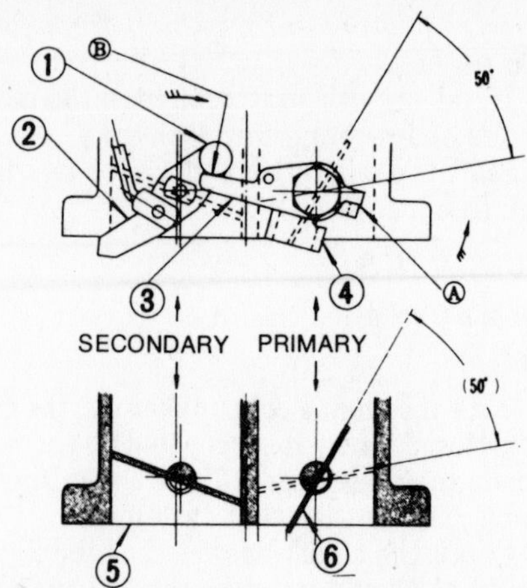

1. Roller
2. Connecting lever
3. Return plate
4. Adjust plate
5. Throttle chamber
6. Throttle valve

Secondary throttle linkage adjustment

Float Level

The fuel level is normal if it is within the lines on the window glass of the float chamber when the vehicle is resting on level ground and the engine is off.

If the fuel level is outside the lines, remove the float housing cover. Have an absorbent cloth under the cover to catch the fuel from the fuel bowl. Adjust the float level by bending the needle seat on the float.

The needle valve should have an effective stroke of about 0.0591 in. (1.5mm). When necessary, the needle valve stroke can be adjusted by bending the float stopper.

NOTE: *Be careful not to bend the needle valve rod when installing the float and baffle plate, if removed.*

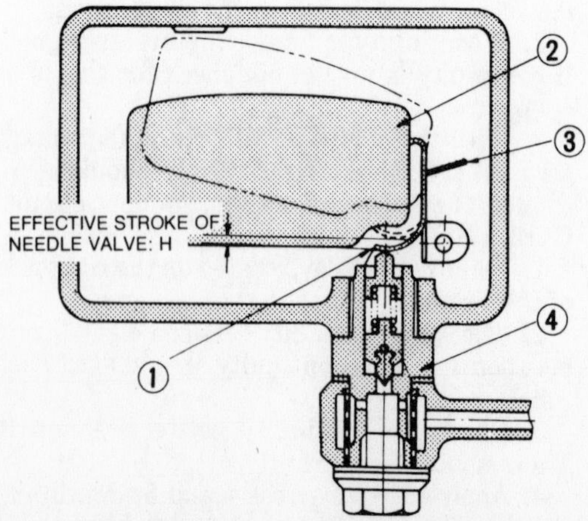

1. Float seat
2. Float
3. Float chamber
4. Needle valve

Float level adjustment

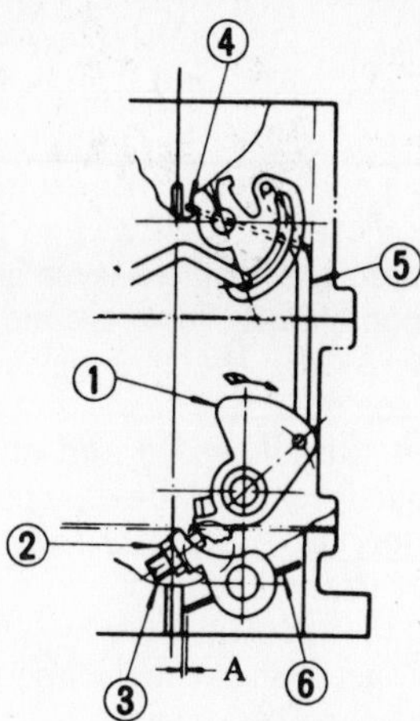

1. Fast idle cam
2. Nut
3. Fast idle screw
4. Choke valve
5. Choke connecting rod
6. Throttle valve

Fast idle adjustment—1970–75

Fast Idle Speed

1. With the carburetor removed from the vehicle, place the upper side of the fast idle screw on the 2nd step (1st step for 1977–82 engines) of the fast idle cam and measure the clearance between the throttle valve and the wall of the throttle valve chamber at the center of the throttle valve. Check it against the following specifications:

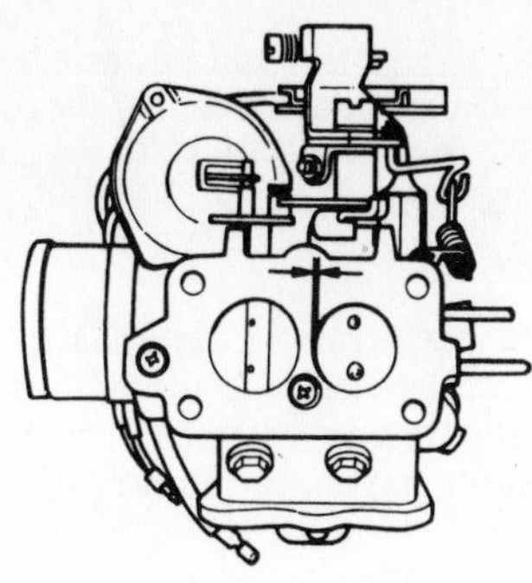

Fast idling cam steps

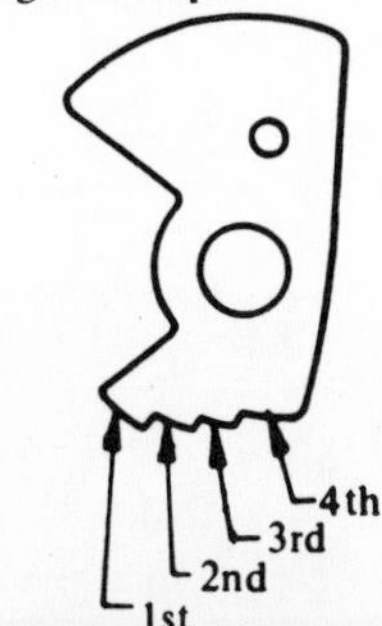

Fast idle adjustment—1976–86

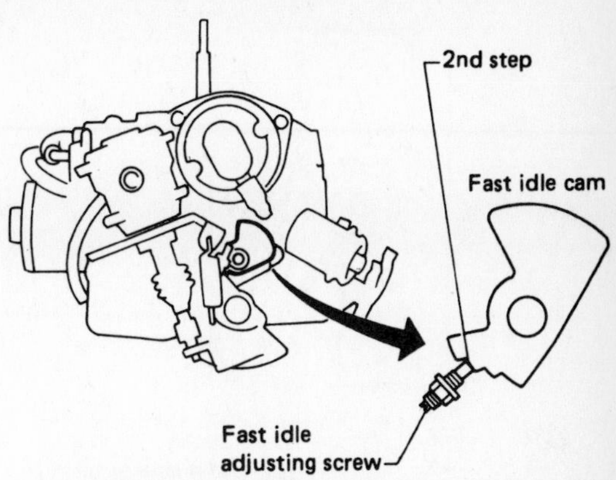

Fast idle adjustment—1984–86

1970-74:
- 0.035–0.039 in. (0.9–1.0mm)–M/T
- 0.044–0.048 in. (1.12–1.22mm)–A/T

1975-76:
- 0.040–0.048 in. (1.01–1.21mm)–M/T
- 0.048–0.052 in. (1.23–1.33mm)–A/T

1977-79:
- 0.052–0.058 in. (1.33–1.47mm)–M/T
- 0.062–0.068 in. (1.58–1.72mm)–A/T

1980:
- 0.032–0.037 in. (0.81–0.95mm)–M/T
- 0.040–0.046 in. (1.02–1.16mm)–A/T

1981:
- 0.032–0.037 in. (0.81–0.95mm)–M/T
- 0.039–0.044 in. (0.98–1.12mm)–A/T (49 State)
- 0.039–0.043 in. (1.00–1.10mm)–A/T (Calif.)

1982-83:
- 0.032–0.037 in. (0.81–0.95mm)–M/T
- 0.038–0.044 in. (0.97–1.11mm)–A/T

1984-86:
- 0.030–0.035 in. (0.76–0.90mm)–M/T (Z20)
- 0.028–0.034 in. (0.71–0.85mm)–M/T (Z24)
- 0.034–0.040 in. (0.87–1.01mm)–A/T

M/T means manual transmission. A/T means automatic transmission.

NOTE: *The first step of the fast idle adjustment procedure is not absolutely necessary.*

2. Install the carburetor on the engine.
3. Start the engine and measure the fast idle rpm with the engine at operating temperature. The cam should be at the 2nd step.

1970-76:
- 1900–2100 rpm–M/T
- 2300–2500 rpm–A/T

1977-80:
- 1900–2800 rpm–M/T
- –2200–3200 rpm–A/T

1981-83:
- 1900–2800 rpm–M/T
- –2200–3200 rpm–A/T

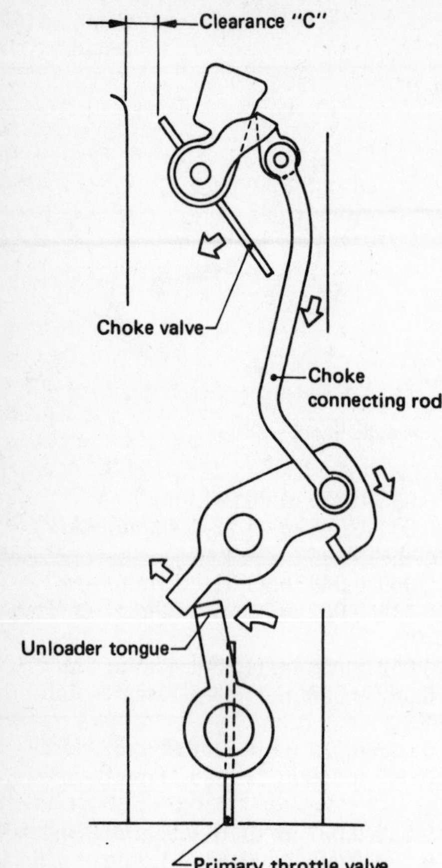

Choke unloader adjustment—1978–86

1984-86:
- 2600–3000 rpm – M/T (Z20)
- 2600–3000 rpm – M/T (Z24)
- 2200–2600 rpm – A/T

4. To adjust the fast idle speed, turn the fast idle adjusting screw counterclockwise to increase the fast idle speed and clockwise to decrease the fast idle speed.

Choke Unloader

1. Close the choke valve completely.
2. Hold the choke valve closed by stretching a rubber band between the choke piston lever and a stationary part of the carburetor.
3. Open the throttle lever fully.
4. With the throttle lever fully open, adjust the clearance between the choke valve and the carburetor body to the figure indicated:
   - 1973-74: 0.1730 in. (4.4mm)
   - 1975-77: 0.0960 in. (2.45mm)
   - 1978-86: 0.0965 in. (2.45mm)

NOTE: *Make sure that the throttle valve opens completely when the carburetor is mounted on the engine.*

Dashpot

The purpose of this device is to prevent the throttle from suddenly snapping shut. The dashpot has a plunger which extends when the throttle is closed suddenly. The plunger contacts a tab on the throttle lever and holds the throttle open slightly for a second, then closes the throttle slowly over the period of another second or so.

1. Adjust the idle speed and mixture before making adjustments to the dashpot. Warm the engine to operating temperature, and connect a tachometer to the engine.
2. Move the throttle lever by hand, and note the engine speed when the dashpot plunger just touches the throttle lever.
3. The engine speed should be as indicated.
   - 1970-72: 1800–2000 rpm – M/T
   - 1973: 1600–1800 rpm – M/T
   - 1974-80: 1900–2100 rpm – M/T; 1650–1850 rpm – A/T
   - 1981-83: 1400–1600 rpm – A/T
   - 1984: 1400–1600 rpm – A/T; 1700–1900 rpm – M/T (Calif.)
   - 1985: 1300–1700 rpm – A/T
   - 1986: 1600–2000 rpm – M/T; 1300–1700 rpm – A/T
4. If not, loosen the locknut and turn the adjusting screw until the engine speed is in the proper range. Tighten the locknut. On 1978-79 models with air conditioning, a different dashpot is used. Adjustment is made by turning the screw on the throttle lever which contacts the plunger.
5. Open the throttle and allow it to close by itself. The dashpot should smoothly reduce the idling speed from 2000 to 1000 rpm in about three seconds.

OVERHAUL

Efficient carburetion depends greatly on careful cleaning and inspection during overhaul, since dirt, gum, water, or varnish in or on the carburetor parts are often responsible for poor performance.

Overhaul your carburetor in a clean, dust-free area. Carefully disassemble the carburetor,

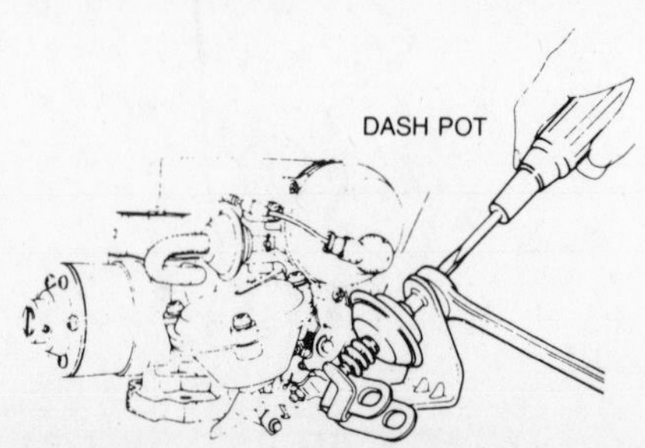

Dashpot adjustment—1972–79 (without A/C)

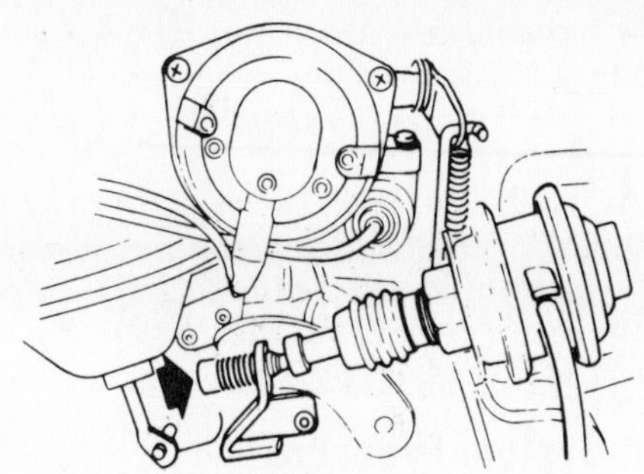

Dashpot adjustment—1978–80 (with A/C)

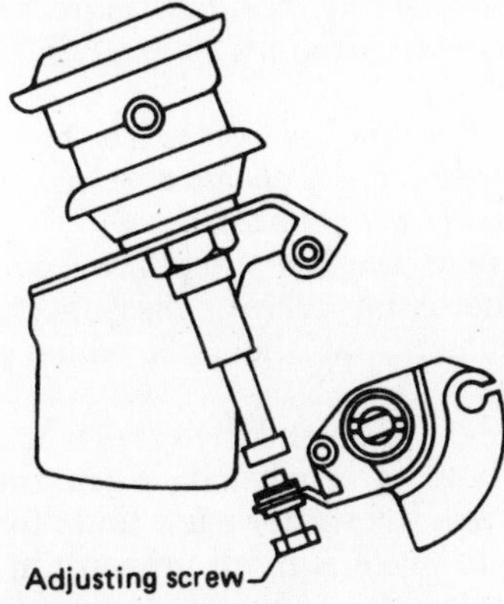

Dashpot adjustment—1981–86

referring often to the exploded views. Keep all similar and look-alike parts segregated during disassembly and cleaning to avoid accidental interchange during assembly. Make a note of all jet sizes.

When the carburetor is disassembled, wash all parts (except diaphragms, electric choke units, pump plunger, and any other plastic, leather, fiber, or rubber parts) in clean carburetor solvent. Do not leave parts in the solvent any longer than is necessary to sufficiently loosen the deposits. Excessive cleaning may remove the special finish from the float bowl and choke valve bodies, leaving these parts unfit for service. Rinse all parts in clean solvent and blow them dry with compressed air to allow them to air dry. Wipe clean all cork, plastic, leather, and fiber parts with a clean, lint-free cloth.

NOTE: *Carburetor solvent is available in various-sized solvent cans, which are designed with a removable small parts basket in the top. The carburetor choke chamber and body, and all small parts can be soaked in this can until clean. These solvent cans are available at most auto parts stores, and are quite handy for soaking other small engine parts.*

Blow out all passages and jets with compressed air and be sure that there are not restrictions or blockages. Never use wire or similar tools to clean jets, fuel passages, or air bleeds. Clean all jets and valves separately to avoid accidental interchange.

Check all parts for wear or damage. If wear or damage is found, replace the defective parts. Especially check the following:

1. Check the float needle and seat for wear. If wear is found, replace the complete assembly.
2. Check the float hinge pin for wear and the float(s) for dents or distortion. Replace the float if fuel has leaked into it.
3. Check the throttle and choke shaft bores for wear or an out-of-round condition. Damage or wear to the throttle arm, shaft, or shaft bore will often require replacement of the throttle body. These parts require a close tolerance of fit; wear may allow air leakage, which could affect starting and idling.

NOTE: *Throttle shafts and bushings are not included in overhaul kits. They can be purchased separately.*

4. Inspect the idle mixture adjusting needles for burrs or grooves. Any such condition requires replacement of the needle, since you will not be able to obtain a satisfactory idle.
5. Test the accelerator pump check valves. They should pass air one way but not the other. Test for proper seating by blowing and sucking on the valve. Replace the valve if necessary. If the valve is satisfactory, wash the valve again to remove breath moisture.
6. Check the bowl cover for warped surfaces with a straight edge.
7. Closely inspect the valves and seats for wear and damage, replacing as necessary.
8. After the carburetor is assembled, check the choke valve for freedom of operation.

Carburetor overhaul kits are recommended for each overhaul. These kits contain all gaskets and new parts to replace those that deteriorate most rapidly. Failure to replace all parts supplied with the kit (especially gaskets) can result in poor performance and a leaky carburetor later.

Most carburetor manufacturers supply overhaul kits in at least one of three basic types: minor repair; major repair; and gasket kits. Basically, they contain the following, and are available at most auto parts jobbers and Toyota dealers:

Minor Repair Kits:
- All gaskets
- Float needle valve
- Volume control screw
- All diaphragms
- Spring for the pump diaphragm

Major Repair Kits:
- All jets and gaskets
- All diaphragms

Float needle valve
Volume control screw
Pump ball valve
Main jet carrier
Float

Gasket Kits:

All gaskets

After cleaning and checking all components, reassemble the carburetor, using new parts and referring to the exploded view. When reassembling, make sure that all screws and jets are tight in their seats, but do not overtighten as the tips will be distorted. Tighten all screws gradually in rotation. Do not tighten needle valves into their seats; uneven jetting will result. Always use new gaskets. Be sure to adjust the float level when reassembling.

GASOLINE FUEL INJECTION SYSTEM

NOTE: *This book contains testing and service procedures for your truck's fuel injection system. More comprehensive testing and diagnostic procedures may be found in CHILTON'S GUIDE TO FUEL INJECTION AND FEEDBACK CARBURETORS, book part number 7488, available at your local retailer, or direct from Chilton.*

TROUBLESHOOTING

Engine troubles are not usually caused by the EFI system. When troubleshooting, always check first the condition of all other related systems.

Many times the most frequent cause of problems is a bad contact in a wiring connector, so always make sure that the connections are secure. When inspecting the connector, pay particular attention to the following

1. Check to see that the terminals are not bent.
2. Check to see that the connector is pushed in all the way and locked.
3. Check that there is no change in signal when the connector is tapped or wiggled.

Actual troubleshooting of the EFI system and the EFI computer is a complex process which requires the use of a few expensive and hard to find tools. Other than checking the operation of the main components individually, we suggest that you leave any further troubleshooting to an authorized service facility.

NOTE: *The worst enemy of any fuel injection system is water or moisture. The best (i.e., cheapest and simplest) insurance for your truck's injection system is to change the fuel filter as frequently as the maintenance schedule recommends. When you follow the filter change interval strictly, many possible expensive injection system problems are eliminated.*

CAUTION: *Before disconnecting the fuel lines or any of the fuel system components, it is important to release the fuel system pressure. Please refer to the Fuel System Pressure Release procedure, which follows.*

Fuel System Pressure

RELEASE PROCEDURE

CAUTION: *Never smoke when working around gasoline! Avoid all sources of sparks or ignition. Gasoline vapors are EXTREMELY volatile!*

Any time the fuel system is being worked on always keep a dry chemical (Class B) fire extinguisher near the work area.

1. Remove the fuel pump fuse from the fuse block, fuel pump relay or disconnect the harness connector at the tank while engine is running.
2. It should run and then stall when the fuel in the lines is exhausted. When the engine stops, crank the starter a few times for about 5 seconds to make sure all pressure in the fuel lines is released.
3. Install the fuel pump fuse, relay or harness connector after repair is made.
4. On some late models the "Check Engine

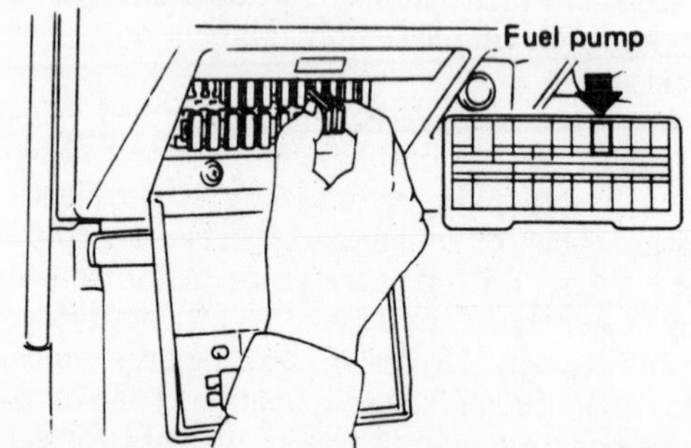

Remove the fuel pump fuse when releasing the fuel pressure

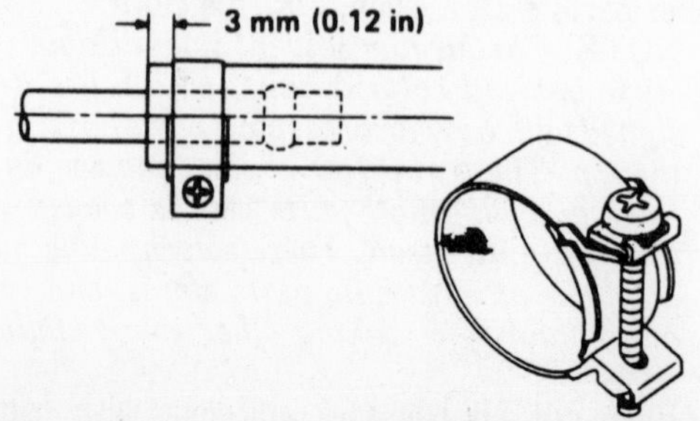

Make sure that the fuel line hose clamps are installed properly

Light" will stay on after test has been completed. The memory code in the control unit must be erased. To erase the code disconnect the battery cable for 10 seconds then reconnect.

Electric Fuel Pump

DESCRIPTION

The fuel pump with a damper is located in the fuel tank. The vane rollers are directly coupled to the motor which is cooled by fuel. a relief valve in the pump is designed to open at 44–64 psi, should a malfunction arise.

REMOVAL AND INSTALLATION

1. Before disconnecting the fuel lines or any of the fuel system components, refer to Fuel Pressure Release procedures and release the fuel pressure. *Reducing the fuel pressure to zero is a very important step for correct removal of the electric fuel pump.* See Fuel Pressure Release procedures in this section.
2. Disconnect the negative battery cable. Disconnect the fuel gauge electrical connector and remove the fuel tank inspection cover.

   NOTE: *If the truck has no fuel tank inspection cover the fuel tank must be lowered or removed to gain access to the in-tank fuel pump.*
3. Disconnect the fuel outlet and the return hoses. Remove the fuel tank if necessary.
4. Remove the ring retaining bolts and the O-ring, then lift the fuel pump assembly from the fuel tank. Plug the opening with a clean rag to prevent dirt from entering the system.

   NOTE: *When removing or installing the fuel pump assembly, be careful not to damage or deform it. Always install a new O-ring.*
5. Install the fuel pump assembly in the fuel tank with a *new* O-ring. Install the ring retaining bolts. Install the fuel tank if removed.
6. Reconnect the fuel lines and the electrical connection.
7. Connect battery cable, start engine and check for fuel leaks.

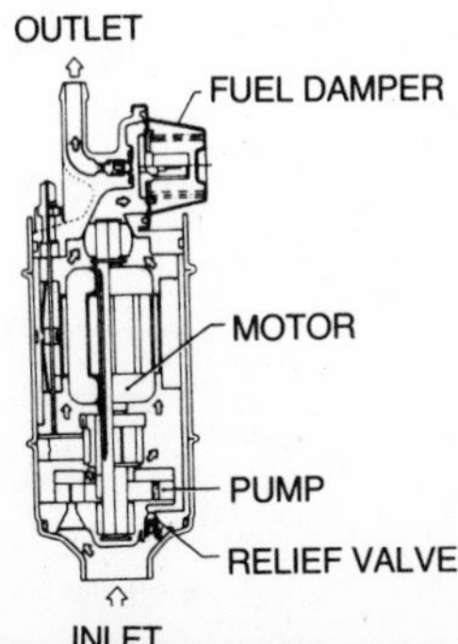

Internal view of the electric fuel pump

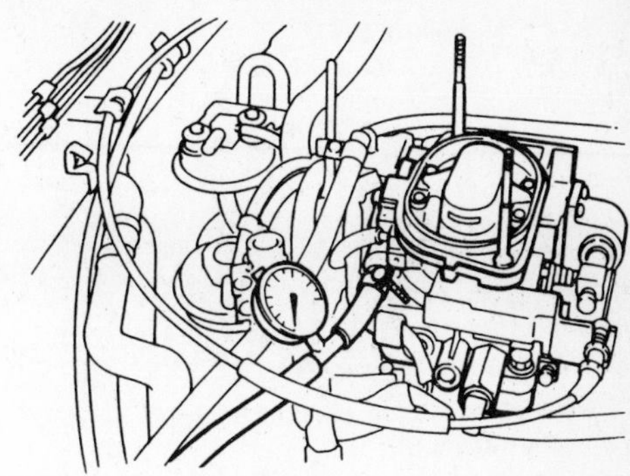

Fuel system pressure test

NOTE: *On some late models the "Check Engine Light" will stay on after installation is completed. The memory code in the control unit must be erased. To erase the code disconnect the battery cable for 10 seconds then reconnect after installation of fuel pump.*

TESTING

1. Release the fuel pressure. Connect a fuel pressure gauge between the fuel filter outlet and fuel feed pipe.
2. Start the engine and check that the pressure is approximately 37 psi.

   NOTE: *Make sure that the fuel filter is not blocked before replacing any fuel system components.*
3. If pressure is not as specified, replace the pressure regulator and repeat the test. If the pressure is still incorrect, check for clogged or deformed fuel lines, then replace the fuel pump.

Throttle Body/Chamber

REMOVAL AND INSTALLATION

CAUTION: *Never smoke when working around gasoline! Avoid all sources of sparks or ignition. Gasoline vapors are EXTREMELY volatile!*

1. Disconnect the negative battery cable and remove the intake duct from the throttle chamber.

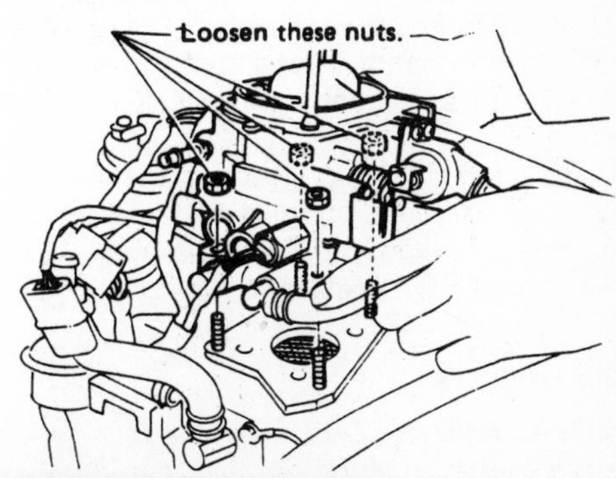

Removing the throttle body

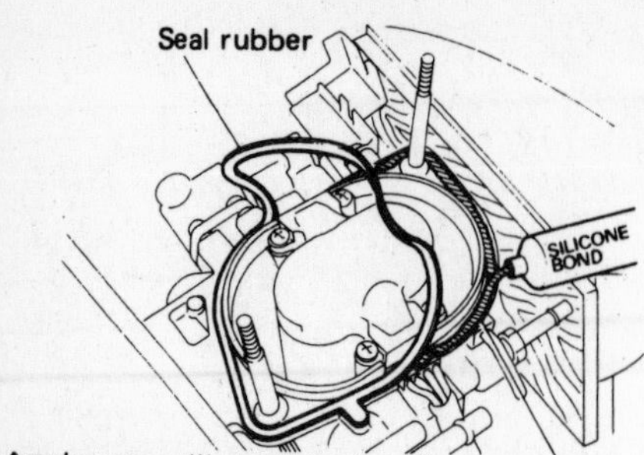

Installing the throttle body seal

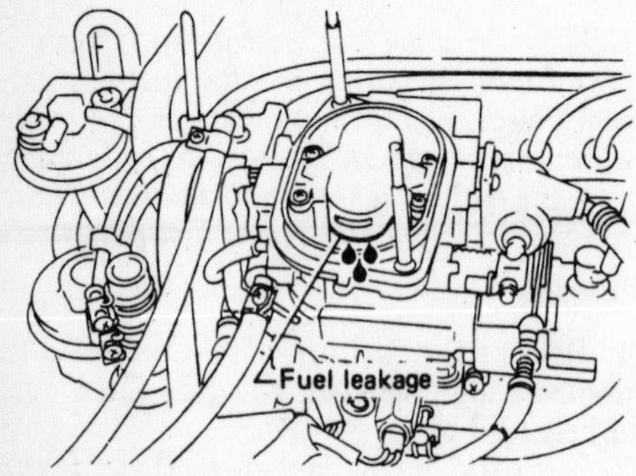

Check for leaks

2. Disconnect the vacuum hoses and the electrical harness connector from the throttle chamber. Disconnect the accelerator cable from the throttle chamber.

3. Remove the mounting bolts and the throttle chamber from the intake manifold.

4. To install, use a new gasket and reverse the removal procedures. Torque the throttle chamber bolts to 9–13 ft. lbs. (12–18 Nm). Adjust the throttle cable if necessary.

Check the throttle for smooth operation and make sure the by-pass port is free of obstacles and is clean. Check to make sure the idle speed adjusting screw moves smoothly.

Do not touch the EGR vacuum port screw or, on some later models, the throttle valve stopper screw, as they are factory adjusted.

Because of the sensitivity of the air flow meter, there cannot be any air leaks in the fuel system. Even the smallest leak could unbalance the system and affect the performance of the vehicle.

During every check pay attention to hose connections, dipstick and oil filler cap for evidence of air leaks. Should you encounter any, take steps to correct the problem.

Fuel Injectors

REMOVAL AND INSTALLATION

1. Remove the throttle body assembly as outlined earlier.

2. Remove the rubber seal and the injector harness grommet from the top of the injection body.

3. Remove the injector cover.

4. Use a hollow bar with an inside diameter of not less than 5.5mm (0.217 in.) and with the throttle valve kept fully open, tap the bottom of the fuel injector with the hollow bar and plastic hammer.

5. Disconnect the harness of the injector from the harness connector.

NOTE: *The Z24i uses one injector, while the VG30i uses two injectors.*

a. Remove the terminal retainer.

b. Using a small screwdriver, tilt the lock tongue, and at the same time push out the terminal.

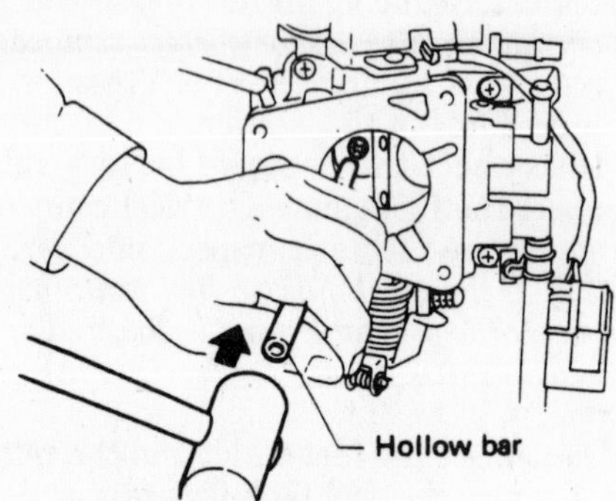

Tap the bottom of the fuel injector

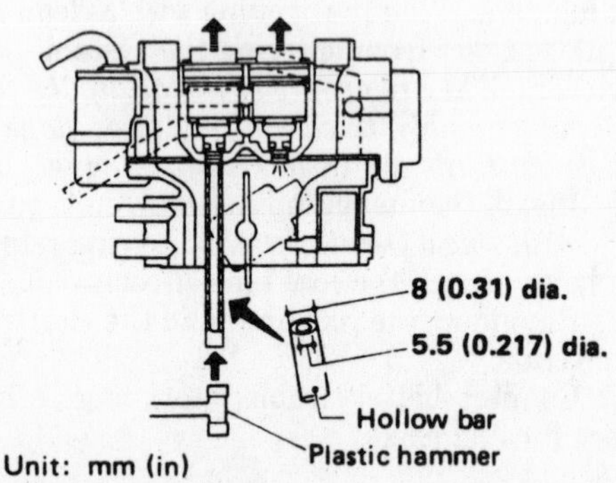

Always use an hollow bar

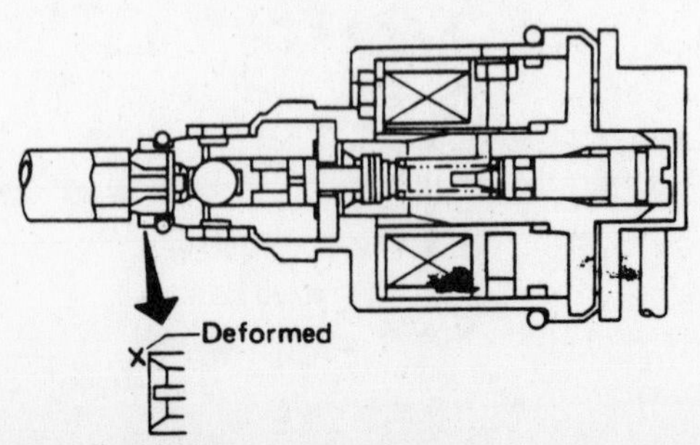

Check the injector for deformities

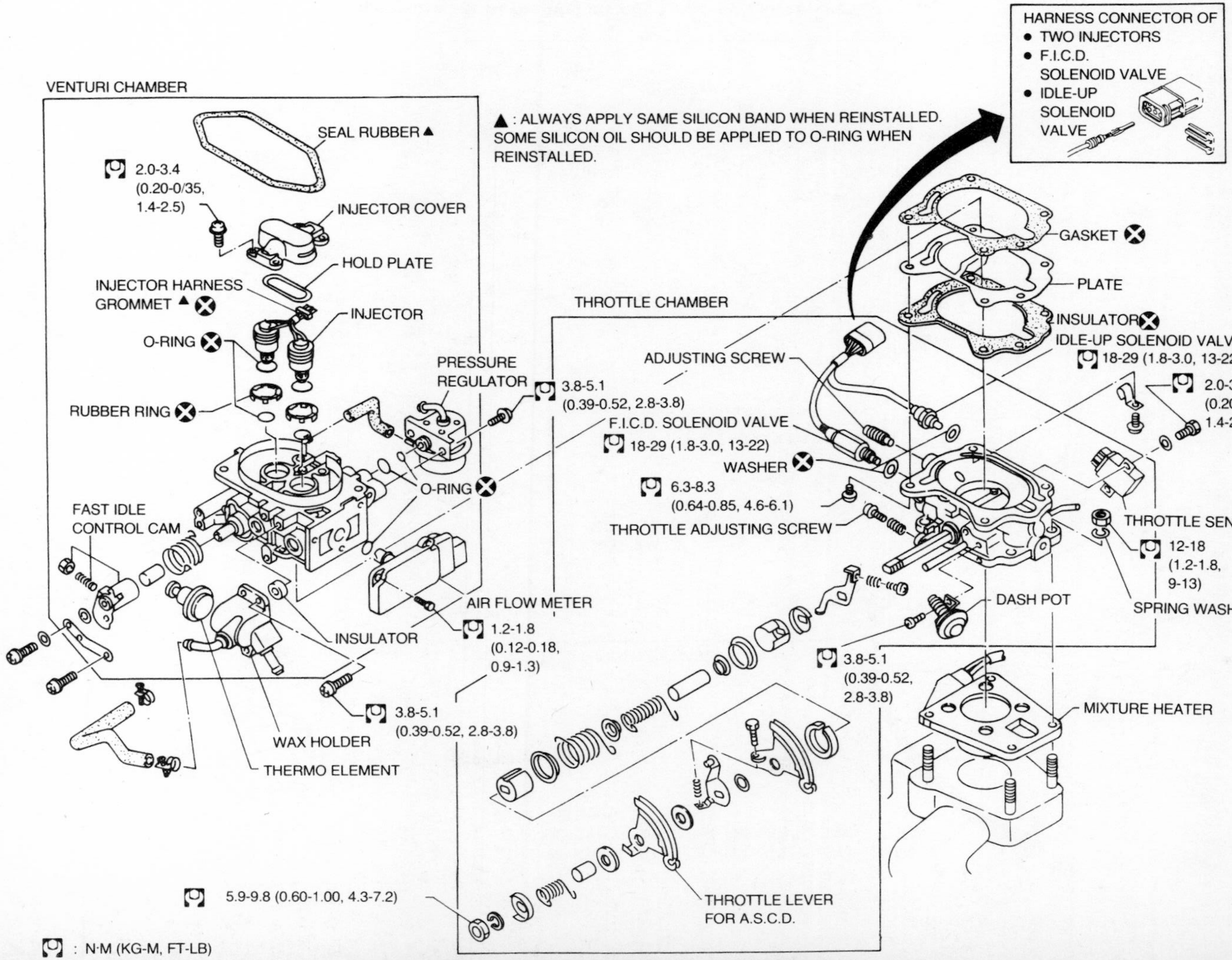

VENTURI CHAMBER
SEAL RUBBER ▲
2.0-3.4 (0.20-0/35, 1.4-2.5)
INJECTOR COVER
HOLD PLATE
INJECTOR HARNESS GROMMET ▲ ⊗
INJECTOR
O-RING ⊗
RUBBER RING ⊗
PRESSURE REGULATOR
3.8-5.1 (0.39-0.52, 2.8-3.8)
O-RING ⊗
FAST IDLE CONTROL CAM
AIR FLOW METER
1.2-1.8 (0.12-0.18, 0.9-1.3)
INSULATOR
3.8-5.1 (0.39-0.52, 2.8-3.8)
WAX HOLDER
THERMO ELEMENT
5.9-9.8 (0.60-1.00, 4.3-7.2)
: N·M (KG-M, FT-LB)

▲ : ALWAYS APPLY SAME SILICON BAND WHEN REINSTALLED. SOME SILICON OIL SHOULD BE APPLIED TO O-RING WHEN REINSTALLED.

HARNESS CONNECTOR OF
- TWO INJECTORS
- F.I.C.D. SOLENOID VALVE
- IDLE-UP SOLENOID VALVE

THROTTLE CHAMBER
GASKET ⊗
PLATE
INSULATOR ⊗
IDLE-UP SOLENOID VALVE
18-29 (1.8-3.0, 13-22)
2.0-3.4 (0.20-0.35, 1.4-2.5)
ADJUSTING SCREW
F.I.C.D. SOLENOID VALVE
18-29 (1.8-3.0, 13-22)
WASHER ⊗
6.3-8.3 (0.64-0.85, 4.6-6.1)
THROTTLE ADJUSTING SCREW
THROTTLE SENSOR
12-18 (1.2-1.8, 9-13)
SPRING WASHER
DASH POT
3.8-5.1 (0.39-0.52, 2.8-3.8)
MIXTURE HEATER
THROTTLE LEVER FOR A.S.C.D.

Exploded view of the fuel injection unit—Z24i engines

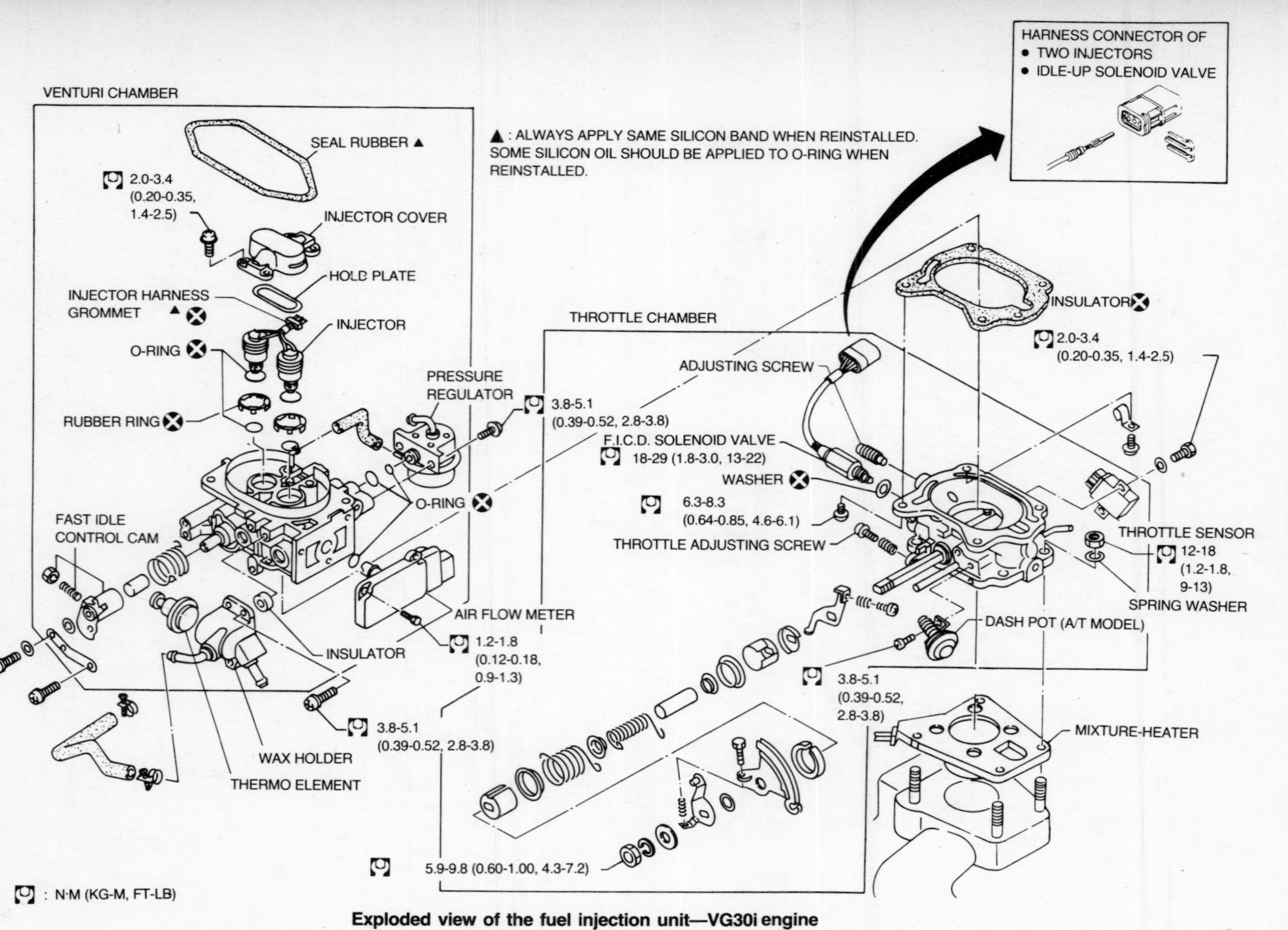

Exploded view of the fuel injection unit—VG30i engine

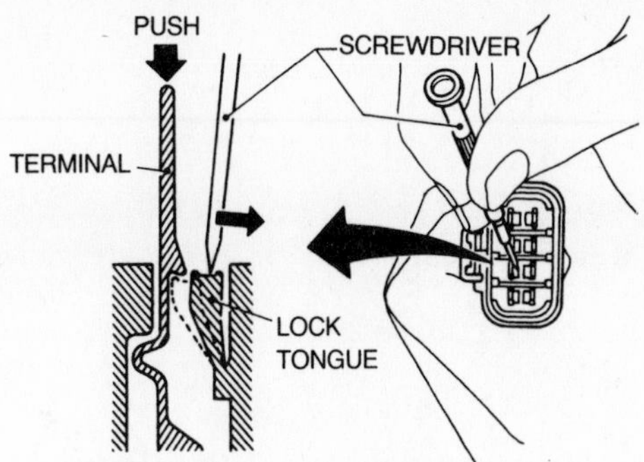

Disconnecting harness connector

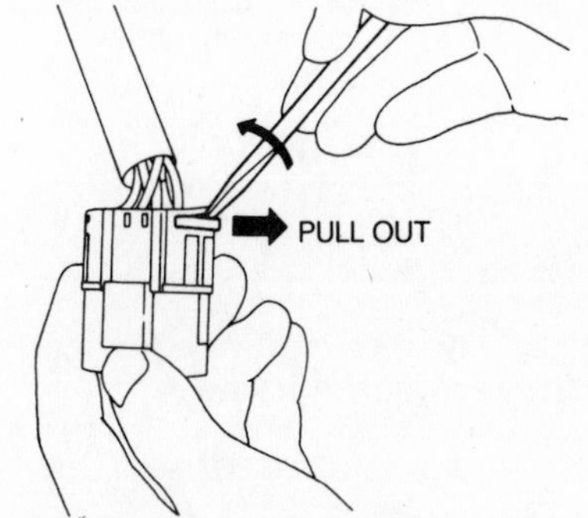

Disconnecting harness connector

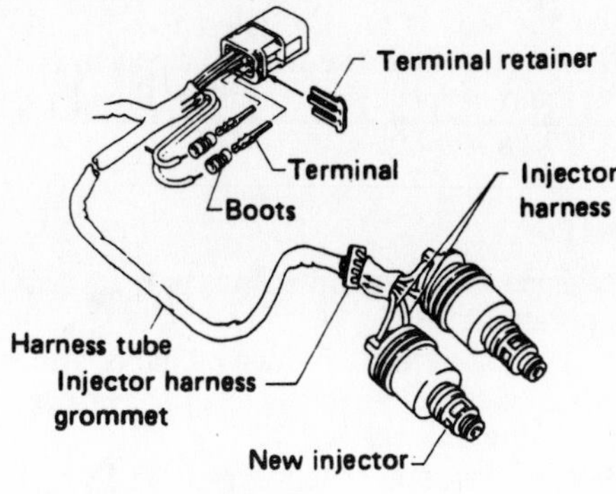

Typical injector assembly

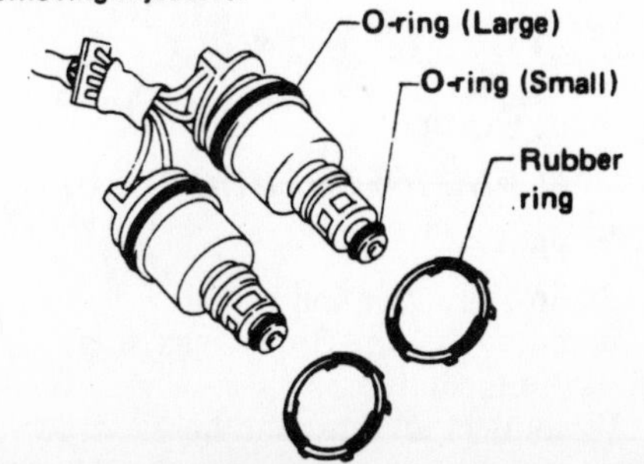

Always replace the O-rings

6. Put the harness of the new injector into a new injector harness grommet and the harness tube.

NOTE: *Every time a harness grommet is removed it should be replaced with a new one. When assembling the connector, pay attention to the harness color and position, otherwise injector damage could occur.*

7. Replace all injector O-rings with new ones coated with some silicone oil and put the injector asssembly into the injection body.

8. Push the injectors into the injector body by hand, until the O-rings are fully seated. Invert the injection body and insure that the injector tips are properly seated.

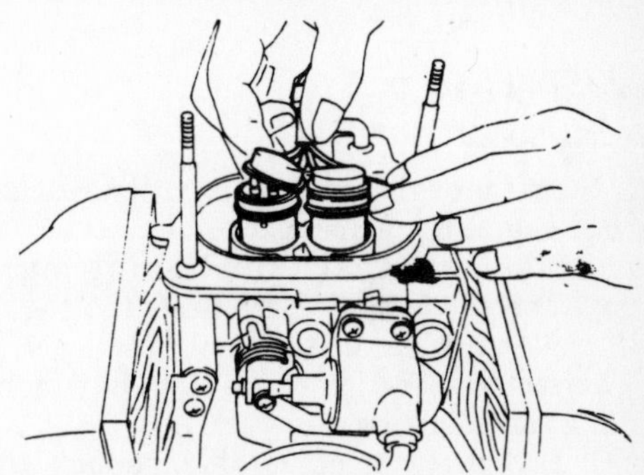
Press the injectors into the throttle body

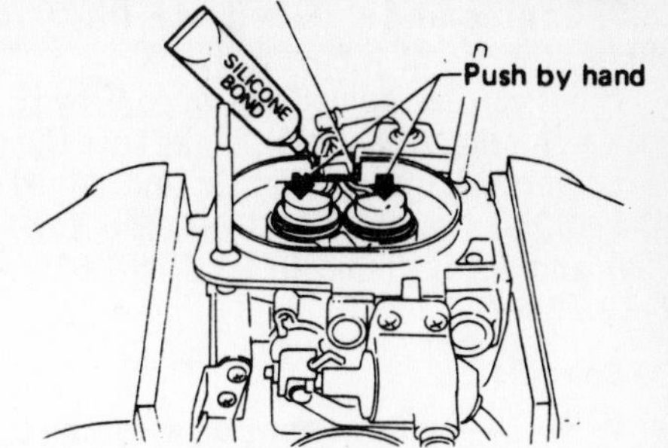

Apply silicone to the harness grommet

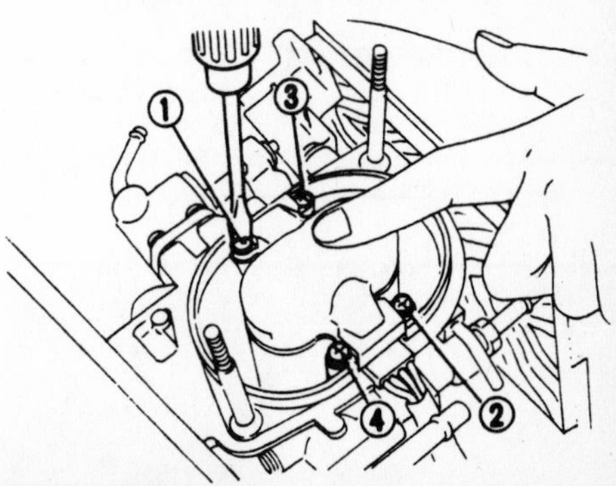

Tighten the injector cover screws in a criss-cross pattern

9. Apply some silicone bond to the injector harness grommet.

NOTE: *Air tight sealing is essential to ensure stable and proper idling condition.*

10. Use locking sealer on the screw threads and reinstall the injector cover. Tighten the screws in a criss-cross pattern to ensure proper seating of the injector and cover.

11. Apply some silicone bond to the bottom of the rubber seal and attach the seal to the top face of the injection body.

NOTE: *Do not reinstall the air cleaner until the silicone bond has hardened.*

12. Install the injection unit to the intake manifold and tighten the bolts to 9–13 ft. lbs. 12–18 Nm).

ADJUSTMENTS

Fast Idle Speed

1. Start the engine and run it until it reaches normal operating temperature.

2. Make sure that the aligning mark stamped on the fast idle cam meets the center of the roller installed on the cam follow lever. If not, correct the location of the fast idle cam by turning the adjusting screw (**S1**).

NOTE:If it is not adjustable, replace the thermo element.

3. Measure the clearance **G** between the roller and the fast idle cam. The clearance should be 0.020–0.118 in. (0.508–2.99mm) for the VG30i engine and 0.028–0.118 in. (0.71–2.99mm) for the Z24i engine.

4. If not correct, adjust clearance **G** by turning the adjusting screw (**S2**). Make sure the engine is warmed up sufficiently and adjust to 0.031–0.047 in. (0.787–1.194mm) for the VG30i and 0.047–0.063 in. (1.194–1.600mm) for the Z24i.

FICD Solenoid

1. With the engine at normal operating temperature, check the idle speed. (Refer to the Tune-Up Specification Chart).

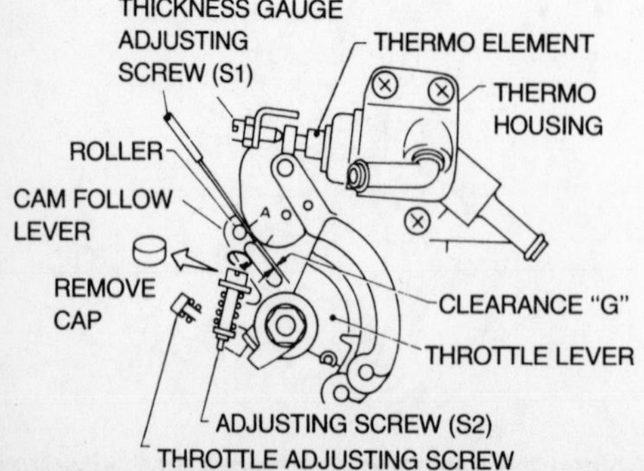

Fast idle adjustment

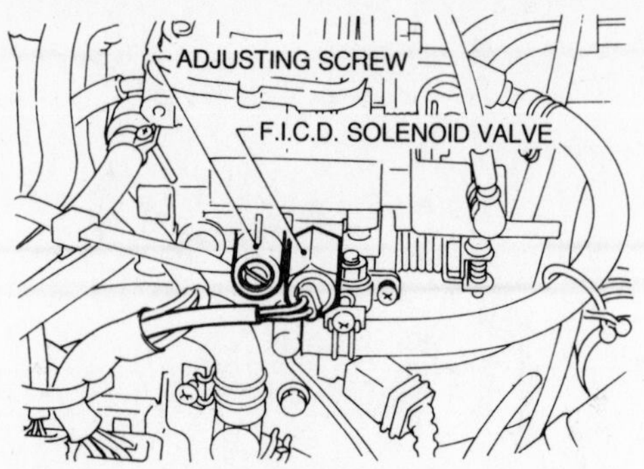

F.I.C.D. solenoid valve adjustment

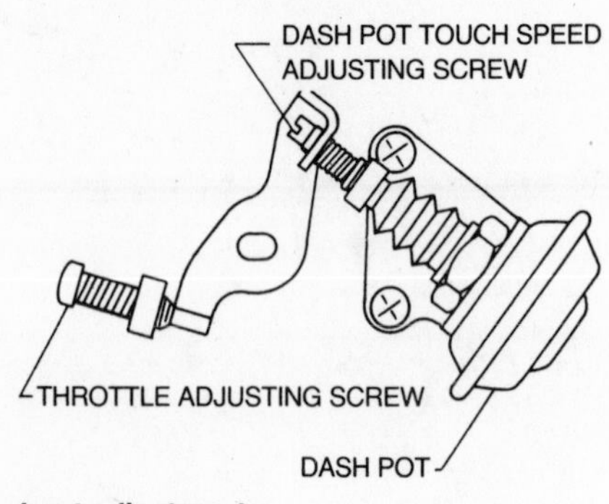

Dashpot adjustment

2. Turn the air conditioner switch **ON**. When the A/C is on, the idle speed should be 850–950 rpm with the transmission in **N**.

3. If out of specification, adjust the idle speed by turning the adjusting screw.

Dash Pot

1. Run the engine to normal operating temperature.

2. Turn the throttle valve by hand, and read the engine speed when the dash pot just touches the adjusting screw.

3. The dashpot touch speed is; 1300–1500 rpm for the VG30i and 1600–2000 rpm for the Z24i.

4. Adjust by turning the adjusting screw.

DIESEL FUEL SYSTEM

Injection Pump

REMOVAL AND INSTALLATION

SD22 Engines

1. Remove the fan and radiator.

2. Remove the injection lines and cap all openings immediately.

3. Disconnect all lines and hoses attached to the pump or in the way of pump removal.

4. Remove the oil filter.

5. Remove the rear pump bracket.
6. Remove the timing gear cover.
7. Remove the timer round nut.
8. Remove the timer assembly using tool #ST1953000.
9. Unbolt and remove the pump.
10. Align the crankshaft timing marks at TDC of the No. 1 piston's compression stroke.
11. Loosely install the injection pump. Mesh the idler gear and pump drive gear at the **Y** mark, then align the gear and keyway on the pump camshaft while turning the crankshaft pulley.
12. Install the timer roundnut and washer. Tighten to 50 ft. lbs.
13. Align the timing mark on the front of the pump with the corresponding mark on the

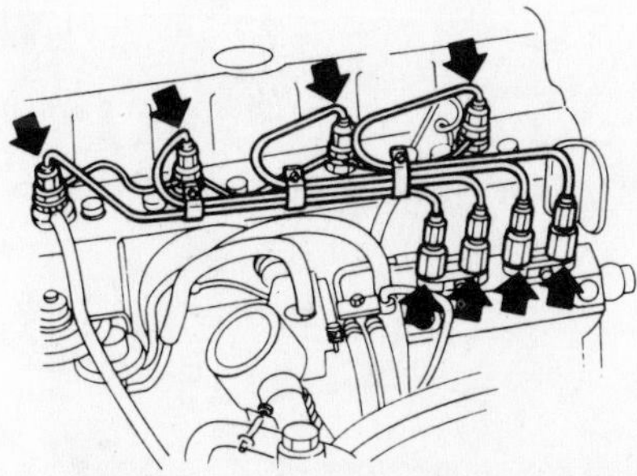

Diesel injection line connection—SD22 engines

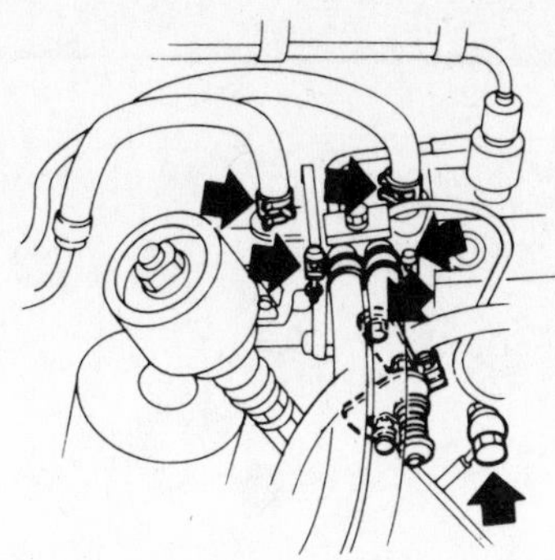

Hose connection points—SD22 engines

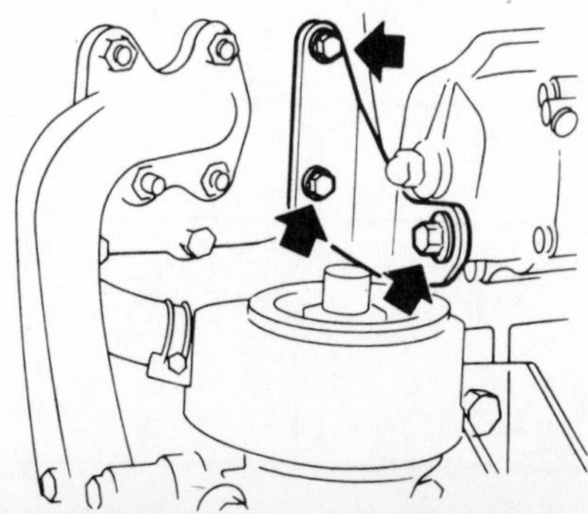

Injection pump rear bracket—SD22 engines

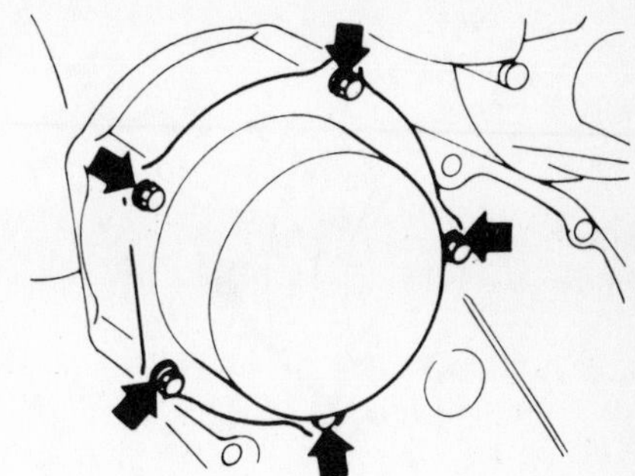

Timer cover—SD22 engines

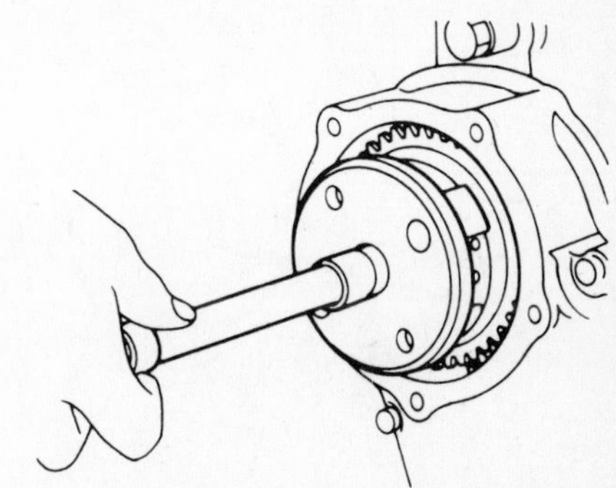

Removing the timer round nut—SD22 engines

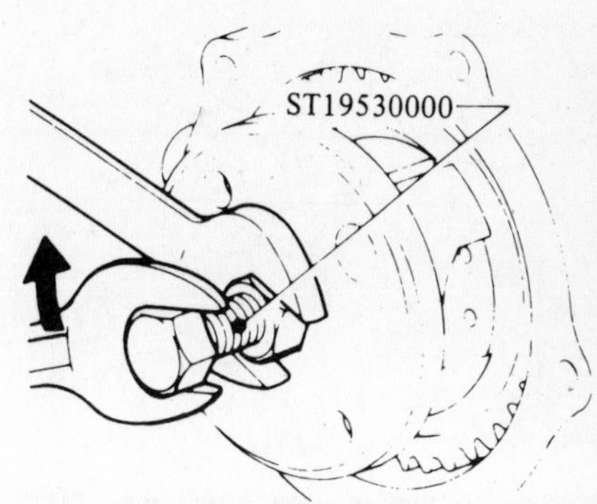

Removing the timer—SD22 engines

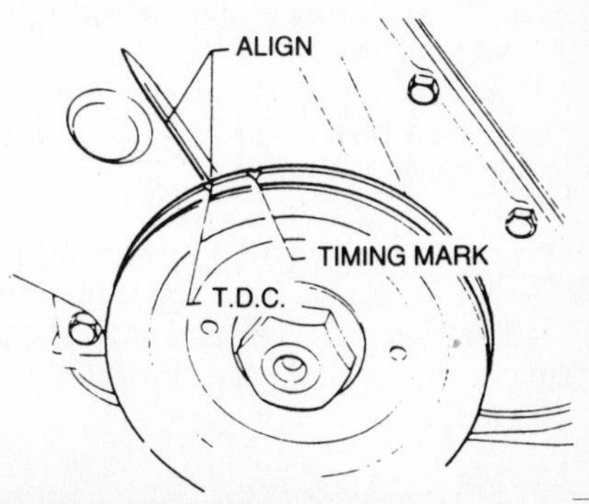

Aligning the crankshaft timing marks—SD22 engines

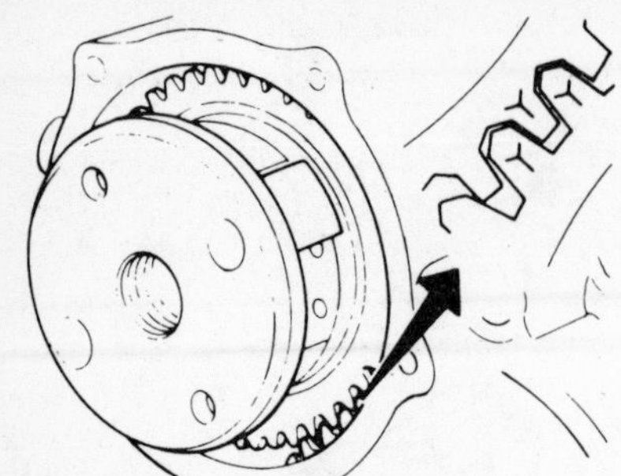

Aligning the timer Y marks—SD22 engines

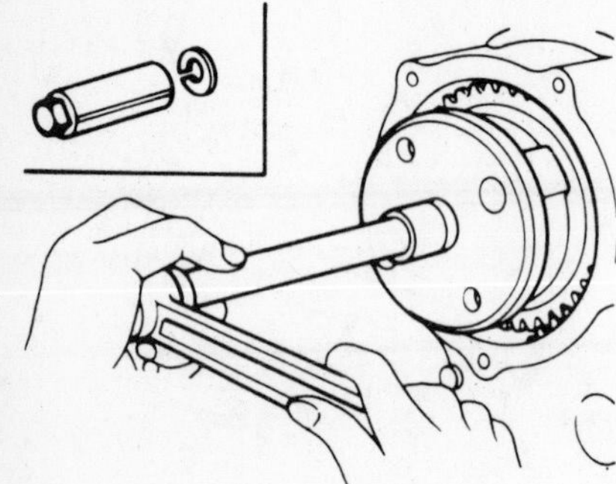

Round nut installation—SD22 engines

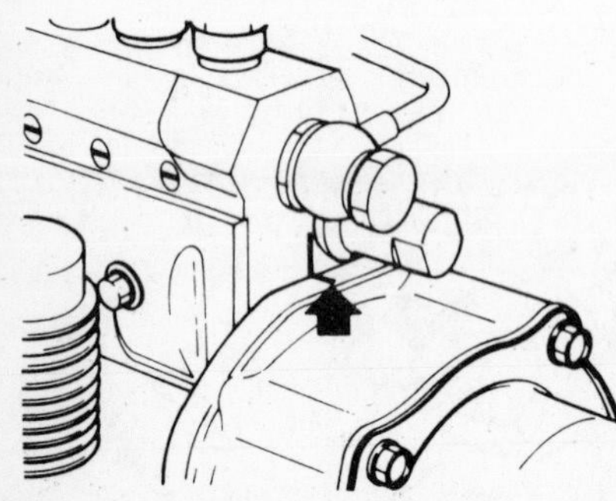

Injection pump timing mark alignment—SD22 engines

front cover. Tighten the pump mounting bolts to 18 ft. lbs.

14. Remove the cap from the priming pump.
15. Turn the priming pump counterclockwise.
16. Loosen the air vent screw.
17. Move the priming pump up and down until no further air comes from the vent screw.
18. Tighten the vent screw and push and turn the priming pump clockwise. Install the cap. Wipe off all spilled fuel.

SD25 Engines

1. Set the No. 1 piston at TDC of its compression stroke.
2. Disconnect the injection tubes. Plug the nozzle openings and be careful not to damage the spill tube.
4. Tag and disconnect the fuel cut solenoid harness.
5. Disconnect the accelerator wire, the overflow hose and the fuel inlet hose (plug this one!). Additionally, disconnect the cold start device water line and the fuel return hose (you guessed it, plug this one too!).
6. Loosen the bolts and remove the injection pump drive gear cover..
7. Loosen the drive gear nut and then remove the gear with a two-armed puller.

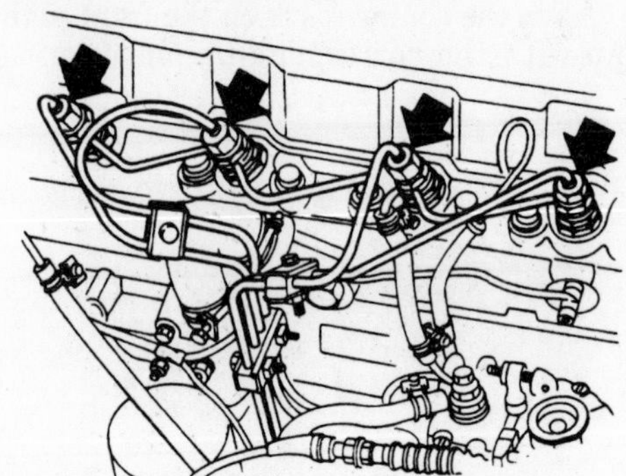

Injection line connections—SD25 engines

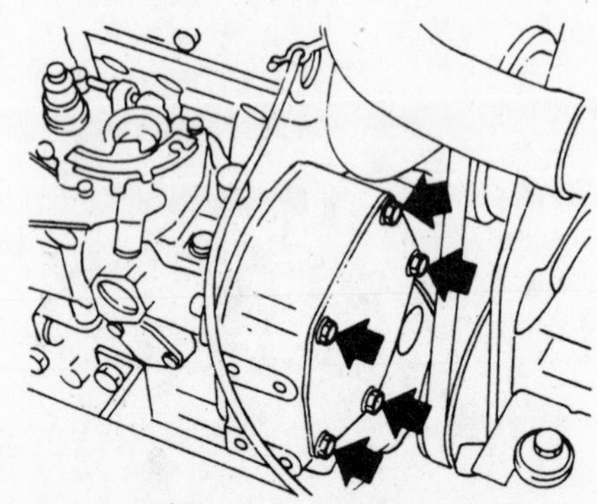

Remove the drive gear cover—SD25 engines

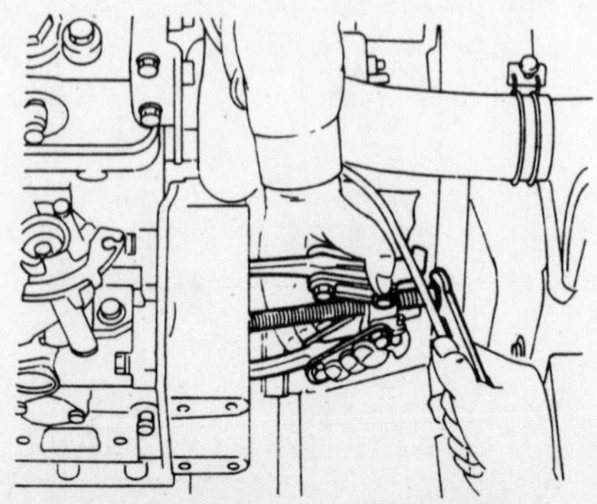

Removing the drive gear nut—SD25 engines

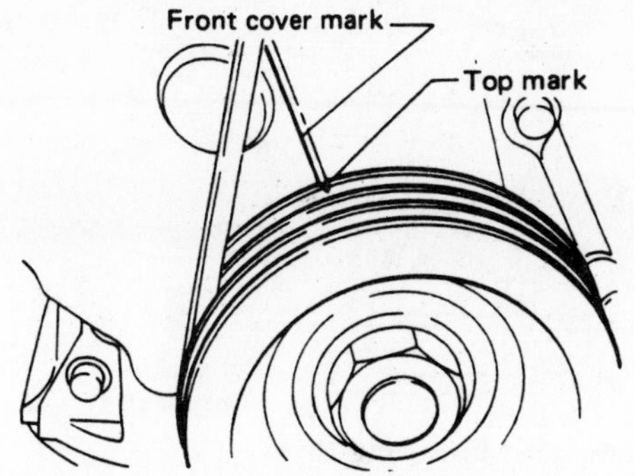

Align the crankshaft timing marks—SD25 engines

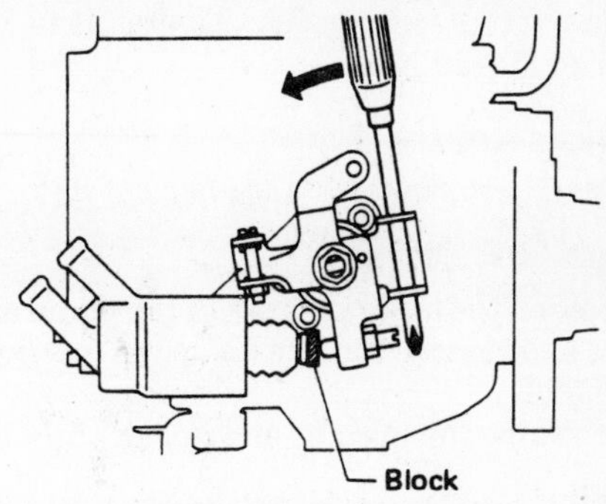

Fabricate a wooden block about 15mm thick—SD25 engines

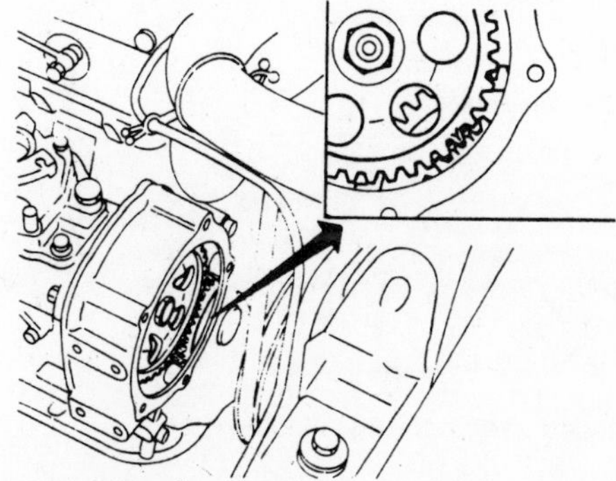
Make sure that the Y marks on the gears are aligned—SD25 engines

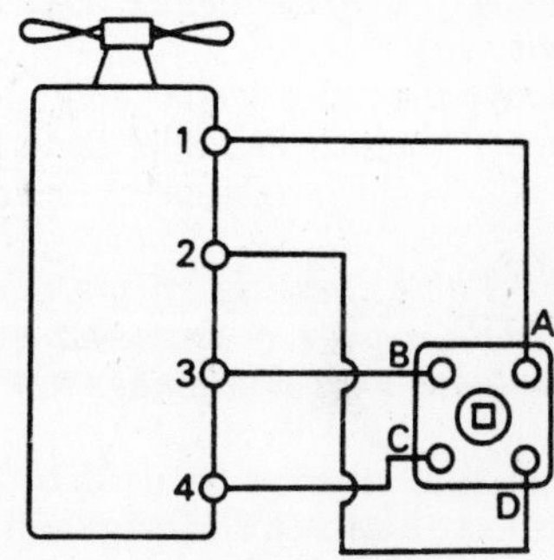

Injection tube routing—SD25 engines

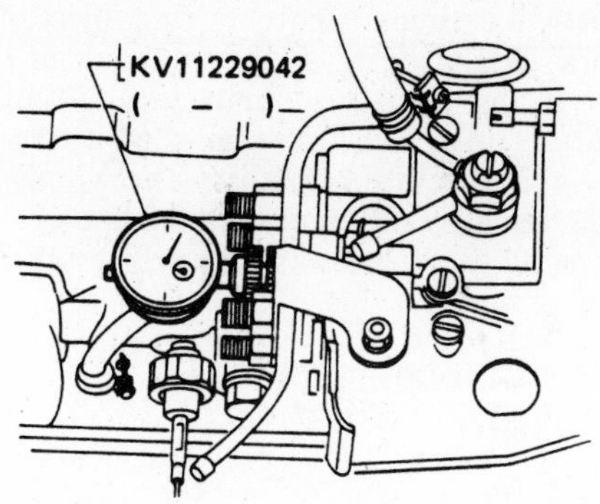

Install a dial gauge in the plug hole to check plunger lift—SD25 engines

8. Loosen the mounting bolts and nuts and remove the injection pump with the injection tubes still attached.

9. Check the the No. 1 piston is still at TDC and then position the injection pump so that the pump flange aligns with the **Y** mark on the front cover. Install the drive gear and tighten the nut to 43–51 ft. lbs. (59–69 Nm).

NOTE: *Be carful not to allow the key to fall into the front cover and be absolutely certain that the Y marks are aligned.*

10. Install the drive gear cover with a new gasket and then adjust the plunger lift.

11. Tighten the injection pump mounting nut to 14–18 ft. lbs. (20–25 Nm) and the bolts to 12–16 ft. lbs. (16–22 Nm).

12. Install the injection tubes to the injectors. Bleed the system.

PLUNGER LIFT ADJUSTMENT

SD25 Engines

1. Remove the plug bolt from the distributor head and install a dial gauge.

2. Rotate the cold start device linkage clockwise and install a block of wood or paper (15mm) between the linkage and the device.

3. Set the No. 1 piston at TDC of the compression stroke and then rotate the crankshaft counterclockwise 20–25 degrees. Check the gauge in this position and then reset it to zero.

4. Rotate the crankshaft clockwise until the No. 1 piston is at TDC again and then read the gauge. Plunger lift should be 0.0374–0.0390 in. (0.95–0.99mm).

5. Adjust the plunger lift by rotating the injection pump until it is within range. Clockwise to decrease the measurement and counterclockwise to increase.

6. Tighten the injection pump mounting bolts. Disconnect the dial gauge and install the

plug bolt with a new washer. Tighten it to 10–14 ft. lbs. (14–20 Nm).

Injection Nozzle

REMOVAL, OVERHAUL AND INSTALLATION

SD22 and SD25 Engines

1. Loosen the injection lines at the pump and nozzles and remove the lines. Cap the openings immediately.
2. Unscrew the injector and holder from the head.
3. Secure the nozzle holder in a vise and remove the lock nut.
4. Remove the nipple.
5. Remove the nozzle holder body from the nozzle nut.
6. Remove the spacer collar and pushrod.
7. Remove the nozzle holder body from the vise and remove the nozzle spring and adjusting shims.

NOTE: *The adjusting shims may be removed with a piece of wire, but great care must be taken to avoid damage to the nozzle tip.*

8. Clean fuel oil may be used to clean all parts. Inspect all parts for damage and good fit.
9. Assemble the nozzle in reverse order of disassembly.

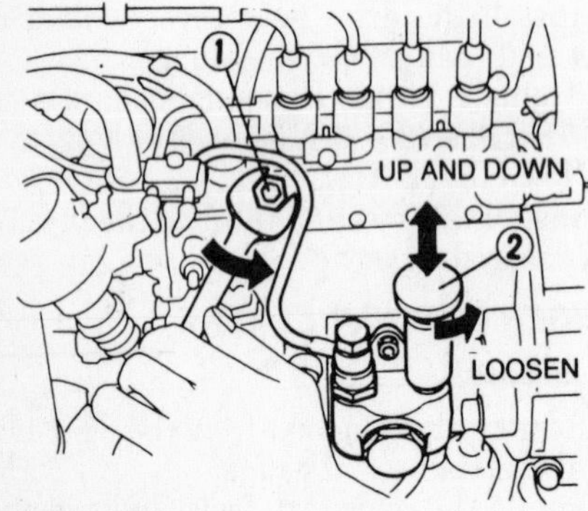

Bleeding the system

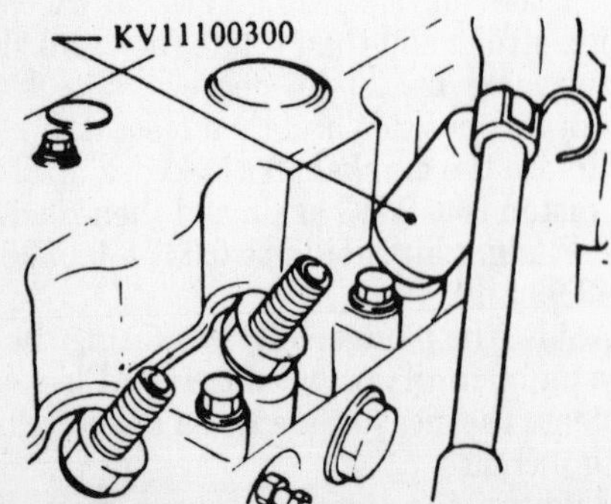

Nozzle removal

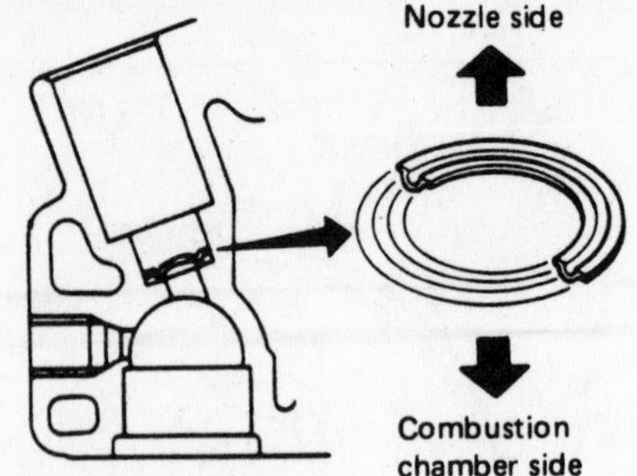

Installing the nozzle gasket

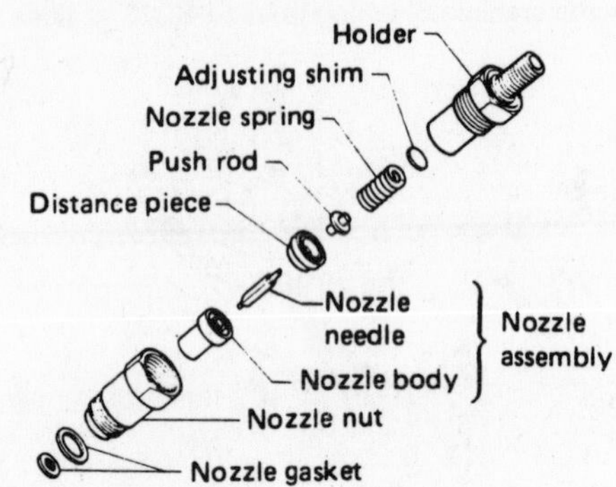

Exploded view of the injection nozzle

10. Install the nozzle in a tester.
11. Operate the tester lever at 1 stroke per second and read the pressure at injection. The pointer will oscillate slightly during injection.
12. Increase or decrease the thickness of the nozzle spring adjusting shims until opening pressure is 1422.3 psi. A total of 31 different shims are available. A shim thickness of 0.05mm equals a difference of 85.338 psi.
13. Install the nozzles and lines. Tighten the nozzles to 50–65 ft. lbs.

Altitude Compensator

ADJUSTMENT

SD22 Engines

NOTE: *This adjustment should be performed with the injection lever in the free position.*

1. Disconnect the pump controller rod.
2. Loosen the locknut and capnut on the compensator.
3. Turn the capnut until it touches the injection lever. Tighten the locknut.
4. Two methods can be used for adjustment depending on your budget:
   a. Using a barometer, measure atmospheric pressure in the immediate area of the pump. Determine how much the capnut should be loosened using the equation, R = 9.878 x 10 [ma] [S3] x (760-P), in which R

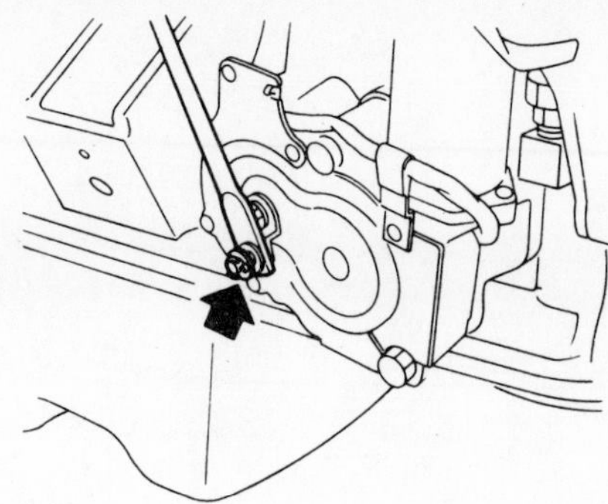

Disconnecting the control rod—SD22 engines

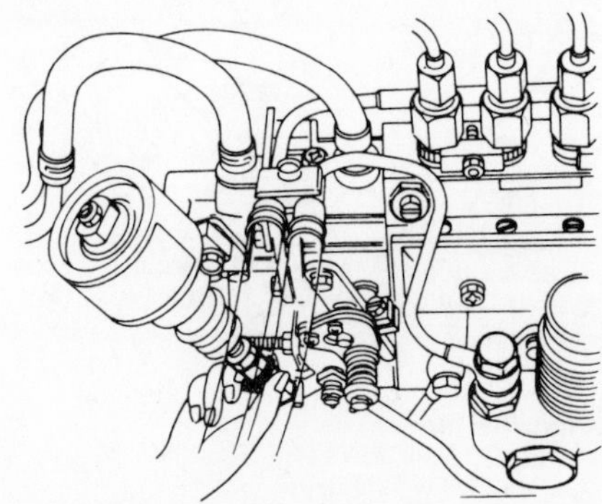

Turning the capscrew—SD22 engines

= the number of revolutions the capnut should be loosened and P = the measured atmospheric pressure in mmHg.

b. The cap nut adjustment can be determined according to altitude above sea level using the following chart:

5. When the adjustment has been made, tighten the locknut.

6. Install the controller rod.

NOTE: *Make certain that the bolt comes into contact with the injection pump lever. If not, loosen and readjust the bolt.*

Governor

RSV AND RAD MECHANICAL TYPE REMOVAL

1. Remove the injection pump and place it in a holding fixture.
2. Install the timer.
3. Drain the cam and governor chambers.
4. Remove the supply pump.
5. Remove the cam cover.
6. Using a special wrench, ST #57916432, on the timer, turn the camshaft until all the tappets are raised to TDC. Place a tappet holder, #57931-210, between the tappet adjusting bolt and nut for each cylinder.
7. Remove the rear cover and dipstick.
8. Loosen the balance idler spring and the auxiliary idler spring lock nut.
9. Loosen the governor cover lock screw.
10. Unbolt and remove the governor cover from the governor body. Remove the link from the control rack.

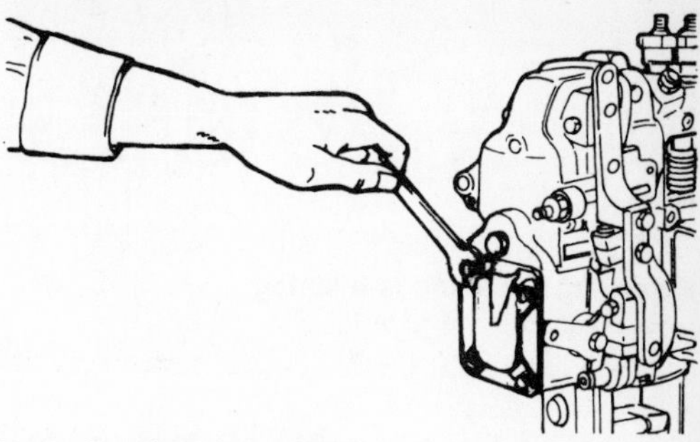

Removing the cam cover

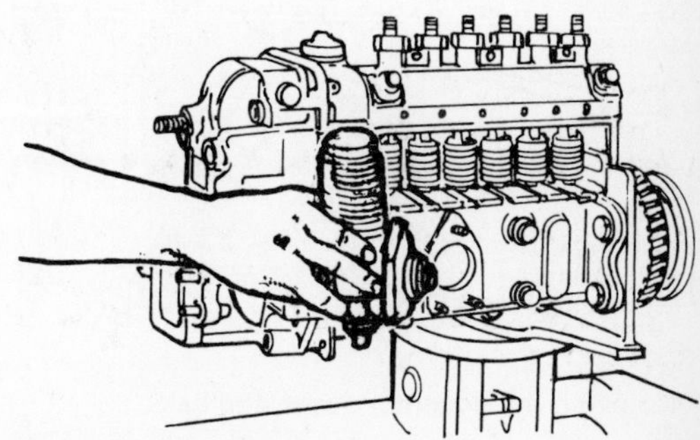

Feed pump removal

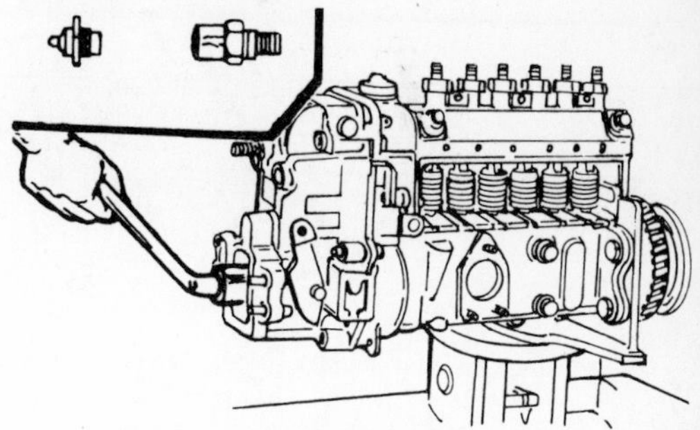

Removing the idling spring, type RAD

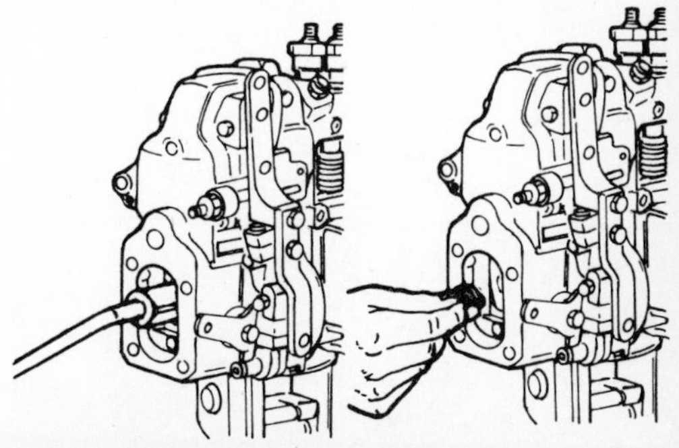

Removing the idling spring, type RSV

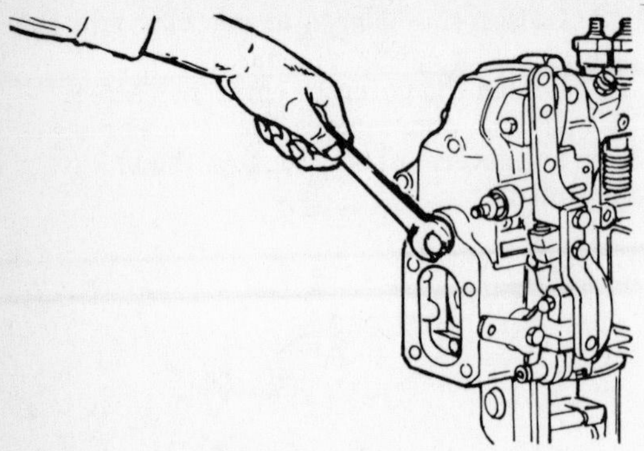

Removing the idling sub spring

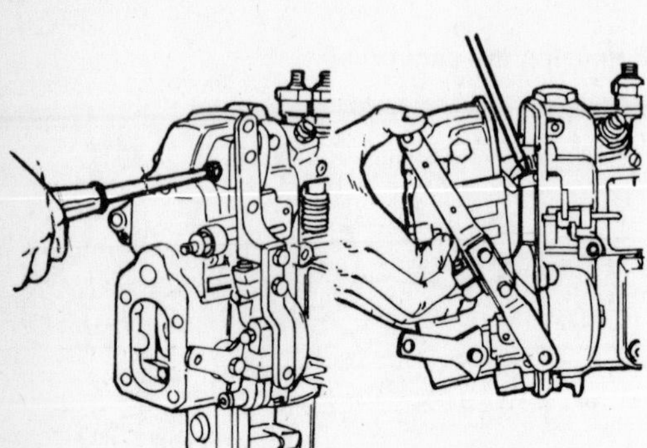

Removing the governor cover and link

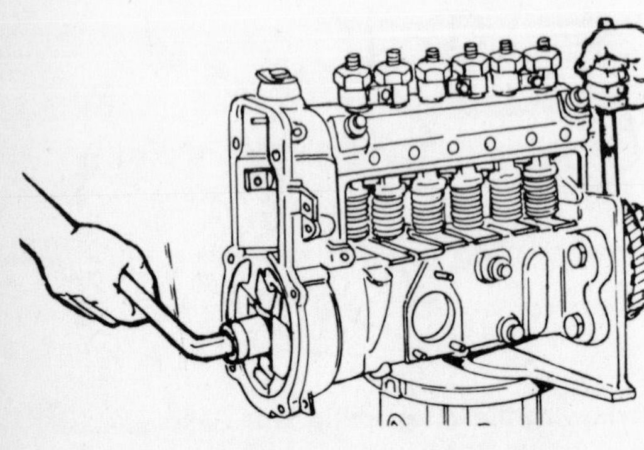

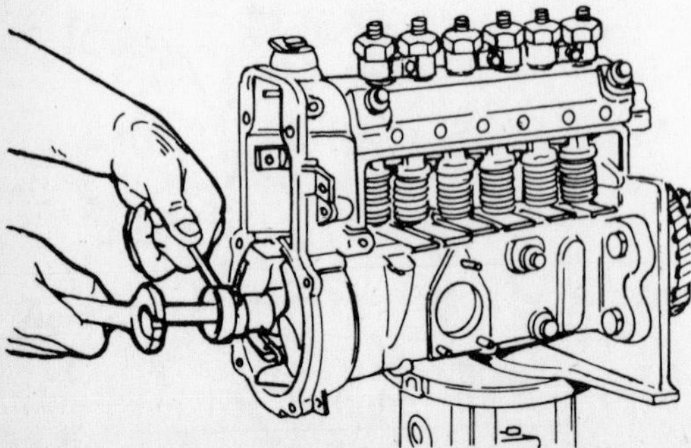

Removing counterweights

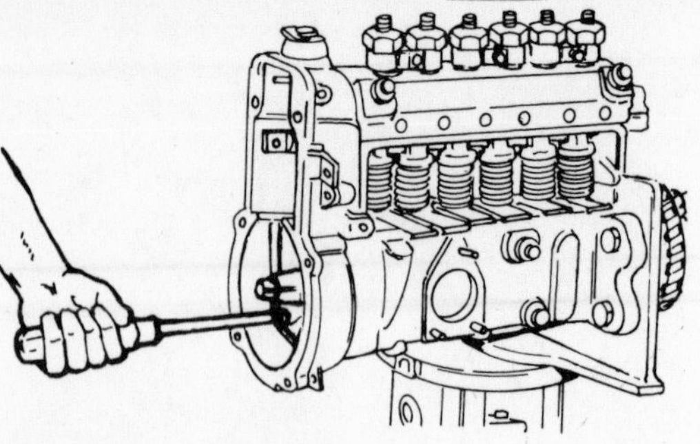

Removing governor body

Removing the timer

11. Remove the start spring from the spring eye.
12. Remove the counterweights from the camshaft.
13. Hold the timer and remove the slotted nuts and lockwasher.
14. Using a puller, ST #57926-512, remove the flyweight assembly.
15. Remove the timer.
16. Unbolt and remove the governor body.

MZ PNEUMATIC TYPE REMOVAL

1. Follow Steps 1–6 of RSV Type Removal.
2. Unbolt and remove the diaphragm housing and main spring.
3. Remove the diaphragm ring with a screwdriver.
4. Remove the cotter pin from the connecting rod bolt with a pair of needlenose pliers.
5. Remove the diaphragm assembly from the control rack.
6. Remove the five set screws and remove the governor body by applying force in the slit between the governor and pump housings.
7. Remove the timer.

RSV TYPE INSTALLATION

1. Apply RTV silicone gasket material to the governor body and install the governor on the injection pump.
2. Tighten the upper spring eye screw holding the starting spring.
3. Install the timer.

4. Install the flyweight assembly.
5. Apply RTV silicone gasket material to the governor cover and install the starting spring on the housing side of the spring eye.
6. Install the link leaf spring in the hole in the end of the control rack.
7. Install the cover and set screws.

MZ TYPE INSTALLATION

1. Apply RTV silicone gasket material to the governor body, position it on the pump body and tap it into position with a plastic mallet. Install the set service.
2. Install the diaphragm and balance spring on the control rack connecting bolt and lock it with a new cotter pin. Apply chassis lube to the diaphragm ring.
3. Insert the main spring and install the diaphragm housing with the four bolts.

Injection Pump Service

REPLACING THE DELIVERY VALVE

1. Thoroughly clean the area around the nozzle tube and delivery valve.
2. Remove the nozzle tube.
3. Remove the delivery valve holder lock plate.
4. Remove the delivery valve holder and spring.
5. Using ST #57930-032, remove the delivery valve.
6. Position the delivery valve in the pump housing making sure no dirt gets between the top of the plunger barrel and the delivery valve.
7. Install a new delivery valve gasket. The gasket is installed with the larger face downward and may be tapped into place through the extractor.
8. Install the delivery valve spring.
9. Install the delivery valve holder and torque it to 22–25 ft. lbs.
10. Loosen the holder and retorque it.

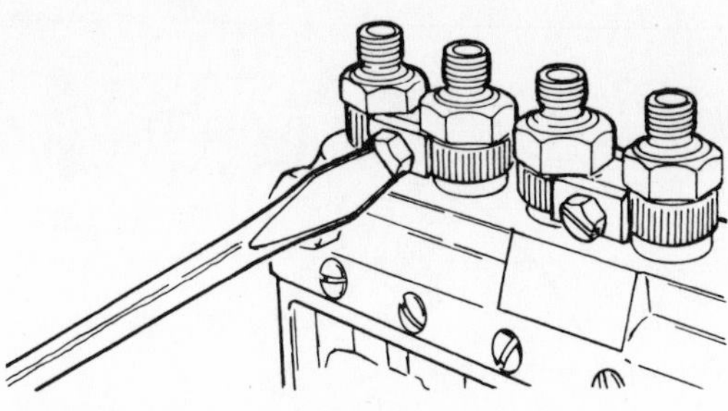

Removing delivery valve holder lock plate

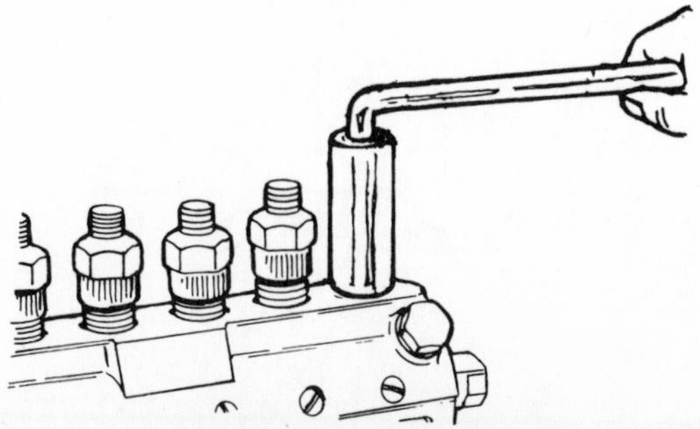

Loosening the delivery valve holder

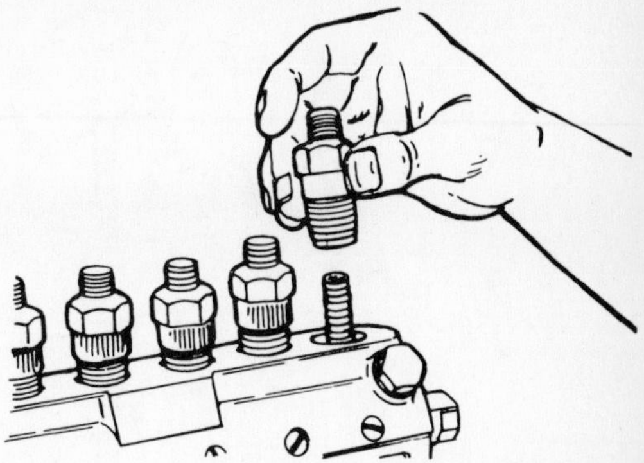

Removing the delivery valve holder and spring

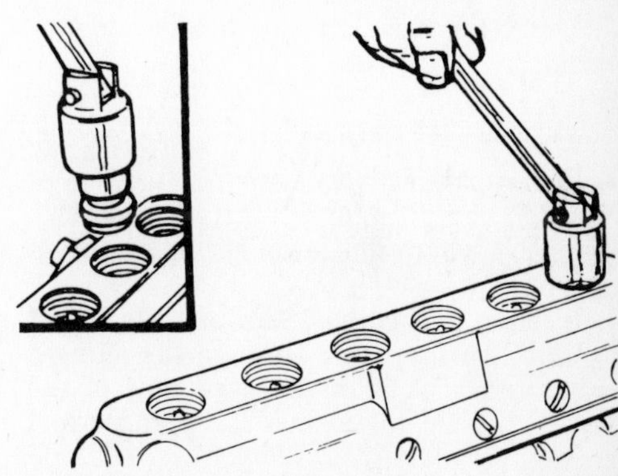

Removing the delivery valve with tool 57930-032

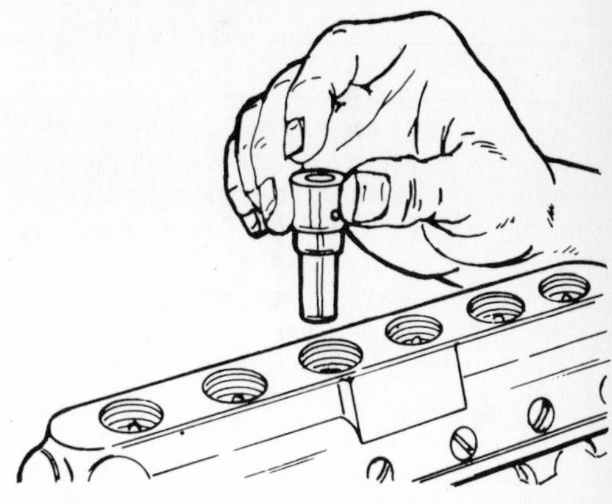

Plunger barrel removal, with delivery valves removed

Inserting the plunger spring holder

11. Install the lock plate, nozzle tube and nozzle clamp.

REPLACING THE PLUNGER

1. Remove the delivery valve.
2. Push the plunger spring up with two prybars and remove the lower spring seat from the plunger.
3. Insert a hooked wire through the top of the pump housing, down through the plunger opening and hook it on the lead unit of the plunger. Pull up to remove the plunger and barrel.
4. Immerse a new plunger in clean fuel oil and thoroughly wash off the rust preventive.

   NOTE: *The plunger was lapped at the factory. Do not hold it by the lapped section!*
5. Operate the plunger in clean fuel oil to check its operation.
6. Slowly insert the plunger and barrel into the pump with the barrel groove and plunger notch facing forward. Make certain the plunger piston pin is properly seated in the groove in the control sleeve.
7. Push the plunger spring up with two prybars and insert the lower spring seat.
8. Install the remaining parts in reverse of disassembly.

CAMSHAFT REMOVAL AND INSTALLATION

1. Remove the key from the camshaft and remove the four setscrews on the drive side of the pump housing. Remove the bearing cover.
2. Lay the pump on its side and remove the screw plugs from the bottom of the housing with tool #57910-112 or a ratchet handle.
3. Remove the set screws from the center bearing.
4. Remove the camshaft from the housing.
5. Install the bearing cover on the timer side of the housing.
6. Install the camshaft so that the alignment mark **A** is toward the timer.

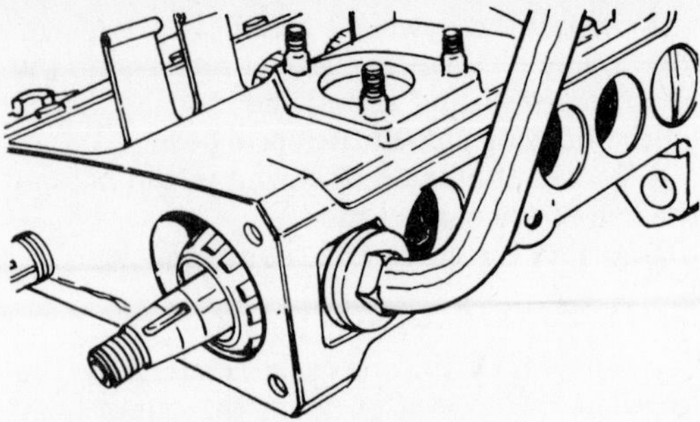

Screw plug removal and installation

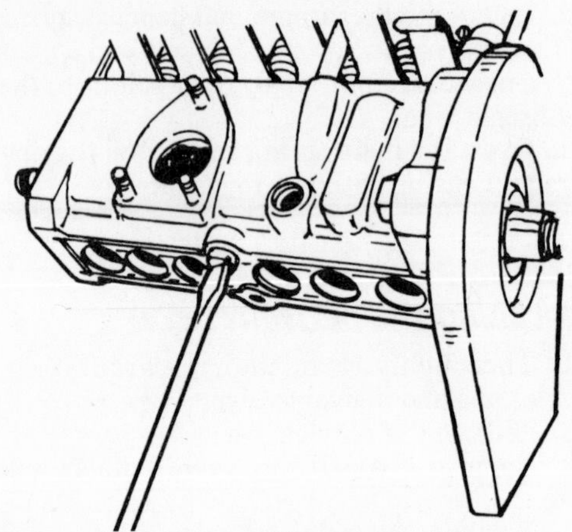

Set screw removal and installation

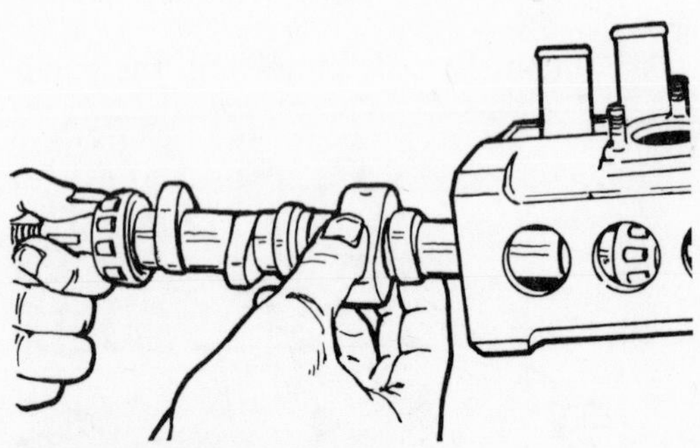

Camshaft removal

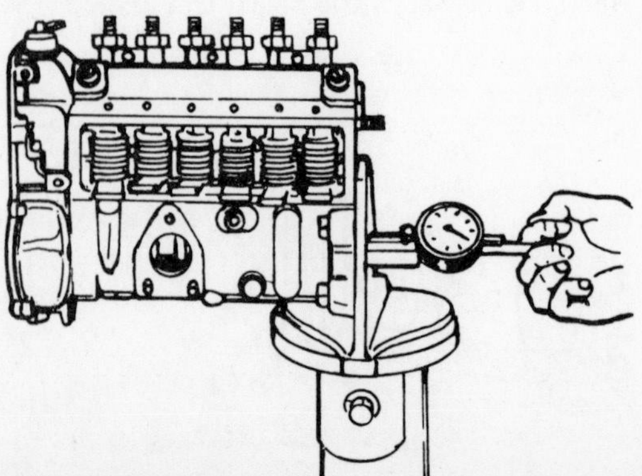

Measuring end play

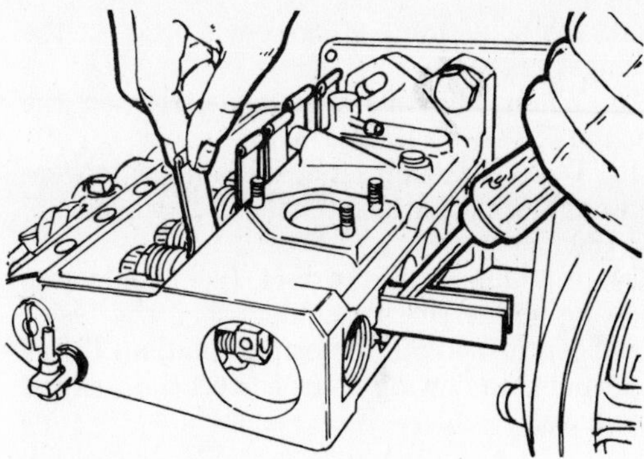

Inserting tappet holder and insert tool

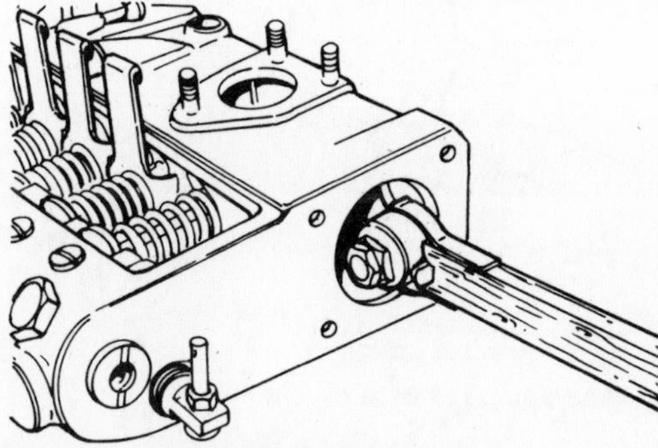

Removing tappet with tappet clamp

7. Check the end play. End play is 0–0.0012 in. (0–0.030mm).

TAPPET REMOVAL AND INSTALLATION

1. Remove the camshaft.
2. Install a tappet insert tool #57912-012 and remove the tappet holder, at the same time, removing the tappet from the holder. Be careful to avoid damaging the housing plug hole threads.
3. Loosen the tappet insert tool, withdraw the tappet assembly into the camshaft chamber and remove the tappet from the housing with a tappet clamp.
4. Installation is the reverse of removal. Make sure that the mechanism works smoothly.

PLUNGER REMOVAL AND INSTALLATION

1. Remove the tappets.
2. Remove the plungers using plunger pinchers #57921-412 or equivalent, together with the lower spring seat.
3. Place any reusable plungers in the corresponding plunger barrels and immerse them in kerosene or safe solvent.
4. Remove the plunger springs, upper spring seats and control sleeves.
5. Lay the housing on it side and position the control rack so that the punch marks on both sides are the same distance from each end of the housing.
6. Install the control sleeve with the gap in the sleeve facing straight upward. At the same time install the spring seats.
7. Install the plunger spring in the housing.

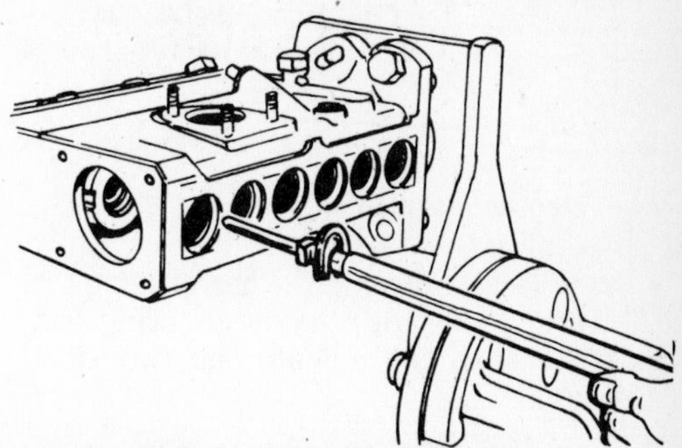

Removing plungers with tool 57921-412

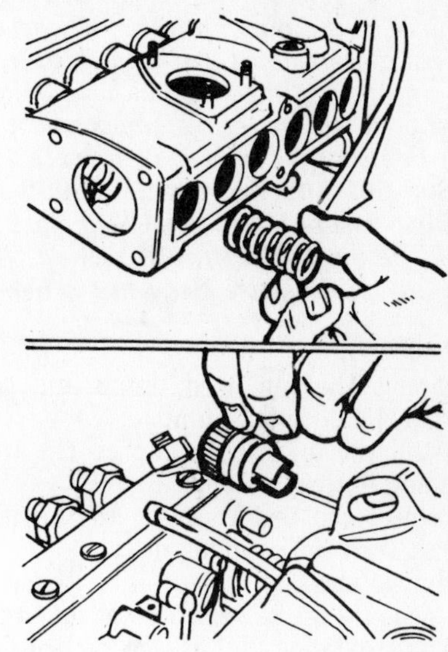

Removing plunger springs, control sleeves and upper spring seats

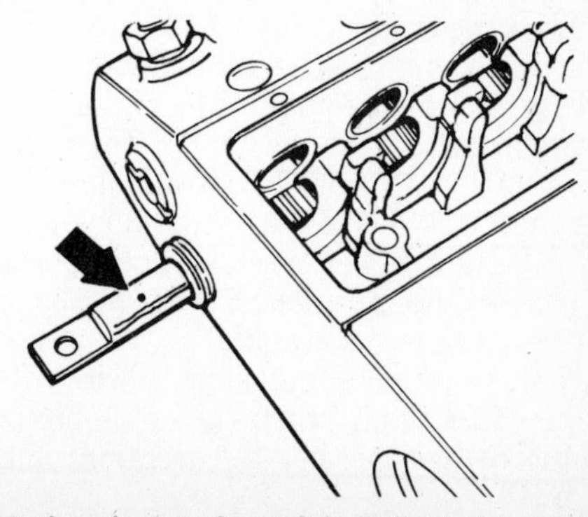

Control rack; punch mark is indicated by arrow

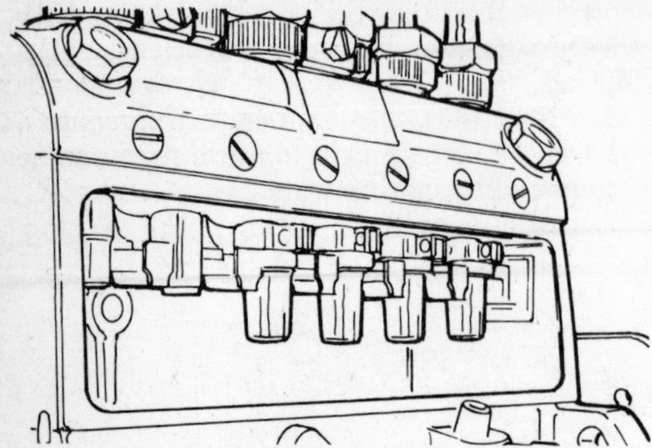

Control sleeves installed

8. Install the plunger in the barrel using tool #57921-412, along with the lower spring seat.

9. Make sure the mechanism functions smoothly.

TESTING AND ADJUSTING THE FUEL INJECTION PUMP

NOTE: *It is necessary to inspect and adjust the pump, using a pump tester, whenever it has been disassembled and assembled, when the plunger or plunger barrel have been replaced or when any of the component parts have been replaced. Use nozzle tube #57805-002 and test nozzle #5000-101, starting pressure 1422.3 psi. Clean No. 2 fuel should be used. Rotating direction, from drive side, is clockwise. Sequence is 1–4–3–2*

Starting Timing

1. Remove the fuel feed pump and cover plate from the injection pump.

2. Install the injection pump on the tester and holding fixture.

3. Connect the test coupling to the tester driveshaft with the coupling disc.

4. Remove the cap and position the tester dial to measure the camshaft rotating angle.

5. Install a tappet lift gauge on the No.1 tappet.

6. Bottom the tappet and set the dial gauge to zero.

7. Bleed the pump at the bleeder screw.

8. Loosen the nozzle holder ball valve.

9. Feed fuel to the pump inlet while slowly turning the pump tester by hand in the normal engine rotation direction. Fuel will flow from the test nozzle. When the fuel stops flowing, the injection point has been reached. The tappet, at this precise point, must be 0.08858–0.09251 in. (2.2249–2.3497mm) above BDC.

10. If the fuel does not stop flowing after 0.0926 in. (2.353mm), turn the adjusting bolt counterclockwise to raise the position of the plunger.

11. If the fuel stops flowing before 0.0886 in., turn the adjusting bolt clockwise to lower the plunger position.

12. When adjustment is made, tighten the locknut to 43–50 ft. lbs.

13. With the pump set at initial injection, set the angle scale mark on the tester flywheel at 0° or 180°.

14. If adjustment is correct, fuel should stop flowing at the No. 4 cylinder when the tester has been turned 60° in normal rotation. If fuel does not stop flowing at the correct time, adjust as above.

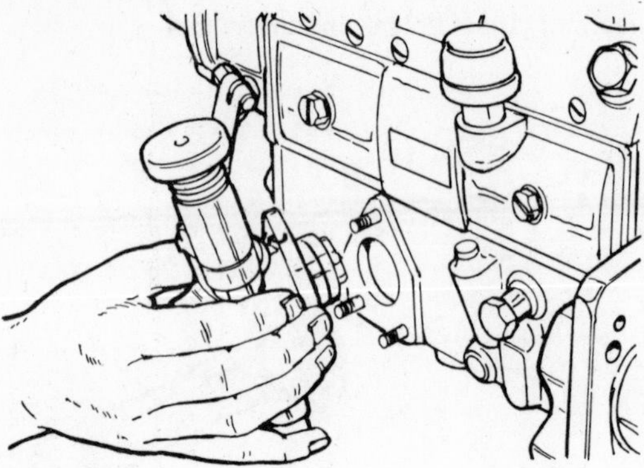

Fuel feed pump removal

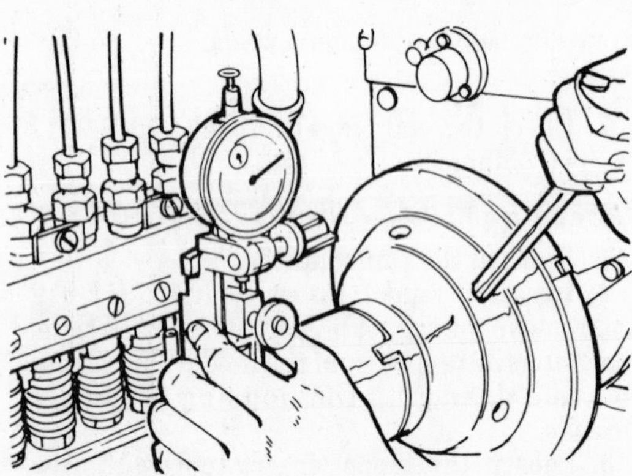

Checking injection start timing with a lift gauge

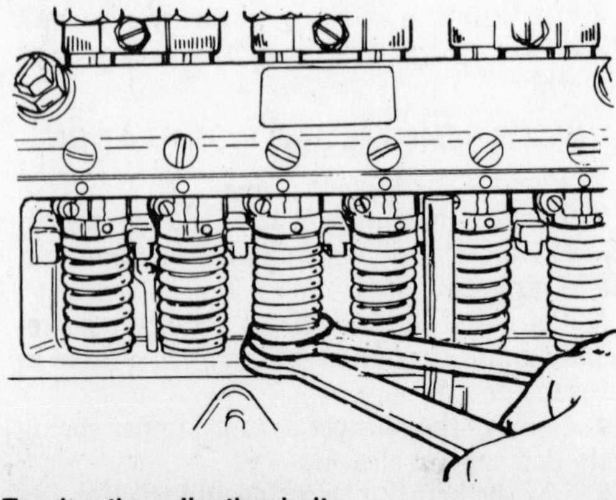

Turning the adjusting bolt

55 WAYS TO IMPROVE FUEL ECONOMY

CHILTON'S FUEL ECONOMY & TUNE-UP TIPS

Tune-up • Spark Plug Diagnosis • Emission Controls

Fuel System • Cooling System • Tires and Wheels

General Maintenance

CHILTON'S FUEL ECONOMY & TUNE-UP TIPS

Fuel economy is important to everyone, no matter what kind of vehicle you drive. The maintenance-minded motorist can save both money and fuel using these tips and the periodic maintenance and tune-up procedures in this Repair and Tune-Up Guide.

There are more than 130,000,000 cars and trucks registered for private use in the United States. Each travels an average of 10-12,000 miles per year, and, and in total they consume close to 70 billion gallons of fuel each year. This represents nearly ⅔ of the oil imported by the United States each year. The Federal government's goal is to reduce consumption 10% by 1985. A variety of methods are either already in use or under serious consideration, and they all affect you driving and the cars you will drive. In addition to "down-sizing", the auto industry is using or investigating the use of electronic fuel delivery, electronic engine controls and alternative engines for use in smaller and lighter vehicles, among other alternatives to meet the federally mandated Corporate Average Fuel Economy (CAFE) of 27.5 mpg by 1985. The government, for its part, is considering rationing, mandatory driving curtailments and tax increases on motor vehicle fuel in an effort to reduce consumption. The government's goal of a 10% reduction could be realized — and further government regulation avoided — if every private vehicle could use just 1 less gallon of fuel per week.

How Much Can You Save?

Tests have proven that almost anyone can make at least a 10% reduction in fuel consumption through regular maintenance and tune-ups. When a major manufacturer of spark plugs sur-

TUNE-UP

1. Check the cylinder compression to be sure the engine will really benefit from a tune-up and that it is capable of producing good fuel economy. A tune-up will be wasted on an engine in poor mechanical condition.
2. Replace spark plugs regularly. New spark plugs alone can increase fuel economy 3%.
3. Be sure the spark plugs are the correct type (heat range) for your vehicle. See the Tune-Up Specifications.

Heat range refers to the spark plug's ability to conduct heat away from the firing end. It must conduct the heat away in an even pattern to avoid becoming a source of pre-ignition, yet it must also operate hot enough to burn off conductive deposits that could cause misfiring.

The heat range is usually indicated by a number on the spark plug, part of the manufacturer's designation for each individual spark plug. The numbers in bold-face indicate the heat range in each manufacturer's identification system.

Manufacturer	Typical Designation
AC	R **45** TS
Bosch (old)	WA **145** T30
Bosch (new)	HR **8** Y
Champion	RBL **15** Y
Fram/Autolite	41**5**
Mopar	P-**62** PR
Motorcraft	BRF-**42**
NGK	BP **5** ES-15
Nippondenso	W **16** EP
Prestolite	14GR **5** 2A

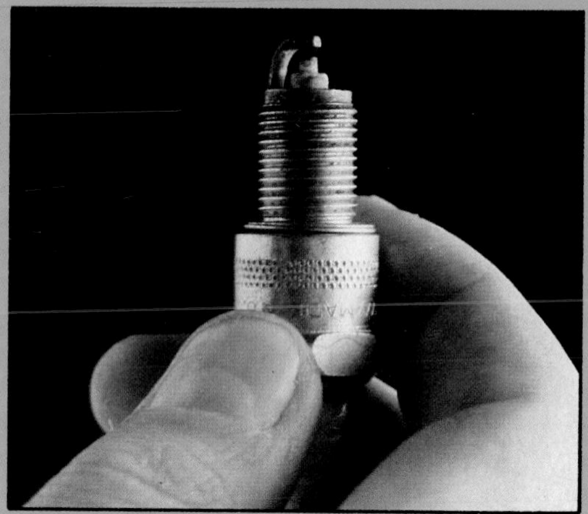

Periodically, check the spark plugs to be sure they are firing efficiently. They are excellent indicators of the internal condition of your engine.

On AC, Bosch (new), Champion, Fram/Autolite, Mopar, Motorcraft and Prestolite, a higher number indicates a hotter plug. On Bosch (old), NGK and Nippondenso, a higher number indicates a colder plug.

4. Make sure the spark plugs are properly gapped. See the Tune-Up Specifications in this book.
5. Be sure the spark plugs are firing efficiently. The illustrations on the next 2 pages show you how to "read" the firing end of the spark plug.
6. Check the ignition timing and set it to specifications. Tests show that almost all cars have incorrect ignition timing by more than 2°.

veyed over 6,000 cars nationwide, they found that a tune-up, on cars that needed one, increased fuel economy over 11%. Replacing worn plugs alone, accounted for a 3% increase. The same test also revealed that 8 out of every 10 vehicles will have some maintenance deficiency that will directly affect fuel economy, emissions or performance. Most of this mileage-robbing neglect could be prevented with regular maintenance.

Modern engines require that all of the functioning systems operate properly for maximum efficiency. A malfunction anywhere wastes fuel. You can keep your vehicle running as efficiently and economically as possible, by being aware of your vehicle's operating and performance characteristics. If your vehicle suddenly develops performance or fuel economy problems it could be due to one or more of the following:

PROBLEM	POSSIBLE CAUSE
Engine Idles Rough	Ignition timing, idle mixture, vacuum leak or something amiss in the emission control system.
Hesitates on Acceleration	Dirty carburetor or fuel filter, improper accelerator pump setting, ignition timing or fouled spark plugs.
Starts Hard or Fails to Start	Worn spark plugs, improperly set automatic choke, ice (or water) in fuel system.
Stalls Frequently	Automatic choke improperly adjusted and possible dirty air filter or fuel filter.
Performs Sluggishly	Worn spark plugs, dirty fuel or air filter, ignition timing or automatic choke out of adjustment.

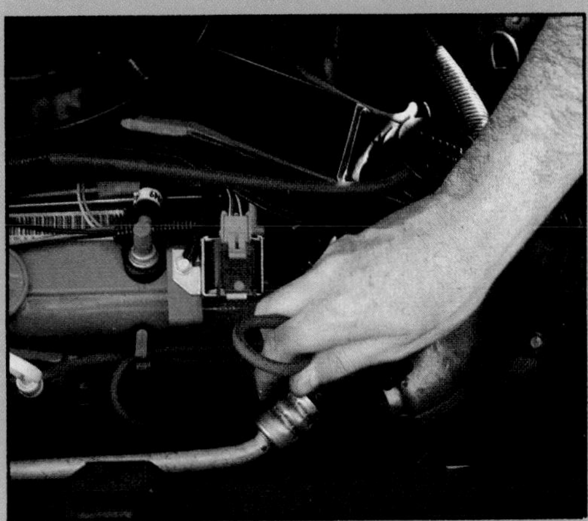

Check spark plug wires on conventional point type ignition for cracks by bending them in a loop around your finger.

Be sure that spark plug wires leading to adjacent cylinders do not run too close together. (Photo courtesy Champion Spark Plug Co.)

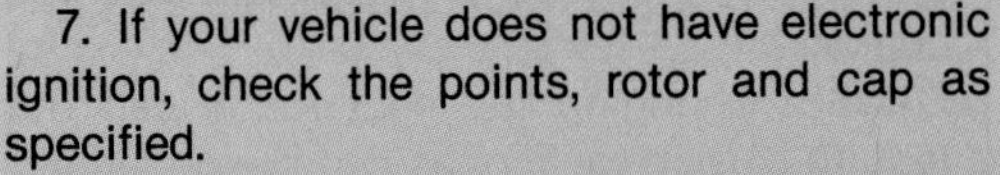

7. If your vehicle does not have electronic ignition, check the points, rotor and cap as specified.

8. Check the spark plug wires (used with conventional point-type ignitions) for cracks and burned or broken insulation by bending them in a loop around your finger. Cracked wires decrease fuel efficiency by failing to deliver full voltage to the spark plugs. One misfiring spark plug can cost you as much as 2 mpg.

9. Check the routing of the plug wires. Misfiring can be the result of spark plug leads to adjacent cylinders running parallel to each other and too close together. One wire tends to pick up voltage from the other causing it to fire "out of time".

10. Check all electrical and ignition circuits for voltage drop and resistance.

11. Check the distributor mechanical and/or vacuum advance mechanisms for proper functioning. The vacuum advance can be checked by twisting the distributor plate in the opposite direction of rotation. It should spring back when released.

12. Check and adjust the valve clearance on engines with mechanical lifters. The clearance should be slightly loose rather than too tight.

SPARK PLUG DIAGNOSIS

Normal

APPEARANCE: This plug is typical of one operating normally. The insulator nose varies from a light tan to grayish color with slight electrode wear. The presence of slight deposits is normal on used plugs and will have no adverse effect on engine performance. The spark plug heat range is correct for the engine and the engine is running normally.
CAUSE: Properly running engine.
RECOMMENDATION: Before reinstalling this plug, the electrodes should be cleaned and filed square. Set the gap to specifications. If the plug has been in service for more than 10-12,000 miles, the entire set should probably be replaced with a fresh set of the same heat range.

Oil Deposits

APPEARANCE: The firing end of the plug is covered with a wet, oily coating.
CAUSE: The problem is poor oil control. On high mileage engines, oil is leaking past the rings or valve guides into the combustion chamber. A common cause is also a plugged PCV valve, and a ruptured fuel pump diaphragm can also cause this condition. Oil fouled plugs such as these are often found in new or recently overhauled engines, before normal oil control is achieved, and can be cleaned and reinstalled.
RECOMMENDATION: A hotter spark plug may temporarily relieve the problem, but the engine is probably in need of work.

Incorrect Heat Range

APPEARANCE: The effects of high temperature on a spark plug are indicated by clean white, often blistered insulator. This can also be accompanied by excessive wear of the electrode, and the absence of deposits.
CAUSE: Check for the correct spark plug heat range. A plug which is too hot for the engine can result in overheating. A car operated mostly at high speeds can require a colder plug. Also check ignition timing, cooling system level, fuel mixture and leaking intake manifold.
RECOMMENDATION: If all ignition and engine adjustments are known to be correct, and no other malfunction exists, install spark plugs one heat range colder.

Carbon Deposits

APPEARANCE: Carbon fouling is easily identified by the presence of dry, soft, black, sooty deposits.
CAUSE: Changing the heat range can often lead to carbon fouling, as can prolonged slow, stop-and-start driving. If the heat range is correct, carbon fouling can be attributed to a rich fuel mixture, sticking choke, clogged air cleaner, worn breaker points, retarded timing or low compression. If only one or two plugs are carbon fouled, check for corroded or cracked wires on the affected plugs. Also look for cracks in the distributor cap between the towers of affected cylinders.
RECOMMENDATION: After the problem is corrected, these plugs can be cleaned and reinstalled if not worn severely.

Photos Courtesy Fram Corporation

MMT Fouled

APPEARANCE: Spark plugs fouled by MMT (Methycyclopentadienyl Maganese Tricarbonyl) have reddish, rusty appearance on the insulator and side electrode.
CAUSE: MMT is an anti-knock additive in gasoline used to replace lead. During the combustion process, the MMT leaves a reddish deposit on the insulator and side electrode.
RECOMMENDATION: No engine malfunction is indicated and the deposits will not affect plug performance any more than lead deposits (see Ash Deposits). MMT fouled plugs can be cleaned, regapped and reinstalled.

High Speed Glazing

APPEARANCE: Glazing appears as shiny coating on the plug, either yellow or tan in color.
CAUSE: During hard, fast acceleration, plug temperatures rise suddenly. Deposits from normal combustion have no chance to fluff-off; instead, they melt on the insulator forming an electrically conductive coating which causes misfiring.
RECOMMENDATION: Glazed plugs are not easily cleaned. They should be replaced with a fresh set of plugs of the correct heat range. If the condition recurs, using plugs with a heat range one step colder may cure the problem.

Ash (Lead) Deposits

APPEARANCE: Ash deposits are characterized by light brown or white colored deposits crusted on the side or center electrodes. In some cases it may give the plug a rusty appearance.
CAUSE: Ash deposits are normally derived from oil or fuel additives burned during normal combustion. Normally they are harmless, though excessive amounts can cause misfiring. If deposits are excessive in short mileage, the valve guides may be worn.
RECOMMENDATION: Ash-fouled plugs can be cleaned, gapped and reinstalled.

Detonation

APPEARANCE: Detonation is usually characterized by a broken plug insulator.
CAUSE: A portion of the fuel charge will begin to burn spontaneously, from the increased heat following ignition. The explosion that results applies extreme pressure to engine components, frequently damaging spark plugs and pistons.

Detonation can result by over-advanced ignition timing, inferior gasoline (low octane) lean air/fuel mixture, poor carburetion, engine lugging or an increase in compression ratio due to combustion chamber deposits or engine modification.
RECOMMENDATION: Replace the plugs after correcting the problem.

Photos Courtesy Champion Spark Plug Co.

EMISSION CONTROLS

13. Be aware of the general condition of the emission control system. It contributes to reduced pollution and should be serviced regularly to maintain efficient engine operation.

14. Check all vacuum lines for dried, cracked or brittle conditions. Something as simple as a leaking vacuum hose can cause poor performance and loss of economy.

15. Avoid tampering with the emission control system. Attempting to improve fuel econ-

FUEL SYSTEM

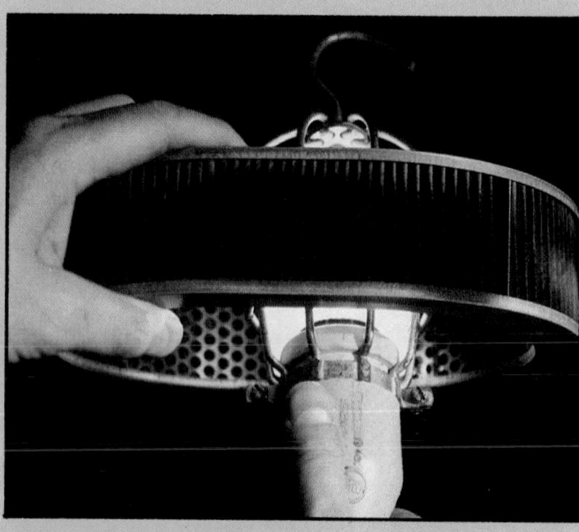

Check the air filter with a light behind it. If you can see light through the filter it can be reused.

Extremely clogged filters should be discarded and replaced with a new one.

18. Replace the air filter regularly. A dirty air filter richens the air/fuel mixture and can increase fuel consumption as much as 10%. Tests show that 1/3 of all vehicles have air filters in need of replacement.

19. Replace the fuel filter at least as often as recommended.

20. Set the idle speed and carburetor mixture to specifications.

21. Check the automatic choke. A sticking or malfunctioning choke wastes gas.

22. During the summer months, adjust the automatic choke for a leaner mixture which will produce faster engine warm-ups.

COOLING SYSTEM

29. Be sure all accessory drive belts are in good condition. Check for cracks or wear.

30. Adjust all accessory drive belts to proper tension.

31. Check all hoses for swollen areas, worn spots, or loose clamps.

32. Check coolant level in the radiator or expansion tank.

33. Be sure the thermostat is operating properly. A stuck thermostat delays engine warm-up and a cold engine uses nearly twice as much fuel as a warm engine.

34. Drain and replace the engine coolant at least as often as recommended. Rust and scale

TIRES & WHEELS

38. Check the tire pressure often with a pencil type gauge. Tests by a major tire manufacturer show that 90% of all vehicles have at least 1 tire improperly inflated. Better mileage can be achieved by over-inflating tires, but never exceed the maximum inflation pressure on the side of the tire.

39. If possible, install radial tires. Radial tires deliver as much as 1/2 mpg more than bias belted tires.

40. Avoid installing super-wide tires. They only create extra rolling resistance and decrease fuel mileage. Stick to the manufacturer's recommendations.

41. Have the wheels properly balanced.

omy by tampering with emission controls is more likely to worsen fuel economy than improve it. Emission control changes on modern engines are not readily reversible.

16. Clean (or replace) the EGR valve and lines as recommended.

17. Be sure that all vacuum lines and hoses are reconnected properly after working under the hood. An unconnected or misrouted vacuum line can wreak havoc with engine performance.

---

23. Check for fuel leaks at the carburetor, fuel pump, fuel lines and fuel tank. Be sure all lines and connections are tight.

24. Periodically check the tightness of the carburetor and intake manifold attaching nuts and bolts. These are a common place for vacuum leaks to occur.

25. Clean the carburetor periodically and lubricate the linkage.

26. The condition of the tailpipe can be an excellent indicator of proper engine combustion. After a long drive at highway speeds, the inside of the tailpipe should be a light grey in color. Black or soot on the insides indicates an overly rich mixture.

27. Check the fuel pump pressure. The fuel pump may be supplying more fuel than the engine needs.

28. Use the proper grade of gasoline for your engine. Don't try to compensate for knocking or "pinging" by advancing the ignition timing. This practice will only increase plug temperature and the chances of detonation or pre-ignition with relatively little performance gain.

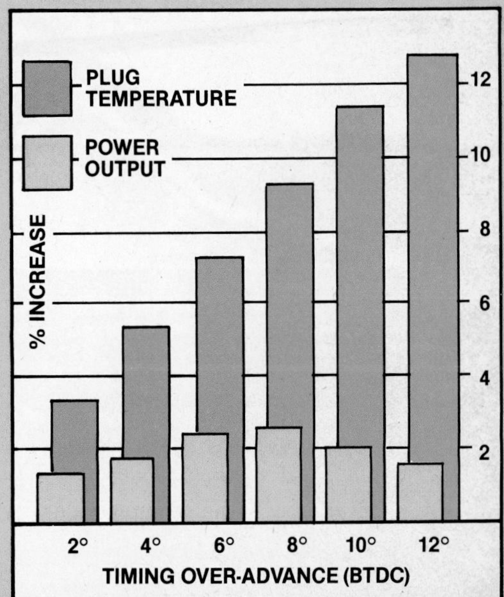

Increasing ignition timing past the specified setting results in a drastic increase in spark plug temperature with increased chance of detonation or preignition. Performance increase is considerably less. (Photo courtesy Champion Spark Plug Co.)

---

that form in the engine should be flushed out to allow the engine to operate at peak efficiency.

35. Clean the radiator of debris that can decrease cooling efficiency.

36. Install a flex-type or electric cooling fan, if you don't have a clutch type fan. Flex fans use curved plastic blades to push more air at low speeds when more cooling is needed; at high speeds the blades flatten out for less resistance. Electric fans only run when the engine temperature reaches a predetermined level.

37. Check the radiator cap for a worn or cracked gasket. If the cap does not seal properly, the cooling system will not function properly.

---

42. Be sure the front end is correctly aligned. A misaligned front end actually has wheels going in differed directions. The increased drag can reduce fuel economy by .3 mpg.

43. Correctly adjust the wheel bearings. Wheel bearings that are adjusted too tight increase rolling resistance.

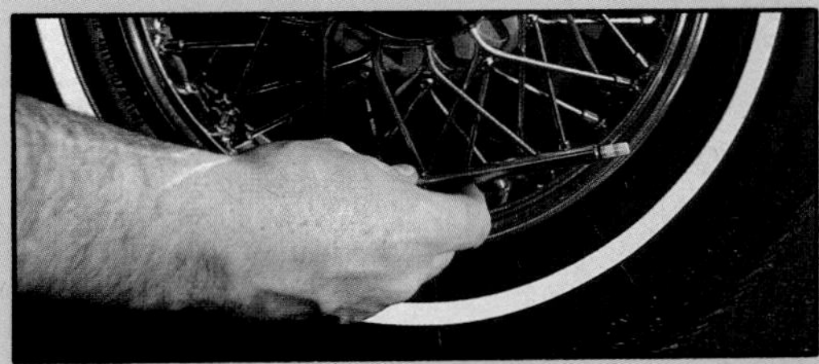
Check tire pressures regularly with a reliable pocket type gauge. Be sure to check the pressure on a cold tire.

GENERAL MAINTENANCE

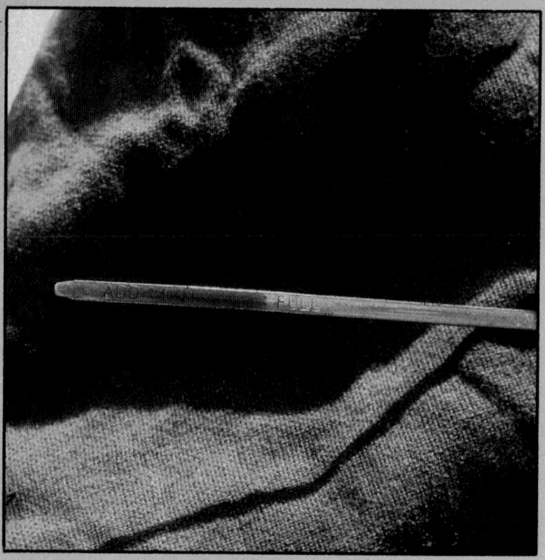

Check the fluid levels (particularly engine oil) on a regular basis. Be sure to check the oil for grit, water or other contamination.

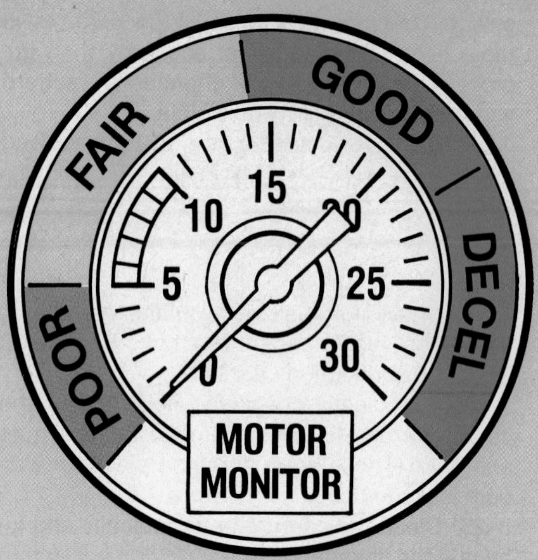

A vacuum gauge is another excellent indicator of internal engine condition and can also be installed in the dash as a mileage indicator.

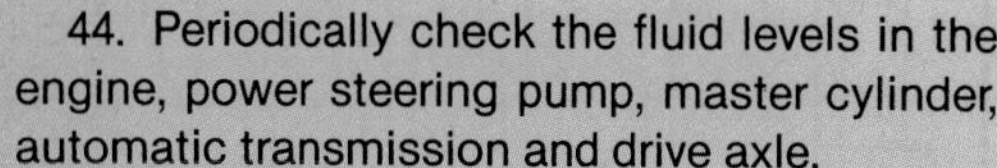

44. Periodically check the fluid levels in the engine, power steering pump, master cylinder, automatic transmission and drive axle.

45. Change the oil at the recommended interval and change the filter at every oil change. Dirty oil is thick and causes extra friction between moving parts, cutting efficiency and increasing wear. A worn engine requires more frequent tune-ups and gets progressively worse fuel economy. In general, use the lightest viscosity oil for the driving conditions you will encounter.

46. Use the recommended viscosity fluids in the transmission and axle.

47. Be sure the battery is fully charged for fast starts. A slow starting engine wastes fuel.

48. Be sure battery terminals are clean and tight.

49. Check the battery electrolyte level and add distilled water if necessary.

50. Check the exhaust system for crushed pipes, blockages and leaks.

51. Adjust the brakes. Dragging brakes or brakes that are not releasing create increased drag on the engine.

52. Install a vacuum gauge or miles-per-gallon gauge. These gauges visually indicate engine vacuum in the intake manifold. High vacuum = good mileage and low vacuum = poorer mileage. The gauge can also be an excellent indicator of internal engine conditions.

53. Be sure the clutch is properly adjusted. A slipping clutch wastes fuel.

54. Check and periodically lubricate the heat control valve in the exhaust manifold. A sticking or inoperative valve prevents engine warm-up and wastes gas.

55. Keep accurate records to check fuel economy over a period of time. A sudden drop in fuel economy may signal a need for tune-up or other maintenance.

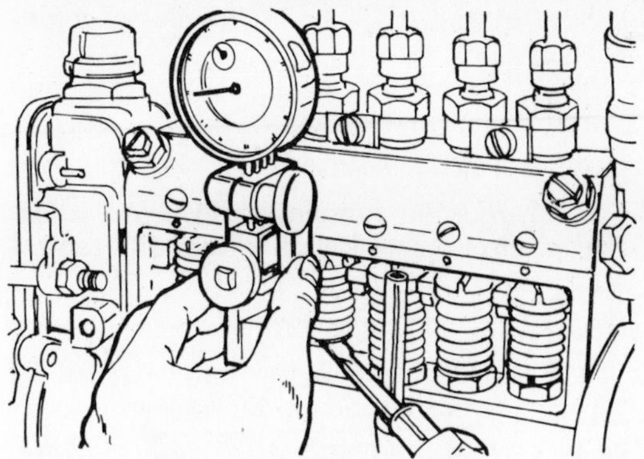

Checking tappet clearance

15. Check and adjust each cylinder in turn.

16. When timing for each cylinder is correct, position the cam at TDC, check the plunger piston pin-to-plunger barrel clearance and make sure that the tappet vertical clearance is at least 0.0118 in. (0.3mm) for each tappet.

Standard Fuel Injection Volume Adjustment

1. Determine the zero position of the control by attaching the measuring device to the pump and pushing the index all the way to governor side. Match the scale on the left end of the index and set the 0 (zero) position of the scale at the position at which the measuring device index stops. On RSV mechanical governors, loosen the stop bolt to align this index.

2. Remove the rack guide screw from the rear of the pump housing and supply the lock screw attached to the tester. Secure the control rack in the standard position for adjustment.

NOTE: *The lock screw should be tightened by hand; overtightening will bend the rack.*

3. Start the tester and run the pump at rated speed.

4. Set the pump feed pressure at 21.3–22.75 psi and measure the injection volume at the rated stroke of the female cylinder.

5. In the same manner, measure the injection volume at rated speed and standard rack position. Compute the rate of unevenness of the injection.

6. If the results show that the mean injection volume and rate of unevenness are not within the limits, adjust by changing the relative position of the control pinion and control sleeve. This may be done by:

a. Loosen the pinion set screw.

b. Place a pin in the hole in the control sleeve and adjust by moving the control sleeve along the control rack a little at a time.

c. When adjustment is completed, secure the pinion set screw.

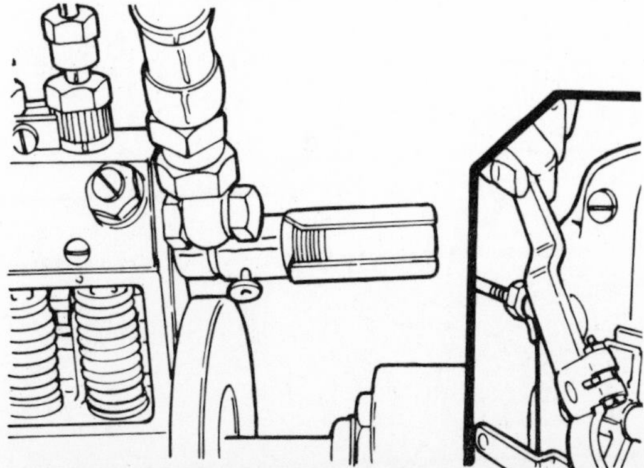

Attaching a measuring device to the pump

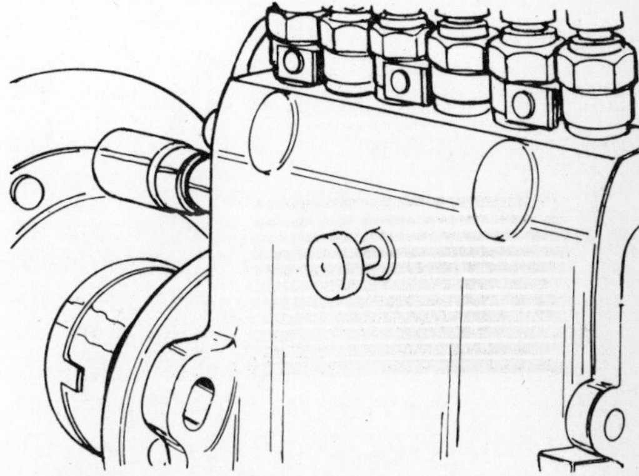

Installing the tester lock screw

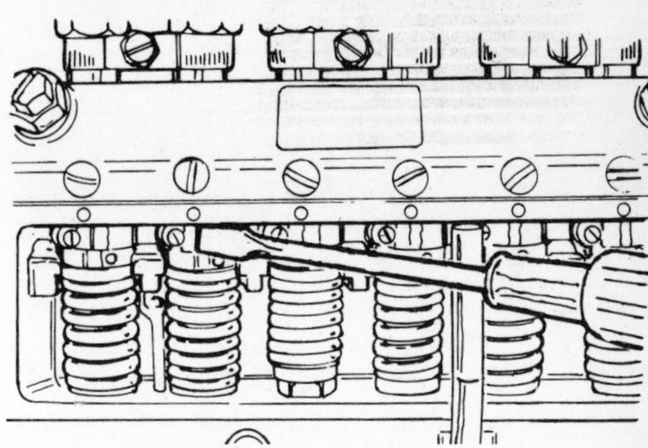

Loosening the pinion set screw

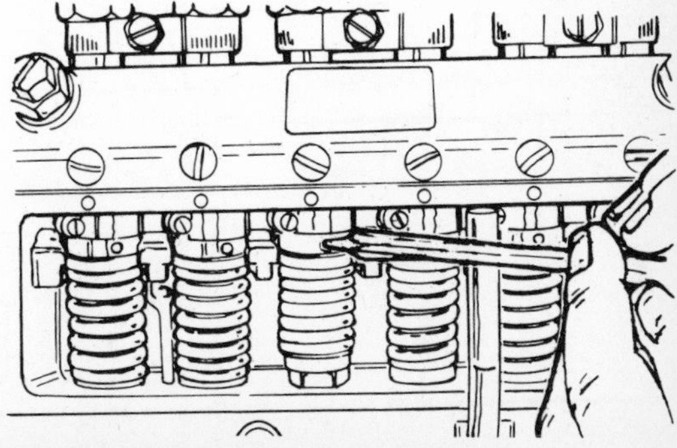

Installing the appropriate sized pin

d. Remove the lock screw from the control rack and reinstall the guide screw.

TESTING AND ADJUSTING THE GOVERNOR

RSV and RAD Mechanical Governor

1. Match the adjusting device index to the zero point on the scale and set the control rack to the zero position.
2. Operate the control lever and make certain the full stroke of the rack is 0.827 in. (21mm).
3. Make certain that the rack moves freely in the direction for maximum fuel injection by the spring force of the starting spring.
4. Set the stop bolt to remove any significant load on the governor linkage.
5. Set the stop bolt to give a control rack setting of 0.0197–0.03937 in. (0.5–1.0mm).

HIGH SPEED ADJUSTMENT

6. Remove the governor rear cover.
7. Loosen the full load stop lock nut and adjust the full load stop so that its setting corresponds to an **A** rack position between **K** rotation and **BC**. See the accompanying chart. Uneveness = max. or min. injection volume for each plunger minus the main injection volume, divided by the mean injection volume, multiplied by 100.
8. To increase the volume, turn the stop to the right; left to decrease.

MAXIMUM SPEED ADJUSTMENT

9. Operate the pump at speed **G** and adjust the maximum speed stop so that the control rack position is **G** mm.

SPEED FLUCTUATION ADJUSTMENT

10. Speed fluctuation can be controlled by varying the spring rate on RSV governors.

BALANCE SPRING ADJUSTMENT

11. Set the control lever to the point where it contacts the maximum speed stop and operate the pump at a rate of **F**, between **A** and **B**.
12. Install the balance spring assembly under the tension lever.
13. Tighten the balance spring assembly with tool #57916-212 until the control rack position **G** is **H** mm, and secure the lock nut.
14. Gradually accelerate the engine from

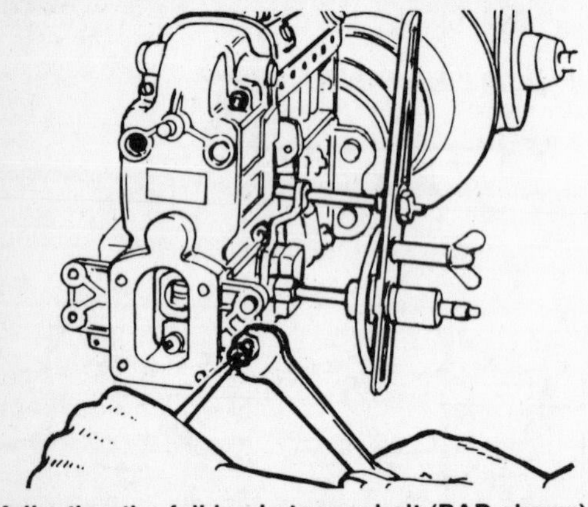

Adjusting the full load stopper bolt (RAD shown)

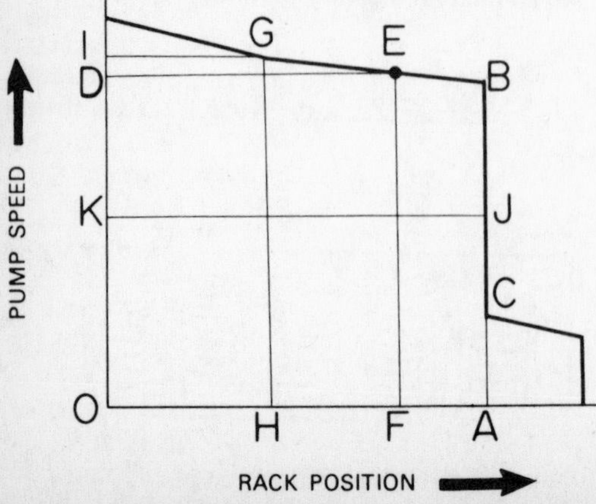

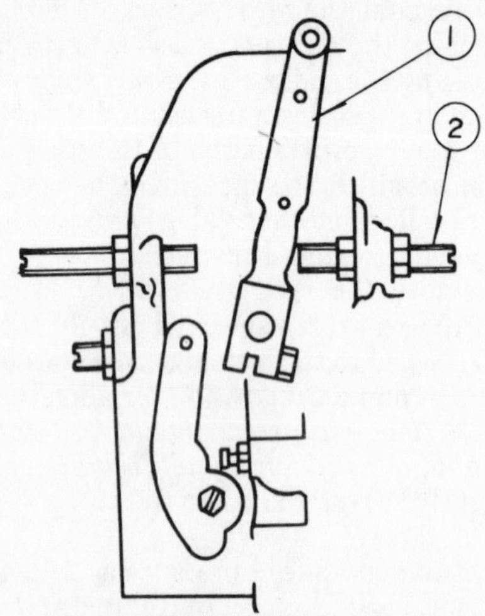

1. Speed control lever
2. Speed adjusting bolt (stopper bolt)

Adjusting the speed adjustment bolt (RSV shown)

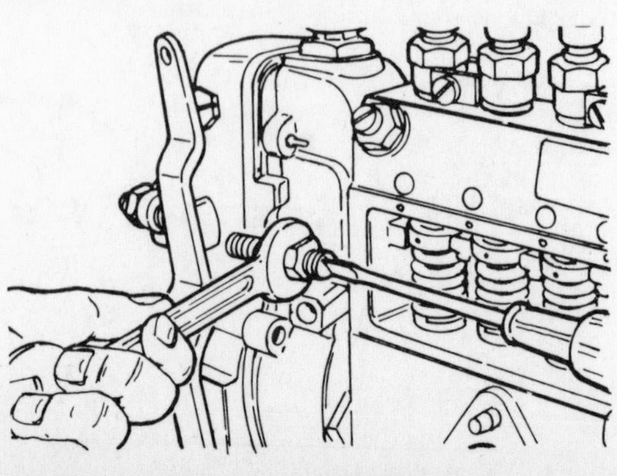

Maximum speed stopper adjustment

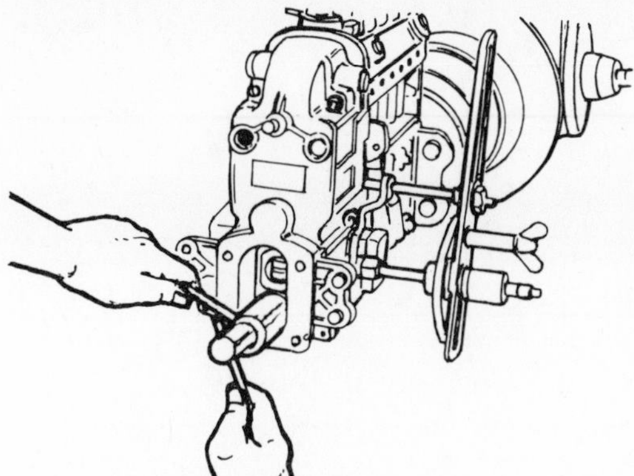

Adjusting the idling spring

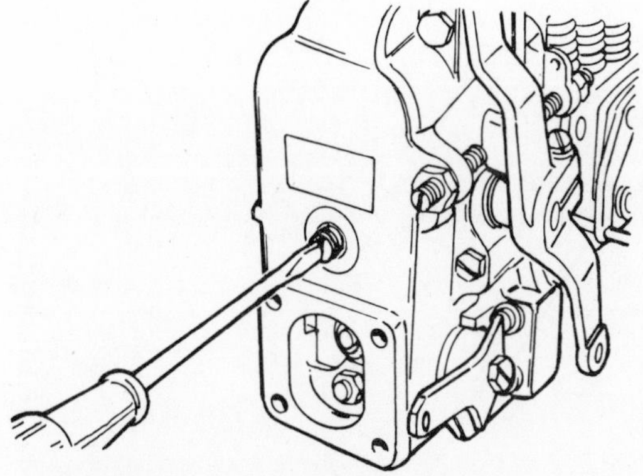

Auxiliary idle spring adjustment

speed **D** and make certain that the control rack is at **G** mm when the action of the spring ends at speed **E**.

IDLE SPEED ADJUSTMENT

15. Set the control lever at the stop position so that the control rack is at point **B**.

16. Set the speed to **D** and tighten the idle auxiliary spring so that the position of the rack is **C** mm. Secure with the lock nut.

NOTE: *Do not tighten the auxiliary idle spring too much or overspeeding will result.*

Testing and Adjusting the Timer

1. Install a timing light, such as tool #5783-001 on the tester using the cover plate attaching bolts, so that the synchronizer lever attachment is applied to the tappet.
2. Start the pump and turn on the timing light.
3. Direct the light at the angle scale on the flywheel and measure the angular change based on variations in pump speed.
4. If the tester does not have an angle scale:

   a. Attach an angle scale to the timer coupling and mount a pointer on the tester driveshaft.

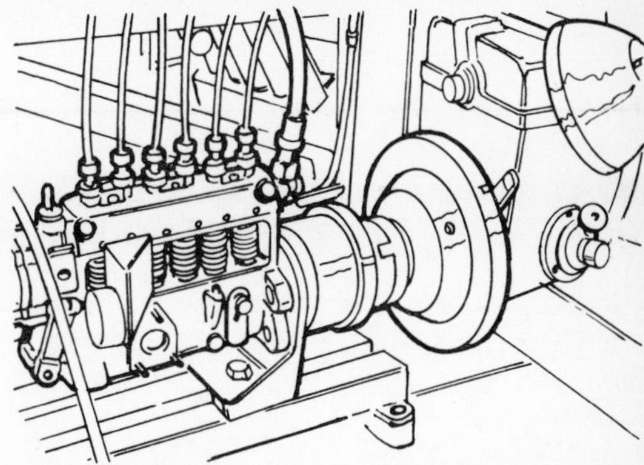

Pump installed on the tester, with synchronizer and strobe light

   b. Operate the pump and direct the light on the scale.

5. If the angular change is not within limits, disassembly the timer and adjust the spring force by increasing or decreasing the shim, or if necessary, replace the spring.

FUEL TANK

The fuel tank is located under the floor of the bed on the right side, directly behind the cab.

REMOVAL AND INSTALLATION

1. Disconnect the negative cable from the battery.
2. Remove the drain plug at the bottom of the tank and drain the fuel into a suitable container.
3. Disconnect the filler tube from the filler hose.
4. Disconnect the ventilation hoses, the fuel return hose and fuel outlet hose from the tank. Disconnect the gauge unit wires at the electrical connector.
5. Remove the mounting bolts and remove the fuel tank.
6. When installing, tighten the clamps securely, but do not crimp any of the lines. Install the clips holding the fuel tube to the underbody securely. Do not attach the filler hose to the tube until the tank is in place. Failure to do this will cause leaks around the connection.

Gauge Unit

The fuel tank must be removed for access to the gauge unit. The unit is installed into the tank with a bayonet type of mount. Turn it counterclockwise with a screwdriver to remove. Use a new O-ring when installing, aligning the tab in the unit with the notch in the tank.

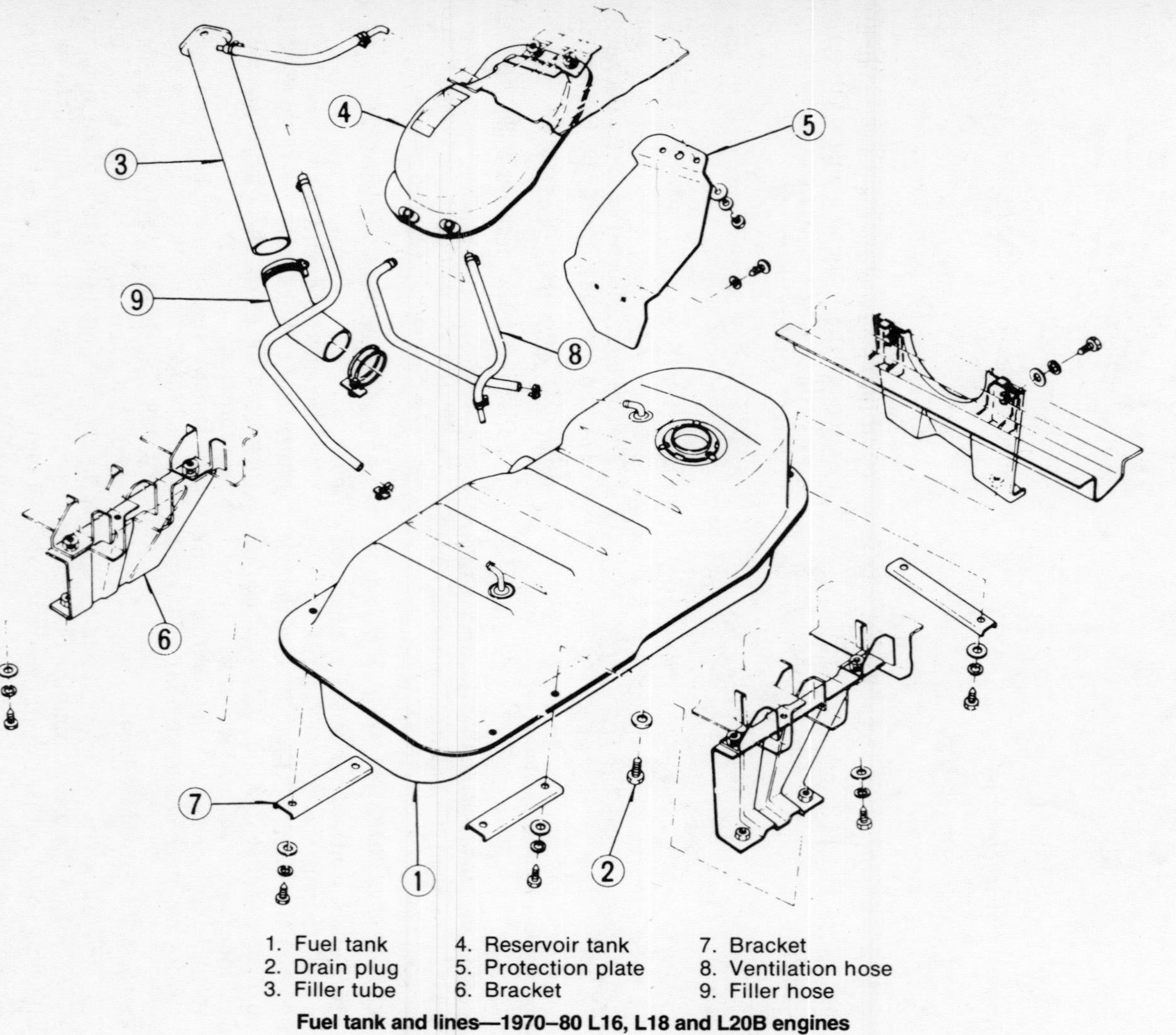

1. Fuel tank
2. Drain plug
3. Filler tube
4. Reservoir tank
5. Protection plate
6. Bracket
7. Bracket
8. Ventilation hose
9. Filler hose

Fuel tank and lines—1970–80 L16, L18 and L20B engines

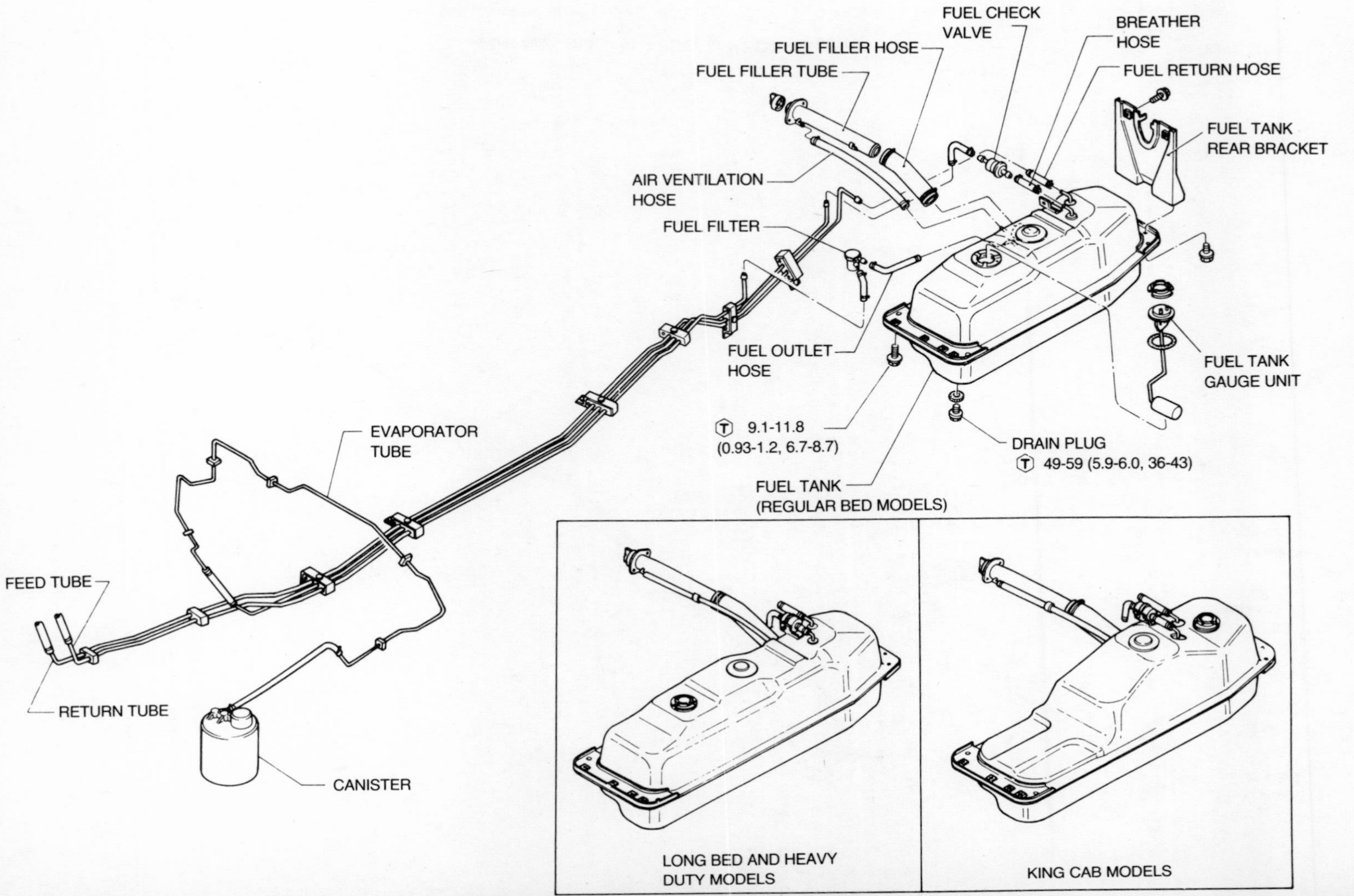

Fuel tank and lines—1981–86 Z20, Z22 and Z24 engines

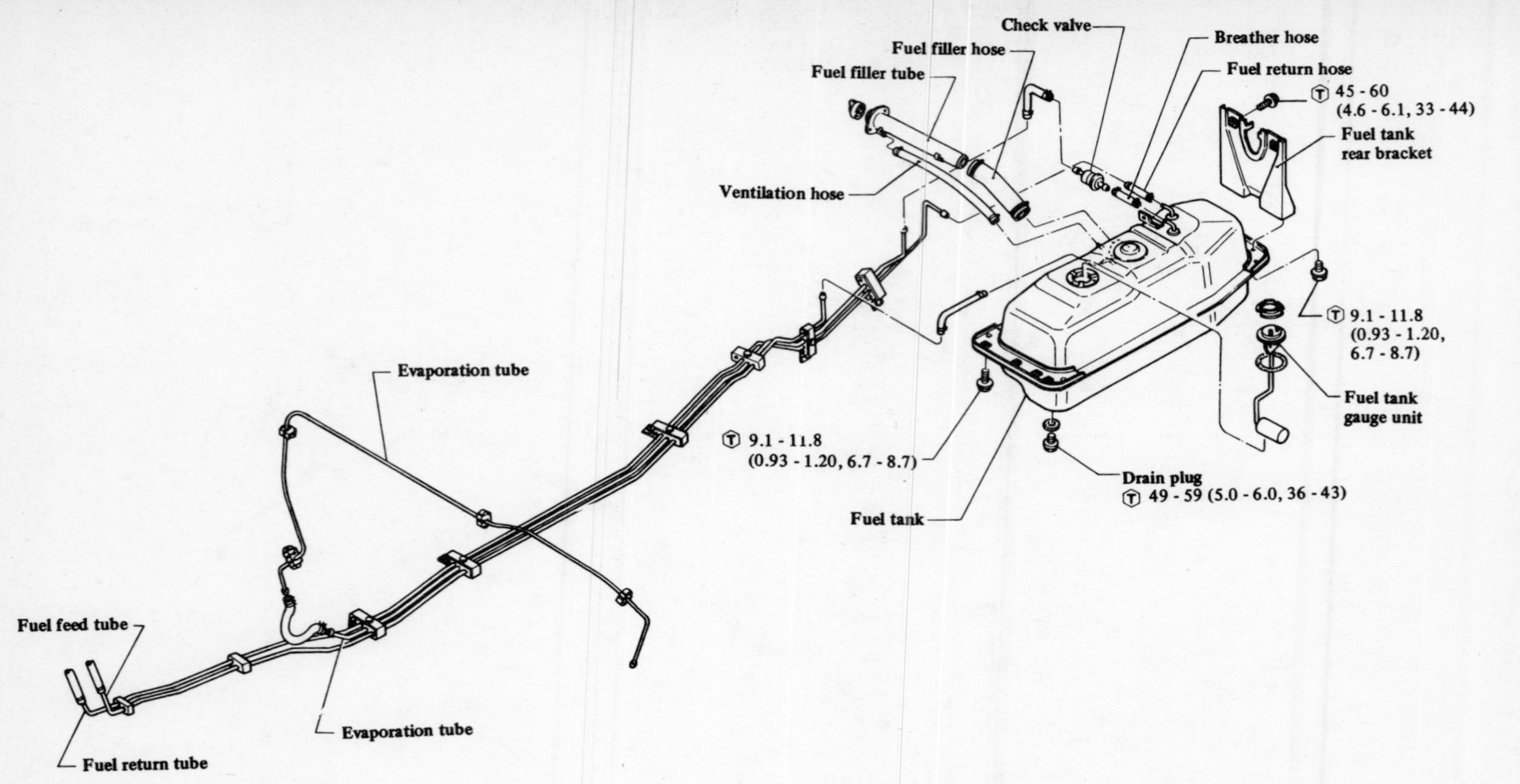

Fuel tank and lines—SD22 and SD25 engines

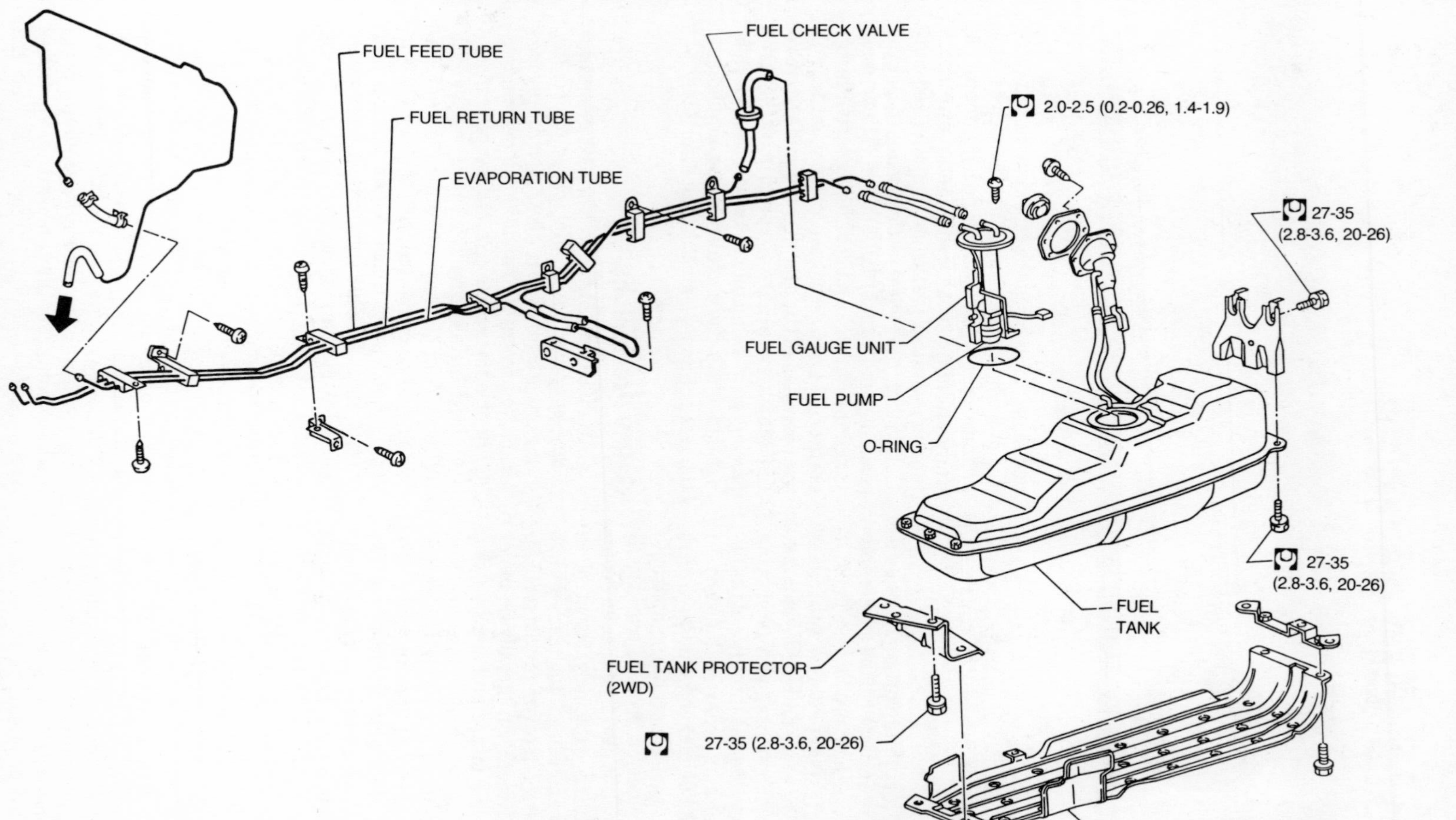

Fuel tank and lines—1986–89 Z24i and VG30i engine

Chassis Electrical

UNDERSTANDING AND TROUBLESHOOTING ELECTRICAL SYSTEMS

At the rate which both import and domestic manufacturers are incorporating electronic control systems into their production lines, it won't be long before every new vehicle is equipped with one or more on-board computer. These electronic components (with no moving parts) should theoretically last the life of the vehicle, provided nothing external happens to damage the circuits or memory chips.

While it is true that electronic components should never wear out, in the real world malfunctions do occur. It is also true that any computer-based system is extremely sensitive to electrical voltages and cannot tolerate careless or haphazard testing or service procedures. An inexperienced individual can literally do major damage looking for a minor problem by using the wrong kind of test equipment or connecting test leads or connectors with the ignition switch **ON**. When selecting test equipment, make sure the manufacturers instructions state that the tester is compatible with whatever type of electronic control system is being serviced. Read all instructions carefully and double check all test points before installing probes or making any test connections.

The following section outlines basic diagnosis techniques for dealing with computerized automotive control systems. Along with a general explanation of the various types of test equipment available to aid in servicing modern electronic automotive systems, basic repair techniques for wiring harnesses and connectors is given. Read the basic information before attempting any repairs or testing on any computerized system, to provide the background of information necessary to avoid the most common and obvious mistakes that can cost both time and money. Although the replacement and testing procedures are simple in themselves, the systems are not, and unless one has a thorough understanding of all components and their function within a particular computerized control system, the logical test sequence these systems demand cannot be followed. Minor malfunctions can make a big difference, so it is important to know how each component affects the operation of the overall electronic system to find the ultimate cause of a problem without replacing good components unnecessarily. It is not enough to use the correct test equipment; the test equipment must be used correctly.

Safety Precautions

CAUTION: *Whenever working on or around any computer based microprocessor control system, always observe these general precautions to prevent the possibility of personal injury or damage to electronic components.*

- Never install or remove battery cables with the key **ON** or the engine running. Jumper cables should be connected with the key **OFF** to avoid power surges that can damage electronic control units. Engines equipped with computer controlled systems should avoid both giving and getting jump starts due to the possibility of serious damage to components from arcing in the engine compartment when connections are made with the ignition **ON**.
- Always remove the battery cables before charging the battery. Never use a high output charger on an installed battery or attempt to use any type of "hot shot" (24 volt) starting aid.
- Exercise care when inserting test probes into connectors to insure good connections without damaging the connector or spreading the pins. Always probe connectors from the rear (wire) side, NOT the pin side, to avoid accidental shorting of terminals during test procedures.

• Never remove or attach wiring harness connectors with the ignition switch **ON**, especially to an electronic control unit.

• Do not drop any components during service procedures and never apply 12 volts directly to any component (like a solenoid or relay) unless instructed specifically to do so. Some component electrical windings are designed to safely handle only 4 or 5 volts and can be destroyed in seconds if 12 volts are applied directly to the connector.

• Remove the electronic control unit if the vehicle is to be placed in an environment where temperatures exceed approximately 176°F (80°C), such as a paint spray booth or when arc or gas welding near the control unit location in the truck.

ORGANIZED TROUBLESHOOTING

When diagnosing a specific problem, organized troubleshooting is a must. The complexity of a modern automobile demands that you approach any problem in a logical, organized manner. There are certain troubleshooting techniques that are standard:

1. Establish when the problem occurs. Does the problem appear only under certain conditions? Were there any noises, odors, or other unusual symptoms?

2. Isolate the problem area. To do this, make some simple tests and observations; then eliminate the systems that are working properly. Check for obvious problems such as broken wires, dirty connections or split or disconnected vacuum hoses. Always check the obvious before assuming something complicated is the cause.

3. Test for problems systematically to determine the cause once the problem area is isolated. Are all the components functioning properly? Is there power going to electrical switches and motors? Is there vacuum at vacuum switches and/or actuators? Is there a mechanical problem such as bent linkage or loose mounting screws? Doing careful, systematic checks will often turn up most causes on the first inspection without wasting time checking components that have little or no relationship to the problem.

4. Test all repairs after the work is done to make sure that the problem is fixed. Some causes can be traced to more than one component, so a careful verification of repair work is important to pick up additional malfunctions that may cause a problem to reappear or a different problem to arise. A blown fuse, for example, is a simple problem that may require more than another fuse to repair. If you don't look for a problem that caused a fuse to blow, for example, a shorted wire may go undetected.

Experience has shown that most problems tend to be the result of a fairly simple and obvious cause, such as loose or corroded connectors or air leaks in the intake system; making careful inspection of components during testing essential to quick and accurate troubleshooting. Special, hand held computerized testers designed specifically for diagnosing the EEC-IV system are available from a variety of aftermarket sources, as well as from the vehicle manufacturer, but care should be taken that any test equipment being used is designed to diagnose that particular computer controlled system accurately without damaging the control unit (ECU) or components being tested.

NOTE: *Pinpointing the exact cause of trouble in an electrical system can sometimes only be accomplished by the use of special test equipment. The following describes commonly used test equipment and explains how to put it to best use in diagnosis. In addition to the information covered below, the manufacturer's instructions booklet provided with the tester should be read and clearly understood before attempting any test procedures.*

TEST EQUIPMENT

Jumper Wires

Jumper wires are simple, yet extremely valuable, pieces of test equipment. Jumper wires are merely wires that are used to bypass sections of a circuit. The simplest type of jumper wire is merely a length of multistrand wire with an alligator clip at each end. Jumper wires are usually fabricated from lengths of standard automotive wire and whatever type of connector (alligator clip, spade connector or pin connector) that is required for the particular vehicle being tested. The well equipped tool box will have several different styles of jumper wires in several different lengths. Some jumper wires are made with three or more terminals coming from a common splice for special purpose testing. In cramped, hard-to-reach areas it is advisable to have insulated boots over the jumper wire terminals in order to prevent accidental grounding, sparks, and possible fire, especially when testing fuel system components.

Jumper wires are used primarily to locate open electrical circuits, on either the ground (–) side of the circuit or on the hot (+) side. If an electrical component fails to operate, connect the jumper wire between the component and a good ground. If the component operates only with the jumper installed, the ground circuit is open. If the ground circuit is good, but the component does not operate, the circuit between the power feed and component is open. You can sometimes connect the jumper wire directly from the battery to the hot terminal of the component, but first make sure the component uses

12 volts in operation. Some electrical components, such as fuel injectors, are designed to operate on about 4 volts and running 12 volts directly to the injector terminals can burn out the wiring. By inserting an inline fuseholder between a set of test leads, a fused jumper wire can be used for bypassing open circuits. Use a 5 amp fuse to provide protection against voltage spikes. When in doubt, use a voltmeter to check the voltage input to the component and measure how much voltage is being applied normally. By moving the jumper wire successively back from the lamp toward the power source, you can isolate the area of the circuit where the open is located. When the component stops functioning, or the power is cut off, the open is in the segment of wire between the jumper and the point previously tested.

CAUTION: *Never use jumpers made from wire that is of lighter gauge than used in the circuit under test. If the jumper wire is of too small gauge, it may overheat and possibly melt. Never use jumpers to bypass high resistance loads (such as motors) in a circuit. Bypassing resistances, in effect, creates a short circuit which may, in turn, cause damage and fire. Never use a jumper for anything other than temporary bypassing of components in a circuit.*

12 Volt Test Light

The 12 volt test light is used to check circuits and components while electrical current is flowing through them. It is used for voltage and ground tests. Twelve volt test lights come in different styles but all have three main parts; a ground clip, a probe, and a light. The most commonly used 12 volt test lights have pick-type probes. To use a 12 volt test light, connect the ground clip to a good ground and probe wherever necessary with the pick. The pick should be sharp so that it can penetrate wire insulation to make contact with the wire, without making a large hole in the insulation. The wrap-around light is handy in hard to reach areas or where it is difficult to support a wire to push a probe pick into it. To use the wrap around light, hook the wire to probed with the hook and pull the trigger. A small pick will be forced through the wire insulation into the wire core.

CAUTION: *Do not use a test light to probe electronic ignition spark plug or coil wires. Never use a pick-type test light to probe wiring on computer controlled systems unless specifically instructed to do so. Any wire insulation that is pierced by the test light probe should be taped and sealed with silicone after testing.*

Like the jumper wire, the 12 volt test light is used to isolate opens in circuits. But, whereas the jumper wire is used to bypass the open to operate the load, the 12 volt test light is used to locate the presence of voltage in a circuit. If the test light glows, you know that there is power up to that point; if the 12 volt test light does not glow when its probe is inserted into the wire or connector, you know that there is an open circuit (no power). Move the test light in successive steps back toward the power source until the light in the handle does glow. When it does glow, the open is between the probe and point previously probed.

NOTE: *The test light does not detect that 12 volts (or any particular amount of voltage) is present; it only detects that some voltage is present. It is advisable before using the test light to touch its terminals across the battery posts to make sure the light is operating properly.*

Self-Powered Test Light

The self-powered test light usually contains a 1.5 volt penlight battery. One type of self-powered test light is similar in design to the 12 volt test light. This type has both the battery and the light in the handle and pick-type probe tip. The second type has the light toward the open tip, so that the light illuminates the contact point. The self-powered test light is dual purpose piece of test equipment. It can be used to test for either open or short circuits when power is isolated from the circuit (continuity test). A powered test light should not be used on any computer controlled system or component unless specifically instructed to do so. Many engine sensors can be destroyed by even this small amount of voltage applied directly to the terminals.

Open Circuit Testing

To use the self-powered test light to check for open circuits, first isolate the circuit from the vehicle's 12 volt power source by disconnecting the battery or wiring harness connector. Connect the test light ground clip to a good ground and probe sections of the circuit sequentially with the test light. (start from either end of the circuit). If the light is out, the open is between the probe and the circuit ground. If the light is on, the open is between the probe and end of the circuit toward the power source.

Short Circuit Testing

By isolating the circuit both from power and from ground, and using a self-powered test light, you can check for shorts to ground in the circuit. Isolate the circuit from power and ground. Connect the test light ground clip to a good ground and probe any easy-to-reach test point in the circuit. If the light comes on, there is a short somewhere in the circuit. To isolate the short, probe a test point at either end of the isolated circuit (the light should be on). Leave the test light probe connected and open connectors, switches, remove parts, etc., sequentially, until the light goes out. When the light goes out, the short is between the last circuit component opened and the previous circuit opened.

NOTE: *The 1.5 volt battery in the test light does not provide much current. A weak battery may not provide enough power to illuminate the test light even when a complete circuit is made (especially if there are high resistances in the circuit). Always make sure that the test battery is strong. To check the battery, briefly touch the ground clip to the probe; if the light glows brightly the battery is strong enough for testing. Never use a self-powered test light to perform checks for opens or shorts when power is applied to the electrical system under test. The 12 volt vehicle power will quickly burn out the 1.5 volt light bulb in the test light.*

Voltmeter

A voltmeter is used to measure voltage at any point in a circuit, or to measure the voltage drop across any part of a circuit. It can also be used to check continuity in a wire or circuit by indicating current flow from one end to the other. Voltmeters usually have various scales on the meter dial and a selector switch to allow the selection of different voltages. The voltmeter has a positive and a negative lead. To avoid damage to the meter, always connect the negative lead to the negative (–) side of circuit (to ground or nearest the ground side of the circuit) and connect the positive lead to the positive (+) side of the circuit (to the power source or the nearest power source). Note that the negative voltmeter lead will always be black and that the positive voltmeter will always be some color other than black (usually red). Depending on how the voltmeter is connected into the circuit, it has several uses.

A voltmeter can be connected either in parallel or in series with a circuit and it has a very high resistance to current flow. When connected in parallel, only a small amount of current will flow through the voltmeter current path; the rest will flow through the normal circuit current path and the circuit will work normally. When the voltmeter is connected in series with a circuit, only a small amount of current can flow through the circuit. The circuit will not work properly, but the voltmeter reading will show if the circuit is complete or not.

Available Voltage Measurement

Set the voltmeter selector switch to the 20V position and connect the meter negative lead to the negative post of the battery. Connect the positive meter lead to the positive post of the battery and turn the ignition switch **ON** to provide a load. Read the voltage on the meter or digital display. A well charged battery should register over 12 volts. If the meter reads below 11.5 volts, the battery power may be insufficient to operate the electrical system properly. This test determines voltage available from the battery and should be the first step in any electrical trouble diagnosis procedure. Many electrical problems, especially on computer controlled systems, can be caused by a low state of charge in the battery. Excessive corrosion at the battery cable terminals can cause a poor contact that will prevent proper charging and full battery current flow.

Normal battery voltage is 12 volts when fully charged. When the battery is supplying current to one or more circuits it is said to be "under load". When everything is off the electrical system is under a "no-load" condition. A fully charged battery may show about 12.5 volts at no load; will drop to 12 volts under medium load; and will drop even lower under heavy load. If the battery is partially discharged the voltage decrease under heavy load may be excessive, even though the battery shows 12 volts or more at no load. When allowed to discharge further, the battery's available voltage under load will decrease more severely. For this reason, it is important that the battery be fully charged during all testing procedures to avoid errors in diagnosis and incorrect test results.

Voltage Drop

When current flows through a resistance, the voltage beyond the resistance is reduced (the larger the current, the greater the reduction in voltage). When no current is flowing, there is no voltage drop because there is no current flow. All points in the circuit which are connected to the power source are at the same voltage as the power source. The total voltage drop always equals the total source voltage. In a long circuit with many connectors, a series of small, unwanted voltage drops due to corrosion at the connectors can add up to a total loss of voltage which impairs the operation of the normal loads in the circuit.

INDIRECT COMPUTATION OF VOLTAGE DROPS

1. Set the voltmeter selector switch to the 20 volt position.
2. Connect the meter negative lead to a good ground.

3. Probe all resistances in the circuit with the positive meter lead.

4. Operate the circuit in all modes and observe the voltage readings.

DIRECT MEASUREMENT OF VOLTAGE DROPS

1. Set the voltmeter switch to the 20 volt position.

2. Connect the voltmeter negative lead to the ground side of the resistance load to be measured.

3. Connect the positive lead to the positive side of the resistance or load to be measured.

4. Read the voltage drop directly on the 20 volt scale.

Too high a voltage indicates too high a resistance. If, for example, a blower motor runs too slowly, you can determine if there is too high a resistance in the resistor pack. By taking voltage drop readings in all parts of the circuit, you can isolate the problem. Too low a voltage drop indicates too low a resistance. If, for example, a blower motor runs too fast in the **MED** and/or **LOW** position, the problem can be isolated in the resistor pack by taking voltage drop readings in all parts of the circuit to locate a possibly shorted resistor. The maximum allowable voltage drop under load is critical, especially if there is more than one high resistance problem in a circuit because all voltage drops are cumulative. A small drop is normal due to the resistance of the conductors.

HIGH RESISTANCE TESTING

1. Set the voltmeter selector switch to the 4 volt position.

2. Connect the voltmeter positive lead to the positive post of the battery.

3. Turn on the headlights and heater blower to provide a load.

4. Probe various points in the circuit with the negative voltmeter lead.

5. Read the voltage drop on the 4 volt scale. Some average maximum allowable voltage drops are:

FUSE PANEL – 7 volts
IGNITION SWITCH – 5volts
HEADLIGHT SWITCH – 7 volts
IGNITION COIL (+) – 5 volts
ANY OTHER LOAD – 1.3 volts

NOTE: *Voltage drops are all measured while a load is operating; without current flow, there will be no voltage drop.*

Ohmmeter

The ohmmeter is designed to read resistance (ohms) in a circuit or component. Although there are several different styles of ohmmeters, all will usually have a selector switch which permits the measurement of different ranges of resistance (usually the selector switch allows the multiplication of the meter reading by 10, 100, 1000, and 10,000). A calibration knob allows the meter to be set at zero for accurate measurement. Since all ohmmeters are powered by an internal battery (usually 9 volts), the ohmmeter can be used as a self-powered test light. When the ohmmeter is connected, current from the ohmmeter flows through the circuit or component being tested. Since the ohmmeter's internal resistance and voltage are known values, the amount of current flow through the meter depends on the resistance of the circuit or component being tested.

The ohmmeter can be used to perform continuity test for opens or shorts (either by observation of the meter needle or as a self-powered test light), and to read actual resistance in a circuit. It should be noted that the ohmmeter is used to check the resistance of a component or wire while there is no voltage applied to the circuit. Current flow from an outside voltage source (such as the vehicle battery) can damage the ohmmeter, so the circuit or component should be isolated from the vehicle electrical system before any testing is done. Since the ohmmeter uses its own voltage source, either lead can be connected to any test point.

NOTE: *When checking diodes or other solid state components, the ohmmeter leads can only be connected one way in order to measure current flow in a single direction. Make sure the positive (+) and negative (–) terminal connections are as described in the test procedures to verify the one-way diode operation.*

In using the meter for making continuity checks, do not be concerned with the actual resistance readings. Zero resistance, or any resistance readings, indicate continuity in the circuit. Infinite resistance indicates an open in the circuit. A high resistance reading where there should be none indicates a problem in the circuit. Checks for short circuits are made in the same manner as checks for open circuits except that the circuit must be isolated from both power and normal ground. Infinite resistance indicates no continuity to ground, while zero resistance indicates a dead short to ground.

RESISTANCE MEASUREMENT

The batteries in an ohmmeter will weaken with age and temperature, so the ohmmeter must be calibrated or "zeroed" before taking measurements. To zero the meter, place the selector switch in its lowest range and touch the two ohmmeter leads together. Turn the calibration knob until the meter needle is exactly on zero.

NOTE: *All analog (needle) type ohmmeters*

must be zeroed before use, but some digital ohmmeter models are automatically calibrated when the switch is turned on. Self-calibrating digital ohmmeters do not have an adjusting knob, but its a good idea to check for a zero readout before use by touching the leads together. All computer controlled systems require the use of a digital ohmmeter with at least 10 meagohms impedance for testing. Before any test procedures are attempted, make sure the ohmmeter used is compatible with the electrical system or damage to the onboard computer could result.

To measure resistance, first isolate the circuit from the vehicle power source by disconnecting the battery cables or the harness connector. Make sure the key is **OFF** when disconnecting any components or the battery. Where necessary, also isolate at least one side of the circuit to be checked to avoid reading parallel resistances. Parallel circuit resistances will always give a lower reading than the actual resistance of either of the branches. When measuring the resistance of parallel circuits, the total resistance will always be lower than the smallest resistance in the circuit. Connect the meter leads to both sides of the circuit (wire or component) and read the actual measured ohms on the meter scale. Make sure the selector switch is set to the proper ohm scale for the circuit being tested to avoid misreading the ohmmeter test value.

WARNING: *Never use an ohmmeter with power applied to the circuit. Like the self-powered test light, the ohmmeter is designed to operate on its own power supply. The normal 12 volt automotive electrical system current could damage the meter!*

Ammeters

An ammeter measures the amount of current flowing through a circuit in units called amperes or amps. Amperes are units of electron flow which indicate how fast the electrons are flowing through the circuit. Since Ohms Law dictates that current flow in a circuit is equal to the circuit voltage divided by the total circuit resistance, increasing voltage also increases the current level (amps). Likewise, any decrease in resistance will increase the amount of amps in a circuit. At normal operating voltage, most circuits have a characteristic amount of amperes, called "current draw" which can be measured using an ammeter. By referring to a specified current draw rating, measuring the amperes, and comparing the two values, one can determine what is happening within the circuit to aid in diagnosis. An open circuit, for example, will not allow any current to flow so the ammeter reading will be zero. More current flows through a heavily loaded circuit or when the charging system is operating.

An ammeter is always connected in series with the circuit being tested. All of the current that normally flows through the circuit must also flow through the ammeter; if there is any other path for the current to follow, the ammeter reading will not be accurate. The ammeter itself has very little resistance to current flow and therefore will not affect the circuit, but it will measure current draw only when the circuit is closed and electricity is flowing. Excessive current draw can blow fuses and drain the battery, while a reduced current draw can cause motors to run slowly, lights to dim and other components to not operate properly. The ammeter can help diagnose these conditions by locating the cause of the high or low reading.

Multimeters

Different combinations of test meters can be built into a single unit designed for specific tests. Some of the more common combination test devices are known as Volt/Amp testers, Tach/Dwell meters, or Digital Multimeters. The Volt/Amp tester is used for charging system, starting system or battery tests and consists of a voltmeter, an ammeter and a variable resistance carbon pile. The voltmeter will usually have at least two ranges for use with 6, 12 and 24 volt systems. The ammeter also has more than one range for testing various levels of battery loads and starter current draw and the carbon pile can be adjusted to offer different amounts of resistance. The Volt/Amp tester has heavy leads to carry large amounts of current and many later models have an inductive ammeter pickup that clamps around the wire to simplify test connections. On some models, the ammeter also has a zero-center scale to allow testing of charging and starting systems without switching leads or polarity. A digital multimeter is a voltmeter, ammeter and ohmmeter combined in an instrument which gives a digital readout. These are often used when testing solid state circuits because of their high input impedance (usually 10 megohms or more).

The tach/dwell meter combines a tachometer and a dwell (cam angle) meter and is a specialized kind of voltmeter. The tachometer scale is marked to show engine speed in rpm and the dwell scale is marked to show degrees of distributor shaft rotation. In most electronic ignition systems, dwell is determined by the control unit, but the dwell meter can also be used to check the duty cycle (operation) of some electronic engine control systems. Some tach/dwell meters are powered by an internal battery, while others take their power from the truck battery in use. The battery powered testers usually require calibration much like an ohmmeter before testing.

Special Test Equipment

A variety of diagnostic tools are available to help troubleshoot and repair computerized engine control systems. The most sophisticated of these devices are the console type engine analyzers that usually occupy a garage service bay, but there are several types of aftermarket electronic testers available that will allow quick circuit tests of the engine control system by plugging directly into a special connector located in the engine compartment or under the dashboard. Several tool and equipment manufacturers offer simple, hand held testers that measure various circuit voltage levels on command to check all system components for proper operation. Although these testers usually cost about $300-500, consider that the average computer control unit (or ECM) can cost just as much and the money saved by not replacing perfectly good sensors or components in an attempt to correct a problem could justify the purchase price of a special diagnostic tester the first time it's used.

These computerized testers can allow quick and easy test measurements while the engine is operating or while the truck is being driven. In addition, the on-board computer memory can be read to access any stored trouble codes; in effect allowing the computer to tell you where it hurts and aid trouble diagnosis by pinpointing exactly which circuit or component is malfunctioning. In the same manner, repairs can be tested to make sure the problem has been corrected. The biggest advantage these special testers have is their relatively easy hookups that minimize or eliminate the chances of making the wrong connections and getting false voltage readings or damaging the computer accidentally.

NOTE: *It should be remembered that these testers check voltage levels in circuits; they don't detect mechanical problems or failed components if the circuit voltage falls within the preprogrammed limits stored in the tester PROM unit. Also, most of the hand held testers are designed to work only on one or two systems made by a specific manufacturer.*

A variety of aftermarket testers are available to help diagnose different computerized control systems. Owatonna Tool Company (OTC), for example, markets a device called the OTC Monitor which plugs directly into the assembly line diagnostic link (ALDL). The OTC tester makes diagnosis a simple matter of pressing the correct buttons and, by changing the internal PROM or inserting a different diagnosis cartridge, it will work on any model from full size to subcompact, over a wide range of years. An adapter is supplied with the tester to allow connection to all types of ALDL links, regardless of the number of pin terminals used. By inserting an updated PROM into the OTC tester, it can be easily updated to diagnose any new modifications of computerized control systems.

Wiring Harnesses

The average automobile contains about ½ mile of wiring, with hundreds of individual connections. To protect the many wires from damage and to keep them from becoming a confusing tangle, they are organized into bundles, enclosed in plastic or taped together and called wire harnesses. Different wiring harnesses serve different parts of the vehicle. Individual wires are color coded to help trace them through a harness where sections are hidden from view.

A loose or corroded connection or a replacement wire that is too small for the circuit will add extra resistance and an additional voltage drop to the circuit. A ten percent voltage drop can result in slow or erratic motor operation, for example, even though the circuit is complete. Automotive wiring or circuit conductors can be in any one of three forms:

1. Single strand wire
2. Multi-strand wire
3. Printed circuitry

Single strand wire has a solid metal core and is usually used inside such components as alternators, motors, relays and other devices. Multistrand wire has a core made of many small strands of wire twisted together into a single conductor. Most of the wiring in an automotive electrical system is made up of multistrand wire, either as a single conductor or grouped together in a harness. All wiring is color coded on the insulator, either as a solid color or as a colored wire with an identification stripe. A printed circuit is a thin film of copper or other conductor that is printed on an insulator backing. Occasionally, a printed circuit is sandwiched between two sheets of plastic for more protection and flexibility. A complete printed circuit, consisting of conductors, insulating material and connectors for lamps or other components is called a printed circuit board. Printed circuitry is used in place of individual wires or harnesses in places where space is limited, such as behind instrument panels.

Wire Gauge

Since computer controlled automotive electrical systems are very sensitive to changes in resistance, the selection of properly sized wires is critical when systems are repaired. The wire gauge number is an expression of the cross section area of the conductor. The most common system for expressing wire size is the American Wire Gauge (AWG) system.

Wire cross section area is measured in circular mils. A mil is $^1/_{1000}$ in. (0.001 in.); a circular mil is the area of a circle one mil in diameter. For example, a conductor ¼ in. in diameter is 0.250 in. or 250 mils. The circular mil cross section area of the wire is 250 squared (250^2)or 62,500 circular mils. Imported truck models usually use metric wire gauge designations, which is simply the cross section area of the conductor in square millimeters (mm^2).

Gauge numbers are assigned to conductors of various cross section areas. As gauge number increases, area decreases and the conductor becomes smaller. A 5 gauge conductor is smaller than a 1 gauge conductor and a 10 gauge is smaller than a 5 gauge. As the cross section area of a conductor decreases, resistance increases and so does the gauge number. A conductor with a higher gauge number will carry less current than a conductor with a lower gauge number.

NOTE: *Gauge wire size refers to the size of the conductor, not the size of the complete wire. It is possible to have two wires of the same gauge with different diameters because one may have thicker insulation than the other.*

12 volt automotive electrical systems generally use 10, 12, 14, 16 and 18 gauge wire. Main power distribution circuits and larger accessories usually use 10 and 12 gauge wire. Battery cables are usually 4 or 6 gauge, although 1 and 2 gauge wires are occasionally used. Wire length must also be considered when making repairs to a circuit. As conductor length increases, so does resistance. An 18 gauge wire, for example, can carry a 10 amp load for 10 feet without excessive voltage drop; however if a 15 foot wire is required for the same 10 amp load, it must be a 16 gauge wire.

An electrical schematic shows the electrical current paths when a circuit is operating properly. It is essential to understand how a circuit works before trying to figure out why it doesn't. Schematics break the entire electrical system down into individual circuits and show only one particular circuit. In a schematic, no attempt is made to represent wiring and components as they physically appear on the vehicle; switches and other components are shown as simply as possible. Face views of harness connectors show the cavity or terminal locations in all multi-pin connectors to help locate test points.

If you need to backprobe a connector while it is on the component, the order of the terminals must be mentally reversed. The wire color code can help in this situation, as well as a keyway, lock tab or other reference mark.

NOTE: *Wiring diagrams are not included in this book. As trucks have become more complex and available with longer option lists, wiring diagrams have grown in size and complexity. It has become almost impossible to provide a readable reproduction of a wiring diagram in a book this size. Information on ordering wiring diagrams from the vehicle manufacturer can be found in the owner's manual.*

WIRING REPAIR

Soldering is a quick, efficient method of joining metals permanently. Everyone who has the occasion to make wiring repairs should know how to solder. Electrical connections that are soldered are far less likely to come apart and will conduct electricity much better than connections that are only "pig-tailed" together. The most popular (and preferred) method of soldering is with an electrical soldering gun. Soldering irons are available in many sizes and wattage ratings. Irons with higher wattage ratings deliver higher temperatures and recover lost heat faster. A small soldering iron rated for no more than 50 watts is recommended, especially on electrical systems where excess heat can damage the components being soldered.

There are three ingredients necessary for successful soldering; proper flux, good solder and sufficient heat. A soldering flux is necessary to clean the metal of tarnish, prepare it for soldering and to enable the solder to spread into tiny crevices. When soldering, always use a resin flux or resin core solder which is non-corrosive and will not attract moisture once the job is finished. Other types of flux (acid core) will leave a residue that will attract moisture and cause the wires to corrode. Tin is a unique metal with a low melting point. In a molten state, it dissolves and alloys easily with many metals. Solder is made by mixing tin with lead. The most common proportions are 40/60, 50/50 and 60/40, with the percentage of tin listed first. Low priced solders usually contain less tin, making them very difficult for a beginner to use because more heat is required to melt the solder. A common solder is 40/60 which is well suited for all-around general use, but 60/40 melts easier, has more tin for a better joint and is preferred for electrical work.

Soldering Techniques

Successful soldering requires that the metals to be joined be heated to a temperature that will melt the solder—usually 360–460°F (182–238°C). Contrary to popular belief, the purpose of the soldering iron is not to melt the solder itself, but to heat the parts being soldered to a temperature high enough to melt the solder when it is touched to the work. Melting flux-cored solder on the soldering iron will usually destroy the effectiveness of the flux.

NOTE: *Soldering tips are made of copper for good heat conductivity, but must be "tinned" regularly for quick transference of heat to the project and to prevent the solder from sticking to the iron. To "tin" the iron, simply heat it and touch the flux-cored solder to the tip; the solder will flow over the hot tip. Wipe the excess off with a clean rag, but be careful as the iron will be hot.*

After some use, the tip may become pitted. If so, simply dress the tip smooth with a smooth file and "tin" the tip again. An old saying holds that "metals well cleaned are half soldered." Flux-cored solder will remove oxides but rust, bits of insulation and oil or grease must be removed with a wire brush or emery cloth. For maximum strength in soldered parts, the joint must start off clean and tight. Weak joints will result in gaps too wide for the solder to bridge.

If a separate soldering flux is used, it should be brushed or swabbed on only those areas that are to be soldered. Most solders contain a core of flux and separate fluxing is unnecessary. Hold the work to be soldered firmly. It is best to solder on a wooden board, because a metal vise will only rob the piece to be soldered of heat and make it difficult to melt the solder. Hold the soldering tip with the broadest face against the work to be soldered. Apply solder under the tip close to the work, using enough solder to give a heavy film between the iron and the piece being soldered, while moving slowly and making sure the solder melts properly. Keep the work level or the solder will run to the lowest part and favor the thicker parts, because these require more heat to melt the solder. If the soldering tip overheats (the solder coating on the face of the tip burns up), it should be retinned. Once the soldering is completed, let the soldered joint stand until cool. Tape and seal all soldered wire splices after the repair has cooled.

Wire Harness and Connectors

The on-board computer (ECM) wire harness electrically connects the control unit to the various solenoids, switches and sensors used by the control system. Most connectors in the engine compartment or otherwise exposed to the elements are protected against moisture and dirt which could create oxidation and deposits on the terminals. This protection is important because of the very low voltage and current levels used by the computer and sensors. All connectors have a lock which secures the male and female terminals together, with a secondary lock holding the seal and terminal into the connector. Both terminal locks must be released when disconnecting ECM connectors.

These special connectors are weather-proof and all repairs require the use of a special terminal and the tool required to service it. This tool is used to remove the pin and sleeve terminals. If removal is attempted with an ordinary pick, there is a good chance that the terminal will be bent or deformed. Unlike standard blade type terminals, these terminals cannot be straightened once they are bent. Make certain that the connectors are properly seated and all of the sealing rings in place when connecting leads. On some models, a hinge-type flap provides a backup or secondary locking feature for the terminals. Most secondary locks are used to improve the connector reliability by retaining the terminals if the small terminal lock tangs are not positioned properly.

Molded-on connectors require complete replacement of the connection. This means splicing a new connector assembly into the harness. All splices in on-board computer systems should be soldered to insure proper contact. Use care when probing the connections or replacing terminals in them as it is possible to short between opposite terminals. If this happens to the wrong terminal pair, it is possible to damage certain components. Always use jumper wires between connectors for circuit checking and never probe through weatherproof seals.

Open circuits are often difficult to locate by sight because corrosion or terminal misalignment are hidden by the connectors. Merely wiggling a connector on a sensor or in the wiring harness may correct the open circuit condition. This should always be considered when an open circuit or a failed sensor is indicated. Intermittent problems may also be caused by oxidized or loose connections. When using a circuit tester for diagnosis, always probe connections from the wire side. Be careful not to damage sealed connectors with test probes.

All wiring harnesses should be replaced with identical parts, using the same gauge wire and connectors. When signal wires are spliced into a harness, use wire with high temperature insulation only. With the low voltage and current levels found in the system, it is important that the best possible connection at all wire splices be made by soldering the splices together. It is seldom necessary to replace a complete harness. If replacement is necessary, pay close attention to insure proper harness routing. Secure the harness with suitable plastic wire clamps to prevent vibrations from causing the harness to wear in spots or contact any hot components.

NOTE: *Weatherproof connectors cannot be replaced with standard connectors. Instruc-*

tions are provided with replacement connector and terminal packages. Some wire harnesses have mounting indicators (usually pieces of colored tape) to mark where the harness is to be secured.

In making wiring repairs, it's important that you always replace damaged wires with wires that are the same gauge as the wire being replaced. The heavier the wire, the smaller the gauge number. Wires are color-coded to aid in identification and whenever possible the same color coded wire should be used for replacement. A wire stripping and crimping tool is necessary to install solderless terminal connectors. Test all crimps by pulling on the wires; it should not be possible to pull the wires out of a good crimp.

Wires which are open, exposed or otherwise damaged are repaired by simple splicing. Where possible, if the wiring harness is accessible and the damaged place in the wire can be located, it is best to open the harness and check for all possible damage. In an inaccessible harness, the wire must be bypassed with a new insert, usually taped to the outside of the old harness.

When replacing fusible links, be sure to use fusible link wire, NOT ordinary automotive wire. Make sure the fusible segment is of the same gauge and construction as the one being replaced and double the stripped end when crimping the terminal connector for a good contact. The melted (open) fusible link segment of the wiring harness should be cut off as close to the harness as possible, then a new segment spliced in as described. In the case of a damaged fusible link that feeds two harness wires, the harness connections should be replaced with two fusible link wires so that each circuit will have its own separate protection.

NOTE: *Most of the problems caused in the wiring harness are due to bad ground connections. Always check all vehicle ground connections for corrosion or looseness before performing any power feed checks to eliminate the chance of a bad ground affecting the circuit.*

Repairing Hard Shell Connectors

Unlike molded connectors, the terminal contacts in hard shell connectors can be replaced. Weatherproof hard-shell connectors with the leads molded into the shell have non-replaceable terminal ends. Replacement usually involves the use of a special terminal removal tool that depress the locking tangs (barbs) on the connector terminal and allow the connector to be removed from the rear of the shell. The connector shell should be replaced if it shows any evidence of burning, melting, cracks, or breaks. Replace individual terminals that are burnt, corroded, distorted or loose.

NOTE: *The insulation crimp must be tight to prevent the insulation from sliding back on the wire when the wire is pulled. The insulation must be visibly compressed under the crimp tabs, and the ends of the crimp should be turned in for a firm grip on the insulation.*

The wire crimp must be made with all wire strands inside the crimp. The terminal must be fully compressed on the wire strands with the ends of the crimp tabs turned in to make a firm grip on the wire. Check all connections with an ohmmeter to insure a good contact. There should be no measurable resistance between the wire and the terminal when connected.

Mechanical Test Equipment

Vacuum Gauge

Most gauges are graduated in inches of mercury (in.Hg), although a device called a manometer reads vacuum in inches of water (in. H_2O). The normal vacuum reading usually varies between 18 and 22 in.Hg at sea level. To test engine vacuum, the vacuum gauge must be connected to a source of manifold vacuum. Many engines have a plug in the intake manifold which can be removed and replaced with an adapter fitting. Connect the vacuum gauge to the fitting with a suitable rubber hose or, if no manifold plug is available, connect the vacuum gauge to any device using manifold vacuum, such as EGR valves, etc. The vacuum gauge can be used to determine if enough vacuum is reaching a component to allow its actuation.

Hand Vacuum Pump

Small, hand-held vacuum pumps come in a variety of designs. Most have a built-in vacuum gauge and allow the component to be tested without removing it from the vehicle. Operate the pump lever or plunger to apply the correct amount of vacuum required for the test specified in the diagnosis routines. The level of vacuum in inches of Mercury (in.Hg) is indicated on the pump gauge. For some testing, an additional vacuum gauge may be necessary.

Intake manifold vacuum is used to operate various systems and devices on late model vehicles. To correctly diagnose and solve problems in vacuum control systems, a vacuum source is necessary for testing. In some cases, vacuum can be taken from the intake manifold when the engine is running, but vacuum is normally provided by a hand vacuum pump. These hand vacuum pumps have a built-in vacuum gauge that allow testing while the device is still attached to the component. For some tests, an additional vacuum gauge may be necessary.

HEATING AND AIR CONDITIONING

Please refer to Chapter 1 for all discharging, evacuating and charging procedures for the air conditioning system.

Heater Assembly

REMOVAL AND INSTALLATION

1970-79

1. Disconnect the negative battery cable.
2. Drain the engine coolant.
3. Remove the defroster hoses.
4. Remove the three cable retaining clips and disconnect the control cables from the valves and water cock.
5. Disconnect the two fan motor leads from each connector.
6. Disconnect the two resistor lead wires from each connector.
7. Disconnect the water hoses from the heater core and water cock.
8. Remove the three heater housing mounting bolts and remove the heater assembly from the vehicle.

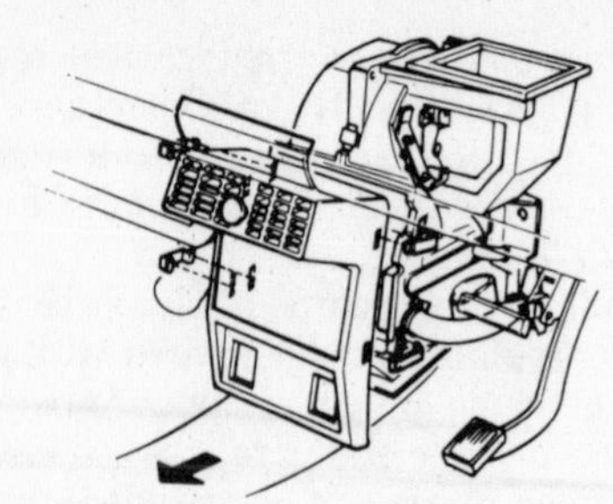

Removing the heater assembly front cover on 1970–79 models

9. Install the heater assembly and tighten the mounting screws.
10. Connect the heater hoses at the core. Connect the two resistor wires and the fan motor leads.
11. Connect the control cables to the valves and water cock.
12. Fill the engine with coolant, connect the battery cable and start the engine. Check for any leaks.

1980-86 720-D Series

1. Disconnect the negative battery cable.
2. Drain the cooling system.

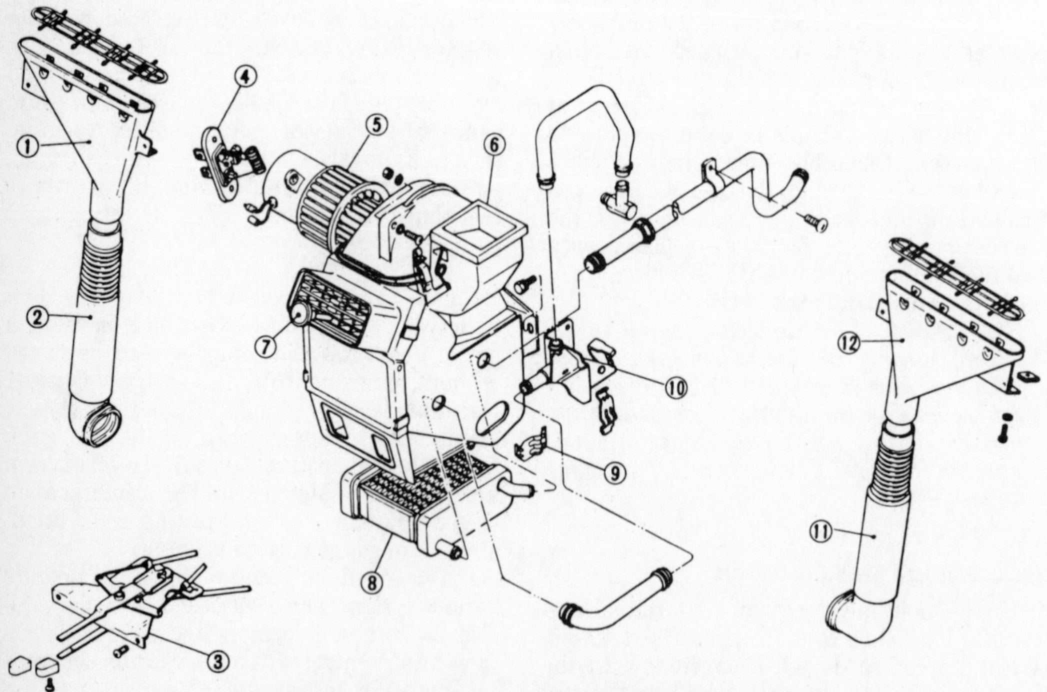

1. Defroster nozzle (L.H.)
2. Defroster duct (L.H.)
3. Heater control
4. Resistor
5. Heater motor
6. Heater case
7. Ventilator knob
8. Heater core
9. Control cable clip
10. Heater cock
11. Defroster duct (R.H.)
12. Defroster nozzle (R.H.)

Heater assembly—1972–79

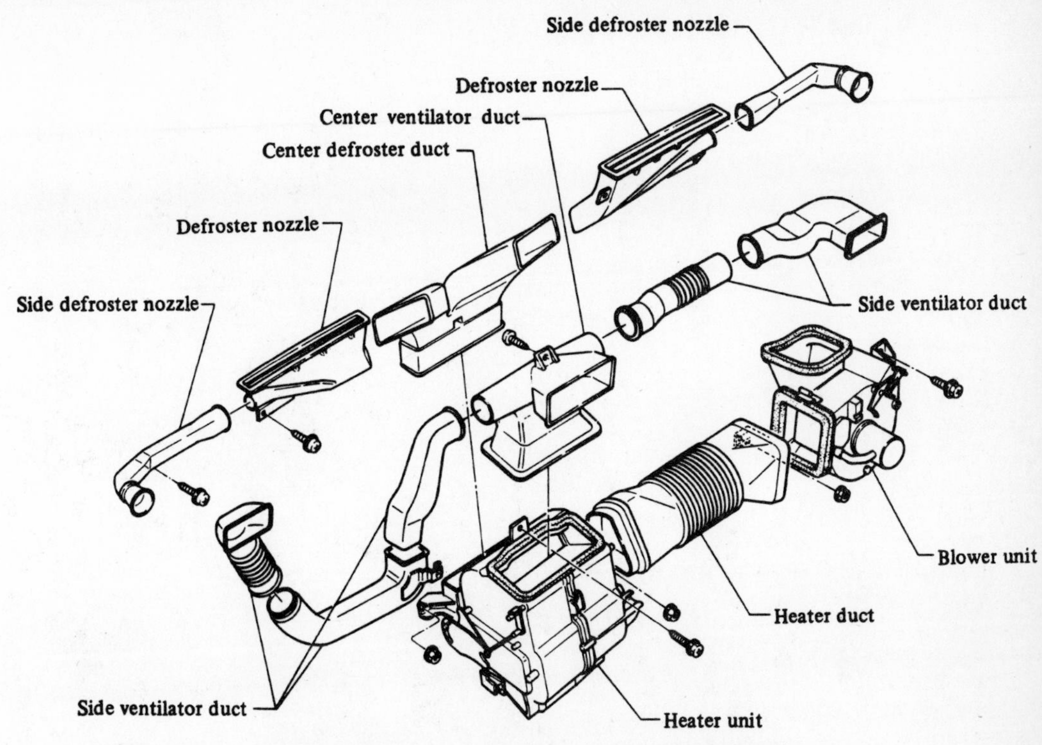

Heater assembly—1980–86 without A/C (720-D series)

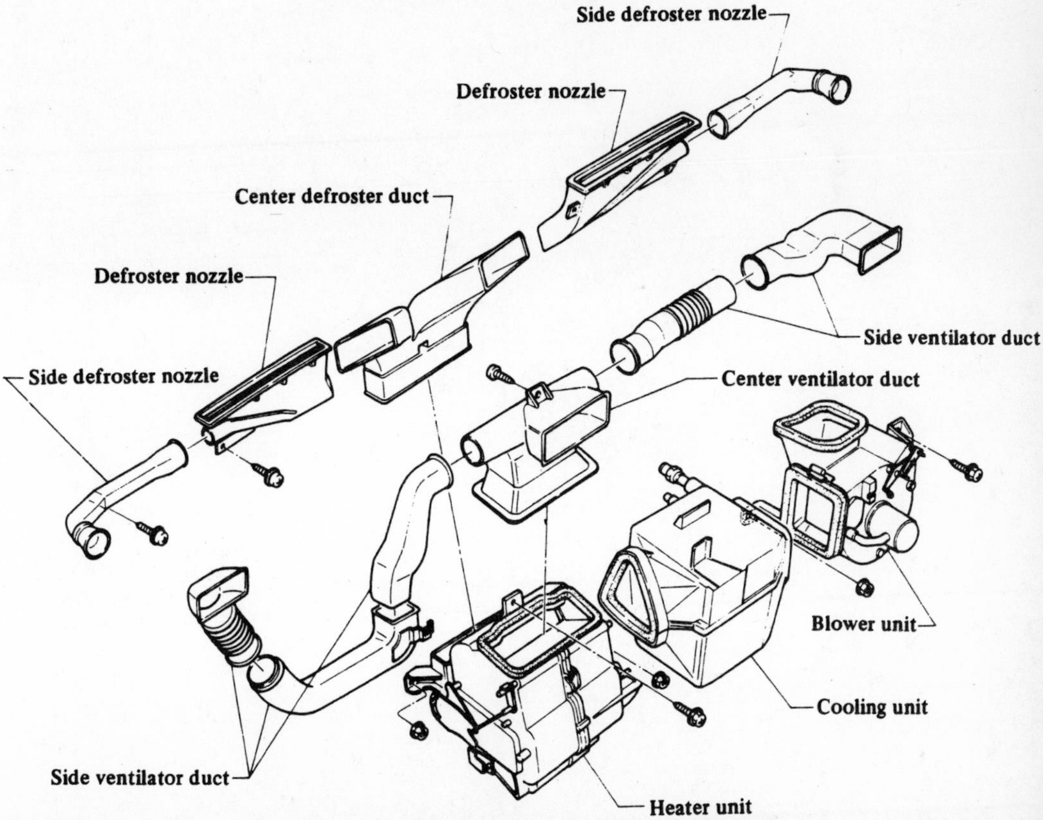

Heater assembly—1980–86 with A/C (720-D series)

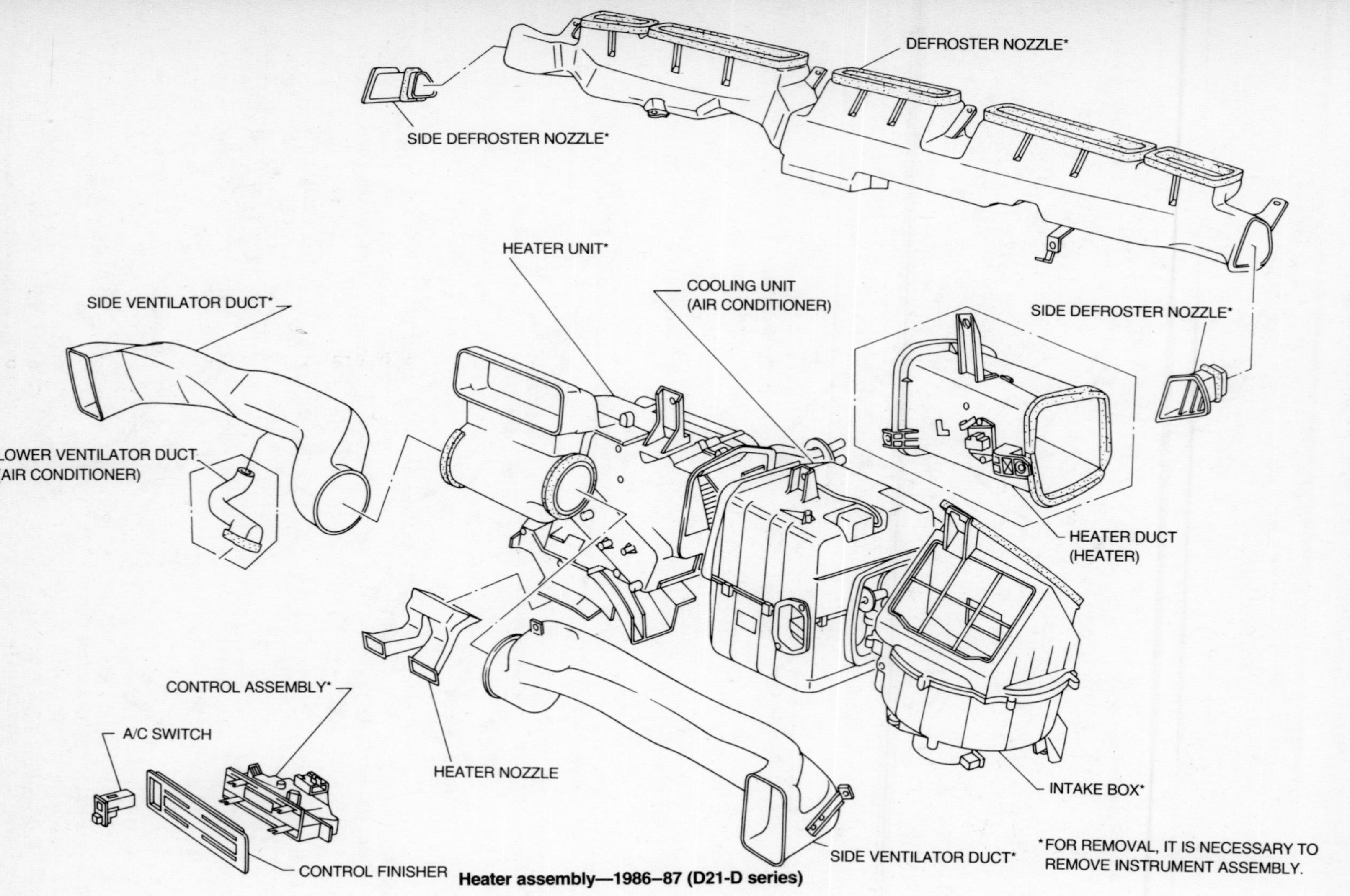

Heater assembly—1986–87 (D21-D series)

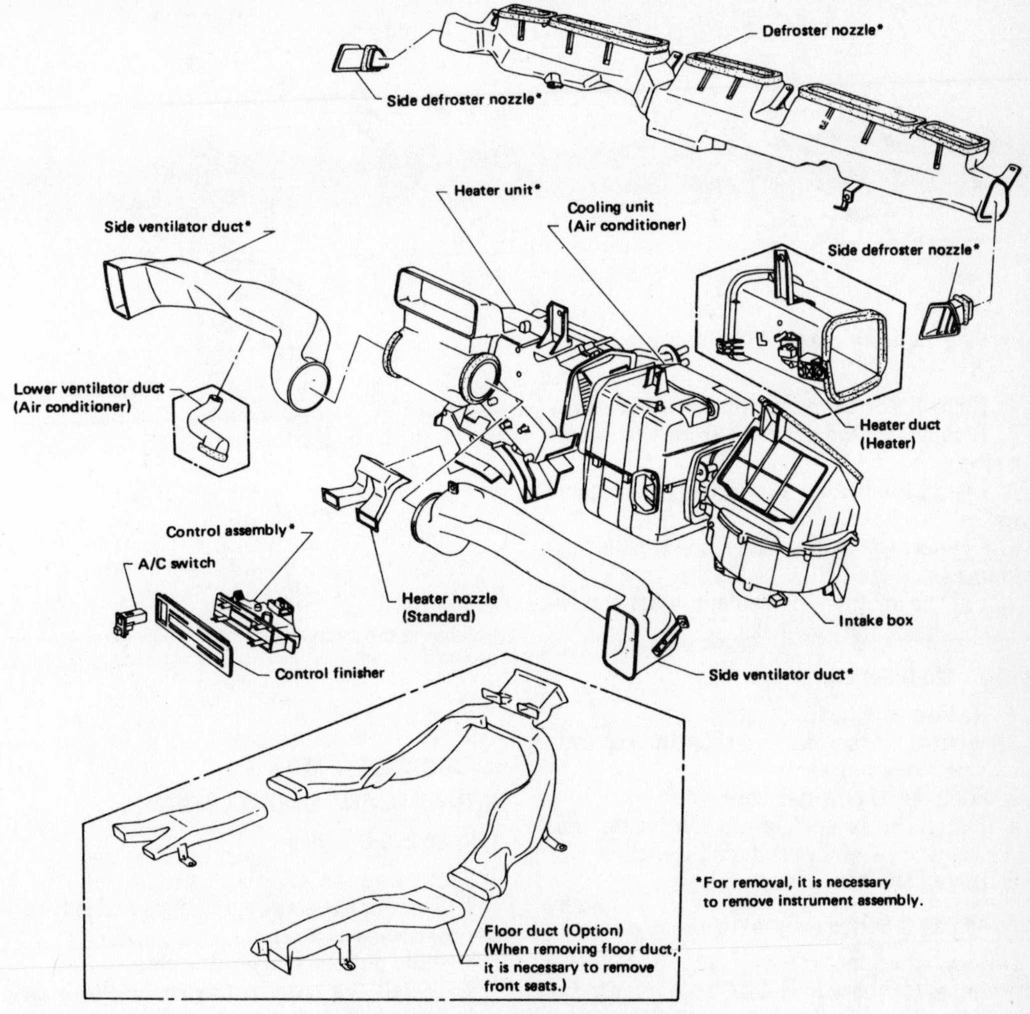

Heater assembly—1988–89 (D21-D series)

3. On models with air conditioning, disconnect the heater hose from the engine.
4. On models without air conditioning, remove the heater duct and disconnect the heater hose at the heater.
5. Remove the console box and instrument panel assembly.
6. Disconnect the air intake control cable from the blower motor.
7. On models equipped with A/C, remove the blower. Remove the evaporator unit nuts and bolts, but do not remove the evaporator unit.
8. Remove the heater assembly.
9. Installation the heater assembly and tighten the mounting screws.
10. Install the blower on A/C models and connect the air intake control cable.
11. Install the instrument panel and the console box.
12. Install the heater duct.
13. Connect the heater hoses and fill the engine with coolant. Adjust the control cable for proper operation. Start the engine and check for any leaks.

1986-89 D21-D Series

Nissan offers no removal and installation procedures for these models. Please refer to the procedures listed for the 720-D series as a general guideline and refer to the illustrations.

Heater Core

REMOVAL AND INSTALLATION

1970-79

1. Drain the engine coolant.
2. Remove the defroster hoses.
3. Disconnect the water hoses from the inlet and outlet pipes of the heater core.

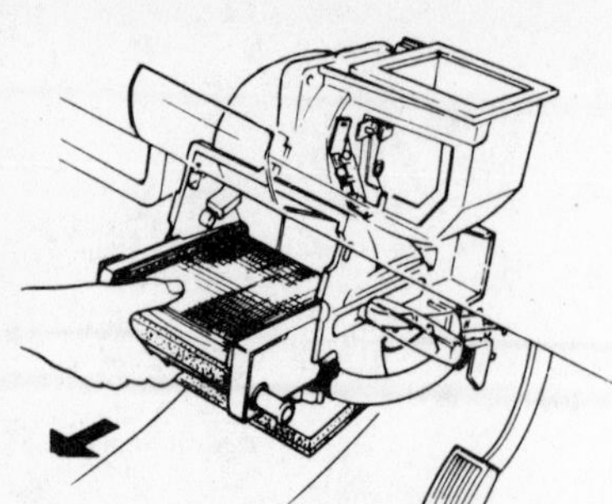

Removing the heater core—1970–79

4. Remove the four clips and front cover.
5. Remove the heater core from the heater housing.
6. Install the heater core in the housing and press in the clips.
7. Connect the heater hoses and the defroster ducts.
8. Fill the engine with coolant, start the engine and check for any leaks.

1980-86 720-D Series

1. Remove the heater assembly.
2. Remove the screws and clips and separate the heater case halves.
3. Slide out the heater core.
4. Install the heater core in the heater case and close the two halves. Install the clips.
5. Install the heater assembly.

1986-89 D21-D Series

Nissan offers no removal and installation procedures for these models. Please refer to the procedures listed for the 720-D series as a general guideline and refer to the illustrations.

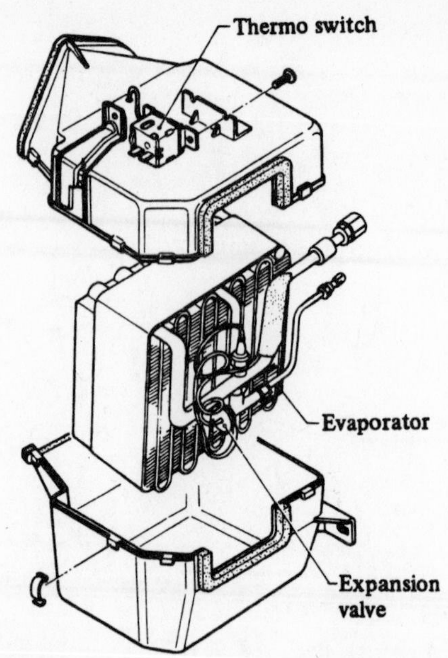

Removing the evaporator core—1980–86 (720-D series)

Evaporator Core

REMOVAL AND INSTALLATION

1981-86 720-D Series

1. Remove the A/C cooling unit.
2. Remove the screws and clips and separate the case halves.
3. Slide out the evaporator core.
4. Install the core in the cooling unit case and close the two halves. Install the clips.
5. Install the A/C cooling unit.

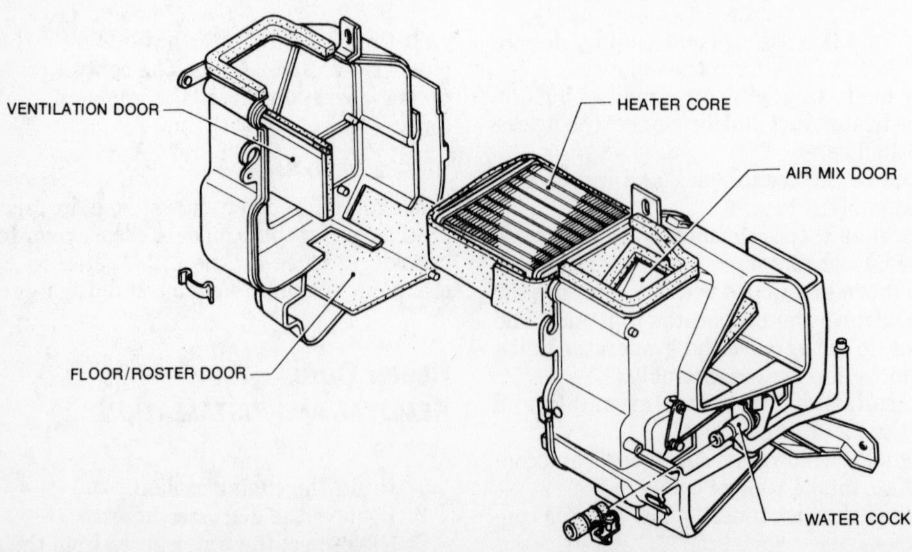

Removing the heater core—1980–86 (720-D series)

1986-89 D21-D Series

Nissan offers no removal and installation procedures for these models. Please refer to the procedures listed for the 720-D series as a general guideline and refer to the illustrations.

Blower Motor

REMOVAL AND INSTALLATION

1970-79

1. Remove the heater assembly from the vehicle as previously outlined.
2. Remove the nine spring clips and disassemble the heater housing.
3. Remove the fan from the electric motor.
4. Remove the fan motor retaining screws and remove the motor.
5. Install the blower motor into the heater assembly and then install the heater assembly.

1980-86 720-D Series

1. Disconnect the negative battery cable.
2. Remove the package tray.
3. Remove the heater duct on models without air conditioning.
4. Remove the resistor connector and disconnect the control cable.
5. Remove the blower.
6. Install the blower motor and connect the control cable and resistor.
7. Install the heater ducts and the package tray.
8. Connact the battery cable. Adjust the control cable for proper operation.

1986-89 D21-D Series

Nissan offers no removal and installation procedures for these models. Please refer to the procedures listed for the 720-D series as a general guideline and refer to the illustrations.

A/C Cooling Unit

REMOVAL AND INSTALLATION

1981-86 720-D Series

1. Disconnect the negative battery cable.
2. Disconnect the refrigerant line at the cooling unit. Remove the tube mounting bolt.
3. Remove the instrument panel assembly.
4. Remove the blower unit.
5. Remove the cooling unit.
6. Install the cooling unit. Install the blower unit.
7. Install the instrument panel.
8. Connect the refrigerant line and battery cable. Adjust the heater control cable.

1986-89 D21-D Series

Nissan offers no removal and installation procedures for these models. Please refer to the procedures listed for the 720-D series as a general guideline and refer to the illustrations.

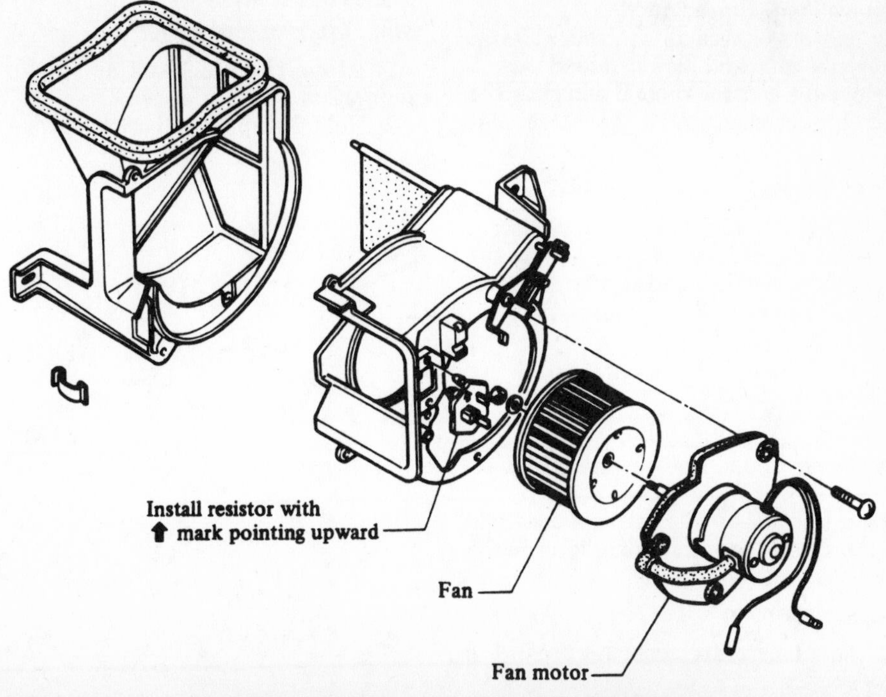

Removing the blower motor—1980–86 (720-D series)

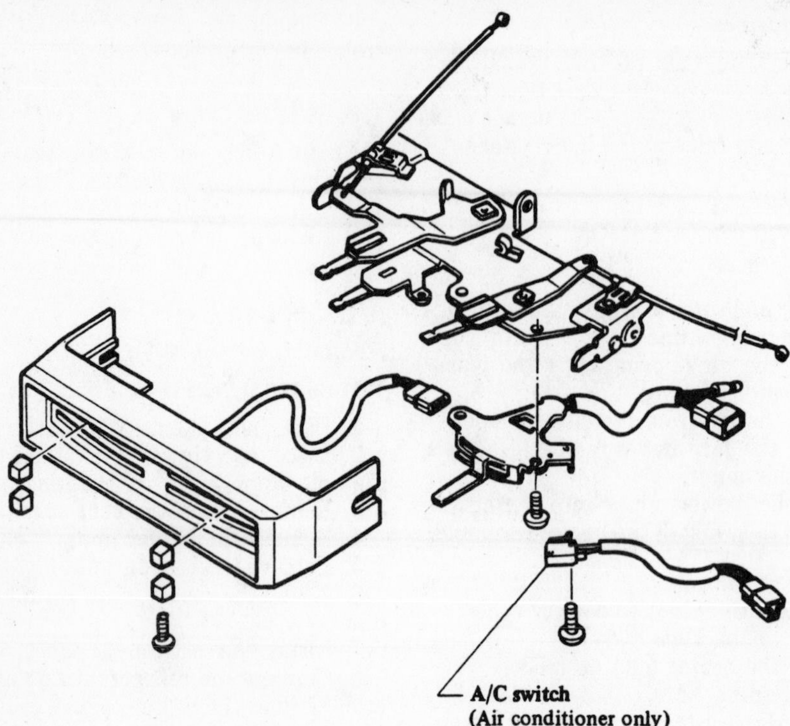

Control head assembly—1980–86 (720-D series)

Control Head

REMOVAL AND INSTALLATION

1970-86 521, 620 and 720-D Series

1. Disconnect the negative battery cable.
2. Remove the package tray.
3. Tag and disconnect all control cables at the heater assembly and blower motor.
4. Remove the control knob(s) and slide the panel out through the front of the instrument panel.

1986-89 D21-D Series

Nissan offers no removal and installation procedures for these models. Please refer to the procedures listed for the 720-D series as a general guideline and refer to the illustrations.

ADJUSTMENT

1970-86 521, 620 and 720-D Series

AIR INTAKE DOOR

1. Set the air intake lever in the **RECIRC** position.
2. Clamp the cable while at the same time pushing the sheathing and the door lever in the direction as shown.

AIR MIX DOOR/WATER COCK

1. Set the temperature control lever in the **COLD** position.
2. Pull the control cable sheathing in the direction shown in the illustration until the clearance between the ends of the rod and water cock lever is approximately 0.08 in. (2mm).
3. Clamp the cable in position.

1986-89 D21-D Series

VENTILATOR DOOR CONTROL ROD

1. Move the side link as shown in the illustration.
2. Hold the upper and lower doors as shown

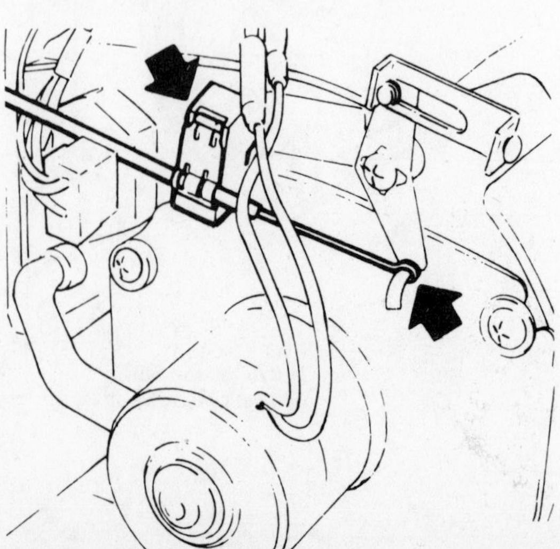
Control cable positioning

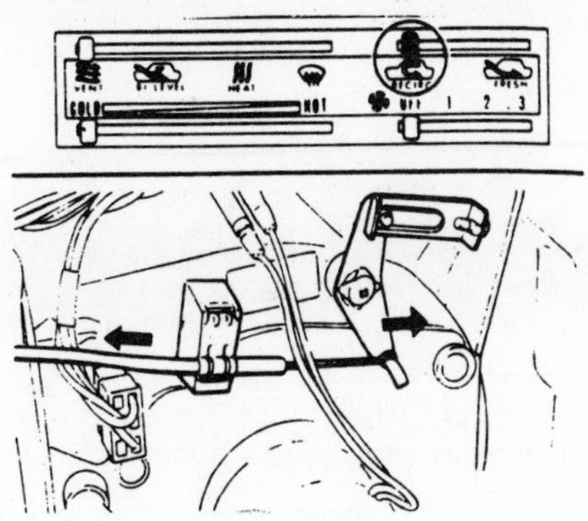

Air intake door control adjustment—1980–86 (720-D series)

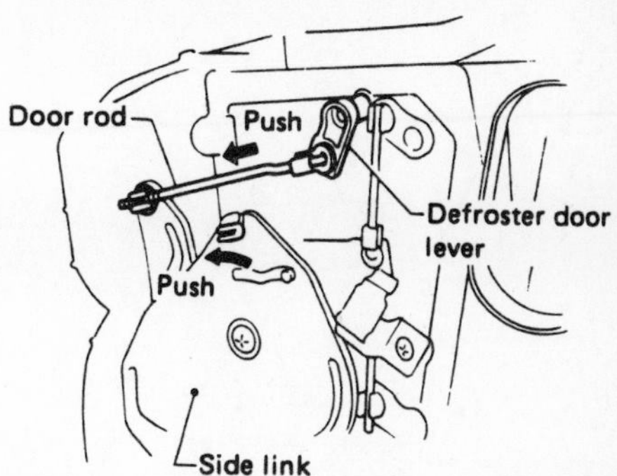

Defroster door control rod adjustment—1986–89 (D21-D series)

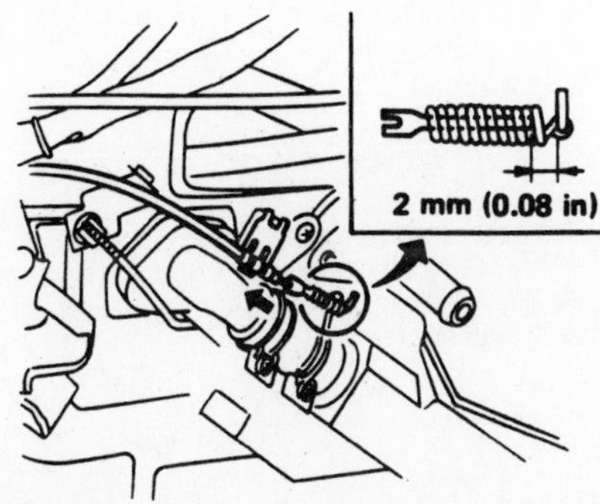

Air mix door/water cock adjustment—1980–86 (720-D series)

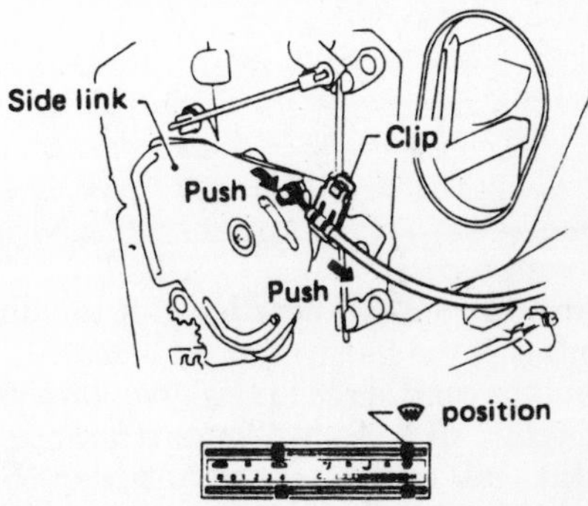

Air control cable adjustment—1986–89 (D21-D series)

and then connect the rods to their respective doors.

DEFROSTER DOOR CONTROL ROD

1. Move the side link as shown in the illustration.
2. Connect the rod to the side link to the rod while pushing the door lever as shown.

AIR CONTROL CABLE

Push the cable sheathing and side link in the direction illustrated and tighten the clamp.

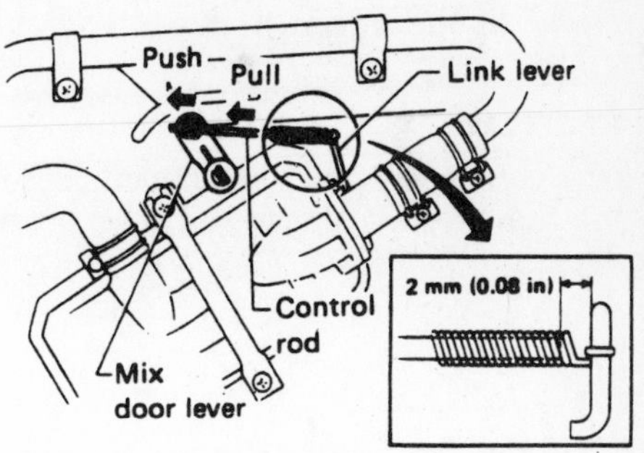

Water cock control rod adjustment—1986–89 (D21-D series)

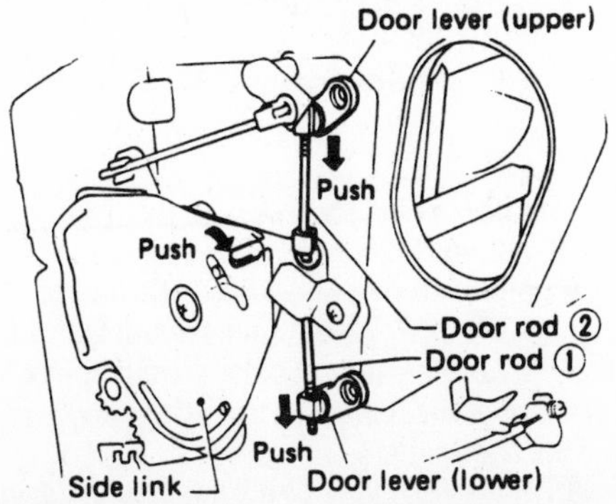

Ventilation door control rod adjustment—1986–89 (D21-D series)

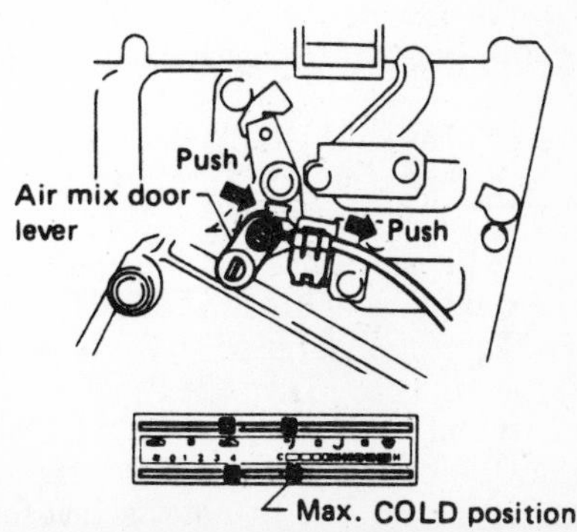

Temperature control cable adjustment—1986–89 (D21-D series)

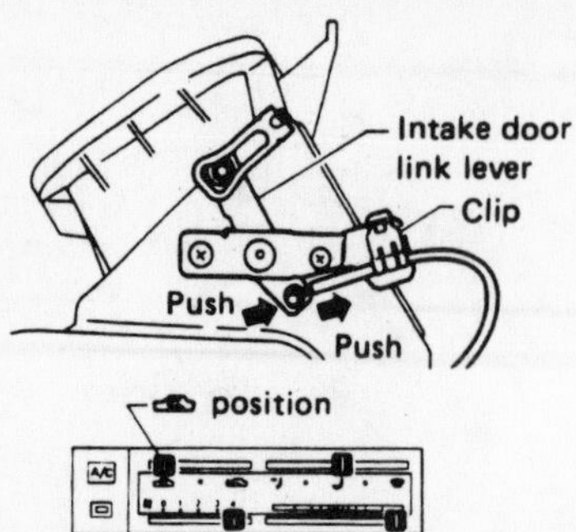

Intake door control cable adjustment—1986–89 (D21-D series)

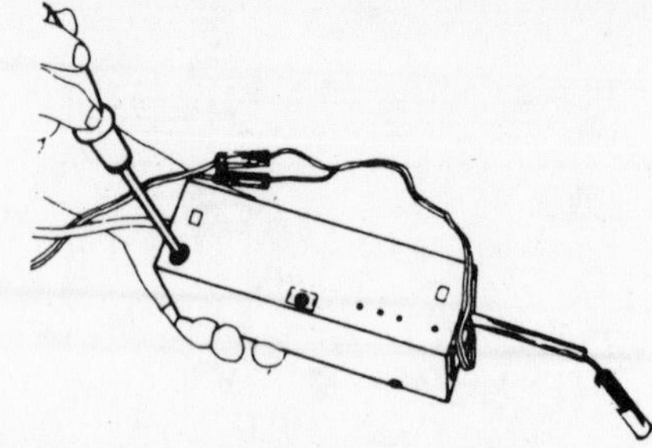

Antenna trimmer adjustment—1972–78

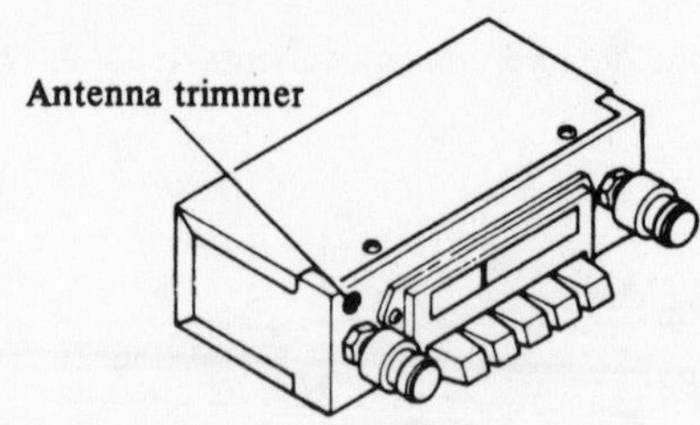

Antenna trimmer adjustment—1979

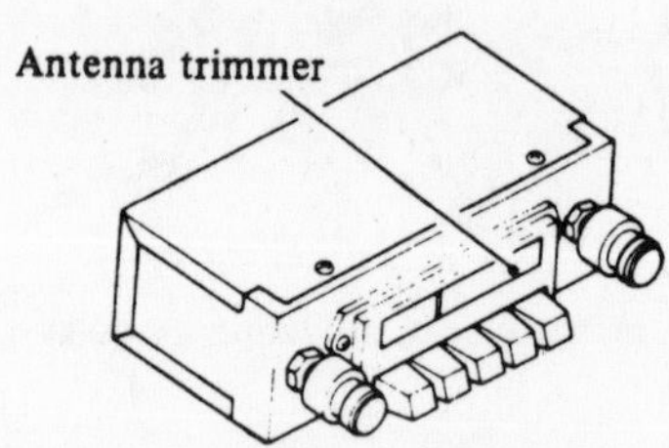

Antenna trimmer adjustment—1980–86 (720-D series)

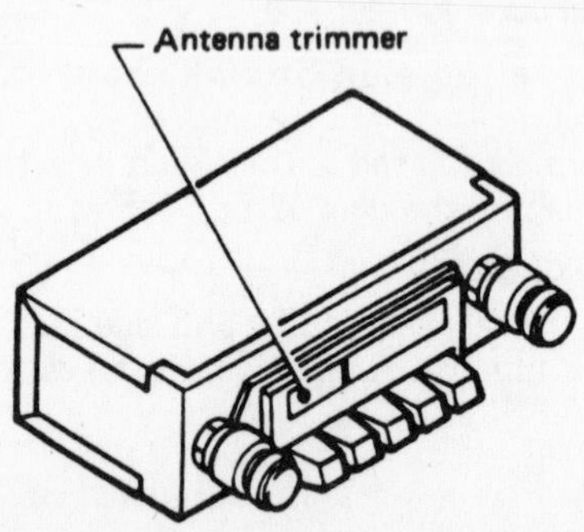

Antenna trimmer adjustment—1986–89 (D21-D series)

WATER COCK CONTROL ROD

NOTE: *When adjusting the control rod, disconnect the temoerature control cable at the air mix door lever and then adjust air mix door control cable and then the control rod. Reconnect the temperature control cable and then readjust it.*

1. Push the air mix door lever in the direction shown in the illustration.
2. Pull the control rod in the direction shown until there is an 0.08 in. (2mm) clearance between the ends of the rod and link lever. Connect the rod to the door lever.

TEMPERATURE CONTROL CABLE

Push the cable sheathing and the air mix door lever in the direction shown and then tighten the clamp.

INTAKE DOOR CABLE

Push the cable sheathing and the intake door lever in the direction shown and then tighten the clamp.

RADIO

ADJUSTMENTS

Observe the following cautions when working on the radio:

1. Always observe the proper polarity of the connections (positive to positive and negative to negative).
2. Never operate the radio without a speaker, to prevent damage to the output transistors. If a new speaker is installed, make sure it has the correct impedance (ohms) for the radio.

If a new antenna or antenna cable is used, or if poor AM reception is noted, the antenna trimmer can be adjusted. Turn the radio to a weak station around 1400 kHz. Adjust the trimmer screw until best reception and maximum volume are obtained. The trimmer screw for the factory installed radio is located on the bottom in the left rear corner on 1970-71 models, in the lower left corner of the rear of the radio case 1972-78, above the left knob on the front of the radio in 1979, above the right station pre-set button on 1980-86 720-D series models, and on 1986-89 D21-D series models, either above the left station pre-set button or in the lower left corner of the facia.

NOTE: *Never turn the antenna trimmer more than ½ turn on 1980-89 models!*

For best FM reception, raise the antenna to

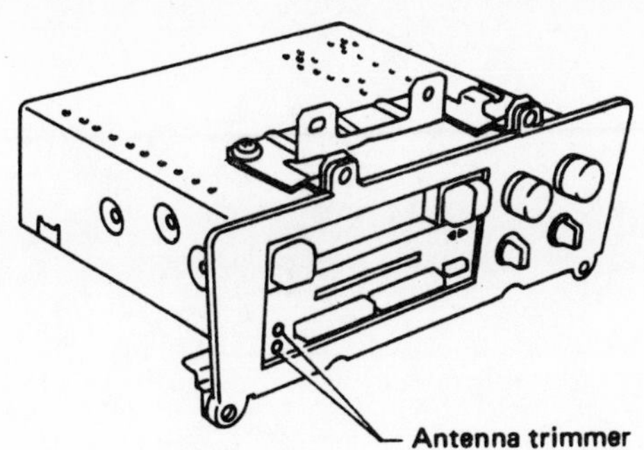

Antenna trimmer adjustment—1986–89 (D21-D series)

31 in. For best AM reception, raise the antenna to its full height.

REMOVAL AND INSTALLATION

1970-79

1. Carefully pull the knobs off the radio control shafts.
2. Remove the radio retaining nuts and washer from the radio control shafts.
3. Remove the bezel plate from the front of the radio.
4. Disconnect the antenna cable and the power and speaker wires from under the instrument panel.
5. Remove the radio from the instrument panel.
6. Install the radio in the instrument panel.
7. Connect the speaker and power leads, plug the antenna in and then position the bezel.
8. Slide the washers over the control shafts and then tighten the retaining nuts.
9. Press the knobs back onto the control shafts.

1980-86 720-D Series

1. Disconnect the negative battery cable.
2. Remove the ash tray and heater/air conditioner control panel.

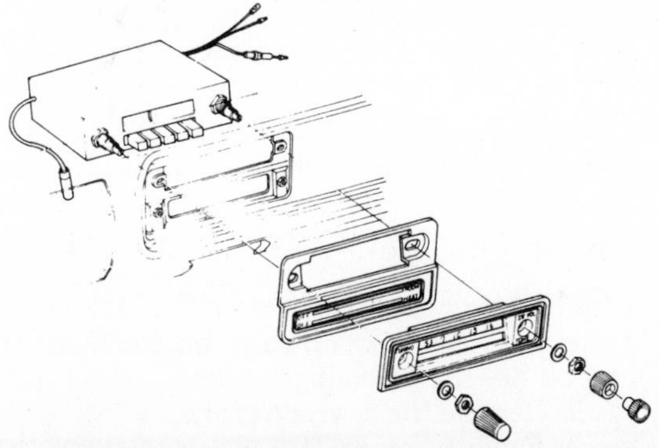

Removing the radio—1970–79

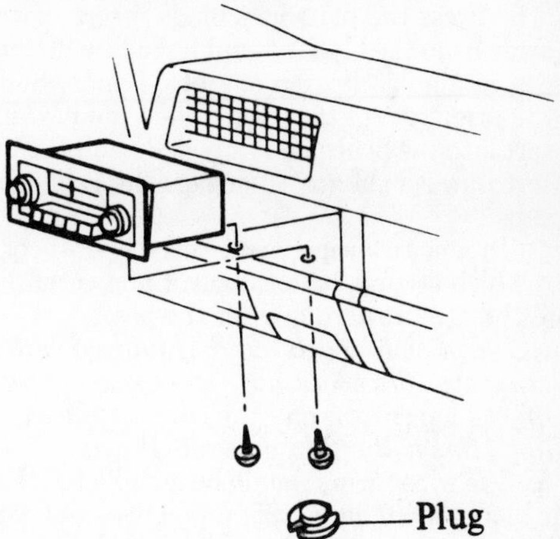

Removing the radio—1980–86 (720-D series)

3. Disconnect the wiring plug at the back of the radio.
4. Remove the plug covering the mounting screws, remove the screws and pull the radio from the dash.
5. Disconnect the wiring harness and the antenna.
6. Reconnect the wiring harness into the rear of the radio and then slide the radio into the instrument panel.
7. Install and tighten the radio mounting screws and then press the plug into position.
8. Reach through the control head opening and connect the antenna and any electrical leads.
9. Install the control head and connect the battery cable. Adjust the heater control head if necessary.

1986-89 D21-D Series

Nissan offers no removal and installation procedures for these models. Please refer to the procedures listed for the 720-D series as a general guideline and refer to the illustrations.

WINDSHIELD WIPERS

Blade and Arm

REMOVAL AND INSTALLATION

NOTE: *Wiper blade element replacement is covered in Chapter 1.*

1. To remove the wiper blades, lift up on the spring release tab on the wiper blade-to-wiper arm connector.
2. Pull the blade assembly off the wiper arm.
3. There are two types of replacements for Nissans:
   a. Replace the entire wiper blade as an assembly. Simply snap the replacement into place on the arm.

b. Press the old wiper blade insert down, away from the blade assembly, to free it from the retaining clips on the blade ends. Slide the insert out of the blade. Slide the new insert into the blade assembly and bend the insert upward slightly to engage the retaining clips.

4. To replace a wiper arm, unscrew the acorn nut which secures it to the pivot and carefully pull the arm upward and off the pivot.

NOTE: *Some models may be equipped with a cover over the acorn nut. To expose the nut, lift the wiper arm and the cover at the same time; this will afford access to the nut.*

5. The wiper arms should be installed so that the blades are 0.98 in. (25mm) above, and parallel to, the windshield molding. If the motor has been run, be sure the motor and linkage is in its parked position before installing the wiper arms. To do this, turn the ignition switch **ON**, and cycle the motor three or four times. Shut off the motor with the wiper switch (not the ignition switch), and allow the motor to return to the park position.

Windshield Wiper Motor

REMOVAL AND INSTALLATION

1. Remove the wiper blades and arms as an assembly from the pivots. The arms are retained to the pivots by nuts. Remove the nuts and pull the arms straight off.
2. Remove the cowl top grille. It is retained by four screws at its front edge. Remove the screws and pull the grille forward to disengage the tabs at the rear.
3. Remove the stop ring which connects the wiper motor arm to the connecting rod.

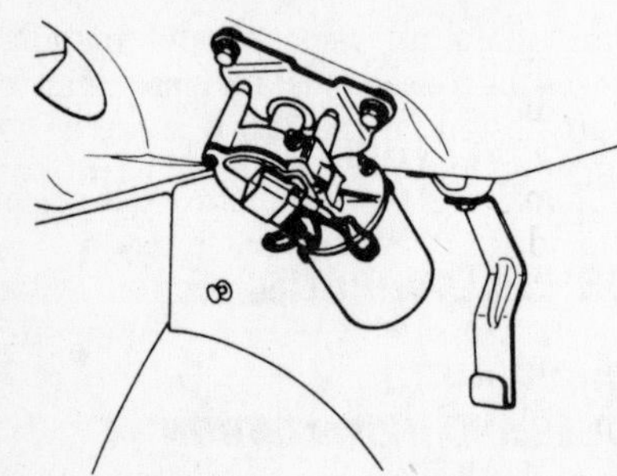

Windshield wiper motor removal

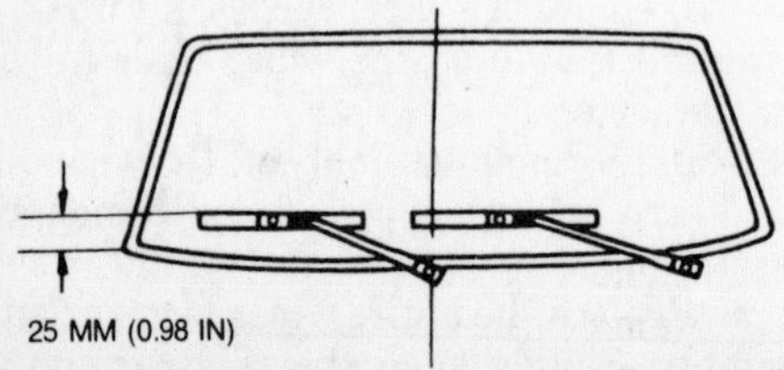

Wiper arm installation

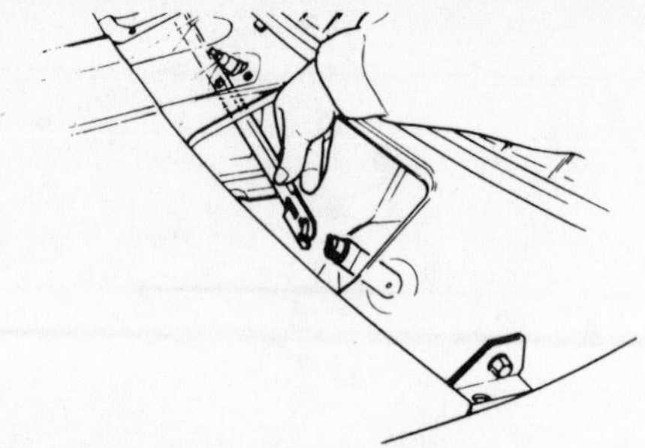

Windshield wiper linkage removal

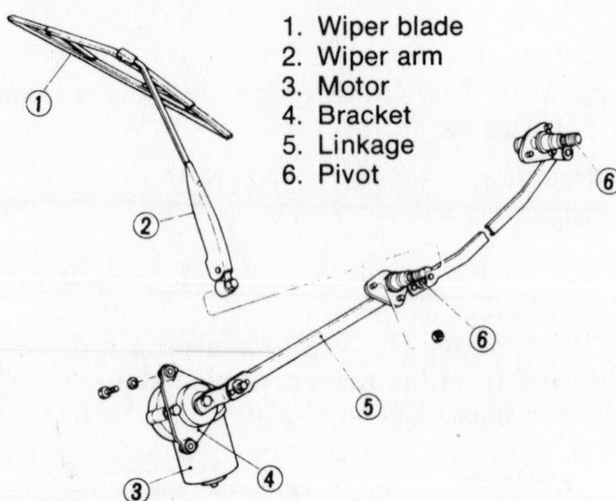

Windshield wiper motor and linkage—1975–79

4. Disconnect the wiper motor harness at the connector on the wiper motor body from under the instrument panel.
5. Remove the three retaining screws and pull the wiper motor outward and remove the motor from the vehicle.
6. Install the wiper motor and connect the harness.
7. Connect the linkage to the motor arm and then install the cowling.
8. The wiper arms should be installed so that the blades are 0.98 in. (25mm) above, and parallel to, the windshield molding. If the motor has been run, be sure the motor and linkage is in its parked position before installing the wiper arms. To do this, turn the ignition switch **ON**, and cycle the motor three or four times. Shut off the motor with the wiper switch (not the ignition switch), and allow the motor to return to the park position.

Wiper Linkage

REMOVAL AND INSTALLATION

1. Remove the wiper blade and arm from the pivot. See the preceding section.
2. Remove the cowl top grille.
3. Remove the two flange nuts retaining the wiper linkage pivot to the cowl top.

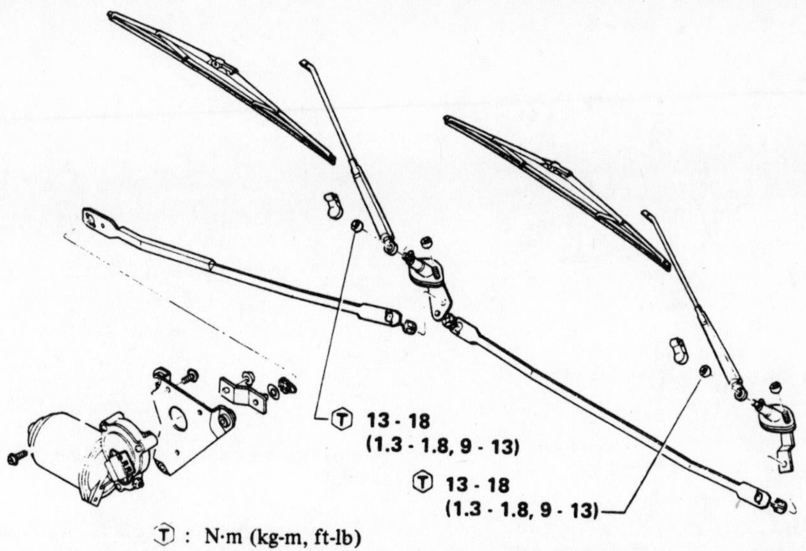

Windshield wiper motor and linkage—1980–86 (720-D series)

4. Remove the stop ring which retains the connecting rod to the wiper motor arm.
5. Remove the wiper motor linkage assembly from the truck.
6. Install the linkage in the reverse order of removal.

Rear Wiper

REMOVAL AND INSTALLATION

Pathfinder

1. Disconnect the negative battery cable.
2. Pop up the acorn nut cover, remove the nut and pull off the rear wiper.
3. Remove the pivot nut.
4. Inside, pop out the 4 clips and remove the wiper motor cover.
5. Disconnect the electrical lead and the washer hose, remove the mounting bolts and lift out the wiper motor.
6. Position the wiper motor and install the mounting bolts.
7. Connect the lead and the washer hose.
8. Position the wiper motor cover over the opening and press in the retaining clips.
9. Install the pivot nut.
10. Install the wiper arm and tighten the acorn nut. Connect the battery cable.

INSTRUMENT AND SWITCHES

Instrument Cluster

REMOVAL AND INSTALLATION

1970-79

1. Disconnect the negative battery cable.
2. Working through the openings of the instrument cluster cover, remove the screws retaining the cluster cover to the instrument panel and remove the cover.
3. From underneath the instrument panel, remove the screw retaining the cluster assembly to the lower instrument panel.
4. Withdraw the cluster lid slightly. Press the windshield wiper control knob in, turn it counterclockwise and pull it off the switch. Remove the headlight/parking light switch knob in the same manner.
5. From behind the instrument cluster, disconnect the speedometer cable at the speedometer head and the multiple connector from the printed circuit.
6. On vehicles with a clock, disconnect the wires at each connection on the instrument panel printed circuit.
7. Remove the screws retaining the cluster assembly to the cluster lid.
8. Remove the instrument cluster assembly from under the instrument panel.
9. Install the instrument cluster into the instrument panel and tighten the cluster-to-lid screws.
10. Connect the clock, speedometer cable and multi-connector.
11. Install the headlight and windshield wiper control knobs.
12. Tighten the cluster-to-panel retaining screws and then reconnect the battery cable.

1980-86

1. Disconnect the negative battery cable.
2. Remove the cluster lid.
3. Remove the cluster assembly.
4. Remove the gauges from the cluster, individually.

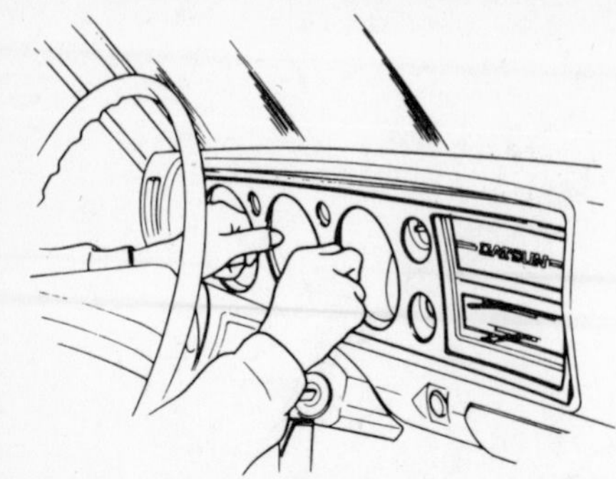

Removing the instrument cluster lid—1970–79

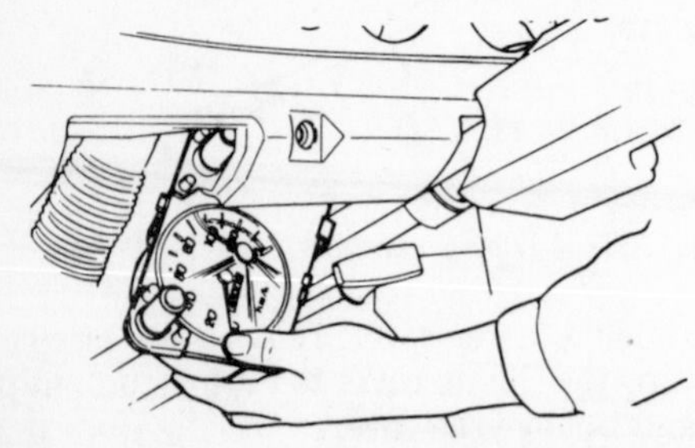

Remove the instrument cluster from under the panel—1970–79

Removing the instrument cluster lid—1980–86 (720-D series)

5. Installation the into the cluster and then position the cluster in the instrument panel.

6. Install the cluster lid and connect the battery cable.

Windshield Wiper Switch

REMOVAL AND INSTALLATION

1970-79

1. Disconnect the negative battery cable.
2. Press the wiper control knob in and turn it counterclockwise. Remove the switch.

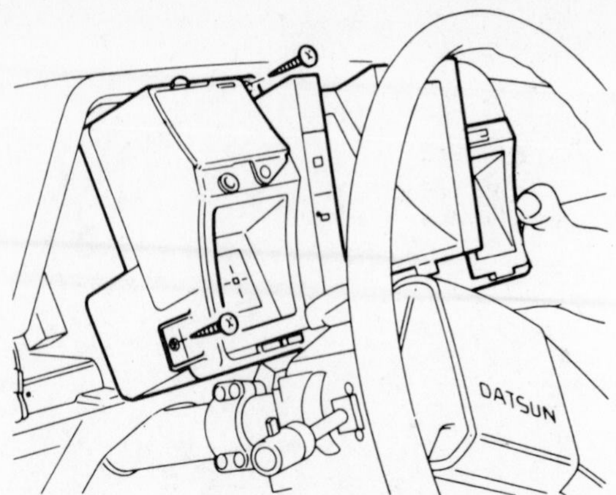

Removing the instrument cluster—1980–86 (720-D series)

3. Install the wiper control knob and connect the battery cable.

1980-89

1. Disconnect the negative battery cable.
2. Pry out the horn pad and remove the steering wheel.
3. Remove the terminals from the connector.
4. Slide the switch assembly off the steering column.
5. Install the switch on the steering column and connect the electrical leads.
6. Press the steering wheel onto the column and install the horn pad.

Headlight Switch

REMOVAL AND INSTALLATION

1970-79

1. Disconnect the negative battery cable.
2. Press the headlight control knob in and turn it counterclockwise. Remove the switch.
3. Install the headlight control knob and connect the battery cable.

1980-89

1. Disconnect the negative battery cable.
2. Pry out the horn pad and remove the steering wheel.
3. Remove the terminals from the connector.
4. Slide the switch assembly off the steering column.
5. Install the switch on the steering column and connect the electrical leads.
6. Press the steering wheel onto the column and install the horn pad.

Turn Signal/Combination Switch

REMOVAL AND INSTALLATION

All removal and installation procedures are detailed in Chapter 8.

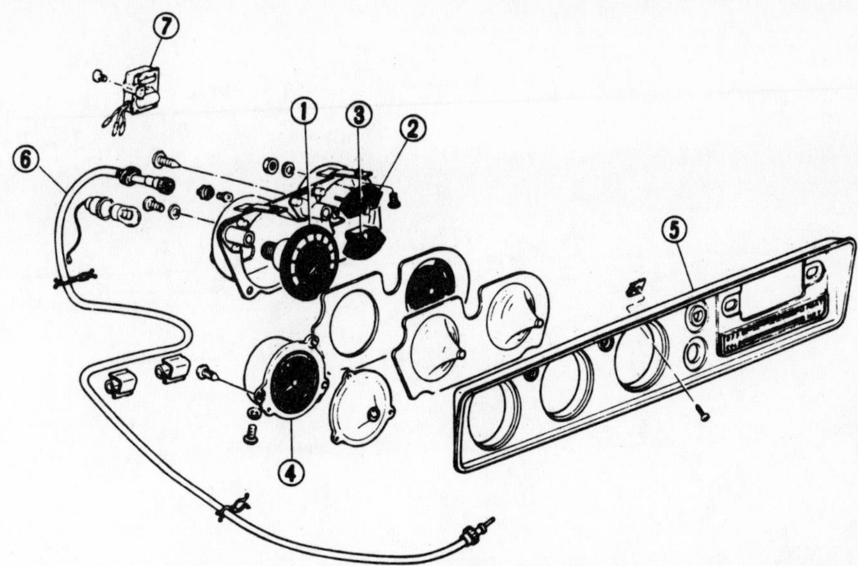

Exploded view of the instrument cluster—1970–79

Ignition Switch

REMOVAL AND INSTALLATION

All removal and installation procedures are detailed in Chapter 8.

Back-Up Light Switch

REMOVAL AND INSTALLATION

All removal and installation procedures are detailed in Chapter 7.

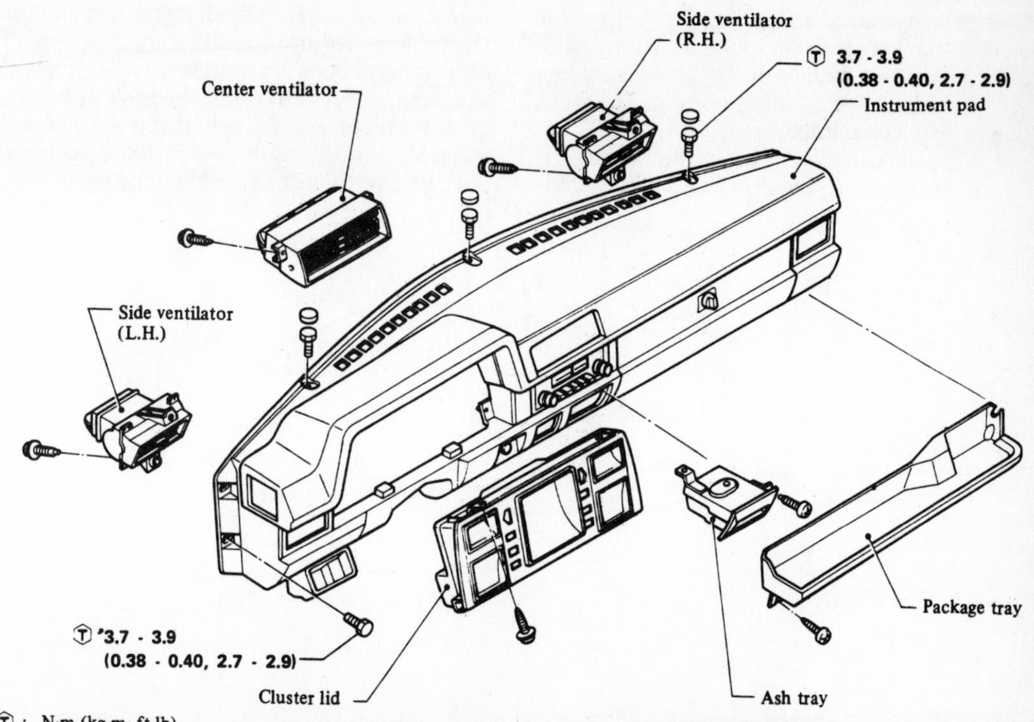

Exploded view of the instrument panel—1980–86 (720-D series)

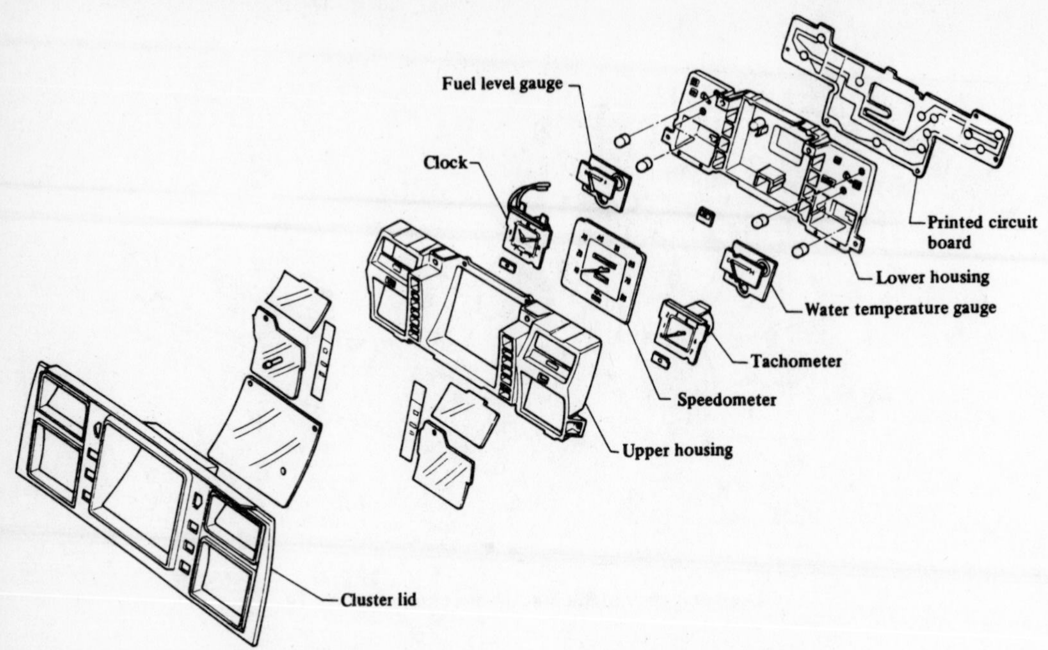

Exploded view of the instrument cluster—1980–86 (720-D series)

Speedometer Cable

REPLACEMENT

1. Reach up under the instrument panel and disconnect the cable housing from the back of the speedometer. It is attached by a knurled knob which simply unscrews. On many later models, the speedometer cable is connected to the speedometer by means of a press-fit. When you remove the combination meter (cluster), they simply come unplugged.

2. Pull the cable from the cable housing. If the cable is broken, the other half of the cable will have to be removed from the transmission end. Unscrew the retaining knob and remove the cable from the transmission extension housing.

3. Lubricate the cable with graphite powder (sold as speedometer cable lubricant, curiously enough) and feed the cable into the housing. It is best to start at the speedometer end and feed the cable down towards the transmission. It is also usually necessary to unscrew the transmission connection and install the cable end to the gear, then reconnect the housing to the transmission. Slip the cable end into the speedometer, and reconnect the cable housing.

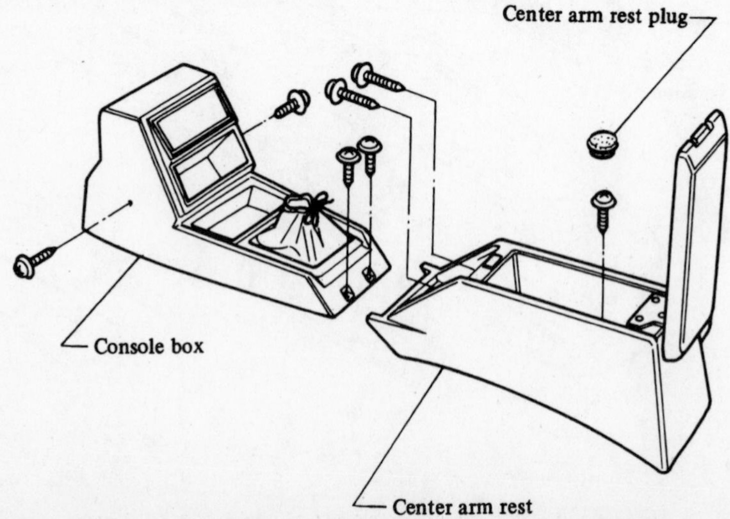

Center console and armrest removal and installation—1970–86

LIGHTING

Headlights

REMOVAL AND INSTALLATION

1. Remove the radiator grille retaining screws and remove the radiator grille (if necessary).
2. Loosen and remove, if necessary, the retaining ring screws. Do not disturb the aiming adjusting screws.
3. Remove the retaining ring. On round headlamp systems, rotate the ring clockwise to remove it.
4. Remove the headlight from the mounting ring and disconnect the electrical connector from behind the light.
5. Change the headlight and connect the wiring connector to the new light.
6. Place the headlight in position so that the three locating tabs behind the light fit in the three holes on the mounting ring.

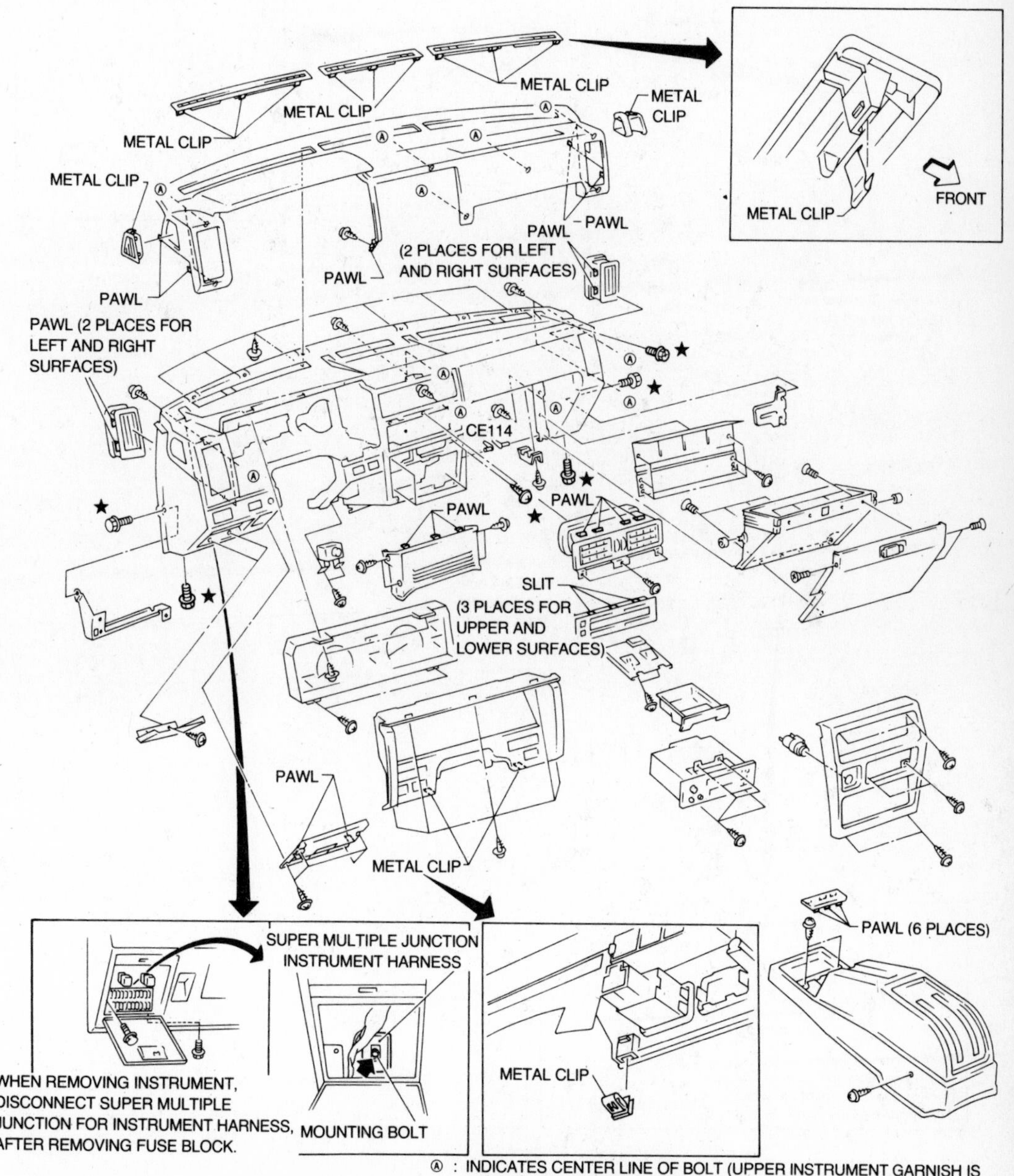

Exploded view of the instrument panel—1986–89 (D21-D series)

7. Install the headlight retaining ring and tighten the retaining screws.
8. Install the radiator grille.

Signal And Marker Lights

REMOVAL AND INSTALLATION

Front Turn Signal And Parking Lights

1. Remove turn signal/parking light lens with retaining screws.
2. Slightly depress the bulb and turn it counterclockwise to release it.
3. To install the bulb, carefully push down and turn bulb clockwise at the same time.
4. Install the turn signal/parking light lens with retaining screws.

Side Marker Lights

1. Remove side marker light lens with retaining screws.
2. Turn the bulb socket counterclockwise to release it from lens.

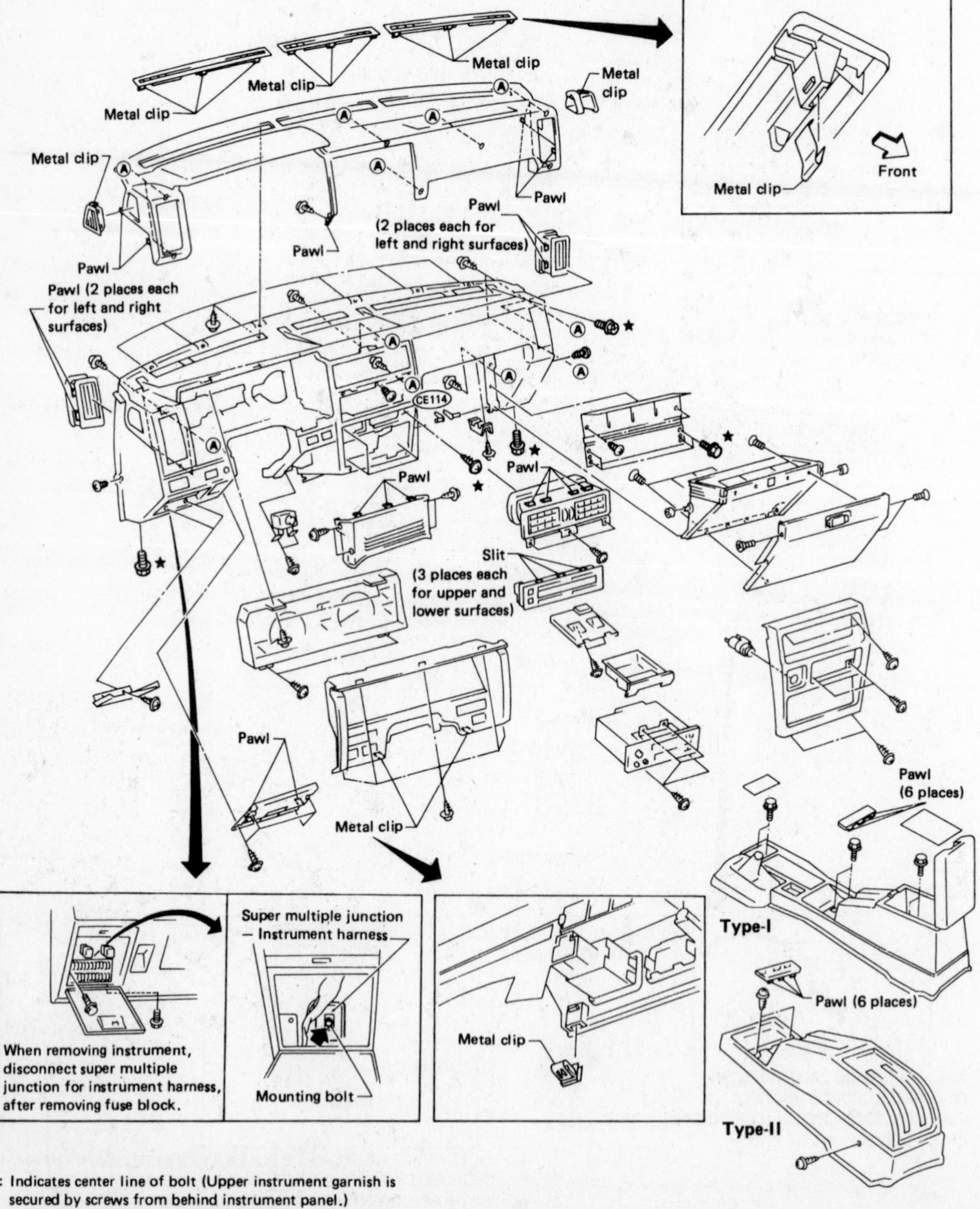

Exploded view of the instrument cluste—1986–89 (D21-D series)

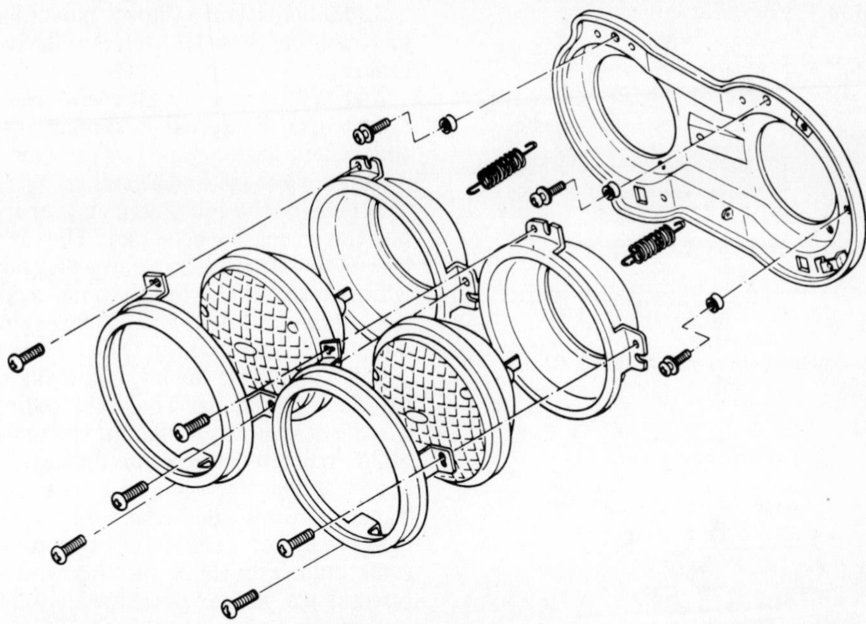

Headlamp assembly—1970–79

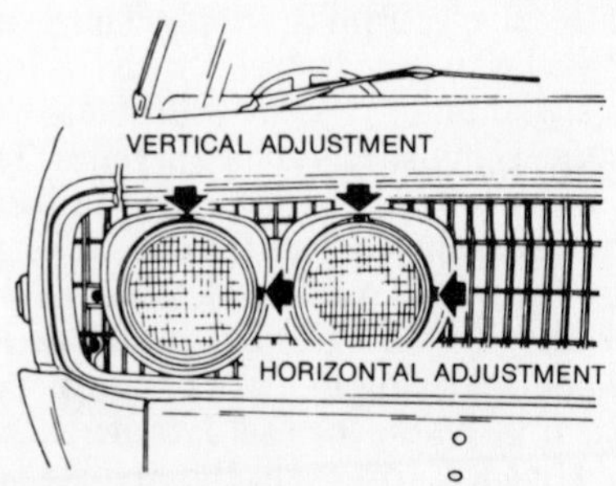

Headlamp adjustment screws—1970–79

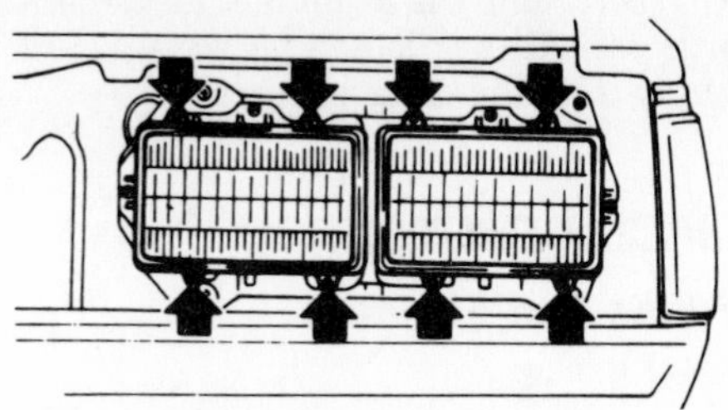

Headlamp retaining screws—1980–86 (720-D series)

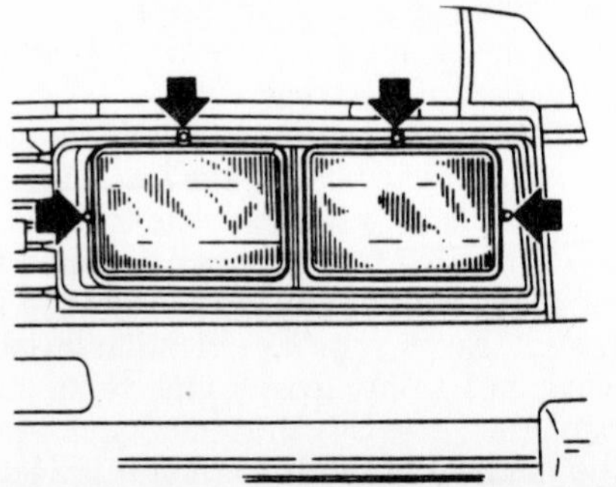

Headlamp adjusting screws—1980–86 (720-D series)

3. Pull bulb straight out.
4. To install the bulb, carefully push straight in.
5. Turn the bulb socket clockwise to install it in lens.
6. Install the side marker light lens with retaining screws.

Rear Turn Signal, Brake And Parking Lights

1. Remove rear trim panel if necessary to gain access to the bulb socket.
2. Slightly depress the bulb and turn it counterclockwise to release it.
3. To install the bulb, carefully push down and turn the bulb clockwise at the same time.
4. Install the trim panel if necessary.

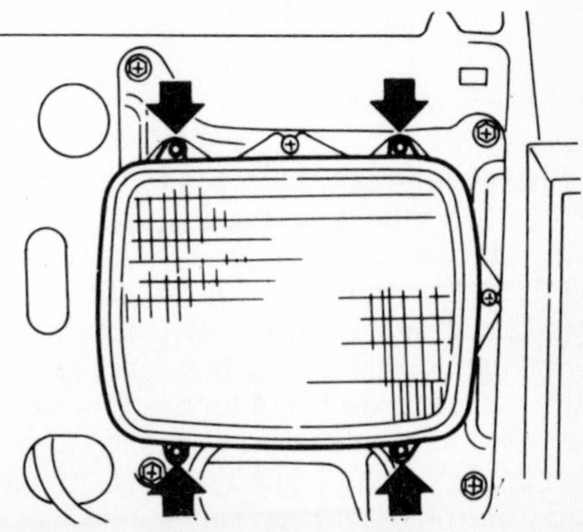

Headlamp retaining screws—1986–89 (D21-D series)

Headlamp adjusting screws—1986–89 (D21-D series)

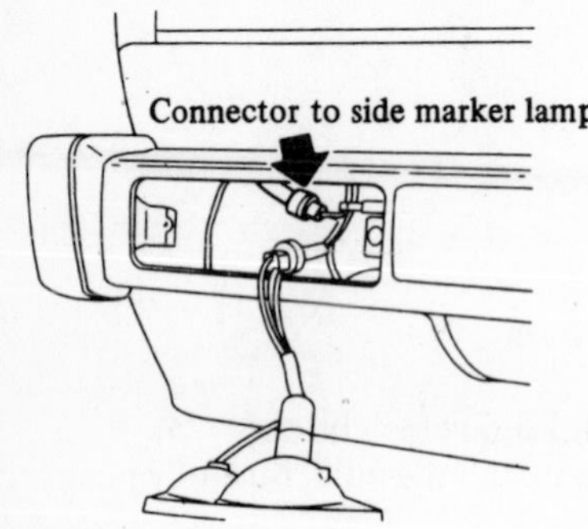

Removing the front turn signal

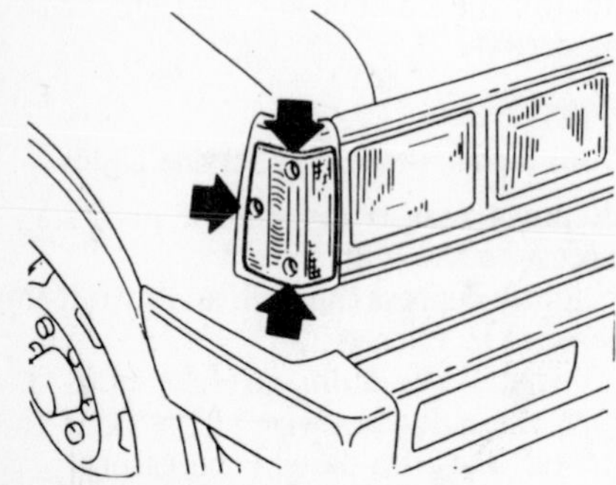

Removing the front side marker lamp

TRAILER WIRING

Wiring the truck for towing is fairly easy. There are a number of good wiring kits available and these should be used, rather than trying to design your own. All trailers will need brake lights and turn signals as well as tail lights and side marker lights. Most states require extra marker lights for overly wide trailers. Also, most states have recently required back-up lights for trailers, and most trailer manufacturers have been building trailers with back-up lights for several years.

Additionally, some Class I, most Class II and just about all Class III trailers will have electric brakes.

Add to this number an accessories wire, to operate trailer internal equipment or to charge the trailer's battery, and you can have as many as seven wires in the harness.

Determine the equipment on your trailer and buy the wiring kit necessary. The kit will contain all the wires needed, plus a plug adapter set which included the female plug, mounted on the bumper or hitch, and the male plug, wired into, or plugged into the trailer harness.

When installing the kit, follow the manufacturer's instructions. The color coding of the wires is standard throughout the industry.

One point to note, some domestic vehicles, and most imported vehicles, have separate turn signals. On most domestic vehicles, the brake lights and rear turn signals operate with the same bulb. For those vehicles with separate turn signals, you can purchase an isolation unit so that the brake lights won't blink whenever the turn signals are operated, or, you can go to your local electronics supply house and buy four diodes to wire in series with the brake and turn signal bulbs. Diodes will isolate the brake and turn signals. The choice is yours. The isolation units are simple and quick to install, but far more expensive than the diodes. The diodes, however, require more work to install properly, since they require the cutting of each bulb's wire and soldering in place of the diode.

One final point, the best kits are those with a spring loaded cover on the vehicle mounted socket. This cover prevents dirt and moisture from corroding the terminals. Never let the vehicle socket hang loosely. Always mount it securely to the bumper or hitch.

CIRCUIT PROTECTION

Fuses And Flashers

FUSES

Fuses protect all the major electrical systems in the truck. In case of an electrical overload, the fuse melts, breaking the circuit and stopping the flow of electricity.

If a fuse blows, the cause should be investigated and corrected before the installation of a new fuse. This, however, is easier to say than to do. Because each fuse protects a limited number of components, your job is narrowed down somewhat. Begin your investigation by looking for obvious fraying, loose connections, breaks in insulation, etc. Use the techniques outlined at the beginning of this chapter. Electrical problems are almost always a real headache to

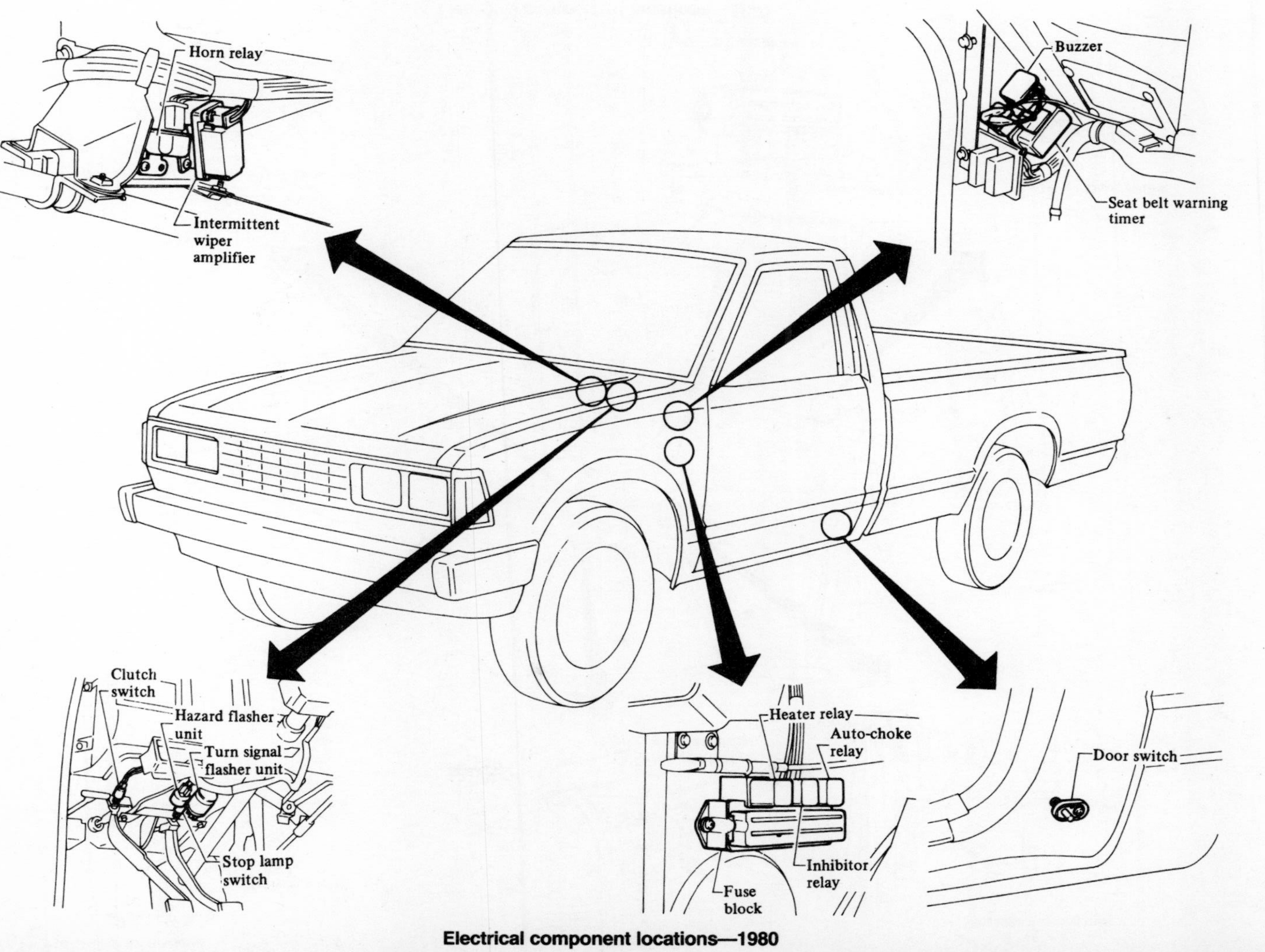

Electrical component locations—1980

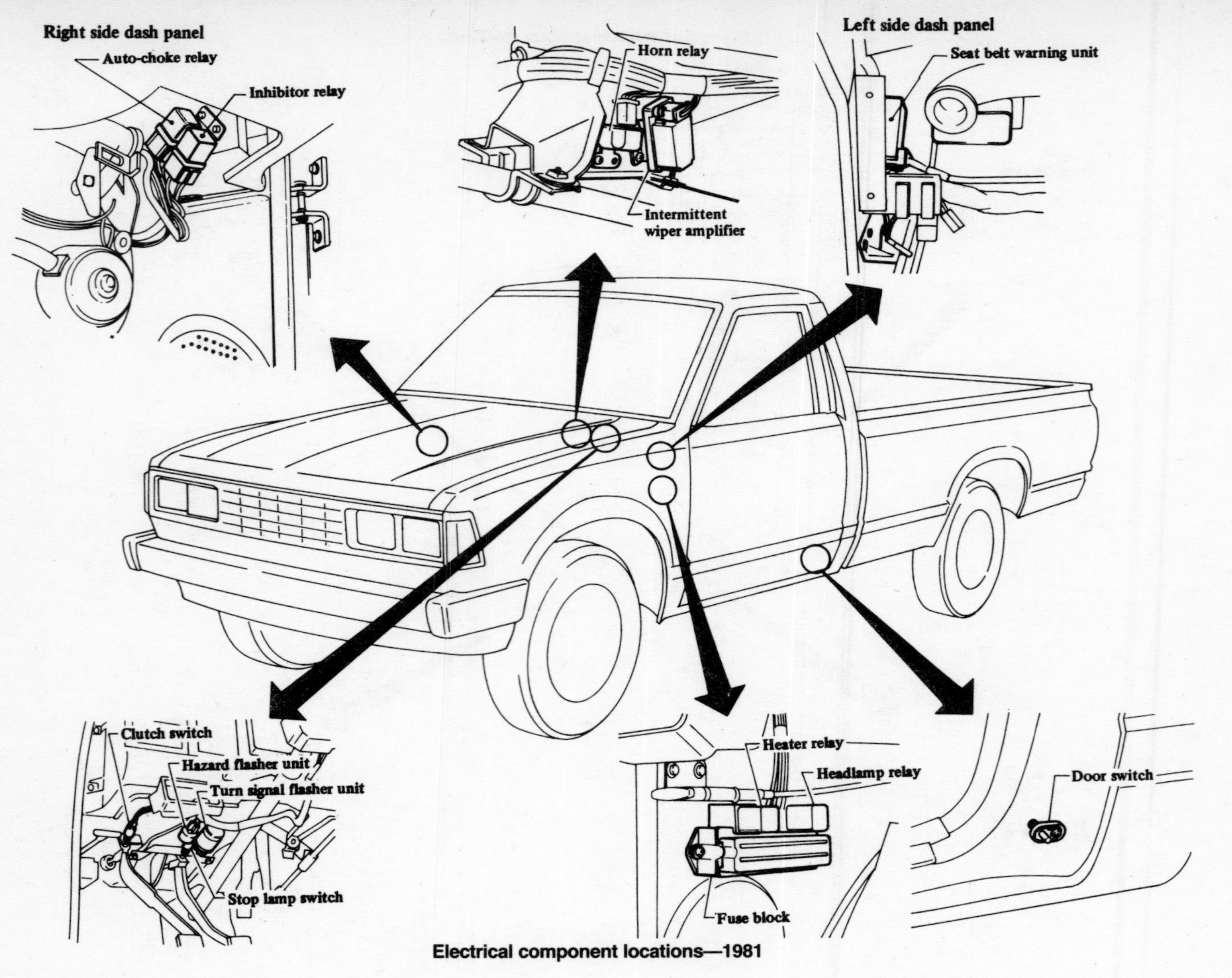

Electrical component locations—1981

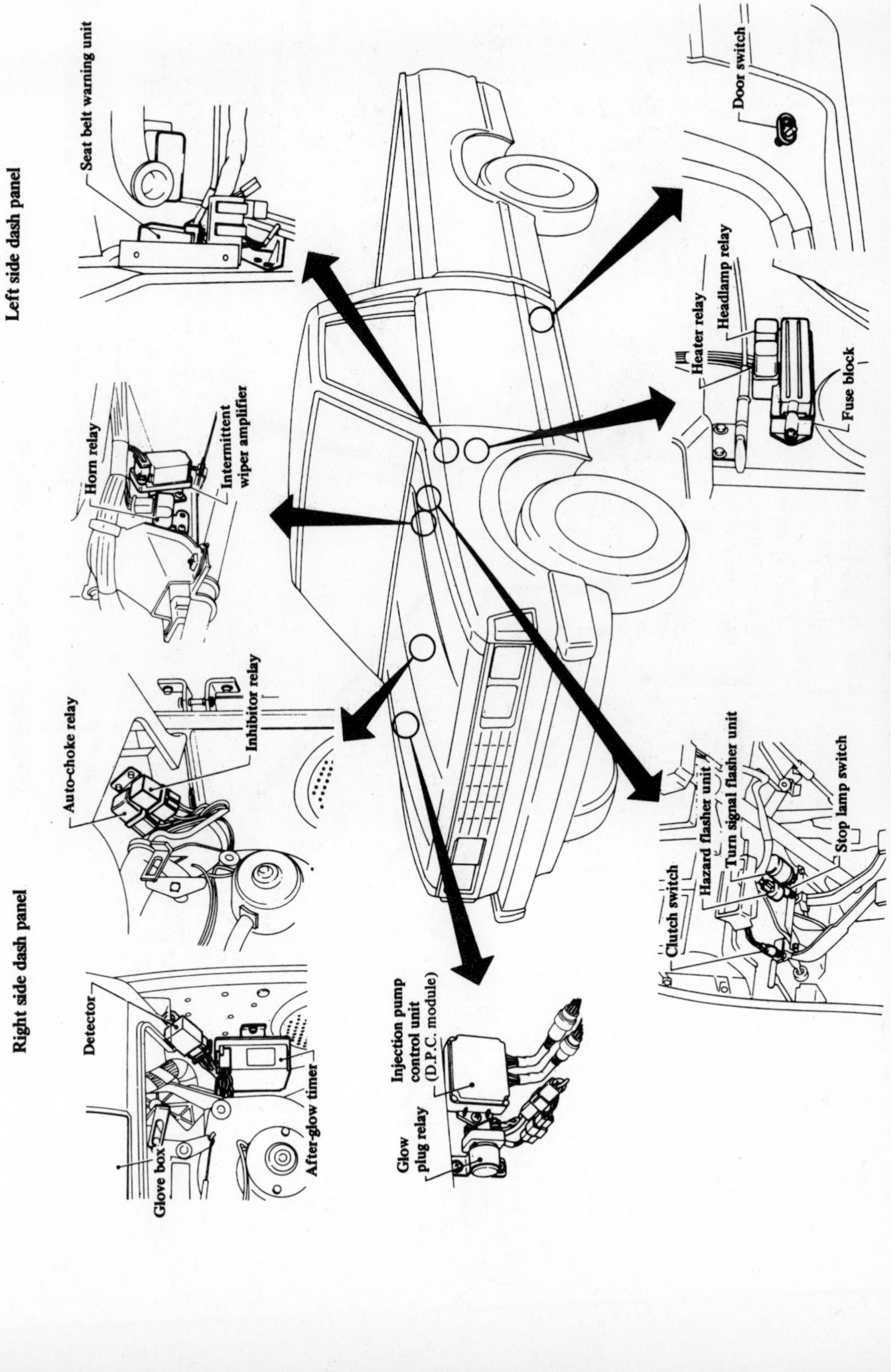

Left side dash panel

Seat belt warning unit

Horn relay

Intermittent wiper amplifier

Door switch

Heater relay

Headlamp relay

Fuse block

Right side dash panel

Auto-choke relay

Inhibitor relay

Detector

Glove box

After-glow timer

Glow plug relay

Injection pump control unit (D.P.C. module)

Clutch switch

Hazard flasher unit

Turn signal flasher unit

Stop lamp switch

Electrical component locations—1982

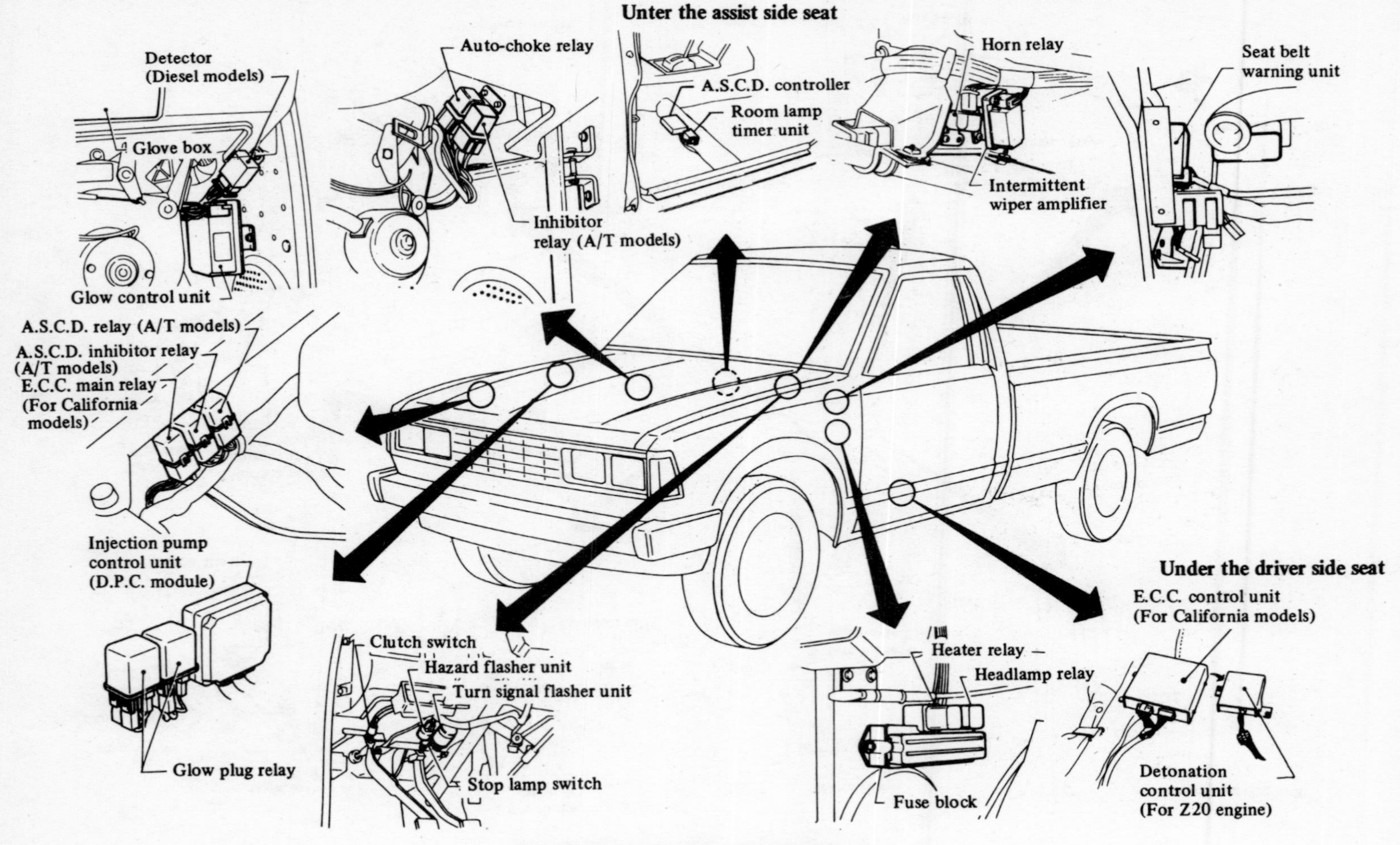

Electrical component locations—1983–84

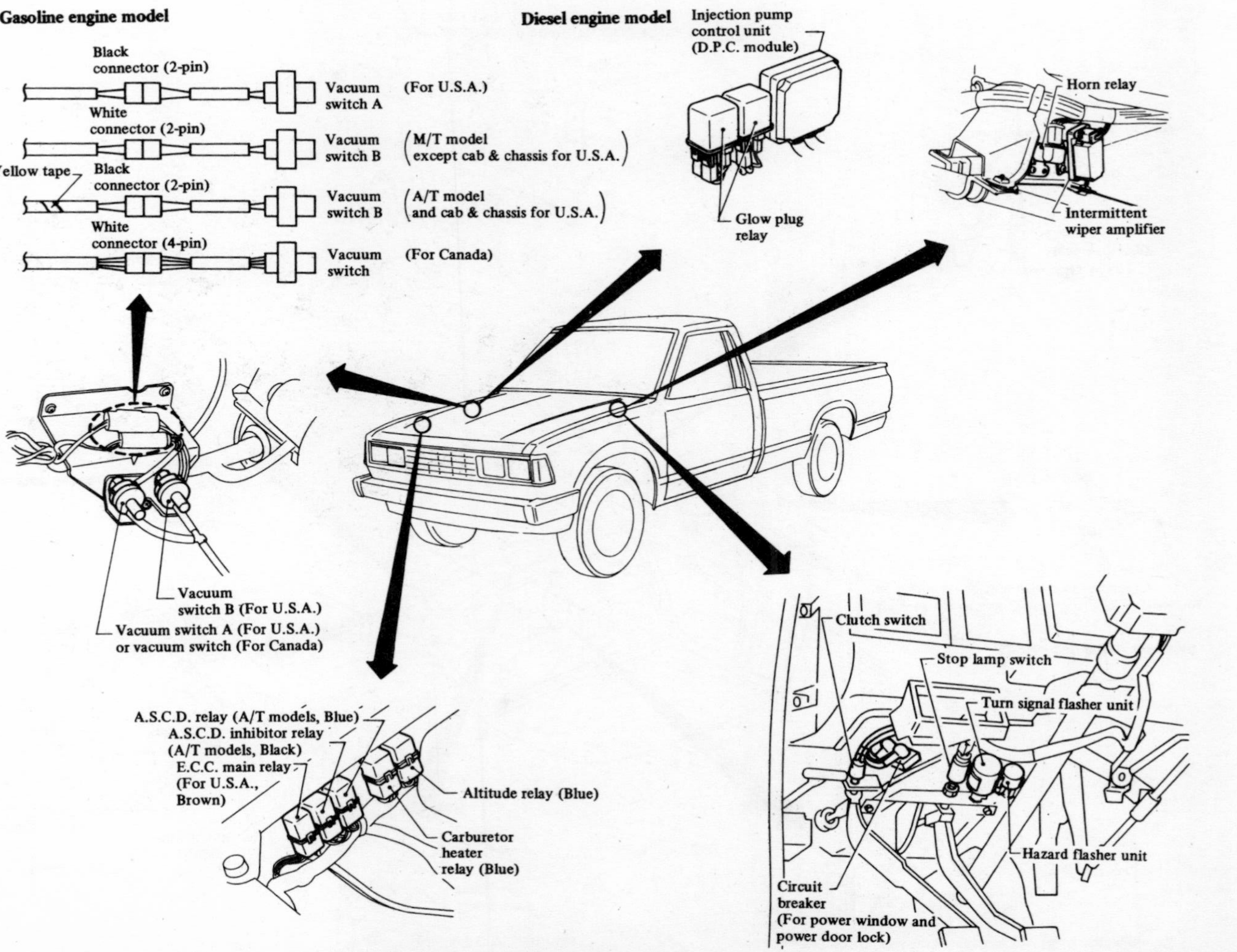

Electrical component locations—1985

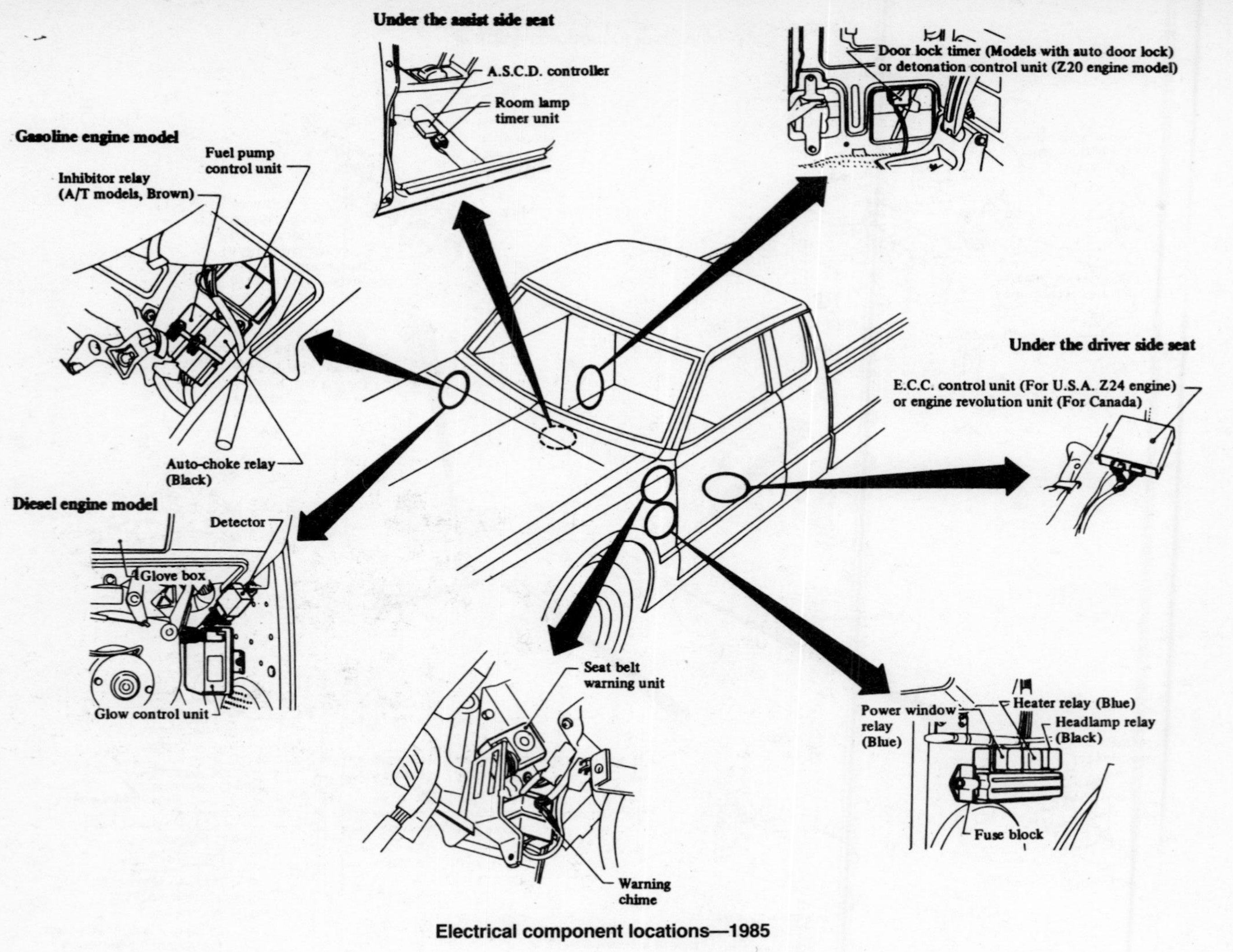

Electrical component locations—1985

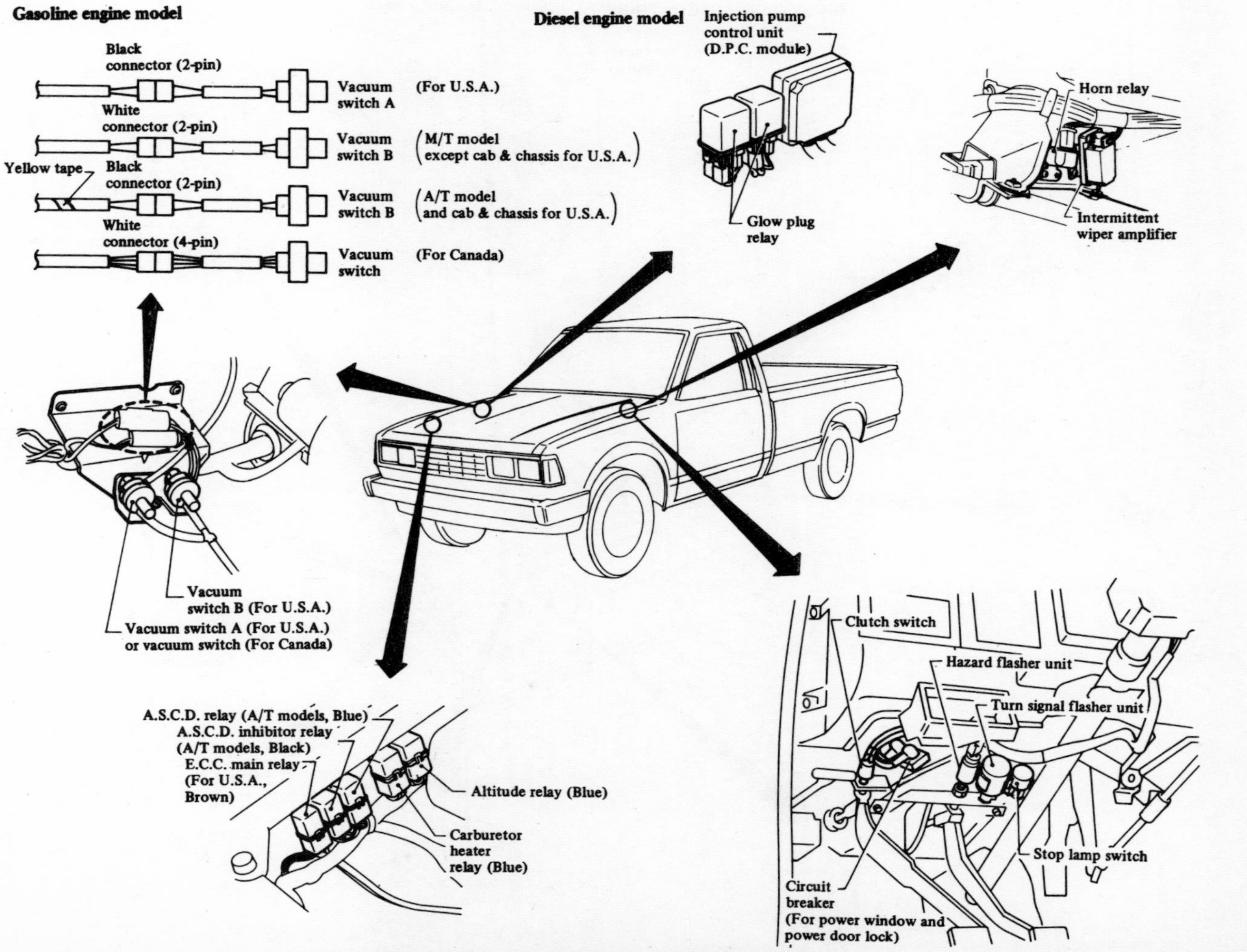

Electrical component locations—1986 (720-D series)

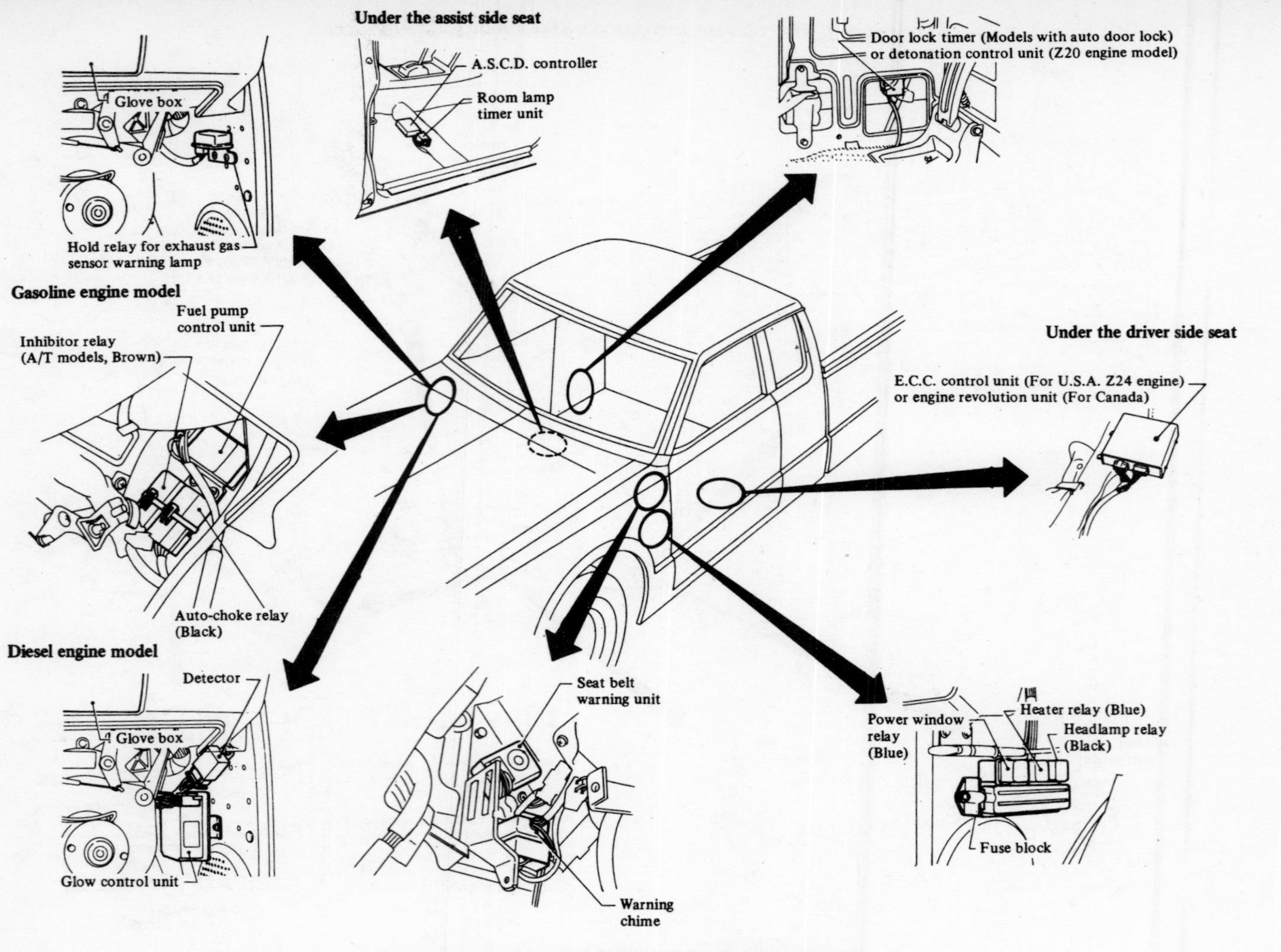

Electrical component locations—1986 (720-D series)

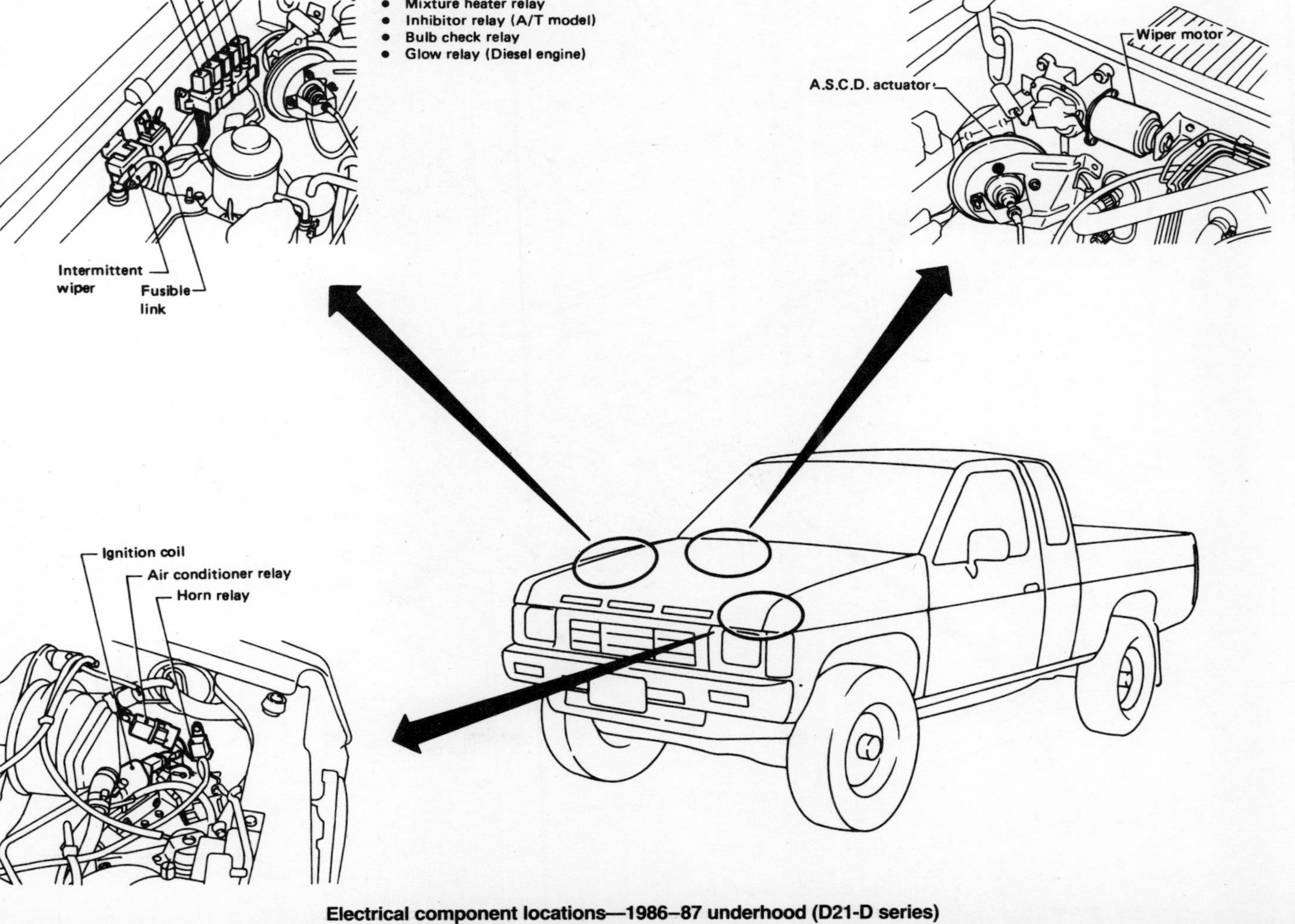

Electrical component locations—1986–87 underhood (D21-D series)

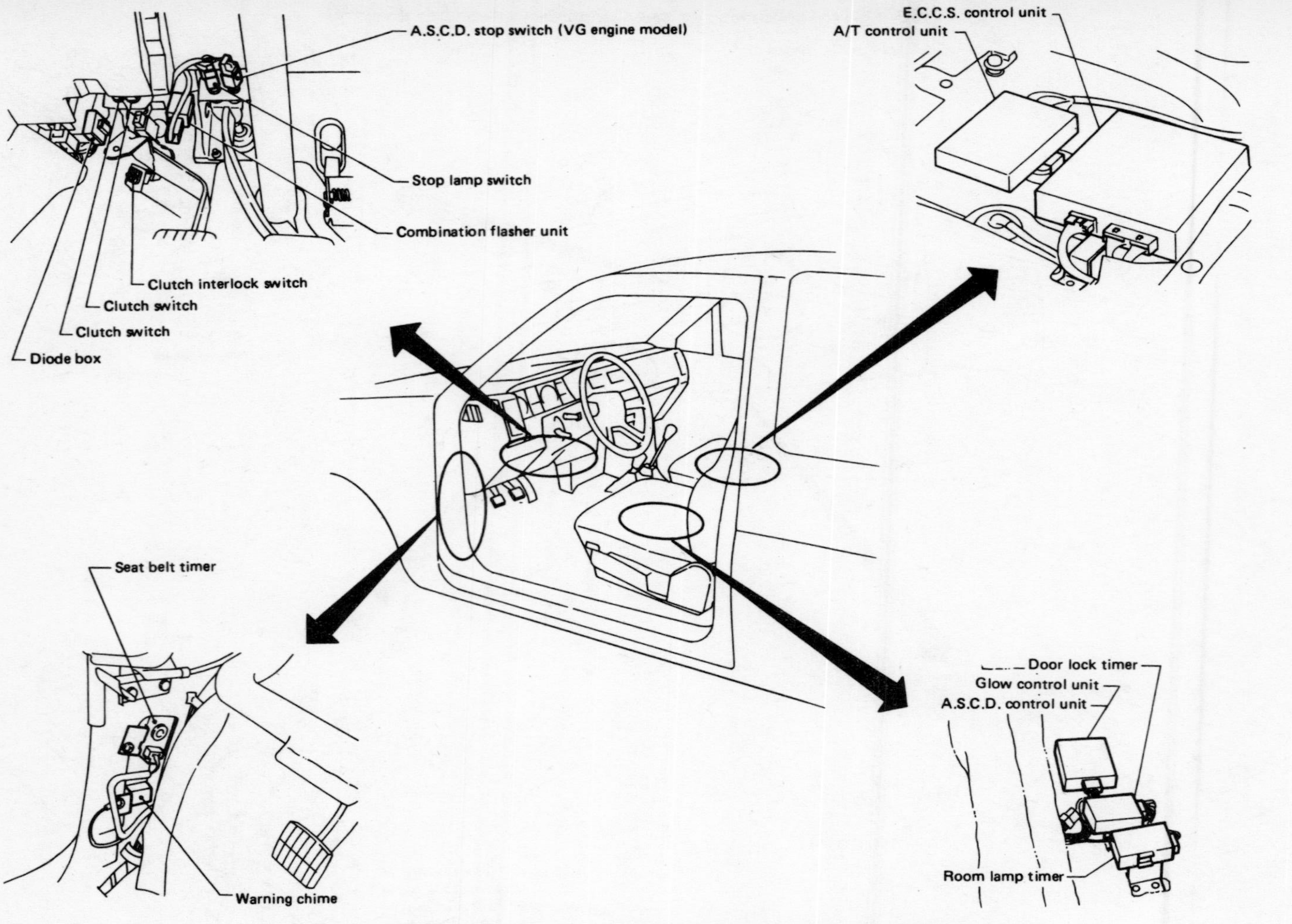

Electrical component locations—1986–87 passenger compartment (D21-D series)

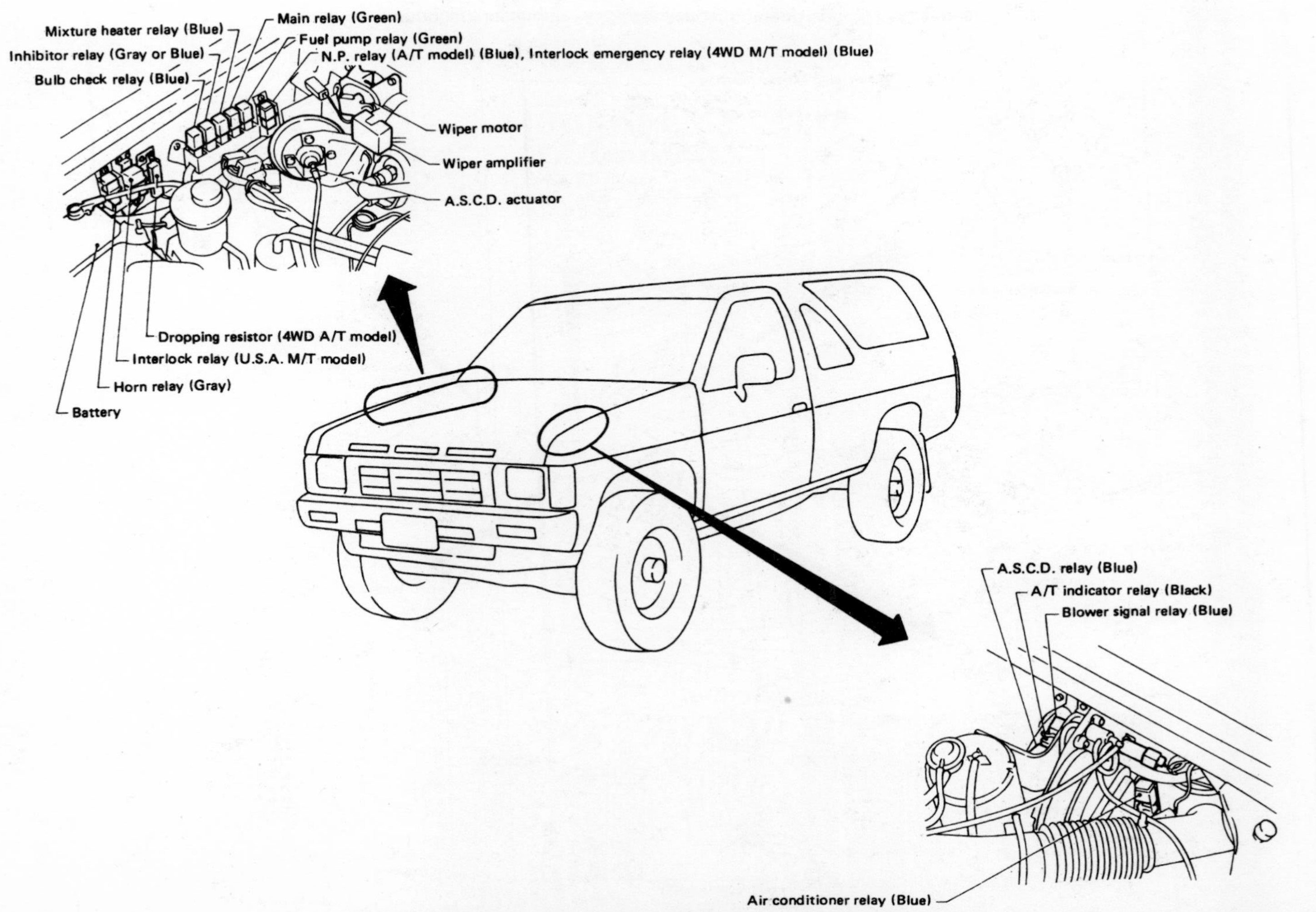

Electrical component locations—1986–87 underhood (D21-D series)

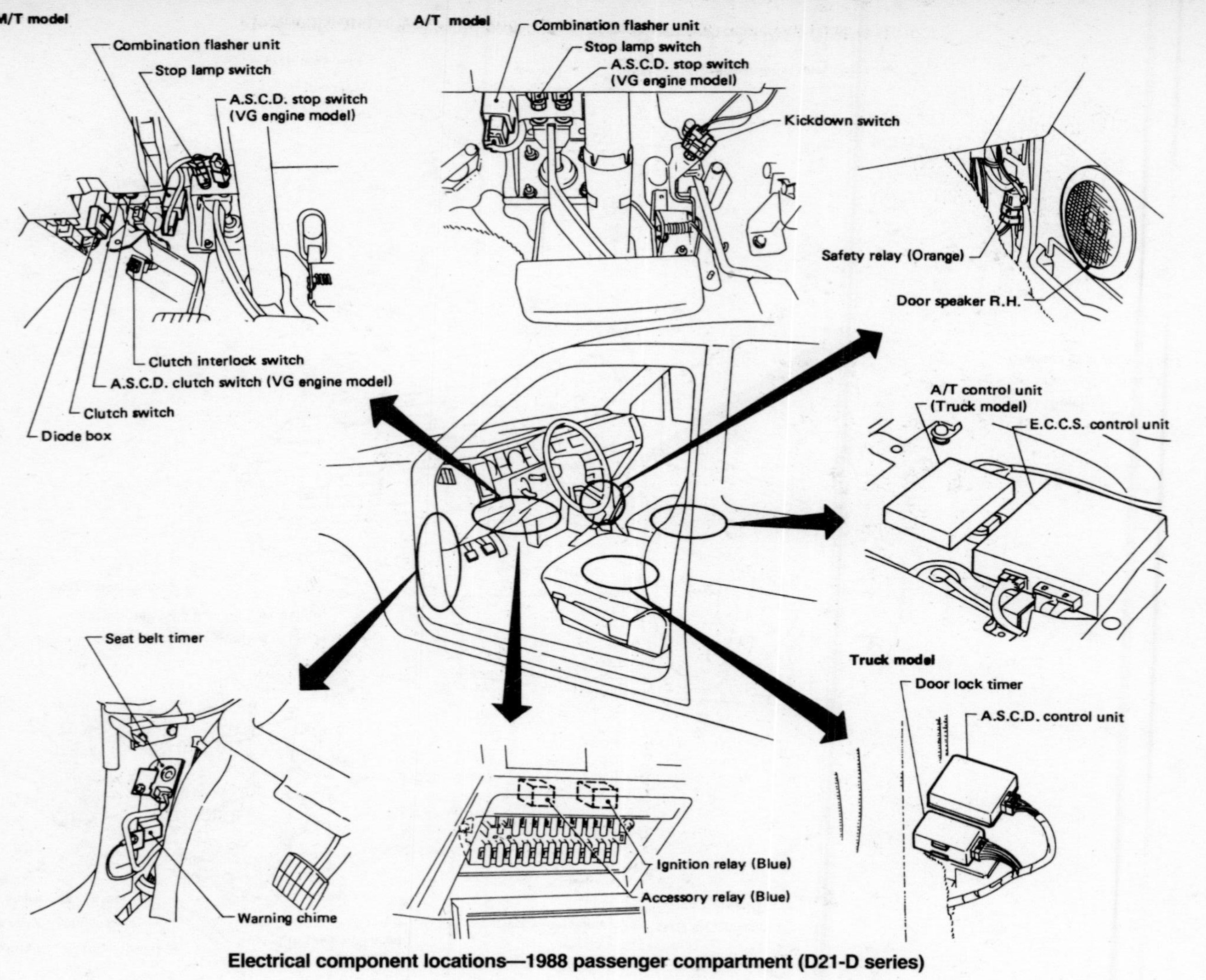

Electrical component locations—1988 passenger compartment (D21-D series)

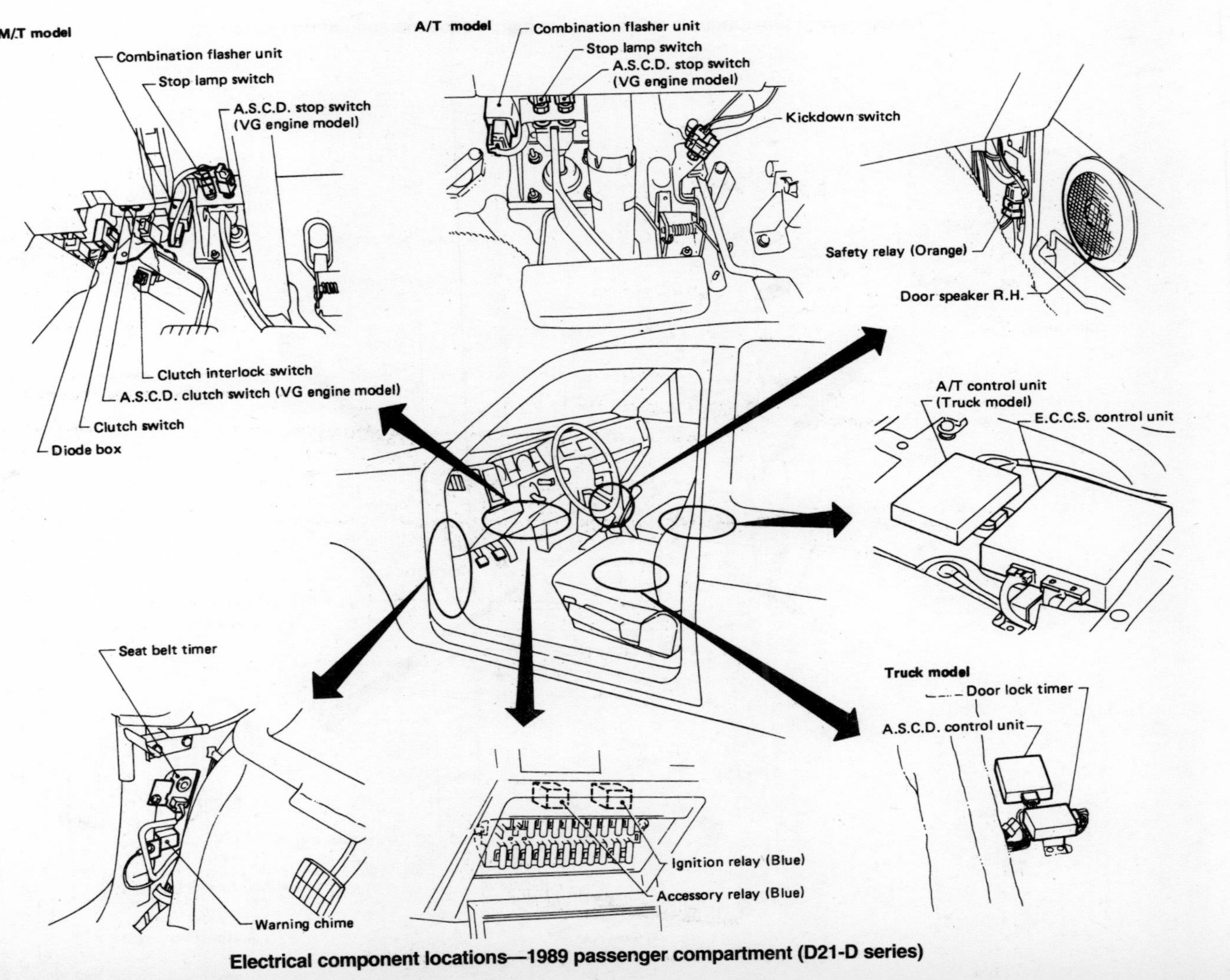

Electrical component locations—1989 passenger compartment (D21-D series)

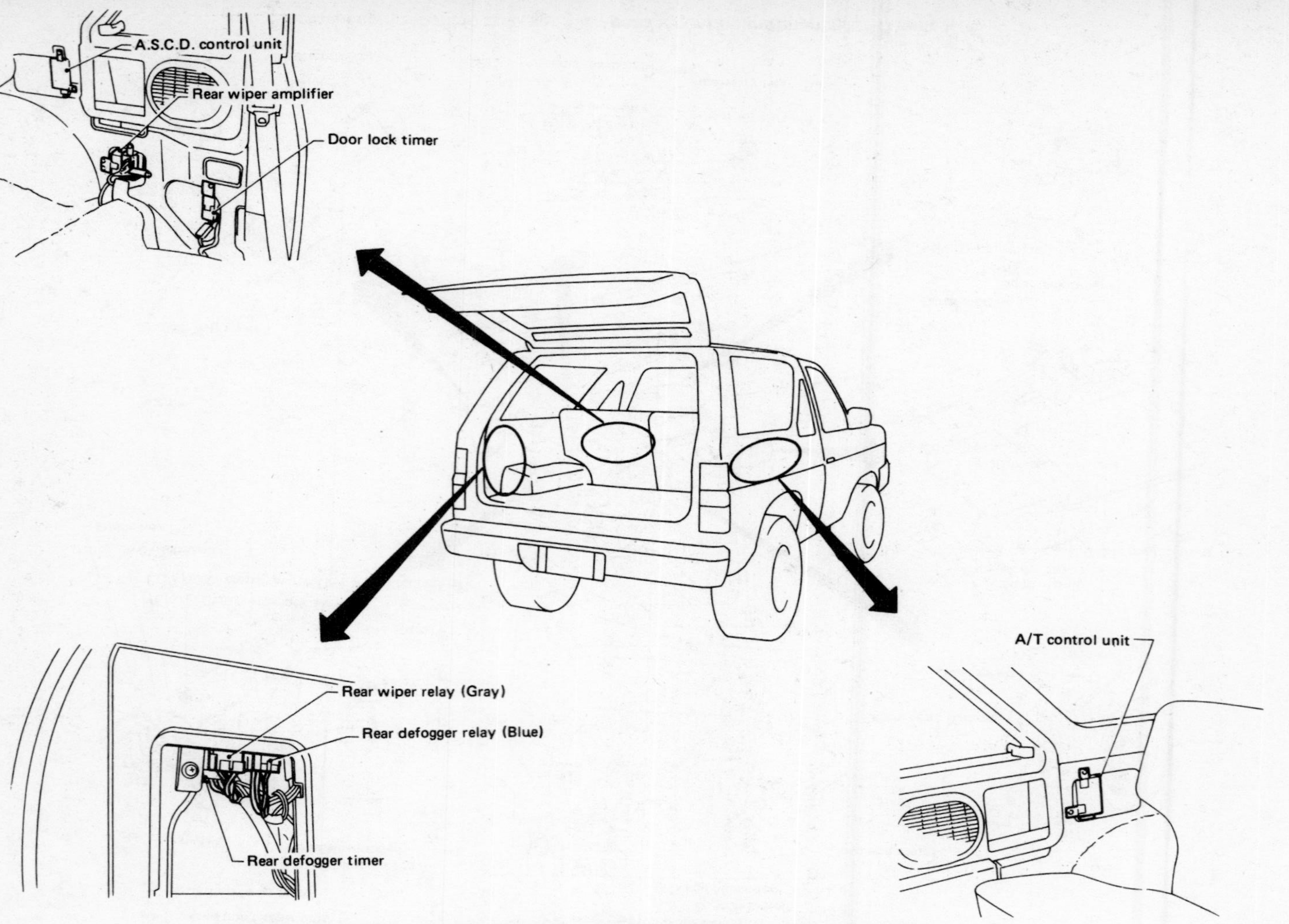

Electrical component locations—1988–89 passenger compartment (D21-D series)

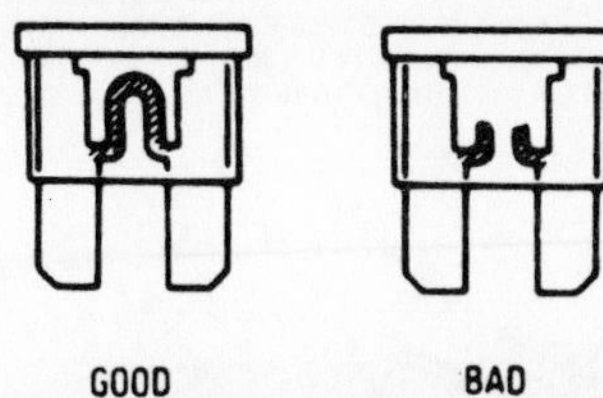

Always replace a bad fuse with one of equal amperage

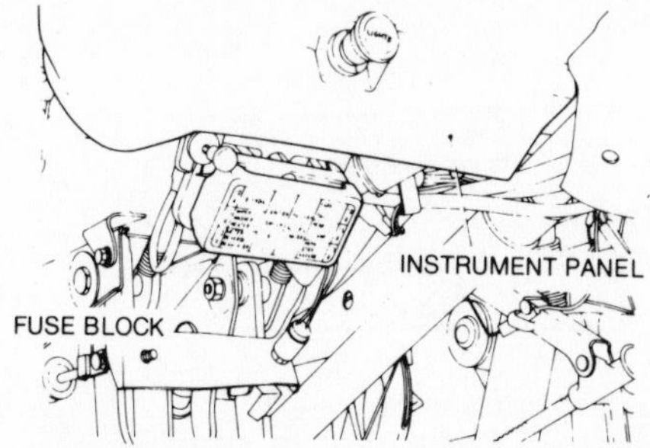

Fuse box location

solve, but patience and persistence, coupled with logic, usually provide a solution.

The amperage of each fuse and the circuit it protects are marked on the cover of the fuse box, which is located under the instrument panel next to the steering column on but 1970-71 trucks where the fuse box is in the engine compartment on the firewall.

NOTE: *NEVER USE A FUSE OF HIGHER AMPERAGE THAN RECOMMENDED!*

FLASHERS AND RELAYS

The turn signal and four-way hazard flashers are located under the instrument panel on opposite sides of the steering column. The turn signal flasher is the larger of the two. Replacement is made by unplugging the old flasher and plugging in the new one. Later model pick-ups may combine the two flashers into one.

Relays are used for the horn, headlights, wiper, heater, choke heater, catalyst floor sensor, air conditioner compressor, and transmission switches, although obviously not all relay are used on all models. All relays used are grouped together, and mounted on the right fender in the engine compartment.

Fusible Link

There is only one fusible link used on all 1972-86 pick-ups (620 and 720-D series) and that is the thinner of the two wires connected to the positive battery terminal. On 1986-89 D21-D series trucks there is also a brown one used in the headlight circuit, brown one used in the ignition switch, green one used in the power windows, brown one used in the EFI control unit and a brown one used with the EFI injector. Replacements are simply plugged into the connectors in this wire.

CAUTION: *Use only replacements of the same electrical capacity as the original, available from your dealer. Replacements of a different electrical value will not provide adequate system protection.*

NOTE: *1970-71 trucks (521 series) do not have a fusible link.*

FUSE LINK

The fuse link is a short length of special, Hypalon (high temperature) insulated wire, integral with the engine compartment wiring harness and should not be confused with standard wire. It is several wire gauges smaller than the circuit which protects. Under no circumstances should a fuse link replacement repair be made using a length of standard wire out from bulk stock or from another wiring harness.

To repair any blown fuse link use the following procedure:

1. Determine which circuit is damaged, its location and the cause of the open fuse link. If the damaged fuse link is one of three fed by a common No. 10 or 12 gauge feed wire, determine the specific affected circuit.
2. Disconnect the negative battery cable.

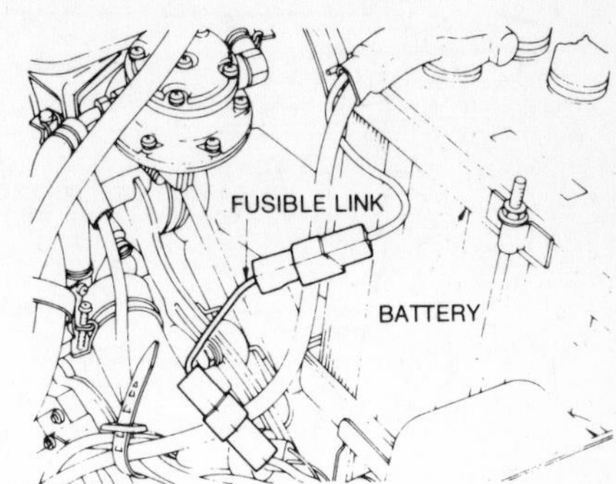

Fusible link

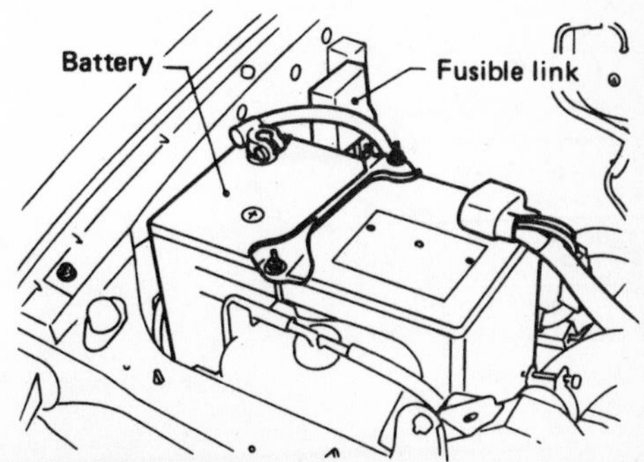

Fusible link

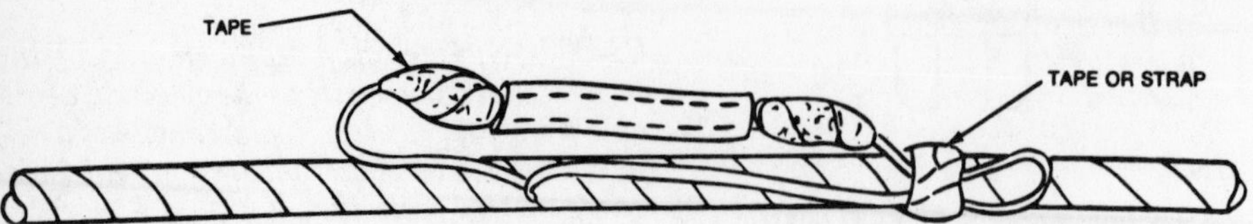

TYPICAL REPAIR USING THE SPECIAL #17 GA. (9.00" LONG-YELLOW) FUSE LINK REQUIRED FOR THE AIR/COND. CIRCUITS (2) #687E and #261A LOCATED IN THE ENGINE COMPARTMENT

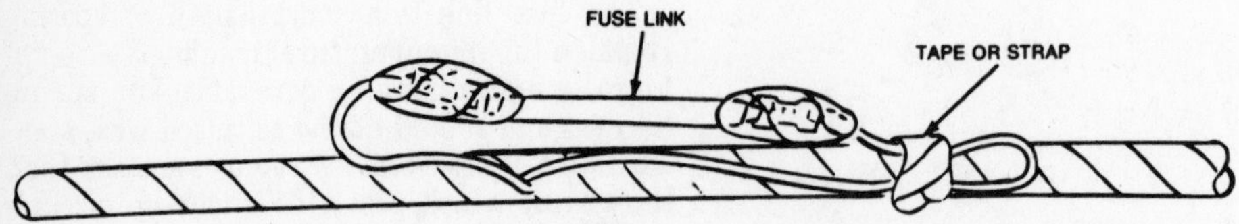

TYPICAL REPAIR FOR ANY IN-LINE FUSE LINK USING THE SPECIFIED GAUGE FUSE LINK FOR THE SPECIFIC CIRCUIT

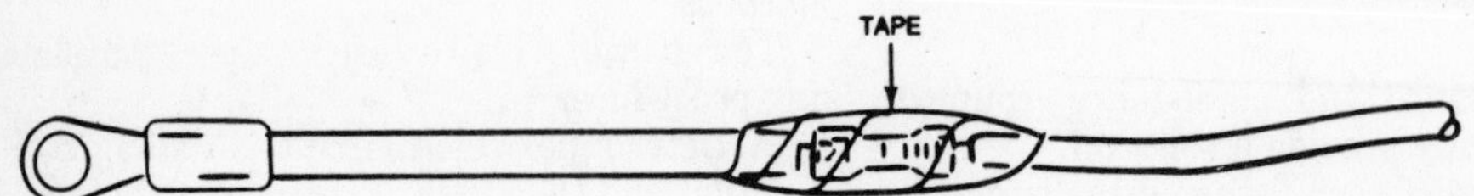

TYPICAL REPAIR USING THE EYELET TERMINAL FUSE LINK OF THE SPECIFIED GAUGE FOR ATTACHMENT TO A CIRCUIT WIRE END

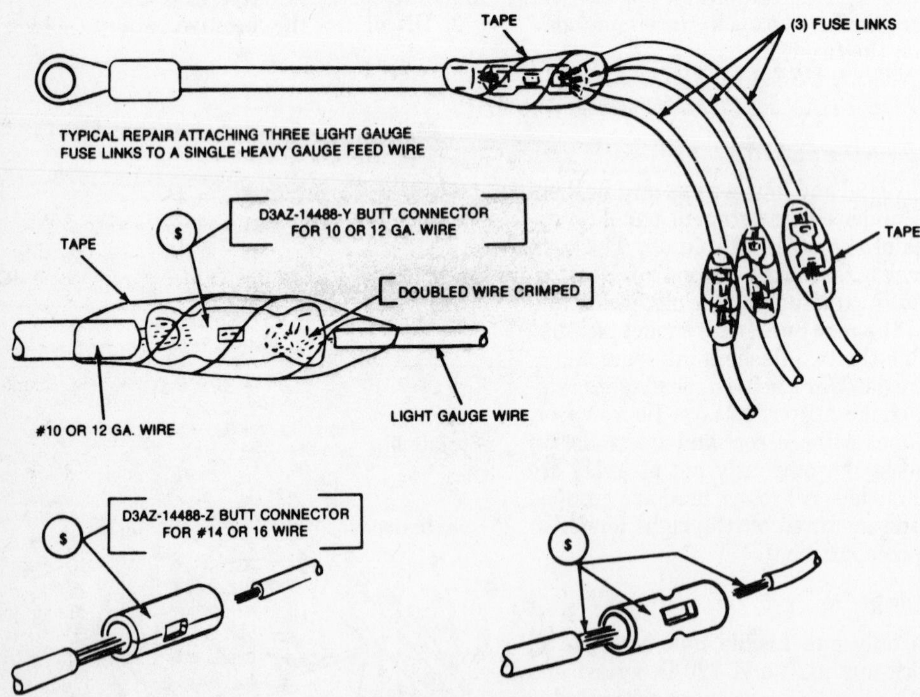

General fuse link repair procedure

Troubleshooting Basic Turn Signal and Flasher Problems

Most problems in the turn signals or flasher system, can be reduced to defective flashers or bulbs, which are easily replaced. Occasionally, problems in the turn signals are traced to the switch in the steering column, which will require professional service.
F = Front R = Rear • = Lights off ○ = Lights on

Problem	Solution
Turn signals light, but do not flash	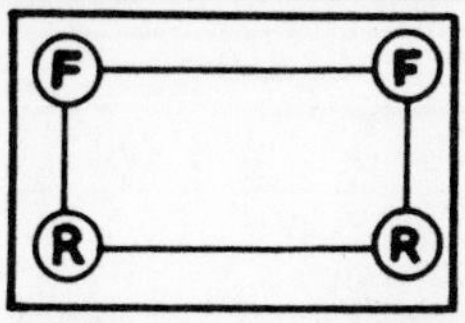 • Replace the flasher
No turn signals light on either side	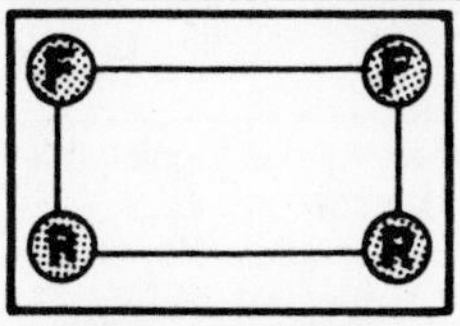 • Check the fuse. Replace if defective. • Check the flasher by substitution • Check for open circuit, short circuit or poor ground
Both turn signals on one side don't work	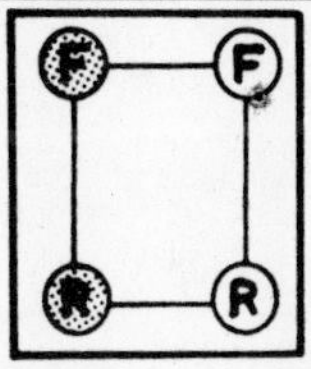 • Check for bad bulbs • Check for bad ground in both housings
One turn signal light on one side doesn't work	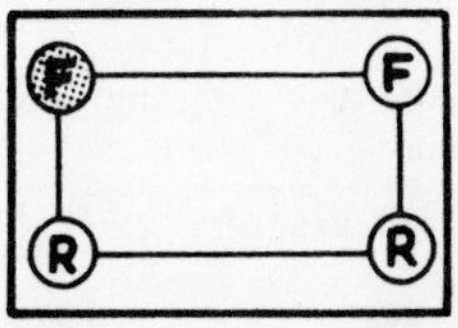 • Check and/or replace bulb • Check for corrosion in socket. Clean contacts. • Check for poor ground at socket
Turn signal flashes too fast or too slow	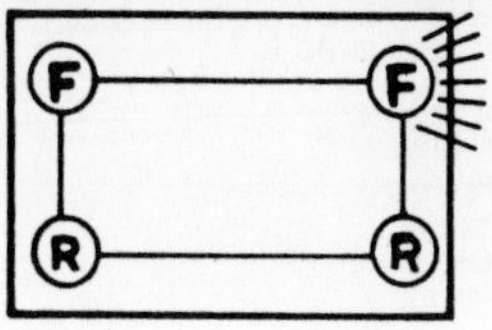 • Check any bulb on the side flashing too fast. A heavy-duty bulb is probably installed in place of a regular bulb. • Check the bulb flashing too slow. A standard bulb was probably installed in place of a heavy-duty bulb. • Check for loose connections or corrosion at the bulb socket
Indicator lights don't work in either direction	 • Check if the turn signals are working • Check the dash indicator lights • Check the flasher by substitution
One indicator light doesn't light	 • On systems with 1 dash indicator: See if the lights work on the same side. Often the filaments have been reversed in systems combining stoplights with taillights and turn signals. Check the flasher by substitution • On systems with 2 indicators: Check the bulbs on the same side Check the indicator light bulb Check the flasher by substitution

Troubleshooting Basic Lighting Problems

Problem	Cause	Solution
Lights		
One or more lights don't work, but others do	• Defective bulb(s) • Blown fuse(s) • Dirty fuse clips or light sockets • Poor ground circuit	• Replace bulb(s) • Replace fuse(s) • Clean connections • Run ground wire from light socket housing to car frame
Lights burn out quickly	• Incorrect voltage regulator setting or defective regulator • Poor battery/alternator connections	• Replace voltage regulator • Check battery/alternator connections
Lights go dim	• Low/discharged battery • Alternator not charging • Corroded sockets or connections • Low voltage output	• Check battery • Check drive belt tension; repair or replace alternator • Clean bulb and socket contacts and connections • Replace voltage regulator
Lights flicker	• Loose connection • Poor ground • Circuit breaker operating (short circuit)	• Tighten all connections • Run ground wire from light housing to car frame • Check connections and look for bare wires
Lights "flare"—Some flare is normal on acceleration—if excessive, see "Lights Burn Out Quickly"	• High voltage setting	• Replace voltage regulator
Lights glare—approaching drivers are blinded	• Lights adjusted too high • Rear springs or shocks sagging • Rear tires soft	• Have headlights aimed • Check rear springs/shocks • Check/correct rear tire pressure
Turn Signals		
Turn signals don't work in either direction	• Blown fuse • Defective flasher • Loose connection	• Replace fuse • Replace flasher • Check/tighten all connections
Right (or left) turn signal only won't work	• Bulb burned out • Right (or left) indicator bulb burned out • Short circuit	• Replace bulb • Check/replace indicator bulb • Check/repair wiring
Flasher rate too slow or too fast	• Incorrect wattage bulb • Incorrect flasher	• Flasher bulb • Replace flasher (use a variable load flasher if you pull a trailer)
Indicator lights do not flash (burn steadily)	• Burned out bulb • Defective flasher	• Replace bulb • Replace flasher
Indicator lights do not light at all	• Burned out indicator bulb • Defective flasher	• Replace indicator bulb • Replace flasher

Troubleshooting Basic Dash Gauge Problems

Problem	Cause	Solution
Coolant Temperature Gauge		
Gauge reads erratically or not at all	• Loose or dirty connections • Defective sending unit	• Clean/tighten connections • Bi-metal gauge: remove the wire from the sending unit. Ground the wire for an instant. If the gauge registers, replace the sending unit.
	• Defective gauge	• Magnetic gauge: disconnect the wire at the sending unit. With ignition ON gauge should register COLD. Ground the wire; gauge should register HOT.
Ammeter Gauge—Turn Headlights ON (do not start engine). Note reaction		
Ammeter shows charge	• Connections reversed on gauge	• Reinstall connections
Ammeter shows discharge	• Ammeter is OK	• Nothing
Ammeter does not move	• Loose connections or faulty wiring • Defective gauge	• Check/correct wiring • Replace gauge
Oil Pressure Gauge		
Gauge does not register or is inaccurate	• On mechanical gauge, Bourdon tube may be bent or kinked	• Check tube for kinks or bends preventing oil from reaching the gauge
	• Low oil pressure	• Remove sending unit. Idle the engine briefly. If no oil flows from sending unit hole, problem is in engine.
	• Defective gauge	• Remove the wire from the sending unit and ground it for an instant with the ignition ON. A good gauge will go to the top of the scale.
	• Defective wiring	• Check the wiring to the gauge. If it's OK and the gauge doesn't register when grounded, replace the gauge.
	• Defective sending unit	• If the wiring is OK and the gauge functions when grounded, replace the sending unit
All Gauges		
All gauges do not operate	• Blown fuse • Defective instrument regulator	• Replace fuse • Replace instrument voltage regulator
All gauges read low or erratically	• Defective or dirty instrument voltage regulator	• Clean contacts or replace
All gauges pegged	• Loss of ground between instrument voltage regulator and car • Defective instrument regulator	• Check ground • Replace regulator
Warning Lights		
Light(s) do not come on when ignition is ON, but engine is not started	• Defective bulb • Defective wire	• Replace bulb • Check wire from light to sending unit
	• Defective sending unit	• Disconnect the wire from the sending unit and ground it. Replace the sending unit if the light comes on with the ignition ON.
Light comes on with engine running	• Problem in individual system • Defective sending unit	• Check system • Check sending unit (see above)

Troubleshooting the Heater

Problem	Cause	Solution
Blower motor will not turn at any speed	• Blown fuse • Loose connection • Defective ground • Faulty switch • Faulty motor • Faulty resistor	• Replace fuse • Inspect and tighten • Clean and tighten • Replace switch • Replace motor • Replace resistor
Blower motor turns at one speed only	• Faulty switch • Faulty resistor	• Replace switch • Replace resistor
Blower motor turns but does not circulate air	• Intake blocked • Fan not secured to the motor shaft	• Clean intake • Tighten security
Heater will not heat	• Coolant does not reach proper temperature • Heater core blocked internally • Heater core air-bound • Blend-air door not in proper position	• Check and replace thermostat if necessary • Flush or replace core if necessary • Purge air from core • Adjust cable
Heater will not defrost	• Control cable adjustment incorrect • Defroster hose damaged	• Adjust control cable • Replace defroster hose

Troubleshooting Basic Windshield Wiper Problems

Problem	Cause	Solution
Electric Wipers		
Wipers do not operate— Wiper motor heats up or hums	• Internal motor defect • Bent or damaged linkage • Arms improperly installed on linking pivots	• Replace motor • Repair or replace linkage • Position linkage in park and reinstall wiper arms
Wipers do not operate— No current to motor	• Fuse or circuit breaker blown • Loose, open or broken wiring • Defective switch • Defective or corroded terminals • No ground circuit for motor or switch	• Replace fuse or circuit breaker • Repair wiring and connections • Replace switch • Replace or clean terminals • Repair ground circuits
Wipers do not operate— Motor runs	• Linkage disconnected or broken	• Connect wiper linkage or replace broken linkage
Vacuum Wipers		
Wipers do not operate	• Control switch or cable inoperative • Loss of engine vacuum to wiper motor (broken hoses, low engine vacuum, defective vacuum/fuel pump) • Linkage broken or disconnected • Defective wiper motor	• Repair or replace switch or cable • Check vacuum lines, engine vacuum and fuel pump • Repair linkage • Replace wiper motor
Wipers stop on engine acceleration	• Leaking vacuum hoses • Dry windshield • Oversize wiper blades • Defective vacuum/fuel pump	• Repair or replace hoses • Wet windshield with washers • Replace with proper size wiper blades • Replace pump

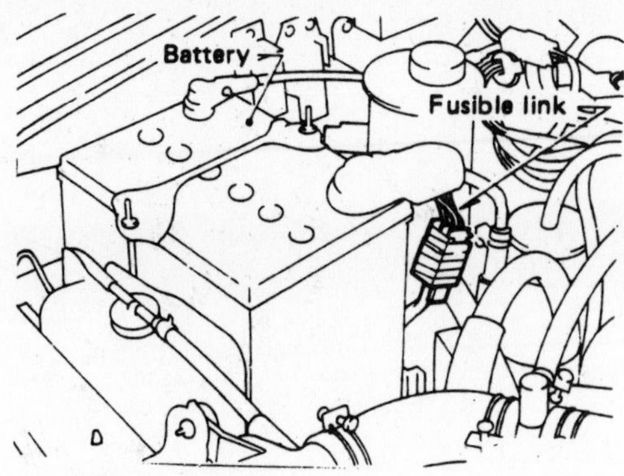

Fusible link

3. Cut the damaged fuse link from the wiring harness and discard it. If the fuse link is one of three circuits fed by a single feed wire, cut it out of the harness at each splice end and discard it.

4. Identify and procure the proper fuse link and butt connectors for attaching the fuse link to the harness.

5. To repair any fuse link in a 3-link ground with one feed:

a. After cutting the open link out of the harness, cut each of the remaining undamaged fuse links closed to the feed wire weld.

b. Strip approximately ½ in. of insulation from the detached ends of the two good fuse links. Then insert two wire ends into one end of a butt connector and carefully push one strip end of the replacement fuse link into the same end of the butt connector and crimp all three firmly together.

NOTE: *Care must be taken when fitting the three fuse links into the butt connector as the internal diameter is a snug fit for three wires. Make sure to use a proper crimping tool. Pliers, side cutters, etc., will not apply the proper crimp to retain the wires and withstand a pull test.*

c. After crimping the butt connector to the three fuse links, cut the weld portion from the feed wire and strip approximately $^1/_2$ inch of insulation from the end cut. Insert the stripped end into the open end of the butt connector and crimp very firmly.

d. To attach the remaining end of the replacement fuse link, strip approximately ½ in. of insulation from the wire end of the circuit from which the blown fuse link was removed, and firmly crimp a butt connector or equivalent to the stripped wire. Then, insert the end of the replacement link into the other end of the butt connector and crimp firmly.

e. Using resin core solder with a consistency of 60 percent tin and 40 percent lead, solder the connectors and the wires at the repairs and insulate with electrical tape.

6. To replace any fuse link on a single circuit in a harness, cut out the damaged portion, strip approximately ½ in. of insulation from the two wire ends and attach the appropriate replacement fuse link to the stripped wire ends with two proper size butt connectors. Solder the connectors and wires and insulate with tape.

7. To repair any fuse link which has an eyelet terminal on one end of such as the charging circuit, cut off the open fuse link behind the weld, strip approximately ½ in. of insulation from the cut end and attach the appropriate new eyelet fuse link to the cut stripped wire with an appropriate size butt connector. Solder the connectors and wires at the repair and insulate with tape.

8. Connect the negative battery cable to the battery and test the system for proper operation.

NOTE: *Do not mistake a resistor wire for a fuse link. The resistor wire is generally longer and has print stating, resistor—don't cut or splice. When attaching a single No. 16, 17, 18, or 20 gauge fuse link to a heavy gauge wire, always double the stripped wire end of the fuse link before inserting and crimping it into the butt connector for positive wire retention.*

Circuit Breakers

Circuit breakers are also located in the fuse block. A circuit breaker is an electrical switch which breaks the circuit during an electrical overload. The circuit breaker will remain open until the short or overload condition in the circuit is corrected.

Drive Train

7

UNDERSTANDING THE MANUAL TRANSMISSION

Because of the way an internal combustion engine breathes, it can produce torque, or twisting force, only within a narrow speed range. Most modern, overhead valve engines must turn at about 2500 rpm to produce their peak torque. By 4500 rpm they are producing so little torque that continued increases in engine speed produce no power increases.

The torque peak on overhead camshaft engines is, generally, much higher, but much narrower.

The manual transmission and clutch are employed to vary the relationship between engine speed and the speed of the wheels so that adequate engine power can be produced under all circumstances. The clutch allows engine torque to be applied to the transmission input shaft gradually, due to mechanical slippage. The car can, consequently, be started smoothly from a full stop.

The transmission changes the ratio between the rotating speeds of the engine and the wheels by the use of gears. 4 speed or 5 speed transmissions are most common. The lower gears allow full engine power to be applied to the rear wheels during acceleration at low speeds.

The clutch drive plate is a thin disc, the center of which is splined to the transmission input shaft. Both sides of the disc are covered with a layer of material which is similar to brake lining and which is capable of allowing slippage without roughness or excessive noise.

The clutch cover is bolted to the engine flywheel and incorporates a diaphragm spring which provides the pressure to engage the clutch. The cover also houses the pressure plate. The driven disc is sandwiched between the pressure plate and the smooth surface of the flywheel when the clutch pedal is released, thus forcing it to turn at the same speed as the engine crankshaft.

The transmission contains a mainshaft which passes all the way through the transmission, from the clutch to the driveshaft. This shaft is separated at one point, so that front and rear portions can turn at different speeds.

Power is transmitted by a countershaft in the lower gears and reverse. The gears of the countershaft mesh with gears on the mainshaft, allowing power to be carried from one to the other. All the countershaft gears are integral with that shaft, while several of the mainshaft gears can either rotate independently of the shaft or be locked to it. Shifting from one gear to the next causes one of the gears to be freed from rotating with the shaft and locks another to it. Gears are locked and unlocked by internal dog clutches which slide between the center of the gear and the shaft. The forward gears usually employ synchronizers; friction members which smoothly bring gear and shaft to the same speed before the toothed dog clutches are engaged.

The clutch is operating properly if:

1. It will stall the engine when released with the vehicle held stationary.

2. The shift lever can be moved freely between 1st and reverse gears when the vehicle is stationary and the clutch disengaged.

A clutch pedal free-play adjustment is incorporated in the linkage. If there is about 25-50mm of motion before the pedal begins to release the clutch, it is adjusted properly. Inadequate free-play wears all parts of the clutch releasing mechanisms and may cause slippage. Excessive free-play may cause inadequate release and hard shifting of gears.

Some clutches use a hydraulic system in place of mechanical linkage. If the clutch fails to release, fill the clutch master cylinder with flu-

Troubleshooting the Manual Transmission and Transfer Case

Problem	Cause	Solution
Transmission shifts hard	• Clutch adjustment incorrect	• Adjust clutch
	• Clutch linkage or cable binding	• Lubricate or repair as necessary
	• Shift rail binding	• Check for mispositioned selector arm roll pin, loose cover bolts, worn shift rail bores, worn shift rail, distorted oil seal, or extension housing not aligned with case. Repair as necessary.
	• Internal bind in transmission caused by shift forks, selector plates, or synchronizer assemblies	• Remove, dissemble and inspect transmission. Replace worn or damaged components as necessary.
	• Clutch housing misalignment	• Check runout at rear face of clutch housing
	• Incorrect lubricant	• Drain and refill transmission
	• Block rings and/or cone seats worn	• Blocking ring to gear clutch tooth face clearance must be 0.030 inch or greater. If clearance is correct it may still be necessary to inspect blocking rings and cone seats for excessive wear. Repair as necessary.
Gear clash when shifting from one gear to another	• Clutch adjustment incorrect	• Adjust clutch
	• Clutch linkage or cable binding	• Lubricate or repair as necessary
	• Clutch housing misalignment	• Check runout at rear of clutch housing
	• Lubricant level low or incorrect lubricant	• Drain and refill transmission and check for lubricant leaks if level was low. Repair as necessary.
	• Gearshift components, or synchronizer assemblies worn or damaged	• Remove, disassemble and inspect transmission. Replace worn or damaged components as necessary.
Transmission noisy	• Lubricant level low or incorrect lubricant	• Drain and refill transmission. If lubricant level was low, check for leaks and repair as necessary.
	• Clutch housing-to-engine, or transmission-to-clutch housing bolts loose	• Check and correct bolt torque as necessary
	• Dirt, chips, foreign material in transmission	• Drain, flush, and refill transmission
	• Gearshift mechanism, transmission gears, or bearing components worn or damaged	• Remove, disassemble and inspect transmission. Replace worn or damaged components as necessary.
	• Clutch housing misalignment	• Check runout at rear face of clutch housing
Jumps out of gear	• Clutch housing misalignment	• Check runout at rear face of clutch housing
	• Gearshift lever loose	• Check lever for worn fork. Tighten loose attaching bolts.
	• Offset lever nylon insert worn or lever attaching nut loose	• Remove gearshift lever and check for loose offset lever nut or worn insert. Repair or replace as necessary.
	• Gearshift mechanism, shift forks, selector plates, interlock plate, selector arm, shift rail, detent plugs, springs or shift cover worn or damaged	• Remove, disassemble and inspect transmission cover assembly. Replace worn or damaged components as necessary.
	• Clutch shaft or roller bearings worn or damaged	• Replace clutch shaft or roller bearings as necessary

Troubleshooting the Manual Transmission and Transfer Case (cont.)

Problem	Cause	Solution
Jumps out of gear (cont.)	• Gear teeth worn or tapered, synchronizer assemblies worn or damaged, excessive end play caused by worn thrust washers or output shaft gears	• Remove, disassemble, and inspect transmission. Replace worn or damaged components as necessary.
	• Pilot bushing worn	• Replace pilot bushing
Will not shift into one gear	• Gearshift selector plates, interlock plate, or selector arm, worn, damaged, or incorrectly assembled	• Remove, disassemble, and inspect transmission cover assembly. Repair or replace components as necessary.
	• Shift rail detent plunger worn, spring broken, or plug loose	• Tighten plug or replace worn or damaged components as necessary
	• Gearshift lever worn or damaged	• Replace gearshift lever
	• Synchronizer sleeves or hubs, damaged or worn	• Remove, disassemble and inspect transmission. Replace worn or damaged components.
Locked in one gear—cannot be shifted out	• Shift rail(s) worn or broken, shifter fork bent, setscrew loose, center detent plug missing or worn	• Inspect and replace worn or damaged parts
	• Broken gear teeth on countershaft gear, clutch shaft, or reverse idler gear	• Inspect and replace damaged part
	Gearshift lever broken or worn, shift mechanism in cover incorrectly assembled or broken, worn damaged gear train components	• Disassemble transmission. Replace damaged parts or assemble correctly.
Transfer case difficult to shift or will not shift into desired range	• Vehicle speed too great to permit shifting	• Stop vehicle and shift into desired range. Or reduce speed to 3–4 km/h (2–3 mph) before attempting to shift.
	• If vehicle was operated for extended period in 4H mode on dry paved surface, driveline torque load may cause difficult shifting	• Stop vehicle, shift transmission to neutral, shift transfer case to 2H mode and operate vehicle in 2H on dry paved surfaces
	• Transfer case external shift linkage binding	• Lubricate or repair or replace linkage, or tighten loose components as necessary
	• Insufficient or incorrect lubricant	• Drain and refill to edge of fill hole with SAE 85W-90 gear lubricant only
	• Internal components binding, worn, or damaged	• Disassemble unit and replace worn or damaged components as necessary
Transfer case noisy in all drive modes	• Insufficient or incorrect lubricant	• Drain and refill to edge of fill hole with SAE 85W-90 gear lubricant only. Check for leaks and repair if necessary. Note: If unit is still noisy after drain and refill, disassembly and inspection may be required to locate source of noise.
Noisy in—or jumps out of four wheel drive low range	• Transfer case not completely engaged in 4L position	• Stop vehicle, shift transfer case in Neutral, then shift back into 4L position
	• Shift linkage loose or binding	• Tighten, lubricate, or repair linkage as necessary
	• Shift fork cracked, inserts worn, or fork is binding on shift rail	• Disassemble unit and repair as necessary
Lubricant leaking from output shaft seals or from vent	• Transfer case overfilled	• Drain to correct level
	• Vent closed or restricted	• Clear or replace vent if necessary

Troubleshooting the Manual Transmission and Transfer Case (cont.)

Problem	Cause	Solution
Lubricant leaking from output shaft seals or from vent (cont.)	• Output shaft seals damaged or installed incorrectly	• Replace seals. Be sure seal lip faces interior of case when installed. Also be sure yoke seal surfaces are not scored or nicked. Remove scores, nicks with fine sandpaper or replace yoke(s) if necessary.
Abnormal tire wear	• Extended operation on dry hard surface (paved) roads in 4H range	• Operate in 2H on hard surface (paved) roads

id to the proper level and pump the clutch pedal to fill the system with fluid. Bleed the system in the same way as a brake system. If leaks are located, tighten loose connections or overhaul the master or slave cylinder as necessary.

MANUAL TRANSMISSION

Identification

All models covered in this book have the manual transmission serial number stamped on the front upper face of the transmission case.

1970-74 models use an F4W63 4-speed transmission.

1975-83 models use an F4W71B 4-speed transmission. or an optional FS5W71B 5-speed transmission.

1984-86 models (720-D series) also use the FS5W71B5 5-speed transmission

1986-87 models (D21-D series) with the Z24i or SD25 engines use an FS5W71C 5-speed transmission, while 1988-89 models use an F4W71C 4-speed transmission or the FS5W71C 5-speed transmission.

1986-89 models with the VG30i engines use an FS5R30A 5-speed transmission.

The F4W63 is a bottom cover unit, with an extension housing for the shift rail, while all other models have a one piece case, an adapter plate which supports the mainshaft and countershaft, and an extension housing.

Adjustments

Most models utilize a floor-mounted shifter and an internally-mounted shift linkage.

No external adjustments are either necessary or possible.

Back-Up Light Switch

REMOVAL AND INSTALLATION

All Models

1. Raise vehicle and support it safely with floor stands.
2. Disconnect the electrical connections from the switch.
3. Unscrew the switch and remove it from the transmission housing. When removing, be sure to position a drain pan under the transmission to catch any leaking fluid.
4. Install the switch and connect the electrical lead. Lower the truck and check the fluid level.

Transmission

REMOVAL AND INSTALLATION

1970-86 (521, 620 and 720-D Series)

F4W63, F4W71B and FS5W71B

1. Disconnect the negative battery cable.
2. On 1975-86 models only, remove the shift lever from inside the cab. It is retained to the shaft rail by a C-clip, accessible under the boot. Remove the C-clip and retaining pin, and remove the lever.
3. Raise the vehicle and support it with jackstands.
4. On 1970-74 models, unscrew the nut securing the bottom of the shifter to the transmission shifting mechanism.
5. Disconnect the exhaust pipe from the exhaust manifold. On trucks with a catalytic converter, also remove the exhaust pipe bracket next to the speedometer cable by unscrewing the two mounting bolts.
6. Remove the clutch slave cylinder from the transmission case.
7. Disconnect the speedometer cable from the transmission extension housing and the back-up light and transmission switch wires at the switch(es).
8. Remove the bracket holding the center bearing of the driveshaft on the third crossmember of the frame.
9. Remove the driveshaft(s).

NOTE: *On 4wd models, this requires removal of the transfer case, which should be performed at this time.*

10. Support the engine with a floor jack locat-

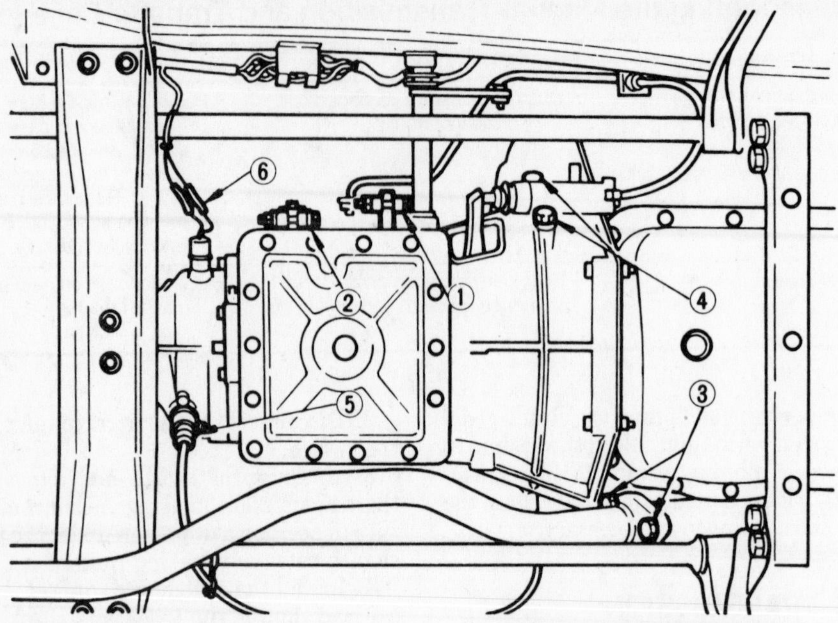

1. Neutral safety switch
2. Downshift solenoid
3. Exhaust pipe-to-flange attaching nuts
4. Clutch slave cylinder attaching bolts
5. Speedometer cable
6. Back-up light switch wires

Bottom view of the transmission—1970–74 F4W63

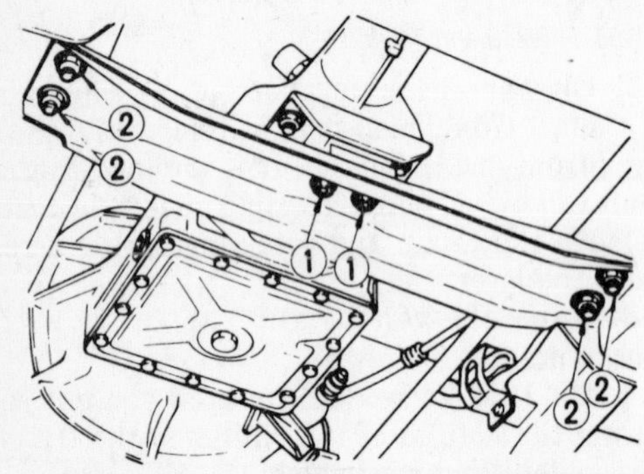

1. Transmission-to-crossmember attaching nuts and bolts
2. Crossmember-to-frame attaching nuts and bolts

Remove the engine crossmember—1970–74 F4W63

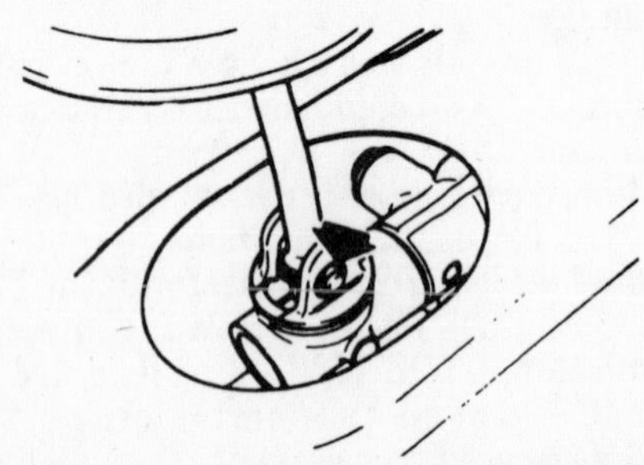

Removing the shift lever—1975–86 FS4W71B and FS5W71B

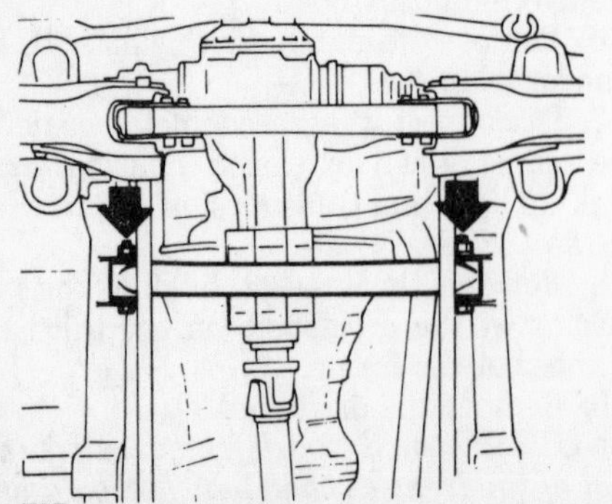

Remove the differential carrier crossmember—1975–86 FS4W71B and FS5W71B

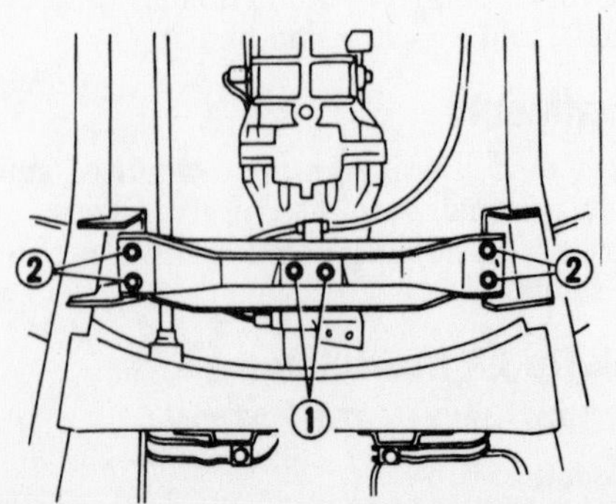

Remove the engine crossmember—1975–86 FS4W71B and FS5W71B

ed under the oil pan. Place a block of wood between the jack and the oil pan to prevent damage to the oil pan. Support the transmission with a jack.

11. Remove the rear engine mount securing bolts and the crossmember mounting bolts. 1970-71 models (521 series) do not have a removable crossmember; only the rear engine/transmission extension housing mount is removable from the crossmember.

12. Remove the starter motor.

13. Remove the bolts securing the transmission to the engine, pull the transmission toward the rear until the transmission mainshaft is free of the back of the engine.

On 1970-71 models, place the rear of the transmission on the crossmember and then pull the transmission down toward the front of the truck and out from under the vehicle.

On 1972-86 models, separate the transmission from the engine, then lower the transmission out from under the truck.

14. Before installing the transmission, clean the mating surfaces of the engine and transmission thoroughly. Lightly coat the input shaft splines with grease. Tighten the engine-to-transmission bolts to 17–20 ft. lbs. (1970-73); 29–36 ft. lbs. (1974-76); or 32–43 ft. lbs. (1977-86).

NOTE: *On the 5-speed transmission, the two bottom bolts are tightened to 7–9 ft. lbs.*

15. Tighten the crossmember-tochassis bolts to 20–27 ft. lbs. and the clutch slave cylinder mounting bolts to 18–22 ft. lbs. Be sure to align the marks made earlier on the U-joint and differential flange when installing the driveshaft, to maintain driveline balance.

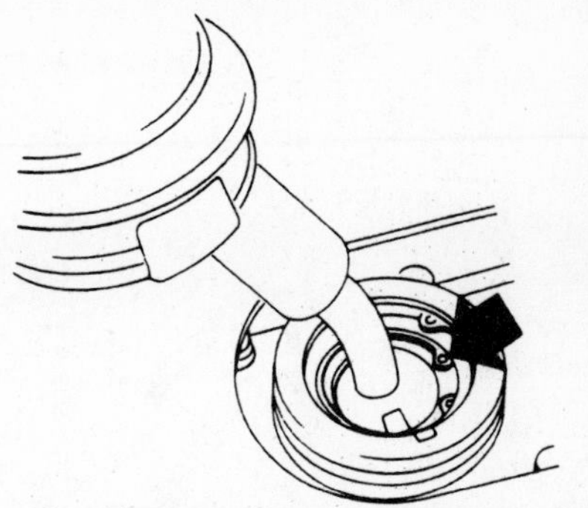

Shift lever removal—2wd models with F4W71C, FS5W71C or FS5R30A

1986-89 (D21-D Series)

F4W71C, FS5W71C AND FS5R30A

1. Disconnect the negative battery cable.
2. Disconnect the accelerator linkage if necessary.
3. Raise the front of the truck and support it with jack stands.
4. Disconnect the exhaust pipe from the manifold and bracket if necessary to gain clearance for transmission removal.
5. Tag and disconnect any switches that are connected to the transmission case (back-up, neutral, top gear or overdrive).

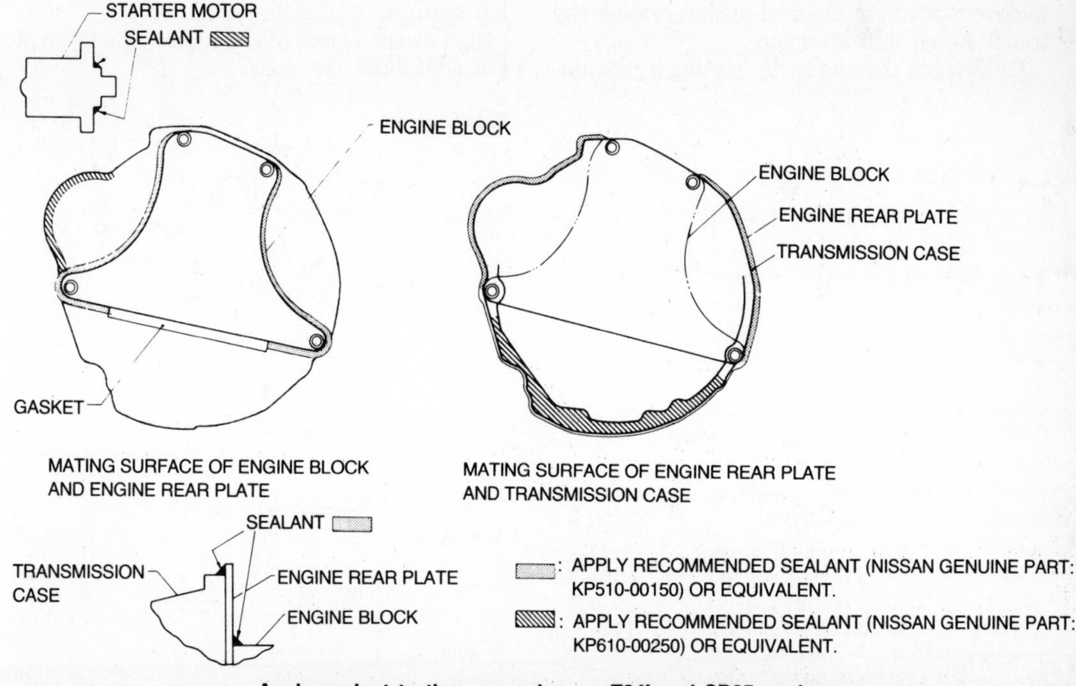

Apply sealant to the areas shown—Z24i and SD25 engines

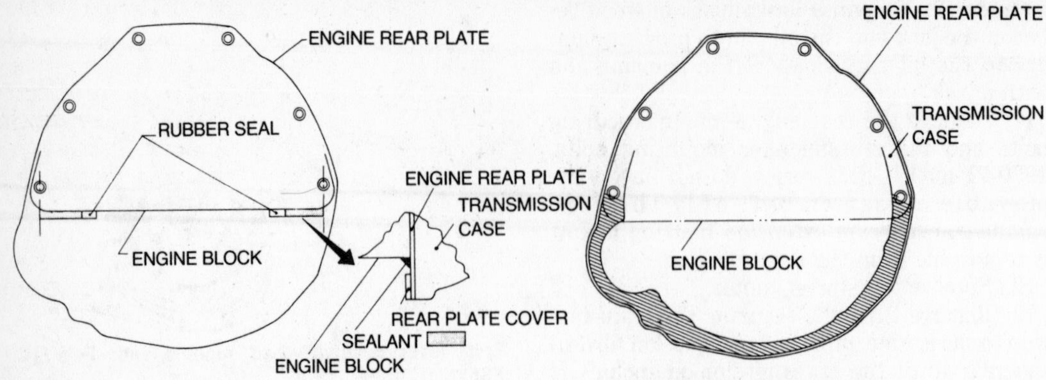

Apply sealant to the areas shown—VG30i engines

6. Disconnect the speedometer cable where it attaches to the transmission.

7. Remove the driveshaft(s). Don't forget to plug the opening in the rear extension so that oil won't flow out.

8. Remove the clutch slave cylinder.

9. Remove the rubber boot and console box (if so equipped). Place the shift lever in neutral, remove the E-ring (later models only) and then remove the shifter. On 4wd models remove the transfer case shift lever also.

10. Support the engine by placing a jack under the oil pan with a wooden block used between the jack and the pan.

NOTE: *Never position the jack directly under the oil pan drain plug.*

11. Support the transmission with a transmission jack.

12. Loosen the rear engine mount securing nuts temporarily and then remove the crossmember. On 4wd models, remove the torsion bar springs.

13. Lower the rear of the engine slightly to allow additional clearance.

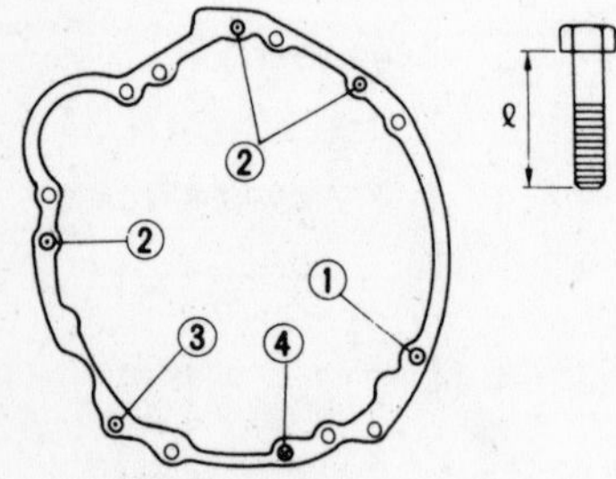

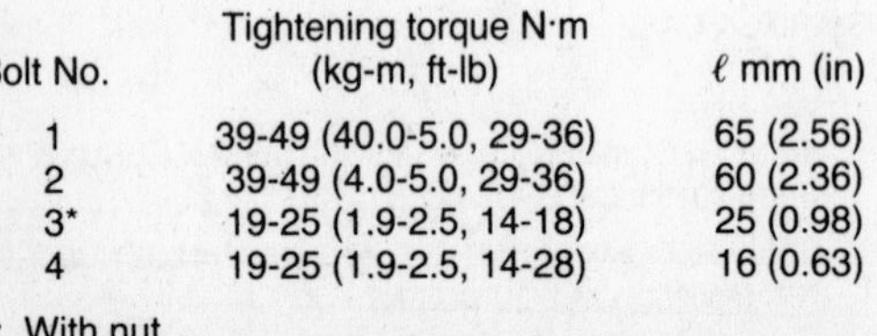

Bolt No.	Tightening torque N·m (kg-m, ft-lb)	ℓ mm (in)
1	39-49 (40.0-5.0, 29-36)	65 (2.56)
2	39-49 (4.0-5.0, 29-36)	60 (2.36)
3*	19-25 (1.9-2.5, 14-18)	25 (0.98)
4	19-25 (1.9-2.5, 14-28)	16 (0.63)

*: With nut

Transmission bolt installation—Z24i engines

⊙ M/T to engine
⊗ Engine rear plate to M/T

Bolt No.	Tightening torque N·m (kg-m, ft-lb)	ℓ mm (in)
1	39-49 (4.0-5.0, 29-36)	65 (2.56)
2	39-49 (4.0-5.0, 29-36)	60 (2.36)
3*	9.1-11.8 (9.93-1.2, 6.7-8.7)	25 (0.98)

*: With nut

Transmission bolt installation—SD25 engines

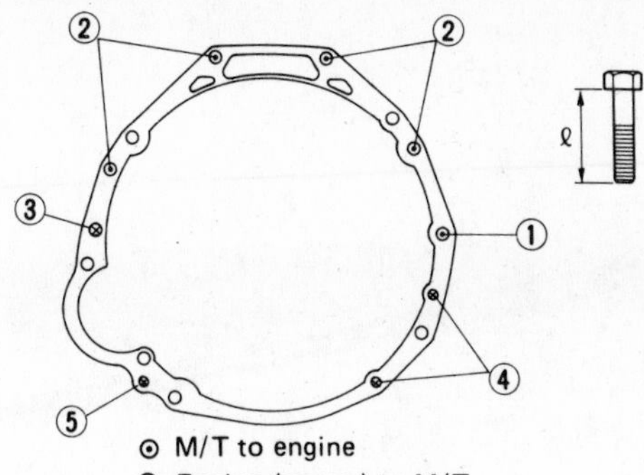

Bolt No.	Tightening torque N·m (kg-m, ft-lb)	ℓ mm (in)
1	39-49 (4.9-5.0, 29-36)	65 (2.56)
2	39-49 (4.0-5.0, 29-36)	60 (2.36)
3	29-39 (3.0-4.0, 22-29)	55 (2.17)
4	29-39 (3.0-4.0, 22-29)	30 (1.18)
5	29-39 (3.0-4.0, 22-29)	25 (0.98)

Transmission bolt installation—VG30i engines

14. Remove the starter electrical connections and the starter motor.
15. Remove the transmission-to-engine mounting bolts, lower the transmission and remove it toward the rear.
16. Install the transmission in the correct position. Tighten all the transmission-to-engine mounting bolts.
    a. On Z24i engines, tighten the 4 longest bolts (1 - 65mm and 3 - 60mm) to 29–36 ft. lbs. (39–49 Nm); tighten the 2 shortest bolts (1 - 25mm with nut and 1 - 16mm) to 14–18 ft. lbs. (19–25 Nm).
    b. On VG30i engines, tighten the 5 longest bolts (1 - 65mm and 4 - 60mm) to 29–36 ft. lbs. (39–49 Nm); tighten the 4 shortest bolts (1 - 55mm, 2 - 30mm and 1 -16mm) to 22–29 ft. lbs. (29–39 Nm).
    c. On SD25 engines, tighten the 4 longest bolts (1 - 65mm and 3 - 60mm) to 29–36 ft. lbs. (39 – 49 Nm); tighten the 2 shortest bolts and nuts (2 - 25mm) to 7–9 ft. lbs. (9–12 Nm).
17. Install the starter motor and electrical connections.
18. Install the crossmember assembly and tighten all retaining nuts to crossmember and rear engine mounts. Install the torsion bars on 4wd models.
19. Install the shifter. Install the rubber boot and console box if so equipped.
20. Install the clutch slave cylinder.
21. Install the driveshaft(s) and connect the speedometer cable.
22. Connect any switches that are connected to the transmission case (back-up, neutral, top gear or overdrive).
23. Connect the exhaust pipe to the manifold and bracket if necessary.
24. Connect the accelerator linkage.
25. Connect the negative battery cable. Bleed the clutch hydraulic system if necessary. Road test the vehicle for proper shift pattern operation.

OVERHAUL

Model F4W63 (4 Speed)

DISASSEMBLY

1. Make sure all transmission fluid is fully drained.
2. Remove the clutch housing dust cover. Remove the clutch release lever and bearing.
3. Remove the front cover retaining bolts and lift out the front cover.
4. Remove the bottom cover from the transmission case.
5. Unscrew the back-up light switch and the speedometer and remove them.
6. Loosen the extension housing-to-transmission case bolts and pull off the housing. It may require a bit of assistance with a rubber mallet!
7. Unscrew the check ball plugs and take out the 3 locking springs and 3 check bolts. Be sure you don't lose these.
8. Remove the cross shaft and operating lever lock pins by prying off the snaprings. Remove the shafts together with their outer levers and then remove the arm and rod assembly.

NOTE: *When removing the cross shafts, be careful not to damage the lips and grooves of the oil seals with the snapring.*

9. Mseh the gears in two places, straighten the lockwasher and then loosen the locknut on the mainshaft.
10. Drive the countershaft out through the rear of the transmission case and then remove the countershaft along with the countershaft guide. Be careful not to drop the counter gear needle bearings.

NOTE: *Always remove the washers between the counter gear and the transmission case.*

11. Pry off the reverse idler gear (helical gear) snapring. Remove the reverse idler gear from the idler gear shaft and then remove the shaft (with the spur gear) from the transmission case.
12. Use a fork rod pin punch and drive out the rod retaining pins. Drive out the fork rods so that the shift forks and fork rod brackets are also removed.
13. Remove the mainshaft bearing retainer bolts and then remove the mainshaft assembly from the rear. This might also require the assistance of a rubber mallet; just tap the case a few times.
14. Remove the snapring at the front of the

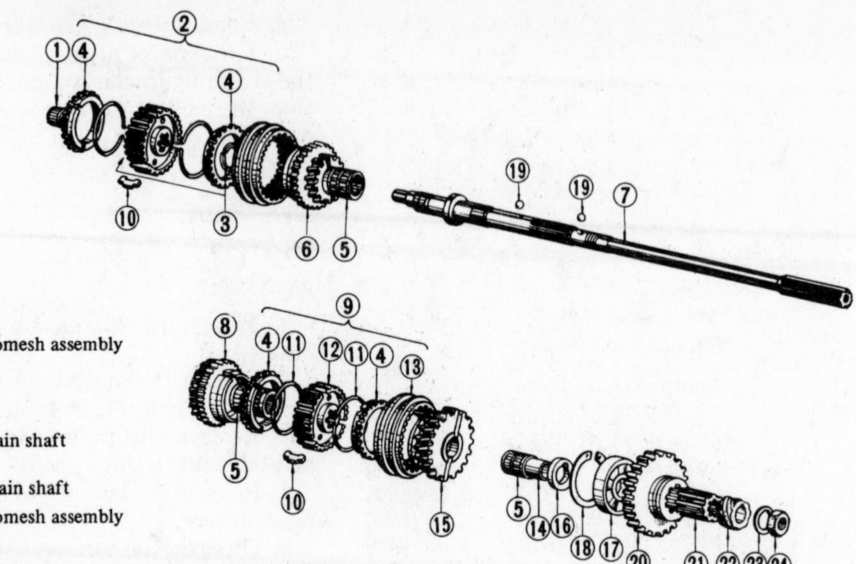

1 Pilot bearing
2 3rd & 4th synchromesh assembly
3 Snap ring
4 Baulk ring
5 Needle bearing
6 3rd speed gear, main shaft
7 Main shaft
8 2nd speed gear, main shaft
9 1st & 2nd synchromesh assembly
10 Shifting insert
11 Spread spring
12 Synchronizer hub
13 Coupling sleeve
14 Bush, 1st gear
15 1st speed gear, main shaft
16 Thrust washer, main shaft
17 Main shaft bearing
18 Snap ring, main shaft bearing
19 Steel ball
20 Reverse gear
21 Reverse hub
22 Speedometer drive gear
23 Lock plate
24 Nut

Exploded view of the mainshaft assembly—F4W63

mainshaft assembly and then slide off the 3-4 syncro assembly and 3rd gear.

15. Remove the mainshaft locknut, lock washer, speedometer drive gear, steel ball, reverse gear and the reverse hub.

16. Remove the mainshaft bearing, retainer, thrust washer and 1st gear at the same time with a press. Take out the steel ball, needle roller bearing and the baulk ring. Never apply the press to the 2nd gear!

17. Use a press and remove the 1-2 syncro assembly and the 2nd gear.

18. Remove the spreader springs and shifting inserts. Separate the coupling sleeve from the syncro hub and then remove the synchromesh assembly.

19. Remove the snapring from the front side of the main drive gear bearing and then remove the spacer. Using a bearing puller and a press, remove the main drive gear bearing.

Model F4W71B (4 Speed)

DISASSEMBLY

This transmission is constructed in three sections: clutch housing, transmission housing and extension housing. There are no case cover plates. There is a cast iron adapter plate between the transmission and extension housings.

1. Remove the clutch housing dust cover. Remove the retaining spring, release bearing sleeve and lever.

2. Remove the back-up light/neutral safety switch.

3. Unbolt and remove the clutch housing, rapping with a soft hammer if necessary. Remove the gasket, mainshaft bearing shim, and countershaft bearing shim.

4. Remove the speedometer pinion sleeve.

5. Remove the striker rod pin from the rod. Separate the striker rod from the shift lever bracket.

6. Unbolt and remove the rear extension. It may be necessary to rap the housing with a soft hammer.

7. Remove the mainshaft bearing snap-ring.

8. Remove the adapter plate and gear assembly from the transmission case.

9. Punch out the shift fork retaining pins. Remove the shift rod snap-rings. Remove the detent plugs, springs and balls from the adapter plate. Remove the shift rods, being careful not to lose the interlock balls.

10. Remove the snapring, speedometer drive gear and locating ball.

11. Remove the nut, lockwasher, thrust washer, reverse hub and reverse gear.

12. Remove the snapring and countershaft reverse gear. Remove the snapring, reverse idler gear, thrust washer and needle bearing.

13. Support the gear assembly while rapping on the rear of the mainshaft with a soft hammer.

14. Remove the setscrew from the adapter

plate. Remove the shaft nut, spring washer, plain washer and reverse idler shaft.

15. Remove the bearing retainer and the mainshaft rear bushing.

16. To disassemble the mainshaft (rear section), remove the front snapring, 3–4 synchronizer assembly, 3rd gear and needle bearing. From the rear, remove the thrust washer, locating ball, 1st gear, needle bearing, 1st gear bushing, 1–2 synchronizer assembly, 2nd gear, and needle bearing.

17. To disassemble the clutch shaft, remove the snapring and bearing spacer and press off the bearing.

18. To disassemble the countershaft, press off the front bearing. Press off the rear bearing, press off the gears and remove the keys.

19. Remove the retaining pin, control arm pin and shift control arm from the rear of the extension housing.

ASSEMBLY

1. Place the O-ring in the front cover. Install the front cover to the clutch housing with a press. Put in the front cover oil seal.

2. Install the rear extension oil seal.

3. Assemble the 1–2 and 3–4 synchronizer

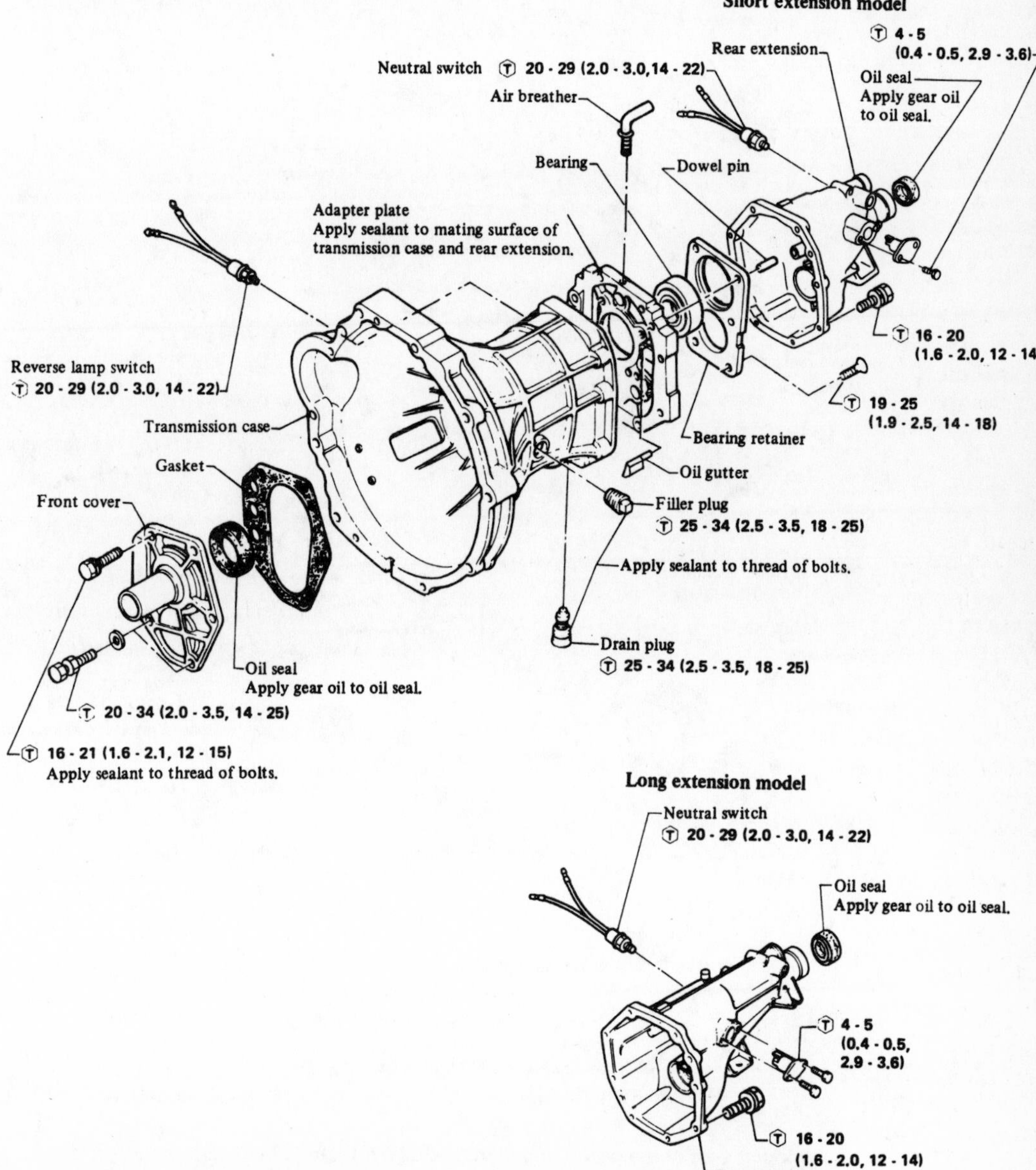

Exploded view of the transmission case—FS4W71B and FS5W71B

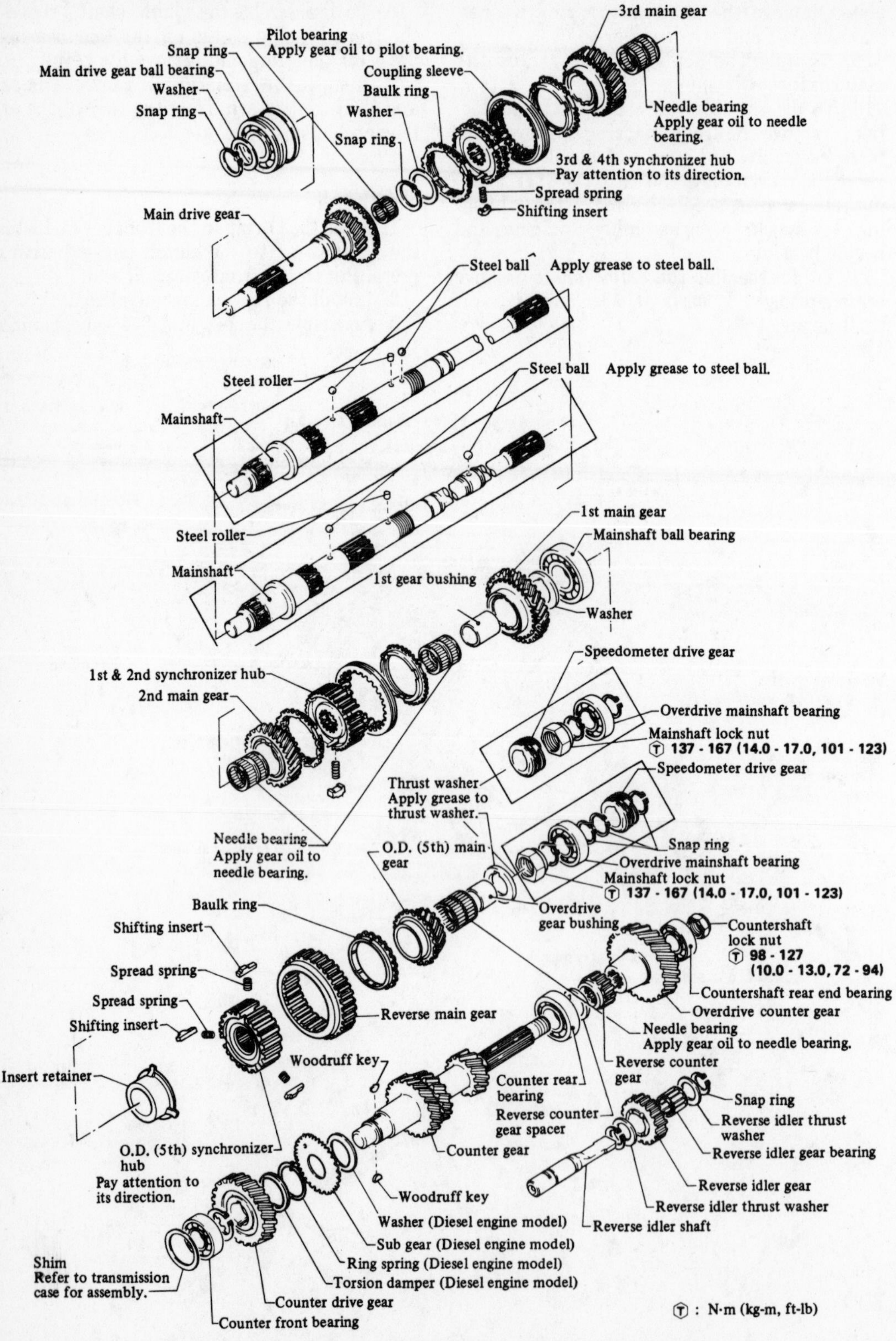

Exploded view of the gear components—FS4W71B and FS5W71B

assemblies. Make sure that the ring gaps are not both on the same side of the unit.

4. On the rear end of the mainshaft, install the needle bearing, 2nd gear, baulk ring, 1–2 synchronizer assembly, baulk ring, 1st gear bushing, needle bearing, 1st gear, locating ball and thrust washer.

5. Drive or press on the mainshaft rear bearing.

6. Install the countershaft rear bearing to the adapter plate. Drive or press the mainshaft rear bearing into the adapter plate until the bearing snapring groove comes through the rear side of the plate. Install the snapring. If it is not tight against the plate, press the bearing back in slightly.

7. Insert the countershaft bearing ring between the countershaft rear bearing and bearing retainer. Install the bearing retainer to the adapter plate. Stake both ends of the screws.

8. Insert the reverse idler shaft from the rear of the adapter plate. Install the spring washer and plain washer to the idler shaft.

9. Place the two keys on the countershaft and oil the shaft lightly. Press on 3rd gear and install a snapring.

10. Install the countershaft into its rear bearing.

11. From the front of the mainshaft, install the needle bearing, 3rd gear, baulk ring, 3–4 synchronizer assembly and snapring. Snaprings are available in thicknesses from 1.4-1.6mm to adjust gear end play.

12. Press the main drive bearing onto the clutch shaft. Install the main drive gear spacer and a snapring. Snaprings are available in thicknesses from 1.8-2.0mm to adjust gear end play.

13. Insert a key into the countershaft drive gear with 4th gear and drive on the countershaft 4th gear with a drift. The rear end of the countershaft should be held steady while driv-

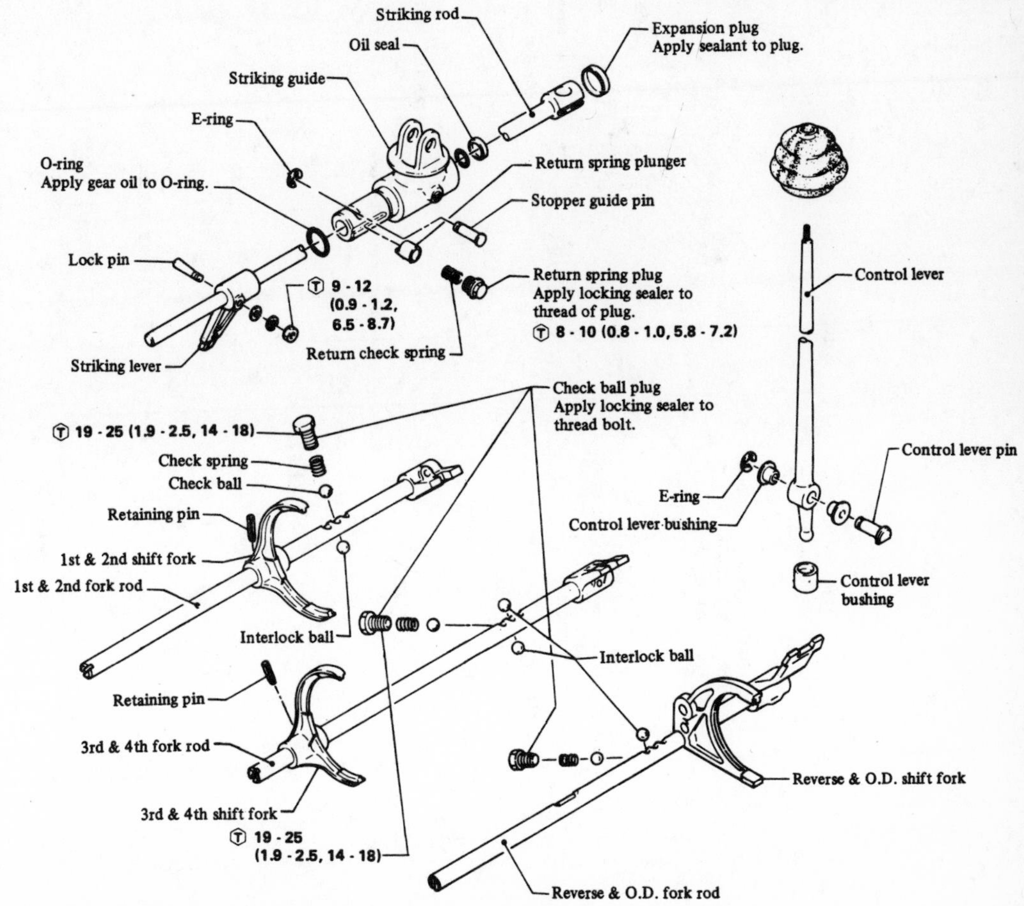

Exploded view of the shift control components—FS4W71B and FS5W71B

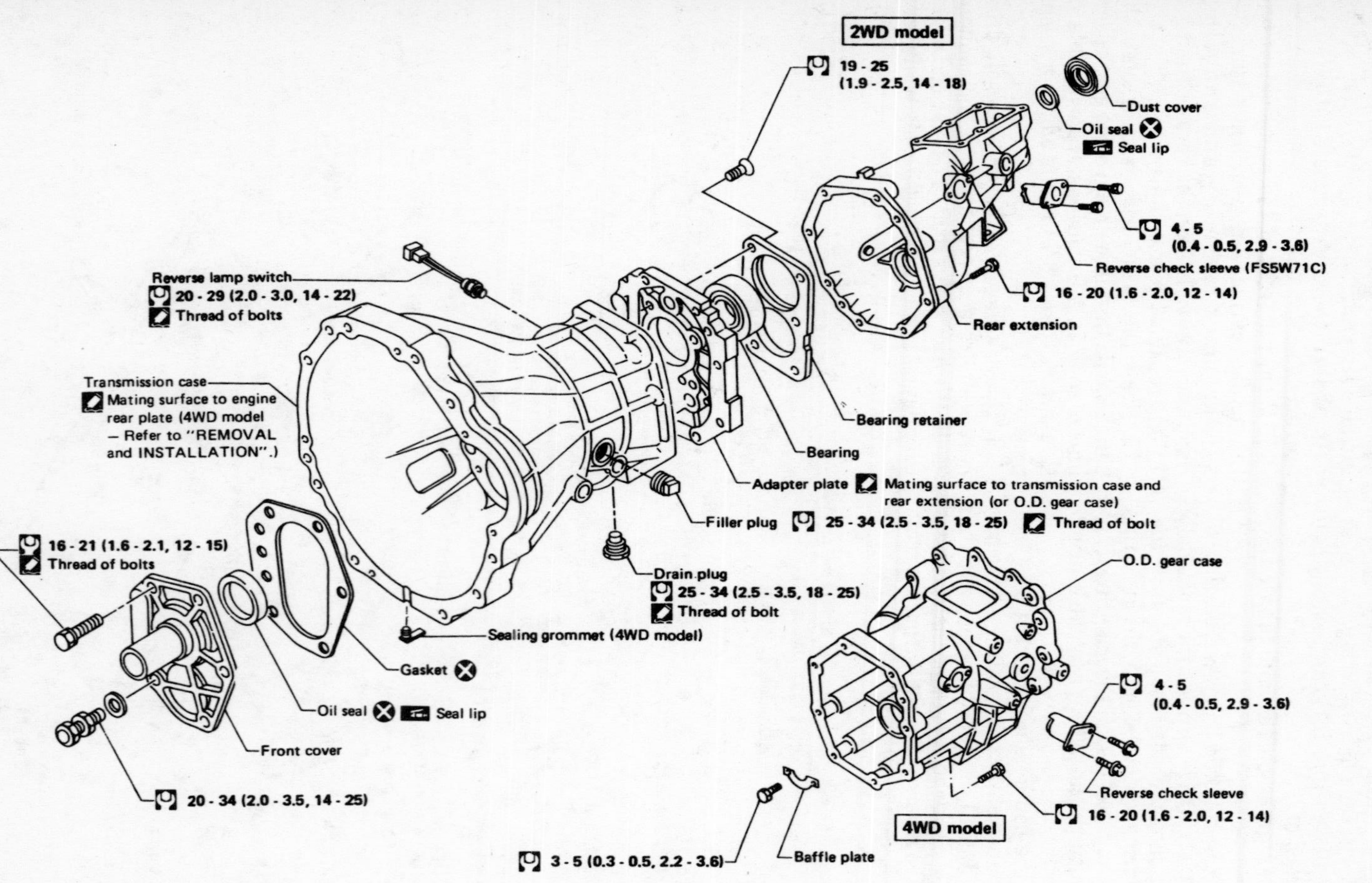

Exploded view of the transmission case—F4W71C and FS5W71C

ing on the gear, to prevent rear bearing damage.

14. Install the reverse hub, reverse gear, thrust washer, and lock tab on the rear of the mainshaft. Install the shaft nut temporarily.

15. Install the needle bearing, reverse idler gear, thrust washer, and snapring.

16. Place the countershaft reverse gear and snapring on the rear of the countershaft. Snaprings are available in thicknesses from 1.0-1.5mm to adjust gear end play.

17. Engage both 1st and 2nd gears to lock the shaft.

18. On the rear of the mainshaft, install the

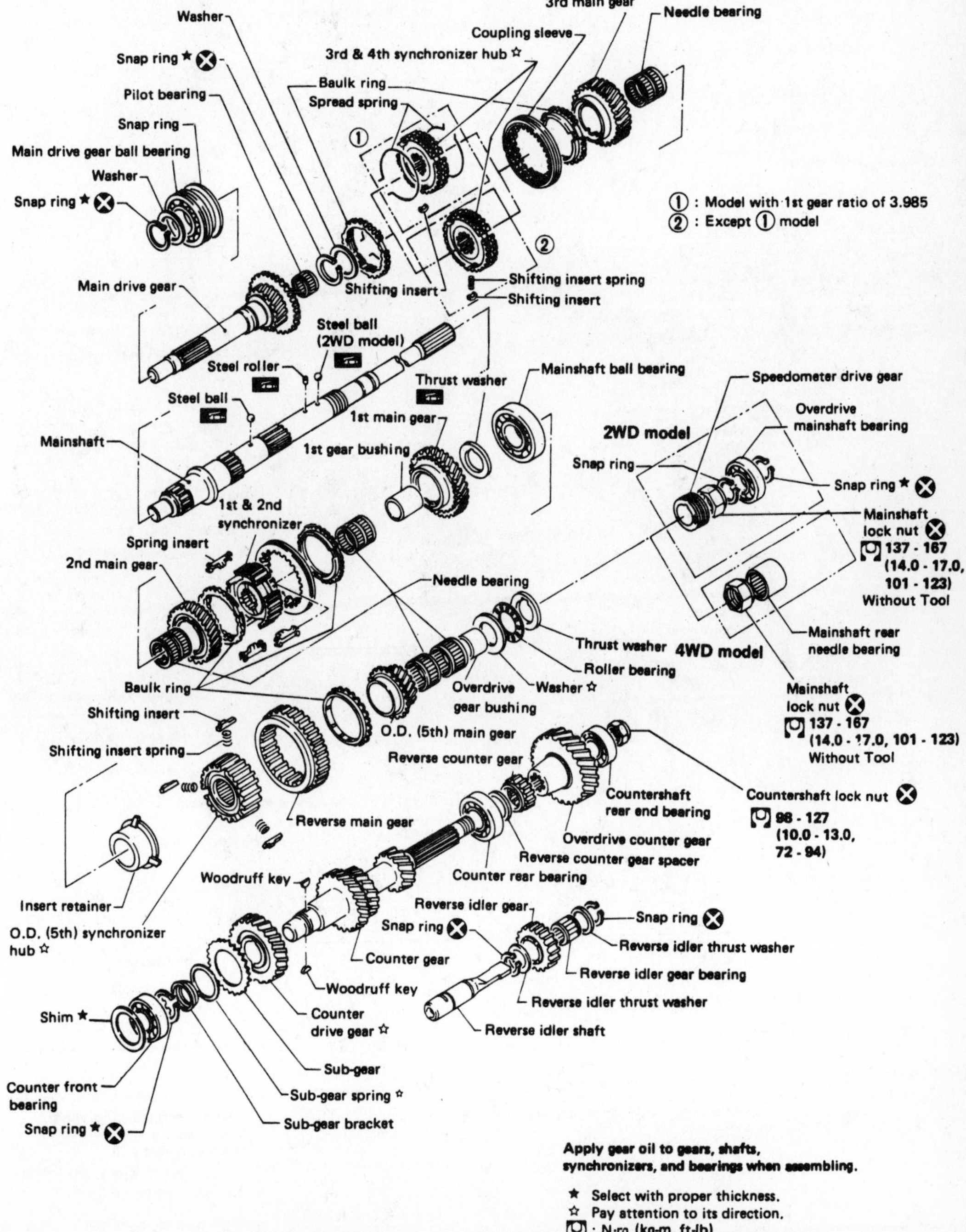

Exploded view of the gear components—FS5W71C

snapring, locating ball, speedometer drive gear, and snapring. Snaprings are available in thicknesses from 1.1-1.5mm.

19. Recheck end play and backlash of all gears.

20. Place the reverse shift fork on the reverse gear and install the reverse shift rod. Install the detent ball, spring and plug. Install the fork retaining pin. Place 2 interlock balls between the reverse shift rod and the 3–4 shift rod location. Install the 3–4 gears and rod. Install the detent ball, spring and plug. This plug is shorter than the other two. Install the fork retaining pin. Place 2 interlock balls between the 1–2 shift rod

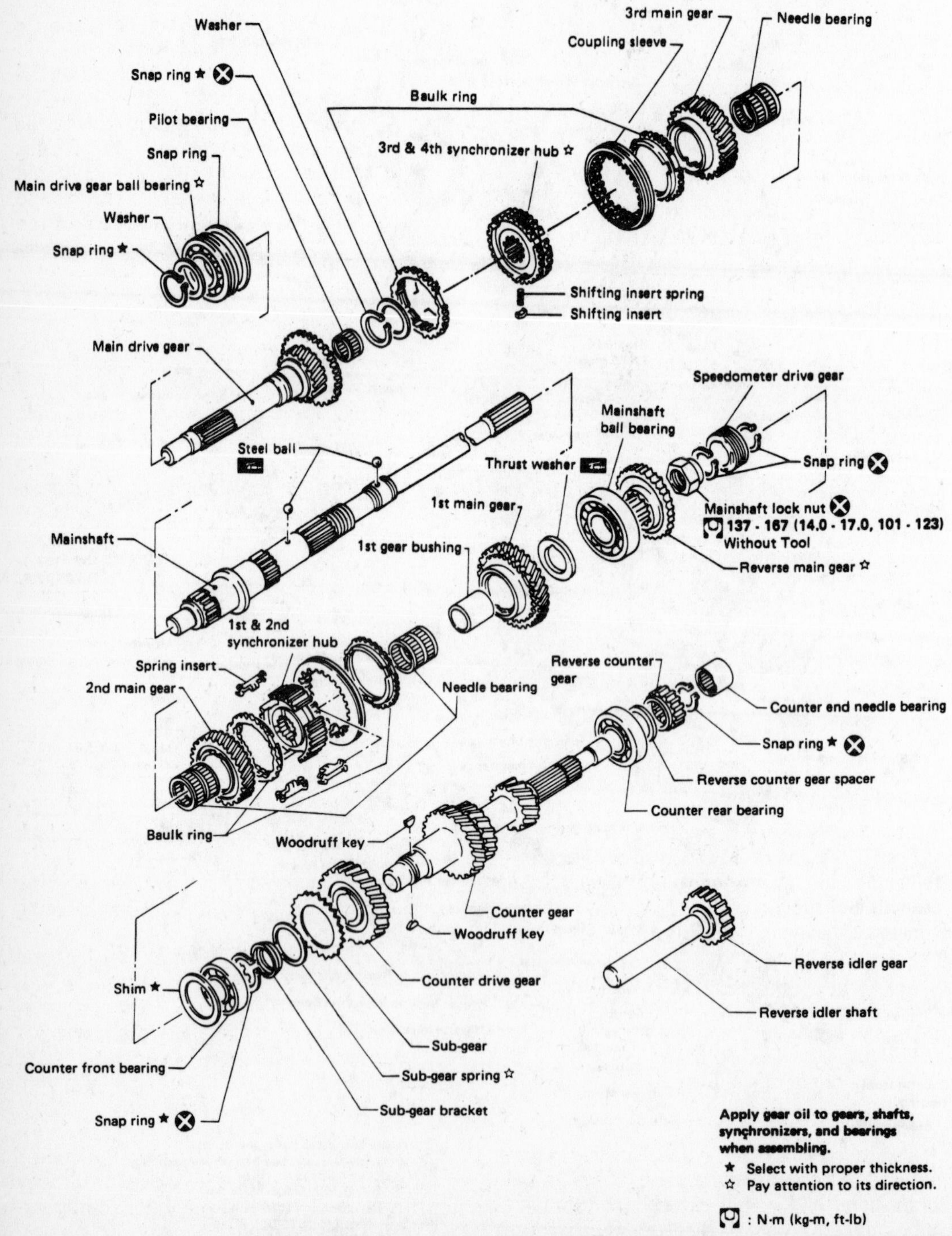

Exploded view of the gear components—F4W71C

location and the 3–4 shift rod. Install the 1–2 shift fork and rod. Install the detent ball, spring and plug.

21. Install the shift rod snaprings.

22. Apply sealant sparingly to the adapter plate and transmission housing. Install the transmission housing to the adapter plate and bolt it down temporarily.

23. Drive in the countershaft front bearing with a drift. Place the snapring in the mainshaft front bearing.

24. Apply sealant sparingly to the adapter plate and extension housing. Align the shift rods in the neutral positions. Position the striker rod to the shift rods and bolt down the extension housing.

25. Insert the striker rod pin, connect the rod to the shift lever bracket and install the striker rod pin retaining ring. Replace the shift control arm.

26. To select the proper mainshaft bearing shim, first measure the amount the bearing protrudes from the front of the transmission case. Then, measure the depth of the bearing recess in the rear of the clutch housing. Required shim thickness is found by subtracting, the difference is required shim size. Shims are available in thicknesses of 1.4-1.6mm.

27. To select the proper countershaft front bearing shim, measure the amount that the bearing is recessed into the transmission case. Shim thickness should equal this measurement. Shims are available in thicknesses from 0.4-1.0mm.

28. Apply sealant sparingly to the clutch and transmission housing mating surfaces.

29. Replace the clutch operating mechanism.

30. Install the shift lever temporarily and check shifting action.

Model FS5W71B (5 Speed)

This transmission is similar to the F4W71B (4 speed). The overhaul can be accomplished by following the outline for the disassembly and assembly of the 4 speed.

Servo type synchromesh is used, instead of the Borg Warner type in the four speed. Shift linkage and interlock arrangements are the same, except the reverse shift rod also operates fifth gear. Most service procedures are identical to those for the 4 speed unit.

Those unique to the 5 speed follow:

DISASSEMBLY

To disassemble the synchronizers, remove the circlip, synchronizer ring, thrust block, brake band, and anchor block. Be careful not to mix parts of the different synchronizer assemblies.

ASSEMBLY

1. The synchronizer assemblies for 2nd, 3rd and 4th are identical. When assembling the first gear synchronizer, be sure to install the 2.2mm thick brake band at the bottom.

2. When assembling the mainshaft, select a 3rd gear synchronizer hub snapring to minimize hub end play. Snaprings are available in thicknesses of 1.5-1.6mm, 1.50-1.55mm and 1.45-1.50mm. The synchronizer hub must be installed with the longer boss to the rear.

3. When reassembling the gear train, install the mainshaft, countershaft, and gears to the adapter plate. Hold the rear nut and force the front nut against it to a torque of 217 ft. lbs. for 1977-79 models and 123 ft. lbs. for 1980 and later models. Select a snapring to minimize end play of the 5th gear bearing at the rear of the mainshaft. Snaprings are available in thicknesses from 1.1-1.4mm.

Model F4W71C (4 Speed)
Model FS5W71C (5 Speed)

DISASSEMBLY

1. Remove the control housing, check ball, return spring plug, select check plunger and return springs from the extension housing. Tap the housing lightly with a rubber mallet and remove it from the adapter plate (2wd) or overdrive case (4wd).

2. Remove the front cover, oil seal and gasket. Remove the countershaft front bearing shim and the main drive gear ball bearing snapring.

3. Tap the transmission case lightly with a rubber mallet and separate the case from the adapter plate.

4. Secure the adapter plate in a soft-jawed vise and remove the check ball plugs, check springs and check balls.

5. Drive out the fork rod retaining pins. Lift out the fork rods and remove the interlock balls.

6. On 4wd models with a mainshaft braking mechanism, remove the lever bracket securing bolt.

7. On 4wd models, remove the 3–4 fork rod and then remove the overdrive–reverse fork rod. Rotate the OD–reverse bracket counterclockwise and then remove the fork shaft.

8. Measure the end play at all gear assemblies:
   a. 1st gear: 0.31–0.41mm
   b. 2nd and 3rd gears: 0.11–0.21mm
   c. Overdrive (FS5W71C): 0.24–0.41mm

9. Turn 2nd and reverse gears until they mesh and then remove the counter front bearing with a suitable puller.

10. Remove the sub-gear snapring and then

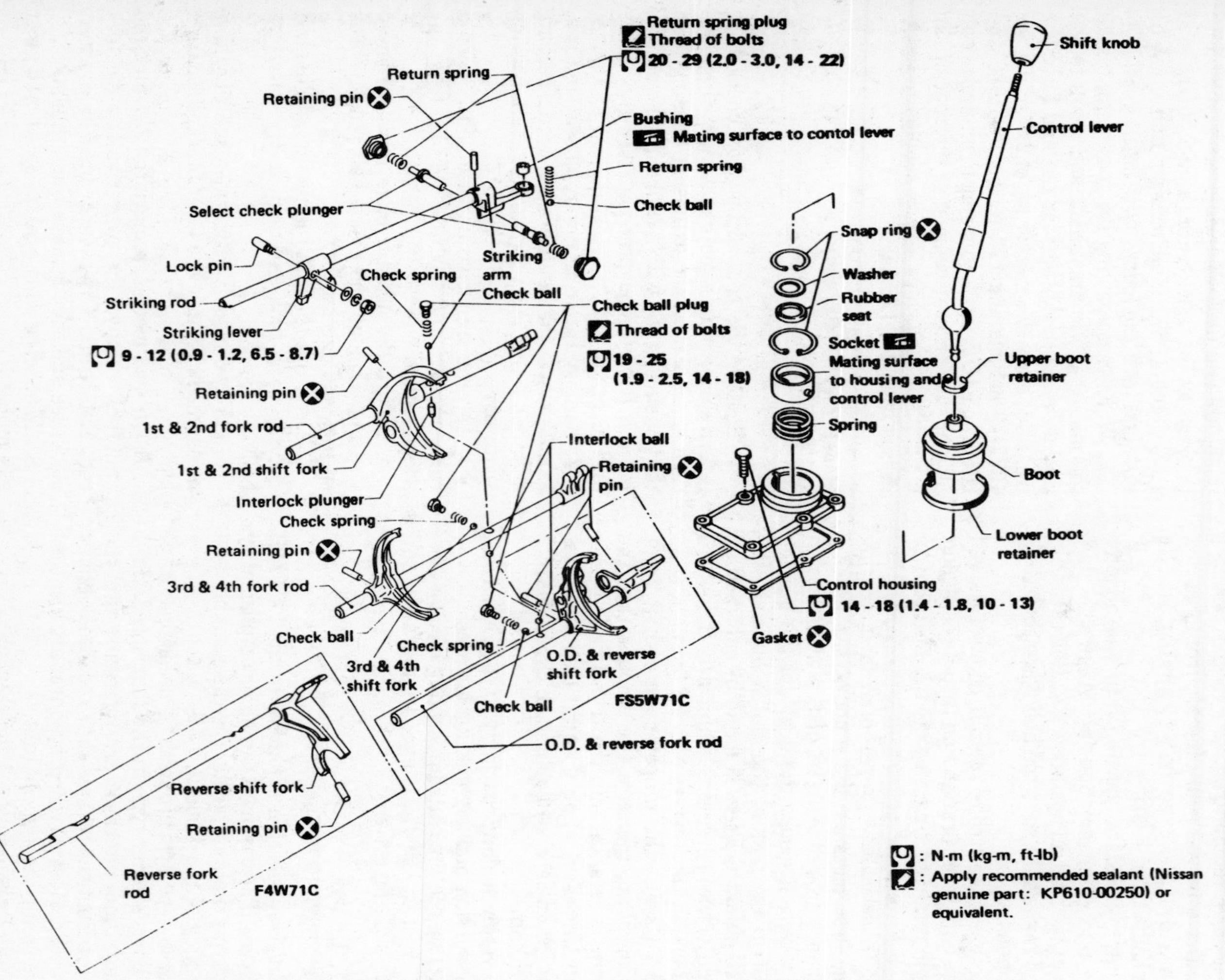

Exploded view of the shift control components—2wd models with F4W71C or FS5W71C

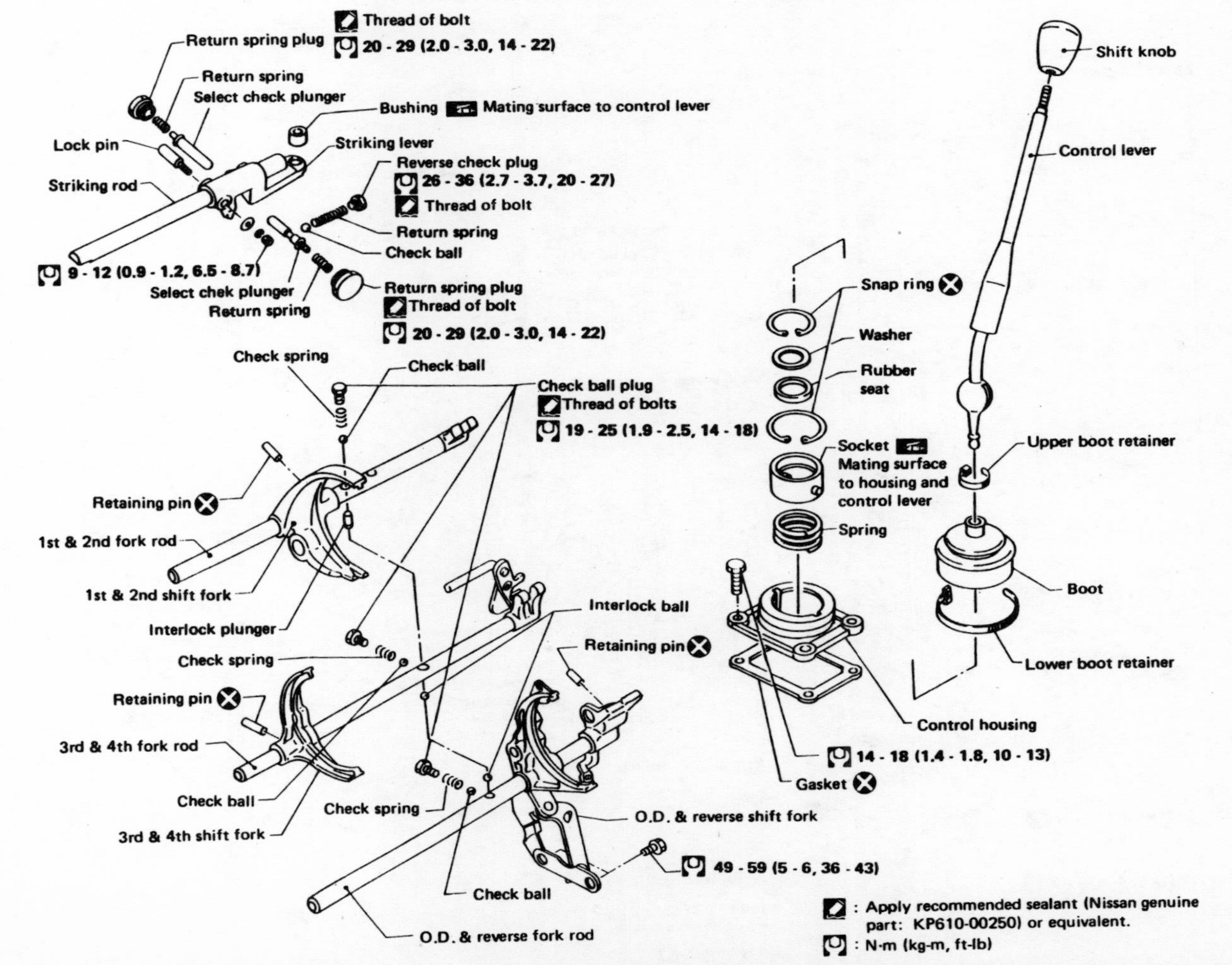

Exploded view of the shift control components—4wd models with F4W71C or FS5W71C

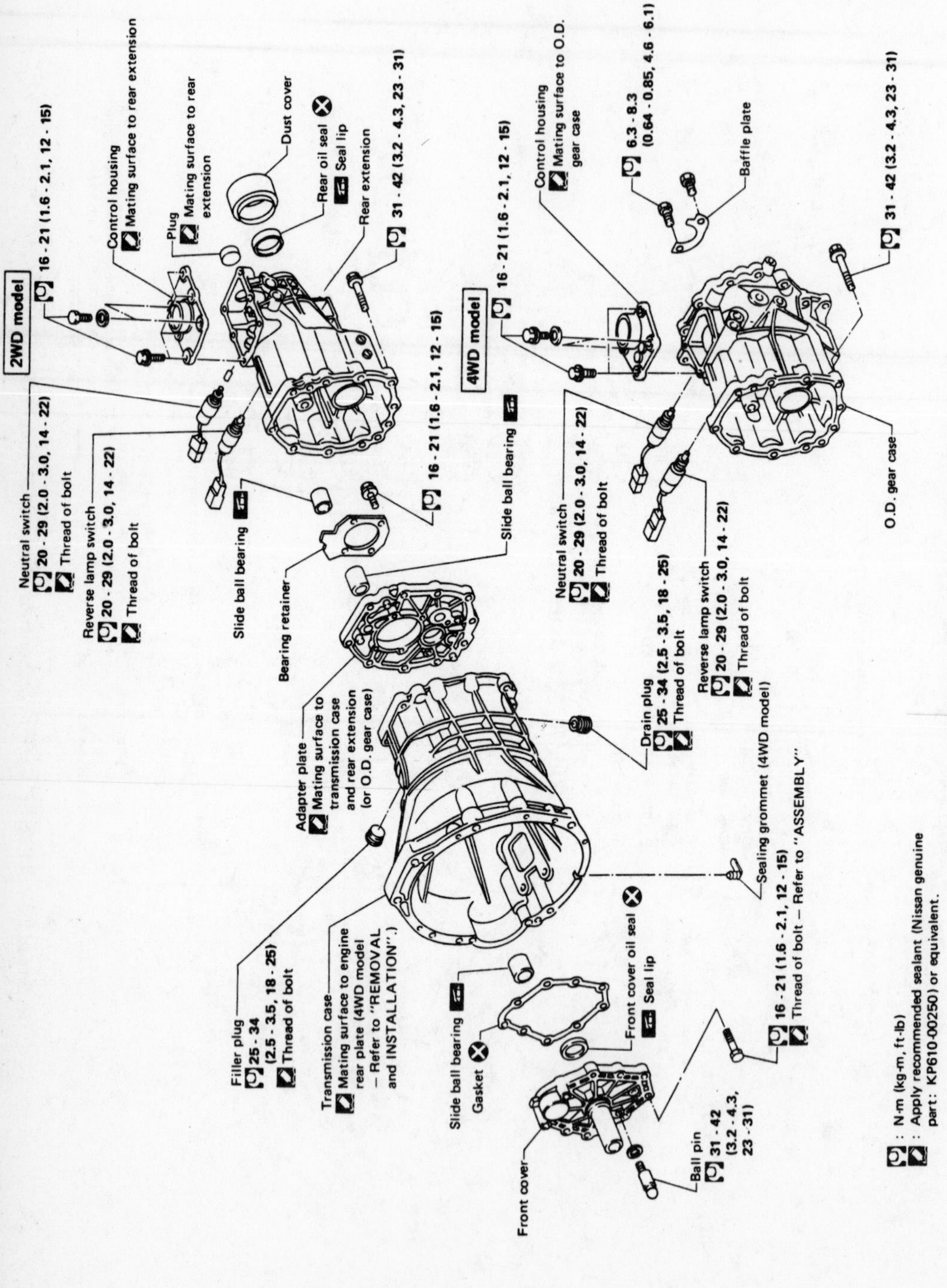

2WD model

Neutral switch
20 - 29 (2.0 - 3.0, 14 - 22)
Thread of bolt

Reverse lamp switch
20 - 29 (2.0 - 3.0, 14 - 22)
Thread of bolt

16 - 21 (1.6 - 2.1, 12 - 15)

Control housing
Mating surface to rear extension

Plug
Mating surface to rear extension

Slide ball bearing

Bearing retainer

Dust cover

Rear oil seal
Seal lip

Rear extension

31 - 42 (3.2 - 4.3, 23 - 31)

16 - 21 (1.6 - 2.1, 12 - 15)

Filler plug
25 - 34
(2.5 - 3.5, 18 - 25)
Thread of bolt

Adapter plate
Mating surface to transmission case and rear extension (or O.D. gear case)

Transmission case
Mating surface to engine rear plate (4WD model – Refer to "REMOVAL and INSTALLATION".)

Slide ball bearing

Gasket

Front cover

Front cover oil seal
Seal lip

Ball pin
31 - 42
(3.2 - 4.3,
23 - 31)

16 - 21 (1.6 - 2.1, 12 - 15)
Thread of bolt – Refer to "ASSEMBLY"

Sealing grommet (4WD model)

Drain plug
25 - 34 (2.5 - 3.5, 18 - 25)
Thread of bolt

Slide ball bearing

4WD model

16 - 21 (1.6 - 2.1, 12 - 15)

Control housing
Mating surface to O.D. gear case

Neutral switch
20 - 29 (2.0 - 3.0, 14 - 22)
Thread of bolt

6.3 - 8.3
(0.64 - 0.85, 4.6 - 6.1)

Reverse lamp switch
20 - 29 (2.0 - 3.0, 14 - 22)
Thread of bolt

Baffle plate

O.D. gear case

31 - 42 (3.2 - 4.3, 23 - 31)

: N·m (kg-m, ft-lb)
: Apply recommended sealant (Nissan genuine part: KP610-00250) or equivalent.

Exploded view of the transmission case—FS5R30A

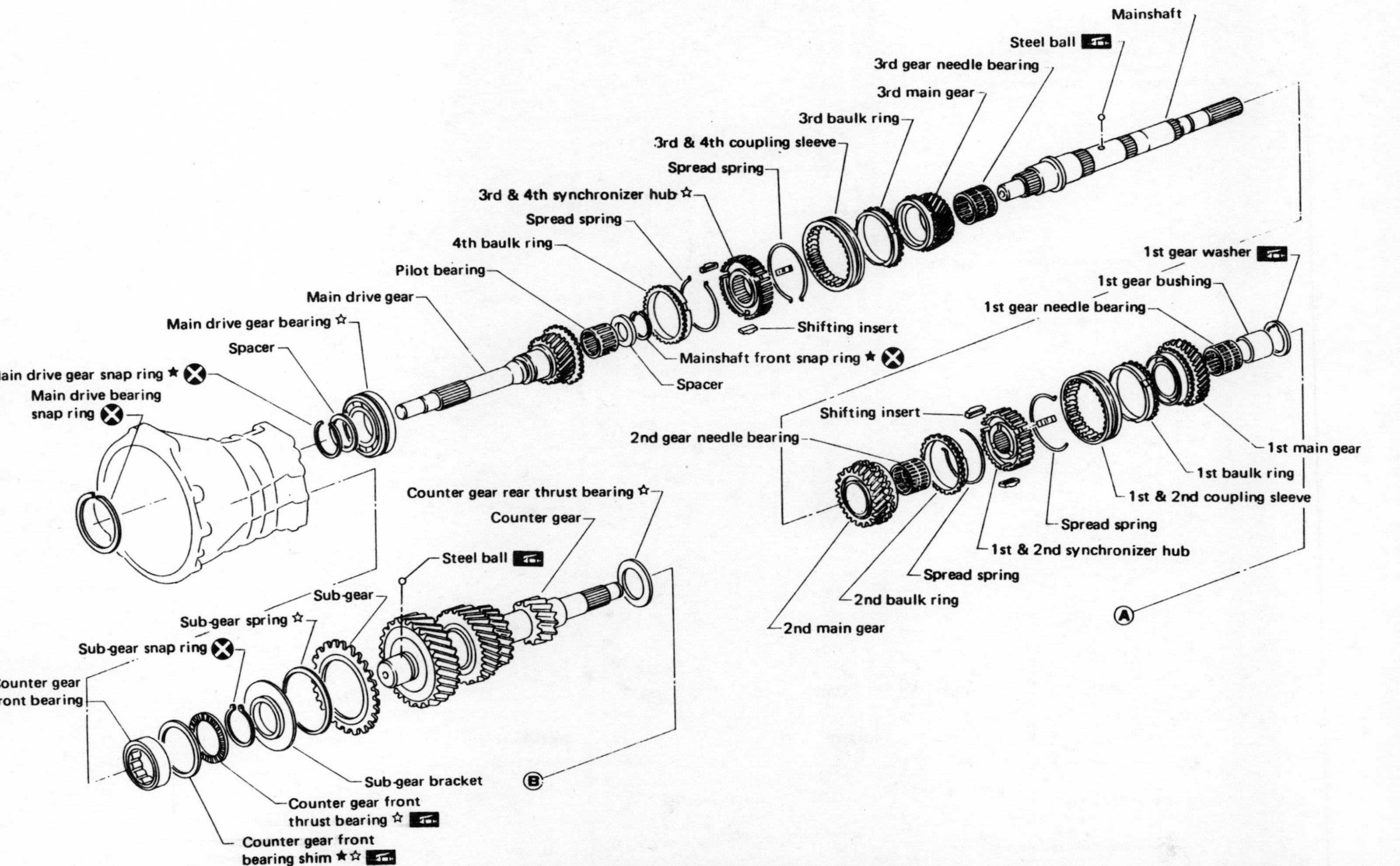

Exploded view of the gear components—FS5R30A

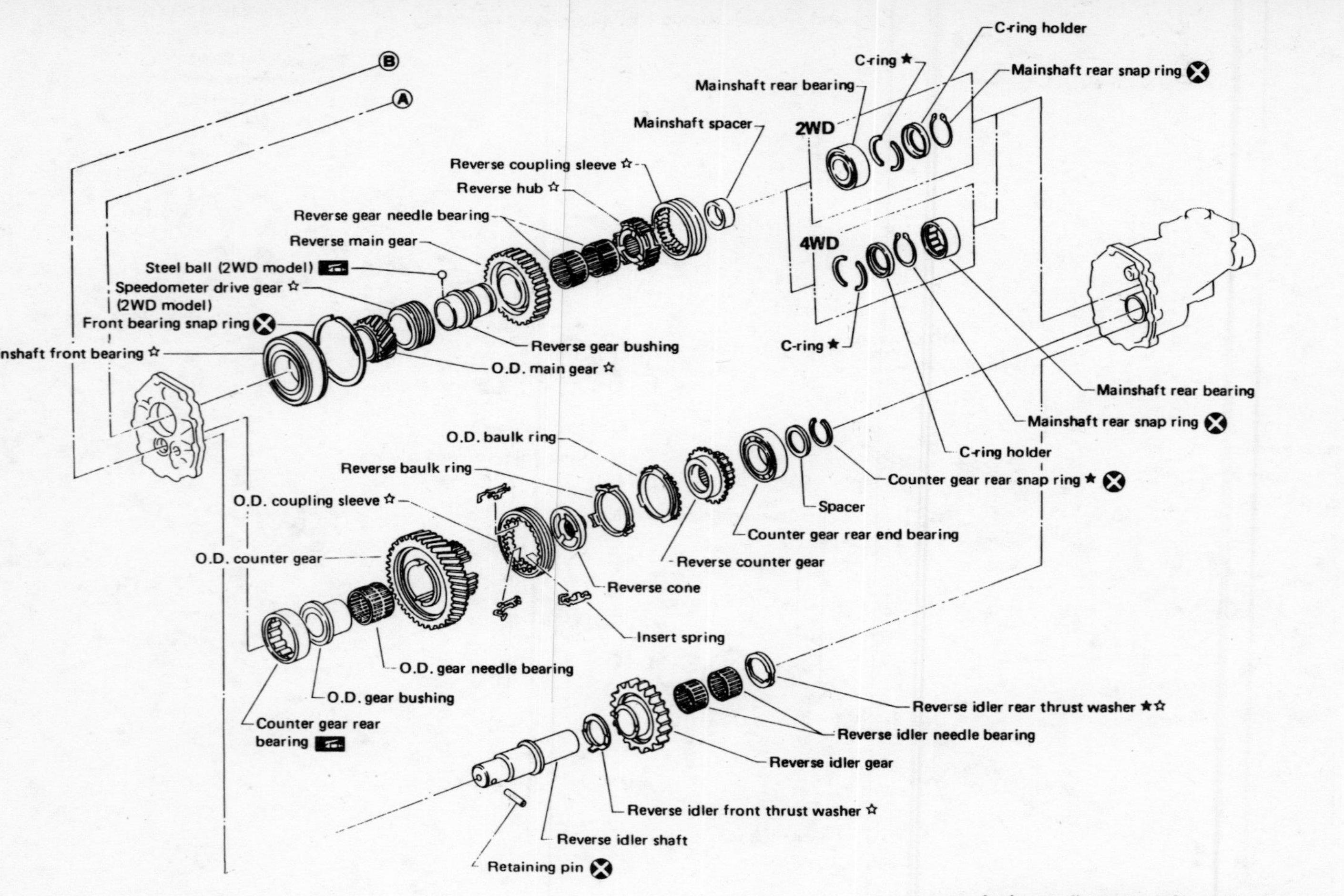

Apply gear oil to gears, shafts, synchronizers and bearings when assembling.

★ : Select with proper thickness

☆ : Pay attention to its direction

Exploded view of the gear components—FS5R30A

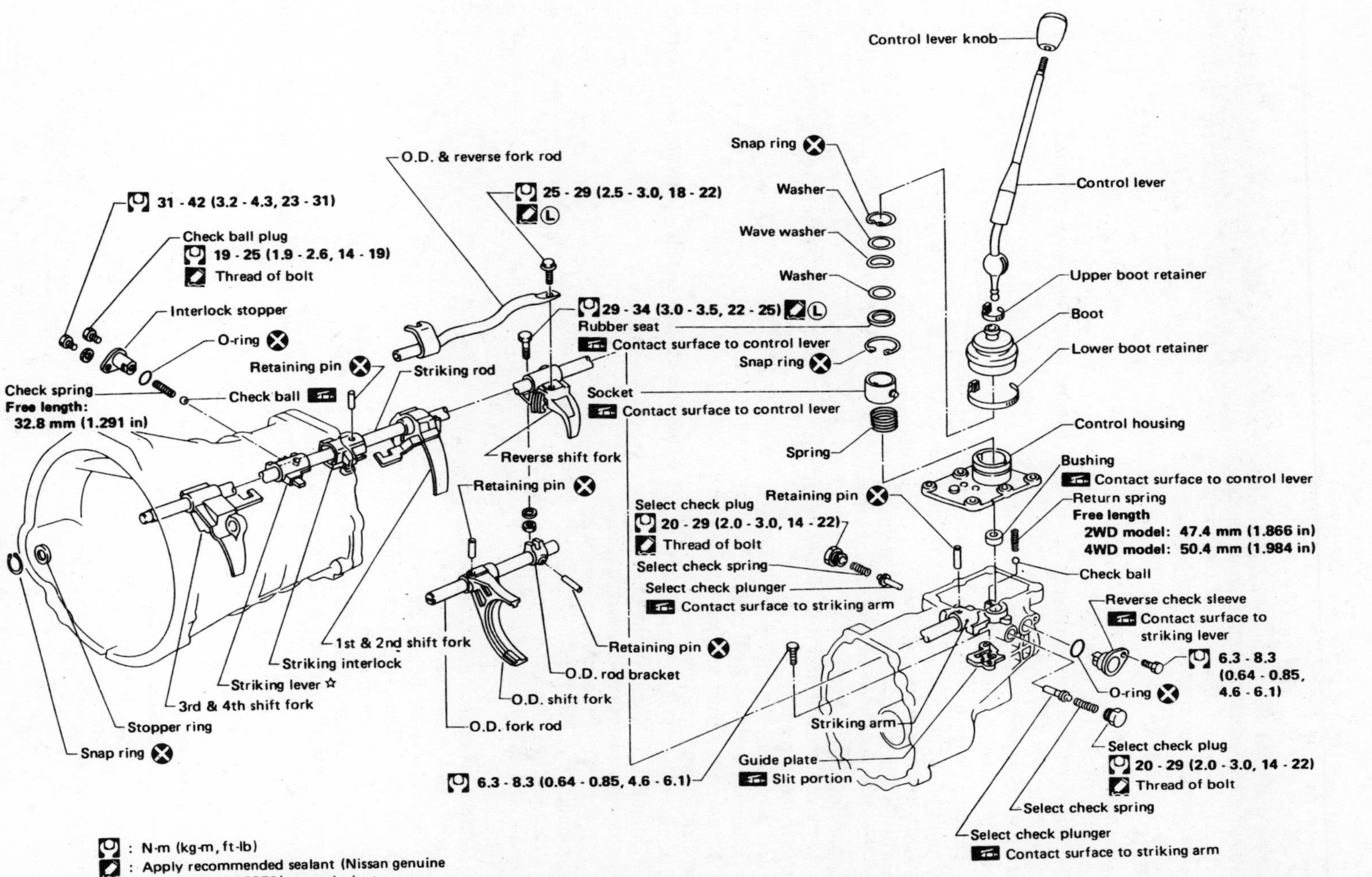

Exploded view of the shift control components—FS5R30A

slide the sub-gear bracket, spring and gear off the shaft.

11. Remove the counter drive gear along with the main drive gear assembly with a suitable puller. Be careful that the pilot bearing and baulk ring don't fall off.

12. Remove the snapring and then slide the 3–4 synchronizer (and 3rd gear) off the shaft.

13. Disassemble the rear of the adapter plate as follows:

FS5W71C:

a. Release the staking and then loosen the countershaft and mainshaft nuts. The mainshaft nut is a *lefthand* thread!

b. Remove the OD counter gear and its bearing with a puller. Remove the reverse counter gear and spacer.

c. Remove the snaprings from the reverse idler shaft and then slide off the reverse idler gear, thrust washers and bearing.

d. On 2wd models, remove the snapring and slide the overdrive mainshaft bearing and snapring off the shaft.

e. Remove the mainshaft nut. Remember, its a *lefthand* thread!

f. On 2wd models, remove the speedometer drive gear and and steel ball.

g. Remove the thrust washer, steel roller, roller bearing and washer.

h. Remove the OD main gear, needle bearing and baulk ring. Remove the OD coupling sleeve, shifting inserts and insert springs.

i. Tap the rear of the counter gear with a rubber mallet and remove it.

j. Press out the OD gear bushing, insert retainer and the OD synchronizer hub.

F4W71C:

a. Remove the snaprings, the speedometer drive gear and the steel ball.

b. Release the staking on the mainshaft nut and loosen it. Remove the mainshaft nut and slide off the reverse main gear.

c. Remove the snapring at the rear of the countershaft and then remove the reverse counter gear.

d. Remove the reverse idler gear.

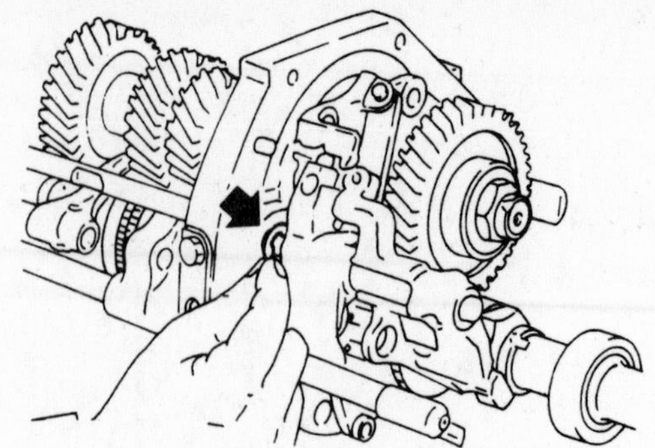

Remove the E-ring—FS5W71C (4wd)

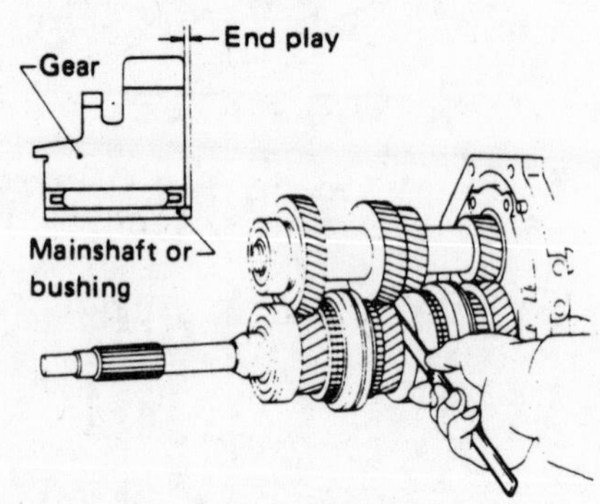

Measure the gear end play—F4W71C and FS5W71C

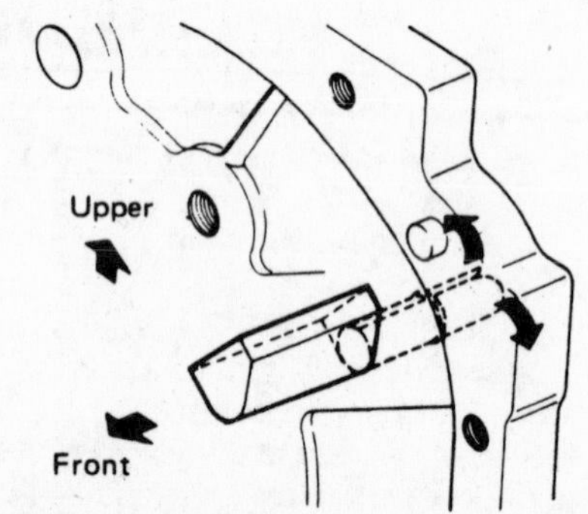

Intall the oil gutter on the adapter plate—F4W71C and FS5W71C

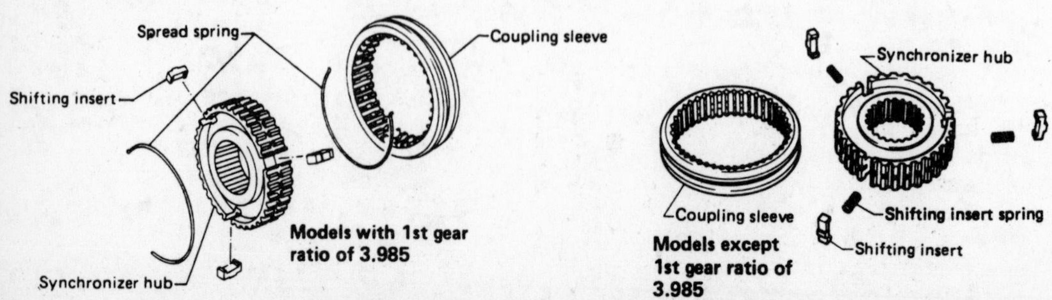

3–4 synchronizer assembly—F4W71C and FS5W71C

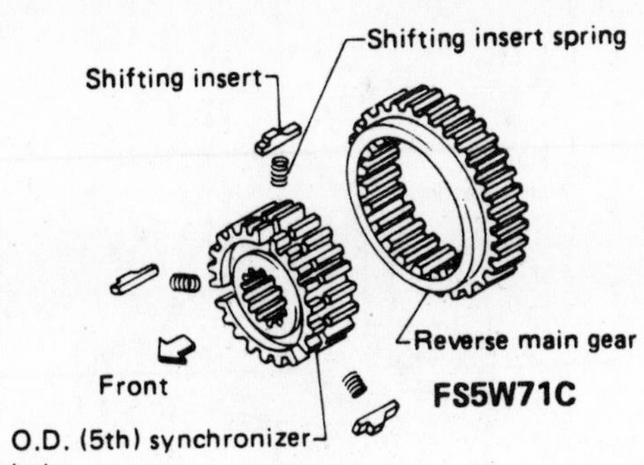

OD synchronizer assembly—FS5W71C

e. Tap the rear of the counter gear with a rubber mallet and slide it off the shaft.

f. Tap the rear of the mainshaft assembly with a rubber mallet and slide the assembly out of the adapter plate.

14. Remove the thrust washer, steel ball and the 1st main gear with needle bearing.

15. Press the 1st mainshaft bushing together with the 2nd main gear with a suitable tool and then remove the 2nd gear needle bushing.

16. Remove the main drive gear bearing snapring and washer and then slide off the bearing.

ASSEMBLY

1. Install all bearings into the case components as illustrated.
2. Install the oil gutter on the adapter plate so that it is expanded on the rear side. Insert the reverse shaft and then install the bearing retainer; tighten each screw and then stake at two points.
3. Press in the main drive gear bearing and install the spacer. Install a snapring so that the clearance of the groove is 0–0.14mm. Snaprings come in sizes from 1.73mm to 2.08mm.
4. Assemble the synchronizers as illustrated.
5. Assemble the 2nd main gear, needle bearing and the 1–2 syncro assembly and then press the 1st gear bushing onto the mainshaft.
6. Coat the steel ball and thrust washer with grease and then install them and the 1st main gear to the mainshaft.
7. Install the counter rear bearing to the adapter plate.
8. Press the mainshaft assembly and the counter gear into the adapter plate.
9. Install the 3rd main gear and the 3–4 syncro assembly. Install the synchro assembly as illustrated.
10. Install the mainshaft thrust washer and secure it with the proper size snapring. There should be minimal clearance in the groove.
11. Coat the pilot bearing with gear oil and install it on the mainshaft.
12. Press the counter drive gear (along with the main drive gear) onto the shaft.
13. Install the sub-gear and bracket on the counter drive gear and install a snapring that will minimize groove clearance. Snaprings come in 3 sizes; 1.4mm, 1.5mm and 1.6mm. Remove the snapring, sub-gear bracket and sub-gear from the counter gear and then reinstall them with the sub-gear spring between them.
14. Install the front bearing onto the counter gear.
15. Assemble the parts at the rear of the adapter plate as detailed in the Disassembly procedure.
16. Make sure that the 2nd and reverse gears are meshed and then tighten the locknut. On the FS5W71C, install a new countershaft locknut and tighten it. Stake both nuts with a punch.
17. Measure the gear endplay.
18. Install the shift rods, interlock plunger, interlock balls and check balls.
19. On 4wd models, rotate the OD–reverse bracket clockwise and install the fork shaft. Install the E-ring on the fork rod and then install the lever bracket bolt.
20. Coat the lip of a new oil seal with grease and install it in the front cover.
21. Apply sealant ot the transmission case mating surface and then slide the gear assembly onto the adapter plate.
22. Apply sealant to the adapter plate mating surface and then install the extension housing. Install the main drive bearing snapring.
23. Install a counter front bearing shim. Install a new gasket and the front cover.
24. Install the return spring plugs, check ball, return springs and check plunger.
25. Install the control housing with a new gasket.

Model FS5R30A (5 Speed)

DISASSEMBLY

1. Remove the check ball plug, check spring and check ball. Remove the interlock stopper. Don't let the check ball fall into the transmission case.
2. Remove the control housing, return spring and check ball.
3. Drive out the striking arm retaining pin with a punch.
4. Tap the extension housing (or OD case) lightly with a rubber mallet and remove it along with the striking arm.
5. Remove the front cover and its gasket.
6. Remove the stopper ring and the main drive bearing snapring.
7. Tap the transmission case lightly with a rubber mallet and remove it. Remove the front cover oil seal.

8. Mount the adapter plate in a soft-jawed vise and then remove the OD and reverse fork rod.

9. Drive the striking lever retaining pin out with a punch. While pulling out the striking rod, remove the lever and interlock. Then, remove 1–2 and 3–4 gears and the reverse shift fork.

10. Drive the OD shift fork retaining pin out with a punch, pull out the OD fork and then remove the OD shift fork.

11. Measure the end play at each gear. It should be 0.23–0.33mm at all gears except reverse which should be 0.33–0.43mm.

12. Remove the reverse coupling sleeve. Remove the snaprings from the rear of the mainshaft and counter gear.

13. Remove the C-ring holder and then the C-rings on the mainshaft. Use a hammer and punch.

14. Remove the mainshaft rear bearing on 2wd models.

15. Remove the reverse main gear along with the mainshaft spacer and the reverse synchronizer hub. Remove the reverse gear needle bearings.

16. Remove the reverse counter gear. Remove the OD coupling sleeve along with the OD and reverse baulk rings and the spring inserts.

17. Remove the reverse gear bushing. Remove the OD counter gear along with the reverse cone.

18. Press out the mainshaft and counter gear *alternately*.

19. From the mainshaft, remove the 1st gear washer and steel ball, 1st main gear and needle bearing. Remove the 2nd main gear along with the 1st gear bushing and the 1–2 syncro assembly. Remove the front snapring. Press out the 3rd main gear along with the 3–4 syncro assembly and the 3rd gear needle bearing.

20. From the counter gear, remove the rear thrust bearing and the sub-gear components.

21. Remove the main drive gear snapring and washer and the remove the bearing itself.

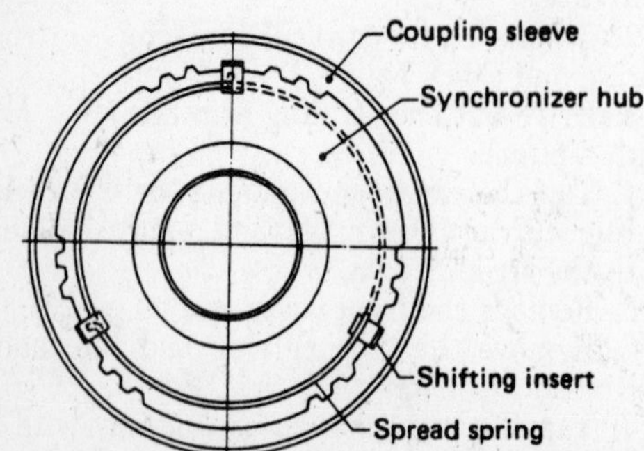

1–2 synchronizer assembly—FS5R30A

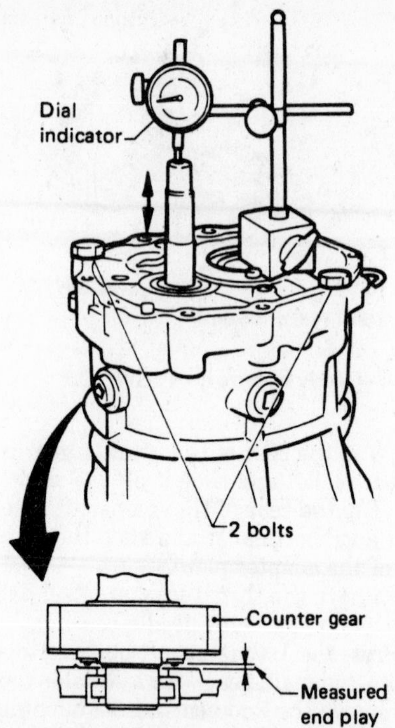

Measure the countergear end play—FS5R30A

ASSEMBLY

1. Install all bearing into the case components. Install the main drive gear bearing and snapring so that the groove clearance is 0–0.1mm. Snaprings come in sizes ranging from 1.89mm to 2.19mm.

2. Install the components on the counter gear. Remember to tap the sub-gear snapring into place on the counter gear.

3. Assemble the 1–2 and 3–4 synchronizers. Install the 3–4 syncro assembly together with the 3rd main gear and needle bearing onto the mainshaft.

4. Press the 1–2 syncro assembly along with the 2nd main gear and needle bearing onto the mainshaft.

5. Press the 1st gear bushing and washer, the 1st main gear and needle bearing, the steel ball and the 1st gear washer onto the mainshaft.

6. Install the counter gear along with the sub-gear components and the thrust washers onto the adapter plate. Remove the counter gear front bearing shim from the transmission case and then position the counter gear assembly into the inverted transmission case.

7. Secure the adapter plate to the case with 2 bolts and install a dial indicator on the rear end of the counter gear. Move the gear up and down while measuring the deflection. End play should be 0.10–0.25mm. Select the proper shim from the following chart:

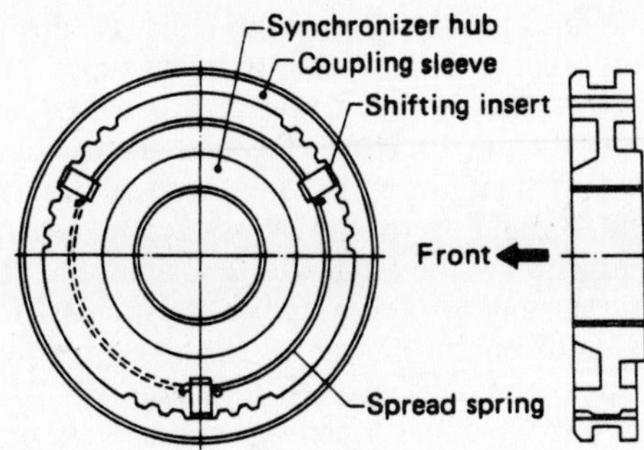

3–4 synchronizer assembly—FS5R30A

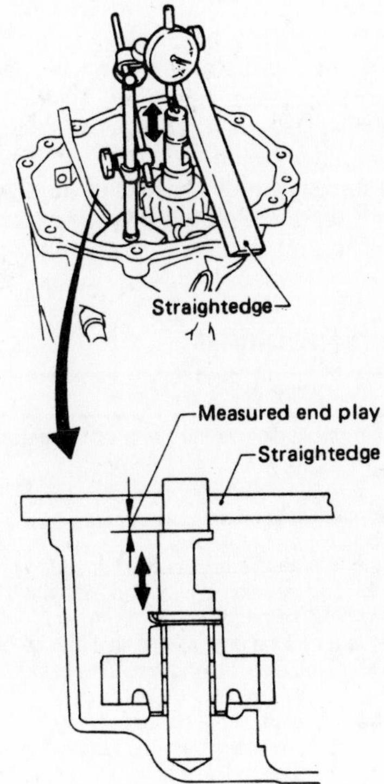

Measure the reverse idler gear end play—FS5R30A

8. Install the reverse idler gear, reverse idler needle bearings, reverse idler thrust washers and the reverse idler shaft to the extension housing (or OD case). Install a dial indicator on the front end of the shaft. Install a straightedge across the extension housing (or OD case) flange as a stopper and then move the shaft up and down to measure end play. It should be 0.30–0.53mm. Adjustment is made by changing the thrust washer; there are 2 sizes: 1.97mm and 2.07mm.

9. Install the mainshaft and counter gear on the adapter plate and then install the main drive gear on the mainshaft.

10. Install the rear side components on the mainshaft and counter gear as detailed in the Disassembly procedures.

11. Install the OD fork rod and shift fork and then press the retaining pin into the shift fork with a punch.

12. Install the 1–2, 3–4 and reverse shift forks onto the coupling sleeve.

13. Install the striking rod into the shift fork, striking lever and interlock hole and then press the retaining pin into the striking lever. Check for smooth movement of the lever.

14. Coat the lip of a new oil seal with grease and install it in the front cover.

15. Coat the selected counter gear front bearing shim with grease and install it in the transmission case.

16. Apply sealant to the case mating surface and install the gear assembly.

17. Coat the check ball with grease and then install it along with the check spring into the interlock stopper.

18. Install the interlock stopper assembly and then tighten the check ball plug. Be sure to coat the threads of the plug with sealant.

19. Install the stopper ring and the main drive bearing snapring.

20. Install the front cover with a new gasket. Apply sealant to the threads of the 3 lower bolts.

Dial indicator deflection mm (in)	Thickness of proper washer mm (in)	Part number
0.93 - 1.02 (0.0366 - 0.0402)	0.88 (0.0346)	32218-01G11
1.03 - 1.12 (0.0406 - 0.0441)	0.96 (0.0378)	32218-01G12
1.13 - 1.22 (0.0445 - 0.0480)	1.04 (0.0409)	32218-01G13
1.23 - 1.32 (0.0484 - 0.0520)	1.12 (0.0441)	32218-01G14
1.33 - 1.42 (0.0524 - 0.0559)	1.28 (0.0504)	32218-01G15
1.43 - 1.52 (0.0563 - 0.0598)	1.36 (0.0535)	32218-01G16
1.53 - 1.62 (0.0602 - 0.0638)	1.44 (0.0567)	32218-01G17

21. Install the extension housing (or OD case) along with the striking arm. Install the striking arm retaining pin with a punch.
22. Install the return spring and check ball and then install the control housing.
23. Tighten the control housing bolts to 12–15 ft. lbs. (16–21 Nm).

CLUTCH

CAUTION: *The clutch driven disc contains asbestos, which has been determined to be a cancer causing agent. Never clean clutch surfaces with compressed air! Avoid inhaling any dust from any clutch surface! When cleaning clutch surfaces, use a commercially available brake cleaning fluid.*

Understanding the Clutch

The purpose of the clutch is to disconnect and connect engine power from the transmission. A car at rest requires a lot of engine torque to get all that weight moving. An internal combustion engine does not develop a high starting torque (unlike steam engines), so it must be allowed to operate without any load until it builds up enough torque to move the car. Torque increases with engine rpm. The clutch allows the engine to build up torque by physically disconnecting the engine from the transmission, relieving the engine of any load or resistance. The transfer of engine power to the transmission (the load) must be smooth and gradual; if it weren't, drive line components would wear out or break quickly. This gradual power transfer is made possible by gradually releasing the clutch pedal. The clutch disc and pressure plate are the connecting link between the engine and transmission. When the clutch pedal is released, the disc and plate contact each other (clutch engagement), physically joining the engine and transmission. When the pedal is pushed in, the disc and plate separate (the clutch is disengaged), disconnecting the engine from the transmission.

The clutch assembly consists of the flywheel, the clutch disc, the clutch pressure plate, the throwout bearing and fork, the actuating link-

Troubleshooting Basic Clutch Problems

Problem	Cause
Excessive clutch noise	Throwout bearing noises are more audible at the lower end of pedal travel. The usual causes are: • Riding the clutch • Too little pedal free-play • Lack of bearing lubrication A bad clutch shaft pilot bearing will make a high pitched squeal, when the clutch is disengaged and the transmission is in gear or within the first 2″ of pedal travel. The bearing must be replaced. Noise from the clutch linkage is a clicking or snapping that can be heard or felt as the pedal is moved completely up or down. This usually requires lubrication. Transmitted engine noises are amplified by the clutch housing and heard in the passenger compartment. They are usually the result of insufficient pedal free-play and can be changed by manipulating the clutch pedal.
Clutch slips (the car does not move as it should when the clutch is engaged)	This is usually most noticeable when pulling away from a standing start. A severe test is to start the engine, apply the brakes, shift into high gear and SLOWLY release the clutch pedal. A healthy clutch will stall the engine. If it slips it may be due to: • A worn pressure plate or clutch plate • Oil soaked clutch plate • Insufficient pedal free-play
Clutch drags or fails to release	The clutch disc and some transmission gears spin briefly after clutch disengagement. Under normal conditions in average temperatures, 3 seconds is maximum spin-time. Failure to release properly can be caused by: • Too light transmission lubricant or low lubricant level • Improperly adjusted clutch linkage
Low clutch life	Low clutch life is usually a result of poor driving habits or heavy duty use. Riding the clutch, pulling heavy loads, holding the car on a grade with the clutch instead of the brakes and rapid clutch engagement all contribute to low clutch life.

age and the pedal. The flywheel and clutch pressure plate (driving members) are connected to the engine crankshaft and rotate with it. The clutch disc is located between the flywheel and pressure plate, and splined to the transmission shaft. A driving member is one that is attached to the engine and transfers engine power to a driven member (clutch disc) on the transmission shaft. A driving member (pressure plate) rotates (drives) a driven member (clutch disc) on contact and, in so doing, turns the transmission shaft. There is a circular diaphragm spring within the pressure plate cover (transmission side). In a relaxed state (when the clutch pedal is fully released), this spring is convex; that is, it is dished outward toward the transmission. Pushing in the clutch pedal actuates an attached linkage rod. Connected to the other end of this rod is the throwout bearing fork. The throwout bearing is attached to the fork. When the clutch pedal is depressed, the clutch linkage pushes the fork and bearing forward to contact the diaphragm spring of the pressure plate. The outer edges of the spring are secured to the pressure plate and are pivoted on rings so that when the center of the spring is compressed by the throwout bearing, the outer edges bow outward and, by so doing, pull the pressure plate in the same direction - away from the clutch disc. This action separates the disc from the plate, disengaging the clutch and allowing the transmission to be shifted into another gear. A coil type clutch return spring attached to the clutch pedal arm permits full release of the pedal. Releasing the pedal pulls the throwout bearing away from the diaphragm spring resulting in a reversal of spring position. As bearing pressure is gradually released from the spring center, the outer edges of the spring bow outward, pushing the pressure plate into closer contact with the clutch disc. As the disc and plate move closer together, friction between the two increases and slippage is reduced until, when full spring pressure is applied (by fully releasing the pedal), The speed of the disc and plate are the same. This stops all slipping, creating a direct connection between the plate and disc which results in the transfer of power from the engine to the transmission. The clutch disc is now rotating with the pressure plate at engine speed and, because it is splined to the transmission shaft, the shaft now turns at the same engine speed. Understanding clutch operation can be rather difficult at first; if you're still confused after reading this, consider the following analogy. The action of the diaphragm spring can be compared to that of an oil can bottom. The bottom of an oil can is shaped very much like the clutch diaphragm spring and pushing in on the can bottom and then releasing it produces a similar effect. As mentioned earlier, the clutch pedal return spring permits full release of the pedal and reduces linkage slack due to wear. As the linkage wears, clutch free-pedal travel will increase and free-travel will decrease as the clutch wears. Free-travel is actually throwout bearing lash.

The diaphragm spring type clutches used are available in two different designs: flat diaphragm springs or bent spring. The bent fingers are bent back to create a centrifugal boost ensuring quick re-engagement at higher engine speeds. This design enables pressure plate load to increase as the clutch disc wears and makes low pedal effort possible even with a heavy-duty clutch. The throwout bearing used with the bent finger design is 32mm long and is shorter than the bearing used with the flat finger design. These bearings are not interchangeable. If the longer bearing is used with the bent finger clutch, free-pedal travel will not exist. This results in clutch slippage and rapid wear.

The transmission varies the gear ratio between the engine and rear wheels. It can be shifted to change engine speed as driving conditions and loads change. The transmission allows disengaging and reversing power from the engine to the wheels.

Adjustments

PEDAL HEIGHT

The pedal height measurement is gauged from the angle section of the floorboard to the center of the clutch pedal pad.

Adjust the pedal height by loosening the locknut on the pedal stopper, clutch switch or ASCD switch and turning the adjusting bolt to provide the following specified heights:

- 1970-73: 150mm
- 1974-77: 153mm
- 1978-80: 163mm
- 1981-82 Z22: 171mm
- 1981-82 SD22: 182mm
- 1983 Z22 168mm
- 1983 SD22: 179mm
- 1984-86 Z20 and Z24: 184mm
- 1986-89 Z24i and SD25: 236–246mm
- 1986-89 VG30i: 227–237mm

PEDAL FREE PLAY

The free-play measurement is the total travel of the clutch pedal from the fully released position to where resistance is felt as the pedal is pushed downward.

Adjust the pedal free play by loosening the pushrod locknut and turning the clevis. Free play is as follows:

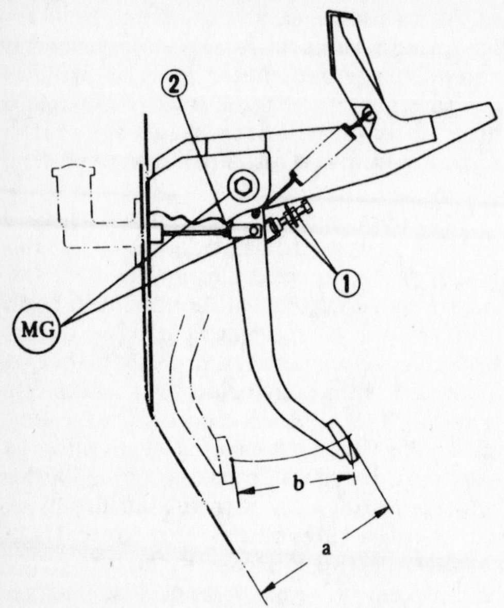

Clutch pedal adjustment points—1970–79

- 1970-77: 2mm
- 1978-84: 3mm
- 1985-89: 1–1.5mm

CLUTCH INTERLOCK

1986-89 (D21-D Series)

Check the clearance between the threaded end of the clutch interlock switch and the pedal stopper bracket when the clutch pedal is fully depressed. Clearance should be 0.3–1.0mm.

Driven Disc And Pressure Plate

The clutch is a hydraulically operated single plate, dry friction disc, diaphragm spring type.

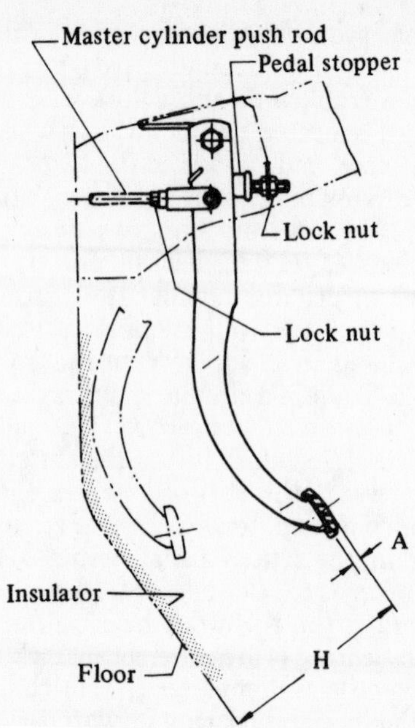

Clutch pedal adjustment points—1980–86 (720-D series)

The clutch is operated by a clutch pedal which is mechanically connected to a clutch master cylinder. When the pedal is depressed, the piston in the master cylinder is moved in the master cylinder bore. This movement compresses the hydraulic fluid in the master cylinder causing pressure which is transferred through a tube to the slave cylinder. The slave cylinder is mounted to the clutch housing with its piston connected to the clutch release lever. The hydraulic pressure in the slave cylinder forces the slave cylinder piston to travel out the

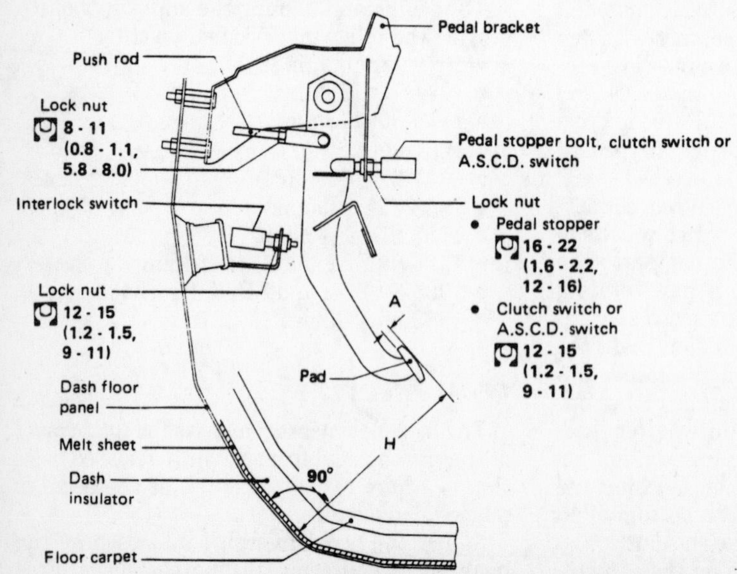

Clutch pedal adjustment points—1986–89 (D21-D series)

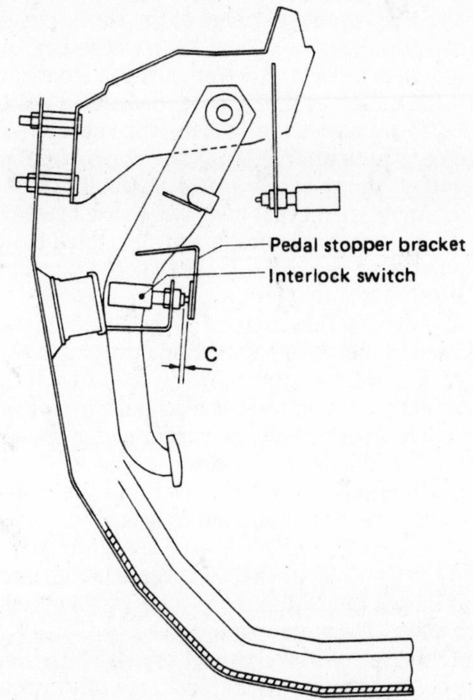

Clutch interlock adjustment—1986–89 (D21-D series)

cylinder bore and move the clutch release lever, disengaging the clutch.

REMOVAL AND INSTALLATION

CAUTION: *The clutch driven disc contains asbestos, which has been determined to be a cancer causing agent. Never clean clutch surfaces with compressed air! Avoid inhaling any dust from any clutch surface! When cleaning clutch surfaces, use a commercially available brake cleaning fluid.*

1. Raise the vehicle and support it with floor stands.
2. Remove the transmission. On 1970-71 models with the non-removable crossmember, you can move the transmission back and rest it on the crossmember while working on the clutch, if you prefer. You won't have much working area, but it will save you the trouble of getting the transmission out from under the truck.
3. Mark the clutch assembly-to-flywheel relationship with paint or a center punch so that the clutch assembly can be reassembled in the same position from which it is removed. Insert a clutch aligning tool (dummy shaft) into the hub. This tool is available from your local Nissan dealer or an auto parts store. It is important to support the weight of the clutch while the retaining bolts are being removed.
4. Loosen the clutch cover-to-flywheel attaching bolts, one turn at a time in an alternating sequence, until the spring tension is relieved to avoid distorting or bending the clutch cover. Remove the clutch assembly.
5. Inspect the flywheel for scoring, roughness, or signs of overheating. Light scoring may be cleaned up with emery cloth, but any deep grooves or scoring warrant replacement or refacing (if possible) of the flywheel. If the clutch

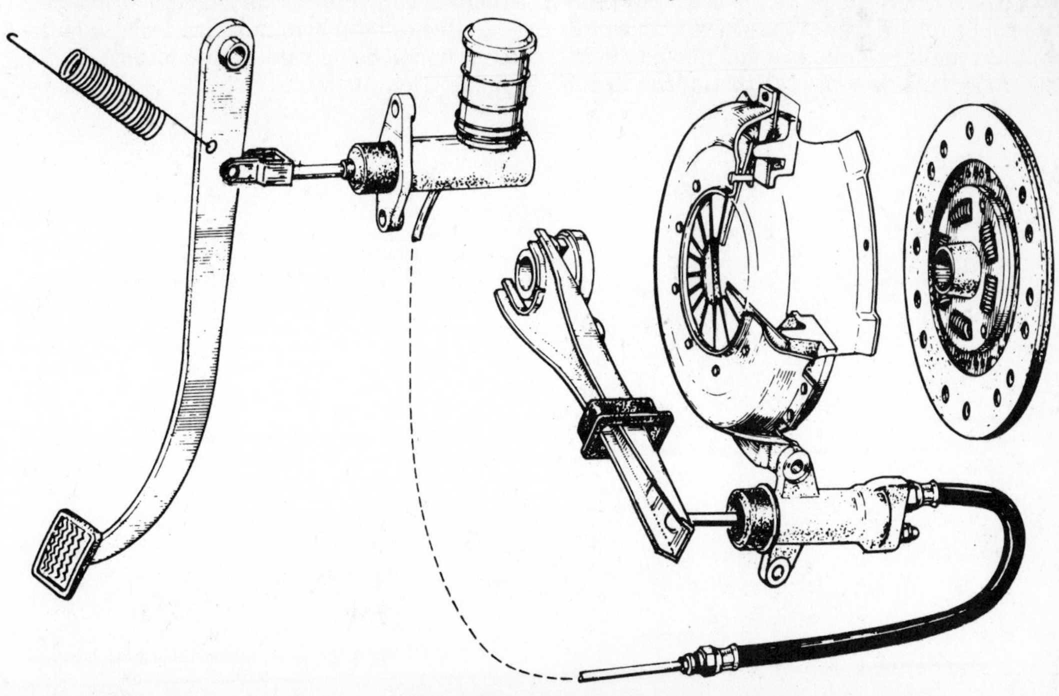
Typical clutch operating system

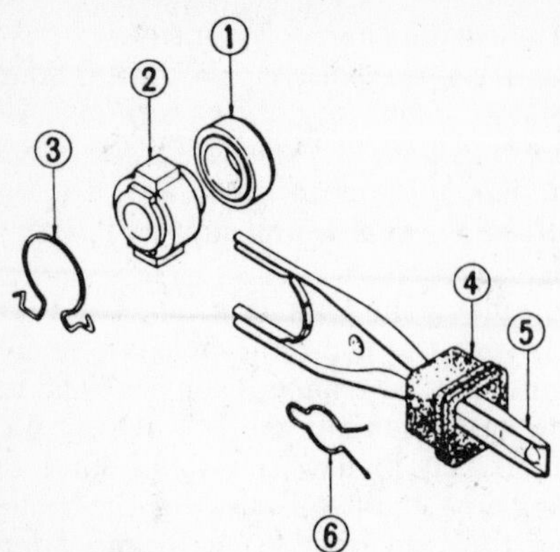

1. Release (throwout) bearing
2. Bearing sleeve
3. Sleeve spring
4. Boot
5. Release lever
6. Retaining spring

Typical clutch release mechanism

facings or flywheel are oily, inspect the transmission front cover oil seal, the pilot bushing, and engine rear seals, etc. for leakage, and correct before replacing the clutch. If the pilot bushing in the crankshaft is worn, replace it. Install it using a soft hammer. The factory supplied part does not have to be oiled, but check the procedure if you are using an aftermarket part. Inspect the clutch cover for wear or scoring, and replace as necessary. The pressure plate and spring cannot be disassembled; you must replace the clutch cover as an assembly.

6. Inspect the clutch release bearing. If it is rough or noisy, it should be replaced. The bearing can be removed from the sleeve with a puller; this requires a press to install the new bearing. After installation, coat the groove in the sleeve, the contact surfaces of the release lever, pivot pin and sleeve, and the release bearing contact surfaces on the transmission front cover with a light coat of grease. Be careful not to use too much grease, which will run at high temperatures and get onto the clutch facings. Reinstall the release bearing on the lever.

7. Apply a thin coat of grease to the pressure plate wire ring, diaphragm spring, clutch cover grooves and the drive bosses on the pressure plate.

8. Apply a thin coat of Lubriplate® to the splines in the driven plate. Slide the clutch disc onto the splines, and move it back and forth several times. Remove the disc and wipe off the excess lubricant. Be very careful not to get any grease on the clutch facings.

9. Assemble the clutch cover and the clutch plate on the clutch alignment arbor.

10. Align the marks made on the clutch cover and the flywheel (if the old cover is being used) and install the clutch cover-to-flywheel attaching bolts. Three dowels are used to locate the clutch cover on the flywheel properly. Tighten the bolts in an alternating sequence one turn at a time to 12–15 ft. lbs. (17–22 Nm) on 1970-79 modelsand 16–22 ft. lbs. (22–29 Nm) on 1980-89 models. Remove the aligning arbor.

11. Install the transmission.

Clutch Master Cylinder

REMOVAL AND INSTALLATION

1. Disconnect the master cylinder pushrod from the clutch pedal.

2. Remove the hydraulic line from the master cylinder being careful not to damage the compression fitting.

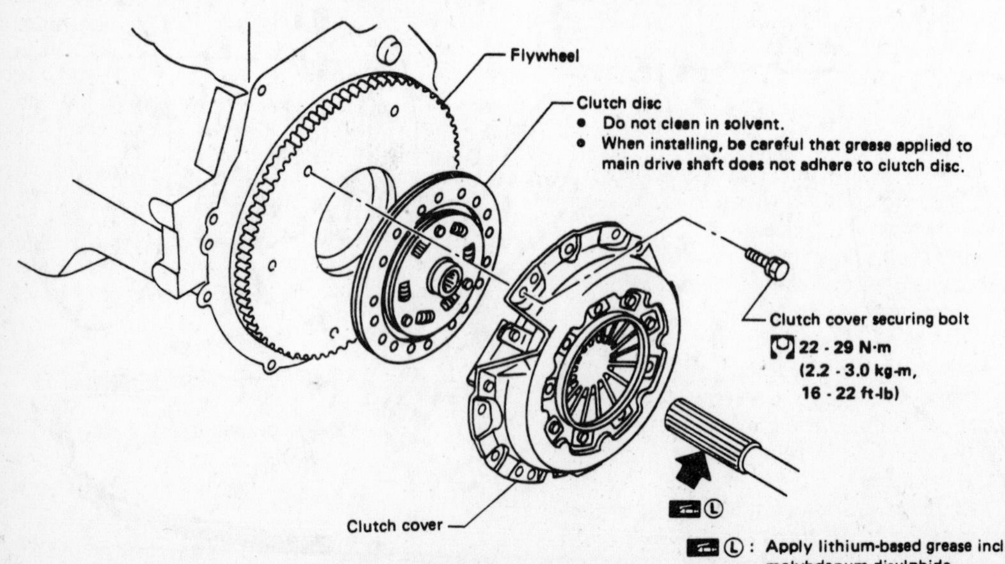

Typical clutch installation

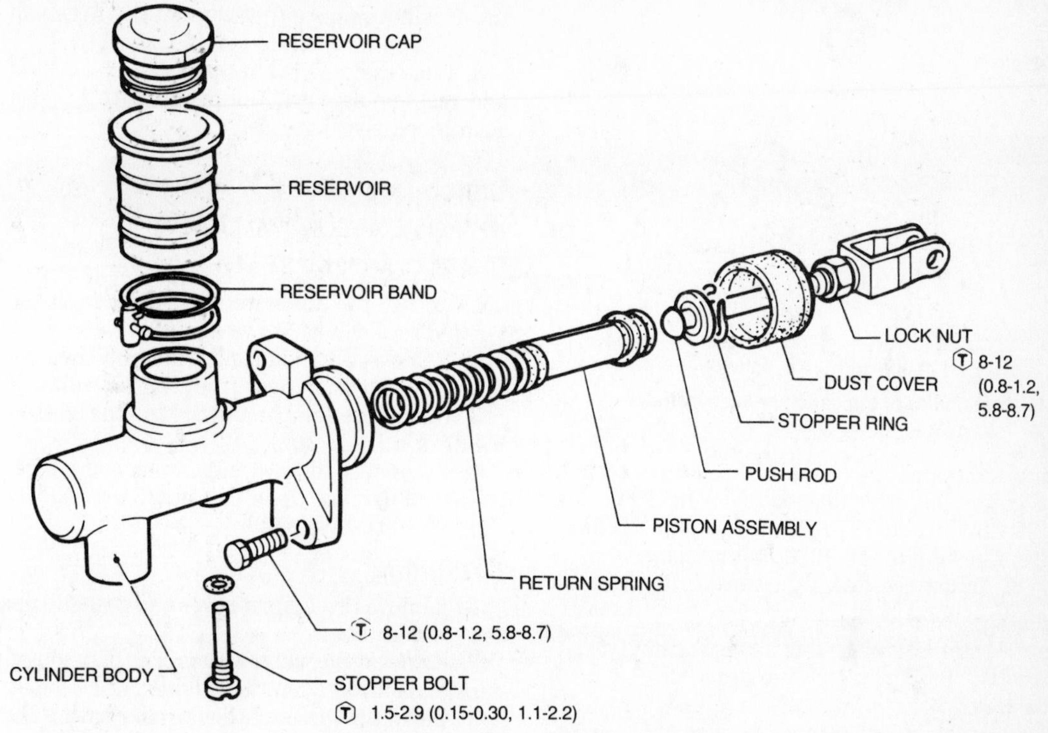

Exploded view of the clutch master cylinder

3. Remove the two bolts holding the master cylinder to the engine compartment.

CAUTION: *Brake fluid dissolves paint. Do not allow it to drip onto the body when removing the master cylinder.*

4. Install the master cylinder. Partially tighten the hydraulic line and then tighten the cylinder mounting bolts.
5. Connect the pushrod to the clutch pedal.
6. Adjust the clutch pedal and bleed the system.

OVERHAUL

1. Disassemble the master cylinder by unscrewing the clutch pedal clevis from the pushrod. Also remove the locknut.
2. Pull off the rubber boot to expose an internal snapring. Remove the snapring and withdraw the piston and compression spring.
3. Take a clean rag and wipe out the inside of the cylinder. Inspect the inside of the cylinder for scoring and deposits. Use crocus cloth or a small hone to refinish the inside of the cylinder. If light honing will not remove score marks replace the cylinder.

NOTE: *Be careful not to remove too much from the cylinder walls as the cups will not be able to seal the cylinder if the diameter is enlarged excessively.*

4. Wash all metal parts in solvent.
5. Further disassembly should be avoided unless the reservoir is leaking. If the reservoir needs to be replaced, remove the cap and remove the master cylinder reservoir bolt located at the bottom of the reservoir. Tighten the bolt upon reassembly.
6. With new parts from the rebuilding kit assemble the master cylinder. Coat the cylinder wall with brake fluid so that the edges of the new cups will not be damaged. Coat the piston with lithium soap based glycol grease.

Clutch Release Cylinder

REMOVAL AND INSTALLATION

1. Raise the front of the truck and support it on jackstands.
2. Remove the tension spring on the clutch fork.
3. Remove the hydraulic line from the release cylinder. Be careful not to damage the fitting.
4. Turn the release cylinder pushrod in sufficiently to gain clearance from the fork.
5. Remove the mounting bolts and withdraw the cylinder.
6. Install the hydraulic line from the master cylinder.
7. Position the cylinder on the clutch hous-

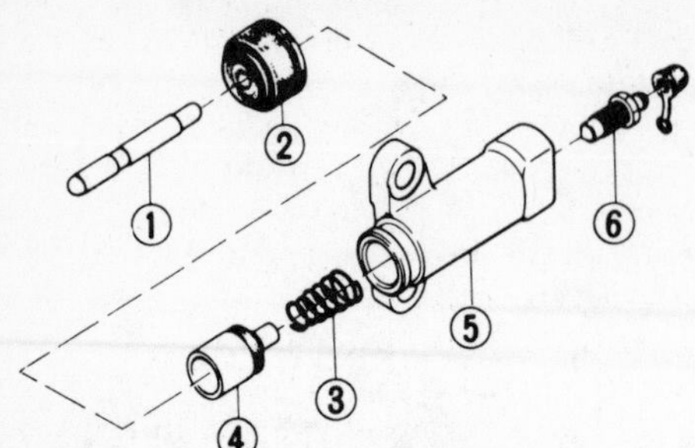

Exploded view of the clutch release cylinder

ing and install the clamp and retaining screws. Tighten the attaching bolts to 18–25 ft. lbs. (25–35 Nm) on 1970-79 models and 22–30 ft. lbs. (30–40 Nm) on 1980-89 models.

8. Adjust the fork tip clearance to 2mm on 1970-71 models

NOTE: *The system must be bled after the cylinder is reinstalled.*

OVERHAUL

1. Remove the pushrod, rubber boot, piston and cups from the cylinder.

2. Clean the inside of the cylinder with a rag and inspect for scoring. If there is no serious damage, hone the cylinder just enough to remove deposits. Replace the cylinder if light honing does not remove the score marks. Wash all the parts in brake fluid before assembly.

3. Coat the new rubber parts in brake fluid and reassemble. Coat the piston with lithium soap based glycol grease.

Clutch Damper

REMOVAL AND INSTALLATION

1986-89 Only (D21-D Series)

1. Loosen the union nuts and disconnect the two hydraulic lines at the damper.

2. Remove the mounting bolts and then remove the clutch damper from the firewall.

3. Install the damper and tighten the bolts to 6–8 ft. lbs. (8–11 Nm).

4. Reconnect the hydraulic lines being careful not to damage the union nuts.

5. Bleed the system.

OVERHAUL

1. Remove the damper cover and gasket from the cylinder body.

2. Remove the rubber damper, piston and cups and spring from the cylinder.

3. Clean the inside of the cylinder with a rag and inspect for scoring. If there is no serious damage, hone the cylinder just enough to remove deposits. Replace the cylinder if light honing does not remove the score marks. Wash all the parts in brake fluid before assembly.

4. Coat the new rubber parts in brake fluid

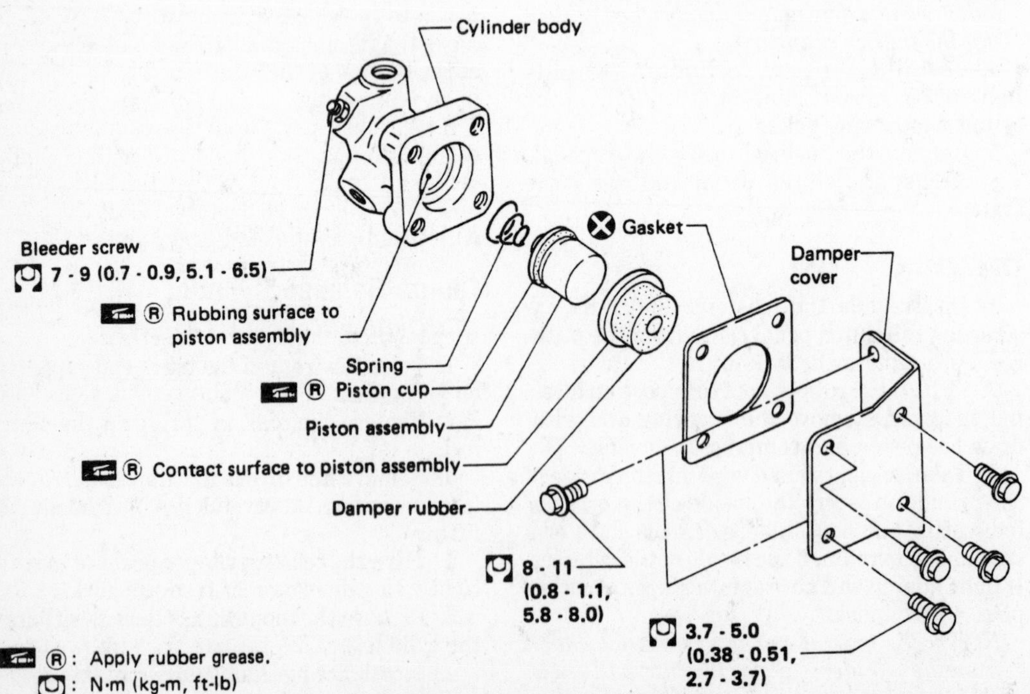

Exploded view of the clutch damper

and reassemble. Coat the piston with lithium soap based glycol grease.

5. Install a new gasket and tighten the damper cover to 3–4 ft. lbs. (3–5 Nm).

Bleeding the Clutch Hydraulic System

NOTE: *This procedure may be utilized when either the clutch master or release cylinder has been removed or if any of the hydraulic lines have been disturbed.*

CAUTION: *Do not spill brake fluid on the body of the vehicle as it will destroy the paint.*

1. Fill the master cylinder reservoir with brake fluid.

NOTE: *On 1986-89 models that incorporate a clutch damper in the hydraulic system, perform Steps 1–10 for the clutch damper and then move on to the release cylinder.*

2. Remove the cap and loosen the bleeder screw on the clutch release cylinder. Cover the hole with your finger.

3. Have an assistant pump the clutch pedal several times. Take your finger off the hole while the pedal is being depressed so that the air in the system can be released. Put your finger back on the hole and release the pedal.

4. After fluid pressure can be felt (with your finger) tighten the bleeder screw.

5. Put a short length of hose over the bleeder screw and place the other end into a jar half full of clean brake fluid.

6. Depress the clutch pedal and loosen the bleeder screw. Allow the fluid to flow into the jar.

7. Tighten the plug and then release the clutch pedal.

8. Repeat Steps 6–7 until no air bubbles are visible in the bleeder tube.

9. When there are no more air bubbles in the system, tighten the plug fully with the pedal depressed. Replace the plastic cap.

10. Fill the master cylinder to the correct level with brake fluid.

11. Check the system for leaks.

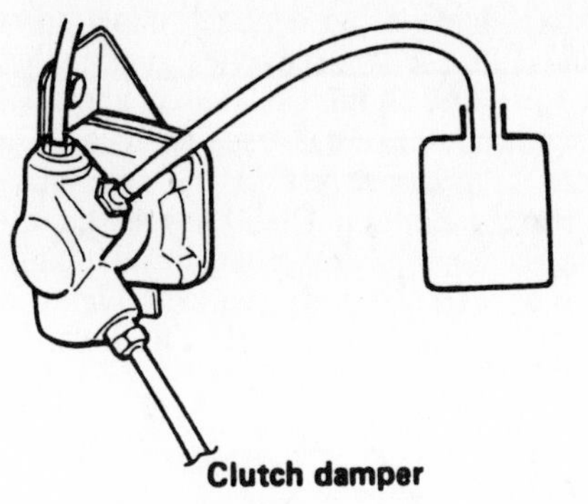

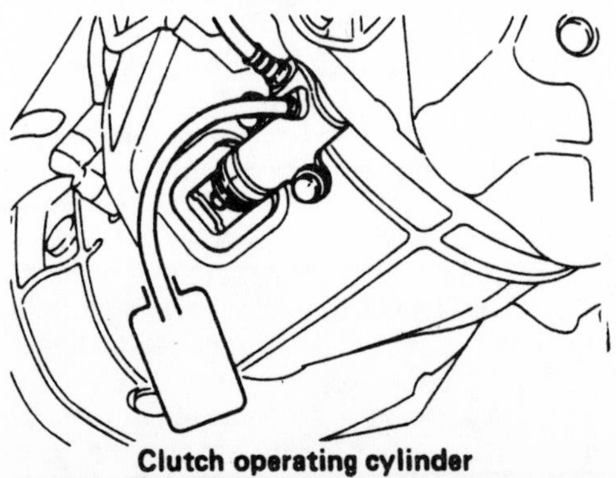

Bleeding the clutch

AUTOMATIC TRANSMISSION

Understanding Automatic Transmissions

The automatic transmission allows engine torque and power to be transmitted to the rear wheels within a narrow range of engine operating speeds. The transmission will allow the engine to turn fast enough to produce plenty of power and torque at very low speeds, while keeping it at a sensible rpm at high vehicle speeds. The transmission performs this job entirely without driver assistance. The transmission uses a light fluid as the medium for the transmission of power. This fluid also works in the operation of various hydraulic control circuits and as a lubricant. Because the transmission fluid performs all of these three functions, trouble within the unit can easily travel from one part to another. For this reason, and because of the complexity and unusual operating principles of the transmission, a very sound understanding of the basic principles of operation will simplify troubleshooting.

THE TORQUE CONVERTER

The torque converter replaces the conventional clutch. It has three functions:

1. It allows the engine to idle with the vehicle at a standstill, even with the transmission in gear.

2. It allows the transmission to shift from range to range smoothly, without requiring that the driver close the throttle during the shift.

3. It multiplies engine torque to an increasing extent as vehicle speed drops and throttle opening is increased. This has the effect of making the transmission more responsive and reduces the amount of shifting required.

The torque converter is a metal case which is shaped like a sphere that has been flattened on opposite sides. It is bolted to the rear end of the engine's crankshaft. Generally, the entire metal case rotates at engine speed and serves as the engine's flywheel.

The case contains three sets of blades. One set is attached directly to the case. This set forms the torus or pump. Another set is directly onnected to the output shaft, and forms the turbine. The third set is mounted on a hub which, in turn, is mounted on a stationary shaft through a one-way clutch. This third set is known as the stator.

A pump, which is driven by the converter hub at engine speed, keeps the torque converter full of transmission fluid at all times. Fluid flows continuously through the unit to provide cooling.

Under low speed acceleration, the torque converter functions as follows:

The torus is turning faster than the turbine. It picks up fluid at the center of the converter and, through centrifugal force, slings it outward. Since the outer edge of the converter moves faster than the portions at the center, the fluid picks up speed.

The fluid then enters the outer edge of the turbine blades. It then travels back toward the center of the converter case along the turbine blades. In impinging upon the turbine blades, the fluid loses the energy picked up in the torus.

If the fluid were now to immediately be returned directly into the torus, both halves of the converter would have to turn at approximately the same speed at all times, and torque input and output would both be the same.

In flowing through the torus and turbine, the fluid picks up two types of flow, or flow in two separate directions. It flows through the turbine blades, and it spins with the engine. The stator, whose blades are stationary when the vehicle is being accelerated at low speeds, converts one type of flow into another. Instead of allowing the fluid to flow straight back into the torus, the stator's curved blades turn the fluid almost 90° toward the direction of rotation of the engine. Thus the fluid does not flow as fast toward the torus, but is already spinning when the torus picks it up. This has the effect of allowing the torus to turn much faster than the turbine. This difference in speed may be compared to the difference in speed between the smaller and larger gears in any gear train. The result is that engine power output is higher, and engine torque is multiplied.

As the speed of the turbine increases, the fluid spins faster and faster in the direction of engine rotation. As a result, the ability of the stator to redirect the fluid flow is reduced. Under cruising conditions, the stator is eventually forced to rotate on its one-way clutch in the direction of engine rotation. Under these conditions, the torque converter begins to behave almost like a solid shaft, with the torus and turbine speeds being almost equal.

THE PLANETARY GEARBOX

The ability of the torque converter to multiply engine torque is limited. Also, the unit tends to be more efficient when the turbine is rotating at relatively high speeds. Therefore, a planetary gearbox is used to carry the power output of the turbine to the driveshaft.

Planetary gears function very similarly to conventional transmission gears. However, their construction is different in that three elements make up one gear system, and, in that all three elements are different from one another. The three elements are: an outer gear that is shaped like a hoop, with teeth cut into the inner surface; a sun gear, mounted on a shaft and located at the very center of the outer gear; and a set of three planet gears, held by pins in a ring-like planet carrier, meshing with both the sun gear and the outer gear. Either the outer gear or the sun gear may be held stationary, providing more than one possible torque multiplication factor for each set of gears. Also, if all three gears are forced to rotate at the same speed, the gearset forms, in effect, a solid shaft.

Most modern automatics use the planetary gears to provide either a single reduction ratio of about 1.8:1, or two reduction gears: a low of about 2.5:1, and an intermediate of about 1.5:1. Bands and clutches are used to hold various portions of the gearsets to the transmission case or to the shaft on which they are mounted. Shifting is accomplished, then, by changing the portion of each planetary gearset which is held to the transmission case or to the shaft.

THE SERVOS AND ACCUMULATORS

The servos are hydraulic pistons and cylinders. They resemble the hydraulic actuators used on many familiar machines, such as bulldozers. Hydraulic fluid enters the cylinder, under pressure, and forces the piston to move to engage the band or clutches.

The accumulators are used to cushion the engagement of the servos. The transmission fluid must pass through the accumulator on the way to the servo. The accumulator housing contains a thin piston which is sprung away from the discharge passage of the accumulator. When fluid passes through the accumulator on the way to the servo, it must move the piston against spring pressure, and this action smooths out the action of the servo.

THE HYDRAULIC CONTROL SYSTEM

The hydraulic pressure used to operate the servos comes from the main transmission oil pump. This fluid is channeled to the various servos through the shift valves. There is generally a manual shift valve which is operated by the transmission selector lever and an automatic shift valve for each automatic upshift the transmission provides: i.e., 2 speed automatics have a low/high shift valve, while 3 speeds have a 1–2 valve, and a 2–3 valve.

There are two pressures which effect the operation of these valves. One is the governor pressure which is affected by vehicle speed. The other is the modulator pressure which is affected by intake manifold vacuum or throttle position. Governor pressure rises with an increase in vehicle speed, and modulator pressure rises as the throttle is opened wider. By responding to these two pressures, the shift valves cause the upshift points to be delayed with increased throttle opening to make the best use of the engine's power output.

Most transmissions also make use of an auxiliary circuit for downshifting. This circuit may be actuated by the throttle linkage or the vacuum line which actuates the modulator, or by a cable or solenoid. It applies pressure to a special downshift surface on the shift valve or valves.

The transmission modulator also governs the line pressure, used to actuate the servos. In this way, the clutches and bands will be actuated with a force matching the torque output of the engine.

Identification

The optional automatic transmission is a JATCO (Japan Automatic Transmission Co., Ltd.) Model L3N71B It is used on all models except the D21-D series truck. The D21-D series trucks introduced in 1986 use a model L4N71B with the Z24i engine, a model E4N71B with the VG30i engine in 1986-87, and in 1988-89, a model E4N71B for 2wd models with the VG30i engine and a model RE4R01A for 4wd models.

They are fully automatic units, with a three element torque converter and tow planetary

Troubleshooting Basic Automatic Transmission Problems

Problem	Cause	Solution
Fluid leakage	• Defective pan gasket • Loose filler tube • Loose extension housing to transmission case • Converter housing area leakage	• Replace gasket or tighten pan bolts • Tighten tube nut • Tighten bolts • Have transmission checked professionally
Fluid flows out the oil filler tube	• High fluid level • Breather vent clogged • Clogged oil filter or screen • Internal fluid leakage	• Check and correct fluid level • Open breather vent • Replace filter or clean screen (change fluid also) • Have transmission checked professionally
Transmission overheats (this is usually accompanied by a strong burned odor to the fluid)	• Low fluid level • Fluid cooler lines clogged • Heavy pulling or hauling with insufficient cooling • Faulty oil pump, internal slippage	• Check and correct fluid level • Drain and refill transmission. If this doesn't cure the problem, have cooler lines cleared or replaced. • Install a transmission oil cooler • Have transmission checked professionally
Buzzing or whining noise	• Low fluid level • Defective torque converter, scored gears	• Check and correct fluid level • Have transmission checked professionally
No forward or reverse gears or slippage in one or more gears	• Low fluid level • Defective vacuum or linkage controls, internal clutch or band failure	• Check and correct fluid level • Have unit checked professionally
Delayed or erratic shift	• Low fluid level • Broken vacuum lines • Internal malfunction	• Check and correct fluid level • Repair or replace lines • Have transmission checked professionally

Lockup Torque Converter Service Diagnosis

Problem	Cause	Solution
No lockup	• Faulty oil pump • Sticking governor valve • Valve body malfunction (a) Stuck switch valve (b) Stuck lockup valve (c) Stuck fail-safe valve • Failed locking clutch • Leaking turbine hub seal • Faulty input shaft or seal ring	• Replace oil pump • Repair or replace as necessary • Repair or replace valve body or its internal components as necessary • Replace torque converter • Replace torque converter • Repair or replace as necessary
Will not unlock	• Sticking governor valve • Valve body malfunction (a) Stuck switch valve (b) Stuck lockup valve (c) Stuck fail-safe valve	• Repair or replace as necessary • Repair or replace valve body or its internal components as necessary
Stays locked up at too low a speed in direct	• Sticking governor valve • Valve body malfunction (a) Stuck switch valve (b) Stuck lockup valve (c) Stuck fail-safe valve	• Repair or replace as necessary • Repair or replace valve body or its internal components as necessary
Locks up or drags in low or second	• Faulty oil pump • Valve body malfunction (a) Stuck switch valve (b) Stuck fail-safe valve	• Replace oil pump • Repair or replace valve body or its internal components as necessary
Sluggish or stalls in reverse	• Faulty oil pump • Plugged cooler, cooler lines or fittings • Valve body malfunction (a) Stuck switch valve (b) Faulty input shaft or seal ring	• Replace oil pump as necessary • Flush or replace cooler and flush lines and fittings • Repair or replace valve body or its internal components as necessary
Loud chatter during lockup engagement (cold)	• Faulty torque converter • Failed locking clutch • Leaking turbine hub seal	• Replace torque converter • Replace torque converter • Replace torque converter
Vibration or shudder during lockup engagement	• Faulty oil pump • Valve body malfunction • Faulty torque converter • Engine needs tune-up	• Repair or replace oil pump as necessary • Repair or replace valve body or its internal components as necessary • Replace torque converter • Tune engine
Vibration after lockup engagement	• Faulty torque converter • Exhaust system strikes underbody • Engine needs tune-up • Throttle linkage misadjusted	• Replace torque converter • Align exhaust system • Tune engine • Adjust throttle linkage
Vibration when revved in neutral Overheating: oil blows out of dip stick tube or pump seal	• Torque converter out of balance • Plugged cooler, cooler lines or fittings • Stuck switch valve	• Replace torque converter • Flush or replace cooler and flush lines and fittings • Repair switch valve in valve body or replace valve body
Shudder after lockup engagement	• Faulty oil pump • Plugged cooler, cooler lines or fittings • Valve body malfunction • Faulty torque converter • Fail locking clutch • Exhaust system strikes underbody • Engine needs tune-up • Throttle linkage misadjusted	• Replace oil pump • Flush or replace cooler and flush lines and fittings • Repair or replace valve body or its internal components as necessary • Replace torque converter • Replace torque converter • Align exhaust system • Tune engine • Adjust throttle linkage

Transmission Fluid Indications

The appearance and odor of the transmission fluid can give valuable clues to the overall condition of the transmission. Always note the appearance of the fluid when you check the fluid level or change the fluid. Rub a small amount of fluid between your fingers to feel for grit and smell the fluid on the dipstick.

If the fluid appears:	It indicates:
Clear and red colored	• Normal operation
Discolored (extremely dark red or brownish) or smells burned	• Band or clutch pack failure, usually caused by an overheated transmission. Hauling very heavy loads with insufficient power or failure to change the fluid, often result in overheating. Do not confuse this appearance with newer fluids that have a darker red color and a strong odor (though not a burned odor).
Foamy or aerated (light in color and full of bubbles)	• The level is too high (gear train is churning oil) • An internal air leak (air is mixing with the fluid). Have the transmission checked professionally.
Solid residue in the fluid	• Defective bands, clutch pack or bearings. Bits of band material or metal abrasives are clinging to the dipstick. Have the transmission checked professionally.
Varnish coating on the dipstick	• The transmission fluid is overheating

gear sets. The transmission shifts gears in response to signals of both engine speed and manifold vacuum.

While it is unlikely that you will ever disassemble the transmission yourself, there are a few adjustments you can perform which will prolong the transmission's life if performed accurately. The most important thing is to change the fluid regularly, which is covered in Chapter One.

Fluid Pan

REMOVAL AND INSTALLATION

1. Raise the front of the truck and support it safely on stands.
2. Slide a drain pan under the transmission. Loosen the rear oil pan bolts first, then drop the rear of the pan slightly so as to allow most of the fluid to drain off without making a mess on your garage floor.
3. Remove the remaining bolts, drop the pan and remove the gasket.
4. The pan may be washed in solvent for cleaning but must be absolutely dry when it is reinstalled. Do not wipe it out with a rag, or you will risk leaving bits of lint inside the transmission.
5. Remove all traces of the old gasket from the pan and from the transmission. Install a new gasket on the pan using small quantities of sealer around the bolt holes.

Clean the pan thoroughly and then allow it to air dry

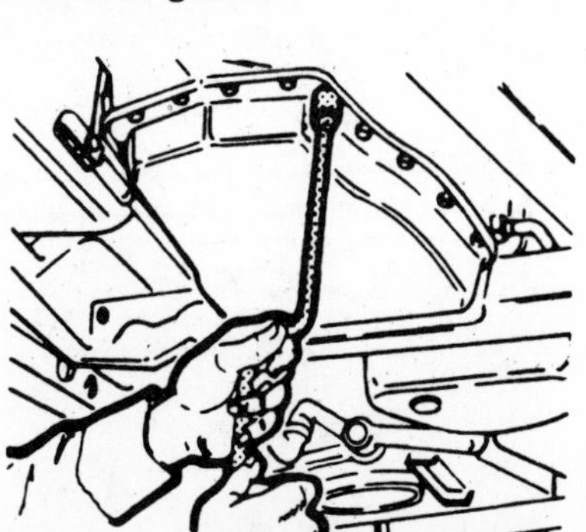

Removing the pan retaining bolts

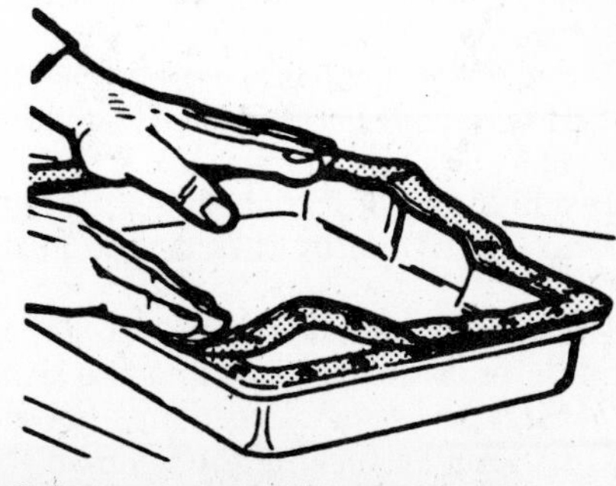

Install the new pan gasket without sealer

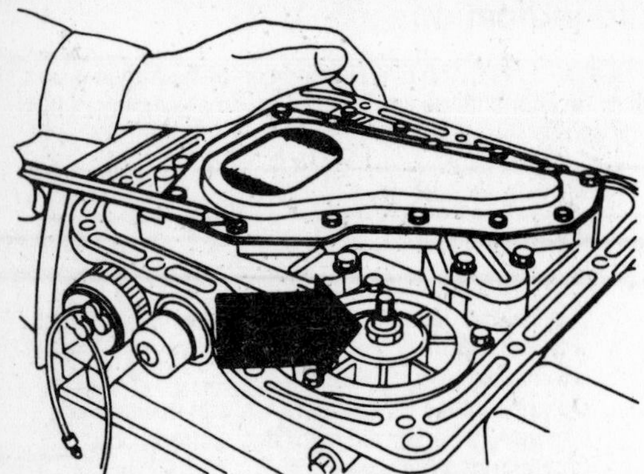

Brake band piston stem and locknut (arrow)

6. Replace the transmission filter or strainer at this time, if necessary.

7. Install the pan and tighten the retaining bolts in a crisscross pattern starting at the center.

NOTE: *The transmission case is aluminum, so don't exert too much force on the bolts. Tighten the bolts to 3.6–5.1 ft. lbs. (5–8 Nm).*

8. Refill the transmission through the dipstick tube and check the fluid level.

Adjustments

BRAKE BAND

L3N71B Only

1. Remove the fluid pan.
2. Loosen the locknut on the piston stem. Tighten the piston stem to 9–11 ft. lbs.
3. Loosen the piston stem *exactly* two (2) turns. Hold the stem and tighten the locknut to 20 ft. lbs. (1973-79) or 14 ft. lbs. (1980-86). If the stem turns when the locknut is tightened, loosen the locknut and repeat the adjustment.
4. Replace the fluid pan and refill the transmission.

SHIFT LINKAGE

1973-79

Adjustment of the shift linkage is a critical operation. If the adjustment is made sloppily, the result will be partial application of the band or clutches, and will eventually burn up the transmission.

1. If the control knob is removed prior to installation set dimension **A** in the illustration to 11–12mm.
2. Install the control knob, adjusting dimension **B** to 0.1–1.1mm by turning the pushing rod (2).
3. Loosen the adjusting nuts (H). Set both the shift lever (3) and the transmission selector lever (4) into the neutral positions. Set clearance **C** to 1mm by turning the adjusting nuts which connect to the selector rod (6).

After making the adjustments, check for proper engagement in each gear, and that the mechanism operates without binding. Readjust as necessary.

1980-86 (720-D Series)

Adjustment is made at the locknuts at the base of the shifter, which control the length of the shift control rod.

1. Place the shift lever in **D**.
2. Loosen the locknuts and move the shift lever until it is firmly in the **D** range, the pointer is aligned, and the transmission is in **D** range.
3. Tighten the locknuts.
4. Check the adjustment. Start the car and apply the parking brake. Shift through all the ranges, starting in **P**. As the lever is moved from **P** to **1**, you should be able to feel the detents in each range. If proper adjustment is not possible, the grommets are probably worn and should be replaced.

1986-89 (D21-D Series)

L4N71B AND E4N71B–FLOOR SHIFT MODELS

Move the gear selector lever slowly throught the ranges from **P** to **1**. You should be able to feel the detents in each range. If the detents can't be felt, or if the indicator point is out of alignment, the linkage needs adjustment.

1. Position the selector lever in **P**.
2. Loosen the locknuts.
3. Tighten the locknut **X** until it touches the trunnion, pulling the selector lever toward the **R** side without pushing the button.
4. Back off the locknut **X** ¼–½ turn (1986-87) or 1 turn (1988-89) and tighten the lock nut **Y** to 6–8 ft. lbs. (8–11 Nm) on 1986-87 models; 8–11 ft. lbs. (11–15 Nm) on 1988-89 models.
5. Move the selector lever from the **P** range to the **1** range. Make sure the selector lever moves smoothly.

L4N71B AND E4N71B–COLUMN SHIFT MODELS

Move the gear selector lever slowly throught the ranges from **P** to **1**. You should be able to feel the detents in each range. If the detents

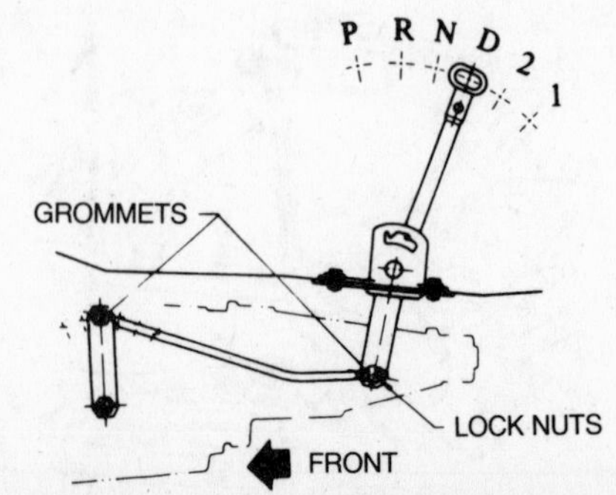

Shift linkage adjustment—1980–86 (720-D series)

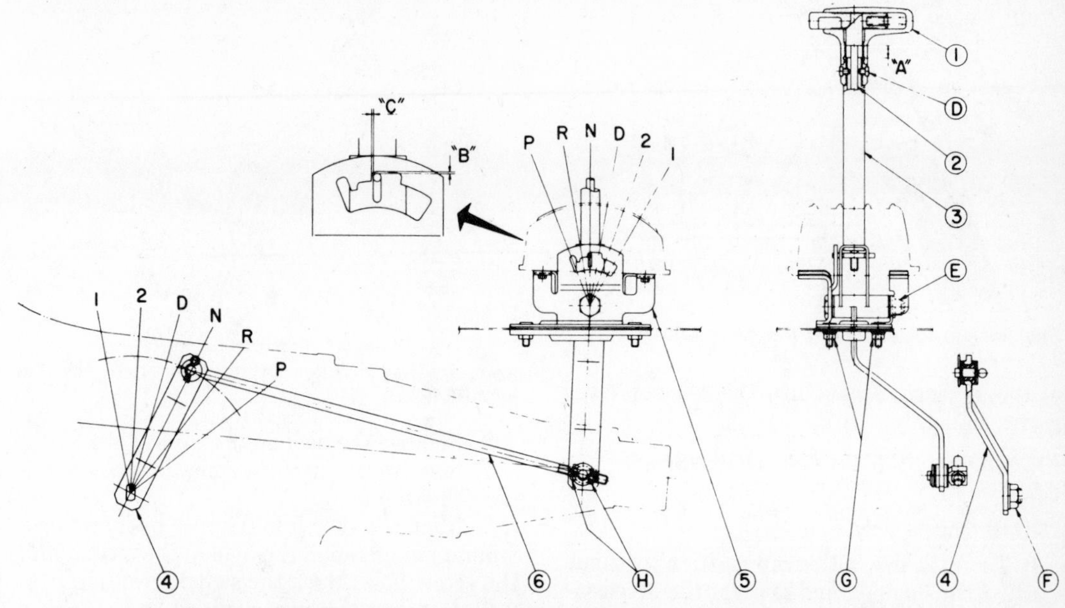

Shift linkage adjustment—1970–79

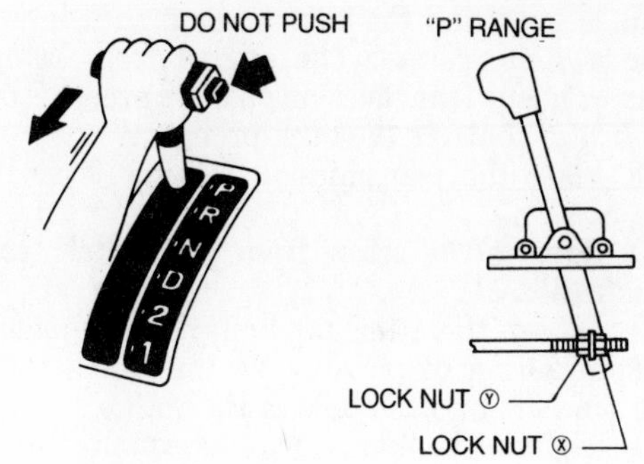

Shift linkage adjustment—1986–89 (D21-D series) L4N71B and E4N71B (floor shift)

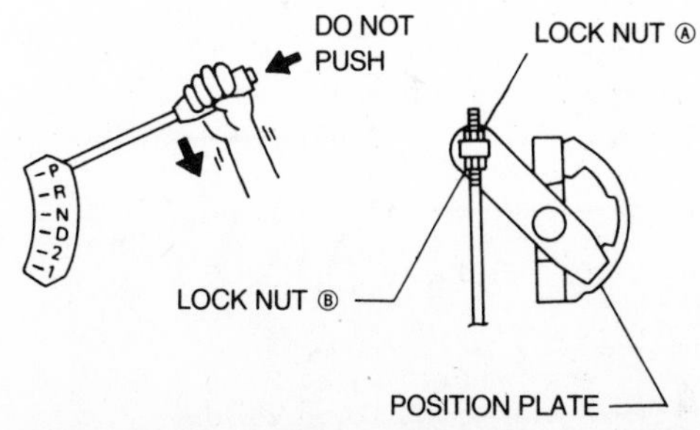

Shift linkage adjustment—1986–89 (D21-D series) L4N71B and E4N71B (column shift)

can't be felt, or if the indicator point is out of alignment, the linkage needs adjustment.

1. Position the selector lever in **P**.
2. Loosen the locknuts.
3. Tighten the locknut **A** until it touches the trunnion, pulling the selector lever toward the **R** side without pushing the button.
4. Back off the locknut **A** 2 turns and tighten the locknut **B** to 6–8 ft. lbs. (8–11 Nm) on 1986-87 models; 8–11 ft. lbs. (11–15 Nm) on 1988-89 models.
5. Move the selector lever from the **P** range to the **1** range. Make sure the selector lever moves smoothly.

RE4R01A – FLOOR SHIFT MODELS

Move the gear selector lever slowly throught the ranges from **P** to **1**. You should be able to feel the detents in each range. If the detents can't be felt, or if the indicator point is out of alignment, the linkage needs adjustment.

1. Position the selector lever in **P**.
2. Loosen the locknuts.
3. Tighten the turnbuckle until it aligns with the inner cable, pulling the selector lever toward the **R** side without pushing the button.
4. Back off the turnbuckle 1 turn and tighten the locknuts to 3.3–4.3 ft. lbs. (4.4–5.9 Nm).
5. Move the selector lever from the **P** range

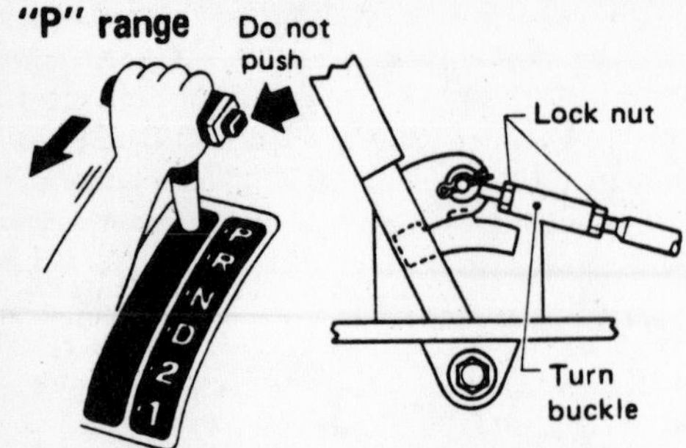

Shift linkage adjustment—1988–89 RE4R01A

to the **1** range. Make sure the selector lever moves smoothly.

KICKDOWN SWITCH AND DOWNSHIFT SOLENOID

L3N71B Models Only

1. Turn the key to the **ON** position (without starting the engine), and depress the accelerator all the way. The solenoid in the transmission should make an audible click.
2. If the solenoid does not work, inspect the wiring, and test it electrically to determine whether the problem is in the wiring, the kickdown switch, or the solenoid.
3. If the solenoid requires replacement, drain a little over 2 pts (1 liter) of fluid from the transmission before removing it.

NEUTRAL SAFETY/INHIBITOR SWITCH

1973-86 (620 and 720-D Series)

The switch unit is bolted to the left side of the transmission case, behind the transmission shift lever. The switch prevents the engine from being started in any transmission position except **P** or **N**. It also controls the back-up lights.

1. Apply the brakes and check to see that the starter works only in the **P** and **N** transmission ranges. If the starter works with the transmission in gear, adjust the switch as described below.
2. Remove the transmission shift lever retaining nut and the lever.

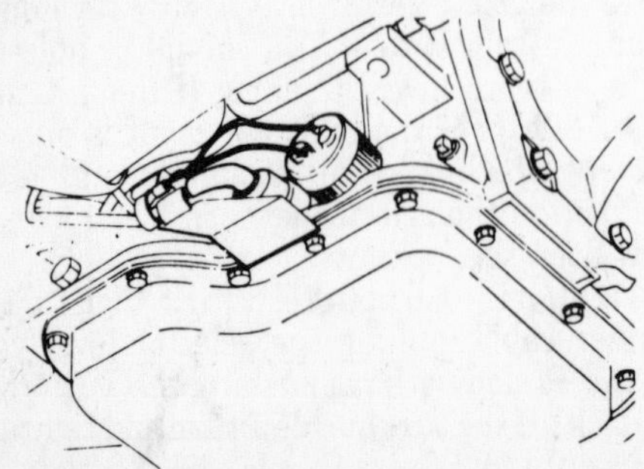

The downshift solenoid

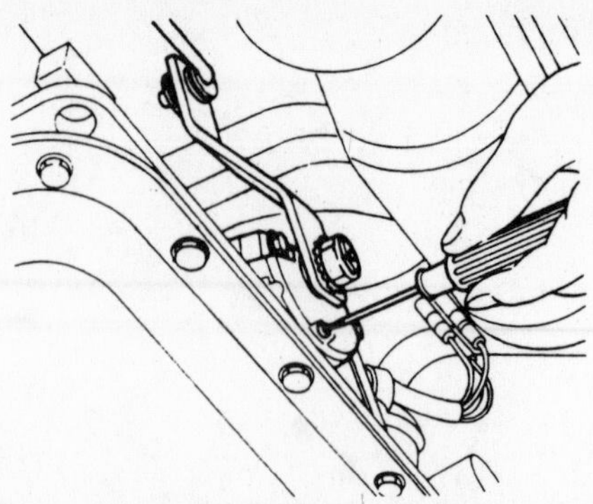

Neutral safety/inhibitor switch adjustment—all except RE4R01A

3. Remove the switch.
4. Remove the machine screw in the case under the switch.
5. Align the switch to the case by inserting a 1.5mm pin, through the hole in the switch into the screw hole. Mark the switch location.
6. Remove the pin, replace the machine screw, install the switch as marked, and replace the transmission shift lever and retaining nut.
7. Make sure while holding the brakes on, that the engine will start only in **P** or **N**. Check that the back-up lights go on only in **R**.

1986-89 (D21-D Series)

The switch unit is bolted to the the transmission case, behind the transmission shift lever. The switch prevents the engine from being started in any transmission position except **P** or **N**. It also controls the back-up lights.

1. Place the transmission selector lever in the **N**.
2. Remove the screw from the switch (see illustration).
3. Loosen the attaching bolts. With a aligning pin, 2.0mm diameter, move the switch until the pin falls into the hole in the rotor.
4. Tighten the attaching bolts equally.
5. Make sure while holding the brakes on, that the engine will start only in **P** or **N**. Check that the back-up lights go on only in **R**.

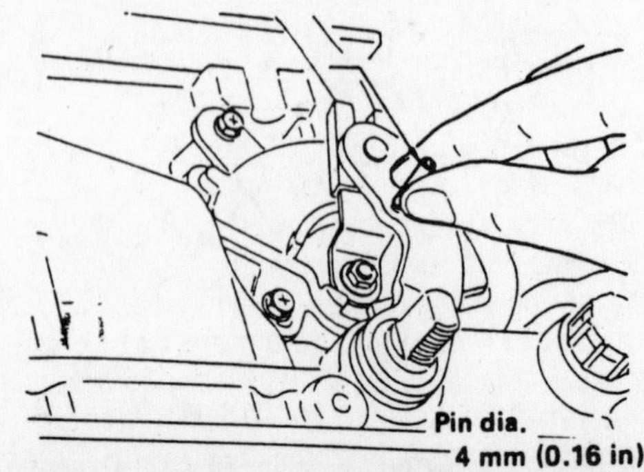

Neutral safety/inhibitor switch adjustment—RE4R01A

Transmission

REMOVAL AND INSTALLATION

1. Disconnect the negative battery cable.
2. Disconnect the shaft from the accelerator linkage.
3. Raise the truck and support it safely on floor stands.
4. Matchmark the U-joint and differential flange and disconnect them. Remove the center bearing mounting bolts and remove the driveshaft. Plug the transmission extension housing.
5. Disconnect the exhaust pipe from the manifold and discard the gasket. Use a new gasket upon assembly. On trucks with a catalytic converter, disconnect the exhaust pipe bracket.
6. Disconnect the shift linkage at the transmission.
7. Disconnect the neutral safety (inhibitor) switch wires. Disconnect the vacuum hose from the diaphragm, and the wire from the downshift solenoid. Disconnect the speedometer cable from the extension housing.
8. Remove the fluid filler tube.
9. Disconnect the fluid cooler lines at the transmission. Use a flare nut wrench if one is available.
10. Support the engine with a jack under the oil pan, placing a wooden block between the pan and the jack as a buffer. Also support the transmission with a jack.
11. Remove the torque converter cover. Matchmark the converter and the drive plate for reassembly; they were balanced as a unit at the factory. Remove the bolts attaching the converter to the drive plate (flywheel). You will have to rotate the engine to do this, using a wrench on the crankshaft pulley bolt.
12. Remove the bolts for the rear engine mount and the crossmember. Remove the crossmember.
13. Remove the starter.
14. Remove the transmission-to-engine bolts. Lower the transmission back and down, out from under the truck.
15. Before installing the transmission, check the drive plate runout with a dial indicator. Turn the crankshaft one full turn. Maximum allowable runout is 0.3mm. Replace the drive plate if runout exceeds 0.5mm; otherwise, reface it.
16. After connecting the torque converter to the transmission, lay a straight-edge across the face of the transmission and measure the distance from the top of the mounting bolt to the straight-edge. It should be at least 35mm on all transmissions except the RE4R01A, where it should be at least 26mm.
17. When installing the torque converter, be sure to line up the notch in the converter with the projection on the oil pump. Align the marks made during removal and bolt the converter to the drive plate, tightening the bolts to 29–36 ft. lbs. (39–49 Nm). Then rotate the engine a few turns to make sure the transmission rotates freely without binding. The engine-to-transmission bolt torque is 29–36 ft. lbs. (39–49 Nm). Adjust the shift linkage and neutral safety switches and check the transmission fluid level.

TRANSFER CASE

Transfer Case

REMOVAL AND INSTALLATION

1981-86 Model T100L (720-D Series)

1. Disconnect the negative battery cable.
2. Raise the vehicle and support it with jackstands.
3. Remove the transfer case shield.
4. Remove the primary driveshaft securing nuts.
5. Remove the front and rear driveshafts.
6. Disconnect the 4wd switch wire.
7. Disconnect the speedometer cable.
8. Remove the exhaust pipe.
9. Support the transfer case with a jack.
10. Temporarily loosen the transfer case insulator bolts.
11. Remove the shift lever rubber boot from the floor.
12. Unbolt and remove the transfer case and primary driveshaft from the vehicle. Remove the insulators from the transfer case.
13. Install the insulators on the transfer case and then install the case itself. Tighten all bolts to 20–26 ft. lbs. (27–35 Nm).
14. Install the shift lever boot.
15. Connect the exhaust pipe to the manifold.

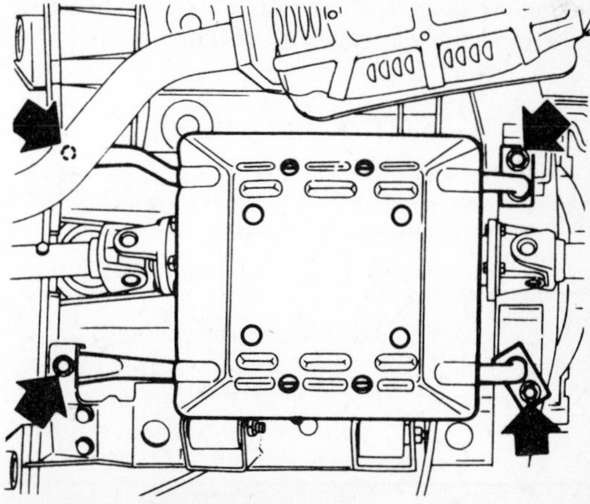

Transfer case shield bolts—T100L

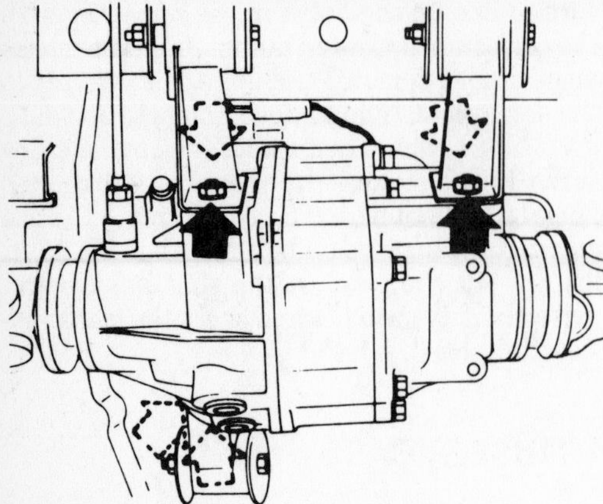

Transfer case mounting bolts—T100L

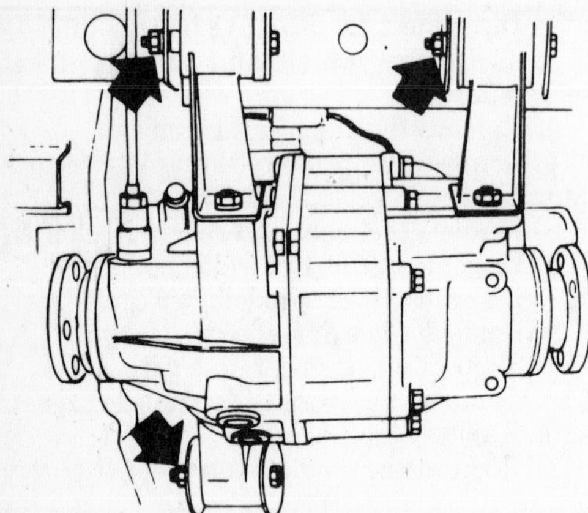

Transfer case insulator cover—T100L

16. Connect the speedometer cable and the 4wd switch.
17. Install the fron and rear driveshafts and tighten the primary driveshaft nuts.
18. Install the case shield. Refill the transfer case with fluid, lower the truck and connect the battery cable. Road test the truck and check for any leaks of improper operation.

1986-89 Model TX100 (D21-D Series)

1. Disconnect the negative battery cable.
2. Raise the front of the vehicle and support it with jackstands.
3. Drain the fluid from the transmission and transfer cases.
4. Remove the front and rear driveshafts. Be sure to plug the oil seal openings after removal.

NOTE: *Be very careful not to damage the transfer case spline, yoke or oil seal while removing the driveshafts.*

5. Remove the torsion bar spring.
6. Remove the second crossmember.
7. Disconnect the transfer control lever at the outer shift lever ball joint and position it out of the way.
8. Position a floor jack underneath the transfer case and remove the case-to-transmission mounting bolts. Separate the transfer case from the transmission and slowly lower it out and away from the transmission.
9. Carefully position the transfer case so that it mates with the transmission and tighten the mounting bolts to 23–30 ft. lbs. (31–41 Nm). On models with manual transmissions, be sure to coat the case mating surface with sealant.
10. Connect the transfer control lever to the outer shift lever and tighten the nut to 18–22 ft. lbs. (25–30 Nm).
11. Install the second crossmember and tighten the bolts to 43–58 ft. lbs. (59–78 Nm). Install the torsion bar spring.
12. Unplug the oil seals and install the two driveshafts.
13. Refill the transmission and transfer case with fluid, lower the vehicle and connect the battery cable. Road test the truck and check for any leaks or improper operation.

DRIVELINE

Front Driveshaft And U-Joints

REMOVAL AND INSTALLATION

4wd Models Only

1981-86 720-D SERIES – PRIMARY DRIVESHAFT

1. Matchmark the flanges and separate the primary driveshaft from the transfer case.
2. Remove the transfer case.
3. Pull the primary shaft from the transmission and plug the opening.
4. Slide the front end of the driveshaft into the transmission and support the driveshaft with wire.
5. Install the transfer case.
6. Position the rear end of the driveshaft at the transfer case so the marks made previously align and then tighten the flange bolts to 58–65 ft. lbs. (78–88 Nm).

1981-86 720-D SERIES – FRONT DRIVESHAFT

1. Matchmark the flanges and unbolt the front driveshaft at the front differential.
2. Matchmark the flanges and unbolt the front driveshaft at the transfer case.
3. Align the matchmarks at the transfer case and install the driveshaft. Tighten the flange bolts to 25–33 ft. lbs. (34–44 Nm).
4. Align the matchmarks at the front differential and install the driveshaft. Tighten the flange bolts to 25–33 ft. lbs. (34–44 Nm).

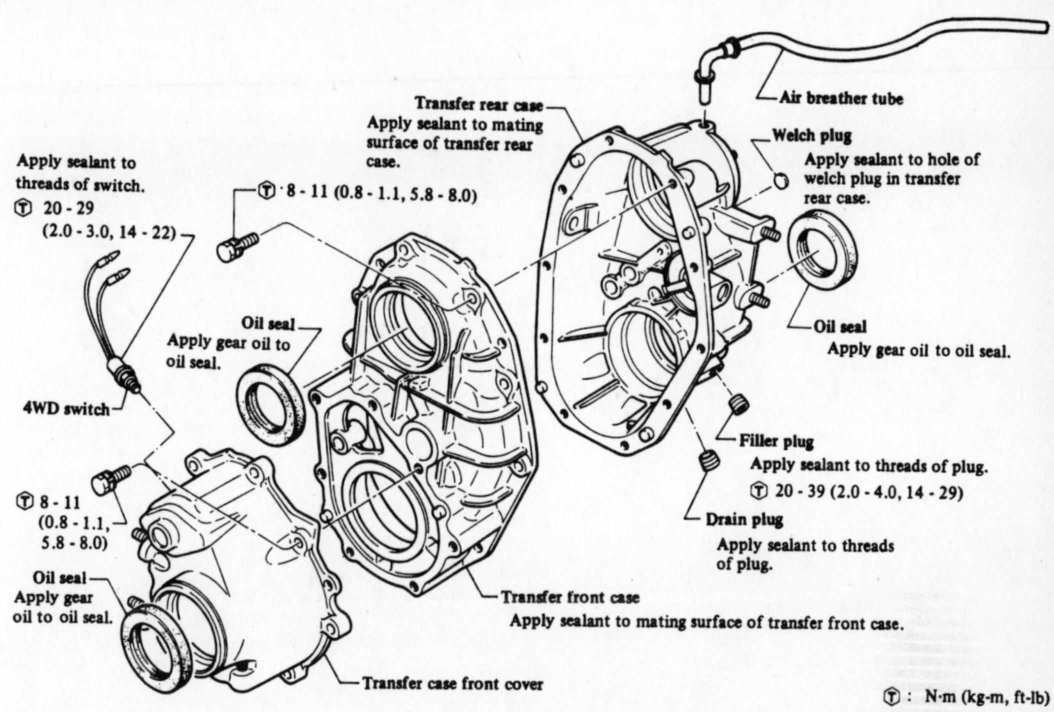

Exploded view of the transfer case—T100L

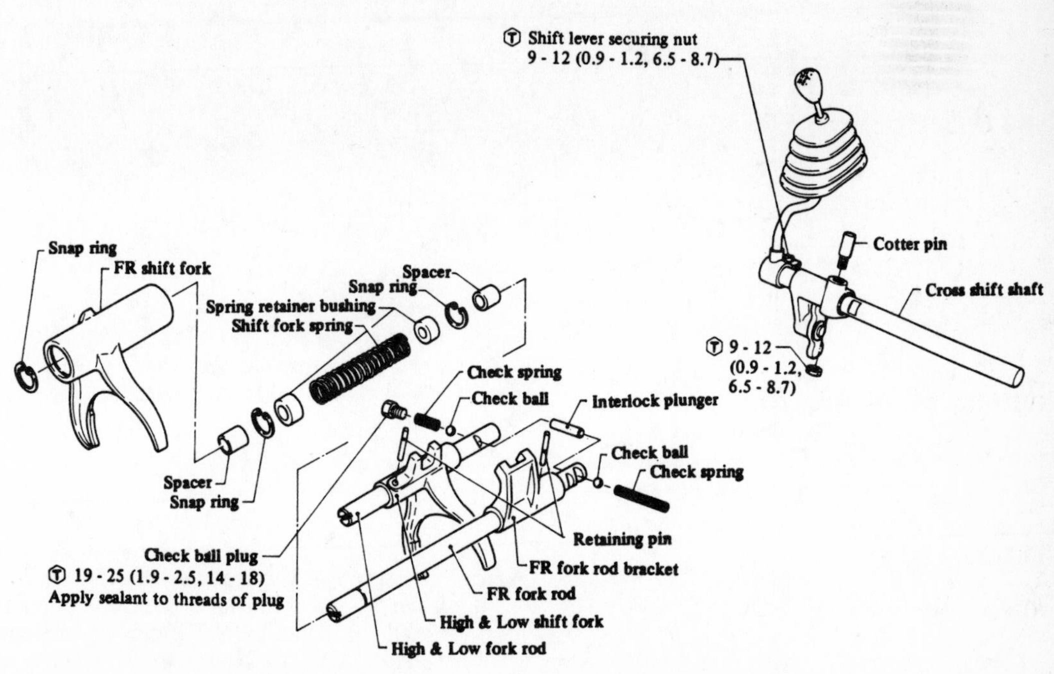

Exploded view of the transfer case shift control components—T100L

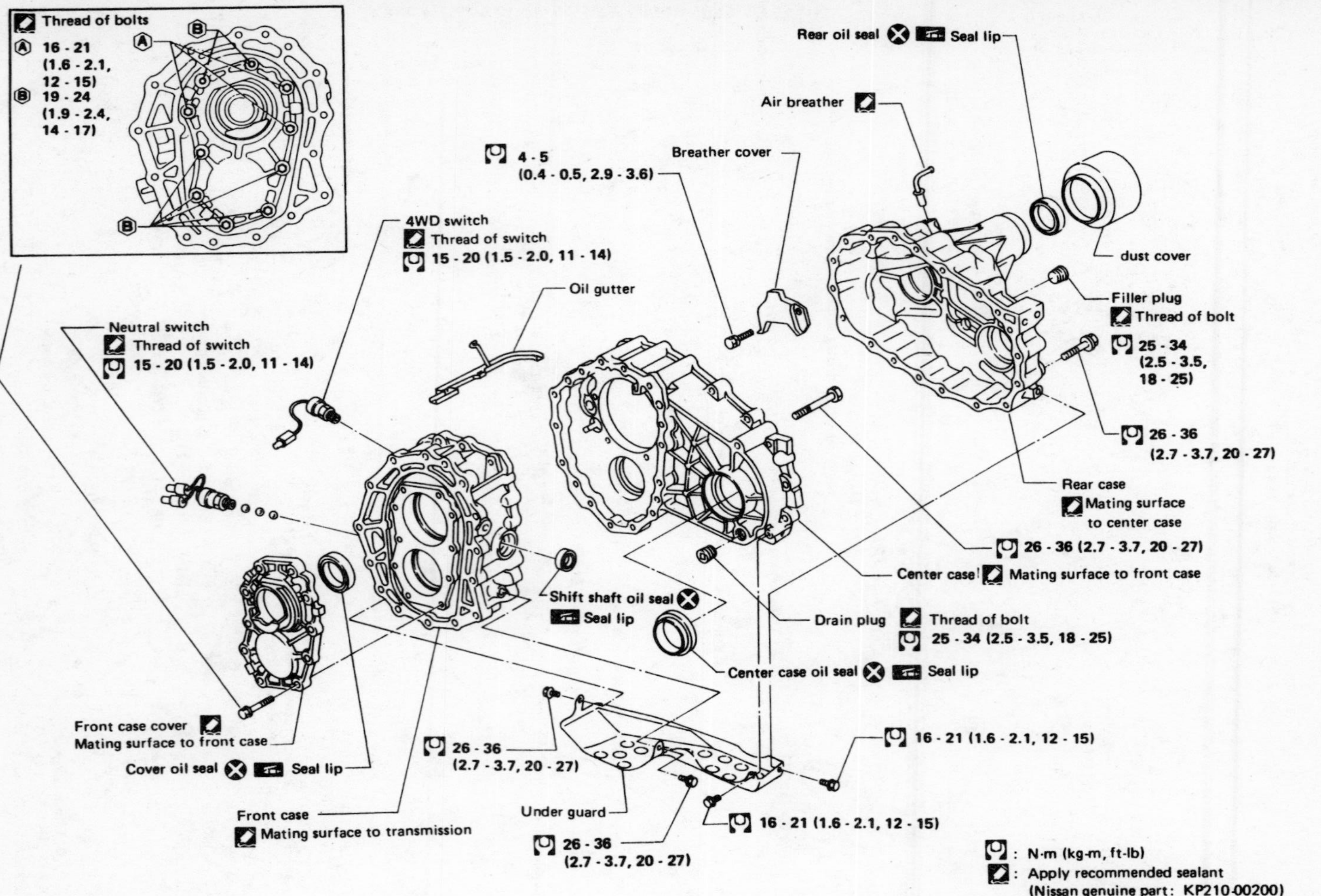

Exploded view of the transfer case—1986–87 TX100

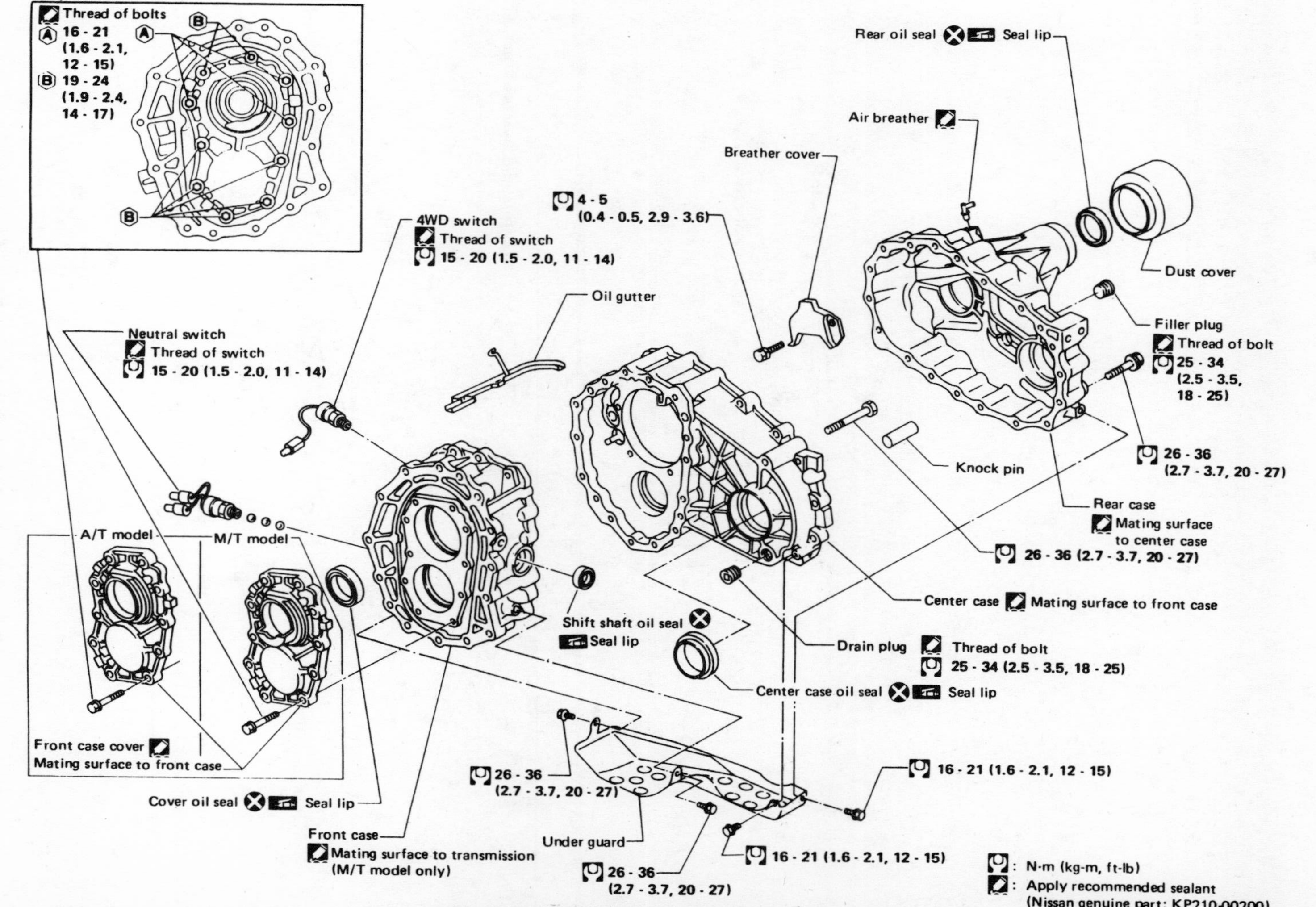

Exploded view of the transfer case—1988–89 TX100

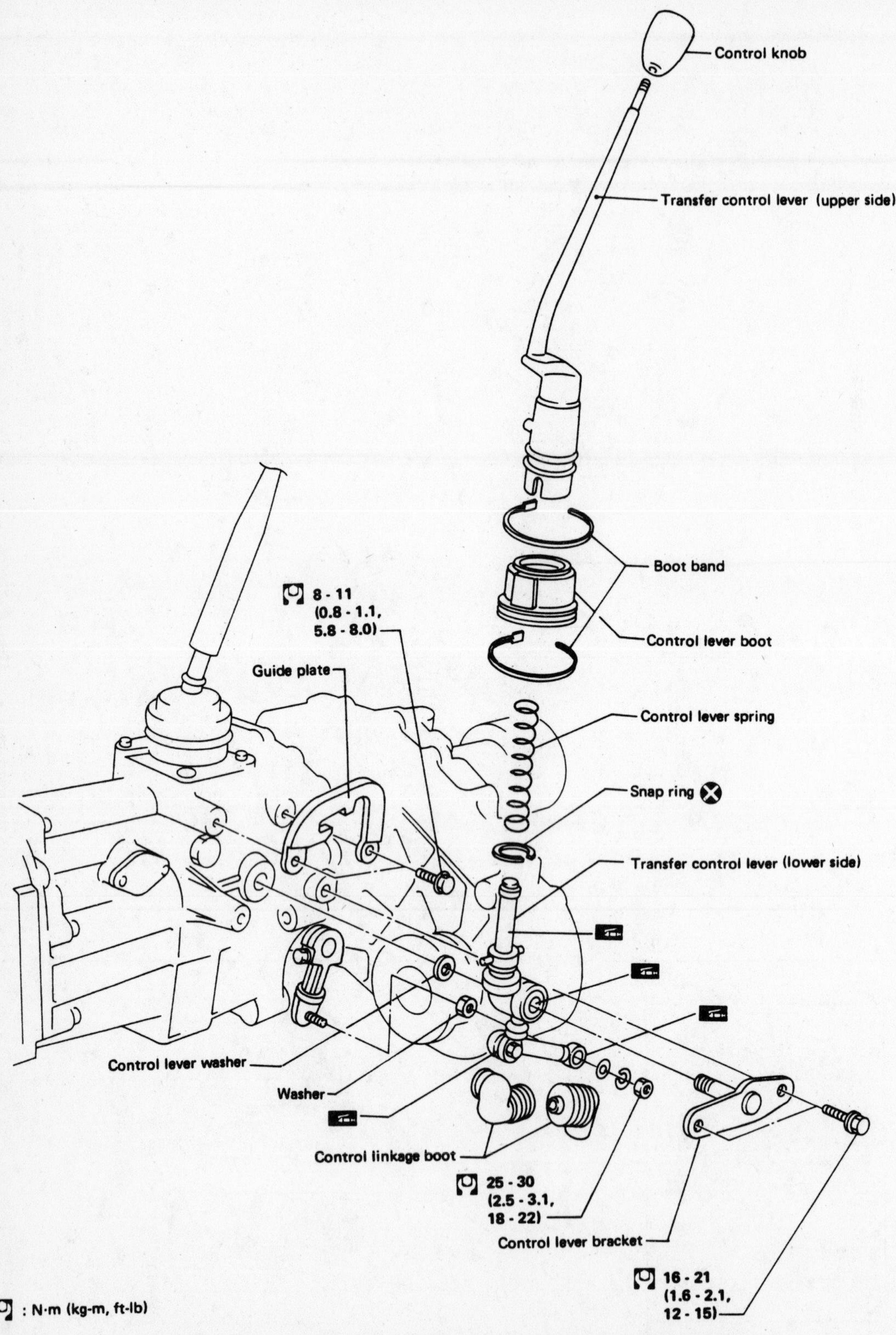

Exploded view of the transfer case shift control components—1986–87 TX100

1986-89 D21-D SERIES

1. Matchmark the flanges and unbolt the front driveshaft at the front differential.
2. Matchmark the flanges and unbolt the front driveshaft at the transfer case.
3. Align the matchmarks at the transfer case and install the driveshaft. Tighten the flange bolts to 29–33 ft. lbs. (39–44 Nm).
4. Align the matchmarks at the front differential and install the driveshaft. Tighten the flange bolts to 29–33 ft. lbs. (39–44 Nm).

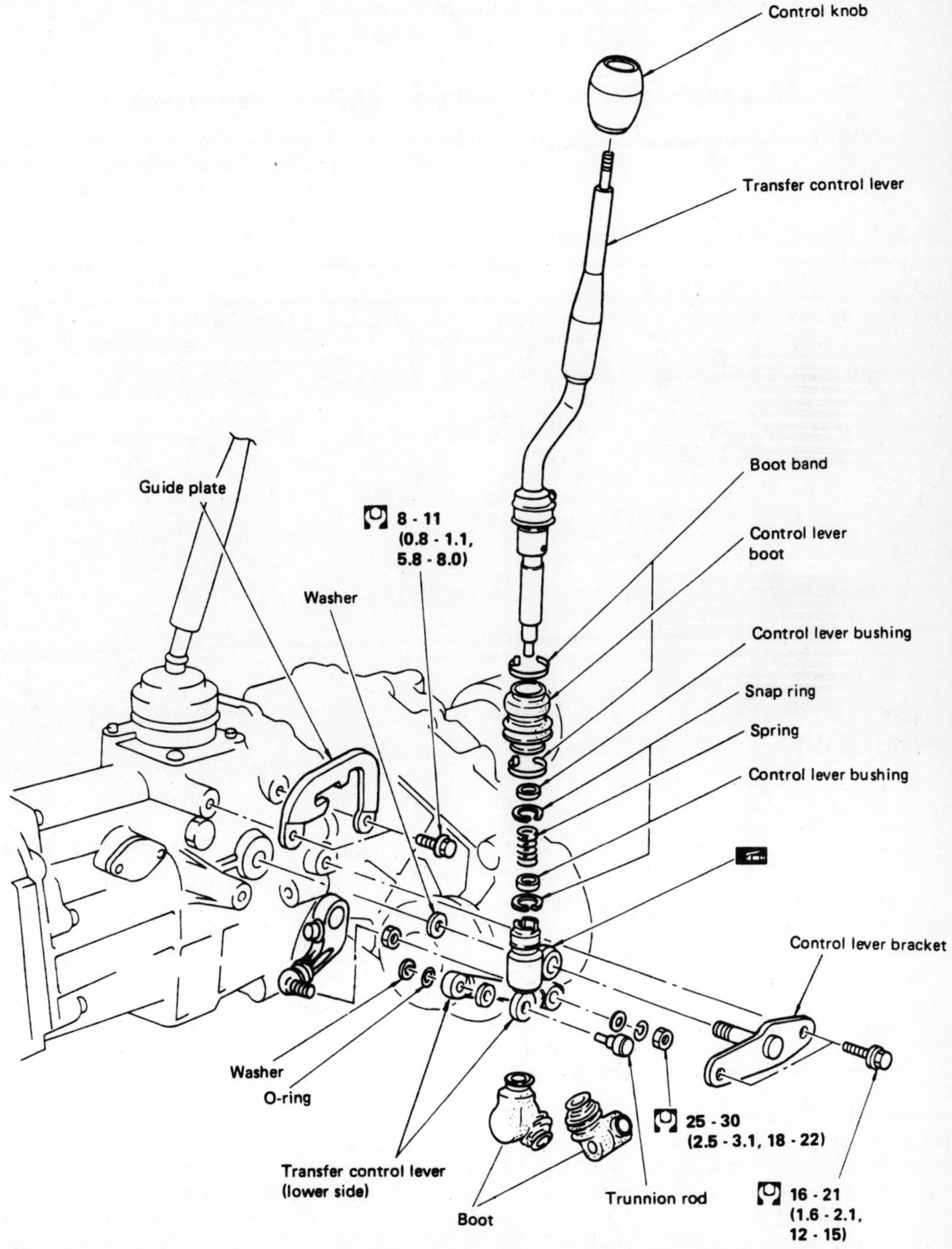

Exploded view of the transfer case shift control components—1988–89 TX100

U-JOINT OVERHAUL

1. Matchmark the yoke and the driveshaft.
2. Remove the snaprings from the bearings.
3. Position the yoke on vise jaws. Using a bearing remover and a hammer, gently tap the remover until the bearing is driven out of the yoke about 25mm.
4. Place the tool in the vise and drive the yoke away from the tool until the bearing is removed.
5. Repeat Steps 3 and 4 for the other bearings.
6. Check for worn or damaged parts. Inspect the bearing journal surfaces for wear.

To assemble:

7. Install the bearing cups, seals, and O-rings in the spider.

Troubleshooting Basic Driveshaft and Rear Axle Problems

When abnormal vibrations or noises are detected in the driveshaft area, this chart can be used to help diagnose possible causes. Remember that other components such as wheels, tires, rear axle and suspension can also produce similar conditions.

BASIC DRIVESHAFT PROBLEMS

Problem	Cause	Solution
Shudder as car accelerates from stop or low speed	• Loose U-joint • Defective center bearing	• Replace U-joint • Replace center bearing
Loud clunk in driveshaft when shifting gears	• Worn U-joints	• Replace U-joints
Roughness or vibration at any speed	• Out-of-balance, bent or dented driveshaft • Worn U-joints • U-joint clamp bolts loose	• Balance or replace driveshaft • Replace U-joints • Tighten U-joint clamp bolts
Squeaking noise at low speeds	• Lack of U-joint lubrication	• Lubricate U-joint; if problem persists, replace U-joint
Knock or clicking noise	• U-joint or driveshaft hitting frame tunnel • Worn CV joint	• Correct overloaded condition • Replace CV joint

BASIC REAR AXLE PROBLEMS

First, determine when the noise is most noticeable.

Drive Noise: Produced under vehicle acceleration.

Coast Noise: Produced while the car coasts with a closed throttle.

Float Noise: Occurs while maintaining constant car speed (just enough to keep speed constant) on a level road.

Road Noise

Brick or rough surfaced concrete roads produce noises that seem to come from the rear axle. Road noise is usually identical in Drive or Coast and driving on a different type of road will tell whether the road is the problem.

Tire Noise

Tire noises are often mistaken for rear axle problems. Snow treads or unevenly worn tires produce vibrations seeming to originate elsewhere. **Temporarily** inflating the tires to 40 lbs will significantly alter tire noise, but will have no effect on rear axle noises (which normally cease below about 30 mph).

Engine/Transmission Noise

Determine at what speed the noise is most pronounced, then stop the car in a quiet place. With the transmission in Neutral, run the engine through speeds corresponding to road speeds where the noise was noticed. Noises produced with the car standing still are coming from the engine or transmission.

Front Wheel Bearings

While holding the car speed steady, lightly apply the footbrake; this will often decease bearing noise, as some of the load is taken from the bearing.

Rear Axle Noises

Eliminating other possible sources can narrow the cause to the rear axle, which normally produces noise from worn gears or bearings. Gear noises tend to peak in a narrow speed range, while bearing noises will usually vary in pitch with engine speeds.

NOISE DIAGNOSIS

The Noise Is	Most Probably Produced By
• Identical under Drive or Coast	• Road surface, tires or front wheel bearings
• Different depending on road surface	• Road surface or tires
• Lower as the car speed is lowered	• Tires
• Similar with car standing or moving	• Engine or transmission
• A vibration	• Unbalanced tires, rear wheel bearing, unbalanced driveshaft or worn U-joint
• A knock or click about every 2 tire revolutions	• Rear wheel bearing
• Most pronounced on turns	• Damaged differential gears
• A steady low-pitched whirring or scraping, starting at low speeds	• Damaged or worn pinion bearing
• A chattering vibration on turns	• Wrong differential lubricant or worn clutch plates (limited slip rear axle)
• Noticed only in Drive, Coast or Float conditions	• Worn ring gear and/or pinion gear

8. Grease the spider and the bearings.
9. Position the spider in the yoke.
10. Start the bearings in the yoke and then press them into place, using a vise.
11. Repeat Step 4 for the other bearings.
12. If the axial play of the spider is greater than 0.02mm, select snaprings which will provide the correct play. Be sure that the snaprings are the same size on both sides or driveshaft noise and vibration will result.

Rear Driveshaft and U-Joints

REMOVAL AND INSTALLATION

2wd Models Only

ONE-PIECE DRIVESHAFT

1. Jack up the rear of the truck and support the rear axle housing with jackstands.
2. Paint a mating mark on the two halves of the rear universal joint flange.
3. Remove the bolts which hold the rear flange together.
4. Remove the splined end of the driveshaft from the transmission.

NOTE: *If you don't want to lose a lot of gear oil, plug the end of the transmission with a rag.*

● : Transfer to M/T
● M/T to transfer

Transfer case bolt installation—TX100

5. Remove the driveshaft from under the truck.

To install:

6. Apply multipurpose grease to the splined end of the shaft.
7. Insert the driveshaft sleeve into the transmission.

NOTE: *Be careful not to damage the extension housing grease seal.*

8. Align the mating marks on the rear flange and replace the bolts. Tighten to 58–65 ft. lbs. (78–88 Nm).
9. Remove the jackstands and lower the vehicle.

TWO-PIECE DRIVESHAFT W/CENTER BEARING

1. Raise the rear of the truck and support the rear axle housing on jackstands.
2. Before you begin to disassemble the driveshaft components, you must first paint accurate alignment marks on the mating flangers. Do this on the rear universal joint flange, the center flange, and on the transmission flange.
3. Remove the bolts attaching the rear universal joint flange to the drive pinion flange.
4. Drop the rear section of the shaft slightly and pull the unit out of the center bearing sleeve yoke.
5. Remove the center bearing support from the crossmember.
6. Separate the transmission output flange and remove the front half of the driveshaft together with the center bearing assembly.

To install:

7. Connect the output flange of the transmission to the flange on the front half of the shaft.
8. Install the center bearing support to the crossmember, but do not fully tighten the bolts.
9. Install the rear section of the shaft making sure that all mating marks are aligned.
10. Tighten all flange bolts to 17–24 ft. lbs. (24–32 Nm) on 1974-86 models. On 1986-89 models (D21-D series), tighten the bolts to 29–

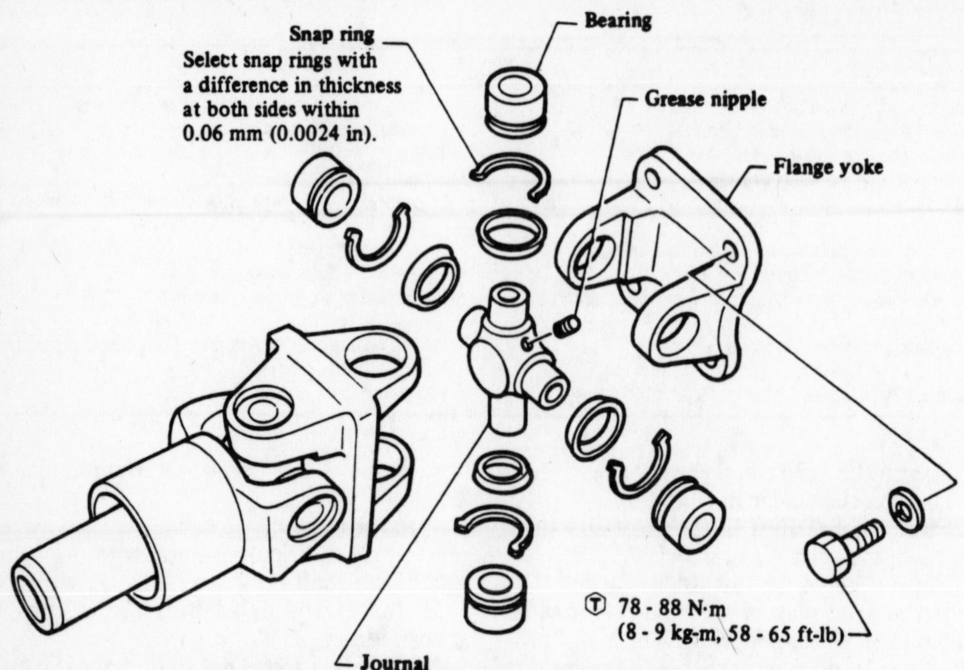

Front driveshaft (primary)—1981–86 4wd models (720-D series)

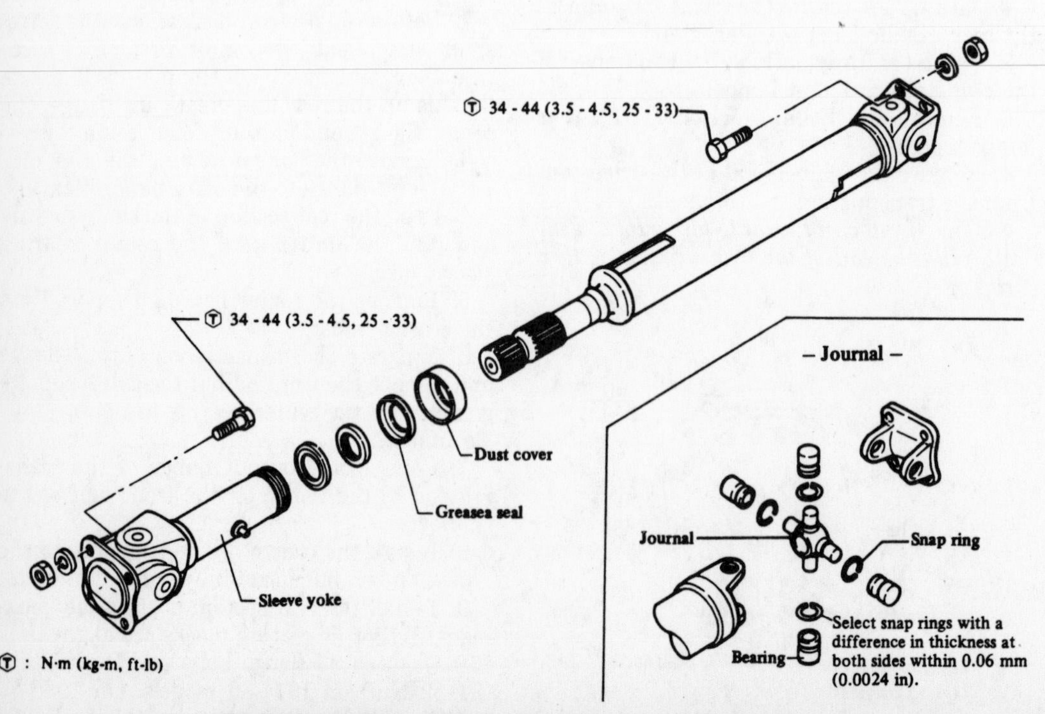

Front driveshaft (front)—1981–86 4wd models (720-D series)

Greasing point
Flange yoke
39 - 44 (4.0 - 4.5, 29 - 33)
Propeller shaft tube
Journal
Journal bearing
Snap ring ★
39 - 44 (4.0 - 4.5, 29 - 33)
★: Adjustment is required.
: N·m (kg-m, ft-lb)

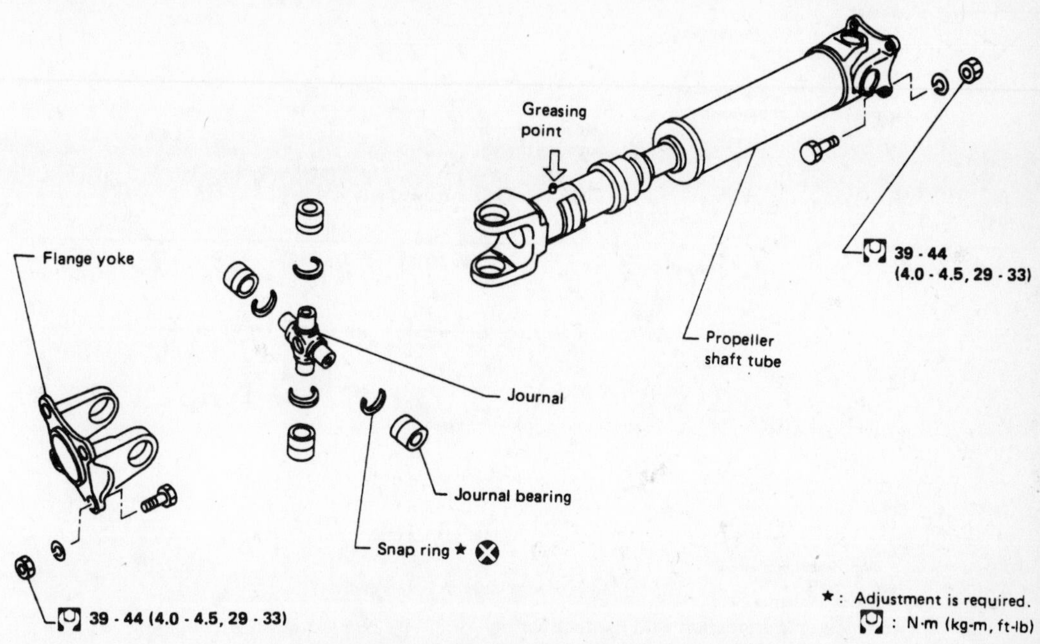

Front driveshaft—1986–89 4wd models (D21-D series)

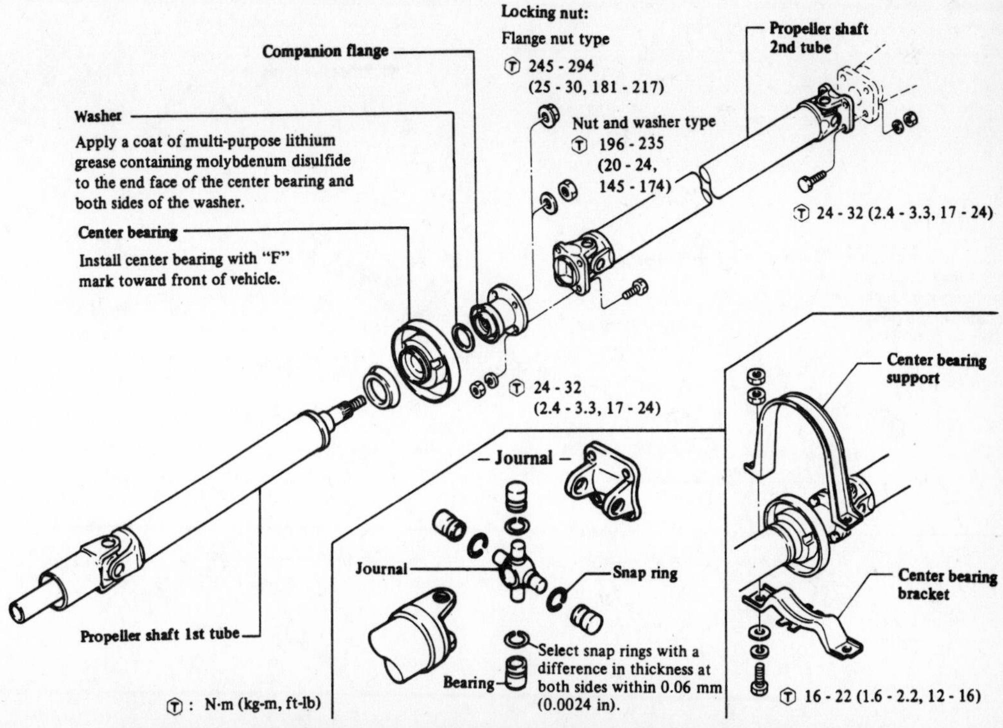

Locking nut:
Flange nut type
245 - 294 (25 - 30, 181 - 217)
Nut and washer type
196 - 235 (20 - 24, 145 - 174)
Companion flange
Propeller shaft 2nd tube
Washer
Apply a coat of multi-purpose lithium grease containing molybdenum disulfide to the end face of the center bearing and both sides of the washer.
Center bearing
Install center bearing with "F" mark toward front of vehicle.
24 - 32 (2.4 - 3.3, 17 - 24)
24 - 32 (2.4 - 3.3, 17 - 24)
Center bearing support
Center bearing bracket
Journal
Journal
Snap ring
Select snap rings with a difference in thickness at both sides within 0.06 mm (0.0024 in).
Bearing
Propeller shaft 1st tube
: N·m (kg-m, ft-lb)
16 - 22 (1.6 - 2.2, 12 - 16)

Two piece rear driveshaft with center bearing—1981–86 2wd models (720-D series)

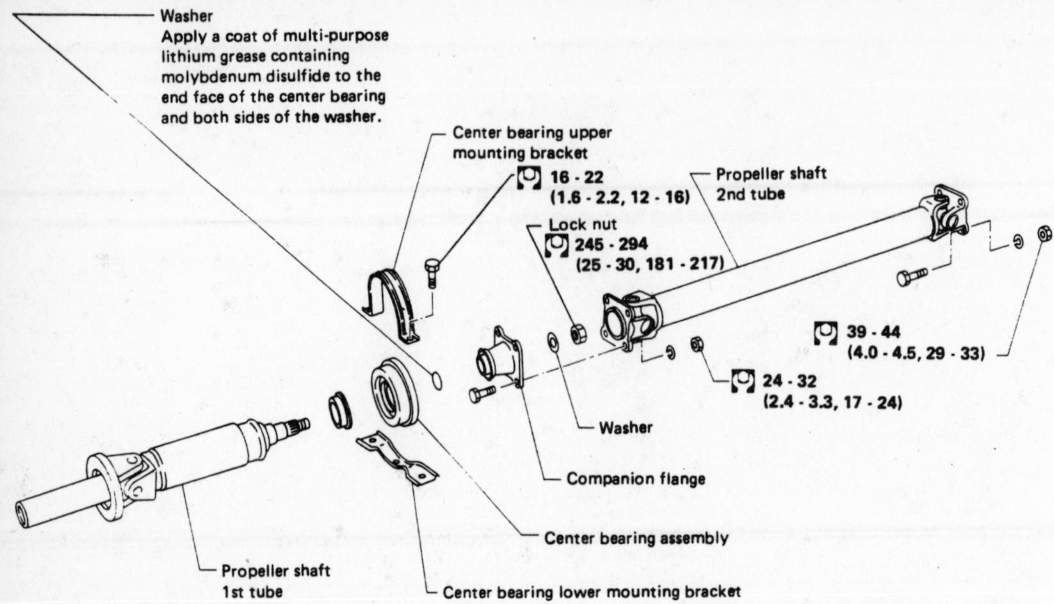

Two piece rear driveshaft with center bearing—1986–89 2wd models (Z24i engine)

33 ft. lbs. (39–44 Nm) – Z24i engines; or 58–65 ft. lbs. (78–88 Nm) – VG30i engines.

11. Tighten the center bearing support bolts to 12–16 ft. lbs. (16–22 Nm).

4wd Models Only

ONE-PIECE DRIVESHAFT

1. Raise the rear of the truck and support the rear axle housing with jackstands.
2. Paint a mating mark on the two halves of the rear universal joint flange.
3. Remove the bolts which hold the rear flange together.
4. Remove the splined end of the driveshaft from the transmission. If you don't want to lose a lot of gear oil, plug the end of the transmission with a rag.

NOTE: *The rear driveshaft on 1981-86 mod-*

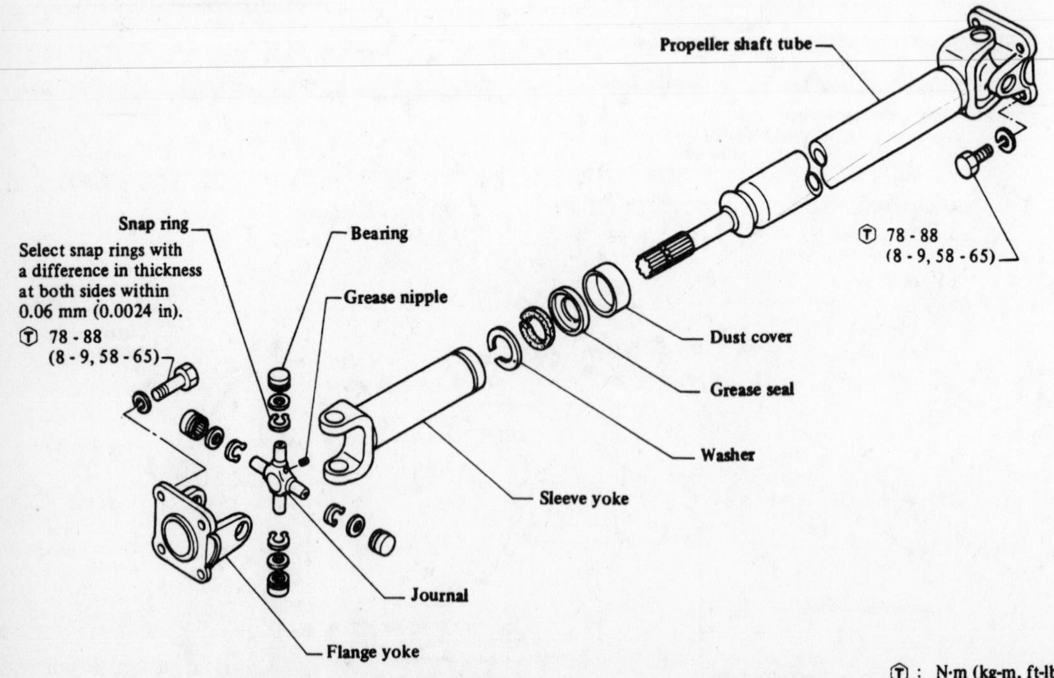

One piece rear driveshaft—1981–86 4wd models (720-D series)

Propeller shaft tube
Snap ring ★
Journal bearing
78 - 88 N·m
(8 - 9 kg-m, 58 - 65 ft-lb)
Journal
Flange yoke
★: Adjustment is required.

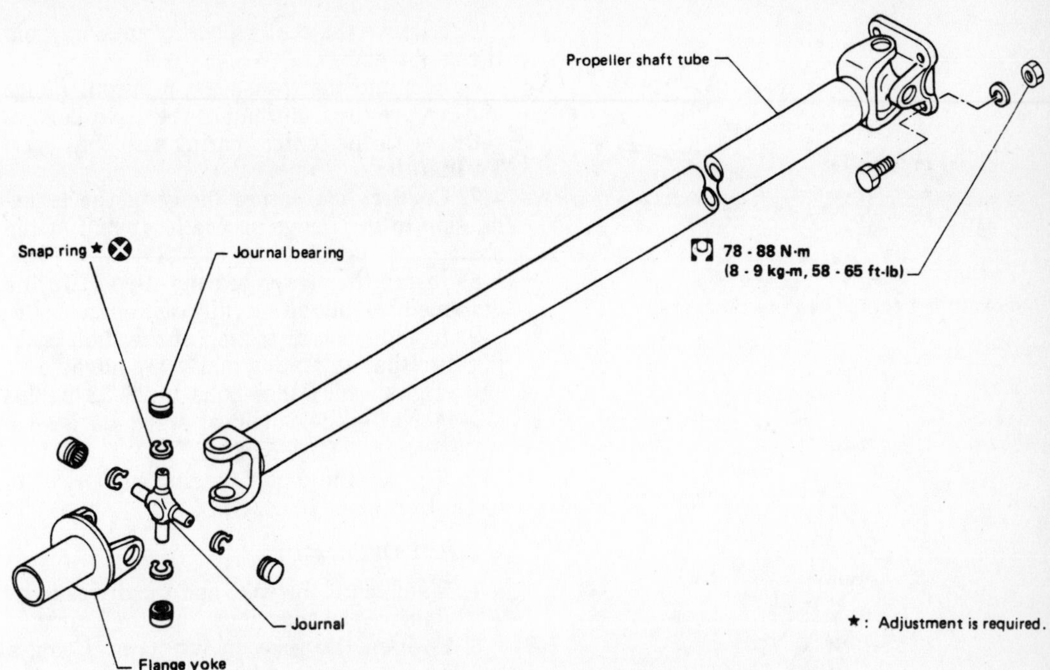

One piece rear driveshaft—1986–89 4wd models (D21-D series)

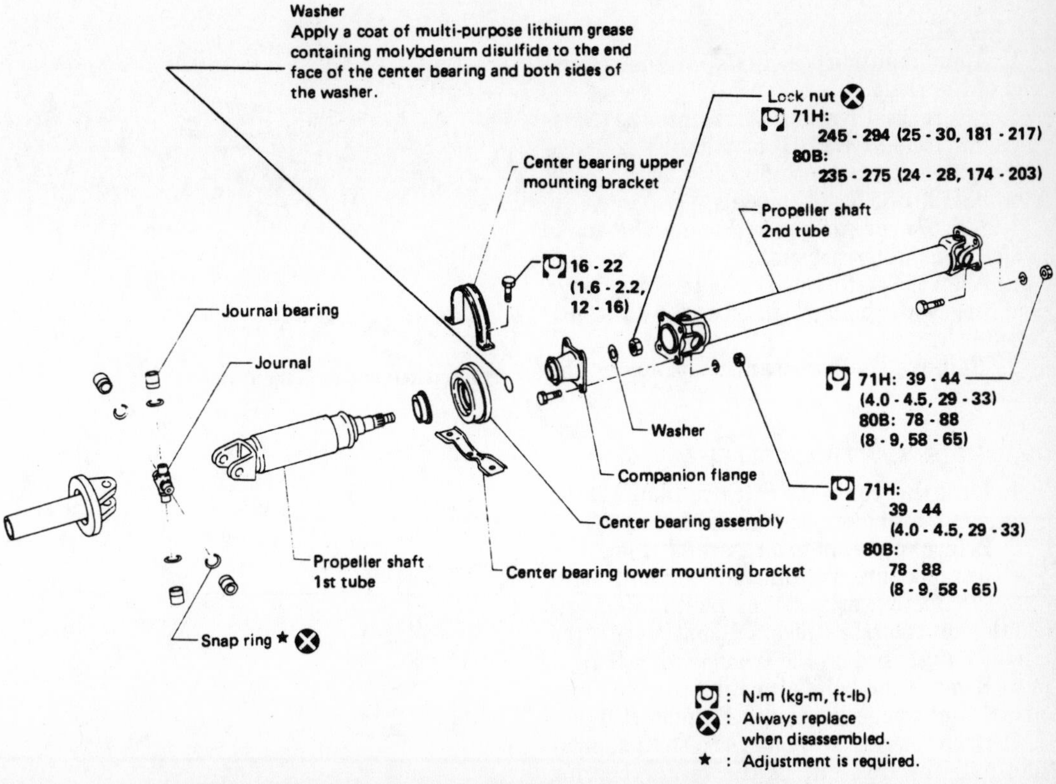

Washer
Apply a coat of multi-purpose lithium grease containing molybdenum disulfide to the end face of the center bearing and both sides of the washer.
Lock nut
71H:
245 - 294 (25 - 30, 181 - 217)
80B:
235 - 275 (24 - 28, 174 - 203)
Center bearing upper mounting bracket
Propeller shaft 2nd tube
16 - 22
(1.6 - 2.2,
12 - 16)
Journal bearing
Journal
71H: 39 - 44
(4.0 - 4.5, 29 - 33)
80B: 78 - 88
(8 - 9, 58 - 65)
Washer
Companion flange
71H:
39 - 44
(4.0 - 4.5, 29 - 33)
80B:
78 - 88
(8 - 9, 58 - 65)
Center bearing assembly
Propeller shaft 1st tube
Center bearing lower mounting bracket
Snap ring ★
: N·m (kg-m, ft-lb)
: Always replace when disassembled.
★ : Adjustment is required.

Two piece rear driveshaft with center bearing—1986–89 models (VG30i engines)

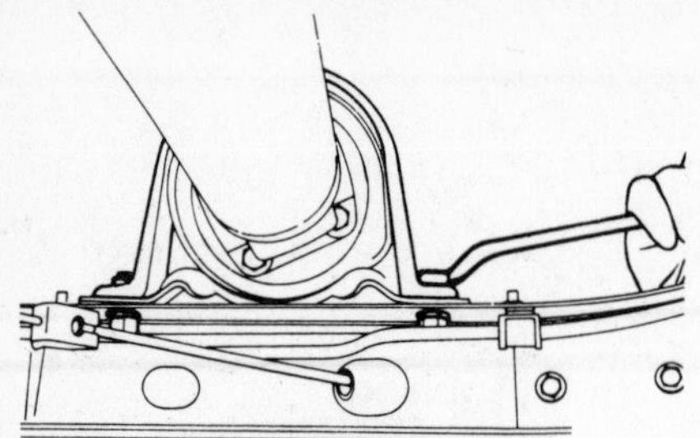

Removing the center bearing bracket

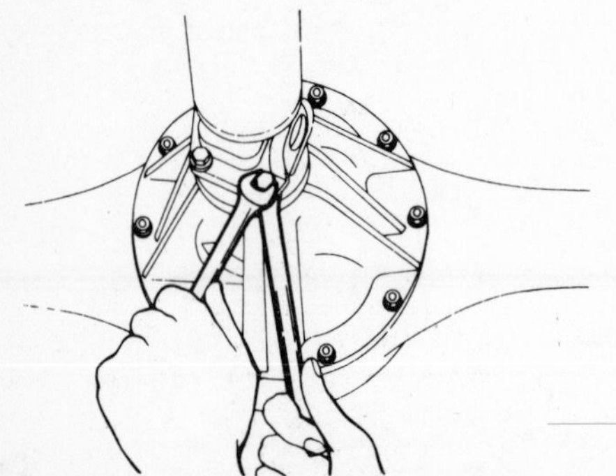

Disconnecting the driveshaft from the differential flange

els is connected to the transfer case by means of a flange, simply unbolt it.

5. Remove the driveshaft from under the truck.

To install:

6. Apply multipurpose grease to the splined end of the shaft.

7. Insert the driveshaft sleeve into the transmission (1986-89 D21-D) or mount the flange and tighten the bolts to 58–65 ft. lbs. (78–88 Nm) on 1981-86 720-D models.

NOTE: *Be careful not to damage the extension housing grease seal.*

8. Align the mating marks on the rear flange and replace the bolts. Tighten to 58–65 ft. lbs. (78–88 Nm).

9. Remove the jackstands and lower the vehicle.

TWO-PIECE DRIVESHAFT W/CENTER BEARING

1. Raise the rear of the truck and support the rear axle housing on jackstands.

2. Before you begin to disassemble the driveshaft components, you must first paint accurate alignment marks on the mating flangers. Do this on the rear universal joint flange, the center flange, and on the transmission flange.

3. Remove the bolts attaching the rear universal joint flange to the drive pinion flange.

4. Drop the rear section of the shaft slightly and pull the unit out of the center bearing sleeve yoke.

5. Remove the center bearing support from the crossmember.

6. Separate the transmission output flange and remove the front half of the driveshaft together with the center bearing assembly.

To install:

7. Connect the output flange of the transmission to the flange on the front half of the shaft.

8. Install the center bearing support to the crossmember, but do not fully tighten the bolts.

9. Install the rear section of the shaft making sure that all mating marks are aligned.

10. Tighten all flange bolts to 29–33 ft. lbs. (39–44 Nm)—Z24i engines; or 58–65 ft. lbs. (78–88 Nm)—VG30i engines.

11. Tighten the center bearing support bolts to 12–16 ft. lbs. (16–22 Nm).

U-JOINT OVERHAUL

1. Matchmark the yoke and the driveshaft.

2. Remove the snaprings from the bearings.

3. Position the yoke on vise jaws. Using a bearing remover and a hammer, gently tap the remover until the bearing is driven out of the yoke about 25mm.

4. Place the tool in the vise and drive the yoke away from the tool until the bearing is removed.

5. Repeat Steps 3 and 4 for the other bearings.

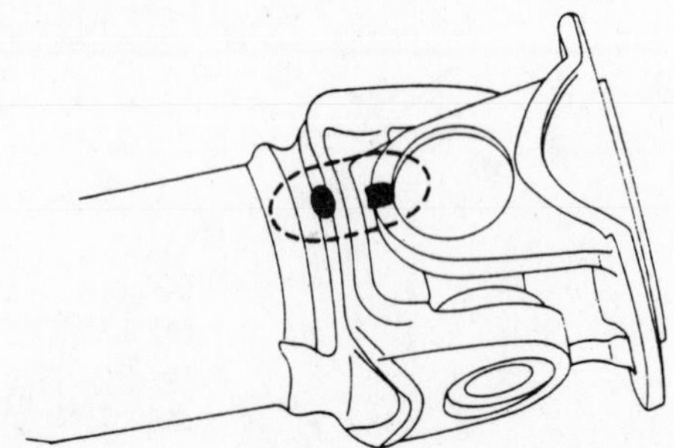

Paint matchmarks on the flanges

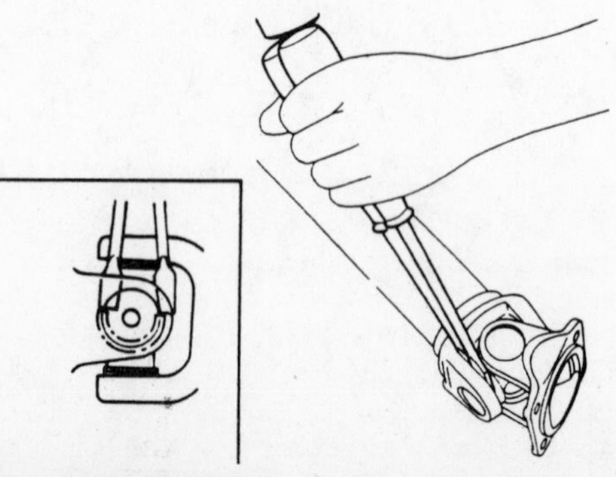

Remove the snapring

6. Check for worn or damaged parts. Inspect the bearing journal surfaces for wear.

To assemble:

7. Install the bearing cups, seals, and O-rings in the spider.
8. Grease the spider and the bearings.
9. Position the spider in the yoke.
10. Start the bearings in the yoke and then press them into place, using a vise.
11. Repeat Step 4 for the other bearings.
12. If the axial play of the spider is greater than 0.02mm, select snaprings which will provide the correct play. Be sure that the snaprings are the same size on both sides or driveshaft noise and vibration will result.

Center Bearing

REMOVAL AND INSTALLATION

NOTE: *The following procedure requires the use of special lock nut removal tool, a puller to remove the companion flange, and a press to remove the center bearing. The center bearing is a sealed unit which must be replaced as an assembly if defective.*

1. Remove the driveshaft.
2. Matchmark the flange yoke and the companion flange which connect the front half of the driveshaft to the rear. Also matchmark the companion flange and the front driveshaft. Remove the bolts and separate the shafts.
3. You must devise a way to hold the driveshaft while unbolting the companion flange from the front driveshaft. Do not place the front driveshaft tube in a vise, because the chances are it will get crushed. The best way is to grip the flange somehow while loosening the nut. It is going to require some strength to remove. There are special lock nut removal tools available. Use Tool No. ST315300 for models through 1986 (except D21-D series). On D21-D series trucks with 2wd use Tool No. ST38060002, on 4wd models use tool No. KV38104700.
4. Remove the companion flange off the front driveshaft with a puller and press the center bearing from its mount.
5. The new bearing is already lubricated. Install it into the mount, making sure that the seals and so on are facing the same way as then removed.
6. Slide the companion flange onto the front driveshaft, aligning the marks made during removal. Install the washer and locknut. Tighten the nut to 145–175 ft. lbs. on all 1970-80 models. On 1981-86 trucks (720-D), tighten to 181–217 ft. lbs. (245–294 Nm). On 1986-89 models with the Z24i engine, tighten to 181–217 ft. lbs. (245–294 Nm). On models with the VG30i engines, tighten to 174–203 ft. lbs. (235–275 Nm).

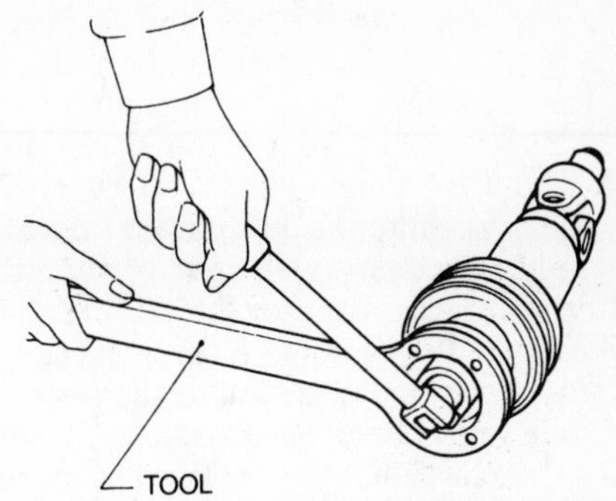

Removing the center bearing locking nut with the special tool

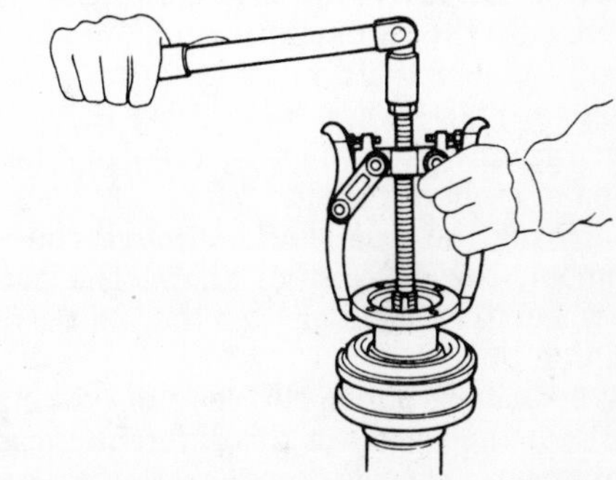

Removing the companion flange with a puller

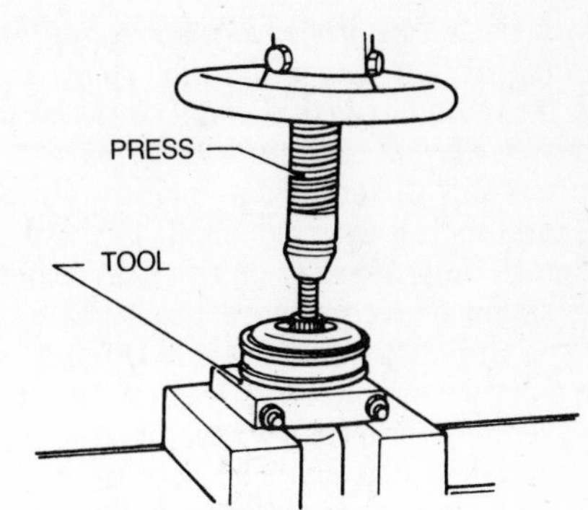

Pressing off the center bearing

Check that the bearing rotates freely around the driveshaft.

7. Connect the companion flange to the flange yoke, aligning the marks made during disassembly.
8. Install the driveshaft, aligning the marks made at the axle flange (and the transmission flange on 521 models) during removal.

REAR DRIVE AXLE

Understanding Drive Axles

The drive axle is a special type of transmission that reduces the speed of the drive from the engine and transmission and divides the power to the wheels. Power enters the axle from the driveshaft via the companion flange. The flange is mounted on the drive pinion shaft. The drive pinion shaft and gear which carry the power into the differential turn at engine speed. The gear on the end of the pinion shaft drives a large ring gear the axis of rotation of which is 90 degrees away from the of the pinion. The pinion and gear reduce the gear ratio of the axle, and change the direction of rotation to turn the axle shafts which drive both wheels. The axle gear ratio is found by dividing the number of pinion gear teeth into the number of ring gear teeth.

The ring gear drives the differential case. The case provides the two mounting points for the ends of a pinion shaft on which are mounted two pinion gears. The pinion gears drive the two side gears, one of which is located on the inner end of each axle shaft.

By driving the axle shafts through the arrangement, the differential allows the outer drive wheel to turn faster than the inner drive wheel in a turn.

The main drive pinion and the side bearings, which bear the weight of the differential case, are shimmed to provide proper bearing preload, and to position the pinion and ring gears properly.

WARNING: *The proper adjustment of the relationship of the ring and pinion gears is critical. It should be attempted only by those with extensive equipment and/or experience.*

Limited-slip differentials include clutches which tend to link each axle shaft to the differential case. Clutches may be engaged either by spring action or by pressure produced by the torque on the axles during a turn. During turning on a dry pavement, the effects of the clutches are overcome, and each wheel turns at the required speed. When slippage occurs at either wheel, however, the clutches will transmit some of the power to the wheel which has the greater amount of traction. Because of the presence of clutches, limited-slip units require a special lubricant.

Determining Axle Ratio

The drive axle of a truck is said to have a certain axle ratio. This number (usually a whole number and a decimal fraction) is actually a comparison of the number of gear teeth on the ring gear and the pinion gear. For example, a 4.11 rear means that theoretically, there are 4.11 teeth on the ring gear and one tooth on the pinion gear or, put another way, the driveshaft must turn 4.11 times to turn the wheels once. Actually, on a 4.11 rear, there might be 37 teeth on the ring gear and 9 teeth on the pinion gear. By dividing the number of teeth on the ring gear, the numerical axle ratio (4.11) is obtained. This also provides a good method of ascertaining exactly which axle ratio one is dealing with.

Another method of determining gear ratio is to jack up and support the truck so that both rear wheels are off the ground. Make a chalk mark on the rear wheel and the driveshaft. Put the transmission in neutral. Turn the rear wheel one complete turn and count the number of turns that the driveshaft makes. The number of turns that the driveshaft makes in one complete revolution of the rear wheel is an approximation of the rear axle ratio.

Axle Shaft, Bearing and Seal

REMOVAL AND INSTALLATION

Single Rear Wheels

1. Raise the rear of the vehicle and support it. Remove the rear wheel and tire.
2. Disconnect the rear parking brake cable by removing the adjusting nut and clamps.
3. Disconnect the brake tube at the rear brake backing plate. Plug the end of the brake tube to prevent loss of brake fluid.
4. Remove the brake drum.
5. Remove the nuts securing the wheel bearing retainer to the brake backing plate.
6. Pull out the axle shaft assembly together with the brake backing plate using a slide hammer.
7. Remove the oil seal in the axle housing if necessary. It can be pried out with a screwdriver. Oil the lips of the new seal and install it carefully to avoid damage to the lip.
8. To replace the bearing, unbend and discard the lockwasher. Remove the locknut with a soft drift and a hammer.
9. Press the old bearing and cage off the shaft.
10. Remove the oil seal in the cage. Use a brass drift to remove the bearing cup after the seal has been removed.
11. Install the new cup with a brass drift. Install a new oil seal over the bearing cup. Lubricate the area between the seal lips with grease after installation.
12. Place the bearing cage and spacer on the axle shaft, then fit the bearing, tapping it into place with a soft drift and light hammer blows.
13. Place the flat bearing lockwasher over the bearing, then the new nut lockwasher. Install the locknut, tightening to 108 ft. lbs. (147 Nm). Continue to tighten after that until the grooves line up with the lockwasher tabs. The nut can be tightened up to 145 ft. lbs. (196 Nm). Bend the lockwasher tabs into place.

14. Lubricate the bearing and recess in the axle housing with wheel bearing grease. Coat the axle splines with gear oil. Coat the seal surface of the shaft with grease.

15. Install the axle shaft and then check the axle end play. It should be 0.3–0.9mm on 1970-74 models; 0.02–0.15mm on 1975-89 models. The end play is adjusted by adding or removing shims behind the brake backing plate. Tighten the backing plate attaching nuts to 27–35 ft. lbs. on 1970-73 models, or 39–46 ft. lbs. (53–63 Nm) on 1974-89 models.

Dual Rear Wheels

1. Follow Steps 1–6 of the procedure for single rear wheels.

2. Remove the attaching screws and detach

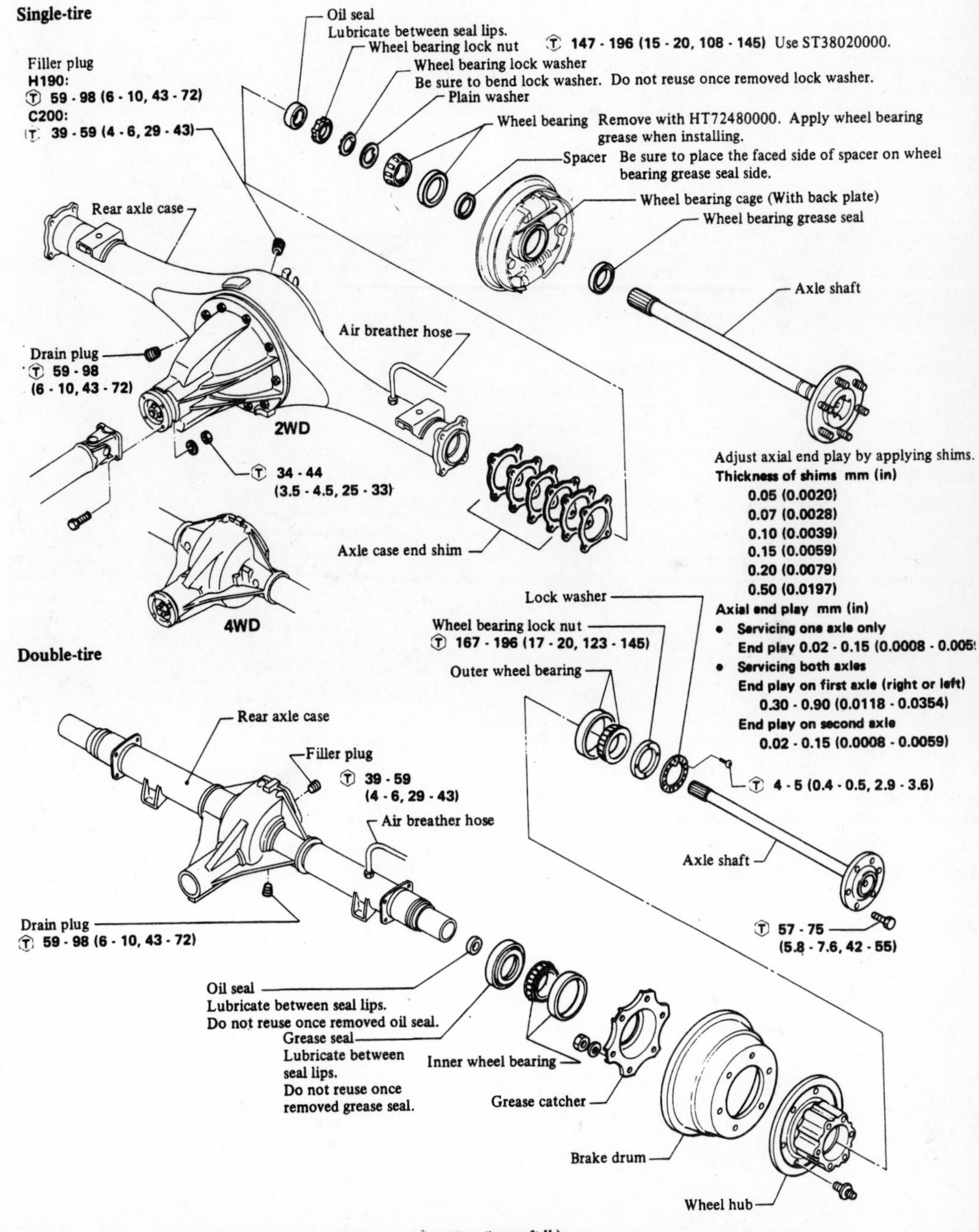

Exploded view of the rear drive axle—1970–86 (521, 620 and 720-S series)

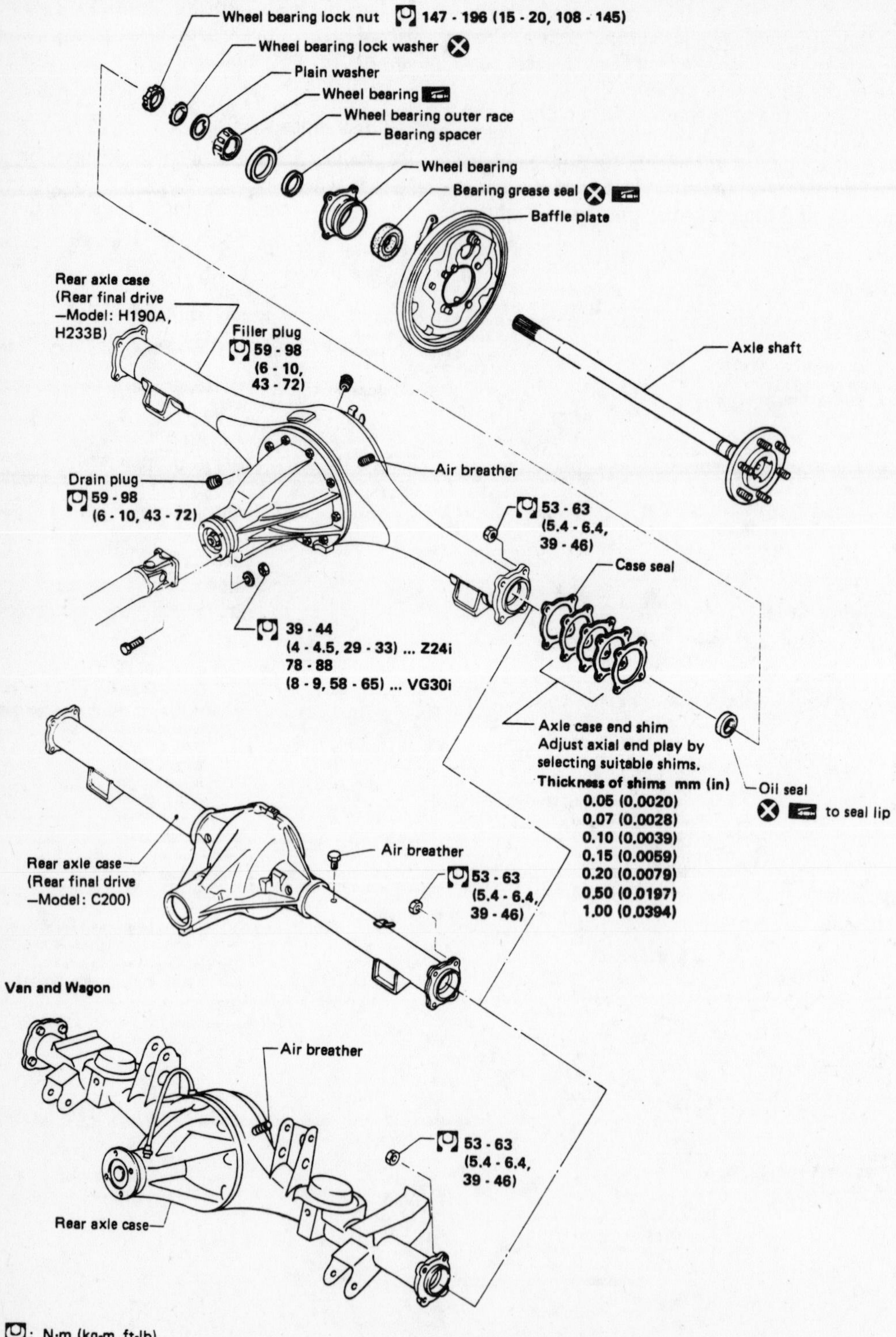

Exploded view of the rear drive axle—1986–89 (D21-D series)

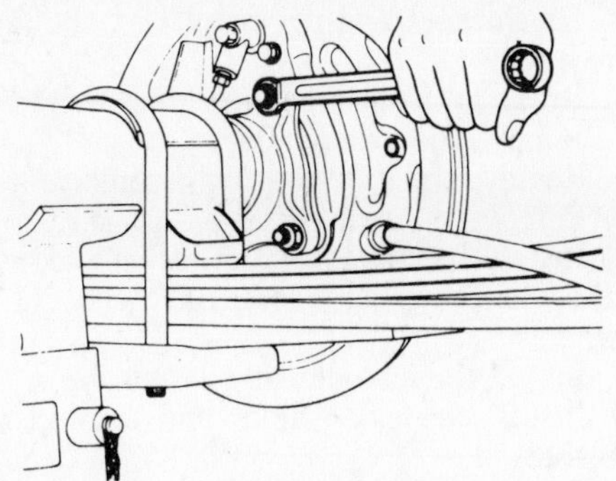

Disconnecting the brake backing plate from the axle housing

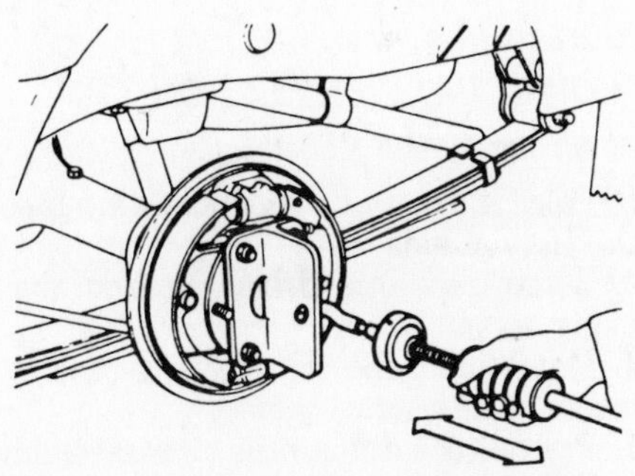

Remove the axle shaft with a slide hammer

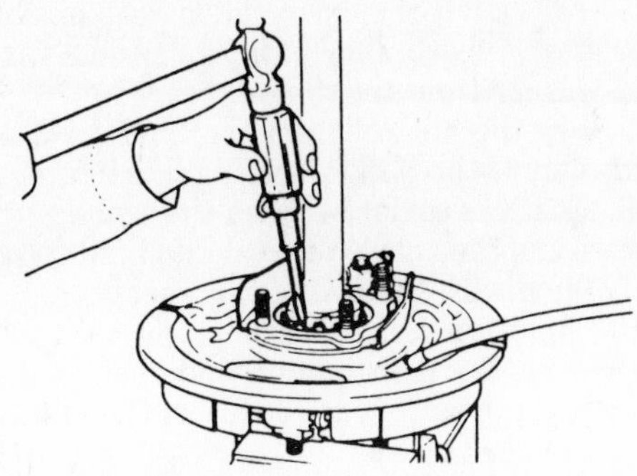

Unbend the lockwasher to remove the bearing locknut; use a new one for installation

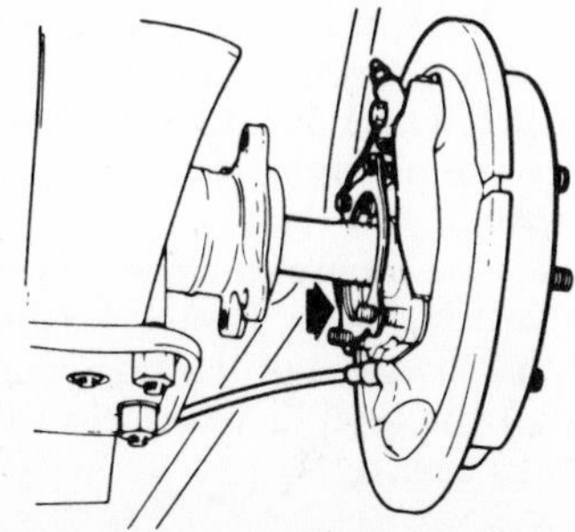

Axle shaft end-play is adjusted by the addition or subtraction of shims behind the brake backing plate

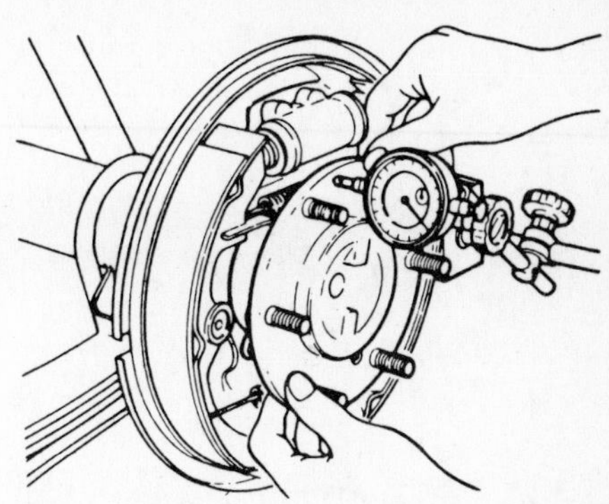

Measure the axial end play with a dial indicator

the lockwasher from the rear wheel bearing nut.

3. Remove the rear wheel bearing nut.
4. Remove the bearing and seal and drive out the races with a brass drift.
5. Coat the axles shaft splines with 90W gear oil and coat the seal lip with chassis lube.
6. Install new bearing races with an installing drift and pack the hub with chassis lube.
7. Pack each bearing and the O-ring with chassis lube.
8. Install the bearings and axle shaft. Be careful not to damage the seal with the shaft. Always use new seals. Make sure that the axle shaft end play is 0.08mm. Observe the following torques:

- Wheel bearing locknut: 123–145 ft. lbs (167–196 Nm).

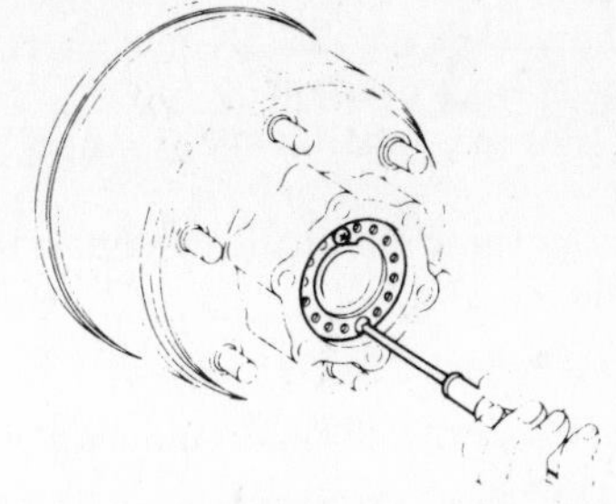

Removing lockwasher attaching screws from rears with dual rear wheels

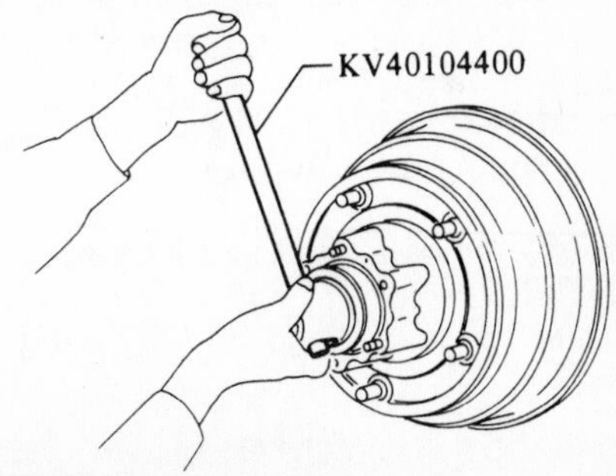

Removing bearing locknut from rears with dual rear wheels

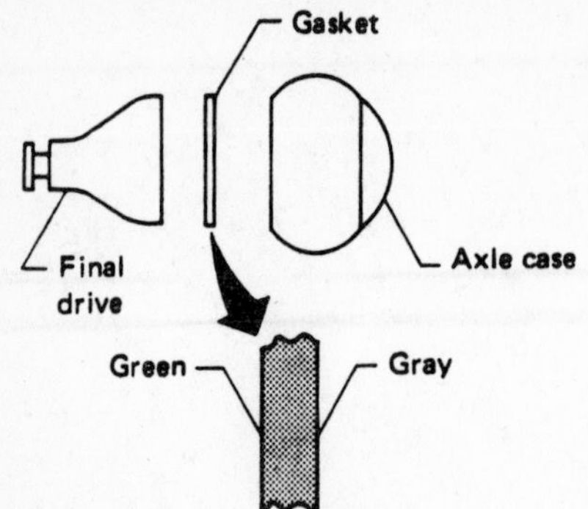

Gasket installation on the H233B

- Backing plate nut: 62–80 ft. lbs. (84–108 Nm).
- Wheel lugs: 159–188 ft. lbs. (216–255 Nm).

Final Drive

REMOVAL AND INSTALLATION

All Except C200 Models

1. Raise the rear of the truck and support it with safety stands.
2. Disconnect the driveshaft at the final drive unit.
3. Drain all fluid from the final drive and then remove the axle shafts.
4. Loosen the final drive-to-axle housing mounting bolts and remove the final drive.
5. Install the final drive and tighten the mounting bolts to 12–18 ft. lbs. (17–25 Nm). Be sure that the gasket on H233B models is installed in the correct position.
6. Install the axle shafts and connect the driveshaft.
7. Lower the vehicle and fill the final drive with gear oil.

1984-86 (720-D Series) C200 Models

1. Raise the rear of the truck and support it with safety stands.
2. Disconnect the driveshaft at the final drive unit.
3. Drain all fluid from the final drive and then remove the axle shafts.
4. Remove the rear cover and gasket.
5. Install the rear cover and gasket and tighten the mounting bolts to 8–10 ft. lbs. (11–14 Nm).
6. Install the axle shafts and connect the driveshaft.
7. Lower the vehicle and fill the final drive with gear oil.

1986-89 (D21-D Series) C200 Models

1. Raise the rear of the truck and support it with safety stands.
2. Disconnect the driveshaft at the final drive unit.
3. Drain all fluid from the final drive and then remove the axle shafts.
4. Remove the axle housing assembly.
5. Remove the rear cover and gasket.
6. Install the rear cover and gasket and tighten the mounting bolts to 8–10 ft. lbs. (11–14 Nm).
7. Install the axle housing assembly.
8. Install the axle shafts and connect the driveshaft.
9. Lower the vehicle and fill the final drive with gear oil.

Pinion Seal

REMOVAL AND INSTALLATION

H190-ML and H190A Models

1. Paise the rear of the vehicle and support it with safety stands.
2. Remove the final drive unit from the axle housing assembly.
3. Matchmark the side bearing caps to the case and then remove them.
4. Pry out the differential case assembly.
5. Remove the pinion nut.
6. Remove the companion flange with a suitable puller.
7. Knock out the drive pinion with a rubber mallet and then remove the collapsible spacer and washer from the pinion.
8. Pry the oil seal from the final drive unit and remove the pinion bearing inner race.
9. Coat the cavity between the seal lips with grease and then drive the seal into final drive so it is flush with the end of the housing.
10. Position a *new* washer and collapsible spacer on the drive pinion and then coat the rear bearing with gear oil. Insert the assembly into the gear carrier.
11. Install the companion flange and hold it firmly while tapping the drive pinion in with a rubber mallet.
12. Hold the companion flange and tighten the pinion nut until there is no axial play. Tighten the nut gradually until the pre-load is 9.5–13.9 inch lbs. (1.1–1.6 Nm). After tightening, rotate the pinion several times to set the bearing rollers.
13. Install the differential case assembly and the side bearing rollers into the final drive housing and then install the side bearing cap.
14. Install the final drive. Lower the vehicle and fill with gear oil.

C200 Models

1. Paise the rear of the vehicle and support it with safety stands.

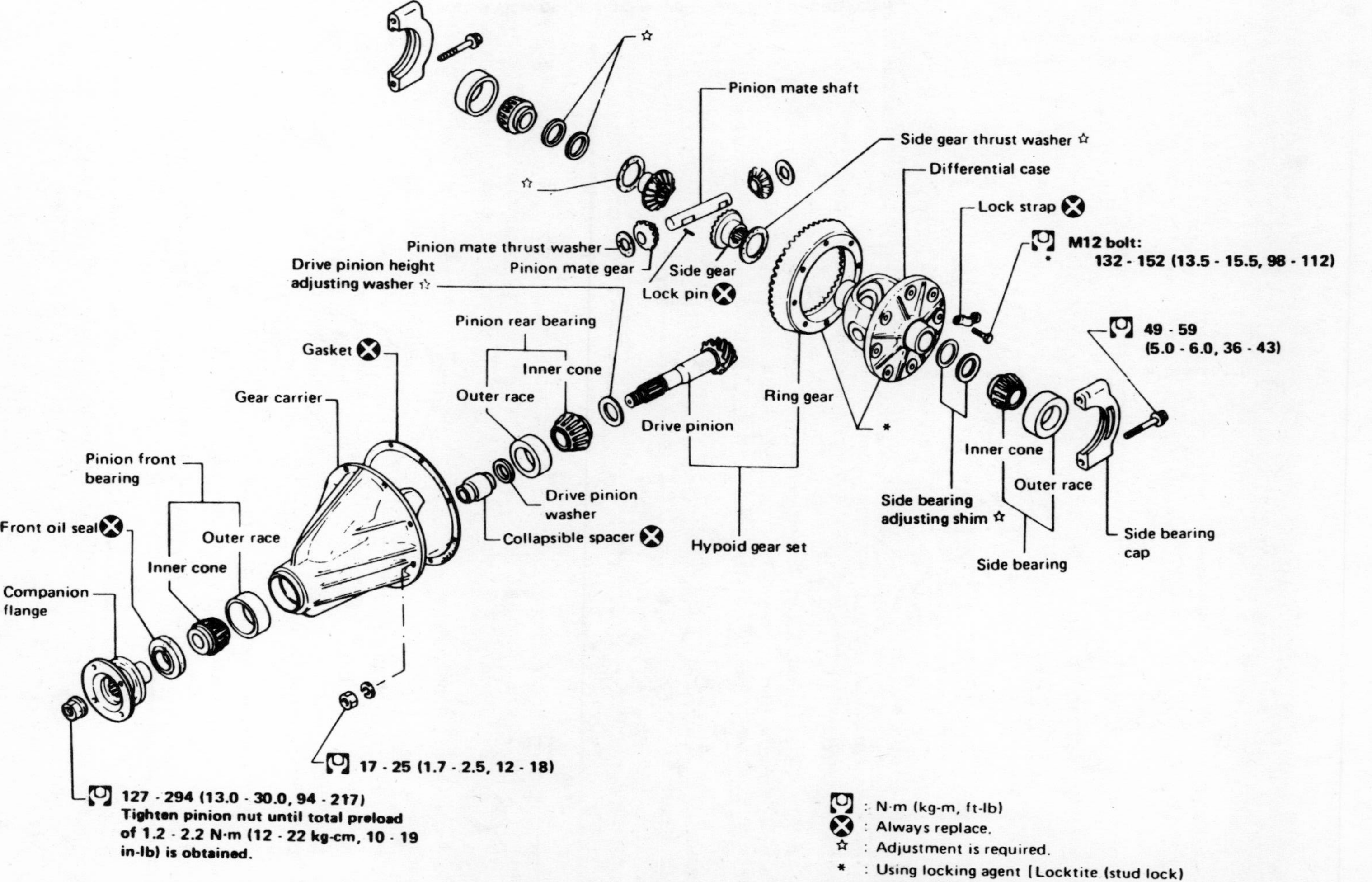

Exploded view of the final drive—H190A and H190-ML

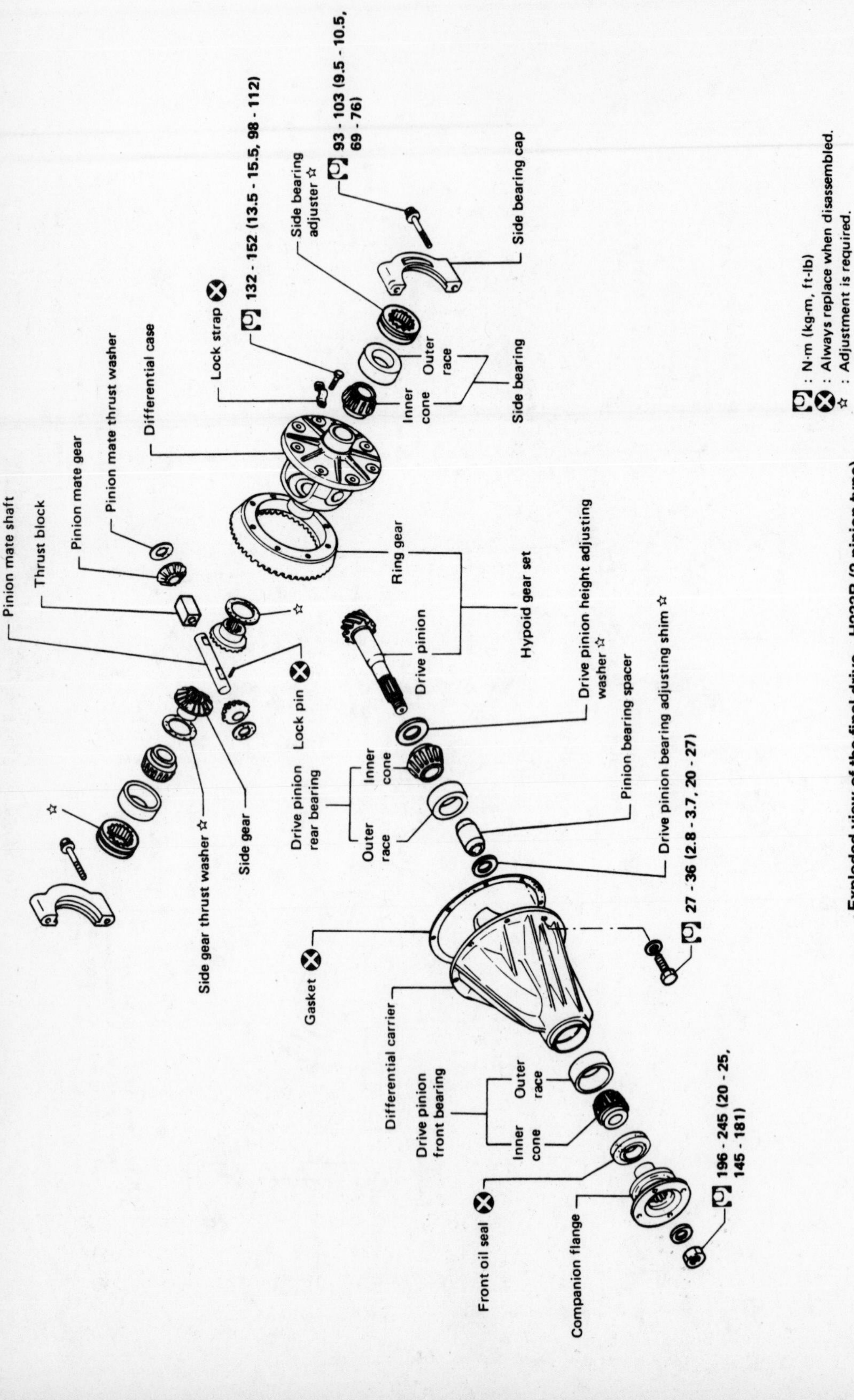

Pinion mate shaft
Thrust block
Pinion mate gear
Pinion mate thrust washer
Differential case
Lock strap ⊗
132 - 152 (13.5 - 15.5, 98 - 112)
Side bearing adjuster ☆
93 - 103 (9.5 - 10.5, 69 - 76)
Side bearing cap
Inner cone
Outer race
Side bearing
Ring gear
Drive pinion
Hypoid gear set
Lock pin ⊗
Side gear thrust washer ☆
Side gear
Drive pinion rear bearing
Inner cone
Outer race
Drive pinion height adjusting washer ☆
Pinion bearing spacer
Drive pinion bearing adjusting shim ☆
Gasket ⊗
27 - 36 (2.8 - 3.7, 20 - 27)
Differential carrier
Drive pinion front bearing
Outer race
Inner cone
Front oil seal ⊗
Companion flange
196 - 245 (20 - 25, 145 - 181)

: N·m (kg-m, ft-lb)
⊗ : Always replace when disassembled.
☆ : Adjustment is required.

Exploded view of the final drive—H233B (2 pinion type)

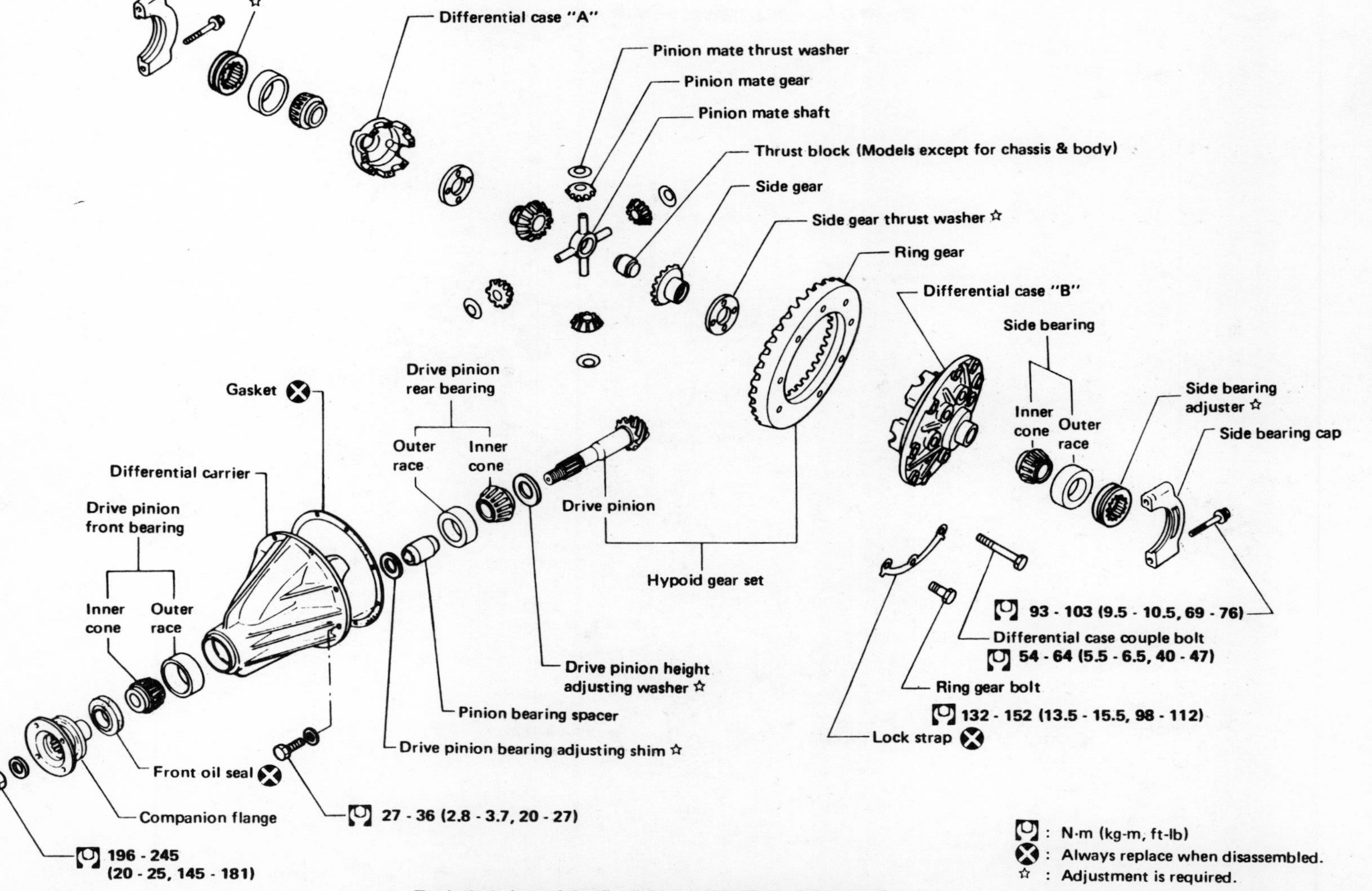

Exploded view of the final drive—H233B (4 pinion type)

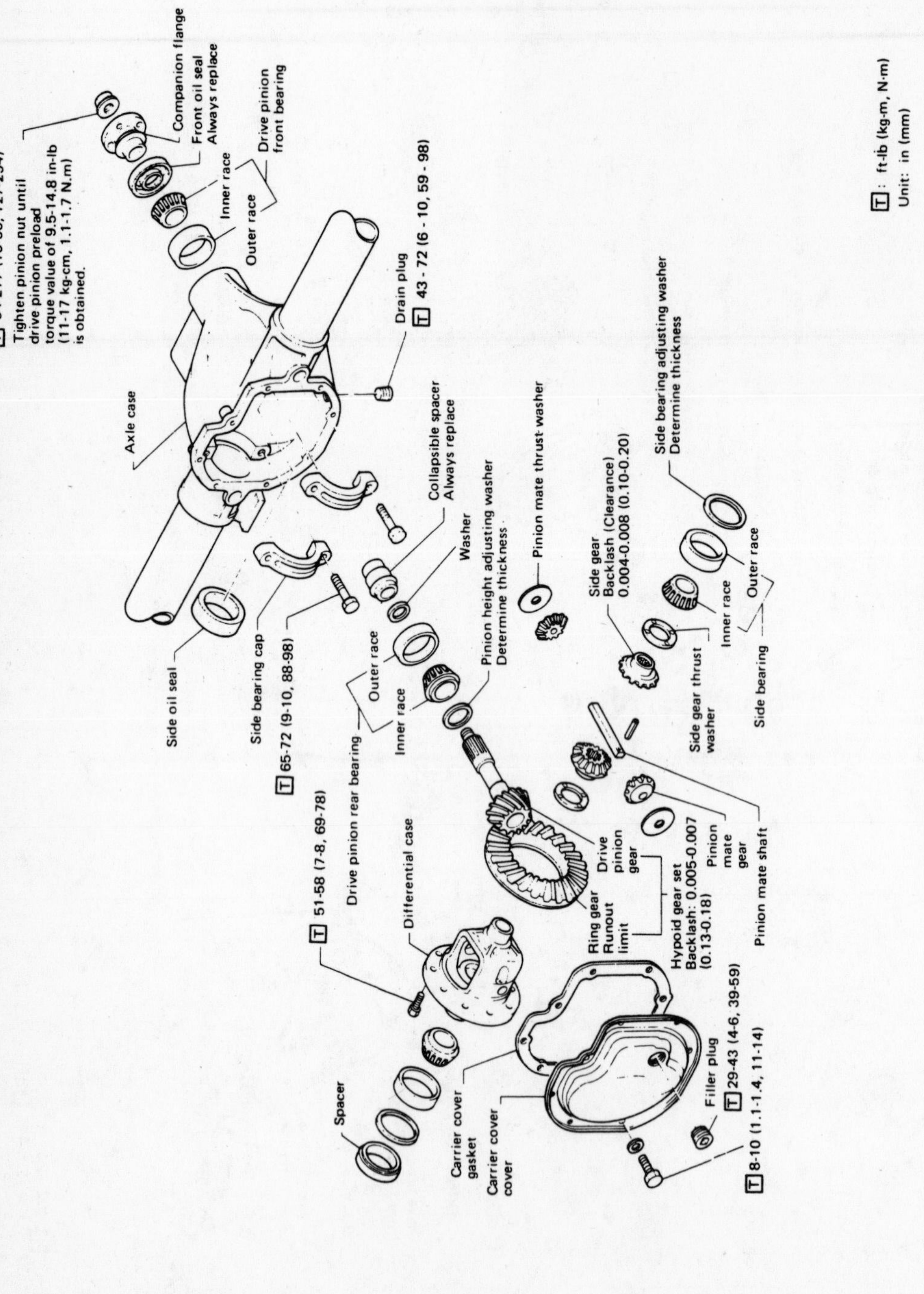

T 94-217 (13-30, 127-294)
Tighten pinion nut until drive pinion preload torque value of 9.5-14.8 in-lb (11-17 kg-cm, 1.1-1.7 N.m) is obtained.

Axle case
Companion flange
Front oil seal
Always replace
Inner race
Outer race
Drive pinion front bearing
Side oil seal
Side bearing cap
T 65-72 (9-10, 88-98)
T 51-58 (7-8, 69-78)
Spacer
Drive pinion rear bearing
Outer race
Inner race
Differential case
Drain plug
T 43 - 72 (6 - 10, 59 - 98)
Collapsible spacer
Always replace
Washer
Carrier cover gasket
Carrier cover cover
Pinion height adjusting washer
Determine thickness
Pinion mate thrust washer
Ring gear
Runout limit
Drive pinion gear
Side gear
Backlash (Clearance)
0.004-0.008 (0.10-0.20)
Side bearing adjusting washer
Determine thickness
Hypoid gear set
Backlash: 0.005-0.007 (0.13-0.18)
Filler plug
T 29-43 (4-6, 39-59)
T 8-10 (1.1-1.4, 11-14)
Pinion mate gear
Pinion mate shaft
Side gear thrust washer
Inner race
Outer race
Side bearing

T: ft-lb (kg-m, N·m)
Unit: in (mm)

Exploded view of the final drive—1984–86 C200 (720-D series)

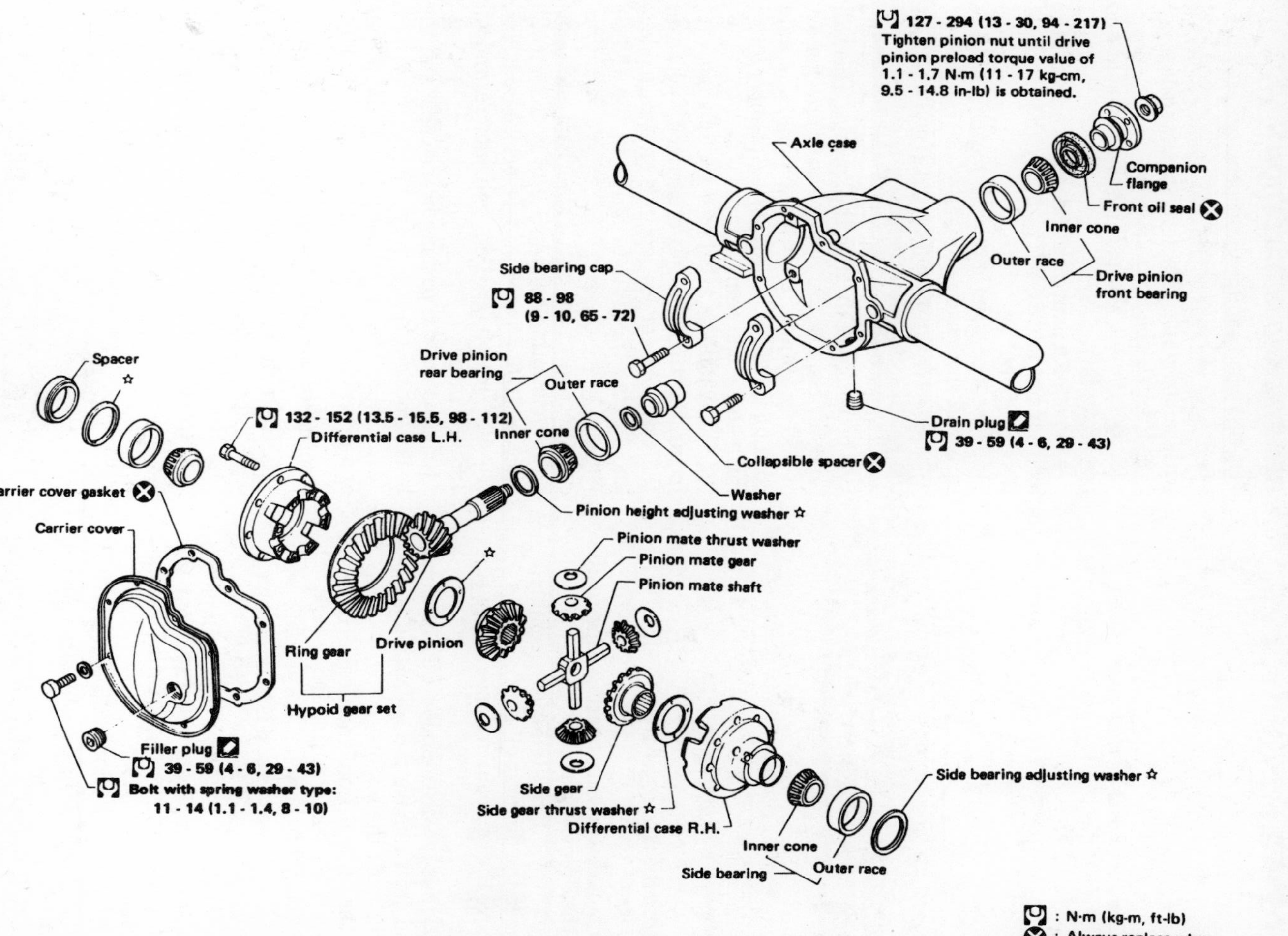

Exploded view of the final drive—1986–89 C200 (D21-D series)

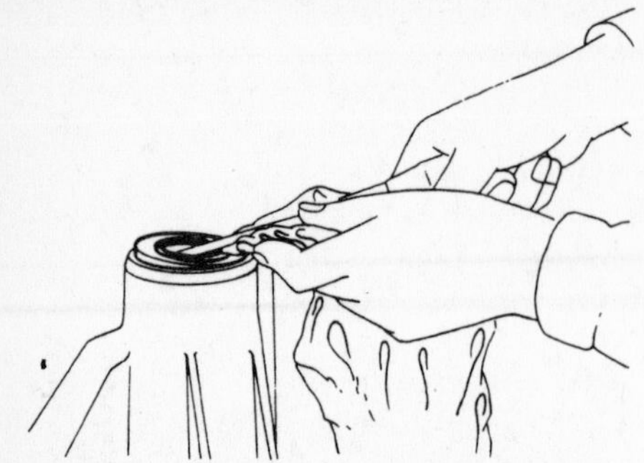

Removing the pinion seal—H190A and H190-ML

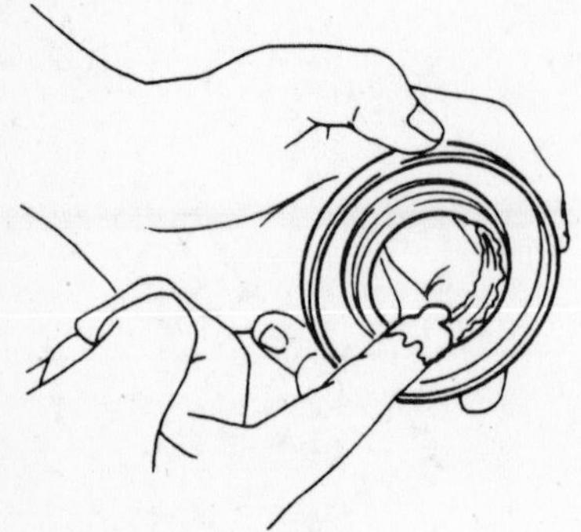

Coat the new seal with grease

2. Remove the rear cover from the final drive unit.

3. Matchmark the side bearing caps to the case and then remove them.

4. Pry out the differential case assembly.

5. Remove the pinion nut.

6. Remove the companion flange with a suitable puller.

7. Knock out the drive pinion with a rubber mallet and then remove the collapsible spacer and washer from the pinion.

8. Pry the oil seal from the final drive unit and remove the pinion bearing inner race.

9. Coat the cavity between the seal lips with grease and then drive the seal into final drive so it is flush with the end of the housing.

10. Position a *new* washer and collapsible spacer on the drive pinion and then coat the rear bearing with gear oil. Insert the assembly into the gear carrier.

11. Install the companion flange and hold it firmly while tapping the drive pinion in with a rubber mallet.

12. Hold the companion flange and tighten the pinion nut until there is no axial play. Tighten the nut gradually until the pre-load is 9.5–14.8 inch lbs. (1.1–1.7 Nm). After tightening, rotate the pinion several times to set the bearing rollers.

13. Install the differential case assembly and the side bearing rollers into the final drive housing and then install the side bearing caps. Tighten to 65–72 ft. lbs. (88–98 Nm).

14. Install the rear cover with a *new* gasket. Lower the vehicle and fill with gear oil.

Axle Housing

REMOVAL AND INSTALLATION

Pick-Ups with Leaf Spring Suspension

1. Raise the rear of the vehicle and support it with safety stands. Remove the rear wheels.

2. Remove the driveshaft.

3. Disconnect the parking brake cable and the brake line.

4. Postion a floor jack under the center of the axle housing and raise it just enough to support the assembly.

5. Disconnect the lower end of each shock absorber at the spring carrier.

6. Remove the spring carrier U-bolts and let the springs drop down slightly.

7. On 2wd models, carefully maneuever the axle housing out through the springs. This will probably require two floor jacks or another set of safety stands. On 4wd models, the axle hosuing is below the leaf springs; simply lower the housing and remove it.

8. Reinstall the axle housing and support it in position. Slide the spring carrier U-bolts over the axle tube (or leaf springs on 4wd models) and tighten the nuts to 65–72 ft. lbs. (88–98 Nm).

9. Reconnect the shock absorbers and tighten the mounting bolts to 12–16 ft. lbs. (16–22 Nm) on 1970-86 2wd models; or, 22–30 ft. lbs. (30–40 Nm) on 1981-86 4wd models and all 1986-89 models.

10. Connect the parking brake cable and the brake lines.

11. Connect the driveshaft, install the wheels and lower the vehicle.

Pathfinders with 5-Link Suspension

1. Raise the rear of the vehicle and support it with safety stands. Remove the rear wheels.

2. Remove the driveshaft.

3. Disconnect the parking brake cable and the brake line.

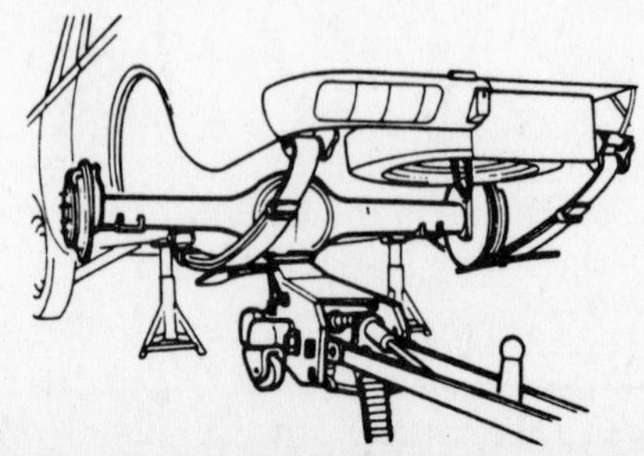

Slide the axle housing out through the leaf springs

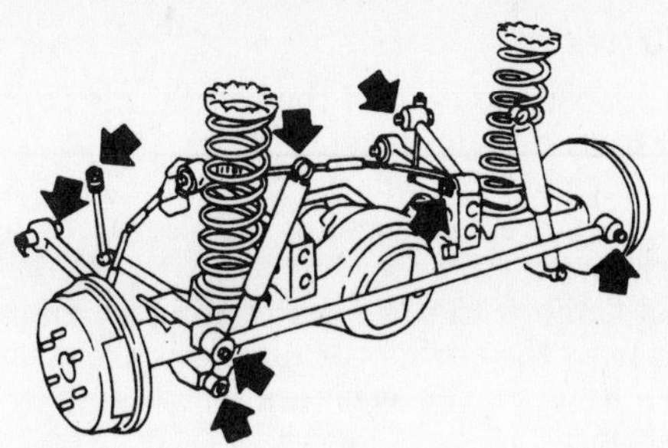

The axle housing on the Pathfinder is removed with the suspension intact

4. Postion a floor jack under the center of the axle housing and raise it just enough to support the assembly.
5. Remove the stabilizer-to-body mounting bolts.
6. Disconnect the upper and lower links at the body.
7. Disconnect the panhard rod at the body.
8. Remove the upper shock absorber mounting nuts.
9. Lower the entire axle housing assembly (suspension and all!) out and away from the vehicle.
10. Position the axle housing assembly under the body of the truck and raise it until the upper ends of the shock absorbers can be connected. Tighten the bolts to 22–30 ft. lbs. (30–40 Nm).
11. Connect the panhard rod and tighten the bolts to 80–108 ft. lbs. (108–147 Nm).
12. Reconnect the upper and lower links and then tighten the bolts to 80–108 ft. lbs. (108–147 Nm).
13. Connect the stabilizer bar to the body and tighten the bolts to 30–35 ft. lbs. (41–47 Nm).
14. Connect the parking brake cable and the brake lines.
15. Install the driveshaft. Install the wheels and then lower the vehicle.

FRONT DRIVE AXLE

Free Running Hub

REMOVAL AND INSTALLATION

1981-83

1. Raise the front of the vehicle and support the front axle on stands.
2. Set the hub in the **Lock** position.
3. Remove the driven clutch by turning it clockwise.

NOTE: *A pin is located inside the hub case to lock the driven clutch. Pull and turn the clutch while attracting the pin with a magnet.*

4. Remove the lockpin.
5. Set the hub at the **Free** position.
6. Screw the driven clutch into place by turning it counterclockwise until it bottoms.
7. Turn it clockwise until it aligns with the bolt hole.
8. Install the lockpin.

1984-86 (720-D Series)

MANUAL LOCK

1. Raise the front of the vehicle and support the front axle on stands.

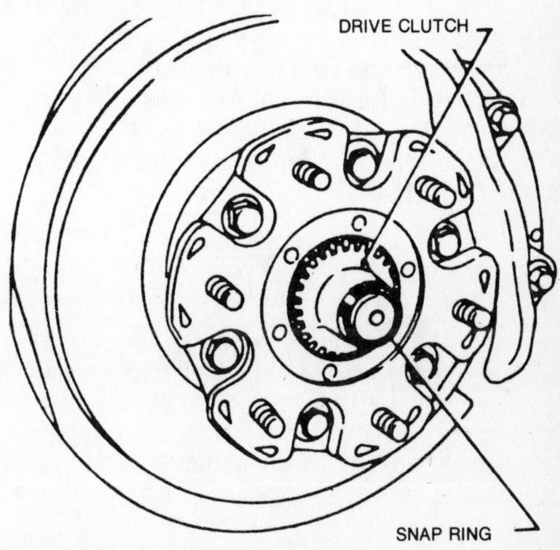

Snapring and driven clutch—1981–83 free running hub

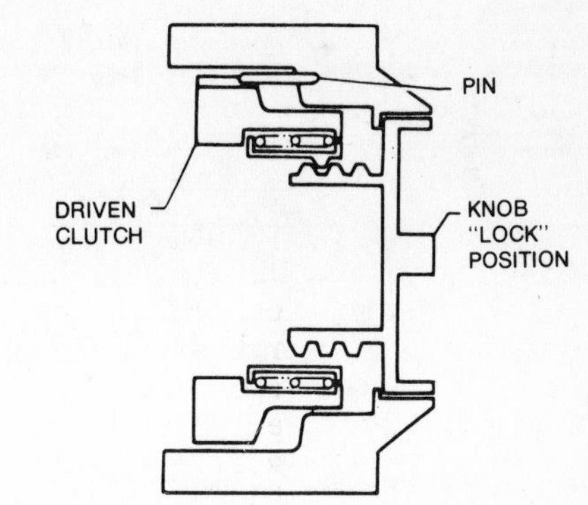

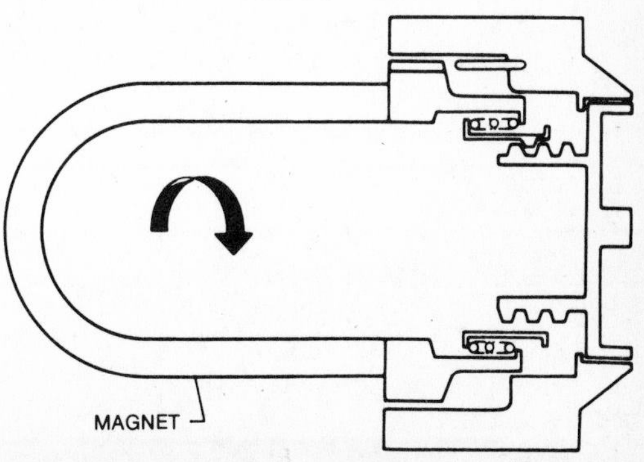

Hub removal sequence—1981–83 free running hub

2. Remove the wheels.
3. Remove the locking hub cover using a Torx® wrench.
4. Pull out the free running hub.
5. Remove the snapring and pull out the drive clutch.
6. Remove the snapring and lock washer and then remove the wheel bearing locknut using tool KV40104300, or its equivalent.
5. Install the wheel bearing locknut. Install a new lock washer and snapring.
6. Press on the driven clutch and install a new snapring.
7. Press on the free running hub.
8. Install the hub cover and tighten the screws to 18–25 ft. lbs. (25–34 Nm).
9. Install the wheels, remove the stands and lower the vehicle.

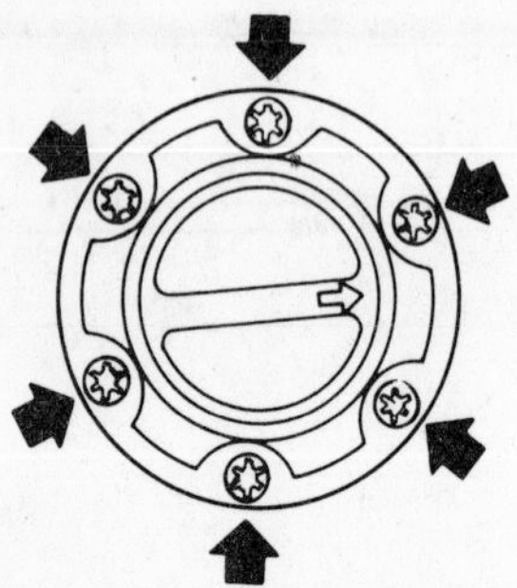

Front locking hub cap Torx® screws

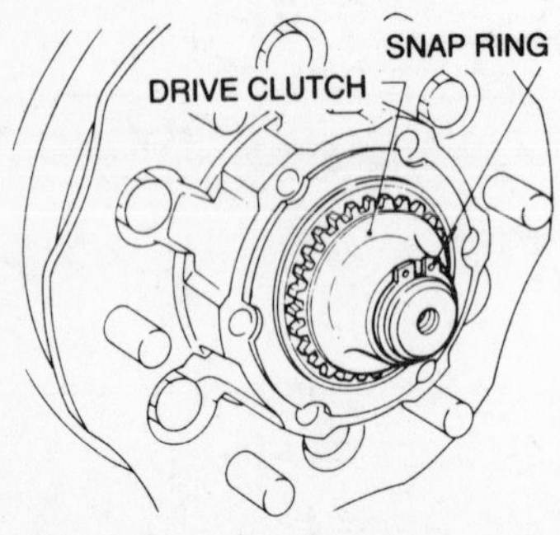

Snapring and driven clutch—1981–83 manual lock hub

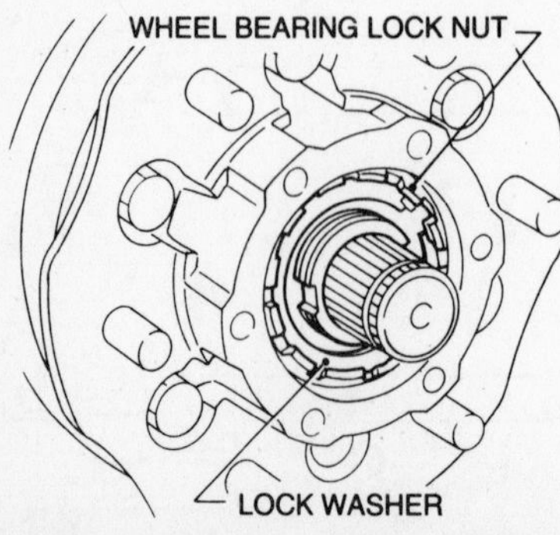

Lock washer and locknut—manual lock hub

AUTO LOCK

1. Raise the front of the vehicle and support the front axle on jackstands.
2. Remove the wheels.
3. Remove the locking hub cover using a Torx® wrench.
4. Remove the the automatic free running hub with the O-ring spring and brake **A**.
5. Remove the washers then remove the snapring.
6. Remove the large snapring, lock washer and wheel bearing lock nut, using tool No. KV40104300, or its equivalent.
7. Install the wheel bearing locknut. Install a new lock washer and large snapring.
8. Install the snapring and then the washers.
9. Install the free running hub along with the brake and O-ring spring.
10. Install the hub cover.
11. Install the wheels, remove the stands and lower the vehicle.

1986-89 (D21-D Series)

MANUAL LOCK

1. Raise the front of the vehicle and support the front axle on stands.
2. Remove the wheels.
3. Set the knob of the manual lock to the **FREE** position.
4. Remove the locking hub cover using a Torx® wrench, while the brake pedal is depressed.
5. Remove the snapring and pull out the drive clutch.
6. Install the drive clutch and snapring. Make sure the hub is in the **FREE** position.
7. Install the hub cover and tighten the bolts to 18–25 ft. lbs. (25–34 Nm).
8. Install the wheels, remove the stands and lower the vehicle.

AUTO LOCK

1. Raise the front of the vehicle and support the front axle on jackstands.
2. Remove the wheels.
3. Set the knob of the auto lock to the **FREE** position.
4. Remove the locking hub cover using a Torx® wrench, while the brake pedal is depressed.
5. Remove the snapring.
6. Remove washer **B**, washer **A** and brake **B**.
7. Make sure the hub is in the **FREE** position and then install washer **B**, washer **A** and brake **B**.
8. Install the snapring.
9. Install the hub cover and tighten the bolts to 18–25 ft. lbs. (25–34 Nm).
10. Install the wheels, remove the stands and then lower the vehicle.

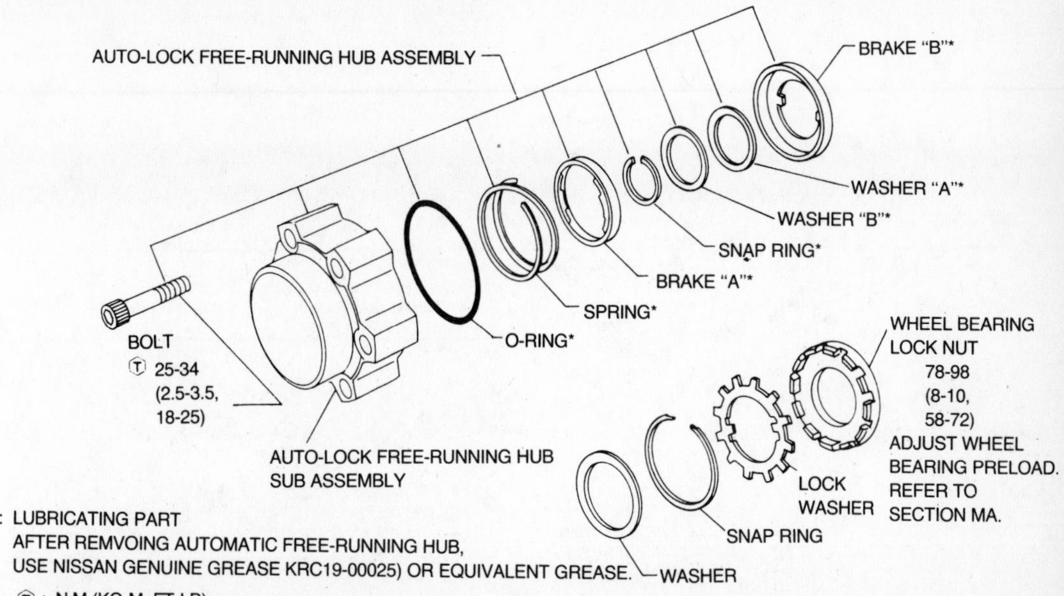

Exploded view of the auto lock hub—1985–86 (720-D series)

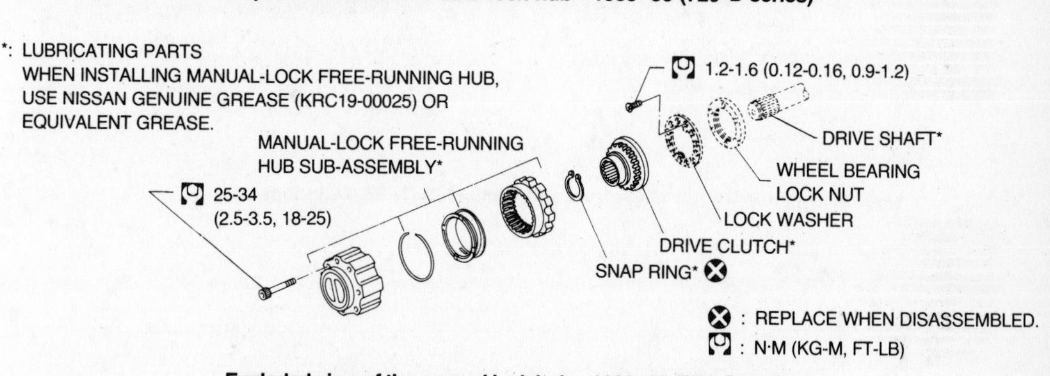

Exploded view of the manual lock hub—1986–89 (D21-D series)

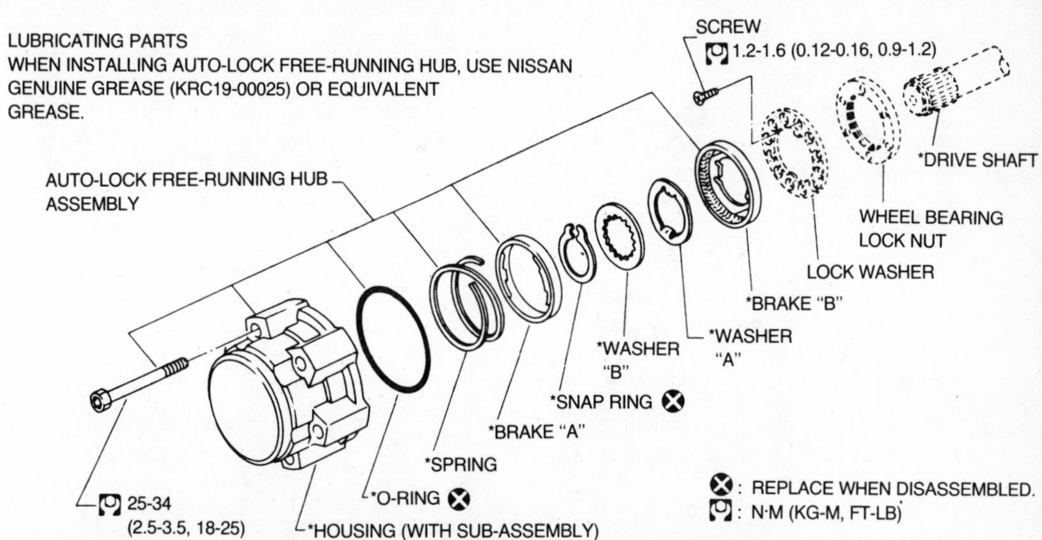

Exploded view of the auto lock hub—1986–89 (D21-D series)

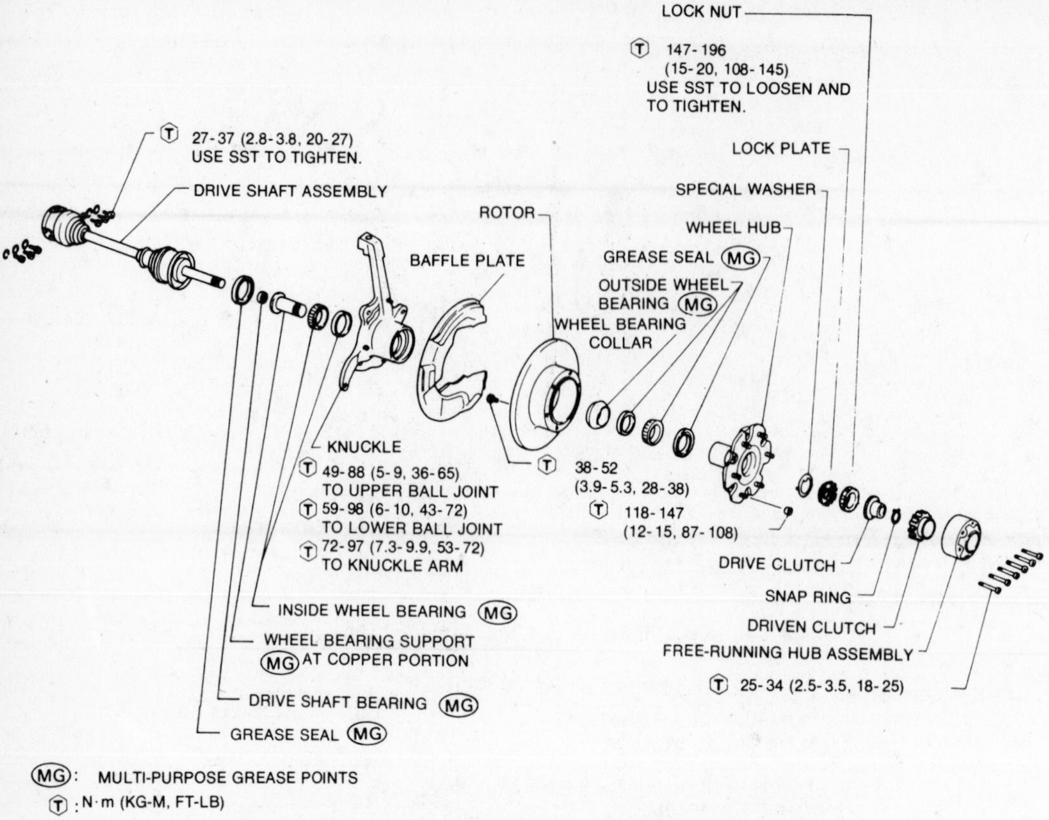

LOCK NUT
(T) 147-196
(15-20, 108-145)
USE SST TO LOOSEN AND
TO TIGHTEN.
(T) 27-37 (2.8-3.8, 20-27)
USE SST TO TIGHTEN.
LOCK PLATE
DRIVE SHAFT ASSEMBLY
SPECIAL WASHER
ROTOR
WHEEL HUB
BAFFLE PLATE
GREASE SEAL (MG)
OUTSIDE WHEEL
BEARING (MG)
WHEEL BEARING
COLLAR
KNUCKLE
(T) 49-88 (5-9, 36-65)
TO UPPER BALL JOINT
(T) 59-98 (6-10, 43-72)
TO LOWER BALL JOINT
(T) 72-97 (7.3-9.9, 53-72)
TO KNUCKLE ARM
(T) 38-52
(3.9-5.3, 28-38)
(T) 118-147
(12-15, 87-108)
DRIVE CLUTCH
SNAP RING
DRIVEN CLUTCH
FREE-RUNNING HUB ASSEMBLY
(T) 25-34 (2.5-3.5, 18-25)
INSIDE WHEEL BEARING (MG)
WHEEL BEARING SUPPORT
(MG) AT COPPER PORTION
DRIVE SHAFT BEARING (MG)
GREASE SEAL (MG)
(MG): MULTI-PURPOSE GREASE POINTS
(T): N·m (KG-M, FT-LB)

Exploded view of the front drive axle—1981–83 4wd models

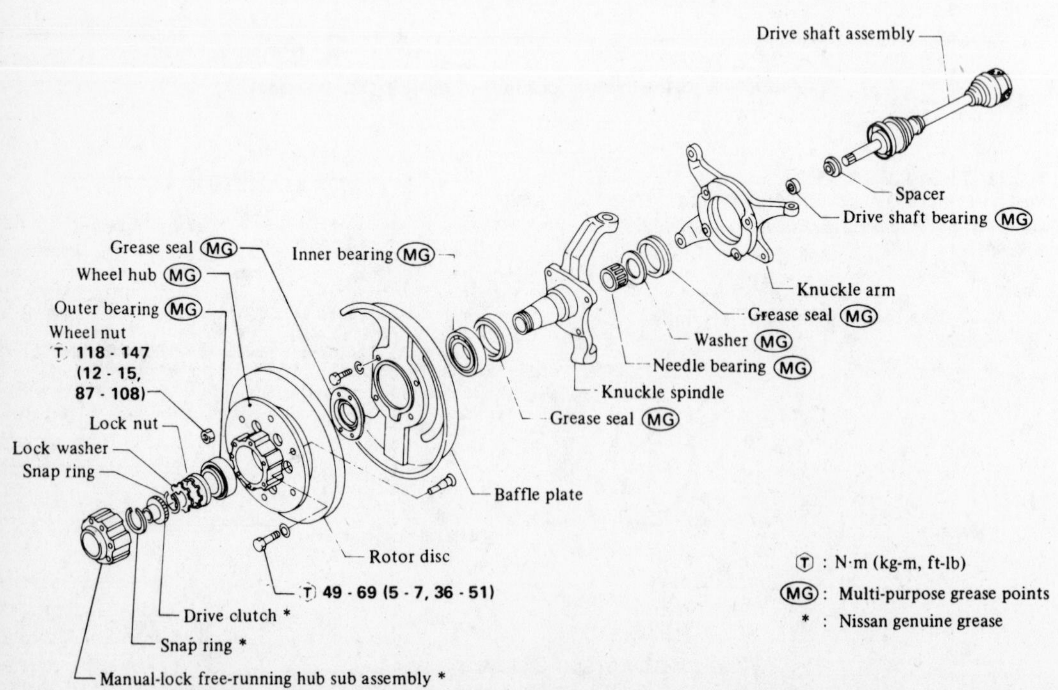

Drive shaft assembly
Spacer
Drive shaft bearing (MG)
Grease seal (MG)
Inner bearing (MG)
Wheel hub (MG)
Outer bearing (MG)
Wheel nut
(T) 118 - 147
(12 - 15,
87 - 108)
Knuckle arm
Grease seal (MG)
Washer (MG)
Needle bearing (MG)
Knuckle spindle
Grease seal (MG)
Lock nut
Lock washer
Snap ring
Baffle plate
Rotor disc
(T) 49 - 69 (5 - 7, 36 - 51)
Drive clutch *
Snap ring *
Manual-lock free-running hub sub assembly *
(T): N·m (kg-m, ft-lb)
(MG): Multi-purpose grease points
*: Nissan genuine grease

Exploded view of the front drive axle—1984–86 4wd models (720-D series)

Axle Shaft

REMOVAL AND INSTALLATION

1981-83

1. Remove the free running hub.
2. Remove the snapring and remove the driven clutch.
3. Remove the front rebound bumper.
4. Disconnect the stabilizer bar at the lower link.
5. Remove the bolts attaching the axle shaft to the carrier. DO NOT REMOVE THE RUBBER BOOTS!
6. Lower the inner end of the axle shaft and then pull the shaft out of the wheel assembly.
7. Install the outer end of the axle shaft into

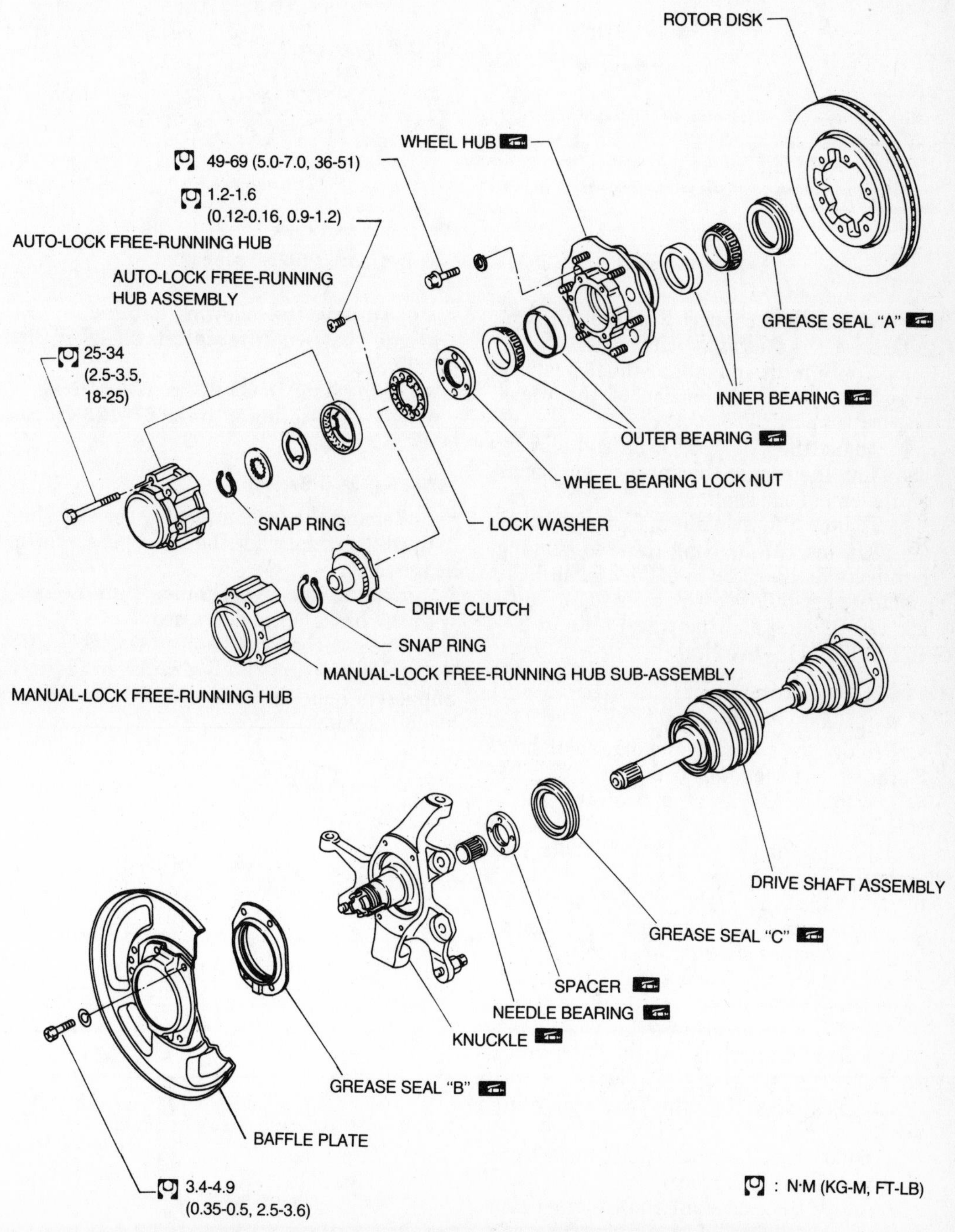

Exploded view of the front drive axle—1986–89 4wd models (D21-D series)

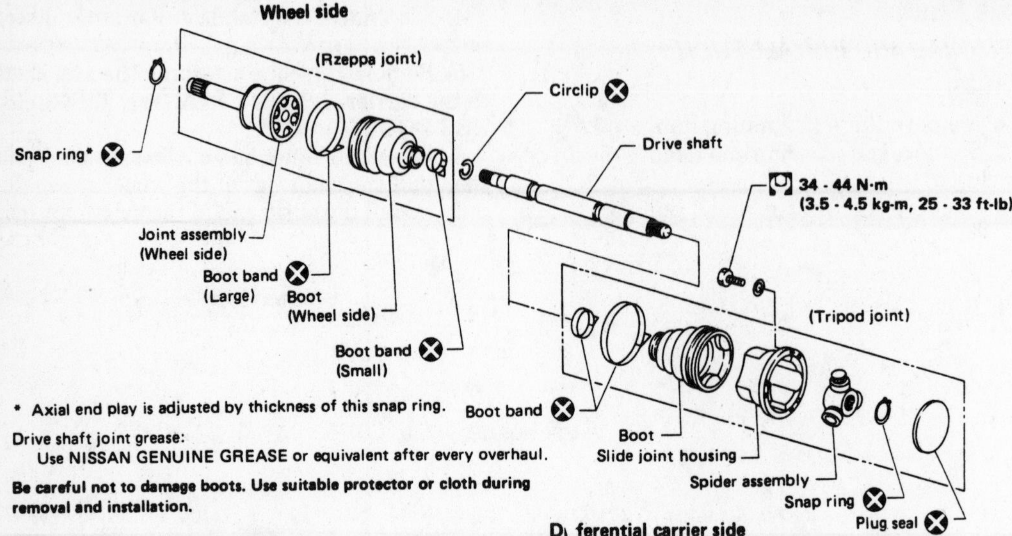

Exploded view of the axle shaft—1986–89 4wd models (D21-D series)

the wheel and then connect it to the differential. Observe the following points:

a. Apply multi-purpose wheel bearing grease to the copper portion of the wheel bearing support.

b. Adjust the axle shaft axial end play by installing the proper thickness of snaprings on the end of the shaft.

c. Tighten the axle shaft flange bolts to 20–27 ft. lbs. (27–37 Nm); the free running hub bolts to 18–25 ft. lbs. (25–34 Nm); the stabilizer bar-to-lower link bolts to 12–16 ft. lbs. (16–22 Nm) and the wheel nuts to 87–108 ft. lbs. (118–147 Nm).

1984-86 (720-D Series)

1. Remove the locking hub.
2. Remove the snapring and drive clutch.
3. Disconnect the lower ball joint.
4. Disconnect the lower end of the shock absorber.
5. Disconnect the axle shaft from the differential.
6. Lower the inner end of the axle shaft and then pull the axle shaft from the wheel housing. It helps to turn the steering wheel to the right when pulling the right shaft and left when pulling the left shaft.
7. Install the axle shaft into the wheel housing and then connect it to the differential. Please note the following:

a. Apply chassis lube to all bearing surfaces.

b. Before installing the shaft make sure that the spacer is in place.

c. Adjust the axle shaft end play by using various thicknesses of snaprings. The end play should be 0.1–0.3mm.

d. Observe the following torques:

- axle shaft-to-differential: 20–27 ft. lbs. (27–37 Nm).
- locking hub: 18–25 ft. lbs. (25–34 Nm).
- ball joint-to-lower link: 87–123 ft. lbs. (118–165 Nm).

1986-89 (D21-D Series)

1. Remove the bolts attaching the axle shaft to the differential while the brake pedal is being depressed.
2. Remove the free running hub assembly with the brake pedal depressed.
3. Remove the brake caliper assembly without disconnecting the hydraulic brake line. Support or hang the brake caliper with a wire to avoid breaking the hose.

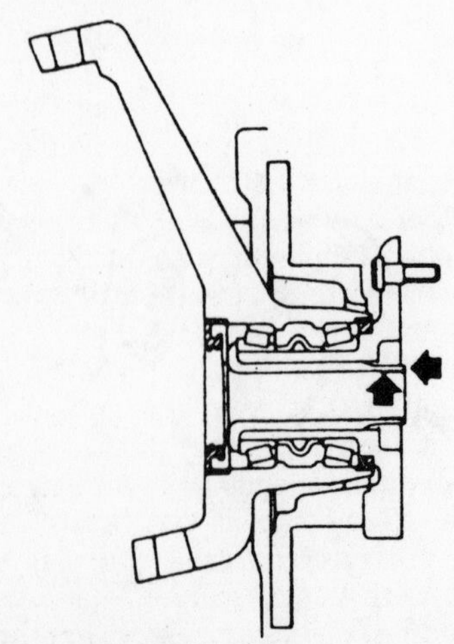

Copper wheel bearing support greasing locations, through 1983

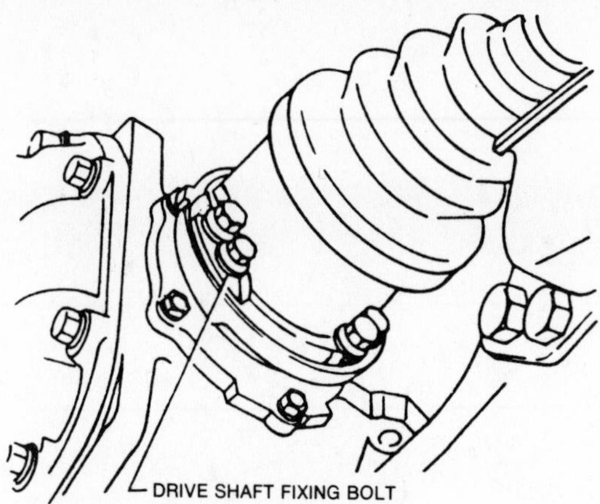

Axle shaft-to-carrier bolts

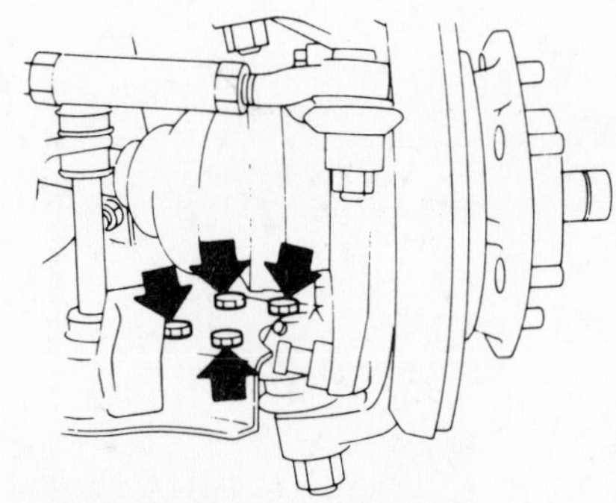

Lower ball joint attachment points

4. Remove the tie rod ball joint.
5. Support the lower link with a jack and remove the nuts attaching the lower ball joint on the lower link.
6. Remove the upper ball joint attaching bolts.
7. Remove the shock absorber lower attaching bolt.
8. Cover the axle shaft boot with a suitable protector, and then remove the axle shaft with the knuckle atill attached.
9. Separate the axle shaft from the knuckle by lightly tapping it with a rubber mallet.
10. Install the axle shaft into the knuckle and then install the assembly.
11. When installing the bearing spacer onto the axle shaft, make sure that the bearing spacer is facing in the proper direction. Temporarily install a new snapring on the axle shaft at the same thickness as it was before removal and then measure the axial end play of the axle shaft with a dial gauge. The axial end play should be 0.1–0.3mm. Select another snapring if not within specifications.
12. Connect the shock absorber and tighten the bolt to 43–58 ft. lbs. (59–78 Nm).
13. Connect the upper ball joint and tighten the bolts to 12–15 ft. lbs. (16–21 Nm).
14. Connect the lower ball joint to the lower link and tighten the nuts to 35–45 ft. lbs. (47–61 Nm).
15. Install the tie rod ball joint and the brake caliper.
16. Install the hub and then connect the axle shaft to the differential and tighten the bolts to 25–33 ft. lbs. (34–44 Nm).
17. Install the wheels, remove the stands and lower the vehicle.

Differential Carrier

REMOVAL AND INSTALLATION

1981-86 (720-D Series)

1. Raise the front of the vehicle and support it with safety stands.
2. Remove the drain plug and drain the differential gear oil.
3. Disconnect the axle shafts at the differential.
4. Remove the front driveshaft.
5. Position a floor jack under the differential and raise it just enough to support the carrier. Remove the five carrier-to-crossmember mounting bolts and then lower the differential carrier down and away from the vehicle.
6. Raise the carrier into position and tighten the mounting bolts.
7. Install the driveshaft and axleshafts.
8. Remove the stands and lower the vehicle. Fill the differential with gear oil.

1986-89 (D21-D Series)

1. Raise the front of the vehicle and support it with safety stands.
2. Remove the drain plug and drain the differential gear oil.
3. Disconnect the axle shafts at the differential.
4. Remove the front driveshaft.
5. Position a floor jack under the differential and raise it just enough to support the carrier.
6. Loosen all the engine mount bolts, position another floor jack under the engine and raise it just enough to release the pressure on the mounts.
7. Remove all mounting bolts and lower the differential carrier down and away from the vehicle.
8. Install the carrier and temporarily tighten nuts **A** and **B**. Tighten bolts **C** and **D**, and nuts **A, B** and **E** in order, to 50–64 ft. lbs. (68–87 Nm).
9. Lower the engine and tighten the engine mount bolts.
10. Install the driveshaft and axle shafts.

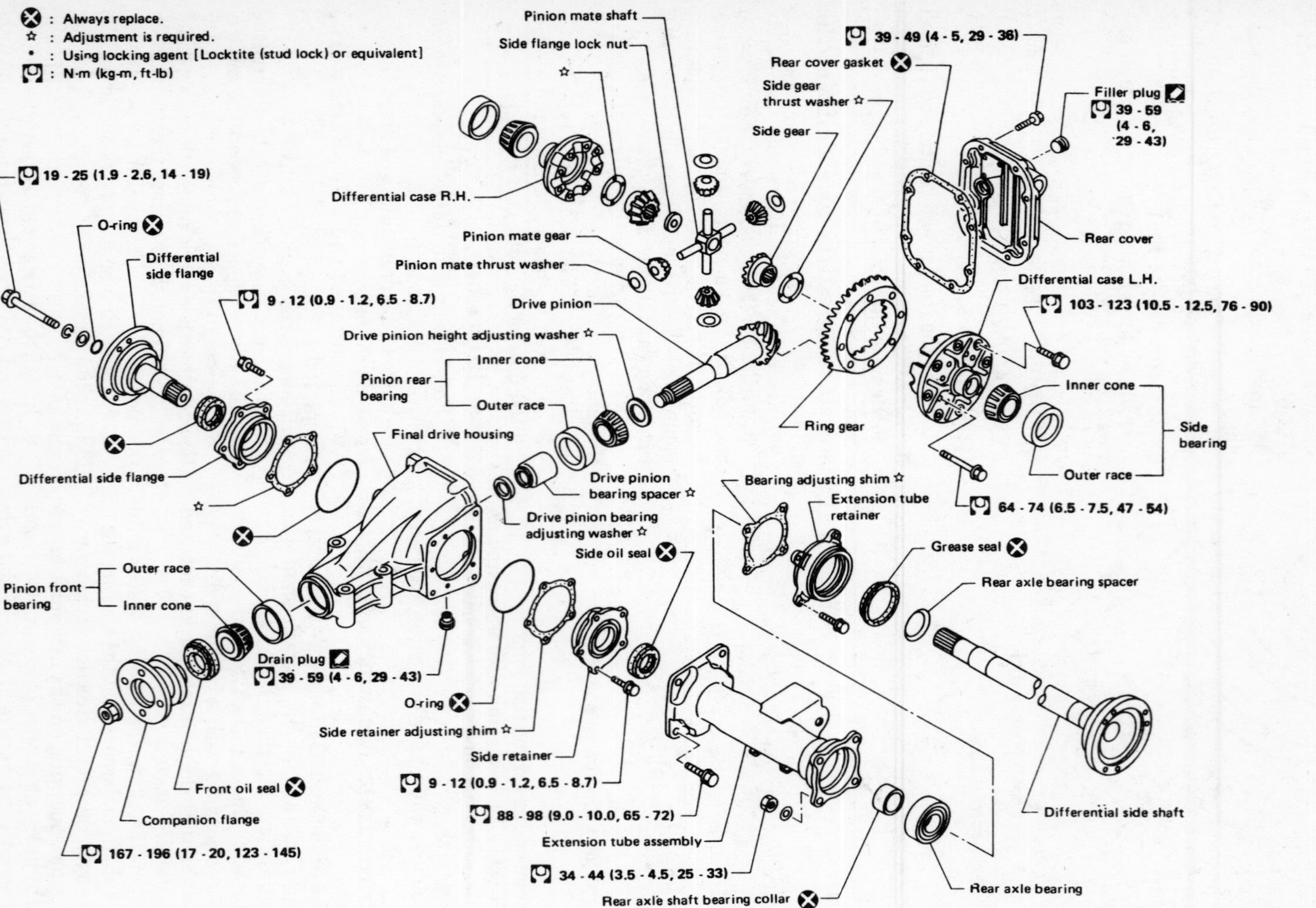

Exploded view of the front differential—R180 shown; others similar

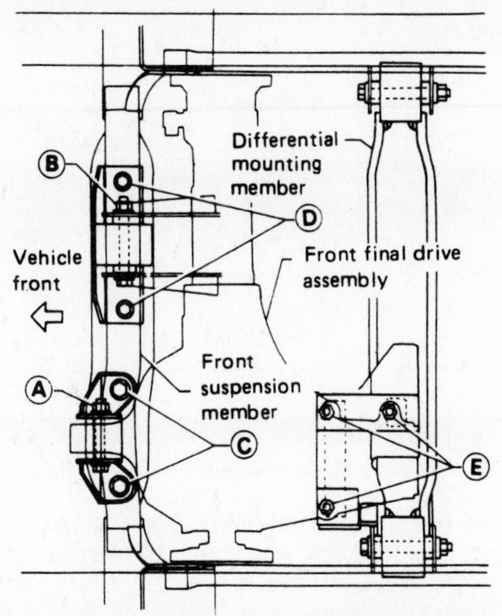

Installing the differential carrier—1986–89 4wd models (D21-D series)

11. Remove the safety stands, lower the vehicle and fill the differential with gear oil.

Pinion Seal

REMOVAL AND INSTALLATION

1. Drain the gear oil from the differential.
2. Raise the front of the vehicle and support it with safety stands.
3. Disconnect the front driveshaft at the differential.
4. Using a flange wrench and a 27mm socket, remove the drive pinion nut.
5. Remove the companion flange and then pry out the oil seal.
6. Coat the cavity between the lips of the oil seal with grease and then install the seal with an oil seal installation tool.
7. Press the companion flange in and install the drive pinion nut. Tighten the nut to 167–196 ft. lbs. (123–145 Nm).
8. Install the driveshaft, remove the stands and lower the vehicle. Refill the differnetial with gear oil.

Suspension and Steering

FRONT SUSPENSION

Torsion Bars

REMOVAL AND INSTALLATION

1970-83 2wd Models

1. Raise the front of the vehicle and support it with jackstands. Remove the wheel.
2. On trucks with a catalytic converter, the converter must be removed if the left torsion bar is being removed.
3. Loosen the ride height adjusting nuts at the anchor (rear) end of the torsion bar, allowing the anchor arm to hang down.
4. Remove the dust cover at the rear end of the torsion bar and remove the snapring.
5. Pull the anchor arm rearward and off the torsion bar.
6. Withdraw the torsion bar from the lower control arm and remove it from under the vehicle.
7. Before installing the torsion bar, apply a light coat of grease to the splines. Install the torsion bar to the lower control arm.

   NOTE: *The torsion bars are marked on the end with an* **L** *(left) or an* **R** *(right). The torsion bars must be installed on the same side from which they are removed.*
8. Install the anchor arm on the rear end of the torsion bar. On 1970-71 models, with the lower arm against the rebound bumper, dimension **A** must be 2.697 in. (68.5mm). On 1972-83 models, dimension **A** must be:

   - 1972-76: 0.20–0.60 in. (5–15mm)–standard bed models; 0.59–0.98 in. (15–25mm)–long bed models.
   - 1977: 0.59–0.98 in. (15–25mm)–all models.
   - 1978-83: 0.28–0.67 in. (7–17mm)–all models.

   NOTE: *There are two different methods used for measuring this distance. Be sure you are using the correct illustration for your truck.*
9. Install a *new* retaining snapring and dust boot to the anchor arm end of the torsion bar.

   NOTE: *Always use a new snapring. Never reinstall the old one.*
10. On 1970-71 models, tighten the adjusting nut until dimension **A** is reached: 3.86 in. (98mm) for standard bed models or 3.62in. (92mm) for long bed models. On all other models, tighten the adjusting nut until the link pro-

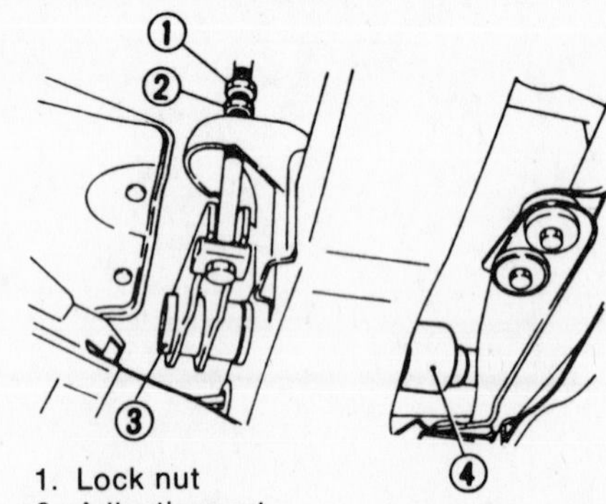

1. Lock nut
2. Adjusting nut
3. Anchor arm
4. Dust cover

Removing the torsion bar anchor—1970–79 2wd models

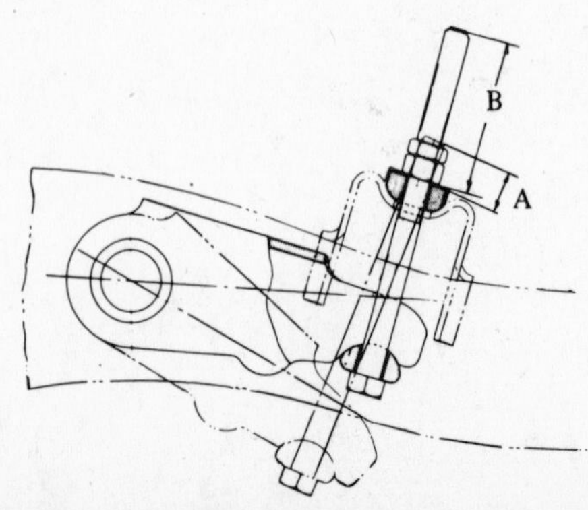

Installing the torsion bar anchor end—1972–79 2wd models

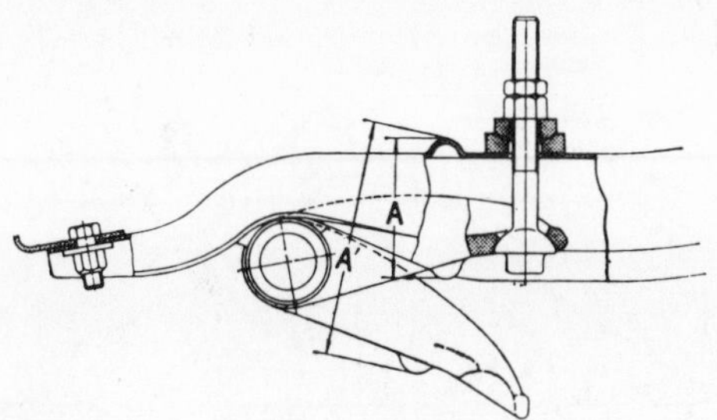

Installing the torsion bar anchor end—1970–71 2wd models

trudes above the support bracket; 2.36–2.76 in. (60–70mm) (dimension **B**). Again, make sure you are looking at the correct illustration for your truck.

11. Install the wheel and lower the vehicle.
12. Adjust the vehicle ride height with the truck at curb weight (full tank of gas and no passengers). Tighten the locknut to 23–30 ft. lbs.

1981-83 4wd Models

1. Raise and support the front end on jackstands.
2. Remove the torsion bar spring anchor bolt.
3. Pull the anchor arm out rearward.
4. Pull the torsion bar spring rearward.
5. Remove the torsion bar.
6. Install the torsion bar to the lower control arm. Tighten the outer bolt to 20–27 ft. lbs. (26–36 Nm) and the inner bolt to 26–33 ft. lbs. (35–45 Nm)
7. Coat the serrated end of the torsion bar with grease and install it into the torque arm.
8. Install the anchor arm to the serrated end of the torsion bar spring and install the anchor arm adjusting bolt. Turn the bolt until the bottom of the nut is about 0.28–0.67 in. (7–17mm) (Dimension **A**) from the end of the bolt.

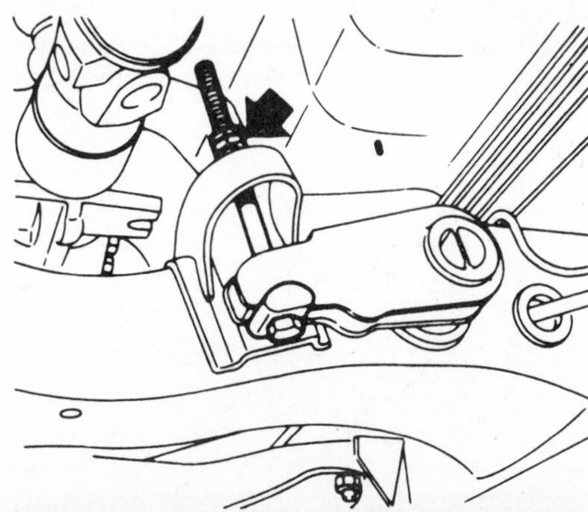
Torsion bar spring anchor bolt—1981–83 4wd models

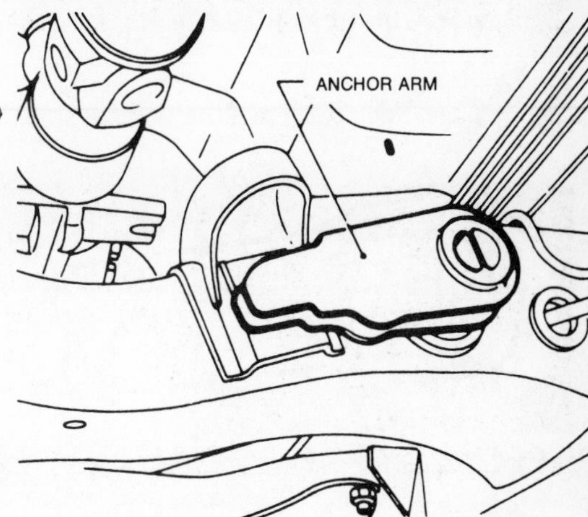

Torsion bar anchor arm—1981–83 4wd models

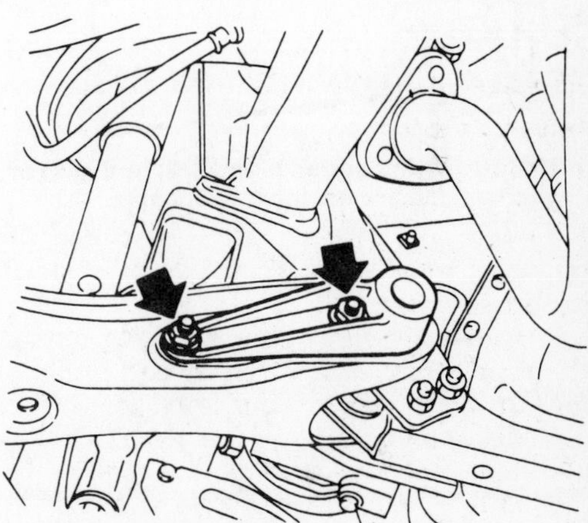
Torsion arm-to-link bolts

9. Install the dust cover.
10. Adjust the anchor arm position until the distance between the end of the dust cover and the bottom of the nut (Dimension **B**) is about 2.36–2.76 in. (60–70mm).
11. Lower the vehicle.
12. Turn the anchor bolt adjusting nut until the center link spindle is 5.28–5.47 in. (134–139mm) above the tension rod attaching bolts. This is dimension **H** in the accompanying figure.

1984-86 2wd Models (720-D Series)

1. Block the rear wheels and raise and support the front end with jackstands under the frame rails.
2. Remove the torsion bar spring anchor bolt.
3. Remove the dust cover and remove the snapring from the anchor arm.
4. Pull the anchor arm off toward the rear.
5. Pull the torsion bar out toward the rear.

6. Remove the torsion bar spring torque arm.

7. Check the torsion bars for wear, cracks or other damage. Replace them if they are suspect.

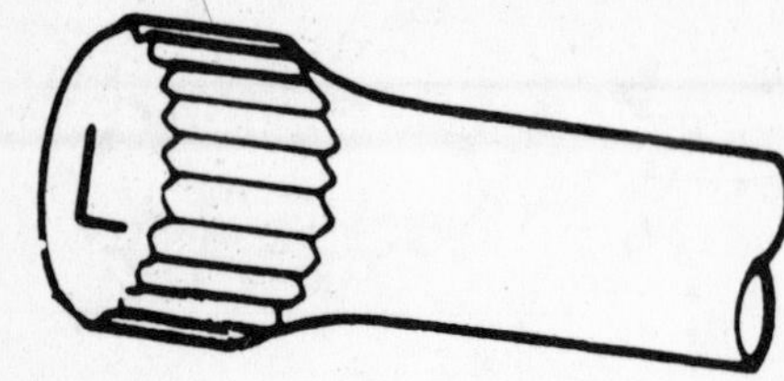

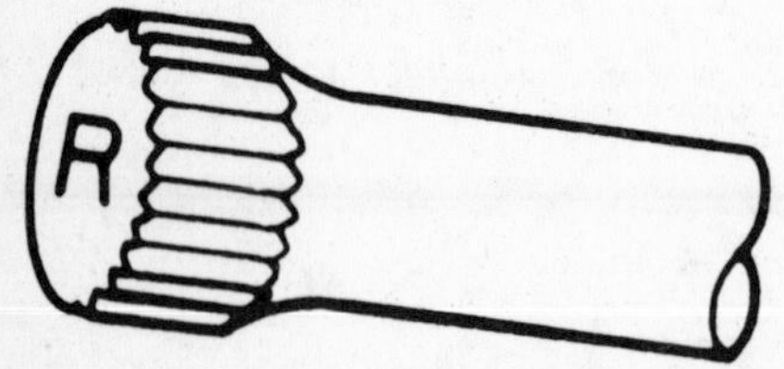

Torsion bar spring serrated ends. Note that they are marked and are not interchangeable

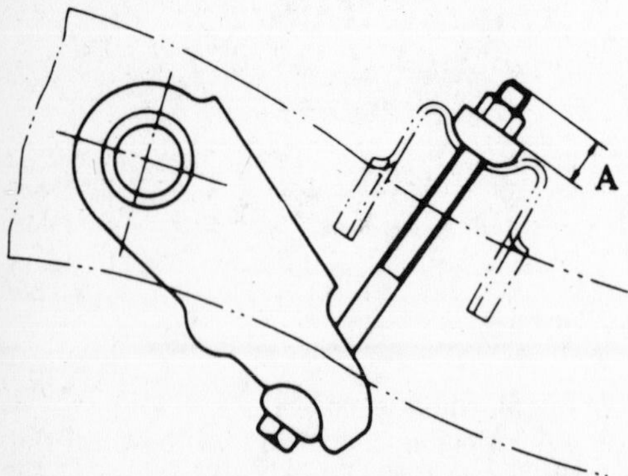

Anchor arm adjusitng bolt measurement—1981–83

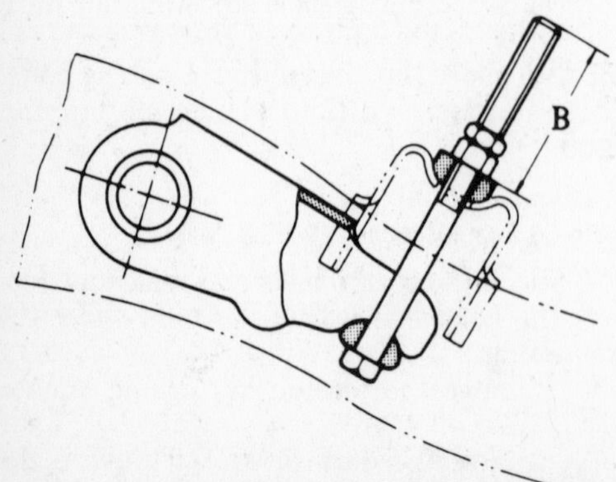

Anchor arm position adjustment—1981–83

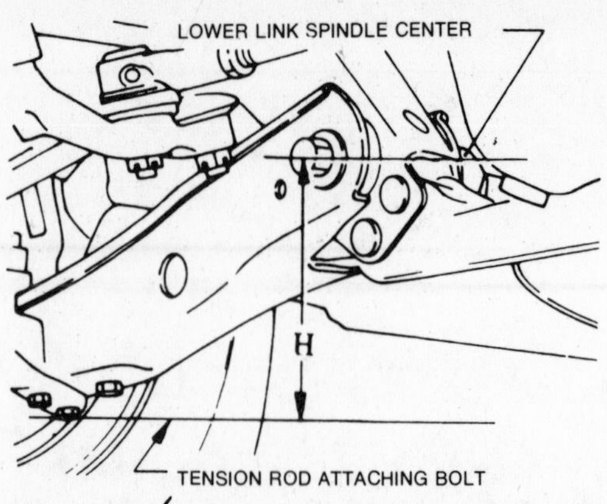

Ride height adjustment—1981–83 4wd models

8. Install the torque arm on the lower link (control arm). Tighten the outer side to 20–27 ft. lbs. (26–36 Nm); the inner side to 26–33 ft. lbs. (35–45 Nm).

9. Install the snapring and dust cover on the torsion bar.

10. Coat the splines on the torsion bar with chassis lube and install it in the torque arm. The torsion bars are marked **L** and **R** and are *not* interchangeable.

11. Place the lower link in position so that clearance between it and the rebound bumper is 0.

12. On 1984 models, install the anchor arm so that dimension **G** in the illustration is:

- Z20 and Z24 engines: left side – 4.33–4.72 in. (110–120mm); right side – 5.12–5.51 in. (130–140mm).
- SD25 engines: left side – 4.53–4.92 in. (115–125mm); right side – 5.31–5.71 in. 135–145mm).

13. On 1985-86 models, install the anchor arm bolt through the seat so that the distance between the seat and the upper end of the bolt is 1.46 in. (37mm).

14. Temporarily tighten the anchor arm bolt so that dimension **H** in the illustration is: 2.72 in. (69mm) on the left side and 2.83 in. (72mm) on the right side for 1984 models. Or 2.36–2.76

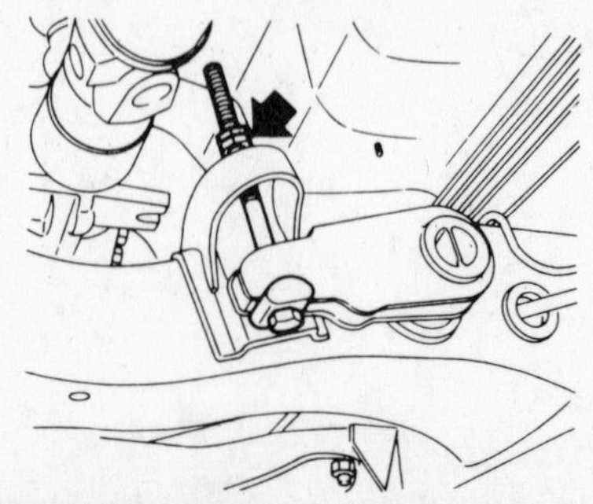

Removing the torsion bar anchor bolt—1984–86 2wd models (720-D series)

in. (60–70mm) for both sides on 1985-86 models.

15. Install the snapring on the anchor arm, turning it to make sure that it is completely in the groove.

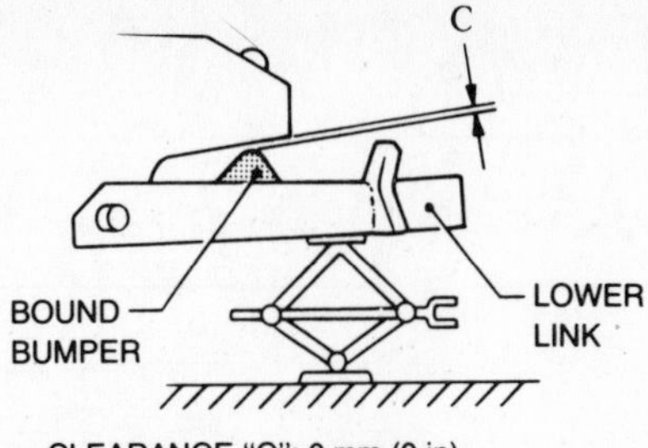

Positioning lower control arm

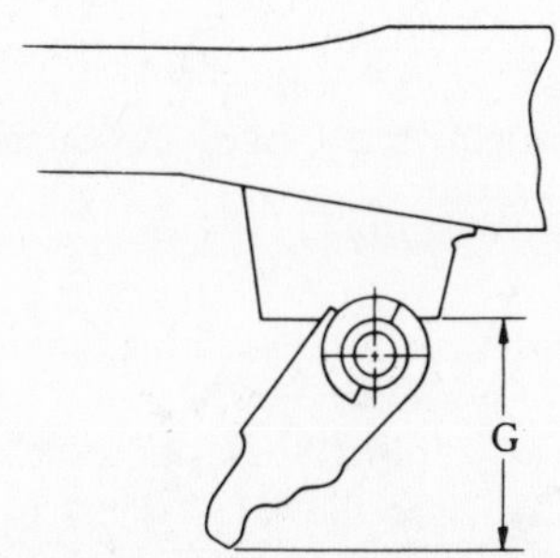

Anchor arm installation—1984 2wd models

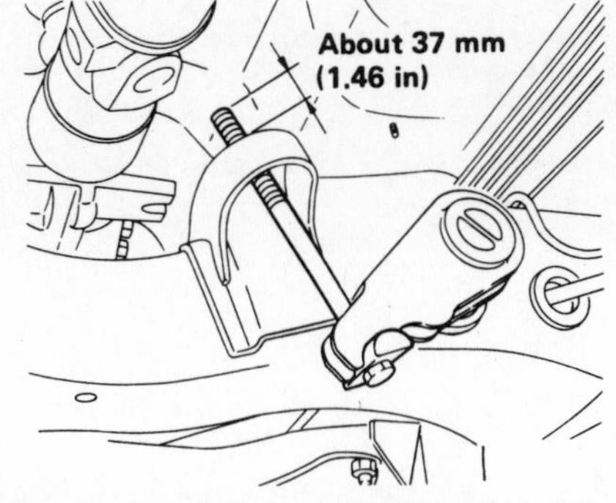

Anchor arm installation—1985–86 2wd models (720-D series)

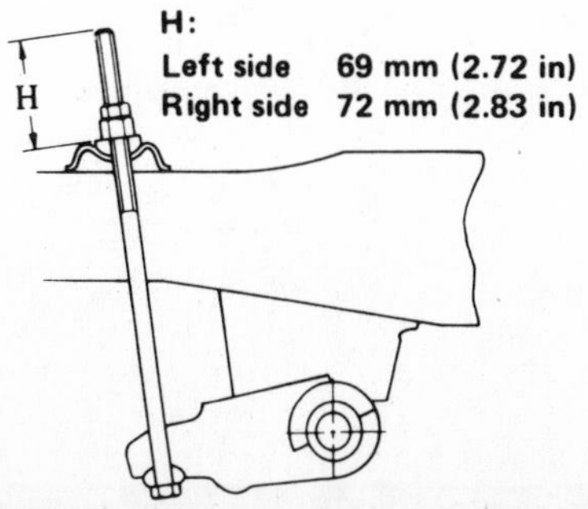

Anchor arm adjustment—1984–86 (720-D series)

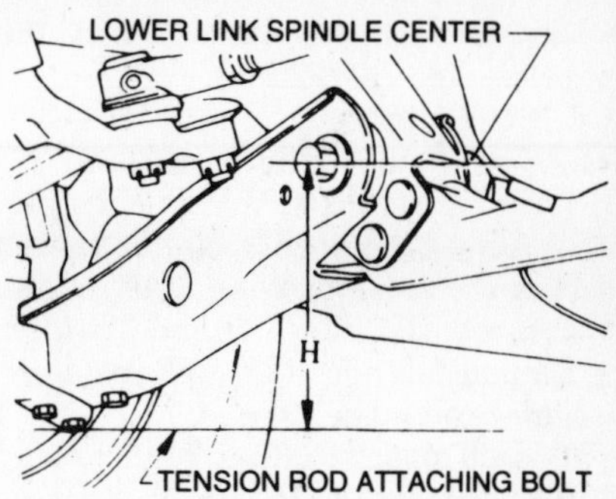

Ride height adjustment—1984–86 (720-D series)

16. Install the dust cover.

17. Lower the truck so that it is resting on its wheels. Turn the anchor bolt adjusting nut so that dimension **H** in the illustration is: 4.65–4.80 in. (118–122mm) on regular cab models and 4.45–4.61 in. (113–117mm) on the King Cab models in 1984. On all 1985-86 models, **H** should be 5.04–5.20 in. (128–132mm). Torque the adjusting nut to 22–30 ft. lbs. (3-–40 Nm).

NOTE: *Dimension* **H** *can be calculated by subtracting dimension* **B** *from dimension* **A**.

1984-86 4wd Models (720-D Series)

1. Raise and support the front end with jackstands under the frame rails.
2. Remove the torsion bar anchor bolt.
3. Pull the anchor arm out toward the rear.
4. Pull the torsion bar out toward the rear.
5. Remove the torque arm.
6. Check the torsion bar for signs of wear and/or damage and replace as necessary.
7. Install the torque arm to the lower link (control arm) and tighten the bolts to 66–87 ft. lbs. (89–118 Nm).
8. Coat the spines on the inner end of the torsion bar with chassis lube and install it into the torque arm.

NOTE: *The torsion bars are marked* **L** *and* **R**. *They are not interchangeable.*

9. Using a floor jack, position the lower link so that there is 0 clearance between it and the rebound bumper.
10. Install the anchor arm so that dimension **G** in the illustration is:

- 1984 Z20 and Z24 engines: left side – 4.33–4.72 in. (110–120mm); right side – 5.12–5.51 in. (130–140mm).
- 1984 SD25 engines: left side – 4.53–4.92 in. (115–125mm); right side – 5.31–5.71 in. (135–145mm).
- 1985-86 models: left side – 3.74 in. (95mm); right side – 4.33 in. (110mm).

11. Temporarily tighten the anchor arm bolt so that dimension **H** is as shown in the accompanying illustration:

• 1984 models: left side–2.72 in. (69mm); right side–2.83 in. (72mm).
• 1985-86 models: left side–3.50 in. (89mm); right side–3.86 in. (98mm).

12. Lower the truck so that it is resting on its wheels. Adjust the anchor bolt so that dimension **H** in the accompanying illustration is:

• 1984 models: 1.54–1.69 in. (39–43mm) for King Cab models and 1.73–1.89 in. (44–48mm) for regular cab models.
• 1985-86 models: 2.09–2.24 in. (53–57mm).

NOTE: *Dimension* **H** *can be calculated by subtracting dimension* **B** *from dimension* **A**.

1986-89 2wd Models (D21-D Series)

1. Block the rear wheels and raise and support the front end with jackstands under the frame rails.
2. Remove the torsion bar spring adjusting nut.
3. Remove the dust cover and remove the snapring from the anchor arm.
4. Pull the anchor arm off toward the rear and then remove the torsion bar spring.
5. Remove the torque arm.
6. Check the torsion bars for wear, cracks or other damage. Replace them if they are suspect.
7. Install the torque arm on the lower link (control arm) and tighten the bolts to 37–50 ft. lbs. (50–68 Nm).
8. Install the snapring and dust cover on the torsion bar.
9. Coat the splines on the inner end of the torsion bar with chassis lube and install it into the torque arm. The torsion bars are marked **L** and **R** and are *not* interchangeable.
10. Position a floor jack under the lower link and raise it so that clearance between the link and the rebound bumper is 0.
11. Install the anchor arm so that dimension **G** in the illustration is 0.24–0.71 in. (6–18mm).
12. Install the snapring to the anchor arm and dust cover. Make sure that the snapring is properly installed in the groove of the anchor arm.
13. Tighten the anchor arm adjusting nut until dimension **L** is 1.38 in. (35mm) for Heavy Duty, Cab/Chassis and STD models; or 1.93 in. (49mm) for all other models.
14. Lower the truck so that it is resting on its wheels and bounce it several times to set the suspension. Turn the anchor bolt adjusting nut so that dimension **H** in the illustration is 4.37–4.53 in. (111–115mm) on 1986-87 models; or 4.25–4.65 in. (108–118mm) on 1988-89 models.

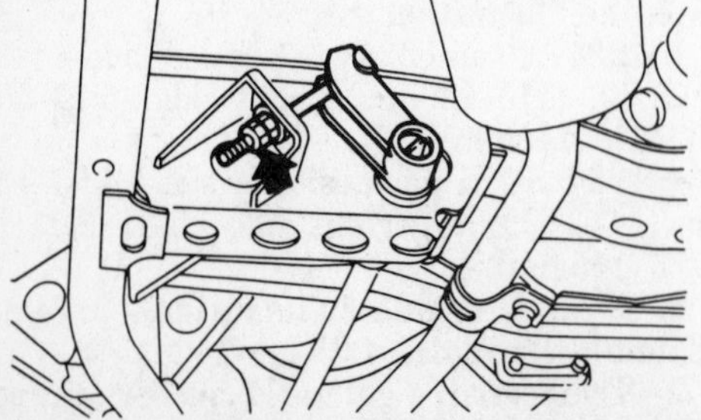
Removing the torsion bar anchor bolt—1986–89 2wd models (D21-D series)

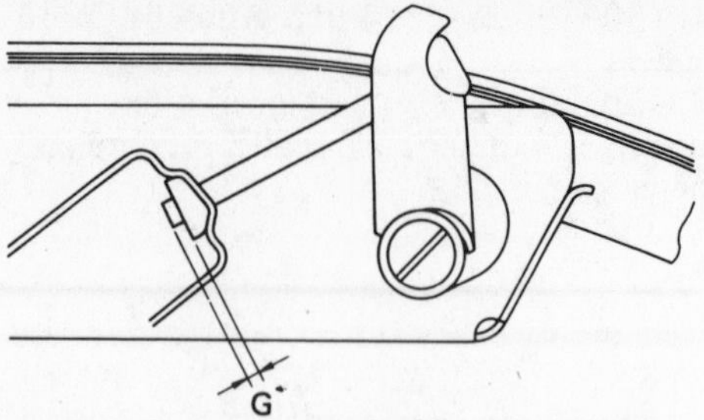

Anchor arm installation—1986–89 2wd models (D21-D series)

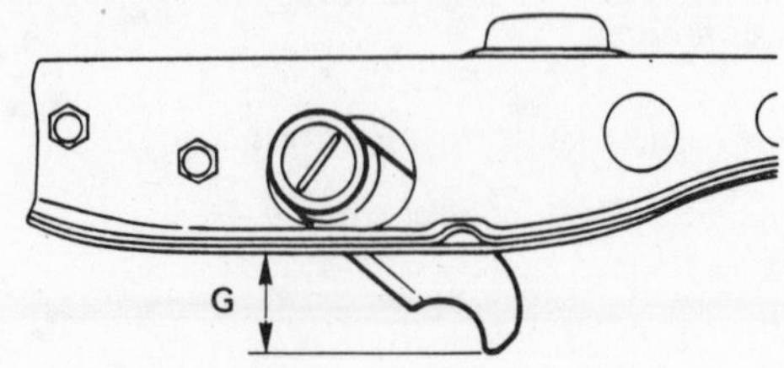

Anchor arm installation—1986–89 4wd models (D21-D series)

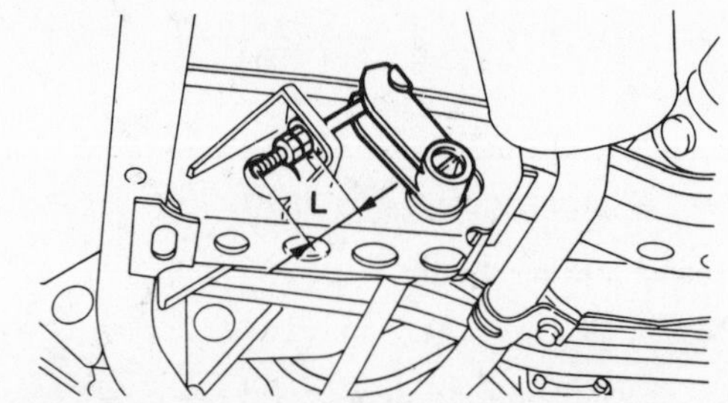

Tighten the anchor arm adjusitng nut—1986–89 2wd models (D21-D series)

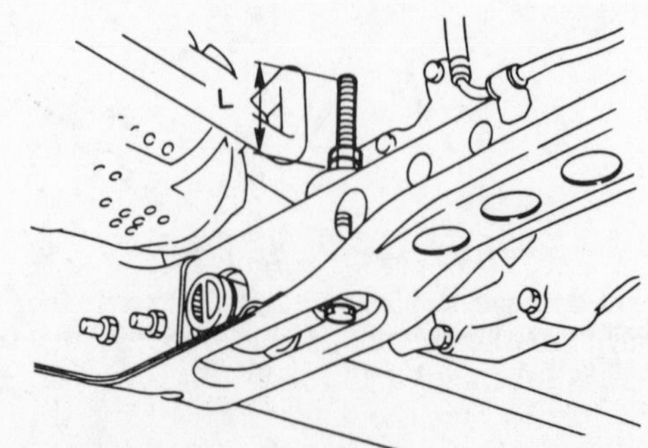

Tighten the anchor arm adjusting nut—1986–89 4wd models (D21-D series)

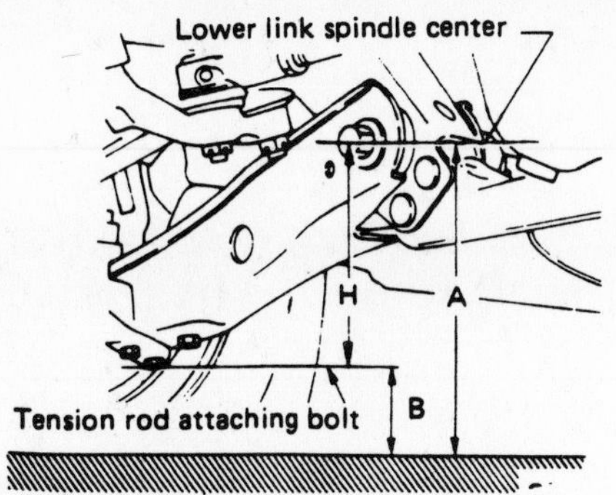

Ride height adjustment—1986–89 2wd models (D21-D series)

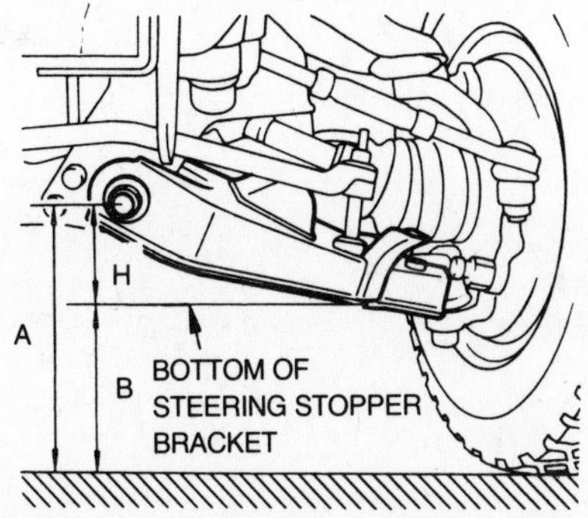

Ride height adjustment—1986–89 4wd models (D21-D series)

1986-89 4wd Models (D21-D Series)

1. Block the rear wheels and raise and support the front end with jackstands under the frame rails.
2. Remove the torsion bar spring adjusting nut.
3. Pull back the dust boot and remove the anchor arm snapring.
4. Remove the torque arm attaching nuts, then withdraw the torsion bar spring forward with the torque arm still attached.
5. Check the torsion bar for wear, cracks or other damage. Replace them if they are suspect.
6. Coat the splines on the torsion bar with chassis lube and install it in the anchor arm. The torsion bars are marked **L** and **R** and are *not* interchangeable.
7. Position a floor jack under the lower link (control arm) and raise it so that the clearance between the link and the rebound bumper is 0.
8. Install the anchor arm so that dimension **G** in the illustration is 1.97–2.36 in. (50–60mm).
9. Install the snapring on the anchor arm and pull the dust boot over it.
10. Tighten the anchor arm adjusting nut until dimension **L** is 3.03 in. (77mm).
11. Lower the truck so that it is resting on its wheels and bounce it several times to set the suspension. Turn the anchor bolt adjusting nut so that dimension **H** in the illustration is 1.73–1.89 in. (44–48mm) on 1986-87 models; or 1.61–2.01 in. (41–51mm) on 1988-89 models.

Shock Absorber

TESTING

The function of the shock absorber is to dampen harsh spring movement and provide a means of controlling the motion of the wheels so that the bumps encountered by the wheels are not totally transmitted to the body of the truck and, therefore, to you and your passengers. As the wheel moves up and down, the shock absorber shortens and lengthens, thereby imposing a restraint on excessive movement by its hydraulic action.

A good way to see if your shock absorbers are working properly is to push on one corner of the truck until it is moving up and down for almost the full suspension travel, then release it and watch its recovery. If the truck bounces slightly about one more time and then comes to a rest, you can be fairly certain that the shock is OK. If the truck continues to bounce excessively, the chocks will probably require replacement.

REMOVAL AND INSTALLATION

1. Raise the front of the vehicle and support it with safety stands. Remove the wheel.
2. Hold the upper stem of the shock absorber and remove the nuts, washer, and rubber bushing.
3. Remove the bolt from the lower end of the shock absorber and remove the shock absorber from the vehicle.
4. Install the shock absorber. Replace all of the rubber bushings with new ones if a new shock absorber is being installed. Install the lower retaining bolt from the front of the truck. Tighten the upper attaching nut to 12–16 ft. lbs. (16–22 Nm) and the lower nut to 23–30 ft. lbs. (30–40 Nm) on 1970-83 models; 43–58 ft. lbs. (59–68 Nm) on 1984-87 2wd models and 1984-89 4wd models; or 36–47 ft. lbs. (49–64 Nm) on 1988-89 2wd models.

Tension Rod and Stabilizer Bar

REMOVAL AND INSTALLATION

2wd Models Only

1. With the truck resting on its wheels, remove the underpan.
2. If the tension rod installation is correct, the white painted marks on the stabilizer bar, at the bushings, should be visible.

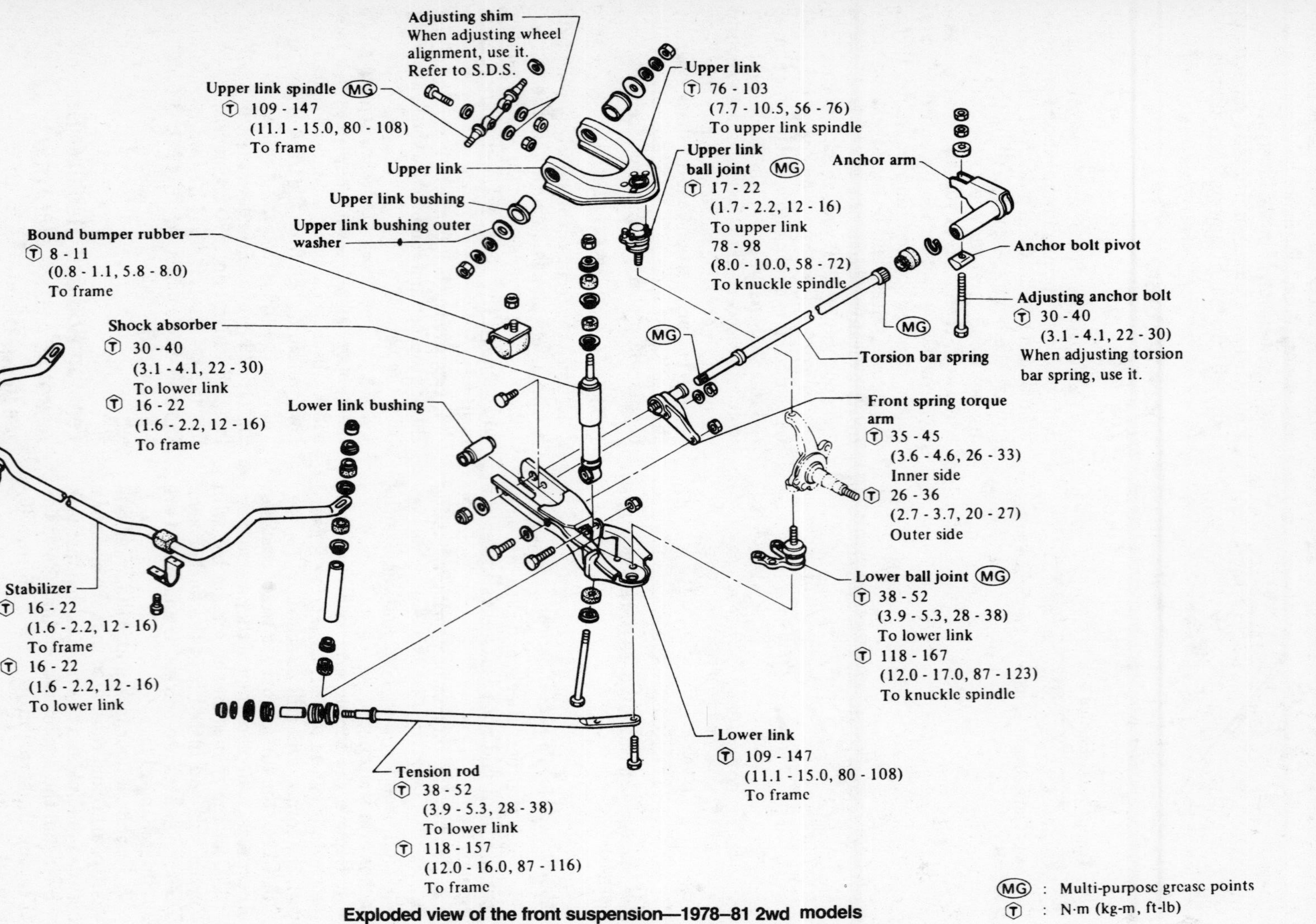

Exploded view of the front suspension—1978–81 2wd models

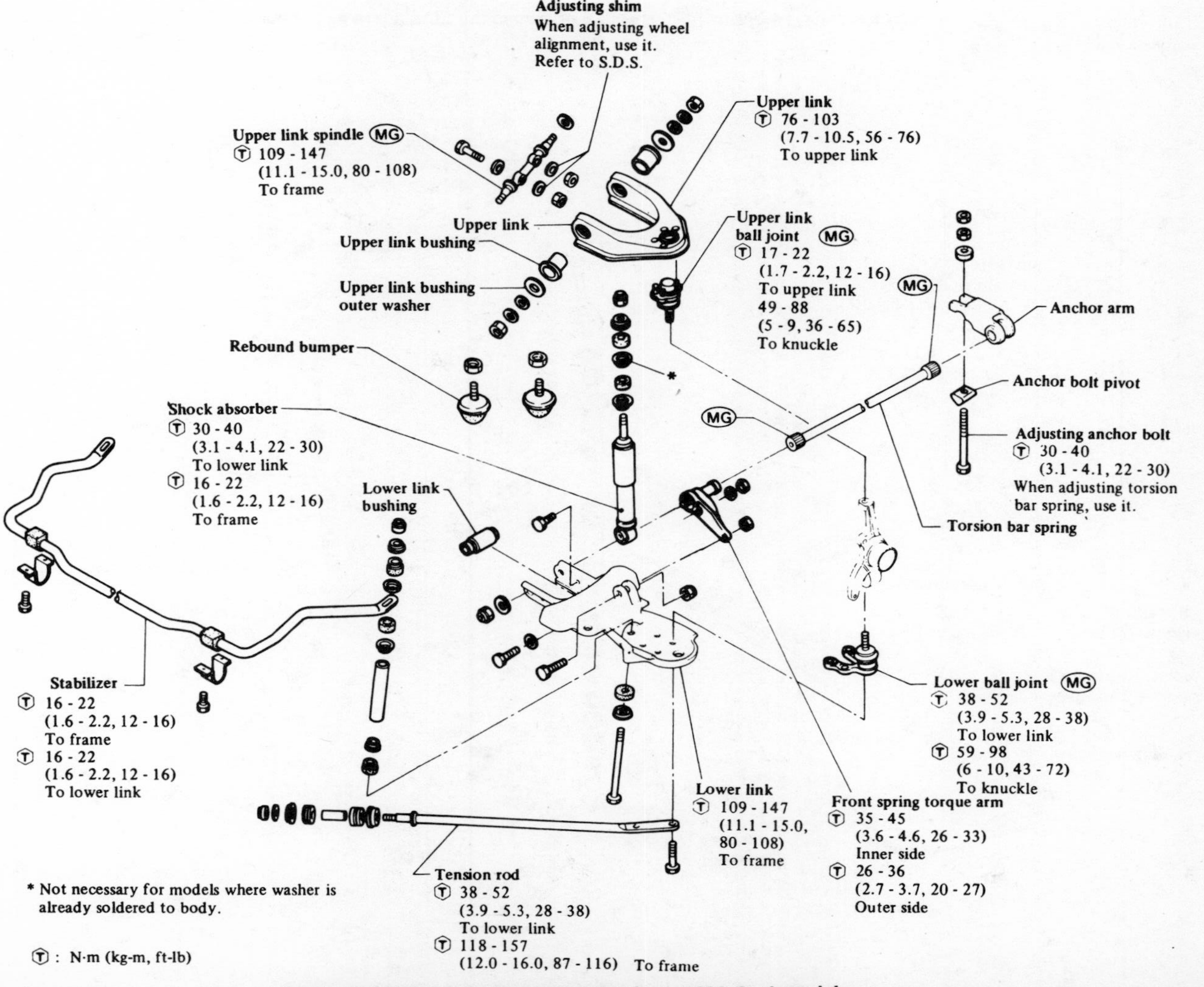

Exploded view of the front suspension—1982 2wd models

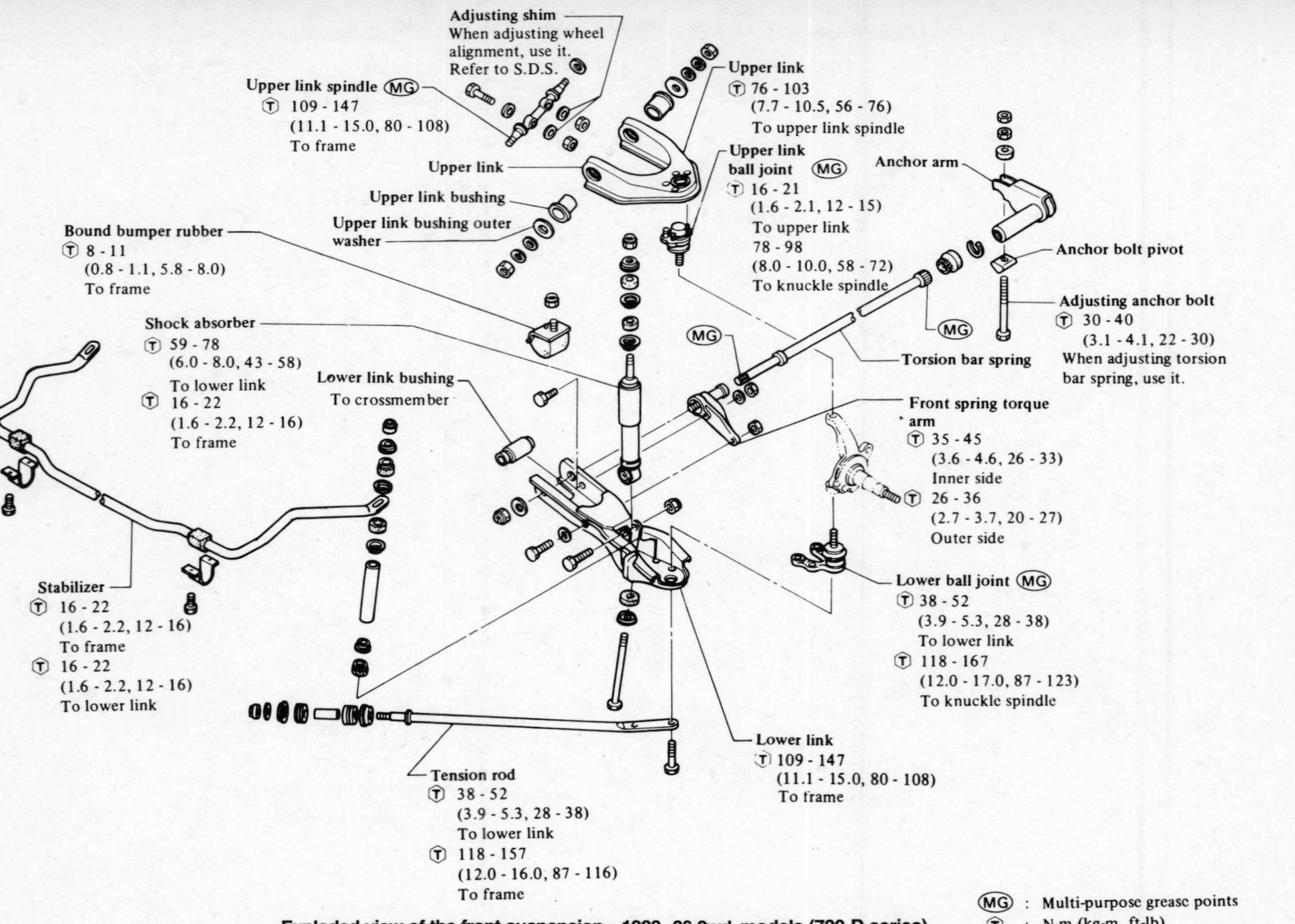

Exploded view of the front suspension—1983–86 2wd models (720-D series)

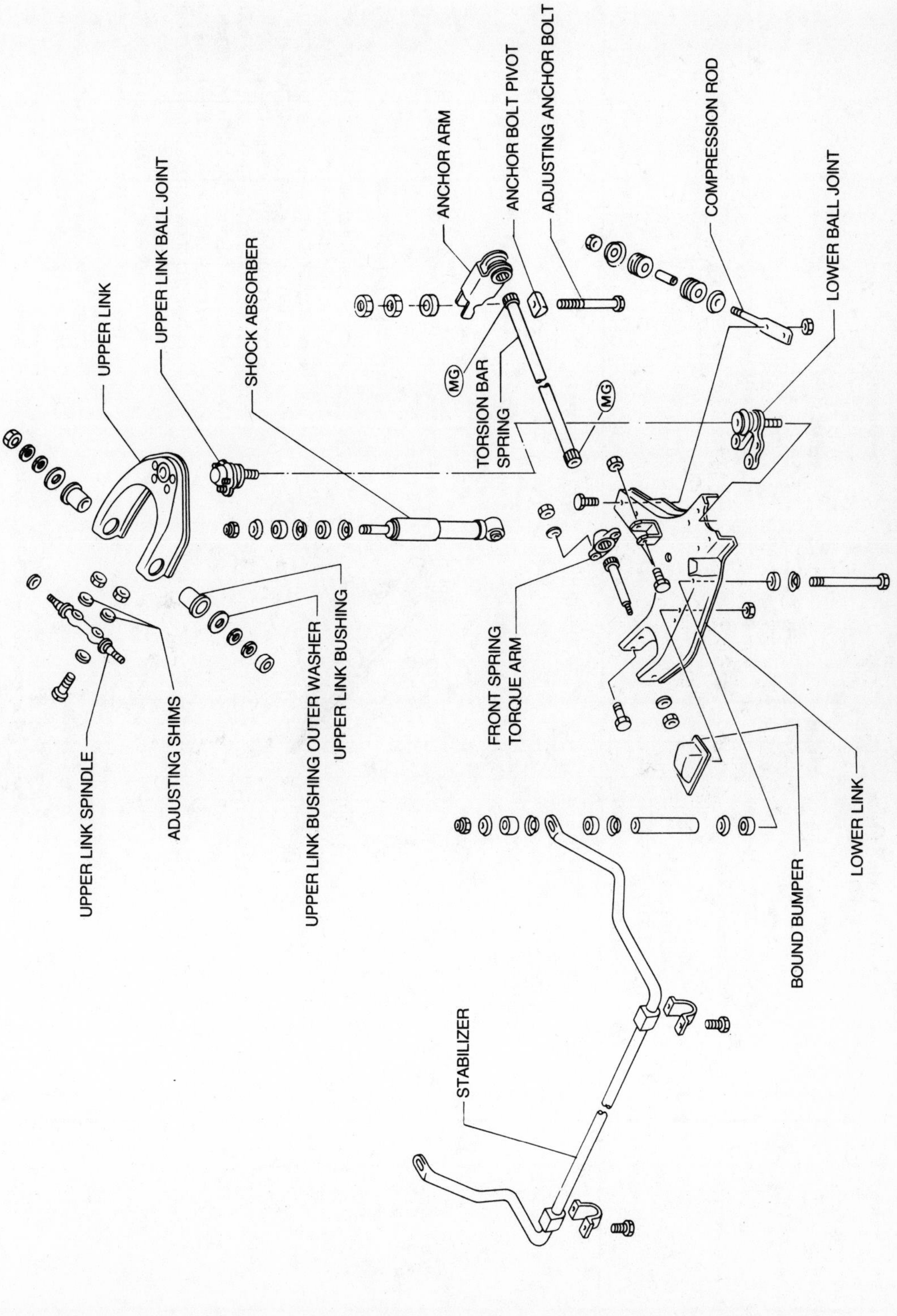

Exploded view of the front suspension—1983–86 4wd models (720-D series)

2WD

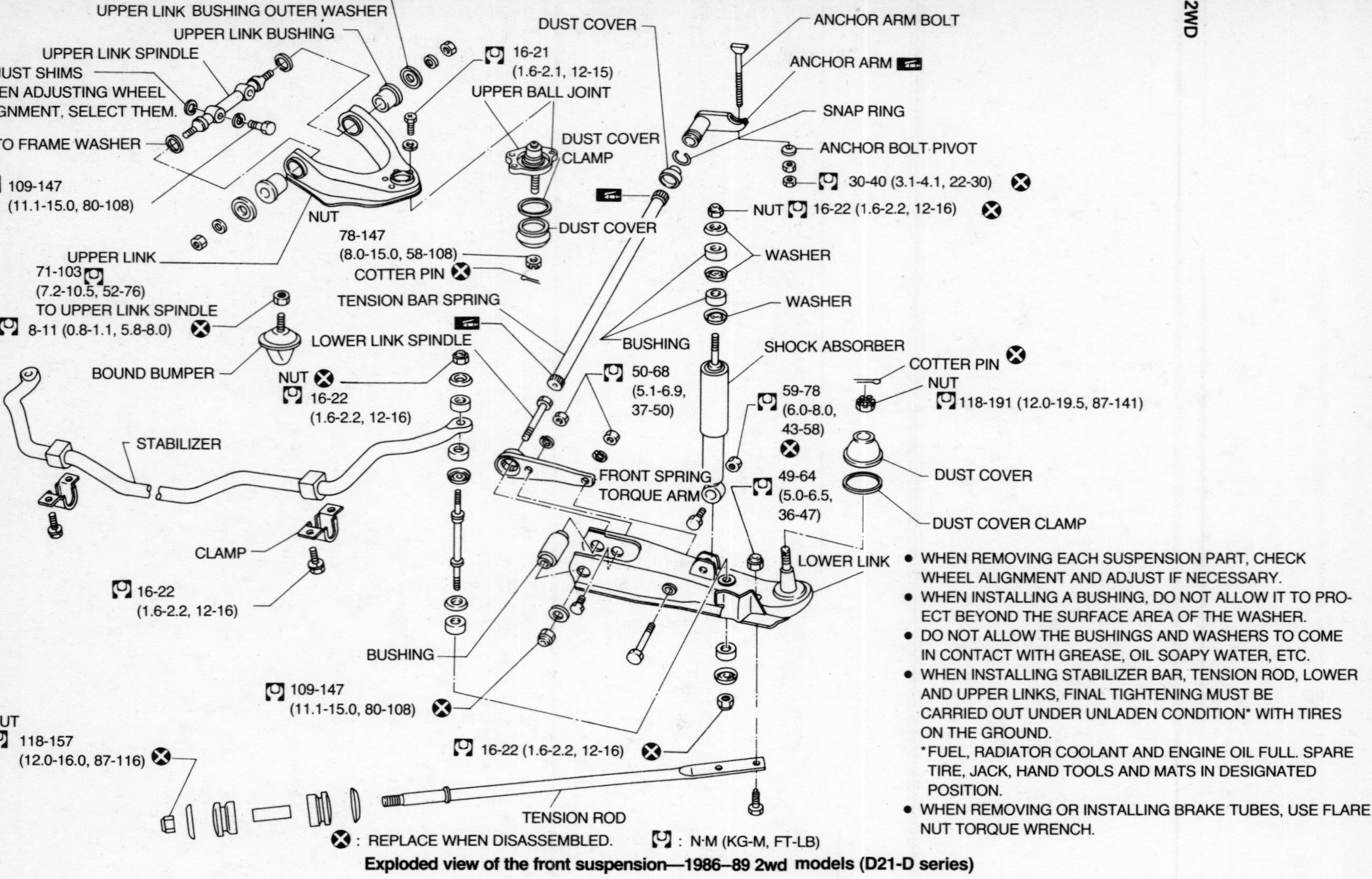

Exploded view of the front suspension—1986–89 2wd models (D21-D series)

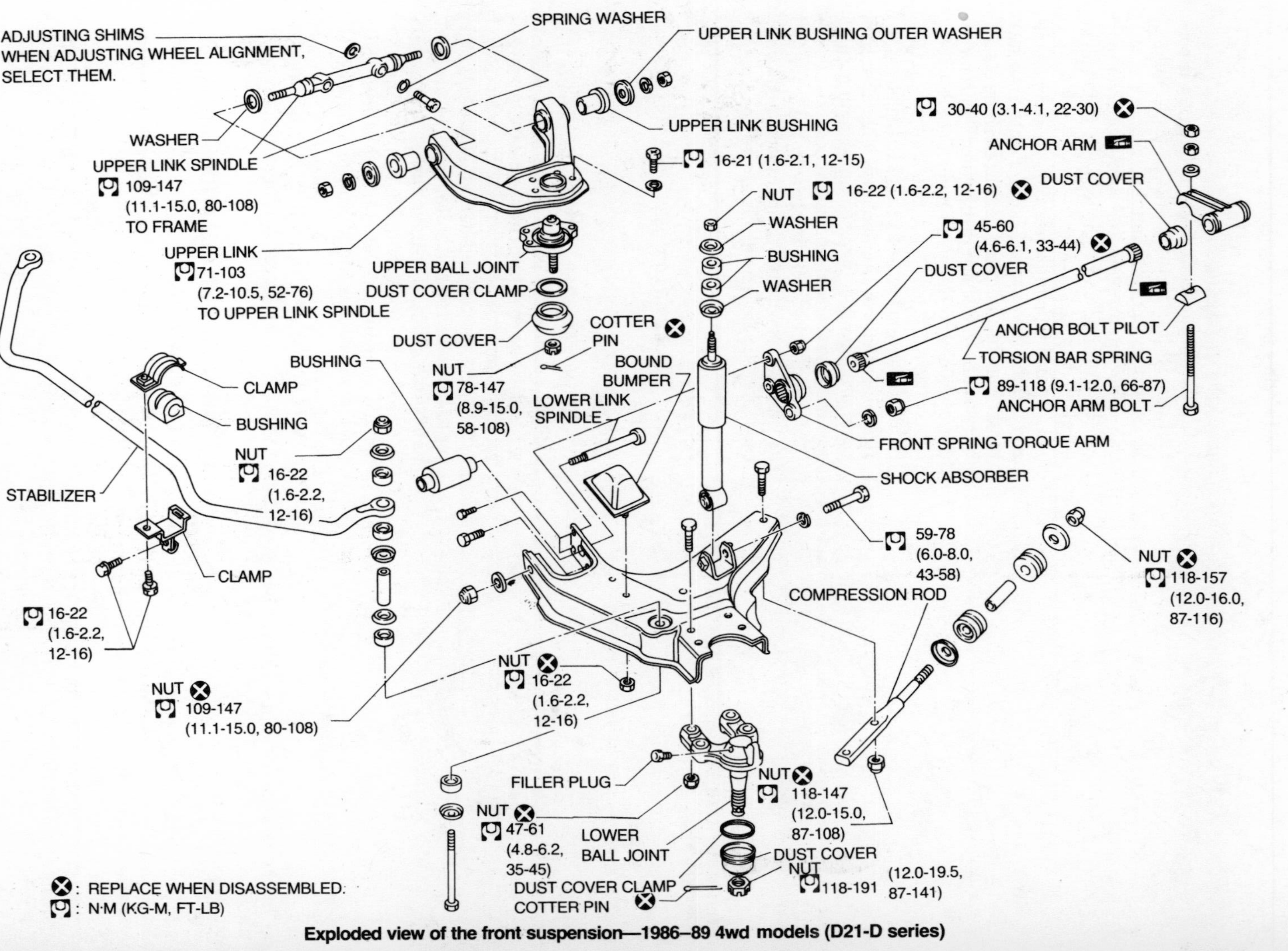

Exploded view of the front suspension—1986–89 4wd models (D21-D series)

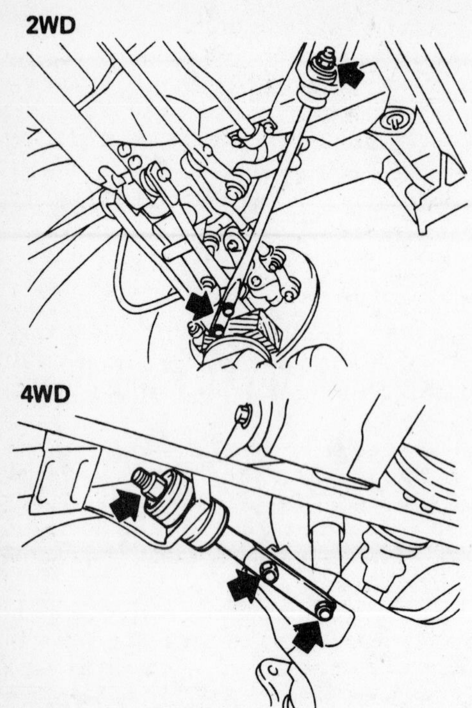

Tenison rod (2wd) and compression rod (4wd) installation

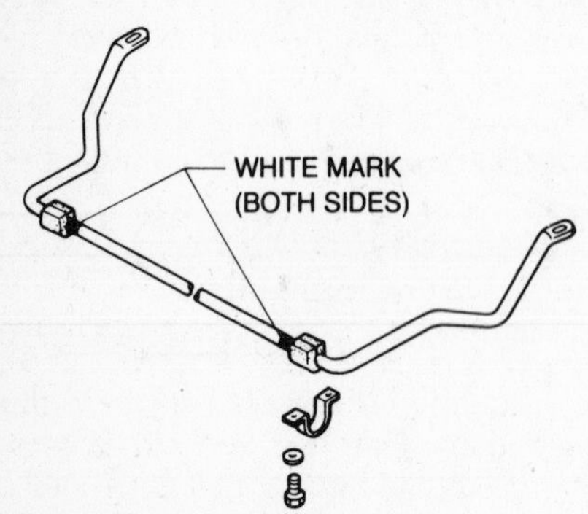

Location of the white painted marks

3. The tension bar and stabilizer bar can be unbolted and removed with the vehicle supported on jackstands.

4. To install, simply position the component and tighten the nuts and bolts. Tighten the stabilizer bar thru-bolt and the bar bushing clamp bolts to 12–16 ft. lbs. (16–22 Nm). Tighten the tension rod-to-lower link bolts to 36–47 ft. lbs. (49–64 Nm); and the tension rod-to-frame anchor nut to 87–116 ft. lbs. (118–157 Nm). Replace the bushings whenever the parts are changed. Replace any bushing that appears dry, cracked or compressed.

5. Check the stabilizer bar with the truck on its wheels to see if both white painted marks on the stabilizer bar are visible at the bushings.

Compression Rod and Stabilizer Bar

REMOVAL AND INSTALLATION

4wd Models Only

1. With the truck resting on its wheels, remove the underpan.

2. If the compression rod installation is correct, the white painted marks on the stabilizer bar, at the bushings, should be visible.

3. The compression rod and stabilizer bar can be unbolted and removed with the vehicle supported on jackstands.

4. To install, simply position the component and tighten the nuts and bolts. Tighten the stabilizer bar thru-bolt and the bar bushing clamp bolts to 12–16 ft. lbs. (16–22 Nm). Tighten the compression rod-to-lower link bolts to 36–47 ft. lbs. (49–64 Nm); and the compression rod-to-frame anchor nut to 87–116 ft. lbs. (118–157 Nm). Replace the bushings whenever the parts are changed. Replace any bushing that appears dry, cracked or compressed.

5. Check the stabilizer bar with the truck on its wheels to see if both white painted marks on the stabilizer bar are visible at the bushings.

Kingpins

NOTE: *Kingpins are used on 1970-77 trucks only.*

INSPECTION

1. Raise the vehicle so that the tire on the side to be checked is off the ground. Adjust wheel bearing preload to the proper specification.

2. Grasp the top and bottom of the tire and try to move the top and bottom of the tire alternately in and out. If there is noticeable play between the steering knuckle/spindle and the spindle support, then it can be assumed that the kingpins or bushings are worn and should be replaced.

NOTE: *Before performing this test make sure that the wheel bearings are properly adjusted.*

REMOVAL AND INSTALLATION

1970-77 Models Only

1. Raise the front of the vehicle and support it by placing jackstands under the frame.

2. Remove the front wheel.

3. Remove the brake hose and connector from the wheel cylinder.

NOTE: *It is not absolutely necessary to remove the drum, hub, brake and backing plate from the spindle, although it will make working with the spindle a great deal easier. If you choose to leave the parts in place, skip down to Step 8.*

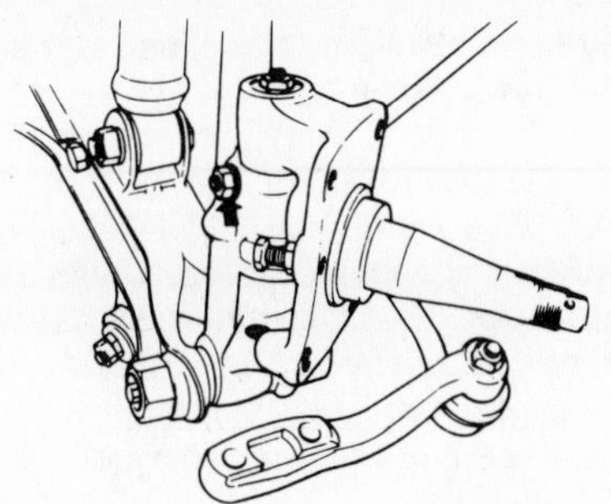

The kingpin lockbolt (arrow); steering arm disconnected

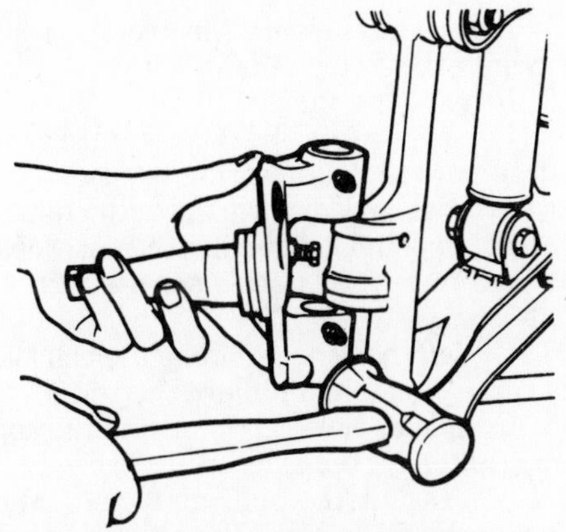

Removing the steering knuckle/spindle

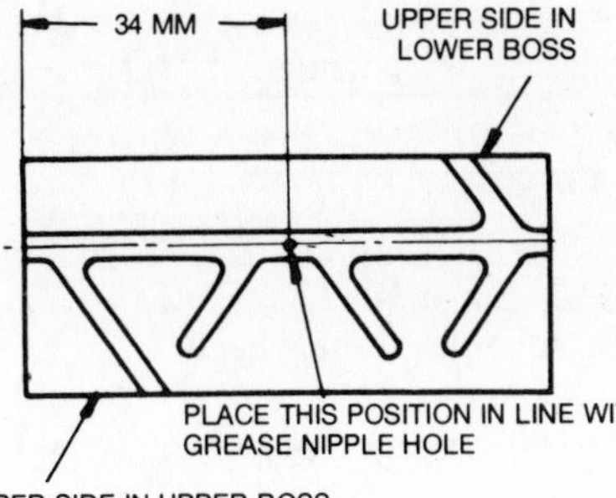

Kingpin bushing to be aligned with the grease nipple hole in the spindle

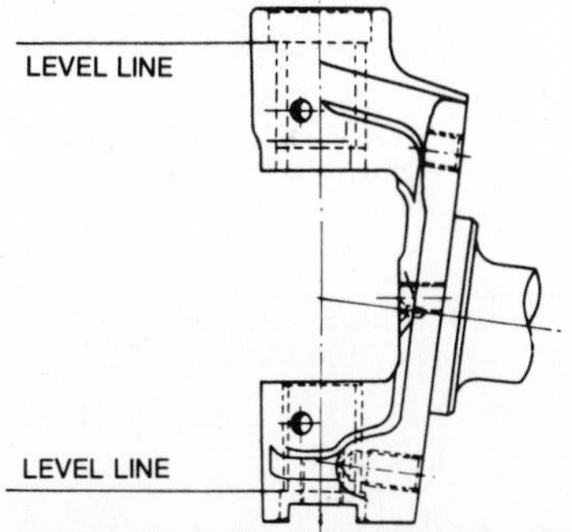

Installation of the kingpin bushings flush with the plug counterbores

4. Remove the brake drum.
5. Remove the hub dust cap, cotter pin, adjusting cap and spindle nut from the spindle.
6. Remove the wheel hub, inner and outer wheel bearings, bearing washer and grease seal from the spindle.
7. Remove the brake backing plate from the knuckle/spindle flange.
8. Remove the knuckle/spindle steering arm from the knuckle/spindle.
9. Remove the kingpin locknut.
10. Remove the plug from the top of the kingpin by drilling a small hole in the plug, screwing a sheet metal screw into the hole, and pulling out the plug.
11. Drive out the kingpin together with the lower plug with a suitable drift and a hammer.
12. Tap the steering knuckle/spindle lightly with a hammer and detach it from knuckle/spindle support. Be careful not to drop the thrust bearing.
13. Drive the steering knuckle/spindle bushing and grease seal out of the kingpin bore with a kingpin bushing driver. Do not try to use a drift, because it will probably score the inner wall of the knuckle spindle.
14. After cleaning the pin bores thoroughly, install the new bushing carefully by using a bushing driver. Position the bushings in the spindle so that they are flush with the counterbores for the plugs. The bushings in the factory rebuilding kit have a grease gallery which should align with the grease nipple hole in the spindle (see the illustration).
15. Remove the grease nipples and drill grease holes through the bushings, placing the drill through the threaded grease nipple hole. The grease hole should be $^1/_8$ in. (3mm) or less. Remove all metal filings and burrs after drilling the grease holes. This step is not necessary if you have used the factory bushings and installed them as outlined in Step 14.
16. Ream the inside of the kingpin bushings, if necessary, to 0.7878–0.7888 in. (20.01–20.03mm). The fit should be such that the kingpin, when greased, can be turned or pushed in or out with thumb pressure. Use the lower bore as a guide for reaming the upper bore, and vice versa, to keep the bores aligned.
17. Press fit the grease seal on the upper bushing. Take care not to damage the grease seal lip.
18. Install the steering knuckle/spindle to the steering knuckle/spindle support as follows:
19. Insert the O-ring in the lower end of the kncukle/spindle support. Install the thrust bearing and shim together with the steering knuckle/spindle to the knuckle/spindle support. Select the spindle shims which will obtain 0.004 in. (0.1mm) or less clearance between the steer-

ing knuckle/spindle and the support. To measure this clearance with a feeler gauge, raise up the bottom of the spindle slightly.

NOTE: *The thrust bearing is installed so that the covered side faces upward. you will probably be able to use the same shims that were originally installed.*

20. Drive the new kingpin into the kingpin bores, securing the steering knuckle/spindle to the support.
21. Align the locking bolt hole of the knuckle/spindle support with the notch in the kingpin and install the lockbolt.
22. Install the upper and lower kingpin plugs.
23. Install the steering knuckle/spindle arm to the steering knuckle/spindle together with a new lockplate. Tighten the steering knuckle arm attaching bolts to 75–88 ft. lbs. Bend the tabs of the lockplate to engage the flats on the bolt head.
24. Install the brake backing plate, hub and wheel bearings, brake drum and wheel. Bleed the brake hydraulic system and grease the newly installed bushings until the grease is visible around the upper and lower grease seals.

Upper Ball Joint

NOTE: *Ball joints are used on all 1978-89 Nissans, replacing the kingpins used in 1970-77.*

INSPECTION

The ball joint should be replaced when play becomes excessive. Nissan does not publish specifications on just what constitutes excessive play, relying instead on a method of determining the force (in inch lbs.) required to keep the ball joint turning. This method is not very helpful to the backyard mechanic since it involves removing the ball joint, which is what we are trying to avoid in the first place. An effective way to determine ball joint play is to raise the truck until the wheel is just a couple of inches off the ground and the ball joint is unloaded, which means that you can't jack directly under the ball joint. Place a long bar under the tire and move the wheel and tire assembly up and down. Keep one hand on top of the tire while doing this. If there is over $\frac{1}{4}$ in. (6mm) of play at the top of the tire, the ball joint is probably bad. This assuming that the wheel bearings are in good shape and properly adjusted. As a double check, have someone watch the ball joint while you move the tire up and down with the bar. If considerable play is seen, besides feeling play at the top of the wheel, the ball joints need to be replaced.

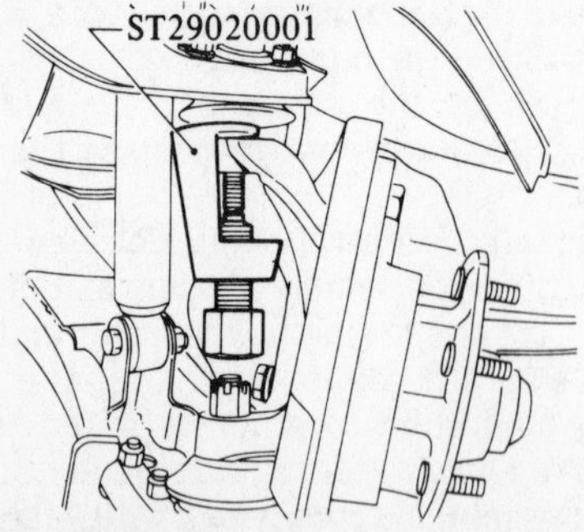

Ball joint separator

REMOVAL AND INSTALLATION

1978-83

1. Raise and support the truck on stands placed on the frame rails.
2. Remove the wheels.
3. Loosen the torsion bar anchor lock and adjusting nuts to relieve spring tension.
4. Remove and discard the cotter pin from the ball joint stud and remove the nut. Separate the stud from the knuckle spindle with a ball joint removal tool.
5. Loosen the bolts retaining the ball joint to the control arm, and remove the joint.
6. Install the new ball joint into the control arm, tightening the bolts to 12–16 ft. lbs. (16–22 Nm). Install the ball joint stud into the knuckle spindle and install the nut. Tighten the nut to 60 ft. lbs., then continue to tighten until the holes align (limit: 72 ft. lbs.). Install a new cotter pin. Install the wheel, lower the truck, and adjust the ride height. Have the alignment checked.

1984-89 Models

1. Raise and support the front end with jackstands under the frame rails.
2. Remove the front wheels.
3. Support the lower control arm with a floor jack and remove the upper ball joint-to-knuckle nut.
4. Using a ball joint separator, such as tool ST29020001, remove the ball joint from the knuckle.
5. Unbolt the ball joint from the upper arm.
6. Install the ball joint in the upper control arm and tighten the bolts to 12–15 ft. lbs. (16–21 Nm). Press the ball stud into the steering knuckle and tighten the nut to 58–72 ft. lbs. (78–98 Nm) on all 1984-86 2wd models (720-D series) or 58–108 ft. lbs. (78–147 Nm) on all 1984-86 4wd models (720-D series) and all 1986-89 models (D21-D series).
7. Have the front end alignment checked.

Lower Ball Joint

NOTE: *Ball joints are used on all 1978-89 Nissans, replacing the kingpins used in 1970-77.*

INSPECTION

The ball joint should be replaced when play becomes excessive. Nissan does not publish specifications on just what constitutes excessive play, relying instead on a method of determining the force (in inch lbs.) required to keep the ball joint turning. This method is not very helpful to the backyard mechanic since it involves removing the ball joint, which is what we are trying to avoid in the first place. An effective way to determine ball joint play is to raise the truck until the wheel is just a couple of inches off the ground and the ball joint is unloaded, which means that you can't jack directly under the ball joint. Place a long bar under the tire and move the wheel and tire assembly up and down. Keep one hand on top of the tire while doing this. If there is over ¼ in. (6mm) of play at the top of the tire, the ball joint is probably bad. This assuming that the wheel bearings are in good shape and properly adjusted. As a double check, have someone watch the ball joint while you move the tire up and down with the bar. If considerable play is seen, besides feeling play at the top of the wheel, the ball joints need to be replaced.

REMOVAL AND INSTALLATION

NOTE: *The lower ball joint on 1986-89 2wd models (D21-D series) is integral with the lower control arm. They are removed and replaced as a unit; please refer to Lower Control Arm for any and all procedures.*

1978-83 Models

1. Perform Steps 1–2 of the Upper Ball Joint removal procedure. Remove the lower shock absorber mounting bolt.
2. Loosen the torsion bar spring anchor lock and adjusting nuts, and remove the anchor arm bolt from the anchor arm.
3. Remove the snapring, then move the anchor arm and torsion bar fully rearward.
4. Disconnect the stabilizer bar from the lower arm, if equipped.
5. Disconnect the tension/compression rod from the lower arm.
6. Remove and discard the cotter pin from the ball joint stud, and remove the nut. Separate the ball joint from the knuckle spindle with a ball joint removal tool.
7. Remove the attaching bolts, and remove the ball joint from the lower arm.
8. Install the new ball joint in the arm and tighten the bolts to 28–38 ft. lbs. (38–52 Nm). Install the ball joint stud into the knuckle spindle and tighten the nut to 87–123 ft. lbs. (118–167 Nm). Continue to tighten until the holes align, then install the new cotter pin (limit: 141 ft. lbs.). The torsion bar ride height must be adjusted after assembly.

1984-86 2wd Models
1984-89 4wd Models

NOTE: *The lower ball joint on 1986-89 2wd models (D21-D series) is integral with the lower control arm. They are removed and replaced as a unit; please refer to Lower Control Arm for any and all procedures.*

1. Raise and support the front of the vehicle on jackstands under the frame rails.
2. Remove the front wheels.
3. Remove the torsion bar as previously described.
4. Unbolt the shock absorber from the lower arm.
5. Remove the ball joint nut.
6. Using a ball joint separator such as tool ST29020001, separate the ball joint from the knuckle.
7. Unbolt the ball joint from the lower arm.
8. Install the ball joint to the lower arm and tighten the nuts to 28–38 ft. lbs. (38–52 Nm) on all 1984-86 models (720-D series); or 35–45 ft. lbs. (47–61 Nm) on all 1986-89 4wd models (D21-D series).
9. Press the ball stud into the knuckle and tighten the nut to 87–123 ft. lbs. (118–167 Nm) on all 1984-86 models (720-D series); or 87–141 ft. lbs. (118–191 Nm) on all 1986-89 4wd models (D21-D series).

Control Arms

REMOVAL AND INSTALLATION

1970-77 Models

1. Raise the truck on a hoist or jack up the front end and support it with jackstands placed under the frame.
2. Remove the wheel and brake drum.
3. Remove the hub.
4. Remove the brake backing plate from the steering knuckle/spindle support.
5. Remove the steering knuckle/spindle arm, torsion bar, stabilizer bar, shock absorber and strut rod, in this order.
6. Remove the upper fulcrum bolt securing the knuckle/spindle support to the upper control arm assembly and detach the two.
7. Remove the upper control arm bushings from the knuckle/spindle support.
8. Remove the screw bushings from both ends of the lower control arm fulcrum pin.
9. Loosen the nut at the lower end of the knuckle/spindle support from the inside and pull out the cotter pin retaining the fulcrum.
10. Drive the fulcrum pin out of the lower control arm and remove the knuckle/spindle

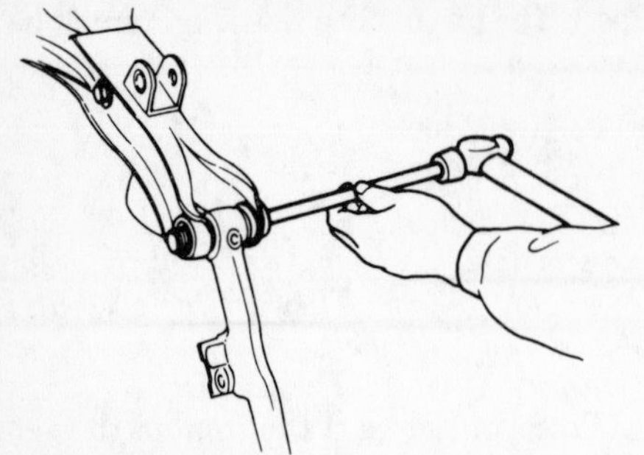

Driving the fulcrum pin out of the lower control arm in order to remove the steering knuckle/spindle support

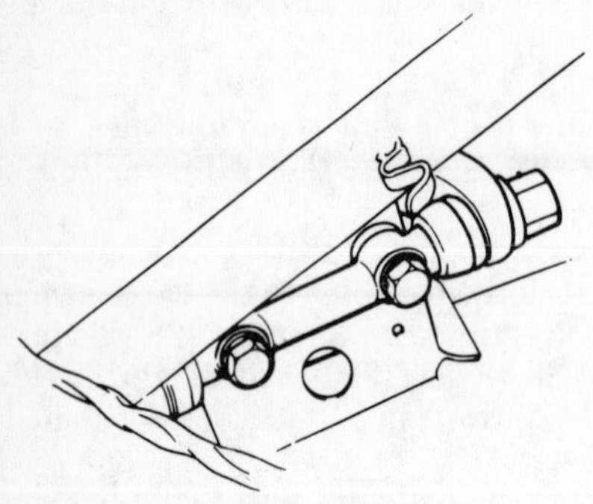

The upper control arm pivot shaft

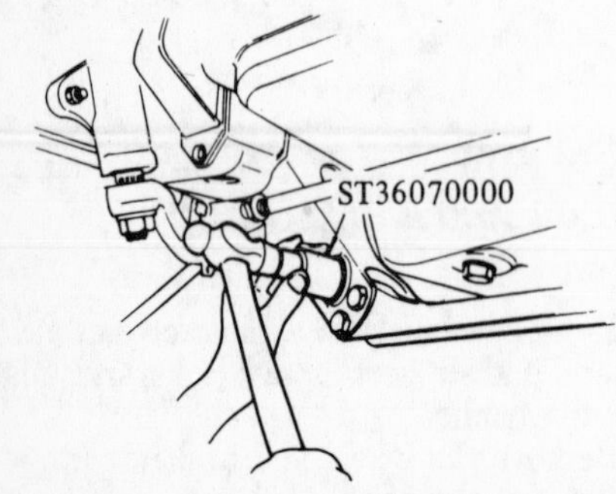

Removing the lower control arm pivot shaft bushing

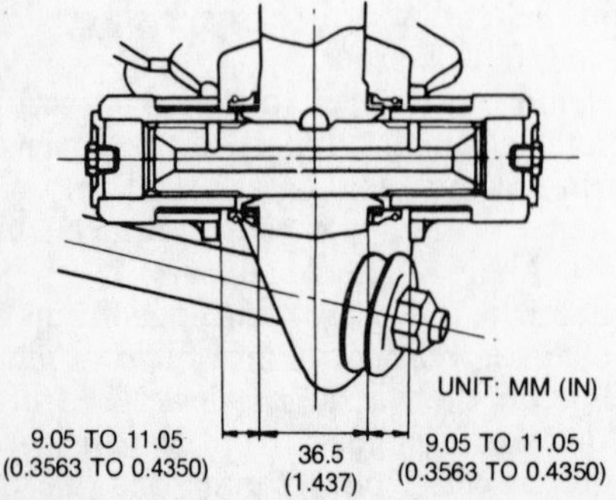

Installation of the lower control arm-to-knuckle screw bushing

support and steering knuckle/spindle from the lower control arm.

11. Remove the bolts retaining the upper control arm pivot shaft and remove the upper control arm pivot shaft with the camber adjusting shims from the body bracket.

12. Remove the nut retaining the lower control arm pivot shaft and remove the lower control arm pivot shaft. Remove the lower control arm, with the torque arm, from the mounting bracket.

13. The lower control arm bushing is removed with a drift and hammer.

14. Install the upper and lower control arms. Tighten the lower control arm attaching nut to 54–58 ft. lbs. Tighten the upper control arm and camber adjusting shim bolts to 51–65 ft. lbs.

15. Coat the threads of the fulcrum pin with grease and line up the notch of the fulcrum pin with the knuckle/spindle support for the insertion of the cotter pin. Install the fulcrum pin to the knuckle/spindle support with a soft hammer, attaching the support to the upper control arm. Install the cotter pin and tighten the locknut to 5.8–8.0 ft. lbs.

16. Coat the inner threaded portion of the screw bushing with grease. Position the support at the center of the lower control arm and install the screw bushings. Check the dimensions of the installed screw bushing against those in the illustration, then tighten the bushing to 145–216 ft. lbs.

17. Replace the grease filler plug with a grease fitting and pump grease in until it comes out around the dust cover. Reinstall the filler plug.

18. Install the upper control arm bushing to the knuckle/spindle support and then connect the knuckle/spindle support to the upper control arm. Insert the connecting bolt from the rear and tighten the nut to 28–38 ft. lbs.

19. Install the strut rod, shock absorber, stabilizer rod, torsion bar and steering knuckle arm.

20. Install the brake backing plate to the steering knuckle/spindle and tighten the attaching bolts to 30–36 ft. lbs.

21. Install the brake drum and wheel and adjust the wheel bearing preload.

Upper Control Arm

REMOVAL AND INSTALLATION

1978-83 Models

1. Perform Steps 1–4 of the Upper Ball Joint removal procedure.

2. Remove the bolts retaining the upper arm pivot shaft and remove the shaft, arm and camber adjusting shims from the body. Note the lo-

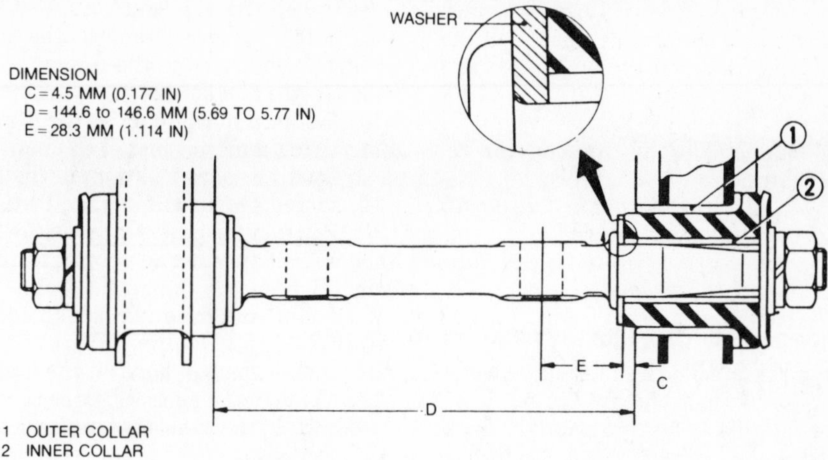

Upper pivot shaft and bushing dimension for 1978–83 models

cation of the shims so that they may be installed in their original positions during assembly.

3. To remove the upper arm shaft and bushings from the arm, remove the nuts and washers from the shaft. Use a press, first on one end of the shaft and then the other, to press out the bushings. Remove the shaft.

4. To install, coat the bushing with soapy water and press it into the upper arm. Install the washers onto the shaft and install the shaft into the arm. Be sure the chamferred side of the washer is against the shaft flange. Measure the distance between the outer collar on the bushing and the washer on the shaft (dimension **C** in the illustration); it should exceed 0.177 in. (4.5mm).

5. Press the other bushing into the arm, and check dimension **C**. Also check the distance between the outer collars of both bushings (dimension **D**) and the distance between the end of the bushing and the centerline of the shaft mounting bolt bore (dimension **E**). **D** should be 5.69–5.77 in. (144.6–146.6mm); **E** should be 1.114 in. (28.3mm).

6. Rotate the pivot shaft in the arm until the angle is as specified in the illustration. Install the nuts and washers on the shaft. Tighten the bushings to 56–76 ft. lbs.

7. Install the upper arm and shaft assembly to the body, replacing the camber shims in their original locations. Tighten the bolts to 80–108 ft. lbs.

8. Follow Step 6 of the upper ball joint removal procedure.

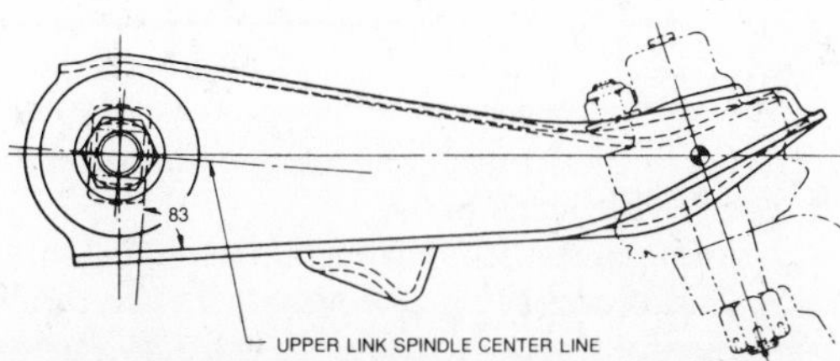

1978–83 upper arm pivot shaft installation before tightening shaft nuts

1984-89 Models

1. Separate the upper ball joint from the knuckle as previously described.

2. Disconnect the shock absorber at the upper end.

3. Unbolt the control arm spindle. Lift out the control arm.

4. The bushings may now be pressed out form both sides of the control arm.

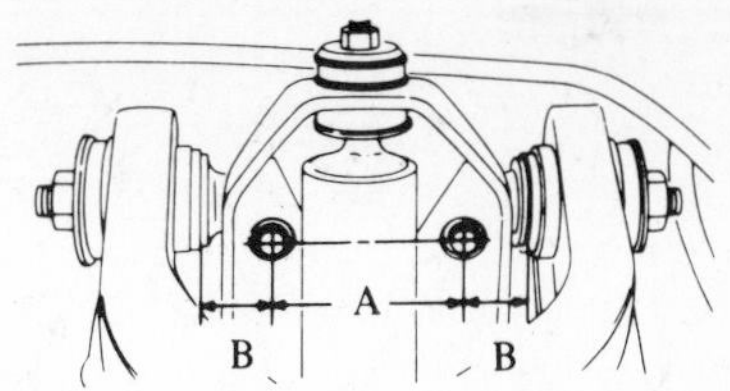

Upper control arm measuring points—1984–86 (720-D series)

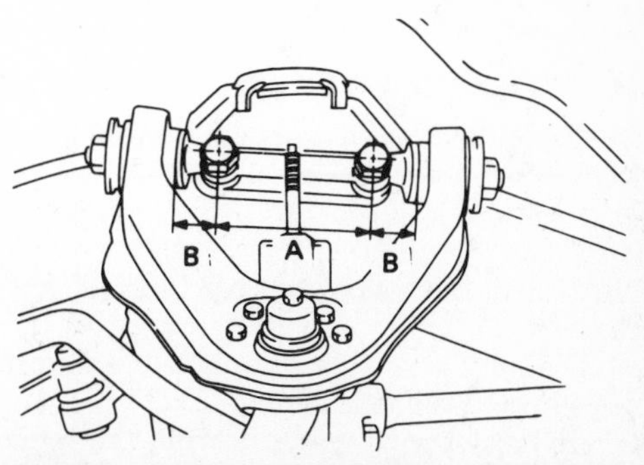

Upper control arm measuring points—1986–89 (D21-D series)

5. Apply a soapy solution to new bushings and press them into position in one end of the arm, so that the flange on the bushing firmly contacts the end surface of the upper link collar.

6. Install the spindle and press in the remaining bushings.

NOTE: *The inner washers are installed with the rounded edges facing inward.*

7. Temporarily tighten the spindle end nuts.

8. Install the upper ball joint.

9. Bolt the control arm to the frame. Tighten the bolts to 80–108 ft. lbs. (109–147 Nm).

10. Tighten the spindle end nut with camber adjusting shims. Torque the nuts to 52–76 ft. lbs. (71–83 Nm). Check the dimensions **A** and **B** in the illustration. Dimension **A** should be 5.34–5.42 in. (135.6–137.6mm) for 1984-86 models (720-D series); or 4.33 (110mm) for 1986-89 models (D21-D series). Dimension **B** should be 1.114 in. (28.3mm) for the 720-D series; or 1.26 in. (32mm) for the D21-D series.

10. Install the ball joint to the knuckle and check the front end alignment.

Lower Control Arm

REMOVAL AND INSTALLATION

NOTE: *The lower ball joint on 1986-89 2wd models (D21-D series) is integral with the lower control arm. They are removed and replaced as a unit.*

1978-83 Models

1. Perform Steps 1–6 of the Lower Ball Joint removal procedure.

2. Remove the lower arm pivot shaft bolt and washer. Tap the pivot shaft out of the bushing. Push down on the torsion bar and remove the lower arm.

3. Use a bushing driver to tap the lower arm bushing from the frame.

4. Drive the new bushing into the frame.

5. Install the arm and pivot shaft, tightening the nut to 80–108 ft. lbs.

6. Follow Step 8 of the lower ball joint removal procedure.

1984-86 Models (720-D Series)

1. Disconnect the lower ball joint from the knuckle as previously described.

2. Remove the torsion bar as previously described.

3. Unbolt the shock absorber from the lower arm.

4. Unbolt the stabilizer bar and tension/compression rod from the arm.

5. Remove the torque arm from the control arm.

6. Unbolt the control arm from the frame.

7. Unbolt the ball joint.

8. Using a driver, remove the lower arm spindle bushings from the frame.

9. Obtain new bushings.

10. Install the ball joint on the lower arm.

11. Using a driver, install the new bushings, coated with a soapy solution, in the frame.

12. Install the torque arm on the torsion bar.

13. Position the control arm on the frame and then install the torque arm onto the control arm. Tighten the inner bolt to 26–33 ft. lbs. (35–45 Nm) and the outer side to 20–27 ft. lbs. (26–36 Nm).

14. Install the ball joint on the knuckle.

15. Connect the shock absorber.

16. Install the tension/compression rod and stabilizer bar.

17. Lower the truck so that it is resting normally on its wheels.

18. Check wheel alignment.

1986-89 Models (D21-D Series)

NOTE: *The lower ball joint on 1986-89 2wd models (D21-D series) is integral with the lower control arm. They are removed and replaced as a unit.*

1. Make matching marks on the anchor arm crossmember when loosening the adjusting nut until there is no tension on the torsion bar and remove the torsion bar.

2. Separate the lower ball joint from the knuckle spindle on 2wd models. On 4wd models, separate it from the control arm.

3. Remove the front lower control arm attaching nut.

4. If necessary, remove the bushing of the lower control arm spindle from the frame using a suitable tool.

5. Coat the control arm bushing with soapy water and then install the arm to the frame. Tighten the bolt to 80–108 ft. lbs. (109–147 Nm).

6. Connect the ball joint to the knuckle on 2wd models or to the control arm on 4wd models.

7. Install the torsion bar and lower the vehicle.

8. Check the front end alignment.

Steering Knuckle And Spindle

REMOVAL AND INSTALLATION

1970-79 2wd Models

1. Raise the front of the vehicle and support it safely with jackstands.

2. Remove the front wheels.

3. Disconnect the brake hose from the steering knuckle at the bracket.

4. Remove the brake caliper.

5. Remove the wheel hub cap, and then re-

move the cotter pin, adjusting cap and spindle nut from the knuckle spindle.

6. Remove the wheel hub and rotor assembly.

7. Remove the hub from the rotor assembly.

8. Remove the outer bearing cone with fingers and remove the inner bearing cone by prying out the grease seal. Discard the grease seal.

9. If it is necessary to replace the bearing outer race, drive it out from the hub with a brass drift and mallet. Evenly tap the bearing outer race through the hole inside the hub.

10. Remove the baffle plate.

11. Separate the knuckle from the spindle arm.

12. Loosen the torsion bar spring anchor nut. and adjusting nut to cancel the torsion of the torsion bar spring.

13. Remove the upper and lower ball joint securing nuts and then remove the ball joints from the knuckle spindle using ball joint removal Tool ST29020001.

To install:

1. Install the knuckle spindle to the upper and lower ball joints. Tighten the upper ball stud nut to 58–72 ft. lbs. and the lower ball stud nut to 124–141 ft. lbs.

2. Tighten the anchor arm adjusting bolt and lock nut to the dimensions show in the illustration.

3. Install the baffle plate.

4. Install and grease the inner and outer bearings and seal if removed. Refer to Chapter One.

5. Install the knuckle arm and caliper and tighten all retaining bolts to 53–72 ft. lbs.

1980-89 2wd Models

1. Raise the front of the vehicle and support it safely with jackstands.

2. Remove the front wheels.

3. Disconnect the brake hose from the knuckle at the bracket.

4. Remove the brake caliper.

5. Remove the wheel hub cap, and then remove the cotter pin, adjusting cap and spindle nut from the knuckle spindle.

6. Remove the wheel hub and rotor assembly.

7. Remove the hub from the rotor assembly.

8. Remove the outer bearing cone with fingers and remove the inner bearing cone by prying out the grease seal. Discard the grease seal.

9. If it is necessary to replace the bearing outer race, drive it out from the hub with a brass drift and mallet. Evenly tap the bearing outer race through the hole inside the hub.

10. Remove the baffle plate.

11. Loosen but do not remove the upper and lower ball joint tightening nut.

12. Separate the upper and lower ball joint from the knuckle spindle.

NOTE: *During Step 12, never remove the ball joint nut which was loosened in Step 11.*

13. Jack up the lower control arm (link), then remove the ball joint tightening nut.

14. Separate the knuckle spindle from the upper and lower control arms (links).

15. Installation is the reverse of removal with the following exceptions:

   a. While jacking up the lower link, install the knuckle spindle to the upper and lower ball joints.

   b. When installing the knuckle arm, torque the retaining bolts to 53–72 ft. lbs.

   c. Install the front hub wheel bearings as outlined in Chapter One.

   d. When attaching the disc rotor to the hub, torque the bolts to 36–51 ft. lbs.

1981-83 4wd Models

1. Block the rear wheels, raise and support the front of the vehicle on jackstands.

2. Remove the wheels.

3. Remove the brake caliper and suspend it out of the way. DO NOT DISCONNECT THE BRAKE HOSE!

4. Remove the axle shaft.

5. Remove the bolt securing the knuckle arm to the knuckle.

6. Loosen, but do not remove the upper and lower ball joint tightening nuts.

7. Separate the ball joints from the knuckle with a ball joint removing tool.

CAUTION: *NEVER REMOVE THE BALL JOINT NUT IN THE ABOVE STEP!*

8. Jack up the lower link and remove the ball joint tightening nut.

9. Remove the knuckle.

10. Unbend the lockwasher with a small prybarr and remove the front hub locknut.

11. Remove the lockwasher and special washer.

12. Push the wheel bearing support out of the hub.

13. Separate the knuckle from the hub with a puller.

14. Remove the bearing collar.

15. Remove the inside bearing and seal. Drive the race out with a brass driver.

16. Separate the hub from the rotor.

17. Knock the hub on a wood block to move the outer bearing away from the hub surface, then pull it the rest of the way with a bearing puller. Remove the grease seal.

18. Remove the axle shaft bearing from the bearing support with a brass driver.

19. Clean and thoroughly repack the bearings.

20. When assembling, note the following points:

a. Install the bearing outer race into each side of the knuckle with a brass driver.

b. Install the outer grease seal and bearing with a brass driver.

c. Pack the seal lip with wheel bearing grease. Be sure that the seal faces the right direction.

d. The wheel bearing collar thickness determines end play. Determine what thickness to use as follows:

- Install the collar which was removed.
- Install the inside bearing with a brass driver.
- Install the special washer and lockwasher.
- Tighten the locknut to 108–145 ft. lbs.
- Turn the hub several times in both directions to seat the bearings.
- Using a spring scale as shown, check the preload to see that it falls between 2.2 and 9.5 ft. lbs.
- If not, adjust by replacing the collar with one of a different thickness, as shown by the number stamped on the collar. The larger the number, the thickness the collar.
- When preload has been correctly set, secure the nut by bending the lockwasher tip.

e. Observe the following torques:

- Upper ball joint-to-knuckle: 36–65 ft. lbs.
- Lower ball joint-to-knuckle: 43–72 ft. lbs.
- Knuckle arm-to-knuckle: 53–72 ft. lbs.
- Caliper-to-knuckle: 53–72 ft. lbs.
- Axle shaft-to-carrier: 20–27 ft. lbs.

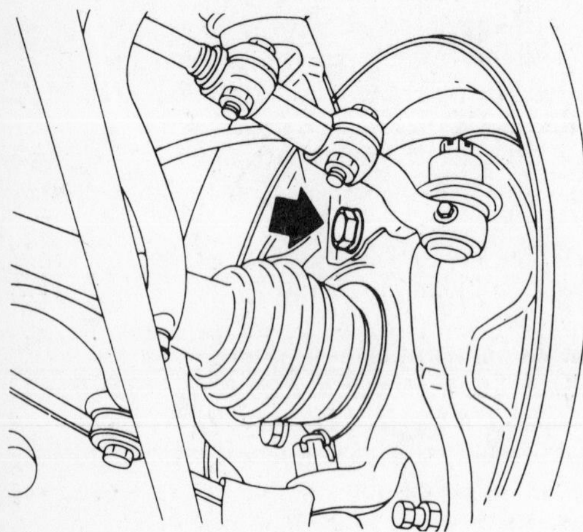

Knuckle arm attaching bolt

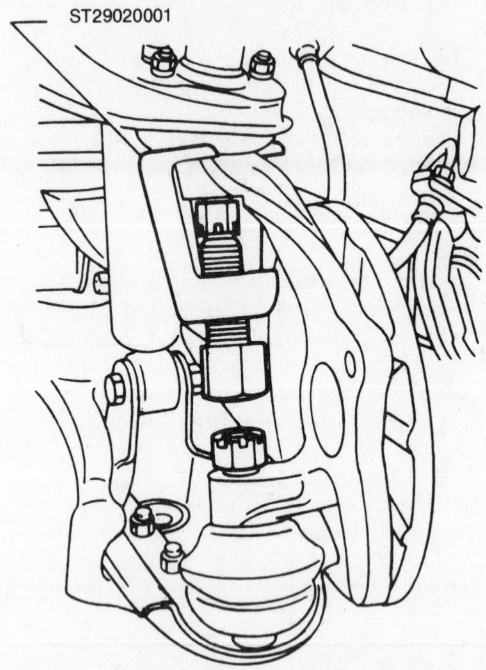

Removing the ball joints with a ball joint tool

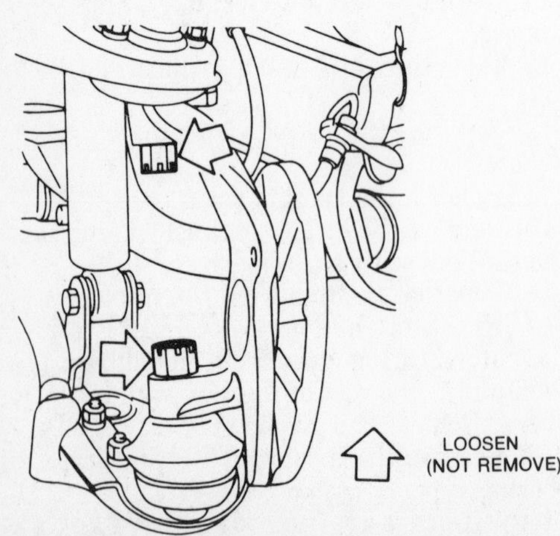

Upper and lower ball joint nuts

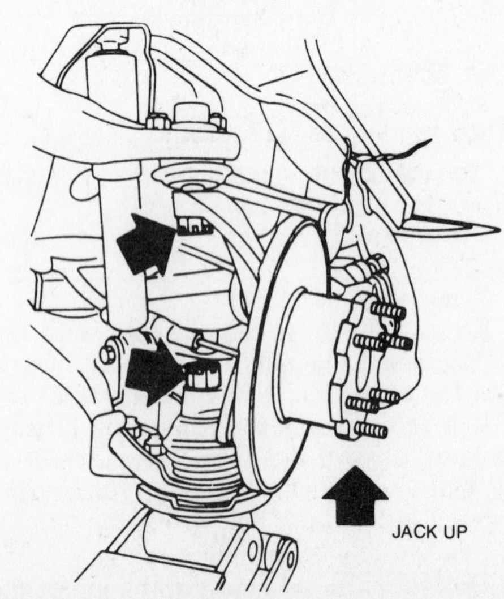

Removing the ball joint tightening nuts

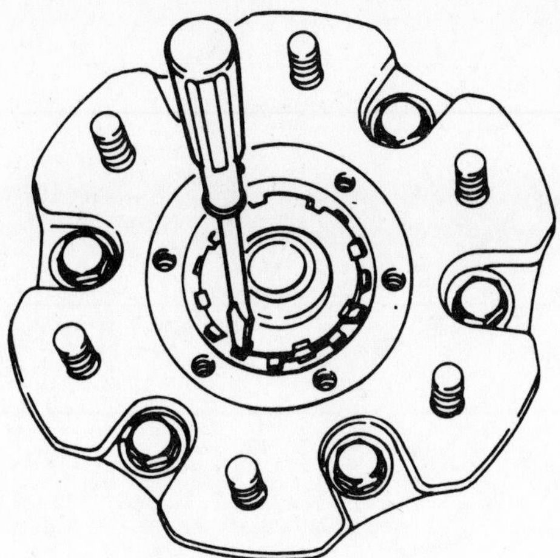
Unbending the lockwasher

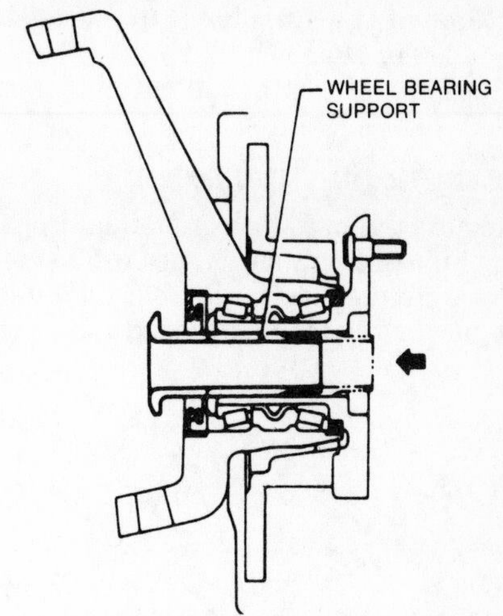

Wheel bearing support greasing location

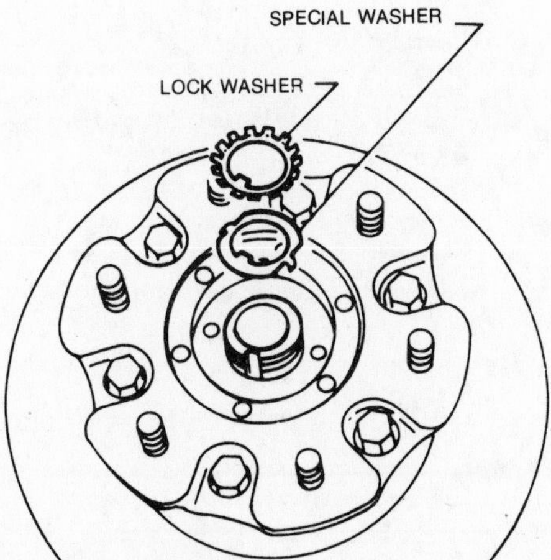

Removing the special washer and lock washer

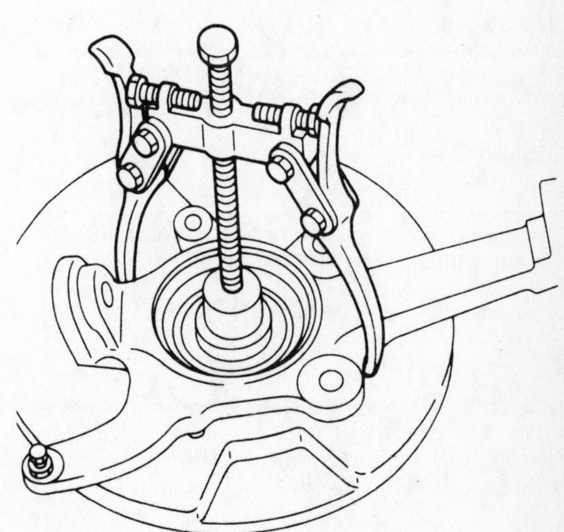
Using a puller to separate the hub from the knuckle

- Free running hub: 18–25 ft. lbs.
- Stabilizer bar: 12–16 ft. lbs.
- Wheel nut: 87–108 ft. lbs.

1984-86 4wd Models (720-D Series)

1. Raise and support the front end with jackstands under the frame rails.
2. Remove the front wheels.
3. Remove the calipers and suspend them out of the way.
4. Remove the locking hub assembly.
5. Remove the tie rod using tool HT2520000, or equivalent.
6. Unbolt the knuckle arm from the knuckle.
7. Support the lower control arm with a floor jack and remove the upper and lower ball joint-to-knuckle nuts.
8. Separate the ball joints from the knuckle.
9. Remove the snapring and lock washer from the hub.

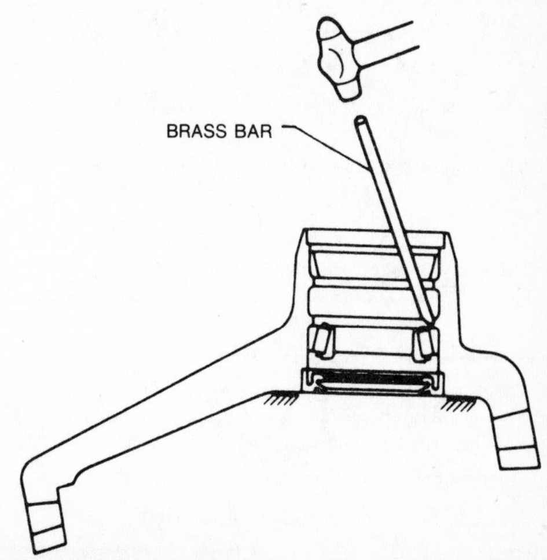

Driving out the inner bearing and seal

10. Remove the hub locknut using tool KV40104300 or equivalent.
11. Separate the hub and rotor from the knuckle.

1986-89 4wd Models (D21-D Series)

1. Remove the Auto-lock or Manual-lock free running hub assembly as detailed in Chapter 7.
2. Separate the axle shaft from the knuckle spindle by slightly tapping the axle shaft end.

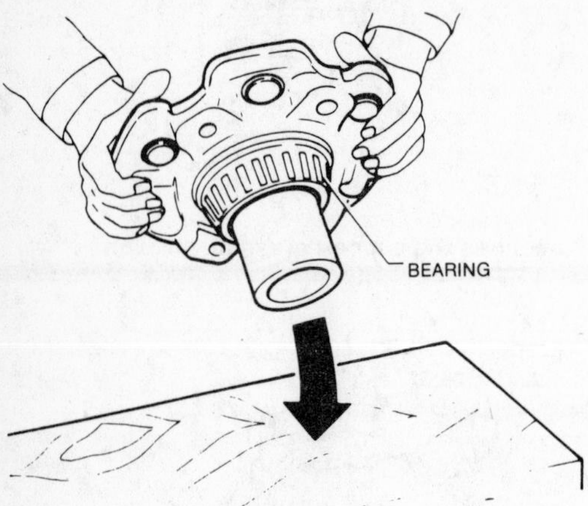

Hit the hub on a block of wood to break the outer bearing loose from the hub face

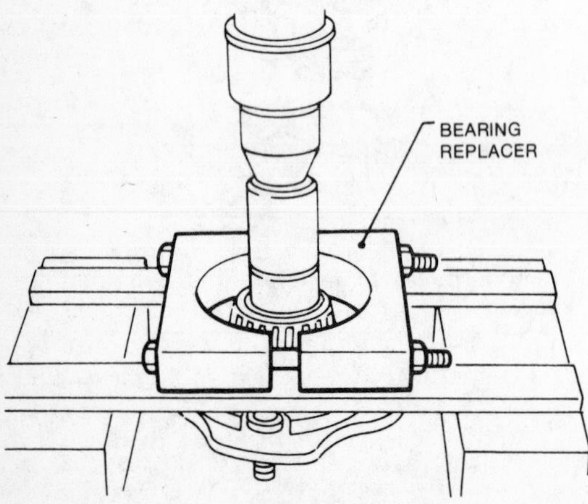

Removing the outer bearing with a puller

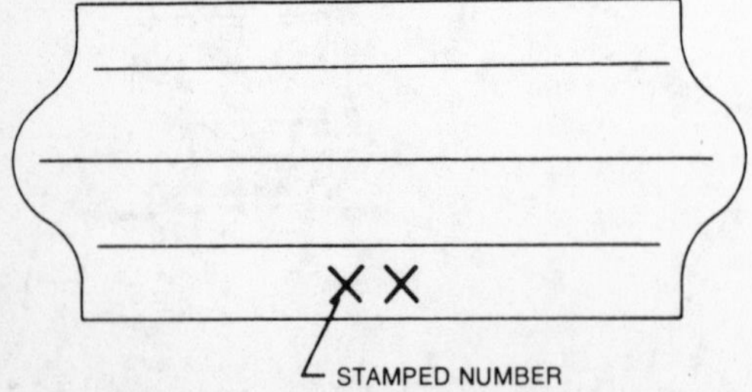

Bearing collars are stamped with a number to indicate thickness

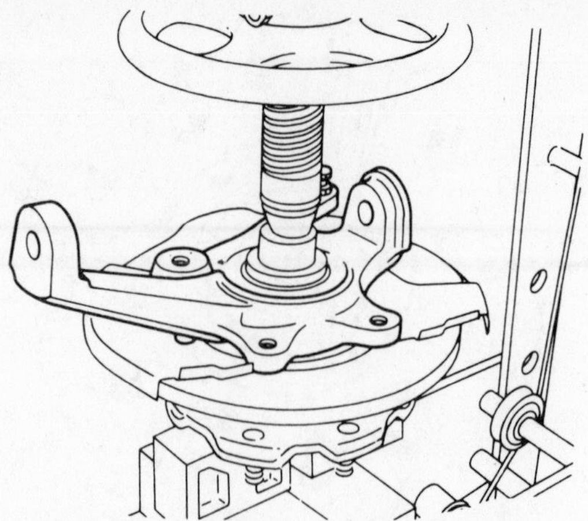

Installing the outer bearing into the knuckle

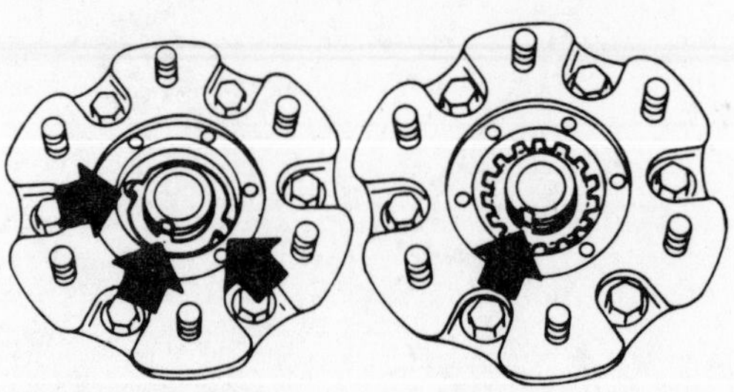

Proper positioning of the lockwasher and special washer

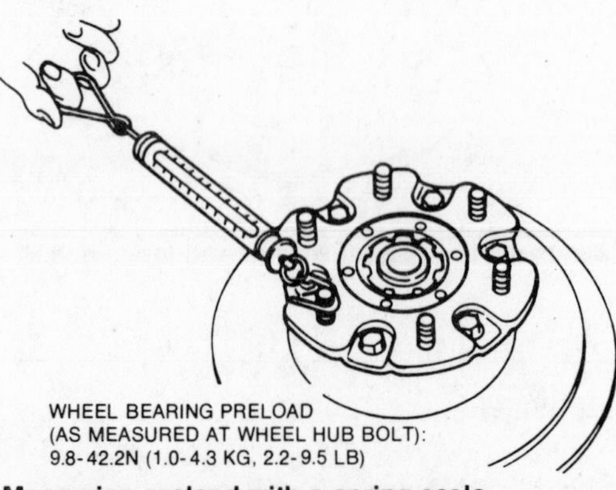

Measuring preload with a spring scale

3. Loosen, but do not remove the upper and lower ball joint-to-spindle nuts.
4. Separate the knuckle spindle from the upper and lower ball joint studs with Tool HT72520000

NOTE: *During Step 4, never remove the ball joint nuts which were loosened in Step 3.*

5. Support the lower control arm with a floor jack and remove the ball joint tightening nuts.
6. Remove the knuckle spindle from the upper and lower control arms.
7. When installing, follow these notes:
   a. When installing the needle bearing into the knuckle spindle, apply multi-purpose

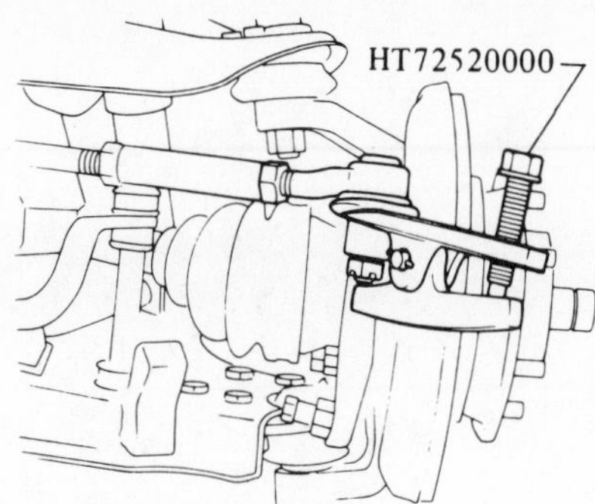

Tie rod removal on 1984 models

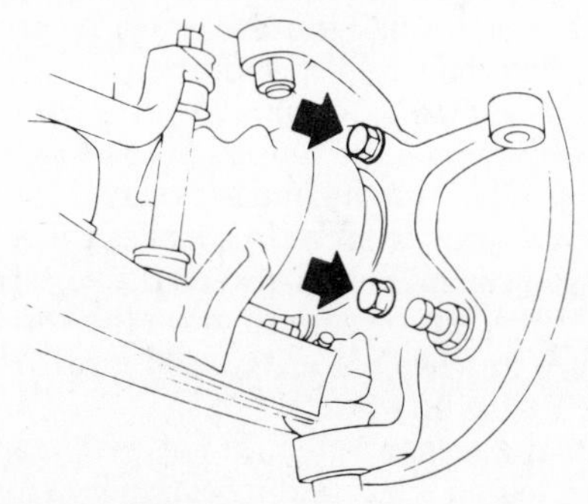

Knuckle arm removal

grease and make sure that the needle bearing is facing in the proper direction.

b. With the lower control arm jacked up, install the knuckle spindle to the upper and lower ball joints.

c. Adjust the wheel bearing preload.

d. When installing the axle shaft, never re-use the snapring, and check axial end play. Refer to Chapter 7.

Front Axle Hub and Wheel Bearing

REMOVAL AND INSTALLATION

2wd Models

1. Raise the front of the truck and support it with safety stands. Remove the wheels.
2. Remove the brake caliper and suspend it with wire, out of the way. Remove the caliper torque plate if equipped.
3. Remove the axle end cap and then remove the cotter pin, nut lock and nut.
4. Pull the hub/disc assembly off the spindle with the outer bearing. Don't let the bearing fall out!
5. Pry the inner oil seal out and remove the inner bearing from the hub.
6. Clean the bearings and outer races and inspect them for wear or cracks.
7. Using a brass drift and a hammer, drive out the bearing outer race. Press a new one into position.
8. Pack the bearings with grease until it oozes out the other side. Coat the inside of the hub and cap with grease.
9. Position the inner bearing into the hub, coat the oil seal with grease and press it into the hub.
10. Press the hub assembly onto the spindle and install the outer bearing and thrust washer.
11. Install the hub nut. Turn the hub a few times to seat the bearings and then loosen the nut until there is 0.5-1.0mm axial play. Using a spring tension gauge, check that the preload is 1.3-4.0 lbs.
12. Install the locknut, new cotter pin and hub grease cap.
13. Install the brake torque plate. Install the brake caliper.
14. Install the wheels and lower the truck.

4wd Models

Hub and bearing removal and installation procedures for these models are detailed in the "Front Drive Axle" section of Chapter 7.

Front End Alignment

Alignment should only be performed after it has been verified that all parts of the steering and suspension systems are in good operating condition. The truck must be empty. The tires must be cold and inflated to the correct pressure and the test surface must be level and horizontal.

Because special, elaborate equipment is required for proper front end alignment, it is recommended that the truck be taken to a reputable alignment shop.

CASTER

Caster is the forward or rearward tilt of the upper end of the kingpin (1970-77), or the upper ball joint (1978-89), which results in a slight tilt of the steering axis forward or backward. Rearward tilt is referred to as positive caster, while forward tilt is referred to as negative caster.

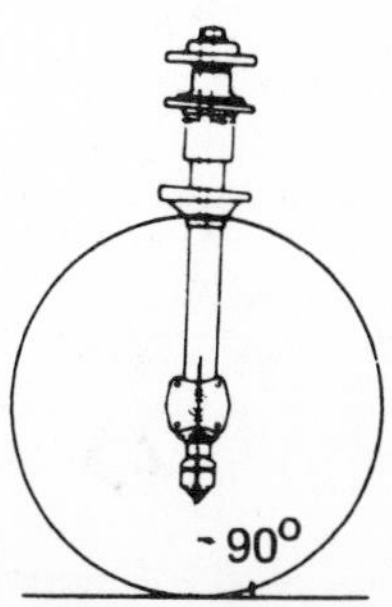

Caster is the forward or backward tilt of the steering axis

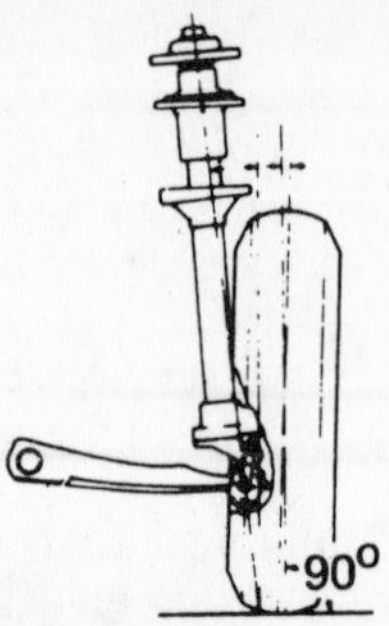

Camber is the slope of the front wheels when viewed from the front of the truck

Caster is adjusted by creating a difference in the total number (thickness) of shims, front and rear, between the upper control arm pivot shaft and its mounting bracket. Adjustment requires the use of special equipment.

CAMBER

Camber is the inward or outward tilt from the vertical, measured in degrees, of the front wheels at the top. An outward tilt gives the wheel positive camber. Proper camber is critical to assure even tire wear.

Camber is adjusted by adding or subtracting the same number and thickness of shims at the front and rear upper arm pivot shaft attaching bolts. Adjustment requires the use of special equipment.

TOE

Toe is the amount measured in a fraction of an inch, that the front wheels are closer together at one end than the other. Toe-in means that the front wheels are closer together at the front of the tire than at the rear; toe-out means that the rear of the tires are closer together than the front.

Although it is recommended that this adjustment be made by your dealer or a qualified shop, you can make it yourself if you make very careful measurement. The wheels must be dead straight ahead. The truck must have a full tank of gas, all fluids must be at their proper levels, all other suspension and steering adjustments must be correct and the tires must be properly inflated to their cold specification.

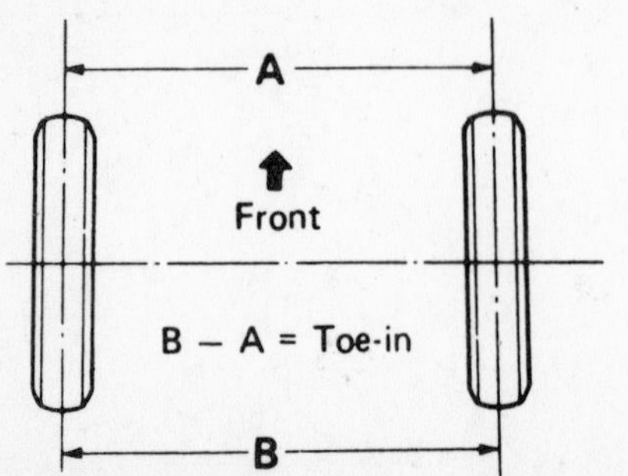

When the fronts of the tires are closer together than the rear, you have toe-in

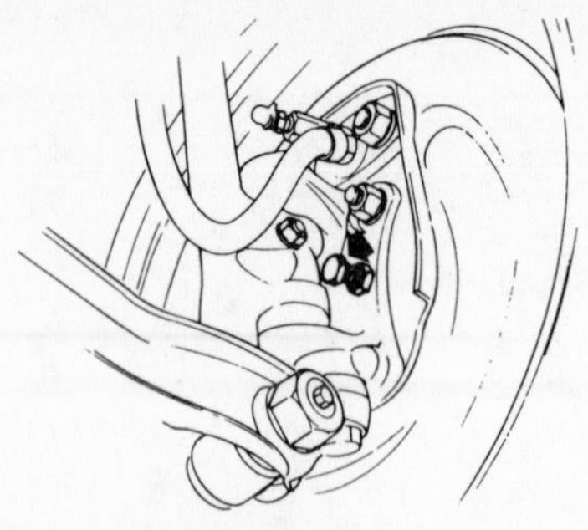

Steering angle adjustment

1. Toe can be determined by measuring the distance between the centers of the tire treads, at the front of the tire and the rear. If the tread pattern of your truck's tires makes this impossible, you can measure between the edges of the wheel rims, but be sure to move the truck and measure in a few places to avoid errors caused by bent rims or wheel runout.
2. If the measurement is not within specifications loosen the retaining clamp lock nuts on the adjustable tie rods.
3. Turn the left and right tie rods EQUAL amounts until the measurements are within specifications.
4. Tighten the lock bolts and then recheck the measurements. Check to see that the steering wheel is still in the proper position. If not, remove it and reposition it as detailed later in this chapter.

STEERING ANGLE ADJUSTMENT

The maximum steering angle is adjusted by stopper bolts located on the inside of the steering knuckle/spindle. Loosen the locknut on the stopper bolt, turn the stopper bolt, turn the stopper bolt in or out as required to obtain the proper maximum steering angle and retighten the locknut.

REAR SUSPENSION

Coil Springs

REMOVAL AND INSTALLATION

CAUTION: *The leaf springs are under a considerable amount of tension. Be very careful when removing or installing them; they can exert enough force to cause serious injuries.*

1988-89 Pathfinder

1. Raise the rear of the truck and remove the rear axle as detailed in Chapter Seven under Rear Axle – 5-Link.

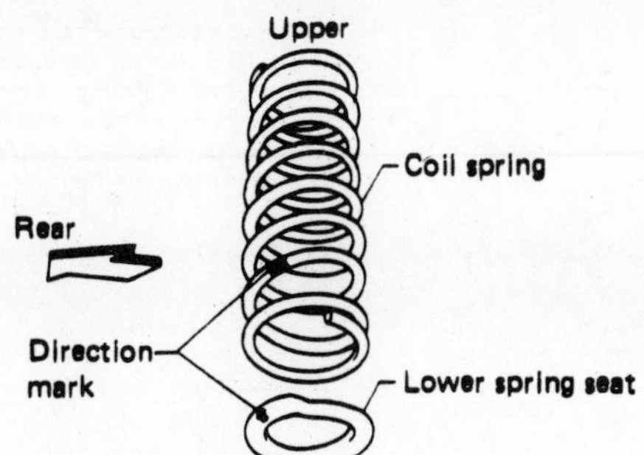

Coil spring installation

2. Remove the coil springs and their spring seats. Be careful to keep all components in their proper order.

3. Install the spring seats on the rear axle in the proper directions and then raise the axle housing until the springs can be inserted.

4. Install the rear axle housing as detailed in Chapter Seven.

Leaf Springs

REMOVAL AND INSTALLATION

CAUTION: *The leaf springs are under a considerable amount of tension. Be very careful when removing or installing them; they can exert enough force to cause serious injuries.*

1970-89 Pick-Ups
1986-87 Pathfinder

1. Raise the rear of the truck and support it with jackstands placed under the frame.

2. Disconnect the shock absorbers at their lower end. Disconnect the parking brake cables from the springs.

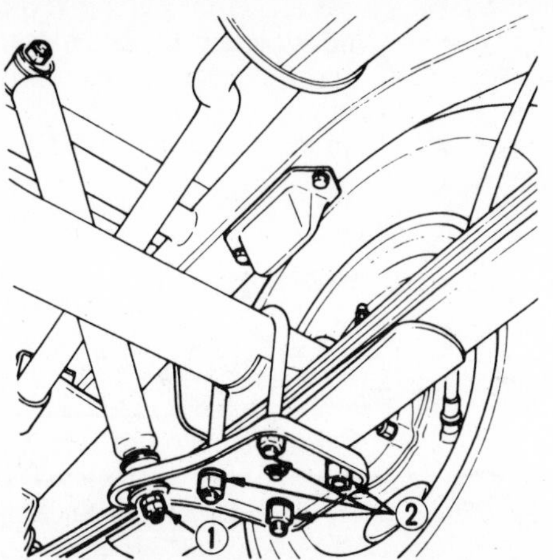

1. Shock absorber lower attaching nut
2. U-bolt attaching nut

Shock absorber lower end and U-bolt attaching nuts

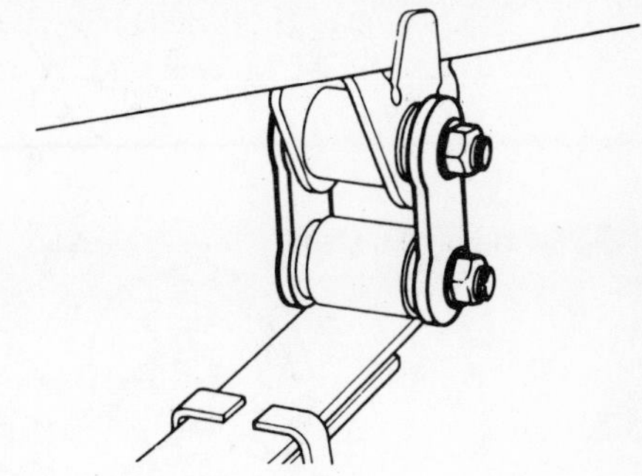

Spring shackle

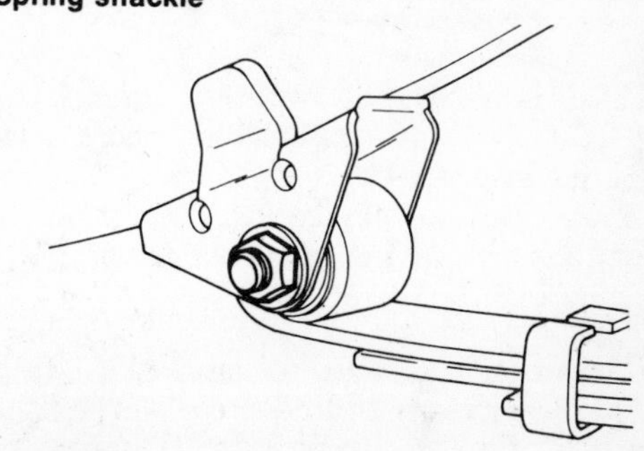

Spring pin

3. Remove the nuts securing the U-bolts around the axle housing.

4. Place a jack under the rear axle housing and raise the housing just enough to remove the weight from the springs.

5. Remove the nuts from the spring shackles, drive out the shackle pins and remove the spring from the vehicle.

6. Install the spring in the reverse order of removal. The weight of the truck must be on the rear wheels before tightening the front pin, shackle, and shock absorber attaching nuts. Bounce the truck several times to set the suspension and then tighten the front pin and shackle nuts to 83–94 ft. lbs. on 1970-77 models; 37–50 ft. lbs. (50–68 Nm) on 1978-86 models (720-D series) and for the spring shackle nuts only on 1986-89 2wd models (D21-D series); or 58–72 ft. lbs. (78–98 Nm) on 1986-89 models (D21-D series) except the shackle nuts on 2wd models. Tighten the U-bolt nuts to 65–72 ft. lbs. (88–98 Nm). Tighten the shock absorber lower end nut to 12–16 ft. lbs. (16–22 Nm) on all 1970-86 2wd models (720-D series) or 22–30 ft. lbs. (30–40 Nm) on all 1981-86 4wd models (720-D series) and all 1986-89 models (D21-D series).

Shock Absorbers

INSPECTION AND TESTING

Inspect and test the rear shock absorbers in the same manner as outlined for the front shock absorbers.

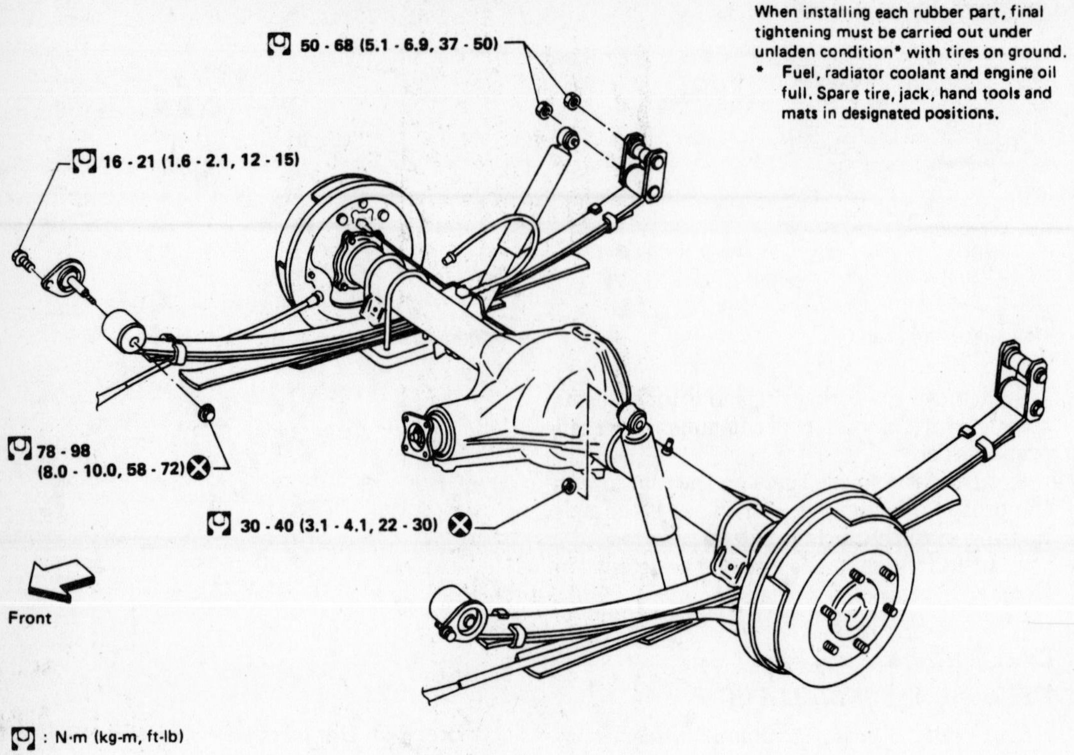

When installing each rubber part, final tightening must be carried out under unladen condition* with tires on ground.

* Fuel, radiator coolant and engine oil full. Spare tire, jack, hand tools and mats in designated positions.

50 - 68 (5.1 - 6.9, 37 - 50)

16 - 21 (1.6 - 2.1, 12 - 15)

78 - 98 (8.0 - 10.0, 58 - 72)

30 - 40 (3.1 - 4.1, 22 - 30)

Front

: N·m (kg-m, ft-lb)

Rear suspension—2wd Pick-Ups

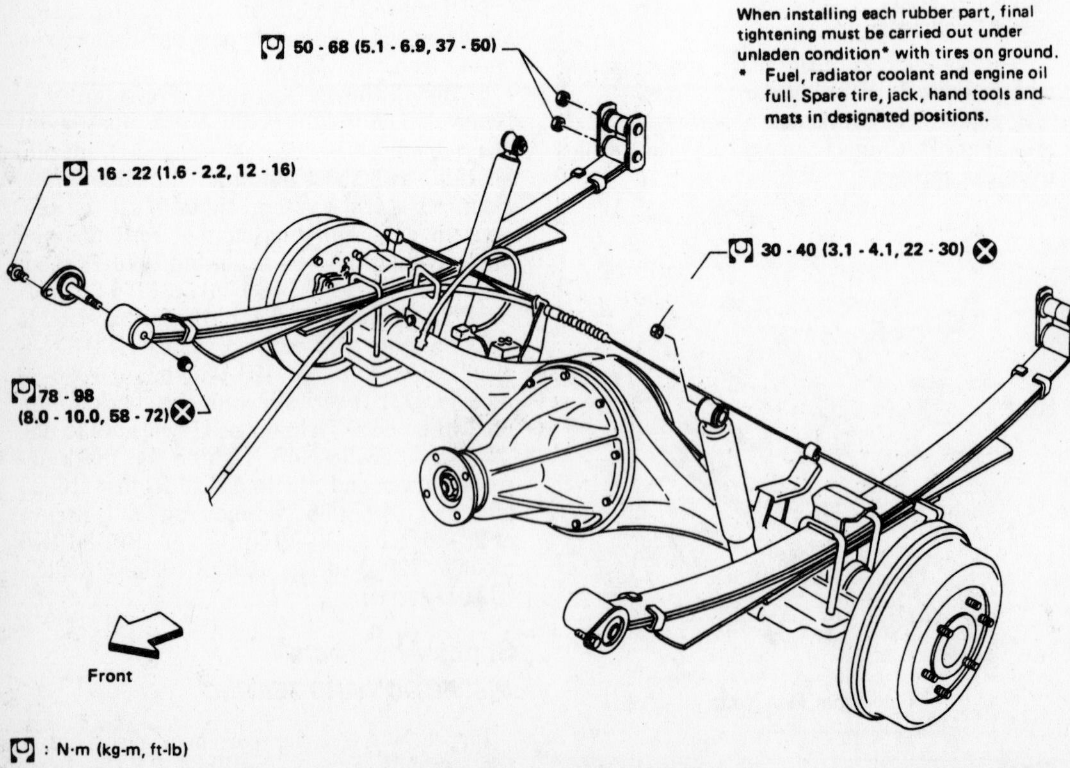

When installing each rubber part, final tightening must be carried out under unladen condition* with tires on ground.

* Fuel, radiator coolant and engine oil full. Spare tire, jack, hand tools and mats in designated positions.

50 - 68 (5.1 - 6.9, 37 - 50)

16 - 22 (1.6 - 2.2, 12 - 16)

30 - 40 (3.1 - 4.1, 22 - 30)

78 - 98 (8.0 - 10.0, 58 - 72)

Front

: N·m (kg-m, ft-lb)

Rear suspension—4wd Pick-Ups

REMOVAL AND INSTALLATION

1. Raise the rear of the vehicle.
2. Support the rear axle housing with jackstands.
3. Unfasten the upper shock absorber retaining nuts and/or bolts from the upper frame member.
4. Depending upon the type of rear spring used, either disconnect the lower end of the shock absorber from the spring seat, or the rear axle housing, by removing its cotter pins, nuts and/or bolts.
5. Remove the shock absorber. Inspect the shock for wear, leaks, or other signs of damage.
6. Install the shock absorber and tighten the upper bolts to 22–30 ft. lbs. (30–40 Nm). Tighten the shock absorber lower bolt to 12–16 ft. lbs. (16–22 Nm) on all 1970-86 2wd models (720-D series) or 22–30 ft. lbs. (30–40 Nm) on all 1981-86 4wd models (720-D series) and all 1986-89 models (D21-D series).

Control Arms

REMOVAL AND INSTALLATION

1988-89 Pathfinder

Control arm removal and installation is fairly simple; raise the vehicle and support the rear axle housing and then unbolt the control arms. Always install the bolts in the same direction that they were removed. Always install the bolts in the same direction that they were removed. All bolts should be tightened to 80–108 ft. lbs. (108–147 Nm) with the vehicle on the ground. Bounce the truck several times to set the suspension.

Panhard Rod

REMOVAL AND INSTALLATION

1988-89 Pathfinder

Panhard rod removal and installation is fairly simple; raise the vehicle and support the rear axle housing and then unbolt the rod. Tighten the right side bolt to 80–108 ft. lbs. (108–147 Nm) and the left side bolt to 36–51 ft. lbs. (49–69 Nm) with the vehicle on the ground. Bounce the truck several times to set the suspension.

Stabilizer Bar

REMOVAL AND INSTALLATION

1988-89 Pathfinder

1. Raise the truck and support it with safety stands.
2. Disconnect the stabilizer bar connecting rod at the body. Remove the retainer and cushion from the link.
3. Disconnect the stabilizer bar bracket and cushion from the axle housing.
4. Remove the stabilizer bar.

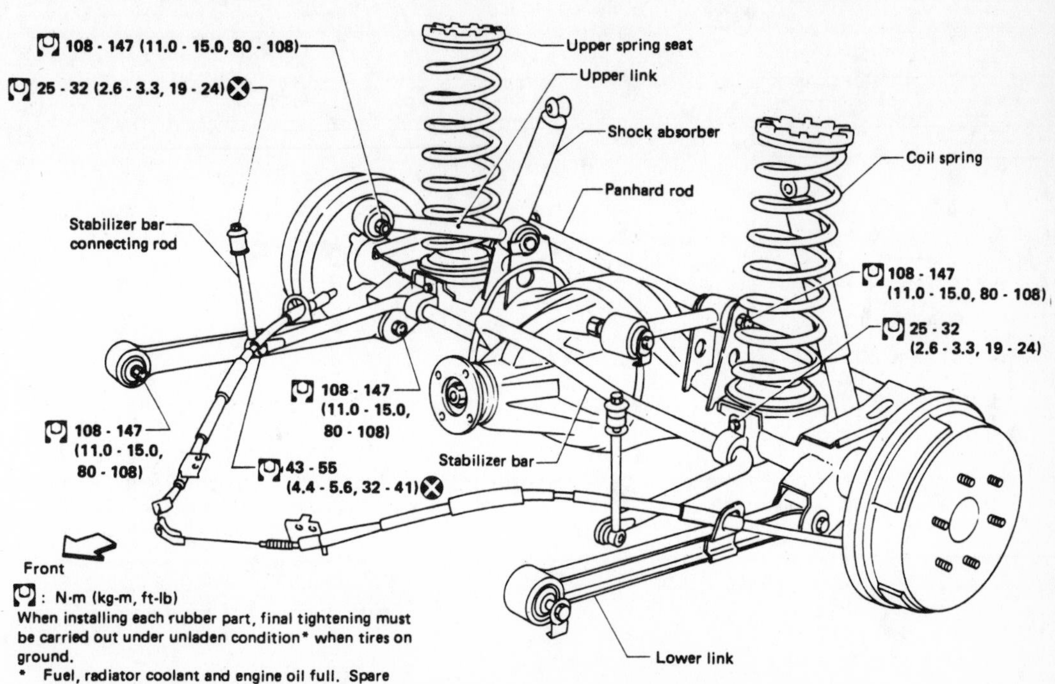

Rear suspension—1988–89 Pathfinders

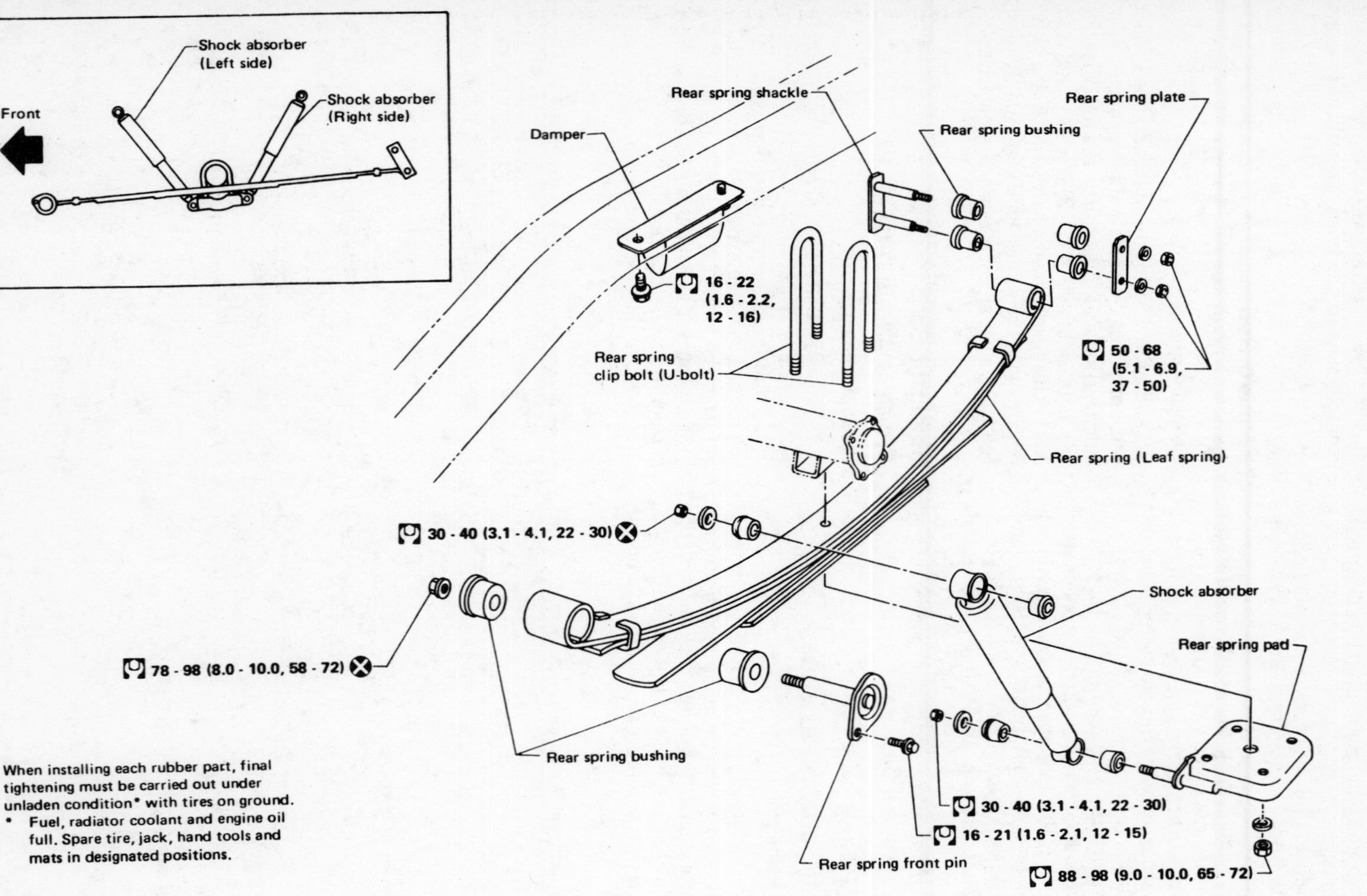

Exploded view of the rear suspension (leaf spring)—2wd models

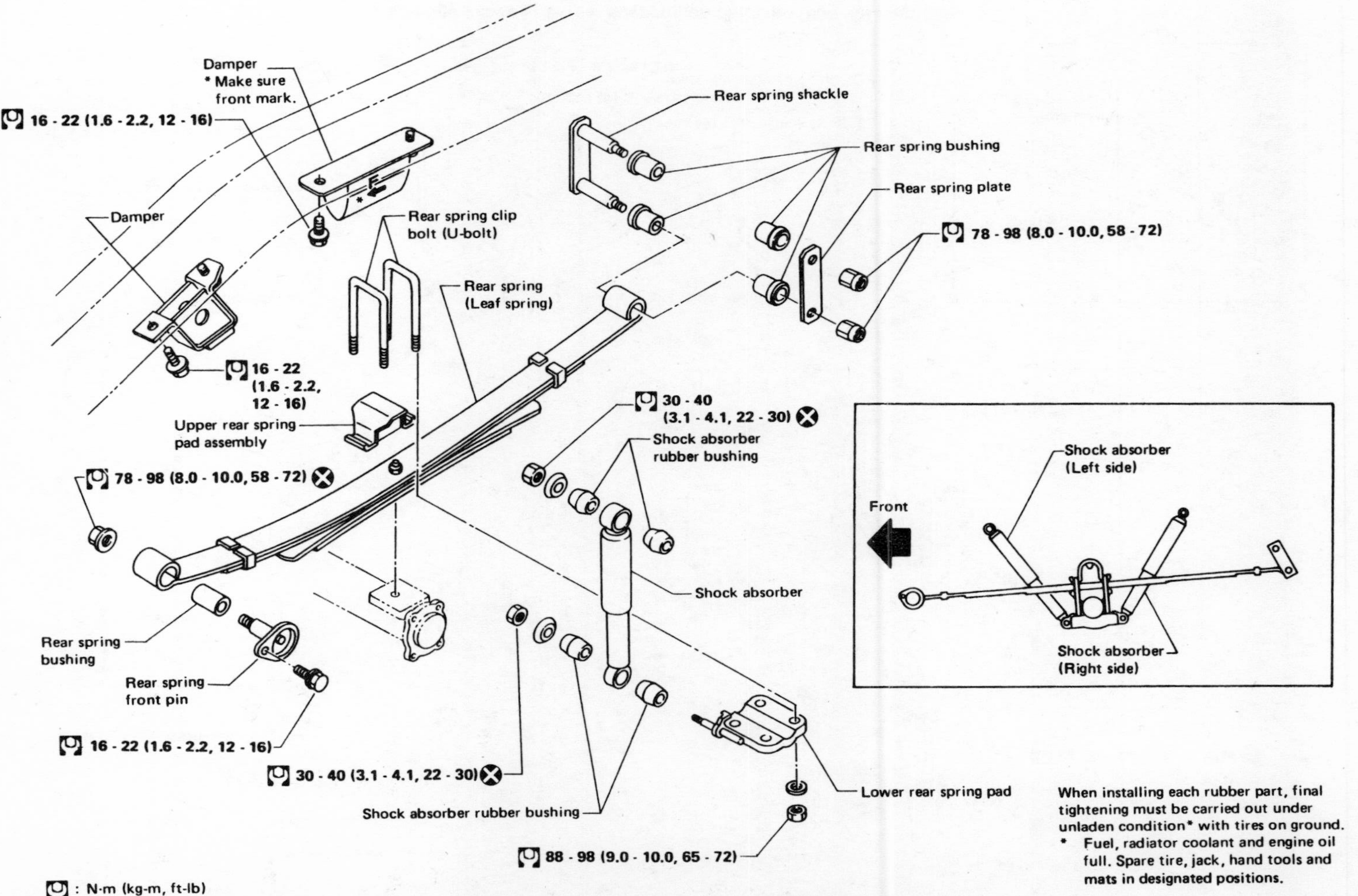

Exploded view of the rear suspension (leaf spring)—4wd models

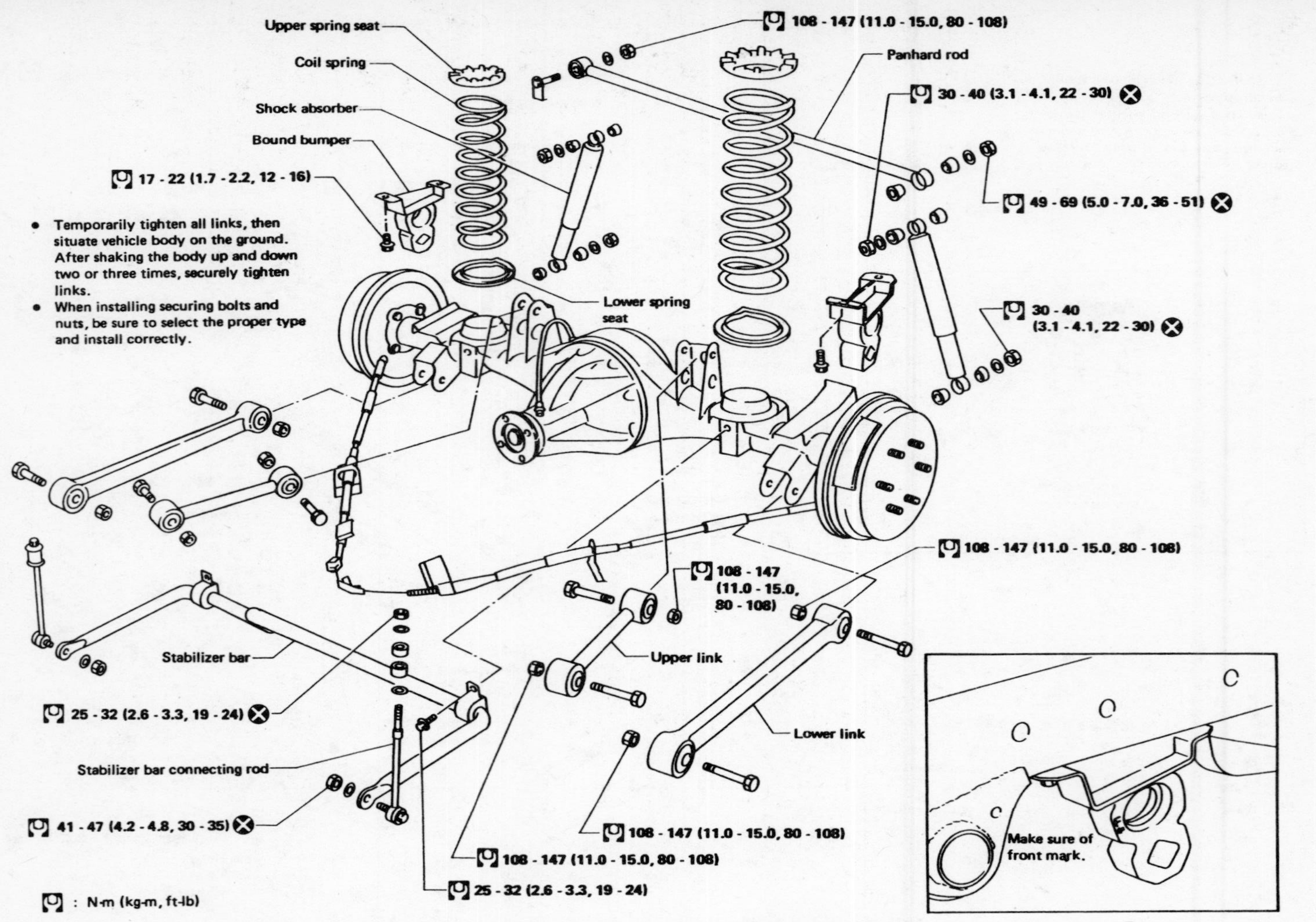

Exploded view of the rear suspension (5-link)—1988–89 Pathfinder

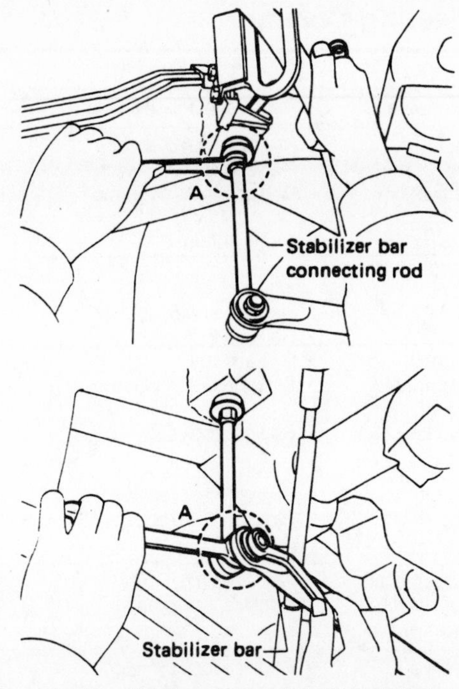

Removing the stabilizer bar—1988–89 Pathfinder

5. Position the stabilizer bar at the axle housing and install the bracket and cushion. Tighten the mounting bolts to 19–24 ft. lbs. (25–32 Nm).

6. Install the connecting rod to the body with the retainers and cushion. Tighten the mounting bolts to 19–24 ft. lbs. (25–32 Nm).

7. Lower the truck.

STEERING

Steering Wheel

REMOVAL AND INSTALLATION

1. Position the wheels in the straight ahead position.

2. Disconnect the negative battery cable.

3. Remove the horn pad by unscrewing the two screws from the rear side of the steering wheel crossbar.

4. Punchmark the top of the steering column shaft and the steering wheel flange.

5. Remove the attaching nut and remove the steering wheel with a puller.

CAUTION: *Do not strike the shaft with a*

Troubleshooting Basic Steering and Suspension Problems

Problem	Cause	Solution
Hard steering (steering wheel is hard to turn)	• Low or uneven tire pressure • Loose power steering pump drive belt • Low or incorrect power steering fluid • Incorrect front end alignment • Defective power steering pump • Bent or poorly lubricated front end parts	• Inflate tires to correct pressure • Adjust belt • Add fluid as necessary • Have front end alignment checked/adjusted • Check pump • Lubricate and/or replace defective parts
Loose steering (too much play in the steering wheel)	• Loose wheel bearings • Loose or worn steering linkage • Faulty shocks • Worn ball joints	• Adjust wheel bearings • Replace worn parts • Replace shocks • Replace ball joints
Car veers or wanders (car pulls to one side with hands off the steering wheel)	• Incorrect tire pressure • Improper front end alignment • Loose wheel bearings • Loose or bent front end components • Faulty shocks	• Inflate tires to correct pressure • Have front end alignment checked/adjusted • Adjust wheel bearings • Replace worn components • Replace shocks
Wheel oscillation or vibration transmitted through steering wheel	• Improper tire pressures • Tires out of balance • Loose wheel bearings • Improper front end alignment • Worn or bent front end components	• Inflate tires to correct pressure • Have tires balanced • Adjust wheel bearings • Have front end alignment checked/adjusted • Replace worn parts
Uneven tire wear	• Incorrect tire pressure • Front end out of alignment • Tires out of balance	• Inflate tires to correct pressure • Have front end alignment checked/adjusted • Have tires balanced

Troubleshooting the Steering Column

Problem	Cause	Solution
Will not lock	• Lockbolt spring broken or defective	• Replace lock bolt spring
High effort (required to turn ignition key and lock cylinder)	• Lock cylinder defective • Ignition switch defective • Rack preload spring broken or deformed • Burr on lock sector, lock rack, housing, support or remote rod coupling • Bent sector shaft • Defective lock rack • Remote rod bent, deformed • Ignition switch mounting bracket bent • Distorted coupling slot in lock rack (tilt column)	• Replace lock cylinder • Replace ignition switch • Replace preload spring • Remove burr • Replace shaft • Replace lock rack • Replace rod • Straighten or replace • Replace lock rack
Will stick in "start"	• Remote rod deformed • Ignition switch mounting bracket bent	• Straighten or replace • Straighten or replace
Key cannot be removed in "off-lock"	• Ignition switch is not adjusted correctly • Defective lock cylinder	• Adjust switch • Replace lock cylinder
Lock cylinder can be removed without depressing retainer	• Lock cylinder with defective retainer • Burr over retainer slot in housing cover or on cylinder retainer	• Replace lock cylinder • Remove burr
High effort on lock cylinder between "off" and "off-lock"	• Distorted lock rack • Burr on tang of shift gate (automatic column) • Gearshift linkage not adjusted	• Replace lock rack • Remove burr • Adjust linkage
Noise in column	• One click when in "off-lock" position and the steering wheel is moved (all except automatic column) • Coupling bolts not tightened • Lack of grease on bearings or bearing surfaces • Upper shaft bearing worn or broken • Lower shaft bearing worn or broken • Column not correctly aligned • Coupling pulled apart • Broken coupling lower joint • Steering shaft snap ring not seated • Shroud loose on shift bowl. Housing loose on jacket—will be noticed with ignition in "off-lock" and when torque is applied to steering wheel.	• Normal—lock bolt is seating • Tighten pinch bolts • Lubricate with chassis grease • Replace bearing assembly • Replace bearing. Check shaft and replace if scored. • Align column • Replace coupling • Repair or replace joint and align column • Replace ring. Check for proper seating in groove. • Position shroud over lugs on shift bowl. Tighten mounting screws.
High steering shaft effort	• Column misaligned • Defective upper or lower bearing • Tight steering shaft universal joint • Flash on I.D. of shift tube at plastic joint (tilt column only) • Upper or lower bearing seized	• Align column • Replace as required • Repair or replace • Replace shift tube • Replace bearings
Lash in mounted column assembly	• Column mounting bracket bolts loose • Broken weld nuts on column jacket • Column capsule bracket sheared	• Tighten bolts • Replace column jacket • Replace bracket assembly

Troubleshooting the Steering Column (cont.)

Problem	Cause	Solution
Lash in mounted column assembly (cont.)	· Column bracket to column jacket mounting bolts loose · Loose lock shoes in housing (tilt column only) · Loose pivot pins (tilt column only) · Loose lock shoe pin (tilt column only) · Loose support screws (tilt column only)	· Tighten to specified torque · Replace shoes · Replace pivot pins and support · Replace pin and housing · Tighten screws
Housing loose (tilt column only)	· Excessive clearance between holes in support or housing and pivot pin diameters · Housing support-screws loose	· Replace pivot pins and support · Tighten screws
Steering wheel loose—every other tilt position (tilt column only)	· Loose fit between lock shoe and lock shoe pivot pin	· Replace lock shoes and pivot pin
Steering column not locking in any tilt position (tilt column only)	· Lock shoe seized on pivot pin · Lock shoe grooves have burrs or are filled with foreign material · Lock shoe springs weak or broken	· Replace lock shoes and pin · Clean or replace lock shoes · Replace springs
Noise when tilting column (tilt column only)	· Upper tilt bumpers worn · Tilt spring rubbing in housing	· Replace tilt bumper · Lubricate with chassis grease
One click when in "off-lock" position and the steering wheel is moved	· Seating of lock bolt	· None. Click is normal characteristic sound produced by lock bolt as it seats.
High shift effort (automatic and tilt column only)	· Column not correctly aligned · Lower bearing not aligned correctly · Lack of grease on seal or lower bearing areas	· Align column · Assemble correctly · Lubricate with chassis grease
Improper transmission shifting—automatic and tilt column only	· Sheared shift tube joint · Improper transmission gearshift linkage adjustment · Loose lower shift lever	· Replace shift tube · Adjust linkage · Replace shift tube

Troubleshooting the Ignition Switch

Problem	Cause	Solution
Ignition switch electrically inoperative	· Loose or defective switch connector · Feed wire open (fusible link) · Defective ignition switch	· Tighten or replace connector · Repair or replace · Replace ignition switch
Engine will not crank	· Ignition switch not adjusted properly	· Adjust switch
Ignition switch wil not actuate mechanically	· Defective ignition switch · Defective lock sector · Defective remote rod	· Replace switch · Replace lock sector · Replace remote rod
Ignition switch cannot be adjusted correctly	· Remote rod deformed	· Repair, straighten or replace

Troubleshooting the Turn Signal Switch

Problem	Cause	Solution
Turn signal will not cancel	• Loose switch mounting screws • Switch or anchor bosses broken • Broken, missing or out of position detent, or cancelling spring	• Tighten screws • Replace switch • Reposition springs or replace switch as required
Turn signal difficult to operate	• Turn signal lever loose • Switch yoke broken or distorted • Loose or misplaced springs • Foreign parts and/or materials in switch • Switch mounted loosely	• Tighten mounting screws • Replace switch • Reposition springs or replace switch • Remove foreign parts and/or material • Tighten mounting screws
Turn signal will not indicate lane change	• Broken lane change pressure pad or spring hanger • Broken, missing or misplaced lane change spring • Jammed wires	• Replace switch • Replace or reposition as required • Loosen mounting screws, reposition wires and retighten screws
Turn signal will not stay in turn position	• Foreign material or loose parts impeding movement of switch yoke • Defective switch	• Remove material and/or parts • Replace switch
Hazard switch cannot be pulled out	• Foreign material between hazard support cancelling leg and yoke	• Remove foreign material. No foreign material impeding function of hazard switch—replace turn signal switch.
No turn signal lights	• Inoperative turn signal flasher • Defective or blown fuse • Loose chassis to column harness connector • Disconnect column to chassis connector. Connect new switch to chassis and operate switch by hand. If vehicle lights now operate normally, signal switch is inoperative • If vehicle lights do not operate, check chassis wiring for opens, grounds, etc.	• Replace turn signal flasher • Replace fuse • Connect securely • Replace signal switch • Repair chassis wiring as required
Instrument panel turn indicator lights on but not flashing	• Burned out or damaged front or rear turn signal bulb • If vehicle lights do not operate, check light sockets for high resistance connections, the chassis wiring for opens, grounds, etc. • Inoperative flasher • Loose chassis to column harness connection • Inoperative turn signal switch • To determine if turn signal switch is defective, substitute new switch into circuit and operate switch by hand. If the vehicle's lights operate normally, signal switch is inoperative.	• Replace bulb • Repair chassis wiring as required • Replace flasher • Connect securely • Replace turn signal switch • Replace turn signal switch
Stop light not on when turn indicated	• Loose column to chassis connection • Disconnect column to chassis connector. Connect new switch into system without removing old.	• Connect securely • Replace signal switch

Troubleshooting the Turn Signal Switch (cont.)

Problem	Cause	Solution
Stop light not on when turn indicated (cont.)	Operate switch by hand. If brake lights work with switch in the turn position, signal switch is defective. • If brake lights do not work, check connector to stop light sockets for grounds, opens, etc.	• Repair connector to stop light circuits using service manual as guide
Turn indicator panel lights not flashing	• Burned out bulbs • High resistance to ground at bulb socket • Opens, ground in wiring harness from front turn signal bulb socket to indicator lights	• Replace bulbs • Replace socket • Locate and repair as required
Turn signal lights flash very slowly	• High resistance ground at light sockets • Incorrect capacity turn signal flasher or bulb • If flashing rate is still extremely slow, check chassis wiring harness from the connector to light sockets for high resistance • Loose chassis to column harness connection • Disconnect column to chassis connector. Connect new switch into system without removing old. Operate switch by hand. If flashing occurs at normal rate, the signal switch is defective.	• Repair high resistance grounds at light sockets • Replace turn signal flasher or bulb • Locate and repair as required • Connect securely • Replace turn signal switch
Hazard signal lights will not flash—turn signal functions normally	• Blow fuse • Inoperative hazard warning flasher • Loose chassis-to-column harness connection • Disconnect column to chassis connector. Connect new switch into system without removing old. Depress the hazard warning lights. If they now work normally, turn signal switch is defective. • If lights do not flash, check wiring harness "K" lead for open between hazard flasher and connector. If open, fuse block is defective	• Replace fuse • Replace hazard warning flasher in fuse panel • Conect securely • Replace turn signal switch • Repair or replace brown wire or connector as required

Troubleshooting the Manual Steering Gear

Problem	Cause	Solution
Hard or erratic steering	• Incorrect tire pressure • Insufficient or incorrect lubrication • Suspension, or steering linkage parts damaged or misaligned • Improper front wheel alignment • Incorrect steering gear adjustment • Sagging springs	• Inflate tires to recommended pressures • Lubricate as required (refer to Maintenance Section) • Repair or replace parts as necessary • Adjust incorrect wheel alignment angles • Adjust steering gear • Replace springs

Troubleshooting the Manual Steering Gear (cont.)

Problem	Cause	Solution
Play or looseness in steering	• Steering wheel loose	• Inspect shaft spines and repair as necessary. Tighten attaching nut and stake in place.
	• Steering linkage or attaching parts loose or worn	• Tighten, adjust, or replace faulty components
	• Pitman arm loose	• Inspect shaft splines and repair as necessary. Tighten attaching nut and stake in place
	• Steering gear attaching bolts loose	• Tighten bolts
	• Loose or worn wheel bearings	• Adjust or replace bearings
	• Steering gear adjustment incorrect or parts badly worn	• Adjust gear or replace defective parts
Wheel shimmy or tramp	• Improper tire pressure	• Inflate tires to recommended pressures
	• Wheels, tires, or brake rotors out-of-balance or out-of-round	• Inspect and replace or balance parts
	• Inoperative, worn, or loose shock absorbers or mounting parts	• Repair or replace shocks or mountings
	• Loose or worn steering or suspension parts	• Tighten or replace as necessary
	• Loose or worn wheel bearings	• Adjust or replace bearings
	• Incorrect steering gear adjustments	• Adjust steering gear
	• Incorrect front wheel alignment	• Correct front wheel alignment
Tire wear	• Improper tire pressure	• Inflate tires to recommended pressures
	• Failure to rotate tires	• Rotate tires
	• Brakes grabbing	• Adjust or repair brakes
	• Incorrect front wheel alignment	• Align incorrect angles
	• Broken or damaged steering and suspension parts	• Repair or replace defective parts
	• Wheel runout	• Replace faulty wheel
	• Excessive speed on turns	• Make driver aware of conditions
Vehicle leads to one side	• Improper tire pressures	• Inflate tires to recommended pressures
	• Front tires with uneven tread depth, wear pattern, or different cord design (i.e., one bias ply and one belted or radial tire on front wheels)	• Install tires of same cord construction and reasonably even tread depth, design, and wear pattern
	• Incorrect front wheel alignment	• Align incorrect angles
	• Brakes dragging	• Adjust or repair brakes
	• Pulling due to uneven tire construction	• Replace faulty tire

Troubleshooting the Power Steering Gear

Problem	Cause	Solution
Hissing noise in steering gear	• There is some noise in all power steering systems. One of the most common is a hissing sound most evident at standstill parking. There is no relationship between this noise and performance of the steering. Hiss may be expected when steering wheel is at end of travel or when slowly turning at standstill.	• Slight hiss is normal and in no way affects steering. Do not replace valve unless hiss is extremely objectionable. A replacement valve will also exhibit slight noise and is not always a cure. Investigate clearance around flexible coupling rivets. Be sure steering shaft and gear are aligned so flexible coupling rotates in a flat plane and is not distorted as shaft rotates. Any metal-to-metal

Troubleshooting the Power Steering Gear (cont.)

Problem	Cause	Solution
Hissing noise in steering gear cont.		contacts through flexible coupling will transmit valve hiss into passenger compartment through the steering column.
Rattle or chuckle noise in steering gear	• Gear loose on frame	• Check gear-to-frame mounting screws. Tighten screws to 88 N·m (65 foot pounds) torque.
	• Steering linkage looseness	• Check linkage pivot points for wear. Replace if necessary.
	• Pressure hose touching other parts of car	• Adjust hose position. Do not bend tubing by hand.
	• Loose pitman shaft over center adjustment **NOTE:** A slight rattle may occur on turns because of increased clearance off the "high point." This is normal and clearance must not be reduced below specified limits to eliminate this slight rattle.	• Adjust to specifications
	• Loose pitman arm	• Tighten pitman arm nut to specifications
Squawk noise in steering gear when turning or recovering from a turn	• Damper O-ring on valve spool cut	• Replace damper O-ring
Poor return of steering wheel to center	• Tires not properly inflated	• Inflate to specified pressure
	• Lack of lubrication in linkage and ball joints	• Lube linkage and ball joints
	• Lower coupling flange rubbing against steering gear adjuster plug	• Loosen pinch bolt and assemble properly
	• Steering gear to column misalignment	• Align steering column
	• Improper front wheel alignment	• Check and adjust as necessary
	• Steering linkage binding	• Replace pivots
	• Ball joints binding	• Replace ball joints
	• Steering wheel rubbing against housing	• Align housing
	• Tight or frozen steering shaft bearings	• Replace bearings
	• Sticking or plugged valve spool	• Remove and clean or replace valve
	• Steering gear adjustments over specifications	• Check adjustment with gear out of car. Adjust as required.
	• Kink in return hose	• Replace hose
Car leads to one side or the other (keep in mind road condition and wind. Test car in both directions on flat road)	• Front end misaligned	• Adjust to specifications
	• Unbalanced steering gear valve **NOTE:** If this is cause, steering effort will be very light in direction of lead and normal or heavier in opposite direction	• Replace valve
Momentary increase in effort when turning wheel fast to right or left	• Low oil level	• Add power steering fluid as required
	• Pump belt slipping	• Tighten or replace belt
	• High internal leakage	• Check pump pressure. (See pressure test)
Steering wheel surges or jerks when turning with engine running especially during parking	• Low oil level	• Fill as required
	• Loose pump belt	• Adjust tension to specification
	• Steering linkage hitting engine oil pan at full turn	• Correct clearance
	• Insufficient pump pressure	• Check pump pressure. (See pressure test). Replace relief valve if defective.

Troubleshooting the Power Steering Gear (cont.)

Problem	Cause	Solution
Steering wheel surges or jerks when turning with engine running especially during parking cont.	• Pump flow control valve sticking	• Inspect for varnish or damage, replace if necessary
Excessive wheel kickback or loose steering	• Air in system	• Add oil to pump reservoir and bleed by operating steering. Check hose connectors for proper torque and adjust as required.
	• Steering gear loose on frame	• Tighten attaching screws to specified torque
	• Steering linkage joints worn enough to be loose	• Replace loose pivots
	• Worn poppet valve	• Replace poppet valve
	• Loose thrust bearing preload adjustment	• Adjust to specification with gear out of vehicle
	• Excessive overcenter lash	• Adjust to specification with gear out of car
Hard steering or lack of assist	• Loose pump belt	• Adjust belt tension to specification
	• Low oil level **NOTE:** Low oil level will also result in excessive pump noise	• Fill to proper level. If excessively low, check all lines and joints for evidence of external leakage. Tighten loose connectors.
	• Steering gear to column misalignment	• Align steering column
	• Lower coupling flange rubbing against steering gear adjuster plug	• Loosen pinch bolt and assemble properly
	• Tires not properly inflated	• Inflate to recommended pressure
Foamy milky power steering fluid, low fluid level and possible low pressure	• Air in the fluid, and loss of fluid due to internal pump leakage causing overflow	• Check for leak and correct. Bleed system. Extremely cold temperatures will cause system aeriation should the oil level be low. If oil level is correct and pump still foams, remove pump from vehicle and separate reservoir from housing. Check welsh plug and housing for cracks. If plug is loose or housing is cracked, replace housing.
Low pressure due to steering pump	• Flow control valve stuck or inoperative	• Remove burrs or dirt or replace. Flush system.
	• Pressure plate not flat against cam ring	• Correct
Low pressure due to steering gear	• Pressure loss in cylinder due to worn piston ring or badly worn housing bore	• Remove gear from car for disassembly and inspection of ring and housing bore
	• Leakage at valve rings, valve body-to-worm seal	• Remove gear from car for disassembly and replace seals

Troubleshooting the Power Steering Pump

Problem	Cause	Solution
Chirp noise in steering pump	• Loose belt	• Adjust belt tension to specification
Belt squeal (particularly noticeable at full wheel travel and stand still parking)	• Loose belt	• Adjust belt tension to specification

Troubleshooting the Power Steering Pump (cont.)

Problem	Cause	Solution
Growl noise in steering pump	• Excessive back pressure in hoses or steering gear caused by restriction	• Locate restriction and correct. Replace part if necessary.
Growl noise in steering pump (particularly noticeable at stand still parking)	• Scored pressure plates, thrust plate or rotor • Extreme wear of cam ring	• Replace parts and flush system • Replace parts
Groan noise in steering pump	• Low oil level • Air in the oil. Poor pressure hose connection.	• Fill reservoir to proper level • Tighten connector to specified torque. Bleed system by operating steering from right to left—full turn.
Rattle noise in steering pump	• Vanes not installed properly • Vanes sticking in rotor slots	• Install properly • Free up by removing burrs, varnish, or dirt
Swish noise in steering pump	• Defective flow control valve	• Replace part
Whine noise in steering pump	• Pump shaft bearing scored	• Replace housing and shaft. Flush system.
Hard steering or lack of assist	• Loose pump belt • Low oil level in reservoir **NOTE:** Low oil level will also result in excessive pump noise • Steering gear to column misalignment • Lower coupling flange rubbing against steering gear adjuster plug • Tires not properly inflated	• Adjust belt tension to specification • Fill to proper level. If excessively low, check all lines and joints for evidence of external leakage. Tighten loose connectors. • Align steering column • Loosen pinch bolt and assemble properly • Inflate to recommended pressure
Foaming milky power steering fluid, low fluid level and possible low pressure	• Air in the fluid, and loss of fluid due to internal pump leakage causing overflow	• Check for leaks and correct. Bleed system. Extremely cold temperatures will cause system aeriation should the oil level be low. If oil level is correct and pump still foams, remove pump from vehicle and separate reservoir from body. Check welsh plug and body for cracks. If plug is loose or body is cracked, replace body.
Low pump pressure	• Flow control valve stuck or inoperative • Pressure plate not flat against cam ring	• Remove burrs or dirt or replace. Flush system. • Correct
Momentary increase in effort when turning wheel fast to right or left	• Low oil level in pump • Pump belt slipping • High internal leakage	• Add power steering fluid as required • Tighten or replace belt • Check pump pressure. (See pressure test)
Steering wheel surges or jerks when turning with engine running especially during parking	• Low oil level • Loose pump belt • Steering linkage hitting engine oil pan at full turn • Insufficient pump pressure • Sticking flow control valve	• Fill as required • Adjust tension to specification • Correct clearance • Check pump pressure. (See pressure test). Replace flow control valve if defective. • Inspect for varnish or damage, replace if necessary

Troubleshooting the Power Steering Gear (cont.)

Problem	Cause	Solution
Excessive wheel kickback or loose steering	• Air in system	• Add oil to pump reservoir and bleed by operating steering. Check hose connectors for proper torque and adjust as required.
Low pump pressure	• Extreme wear of cam ring	• Replace parts. Flush system.
	• Scored pressure plate, thrust plate, or rotor	• Replace parts. Flush system.
	• Vanes not installed properly	• Install properly
	• Vanes sticking in rotor slots	• Freeup by removing burrs, varnish, or dirt
	• Cracked or broken thrust or pressure plate	• Replace part

hammer, which may cause the column to collapse.

6. Install the steering wheel so that the punchmarks are aligned. Tighten the steering wheel attaching nut to 51–54 ft. lbs. for 1970-79 models; 29–36 ft. lbs. (39–49 Nm) on 1980-86 models (720-D series); and 22–29 ft. lbs. (29–39 Nm) on 1986-89 models (D21-D series).
7. Install the hor pad.

Turn Signal and Dimmer Switch

REMOVAL AND INSTALLATION

1970-79 Models

1. Disconnect the negative battery cable.
2. Remove the steering wheel.

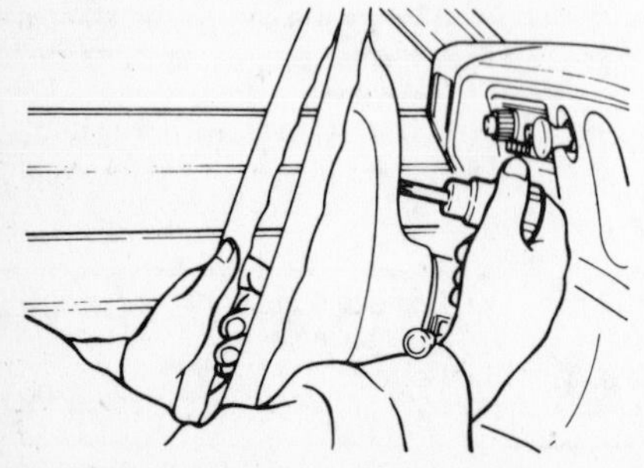

Removing the horn pad from the steering wheel

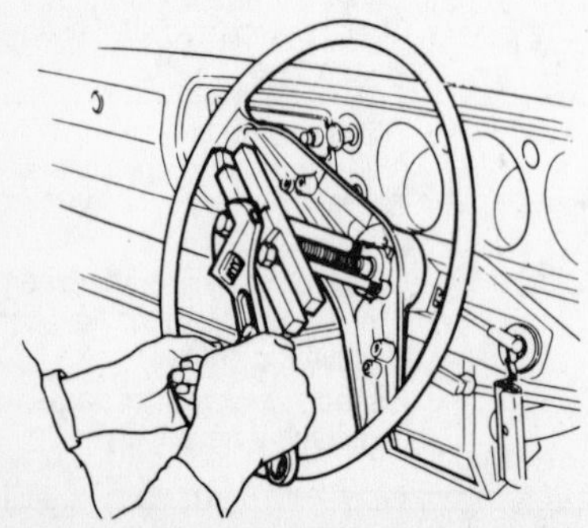

Removing the steering wheel with a puller

3. Disconnect the wiring harness from the clip which retains it to the lower instrument panel.
4. Disconnect the multi-connector and lead wire from the instrument panel wiring harness.
5. Remove the steering column shell covers (upper and lower).
6. Loosen the 2 screws attaching the switch assembly to the steering column jacket and remove the switch assembly.
7. Install the turn signal and dimmer switch and connect the electrical leads.
8. Install the steering column covers and the steering wheel.

Combination Switch

REMOVAL AND INSTALLATION

1980-89

1. Disconnect the negative battery cable.
2. Unscrew the two retaining bolts and remove the steering column garnish.
3. Remove the upper and lower steering column covers.
4. Remove the steering wheel as detailed previously.
5. Trace the switch wiring harness to the multi-connector. Push in the lock levers and pull apart the connector.
6. Unscrew the mounting screws and remove the switch.

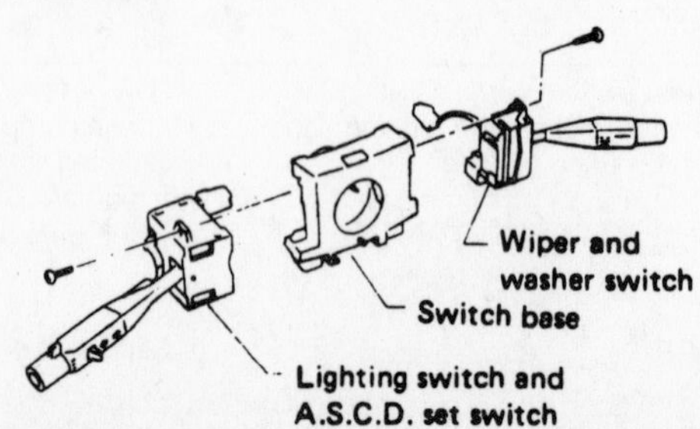

Switches can be removed without removing the switch base

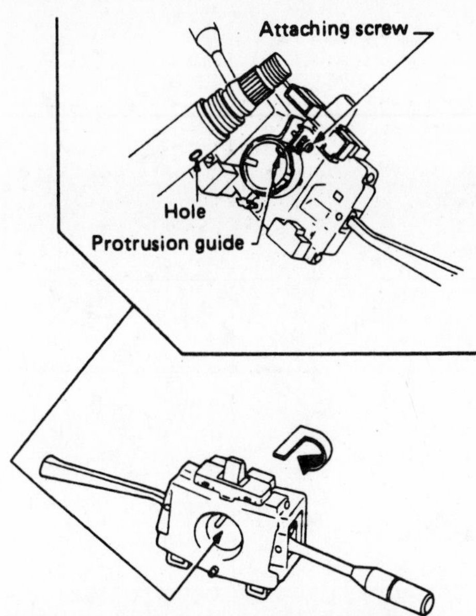

Combination switch installation—1980–89

7. Install the switch and tighten the mounting screws. Be sure to align the protrusion on the switch body with the hole in the steering column.
8. Connect the switch multi-connector.
9. Install the steering wheel and column covers. Connect the negative battery cable.

NOTE: *On 1986-89 models (D21-D series), the lighting switch, wiper and washer switch and the A.S.C.D. switch can be replaced without removing the combination switch base.*

Ignition Switch

REMOVAL AND INSTALLATION

1970-79

1. Disconnect the negative cable from the battery.
2. Unscrew and remove the escutcheon from the front of the ignition switch.
3. Remove the ignition switch and wiring harness with spacer from the steering shell cover.
4. Disconnect the wiring connector from the back of the ignition switch.
5. Install the ignition switch and connect the electrical lead.
6. Screw the escutcheon onto the switch and connect the battery cable.

Ignition Lock/Switch

REMOVAL AND INSTALLATION

1980-89

1. Disconnect the battery ground cable.
2. Remove the steering wheel and the column covers.

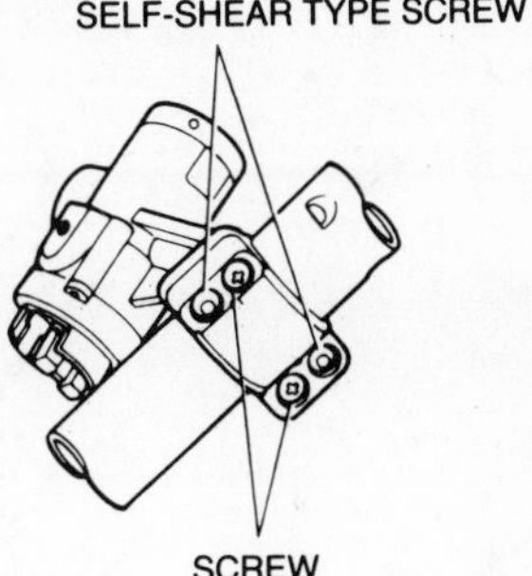

Ignition lock screws

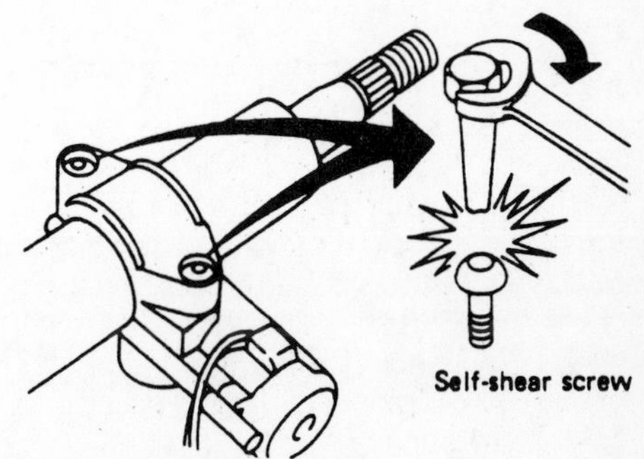

Breaking off the shear screws

3. Drill out the shear bolts holding the lock assembly in place and remove the conventional bolts.
4. Disconnect the wiring from the switch and remove the assembly.
5. Unscrew the retaining bolts in the lock cylinder and separate the switch from the lock.
6. Connect the switch to the lock cylinder and tighten the retaining screws.
7. Make sure that the hole in the column and the mating part of the lock cylinder are aligned. Install new shear bolts and break off their heads.
8. Connect the electrical lead to the switch and then install the column covers.
9. Install the steering wheel and connect the battery cable.

Steering Column

REMOVAL AND INSTALLATION

1970-79 Models

1. Disconnect the negative battery cable.
2. Remove the steering wheel.
3. Remove the upper and lower steering column shell covers.
4. Remove the turn signal switch assembly.
5. Remove the 2 column clamp bolts.
6. Remove the 4 bolts securing the steering column grommet to the instrument panel and remove the steering column.

1. Steering wheel
2. Column clamp
3. Post grommet
4. Steering column jacket
5. Steering column shaft
6. Knuckle arm
7. Idler arm assembly
8. Cross rod socket
9. Cross rod
10. Steering gear assembly
11. Steering gear arm
12. Side rod
13. Knuckle arm

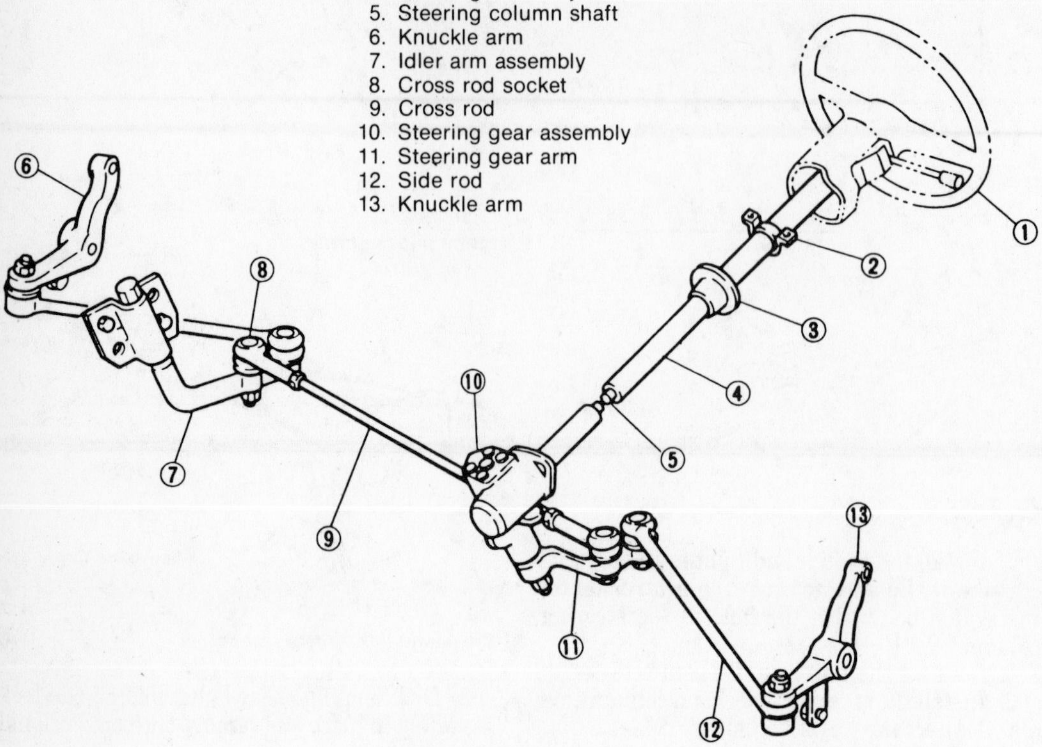

Steering system—1970–79

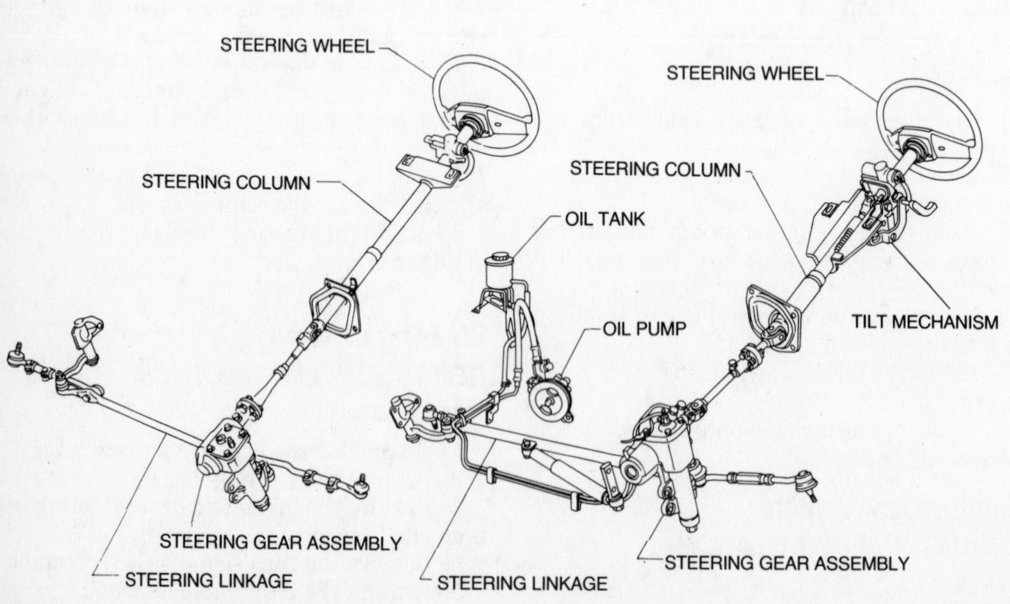

Steering system—1980–86 (720-D series)

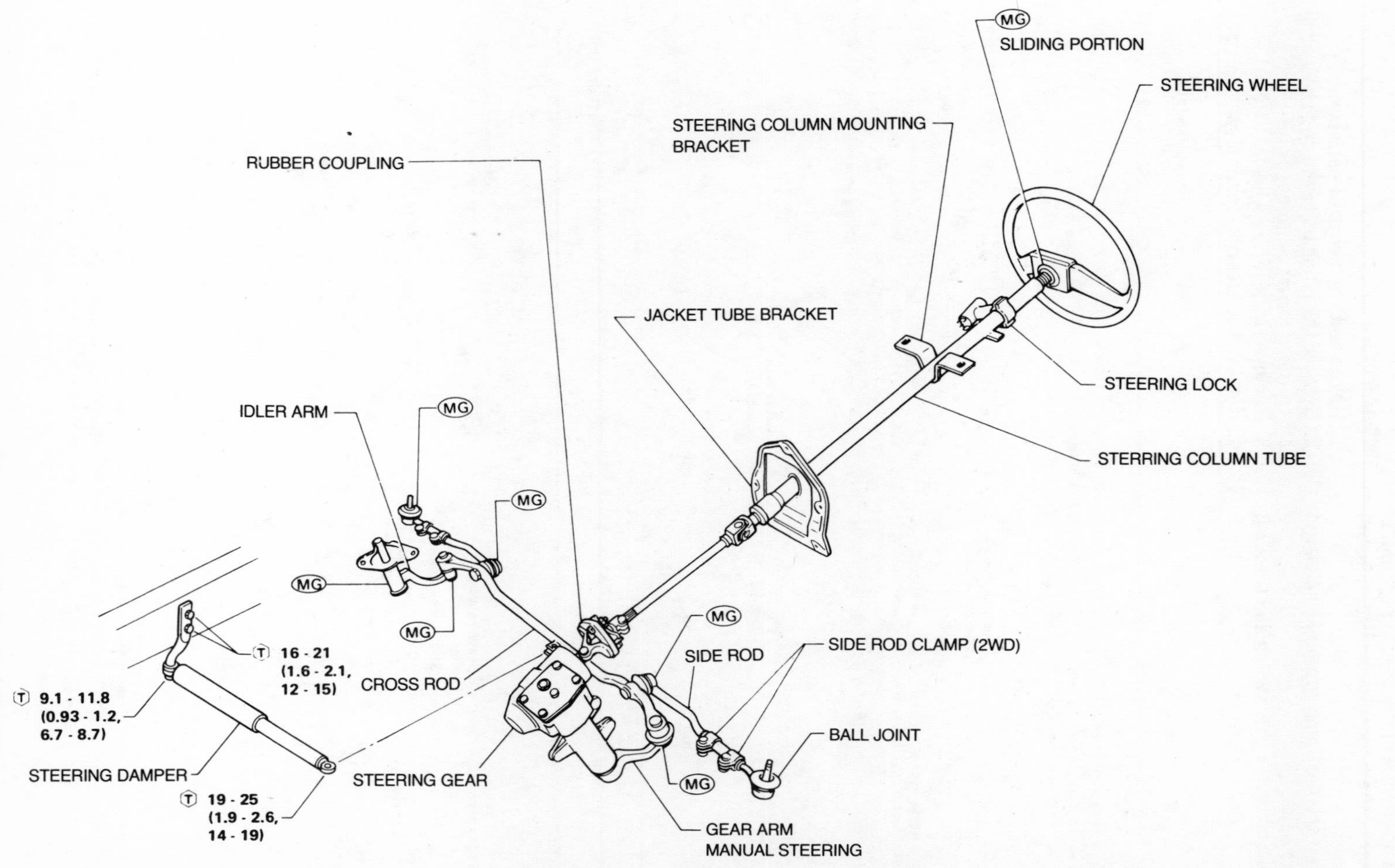

Steering system—1986–89 (D21-D series)

7. Set the front wheels in the straight-ahead position and make sure that the punchmark on the upper end surface of the steering column is at the center of the upper side and then install the column.
8. Tighten the 4 column grommet bolts and the 2 clamp bolts.
9. Install the turn signal switch and the shell covers.
10. Install the steering wheel and connect the battery cable.

1980-82 Models

1. Disconnect the negative battery cable.
2. Remove the pinch bolt securing the worm shaft to the steering coupling.
3. Remove the steering wheel.
4. Remove the steering column shell covers.

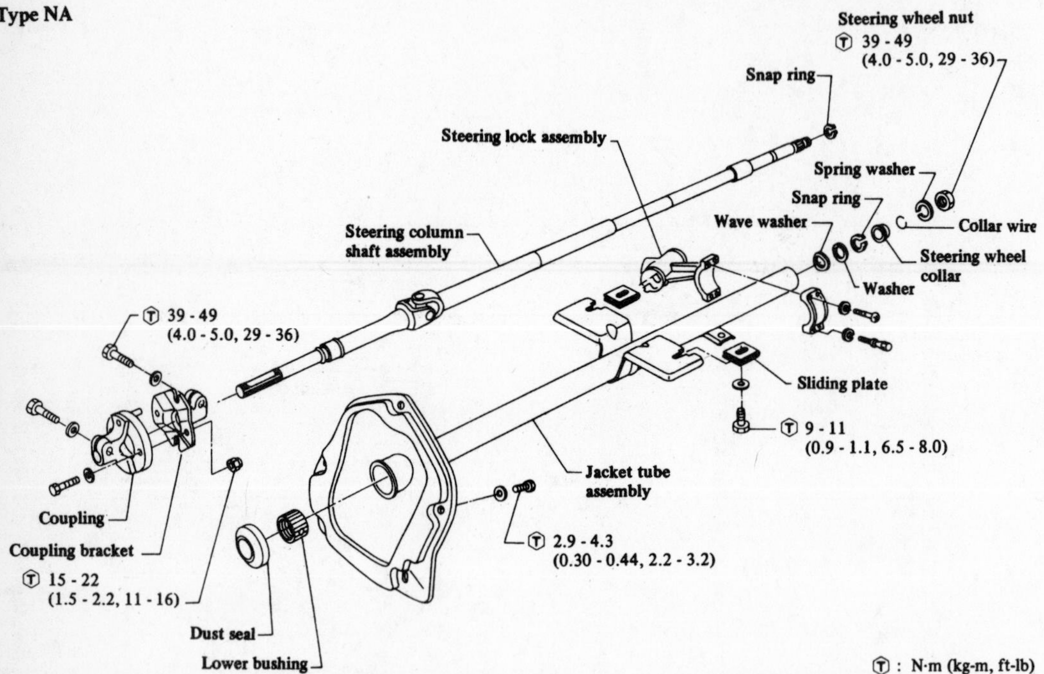

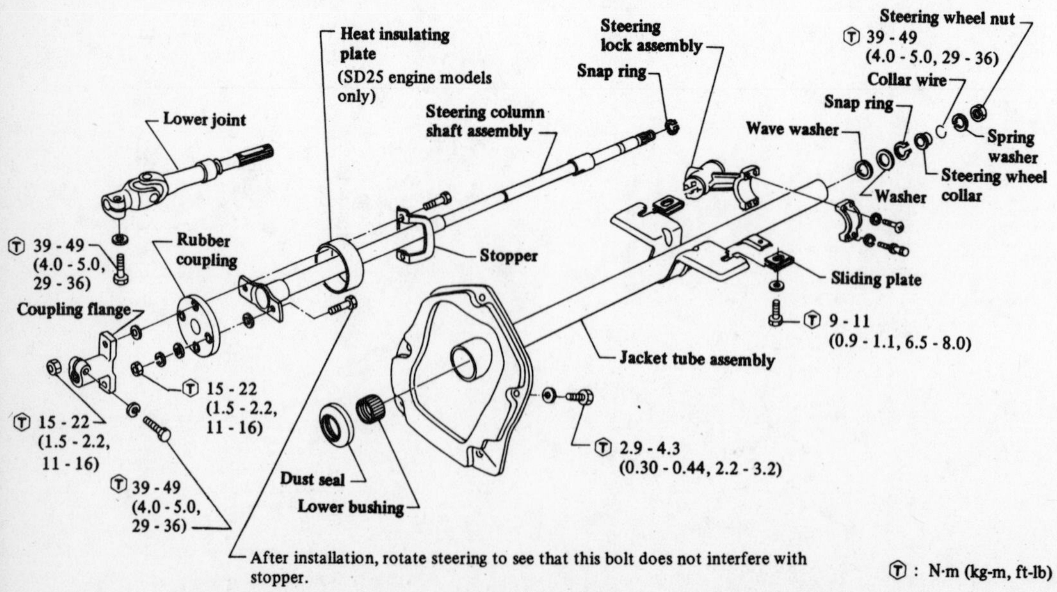

Exploded view of the steering column (non-tilt)—1980–86 (720-D series)

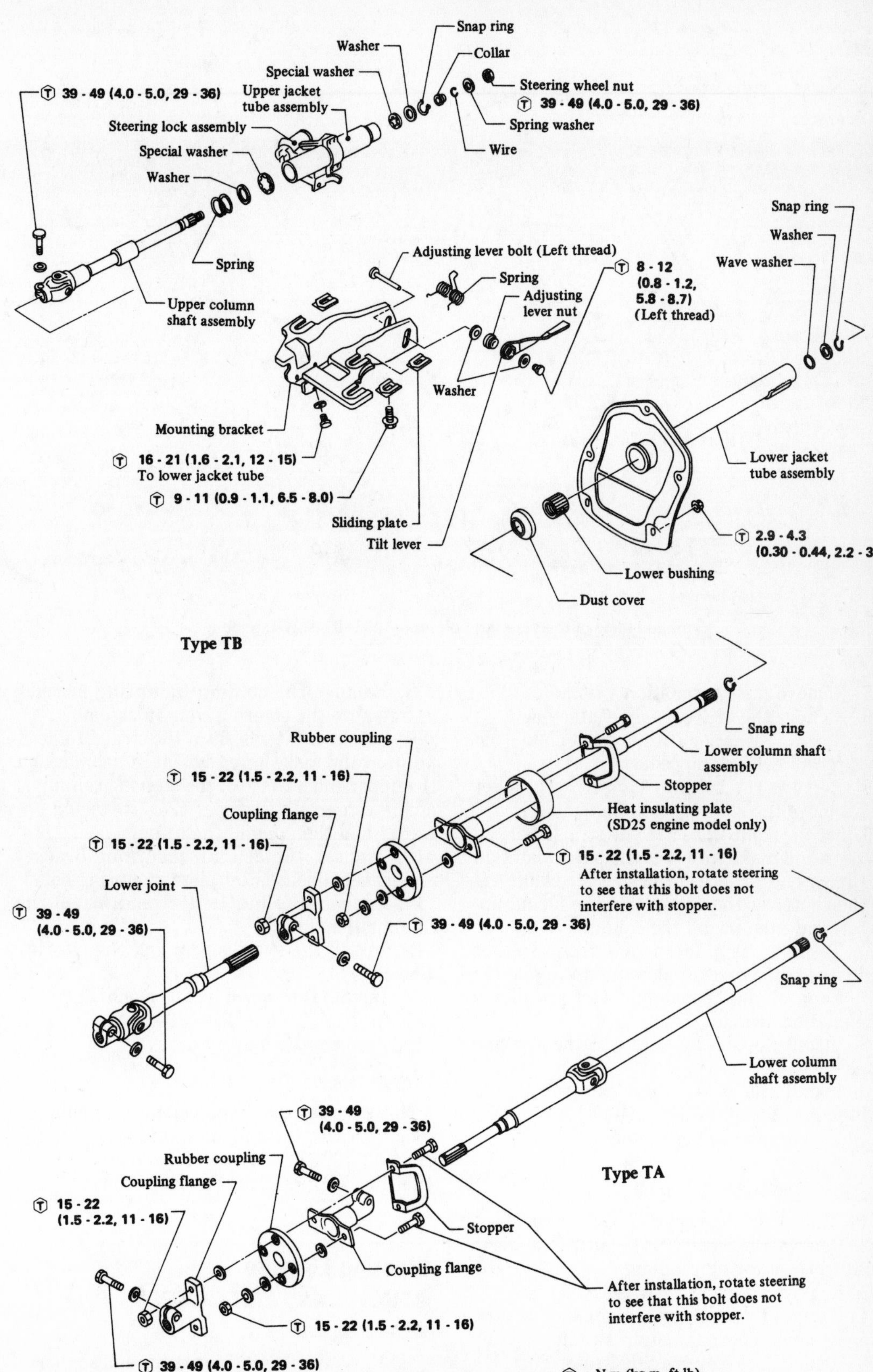

Exploded view of the steering column (tilt)—1980–86 (720-D series)

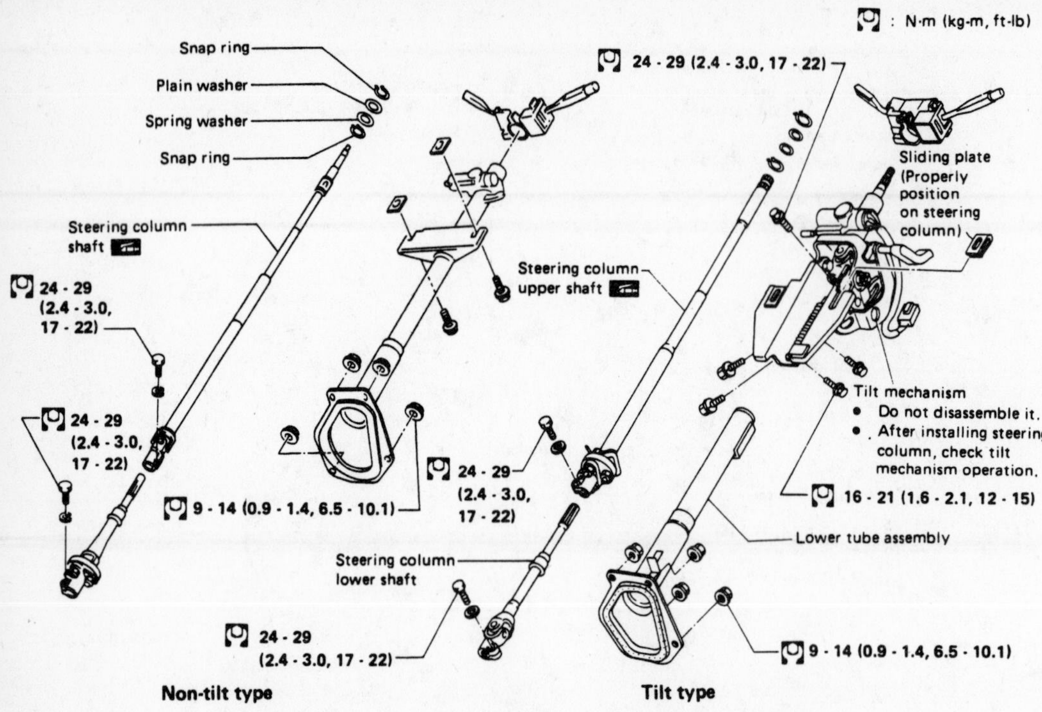

Exploded view of the steering column—1986–89 (D21-D series)

5. Remove the combination switch.
6. Remove the driver's side heater duct.
7. Remove the jacket tube bracket plate from the firewall behind the pedals.
8. Remove the column mounting bracket and remove the steering column assembly.
9. Set the front wheels in the straight-ahead position and make sure that the punchmark on the upper end surface of the steering column is at the center of the upper side (its facing upward!) and then install the column.
10. Tighten the column mounting bracket and jacket tube bracket plate mounting bolts.
11. Connect the heater duct and install the combination switch.
12. Install the sheel covers and the steering wheel.
13. Install the worm shaft pinch bolt and tighten it to 29–36 ft. lbs. (39–49 Nm).
14. Connect the battery cable.

1983-86 Models (720-D Series)

1. Disconnect the negative battery cable.
2. Remove the pinch bolt securing the worm shaft to the steering coupling.
3. Remove the steering wheel.
4. Remove the steering column shell covers.
5. Remove the combination switch.
6. Remove the driver's side heater duct.
7. Remove the jacket tube bracket plate from the firewall behind the pedals.
8. Remove the column mounting bracket and remove the steering column assembly.
9. Set the front wheels in the straight-ahead position and make sure that the punchmark on the upper end surface of the steering column is at the center of the upper side (its facing upward!) and then install the column.
10. Tighten the column mounting bracket and jacket tube bracket plate mounting bolts.
11. Connect the heater duct and install the combination switch.
12. Install the sheel covers and the steering wheel.
13. Install the worm shaft pinch bolt and tighten it to 29–36 ft. lbs. (39–49 Nm).
14. Connect the battery cable.

1986-89 Models (D21-D Series)

Nissan offers no removal and installation procedures for these models. Please refer to the 1984-86 720-D series procedures as a general guideline and refer to the illustrations.

Steering Linkage

REMOVAL AND INSTALLATION

1970-79 Models

1. Raise the front of the truck and support it with jackstands placed under the frame.
2. Remove the cotter pins and nuts securing

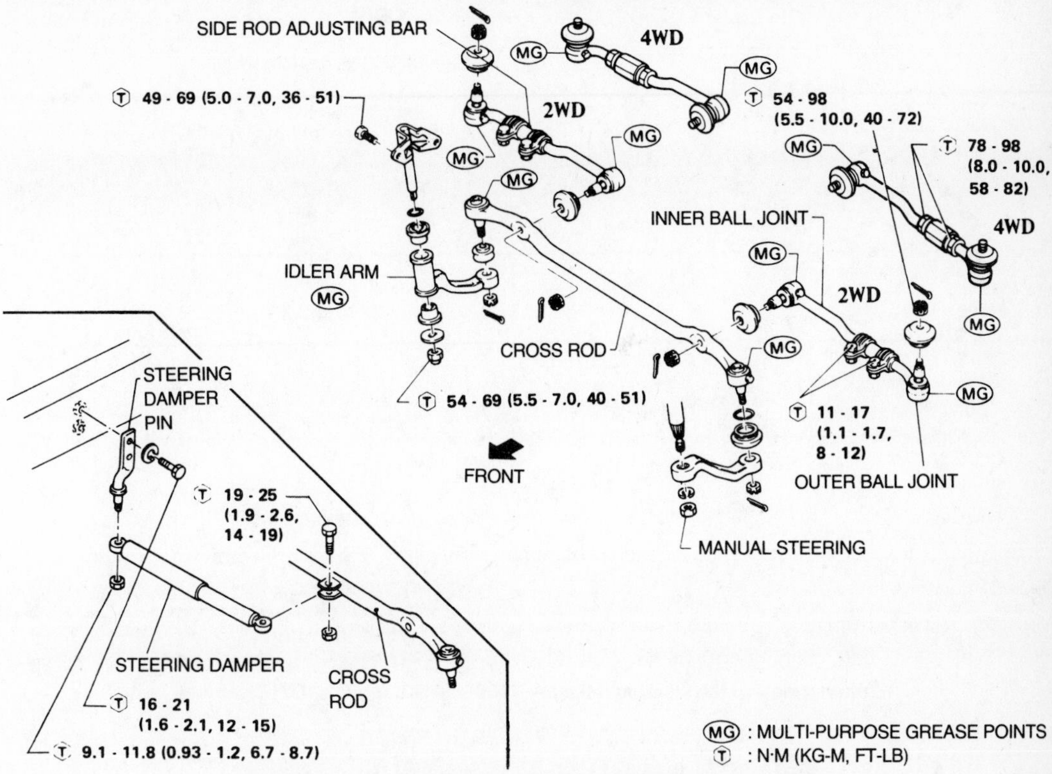

SIDE ROD ADJUSTING BAR
4WD
MG
MG
T 49 - 69 (5.0 - 7.0, 36 - 51)
T 54 - 98
(5.5 - 10.0, 40 - 72)
2WD
MG
MG
MG
T 78 - 98
(8.0 - 10.0,
58 - 82)
MG
INNER BALL JOINT
4WD
MG
IDLER ARM
MG
2WD
MG
CROSS ROD
MG
STEERING
DAMPER
PIN
T 54 - 69 (5.5 - 7.0, 40 - 51)
MG
T 11 - 17
(1.1 - 1.7,
8 - 12)
FRONT
OUTER BALL JOINT
T 19 - 25
(1.9 - 2.6,
14 - 19)
MANUAL STEERING
STEERING DAMPER
CROSS
ROD
T 16 - 21
(1.6 - 2.1, 12 - 15)
T 9.1 - 11.8 (0.93 - 1.2, 6.7 - 8.7)
MG : MULTI-PURPOSE GREASE POINTS
T : N·M (KG-M, FT-LB)

Exploded view of the steering linkage—1980–86 (720- D series)

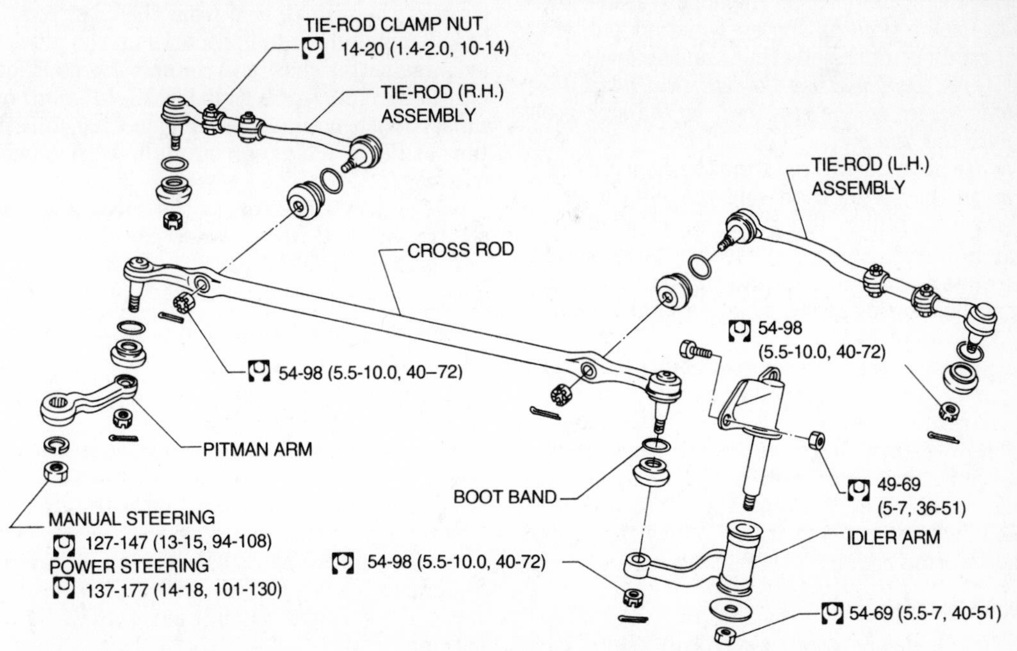

Exploded view of the steering linkage—1986–89 2wd models (D21-D series)

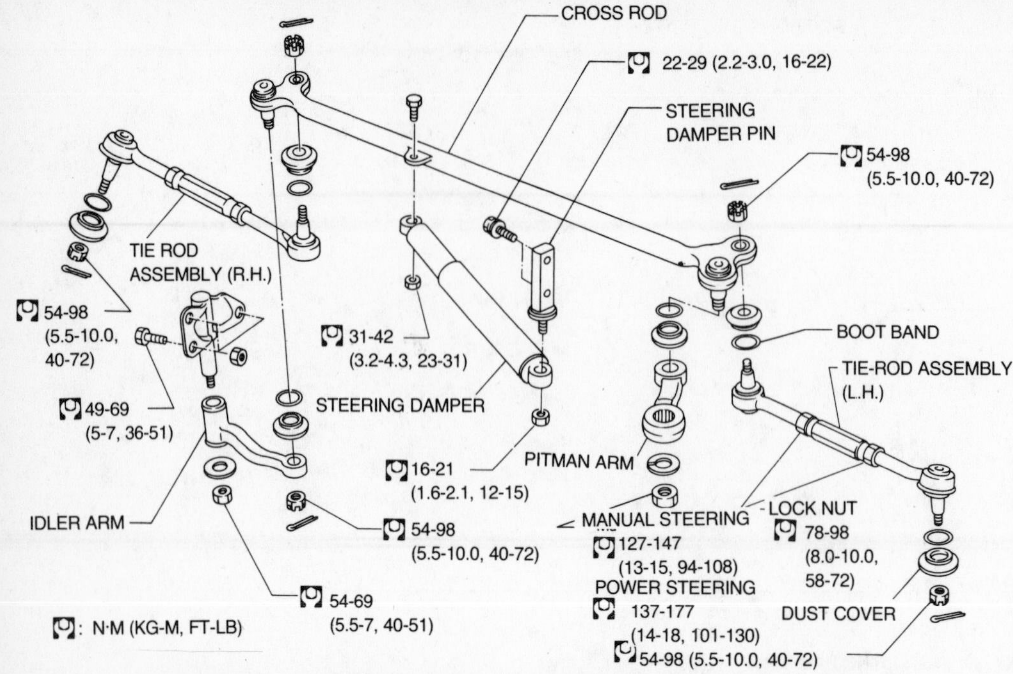

Exploded view of the steering linkage—1986–89 4wd models (D21-D series)

the side rod ball studs to the steering knuckle/spindle arms.

3. Use a puller to disconnect the side rod ball studs from the steering knuckle arms. If a puller is not available, strike the side of the steering knuckle arm boss with a hammer, backing it up with a heavy hammer on the opposite side, and at the same time having an assistant pull the ball stud out of the steering knuckle arm.

NOTE: *Do not strike the ball stud head, the ball socket on the side rod, or the side rod with the hammer.*

4. Remove the nut securing the steering gear arm on the sector shaft and remove the gear arm with a puller. If a puller is not available, and the steering gear arm need not be removed, disconnect the side arm and tie rod ball studs from the steering gear arm in the same manner as outlined in Step 3.

5. Remove the idler arm assembly from the frame by unscrewing the two attaching nuts.

6. Install the steering linkage in the reverse order of removal. Tighten the ball stud nuts to 40–55 ft. lbs., idler arm assembly attaching nuts to 23–27 ft. lbs., and the tie rod adjustment locknuts to 58–72 ft. lbs. Adjust the toe-in and steering angle.

1980-89 Models

NOTE: *Before working on any of the following steering linkage components, disconnect the battery cable, raise the front of the truck and support it with safety stands.*

PITMAN ARM

1. Remove the strut bar.
2. Loosen the pitman arm nut.
3. Using a tie rod end puller or the like, disconnect the pitman arm from the sector shaft.
4. Using a tie rod end puller or the like, disconnect the pitman arm from the cross rod.
5. To install, align the marks on the pitman arm and sector shaft and connect them. Tighten the nut to 94–108 ft. lbs. (127–147 Nm) on models with manual steering; or 101–130 ft. lbs. (137–177 Nm) on models with power steering.
6. Connect the arm to the cross rod and tighten the nut. Install a new cotter pin.
7. Install the strut bar.

TIE ROD

1. Using a tie rod end puller, disconnect the tie rod from the cross rod.
2. Using a tie rod end puller, disconnect the tie rod from the knuckle arm.
3. Remove the tie rod and remove the tie rod ends.
4. Screw the tie rod ends onto the tie rod. The tie rod length should be:

- 1980-86 2wd (720-D series): 13.07 in. (332mm).
- 1986-89 2wd (D21-D series): 13.54 in. (344mm).
- 1981-83 4wd: 10.83 in. (275mm).
- 1984-86 4wd (720-D series): 11.54 in. (293mm).

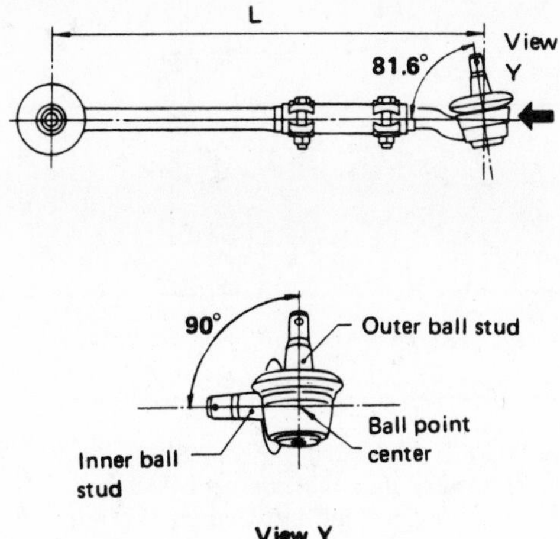

Tie rod length and angle measurement—1986–89 2wd mdoels; other years similar

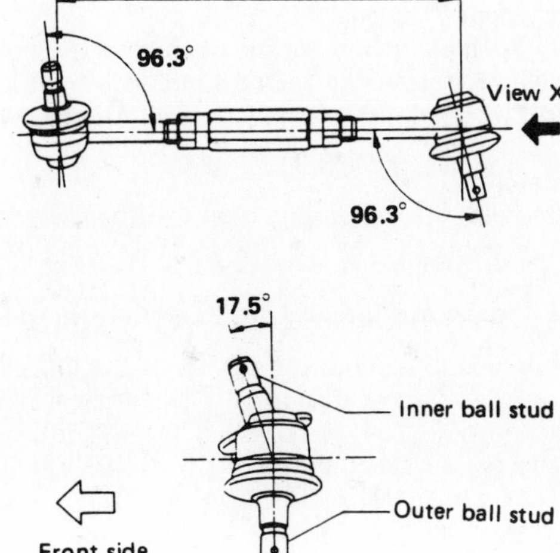

Tie rod length and angle measurement—1986–89 4wd models; other years similar

- 1986-89 4wd (D21-D series): 11.06 in. (281mm).

The remaining length of threads on both ends should always be equal. On 1986-89 models (D21-D series), the tie rod ends should always be screwed on at least 1.38 in. (35mm).

5. Turn the tie rod ends so they cross at about 90° (17.5° on 1986-89 4wd models). Tighten the clamp nuts to 8–12 ft. lbs. (11–17 Nm) on 1980-86 2wd models (720-D series); or 10–14 ft. lbs (14–20 Nm) on 1986-89 2wd models (D21-D series). Tighten the locknuts to 58–72 ft. lbs. (78–98 Nm) on all 4wd models.

6. Connect the tie rod to the knuckle arm and cross rod and tighten the mounting nuts to 40–72 ft. lbs. (54–98 Nm).

CROSS ROD

1. Disconnect the tie rod ends from the crossrod.
2. Using a tie rod end puller, disconnect the pitman arm from the cross rod.
3. Using a tie rod end puller, disconnect the idler arm from the cross rod.
4. Remove the rod and inspect it for cracks or other damage.
5. Connect the cross rod to the idler arm and tighten the nut 40–72 ft. lbs. (54–98 Nm).
6. Connect the cross rod to the pitman arm and tighten the nut to 40–72 ft. lbs. (54–98 Nm).
7. Connect the tie rod ends to the cross rod and tighten the nuts to 40–72 ft. lbs. (54–98 Nm).

STEERING DAMPER

1. Disconnect the steering damper at the cross rod.
2. Disconnect the damper at the frame and remove the damper with all washers and cushions.
3. Install the damper to the frame bracket and tighten the nut to 7–8 ft. lbs. (9–12 Nm) on 1981-86 models (720-D series), or 13–17 ft. lbs. (18–24 Nm) on 1986-89 models (D21-D series).
4. Connect the other end of the steering damper to the cross rod and tighten the nut to 14–19 ft. lbs. (19–25 Nm) on 1981-86 models (720-D series), or 27–36 ft. lbs. (37–49 Nm) on 1986-89 models (D21-D series).

IDLER ARM BRACKET

1. Disconnect the cross rod from the idler arm.
2. Remove the mounting bolts and remove the idler arm bracket with the arm attached.
3. Position the bracket and arm on the frame and tighten the bolts to 36–51 ft. lbs. (49–69 Nm) on 1981-86 models (720-D series), or 58–72 ft. lbs. (78–98 Nm) on 1986-89 models (D21-D series).
4. Connect the idler arm to the cross rod and tighten the nut to 40–72 ft. lbs. (54–98 Nm). Install a new cotter pin.

Manual Steering Gear

ADJUSTMENTS

Adjustments to the manual steering gear are not necessary during normal service. Adjustments are performed only as part of overhaul.

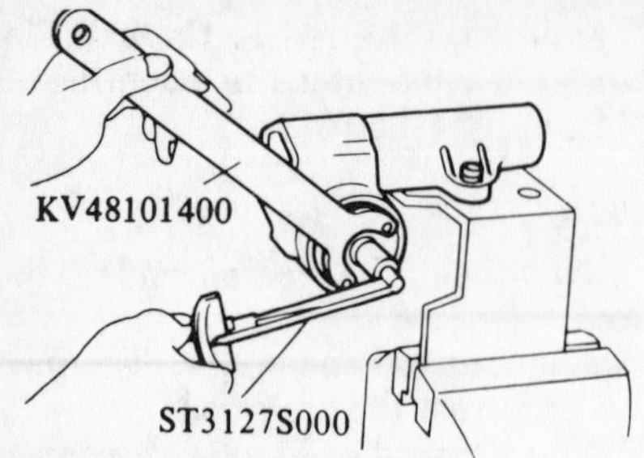

Measuring worm bearing preload

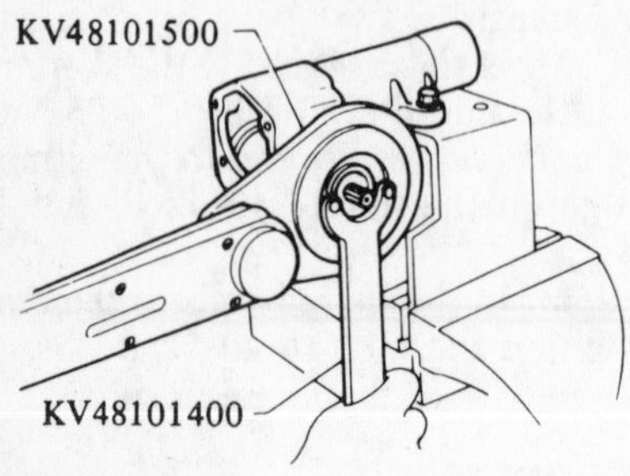

Tightening the locknut

Worm Bearing Preload

1. Mount the gear in a vise.
2. Using an inch lbs. torque wrench and spanner KV48101400, or its equivalent, rotate the worm shaft a few turns in each direction to settle the bearing and measure the existing preload.
3. If preload is not 1.7–5.2 inch lbs., loosen the locknut and turn the adjusting plug with the spanner, in a clockwise rotation ONLY. Never adjust preload by turning the adjusting plug counterclockwise! If preload cannot be obtained in this manner, rebuild the gear.
4. Apply liquid sealer on the shaft threads and tighten the locknut to 181–231 ft. lbs. (245–314 Nm).

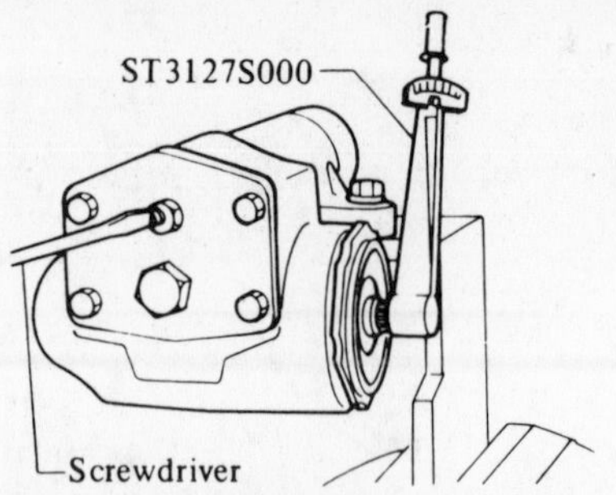

Measuring overcenter preload

Overcenter Preload

1. Mount the gear in a vise.
2. With an inch lb. torque wrench on the sector shaft, rotate the sector shaft lock-to-lock, counting the total number of turns. Divide the total by two and position the shaft at this midpoint.
3. Rotate the shaft one turn to either side of center using the torque wrench and noting the preload.
4. Adjust the preload by loosening the ad-

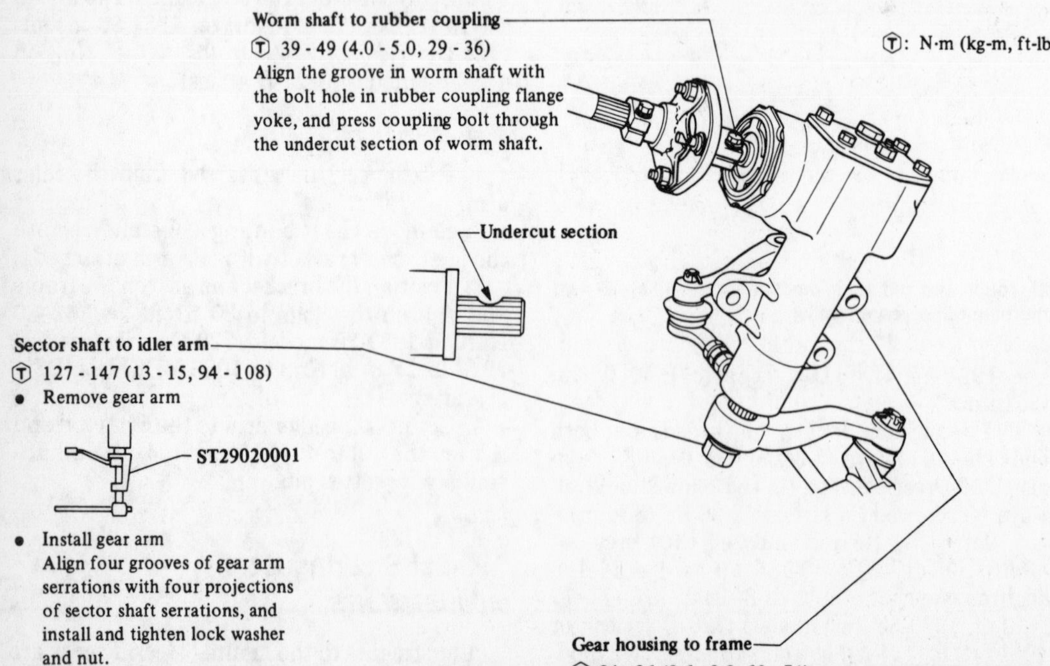

Typical manual steering gear assembly

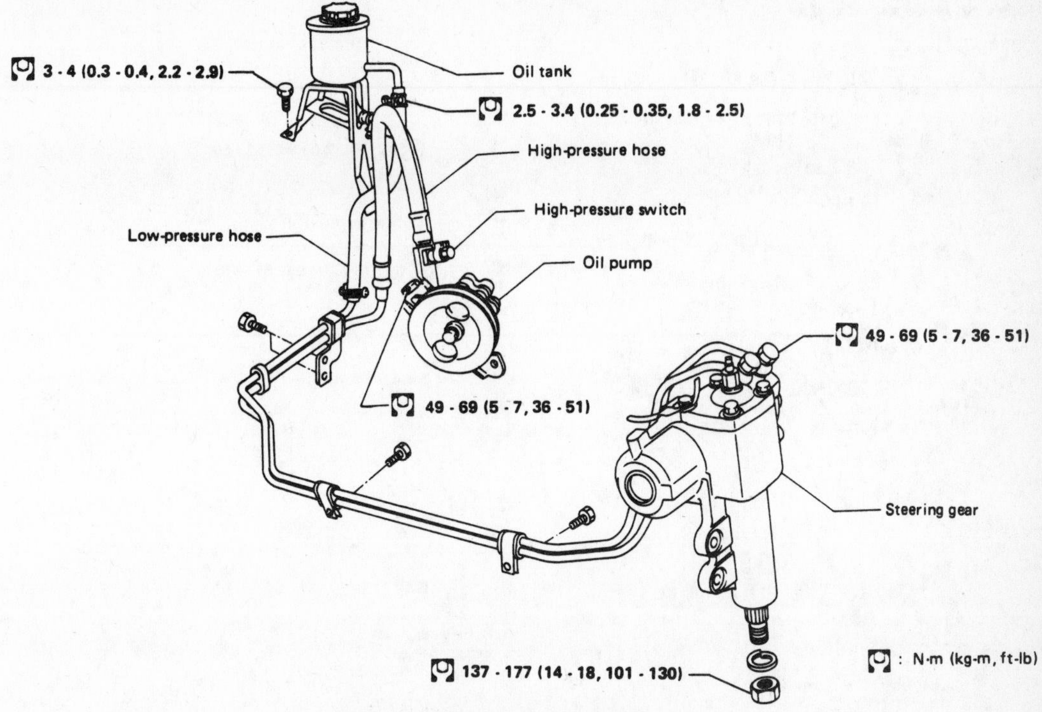

Typical power steering gear assembly

justing screw locknut and turning the adjusting screw in a clockwise rotation ONLY. Preload should be 5.2–8.7 inch lbs.

5. If adjustment will not correct preload, the unit must be rebuilt.

REMOVAL AND INSTALLATION

1. Raise and support the truck on jackstands.
2. Unbolt the wormshaft pinch bolt at the rubber coupling.
3. Matchmark the pitman arm and sector shaft, and with the wheels in a straight ahead position, remove the pitman arm with a puller.
4. Unbolt and remove the gear from the frame.
5. Install the gear and tighten the bolts to 62–71 ft. lbs. (84–96 Nm).
6. Press the pitman arm onto the sector shaft so that the marks are aligned and then tighten the nut to 94–108 ft. lbs. (127–147 Nm).
7. Slide the worm shaft into the coupling pinch bolt and tighten the bolt to 29-36 ft. lbs. (39–49 Nm) except on 1986-89 models (D21-D series) where it should be 17–22 ft. lbs. (24–29 Nm).

Power Steering Gear

ADJUSTMENT

Turning Torque

1. Mount the gear on a holding fixture in a vise.
2. Turn the stub shaft (the shaft that connects with the steering column) several turns in either direction.
3. Mount an inch lb. torque wrench on the stub shaft and turn it lock-to-lock, counting the total number of turns. Divide that number by 2

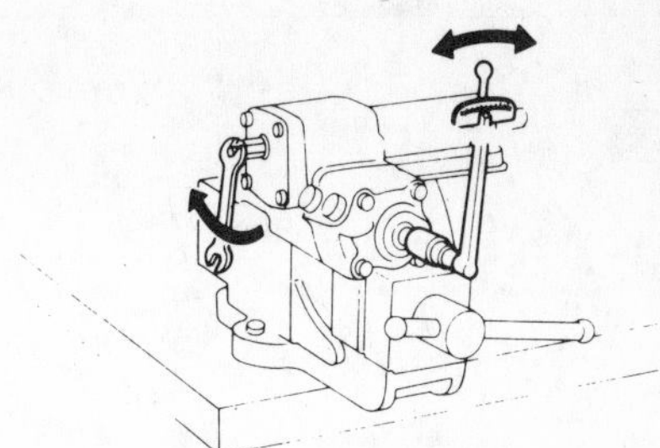

Measuring power steering gear turning torque

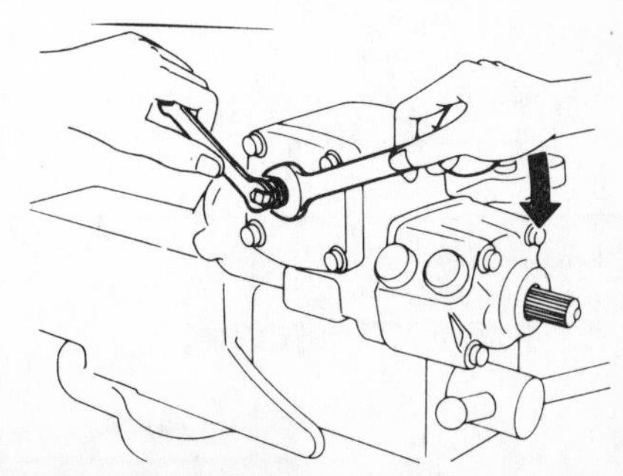

Adjusting turning torque

Models equipped with Z engine

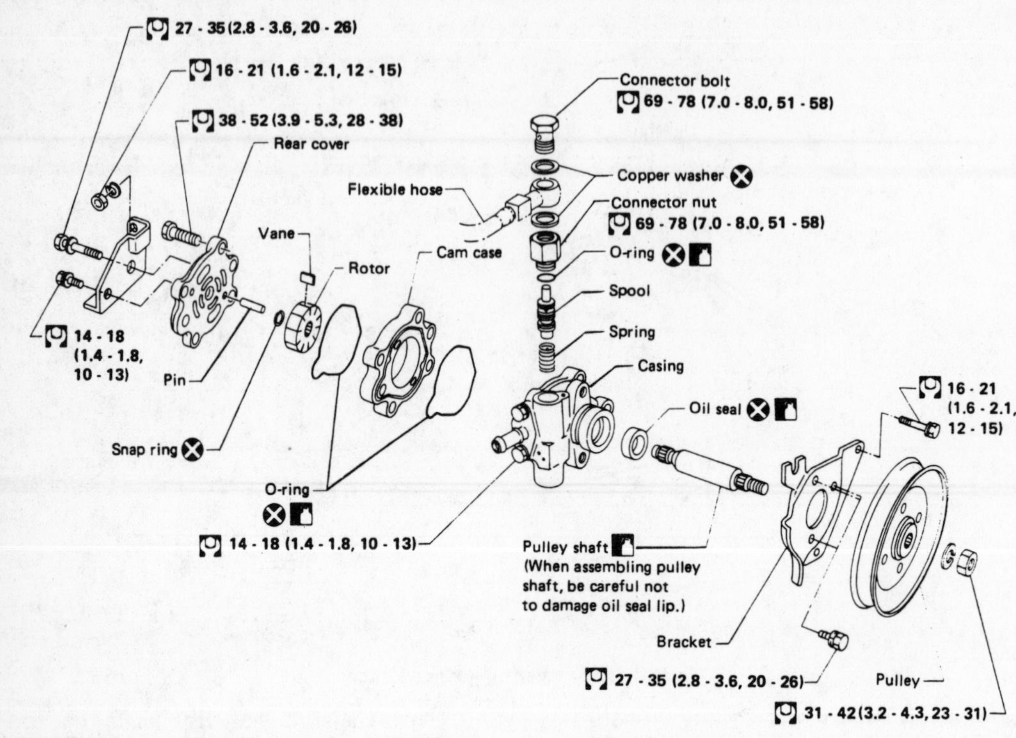

Models equipped with VG engine

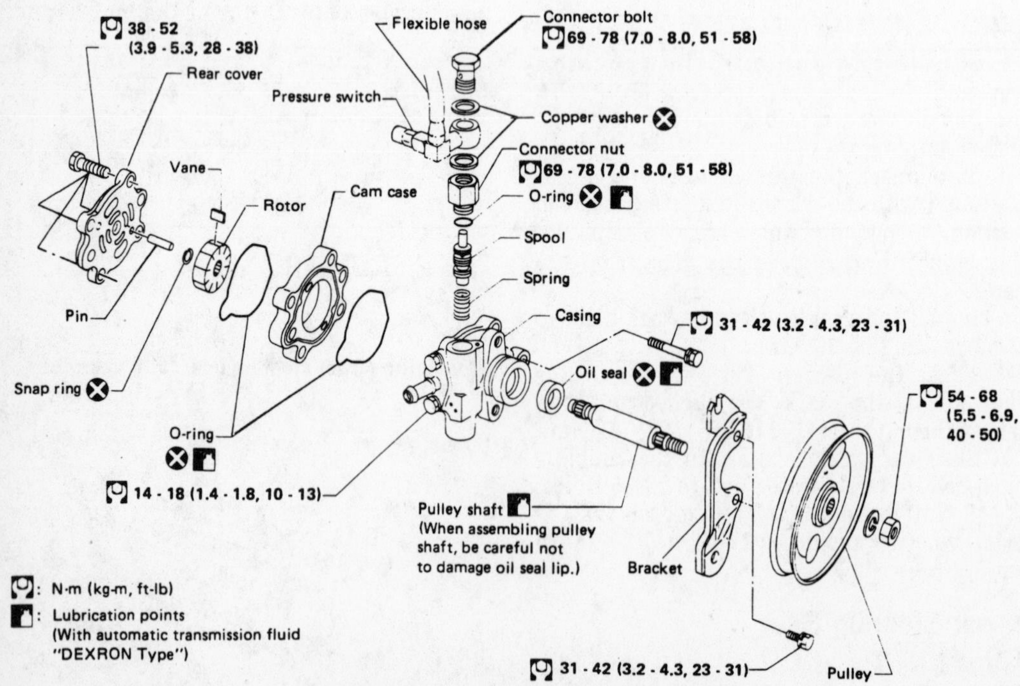

Exploded view of the power steering pump

Wheel Alignment Specifications

Year	Model	Caster (deg.)		Camber (deg.)		Toe-in (in.)	Steering Angle (deg.)	
		Range	Pref.	Range	Pref.		Inner	Outer
1970	Pick-Up	1⅙P–2½P	2P	¼P–2¼P	1¼P	0.125	36	31
1971	Pick-Up	1⅙P–2½P	2P	¼P–2¼P	1¼P	0.125	36	31
1972	Pick-Up	1⅙P–2½P	2P	¼P–2¼P	1¼P	0.125	36	31
1973	Pick-Up	1⅙P–2½P	2P	¼P–2¼P	1¼P	0.125	36	31
1974	Pick-Up	1⅙P–2½P	2P	¼P–2¼P	1¼P	0.125	36	31
1975	Pick-Up	1⅙P–2½P	2P	¼P–2¼P	1¼P	0.125	36	31
1976	Pick-Up	1⅙P–2½P	2P	¼P–2¼P	1¼P	0.125	36	31
1977	Pick-Up	1⅙P–2½P	2P	¼P–2¼P	1¼P	0.125	36	31
1978	Pick-Up	½P–2½P	1½P	¼P–1¼P	¾P	0.250	35	30.5
1979	Pick-Up	½P–2½P	1½P	¼P–1¼P	¾P	0.250	35	30.5
1980	Pick-Up	13/16P–1 13/16P	1 5/16P	0–1P	½P	0.250	35	31
1981	Pick-Up (2wd)	13/16P–1 13/16P	1 5/16P	0–1P	½P	0.250	35	31
	Pick-Up (4wd)	1 3/16P–2 3/16P	1 11/16P	0–1P	½P	0.250	31	28
1982	Pick-Up (2wd)	13/16P–1 13/16P	1 5/16P	0–1P	½P	0.250	35	31
	Pick-Up (4wd)	1 3/16P–2 3/16P	1 11/16P	0–1P	½P	0.250	31	28
1983	Pick-Up (2wd)	13/16P–1 13/16P	1 5/16P	0–1P	½P	0.250	35	31
	Pick-Up (4wd)	1 3/16P–2 3/16P	1 11/16P	0–1P	½P	0.250	31	28
1984	Pick-Up (2wd)	13/16P–1 13/16P	1 5/16P	0–1P	½P	①	35	31
	Pick-Up (4wd)	15/16P–1 15/16P	1 7/16P	1P–1 3/16P	1 1/16P	0.125	32	31
1985	Pick-Up (2wd)	13/16P–1 13/16P	1 5/16P	0–1P	½P	①	35	31
	Pick-Up (4wd)	15/16P–1 15/16P	1 7/16P	1P–1 3/16P	1 1/16P	0.125	32	31
1986 ②	Pick-Up (2wd)	13/16P–1 13/16P	1 5/16P	0–1P	½P	①	35	31
	Pick-Up (4wd)	15/16P–1 15/16P	1 7/16P	1P–1 3/16P	1 1/16P	0.125	32	31
1986 ③	Pick-Up (2wd)	⅛N–⅞P	½P	1/16N–15/16P	5/16P	④	37	34
	Pick-Up (4wd)	13/16P–1 13/16P	1 5/16P	3/16P–1 3/16P	11/16P	⑤	34 ⑥	32
1987	Pick-Up (2wd)	⅛N–⅞P	½P	1/16N–15/16P	5/16P	④	37	34
	Pick-Up (4wd)	13/16P–1 13/16P	1 5/16P	3/16P–1 3/16P	11/16P	⑤	34 ⑥	32
1988	Pick-Up (2wd)	⅛N–⅞P	½P	1/16N–15/16P	5/16P	④	37	34
	Pick-Up (4wd)	13/16P–1 13/16P	1 5/16P	3/16P–1 3/16P	11/16P	⑤	34 ⑥	32
1989	Pick-Up (2wd)	⅛N–⅞P	½P	1/16N–15/16P	5/16P	④	37	34
	Pick-Up (4wd)	13/16P–1 13/16P	1 5/16P	3/16P–1 3/16P	11/16P	⑤	34 ⑥	32

P Positive
N Negative
① Radial: 0.125
Bias: 0.250
② 720-D series
③ D21-D series
④ Radial: 0.08–0.16
Bias: 0.16–0.24
⑤ Radial: 0.12–0.20
Bias: 0.16–0.24
⑥ 31X10.5R15 tires: inner—28; outer—26

and position the torque wrench and shaft at the mid-point.

4. Measure the amount of force needed to turn the shaft past the midpoint in both directions. The force should be 3.5 inch lbs.

5. To correct the adjustment, loosen the locknut on the adjusting screw and turn the screw to give the correct torque. Tighten the locknut to 21–25 ft. lbs. (28–34 Nm) on all except 1986-89 models (D21-D series) where it should be 25–29 ft. lbs. (34–39 Nm).

REMOVAL AND INSTALLATION

1. Matchmark and remove the pitman arm from the sector shaft, using a puller such as special tool 290200001.

2. Matchmark and disconnect the steering stub shaft from the gear at the coupling.

3. Disconnect the fluid lines from the gear and cap the lines and openings in the gear.

4. Unbolt and remove the gear assembly from the frame.

5. When installing, observe the following torques:

- Gear housing-to-frame: 62–71 ft. lbs. (84–96 Nm).
- Steering stub shaft-to-coupling: 29–36 ft. lbs. (39–49 Nm) – except 1986-89 models (D21-D series); 17–22 ft. lbs. (24–29 Nm) – 1986-89 models (D21-D series).
- Pitman arm-to-sector shaft: 101–130 ft. lbs. (137–177 Nm).

Power Steering Pump

REMOVAL AND INSTALLATION

1. Remove the fan shroud.

2. Unfasten the nut from the center of the pump pulley.

NOTE: *Use the drive belt as a brake to keep the pulley from rotating.*

3. Remove the drive belt.

4. Remove the pulley and the bracketfrom the pump shaft.

5. Detach the intake and outlet hoses from the pump reservoir.

NOTE: *Tie the hose ends up high so the fluid cannot flow out of them. Drain or plug the pump to prevent fluid leakage.*

6. Remove the bolt from the rear mounting brace.

7. Remove the bracket bolts and then remove the pump.

8. Install the pump and tighten the pump pulley mounting bolt to 23–31 ft. lbs. (31–42 Nm).

9. Adjust the pump drive belt tension. The belt should deflect 8-10mm under thumb pressure applied midway between the air pump and power steering pump.

10. Fill the reservoir with Dexron®II automatic transmission fluid. Bleed the air from the system.

BLEEDING

1. Raise the front of the truck and support it securely with jackstands.

2. Fill the pump reservoir with Dexron®II automatic transmission fluid.

3. Rotate the steering wheel from lock-to-lock several times. Add fluid as necessary.

NOTE: *Never hold the steering wheel in the lock position for more than 15 seconds.*

4. Repeat Step 3 until the fluid level in the reservoir remains the same.

5. Start the engine. With the engine idling, turn the steering wheel from lock-to-lock several times.

6. Lower the front of the truck and repeat Step 5.

7. Center the wheel at the midpoint of its travel. Stop the engine.

8. The fluid level should not have risen more than 5mm If it does, repeat Step 6.

9. Check for fluid leakage.

Brakes

9

BASIC OPERATING PRINCIPLES

Hydraulic systems are used to actuate the brakes of all automobiles. The system transports the power required to force the frictional surfaces of the braking system together from the pedal to the individual brake units at each wheel. A hydraulic system is used for two reasons.

First, fluid under pressure can be carried to all parts of an automobile by small pipes and flexible hoses without taking up a significant amount of room or posing routing problems.

Second, a great mechanical advantage can be given to the brake pedal end of the system, and the foot pressure required to actuate the brakes can be reduced by making the surface area of the master cylinder pistons smaller than that of any of the pistons in the wheel cylinders or calipers.

The master cylinder consists of a fluid reservoir and a double cylinder and piston assembly. Double type master cylinders are designed to separate the front and rear braking systems hydraulically in case of a leak.

Steel lines carry the brake fluid to a point on the vehicle's frame near each of the vehicle's wheels. The fluid is then carried to the calipers and wheel cylinders by flexible tubes in order to allow for suspension and steering movements.

In drum brake systems, each wheel cylinder contains two pistons, one at either end, which push outward in opposite directions.

In disc brake systems, the cylinders are part of the calipers. One cylinder in each caliper is used to force the brake pads against the disc.

All pistons employ some type of seal, usually made of rubber, to minimize fluid leakage. A rubber dust boot seals the outer end of the cylinder against dust and dirt. The boot fits around the outer end of the piston on disc brake calipers, and around the brake actuating rod on wheel cylinders.

The hydraulic system operates as follows: When at rest, the entire system, from the piston(s) in the master cylinder to those in the wheel cylinders or calipers, is full of brake fluid. Upon application of the brake pedal, fluid trapped in front of the master cylinder piston(s) is forced through the lines to the wheel cylinders. Here, it forces the pistons outward, in the case of drum brakes, and inward toward the disc, in the case of disc brakes. The motion of the pistons is opposed by return springs mounted outside the cylinders in drum brakes, and by spring seals, in disc brakes.

Upon release of the brake pedal, a spring located inside the master cylinder immediately returns the master cylinder pistons to the normal position. The pistons contain check valves and the master cylinder has compensating ports drilled in it. These are uncovered as the pistons reach their normal position. The piston check valves allow fluid to flow toward the wheel cylinders or calipers as the pistons withdraw. Then, as the return springs force the brake pads or shoes into the released position, the excess fluid reservoir through the compensating ports. It is during the time the pedal is in the released position that any fluid that has leaked out of the system will be replaced through the compensating ports.

Dual circuit master cylinders employ two pistons, located one behind the other, in the same cylinder. The primary piston is actuated directly by mechanical linkage from the brake pedal through the power booster. The secondary piston is actuated by fluid trapped between the two pistons. If a leak develops in front of the secondary piston, it moves forward until it bottoms against the front of the master cylinder, and the fluid trapped between the pistons will operate the rear brakes. If the rear brakes develop a leak, the primary piston will move forward until direct contact with the secondary piston takes place, and it will force the secondary piston to actuate the front brakes. In either case, the brake pedal moves farther when the brakes are applied, and less braking power is available.

All dual circuit systems use a switch to warn the driver when only half of the brake system is operational. This switch is located in a valve body which is mounted on the firewall or the frame below the master cylinder. A hydraulic piston receives pressure from both circuits, each circuit's pressure being applied to one end of the piston. When the pressures are in balance, the piston remains stationary. When one circuit has a leak, however, the greater pressure in that circuit during application of the brakes will push the piston to one side, closing the switch and activating the brake warning light.

In disc brake systems, this valve body also contains a metering valve and, in some cases, a proportioning valve. The metering valve keeps pressure from traveling to the disc brakes on the front wheels until the brake shoes on the rear wheels have contacted the drums, ensuring that the front brakes will never be used alone. The proportioning valve controls the pressure to the rear brakes to lessen the chance of rear wheel lock-up during very hard braking.

Warning lights may be tested by depressing the brake pedal and holding it while opening one of the wheel cylinder bleeder screws. If this does not cause the light to go on, substitute a new lamp, make continuity checks, and, finally, replace the switch as necessary.

The hydraulic system may be checked for leaks by applying pressure to the pedal gradually and steadily. If the pedal sinks very slowly to the floor, the system has a leak. This is not to be confused with a springy or spongy feel due to the compression of air within the lines. If the system leaks, there will be a gradual change in the position of the pedal with a constant pressure.

Check for leaks along all lines and at wheel cylinders. If no external leaks are apparent, the problem is inside the master cylinder.

Disc Brakes

BASIC OPERATING PRINCIPLES

Instead of the traditional expanding brakes that press outward against a circular drum, disc brake systems utilize a disc (rotor) with brake pads positioned on either side of it. Braking effect is achieved in a manner similar to the way you would squeeze a spinning phonograph record between your fingers. The disc (rotor) is a casting with cooling fins between the two braking surfaces. This enables air to circulate between the braking surfaces making them less sensitive to heat buildup and more resistant to fade. Dirt and water do not affect braking action since contaminants are thrown off by the centrifugal action of the rotor or scraped off the by the pads. Also, the equal clamping action of the two brake pads tends to ensure uniform, straight line stops. Disc brakes are inherently self-adjusting.

There are three general types of disc brake:

1. A fixed caliper.
2. A floating caliper.
3. A sliding caliper.

The fixed caliper design uses two pistons mounted on either side of the rotor (in each side of the caliper). The caliper is mounted rigidly and does not move.

The sliding and floating designs are quite similar. In fact, these two types are often lumped together. In both designs, the pad on the inside of the rotor is moved into contact with the rotor by hydraulic force. The caliper, which is not held in a fixed position, moves slightly, bringing the outside pad into contact with the rotor. There are various methods of attaching floating calipers. Some pivot at the bottom or top, and some slide on mounting bolts. In any event, the end result is the same.

Drum Brakes

BASIC OPERATING PRINCIPLES

Drum brakes employ two brake shoes mounted on a stationary backing plate. These shoes are positioned inside a circular drum which rotates with the wheel assembly. The shoes are held in place by springs. This allows them to slide toward the drums (when they are applied) while keeping the linings and drums in alignment. The shoes are actuated by a wheel cylinder which is mounted at the top of the backing plate. When the brakes are applied, hydraulic pressure forces the wheel cylinder's actuating links outward. Since these links bear directly against the top of the brake shoes, the tops of the shoes are then forced against the inner side of the drum. This action forces the bottoms of the two shoes to contact the brake drum by rotating the entire assembly slightly (known as servo action). When pressure within the wheel cylinder is relaxed, return springs pull the shoes back away from the drum.

Most modern drum brakes are designed to self-adjust themselves during application when the vehicle is moving in reverse. This motion causes both shoes to rotate very slightly with the drum, rocking an adjusting lever, thereby causing rotation of the adjusting screw.

Power Boosters

Power brakes operate just as non-power brake systems except in the actuation of the master cylinder pistons. A vacuum diaphragm is located on the front of the master cylinder and assists the driver in applying the brakes, reducing both the effort and travel he must put into moving the brake pedal.

The vacuum diaphragm housing is connected to the intake manifold by a vacuum hose. A check valve is placed at the point where the hose enters the diaphragm housing, so that during periods of low manifold vacuum brake assist vacuum will not be lost.

Depressing the brake pedal closes off the vacuum source and allows atmospheric pressure to enter on one side of the diaphragm. This causes the master cylinder pistons to move and apply the brakes. When the brake pedal is released, vacuum is applied to both sides of the diaphragm, and return springs return the diaphragm and master cylinder pistons to the released position. If the vacuum fails, the brake pedal rod will butt against the end of the master cylinder actuating rod, and direct mechanical application will occur as the pedal is depressed.

The hydraulic and mechanical problems that apply to conventional brake systems also apply to power brakes, and should be checked for if the tests below do not reveal the problem.

Test for a system vacuum leak as described below:

1. Operate the engine at idle without touching the brake pedal for at least one minute.
2. Turn off the engine, and wait one minute.
3. Test for the presence of assist vacuum by depressing the brake pedal and releasing it several times. Light application will produce less and less pedal travel, if vacuum was present. If there is no vacuum, air is leaking into the system somewhere.

Test for system operation as follows:

1. Pump the brake pedal (with engine off) until the supply vacuum is entirely gone.
2. Put a light, steady pressure on the pedal.
3. Start the engine, and operate it at idle. If the system is operating, the brake pedal should fall toward the floor if constant pressure is maintained on the pedal.

Power brake systems may be tested for hydraulic leaks just as ordinary systems are tested.

BRAKE SYSTEM

CAUTION: *Brake shoes contain asbestos, which has been determined to be a cancer causing agent. Never clean the brake surfaces with compressed air! Avoid inhaling any dust from any brake surface! When cleaning brake surfaces, use a commercially available brake cleaning fluid.*

Adjustments

DISC BRAKES

All disc brakes are inherently self-adjusting. No periodic adjustment is either necessary or possible.

On moodels with rear disc brakes, the parking brake is actuated by means of conventional drum brake shoes. For adjustment of these shoes, please refer to Parking Brake at the end of this chapter.

DRUM BRAKES

Front

1970-77

1. Jack up the wheel to be adjusted until it completely clears the ground.
2. Make sure that the parking brake is completely released if the rear brakes are being adjusted.
3. Remove the rubber boot from the rear of the brake backing plate.
4. Lightly tap the adjuster housing forward with a hammer and screwdriver.
5. Turn the adjuster wheel downward with a screwdriver to spread the brake shoes. Stop turning the adjuster wheel when the brake drum is locked and the wheel cannot be turned by hand.
6. Turn the adjuster wheel upward, backing off the shoes from the brake drum 12 notches, to obtain the correct clearance between the brake shoes and drum. Turn the wheel to make sure that the brake drum turn without dragging.
7. Install the rubber boot.

Rear

1970-83

NOTE: *1984-89 Nissan trucks utilize self-adjusting brakes. The following procedure is necessary only after the brake shoes have been changed.*

1. Raise and support the rear of the vehicle until the wheel to be adjusted completely clears the ground.
2. Make sure that the parking brake is completely released.
3. Remove the rubber boot from the rear of the brake backing plate.
4. Lightly tap the adjuster housing forward with a hammer and screwdriver.

Troubleshooting the Brake System

Problem	Cause	Solution
Low brake pedal (excessive pedal travel required for braking action.)	• Excessive clearance between rear linings and drums caused by inoperative automatic adjusters	• Make 10 to 15 alternate forward and reverse brake stops to adjust brakes. If brake pedal does not come up, repair or replace adjuster parts as necessary.
	• Worn rear brakelining	• Inspect and replace lining if worn beyond minimum thickness specification
	• Bent, distorted brakeshoes, front or rear	• Replace brakeshoes in axle sets
	• Air in hydraulic system	• Remove air from system. Refer to Brake Bleeding.
Low brake pedal (pedal may go to floor with steady pressure applied.)	• Fluid leak in hydraulic system	• Fill master cylinder to fill line; have helper apply brakes and check calipers, wheel cylinders, differential valve tubes, hoses and fittings for leaks. Repair or replace as necessary.
	• Air in hydraulic system	• Remove air from system. Refer to Brake Bleeding.
	• Incorrect or non-recommended brake fluid (fluid evaporates at below normal temp).	• Flush hydraulic system with clean brake fluid. Refill with correct-type fluid.
	• Master cylinder piston seals worn, or master cylinder bore is scored, worn or corroded	• Repair or replace master cylinder
Low brake pedal (pedal goes to floor on first application—o.k. on subsequent applications.)	• Disc brake pads sticking on abutment surfaces of anchor plate. Caused by a build-up of dirt, rust, or corrosion on abutment surfaces	• Clean abutment surfaces
Fading brake pedal (pedal height decreases with steady pressure applied.)	• Fluid leak in hydraulic system	• Fill master cylinder reservoirs to fill mark, have helper apply brakes, check calipers, wheel cylinders, differential valve, tubes, hoses, and fittings for fluid leaks. Repair or replace parts as necessary.
	• Master cylinder piston seals worn, or master cylinder bore is scored, worn or corroded	• Repair or replace master cylinder
Decreasing brake pedal travel (pedal travel required for braking action decreases and may be accompanied by a hard pedal.)	• Caliper or wheel cylinder pistons sticking or seized	• Repair or replace the calipers, or wheel cylinders
	• Master cylinder compensator ports blocked (preventing fluid return to reservoirs) or pistons sticking or seized in master cylinder bore	• Repair or replace the master cylinder
	• Power brake unit binding internally	• Test unit according to the following procedure: (a) Shift transmission into neutral and start engine (b) Increase engine speed to 1500 rpm, close throttle and fully depress brake pedal (c) Slow release brake pedal and stop engine (d) Have helper remove vacuum check valve and hose from power unit. Observe for backward movement of brake pedal. (e) If the pedal moves backward, the power unit has an internal bind—replace power unit

Troubleshooting the Brake System (cont.)

Problem	Cause	Solution
Spongy brake pedal (pedal has abnormally soft, springy, spongy feel when depressed.)	• Air in hydraulic system	• Remove air from system. Refer to Brake Bleeding.
	• Brakeshoes bent or distorted	• Replace brakeshoes
	• Brakelining not yet seated with drums and rotors	• Burnish brakes
	• Rear drum brakes not properly adjusted	• Adjust brakes
Hard brake pedal (excessive pedal pressure required to stop vehicle. May be accompanied by brake fade.)	• Loose or leaking power brake unit vacuum hose	• Tighten connections or replace leaking hose
	• Incorrect or poor quality brakelining	• Replace with lining in axle sets
	• Bent, broken, distorted brakeshoes	• Replace brakeshoes
	• Calipers binding or dragging on mounting pins. Rear brakeshoes dragging on support plate.	• Replace mounting pins and bushings. Clean rust or burrs from rear brake support plate ledges and lubricate ledges with molydisulfide grease. **NOTE:** If ledges are deeply grooved or scored, do not attempt to sand or grind them smooth—replace support plate.
	• Caliper, wheel cylinder, or master cylinder pistons sticking or seized	• Repair or replace parts as necessary
	• Power brake unit vacuum check valve malfunction	• Test valve according to the following procedure: (a) Start engine, increase engine speed to 1500 rpm, close throttle and immediately stop engine (b) Wait at least 90 seconds then depress brake pedal (c) If brakes are not vacuum assisted for 2 or more applications, check valve is faulty
	• Power brake unit has internal bind	• Test unit according to the following procedure: (a) With engine stopped, apply brakes several times to exhaust all vacuum in system (b) Shift transmission into neutral, depress brake pedal and start engine (c) If pedal height decreases with foot pressure and less pressure is required to hold pedal in applied position, power unit vacuum system is operating normally. Test power unit. If power unit exhibits a bind condition, replace the power unit.
	• Master cylinder compensator ports (at bottom of reservoirs) blocked by dirt, scale, rust, or have small burrs (blocked ports prevent fluid return to reservoirs).	• Repair or replace master cylinder **CAUTION:** Do not attempt to clean blocked ports with wire, pencils, or similar implements. Use compressed air only.
	• Brake hoses, tubes, fittings clogged or restricted	• Use compressed air to check or unclog parts. Replace any damaged parts.
	• Brake fluid contaminated with improper fluids (motor oil, transmission fluid, causing rubber components to swell and stick in bores	• Replace all rubber components, combination valve and hoses. Flush entire brake system with DOT 3 brake fluid or equivalent.
	• Low engine vacuum	• Adjust or repair engine

Troubleshooting the Brake System (cont.)

Problem	Cause	Solution
Grabbing brakes (severe reaction to brake pedal pressure.)	• Brakelining(s) contaminated by grease or brake fluid	• Determine and correct cause of contamination and replace brakeshoes in axle sets
	• Parking brake cables incorrectly adjusted or seized	• Adjust cables. Replace seized cables.
	• Incorrect brakelining or lining loose on brakeshoes	• Replace brakeshoes in axle sets
	• Caliper anchor plate bolts loose	• Tighten bolts
	• Rear brakeshoes binding on support plate ledges	• Clean and lubricate ledges. Replace support plate(s) if ledges are deeply grooved. Do not attempt to smooth ledges by grinding.
	• Incorrect or missing power brake reaction disc	• Install correct disc
	• Rear brake support plates loose	• Tighten mounting bolts
Dragging brakes (slow or incomplete release of brakes)	• Brake pedal binding at pivot	• Loosen and lubricate
	• Power brake unit has internal bind	• Inspect for internal bind. Replace unit if internal bind exists.
	• Parking brake cables incorrrectly adjusted or seized	• Adjust cables. Replace seized cables.
	• Rear brakeshoe return springs weak or broken	• Replace return springs. Replace brakeshoe if necessary in axle sets.
	• Automatic adjusters malfunctioning	• Repair or replace adjuster parts as required
	• Caliper, wheel cylinder or master cylinder pistons sticking or seized	• Repair or replace parts as necessary
	• Master cylinder compensating ports blocked (fluid does not return to reservoirs).	• Use compressed air to clear ports. Do not use wire, pencils, or similar objects to open blocked ports.
Vehicle moves to one side when brakes are applied	• Incorrect front tire pressure	• Inflate to recommended cold (reduced load) inflation pressure
	• Worn or damaged wheel bearings	• Replace worn or damaged bearings
	• Brakelining on one side contaminated	• Determine and correct cause of contamination and replace brakelining in axle sets
	• Brakeshoes on one side bent, distorted, or lining loose on shoe	• Replace brakeshoes in axle sets
	• Support plate bent or loose on one side	• Tighten or replace support plate
	• Brakelining not yet seated with drums or rotors	• Burnish brakelining
	• Caliper anchor plate loose on one side	• Tighten anchor plate bolts
	• Caliper piston sticking or seized	• Repair or replace caliper
	• Brakelinings water soaked	• Drive vehicle with brakes lightly applied to dry linings
	• Loose suspension component attaching or mounting bolts	• Tighten suspension bolts. Replace worn suspension components.
	• Brake combination valve failure	• Replace combination valve
Chatter or shudder when brakes are applied (pedal pulsation and roughness may also occur.)	• Brakeshoes distorted, bent, contaminated, or worn	• Replace brakeshoes in axle sets
	• Caliper anchor plate or support plate loose	• Tighten mounting bolts
	• Excessive thickness variation of rotor(s)	• Refinish or replace rotors in axle sets
Noisy brakes (squealing, clicking, scraping sound when brakes are applied.)	• Bent, broken, distorted brakeshoes	• Replace brakeshoes in axle sets
	• Excessive rust on outer edge of rotor braking surface	• Remove rust

Troubleshooting the Brake System (cont.)

Problem	Cause	Solution
Noisy brakes (squealing, clicking, scraping sound when brakes are applied.) (cont.)	• Brakelining worn out—shoes contacting drum of rotor	• Replace brakeshoes and lining in axle sets. Refinish or replace drums or rotors.
	• Broken or loose holdown or return springs	• Replace parts as necessary
	• Rough or dry drum brake support plate ledges	• Lubricate support plate ledges
	• Cracked, grooved, or scored rotor(s) or drum(s)	• Replace rotor(s) or drum(s). Replace brakeshoes and lining in axle sets if necessary.
	• Incorrect brakelining and/or shoes (front or rear).	• Install specified shoe and lining assemblies
Pulsating brake pedal	• Out of round drums or excessive lateral runout in disc brake rotor(s)	• Refinish or replace drums, re-index rotors or replace

5. Turn the adjuster wheel downward with a screwdriver to spread the brake shoes. Stop turning the adjuster wheel when the brake drum is locked and the wheel cannot be turned by hand.
6. Turn the adjuster wheel upward, backing off the shoes from the brake drum 12 notches, to obtain the correct clearance between the brake shoes and drum. Turn the wheel to make sure that the brake drum will turn without dragging.
7. Install the rubber boot.
8. Adjust the other wheel in the same manner.
9. Lower the vehicle.

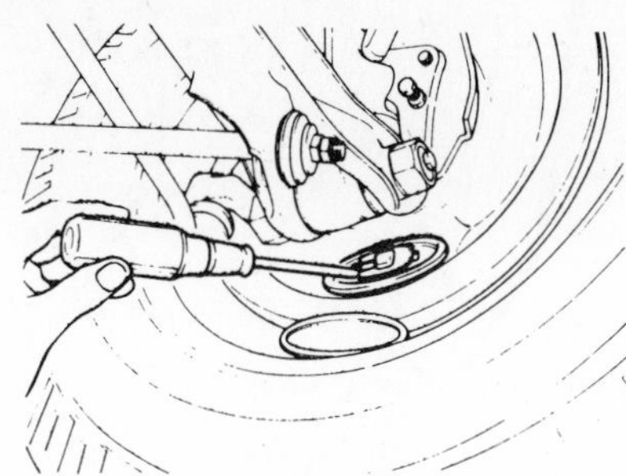
Adjusting the front drum brake

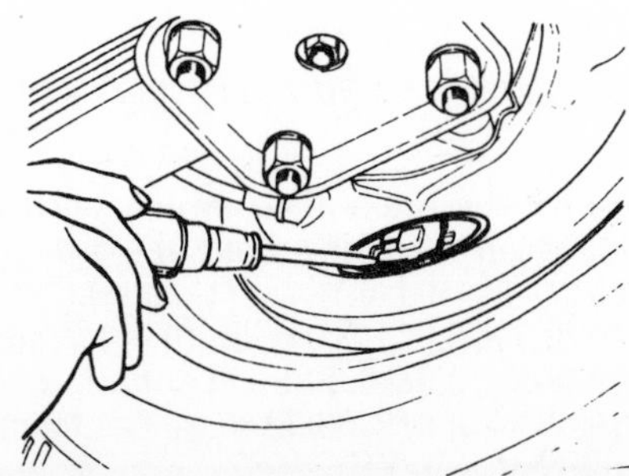
Adjusting the rear drum brake

BRAKE PEDAL

Pedal Height

1970-71

These models have non-adjustable master cylinder pushrods. The freeplay must be adjusted by the use of shims between the master cylinder and the firewall.

1. Loosen the pedal stopper so that it does not contact the pedal arm.
2. With the master cylinder pushrod completely extended, the pedal should be 5.45 in. (139mm) from the tow board (rugs removed). The distance can be adjusted with shims. Use the same thickness of shim for both the upper and lower master cylinder mounting bolts.

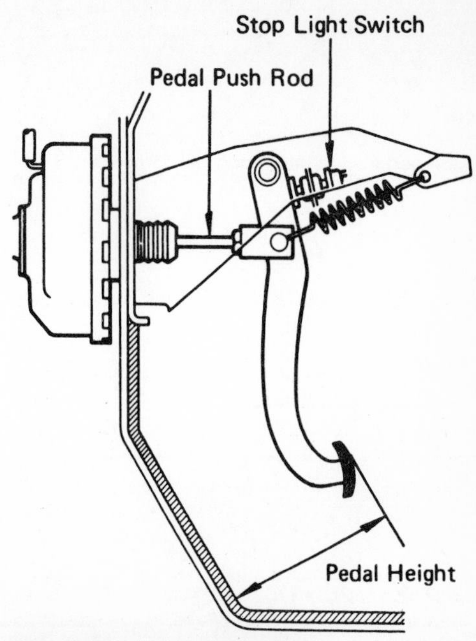

Adjusting the brake pedal height

1972-89

1. Measure the distance between the center (upper surface) of the pedal pad and the floor pad.
2. If out of specifications, loosen the brake light switch.
3. Turn the pedal pushrod (input rod) until the pedal height is within specifications.
   - 1972-75: 5.5 in. (140mm).
   - 1976-77: 5.8 in. (147mm).
   - 1978-79: 6.06 in. (154mm).
   - 1980-83: 6.7 in. (170mm).
   - 1984-86 (720-D series): 7.125 in. (181mm).
   - 1986-89 (D21-D series): AT – 8.35–8.74 in. (212–222mm); MT – 8.23–8.62 in. (209–219mm).

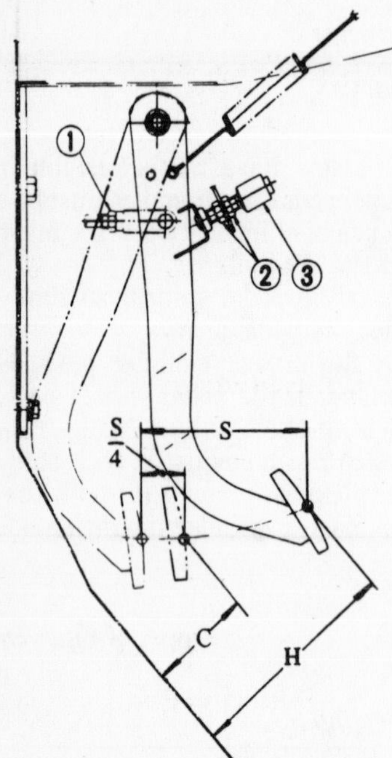

Clutch pedal adjustment points—1972–79

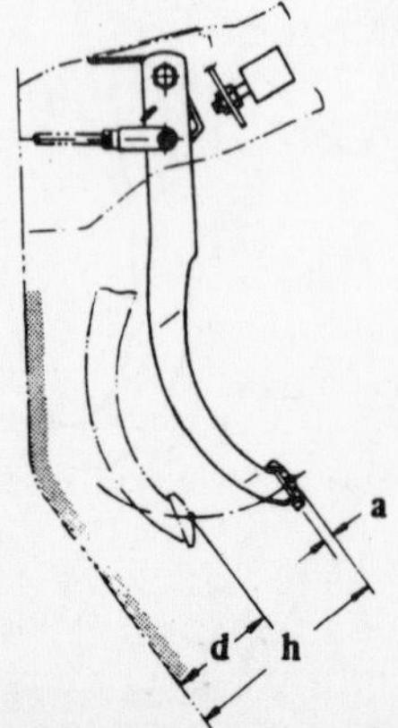

Clutch pedal adjustment points—1980–83

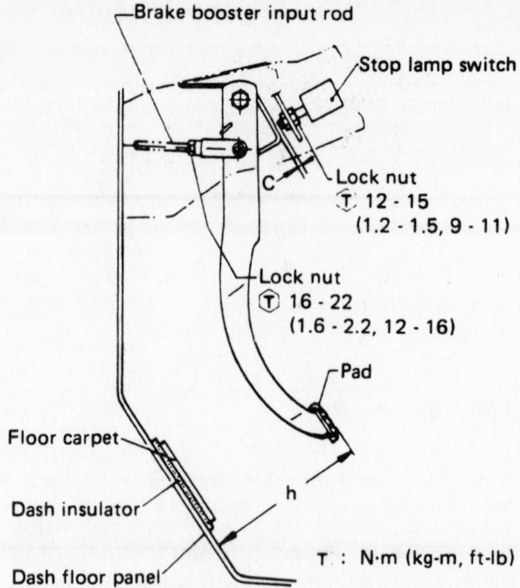

Clutch pedal adjustment points—1984–86 (720-D series)

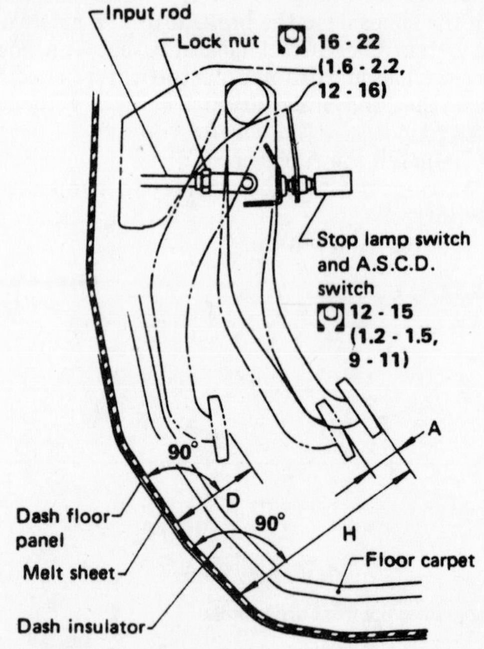

Clutch pedal adjustment points—1986–89 (D21-D series)

4. Move the brake light switch until clearance between the plunger and the pedal is:
   - 1972-75: 0.04–0.12 in. (1–3mm).
   - 1976-77: 0.024–0.047 in. (0.6–1.2mm).
   - 1978-83: 0.04–0.20 in. (1–5mm).
   - 1984-89: 0.012–0.039 in. (0.3–1.0mm).

   Tighten the switch.
5. Check the brake pedal free-play.

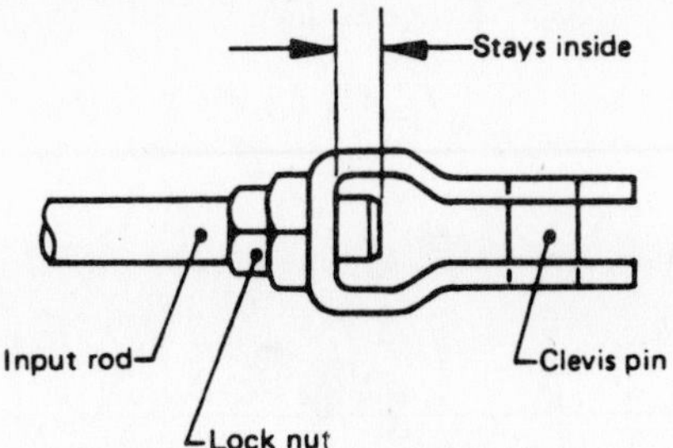

When adjusting the pedal height; make sure the tip of the pushrod stays inside the bracket

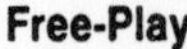

Free-Play

1970-71

Depress the brake pedal until resistance is felt. Adjust the pedal height with the stopper, so that the front of the pedal pad is 5.33 in. (135mm) from the toe board.

1972-89

1. With the engine turned off, depress the brake pedal several times until there is no vacuum left in the brake booster.
2. Push the pedal down until resistance is first felt. Measure this distance; it should be 0.04–0.12 in. (1–3mm).
3. Adjust the free-play by turning the pedal pushrod.
4. Start the engine and recheck the free-play.
5. Recheck the pedal height.

Reserve Distance

Depress the brake pedal to the bottom of the pedal travel and measure the distance from the center (upper surface) of the pedal pad to the floor mat. If the distance is out of specifications, recheck the other pedal adjustments and the master cylinder. Pedal depressed height should be:

- 1970-77: 1.69–1.93 in. (43–49mm).
- 1978: at least 2.95 in. (75mm).
- 1979: at least 2.56 in. (65mm).
- 1980-83: at least 3.23 in. (82mm).
- 1984-86 (720-D series): at least 3.35 in. (85mm).
- 1986-89 (D21-D series): at least 4.72 in. (120mm).

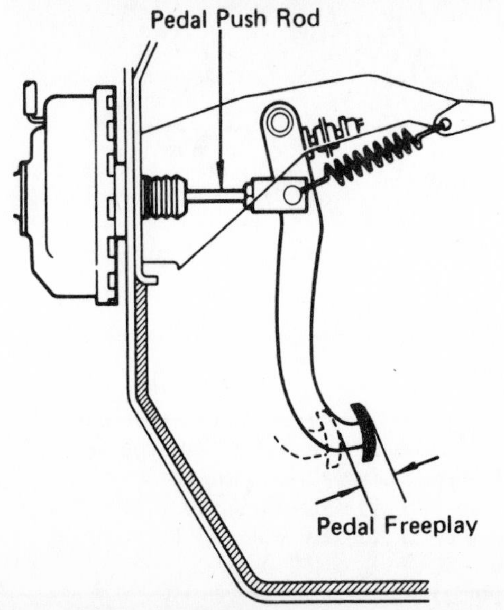

Adjusting the brake pedal free-play

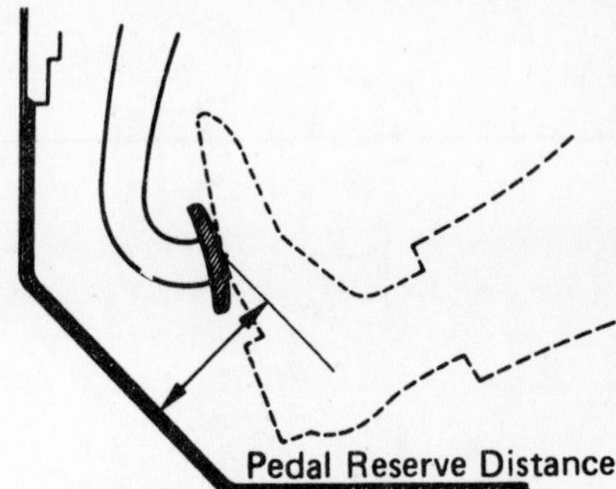

Adjusting the brake pedal reserve distance

Brake Light Switch

REMOVAL AND INSTALLATION

1. Disconnect the electrical harness at the switch.
2. Remove the mounting bolt and slide the switch up and down. Remove the switch from the brake pedal.

NOTE: *It is not necessary to remove the pushrod from the stud.*

Master Cylinder

REMOVAL AND INSTALLATION

CAUTION: *Be careful not to spill brake fluid on the painted surfaces of the vehicle; it will damage the paint.*

1. Unfasten the hydraulic lines from the master cylinder. On early models, disconnect the lines running to the master cylinder reservoir.
2. Disconnect the hydraulic fluid pressure differential switch wiring connectors. On models with fluid level sensors, disconnect the fluid level sensor wiring connectors, as well.
3. Loosen the master cylinder reservoir mounting bolts.
4. Then do one of the following:
   a. On models with manual brakes, remove the master cylinder securing bolts and the clevis pin from the brake pedal. Remove the master cylinder;

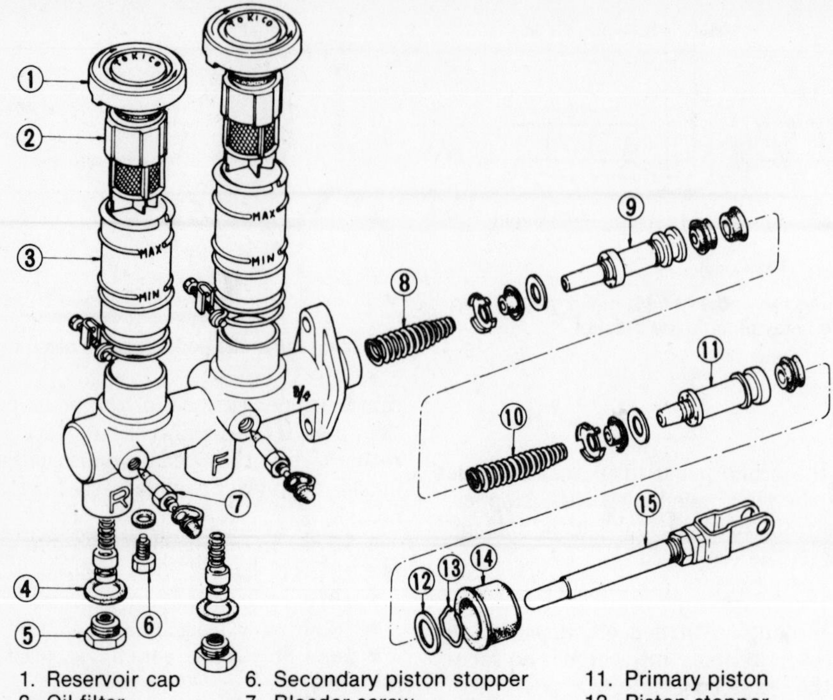

1. Reservoir cap	6. Secondary piston stopper	11. Primary piston
2. Oil filter	7. Bleeder screw	12. Piston stopper
3. Oil reservoir	8. Secondary return spring	13. Piston stopper ring
4. Packing	9. Secondary piston	14. Dust cover
5. Valve cap	10. Primary return spring	15. Pushrod

Exploded view of the master cylinder—1972–77

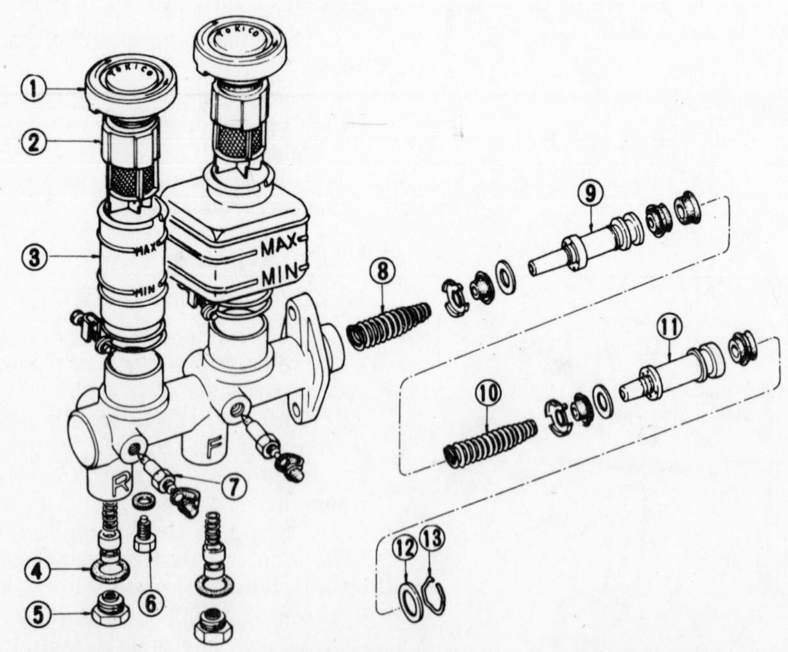

1 Reservoir cap	6 Secondary piston stopper	11 Primary piston
2 Oil filter	7 Bleeder screw	12 Piston stopper
3 Oil reservoir	8 Secondary return spring	13 Piston stopper ring
4 Packing	9 Secondary piston	
5 Valve cap	10 Primary return spring	

Exploded view of the master cylinder—1978–80

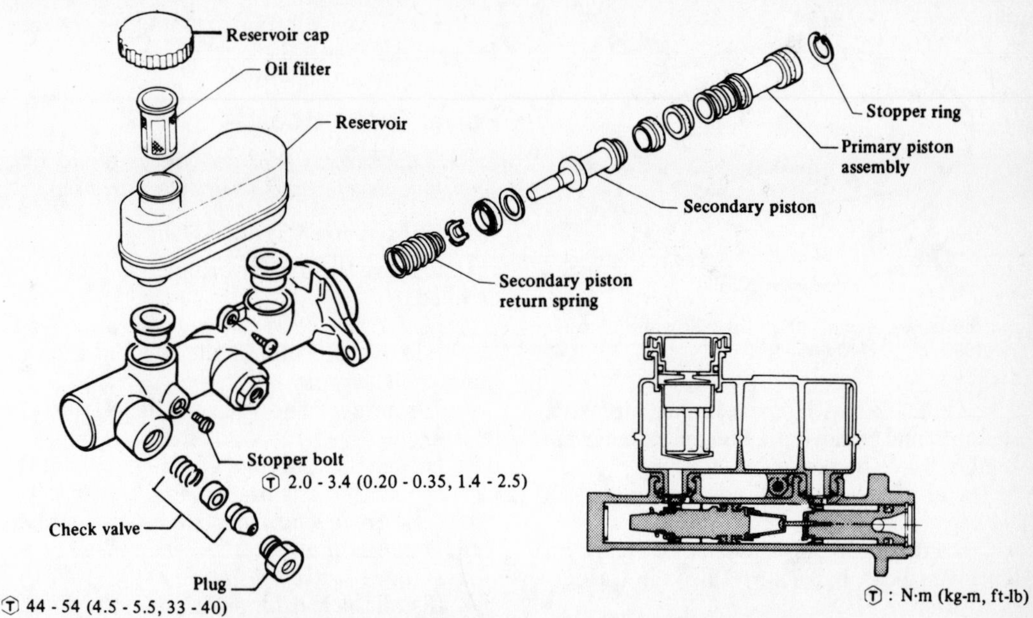

Reservoir cap
Oil filter
Reservoir
Stopper ring
Primary piston assembly
Secondary piston
Secondary piston return spring
Stopper bolt
Ⓣ 2.0 - 3.4 (0.20 - 0.35, 1.4 - 2.5)
Check valve
Plug
Ⓣ 44 - 54 (4.5 - 5.5, 33 - 40)
Ⓣ : N·m (kg-m, ft-lb)

Exploded view of the master cylinder—1981–86 (720-D series)

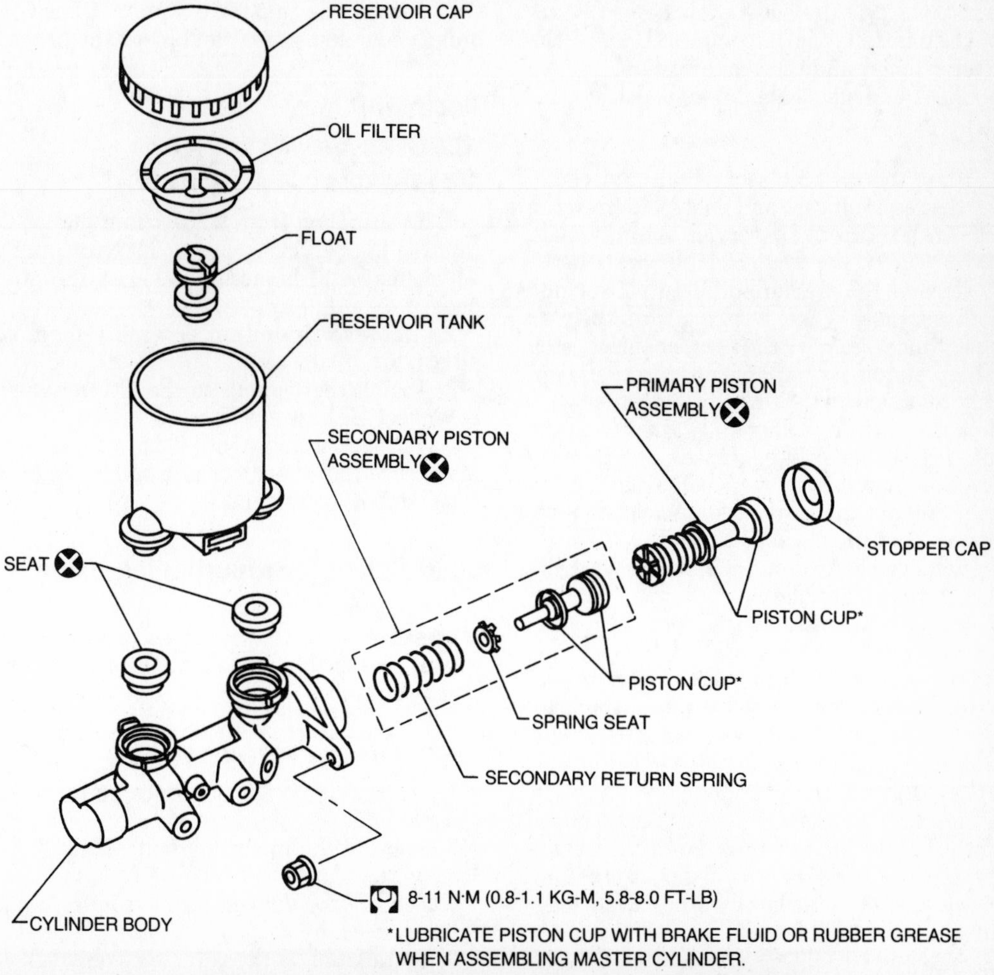

RESERVOIR CAP
OIL FILTER
FLOAT
RESERVOIR TANK
PRIMARY PISTON ASSEMBLY
SECONDARY PISTON ASSEMBLY
STOPPER CAP
SEAT
PISTON CUP*
PISTON CUP*
SPRING SEAT
SECONDARY RETURN SPRING
CYLINDER BODY
8-11 N·M (0.8-1.1 KG-M, 5.8-8.0 FT-LB)
*LUBRICATE PISTON CUP WITH BRAKE FLUID OR RUBBER GREASE WHEN ASSEMBLING MASTER CYLINDER.

Exploded view of the master cylinder—1986–89 (D21-D series)

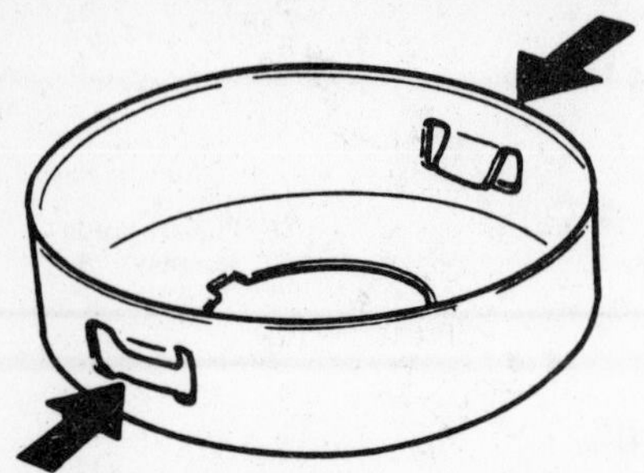

Bend the claws inward when installing the stopper cap—1986–89 (D21-D series)

b. On models with power brakes, unfasten the nuts and remove the master cylinder assembly from the power brake unit.

5. Install the master cylinder and note the following:

- Certain models may have an **UP** mark on the cylinder boot, make sure this is in the correct position.
- Before tightening the master cylinder mounting nuts or bolts, screw the hydraulic line into the cylinder body a few turns.
- After installation is completed, bleed the master cylinder and the brake system.
- Check and adjust the brake pedal.

OVERHAUL

1. Place the cylinder securely in a vise. Remove the reservoir caps and floats. Unscrew the bolts which secure the reservoir(s) to the main body.
2. Remove the pressure differential warning switch assembly. Then, working from the rear of the cylinder, remove the boot, snapring, stop washer, piston No. 1, spacer, cylinder cup, spring retainer, and spring, in that order.
3. Remove the end plug and gasket from the front of the cylinder (if equipped), and then remove the front piston stop bolt from underneath. Pull out the spring, retainer, piston No. 2, spacer, and the cylinder cup.
4. Remove the two outlet fittings, washers, check valves and springs.
5. Remove the piston cups from their seats only if they are to be replaced.

After washing all parts in clean brake fluid, dry them with compressed air (if available). Drying parts with a shop rag can deposit lint and dirt particles inside the assembled master cylinder. Inspect the cylinder bore for wear, scuff marks, or nicks. Cylinders may be honed slightly, but the limits is 0.15mm. In view of the importance of the master cylinder, it is recommended that it is replaced rather than overhauled if worn or damaged.

6. Absolute cleanliness is essential. Coat all parts with clean brake fluid prior to assembly.
7. Bleed the hydraulic system after the master cylinder is installed.

Power Brake Booster

NOTE: *Vacuum boosters can be found only on models equipped with power brakes.*

REMOVAL AND INSTALLATION

1. Remove the master cylinder as previously detailed.
2. Locate the clevis rod where it attaches to the brake pedal. Pull out the clip and then remove the clevis pin.
3. Disconnect the vacuum hose from the booster.
4. Loosen the four nuts and then pull out the vacuum booster, the bracket and the gasket.

NOTE: *Some 4wd models may have two extra brackets that must be removed when removing the brake booster.*

5. Install the booster and tighten the mounting bolts to 6–8 ft. lbs. (0.8–1.1 Nm).
6. Connect the clevis rod to the brake pedal.
7. Install the master cylinder. Check the brake pedal adjustment and bleed the brakes.

Vacuum Pump

REMOVAL AND INSTALLATION

SD22 and SD25 Diesel Engines Only

1. Drain all oil from the vacuum pump. Rotate the fan belt clockwise to discharge any oil which may still be accumulated in the pump body.
2. Remove the pump assembly from the alternator.
3. Install thew pump to the alternator and reconnect all hoses or lines.
4. Fill the assembly with 0.2 oz. of engine oil. Make sure that the alternator pulley can be rotated smoothly by hand.

Load Sensing Proportioning Valve

The purpose of this valve is to control the fluid pressure applied to the brakes to prevent rear wheel lock-up during weight transfer at high speed stops.

REMOVAL AND INSTALLATION

1. Disconnect the brake lines going to the valve.
2. Remove the mounting bolts, if used, and remove the valve.

NOTE: *This valve can not be rebuilt. It must be replaced.*

3. Installation is the reverse of removal.
4. Bleed the brake system.

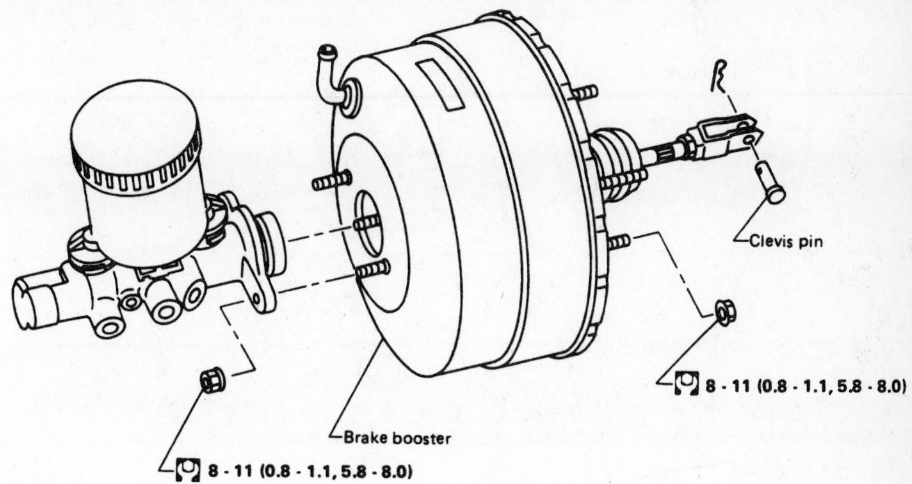

Typical power brake booster

ADJUSTMENT

1986-89 (D21-D Series)

HEAVY DUTY MODELS WITH VG30I ENGINE

1. Position approximately 220 lbs. of weight over the rear axle.
2. Install pressure gauges at the front and rear brakes.
3. Depress the brake pedal until the front brake pressure is approximately 711 lbs. Check that the rear brake pressure is 327–469 lbs.
4. Depress the brake pedal until the front brake pressure is approximately 1422 lbs. Check that the rear brake pressure is 455–654 lbs.
5. If the rear brake pressure is not within specifications, move the spring bracket to the left if the pressure is high or to the right if the pressure is low. Repeat this process until the rear brake pressure is correct.

Brake Hoses and Lines

HYDRAULIC BRAKE LINE CHECK

The hydraulic brake lines and brake linings are to be inspected at the recommended inter-

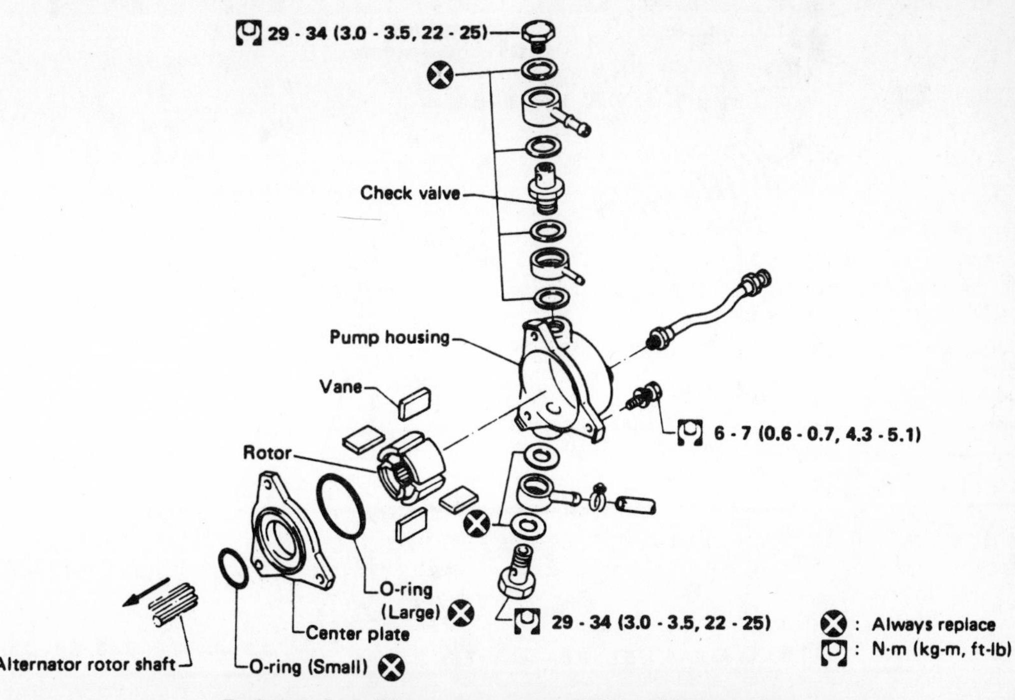

Exploded view of the vacuum pump—SD22 and SD25 engines

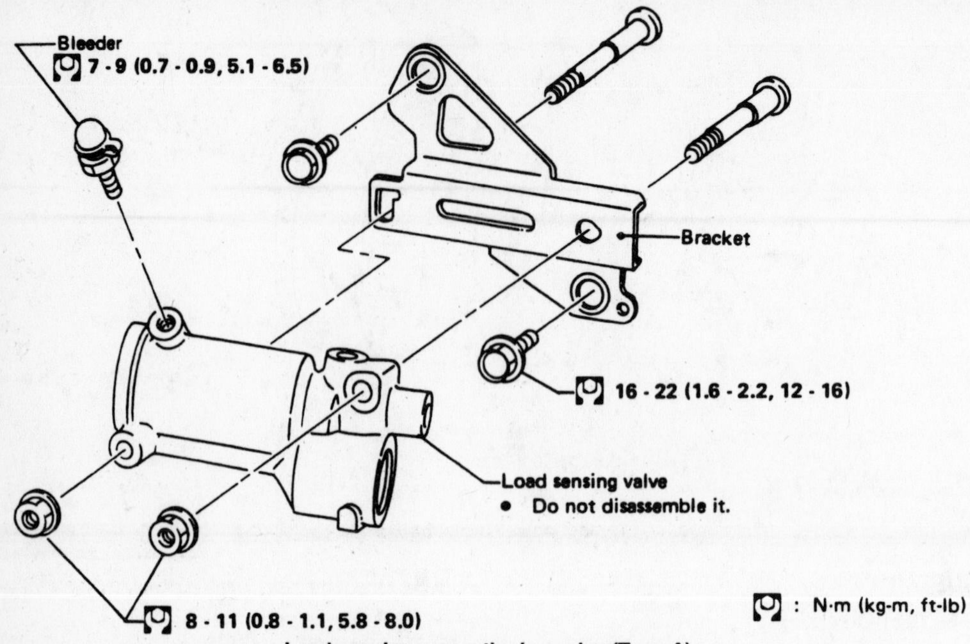

Bleeder
7 - 9 (0.7 - 0.9, 5.1 - 6.5)
Bracket
16 - 22 (1.6 - 2.2, 12 - 16)
Load sensing valve
• Do not disassemble it.
8 - 11 (0.8 - 1.1, 5.8 - 8.0)
: N·m (kg-m, ft-lb)

Load sensing proportioning valve (Type A)

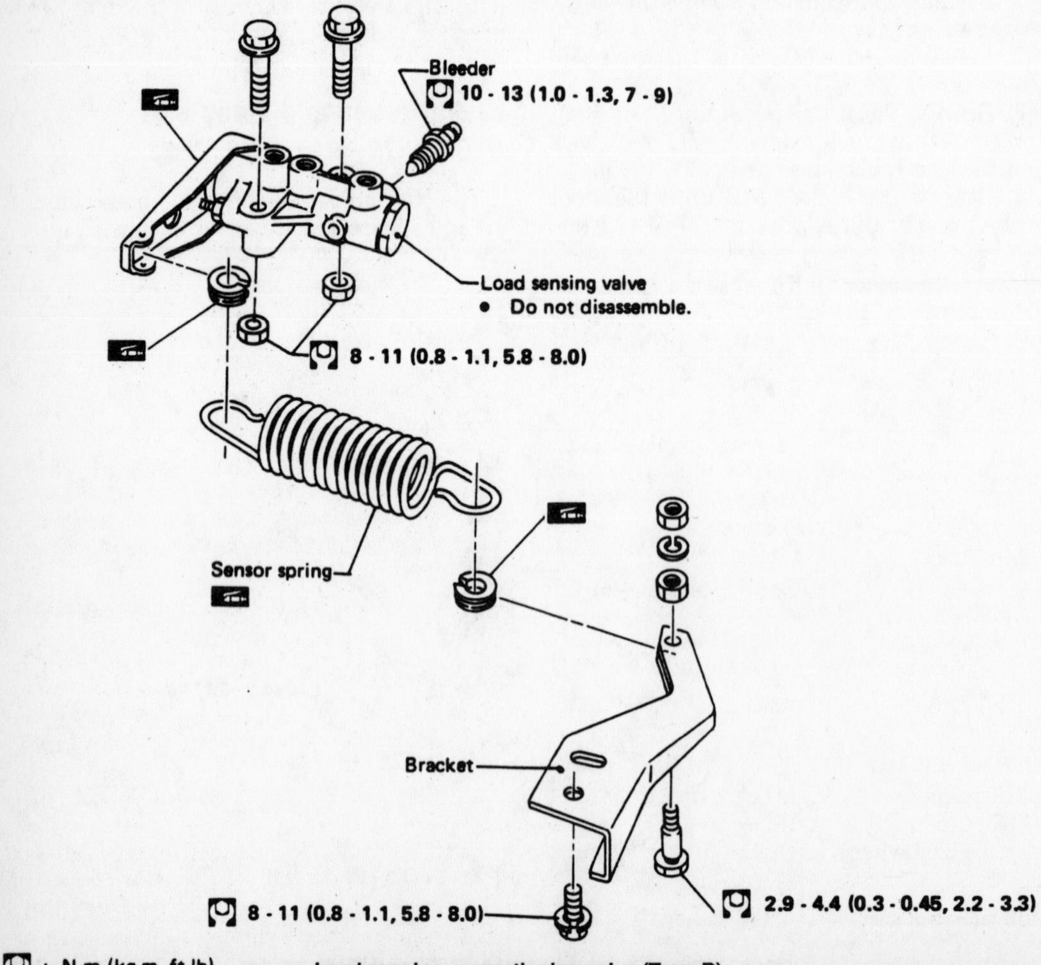

Bleeder
10 - 13 (1.0 - 1.3, 7 - 9)
Load sensing valve
• Do not disassemble.
8 - 11 (0.8 - 1.1, 5.8 - 8.0)
Sensor spring
Bracket
8 - 11 (0.8 - 1.1, 5.8 - 8.0)
2.9 - 4.4 (0.3 - 0.45, 2.2 - 3.3)
: N·m (kg-m, ft-lb)

Load sensing proportioning valve (Type B)

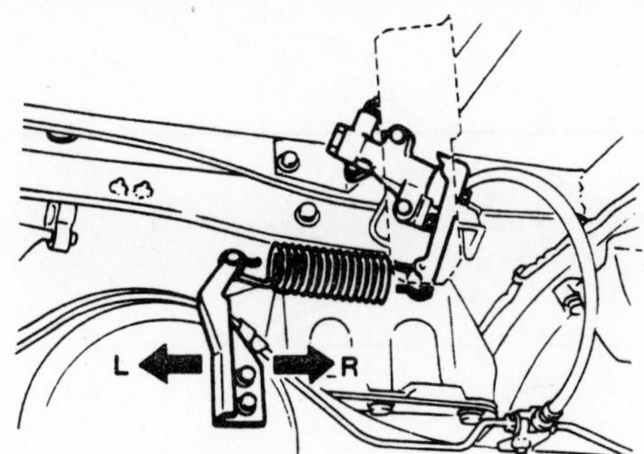

Adjusting the proportioning valve (Type B)—1986–89 HD with VG30i engines

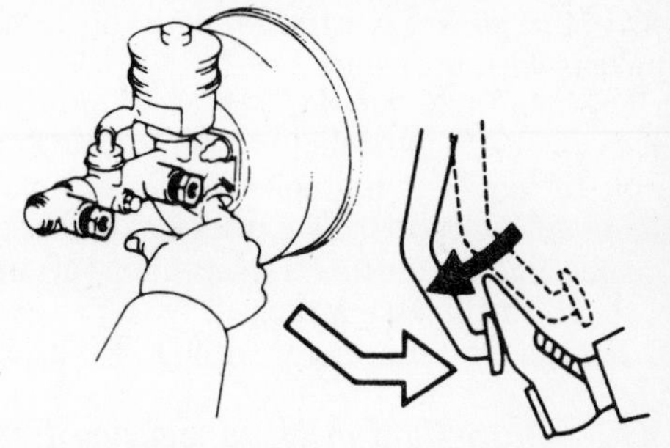

When bleeding the master cylinder, depress the brake pedal and hold it down

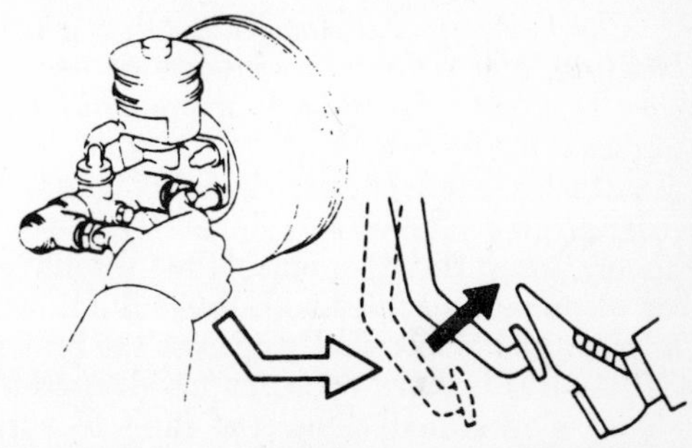

Block the brake line holes with your fingers and release the brake pedal. Repeat this several times

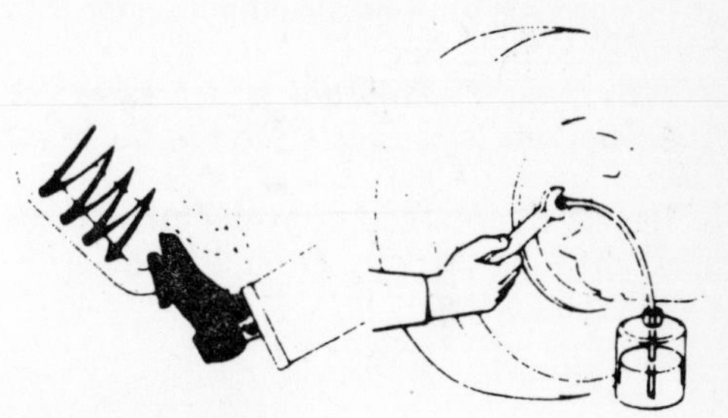

Bleeding the brakes

vals in the maintenance schedule. Follow the steel tubing from the master cylinder to the flexible hose fitting at each wheel. If a section of the tubing is found to be damaged, replace the entire section with tubing of the same type (steel, not copper), size, shape, and length. When installing a new section of brake tubing, flush clean brake fluid or denatured alcohol through to remove any dirt or foreign material from the line. Be sure to flare both ends to provide sound, leak-proof connections. When bending the tubing to fit the underbody contours, be careful not to kink or crack the line. Torque all hydraulic connections to 10-15 lbs.

Check the flexible brake hoses that connect the steel tubing to each wheel cylinder. Replace the hose if it shows any signs of softening, cracking, or other damage. When installing a new front brake hose, position the hose to avoid contact with other chassis parts. Place a new copper gasket over the hose fitting and thread the hose assembly into the front wheel cylinder. A new rear brake hose must be positioned clear of the exhaust pipe or shock absorber. Thread the hose into the rear brake tube connector. When installing either a new front or rear brake hose, engage the opposite end of the hose to the bracket on the frame. Install the horseshoe type retaining clip and connect the tube to the hose with the tube fitting nut.

Always bleed the system after hose or line replacement. Before bleeding, make sure that the master cylinder is topped up with high temperature, extra heavy duty fluid of at least SAE 70R3 quality.

Bleeding

The purpose of bleeding the brakes is to expel air trapped in the hydraulic system. The system must be bled whenever the pedal feels spongy, indicating that compressible air has entered the system. It must also be bled whenever the system has been opened or repaired. You will need a helper for this job.

CAUTION: *Never reuse brake fluid which has been bled from the brake system.*

1. The sequence for bleeding is as follows:

- 1970-71: Right rear, left rear, right front, left front;
- 1972-75: Master cylinder front, master cylinder rear, then the 1970–71 sequence;
- 1976-79: Master cylinder front, master cylinder rear, NLSV front, right front, left front, left rear, right rear, NLSV rear, NLSV center.
- 1980-86 (720-D series): NLSV, rear wheel, front wheel.
- 1986-89 (D21-D series) equipped with LSV: LSV air bleeder, left rear wheel cylinder, right rear wheel cylinder, left front caliper, right front caliper.
- 1986-89 (D21-D series) not equipped with LSV: left rear wheel cylinder, right rear wheel cylinder, left front caliper, right front caliper.

It is not necessary to run the engine on 1972-79 models with a vacuum booster.

2. Clean all the bleeder screws. You may want to give each one a shot of a penetrating lubricant to loosen it up; seizure is a common problem with bleeder screw, which then break off, sometimes requiring replacement of the part to which they are attached.

3. Fill the master cylinder with DOT 3 brake fluid.

NOTE: *Brake fluid picks up moisture from the air. Don't leave the master cylinder or the fluid container uncovered any longer than necessary. Be careful! Brake fluid eats paint.*

Check the level of the fluid often when bleeding, and refill the reservoirs as necessary. Don't let them run dry, or you will have to repeat the process.

4. Attach a length of clear vinyl tubing to the bleeder screw on the wheel cylinder (or master cylinder). Insert the other end of the tube into a clear, clean jar half filled with brake fluid.

5. Have you helper slowly depress the brake pedal. As this is done, open the bleeder screw ⅓–½ of a turn, and allow the fluid to run through the tube. Then close the bleeder screw before the pedal reaches the end of its travel. Have you assistant slowly release the pedal. Repeat this process until no air bubbles appear in the expelled fluid.

NOTE: *If the brake pedal is depressed too fast, small air bubbles will form in the brake fluid.*

6. Repeat the procedure on the other three brakes, checking the level of fluid in the cylinder reservoirs often.

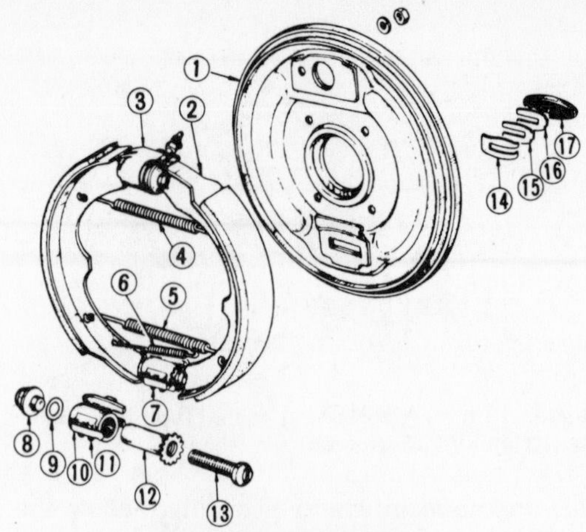

1. Brake backing plate
2. Brake shoe assembly
3. Wheel cylinder assembly
4. Brake shoe upper return spring
5. Brake shoe lower return spring
6. After shoe return spring
7. Adjuster assembly
8. Adjuster head
9. Adjuster head shim
10. Lock spring
11. Adjuster housing
12. Adjuster wheel
13. Adjuster screw
14. Retaining spring
15. Lockplate
16. Adjuster shim
17. Rubber boot

Exploded view of the front drum brake—1970–77

FRONT DRUM BRAKES

CAUTION: *Brake shoes contain asbestos, which has been determined to be a cancer causing agent. Never clean the brake surfaces with compressed air! Avoid inhaling any dust from any brake surface! When cleaning brake surfaces, use a commercially available brake cleaning fluid.*

Brake Drum

REMOVAL AND INSTALLATION

1. Remove the hub cap and loosen the lug nuts.

2. Raise the front of the vehicle and support it on jackstands.

3. Remove the lug nuts, tire and wheel.

4. Remove the axle hub grease cap.

5. Remove the cotter pin, and then loosen the hub nut. When the nut is close to the end of the spindle, pull the drum and hub assembly toward you. If it does not slide off the brake shoes, loosen the brake shoe adjuster star wheels. Remove the spindle nut, brake drum and hub, the washer, and the wheel bearings.

NOTE: *Be careful not to get foreign matter in the wheel bearings. The heavy coating of grease will hold many particles. These will damage the bearings.*

6. Inspect the brake drum as outlined below.

CAUTION: *Do not depress the brake pedal with the brake drum removed.*

7. For instructions on preloading the front wheel bearings, see the appropriate section.

INSPECTION

1. Clean the drum with a rag and a little paint thinner.

CAUTION: *Do not blow the brake dust out of the drum with compressed air or lung power. Brake linings contain asbestos, a known cancer causing agent.*

2. Inspect the drum for cracks, grooves, scoring and out-of-roundness.

3. Light scoring may be removed with fine

emery paper, Heavy scores or grooves will have to be removed by having the drum turned on a lathe. This can be done at many automotive machine shops and some service stations.

4. Before cutting the drum it must be measured to determine whether or not the inside dimension of the drum is within limitations after removing the score marks. The service limits of the brake drums are 10.079 in. (256mm).

5. Check the drum for concentricity. An inside micrometer is necessary for an exact measurement, so unless this tool is available, the drum should be taken to a machine shop to be checked. Any drum which measures more than 0.15mm out of round will result in an inaccurate brake adjustment and other problems, and must be refinished or replaced.

NOTE: *Make all measurements at right angles to each other and at the open and closed edges of the drum machined surface.*

Brake Shoes

INSPECTION

After removing the brake drum, inspect the brake shoes. If the lining is worn down so that the thickness is less than 0.0394 in. (1mm), the brake shoes must be replaced.

NOTE: *This figure may disagree with your state inspection laws.*

If the brake lining is soaked with brake fluid, it must be replaced. Also the brake drum should be sanded with crocus cloth to remove all traces of brake fluid and the wheel cylinders rebuilt. Clean all grit off the brake drum before installing it.

If the brake lining is chipped, cracked, or otherwise damaged, it must be replace with new lining.

NOTE: *Always replace the brake linings (shoes) in sets of two on both ends of the axle. Never replace just one shoe or both shoes on just one side.*

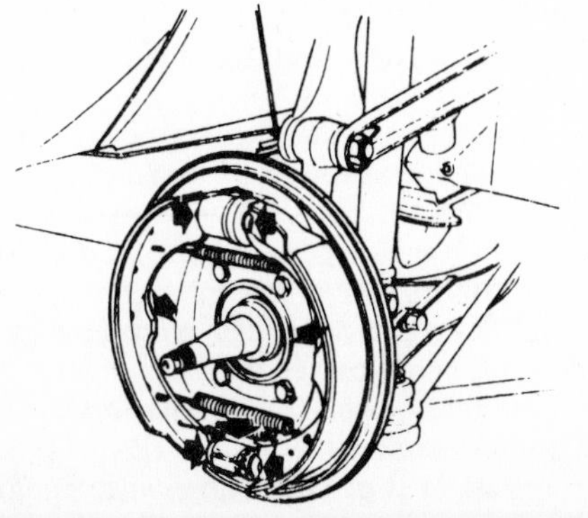

Greasing points on the front brakes indicated by the arrows

Check the condition of the shoes, retracting springs and holddown springs for signs of overheating. If the shoes or springs have a slight blue color, this indicates overheating and replacement of the springs and hoes is recommended. The wheel cylinders should be rebuilt as a precaution against future problems.

REMOVAL AND INSTALLATION

1. Raise and support the vehicle until the wheel which is to be serviced is off the ground. Remove the wheel and brake drum.

NOTE: *It is not absolutely essential to remove the hub assembly from the spindle, but it makes the job a great deal easier. If you can work with the hub in place, skip down to Step 7.*

2. Remove the hub dust cap.

3. Straighten the cotter pin and remove it from the spindle.

4. Unscrew the spindle nut and remove the adjusting cap, spindle nut, and spindle washer.

5. Wiggle the hub assembly until the outer bearing comes unseated and can be removed from the hub. Remove the outer bearing.

6. Pull the hub assembly off the spindle.

7. Unhook the upper, lower, and after shoe return springs, and remove them from the brake assembly.

8. Remove the brake shoes from the wheel cylinder at the top and the adjuster assembly at the bottom.

9. Clean the brake backing plate and adjuster assembly so they are free of all dust and dirt. To remove the adjuster assembly for cleaning, remove the rubber boot at the back of the adjuster assembly and slide the adjuster shim, lockplate and retaining spring off the rear of the adjuster assembly.

10. Check the wheel cylinders by carefully pulling the lower edges of the wheel cylinder boots away from the cylinders. If there is leakage, the inside of the cylinder will be wet with fluid. If leakage exists, a wheel cylinder overhaul is in order. Do not delay, because brake failure could result.

NOTE: *A trace of fluid will be present, which acts as a lubricant for the wheel cylinder pistons.*

11. Apply brake grease to the adjuster assembly housing bore, adjuster wheel, and adjuster screw. Assemble the adjuster assembly with the adjuster screw turned all the way in. Apply brake grease to the sliding surfaces of the adjuster assembly, brake backing plate, and the retaining spring. Install the adjuster assembly to the backing plate in the reverse order of removal.

12. Before installing the brake shoes, apply brake grease to the notches into which the

brake shoes fit on the wheel cylinder and adjuster mechanism, and brake shoe-to-backing plate contact surfaces.

13. Install the brake shoes.

14. Install the hub, brake drum, and wheel in the reverse order of removal and adjust the wheel bearings and the brake shoes. Bleed the brakes. Lower the vehicle and roadtest it.

Wheel Cylinders

REMOVAL AND INSTALLATION

1. Raise the front of the truck and support it with safety stands.
2. Remove the wheel, brake drum, hub assembly, and brake shoes.
3. Disconnect the brake hose from the wheel cylinder.
4. Unscrew the wheel cylinder securing nut and remove the wheel cylinder from the brake backing plate.
5. Install the wheel cylinder, assemble the remaining components, and bleed the brake hydraulic system.

OVERHAUL

NOTE: *This is one of those jobs where it is usually easier just to replace the part rather than rebuild it. If you decide to rebuild the wheel cylinders, be sure you get the correct parts for your truck. Datsun obtains parts from two manufacturers: Nabco and Tokiko. Parts are not interchangeable. The name of the manufacturer is on the part.*

1. Remove the wheel cylinder from the backing plate.
2. Remove the snapring from the piston bore.
3. Remove the dust boot and take out the piston. Discard the piston cup. The dust boot can be reused, if necessary, but it is better to replace it.
4. Wash all of the components in clean brake fluid.

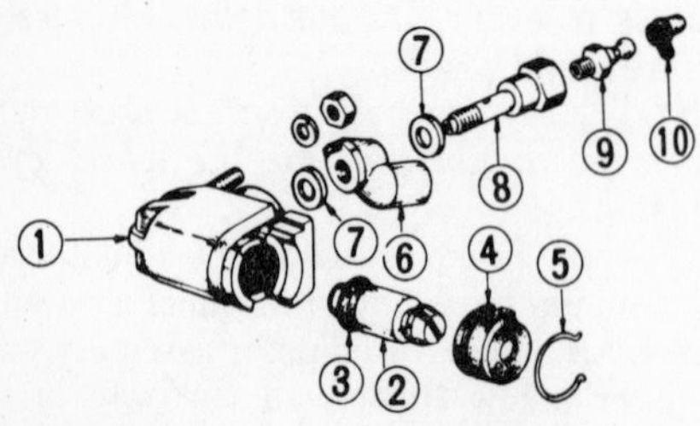

1. Wheel cylinder housing
2. Piston
3. Piston cup
4. Dust cover
5. Snap-ring
6. Connector
7. Packings
8. Connector bolt
9. Bleeder screw
10. Bleeder cap

Exploded view of the front wheel cylinder

5. Inspect the piston and piston bore. Replace any components which are severely corroded, scored, or worn. The piston and piston bore can be polished lightly with crocus cloth. Move the crocus cloth around the piston bore; not in and out of the piston bore.
6. Wash the wheel cylinder and piston thoroughly in clean brake fluid, allowing them to remain lubricated for assembly.
7. Coat all of the new components to be installed in the wheel cylinder with clean brake fluid prior to assembly.
8. Assemble the wheel cylinder and install it to the backing plate. Assemble the remaining components and bleed the brake hydraulic system.

FRONT DISC BRAKES

CAUTION: *Brake shoes contain asbestos, which has been determined to be a cancer causing agent. Never clean the brake surfaces with compressed air! Avoid inhaling any dust from any brake surface! When cleaning brake surfaces, use a commercially available brake cleaning fluid.*

Brake Pads

INSPECTION

The pads should be removed so that the thickness of the remaining friction material can be measured. If the pads are less than 2mm (0.08 in.) thick, they must be replaced. This measurement may disagree with your state inspection laws.

NOTE: *Always replace all pads on both wheels at the same time. The factory kit includes four pads, slips, pins, and springs; all parts should be used.*

REMOVAL AND INSTALLATION

1978-83

1. Raise and support the front of the truck. Remove the wheels.
2. Remove the retaining clip from the outboard pad.
3. Remove the pad pins retaining the anti-squeal springs.
4. Remove the pads.

NOTE: *When replacing the pads, always check the surface of the rotors for scoring or wear. The rotors should be removed for resurfacing if badly worn.*

5. To install, open the bleeder screw slightly and push the outer piston into the cylinder until the dust seal groove aligns with the end of the seal retaining ring, then close the bleeder screw. Be careful, because the piston can be

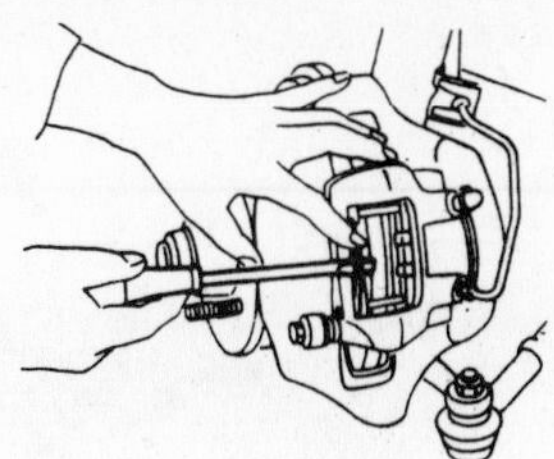

Removing the clip—1978–83

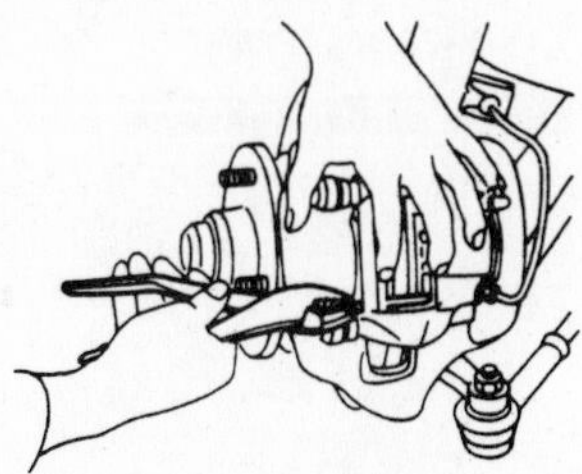

Removing the pad pins—1978–83

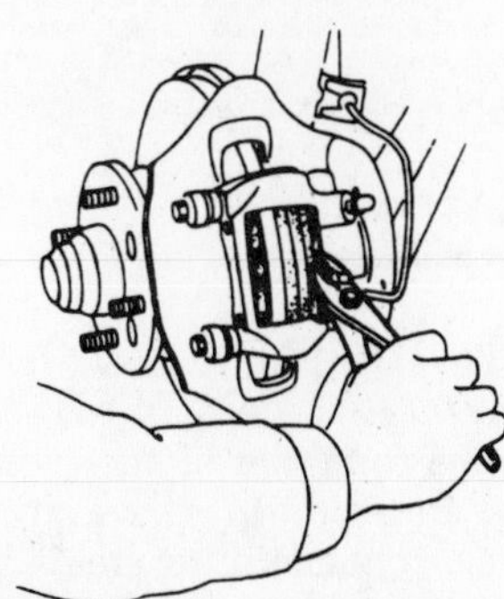

Removing the brake pads—1978–83

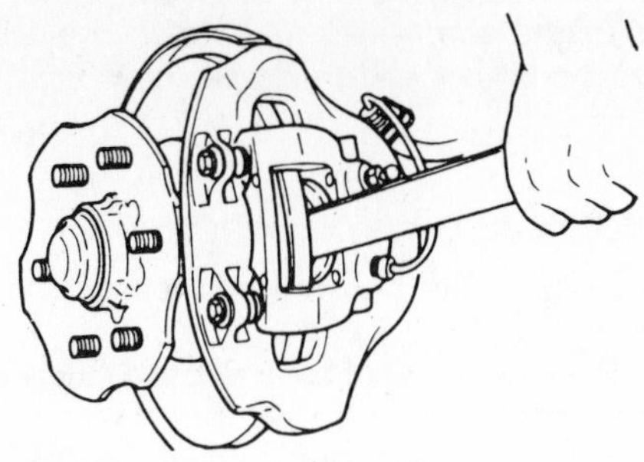

Pressing the piston into place

pads. Check the master cylinder level; add fluid if necessary. Bleed the brakes if necessary.

1984-89

1. Remove the hub cap and loosen the lug nuts.
2. Raise the front of the truck and safely support it with jackstands.
3. Remove the lug nuts and the wheel.
4. Attach a clear vinyl tube onto the bleeder plug on the brake cylinder, and insert the other end into a jar half filled with brake fluid. Bleed off a small amount of brake fluid.
5. Remove the caliper slide pin bolt on the sub-pin (lower) side.
6. Swivel the caliper up and away from the torque plate. Tie the caliper to a suspension member so its out of the way. *Do not* disconnect the brake line.
7. Lift the 2 brake pads out of the torque plate..
8. Remove the inner and outer shims. Remove the 2 pad retainers if they are not still attached to the pads.
9. Check the pad thickness and replace the pads if they are less than 1mm thick.

NOTE: *This minimum thickness measurement may disagree with your state inspection laws.*

To install:

10. Install the inner and outer shims into the torque plate.
11. Install a pad retainer to the bottom of each pad.
12. Install the pads into the torque plate.

CAUTION: *When installing new brake pads, make sure your hands are clean. Do not allow any grease or oil to touch the contact face of the pads or the brakes will not stop the truck properly!*

13. Use a C-clamp or hammer handle and press the caliper piston back into the housing.

NOTE: *Never press the piston into the cali-*

pushed too far, requiring disassembly of the caliper to repair. Install the inner pad.

6. Pull the yoke to push the inner piston into place. Install the outer pad.
7. Lightly coat the areas where the pins touch the pads, and where the pads touch the caliper (at the top) with grease. Do not allow the grease to get on the pad friction surfaces.
8. Install the anti-squeal springs and pad pins. Install the clip.
9. Apply the brakes a few times to seat the

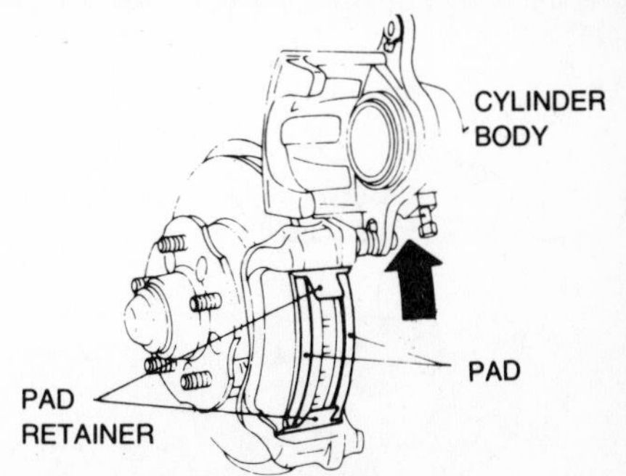

To remove the pads, swivel the caliper upward—1984–86 (720-D series) and 1986–89 2wd models with Z24i engines (D21-D series)

per when the pads are out on both sides of the truck.

14. Untie the caliper and swivel it back into position over the torque plate so that the dust boot is not pinched. Install the slide pin and tighten it to 16–23 ft. lbs. (22–31 Nm) on 1984-

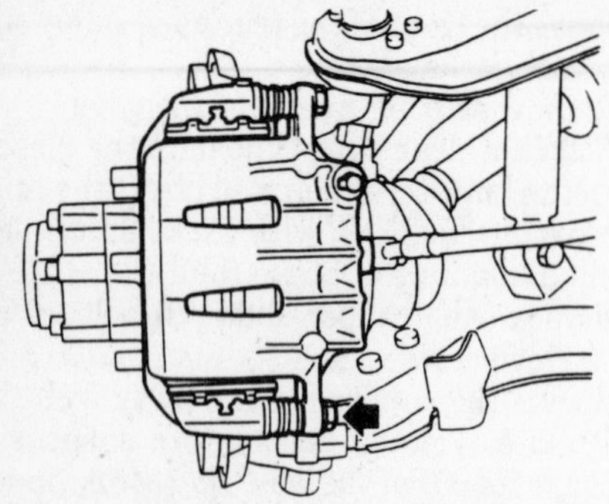

Remove the guide pin bolt—twin piston calipers

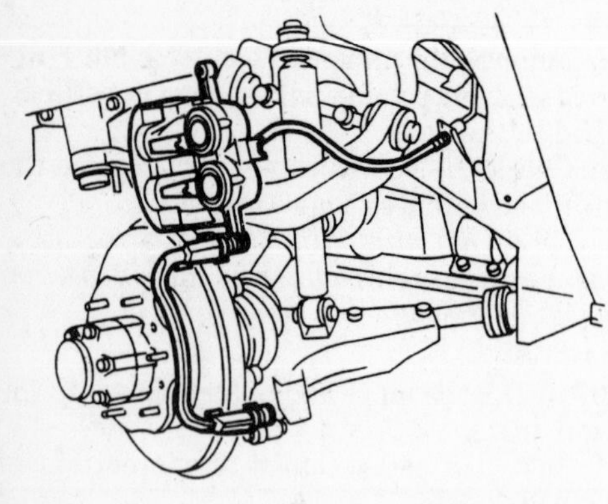

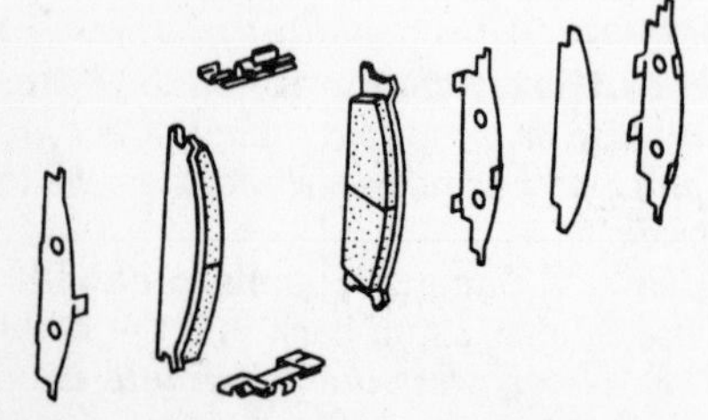

Swivel the caliper upward to remove the pads—twin piston caliper

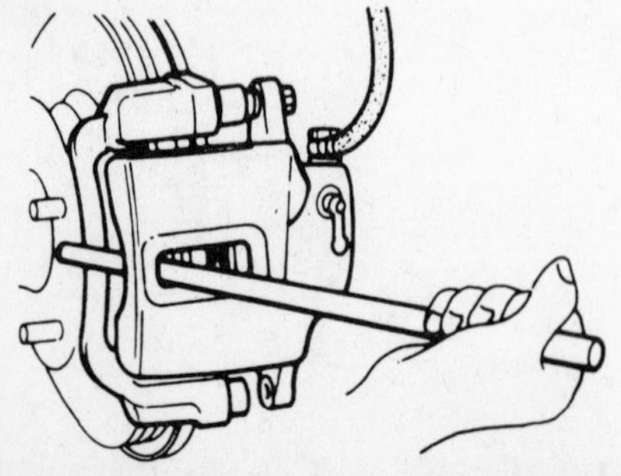

To install the inner pad, lever the cylinder body outward

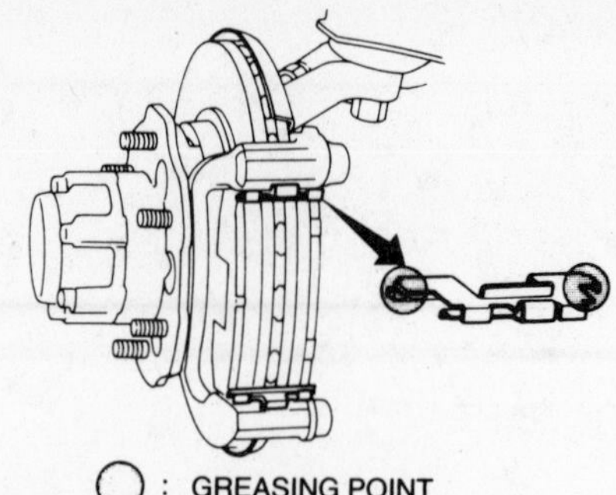

Installing the outer pad and retainer

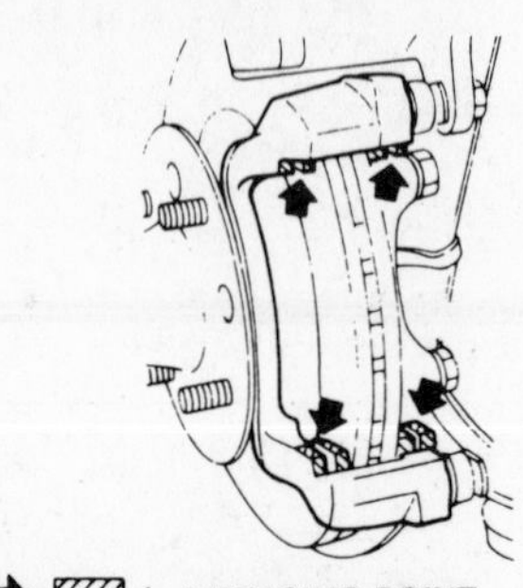

Brake pad greasing points

86 models (720-D series); or 53–72 ft. lbs. (72–97 Nm) on 1986-89 models (D21-D series).

15. Check the condition of the cylinder side bushing boot. Pull on it to relieve any air from the cylinder side pin mounting area. Check that the hole plug on the main pin side is there. Push on the center of the plug to relieve any air from the inner portion of the main pin.

16. Install the wheel and lower the truck. Bleed the brakes and road test the vehicle.

Caliper

REMOVAL AND INSTALLATION

1. Remove the hub cap and loosen the lug nuts.
2. Raise the front of the truck and safely support it with jackstands.
3. Remove the lug nuts and the wheel.
4. Attach a clear vinyl tube onto the bleeder plug on the brake cylinder, and insert the other end into a jar half filled with brake fluid. Bleed off a small amount of brake fluid.
5. Disconnect and plug the brake line.
6. Remove the caliper slide pin bolts and lift out the caliper.
7. Press the caliper piston(s) back into the housing until they are flush and then install the caliper. Tighten the mounting bolts to 16–23 ft. lbs. (22–31 Nm) on 1984-86 models (720-D series); and 53–72 ft. lbs. (72–97 Nm) on 1978-83 models and all 1986-89 models (D21-D series).

OVERHAUL

1978-83

1. Remove the caliper.
2. Remove the pads.
3. Remove the gripper pin attaching nuts and separate the yoke from the caliper body.
4. Remove the yoke holder from the piston and remove the retaining rings and dust seals from the ends of both pistons.
5. Apply air pressure gradually into the fluid chamber of the caliper, to force the pistons from the cylinders.
6. Remove the piston seals.
7. Inspect the parts for wear or damage. Check the inside surface of the cylinder for scoring or wear, and replace the caliper as necessary. Minor damage can be cleaned up with crocus cloth, buy deep pitting or scoring warrants replacement of the caliper. The piston should be examined for wear, but do not polish it with crocus cloth; it has a plated surface which will be damaged by sanding. Replace the piston as necessary.

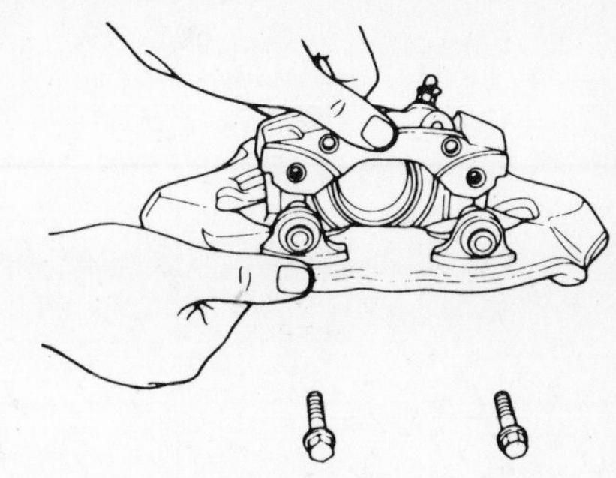

Separate the yoke from the caliper—1978–83

8. To assembly, coat the seals and pistons with clean brake fluid. Install the seals into the cylinder bore.
9. Slide the **A** piston into the cylinder, followed by the **B** piston, so that its yoke groove coincides with the yoke groove of the cylinder.
10. Install the dust seal and secure tightly with the retaining ring.
11. Install the yoke holder onto the **A** piston and install the gripper to the yoke. If you lightly

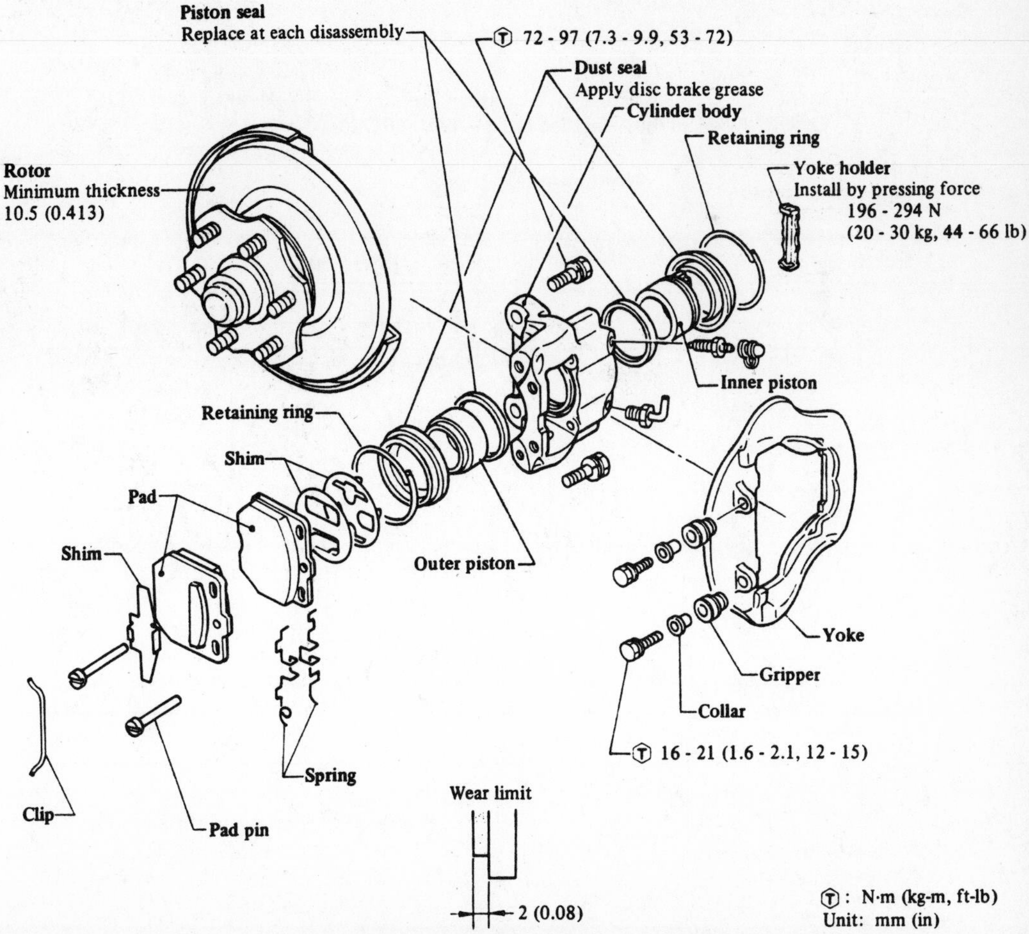

Exploded view of the front disc brake—1978–83

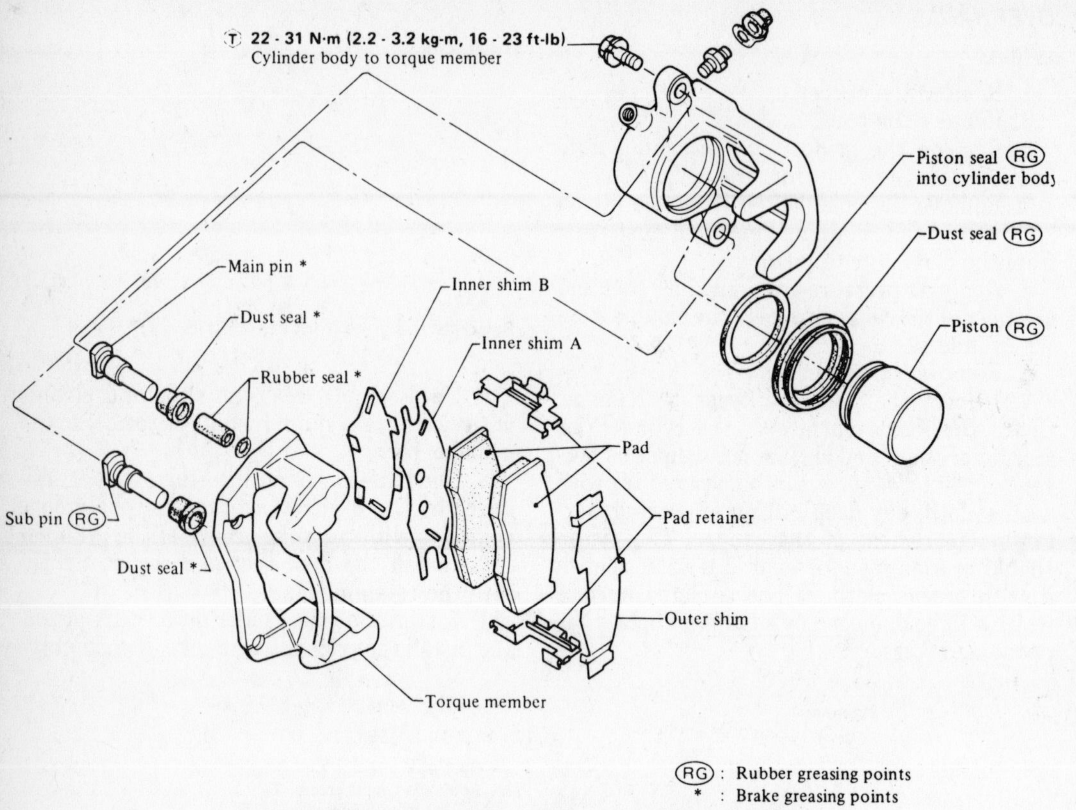

T 22 - 31 N·m (2.2 - 3.2 kg-m, 16 - 23 ft-lb)
Cylinder body to torque member

Piston seal (RG)
into cylinder body

Dust seal (RG)

Piston (RG)

Main pin *

Dust seal *

Inner shim B

Inner shim A

Rubber seal *

Pad

Pad retainer

Sub pin (RG)

Dust seal *

Outer shim

Torque member

(RG) : Rubber greasing points
* : Brake greasing points

Exploded view of the front disc brake—1984–86 (720- D series)

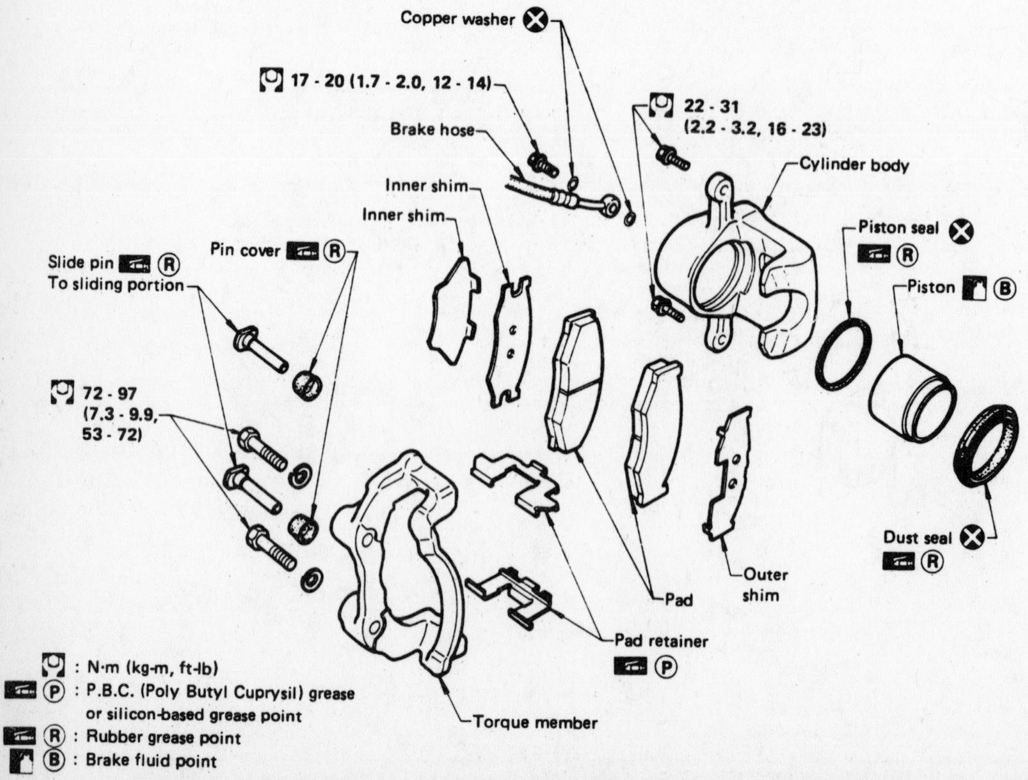

Copper washer ⊗

17 - 20 (1.7 - 2.0, 12 - 14)

22 - 31
(2.2 - 3.2, 16 - 23)

Brake hose

Cylinder body

Inner shim

Inner shim

Piston seal ⊗
(R)

Piston (B)

Pin cover (R)

Slide pin (R)
To sliding portion

72 - 97
(7.3 - 9.9,
53 - 72)

Dust seal ⊗
(R)

Outer
shim

Pad

Pad retainer
(P)

Torque member

: N·m (kg-m, ft-lb)
(P) : P.B.C. (Poly Butyl Cuprysil) grease
or silicon-based grease point
(R) : Rubber grease point
(B) : Brake fluid point

Exploded view of the front disc brake—1986–89 2wd models with the Z24i engine

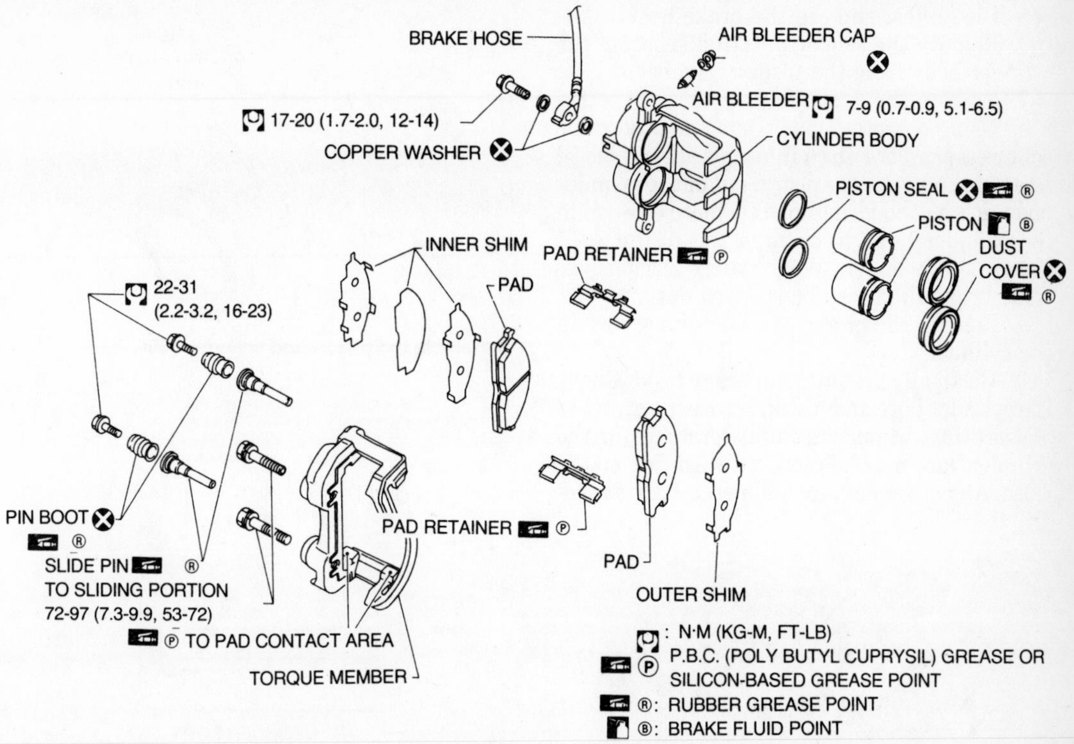

Exploded view of the front disc brake—1986–89 2wd models with SD25 and VG30i engines and all 4wd models

coat the gripper pins with soapy water, they will be easier to install.

12. Support the end of the **B** piston, and press the yoke into the yoke holder. This will require a good deal of force. Be careful to insert the yoke straight into the holder, to avoid cracking the yoke holder.

13. Install the pads, anti-squeal springs, and pad pins and retain with the clip.

14. Tighten the gripper pin attaching nuts to 12–15 ft. lbs. (16–21 Nm), and install the caliper on the spindle.

1984-89

1. Raise and support the truck on jackstands.

2. Remove the wheels.

3. Remove the caliper pin bolts and lift off the caliper.

4. Remove the brake pads.

1. Piston A
2. Piston B
3. Caliper body

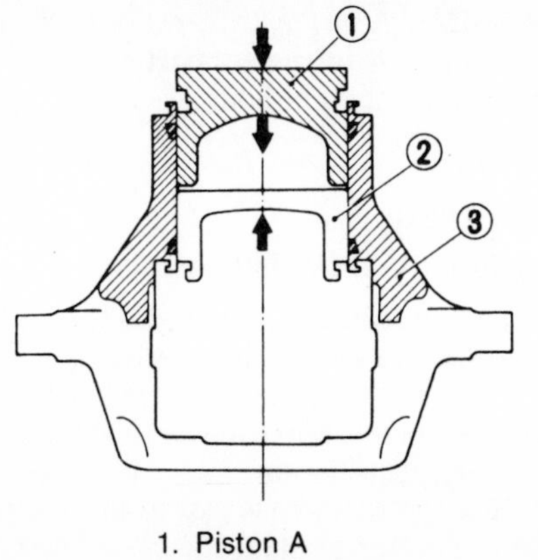

Install the piston in the caliper; the arrows show the direction—1978–83

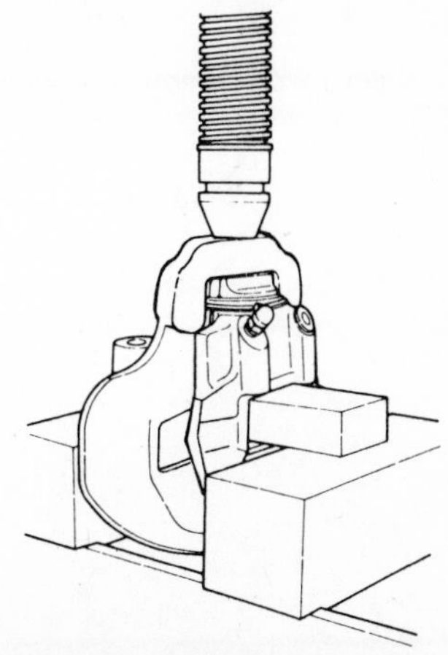

Installing the yoke—1978–83

5. Disconnect and cap the brake hose.

6. Remove the caliper pins and separate the cylinder body from the torque member.

7. Remove the dust cover.

8. Using compressed air, such as a portable compressor, place the air nozzle in the brake line hole and force the piston out of the cylinder body. It's a good idea to place a piece of wood in the cylinder body to cushion the piston as it leaves the cylinder. Wear safety goggles, as some brake fluid may be sprayed out.

9. Remove the piston seal from its groove in the cylinder.

10. Clean all parts in clean brake fluid. Check the cylinder bore and piston for wear, scratches and scoring. Minor rust and scratches in the cylinder bore may be removed with fine emery cloth. Any other damage will necessitate the replacement of the affected cylinder body. Any cracks in the torque member will require replacement of the part. The piston sliding surface is plated. DO NOT USE EMERY CLOTH OR ANY OTHER POLISHING MATERIAL TO REMOVE RUST OR OTHER FOREIGN MATTER. Replace the piston seal and dust boot. If the support pins are damaged at all, replace them.

11. Assembly is the reverse of disassembly. Coat all metal parts with clean brake fluid prior to assembly. Apply a thin coating of silicone brake lubricant to the support pins and bushings. Tighten the pin bolts.

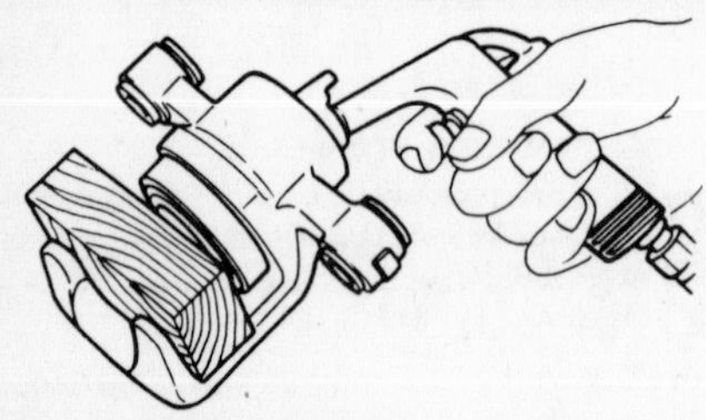

Remove the piston with compressed air—1984–89 models with a single piston

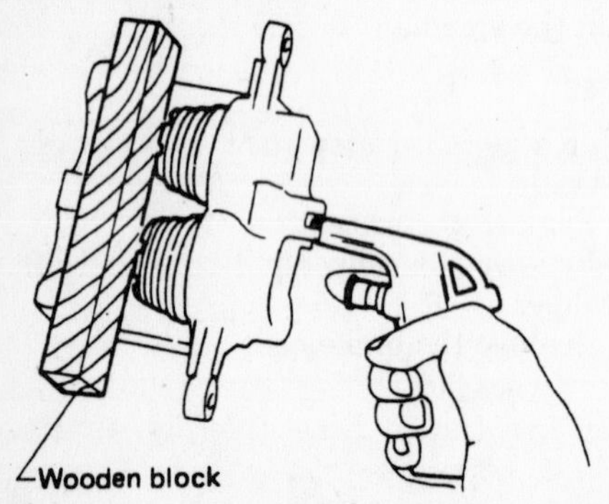

Remove the pistons with compressed air—1984–89 models with twin pistons

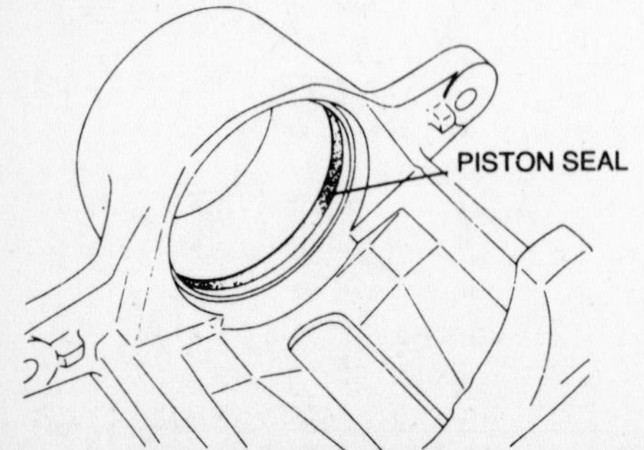

Piston seal in its groove—1984–89

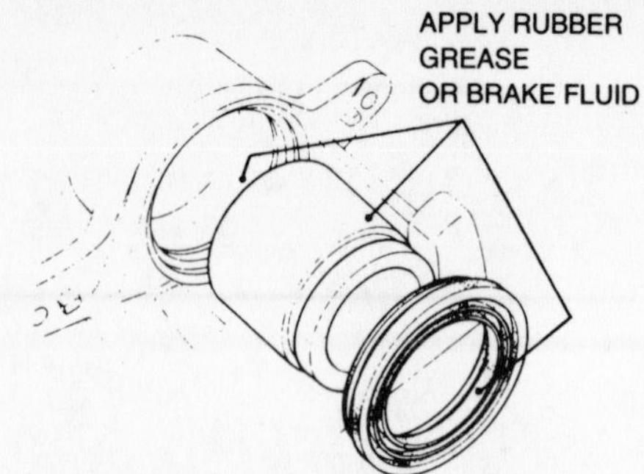

Assemble the piston and caliper—1984–89

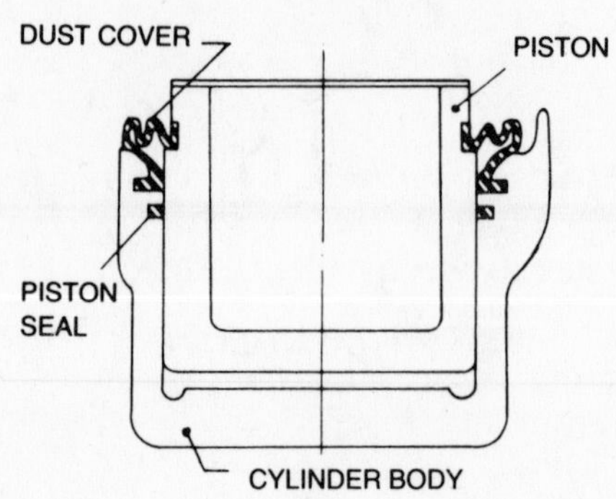

Cross section of the cylinder and piston—1984–89

Brake Disc

REMOVAL AND INSTALLATION

1. Remove the brake pads and the caliper, as detailed in the appropriate section.

2. Check the disc run-out, as detailed following, at this point. Make a note of the results for use during installation.

3. Remove the grease cap from the hub. Remove the cotter pin and the castellated nut.

4. Remove the wheel hub with the brake disc attached.

5. Perform the disc inspection procedure, as outlined in the following section.

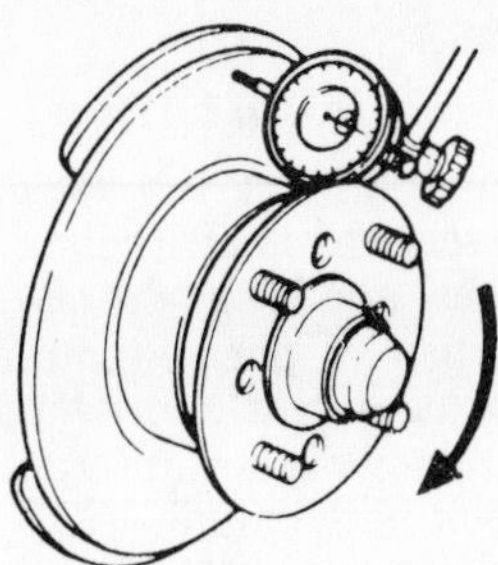

Measure the disc runout with a dial indicator

To install:

1. Coat the hub oil seal lip with multipurpose grease and install the disc/hub assembly.
2. Adjust the wheel bearing preload, as detailed following.
3. Measure the disc run-out. Check it against the specifications in the "Brake Specifications" chart and against the figures noted during removal.

 NOTE: *If the wheel bearing nut is improperly tightened, disc run-out will be affected.*

4. Install the remainder of the components as outlined in the appropriate sections.
5. Bleed the brake system.
6. Road test the truck. Check the wheel bearing preload.

INSPECTION

Examine the disc. If it is worn, warped or scored, it must be replaced. Check the thickness of the disc against the specifications given in the "Brake Specifications" chart. If it is below specifications, replace it. Use a micrometer to measure the thickness.

The disc run-out should be measured before the disc is removed and again, after the disc is installed. Use a dial indicator mounted on a stand to determine run-out. If run-out exceeds 0.0059 in. (0.15mm) on 1978-83 models or 0.0028 in. (0.07mm) on 1984-89 models, replace the disc.

NOTE: *Be sure that the wheel bearing nut is properly tightened. If it is not, an inaccurate run-out reading may be obtained. If different run-out readings are obtained with the same disc, between removal and installation, this is probably the cause.*

For Wheel Bearing removal and installation and adjustment please refer to Chapters 1 or 7.

PRELOAD ADJUSTMENT

1. With the front hub/disc assembly installed, tighten the castellated nut to the torque.
2. Rotate the disc back and forth, two or three times, to allow the bearing to seat properly.
3. Loosen the castellated nut until it is only finger tight.
4. Tighten the nut firmly, using a box wrench. Make sure the disc rotates smoothly.
5. Measure the bearing preload with a spring scale attached to a wheel mounting stud.
6. Install the cotter pin.

 NOTE: *If the hole does not align with the nut (or cap) holes, tighten the nut slightly until it does.*

7. Finish installing the brake components and the wheel.

REAR DRUM BRAKES

Brake Drums

CAUTION: *Brake shoes contain asbestos, which has been determined to be a cancer causing agent. Never clean the brake surfaces with compressed air! Avoid inhaling any dust from any brake surface! When cleaning brake surfaces, use a commercially available brake cleaning fluid.*

INSPECTION

1. Clean the drum with a rag and a little paint thinner.

 CAUTION: *Do not blow the brake dust out of the drum with compressed air or lung power. Brake linings contain asbestos, a known cancer causing agent.*

2. Inspect the drum for cracks, grooves, scoring and out-of-roundness.
3. Light scoring may be removed with fine emery paper, Heavy scores or grooves will have to be removed by having the drum turned on a lathe. This can be done at many automotive machine shops and some service stations.
4. Before cutting the drum it must be measured to determine whether or not the inside dimension of the drum is within limitations after removing the score marks. The service limits of the brake drums are detailed in the "Brake Specifications" chart.
5. Check the drum for concentricity. An inside micrometer is necessary for an exact measurement, so unless this tool is available, the drum should be taken to a machine shop to be checked. Any drum which measures more than 0.15mm out of round will result in an inaccurate brake adjustment and other problems, and must be refinished or replaced.

 NOTE: *Make all measurements at right angles to each other and at the open and closed edges of the drum machined surface.*

REMOVAL AND INSTALLATION

1. Remove the hub cap and loosen the lug nuts.
2. Raise the rear of the vehicle and support it on jackstands.
3. Remove the lug nuts, tire and wheel.
4. Remove the axle hub grease cap.
5. Remove the cotter pin, and then loosen the hub nut. When the nut is close to the end of the spindle, pull the drum and hub assembly toward you. If it does not slide off the brake shoes, loosen the brake shoe adjuster star wheels. Remove the spindle nut, brake drum and hub, the washer, and the wheel bearings.

NOTE: *Be careful not to get foreign matter in the wheel bearings. The heavy coating of grease will hold many particles. These will damage the bearings.*

6. Inspect the brake drum as outlined above.

CAUTION: *Do not depress the brake pedal with the brake drum removed.*

7. For instructions on preloading the front wheel bearings, see the appropriate section.

Brake Shoes

REMOVAL AND INSTALLATION

1. Raise and support the vehicle until the wheel to be serviced is off the ground and remove the wheel and brake drum.
2. With a pair of pliers, remove the brake shoe holddown anti-rattle spring retainers. Depress the retainer while rotating it 90 degrees to align the slot in the retainer with the flanged end of the pin. Remove the retainers, springs, spring seats, and pins.
3. Open the brake shoes outward against the return springs and remove the parking brake extension link.
4. Disconnect the brake shoe return springs.
5. Remove the brake shoes from the backing plate. The secondary (after) brake shoe must be disconnected from the parking brake toggle lever after withdrawing the toggle lever clevis pin.
6. Remove the rubber boot from behind the brake backing plate and slide the adjuster shim, lockplate, and adjuster springs off the back of

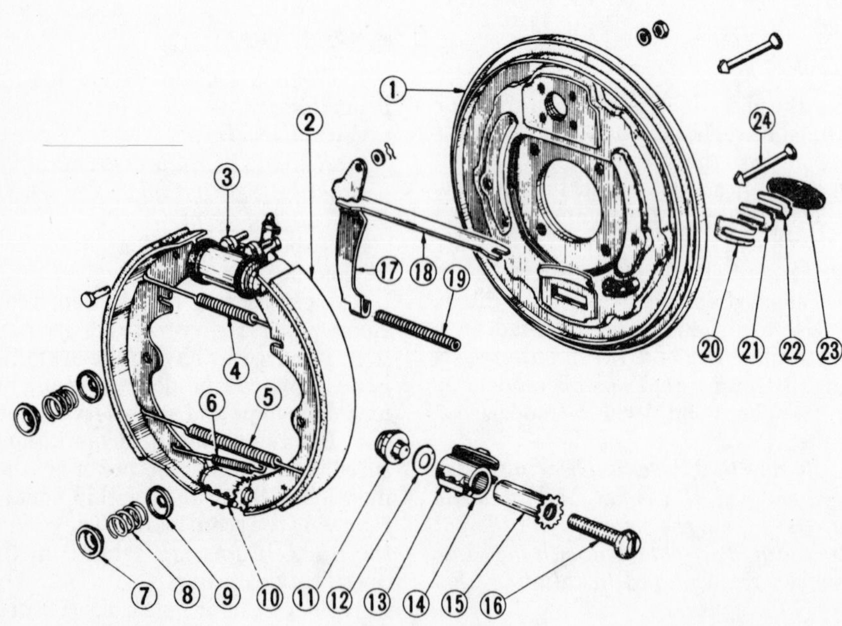

1. Brake backing plate	9. Spring seat	17. Toggle lever
2. Brake shoe	10. Adjuster assembly	18. Extension link
3. Wheel cylinder	11. Adjuster head	19. Return spring
4. Return upper spring	12. Adjuster head shim	20. Adjuster spring
5. Return lower spring	13. Lock-spring	21. Lockplate
6. After shoe return spring	14. Adjuster housing	22. Adjuster shim
7. Retainer	15. Adjuster wheel	23. Rubber boot
8. Anti-rattle spring	16. Adjuster screw	24. Anti-rattle pin

Exploded view of the rear drum brake—1970–79

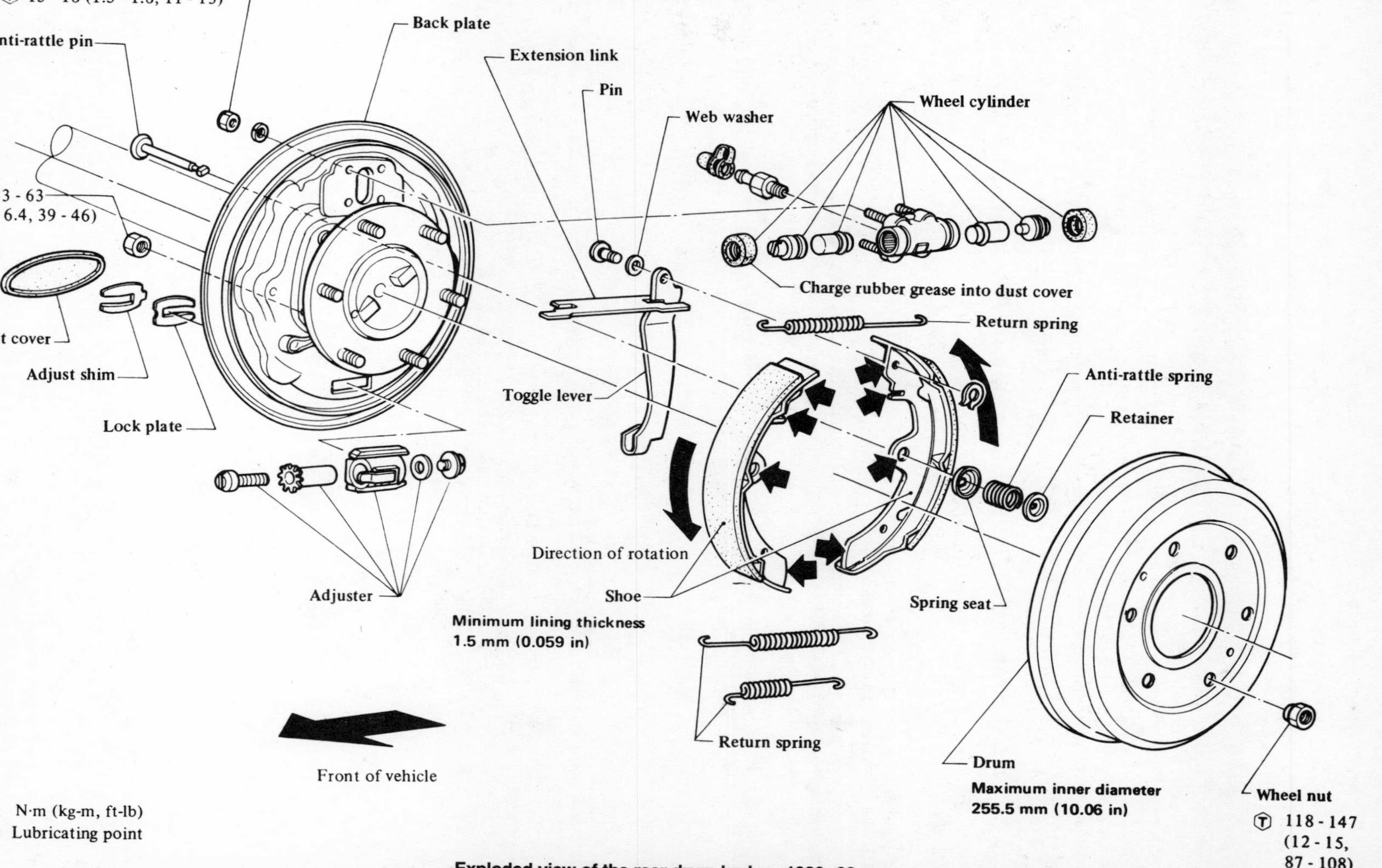

Exploded view of the rear drum brake—1980–83

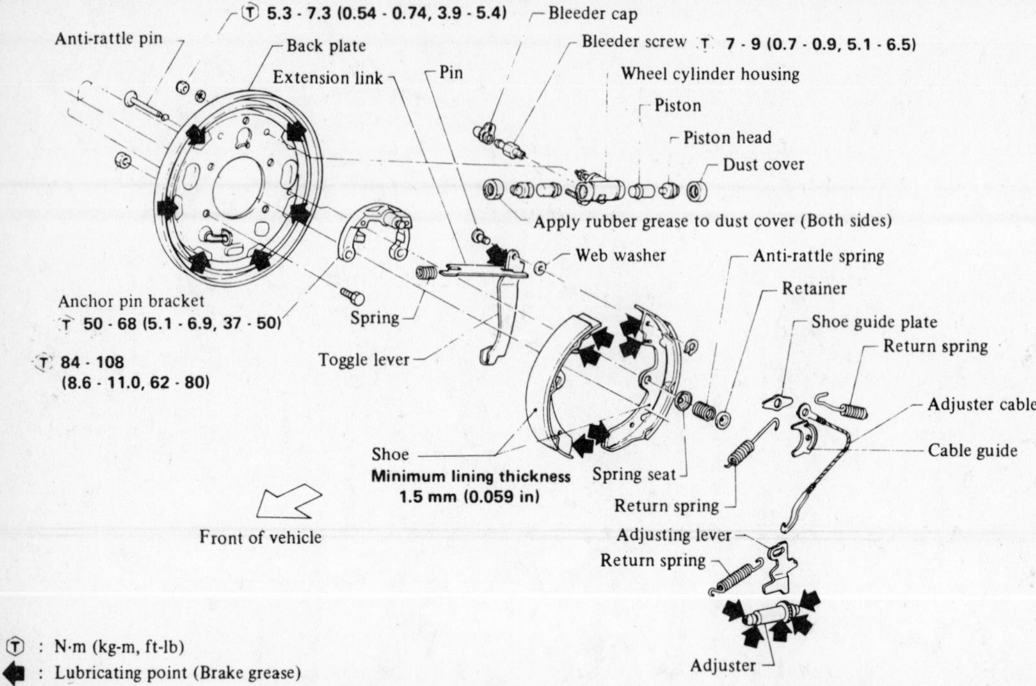

Exploded view of the rear drum brake (DS22 and DS25B)—1984–86 models (720-D series) and 1986–89 2wd HD and C/C models (D21-D series)

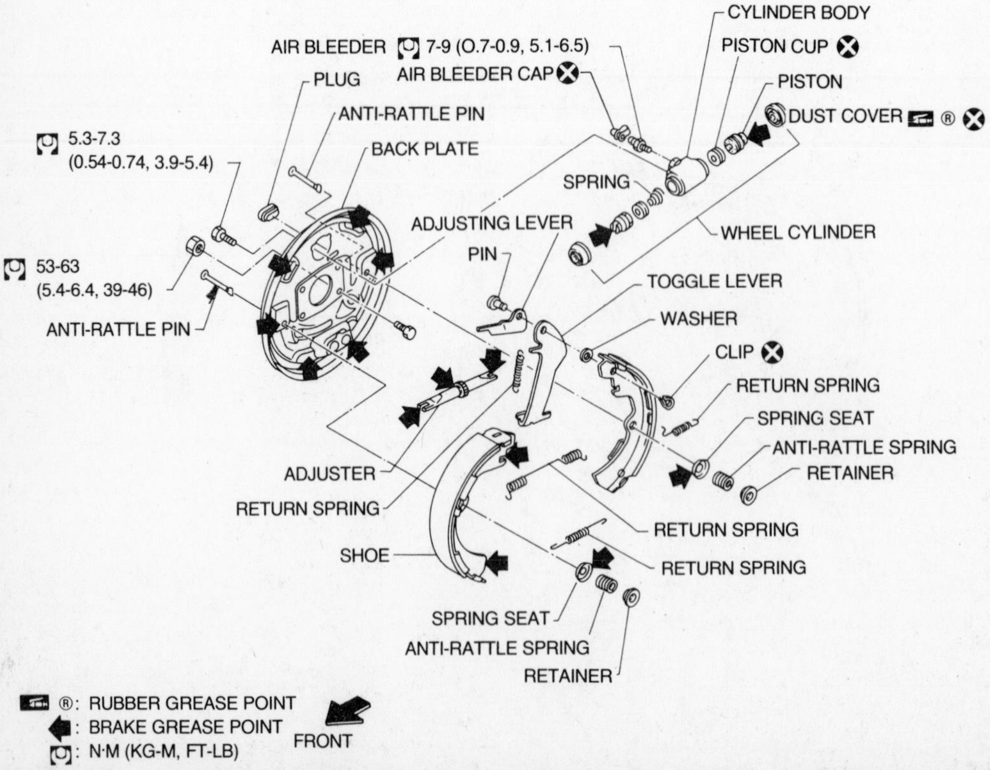

CYLINDER BODY
AIR BLEEDER 7-9 (0.7-0.9, 5.1-6.5)
PISTON CUP
PLUG
AIR BLEEDER CAP
PISTON
ANTI-RATTLE PIN
DUST COVER ®
5.3-7.3
(0.54-0.74, 3.9-5.4)
BACK PLATE
SPRING
ADJUSTING LEVER
WHEEL CYLINDER
PIN
53-63
(5.4-6.4, 39-46)
TOGGLE LEVER
WASHER
ANTI-RATTLE PIN
CLIP
RETURN SPRING
SPRING SEAT
ANTI-RATTLE SPRING
ADJUSTER
RETAINER
RETURN SPRING
RETURN SPRING
SHOE
RETURN SPRING
SPRING SEAT
ANTI-RATTLE SPRING
RETAINER
®: RUBBER GREASE POINT
: BRAKE GREASE POINT
: N·M (KG-M, FT-LB)
FRONT

Exploded view of the rear drum brake (LT26B)—1986– 89 2wd models except HD and C/C (D21-D series)

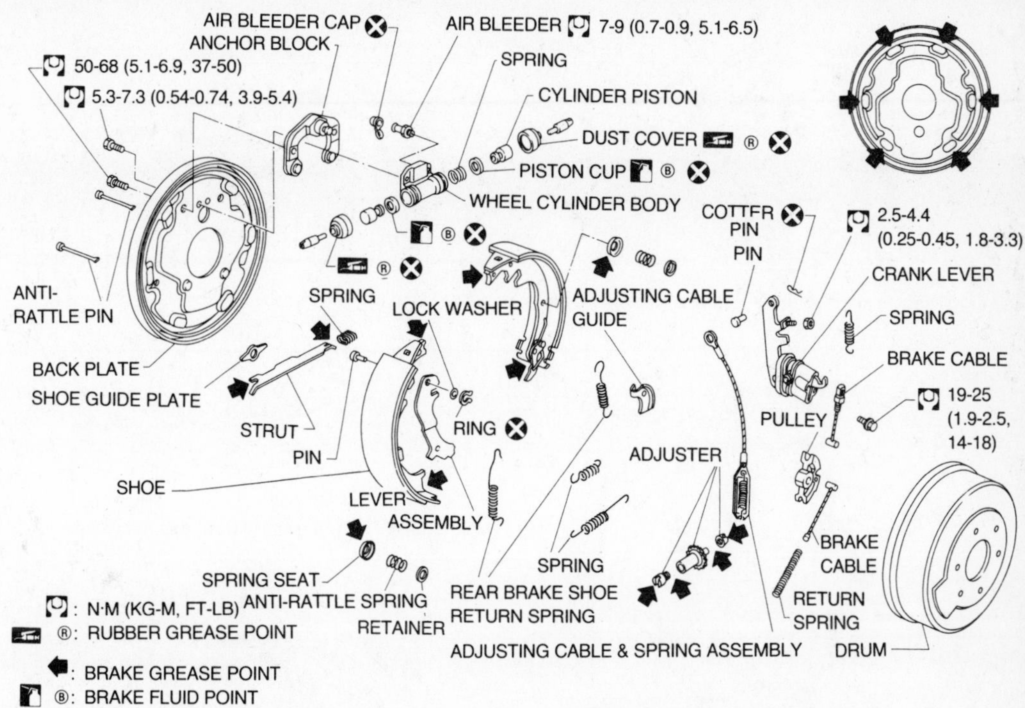

Exploded view of the rear drum brake—1986–89 4wd models (D21-D series)

the adjuster assembly. Remove the adjuster assembly from the backing plate.

7. Clean the backing plate and adjuster assembly so they are free of all dust and dirt.

8. Check the wheel cylinders.

9. Apply brake grease to the adjuster assembly housing bore, adjuster wheel, and adjuster screw. Assemble the adjuster assemble with the adjuster screw turned all the way in. Apply brake grease to the sliding surfaces of the adjuster assembly, brake backing plate, and the retaining spring. Install the adjuster assembly to the backing plate.

NOTE: *On 1986-89 models (D21-D series) with 4wd, after installing the crank lever on the back plate, make sure there is no play between the crank lever and the back plate when pulling the crank lever. If play exists, adjust bolt* **A** *and locknut* **A**.

10. Assemble the secondary (after) brake shoe to the parking brake toggle lever and adjust the clearance between the toggle lever and the brake shoe. On 1970-79 models, use the proper thickness toggle pin washer to adjust the clearance which should be 0.012 in. (0.3mm). Toggle pin washers are available in the following thicknesses: 0.079 in. (2mm), 0.091 in. (2.3mm), 0.102 in. (2.6mm), 0.114 in. (2.9mm), and 0.126 in. (3.2mm).

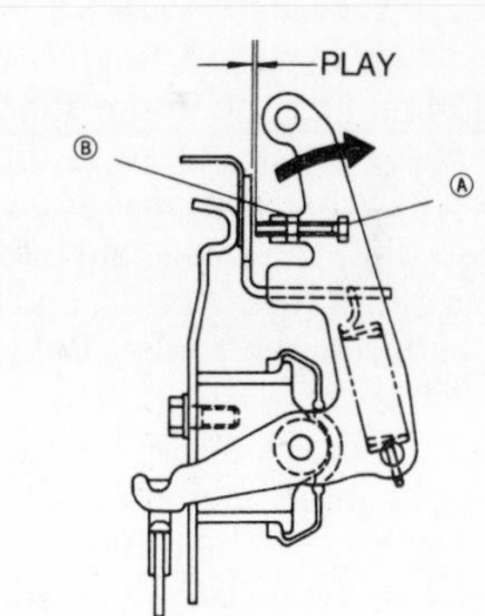

Adjust bolt "A" and locknut "B" to reduce play on Model DS25C brake systems

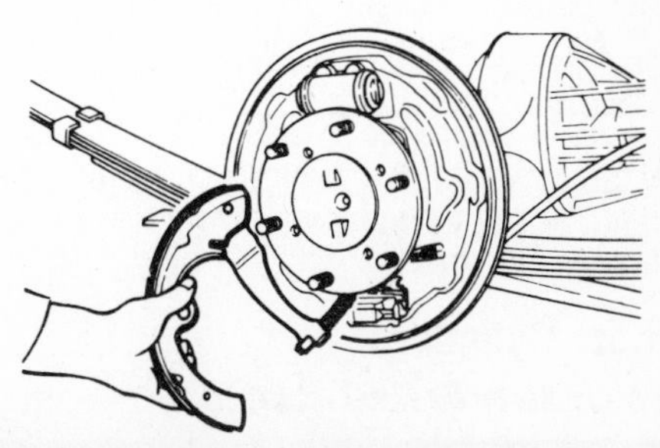

Remove the parking brake toggle lever from the secondary shoe

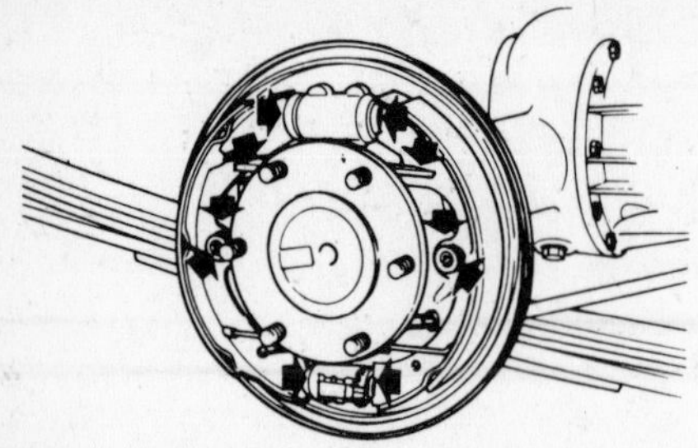

Greasing points on the rear brakes indicated by arrows

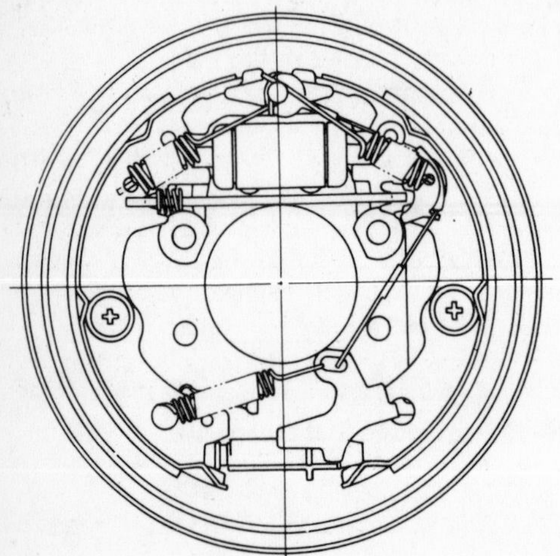

Model DS22, DS25B shoe installation, L.H.wheel

11. Before assembling the brake shoes to the backing plate apply brake grease to the following areas: the brake shoe grooves in the parking brake extension link, the inside surfaces of the anti-rattle (retaining) spring seats, and the contact surfaces between the brake backing plate and the brake shoes.
12. Assemble the brake shoes to the backing plate. Measure the inner diameter of the brake drum and then measure the outer diameter of the shoes (at the center!). The shoe outer diameter should be 0.0098–0.0157 in. (0.25–0.40mm) less than the drume inner diameter; if not, adjust it by rotating the star wheel adjuster.
13. Install the brake drum and the wheel.
14. Adjust the brakes. Bleed the brakes.

NOTE: *On 1980-89 models, adjust the shoe-to-drum clearance by operating the parking brake lever several times. On earlier models refer to the adjustment procedure for drum brakes outlined earlier.*

Wheel Cylinders

REMOVAL AND INSTALLATION

1. Raise the rear of the truck and support it with safety stands.

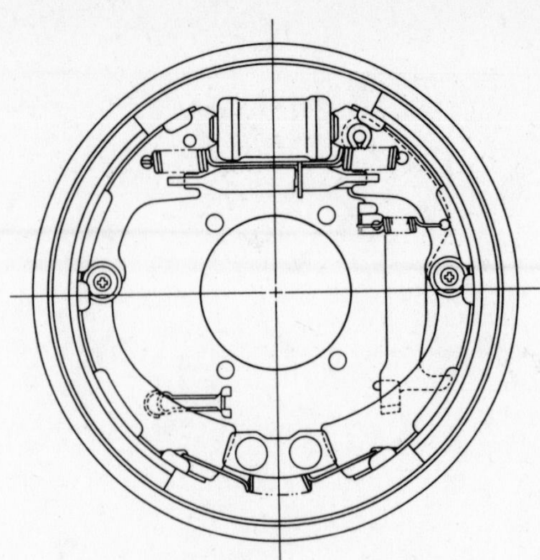

Model LT26B shoe installation, L.H. wheel

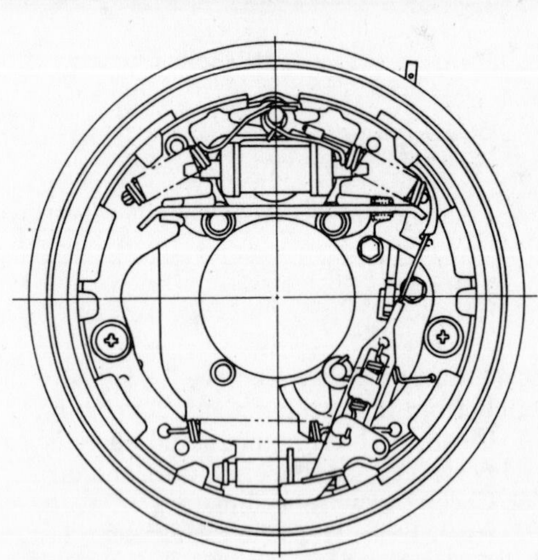

Model DS25C shoe installation, L.H. wheel

2. Remove the wheel, brake drum, hub assembly, and brake shoes.
3. Disconnect the brake hose from the wheel cylinder.
4. Unscrew the wheel cylinder securing nut and remove the wheel cylinder from the brake backing plate.
5. Install the wheel cylinder, assemble the remaining components, and bleed the brake hydraulic system.

OVERHAUL

NOTE: *This is one of those jobs where it is usually easier just to replace the part rather than rebuild it. If you decide to rebuild the wheel cylinders, be sure you get the correct parts for your truck. Datsun obtains parts from two manufacturers: Nabco and Tokiko. Parts are not interchangeable. The name of the manufacturer is on the part.*

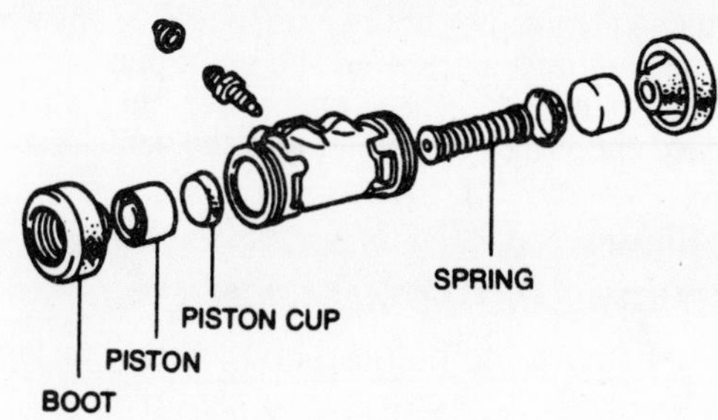

Exploded view of a wheel cylinder

1. Remove the wheel cylinder from the backing plate.
2. Remove the snapring from the piston bore.
3. Remove the dust boot and take out the piston. Discard the piston cup. The dust boot can be reused, if necessary, but it is better to replace it.
4. Wash all of the components in clean brake fluid.
5. Inspect the piston and piston bore. Replace any components which are severely corroded, scored, or worn. The piston and piston bore can be polished lightly with crocus cloth. Move the crocus cloth around the piston bore; not in and out of the piston bore.
6. Wash the wheel cylinder and piston thoroughly in clean brake fluid, allowing them to remain lubricated for assembly.
7. Coat all of the new components to be installed in the wheel cylinder with clean brake fluid prior to assembly.
8. Assemble the wheel cylinder and install it to the backing plate. Assemble the remaining components and bleed the brake hydraulic system.

REAR DISC BRAKES

CAUTION: *Brake shoes contain asbestos, which has been determined to be a cancer causing agent. Never clean the brake surfaces with compressed air! Avoid inhaling any dust from any brake surface! When cleaning brake surfaces, use a commercially available brake cleaning fluid.*

Brake Pads

INSPECTION

The pads should be removed so that the thickness of the remaining friction material can be measured. If the pads are less than 2mm (0.08 in.) thick, they must be replaced. This measurement may disagree with your state inspection laws.

NOTE: *Always replace all pads on both wheels at the same time. The factory kit includes four pads, slips, pins, and springs; all parts should be used.*

REMOVAL AND INSTALLATION

1988-89

1. Remove the hub cap and loosen the lug nuts.
2. Raise the rear of the truck and safely support it with jackstands.
3. Remove the lug nuts and the wheel.
4. Attach a clear vinyl tube onto the bleeder plug on the brake cylinder, and insert the other end into a jar half filled with brake fluid. Bleed off a small amount of brake fluid.
5. Remove the caliper guide pin on the lower side.
6. Swivel the caliper up and away from the torque plate. Tie the caliper to a suspension member so its out of the way. *Do not* disconnect the brake line.
7. Lift the 2 brake pads out of the torque plate.
8. Remove the inner and outer shims and cover. Remove the pad retainer if it is not still attached to the pads.
9. Check the pad thickness and replace the pads if they are less than 1mm thick.

NOTE: *This minimum thickness measure-*

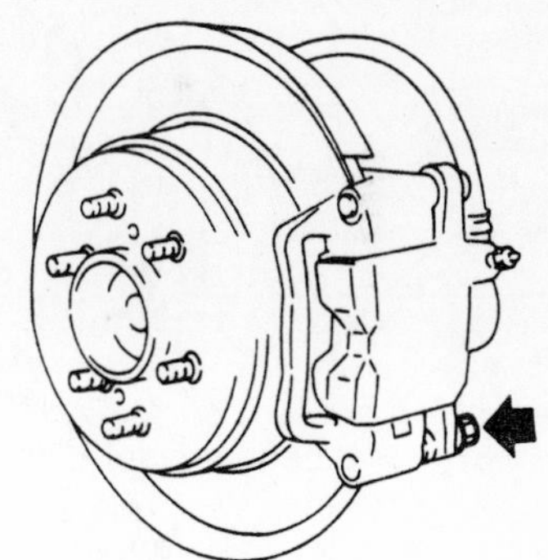
Remove the lever guide pin

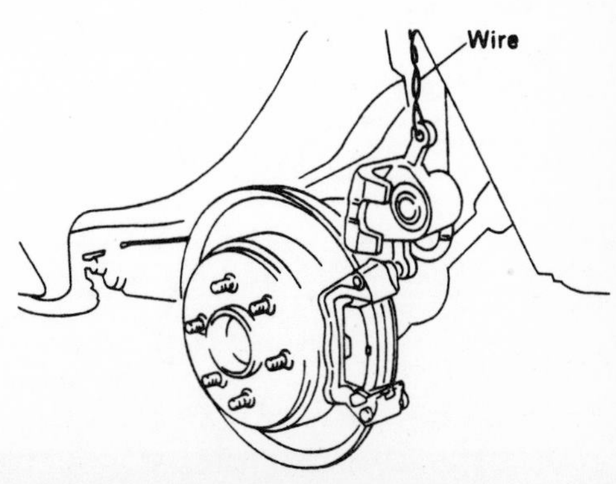

Swivel the calier upward to remove the brake pads

ment may disagree with your state inspection laws.

To install:

10. Install the inner and outer shims into the torque plate.
11. Install the pad retainer.
12. Install the pads into the torque plate.

CAUTION: *When installing new brake pads, make sure your hands are clean. Do not allow any grease or oil to touch the contact face of the pads or the brakes will not stop the truck properly!*

13. Use a C-clamp or hammer handle and press the caliper piston back into the housing.

NOTE: *Never press the piston into the caliper when the pads are out on both sides of the truck.*

14. Untie the caliper and swivel it back into position over the torque plate so that the dust boot is not pinched. Install the guide pin and tighten it to 23–30 ft. lbs. (31–41 Nm).
15. Check the condition of the cylinder side bushing boot. Pull on it to relieve any air from the cylinder side pin mounting area. Check that the hole plug on the main pin side is there. Push on the center of the plug to relieve any air from the inner portion of the main pin.
16. Install the wheel and lower the truck. Bleed the brakes and road test the vehicle.

Caliper

REMOVAL AND INSTALLATION

1. Remove the hub cap and loosen the lug nuts.
2. Raise the rear of the truck and safely support it with jackstands.
3. Remove the lug nuts and the wheel.
4. Disconnect and plug the brake line.
5. Remove the caliper slide pin bolts and lift out the caliper.
6. Press the caliper piston into the housing until it is flush and then install the caliper. Tighten the mounting bolts 23–30 ft. lbs. (31–41 Nm).

OVERHAUL

1. Raise and support the truck on jackstands.
2. Remove the wheels.

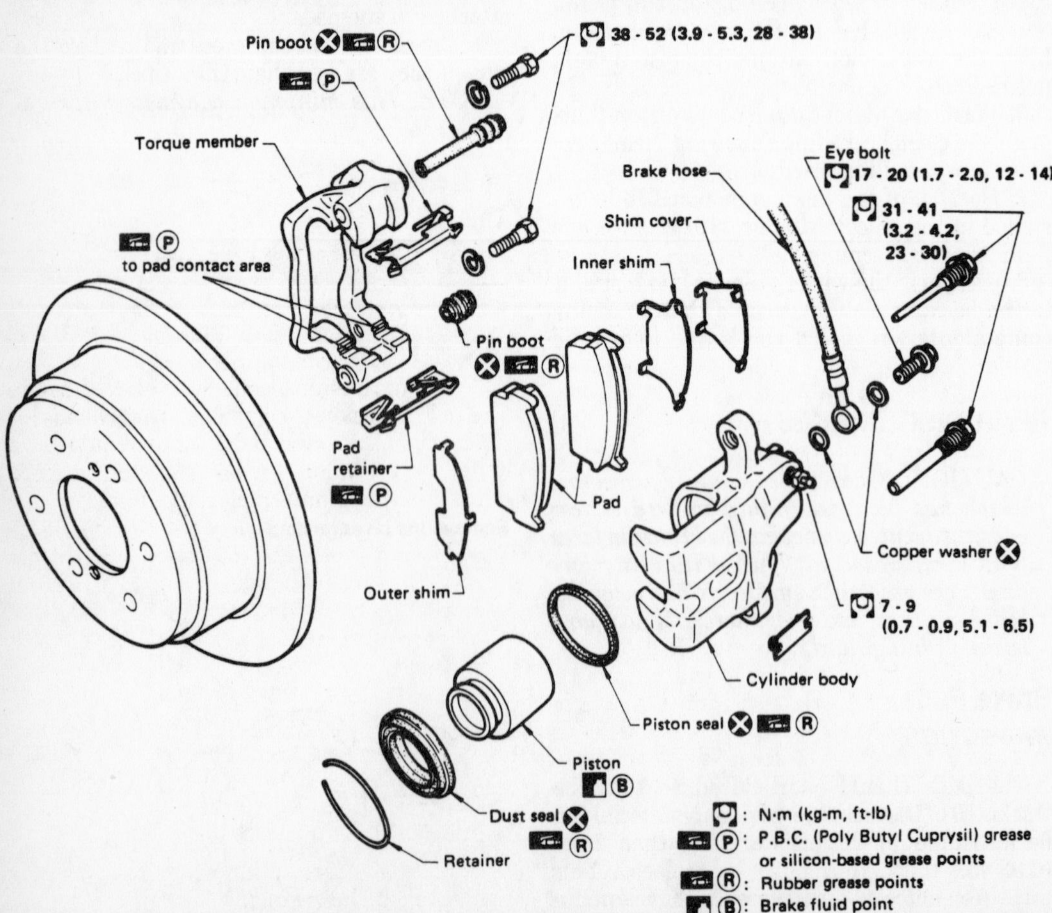

Exploded view of the rear disc brake—1988–89

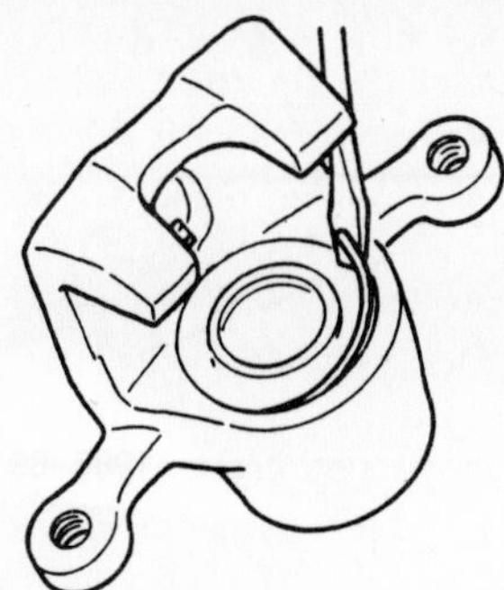

Remove the piston retainer

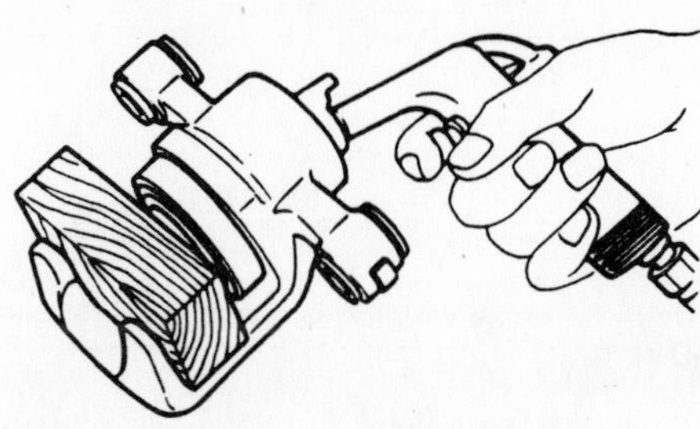

Removing the piston with compressed air

3. Remove the caliper pin bolts and lift off the caliper.
4. Remove the brake pads.
5. Disconnect and cap the brake hose.
6. Remove the caliper pins and separate the cylinder body from the torque member.
7. Remove the piston retainer.
8. Using compressed air, such as a portable compressor, place the air nozzle in the brake line hole and force the piston out of the cylinder body. It's a good idea to place a piece of wood in the cylinder body to cushion the piston as it leaves the cylinder. Wear safety goggles, as some brake fluid may be sprayed out.
9. Remove the piston seal from its groove in the cylinder.
10. Clean all parts in clean brake fluid. Check the cylinder bore and piston for wear, scratches and scoring. Minor rust and scratches in the cylinder bore may be removed with fine emery cloth. Any other damage will necessitate the replacement of the affected cylinder body. Any cracks in the torque member will require replacement of the part. The piston sliding surface is plated. DO NOT USE EMERY CLOTH OR ANY OTHER POLISHING MATERIAL TO REMOVE RUST OR OTHER FOREIGN MATTER. Replace the piston seal and dust boot. If the support pins are damaged at all, replace them.
11. Assembly is the reverse of disassembly. Coat all metal parts with clean brake fluid prior to assembly. Apply a thin coating of silicone brake lubricant to the support pins and bushings. Tighten the pin bolts.

Brake Disc

REMOVAL AND INSTALLATION

1. Remove the brake pads and the caliper, as detailed in the appropriate section.
2. Check the disc run-out, as detailed following, at this point. Make a note of the results for use during installation.
3. Loosen the parking brake shoes by rotating the star wheel upward.
4. Remove the two mounting bolts and then remove the brake disc assembly.
5. Perform the disc inspection procedure, as outlined in the following section.

To install:

1. Install the disc/hub assembly and tighten the mounting bolts.
2. Measure the disc run-out. Check it against the specifications in the "Brake Specifications" chart and against the figures noted during removal.

NOTE: *If the wheel bearing nut is improperly tightened, disc run-out will be affected.*

3. Install the remainder of the components as outlined in the appropriate sections.
4. Bleed the brake system.
5. Road test the truck. Check the wheel bearing preload.

INSPECTION

Examine the disc. If it is worn, warped or scored, it must be replaced. Check the thickness of the disc against the specifications given in the "Brake Specifications" chart. If it is below specifications, replace it. Use a micrometer to measure the thickness.

The disc run-out should be measured before the disc is removed and again, after the disc is installed. Use a dial indicator mounted on a stand to determine run-out. If run-out exceeds 0.0028 in. (0.07mm), replace the disc.

NOTE: *Be sure that the wheel bearing nut is properly tightened. If it is not, an inaccurate run-out reading may be obtained. If different run-out readings are obtained with the same disc, between removal and installation, this is probably the cause.*

PARKING BRAKE

Cables

ADJUSTMENT

1. Raise the rear of the vehicle until the rear wheels clear the ground.
2. Adjust the rear brakes as outlined under Brake System Adjustment.

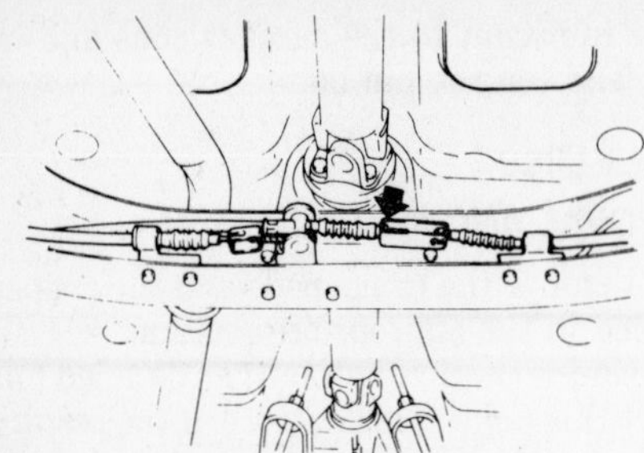

Adjusting the parking brake—1975–79

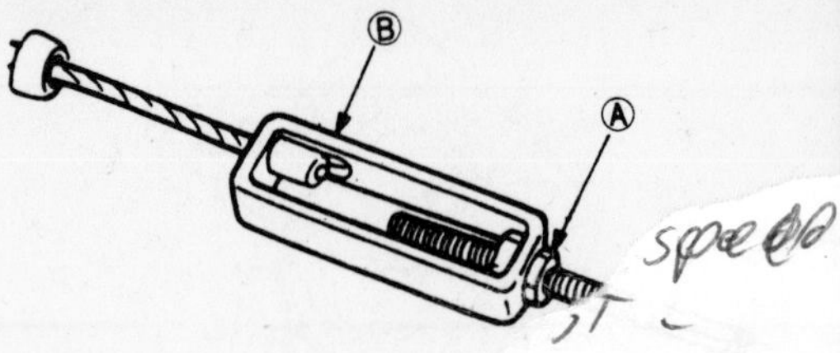

Adjusting the parking bra... ries)

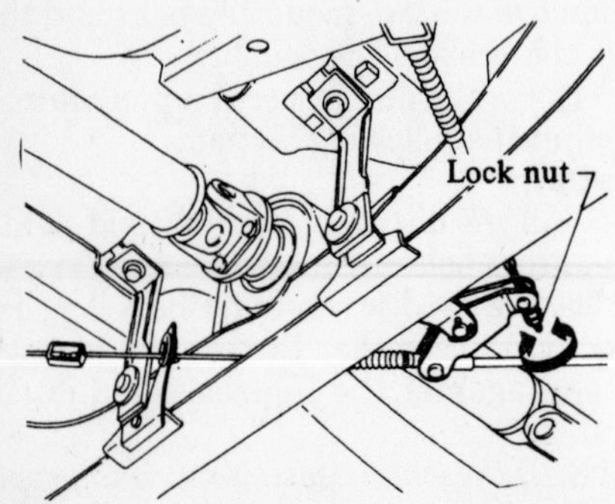

Adjusting the parking brake—1980–86 (720-D series)

Adjusting the brake warning lamp switch—1986–89 (D21-D series)

3. Loosen the locknut at the parking cable lever assembly mounted on the driveshaft center bearing crossmember.

4. Turn the adjusting nut until the parking brake control lever operating stroke is 6–10 notches on 1970-83 models; 13-16 notches 1984-86 models (720-D series); 10–12 notches (center lever and 2wd with stick lever) and 9–11 notches (4wd with stick lever) on 1986-87 models (D21-D series); 1988-89 models are the same except for Pathfinders with a center lever where is should be 7–9 notches. Notches are measured from the rest position (in or down) to the full-on position (out or up).

5. Release the parking brake and make sure that the rear wheels turn freely with no drag.

6. On 1986-89 models (D21-D series), the brake warning light should come on after 1 notch (pick-ups with center lever) or 2 notches (pick-ups with stick lever and Pathfinders with center lever). If not, adjust the switch.

7. Lower the vehicle.

REMOVAL AND INSTALLATION

1. Fully release the parking brake control lever.

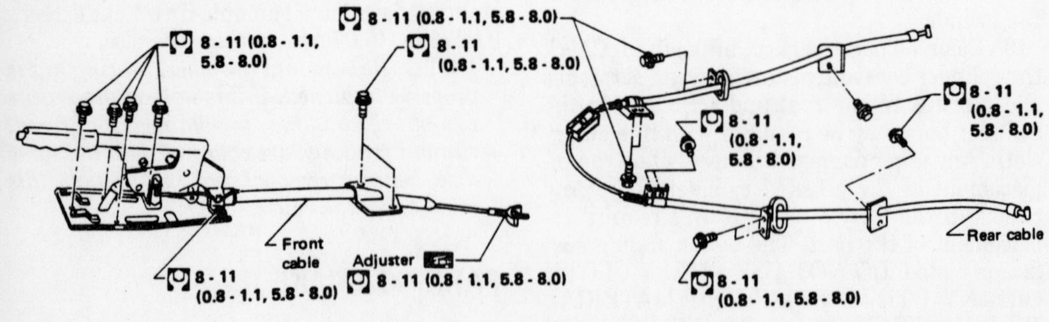

Typical parking brake cable routing—Pathfinder

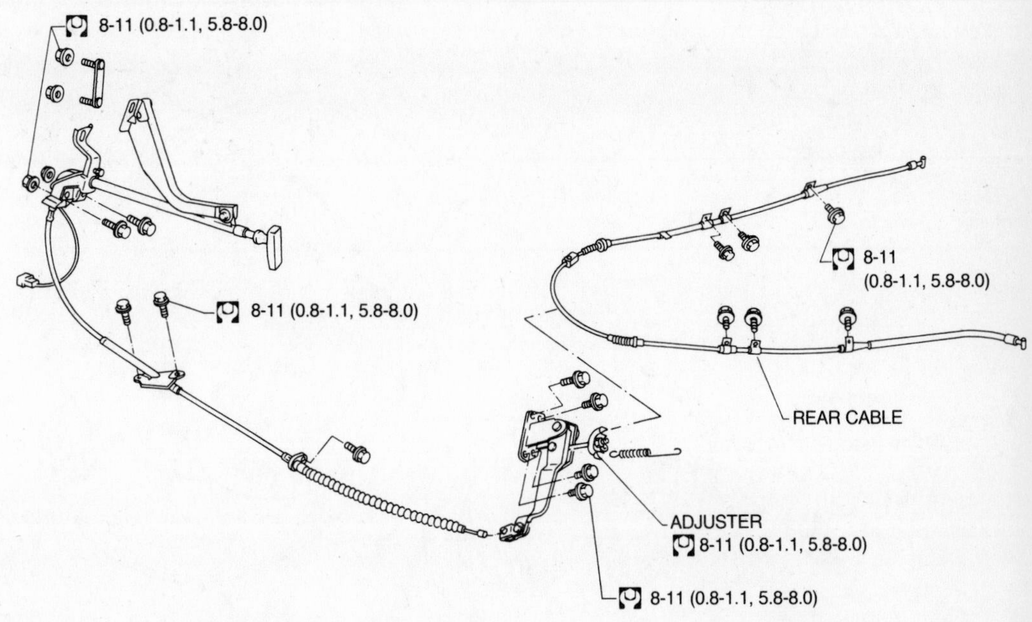

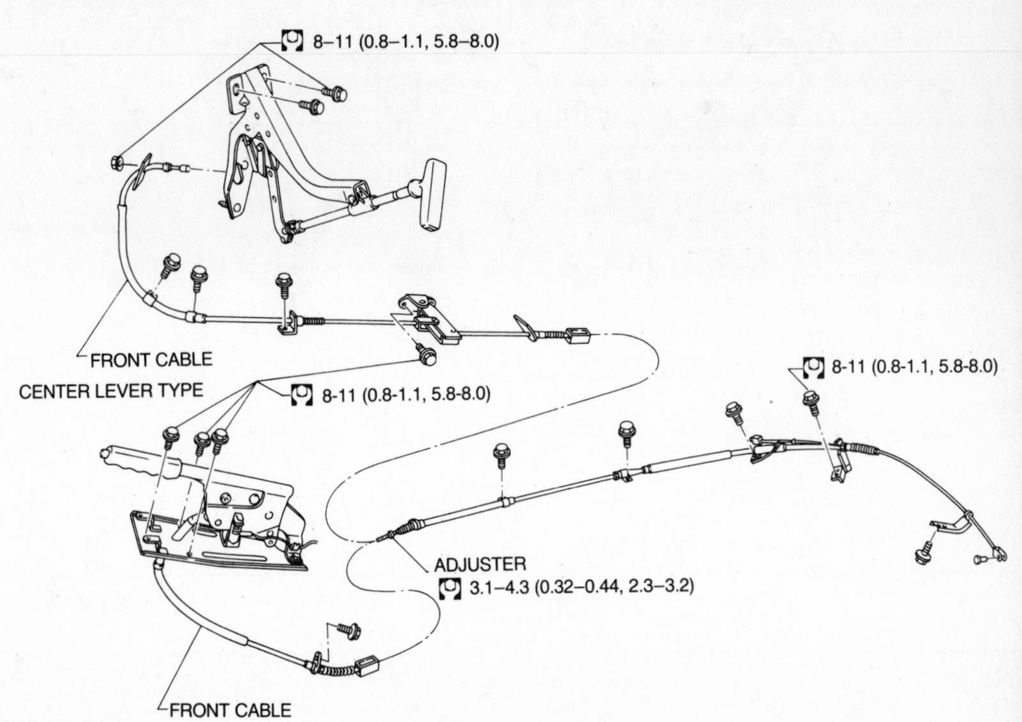

: N·M (KG-M, FT-LB)

Typical parking brake cable routing—Pick-Up

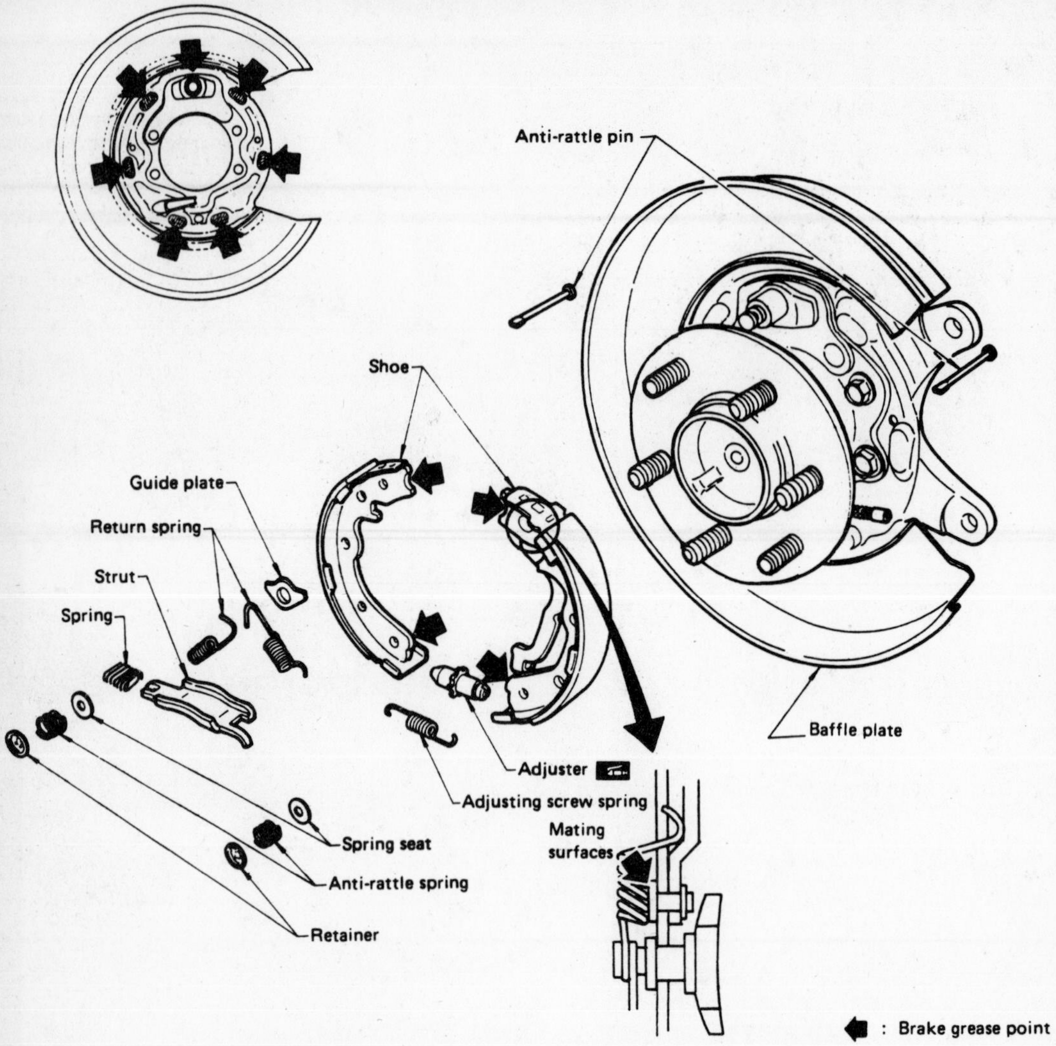

Exploded view of the parking brake—models with rear disc brakes

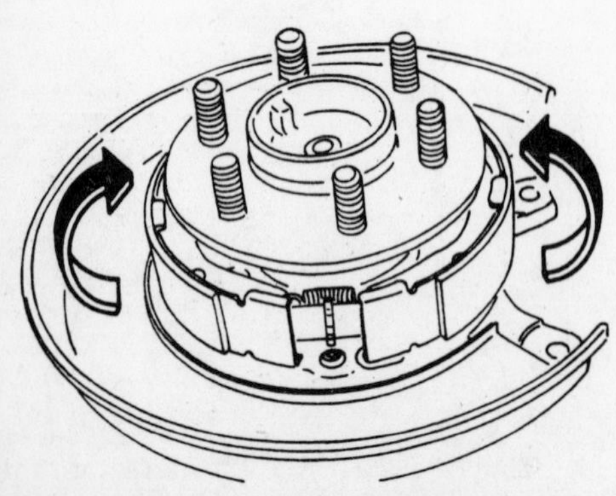

Removing the brake shoes—models with rear disc brakes

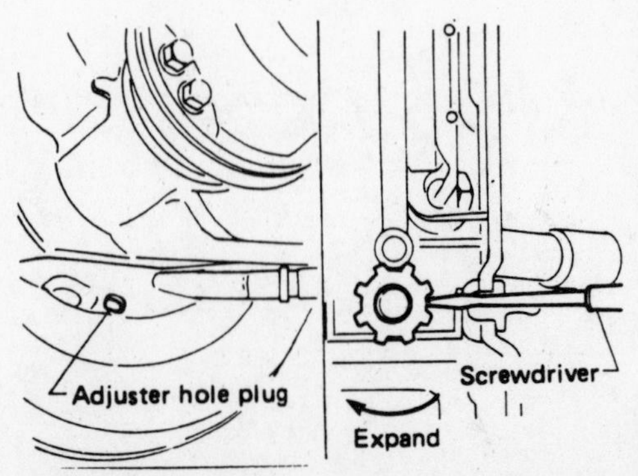

Adjusting the parking brake shoes—models with rear disc brakes

EASY STEP-BY-STEP TIPS FROM PROS

CHILTON'S AUTO BODY REPAIR TIPS

Tools and Materials • Step-by-Step Illustrated Procedures
How To Repair Dents, Scratches and Rust Holes
Spray Painting and Refinishing Tips

With a little practice, basic body repair procedures can be mastered by any do-it-yourself mechanic. The step-by-step repairs shown here can be applied to almost any type of auto body repair.

TOOLS & MATERIALS

You may already have basic tools, such as hammers and electric drills. Other tools unique to body repair — body hammers, grinding attachments, sanding blocks, dent puller, half-round plastic file and plastic spreaders — are relatively inexpensive and can be obtained wherever auto parts or auto body repair parts are sold. Portable air compressors and paint spray guns can be purchased or rented.

Auto Body Repair Kits

The best and most often used products are available to the do-it-yourselfer in kit form, from major manufacturers of auto body repair products. The same manufacturers also merchandise the individual products for use by pros.

Kits are available to make a wide variety of repairs, including holes, dents and scratches and fiberglass, and offer the advantage of buying the materials you'll need for the job. There is little waste or chance of materials going bad from not being used. Many kits may also contain basic body-working tools such as body files, sanding blocks and spreaders. Check the contents of the kit before buying your tools.

BODY REPAIR TIPS

Safety

Many of the products associated with auto body repair and refinishing contain toxic chemicals. Read all labels before opening containers and store them in a safe place and manner.

• Wear eye protection (safety goggles) when using power tools or when performing any operation that involves the removal of any type of material.

• Wear lung protection (disposable mask or respirator) when grinding, sanding or painting.

Sanding

1 Sand off paint before using a dent puller. When using a non-adhesive sanding disc, cover the back of the disc with an overlapping layer or two of masking tape and trim the edges. The disc will last considerably longer.

1

2 Use the circular motion of the sanding disc to grind *into* the edge of the repair. Grinding or sanding away from the jagged edge will only tear the sandpaper.

3 Use the palm of your hand flat on the panel to detect high and low spots. Do not use your fingertips. Slide your hand slowly back and forth.

3

WORKING WITH BODY FILLER

Mixing The Filler

Cleanliness and proper mixing and application are extremely important. Use a clean piece of plastic or glass or a disposable artist's palette to mix body filler.

1 Allow plenty of time and follow directions. No useful purpose will be served by adding more hardener to make it cure (set-up) faster. Less hardener means more curing time, but the mixture dries harder; more hardener means less curing time but a softer mixture.

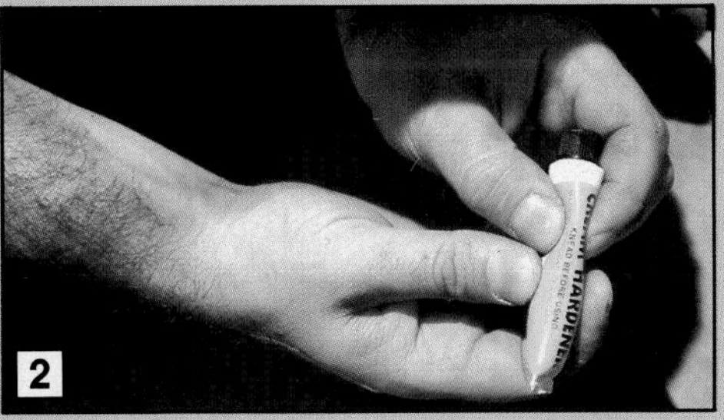

2

2 Both the hardener and the filler should be thoroughly kneaded or stirred before mixing. Hardener should be a solid paste and dispense like thin toothpaste. Body filler should be smooth, and free of lumps or thick spots.

Getting the proper amount of hardener in the filler is the trickiest part of preparing the filler. Use the same amount of hardener in cold or warm weather. For contour filler (thick coats), a bead of hardener twice the diameter of the filler is about right. There's about a 15% margin on either side, but, if in doubt use less hardener.

2

2

3 Mix the body filler and hardener by wiping across the mixing surface, picking the mixture up and wiping it again. Colder weather requires longer mixing times. Do not mix in a circular motion; this will trap air bubbles which will become holes in the cured filler.

3

Applying The Filler

1 For best results, filler should not be applied over 1/4" thick.

Apply the filler in several coats. Build it up to above the level of the repair surface so that it can be sanded or grated down.

The first coat of filler must be pressed on with a firm wiping motion.

Apply the filler in one direction only. Working the filler back and forth will either pull it off the metal or trap air bubbles.

REPAIRING DENTS

Before you start, take a few minutes to study the damaged area. Try to visualize the shape of the panel before it was damaged. If the damage is on the left fender, look at the right fender and use it as a guide. If there is access to the panel from behind, you can reshape it with a body hammer. If not, you'll have to use a dent puller. Go slowly and work the metal a little at a time. Get the panel as straight as possible before applying filler.

1 This dent is typical of one that can be pulled out or hammered out from behind. Remove the headlight cover, headlight assembly and turn signal housing.

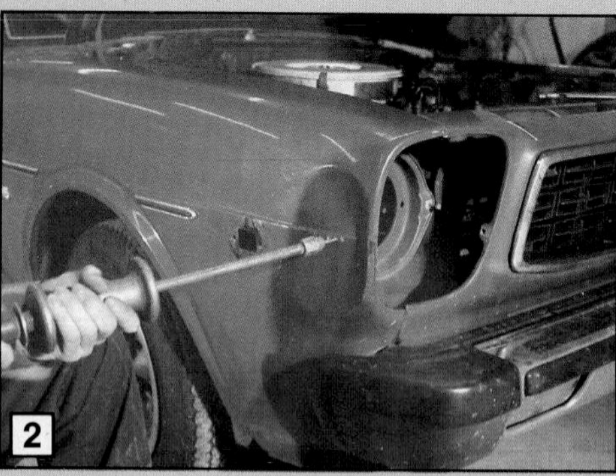

2 Drill a series of holes 1/2 the size of the end of the dent puller along the stress line. Make some trial pulls and assess the results. If necessary, drill more holes and try again. Do not hurry.

3 If possible, use a body hammer and block to shape the metal back to its original contours. Get the metal back as close to its original shape as possible. Don't depend on body filler to fill dents.

4 Using an 80-grit grinding disc on an electric drill, grind the paint from the surrounding area down to bare metal. Use a new grinding pad to prevent heat buildup that will warp metal.

5 The area should look like this when you're finished grinding. Knock the drill holes in and tape over small openings to keep plastic filler out.

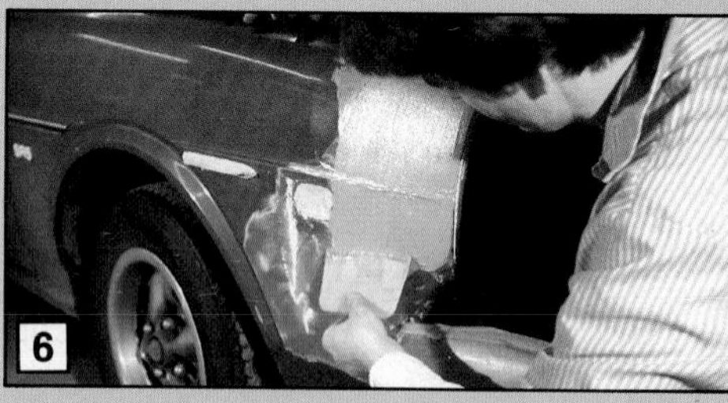

6 Mix the body filler (see Body Repair Tips). Spread the body filler evenly over the entire area (see Body Repair Tips). Be sure to cover the area completely.

7 Let the body filler dry until the surface can just be scratched with your fingernail. Knock the high spots from the body filler with a body file ("Cheese-grater"). Check frequently with the palm of your hand for high and low spots.

8 Check to be sure that trim pieces that will be installed later will fit exactly. Sand the area with 40-grit paper.

9 If you wind up with low spots, you may have to apply another layer of filler.

10 Knock the high spots off with 40-grit paper. When you are satisfied with the contours of the repair, apply a thin coat of filler to cover pin holes and scratches.

11 Block sand the area with 40-grit paper to a smooth finish. Pay particular attention to body lines and ridges that must be well-defined.

12 Sand the area with 400 paper and then finish with a scuff pad. The finished repair is ready for priming and painting (see Painting Tips).

Materials and photos courtesy of Ritt Jones Auto Body, Prospect Park, PA.

REPAIRING RUST HOLES

There are many ways to repair rust holes. The fiberglass cloth kit shown here is one of the most cost efficient for the owner because it provides a strong repair that resists cracking and moisture and is relatively easy to use. It can be used on large and small holes (with or without backing) and can be applied over contoured areas. Remember, however, that short of replacing an entire panel, no repair is a guarantee that the rust will not return.

1 Remove any trim that will be in the way. Clean away all loose debris. Cut away all the rusted metal. But be sure to leave enough metal to retain the contour or body shape.

2

2 Grind away all traces of rust with a 24-grit grinding disc. Be sure to grind back 3-4 inches from the edge of the hole down to bare metal and be sure all traces of paint, primer and rust are removed.

3

3 Block sand the area with 80 or 100 grit sandpaper to get a clear, shiny surface and feathered paint edge. Tap the edges of the hole inward with a ball peen hammer.

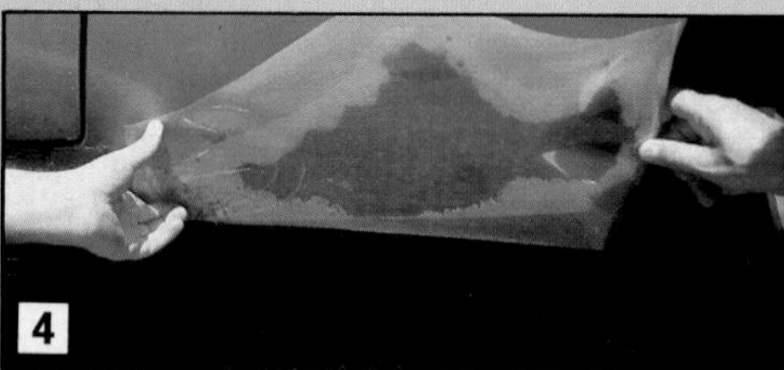

4

4 If you are going to use release film, cut a piece about 2-3″ larger than the area you have sanded. Place the film over the repair and mark the sanded area on the film. Avoid any unnecessary wrinkling of the film.

5

5 Cut 2 pieces of fiberglass matte to match the shape of the repair. One piece should be about 1″ smaller than the sanded area and the second piece should be 1″ smaller than the first. Mix enough filler and hardener to saturate the fiberglass material (see Body Repair Tips).

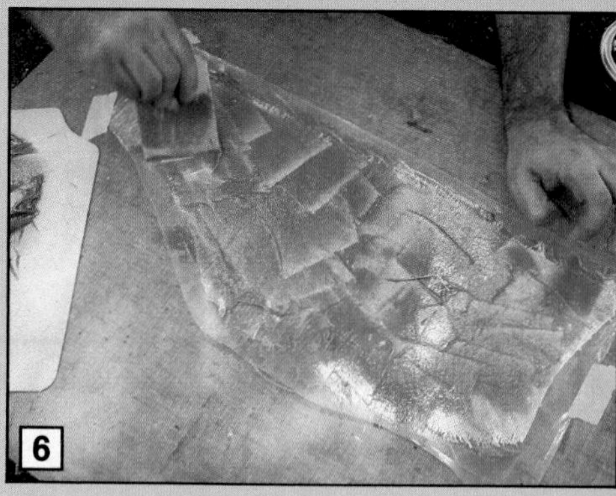

6

6 Lay the release sheet on a flat surface and spread an even layer of filler, large enough to cover the repair. Lay the smaller piece of fiberglass cloth in the center of the sheet and spread another layer of filler over the fiberglass cloth. Repeat the operation for the larger piece of cloth.

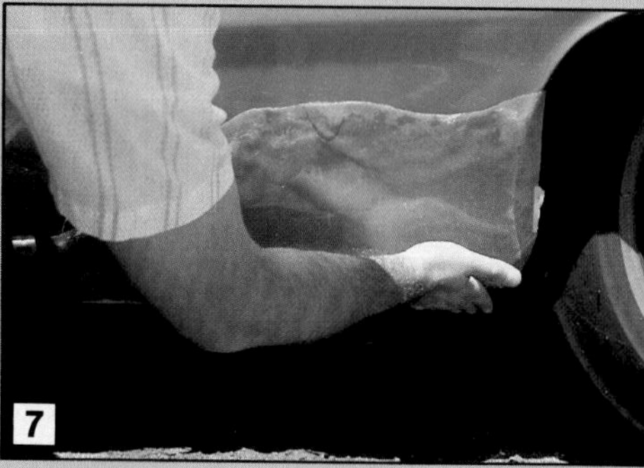

7

7 Place the repair material over the repair area, with the release film facing outward. Use a spreader and work from the center outward to smooth the material, following the body contours. Be sure to remove all air bubbles.

8

8 Wait until the repair has dried tack-free and peel off the release sheet. The ideal working temperature is 60°-90° F. Cooler or warmer temperatures or high humidity may require additional curing time. Wait longer, if in doubt.

9

9 Sand and feather-edge the entire area. The initial sanding can be done with a sanding disc on an electric drill if care is used. Finish the sanding with a block sander. Low spots can be filled with body filler; this may require several applications.

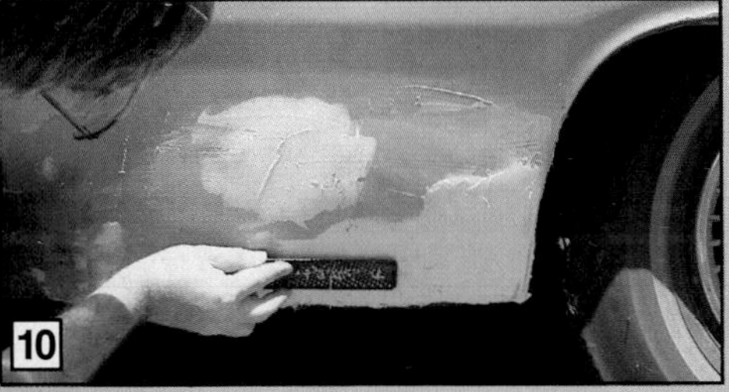

10

10 When the filler can just be scratched with a fingernail, knock the high spots down with a body file and smooth the entire area with 80-grit. Feather the filled areas into the surrounding areas.

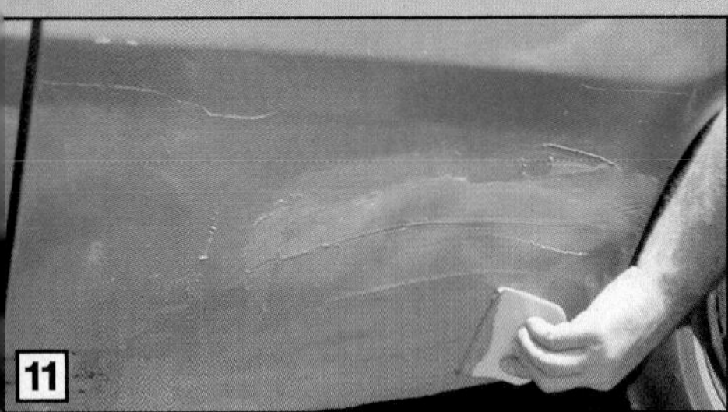

11

11 When the area is sanded smooth, mix some topcoat and hardener and apply it directly with a spreader. This will give a smooth finish and prevent the glass matte from showing through the paint.

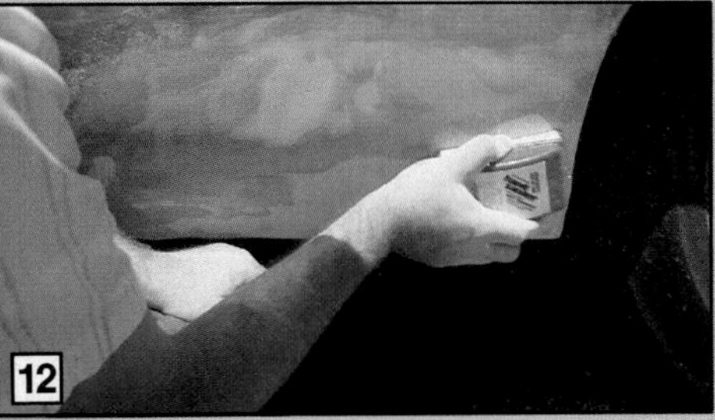

12

12 Block sand the topcoat smooth with finishing sandpaper (200 grit), and 400 grit. The repair is ready for masking, priming and painting (see Painting Tips).

Materials and photos courtesy Marson Corporation, Chelsea, Massachusetts

PAINTING TIPS

Preparation

1 SANDING — Use a 400 or 600 grit wet or dry sandpaper. Wet-sand the area with a 1/4 sheet of sandpaper soaked in clean water. Keep the paper wet while sanding. Sand the area until the repaired area tapers into the original finish.

2 CLEANING — Wash the area to be painted thoroughly with water and a clean rag. Rinse it thoroughly and wipe the surface dry until you're sure it's completely free of dirt, dust, fingerprints, wax, detergent or other foreign matter.

3 MASKING — Protect any areas you don't want to overspray by covering them with masking tape and newspaper. Be careful not get fingerprints on the area to be painted.

4 PRIMING — All exposed metal should be primed before painting. Primer protects the metal and provides an excellent surface for paint adhesion. When the primer is dry, wet-sand the area again with 600 grit wet-sandpaper. Clean the area again after sanding.

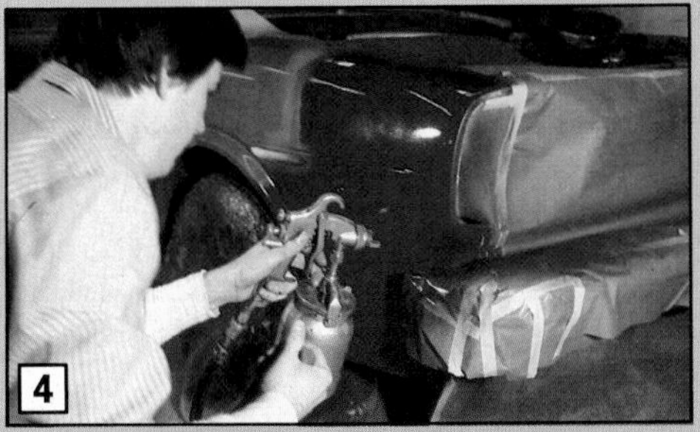

4

Painting Techniques

Paint applied from either a spray gun or a spray can (for small areas) will provide good results. Experiment on an old piece of metal to get the right combination before you begin painting.

SPRAYING VISCOSITY (SPRAY GUN ONLY) — Paint should be thinned to spraying viscosity according to the directions on the can. Use only the recommended thinner or reducer and the same amount of reduction regardless of temperature.

AIR PRESSURE (SPRAY GUN ONLY) — This is extremely important. Be sure you are using the proper recommended pressure.

TEMPERATURE — The surface to be painted should be approximately the same temperature as the surrounding air. Applying warm paint to a cold surface, or vice versa, will completely upset the paint characteristics.

THICKNESS — Spray with smooth strokes. In general, the thicker the coat of paint, the longer the drying time. Apply several thin coats about 30 seconds apart. The paint should remain wet long enough to flow out and no longer; heavier coats will only produce sags or wrinkles. Spray a light (fog) coat, followed by heavier color coats.

DISTANCE — The ideal spraying distance is 8″-12″ from the gun or can to the surface. Shorter distances will produce ripples, while greater distances will result in orange peel, dry film and poor color match and loss of material due to overspray.

OVERLAPPING — The gun or can should be kept at right angles to the surface at all times. Work to a wet edge at an even speed, using a 50% overlap and direct the center of the spray at the lower or nearest edge of the previous stroke.

RUBBING OUT (BLENDING) FRESH PAINT — Let the paint dry thoroughly. Runs or imperfections can be sanded out, primed and repainted.

Don't be in too big a hurry to remove the masking. This only produces paint ridges. When the finish has dried for at least a week, apply a small amount of fine grade rubbing compound with a clean, wet cloth. Use lots of water and blend the new paint with the surrounding area.

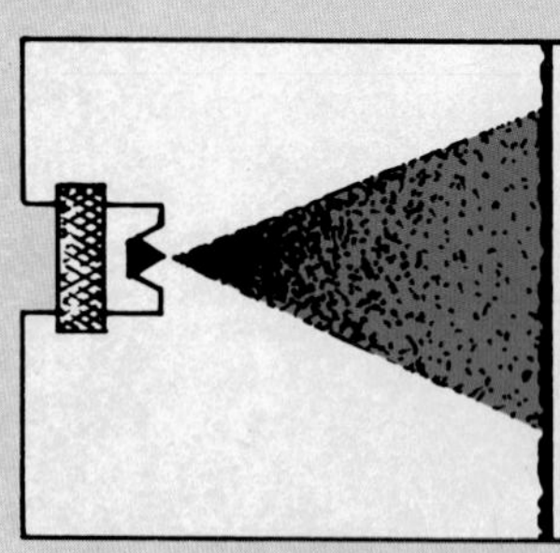

WRONG

Thin coat. Stroke too fast, not enough overlap, gun too far away.

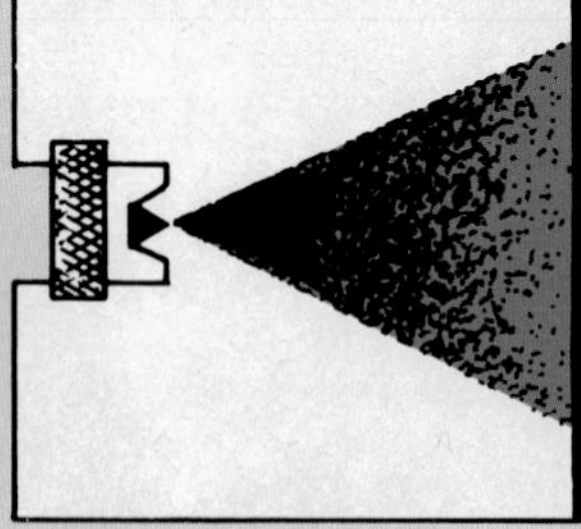

CORRECT

Medium coat. Proper distance, good stroke, proper overlap.

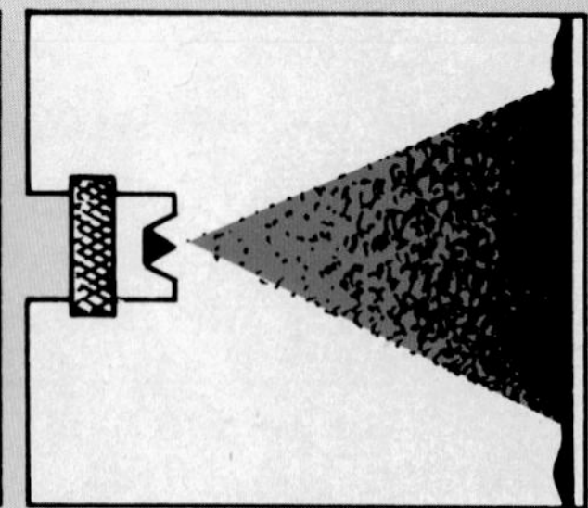

WRONG

Heavy coat. Stroke too slow, too much overlap, gun too close.

2. Loosen the adjusting nut at the cable lever mounted to the frame crossmember.

3. Disconnect the cable from the control lever.

4. Remove the rear brake drums, and disconnect the parking brake cables from the parking brake toggle levers of the rear service brake assemblies.

5. Remove the lockplate, spring and clip, and pull the parking brake cable out toward the cable lever.

6. Remove the cotter pin at the cable lever and disconnect the cable.

7. Install the cables in the reverse order of removal. Apply a light coat of grease to the cables to make sure that they slide properly. Adjust the parking brakes.

Parking Brake Shoes

ADJUSTMENT

Rear Disc Brakes Only

1. Raise the rear of the truck and support it with safety stands.

2. Remove the adjuster hole plug at the rear of the brake backing plate.

3. Make sure that the parking brake is fully released and rotate the star wheel adjuster downward with a brake adjusting tool until the shoes are touching the brake drum.

4. Back off the star wheel 7–8 latches.

5. Install the hole plug and rotate the wheel a few times to ensure that the shoes are not dragging on the drums.

Brake Specifications

(All measurements given are (in.) unless noted

Year	Model	Master Cyl. Bore	Brake Disc		Brake Drum			Minimum Lining Thickness	
			Minimum Thickness	Maximum Run-Out	Diameter	Max. Machine O/S	Max. Wear Limit	Front	Rear
1970	521	0.750	—	—	10.00	10.09	10.06	0.039	0.059
1971	521	0.750	—	—	10.00	10.09	10.06	0.039	0.059
1972	521	0.750	—	—	10.00	10.09	10.06	0.039	0.059
1973	620	0.750	—	—	10.00	10.09	10.06	0.039	0.059
1974	620	0.750	—	—	10.00	10.09	10.06	0.039	0.059
1975	620	0.750	—	—	10.00	10.09	10.06	0.039	0.059
1976	620	0.750	—	—	10.00	10.09	10.06	0.039	0.059
1977	620	0.750	—	—	10.00	10.09	10.06	0.039	0.059
1978	620	0.813	0.413	0.0059	10.00	10.09	10.06	0.079	0.059
1979	720-D	0.813	0.413	0.0059	10.00	10.09	10.06	0.079	0.059
1980	720-D	0.875	0.413	0.0059	10.00	10.09	10.06	0.079	0.059
1981	720-D	0.875	0.413	0.0059	10.00	10.09	10.06	0.079	0.059
1982	720-D	0.875	0.413	0.0059	10.00	10.09	10.06	0.079	0.059
1983	720-D	0.875	0.413	0.0059	10.00	10.09	10.06	0.079	0.059
1984	720-D	0.938	0.787	0.0028	①	②	③	0.079	0.059
1985	720-D	0.938	0.787	0.0028	①	②	③	0.079	0.059
1986	720-D	0.938	0.787	0.0028	①	②	③	0.079	0.059
1986	D21-D	0.938	④	0.0028	⑤	③	⑥	0.079	0.059
1987	D21-D	0.938	④	0.0028	⑤	③	⑥	0.079	0.059
1988	D21-D	0.938	④	0.0028	⑤	③	⑥	0.079	0.059 ⑦
1989	D21-D	0.938	④	0.0028	⑤	③	⑥	0.079	0.059 ⑦

① Single rear wheels: 10.00
Dual rear wheels: 8.66
② Single rear wheels: 10.06
Dual rear wheels: 8.72
③ Single rear wheels: 10.09
Dual rear wheels: 8.75
④ CL28VA: 0.787
CL28VD: 0.945
AD14VB (rear): 0.630
⑤ 2wd exc. HD & C/C: 10.24
2wd C/C: 8.66
2wd HD: 10.00
4wd: 10.00 or 7.48
⑥ 2wd exc. HD & C/C: 10.30
2wd C/C: 8.72
2wd HD: 10.06
4wd: 10.06 or 7.52
⑦ Rear disc: 0.079

Body 10

EXTERIOR

Front Door

REMOVAL AND INSTALLATION

1. With the door in the full open position, place a jack or stand under the door to support its weight when the bolts are removed. Place a rag between the door and the jack or stand to avoid damaging the painted surface.

2. While supporting the door remove the upper and lower hinge attaching bolts and remove the door.

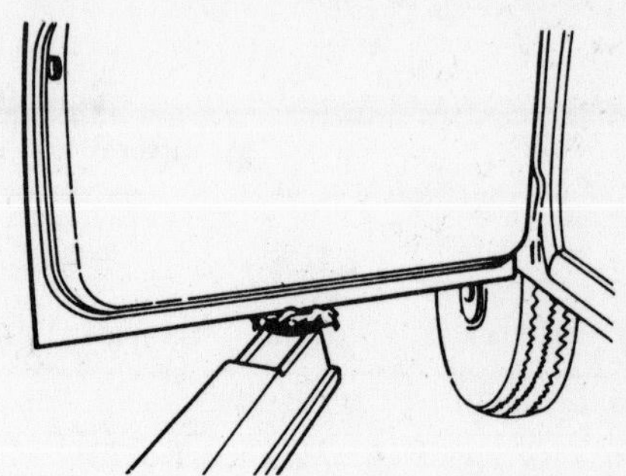

Support the front door for removal and installation

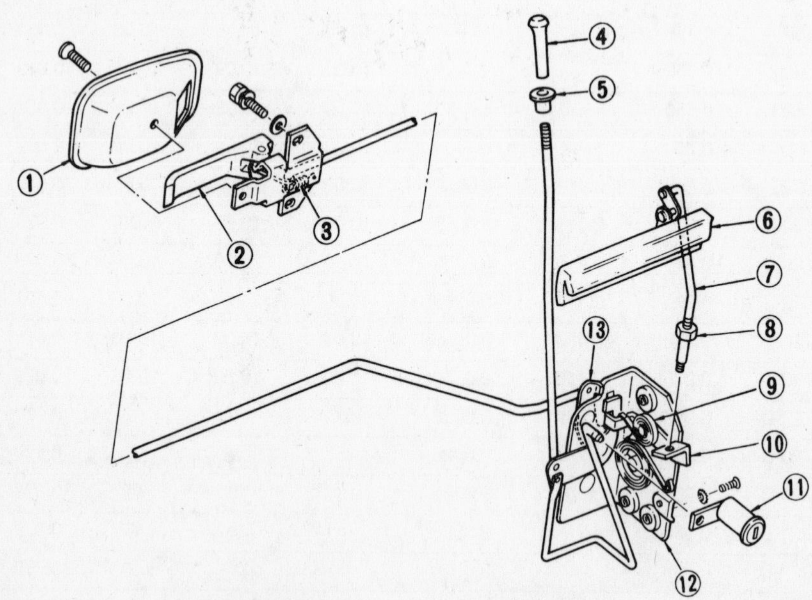

1. Escutcheon
2. Inside handle
3. Spring
4. Door lock knob
5. Knob grommet
6. Outside handle
7. Outside handle rod
8. Nylon nut
9. Locking plate spring
10. Locking plate
11. Door lock cylinder
12. Door lock
13. Stopper

Door lock mechanism, 620 series

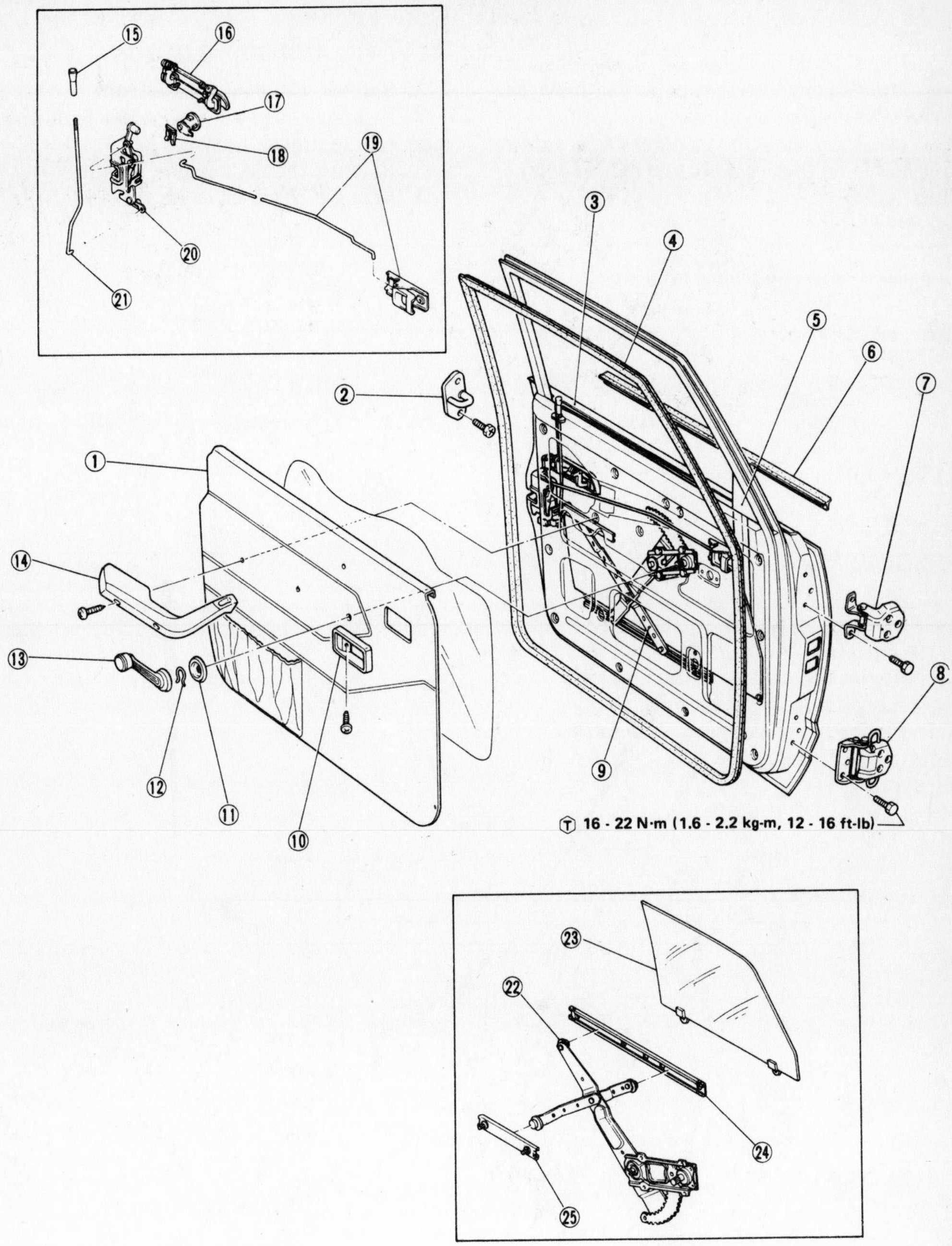

16 - 22 N·m (1.6 - 2.2 kg-m, 12 - 16 ft-lb)

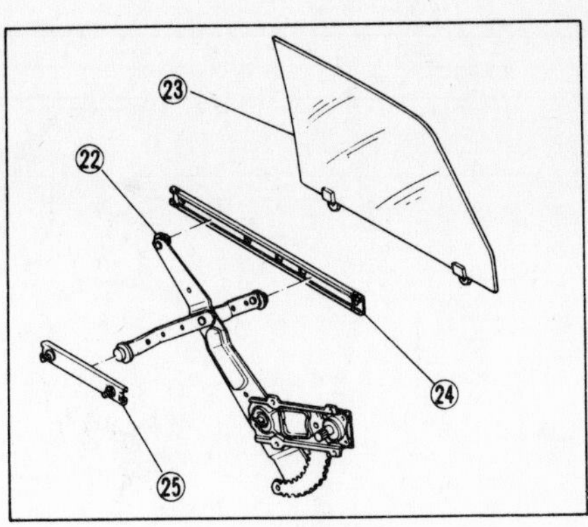

1. Door finisher
2. Door lock striker
3. Door
4. Weatherstrip
5-1. Lower sash
5-2. Ventilator frame (with ventilator model only)
6. Outer side weatherstrip
7. Upper hinge
8. Lower hinge
9. Regulator assembly
10. Remote control escutcheon
11. Regulator seating washer
12. Retaining spring
13. Regulator door handle
14. Arm rest
15. Door lock knob
16. Outside handle
17. Door lock cylinder
18. Retaining clip
19. Remote control assembly
20. Door lock assembly
21. Door lock rod
22. Regulator
23. Door glass
24. Guide channel A
25. Guide channel B

Front door assembly, 720 series

Adjustment

To adjust the door alignment, loosen the door hinge and door lock striker bolts and move the door to the desired position.

NOTE: *Make sure the weatherstrip contacts the body opening evenly to prevent the entry of water.*

Door Locks

REMOVAL AND INSTALLATION

1. Remove the door inside trim.
2. Disengage the the rod holder from the inside handle unlock rod.
3. Remove the door inside handle.
4. Remove the door lock cylinder.

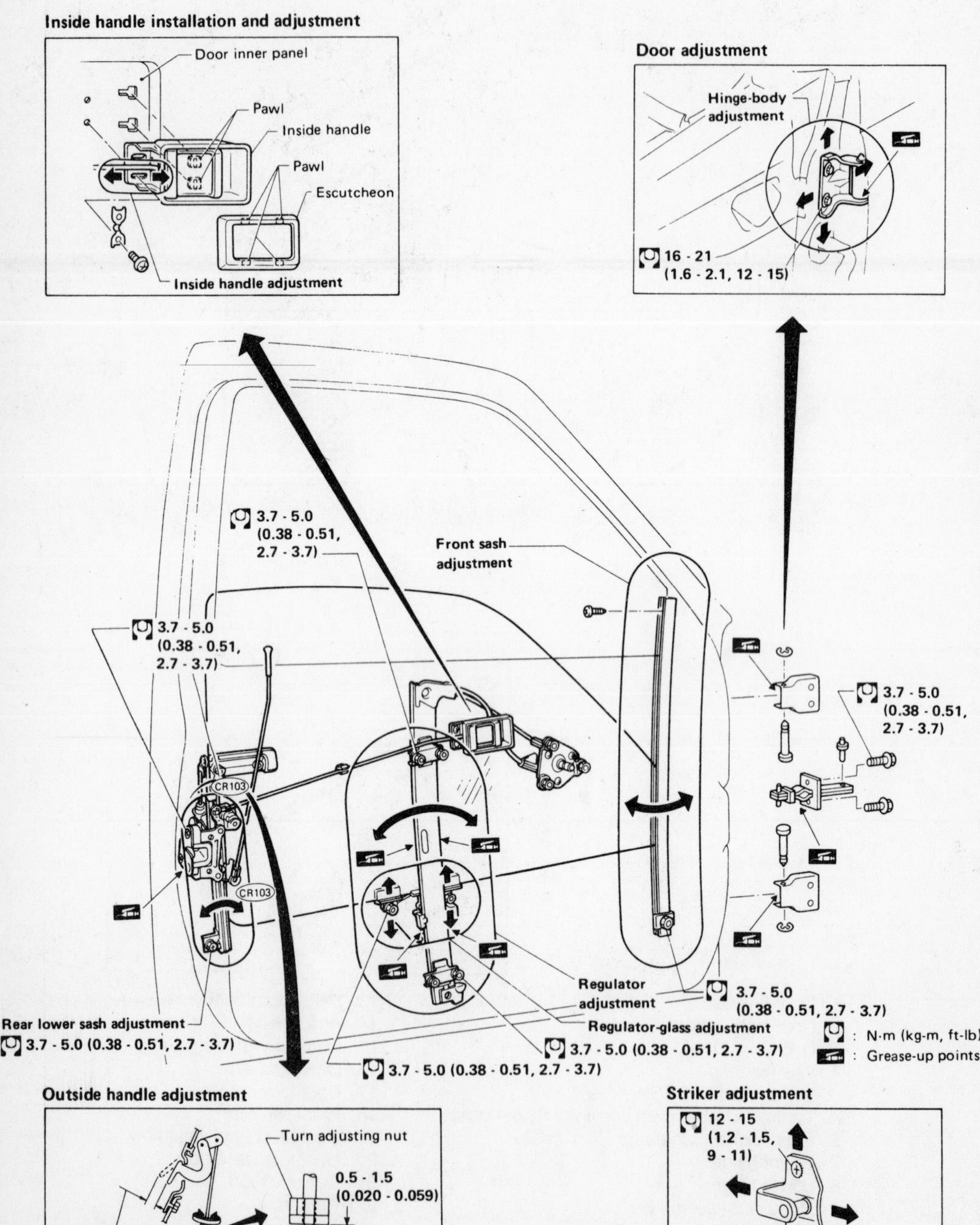

Front door assembly, D21 series

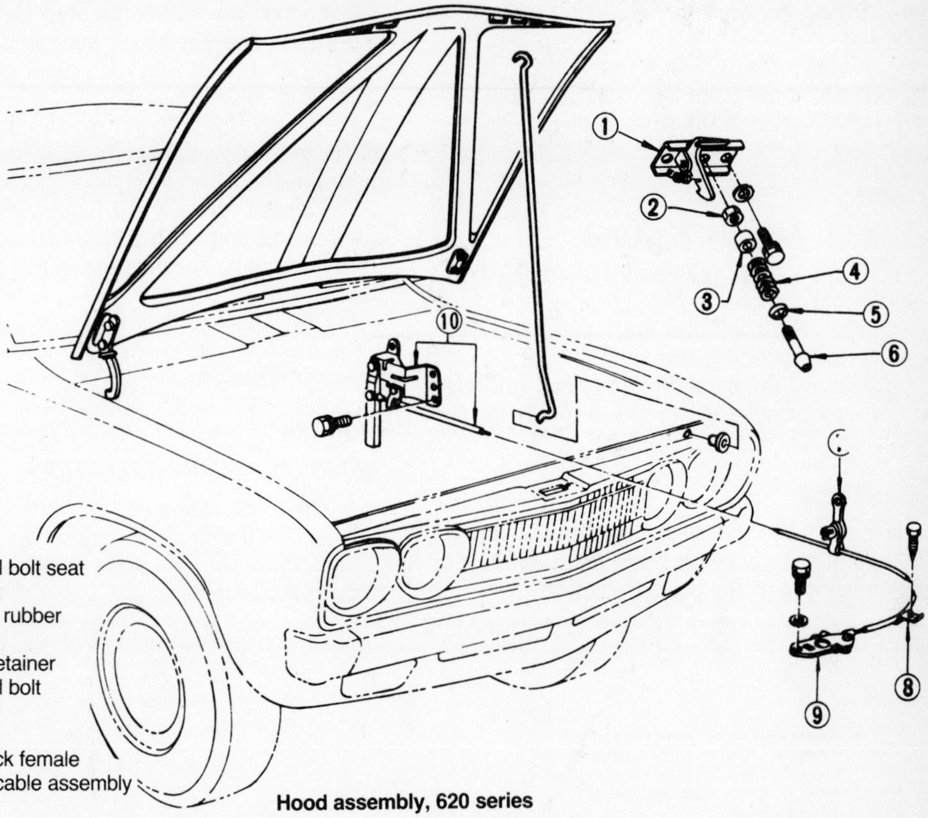

1. Dove-tail bolt seat
2. Lock nut
3. Cushion rubber
4. Spring
5. Spring retainer
6. Dove-tail bolt
7. Clamp
8. Clamp
9. Hood lock female
10. Control cable assembly

Hood assembly, 620 series

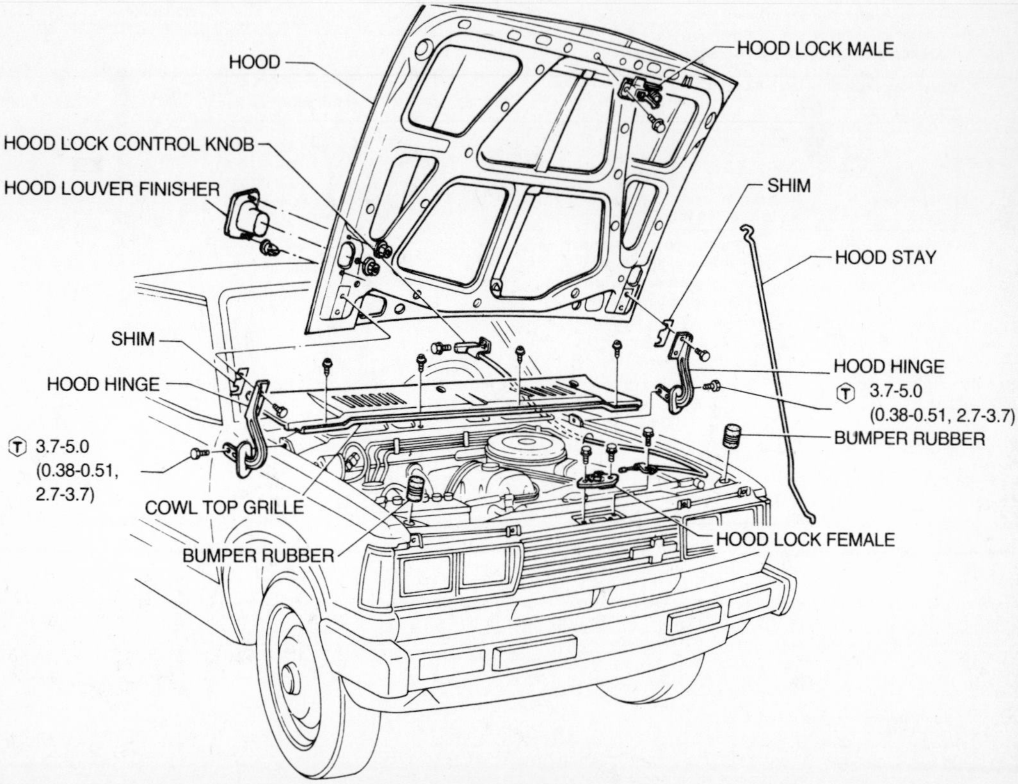

Hood assembly, 720 series

5. Disengage the rod holder from the door lock rod.
6. Remove the door lock assembly.
7. Remove the front door outside handle.
8. Installation is the reverse of removal.

Hood

REMOVAL AND INSTALLATION

1. Place protective covers over the front fender and cowl top grille.
2. Open the hood and mark the hinge locations on the hood for reinstalling.
3. Remove the hood hinge to hood retaining bolts and carefully lift the hood from the vehicle.

Adjustment

1. Loosen the bolts attaching the hood hinge.
2. Adjust the hood back and forth and side to side until it is in the proper position.
3. Loosen the bolts attaching the hood lock and adjust the hood lock back and forth and side to side until it is in the proper position and opens and closes smoothly.
4. Loosen the lock nut on the dovetail bolt and turn the dovetail bolt in or out as necessary to obtain the correct height.
5. Tighten the lock nut firmly while holding the dovetail bolt with a screwdriver to secure the adjustment. Torque the locknut to 14–19 ft. lbs.

NOTE: *Make sure that the saftey catch hooks the hood properly when the hood latch has been disengaged.*

Tailgate

REMOVAL AND INSTALLATION

1. Open the rear gate.
2. On earlier models, remove the gate chain.
3. Remove the gate hinge attaching bolts and remove the rear gate.

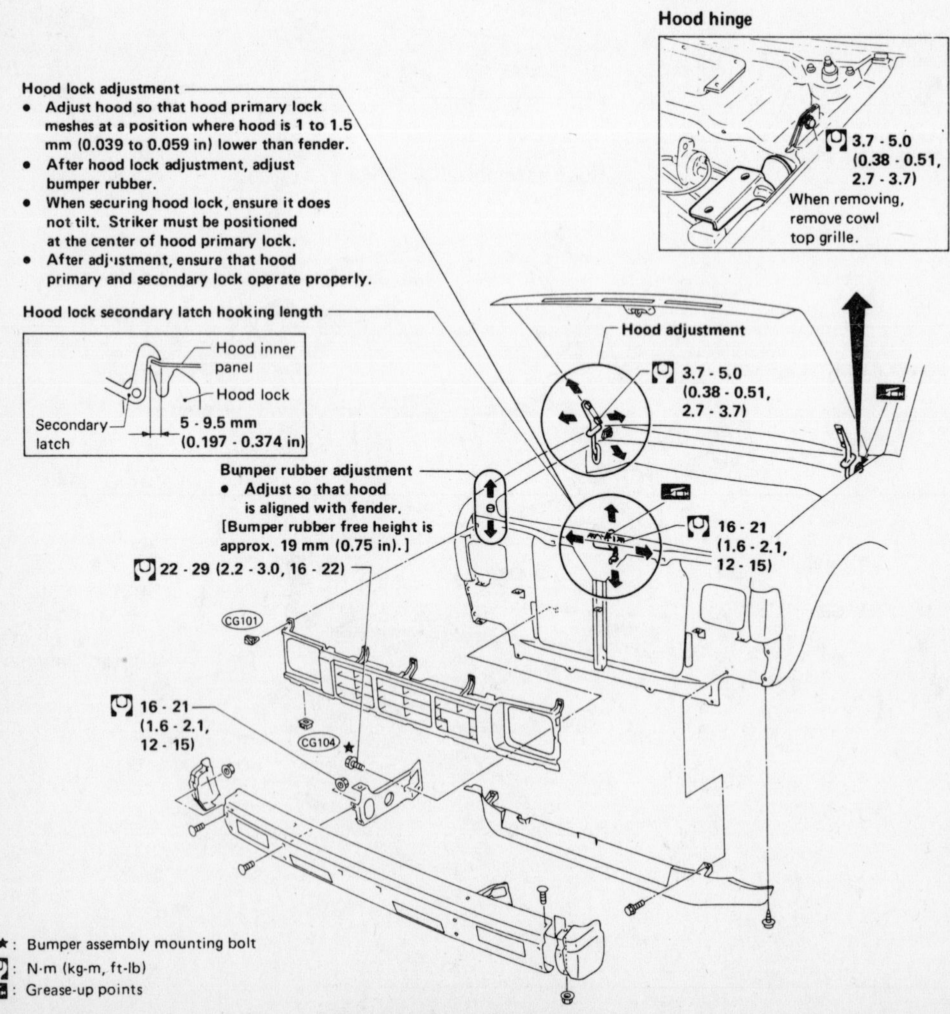

Hood assembly, D21 series

ALIGNMENT

The rear gate may be adjusted by loosening the hinge attaching bolts and moving the gate as required. The height may be adjusted by adding or removing shims at the rear gate hinge.

Windshield

REMOVAL

NOTE: *Removal and installation of the windshield requires two people.*

1. Place protective covers over the hood, front fender, seat and instrument panel.
2. On earlier models remove the inside rear view mirror and sun visor.
3. On 1979 and later models, remove the windshield wiper arms.
4. Remove the windshield moldings by carefully prying them out.
5. On 1979 and later models, remove the cowl top grille, and then remove the windshield retainer, if so equipped.
6. Using a putty knife or similar flat-bladed

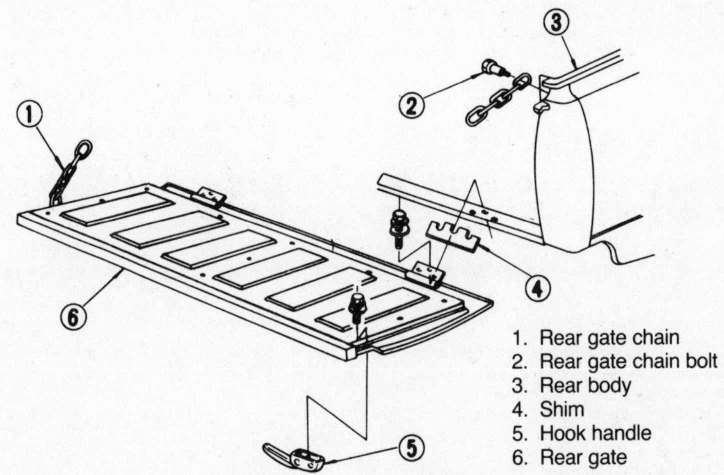

Tailgate assembly, 620 series

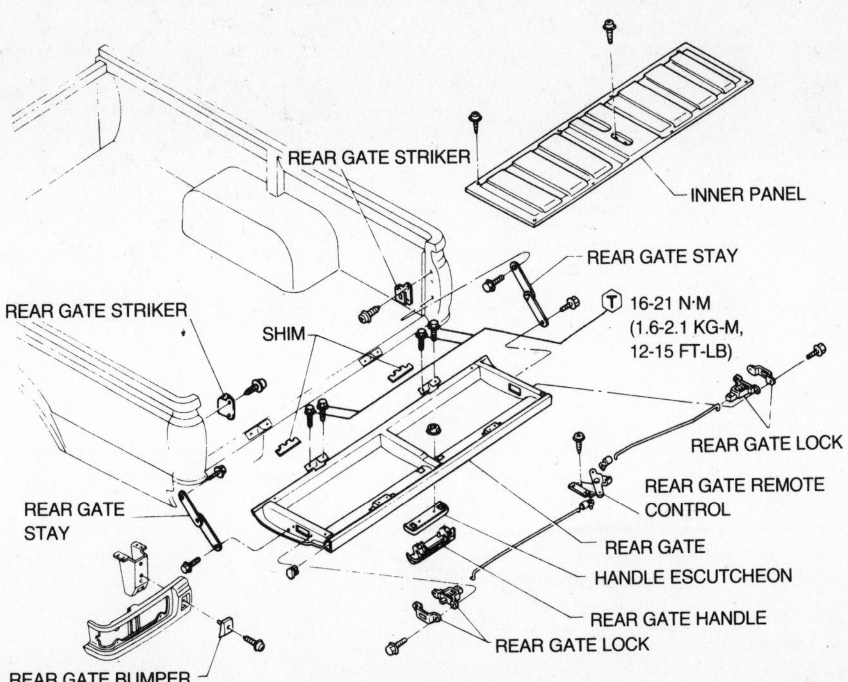

Tailgate assembly, 720 series

tool, pry the lips of the weatherstrip out of place from the top and side flanges of the body opening.

NOTE: *Be careful not to damage the weatherstrip if it is to be reused.*

7. Working from inside the vehicle, push the windshield glass out of the body opening by hand, starting at the right and left upper corners and working out towards the ends.

8. After removing the weatherstrip from the top and sides of the body opening, lift the glass up sufficiently to premit removal of the weatherstrip from the bottom flange; pry the weatherstrip out of position.

INSTALLATION

1. Fit the weatherstrip on the glass, making sure it is correctly seated and positioned.

2. Apply adhesive to the appropriate portions of the weatherstrip.

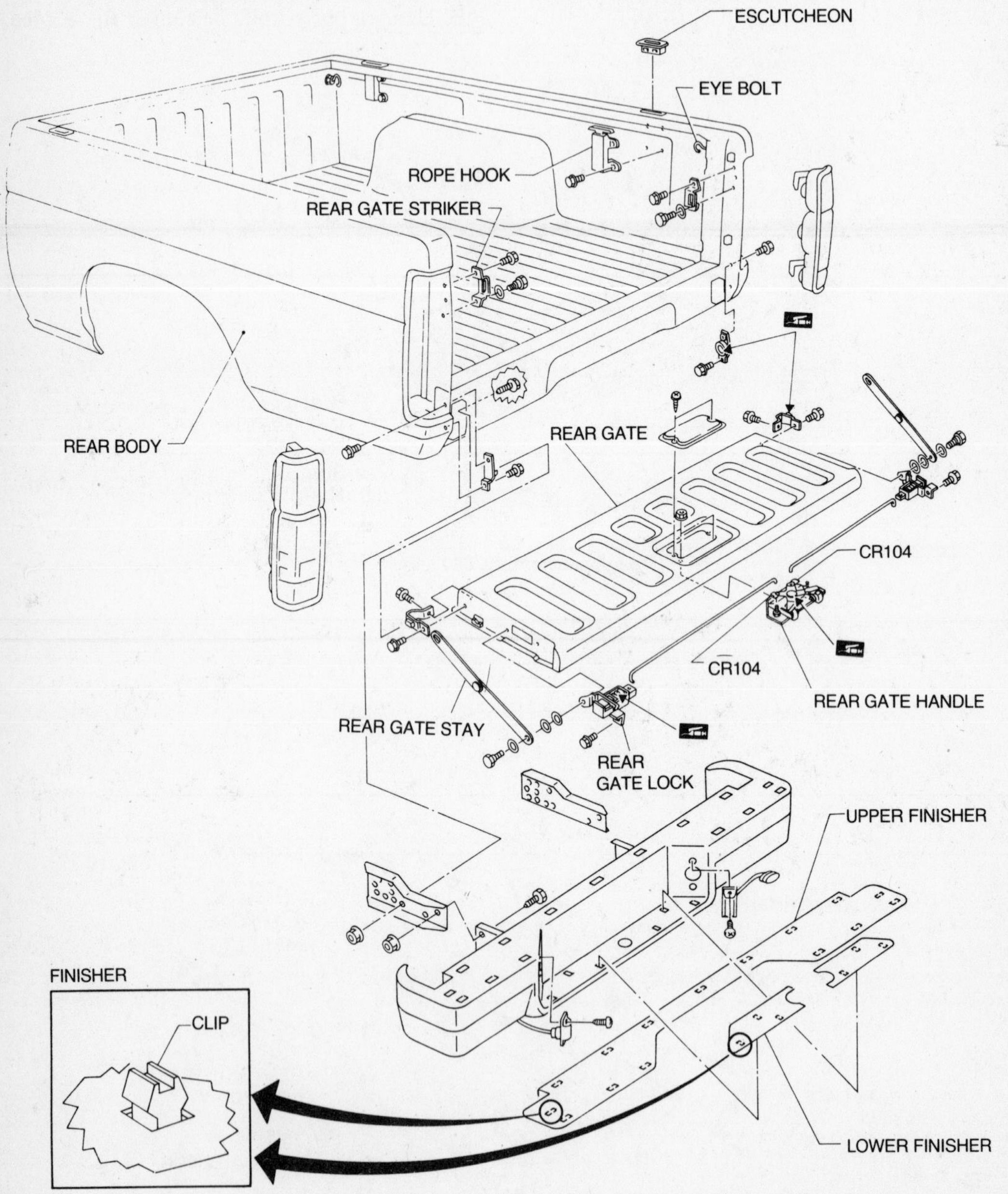

Tailgate assembly—D21-D series (Pick-up)

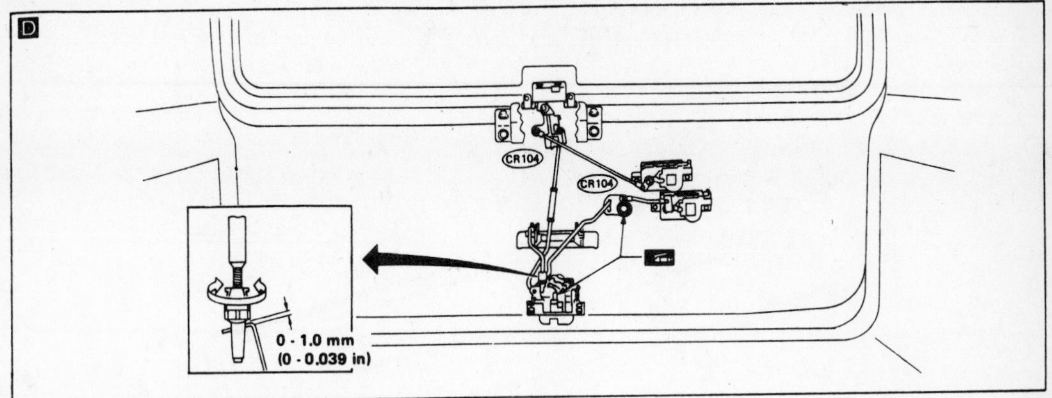

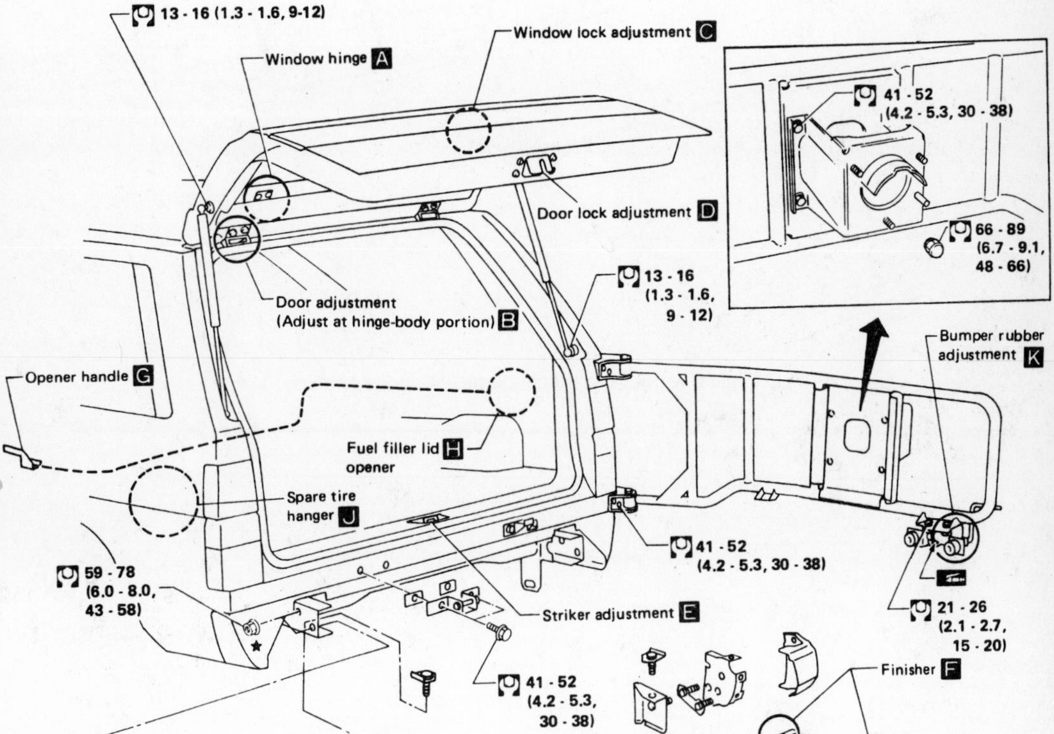

13 - 16 (1.3 - 1.6, 9-12)
Window lock adjustment C
Window hinge A
41 - 52 (4.2 - 5.3, 30 - 38)
Door lock adjustment D
66 - 89 (6.7 - 9.1, 48 - 66)
13 - 16 (1.3 - 1.6, 9 - 12)
Door adjustment (Adjust at hinge-body portion) B
Bumper rubber adjustment K
Opener handle G
Fuel filler lid H opener
Spare tire hanger J
41 - 52 (4.2 - 5.3, 30 - 38)
59 - 78 (6.0 - 8.0, 43 - 58)
Striker adjustment E
21 - 26 (2.1 - 2.7, 15 - 20)
41 - 52 (4.2 - 5.3, 30 - 38)
Finisher F

★ : Bumper assembly mounting bolt
: N·m (kg-m, ft-lb)
: Grease-up points

Tailgate assembly—D21-D series (Pathfinder)

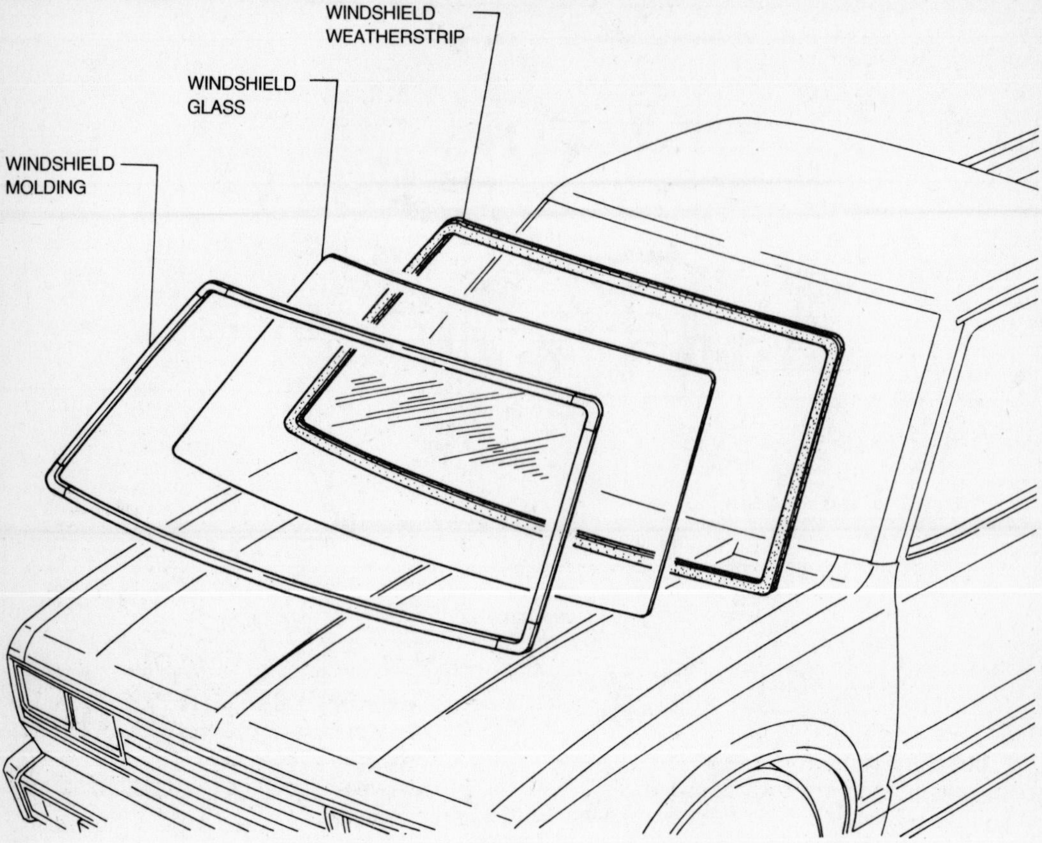

WINDSHIELD WEATHERSTRIP
WINDSHIELD GLASS
WINDSHIELD MOLDING

Typical windshield installation, 720 series shown

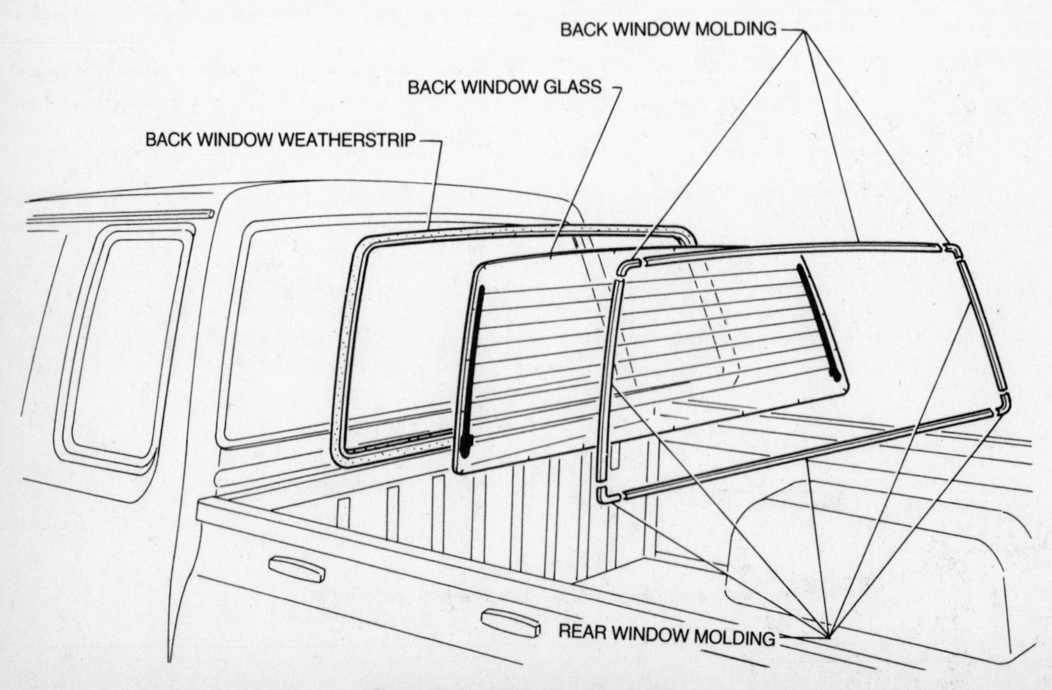

Rear glass assembly, 720 series

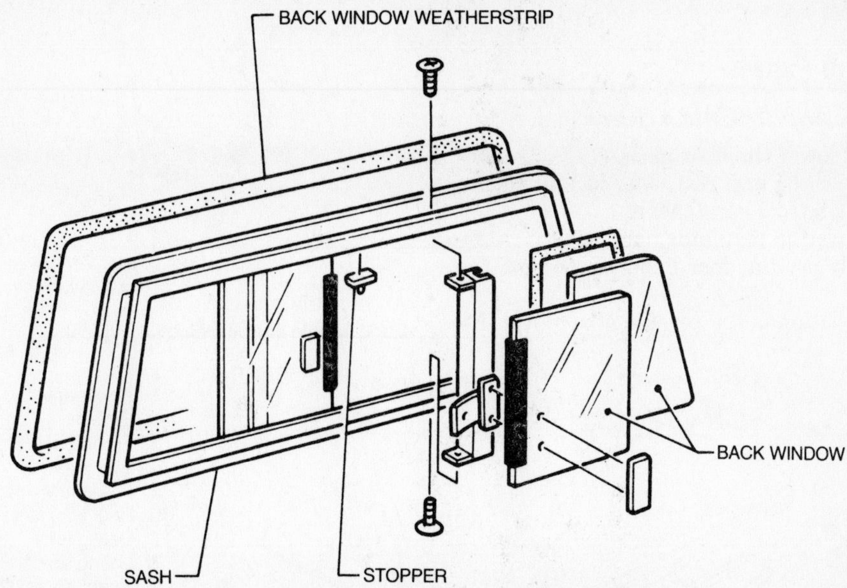

Rear glass assembly, D21 series

NOTE: *On models through 1978 adhesive is not necessary.*

3. Install a strong cord in the groove of the weatherstrip where the body flange fits. Tie the ends of the cord and tape to the inside surface of the glass at the bottom center of the glass.
4. Position and center the windshield glass in the body opening.

NOTE: *Do not tap or hammer at any time to position the glass.*

5. When the glass and weatherstrip are properly positioned in the body opening, slowly pull the ends of the cord, starting at the lower center of the windshield to seat the lip of the weatherstrip over the body flange.
6. The cord should be pulled across the bottom of the windshield, then up each side and finally across the windshield top.
7. The remainder of the installation is the reverse of removal.

Rear Window Glass

REMOVAL AND INSTALLATION

Removal and installation of the rear window glass is the same as for the windshield with the exception that adhesive is not use on the rear window glass weatherstrip. Be sure to disconnect the window defogger harness, if so equipped.

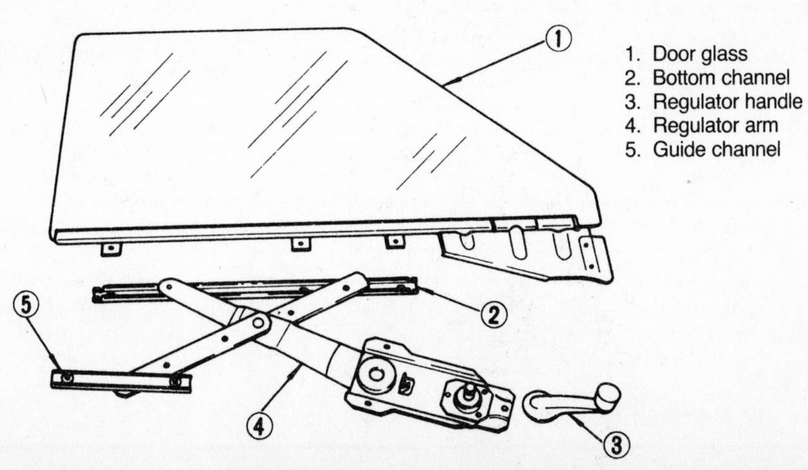

Door glass and regulator, 620 series

INTERIOR

Door Trim Panels

REMOVAL AND INSTALLATION

1. Fully lower the door glass.
2. Remove the arm rest, door lock knob and inside door handle escutcheon.
3. Remove the regulator handle.
4. Gently pry the door panel away from the door.
5. Installation is the reverse of removal. In-

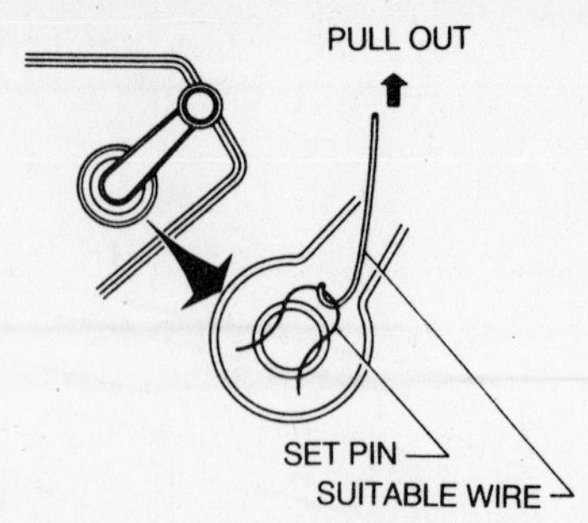

Door handle set pin removal, typical

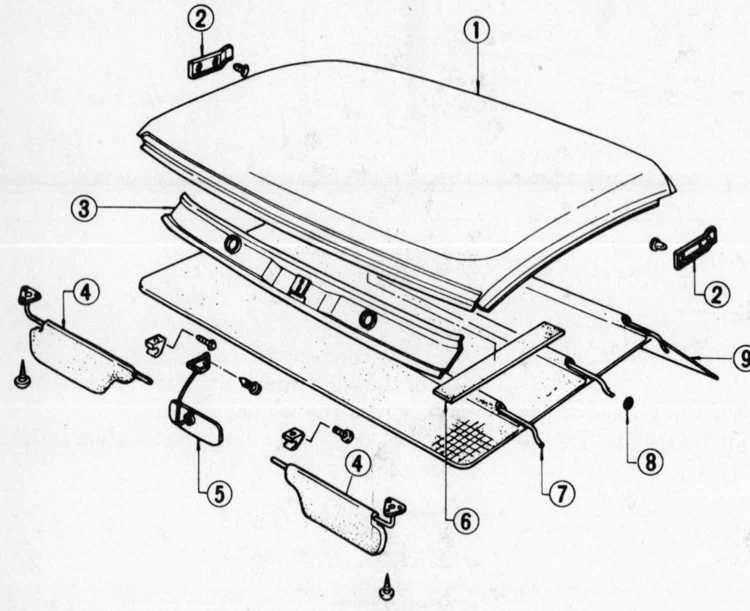

Headliner installation, 620 series

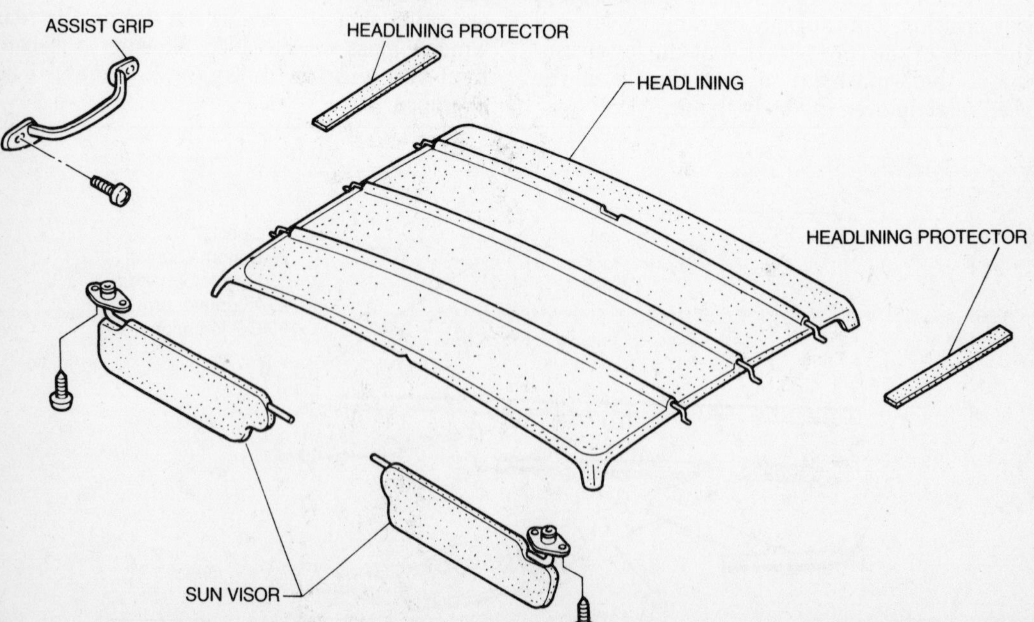

Headliner installation, 720 series

stall the regulator handle with the door glass closed.

Door Glass And Regulator

REMOVAL AND INSTALLATION

1. Remove the door trim panel.
2. Remove the front door lower sash or the front door ventilator frame, if so equipped.
3. Remove the door glass to regulator attaching bolts and remove the door glass by lifting upwards.
4. Remove the regulator attaching bolts from the bottom of the regulator.
5. Remove the regulator through the large access hole in the door inside panel.
6. Installation is the reverse of removal. Grease the regulator sliding surfaces and adjust the door glass and regulator.

ADJUSTMENT

1. In-and-out and fore-and-aft adjustments can be made by moving the front or rear sash and guide channel as required.

The ease with which the window assembly raises and lowers depends on the adjustment of the rear lower sash. The rear lower sash should be parallel with the front lower sash.

2. Fore and aft adjustment is determined by position of the guide channel and front lower sash. Moving the front lower sash backward reduces play in the window assembly.

Headliner

REMOVAL AND INSTALLATION

All Except D21 Series

NOTE: *The headliner assembly is of the suspension type, which is held in place by listing wires.*

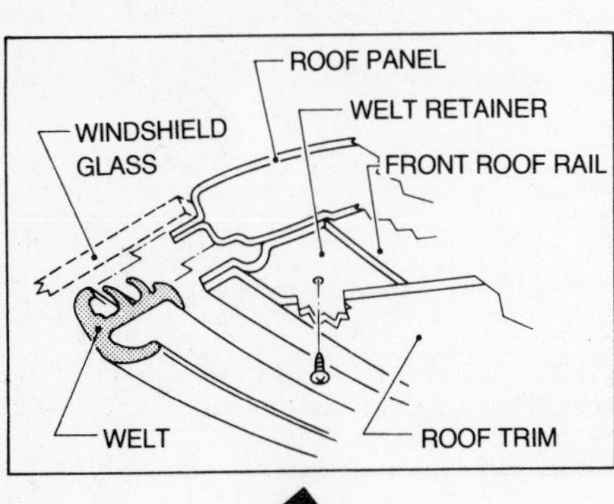

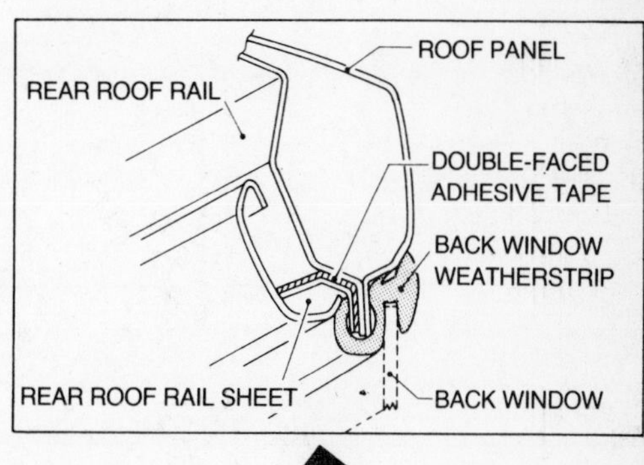

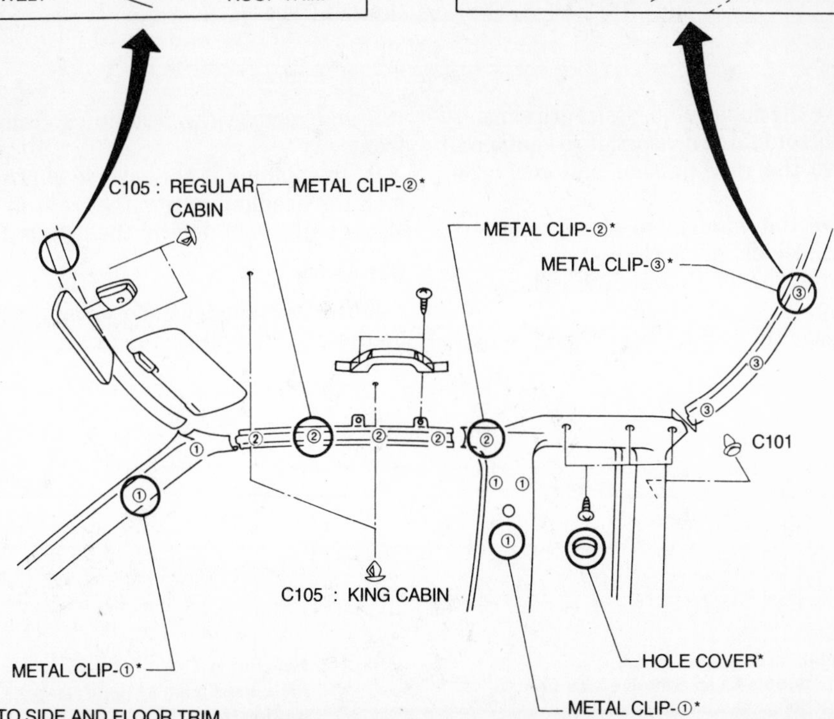

Headliner installation, D21 series (Type I)

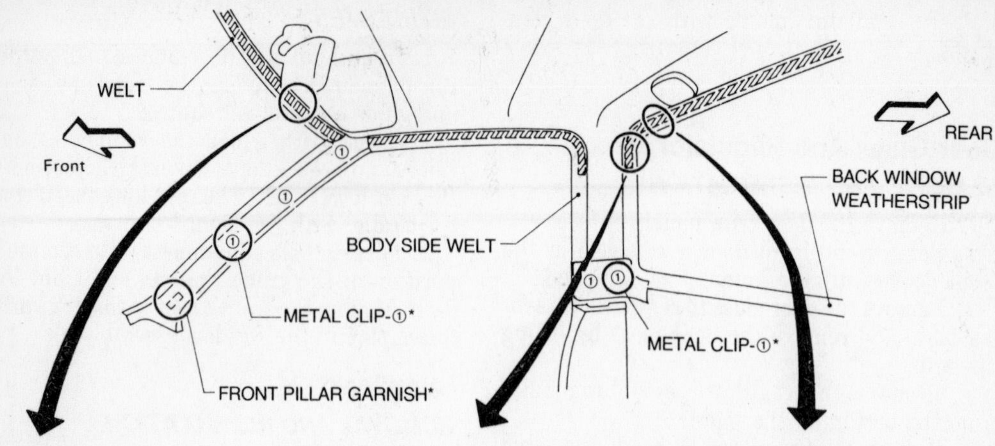

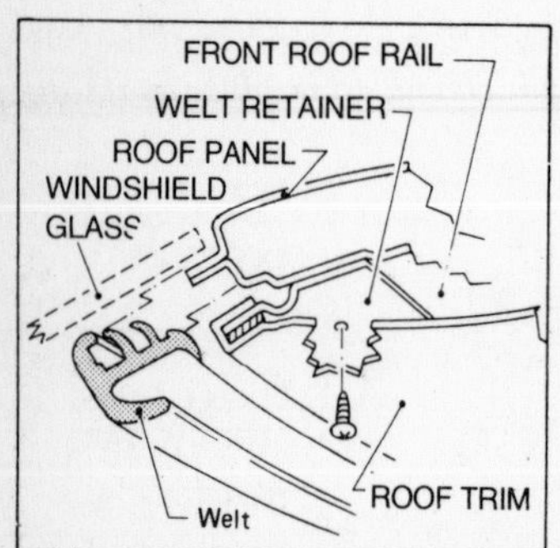

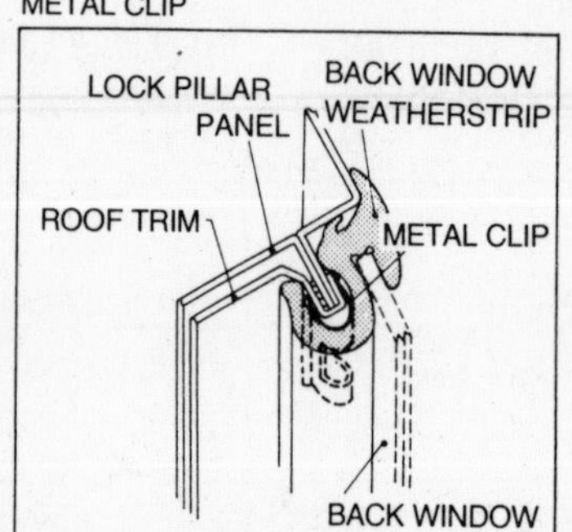

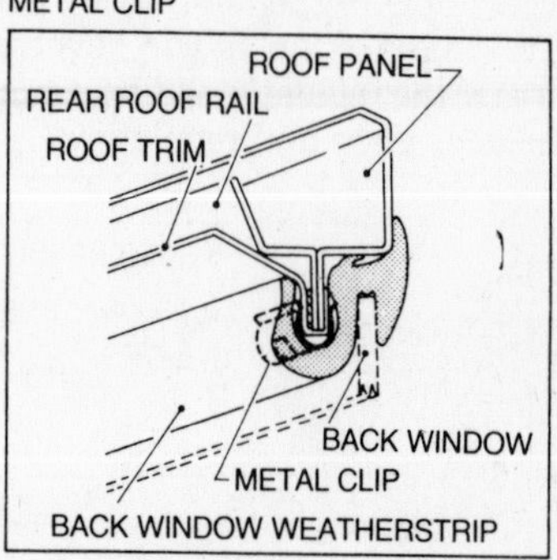

▨: DOUBLE-FACED ADHESIVE TAPE PORTION
*: REFER TO SIDE AND FLOOR TRIM.

Headliner installation, D21 series (Type II)

1. Remove the dome lamp, assist grips inside rear view mirror and sun visors, if so equipped.
2. Remove the rear finisher and rear side finisher.
3. Remove the windshield glass, weatherstrip and windshield pillar cloth.
4. Remove the back window glass and weatherstrip.
5. Disengage the listing wires from the roof rail and remove the headlining from back to front.
6. Installation is the reverse of removal. Install the headlining from the front to the rear. Be careful not to deform the listing wires.

D21 Series

For removal and installation of the headliner on these models please refer to the illustration.

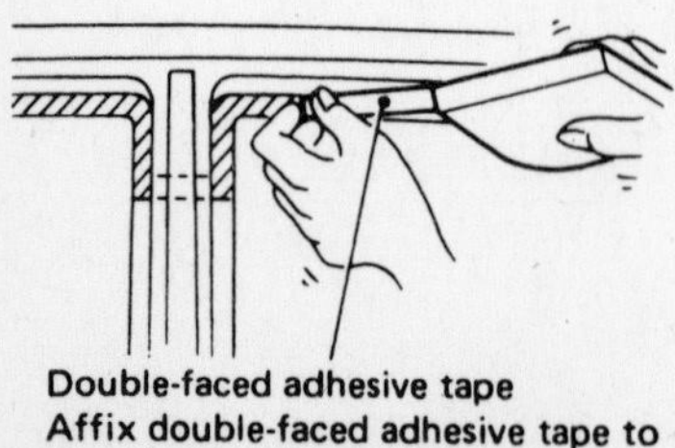

Headliner installation, D21 series (Type II)

Heat gun
Headlining
Affix headlining to body flange starting from corner portion.

Headliner installation, D21 series (Type II)

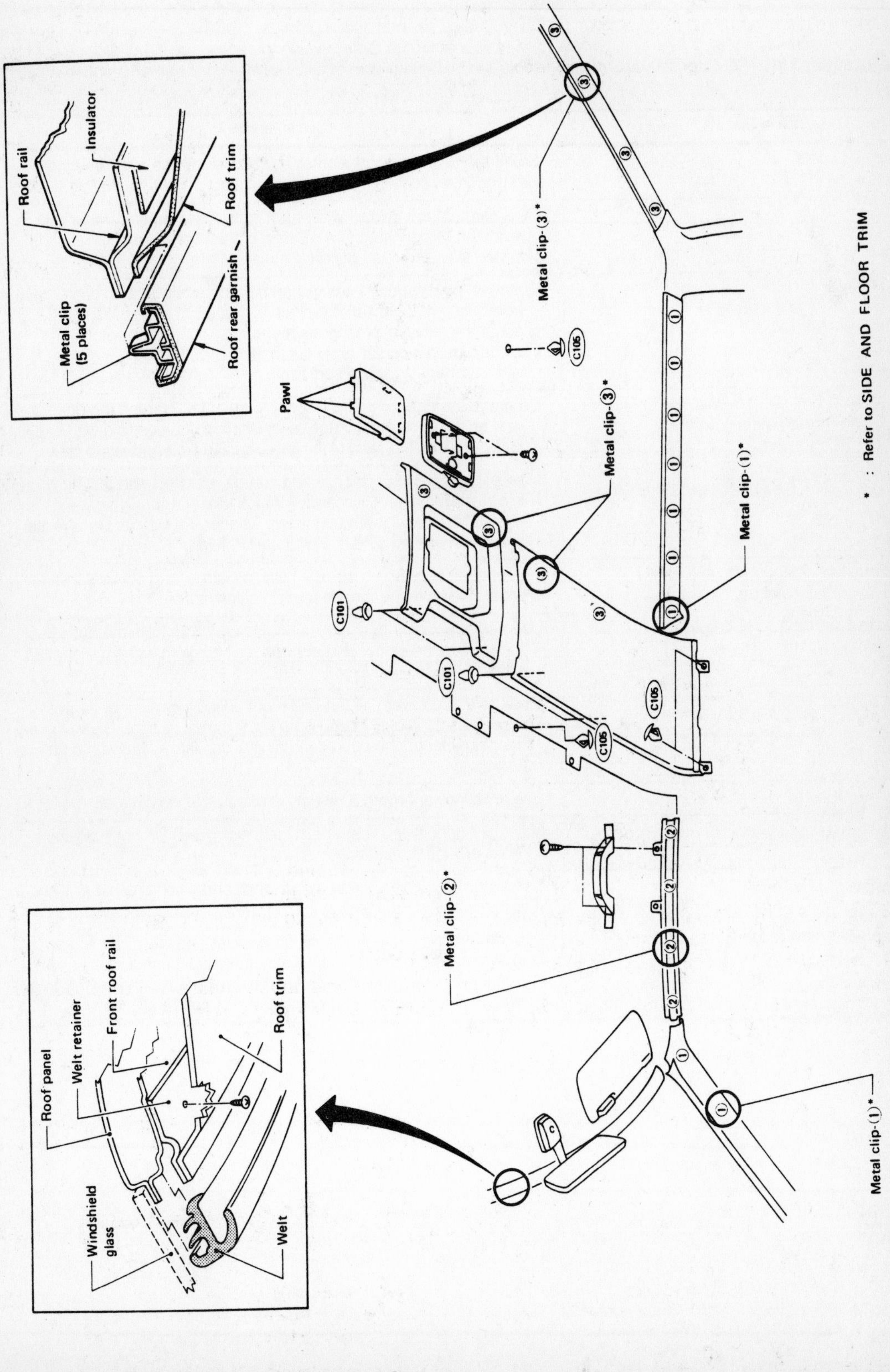

Headliner installation—Pathfinder

How to Remove Stains from Fabric Interior

For rest results, spots and stains should be removed as soon as possible. Never use gasoline, lacquer thinner, acetone, nail polish remover or bleach. Use a 3′ x 3″ piece of cheesecloth. Squeeze most of the liquid from the fabric and wipe the stained fabric from the outside of the stain toward the center with a lifting motion. Turn the cheesecloth as soon as one side becomes soiled. When using water to remove a stain, be sure to wash the entire section after the spot has been removed to avoid water stains. Encrusted spots can be broken up with a dull knife and vacuumed before removing the stain.

Type of Stain	How to Remove It
Surface spots	Brush the spots out with a small hand brush or use a commercial preparation such as K2R to lift the stain.
Mildew	Clean around the mildew with warm suds. Rinse in cold water and soak the mildew area in a solution of 1 part table salt and 2 parts water. Wash with upholstery cleaner.
Water stains	Water stains in fabric materials can be removed with a solution made from 1 cup of table salt dissolved in 1 quart of water. Vigorously scrub the solution into the stain and rinse with clear water. Water stains in nylon or other synthetic fabrics should be removed with a commercial type spot remover.
Chewing gum, tar, crayons, shoe polish (greasy stains)	Do not use a cleaner that will soften gum or tar. Harden the deposit with an ice cube and scrape away as much as possible with a dull knife. Moisten the remainder with cleaning fluid and scrub clean.
Ice cream, candy	Most candy has a sugar base and can be removed with a cloth wrung out in warm water. Oily candy, after cleaning with warm water, should be cleaned with upholstery cleaner. Rinse with warm water and clean the remainder with cleaning fluid.
Wine, alcohol, egg, milk, soft drink (non-greasy stains)	Do not use soap. Scrub the stain with a cloth wrung out in warm water. Remove the remainder with cleaning fluid.
Grease, oil, lipstick, butter and related stains	Use a spot remover to avoid leaving a ring. Work from the outisde of the stain to the center and dry with a clean cloth when the spot is gone.
Headliners (cloth)	Mix a solution of warm water and foam upholstery cleaner to give thick suds. Use only foam—liquid may streak or spot. Clean the entire headliner in one operation using a circular motion with a natural sponge.
Headliner (vinyl)	Use a vinyl cleaner with a sponge and wipe clean with a dry cloth.
Seats and door panels	Mix 1 pint upholstery cleaner in 1 gallon of water. Do not soak the fabric around the buttons.
Leather or vinyl fabric	Use a multi-purpose cleaner full strength and a stiff brush. Let stand 2 minutes and scrub thoroughly. Wipe with a clean, soft rag.
Nylon or synthetic fabrics	For normal stains, use the same procedures you would for washing cloth upholstery. If the fabric is extremely dirty, use a multi-purpose cleaner full strength with a stiff scrub brush. Scrub thoroughly in all directions and wipe with a cotton towel or soft rag.

Mechanic's Data

General Conversion Table

Multiply By	To Convert	To	
	LENGTH		
2.54	Inches	Centimeters	.3937
25.4	Inches	Millimeters	.03937
30.48	Feet	Centimeters	.0328
.304	Feet	Meters	3.28
.914	Yards	Meters	1.094
1.609	Miles	Kilometers	.621
	VOLUME		
.473	Pints	Liters	2.11
.946	Quarts	Liters	1.06
3.785	Gallons	Liters	.264
.016	Cubic inches	Liters	61.02
16.39	Cubic inches	Cubic cms.	.061
28.3	Cubic feet	Liters	.0353
	MASS (Weight)		
28.35	Ounces	Grams	.035
.4536	Pounds	Kilograms	2.20
—	To obtain	From	Multiply by

Multiply By	To Convert	To	
	AREA		
.645	Square inches	Square cms.	.155
.836	Square yds.	Square meters	1.196
	FORCE		
4.448	Pounds	Newtons	.225
.138	Ft./lbs.	Kilogram/meters	7.23
1.36	Ft./lbs.	Newton-meters	.737
.112	In./lbs.	Newton-meters	8.844
	PRESSURE		
.068	Psi	Atmospheres	14.7
6.89	Psi	Kilopascals	.145
	OTHER		
1.104	Horsepower (DIN)	Horsepower (SAE)	.9861
.746	Horsepower (SAE)	Kilowatts (KW)	1.34
1.60	Mph	Km/h	.625
.425	Mpg	Km/1	2.35
—	To obtain	From	Multiply by

Tap Drill Sizes

National Coarse or U.S.S.

Screw & Tap Size	Threads Per Inch	Use Drill Number
No. 5	40	39
No. 6	32	36
No. 8	32	29
No. 10	24	25
No. 12	24	17
1/4	20	8
5/16	18	F
3/8	16	5/16
7/16	14	U
1/2	13	27/64
9/16	12	31/64
5/8	11	17/32
3/4	10	21/32
7/8	9	49/64

National Coarse or U.S.S.

Screw & Tap Size	Threads Per Inch	Use Drill Number
1	8	7/8
1 1/8	7	63/64
1 1/4	7	1 7/64
1 1/2	6	1 11/32

National Fine or S.A.E.

Screw & Tap Size	Threads Per Inch	Use Drill Number
No. 5	44	37
No. 6	40	33
No. 8	36	29
No. 10	32	21

National Fine or S.A.E.

Screw & Tap Size	Threads Per Inch	Use Drill Number
No. 12	28	15
1/4	28	3
6/16	24	1
3/8	24	Q
7/16	20	W
1/2	20	29/64
9/16	18	33/64
5/8	18	37/64
3/4	16	11/16
7/8	14	13/16
1 1/8	12	1 3/64
1 1/4	12	1 11/64
1 1/2	12	1 27/64

Drill Sizes In Decimal Equivalents

Inch	Decimal	Wire	mm	Inch	Decimal	Wire	mm	Inch	Decimal	Wire & Letter	mm	Inch	Decimal	Letter	mm	Inch	Decimal	mm
1/64	.0156		.39		.0730	49			.1614		4.1		.2717		6.9		.4331	11.0
	.0157		.4		.0748		1.9		.1654		4.2		.2720	I		7/16	.4375	11.11
	.0160	78			.0760	48			.1660	19			.2756		7.0		.4528	11.5
	.0165		.42		.0768		1.95		.1673		4.25		.2770	J		29/64	.4531	11.51
	.0173		.44	5/64	.0781		1.98		.1693		4.3		.2795		7.1	15/32	.4688	11.90
	.0177		.45		.0785	47			.1695	18			.2810	K			.4724	12.0
	.0180	77			.0787		2.0	11/64	.1719		4.36	9/32	.2812		7.14	31/64	.4844	12.30
	.0181		.46		.0807		2.05		.1730	17			.2835		7.2		.4921	12.5
	.0189		.48		.0810	46			.1732		4.4		.2854		7.25	1/2	.5000	12.70
	.0197		.5		.0820	45			.1770	16			.2874		7.3		.5118	13.0
	.0200	76			.0827		2.1		.1772		4.5		.2900	L		33/64	.5156	13.09
	.0210	75			.0846		2.15		.1800	15			.2913		7.4	17/32	.5312	13.49
	.0217		.55		.0860	44			.1811		4.6		.2950	M			.5315	13.5
	.0225	74			.0866		2.2		.1820	14			.2953		7.5	35/64	.5469	13.89
	.0236		.6		.0886		2.25		.1850	13		19/64	.2969		7.54		.5512	14.0
	.0240	73			.0890	43			.1850		4.7		.2992		7.6	9/16	.5625	14.28
	.0250	72			.0906		2.3		.1870		4.75		.3020	N			.5709	14.5
	.0256		.65		.0925		2.35	3/16	.1875		4.76		.3031		7.7	37/64	.5781	14.68
	.0260	71			.0935	42			.1890		4.8		.3051		7.75		.5906	15.0
	.0276		.7	3/32	.0938		2.38		.1890	12			.3071		7.8	19/32	.5938	15.08
	.0280	70			.0945		2.4		.1910	11			.3110		7.9	39/64	.6094	15.47
	.0292	69			.0960	41			.1929		4.9	5/16	.3125		7.93		.6102	15.5
	.0295		.75		.0965		2.45		.1935	10			.3150		8.0	5/8	.6250	15.87
	.0310	68			.0980	40			.1960	9			.3160	O			.6299	16.0
1/32	.0312		.79		.0981		2.5		.1969		5.0		.3189		8.1	41/64	.6406	16.27
	.0315		.8		.0995	39			.1990	8			.3228		8.2		.6496	16.5
	.0320	67			.1015	38			.2008		5.1		.3230	P		21/32	.6562	16.66
	.0330	66			.1024		2.6		.2010	7			.3248		8.25		.6693	17.0
	.0335		.85		.1040	37		13/64	.2031		5.16		.3268		8.3	43/64	.6719	17.06
	.0350	65			.1063		2.7		.2040	6		21/64	.3281		8.33	11/16	.6875	17.46
	.0354		.9		.1065	36			.2047		5.2		.3307		8.4		.6890	17.5
	.0360	64			.1083		2.75		.2055	5			.3320	Q		45/64	.7031	17.85
	.0370	63		7/64	.1094		2.77		.2067		5.25		.3346		8.5		.7087	18.0
	.0374		.95		.1100	35			.2087		5.3		.3386		8.6	23/32	.7188	18.25
	.0380	62			.1102		2.8		.2090	4			.3390	R			.7283	18.5
	.0390	61			.1110	34			.2126		5.4		.3425		8.7	47/64	.7344	18.65
	.0394		1.0		.1130	33			.2130	3		11/32	.3438		8.73		.7480	19.0
	.0400	60			.1142		2.9		.2165		5.5		.3445		8.75	3/4	.7500	19.05
	.0410	59			.1160	32		7/32	2188		5.55		.3465		8.8	49/64	.7656	19.44
	.0413		1.05		.1181		3.0		.2205		5.6		.3480	S			.7677	19.5
	.0420	58			.1200	31			.2210	2			.3504		8.9	25/32	.7812	19.84
	.0430	57			.1220		3.1		.2244		5.7		.3543		9.0		.7874	20.0
	.0433		1.1	1/8	.1250		3.17		.2264		5.75		.3580	T		51/64	.7969	20.24
	.0453		1.15		.1260		3.2		.2280	1			.3583		9.1		.8071	20.5
	.0465	56			.1280		3.25		.2283		5.8	23/64	.3594		9.12	13/16	.8125	20.63
3/64	.0469		1.19		.1285	30			.2323		5.9		.3622		9.2		.8268	21.0
	.0472		1.2		.1299		3.3		.2340	A			.3642		9.25	53/64	.8281	21.03
	.0492		1.25		.1339		3.4	15/64	.2344		5.95		.3661		9.3	27/32	.8438	21.43
	.0512		1.3		.1360	29			.2362		6.0		.3680	U			.8465	21.5
	.0520	55			.1378		3.5		.2380	B			.3701		9.4	55/64	.8594	21.82
	.0531		1.35		.1405	28			.2402		6.1		.3740		9.5		.8661	22.0
	.0550	54		9/64	.1406		3.57		.2420	C		3/8	.3750		9.52	7/8	.8750	22.22
	.0551		1.4		.1417		3.6		.2441		6.2		.3770	V			.8858	22.5
	.0571		1.45		.1440	27			.2460	D			.3780		9.6	57/64	.8906	22.62
	.0591		1.5		.1457		3.7		.2461		6.25		.3819		9.7		.9055	23.0
	.0595	53			.1470	26			.2480		6.3		.3839		9.75	29/32	.9062	23.01
	.0610		1.55		.1476		3.75	1/4	.2500	E	6.35		.3858		9.8	59/64	.9219	23.41
1/16	.0625		1.59		.1495	25			.2520		6.		.3860	W			.9252	23.5
	.0630		1.6		.1496		3.8		.2559		6.5		.3898		9.9	15/16	.9375	23.81
	.0635	52			.1520	24			.2570	F		25/64	.3906		9.92		.9449	24.0
	.0650		1.65		.1535		3.9		.2598		6.6		.3937		10.0	61/64	.9531	24.2
	.0669		1.7		.1540	23			.2610	G			.3970	X			.9646	24.5
	.0670	51		5/32	.1562		3.96		.2638		6.7		.4040	Y		31/64	.9688	24.6
	.0689		1.75		.1570	22		17/64	.2656		6.74	13/32	.4062		10.31		.9843	25.0
	.0700	50			.1575		4.0		.2657		6.75		.4130	Z		63/64	.9844	25.0
	.0709		1.8		.1590	21			.2660	H			.4134		10.5	1	1.0000	25.4
	.0728		1.85		.1610	20			.2677		6.8	27/64	.4219		10.71			

AIR/FUEL RATIO: The ratio of air to gasoline by weight in the fuel mixture drawn into the engine.

AIR INJECTION: One method of reducing harmful exhaust emissions by injecting air into each of the exhaust ports of an engine. The fresh air entering the hot exhaust manifold causes any remaining fuel to be burned before it can exit the tailpipe.

ALTERNATOR: A device used for converting mechanical energy into electrical energy.

AMMETER: An instrument, calibrated in amperes, used to measure the flow of an electrical current in a circuit. Ammeters are always connected in series with the circuit being tested.

AMPERE: The rate of flow of electrical current present when one volt of electrical pressure is applied against one ohm of electrical resistance.

ANALOG COMPUTER: Any microprocessor that uses similar (analogous) electrical signals to make its calculations.

ARMATURE: A laminated, soft iron core wrapped by a wire that converts electrical energy to mechanical energy as in a motor or relay. When rotated in a magnetic field, it changes mechanical energy into electrical energy as in a generator.

ATMOSPHERIC PRESSURE: The pressure on the Earth's surface caused by the weight of the air in the atmosphere. At sea level, this pressure is 14.7 psi at 32°F (101 kPa at 0°C).

ATOMIZATION: The breaking down of a liquid into a fine mist that can be suspended in air.

AXIAL PLAY: Movement parallel to a shaft or bearing bore.

BACKFIRE: The sudden combustion of gases in the intake or exhaust system that results in a loud explosion.

BACKLASH: The clearance or play between two parts, such as meshed gears.

BACKPRESSURE: Restrictions in the exhaust system that slow the exit of exhaust gases from the combustion chamber.

BAKELITE: A heat resistant, plastic insulator material commonly used in printed circuit boards and transistorized components.

BALL BEARING: A bearing made up of hardened inner and outer races between which hardened steel ball roll.

BALLAST RESISTOR: A resistor in the primary ignition circuit that lowers voltage after the engine is started to reduce wear on ignition components.

BEARING: A friction reducing, supportive device usually located between a stationary part and a moving part.

BIMETAL TEMPERATURE SENSOR: Any sensor or switch made of two dissimilar types of metal that bend when heated or cooled due to the different expansion rates of the alloys. These types of sensors usually function as an on/off switch.

BLOWBY: Combustion gases, composed of water vapor and unburned fuel, that leak past the piston rings into the crankcase during normal engine operation. These gases are removed by the PCV system to prevent the buildup of harmful acids in the crankcase.

BRAKE PAD: A brake shoe and lining assembly used with disc brakes.

BRAKE SHOE: The backing for the brake lining. The term is, however, usually applied to the assembly of the brake backing and lining.

BUSHING: A liner, usually removable, for a bearing; an anti-friction liner used in place of a bearing.

BYPASS: System used to bypass ballast resistor during engine cranking to increase voltage supplied to the coil.

CALIPER: A hydraulically activated device in a disc brake system, which is mounted straddling the brake rotor (disc). The caliper contains at least one piston and two brake pads. Hydraulic pressure on the piston(s) forces the pads against the rotor.

CAMSHAFT: A shaft in the engine on which are the lobes (cams) which operate the valves. The camshaft is driven by the crankshaft, via a belt, chain or gears, at one half the crankshaft speed.

CAPACITOR: A device which stores an electrical charge.

CARBON MONOXIDE (CO): a colorless, odorless gas given off as a normal byproduct of combustion. It is poisonous and extremely dangerous in confined areas, building up slowly to toxic levels without warning if adequate ventilation is not available.

CARBURETOR: A device, usually mounted on the intake manifold of an engine, which mixes the air and fuel in the proper proportion to allow even combustion.

CATALYTIC CONVERTER: A device installed in the exhaust system, like a muffler, that converts harmful byproducts of combustion into carbon dioxide and water vapor by means of a heat-producing chemical reaction.

CENTRIFUGAL ADVANCE: A mechanical method of advancing the spark timing by using flyweights in the distributor that react to centrifugal force generated by the distributor shaft rotation.

CHECK VALVE: Any one-way valve installed to permit the flow of air, fuel or vacuum in one direction only.

CHOKE: A device, usually a moveable valve, placed in the intake path of a carburetor to restrict the flow of air.

CIRCUIT: Any unbroken path through which an electrical current can flow. Also used to describe fuel flow in some instances.

CIRCUIT BREAKER: A switch which protects an electrical circuit from overload by opening the circuit when the current flow exceeds a predetermined level. Some circuit breakers must be reset manually, while other reset automatically

COIL (IGNITION): A transformer in the ignition circuit which steps of the voltage provided to the spark plugs.

COMBINATION MANIFOLD: An assembly which includes both the intake and exhaust manifolds in one casting.

COMBINATION VALVE: A device used in some fuel systems that routes fuel vapors to a charcoal storage canister instead of venting them into the atmosphere. The valve relieves fuel tank pressure and allows fresh air into the tank as fuel level drops to prevent a vapor lock situation.

COMPRESSION RATIO: The comparison of the total volume of the cylinder and combustion chamber with the piston at BDC and the piston at TDC.

CONDENSER: 1. An electrical device which acts to store an electrical charge, preventing voltage surges.

2. A radiator-like device in the air conditioning system in which refrigerant gas condenses into a liquid, giving off heat.

CONDUCTOR: Any material through which an electrical current can be transmitted easily.

CONTINUITY: Continuous or complete circuit. Can be checked with an ohmmeter.

COUNTERSHAFT: An intermediate shaft which is rotated by a mainshaft and transmits, in turn, that rotation to a working part.

CRANKCASE: The lower part of an engine in which the crankshaft and related parts operate.

CRANKSHAFT: The main driving shaft of an engine which receives reciprocating motion from the pistons and converts it to rotary motion.

CYLINDER: In an engine, the round hole in the engine block in which the piston(s) ride.

CYLINDER BLOCK: The main structural member of an engine in which is found the cylinders, crankshaft and other principal parts.

CYLINDER HEAD: The detachable portion of the engine, fastened, usually, to the top of the cylinder block, containing all or most of the combustion chambers. On overhead valve engines, it contains the valves and their operating parts. On overhead cam engines, it contains the camshaft as well.

DEAD CENTER: The extreme top or bottom of the piston stroke.

DETONATION: An unwanted explosion of the air fuel mixture in the combustion chamber caused by excess heat and compression, advanced timing, or an overly lean mixture. Also referred to as "ping".

DIAPHRAGM: A thin, flexible wall separating two cavities, such as in a vacuum advance unit.

DIESELING: A condition in which hot spots in the combustion chamber cause the engine to run on after the key is turned off.

DIFFERENTIAL: A geared assembly which allows the transmission of motion between drive axles, giving one axle the ability to turn faster than the other.

DIODE: An electrical device that will allow current to flow in one direction only.

DISC BRAKE: A hydraulic braking assembly consisting of a brake disc, or rotor, mounted on an axle, and a caliper assembly containing, usually two brake pads which are activated by hydraulic pressure. The pads are forced against the sides of the disc, creating friction which slows the vehicle.

DISTRIBUTOR: A mechanically driven device on an engine which is responsible for electrically firing the spark plug at a predetermined point of the piston stroke.

DOWEL PIN: A pin, inserted in mating holes in two different parts allowing those parts to maintain a fixed relationship.

DRUM BRAKE: A braking system which consists of two brake shoes and one or two wheel cylinders, mounted on a fixed backing plate, and a brake drum, mounted on an axle, which revolves around the assembly. Hydraulic action applied to the wheel cylinders forces the shoes outward against the drum, creating friction and slowing the vehicle.

DWELL: The rate, measured in degrees of shaft rotation, at which an electrical circuit cycles on and off.

ELECTRONIC CONTROL UNIT (ECU): Ignition module, module, amplifier or igniter. See Module for definition.

ELECTRONIC IGNITION: A system in which the timing and firing of the spark plugs is controlled by an electronic control unit, usually called a module. These systems have not points or condenser.

ENDPLAY: The measured amount of axial movement in a shaft.

ENGINE: A device that converts heat into mechanical energy.

EXHAUST MANIFOLD: A set of cast passages or pipes which conduct exhaust gases from the engine.

FEELER GAUGE: A blade, usually metal, of precisely predetermined thickness, used to measure the clearance between two parts. These blades usually are available in sets of assorted thicknesses.

F-Head: An engine configuration in which the intake valves are in the cylinder head, while the camshaft and exhaust valves are located in the cylinder block. The camshaft operates the intake valves via lifters and pushrods, while it operates the exhaust valves directly.

FIRING ORDER: The order in which combustion occurs in the cylinders of an engine. Also the order in which spark is distributed to the plugs by the distributor.

FLATHEAD: An engine configuration in which the camshaft and all the valves are located in the cylinder block.

FLOODING: The presence of too much fuel in the intake manifold and combustion chamber which prevents the air/fuel mixture from firing, thereby causing a no-start situation.

FLYWHEEL: A disc shaped part bolted to the rear end of the crankshaft. Around the outer perimeter is affixed the ring gear. The starter drive engages the ring gear, turning the flywheel, which rotates the crankshaft, imparting the initial starting motion to the engine.

FOOT POUND (ft.lb. or sometimes, ft. lbs.): The amount of energy or work needed to raise an item weighing one pound, a distance of one foot.

FUSE: A protective device in a circuit which prevents circuit overload by breaking the circuit when a specific amperage is present. The device is constructed around a strip or wire of a lower amperage rating than the circuit it is designed to protect. When an amperage higher than that stamped on the fuse is present in the circuit, the strip or wire melts, opening the circuit.

GEAR RATIO: The ratio between the number of teeth on meshing gears.

GENERATOR: A device which converts mechanical energy into electrical energy.

HEAT RANGE: The measure of a spark plug's ability to dissipate heat from its firing end. The higher the heat range, the hotter the plug fires.

HUB: The center part of a wheel or gear.

HYDROCARBON (HC): Any chemical compound made up of hydrogen and carbon. A major pollutant formed by the engine as a byproduct of combustion.

HYDROMETER: An instrument used to measure the specific gravity of a solution.

INCH POUND (in.lb. or sometimes, in. lbs.): One twelfth of a foot pound.

INDUCTION: A means of transferring electrical energy in the form of a magnetic field. Principle used in the ignition coil to increase voltage.

INJECTION PUMP: A device, usually mechanically operated, which meters and delivers fuel under pressure to the fuel injector.

INJECTOR: A device which receives metered fuel under relatively low pressure and is activated to inject the fuel into the engine under relatively high pressure at a predetermined time.

INPUT SHAFT: The shaft to which torque is applied, usually carrying the driving gear or gears.

INTAKE MANIFOLD: A casting of passages or pipes used to conduct air or a fuel/air mixture to the cylinders.

JOURNAL: The bearing surface within which a shaft operates.

KEY: A small block usually fitted in a notch between a shaft and a hub to prevent slippage of the two parts.

MANIFOLD: A casting of passages or set of pipes which connect the cylinders to an inlet or outlet source.

MANIFOLD VACUUM: Low pressure in an engine intake manifold formed just below the throttle plates. Manifold vacuum is highest at idle and drops under acceleration.

MASTER CYLINDER: The primary fluid pressurizing device in a hydraulic system. In automotive use, it is found in brake and hydraulic clutch systems and is pedal activated, either directly or, in a power brake system, through the power booster.

MODULE: Electronic control unit, amplifier or igniter of solid state or integrated design which controls the current flow in the ignition primary circuit based on input from the pick-up coil. When the module opens the primary circuit, the high secondary voltage is induced in the coil.

NEEDLE BEARING: A bearing which consists of a number (usually a large number) of long, thin rollers.

OHM: (Ω) The unit used to measure the resistance of conductor to electrical flow. One ohm is the amount of resistance that limits current flow to one ampere in a circuit with one volt of pressure.

OHMMETER: An instrument used for measuring the resistance, in ohms, in an electrical circuit.

OUTPUT SHAFT: The shaft which transmits torque from a device, such as a transmission.

OVERDRIVE: A gear assembly which produces more shaft revolutions than that transmitted to it.

OVERHEAD CAMSHAFT (OHC): An engine configuration in which the camshaft is mounted on top of the cylinder head and operates the valve either directly or by means of rocker arms.

OVERHEAD VALVE (OHV): An engine configuration in which all of the valves are located in the cylinder head and the camshaft is located in the cylinder block. The camshaft operates the valves via lifters and pushrods.

OXIDES OF NITROGEN (NOx): Chemical compounds of nitrogen produced as a byproduct of combustion. They combine with hydrocarbons to produce smog.

OXYGEN SENSOR: Used with the feedback system to sense the presence of oxygen in the exhaust gas and signal the computer which can reference the voltage signal to an air/fuel ratio.

PINION: The smaller of two meshing gears.

PISTON RING: An open ended ring which fits into a groove on the outer diameter of the piston. Its chief function is to form a seal between the piston and cylinder wall. Most automotive pistons have three rings: two for compression sealing; one for oil sealing.

PRELOAD: A predetermined load placed on a bearing during assembly or by adjustment.

PRIMARY CIRCUIT: Is the low voltage side of the ignition system which consists of the ignition switch, ballast resistor or resistance wire, bypass, coil, electronic control unit and pick-up coil as well as the connecting wires and harnesses.

PRESS FIT: The mating of two parts under pressure, due to the inner diameter of one being smaller than the outer diameter of the other, or vice versa; an interference fit.

RACE: The surface on the inner or outer ring of a bearing on which the balls, needles or rollers move.

REGULATOR: A device which maintains the amperage and/or voltage levels of a circuit at predetermined values.

RELAY: A switch which automatically opens and/or closes a circuit.

RESISTANCE: The opposition to the flow of current through a circuit or electrical device, and is measured in ohms. Resistance is equal to the voltage divided by the amperage.

RESISTOR: A device, usually made of wire, which offers a preset amount of resistance in an electrical circuit.

RING GEAR: The name given to a ring-shaped gear attached to a differential case, or affixed to a flywheel or as part a planetary gear set.

ROLLER BEARING: A bearing made up of hardened inner and outer races between which hardened steel rollers move.

ROTOR: 1. The disc-shaped part of a disc brake assembly, upon which the brake pads bear; also called, brake disc.
2. The device mounted atop the distributor shaft, which passes current to the distributor cap tower contacts.

SECONDARY CIRCUIT: The high voltage side of the ignition system, usually above 20,000 volts. The secondary includes the ignition coil, coil wire, distributor cap and rotor, spark plug wires and spark plugs.

SENDING UNIT: A mechanical, electrical, hydraulic or electromagnetic device which transmits information to a gauge.

SENSOR: Any device designed to measure engine operating conditions or ambient pressures and temperatures. Usually electronic in nature and designed to send a voltage signal to an on-board computer, some sensors may operate as a simple on/off switch or they may provide a variable voltage signal (like a potentiometer) as conditions or measured parameters change.

SHIM: Spacers of precise, predetermined thickness used between parts to establish a proper working relationship.

SLAVE CYLINDER: In automotive use, a device in the hydraulic clutch system which is activated by hydraulic force, disengaging the clutch.

SOLENOID: A coil used to produce a magnetic field, the effect of which is produce work.

SPARK PLUG: A device screwed into the combustion chamber of a spark ignition engine. The basic construction is a conductive core inside of a ceramic insulator, mounted in an outer conductive base. An electrical charge from the spark plug wire travels along the conductive core and jumps a preset air gap to a grounding point or points at the end of the conductive base. The resultant spark ignites the fuel/air mixture in the combustion chamber.

SPLINES: Ridges machined or cast onto the outer diameter of a shaft or inner diameter of a bore to enable parts to mate without rotation.

TACHOMETER: A device used to measure the rotary speed of an engine, shaft, gear, etc., usually in rotations per minute.

THERMOSTAT: A valve, located in the cooling system of an engine, which is closed when cold and opens gradually in response to engine heating, controlling the temperature of the coolant and rate of coolant flow.

TOP DEAD CENTER (TDC): The point at which the piston reaches the top of its travel on the compression stroke.

TORQUE: The twisting force applied to an object.

TORQUE CONVERTER: A turbine used to transmit power from a driving member to a driven member via hydraulic action, providing changes in drive ratio and torque. In automotive use, it links the driveplate at the rear of the engine to the automatic transmission.

TRANSDUCER: A device used to change a force into an electrical signal.

TRANSISTOR: A semi-conductor component which can be actuated by a small voltage to perform an electrical switching function.

TUNE-UP: A regular maintenance function, usually associated with the replacement and adjustment of parts and components in the electrical and fuel systems of a vehicle for the purpose of attaining optimum performance.

TURBOCHARGER: An exhaust driven pump which compresses intake air and forces it into the combustion chambers at higher than atmospheric pressures. The increased air pressure allows more fuel to be burned and results in increased horsepower being produced.

VACUUM ADVANCE: A device which advances the ignition timing in response to increased engine vacuum.

VACUUM GAUGE: An instrument used to measure the presence of vacuum in a chamber.

VALVE: A device which control the pressure, direction of flow or rate of flow of a liquid or gas.

VALVE CLEARANCE: The measured gap between the end of the valve stem and the rocker arm, cam lobe or follower that activates the valve.

VISCOSITY: The rating of a liquid's internal resistance to flow.

VOLTMETER: An instrument used for measuring electrical force in units called volts. Voltmeters are always connected parallel with the circuit being tested.

WHEEL CYLINDER: Found in the automotive drum brake assembly, it is a device, actuated by hydraulic pressure, which, through internal pistons, pushes the brake shoes outward against the drums.

ABBREVIATIONS AND SYMBOLS

A: Ampere
AC: Alternating current
A/C: Air conditioning
A-h: Ampere hour
AT: Automatic transmission
ATDC: After top dead center
μA: Microampere
bbl: Barrel
BDC: Bottom dead center
bhp: Brake horsepower
BTDC: Before top dead center
BTU: British thermal unit
C: Celsius (Centigrade)
CCA: Cold cranking amps
cd: Candela
cm^2: Square centimeter
cm^3, cc: Cubic centimeter
CO: Carbon monoxide
CO_2: Carbon dioxide
cu.in., in^3: Cubic inch
CV: Constant velocity
Cyl.: Cylinder
DC: Direct current
ECM: Electronic control module
EFE: Early fuel evaporation
EFI: Electronic fuel injection
EGR: Exhaust gas recirculation
Exh.: Exhaust
F: Fahrenheit
F: Farad
pF: Picofarad
μF: Microfarad
FI: Fuel injection
ft.lb., ft. lb., ft. lbs.: foot pound(s)
gal: Gallon
g: Gram
HC: Hydrocarbon
HEI: High energy ignition
HO: High output
hp: Horsepower
Hyd.: Hydraulic
Hz: Hertz
ID: Inside diameter
in.lb.; in. lb.; in. lbs: inch pound(s)
Int.: Intake
K: Kelvin
kg: Kilogram
kHz: Kilohertz
km: Kilometer
km/h: Kilometers per hour
kΩ: Kilohm
kPa: Kilopascal
kV: Kilovolt
kW: Kilowatt
l: Liter
l/s: Liters per second
m: Meter
mA: Milliampere

mg: Milligram

mHz: Megahertz

mm: Millimeter

mm^2: Square millimeter

m^3: Cubic meter

MΩ: Megohm

m/s: Meters per second

MT: Manual transmission

mV: Millivolt

μm: Micrometer

N: Newton

N-m: Newton meter

NOx: Nitrous oxide

OD: Outside diameter

OHC: Over head camshaft

OHV: Over head valve

Ω: Ohm

PCV: Positive crankcase ventilation

psi: Pounds per square inch

pts: Pints

qts: Quarts

rpm: Rotations per minute

rps: Rotations per second

R-12: A refrigerant gas (Freon)

SAE: Society of Automotive Engineers

SO_2: Sulfur dioxide

T: Ton

t: Megagram

TBI: Throttle Body Injection

TPS: Throttle Position Sensor

V: 1. Volt; 2. Venturi

μV: Microvolt

W: Watt

∝: Infinity

<: Less than

>: Greater than

Index

D

E

H

I

J

K

L

M

N

O

P

U

V

W